Gonna Sit At The Welcome Table

Second Edition

Editors

Julian Bond

Andrew Lewis

THOMSON LEARNING™
CUSTOM PUBLISHING

Editor: Nathan Anderson
Production Coordinator: Mary Snelling
Marketing Coordinator: Sara L. Hinckley

Printed in the United States of America

Thomson Learning Custom Publishing
5191 Natorp Blvd.
Mason, Ohio 45040
USA

For information about our products, contact us:
1-800-355-9983
http://www.custom.thomsonlearning.com

International Headquarters
Thomson Learning
International Division
290 Harbor Drive, 2nd Floor
Stamford, CT 06902-7477
USA

UK/Europe/Middle East/South Africa
Thomson Learning
Berkshire House
168-173 High Holborn
London WCIV 7AA

Asia
Thomson Learning
60 Albert Street, #15-01
Albert Complex
Singapore 189969

Canada
Nelson Thomson Learning
1120 Birchmount Road
Toronto, Ontario MIK 5G4
Canada
United Kingdom

Visit us at www.e-riginality.com and learn more about this book and other titles published by Thomson Learning Custom Publishing

ISBN 0-828-10639-8

The Adaptable Courseware Program consists of products and additions to existing Custom Publishing products that are produced from camera-ready copy. Peer review, class testing, and accuracy are primarily the responsibility of the author(s).

ACKNOWLEDGMENTS

"The Legacy of the First Reconstruction" by Manning Marable is reprinted from *Race, Reform and Rebellion: The Second Reconstruction in Black America, 1945–1982.* Copyright © 1982 University Press of Mississippi.

"In Black and White" by Edward Ayers is from Promise of the New South. Copyright © 1992 Oxford University Press.

"The NAACP as a Reform Movement" by August Meier and John Bracey, Jr. is from the February, 1993 issue of *The Journal of Southern History.* Copyright © 1993 Southern Historical Association.

"Marcus Garvey and the Politics of Revitalization" by Lawrence Levine is from *Black Leaders of the 20th Century* by John H. Franklin & August Meier. Copyright © 1982 University of Illinois Press. Used by permission.

"Principles of the UNIA" by Marcus Garvey is taken from *Chronicles of Black Protest.* Copyright © 1968 Bradford Chambers.

"A French Directive" is from the May 1919 issue of *The Crisis.*

"A. Philip Randolph" by Benjamin Quarles is from *Black Leaders of the 20th Century* by John H. Franklin & August Meier. Copyright © 1982 University of Illinois Press. Used by permission.

"Randolph's Demands" by A. Philip Randolph and "The Black Man and Self Defense: 1962" are from *Chronicles of Black Protest* by Bradford Chambers. Copyright © 1968 Bradford Chambers.

"The Richmond Statement," "A Basis for Interracial Cooperation and Development in the South (Durham Conference Statement)," "Statement of Conference of White Southerners on Race Relations (Atlanta Statement)," "An Informal Letter From Harry Ashmore," "Resolutions of the Collaboration Committee," "Selections from The New South," "A Norfolk Sampling and Faulkner On Schools," "Public School Desegregation: Charlottesville, VA, 1955–62," "The Sit-In Movement, 1960–61," "Atlanta: A Second Look," "The Freedom Rides," "The Agony of Albany," "Reflections on the Death of a Child," "Albany, Failure or First Step?," "Homegrown Movement in Macon," "Southern Bombings Jan. 1, 1956–June 1, 1963," "Birmingham and Beyond," "Civil Disobedience and the Law," and "Retrospect and Prospect" are all reprinted from *The New South* and various other publications of the Southern Regional Council. Copyright © 1943, 1955, 1960, 1962, 1963, Southern Regional Council.

The NAACP ad in Unit 4 is Copyright © 1955 *The Crisis.*

"School Segregation" is reprinted from *The Civil Rights Movement: An Eyewitness History* by Sanford Wexler. Copyright © 1993 Facts On File.

The Chuck Grey cartoons in Unit 4 are from the *Richmond Afro-American.* Copyright © 1954, 1955, *The Richmond Afro-American.*

Passages from *What the Negro Wants and How to Get It: The Inward Power of the Masses* by Leslie Pinckney Hill are Copyright © 1944 The University of North Carolina Press.

The Marcus Garvey Cartoon in Unit 2 is from *The Guardian,* August 27, 1910.

"Marcus Garvey & The NAACP" by W.E.B. Du Bois is from the February 1, 1928 issue of *The Crisis.* Copyright © 1928 *The Crisis.*

The NAACP ad in Unit 2 is Copyright © 1933 *The Crisis.*

"Selections from The Crisis," June/July, 1954, Copyright © 1954 *The Crisis*.

The Athens College Letter to the NAACP is from the June/July 1954 issue of *The Crisis*. Copyright © 1954 *The Crisis*.

"Legislative Action is Needed" is reprinted from the Sept. 18, 1958 issue of *The Charlottesville Daily Progress*. Copyright © 1958 *The Charlottesville Daily Progress*.

"Letters to the Editor" are reprinted from the Sept. 22, 1958 issue of *The Charlottesville Daily Progress*. Copyright © 1958 *The Charlottesville Daily Progress*.

"A Box Lunch, A Chair and a Drinking Cup" is from the Oct. 2, 1958 issue of *The Halifax Gazette*. Copyright © 1958 *The Halifax Gazette*.

"Tragedy of a Negro Teacher" is from the Oct. 16, 1956 issue of *The Richmond Times-Dispatch*. Copyright © 1956 *The Richmond Times-Dispatch*.

"Little Rock," "Negro Voting in the South—And The Protest Movement," "Route of the Freedom Riders," and "Maps, Charts, 1964 Civil Rights" are reprinted from *Portrait of a Decade* by Anthony Lewis, published by Bantam Doubleday Dell. Copyright © 1964 Anthony Lewis and the *New York Times*.

"Letter From Women's Political Council" by Joanne Robinson is from *The Montgomery Bus Boycott and the Women Who Started It* by David Garrow. Copyright © 1987 University of Tennessee. Used by permission.

"Holt Street Baptist Church Speech" by Martin Luther King, Jr., is reprinted by arrangement with the Heirs to the Estate of Martin Luther King, Jr., c/o Joan Daves Agency as agent for the proprietor.

"Keep Your Eyes On the Prize," "Ballad of the Student Sit-Ins," "I'm Gonna Sit at the Welcome Table," "Ain't Gonna Let Nobody Turn Me Around," and "Which Side Are You On?" are reprinted from *Songs of the Southern Freedom Movement* published by New Society Publishers. Copyright © 1990 Sing Out Corporation.

"Challenge and Response in the Montgomery Bus Boycott of 1955–56" by J. Mills Thornton III is from the July 1980 issue of *The Alabama Review*. Copyright © 1980 The University of Alabama Press.

"Ask Yourself This Important Question" was published by The Dallas County Citizens Organization.

The Defenders' News and Views was the newsletter for The Defenders of State Sovereignty and Individual Liberties.

Selections from *The Richmond News Leader*, 1955–56 are Copyright © *The Richmond Times-Dispatch*.

"Carleton Putnam Letter to Atty. General Rodgers" is reprinted from *Struggle for Racial Equality* by Henry Steele Commager. Copyright © Harper Collins.

"You Can Help" was printed by The White Citizen's Legal Fund.

"White Citizens Legal Fund is Started Today" is reprinted from the June 24, 1963 issue of *The Greenwood Commonwealth*. Copyright © 1963 *The Greenwood Commonwealth*.

"Directors Chosen for Citizens Fund" is reprinted from the July 9, 1963 issue of the *Memphis Commercial Appeal*. Copyright © 1963 *Memphis Commercial Appeal*.

"Sit-Ins—The Students Report," and "Freedom Ride" are from *Freedom Ride* by James Peck. Copyright © 1962 Simon & Schuster.

"SCLC News Alert, April 11, 1960" is Copyright © 1960 Southern Christian Leadership Conference.

"Statement to the Press" by Martin Luther King, Jr., is reprinted by arrangement with the Heirs to the Estate of Martin Luther King, Jr., c/o Joan Davies Agency as agent for the proprietor.

"SNCC Founding Statement," "Recommendations of the Committee," "Fund Appeal, 1961," "111 Arrests Mark Freedom Day," "The General Condition of the Mississippi Negro," "Mississippi: Structure of the Movement," "Civil Rights Law Compliance Varies," "Freedom Schools," "The Freedom Schools Document," "SNCC Fundraising Letter," "SNCC Position on Women in the Movement," "Should Civil Rights Workers Take A Stand On Vietnam?," "XMAS Boycott Called,"

"From Civil Rights to Black Power: The Case of SNCC, 1960–1966" is from *Twentieth Century America: Recent Interpretation* by Barton J. Bernstein and Allen J. Matusow. Copyright © 1969 Harcourt, Brace, Jovanovich.

"Black Power: Its Need and Substance" is from *Black Power: The Politics of Liberation* by Stokely Carmichael and Charles V. Hamilton, published by Random House. Copyright © 1967 Stokely Carmichael and Charles V. Hamilton.

"The Black Revolution" by Malcolm X is from *Two Speeches by Malcolm X*. Copyright © 1965 Merit Press and Betty Shabazz.

Selections from *The Crisis*, June/July 1955, are Copyright © 1955 The Crisis.

"Of Mr. Booker T. Washington and Others" by W.E.B. Du Bois is reprinted through an exclusive arrangement with The Library of America.

"The Impact of the New Deal on Black Southerners" by Harvard Sitkoff is reprinted from *The New Deal and the South* by James C. Cobb and Michael V. Namorato. Copyright © 1984 University Press of Mississippi.

"The Birth of Jim Crow" by C. Vann Woodward, © 1964 C. Vann Woodward.

"Address to White Liberals" by Lillian Smith is reprinted from *The New Republic*, Sept. 18, 1944. Copyright © 1944 *The New Republic*.

CONTENTS

SELECTIVE CHRONOLOGY xvii
Julian Bond

UNIT 1
SEGREGATION'S ORIGINS 1

INTRODUCTION 2

1-1 • PROLOGUE: THE LEGACY OF THE FIRST RECONSTRUCTION 3
Manning Marable

1-2 • PLESSY V. FERGUSON: THE BIRTH OF JIM CROW 10
C. Vann Woodward

1-3 • IN BLACK AND WHITE 18
Edward Ayers

UNIT 2
AFRICAN AMERICAN THOUGHT AND OPPOSITION TO SEGREGATION 47

INTRODUCTION 48

2-1 • WASHINGTON CARTOON 49

2-2 • ATLANTA EXPOSITION ADDRESS 50
Booker T. Washington

2-3 • OF MR. BOOKER T. WASHINGTON AND OTHERS 53
W.E.B. Du Bois

2-4 • THE NIAGARA MOVEMENT DECLARATION OF PRINCIPLES 61

2-5 • THE NAACP AS A REFORM MOVEMENT, 1909–1965 65
"TO REACH THE CONSCIENCE OF AMERICA"
August Meier and John H. Bracey, Jr.

2-6 • MARCUS GARVEY AND THE POLITICS OF REVITALIZATION 83
Lawrence W. Levine

2-7 • THE OBJECTIVES OF THE UNIVERSAL NEGRO IMPROVEMENT ASSOCIATION 104
Marcus Garvey

2-8 • MARCUS GARVEY AND THE NAACP 106
W.E.B. Du Bois

2-9 • A FRENCH DIRECTIVE 108
ON THE TREATMENT OF BLACK AMERICAN TROOPS

2-10 • NAACP ADVERTISEMENT, 1933 110

UNIT 3
NEW DEAL AND WORLD WAR II 111

INTRODUCTION 112

3-1 • THE IMPACT OF THE NEW DEAL ON BLACK SOUTHERNERS 113
Harvard Sitkoff

3-2 • A. PHILIP RANDOLPH: LABOR LEADER AT LARGE 125
Benjamin Quarles

3-3 • A. PHILIP RANDOLPH'S MARCH ON WASHINGTON: 1941 142
THE BLACK MAN DEMANDS A SHARE IN WORLD WAR II
A. Philip Randolph

3-4 • PRESIDENT ROOSEVELT'S FAIR EMPLOYMENT PRACTICES COMMITTEE 145
EXECUTIVE ORDER 8802, JUNE 25, 1941

3-5 • A BASIS FOR INTERRACIAL COOPERATION AND DEVELOPMENT IN THE SOUTH 147
A STATEMENT BY SOUTHERN NEGROES

3-6 • STATEMENT OF CONFERENCE OF WHITE SOUTHERNERS ON RACE RELATIONS 154

3-7 • RESOLUTIONS OF THE COLLABORATION COMMITTEE 156

3-8 • RESOLUTION LAUNCHING THE SOUTHERN REGIONAL COUNCIL 159

3-9 • ADDRESSED TO WHITE LIBERALS 161
Lillian Smith

3-10 • WHAT THE NEGRO WANTS 164

UNIT 4
BROWN, LITTLE ROCK AND CHARLOTTESVILLE 185

INTRODUCTION 187

4-1 • NAACP ADVERTISEMENT, 1955 188

4-2 • SEGREGATION MAP, MAY 1954 189

4-3 • BROWN V. BOARD OF EDUCATION 199

4-4 • A RANDOM THOUGHT ON THE SEGREGATION CASES 200
William H. Rehnquist

4-5 • **The Opinion of Mankind** 202
The U.S. Secretary of State on Segregation and World Relations
Dean Acheson

4-6 • **Afro-American Cartoons** 204

4-7 • **Excerpts from Informal Memorandum from Harry Ashmore** 209
Dred Scott Ashmore

4-8 • **Editorial** 211
Segregation Decison

4-9 • **SRC Reacts to the Brown Decision** 216
A Statement by the Executive Committee
of the Southern Regional Council

4-10 • **Interpretation of Supreme Court Decision and The NAACP Program** 223
Thurgood Marshall and Roy Wilkins

4-11 • **Opportunity for the South** 229
Marion A. Wright

4-12 • **Letter to NAACP from Athens College** 233

4-13 • **Declaration of Constitutional Principles** 234

4-14 • **Public Opinion and the School Decision** 237

4-15 • **Charlottesville School Closing Letter** 240

4-16 • **Public School Desegregation** 242
Charlottesville, Virginia, 1955–62
Paul M. Gaston and Thomas T. Hammond

4-17 • **Charlottesville Daily Progress** 255
Editorial and Letters to the Editor

4-18 • **A Box Lunch, A Chair and A Drinking Cup** 258

4-19 • **Little Rock** 260
Anthony Lewis

Unit 5
The Montgomery Bus Boycott 275

Introduction 276

5-1 • **Arrest Record, Rosa Parks, December 1, 1955** 277

5-2 • **Challenge and Response in the Montgomery Bus Boycott of 1955–1956** 278
J. Mills Thornton III

5-3 • **A Letter from the Women's Political Council to the Mayor of Montgomery, Alabama** 312

5-4 • SPEECH BY MARTIN LUTHER KING, JR., AT HOLT STREET BAPTIST CHURCH 314
Martin Luther King, Jr.

5-5 • "KEEP YOUR EYES ON THE PRIZE," SONG 316

UNIT 6
SEGREGATION AND ITS ADHERENTS 317

INTRODUCTION 318

6-1 • ASK YOURSELF THIS IMPORTANT QUESTION 319

6-2 • THE CITIZENS' COUNCIL 320
ORGANIZED RESISTANCE TO THE SECOND RECONSTRUCTION, 1954–64
Neil R. McMillen

6-3 • DEFENDERS' NEWS AND VIEWS 338
SELECTIONS, 1955–59

6-4 • RICHMOND TIMES DISPATCH EDITORIAL, OCTOBER 1961 349

6-5 • RICHMOND NEWS LEADER 350
INTERPOSITION EDITORIALS, 1956

6-6 • AN ARGUMENT THAT THE NEGRO IS INHERENTLY INFERIOR 370
Carleton Putnam

6-7 • THE WHITE CITIZENS' COUNCIL 376
POWER FOR THE STATUS QUO

6-8 • YOU CAN HELP . . . 380

UNIT 7
SIT-INS AND THE ESTABLISHMENT OF SNCC 383

INTRODUCTION 385

7-1 • "BALLAD OF THE STUDENT SIT-INS," SONG 386

7-2 • SIT-IN, VOTING MAP, 1960 387

7-3 • THE SIT-IN MOVEMENT,1960–61 388

7-4 • SIT-INS—THE STUDENTS REPORT 392

7-5 • FIRST OCCURRENCE OF SIT-INS IN A LOCALITY 401
Martin Oppenheimer

7-6 • SCLC NEWS ALERT 403

7-7 • BIGGER THAN A HAMBURGER 406
Ella J. Baker

7-8 • STATEMENT TO THE PRESS 408
Dr. Martin Luther King, Jr.

7-9 • Personal Notes from Founding Conference 410
Charles Jones

7-10 • Recommendations 412
Of the Findings and Recommendations Committee Are As Follows

7-11 • SNCC: Founding Statement 414

7-12 • NAACP Memo on Shaw Student Conference 415

7-13 • Roy Wilkins to Martin Luther King 417
Roy Wilkins

7-14 • Roy Wilkins to James Lawson 419
Roy Wilkins

7-15 • Roy Wilkins to Benjamin Mays 422
Roy Wilkins

7-16 • Democratic Convention Statement, July 1960 425
Marion Barry

7-17 • SNCC Fund Appeal, 1961 430

7-18 • "I'm Gonna Sit at the Welcome Table," Song 434

Unit 8
Atlanta: Protest to Politics 435

Introduction 436

8-1 • A Second Look 437
The Negro Citizen in Atlanta

8-2 • An Appeal for Human Rights 447

8-3 • Atlanta Student Movement 448

8-4 • Table of Organization: Atlanta Student Movement 450
From February 4th to the Present

8-5 • Student-Adult Liaison Committee 453

8-6 • "Student Movement and You," #1, #5, #6, and "Freedom and You" 455

8-7 • Christmas Boycott Called! 462

8-8 • 3,000 March in Atlanta 464

8-9 • 'Open City' Drive Begins 467

8-10 • Jails Fill as Protests Rise 468

8-11 • In Struggle: SNCC and the Black Awakening of the 1960s 470
Clayborne Carson

8-12 • Bond Attempts To Hear Voice of People 473

8-13 • BOND CAMPAIGN LITERATURE 475

8-14 • GEORGIA'S NEW ERA 478
THE YOUNG POLITICIANS

8-15 • THE JULIAN BOND CAMPAIGN 481

8-16 • BOND/MARTIN LUTHER KING MARCH 483

8-17 • THE BOND CASE: ITS MEANING TO AMERICA 484

UNIT 9
THE MOVEMENT EXPANDS 489

INTRODUCTION 490

9-1 • FREEDOM RIDE MAP 491

9-2 • THE FREEDOM RIDES 492

9-3 • FREEDOM RIDE—1961 495
James Peck

9-4 • BRINKLEY TAKES STAND AGAINST 'FREEDOM RIDERS' 503

9-5 • THE AGONY OF ALBANY 504

9-6 • THE BLOODY BATTLEGROUND OF ALBANY 509
Slater King

9-7 • THE NEW BLACK RADICALS 515
Charles McLaurin and Randy Battle

9-8 • REFLECTIONS ON THE DEATH OF A CHILD 519
Marion King

9-9 • ALBANY, FAILURE OR FIRST STEP? 521
Wyatt Tee Walker

9-10 • ALBANY POLICE DEPARTMENT 526
Laurie Pritchett

9-11 • HOMEGROWN MOVEMENT IN MACON 528
George A. Doss, Jr.

9-12 • "AIN'T GONNA LET NOBODY TURN ME ROUND," SONG 535

UNIT 10
BIRMINGHAM, SELMA, VIOLENCE AND NONVIOLENCE 537

INTRODUCTION 538

10-1 • SOUTHERN BOMBINGS 539

10-2 • FEAR AND HATRED GRIP BIRMINGHAM 540
RACIAL TENSION SMOLDERING AFTER BELATED SITDOWNS
Harrison E. Salisbury

10-3 • BIRMINGHAM AND BEYOND 544

10-4 • THE SOUTHERN CHRISTIAN LEADERSHIP CONFERENCE AND THE SECOND RECONSTRUCTION, 1957–1973 550
Adam Fairclough

10-5 • RETROSPECT AND PROSPECT 562

10-6 • CIVIL DISOBEDIENCE AND THE LAW 566

10-7 • REPORTS FROM SELMA'S "BLOODY SUNDAY" 570

10-8 • DALLAS COUNTY CHRISTIAN MINISTERS UNION 573

10-9 • THE BLACK MAN AND SELF-DEFENSE: 1962 574
THE CASE FOR ANSWERING VIOLENCE WITH VIOLENCE
Robert F. Williams

10-10 • LETTER FROM BIRMINGHAM CITY JAIL 582
Martin Luther King, Jr.

10-11 • IS VIOLENCE NECESSARY TO COMBAT INJUSTICE? 592
Robert F. Williams and Martin Luther King, Jr.

UNIT 11
MISSISSIPPI, VOTER EDUCATION PROJECT, FREEDOM SUMMER, AND 1964 CIVIL RIGHTS ACT 597

INTRODUCTION 599

11-1 • 111 ARRESTS MARK MISSISSIPPI FREEDOM DAY 600

11-2 • MISSISSIPPI: THE CLOSED SOCIETY 601
James W. Silver

11-3 • THE GENERAL CONDITION OF THE MISSISSIPPI NEGRO 621

11-4 • MISSISSIPPI 642
STRUCTURE OF THE MOVEMENT,
PRESENT OPERATIONS AND PROSPECTUS FOR THIS SUMMER

11-5 • FREEDOM SCHOOLS, MISSISSIPPI 650

11-6 • FREEDOM SCHOOL DOCUMENT 652

11-7 • MISSISSIPPI NEGRO VOTE CURTAILED IN CONGRESSIONAL PRIMARY 659

11-8 • SOVEREIGNTY COMMISSION (MS) MEMO, SEPTEMBER 23, 1965 662

11-9 • FIELD REPORTS—TELLING IT LIKE IT WAS 663

11-10 • SOVEREIGNTY COMMISSION (MS) MEMO, JUNE 26, 1964 678

11-11 • THE ROAD TO MISSISSIPPI 679

11-12 • AFFIDAVITS FROM MISSISSIPPI BLACK PAPER 693

11-13 • LIFE IN MISSISSIPPI — 703
AN INTERVIEW WITH FANNIE LOU HAMER
J. H. O'Dell

11-14 • CIVIL RIGHTS LAW COMPLIANCE VARIES — 710

11-15 • MAPS, CHARTS ON 1964 CIVIL RIGHTS ACT — 712

11-16 • SNCC FUND-RAISING LETTER — 714

UNIT 12
COMPETING FORCES I — 719

INTRODUCTION — 720

12-1 • "WHICH SIDE ARE YOU ON," SONG — 721

12-2 • QUESTIONS RAISED BY MOSES — 722
TRANSCRIPT OF THE TALK GIVEN BY BOB MOSES AT THE 5TH ANNIVERSARY OF SNCC
Bob Moses

12-3 • SNCC POSITION PAPER: WOMEN IN THE MOVEMENT — 725

12-4 • THE ROLE OF BLACK WOMEN IN THE CIVIL RIGHTS MOVEMENT — 727
Anne Standley

12-5 • SHOULD CIVIL RIGHTS WORKERS TAKE A STAND ON VIETNAM? — 741
Howard Zinn

12-6 • THE WAR IN VIETNAM — 743

12-7 • THE FREEDOM MOVEMENT AND THE WAR IN VIETNAM — 745
Robert S. Browne

12-8 • SNCC POSITION PAPER: VIETNAM — 755

12-9 • SNCC VIETNAM COMIC BOOK — 757

UNIT 13
COMPETING FORCES II — 769

INTRODUCTION — 770

13-1 • FROM CIVIL RIGHTS TO BLACK POWER: THE CASE OF SNCC, 1960–1966 — 771
Allen J. Matusow

13-2 • SCLC TACKLES ECONOMIC PROBLEMS — 788

13-3 • A MOVEMENT TURNS TO ECONOMICS — 790
MISSISSIPPI REVISITED
Liz Shirah

13-4 • THE SNCC TRENDS: CHALLENGE TO WHITE AMERICA — 793
Anne Braden

13-5 • BLACK—WHITE RELATIONS: A TIME OF SEARCHING **800**
Virginia Collins and Ed Hamlett

13-6 • BLACK POWER: ITS NEED AND SUBSTANCE **804**
Stokely Carmichael and Charles V. Hamilton

13-7 • LIBERATION BY ANY MEANS NECESSARY **815**
ADDRESS TO A MEETING IN NEW YORK, 1964
Malcolm X

UNIT 1

SEGREGATION'S ORIGINS

INTRODUCTION 2

1-1 • PROLOGUE: THE LEGACY OF THE FIRST RECONSTRUCTION 3
Manning Marable

1-2 • PLESSY V. FERGUSON: THE BIRTH OF JIM CROW 10
C. Vann Woodward

1-3 • IN BLACK AND WHITE 18
Edward Ayers

INTRODUCTION

An understanding of the Civil Rights Movement must begin with an understanding of the origins of segregation. Manning Marable, C. Vann Woodward, and Edward Ayers, three well known historians of African-American life and the South, analyze the institutionalization of Jim Crow in the South. "Prologue" (1-1) describes briefly Reconstruction (1865–1877), the period that followed the Civil War. Marable argues that these 12 years set the tone for the next 100 years of race relations in the United States. C. Vann Woodward's "The Birth of Jim Crow" (1-2) is based on his famous 1955 book *The Strange Career of Jim Crow.* Woodward asserts that segregation was a relatively recent phenomenon, emerging as late as the 1890s. In addition, he postulates that stateways—the segregation laws passed in the 1890s—changed the South's racial folkways—the way people actually acted. Published just after the *Brown v. Board of Education* decision was handed down, Woodward wanted to convince Americans that what the law had done to solidify segregation it could also do to end it. When *Strange Career* appeared in 1955 these ideas were considered revolutionary to most Americans, especially Southerners. "In Black and White" (1-3), a chapter from Edward Ayers's recent book *The Promise of the New South,* is the state-of-the-art interpretation of the development of segregation, combining synthesis with his own sharp insights. Though he appears to share much in common with Woodward, Ayers is dubious about the ability of stateways to change folkways in American life, believing that a more complex interplay exists between stateways and folkways.

UNIT 1-1

PROLOGUE: THE LEGACY OF THE FIRST RECONSTRUCTION

Manning Marable

> In two historic instances, Negro Americans have been beneficiaries—as well as victims—of the national compulsion to level or to blur distinctions. The first leveling ended the legal status of slavery, the second the legal system of segregation. Both abolitions left the beneficiaries still suffering under handicaps inflicted by the system abolished.
>
> —C. Vann Woodward, *The Strange Career of Jim Crow*

> What is the object of writing the history of Reconstruction? Is it to wipe out the disgrace of a people which fought to make slaves of Negroes? Is it to show that the North had higher motives than freeing black men? Is it to prove that Negroes were black angels? No, it is simply to establish the Truth, on which Right in the future may be built.
>
> —W.E.B. Du Bois, *Black Reconstruction in America, 1860–1880*

I

During two brief moments in history, the United States experienced major social movements which, at their core, expressed a powerful vision of multicultural democracy and human equality. The first was developed before the seminal conflict in American history, the Civil War (1861–65), and came to fruition in the twelve-year period of reunion, reconstruction and racial readjustment which followed (1865–77). Almost a century later, a "Second Reconstruction" occurred. Like the former period, the Second Reconstruction was a series of massive confrontations concerning the status of the Afro-American and other national minorities (*e.g.* Indians, Chicanos, Puerto Ricans, Asians) in the nation's economic, social and political institutions. Both movements brought about the end of rigid racial/caste structures which had been used to oppress blacks for many decades. Both elevated articulate and charismatic black leaders from the Afro-American working class and fragile middle class. Both were fought primarily in the Southern U.S., although in certain respects both inspired major socio-economic reforms in the Northern states as well. In both instances, the Federal government was viewed as a 'reluctant ally' of the blacks and their progressive white supporters, whereas the opponents to black equality were primarily white Southern Democrats and substantial numbers of white small-business and working-class people. Both movements pressured the Federal courts and Congress to ratify and to validate legislative measures which promoted greater racial equality and an improvement in the material status of blacks and poor whites. Finally, both movements eventually succumbed to internal contradictions, the loss of Northern white support, and the re-emergence of the South's tradition of inequality and racial prejudice as the dominant theme of U.S. public policies *vis á vis* blacks. History never repeats itself exactly, so it would be foolish to view the period of racial rebellion from 1945 to the present strictly through the prism of the past. Nevertheless, no real understanding of modern America is possible without an analysis of this nation's ongoing burden of race and class, a social and economic dilemma which was created by almost 250 years of chattel slavery. The racial patterns of the present and the possibilities for the future are buried in that past, in the myriad of successes and failures of the Civil War, and the First Reconstruction. It is here that our assessment of modern American race relations must begin.

More than any other modern nation in the world, with the possible exception of South Africa, the United States developed from the beginning a unique socio-economic structure and a political apparatus which was simultaneously racist, stubbornly capitalist, and committed to a limited form of bourgeois democracy: a racist/capitalist state. In electoral politics, free blacks from the eighteenth century onward found it difficult if not impossible to exercise the franchise. North Carolina permitted some blacks to vote in 1667, for example, but repealed the measure in 1715. At the election of George Washington in 1789, no Southern state permitted blacks to vote. In the nineteenth century, Northern states passed anti-black voting restrictions as well. In 1823, New York established a stiff property qualification which effectively eliminated blacks from voting. Pennsylvania and Indiana denied black males the right to vote in 1838 and 1851, respectively. In most states, blacks were forbidden by law to pursue certain vocations. Free blacks in South Carolina, for example, could not work as clerks; Maryland blacks were forbidden to sell wheat, corn or tobacco without a state license after 1805; Georgia's free blacks briefly lost the right to own or sell property in 1818. The primary source for all discriminatory legislation, North and South, prior to the Civil War, was the omnipresence of slavery. The 'peculiar institution' was the South's chief mode of agricultural production, and its existence, and the unquenching demand for servile black labor, directly and indirectly influenced the shape of every state's laws and relations with blacks. The growth of the slavery mode of production generated increasing political and social conflicts within American society over a period of eight decades, which culminated in the Civil War.

The white North did not wage the Civil War 'to free the slaves.' Most Republicans, including Lincoln, expressed absolutely no support for the idea of social and political equality between the races. This was, at first, clearly a "white man's war," fought to preserve Federal authority. Throughout the conflict, blacks in the North continued to experience racist assaults. When blacks were hired to work on riverboats in 1862, for example, white residents of Cincinnati, Ohio, were so outraged that they looted and burned the city's black districts. In July 1863, white New Yorkers destroyed black-owned stores, burned a black orphanage, and lynched black women and men in a four-day racist rampage. It was only after white military casualty figures mounted that an alarmed white public began to accept the suggestion that Northern blacks should be permitted to join the Union army in combat units. The Enlistment Act of July 1862 ordered that black troops should receive half the amount of salary that whites received. Despite this insult, about 186,000 blacks enlisted in the Union army during the conflict. Half of these troops were from the South. In a series of bitter engagements with the Confederate army, they fought with courage and distinction which amazed racists on both sides of the struggle. Partially due to the brutal policy of "no quarter" which many Southern troops exercised when fighting blacks, 38,000 black soldiers were killed in the war.

By the battle of Shiloh in April 1862, it became evident to the Lincoln administration that a disruption of the South's labor force was a necessity in order to win the war. In July 1862, Congress legally freed any slaves who had run away from the plantations to join the Union army. Three months earlier, Congress abolished slavery in Washington, D.C. and provided up to $300 per slave to the former owners. On 1 January 1863, Lincoln freed all slaves who lived in rebel territory not yet controlled by the Union army. Technically, slavery as a legal institution did not end in the United States until the ratification of the Thirteenth Amendment in December 1865. Practically, black emancipation occurred not by fiat, but by the direct actions of the slaves themselves. Thousands waited, watching for the first opportunity to escape. Northern and Southern whites began to understand what virtually every black American, slave or free, had first comprehended. "After the first few months," noted black scholar W.E.B. Du Bois observed, "everybody knew that slavery was done with; that no matter who won, the condition of the slave could never be the same after this disaster of war."[1] As nameless chattels, they had been raped, whipped, sold on the auction block, worked in the hot fields of endless cotton rows from dawn to dreary dusk. As men and women, they departed defiantly, with every expectation that their ordeal would soon end, and the freedom was close at hand. "To win the war," DuBois wrote, "America freed the slave and armed him; and the threat to arm the mass of black workers of the Confederacy stopped the war."[2]

Reconstruction actually began barely one year after the conflict started, when in July 1862, one Union general, Rufus Saxon, confiscated plantations along the Carolina coast and promoted the development of black-owned family farms. General William T. Sherman issued Order No. 15 in January 1865, which seemed to promise land to the former slaves. Other Union officers and politicians held property rights as superior to whatever claims blacks made for a just return for 250 years of unpaid labor power. General Nathaniel P. Banks ordered Louisiana blacks to return to their masters and to accept absurdly low wages. After Lincoln's assassination, President Andrew Johnson, a Southerner, promptly voided most of the land transfers to blacks, and returned the property to wealthy whites. In 1866, the Governor of Mississippi complained that the presence of 9,000 black troops in his state promoted the rumor that former slaves would be given property. President Johnson ordered all black troops out of the state within five months. Despite these and other problems, blacks attempted to purchase land wherever and whenever possible. By the early 1870s, Virginia black farmers had purchased 80,000 to 100,000 acres. A decade after the war, Georgia blacks owned approximately 400,000 acres, worth $1.3 million. The failure of the Federal government to recognize the necessity for massive land redistribution, along the lines of what blacks themselves called "forty acres and a mule," would be the principal reason for the failure of the First Reconstruction. In most Southern counties by the mid-1870s, 5 percent of the white farmers controlled at least 40 percent of the productive agricultural land. The upper one-tenth of the white farmers in most states owned anything from one-half to two-thirds of the farmland. Racial equality could not occur in political and social relations when economic power was held in relatively few hands.

In non-economic matters, however, Reconstruction produced major changes in the social status of blacks. The Federal government launched the Freedmen's Bureau, which provided food and clothing to millions. The Bureau opened 46 hospitals for blacks across the South. By 1870, its educational institutions claimed one-quarter of a million students and almost 10,000 instructors. A number of Bureau sponsored colleges became the basis for Afro-American higher education: Howard University of Washington, D.C., Atlanta University, Fisk University, and Hampton Institute, are among the most prominent examples. Prior to the Civil War, most Southern states had no real public school systems. With blacks as voters and legislators, the public school was made accessible to the poor of both races. Mississippi's constitution of 1868 created a biracial public school system for the entire state, and legislators set about the task of constructing hundreds of school buildings. The delegates at South Carolina's constitutional convention that same year ratified a proposal for universal education, and proposed $900,000 in expenditures for the public schools. Black religious organizations, notably the African Methodist Episcopal Church, were actively involved in educational and health care efforts. From 1865 to 1869, black churches established 257 black schools in North Carolina alone, which served 15,600 black students. State legislatures passed legislation creating orphanages and other public charities for blacks and whites.

The electoral defeat of Congressional Democrats in November 1866, and the subsequent impeachment of Johnson, shifted effective power from the President to the "Radical Republicans." The effect of this political transition was felt almost at once: the passage of the Fourteenth Amendment, which guaranteed blacks civil rights; the Fifteenth Amendment, which allowed black male adults the electoral franchise; and the Federal government's acceptance of black legislative representation, both in the state and nation. Reconstruction state governments, as a rule, tended to have a smaller percentage of blacks as merited by their respective numbers in each state. Only one Southern state, Mississippi, appointed or elected blacks to the U.S. Senate. Only fourteen blacks were elected to the U.S. House of Representatives during Reconstruction. Most of the states' top offices were filled by white Southerners. White historians, dismayed by the phantom of "Negro rule," have tried to claim that these men were unfit for public office. Even their white contemporaries, influenced by the deep racism of the day, knew otherwise. Four of the sixteen elected to Congress had received college diplomas; five were prominent lawyers. Francis L. Cardozo, who served as South Carolina's secretary of state from 1868 to 1872, was a former student of the University of Glasgow. Mississippi's two black U.S. Senators, Hiram R. Revels and Blanche K. Bruce, were superior in intellect and political acumen to most of their counterparts. Revels was trained in an Ohio seminary, and attended Knox College in Illinois. During the war he served as a chaplain in the Union army, and in the late 1860s he emerged as the leader of Natchez, Mississippi's black community. Bruce had served as tax collector, sheriff and state superintendent of schools before his election to the U.S. Senate in 1874. He purchased hundreds of acres of farmland in the state's "blackbelt" region and became one of the most affluent public figures in the South. Between 1869 and 1901, a total of 816 black men were elected as Federal and state legislators. Of these, 63 percent came from just four Southern states: South Carolina (218); Virginia (93); North Carolina (82); and Louisiana (122). Some Southern and border states with substantial black populations had few or no black elected officials: Kentucky (0); Maryland (0); Tennessee (12); West Virginia (1).

The drive for biracial democracy could not be contained in the South. Northern blacks fought for the repeal of every law which discriminated by race. Gradually, Northern states were forced to amend or abolish many racist regulations. In 1865, Illinois finally permitted blacks to testify in courtrooms. Blacks in Washington, D.C., in 1865, led by the fiery abolitionist Sojourner Truth, led a boycott of public transportation facilities which practiced Jim Crow. Philadelphia blacks fought successfully to bar segregation in the city's streetcars. Rhode Island blacks forced state officials to desegregate public schools in 1866. Northern blacks pressured their white Congressmen to ratify the Enforcement Act of May 1870, and the Civil Rights Act of March 1875, which further protected blacks' civil liberties. The period even brought black women leaders to the center of national attention. Frances Ellen Watkins Harper, for instance, travelled and spoke throughout the South from 1865 to 1871, raising capital for black schools and hospitals. In the 1870s, she became Assistant Superintendent of the YMCA school in Philadelphia, and subsequently helped to establish the National Association of Colored Women. Across the nation, blacks in commerce, politics and education were building new institutions with incredible energy. Between 1865 and 1900, to take a single example, over 1200 black-owned newspapers were established. This fact alone, from a population which was 90–95 percent illiterate in 1860, is awesome.

The decline and demise of the First Reconstruction grew apparent before the Panic of 1873 and the economic recession which lasted for four years afterwards. Northern capitalists recognized that they did not have to condone biracial rule in the South in order to develop the predominantly rural region. Conservatives in the Republican Party found that their own interests converged with those of the former planter class to a greater extent than they did with poor blacks. As historian Lawrence Goodwyn observes, "the bankers, manufacturers, shippers, and merchants" who ran the Republican Party "soon wearied of their attempt to build a postwar party in the South based on black suffrage. As elected victories in the 1860s and 1870s proved that the [Republicans] could rule with a basically Northern constituency, Negroes, their morale declining, and white radical abolitionists, their numbers thinning, lost the intra-party debate over Southern policy."[3] White Southern hostility towards blacks expressed itself dramatically with race riots in Meridian, Mississippi, in 1871, and in Savannah, Georgia, and Hamburg, South Carolina, in 1872. White terrorists organized a series of vigilante groups, including the Klu Klux Klan and the Knights of the White Camelia, to intimidate black voters and elected officials. In the disputed presidential election of 1876, the Republicans secured their narrow victory by promising to curtail civil rights measures and to allow the re-establishment of white supremacy in the South. After the so-called Compromise of 1877, Federal troops were eventually ordered to leave the South.

The end of Reconstruction produced a political and social climate of fear and intimidation for every black person in the South. Despite a brief period from the late 1880s, to the mid-1890s when black and white Southern farmers attempted to develop a biracial opposition to the planters through the Populist Party, the conditions of black life and labor deteriorated rapidly. Politically, the Federal government abandoned any commitment to biracial democracy. In 1883, the Supreme Court declared the Civil Rights Act of 1875 unconstitutional. The principle of "separate but equal," America's legal justification for domestic *apartheid*, was ordained by the Supreme Court in the *Plessy v. Ferguson* decision of 1896. By the 1890s, Southern states had begun to rewrite their Reconstruction-era constitutions, denying blacks and many poor whites the right to vote. The effect of these new state constitutions was as striking as it was undemocratic. In Alabama, for example, there were 181,000 blacks who were eligible to vote in 1900; two years later, merely 3000 were noted as registered voters. Republican presidents supported the creation of a "Lily White" wing of their party in the South, which would deny blacks the right to participate even in their own political organizations. Political disfranchisement was also facilitated by extra-legal means. Between 1882 and 1903, 2060 blacks were lynched in the United States. Some of the black victims were children and pregnant women; many were burned alive at the stake; others were castrated with axes or knives, blinded with hot pokers, or decapitated.

II

The experiment in biracial democracy was effectively at an end. For many millions of black farmers, the only hope for political survival and economic self-sufficiency was in an exodus from the South. The earliest migrants left in the 1870s. Benjamin "Pap" Singleton, a black mortician, led over 7000 blacks from Kentucky and Tennessee into Kansas. In 1879, a second wave of 60,000 black farm families walked and rode from the lower Mississippi River Valley into Kansas. Many blacks later migrated to Oklahoma Territory; between 1891 and 1910 more than two dozen all-black settlements were established in the state. The vast majority who fled, however, moved to the North. The flood of black humanity increased steadily: 170,000 migrants in 1900–10; 454,000 in 1910–20; 749,000 in 1920–30. Black migration dropped during the Great Depression decade, 1930–40, with only 349,000. From 1940–50, the movement accelerated again, totalling 1,599,000 for the decade. In the thirty years between 1910 and 1940, the black population in Illinois increased from 109,000 to 387,000; in New York from 134,000 to 571,000; in Pennsylvania from 194,000 to 470,000. In 1940, 22 percent of all blacks lived in the North, compared to 10 percent in 1910. This major demographic shift produced dramatic changes in the labor patterns of blacks. In 1890, 63 percent of all black males were agricultural workers, 22 percent were domestic servants, and only 14 percent worked in transportation, communications, and/or manufacturing. In 1930, the percentage of black male agricultural workers declined to 42 percent. Only 11 percent were domestics, but 36 percent were employed in manufacturing, transportation and communications. The small, black middle class which emerged after slavery had begun to multiply. The number of black public and private schoolteachers more than doubled from 1910–40. The number of black-owned businesses between 1904 and 1929 grew from 20,000 to over 70,000. Between 1900 and 1914, 47 black-owned banks were established. The percentage of black youth between the ages of 5 to 20 enrolled in school increased from 33 percent in 1890 to 65 percent 50 years later. In the same period, black illiteracy dropped from 61 percent to 15 percent. The migration from the rural South to the urban Northeast and Midwest, and the growth of a black urban working class throughout the nation, brought an improvement in health care, education, economic and political life for millions of black people. Nevertheless, the substantial gap between the socio-economic and political status of whites and blacks still existed, and was reinforced across the nation by the rule of Jim Crow.

Even these marginal improvements in the material existence of many blacks did nothing to halt the proliferation of brutal white violence. The Jim Crow system of racial exploitation was, like slavery, both a caste/social order for regimenting cultural and political relations, and an economic structure which facilitated the superexploitation of blacks' labor power. Unlike slavery, Jim Crow was much more clearly capitalistic, since white owners of factories did not have to purchase entire black families in order to obtain the services of a single wage-earner. However, in caste/racial relations, both systems were dependent upon the omnipresence of violence or coercion. Throughout the early twentieth century, white politicians, business leaders and most workers defended the necessity to discipline the black working class via lynchings, public executions, and the like. One particularly brutal moment occurred immediately after World War I, when whites across the country committed an array of bestial acts against blacks, unheard of even in slavery. In the "Red Summer of 1919" 70 blacks were lynched, including ten soldiers who had fought "to preserve democracy against the Kaiser." Eleven of these blacks were burned alive. In the Chicago race riot of 1919, 38 persons were killed, and 537 were injured. Up to 1000 black families were burned out of their homes in the city. Whites in Knoxville, Tennessee, destroyed black property worth $50,000. Dozens of black cotton farmers and laborers were shot in Elaine, Arkansas. An Omaha, Nebraska, white mob attacked a black man suspect accused of raping a white woman. The man was shot over 1,000 times, and the corpse was lynched in the city's central district. Throughout the carnage, the Federal government remained blind and mute. State governments increased stringent segregation laws to the point of high absurdity. South Carolina insisted that black and white textile workers could not use the same doorways, pay windows, bathrooms or even the same water buckets. Many cities passed ordinances which kept blacks out of public parks and white residential districts. Atlanta outlawed black barbers from clipping the hair of white children and women in 1926. There were soon segregated zoos, baseball clubs, buses, taxicabs, restaurants, and race tracks. Historian C. Vann Woodward noted one extreme case: A Birmingham ordinance got down to particulars in 1930 by making it "unlawful for a Negro and a white person to play together or in company with each other" at dominoes or checkers.[4] For all practical purposes, the black American was proscribed by the state from any meaningful political and social activity for two generations. Behind this powerful proscription, as always, was the use of force.

The first four decades of the twentieth century witnessed major social, cultural and economic changes for most black Americans. Yet after two world wars and a devastating economic depression, the barrier of the color line still existed in the United States. Most white Americans, looking backward at Reconstruction, cautioned Negroes not to demand abrupt changes in their caste status too quickly. Jim Crow would gradually be allowed to decline after another century or two of racial improvement and social adjustment. But in growing numbers, blacks and other national minorities looked at America's experiment in multicultural democracy as the harbinger for a better life in the immediate future. In the prophetic words of W.E.B. Du Bois, the campaign for freedom had hardly begun:

> This the American black man knows: his fight here is a fight to the finish. Either he dies or wins. If he wins it will be by no subterfuge or evasion of amalgamation. He will enter modern civilization here in America as a black man on terms of perfect and unlimited equality with any white man, or he will enter not at all. Either extermination root and branch, or absolute equality. There can be no compromise. This is the last great battle of the West.[5]

ENDNOTES

1. W.E.B. Du Bois, *Black Reconstruction in America*, 1860–1880 (New York: Atheneum, 1971), p. 59.

2. *Ibid.*, p. 378.

3. Lawrence Goodwyn, *The Populist Moment: A Short History of the Agrarian Revolt in America* (New York: Oxford University Press, 1978), pp. 5–6.

4. C. Vann Woodward, *The Strange Case of Jim Crow* (New York: Oxford University Press, 1974), p. 118.

5. Du Bois, *Black Revolution*, p. 703.

UNIT 1-2

PLESSY V. FERGUSON: THE BIRTH OF JIM CROW

C. Vann Woodward

In the spring of 1885, Charles Dudley Warner, Mark Twain's friend, neighbor, and onetime collaborator from Hartford, Connecticut, visited the International Exposition at New Orleans. He was astonished to find that "white and colored people mingled freely, talking and looking at what was of common interest," that blacks "took their full share of the parade and the honors," and that the two races associated "in unconscious equality of privileges." During his visit he saw "a colored clergyman in his surplice seated in the chancel of the most important white Episcopal church in New Orleans, assisting in the service."

It was a common occurrence in the 1880s for foreign travellers and northern visitors to comment, sometimes with distaste and always with surprise, on the freedom of association between white and black people in the South. Yankees in particular were unprepared for what they found and sometimes estimated that conditions below the Potomac were better than those above. There was discrimination, to be sure, and blacks were often excluded from first-class public accommodations—as they were in the North. But that was done on the responsibility of private owners or managers and not by requirement of law. According to the Supreme Court's decision in the Civil Rights Cases of 1883 the federal law gave no protection from such private acts.

Where discrimination existed it was often erratic and inconsistent. On trains the usual practice was to exclude blacks from first-class or "ladies'" cars but to permit them to mix with whites in second-class or "smoking" cars. In the old seaboard states of the South, however, blacks were as free to ride first class as whites. In no state was segregation on trains complete, and in none was it enforced by law. The age of Jim Crow was still to come.

The first genuine Jim Crow law requiring railroads to carry blacks in separate cars or behind partitions was adopted by Florida in 1887. Mississippi followed this example in 1888; Texas in 1889; Louisiana in 1890; Alabama, Arkansas, Georgia, and Tennessee in 1891; and Kentucky in 1892. The Carolinas and Virginia did not fall into line until the last three years of the century.

Blacks watched with despair while the legal foundations for the Jim Crow system were laid and the walls of segregation mounted around them. Their disenchantment with the hopes based on the Civil War amendments and the Reconstruction laws was nearly complete by 1890. The American commitment to equality, solemnly attested by three amendments to the Constitution and by elaborate civil rights acts, was virtually repudiated. The "compromise of 1877" between the Hayes Republicans and the southern conservatives had resulted in the withdrawal of federal troops from the South and the formal end of Reconstruction. What had started then as a retreat had within a decade turned into a rout. Northern radicals and liberals had abandoned the cause; the courts had rendered the Constitution helpless; the Republican party had forsaken the cause it had sponsored. A tide of racism was mounting in the country unopposed.

The black community of New Orleans, with its strong infusion of French and other nationalities, was in a strategic position to furnish leadership for the resistance against segregation. Many of these people had culture, education, and some wealth, as well as a heritage of several generations of freedom. Unlike the great majority of blacks, they were city people with an established professional class and a high degree of literacy. By ancestry as well as by residence they were associated with Latin cultures at variance with Anglo-American ideas of race relations. Their forebears had lived under the Code Noir decreed for Louisiana by Louis XIV, and their city faced out upon Latin America.

When the Jim Crow car bill was introduced in the Louisiana legislature, New Orleans blacks organized to fight it. Blacks were still voting in large numbers, and there were sixteen black senators and representatives in the Louisiana General Assembly. On May 24, 1890, that body received "A Protest of the American Citizens' Equal Rights Association of Louisiana Against Class Legislation." An organization of black people, the association protested that the pending bill was "unconstitutional, unamerican, unjust, dangerous and against sound public policy." It would, declared the protest, "be a free license to the evilly-disposed that they might with impunity insult, humiliate, and otherwise maltreat inoffensive persons, and especially women and children who should happen to have a dark skin."

On July 10, 1890, the Assembly passed the bill, the governor signed it, and it became law. Entitled "An Act to promote the comfort of passengers," the new law required railroads "to provide equal but separate accommodations for the white and black races." Two members of the Equal Rights Association, L. A. Martinet, editor of the *New Orleans Crusader,* and R. L. Desdunes, placed heavy blame on the sixteen colored members of the Assembly for the passage of the bill. According to Martinet, "they were completely the masters of the situation." They had but to withhold their support for a bill desired by the powerful Louisiana Lottery Company until the Jim Crow bill was killed. "But in an evil moment," he added, "our Representatives turned their ears to listen to the golden siren," and "did so for a 'consideration.'"

Putting aside recriminations, the *Crusader* declared: "The Bill is now a law. The next thing is what we are going to do?" The editor spoke testily of boycotting the railroads, but concluded that "the next thing is . . . to begin to gather funds to test the constitutionality of this law. We'll make a case, a test case, and bring it before the Federal Courts." On September 1, 1891, a group of eighteen men of color formed a "Citizens' Committee to Test the Constitutionality of the Separate Car Law."

Money came in slowly at first, but by October 11, Martinet could write that the committee had already collected $1,500 and that more could be expected "after we have the case well started." Even before the money was collected, Martinet had opened a correspondence about the case with Albion Winegar Tourgée of Mayville, New York, and on October 10 the Citizens' Committee formally elected Tourgée "leading counsel in the case, from beginning to end, with power to choose associates."

This action called back into the stream of history a name prominent in the annals of Reconstruction. Albion Tourgée was in 1890 probably the most famous surviving carpetbagger. His fame was due not so much to his achievements as a carpetbagger in North Carolina, significant though they were, as to the six novels about his Reconstruction experiences that he had published since 1879. Born in Ohio, of French Huguenot descent, he had served as an officer in the Union Army, and moved to Greensboro, North Carolina, in 1865 to practice law. He soon became a leader of the Radical Republican party, took a prominent part in writing the Radical Constitution of North Carolina, and served as a judge of the superior court for six years with considerable distinction. He brought to the fight against segregation in Louisiana a combination of zeal and ability that the Citizens' Committee of New Orleans would have found it hard to duplicate. They had reason to write him, "we know we have a friend in you & we know your ability is beyond question." He was informed that the committee's decision was made "spontaneously, warmly, & gratefully."

Tourgée's first suggestion was that the person chosen for defendant in the test case be "nearly white," but that proposal raised some doubts. "It would be quite difficult," explained Martinet, "to have a lady *too* nearly white refused admission to a 'white' car." He pointed out that "people of tolerably fair complexion, even if unmistakably colored, enjoy here a large degree of immunity from the accursed prejudice. . . . To make this case would require some tact." He would volunteer himself, "but I am one of those whom a fair complexion favors. I go everywhere, in all public places, though well-known all over the city, & never is anything said to me. On the cars it would be the same thing. In fact, color prejudice, in this respect does not affect me. But, as I have said, we can try it, with another."

Railroad officials proved surprisingly co-operative. The first one approached, however, confessed that his road "did not enforce the law." It provided the Jim Crow car and posted the required sign, but told its conductors to molest no one who ignored instructions. Officers of two other roads "said the law was a bad and mean one; they would like to get rid of it," and asked for time to consult counsel. "They want to help us," said Martinet, "but dread public opinion." The extra expense of separate cars was one reason for railroad opposition to the Jim Crow law.

It was finally agreed that a white passenger should object to the presence of a black in a "white" coach, that the conductor should direct the black passenger to go to the Jim Crow car, and that he should refuse to go. "The conductor will be instructed not to use force or molest," reported Martinet, "& *our* white passenger will swear out the affidavit. This will give us our *habeas corpus* case, I hope." On the appointed day, February 24, 1892, Daniel F. Desdunes, a young black man, bought a ticket for Mobile, boarded the Louisville & Nashville Railroad, and took a seat in the white coach.

All went according to plan. Desdunes was committed for trial to the Criminal District Court in New Orleans and released on bail. On March 21, James C. Walker, a local attorney associated with Tourgée in the case, filed a plea protesting that his client was not guilty and attacking the constitutionality of the Jim Crow law. He wrote Tourgée that he intended to go to trial as early as he could.

Between the lawyers there was not entire agreement on procedure. Walker favored the plea that the law was void because it attempted to regulate interstate commerce, over which the Supreme Court held that Congress had exclusive jurisdiction. Tourgée was doubtful. "What we want," he wrote Walker, "is not a verdict of not guilty, nor a defect in this law but a decision whether such a law can be legally enacted and enforced in any state and we should get everything off the track and out of the way for such a decision." Walker confessed that "it's hard for me to give up my pet hobby that the law is void as a regulation of interstate commerce," and Tourgée admitted that he "may have spoken too lightly of the interstate commerce matter."

The discussion was ended abruptly and the whole approach altered before Desdunes' case came to trial by a decision of the Louisiana Supreme Court handed down on May 25. In this case, which was of entirely independent origin, the court reversed the ruling of a lower court and upheld the Pullman Company's plea that the Jim Crow law was unconstitutional in so far as it applied to interstate passengers.

Desdunes was an interstate passenger holding a ticket to Alabama, but the decision was a rather empty victory. The law still applied to intrastate passengers, and since all states adjacent to Louisiana had by this time adopted similar or identical Jim Crow laws, the exemption of interstate passengers was of no great importance to the blacks of Louisiana, and it left the principle against which they contended unchallenged. On June 1, Martinet wired Tourgée on behalf of the committee, saying that "Walker wants new case wholly within state limits," and asking Tourgée's opinion. Tourgée wired his agreement.

One week later, on June 7, Homer Adolph Plessy bought a ticket in New Orleans, boarded the East Louisiana Railroad bound for Covington, a destination "wholly within the state limits," and took a seat in the white coach. Since Plessy later described himself as "seven-eighths Caucasian and one-eighth African blood," and swore that "the admixture of colored blood is not discernible," it may be assumed that the railroad had been told of the plan and had agreed to co-operate. When Plessy refused to comply with the conductor's request that he move to the Jim Crow car, he was arrested by Detective Christopher C. Cain "and quietly accompanied the officer." The *New Orleans Times-Democrat* remarked that "It is generally believed that Plessy intends testing the law before the courts."

In due course Homer Plessy's case became *Plessy v. Ferguson.* The latter name belonged to John H. Ferguson, Judge of Section A of the Criminal District Court for the Parish of New Orleans, who overruled the plea of Tourgée and Walker, the defendant's counsel, that the Jim Crow law was null and void because it was in conflict with the Constitution of the United States. Plessy then applied to the State Supreme Court for a writ of prohibition and certiorari and was given a hearing in November, 1892. The court recognized that neither the interstate commerce clause nor the question of equality of accommodations was involved and held that "the sole question" was whether a law requiring "separate but equal accommodations" violated the Fourteenth Amendment. Citing numerous decisions of lower federal courts to the effect that accommodations did not have to be identical to be equal, the court as expected upheld the law.

"We have been at pains to expound this statute," added the court, "because the dissatisfaction felt with it by a portion of the people seems to us so unreasonable that we can account for it only on the ground of some misconception."

Chief Justice Francis Redding Tillou Nicholls, heading the court that handed down this decision in 1892, had signed the Jim Crow act as governor when it was passed in 1890. Previously he had served as the "Redeemer" governor who took over Louisiana from the carpetbaggers in 1877 and inaugurated a brief regime of conservative paternalism. In those days Nicholls had denounced race bigotry, appointed blacks to office, and attracted many of them to his party.

L. A. Martinet wrote Tourgée that Nicholls in those years had been "fair & just to colored men" and had, in fact, "secured a degree of protection to the colored people not enjoyed under Republican Governors." But in November, 1892, the wave of Populist rebellion among the white farmers was reaching its crest in the South, and Judge Nicholls' change of course typified the concessions to racism that conservatives of his class made in their efforts to forestall or divert the rebellion. Nonetheless, at a further hearing Nicholls granted Plessy's petition for a writ of error that permitted him to seek redress before the Supreme Court of the United States.

The brief that Albion Tourgée submitted to the Supreme Court in behalf of Plessy breathed a spirit of equalitarianism that was more in tune with his carpetbagger days than with the prevailing spirit of the mid-nineties.

At the very outset, he advanced an argument in behalf of his client that unconsciously illustrated the paradox that had from the start haunted the American attempt to reconcile strong color prejudice with deep equalitarian commitments.

Plessy, he contended, had been deprived of property without due process of law. The "property" in question was the "reputation of being white." It was "the most valuable sort of property, being the master-key that unlocks the golden door of opportunity." Intense race prejudice excluded any man suspected of having black blood "from the friendship and companionship of the white man," and therefore from the avenues to wealth, prestige, and opportunity. "Probably most white persons if given the choice," he held, "would prefer death to life in the United States as *colored persons*."

Since Tourgée had proposed that a person who was "nearly white" be selected for the test case, it may be presumed that he did so with this argument in mind. But this was not a defense of the black man against discrimination by whites, but a defense of the "nearly" white man against the penalties of color. The argument, whatever its merits, apparently did not impress the Court.

Tourgée went on to develop more relevant points. He emphasized especially the incompatibility of the segregation law with the spirit and intent of the Thirteenth and particularly the Fourteenth amendments. Segregation perpetuated distinctions "of a servile character, coincident with the institution of slavery." He held that "slavery was a caste, a legal condition of subjection to the dominant class, a bondage quite separable from the incident of ownership." He scorned the pretense of impartiality and equal protection advanced in the defense of the "separate but equal" doctrine.

"The object of such a law," he declared, "is simply to debase and distinguish against the inferior race. Its purpose has been properly interpreted by the general designation of 'Jim Crow Car' law. Its object is to separate the blacks from the whites in public conveyances for the gratification and recognition of the sentiment of white superiority and white supremacy of right and power." He asked the members of the Court to imagine the tables turned and themselves ordered into a Jim Crow car. "What humiliation, what rage would then fill the judicial mind!" he exclaimed.

The clue to the true intent of the Louisiana statute was that it did not apply "to nurses attending the children of the other race." On this clause Tourgée shrewdly observed:

> The exemption of nurses shows that the real evil lies not in the color of the skin but in the relation the colored person sustains to the white. If he is a dependent it may be endured: if he is not, his presence is insufferable. Instead of being intended to promote the general comfort and moral well-being, this act is plainly and evidently intended to promote the happiness of one class by asserting its supremacy and the inferiority of another class. Justice is pictured blind and her daughter, the Law, ought at least to be color-blind.

Tourgée then asked the Court to look to the future. Should the separate-car law be upheld, he inquired, "what is to prevent the application of the same principle to other relations?" Was there any limit to such laws? "Why not require all colored people to walk on one side of the street and whites on the other? . . . One side of the street may be just as good as the other. . . . The question is not as to the *equality* of the privileges enjoyed, but *the right of the State to label one citizen as white and another as colored* in the common enjoyment of a public highway."

The Supreme Court did not get around to handing down a decision on *Plessy v. Ferguson* until 1896. In the years that intervened between the passage of the Louisiana segregation law in July, 1890, and the time of the eventual decision on its constitutionality in 1896, the retreat from the commitment to equality had quickened its pace in the South and met with additional acquiescence, encouragement, and approval in the North. Two states had already disfranchised the black citizen, and several others, including Louisiana, were planning to take the same course. In 1892 Congress defeated the Lodge Bill, designed to extend federal protection to elections, and in 1894 it wiped from the federal statute books a mass of Reconstruction laws for the protection of equal rights. And then, on September 18, 1895, Booker T. Washington delivered a famous speech embodying the so-called "Atlanta Compromise," which was widely interpreted as an acceptance of subordinate status for the black citizen by the foremost leader of the race.

On May 18, 1896, Justice Henry Billings Brown, a resident of Michigan but a native of Massachusetts, delivered the opinion of the Court in the case of *Plessy v. Ferguson.* His views upholding the defendant's case—that the "separate but equal" doctrine was constitutional—were in accord with those of all his brothers, with the possible exception of Justice David Josiah Brewer, who did not participate, and the certain exception of Justice John Marshall Harlan, who vigorously dissented in phrases that often echoed Tourgée's arguments. In approving, to all intents and purposes, the principle of segregation, Justice Brown followed not only the trend of the times, but a host of state judicial precedents, which he cited at length. That there were no federal judicial precedents to the contrary only added to the technical strength of his position. Just as telling, perhaps, was Brown's mention of the action of Congress in establishing segregated schools for the District of Columbia, an action endorsed by Radical Republicans who had supported the Fourteenth Amendment, and sustained in regular congressional appropriations ever since.

Similar laws, wrote Brown, were adopted by "the legislatures of many states, and have been generally, if not uniformly, sustained by the courts." The validity of such segregation laws, he maintained, depended on their "reasonableness." And in determining reasonableness, the legislature "is at liberty to act with reference to the established usages, customs, and traditions of the people, and with a view to the promotion of their comfort, and the preservation of the public peace and good order."

In addition to judicial precedent and accepted practice, Justice Brown ventured into the more uncertain fields of sociology and psychology for support of his opinion. He wrote:

> We consider the underlying fallacy of the plaintiff's argument to consist in the assumption that the enforced separation of the two races stamps the colored race with a badge of inferiority. If this be so, it is not by reason of anything found in the act, but solely because the colored race chooses to put that construction upon it. . . . The argument also assumes that social prejudices may be overcome by legislation, and that equal rights cannot be secured by the negro except by an enforced commingling of the two races. We cannot accept this proposition. . . . Legislation is powerless to eradicate racial instincts, or to abolish distinctions based upon physical differences, and the attempt to do so can only result in accentuating the difficulties of the present situation. If the civil and political rights of both races be equal, one cannot be inferior to the other civilly or politically. If one race be inferior to the other socially, the constitution of the United States cannot put them upon the same plane.

One of the most fascinating paradoxes in American jurisprudence is that the opinion of a native son of Massachusetts, Brown, should have bridged the gap between the radical equalitarian commitment of 1868 and the reactionary repudiation of that commitment in 1896; and that Harlan, a southerner, should have bridged the greater gap between the repudiation of 1896 and the radical rededication to the equalitarian idealism of 1868 in 1954. For the dissenting opinion of Justice Harlan, embodying many of the arguments of Plessy's ex-carpetbagger counsel, foreshadowed the Court's eventual repudiation of the *Plessy v. Ferguson* decision and the doctrine of "separate but equal" more than half a century later—a repudiation in which, fittingly enough, Harlan's grandson and namesake on the Warren Court wholly concurred.

The elder John Marshall Harlan is correctly described by Robert Cushman as "a Southern gentleman and a slave-holder, and at heart a conservative." A Kentuckian of the Whig persuasion, Harlan had opposed secession and fought in the Union Army, but at the same time he opposed both the emancipation of the slaves and the passage of civil rights laws to protect the rights of the freedmen. Shocked by Ku Klux excesses, he experienced a sudden conversion, renounced his former views, became a Republican in 1868, and was appointed to the Supreme Court by President Hayes in 1877.

After his conversion Harlan became one of the most outspoken champions of black rights of his time, and during his thirty-four years on the bench he lifted his voice repeatedly against denial of those rights by the dominant opinion of the Court. His famous dissent in the Civil Rights Cases of 1883 had denounced the "subtle and ingenious verbal criticism" by which "the substance and spirit of the recent amendments of the Constitution have been sacrificed." And in 1896 he was ready to strike another blow for his adopted cause.

Harlan held the Louisiana segregation law in clear conflict with both the Thirteenth and the Fourteenth amendments. The former "not only struck down the institution of slavery," but also "any burdens or disabilities that constitute badges of slavery or servitude," and segregation was just such a burden or badge. Moreover, the Fourteenth Amendment "added greatly to the dignity and glory of American citizenship, and to the security of personal liberty," and segregation denied to blacks the equal protection of both dignity and liberty. "The arbitrary separation of citizens, on the basis of race, while they are on a public highway," he said, "is a badge of servitude wholly inconsistent with the civil freedom and the equality before the law established by the constitution. It cannot be justified upon any legal grounds."

Harlan was as scornful as Tourgée had been of the claim that the separate-car law did not discriminate against the black citizen. "Every one knows," he declared, that its purpose was "to exclude colored people from coaches occupied by or assigned to white persons." This was simply a poorly disguised means of asserting the supremacy of one class of citizens over another. The justice continued:

> But in view of the constitution, in the eye of the law, there is in this country no superior, dominant, ruling class of citizens. There is no caste here. Our constitution is color-blind, and neither knows nor tolerates classes among citizens. In respect of civil rights, all citizens are equal before the law. The humblest is the peer of the most powerful. The law regards man as man, and takes no account of his surroundings, or of his color when his civil rights as guaranteed by the supreme law of the land are involved. . . . We boast of the freedom enjoyed by our people above all other peoples. But it is difficult to reconcile that boast with a state of law which, practically, puts the brand of servitude and degradation upon a large class of our fellow citizens,—our equals before the law. The thin disguise of "equal" accommodations for passengers in railroad coaches will not mislead any one, nor atone for the wrong this day done.

"The present decision, it may well be apprehended," predicted Harlan, "will not only stimulate aggressions, more or less brutal and irritating, upon the admitted rights of colored citizens, but will encourage the belief that it is possible, by means of state enactments, to defeat the beneficent purposes which the people of the United States had in view when they adopted the recent amendments of the constitution. . . . " For if the state may so regulate the railroads, "why may it not so regulate the use of the streets of its cities and towns as to compel white citizens to keep on one side of a street, and black citizens to keep on the other," or, for that matter, apply the same regulations to streetcars and other vehicles, or to courtroom, the jury box, the legislative hall, or to any other place of public assembly?

"In my opinion," the Kentuckian concluded, "the judgment this day rendered will, in time, prove to be quite as pernicious as the decision made by this tribunal in the Dred Scott Case."

But Harlan was without allies on the Court, and the country as a whole received the news of its momentous decision upholding the "separate but equal" doctrine in relative silence and apparent indifference. Thirteen years earlier the Civil Rights Cases had precipitated pages of news reports, hundreds of editorials, indignant rallies, congressional bills, a Senate report, and much general debate. In striking contrast, the *Plessy* decision was accorded only short, inconspicuous news reports and virtually no editorial comment outside the black press. A great change had taken place, and the Court evidently now gave voice to the dominant mood of the country. Justice Harlan had spoken for the forgotten convictions of a bygone era.

The racial aggressions he foresaw came in a flood after the decision of 1896. Even Harlan indicated by his opinion of 1899 in *Cummings v. Board of Education* that he saw nothing unconstitutional in segregated public schools. Virginia was the last state in the South to adopt the separate-car law, and she resisted it only until 1900. Up to that year this was the only law of the type adopted by a majority of the southern states. But on January 12, 1900, the editor of the *Richmond Times* was in full accord with the new spirit when he asserted: "It is necessary that this principle be applied in every relation of Southern life. God Almighty drew the color line and it cannot be obliterated. The negro must stay on his side of the line and the white man must stay on his side, and the sooner both races recognize this fact and accept it, the better it will be for both."

With a thoroughness approaching the incredible, the color line *was* drawn and the Jim Crow principle was applied even in those areas that Tourgée and Harlan had suggested a few years before as absurd extremes. In sustaining all these new laws, courts universally and confidently cited *Plessy v. Ferguson* as their authority. They continued to do so for more than half a century.

On April 4, 1950, Justice Robert H. Jackson wrote old friends in Jamestown, New York, of his surprise in running across the name of Albion W. Tourgée, once a resident of the nearby village of Mayville, in connection with segregation decisions then pending before the Supreme Court. "The *Plessy* case arose in Louisiana," he wrote, "and how Tourgée got into it I have not learned. In any event, I have gone to his old brief, filed here, and there is no argument made today that he would not make to the Court. He says, 'Justice is pictured blind and her daughter, the Law, ought at least to be color-blind.' Whether this was original with him, it has been gotten off a number of times since as original wit. Tourgée's brief was filed April 6, 1896 and now, just fifty-four years after, the question is again being argued whether his position will be adopted and what was a defeat for him in '96 be a postmortem victory."

Plessy v. Ferguson remained the law of the land for fifty-eight years lacking one day, from May 18, 1896, to May 17, 1954, when the Supreme Court at last renounced it in the school segregation cases of *Brown et al. v. Board of Education of Topeka, et al.* In that decision could indeed be found, at long last, a vindication, "a post-mortem victory"—not only for the ex-carpetbagger Tourgée, but for the ex-slaveholder Harlan as well.

April 1964

UNIT 1-3

IN BLACK AND WHITE

Edward Ayers

Every Human Emotion became entangled in Southern race relations. Booker T. Washington claimed to find "at least one white man who believed implicitly in one Negro, and one Negro who believed implicitly in one white man" wherever he traveled in the South. Yet even when human sympathy and friendship drew people together, the rituals of Southern race relations constrained and distorted the feelings. "There was a part of me in which it did not matter at all that they were black," Harry Crews remembered of his childhood friends, "but there was another part of me in which it had to matter because it mattered to the world I lived in." When Crews referred to a respected black man as "Mr. Jones," Crews's aunt quickly corrected him. "No, son. Robert Jones is a nigger. You don't say 'mister' when you speak of a nigger. You don't say 'Mr. Jones,' you say 'nigger Jones.'" Children soon learned the lesson.[1]

White rituals of black naming conveyed various shades of deference, condescension, affection, and respect, tried to maintain the illusion of personal relationships where none existed. Blacks called white men they did not know "mister," "cap'n," or "boss." Acquainted black men attached "Mr." to a white man's first name; the first name of white women was accompanied by "Miss." Whites never addressed black men they did not know as "mister," but rather as "boy," "Jack," or "George"; black women were never called "Mrs.," but rather "aunt" or their first name. A black person, regardless of age or gender, was referred to in white newspaper accounts as simply a "negro," as in "two men and two women were killed, and four Negroes." According to custom, the two races did not shake hands, walk together, or fraternize in public. Black men removed their hats in public places reserved for whites, while whites did not remove their hats even in black homes. Whites "even segregated days of the week," Mamie Garvin Fields recalled of growing up in South Carolina. White people stayed away from town on Saturday afternoons, setting aside that time for blacks from the countryside to shop and meet. "Those white folks didn't want you to come to town in the weekday at all. . . . Really, certain whites didn't like to think you had leisure to do anything but pick cotton and work in the field."[2]

Some blacks, especially in towns and cities, refused to follow the etiquette. A Louisiana newspaper complained that "the younger generation of negro bucks and wenches have lost that wholesome respect for the white man, without which two races, the one inferior, cannot live in peace and harmony together. . . . Is it not every day manifest when your house-girl informs you that Miss Johnson (your cook) says dinner is ready; that Mr. Jones (your butler) will hitch up the buggy in a minute as he is busy talking to a lady (your washerwoman) at the gate. if you address one of the younger generation with the 'uncle' or 'auntie' the older ones delighted in the chances you will hear 'I aint yah uncle, doggone you.'" According to another white man's diary, the older generation was learning from the young. "We have no servant yet—the colored race are getting most unreliable—freedom has ruined them in every way—only the old ones can be relied on and there is a great demand for them and it makes them uppish and they leave you now without a moment's warning—you never know whether your cook will [be] at your house next morning or not." One South Carolina white woman recorded a revealing line she overheard as a black group passed on the street: "Well, I has no boss; I is *my own darlin' boss*!"[3]

On the other hand, many whites and blacks managed to create humane relationships even in the face of the general distrust and dislike. Kindness toward elderly or worthy blacks was taken as a symbol of good character among whites. At the Belk store in Monroe, North Carolina, one of the jobs of a young clerk named John Parker was to help women coming into the store. One day, William Henry Belk recalled, when "an old colored woman came along and stopped in front of the store, John went out and helped her out of her buggy and held the umbrella over her until she got out of the rain. It was a nice thing to do, and it was just like John to do a thing like that." Another clerk "made some remark about it-not bad, but in a sort of teasing way." Belk's brother, the boss, heard the comment "and he didn't like it. He spoke up right quick. He knew that John wanted to be a lawyer when he grew up. 'Don't let him tease you, John,'" the employer said. "'When he's still clerking you'll be on the Supreme Court, son, and I mean the United States Supreme Court.'"[4]

Stories of white aid to blacks did not happen only in white folklore. Charley White recalled one white man with real affection. White's mother, left alone with their children when abandoned by her husband, supported the family through farm labor, midwifery, and washing. Moving from one farm to the next, they eventually settled on the farm of Prayter Windham. Charley was sick the day they arrived, and Windham brought his young daughter with him. "This is my daughter Tish," the landlord said. "We heard you had a sick boy, and Mrs. Windham sent him this chicken broth." When Charley recovered, Windham recognized that the boy was interested in learning about fanning "and he took to teaching me the right way to do things. . . . And seemed like he'd be as tickled as me when I could do it right." When Windham went out on circuit with the court, he put Charley, then about seventeen years old, in the room next to his wife and ten-year-old daughter. A gun rested under his bed. "Nothing ever happened," White recalled, "But if somebody had tried to come in there I'd a shot him, sure as I lived." Although White's mother soon died and the youngster went to live with relatives, when he first got married White returned to Windham's farm to start out.[5]

Rural race relations often seemed marked by such personal ties, patronizing as well as helpful. The diary of Clive Metcalfe, a young white planter surrounded almost entirely by black people in the Delta region of Mississippi in the 1890s, has about it much of the air of the antebellum plantation. "The negroes worry one's life out of them. It is the devil to be situated in the capacity of having anything to do with such people." Metcalfe took upon himself much of the authority of the planter under slavery. "Caught a negro girl stealing clothes from one of my darkens, and I gave her a good whipping," he wrote in 1890. A few weeks later, he blandly noted that he went coon hunting, "Did not see a coon. Came home and whipped Harrison for feeding the dogs on the gallery." Like the planters of the Old South, Metcalfe mixed his violence with what he took to be patemalistic concern. Metcalfe intervened in a domestic fight. "Came home last night, found that Powell had given his wife a good whipping. Had to go over and settle it for them." On the Fourth of July the next year the planter and a friend "gave the darkies a dinner in the Cold Springs yard, which went off very nicely. There was quite four hundred darkies there." [6]

Another holiday showed the continuity that marked some facets of race relations. For generations, black Southerners had celebrated Christmas as a time of white gift-giving and ritualized freedom. While the practice faded in the highly mobile New South, vestiges of the tradition remained on some plantations. Clive Metcalfe dreaded the season, partly because black sharecroppers moved from one farm to another then ("like a lot of sheep," he spat), and partly because black folk on his place always seemed to be "begging a little something for Xmas. It is just awful to be bothered to death by the black faces from morning until night." The next year, in a softer mood, Metcalfe noted that "the darkies are shooting Xmas guns and having lots of fun." Gifts flowed in the other direction as well: a white widow from Mississippi noted in her diary in 1890 that "our colored tenants Bob Rollins and Sam Houston each sent us this evening a nice piece of fresh pork." William Pickens, who grew up in Pendleton, South Carolina, recalled that "the black folks used to say that 'there is no law for Christmas.' And so the young Negro men, in a good-natured spree, would catch the lone policeman, who was always more a joke than a terror, and lock him in the calaboose to stay a part of Christmas Day, while one of the black men with star and club would strut about the town and play officer." Pickens, himself black, thought that this carnival-like inversion of the early 1890s would in 1911, when he wrote, "summon the militia from the four quarters of almost any state and be heralded an ugly insurrection." [7]

Black people turned to whites when they felt they had no other choice. Adelaide Brown, a black woman living in Savannah, wrote to Mary Camak asking for help as Christmas approached in 1896. "Miss Mary My Dear friend," she began, "I am out on the waves of the world by my self no body to help me at all. Joe has quit me and took up with another woman compleat so I thought I would write you to let you know my troubles. Sometimes I field like I haven got a friend on earth." Brown had been ill "for quite a while" and was still sick. "The white people who I am working with has been very kind to me, but I have got to the place wherein I can hardly go or come when I was throude out of doors by Joe these white people taken me in they help me to meet my Groses bill and I tryes to meet my house rent the best I can." Brown wanted to borrow eight or ten dollars. "I make $14 dollars a month if I live . . . I will . . . surely pay you back soon." Brown was writing to Camak "because you is able if you only will. you all are the only people I have. My mother is dead and if she was living she woulden be able to do this favor." Remember, Brown closed, "you are lendeding to the Lord."

Few laws circumscribed day-to-day rural race relations. Rural roads, country stores, and cotton gins were not segregated; hunters and fishermen respected rules of fair play, regardless of race. Corn shuckings saw black and white men working around the same fire and black and white women cooking over the same food, though members of the two races went to separate tables when it came time to eat. In the diary of Nannie Stillwell Jackson, a white Arkansas woman of moderate means, it is difficult to determine whether the people she describes are white or black. Jackson tells, with affection and gratitude, of the visits and gifts black friends brought her during an illness. She trades with her black neighbors, writes and receives letters for them, sews for them; a black midwife tends to her baby. The best of Southern race relations appeared in such scenes, where individuals developed personal respect for one another beyond the reach of hateful laws. The conditions of the New South, though, often worked against people of good will, whatever their race.[9]

In a quest to channel the relations between the races, white Southerners enacted one law after another to proscribe contact among blacks and whites. Some things about the relations between the races had been established quickly after emancipation. Schools, poor houses, orphanages, and hospitals, founded to help people who had once been slaves, were usually separated by race at their inception. Cities segregated cemeteries and parks; counties segregated court houses. Churches quickly broke into different congregations for blacks and whites. Hotels served one race only; blacks could see plays only from the balcony or separate seats; restaurants served one race or served them in different rooms or from separate windows. In 1885, a Memphis newspaper described how thoroughly the races were separated: "The colored people make no effort to obtrude themselves upon the whites in the public schools, their churches, their fairs, their Sunday-schools, their picnics, their social parties, hotels or banquets. They prefer their own preachers, teachers, schools, picnics, hotels and social gatherings." In the countryside as well as in town, blacks and whites associated with members of their own race except in those situations when interracial association could not be avoided: work, commerce, politics, travel. [10]

Even if the general boundaries of race relations had been drawn early on, though, many decisions had yet to be made by the 1880s. The notion of a completely circumscribed world of white and black had not yet become entrenched; the use of the word "segregation" to describe systematic racial separation did not begin until the early twentieth century. Although most whites seem to have welcomed segregation in general, others saw no need to complicate the business of everyday life with additional distinctions between the races, no need to antagonize friendly and respectable blacks, no need to spend money on separate facilities, no need to risk bringing down Northern interference. Although many blacks fought against the new laws with boycotts, lawsuits, and formal complaints, others saw no use in fighting the whites who had all the power on their side, no use in antagonizing white benefactors or white enemies, no use in going places they were not welcome. The segregation begun in the decade following the end of the Civil War did not spread inexorably and evenly across the face of the South. The 1880s saw much uncertainty and much bargaining, many forays and retreats.[11]

Most of the debates about race relations focused on the railroads of the New South. While some blacks resisted their exclusion from white-owned hotels and restaurants, they could usually find, and often preferred, accommodations in blackrun businesses. Travel was a different story, for members of both races had no choice but to use the same railroads. As the number of railroads proliferated in the 1880s, as the number of stations quickly mounted, as dozens of counties got on a line for the first time, as previously isolated areas found themselves connected to towns and cities with different kinds of black people and different kinds of race relations, segregation became a matter of statewide attention. Prior to the eighties, localities could strike their own compromises in race relations, try their own experiments, tolerate their own ambiguities. Tough decisions forced themselves on the state legislatures of the South after the railroads came. The result was the first wave of segregation laws that affected virtually the entire South in anything like a uniform way, as nine Southern states enacted railroad segregation laws in the years between 1887 and 1891.[12]

By all accounts, the railroads of the 1880s were contested terrain. Trains ran cars of two classes: in the first-class car rode women and men who did not use tobacco, while in the second-class car rode men who chewed or smoked, men unaccompanied by women, and people who could not afford a first-class ticket. To travel in the second-class car was to travel with people, overwhelmingly men, who behaved very differently from those in the car ahead. The floors were thick with spit and tobacco juice, the air thick with smoke and vulgarities. The second class car had hard seats, low ceilings, and no water; frequently, it was merely a part of the baggage car set off by a partition. The second-class car ran right behind the engine, and was often invaded by smoke and soot. The cars saw more crowding of strangers than in any other place in the New South. "The cars were jammed, all the way over here, with the dirtiest, nastiest set I ever rode with," a Louisiana man complained about a trip to Texas.[13]

A first-class or parlor, car contained a diverse group of travelers, but their behavior tended to be more genteel than those in the smoking car. "It was the ordinary car of a Southern railroad," Ellen Glasgow wrote, with "the usual examples of Southern passengers. Across the aisle a slender mother was holding a crying baby, two small children huddling beside her." "A mulatto of the new era" sat nearby, while "further off there were several men returning from business trips, and across from them sat a pretty girl, asleep, her hand resting on a gilded cage containing a startled canary. At intervals she was aroused by the flitting figure of a small boy on the way to the cooler of iced water. From the rear of the car came the amiable drawl of the conductor as he discussed the affairs of the State with a local drummer, whose feet rested upon a square leather case." The seats were covered with soft plush fabric, the floor covered with carpet.[14]

Strangely enough, the scenes of racial contention and conflict on the trains focused on the placid first-class cars rather than on the boisterous cars ahead. Sutton Griggs, a black Virginia novelist, gave a compelling account of the random violence that hovered around blacks who rode in the parlor cars. A young black man on his way to Louisiana to become president of a small black college had traveled all the way from Richmond without incident. Absorbed in a newspaper as the car crossed the line into Louisiana, he did not notice the car gradually filling at each stop. "A white lady entered, and not at once seeing a vacant seat, paused a few seconds to look about for one. She soon espied an unoccupied seat. She proceeded to it, but her slight difficulty had been noted by the white passengers." Before the black man knew what was happening, he found himself surrounded by a group of angry whites. "'Get out of this coach. We don't allow niggers in first-class coaches.'" The black passenger resisted moving, only to be thrown off the train altogether. "Covered from head to foot with red clay, the president-elect of Cadeville College walked down to the next station, two miles away."[15]

This sort of clash was hardly confined to fiction. Andrew Springs, a young black man on the way from North Carolina to Fisk University in Nashville in 1891, told a friend back home about his experiences. "I came very near being locked up by the police at Chattanooga. I wanted some water. I went in to the White Waiting [room] and got it as they didn't have any for Curry to drink. Just time I got the water here come the police just like I were killing some one and said You get out of here you black rascal put that cup down. I got a notion to knock your head off." As so often happened, the black man refused to accept such treatment without protest. "I told him I were no rascal neither were I black. I were very near as white as he was. Great Scott he started for me. . . . He didn't strike tho, but had me started to the lock up." Springs, like many blacks harassed on the railroad, used the law to stop his persecution. "I told him I had my ticket and it was the duty of the R.R. Co. to furnish water for both white (and) black." The officer let him go. The young man then took the dangerous, and atypical, step of threatening the officer: "I told him if ever I catch him in North Carolina I would fix him."[16]

Aggressive single young men were not the only ones who threatened, intentionally and unintentionally, the tenuous racial situation on the railroad. In 1889, Emanuel Love, a leader of the First African Baptist Church of Savannah, was asked by an agent of the East Tennessee, Virginia and Georgia Railroad to travel over the road to a convention in Indianapolis, assuring Love that he and his entourage could have first-class accommodations the entire day. Love assumed the delegation would have a car to themselves so they would not antagonize white first-class passengers who might be on board. As the train pulled out and the pastor walked through the car greeting the other delegates, he soon noticed that there were indeed whites in the first-class car, and they began to whisper among themselves and to the white conductor. A black railway workman warned the delegation that trouble was ahead, but there was little they could do; someone had already telegraphed news of the black effrontery to the next stop. There, al least fifty white men, carrying pistols, clubs, and pieces of iron, pushed their way into the car and assaulted the "well dressed" delegates. Some sought to defend themselves, while most fled. One who could do neither was Mrs. Janie Gamet, a graduate of Atlanta University and a school teacher, who screamed in fear. One of the white men put a cocked pistol to her breast and said "You G—d d—d heffer, if you don't hush your mouth and get out of here, I will blow your G—d d—d brains out." The delegation was treated for their broken bones and bruises and made their way, presumably in a separate car, to Indianapolis. Accounts of the violence directed at blacks often spoke of well-dressed clergymen and well-dressed women as the objects of white anger.[17]

Whites also experienced racial discomfiture that did not necessarily result in violence or even overt conflict. In 1889, a Tennessee newspaper related in a light tone a story that captured some of the risks of the "parlor car." At Nashville, "a bright, good-looking colored girl (or rather an almost white colored girl)" boarded the train. A "flashily-dressed white gentleman, usually known as the 'car masher,'" began an elaborate flirtation with the girl, whom he assumed to be white. She "very modestly" accepted his attentions, "slightly blushing probably out of compassion for the fellow's mistake, but which he evidently took as an indication of a surrender to his charms." He bought his "'lady friend' a lunch, and the two sat for half an hour enjoying their supper tete-a-tete. . . . every passenger on the train enjoying the situation. The girl was entirely innocent of any intention to entrap or deceive the fellow, but he was the victim of his own inordinate conceit and folly." He eventually found out his mistake after she had reached her destination. "He was probably the maddest man in the State when he found it all out. He was mad at the girl, mad at the passengers and doubtless wanted to kick himself all the way home." The account ended, significantly, with the information that "none enjoyed the episode more than the ladies on the train."[18]

If the situation had been reversed, if some "almost white" black man had been flirting with a white girl, deceiving her, eating with her, what then? Such a scene would have invoked the sense of pollution whites associated with blacks, no matter how clean, how well-dressed, how well-mannered they might be. As a New Orleans newspaper argued in 1890, when the state was considering the segregation of its railroad cars, "one is thrown in much closer communication in the car with one's traveling companions than in the theatre or restaurant," which were already segregated. In the railroad car, the article related in suggestive language, whites and blacks would be "crowded together, squeezed close to each other in the same seats, using the same conveniences, and to all intents and purposes in social intercourse." The lesson was clear: "A man that would be horrified at the idea of his wife or daughter seated by the side of a burly negro in the parlor of a hotel or at a restaurant cannot see her occupying a crowded seat in a car next to a negro without the same feeling of disgust." Any man "who believes that the white race should be kept pure from African taint will vote against that commingling of the races inevitable in a 'mixed car' and which must have bad results." A white woman or girl who let herself fall into easy and equal relations with a black man in such an anomalous place as the parlor car would risk her reputation.[19]

The sexual charge that might be created among strangers temporarily placed in intimate surroundings, many whites worried, could not be tolerated in a racially integrated car. In the late nineteenth century, sexual relations did not have to end in intercourse or even physical contact to be considered intimate and dangerous to a woman's reputation and self-respect. In fact, the history of segregation shows a clear connection to gender: the more closely linked to sexuality, the more likely was a place to be segregated. At one extreme was the private home, where the intimacies of the parlor, the dining table, and bedroom were never shared with blacks as equals; it was no accident that blacks were proscribed from entering a white home through its front door. Exclusive hotels, restaurants, and darkened theaters, which mimicked the quiet and privacy of the home, also saw virtually no racial mixing. Schools, where children of both genders associated in terms of intimacy and equality, saw early and consistent segregation. Places where people of only one gender associated with one another, though, tended to have relaxed racial barriers. The kitchen and nursery of a home, which "should" have been off-limits to blacks for white taboos to have remained consistent, in fact saw black women participating in the most private life of white families. Part of the lowered boundary, of course, grew out of the necessity whites perceived to use black labor, but blacks were permitted in the heart of the home because those rooms saw the interaction only of white women and black women. Male preserves, for their part, were often barely segregated at all: bars, race tracks, and boxing rings were notorious, and exciting, for the presence of blacks among whites. Some houses of prostitution profited directly from the sexual attraction black women held for some white men.[20]

The railroad would not have been such a problem, then, had blacks not been seeking first-class accommodations where women as well as men traveled, where blacks appeared not as dirty workers but as well-dressed and attractive ladies and gentlemen. When the Arkansas legislature was debating the need for a separate car in 1891, some whites argued that whites should not be forced to sit next to dirty blacks; other whites argued instead that the worst blacks were those who were educated and relatively well-to-do and who insisted on imposing themselves on the white people. A young black legislator, John Gray Lucas, a recent graduate of Boston University, confronted the white lawmakers with their inconsistency: "Is it true, as charged, that we use less of soap and God's pure water than other people. . . . Or is it the constant growth of a more refined, intelligent, and I might say a more perfumed class, that grow more and more obnoxious as they more nearly approximate to our white friends' habits and plane of life?"[21]

With every year in the 1880s, more blacks fought their way to white standards of "respectability." Black literacy, black wealth, black businesses, black higher education, and black landowning all increased substantially. When whites discussed segregating the railroads, respectable blacks responded in fury and disbelief. "Is it not enough that the two races are hopelessly separated in nearly all the higher relations of life already?" an open letter from seven black clergymen, and teachers from Orangeburg, South Carolina, asked in 1889. "Are you now content with separate places of public entertainment, separate places of public amusement, separate places of public instruction, and even separate places of public worship? Why, in the name of common sense, of common humanity, the common high-bred sensitiveness of every decent person of color, should you wish to force further unnatural separation even upon the thoroughfares of daily travel?"[22]

A Northern traveler in the South observed that "a few colored men are inclined to insist upon enjoying whatever right belongs to them under the law because they believe that any concessions on the part of the black people, any surrender of their legal rights, would invite and produce new injuries and apprehensions." Educated and assertive blacks, especially those of the younger generation, chafed at every restriction against them and looked for opportunities to exercise their legal rights to attack the very assumptions and presumptions of segregation. A black Georgia newspaper reflected this aggressive mentality: "When a conductor orders a colored passenger from the first class car it's a bluff, and if the passenger goes to the forward or smoking car, that ends it; should he refuse, it ends it also, for the trainman will reflect seriously before he lays off violent hands, for he knows that such a rash proceeding makes him amenable to the law."[23]

Mary Church, sixteen years old, boarded a train by herself only to be ushered to a Jim Crow car. She protested to the conductor that she had bought a first class ticket. "'This is first class enough for you,' he replied sarcastically, 'and you just stay where you are,' with a look calculated to freeze the very marrow of my bones." Having heard about "awful tragedies which had overtaken colored girls who had been obliged to travel alone on these cars at night," Church decided to get off the train. The conductor refused to let her pass, wanting to know where she was going. "'I am getting off here,' I replied, 'to wire my father that you are forcing me to ride all night in a Jim Crow car. He will sue the railroad for compelling his daughter who has a first class ticket to ride in a second class car.'" The conductor relented.[24]

Blacks resorted to the law in increasing numbers in the 1880s, taking railroad and railroad employees to court to press for equal accommodations. Blacks actually won several of these cases, even in Southern courts. In 1885, for example a black man named Murphy had bought a first-class ticket for a train from Georgia to Tennessee. His trip was uneventful until two white women boarded the train and their male companions told Murphy to go back to the smoking car. He refused, and the white men then threw Murphy into the other car. Murphy sued the railroad. The federal judge, a former United

States senator, instructed the jury that precedent established in other, Northern, states had shown that under the common law railroads could segregate their cars by race, "so as to avoid complaint and friction." The railroads forfeited that right "when the money of the white man purchases luxurious accommodations and elegant company, and the same amount of money purchases for the black man inferior quarters in a smoking car." The jury therefore awarded the black plaintiff damages—to be paid both by the assailants and by the railroad company whose employees "made no effort to prevent the mischief." Another decision in the same year, this one occasioned by a suit brought by a black woman who had gotten off the train rather than be shunted into the smoking car with its "swearing and smoking and whiskey drinking," also ruled in favor of the black litigant. The court judged that if the railroad provided for white ladies "a car with special privileges of seclusion and other comforts, the same must be substantially furnished for colored ladies."[25]

These 1885 rulings reflected the growing consensus of the nation's appellate and federal courts, Northern and Southern, that equal accommodations had to be provided for those who paid equal amounts for their tickets. Those rulings also stipulated that the railroads could provide separate accommodations for any groups of passengers, as long as the facilities were equal and as long as separation was consistently enforced and publicized before passengers boarded the train. The railroad's case would be strengthened if it could show that separation encouraged "peace, order, convenience, and comfort," by adjusting to dominant customs in the area through which the railroad passed. In the 1880s, black Southerners were able to use this body of law to win more equitable treatment on the railroads of the region, to force the railroads to provide them equal facilities. "There is a plain rule of justice, which ought to be recognized and enforced, viz: that every man is entitled to what he pays for," a defender of the rights of black passengers in 1890 argued. "If there be on the part of the whites an unwillingness to occupy the same cars and to sit in the same seats with the blacks, let them be separate; only let equally good cars be provided for both, if both pay for them." In 1887 and 1889, the new Interstate Commerce Commission ruled that trains crossing state lines had to "give one passenger as good accommodations as another for the same price, but they are not compelled to permit a passenger to take any car or any seat that may please his fancy." The "equality of accommodations" must be "real and not delusive." The federal government simultaneously stressed equality and sanctioned segregation, giving with one hand and taking away with the other.[26]

In the 1880s, then, blacks confronted a dangerous and uncertain situation every time they bought a first-class ticket to ride on a Southern railroad. Each road had its own customs and policy, and the events on the train might depend on the proclivity of the conductor or, worse, the mood and make-up of the white passengers who happened to be on board. Although the courts upheld the rights of several blacks who had the means to take their cases to court, there was no telling how many blacks suffered discrimination, intimidation, and violence in the meantime. Some railroads sought to avoid the problems simply by refusing to sell blacks first-class tickets; the L & N resorted to this policy until blacks threatened to boycott, then it allowed black women to travel first class, then reversed itself again two months later when whites protested. At least one railroad in Alabama, operating in the piney woods along the coast, sought to avoid the potentially costly conflicts by running its own separate and identical car for blacks as early as 1882. "The rule is made for the protection of the blacks as much as for anything else in a part of the country in which they might be subjected to drunken men's insults," a Mobile paper argued."[27]

If other railroads had followed the example of this Alabama company, rail segregation might have remained in the uncertain realm of custom and private business decisions that guided so much else in Southern race relations. Other railroads, however, especially those in parts of the South where blacks did not make up a large part of the clientele, were reluctant to go the considerable expense and trouble of running twice the number of cars. The railroads, unenthusiastic about passenger traffic in any case because, as the L and N's president put it, "You can't make a g—— d—— cent out of it," neither wanted to police Southern race relations and then be sued for it nor to run extra cars. It was clear that white Southerners could not count on the railroads to take matters in hand. Some whites came to blame the railroads for the problem, for it seemed to them that the corporations as usual were putting profits ahead of the welfare of the region.[28]

The first legislative attempt at statewide segregation, in fact, began in an unlikely setting that combined black anger and white frustration at the railroads. Republicans held half the seats in Tennessee's lower house in 1881, and four of their representatives were black men determined to overturn an 1875 state law that prevented black passengers from suing discriminatory railroads. Their straightforward attempt to repeal the law failed by the narrowest of margins, however, and a bill that would have outlawed racial discrimination by the railroads never came to a vote. Another measure raced through both houses, however, and the only votes against it came from the blacks who had worked to prohibit any kind of racial distinction. The new law dictated that "All railroad companies shall furnish separate cars, or portions of cars cut off by partition walls, which all colored passengers who pay first-class rates of fare may have the privilege to enter and occupy." The separate cars or apartments had to be kept "in good repair, with the same conveniences, and subject to the same rules governing other first-class cars for preventing smoking and obscene language." If the railroad failed to enforce the law, "the company shall pay a forfeit of $ 1.00, half to be paid to the person suing, the other half to be paid to the common school fund of the state." The next year, black legislators managed to make the punishment steeper, raising the penalty to $300. In the next two sessions of the legislature, black representatives continued to work for the outright abolition of discrimination, not the half-hearted separate-but-equal law. Although whites may have considered the law a compromise, to militant blacks it was inadequate in theory and practice, full of danger.[29]

Judged by what was to come, the language of this first separate-but-equal law stressed equality and put the burden on railroads who deprived passengers of services for which they had paid; most important, it did not actually require railroads to segregate their passengers, only to provide separate but equal accommodations that blacks had "the privilege to enter and occupy." Like the appellate decisions handed down in the nation's courts in these years, this law could have been construed as a victory of sorts for black passengers. "No white person shall be permitted to ride in a negro car or to insult or annoy any negro in such car," Florida's 1887 railroad segregation law announced.[30]

The earliest railroad segregation laws, therefore, carried an ambiguous message. They took racial division and conflict for granted but placed the blame and the burden of dispelling that conflict on the railroads. Laws demanding separate cars seemed a compromise between white sensibilities and black rights, and, to whites, the only one who seemed to lose was the railroad who had to pay the cost. Mississippi's legislature of 1888 struck the same bargain, putting its first railroad segregation law in the context of an act that created a railroad commission. The focus of the language now shifted from the rights and comforts of blacks to the powers of railroad officials to make the law operate smoothly. Texas continued the trend away from an emphasis on black rights the next year in its law, when it blandly dictated that "Railroad companies shall maintain separate coaches for the white and the colored races. They shall be equal as to comfort. They shall be designated by words or letters, showing the race for whom intended." Not only could "comfort" be open to many interpretations, but the law neglected to stipulate the punishment a railroad or a conductor would suffer for failure to carry out the law.[31]

Despite the shift in emphasis, matters still remained very much in doubt in 1890, as events in Louisiana show. When the Louisiana legislature began considering a separate car law, a New Orleans newspaper felt compelled to attack the railroads who opposed the bill. "In view of the extreme liberality in which the State has treated them, there should have been at least some concessions from the powerful corporations to the people." Blacks clearly did not see a separate car as an equitable solution to the violence they suffered on the trains, and they sought to use their considerable representation in the state legislature to stop passage of the law in Louisiana. The American Citizens' Equal Rights Association of Louisiana, a black organization, sent a memorial to the legislature protesting the law, a memorial that also bore the signatures of the state's eighteen black legislators. Working with white delegates friendly to the railroads, the black lawmakers were able to defeat the bill in the senate. As soon as their votes were no longer needed to override a veto on an unrelated bill, however, the black legislators found themselves betrayed: white delegates joined together to write a separate-car law after all.[32]

Two blacks in New Orleans, furious at the turn of events, decided to make a test case of the Louisiana law. They sought the help of a white Northern lawyer long dedicated to black rights, Albion Tourgde, who responded enthusiastically. "Submission to such outrages," he wrote, tends "only to their multiplication and exaggeration. It is by constant resistance to oppression that the race must ultimately win equality of right." Accordingly, they enlisted a man named Homer Adolph Plessy, seven-eighths white, to board the East Louisiana Railroad and refuse to leave the white car even though officials had been notified earlier of his status as a black. He was arrested, and his case tried in Louisiana in late 1892. "The roads are not in favor of the separate car law, owing to the expense entailed," a lawyer looking into the matter reported, "but they fear to array themselves against it." It took four more years for the United States Supreme Court to hear the Plessy case, by which time segregation had been written into the laws of every Southern state except the Carolinas and Virginia. The years in between saw the political map of the South redrawn.[33]

The timing of the first wave of segregation law is explained, then, by the growing ambition, attainments, and assertiveness of blacks, by the striking expansion and importance of the railroad system in the 1880s, by a widespread distrust and dislike for the railroad corporations, by the course of legal cases at the state and circuit level, and by the example each state set for others. Most white officials who held power in these years played their role in the creation of statewide segregation; it was the product of no particular class, of no wave of hysteria or displaced frustration, no rising tide of abstract racism, no new ideas about race. Like everything else in the New South, segregation grew out of concrete situations, out of technological, demographic, economic, and political changes that had unforeseen and often unintended social consequences.[34]

Railroad segregation was not a throwback to old-fashioned racism; indeed, segregation became, to whites, a badge of sophisticated, modern, managed race relations. John Andrew Rice recalled an incident from his youth in South Carolina in 1892. He visited Columbia, then "an awkward overgrown village, like a country boy come to town all dressed up on a Saturday night." Despite the rawness of the state capital, "the main entrance to the town was the depot, and here was something new, something that marked the town as different from the country and the country depots at Lynchburg and Darlington and Vamville: two doors to two waiting rooms and on these two doors arresting signs, 'White' and 'Colored.'" Soon those signs *would* be in Lynchburg, Darlington, and Vamville as well, for state law would demand it. The railroads took a piece of the city with them wherever they went. The railroad cars and waiting rooms were marked by the same anonymity that was coming to characterize the towns and cities of the South, the same diversity within confined spaces, the same display of class by clothing and demeanor, the same crowding of men and women, the same crowding of different races. In fact, the railroads were even more "modern" than cities themselves, detached from their settings, transitory, volatile.[35]

Segregation laws, of course, could not contain all the conflicts generated by these new social relations. Blacks refused to be satisfied with the "compromise" of segregation, partly because its very existence was insulting and partly because of the way it was implemented. Two black men wrote a furious letter in the wake of Tennessee's 1891 law, charging that the black "first-class" area was in fact merely separated by a partition from the smoking area of the second-class car. As a result, they and their families had to wade through the smoke, tobacco juice, and jeers of white men to get to their section. The black men boldly warned the white South that "the signs of the times unmistakably show that unless public sentiment will cry down such injustice, the future of the two races will be (let us put it mildly) anything but peaceful." Jim Crow cars quickly became known as "universally filthy and uncomfortable," a symbol of "indignity, disgrace, and shame." Lawmakers and railroads merely clamped down more tightly. In Florida, for example, legislators empowered passengers to help conductors carry out their duties, codifying the sort of violence and bullying the segregation laws had been designed to stop in the first place. From Arkansas came word that municipalities, after the passage of the railroad law, began to implement racial restrictions far more than in the past.[36]

After 1891, only Virginia and the Carolinas did not have railroad segregation laws. The same forces working in the rest of the South worked in those states as well, of course, but having failed to put railroad segregation laws on the books in the late eighties and early nineties, they found that the political events of the next few years prevented them from joining their neighboring states. It was not until the late nineties that these states could implement their version of the law, just when the other Southern states began to enact even more kinds of segregation designed to enclose yet more of the machinery of the new age.[37]

In the same years that statewide railroad segregation peaked, the South embarked on the constitutional disfranchisement of black voters. Southern disfranchisement, scattered and isolated in Georgia, South Carolina, and Florida, appeared to be moving into the current of the national mainstream with the adoption of secret ballots in Tennessee in 1888 and 1889. In the latter year, too, North Carolina's legislature tightened registration laws by requiring greater accuracy and detail on age, place of birth, and occupation, requirements that could restrict the vote in ways that sympathetic reformers in the North might appreciate.[38]

The course of Southern voting restriction suddenly veered off in a uniquely Southern direction in Mississippi in 1890. For over a decade, legislators from outside Mississippi's Black Belt had attempted to organize support for a new constitution that would give their counties a more equitable role in state affairs. Rings composed of a few white Democrats in the heavily black counties exploited the inflated representation created by their large black populations, manipulating the votes in their counties, controlling the state government, and ignoring the needs of the majority of Mississippi whites. These despicable politicians, an editor speaking for white hill-country farmers charged, "disregarded the rights of the blacks, incited useless and extravagant expenditures, raised the taxes, plunged the State into debt, and actually dominated the will of the white people through the instrumentality of the stolen negro vote."[39]

The Black Belt delegates and the state leaders they elected resisted any change throughout the 1880s, but suddenly changed their position in 1889. United States Senator James Z. George, a prominent Redeemer and leading politician of the state, predicted that the 1890 census would "show that the black population of Mississippi will exceed that of the whites [by] nearly one-half million." Moreover, the Republicans controlled not only the White House but also both houses of Congress. The Republican ascendency in Washington had produced "an exciting of sectional passions and sectional prejudices." With "all the departments of the government in unfriendly hands," George warned, the "check on bad legislation" offered in the past by a Democratic-controlled House had disappeared. It seemed "almost certain" that the Republican majority would "pass a law taking the federal elections from the control of the state."[40]

Recent events at home showed just how volatile the situation had in fact become. In Mississippi in 1889 and 1890 the Republicans became emboldened by the state of affairs in

Washington. With firm control of the federal government, the Republicans prepared to contest three of Mississippi's seven recent congressional elections. Blacks in fusion arrangements demanded a greater share of the offices. Some blacks even refused to pay their taxes until guaranteed their right to vote. Moreover, the Republican party established a newspaper in Jackson and applauded as Mississippi Republicans who had kept the faith saw their loyalty rewarded by appointments to desirable federal posts. Forty Republicans, including thirty-two blacks, took federal civil service examinations for positions ranging from copyist to meteorological clerk. A convention of Mississippi blacks offered a state fusion ticket with the Democrats; when they were denied, they nominated candidates for all state offices, the first time the state Republican party had run a complete ticket since Redemption. Black leaders from forty counties met in 1889, in what some whites feared as the "largest colored convention" ever held in Mississippi, to denounce the "violent and criminal suppression of the black vote." The convention called for federal intervention to "break up lawlessness and ballot-box stuffing." Clearly, the political situation in Mississippi was anything but settled.[41]

The prospect facing the Democrats was one of perpetual turmoil, violence, dispute, factionalism, and growing opposition if they could not find some way to purge the black vote without bringing down on themselves the Republican controlled power of the federal government. Many white Mississippians had grown weary of the constant fraud and violence they used to check black aspiration. "The old men of the present generation can't afford to die and leave the election to their children and grandchildren, with shot guns in their hands, a lie in their mouths and perjury on their lips in order to defeat the negroes," one Mississippian passionately argued. "There must be devised some legal defensible substitute for the abhorrent and evil methods on which white supremacy lies," another paper agreed. A constitutional convention could break this cycle by doing away with the need for force altogether.[42]

Despite widespread disgust with the current state of Mississippi politics, advocates of a convention barely won in the legislature of 1890. A third of the members of both houses were opposed to the convention, and then only 15 percent of the eligible electorate bothered to show up to vote for delegate—the smallest turnout for a Mississippi statewide election since the Civil War. The object of overt threats, most local Republican organizations did not put candidates in the field; one man brave enough to canvass his district as a Republican candidate was assassinated. Of the 134 delegates, all but four were Democrats; the one Republican was the only black man at the convention. Despite the apparent Democratic unity, delegates from the Black Belt fought against delegates from the white districts on almost every issue.[43]

It soon became clear that no one had a workable idea of how to disfranchise blacks without either disfranchising whites in the process or obviously violating the Fifteenth Amendment and losing federal representation. Delegates from white counties wanted no educational or property requirements, while black-county delegates favored such requirements. "Impose a property test, weigh true manhood against dirty dollars, and for the black problem you will have a white one which will revolutionize the state," ran one warning. An educational or literacy test was no more acceptable to poorer whites. The Black Belt delegates, rich and educated, looked on the compromises they had to make with disgust. "To avoid the disfranchisement of a lot of white ignoramuses we can't have an educational qualification," one Black Belt judge moaned, "and to pander to the prejudices of those who have no property we cannot have a property qualification."[44]

Ironically, the property and educational requirements won the endorsement of the sole black delegate to the convention, Isaiah T. Montgomery. Montgomery, the former slave of Jefferson Davis's brother, had become a well-to-do planter after the war and founded the all-black town of Mound Bayou. Montgomery sought to deflect the pain inflicted by the convention away from at least some blacks by calling for strict adherence to an educational or property qualification. Political conflict and bloodshed could be reduced, he hoped, even as some educated and propertied blacks-up to a third of all black voters-would be able to vote and exert some political influence. As black progress continued, Montgomery felt sure, an increasing percentage of Mississippi blacks would win the right to cast a ballot. "I have stood by, consenting and assisting to strike down the rights and liberties of 123,000 free men," Montgomery told the convention. "It is a fearful sacrifice laid upon the burning altar of liberty. Many of these men I know personally; their hearts are true as steel." Montgomery wanted to tell these men "that the sacrifice has been made to restore confidence, the great missing link between the races; to restore honesty and purity to the ballot box and to confer the boon of political liberty upon the Commonwealth of Mississippi." Whites, Montgomery insisted, must repay black acquiescence by working to settle racial problems "upon the enduring basis of Truth, Justice and Equality." The disfranchisement law promised safety if it promised nothing else: "It is the ship. All else is an open, raging, tempestuous sea."[45]

The bill was an unsound ship, however, its timbers rotten and its sails poorly patched. The thirty-five-member committee on the franchise listened to the ideas of each of its members and then spent weeks assembling those ideas into an acceptable plan. The white counties were granted a majority in the house while the black counties controlled the senate. As for the franchise itself, the convention decided to erect a series of supposedly color-blind obstacles designed to let white voters pass while stopping blacks. Voters had to be registered by state appointed officers (so that blacks could not use local or federal power to appoint black or Republican registrars), and only registered voters could hold any office. A potential voter had to prove he had lived in the state for at least two years and at least one year in his election district-a direct result of "the disposition of young negroes . . . to change their homes or precincts every year." A man presenting himself to vote could not have been convicted of any of a certain range of stereotypically "negro" crimes; arson, bigamy, and petty theft precluded a man from voting, but not murder, rape, or grand larceny, for blacks were supposedly "given rather to furtive offenses than to the robust crimes of the whites." He also had to be on record as having paid all taxes, including a poll tax of two dollars, for the last two years. Each of these provisions, Mississippians knew from the experience of other states, Southern and otherwise, would remove an appreciable number of black voters.[46]

The convention was not satisfied, though, until it had tacked on one final and novel provision: the so-called understanding clause. An aspiring voter had either to be able to read any section of the state constitution or to understand that section when it was read to him "or give a reasonable interpretation thereof." The idea, of course, was that illiterate whites could understand the constitution to the satisfaction of the white registrar while even a literate black man would find it difficult to persuade the official of his understanding. Even illiterate whites supposedly possessed "the aptitude of free government" as an automatic product of their racial heritage, while "if every negro in Mississippi was a graduate of Harvard, and had been elected as class orator . . . he would not be as well fitted to exercise the right of suffrage as the Anglo-Saxon farm laborer."[47]

To their credit, many white Mississippians rejected such rationalizations as the nonsense they were. Only one newspaper in the entire state endorsed the understanding clause before its passage, and that was the newspaper that enjoyed the printing patronage of the convention. More common was this sort of denunciation: "It is evident that the clamor of demagogueism is riding the convention with whip and spur," the Raymond *Gazette* fumed. "The people of Mississippi who are sick and tired of ballot box frauds, perjury and all their attendant demoralization, and the people of the entire nation, are looking on and expecting something higher and more manly than this from a Convention of Mississippi's picked statesmen." Senator George, who entered the convention with the reputation of a bold statesman, left it with his reputation tarnished. The widespread sense was, as a Jackson paper put it, that "time and experience are likely to prove that the opponents of the calling of a Constitutional Convention were wiser than its advocates believed." "Every State suffers more or less from corrupt practices at elections," one paper bitterly observed, "but it was reserved for the State of Mississippi to make its very Constitution the instrument and shield of fraud."[48]

But it was too late to turn back. The convention decided it would be "unnecessary and inexpedient" to allow Mississippi's voters to decide whether they wanted to live under such a constitution. Delegates dared not risk a vote once they saw what kind of popular reception greeted the new document. Mississippi's Democratic papers, full of ridicule and disgust during the convention, fell into line as soon as the work had been done. It was too early to tell if the constitution's provisions would be adequate to control the opposition vote, so it was better to be quiet until the 1890 elections had passed, until the state and federal courts had ruled on the legality of the convention's work, until other Southern states had run the same gauntlet. Too much remained unsettled for whites to admit they disagreed.[49]

A leading black North Carolina politician, George Henry White, thought the "best way to solve what is now regarded as the race problem" was to be attained through "a gradual thinning out" of the black population "to relieve the over crowded agricultural communities, where the supply is far in advance of the demand for labor." A far more vehement statement of the same general principle came from the pen of David Schenck, who confided to his diary that "Negro immigration *somewhere*, is the absorbing topic of the day. How to get rid of this lazy, thieving, detestable race is the problem every thinking man in the South is endeavoring to solve." Nine out of ten white North Carolinians, he thought, "rejoice at the movement and look upon it as the work of Divine Providence who is putting it in the heart of Negroes to leave and thus solve the great race problem in the States." Schenck was convinced that most black emigrants would find their way to Mexico.[50]

A townsman such as Schenck might be able to enjoy such fantasies, but the planters and other employers of black labor watched the black exodus with considerable misgivings. They did not mind too much when a few isolated families left, but the planters became worried when hundreds and even thousands of able-bodied and strong-willed workers abandoned their counties. Some planters might try persuasion or trickery. "The general and George both much exercised about the darkies leaving this section," John B. MacRae of Jackson, North Carolina, observed in his diary in 1890, "and think they can prevent it by using the nigger preacher Anderson Boone, or rather George is inclined to think so." We do not know whether Boone was able to exert much influence on his fellow blacks, but it does appear that black ministers, politicians, and businessmen-for their own reasons—did often try to talk their parishioners, constituents, and customers out of leaving.[51]

Black leaders who attempted such persuasion worked not only against the ambition and hopefulness of rural blacks but also against the efforts of labor agents. A North Carolina newspaper complained in 1892 that hundreds of these agents combed the South Atlantic states, persuading thousands of workers to leave for jobs elsewhere. Some of these recruiters worked for railroads, large planters, or labor agencies that specialized in moving workers long distances. The letterhead of J. P. Justis's Employment and Labor Agency of Richmond, for example, advertised "House Servants, Coal Miners, Farm Hands, etc. forwarded to any part of the United States." Southern states levied prohibitive taxes on such agents and Southern localities did all they could to hinder their actions. They were unable to stanch the flow for long.[52]

One white labor agent, R. A. "Peg-Leg" Williams, recruited for the Illinois Central Railroad. In 1890 Williams claimed that he had helped 80,000 blacks move from the South Atlantic states to Mississippi and Texas; in 1899 he arrived in Greene County, Georgia, to do the same there. Greene was an old plantation county that had seen its best days before the Civil War, and its abundant black population seemed a likely source for a labor agent. At first, Williams worked in harmony with local "leading men"; they agreed not to require him to purchase the usual license, and he promised to unburden the county of a thousand impoverished blacks who had no contracts with white landlords. For several weeks the arrangement worked well, and the local newspaper even applauded his efforts.

Planters eventually decided that things had gone far enough, that enough black residents had left Greene County. Some planters tried to have Williams arrested, but the county prosecutor, pleased with the agent's effect on the community, refused to press the case. Williams simply posted bond and intensified his efforts. Now that whites were resisting, blacks became even more responsive to Williams's message. Some of the best tenants left, while several of those who remained went to their landlords to demand lower rents and higher wages. Violent outbreaks often resulted from these demands, and planters saw to it that Williams was arrested again. Rumors of lynching began to circulate. Seeing that the time had come to leave Greene County, Williams issued statements "To All Colored Farm Hands," informing them that he would be taking no more of them to Mississippi that year. The planters then allowed Williams to depart unharmed.[53]

Once black workers began to leave, however, whites found it almost impossible to stop them for long. "The great trouble," one North Carolina landowner explained, "is the factories, railroads, saw-mills and public works, paying more for hands than farmers can, and will give them short jobs, allow them to be in and out at their pleasure—no system—any hand can quit his job and get another the same day in any neighborhood." The poverty of rural black Southerners led to risky moving as well as resigned stagnation.[54]

Since planters had the power of the law and the law enforcers on their side, any tenant who sought to flee a debt did so at considerable risk—risk of imprisonment, a beating, or formal debt peonage. Yet a family desperate enough might take the risks, and desperation flourished in the New South. William Pickens's family moved from South Carolina to Arkansas, their way paid by a planter eager to get the labor of such hardworking people. Their first two years of labor, however, produced good crops but deepening debt; "if the debt could not be paid in fat years, there was the constant danger that lean years would come and make it bigger." From their perspective, "there was but one recourse—the way of escape." Pickens's father set out on some pretext to visit Little Rock and managed to find a landowner willing to advance fares for the family. "And so one night the young children and some goods were piled into a wagon and the adults went afoot," Pickens remembered years later. "By morning we were in the town of Augusta, twelve or fifteen miles away, where we caught the first train."[55]

From the immediate postwar years on, in growing numbers as the years passed, restless blacks moved short distances and long, to the North as well as to other places in the South, alone and in groups, with and without the aid of agents. As a result, in the 1800s and 1900s every Southern state except Mississippi, Alabama, and Florida registered rates of black outmigration almost as great as in the famed "Great Migration" of the World War I years.[56]

Black mobility came at a cost to black families. For young black men, the best chances to make a decent living appeared where lumber camps, sawmill towns, large Delta plantations, and steel mills used large numbers of wage laborers. Black women found the best jobs in the domestic work available in the small towns of the South, where most white families employed a cook or washerwoman. As a result, the heavily black parts of the South from Virginia to Mississippi contained by far the largest proportion of women relative to men in the entire country. The gender imbalance among blacks throughout the South, furthermore, was far greater than among whites; black men and women were often pulled in strongly divergent directions by the hope of a decent living. When blacks felt secure enough to move as families, whites noted the fact: "there was considerable exodus of colored men from the eastern part of the state to the newly opened turpentine fields of Georgia and Alabama," a Raleigh newspaper observed, and "these men are doing what they have never done before—taking their women with them—which course seems to indicate their purpose to remain."[57]

Once a young black person got old enough to set out on his or her own, virtually any place was better than staying on a sharecropping farm. As a result of the mobility of the young, W.E.B. Du Bois wrote of Dougherty County, Georgia, in the late 1890s, "you will find many families with hosts of babies, and many young couples, but few families with half-grown boys and girls. The whole tendency of the labor system is to separate the family group—the house is too small for them, the young people go to town or hire out on a neighboring farm." Not only were relatively young families thus prematurely divided, but older people sometimes found themselves without nearby kin to care for them.

"Away down at the edge of the woods will live some grizzle-haired black man, digging wearily in the earth for this last crust; or a swarthy fat auntie, supported by an absent daughter, or an old couple living half by charity and half by odd jobs."[58]

Partly in response to the powerful centrifugal forces pulling against the family, blacks adopted flexible domestic arrangements. As young adults left the household, family heads invited in other people to take their place. Almost a quarter of the black households in one study included blood relations other than children, and about a third of all families lived near other relatives. Black families also relied heavily on remarriage to keep households complete, as a life expectancy of only 33 years repeatedly undermined the deepest of commitments.[59]

Sexual relations between the races changed along with other kinds of relationships. In general, interracial sex and marriage came to be far more opposed by the blacks and whites as the decades passed. Whites thought black people were widely infected with venereal disease; that fear discouraged white men who might otherwise have pursued black women. For their part, black women and men strengthened their resistance to the callous abuse of black women by white men as soon as slavery ended. By moving into their own homes and out of the quarters, black families reduced the access white men had to black women. One white man testified before a national commission that there was less intercourse between white men and black women than before the war, not only because of syphilis "but because the negro will not let them have it. The negro buck will go down and will stay right around them." This retired planter from Mississippi told the investigators that "if a woman comes into a store, and there is a white man standing around, there will be a half a dozen colored men in front of the store waiting for her."[60]

Interracial sex by no means ended, though the sexual contact between the races seems to have shifted from plantations to the less well-defined terrain of stores and towns where white men felt freer to proposition black women. "In the towns, where the white population, unlike that of the country, is so largely a floating one, and where the opportunities for a single act of intimacy between white men and negro women, entirely unacquainted with each other and passing at once out of each other's knowledge, are so numerous," Virginian Philip A. Bruce wrote in a London periodical in 1900, "the intercourse is more frequent, as the danger of exposure is very small." In such places, white men harassed black women. "The way in which many respectable, intelligent colored girls are hounded by white men of the baser sort does much to create bitterness among the negroes," a Hampton Institute professor said. Indeed, a black pastor wrote from Alabama, "if one of our men look at a white woman very hard and she complains he is lynched for it; white men on the high ways and in their stores and on the trains will insult our women and we are powerless to resent it as it would only be an invitation for our lives to be taken. The South is a pretty good organized mob and will remain so until bursted by the Federal Government."[61]

For their part, Southern whites were convinced that it was blacks who were dangerous, who bred the violence that hung over the South. Virtually every issue of every Southern newspaper contained an account of black wrongdoing; if no episode from nearby could be found, episodes were imported from as far away as necessary; black crimes perpetrated in the North were especially attractive. Black men were thought to be inclined toward certain kinds of crimes, crimes of passion rather than crimes of cunning.

"The longer I am here, the more I dread and fear the nigger," a white woman from Massachusetts wrote to a relative from her new home in Louisiana. "They have no regard for their own lives, and seem to have no feeling. Consequently if they have some fancied wrong to avenge, the first thing they think of is to kill. You rarely hear of them fighting fist fights. It is always a razor or knife or revolver." A white lumberman recalled how bold a black man might be even to an armed white. The quarter boss of a lumber camp was told that "a bad nigger" had just come in on a boxcar, and it was the boss's job to move him on. The boss overtook the black man, took a .45 pistol from him, and told him to "hit the road." The black man turned and left. "But before the quarter boss got back to town, that black man snuck around and met him and he said, 'Well, we're even now—I let you look good. But you'd rather live than keep that gun, wouldn't you?' And the quarterboss gave up that gun. Then the black man said, 'Now you go back to the quarters and tend to them, and I'll tend to the road.'"[62]

Whites believed that such men were responsible for a rising tide of crime in the South in the late 1880s and early 1890s. "Up to fifteen years ago, tramps of any sort were unknown," an article in the Nation observed in 1893. "Now, whites go by, at some seasons, daily, and gangs of colored wandering beggars have also begun. Usually such negroes are willing to work on odd jobs only. It is probable that these vagrant bands furnish the wretched victims for the horrible lynchings described in so much detail in the local papers." J. Pope Brown told the federal commission on agriculture in 1901 that a neighbor of his had been killed with an ax. "I said right then and there: 'There is one thing you can set down . . . , this crime was not committed by a negro that owned a mule or a foot of land or any other piece of property.'" And, "sure enough, we traced this thing to a couple of negro tramps that followed up and down the railroads and gambled and drank whisky with the negroes after they had been paid off. They are the class that commit the crimes."[63]

Economic change did in fact feed higher rates of black arrests and prison terms. One state after another passed laws in the early 1890s and again in the early 1900s to check black mobility; they piled on restrictions against vagrancy, contract evasion, and labor agents. Black men moving from one place to another, with no white boss to speak up for them or pay their bail, found themselves at the mercy of local police and courts. Planters, railroads, or other employers facing labor shortages were all too happy to purchase, merely by paying a small fine and court-costs, the labor of black men convicted of petty crimes. County officials were eager to arrest black men moving through a county, whether for vagrancy or some other trumped up charge, when they knew they could make money for the county and themselves by farming the prisoners out. The white men who hired convict labor had no incentive to treat the convicts with anything other than enough care to keep them alive and working. County officials looked the other way when mistreatment and even death resulted.[64]

In the decades after emancipation the prison populations of the Southern states had burgeoned with black men convicted of property crimes; the hard times of the 1870s had seen the numbers surge as desperate men resorted to theft and as landowners prosecuted mercilessly, even when guilt was in doubt or the object of the theft low in value. From 1866 on, every Southern government had struggled to find a way to deal with this new prison population, for spending money on black criminals was at the bottom of every white taxpayers' list of priorities. As a result, one state after another turned to the leasing of convicts to private businesses. For a small fee, a railroad builder, a planter, or a mine owner could use the labor of state convicts with littler financial risk and with no labor troubles.[65]

Not surprisingly, such a system bred inhumane travesties. In some of the most forbidding landscapes of the New South terrible scenes of inhumanity were played out: mass sickness, brutal whipping, discarded bodies, near starvation, rape. Time after time, word leaked out about what was happening in the camps in the swamps or the piney woods; time after time, investigations lamely concluded that something would have to be done; time after time, the deaths and exploitation went on. Some of the wealthiest capitalists in the South became convict lessees, and some men with little capital but good political connections became rich off the franchise in the state's felons. The convict camps became places not only of profit but also of political patronage, places where party workers with little ability could be posted with a shotgun, a ledgerbook, or even a doctor's bag. Critics repeatedly raised their voices against this crime committed by the state, but it went on for decades, while thousands died. Southern whites tolerated such barbarities partly because they were persuaded that black crime was out of control. White papers began to speak of "bad niggers" who held white law in contempt, who feared no white man, who longed for revenge against all whites, who held it as a matter of pride that no white boss qualified their freedom. These black men, considering the courts the "white man's law," accorded sheriffs and judges no respect. Whites heard rumors that black criminals were held up as heroes by the black community, championed for their bravery against persistent white injustice. Whites in the cities and the countryside were certain that black crime was rapidly spinning out of control. In the late 1880s, arrests and prison terms for black men began to mount, along with white rhetoric, anxiety, and violence.[66]

The newspapers did more than their share to publicize and exaggerate black crime and white retaliation. A Louisiana paper noted several incidents indicating that "the negroes are becoming overbearing and need toning down. We warn them to be careful, or they will be taught a lesson that they will never forget." The newspapers, taking every opportunity to trumpet such challenges, increased racial tension in the late 1880s and early 1890s. "The negroes are evidently in an excited state—loud talking and gruff looks the order of the day. . . . I feel truly heavy-hearted. This neighborhood is getting more and more disagreeable," Anne Simons Deas of South Carolina wrote in her diary in 1893. "Last night the noise was horrible, for two nights we have not slept much. Friday night we had some ground for suspecting that the house was entered, though nothing was missing. The negroes are in a very excited state. I fear trouble is pending. The newspapers with their intolerable gabble, will be responsible. They seem trying to precipitate trouble."[67]

The New South was a notoriously violent place. Homicide rates among both blacks and whites were the highest in the country, among the highest in the world. Lethal weapons seemed everywhere. Guns as well as life were cheap: two or three dollars would buy a pistol known in the trade as a "nigger killer," or one of its major competitors, the "owl-head" or the "American Bulldog." in a memoir about a Presbyterian picnic, one man recalled that "each young gentleman desired to have a pistol, a jack knife, and a pair of brass knucks," all of which were considered "the proper accoutrements of the young blades of the day." One young man working at a cotton compress on the border between the Carolinas wrote a friend for a favor. "I want you to get me a gun if you know where you can get a good one, and send it to me. This is a tough place up here. I am simply afraid to go out at night without one. They shoot about one hundred times every night."[68]

In the turbulent South of the 1880s and early 1890s, when politics and economic turmoil constantly threw people into conflict, such weaponry and violence could easily spark interracial bloodshed. Most of that violence was directed by whites against blacks, whether in barroom shootings, political assassinations, labor disputes, or because of some real or imaginary breach of the racial code. When blacks did turn against whites, they risked terrible reputation from other whites. That, in itself, was nothing new: black men, in both the antebellum and Postbellum years, had been taken from jail and hanged, tortured, and burned by mobs of white men because a legal execution seemed too good for such criminals. Events of this sort had happened throughout Reconstruction, in high numbers.

The visibility and ferocity of lynching seemed to assume new proportions in the 1880s and 1890s. One peak of lynching appears to have occurred in the early 1880s and another in the years around 1890. Newspaper and magazine articles proliferated both in defense and in denunciation of lynching; a steady stream of more thoughtful articles and books emerged throughout the first decades of the twentieth century which tried to discover the origins and solutions to lynching.[69]

Lynchings were far more likely to occur in some regions of the South than in others, and those patterns call into question easy assumptions about the forces behind lynching. No simple political argument will work. Although North Carolina witnessed the greatest amount of racial conflict in the political realm of any Southern state, including the brutal white supremacy campaign and Wilmington riot of 1898, the heavily black part of the state registered a remarkably low rate of lynching. Although white South Carolina under race-baiting Governor Ben Tillman was given every permission to hate, his state fell far below the regional average in the number of black men lynched. Although white Virginia felt compelled to hold a disfranchisement convention, it recorded one of the lowest lynching rates in the South. Kentucky, on the other hand, largely outside the maelstrom of Populism and disfranchisement, near the border of the North, and with a relatively diversified economy, saw a remarkably high rate of lynching. Even West Virginia, dominated by Republicans, reached the regional average in black lynching. Clearly, something other than the political environment triggered the bloodshed.[70]

Two subregions witnessed especially high rates of lynchings: the Gulf Plain stretching from Florida to Texas, and the cotton uplands of Mississippi, Louisiana, Arkansas, and Texas. While both of these subregions had a high proportion of blacks in their populations, they were by no means the regions with the highest black proportion. Neither did they register a particularly high level of voting against the Democratic regime.

What they did share was a particular demography. These subregions had an extremely low rural population density, often only half that of states in the east. In the last two decades of the nineteenth century they experienced tremendous rates of black population increase. While the average county in the South saw its black population grow by 48 percent between 1880 and 1910, counties in Florida's Gulf Plain grew by 131 percent, Alabama's grew by 119 percent, Mississippi's by 91 percent, and Texas's by 71 percent. The only state whose Gulf Plain area had a relatively low lynching rate, close to that of the region as a whole, was Louisiana's, which did not see great black population change. The subregions with the second and third highest rates of lynching—the cotton uplands and, surprisingly, the mountains of Appalachia—also combined a relatively low population density and high rates of black population growth.[71]

The counties most likely to witness lynchings had scattered farms where many black newcomers and strangers lived and worked. Those counties were also likely to have few towns, weak law enforcement, poor communication with the outside, and high levels of transiency among both races. Such a setting fostered the fear and insecurity that fed lynching at the same time it removed the few checks that helped dissuade would-be lynchers elsewhere. Lynching served as a method of law enforcement in sparsely populated places where white people felt especially insecure. Whites dreaded the idea that black criminals could get away with harming a white person without being punished, worried that the lack of retribution would encourage others to raise their hand against isolated whites on remote plantations, farms, or roads.

The sporadic violence of lynching was a way for white people to reconcile weak governments with a demand for an impossibly high level of racial mastery, a way to terrorize blacks into acquiescence by brutally killing those who intentionally or accidentally stepped over some invisible and shifting line of permissible behavior. The brutality was not generated by crowding and friction; places such as the Black Belt and the Piedmont, with high population densities, saw relatively low rates of lynching. In such places, black people were more likely to know at least a few whites as neighbors or employers. They were also able to turn to black friends and allies should they be pursued by a lynch mob.

Lynchings tended to flourish where whites were surrounded by what they called "strange niggers," blacks with no white to vouch for them, blacks with no reputation in the neighborhood, blacks without even other blacks to aid them. Lynching seemed both more necessary and more feasible in places such as the Gulf Plain, the cotton uplands, and the mountains. In those places most blacks and whites did not know one another, much less share ties of several generations. The black population often moved from one year to the next in search of jobs at lumber camps and large plantations. "The salvation of the negro in this country depends upon drawing the social lines tighter, tighter all the while, North and South," the president of a black college in Alabama warned an Emancipation Day audience in 1901. "The moment they become slack the white man becomes brutal—the negro goes down forever."[72]

Local black leaders, for their own purposes, readily joined whites in blaming vagrant blacks for any crime in the neighborhood. "There never was a respectable colored man lynched in the south, except in a case of murder," a black minister from Montgomery wrote even as he denounced lynching. "I speak from my own experience when I say that in the lynchings I have known about, the victims were always men in the community no one could say a good word for. They came out from the slums at night, like the raccoon, and stole back again." Local blacks had every reason for displacing white anger, for finding some stranger who could bear the brunt of white men determined to wreak vengeance.[73]

Although most lynchings were inflicted in response to alleged murder, most of the rhetoric and justification focused intently on the so-called "one crime" or "usual crime": the sexual assault of white women by blacks. That assault some times involved rape, while at other times a mere look or word was enough to justify death. Black reformers such as Ida B. Wells argued repeatedly that even the accusation of rape made up only a fraction of the reasons giving for lynching: Just as repeatedly, whites argued that violations of white womanhood were the crimes that unleashed the lynching beast. Whites opposed to lynching, Northern and Southern, apparently felt compelled to acquiesce to this argument.

Whites assumed that black men lusted after white women, but there was a widespread suspicion that it was more than lust that drove black men into the alleged assaults. "I think there can be no doubt that a considerable amount of crime on the part of colored men against white men and women is due to a spirit of getting even," a white Southerner observed. "Not getting even with any particular individual, but just an indefinite getting even with white race." Whites could not help but realize that black people chafed under their many injustice, It did not seem far-fetched to whites that furious black men would attack the most vulnerable among the more privileged race. One woman who had grown up in the countryside of middle Tennessee recalled that girls were taught to sew but not cook, "because we were never allowed to enter the kitchen. There was a prohibition because the Negro men on the place that didn't have families were fed in the kitchen." This woman told the younger white woman interviewing her in 1952 that "you can't remember and maybe can't understand the horror that had grown up of any contact with a Negro man."[74]

Just as white girls and women were raised to fear strange black men, so were black boys and men taught to avoid any situation where they might be falsely accused. For generations, young black men learned early in their lives that they could at any time be grabbed by a white mob—whether for murder, looking at a white woman the wrong way, or merely being "smart"—and dragged into the woods or a public street to be tortured, burned, mutilated. It was a poisoned atmosphere, one that permeated life far beyond those counties where a lynching had actually taken place, one that pervaded all the dealings each race had with the other.[75]

Juxtapositions of the modern and the archaic constantly jarred the New South, as Mell Barrett, a young white boy, discovered when he spent a nickel to hear his first Edison talking machine at a country picnic in 1896. "With the tubes in my ears, the Pitchman was now adjusting the needle on the machine. . . . My excitement increased, my heart was pounding so I could hardly hold the tubes in my ears with my shaking hands." At first, he thought he was listening to a recording of a convention of some sort. "'All Right Men. Bring Them Out. Let's Hear What They Have to Say,' were the first words I understood coming from a talking machine." The young boy listened to two men confess to a rape, then beg for mercy. "The sounds of shuffling feet, swearing men, rattle of chains, falling wood, brush, and fagots, then a voice—shrill, strident, angry, called out, 'Who will apply the torch?' 'I will,' came a chorus of high-pitched, angry voices." Barrett could hear "the crackle of flames as it ate its way into the dry tender," and the victims asking God to forgive their tormentors. The crowd fell quiet; only the sound of the flames remained.

My eyes and mouth were dry. I tried to wet my lips, but my tongue, too, parched. Perspiration dripped from my hands. I stood immobile, unable to move. Now the voice of the Pitchman saying, "That's all gentlemen—who's next?" As Barrett took the tubes from his ears, the next man asked, "'What's the matter, Son—sick?'" The Pitchman, "sensing what my trouble was, said, 'Too much cake, too much lemonade. You know how boys are at a picnic.'"[76]

ENDNOTES

1. Washington quoted in Thomas Jackson Woofter, Jr., *Negro Migration: Changes in Rural Organization and Population of the Cotton Belt* (New York: W. D. Gray, 1920), 53; Harry Crews, *A Childhood, the Biography of a Place* (NewYork, Harper and Row, 1978), 57–58. Although Crews grew up in the early twentieth century, the same lesson had surely been passed down the generation before.

2. Bertram Wilbur Doyle, *The Etiquette of Race Relations in the South: A Study in Social Control* (Chicago: Univ. of Chicago Press, 1937), 136–159; Glenn N. Sisk, "Alabama Black Belt: A Social History, 1875–1917" (Ph.D. diss., Duke Univ., 1951), 91–92; Mamie Garvin Fields with Karen Fields, *Lemon Swamp and Other Places: A Carolina Memoir* (New York: Free Press, 1983), 72–73.

3. *Lafayette Gazette* in *St. Landry Clarion*, Oct. 5, 1895; Robert J. Knox Diary, Feb. 19,1897, Knox-Wallace Papers, UVA; Anne Simon Deas JournaL, May 19, 1894, SCa.

4. Parker was in fact nominated for the court, which may have affected the way the story was remembered. LeGette Blythe, *William Henry Belk: Merchant of the South* (Chapel Hill: Univ. of North Carolina Press, 1950), 48.

5. Rev. C. C. White and Ada Morehead Holland, *No Quittin' Sense* (Austin: Univ. of Texas Press, 1969), 55–69.

6. Clive Metcalfe Diary, Feb. 20, 1892, Feb. 17, April 25, Aug. 10, 1890, July 4, 1891, microfilm copy, UNC-SHC. Only about 15 percent of white households had a black resident, according to Barbara F. Agresti, "Town and Country in a Florida Rural County in the Late Nineteenth Century: Some Population and Household Comparisons," *Rural Sociology* 42 (Winter 1977): 562.

7. Clive Metcalfe Diary, Dec. 21, 22, 1890, Dec. 24, 1891, UNC-SHC; Louisa Taylor Diary, Dec. 23, 1890, Taylor Family Papers, LSU; William Pickens, *Bursting Bonds*, enlarged ed., *The Heir of Slaves* (1911; Boston and Jordan and More, 1923), 15–16.

8. Adelaide Brown to Mrs. W. M. Camak, Dec. 23, 1896, Camak Collection, UGA.

9. Jack Temple Kirby, "Black and White in the Rural South, 1915–1954," *Agricultural History* 58 (July 1984): 413–17; Caroline S. Coleman, *Five Petticoats on Sunday* (Greeneville, S.C.: Hiott Press, 1962), 55–56; Margaret J. Bosterli, ed., *Vinegar Pie and Chicken Bread: A Woman's Diary of Life in the Rural South, 1890–1891* (Fayetteville: Univ. of Arkansas Press, 1982), 9–10.

10. Howard N. Rabinowitz, *Race Relations in the Urban South, 1865–1890* (New York: Oxford Univ. Press, 1978), 127–225, passim; Memphis *Commercial Appeal*, Jan. 6, 1885, quoted in Thomas H. Baker, *The Memphis "Commercial Appeal": The History of a Southern Newspaper* (Baton Rouge: LSU Press, 1971), 140. The timing of segregation has been a topic of prolonged debate in Southern history ever since the publication of C. Vann Woodward's classic, *The Strange Career of Jim Crow* (New York: Oxford Univ. Press, 1955). For a thorough overview of the debate, see Howard N. Rabinowitz, "More Than the Woodward Thesis: Assessing *The Strange Career of Jim Crow*," *JAH* 75 (Dec. 1988): 842–56.

11. Woodward stressed the flux of the eighties in *Strange Career*, and subsequent studies have proven him correct. For the most thorough and systematic portrayals of race relations in the decade, see Joel Williamson, *The Crucible of Race: Black-White Relations in the American South Since Emancipation* (New York: Oxford Univ. Press, 1984); Joseph H. Cartwright, *The Triumph of Jim Crow: Tennessee Race Relations in the 1880s* (Knoxville: Univ. of Tennessee Press, 1976); George C. Wright,

Life Behind a Veil: Blacks in Louisville, Kentucky, 1865–1930 (Baton Rouge, LSU Press, 1985), 54; David Paul Bennetts, "Black and White Workers: New Orleans, 1880–1900" (Ph.D. diss., Univ. of Illinois at Urbana-Champaign, 1972), 211; Rabinowitz, *Race Relations.*

Some historians, focusing on law, emphasize the instrumental uses of racial prejudice for whites. From such a perspective, ravings about the black menace appear mainly as campaign rhetoric, smokescreens thrown up to hide more tangible motives of greed and lust for power. Segregation laws look like campaign ploys, ways to win the votes of ignorant voters back home. Some have seen similar desires behind the chilling racial violence of the New South, portraying lynchings as political maneuvers orchestrated to cow black opposition. An instrumental view is usually associated with the tradition of progressive history best embodied in the work of C. Vann Woodward, especially *Tom Watson: Agrarian Rebel* (New York: Macmillan, 1938) and *Origins of the New South, 1877–1913* (Baton Rouge: LSU Press, 1951). Woodward, while painfully aware of the power of race, has seen class and economic divisions as more fundamental; indeed, a considerable part of the power of his interpretations grows from his indignation at the uses of race by those who dominated the South. J. Morgan Kousser employs this perspective in a more insistent fashion in his *The Shaping of Southern Politics: Suffrage Restriction and the Establishment of the One-Party South, 1880–1910* (New Haven: Yale Univ. Press, 1974) and in "Progressivism—For Middle Class Whites Only: North Carolina Education, 1880–1910," *JSH* 46 (May 1980): 169–94. For lynching, see James M. Inveriarity, "Populism and Lynching in Louisiana, 1889–1896: A Test of Erickson's Theory of the Relationship Between Boundary Crises and Repressive Justice," *American Sociological Review* 41 (April 1976): 262–80.

Others have seen racial prejudice in general as false consciousness, an illusion bred by the powerful. John W. Cell argues that "unlike class relations, which have their ultimate origins in contradictions that emerge within and between a society's basic modes of production and exchange, race relations are essentially extrinsic. Their origins are not in production, but in power. They are not inevitable or natural. They must therefore be imposed. In the evolution of history, however, race can and has become so embedded in fundamental institutions that it is virtually inseparable except by means of decisive overthrow or wholesale reordering of the political and social system. Racism is indeed what Lenin called false consciousness. It it nonetheless real and powerful." See *The Highest Stage of White Supremacy: The Origins of Segregation in South Africa and the American South* (New York: Cambridge Univ. Press, 1982), 117.

At the other pole of interpretation are those who focus on racism as a set of motivations that enveloped, subsumed, others. From such a perspective, the manifestations of racial conflict in the New South, whether segregation, disfranchisement, or lynching, were driven by ideas and notions promulgated by influential whites. This racism, in turn, grew out of those whites' personal experiences and conflicts, often intellectual, psychological, or sexual. Events appear caught in tides of irrational fear and resentment. A perspective that explores "the development of intellectualized racist theory and ideology as it was applied directly and programmatically to the 'problem' posed in the white mind by the presence of millions of blacks in the United States" is given its most sophisticated statement in George M. Fredrickson, *The Black Image in the White Mind: The Debate on Afro-American Character and Destiny, 1817–1914* (New York: Harper and Row, 1971); a bold psychological interpretation has been put forward in Joel Williamson's *The Crucible of Race.* As with the historians discussed in the preceding paragraph, both Fredrickson and Williamson portray race and racism in complex ways that cannot be reduced to easy characterization. While many less skilled historians merely invoke racism, Fredrickson and Williamson have explored it.

The present account seeks to show that relations among blacks and whites were so volatile precisely because they were inseparable from class, political, psychological, generational, and gender relations. I have been influenced by Barbara Jeanne Fields, "Ideology and Race in American History," in J. Morgan Kousser and James M. McPherson, eds., *Region, Race, and Reconstruction: Essays in Honor of C. Vann Woodward* (New York: Oxford Univ. Press, 1982), 143–77, and Judith Stein, "'Of Mr. Booker T. Washington and Others': The Political Economy of Racism in the United States," *Science and Society* 38 (Winter 1974–75): 422–53.

12. On the uniqueness of travel, see Stephen J. Riegel, "The Persistent Career of Jim Crow: Lower Federal Courts and the 'Separate but Equal' Doctrine, 1865–1896," *American Journal of Legal History* 28 (Jan. 1984): 25, and Charles A. Lofgren, *The Plessy Case: A Legal-Historical Interpretation* (New York: Oxford Univ. Press, 1987), 17; Rabinowitz, "More Than the Woodward Thesis," 847.

13. "Papa," [J. C. Carpenter] to "My dear boy," Nov. 14, 1891, Carpenter Papers, LSU; Lofgren, *Plessy*, 9–17; also see Annie Perry [Jester] to "Dear Mother," Sept. 29, 1896, Annie Perry Jester Papers, SCa.

14. Ellen Glasgow, *The Voice of the People* (New York: Doubleday, Page, 1900), 309.

15. Sutton E. Griggs, *Imperium in Imperio* (1899; rpt., New York, Arno Press, 1969), 142–44.

16. Andrew W. Springs to Charles N. Hunter, Sept. 26, 1891, Hunter Papers, Duke.

17. James Melvin Washington, "The Origins and Emergence of Black Baptist Separation, 1863–1897" (Ph.D. diss., Yale Univ., 1979), 177–78.

18. *Chattanooga Times* in *Nashville American*, March 19, 1889, in John E. Buser, "After Half a Generation: The South of the 1880s" (Ph.D. diss., Univ. of Texas, 1968), 205–6.

19. *New Orleans Times-Democrat*, July 9, 1890, quoted in Otto Olsen, ed., *The Thin Disguise: Turning Point in Negro History—Plessy v. Ferguson: A Documentary Presentation (1864–1896)* (New York: Humanities Press, 1967), 53.

20. Buser, "After Half a Generation," 67; for a fascinating account of Southern race relations in this period that puts sexuality at the heart of conflict, though in a way that focuses more on changes in white psychology and less on evolving kinds of social interaction, see Williamson, *Crucible of Race*.

21. Quoted in John William Graves, "Town and Country: Race Relations and Urban Development in Arkansas, 1874–1905" (Ph.D. diss., Univ. of Virginia, 1978), 285.

22. A newspaper from Columbia had already suggested part of the answer; when the railroad voluntarily offered to run segregated trains to the state fair, the paper had warmly noted "a very obliging spirit on the part of the railroad authorities, and no doubt many ladies will in consequence come to the Fair who would not otherwise have attended." The governor accepted the offer because race mixing in the cars was often "attended by unpleasant incidents." All quotes from James Hammond Moore, introduction to Isaac DuBose Seabrook, *Before and After: or, The Relations of the Races of the South* (1895; rpt., Baton Rouge: LSU Press, 1967), 14–16.

23. "Studies in the South," *Atlantic Monthly*, 50 (Nov. 1882); 627; *Savannah Tribune*, May 7, 1887, in Horace Calvin Wingo, "Race Relations in Georgia, 1872–1908" (Ph.D. diss., Univ. of Georgia, 1969), 130.

24. Mary Church Terrell, *A Colored Woman in a White World* (1940; rpt., New York: Arno, 1980), 296–98.

25. Riegel, "Persistent Career of Jim Crow," 25–27.

26. Lofgren, *Plessy*, 145–47; Henry M. Field, *Bright Skies and Dark Shadows* (New York: C. Scribner's Sons, 1890), 152; Buser, "After Half a Generation," 163–64, 203–4; Catherine A. Barnes, *Journey from Jim Crow: The Desegregation of Southern Transit* (New York: Columbia Univ. Press, 1983), 6–7.

27. *Mobile Register*, April 18, 1882, in Buser, "After Half a Generation," 56, Wright, *Life Behind a Veil*, 63–64. Also see John Hammond Moore, "Jim Crow in Georgia," *South Atlantic Quarterly* 66 (Autumn 1967), 554–65; Henry C. Dethloff and Robert R. Jones, "Race Relations in Louisiana, 1877–1898," *Louisiana History* 9 (Fall 1968); 322; Wingo, "Race Relations in Georgia," 125–27.

28. Milton Smith, quoted in Maury Klein, *History of the Louisville and Nashville Railroad* (New York: Macmillan, 1972), 331.

29. Cartwright, *Triumph of Jim Crow*, 104–7; Roger L. Hart, *Redeemers, Bourbons, and Populists: Tennessee, 1870–1896* (Baton Rouge: LSU Press, 1975), 28–55; Franklin Johnson, *The Development of State Legislation Concerning the Free Negro* (1918; rpt., Westport: Greenwood, 1979), 184. Stanley Folmsbee, in a 1949 article, argued that this law was "a concession to Negroes," but Cartwright sees the law instead as "an effort by the legislature to sanction racial discrimination on the state's railroads in a more systematic basis than before." The law, it seems, was both an attempt to forestall further black agitation on the issue and an attempt to force the railroads to make more of an effort to appease blacks. See Folmsbee, "The Origins of the First 'Jim Crow' Law," *JSH* 15 (May 1949); 235–47, and Cartwright, *Triumph*, 107.

30. Grady quoted in Dana White, "The Old South Under New Conditions," in Dana F. White and Victor A. Kramer, eds., *Olmsted South: Old South Critic/New South Planner* (Westport: Greenwood Press, 1979), 162; Paul M. Gaston, *The New South Creed: A Study in Southern Mythmaking* (New York: Alfred Knopf, 1970), 148–49; Cell, *Highest Stage of White Supremacy*, 181–83; Buser, "After Half a Generation," 204–5; Lofgren, *Plessy*, 24–25; Florida law in Johnson, *State Legislation*, 86.

31. Johnson, *State Legislation*, 133, 189.

32. Lofgren, *Plessy*, 24–25; Olsen, *The Thin Disguise*, 10–21.

33. Olsen, *The Thin Disguise*, 10–21; Lofgren, *Plessy*, 32.

34. Two very useful works that argue along similar lines are Riegel, "Persistent Career of Jim Crow," and Lofgren, *Plessy*. Rabinowitz's *Race Relations in the Urban South* has played an important role by calling attention to the generational differences among blacks and the growing militancy of the younger blacks. See pp. 334–35. For the role of example, a letter to the governor of South Carolina from a salesman who regularly traveled from Baltimore to Texas pointed out that "I cannot but see the great comfort and advantage to the White people of a state overcrowded with darkies in passing a Law of this Kind. . . . The passage of such a law during your administration would be greatly appreciated by all South Carolinians except RailRoad Lawyers and would be double valued by ladies." George F. Pringle to John Gary Evans, Aug. 21, 1894, Evans Papers, SCa.

35. John Andrew Rice, *I Came Out of the Eighteenth Century* (New York, London: Harper & Bros., 1942), 41–42. An exciting and innovative work on this topic is Cell's *Highest Stage of White Supremacy.* While I find his critique of extant scholarship and his emphasis on the "modernity" of segregation well taken, it seems to me that Cell does not take the context in which power was exercised—the state legislatures—as seriously as he should. Cell emphasizes the capitalist nature of the New South, only to turn to a rather mechanical reliance on a "power elite" in which planters play a large role to explain segregation. Of course men with power wrote the laws, but they possessed a temporary and quite circumscribed kind of power, thoroughly caught in the contingencies of electoral politics. Jeffrey Richards and John M. MacKenzie, *The Railway Station: A Social History* (Oxford: Clarendon, 1986), 137, point out that throughout the world the railroad station "was an extraordinary agent of social mixing. . . . But the stations were in many respects designed to avoid these encounters across class and racial boundaries as much as possible."

36. *Nashville Banner,* June 12, 1891, quoted in Hart, *Redeemers, Bourbons, and Populists,* 164–65; "Jim Crow on Wheels," *Chicago Defender,* Nov. 3, 1917, quoted in Neil R. McMillen, *Dark Journey: Black Mississippians in the Age of Jim Crow* (Urbana: Univ. of Illinois Press, 1989), 293; Kharif, "Refinement of Racial Segregation in Florida," 146–47; Willard B. Gatewood, Jr., "Arkansas Negroes in the 1890s: Documents," *Arkansas Historical Quarterly* 33 (1974): 296–97.

37. Virginia's railroad commissioner did propose a segregation law in 1891, but no action was taken. Charles Wynes argues that "by the end of the nineteenth century it was customary for the races to ride together on most of the railroads in Virginia without confinement to either a Jim Crow or the smoking car." This would mean that Virginia was quite different from the surrounding Southern states. See Wynes, *Race Relations in Virginia, 1870–1902* (Charlottesville: Univ. of Virginia Press, 1961), 73–74. A law was suggested in North Carolina, but a black delegation won assurances from the speaker of the house that he would never allow such a law to pass while he held his office. Frenise Logan documents conflicts and black assertion in North Carolina that resembled those of states that did implement Jim Crow. See Frenise A. Logan, *The Negro in North Carolina, 1876–1894* (Chapel Hill: UNC Press, 1964), 176–80. South Carolina saw railroad segregation laws "introduced and defeated by every legislature in the early 1890s. . . . Economic motives lay behind the opposition, which came largely from businessmen and pro-railroad men." Linda M. Matthews, "Keeping Down Jim Crow: The Railroads and the Separate Coach Bills in South Carolina," *South Atlantic Quarterly* 73 (1974): 121. The forthcoming dissertation by Patricia Minter of the University of Virginia promises to shed new light on the evolution of transportation and segregation law.

38. On North Carolina's efforts, see Eric Anderson, *Race and Politics in North Carolina, 1872–1901: The Black Second* (Baton Rouge: LSU Press, 1981), 166–67, and Frenise A. Logan, "The Movement of Negroes from North Carolina, 1876–1894," *North Carolina Historical Review* 33 (Jan. 1956): 54–55.

39. *Chicksaw Messenger,* quoted in Vernon Lane Wharton, *The Negro in Mississippi, 1865–1890* (Chapel Hill: UNC Press, 1947), 207.

40. Clark Leonard Miller, "'Let Us Die to Make Men Free': Political Terrorism in Post-Reconstruction Mississippi, 1877–1896" (Ph.D. diss., Univ. of Minnesota, 1983), vol. I, pp. 578–79; William F. Holmes, *The White Chief: James Kimble Vardaman* (Baton Rouge: LSU Press, 1970), 44–46.

41. Miller, "'Let Us Die,'" 505–11; McMillen, *Dark Journey,* 53 (quotes); Holmes, *White Chief,* 44–46; Albert D. Kirwan, *Revolt of the Rednecks: Mississippi Politics, 1876–1925* (Lexington: Univ. of Kentucky Press, 1951), 59; Kousser, *Shaping of Southern Politics,* 139–42.

42. William S. McAllister in *Jackson Clarion-Ledger,* Aug. 29, 1889, quoted in Miller, "'Let Us Die,'" 572; last two quotes in William Charles Sallis, "The Color Line in Mississippi Politics, 1865–1915" (Ph.D. diss., Univ. of Kentucky, 1967), 281–82.

43. Wharton, *Negro in Mississippi,* 210–11; Kirwan, *Revolt of the Rednecks,* 65–66; Kousser, *Shaping of Southern Politics,* 142–143.

44. *Greenville Times,* Oct. 11, 1890, in Sallis, "Color Line in Mississippi Politics," 309–10; *Jackson Daily Clarion-Ledger,* Sept. 17, 18, 1890, in Kirwan, *Revolt of the Rednecks,* 66; Janet Sharp Hermann, in *The Pursuit of a Dream* (New York: Oxford Univ. Press, 1981), 227–32, found that Montgomery's town of Mound Bayou received favorable treatment after his actions at the convention.

45. Montgomery in Miller, "'Let Us Die,'" 606–9; *Aberdeen Weekly Examiner,* Sept. 19, 1890, quoted in Sallis, "Color Line," 317–18. For the "ambivalent" black response to Montgomery's stand, see McMillen, *Dark Journey,* 50–52.

46. For the quote on crimes, see McMillen, *Dark Journey,* 43.

47. Wharton, *Negro in Mississippi,* 213–14; Kirwan, *Revolt of the Rednecks,* 67; Kousser, *Shaping of Southern Politics,* 143; Sallis, "Color Line," 316.

48. First two papers quoted in Sallis, "Color Line," 310–14; last quote from Wharton, *Negro in Mississippi*, 214.

49. Sallis, "Color Line," 320; Wharton, *Negro in Mississippi*, 214.

50. White in *Report of the Industrial Commission on Agriculture and Agricultural Labor,* vol. 10 (Washington, D.C.: Government Printing Office, 1901), 428; David Schenck diary, Jan. 20, 1890, UNC-SHC. One white author heralded black population movement, especially to the cities of the North, as "The Unaided Solution of the Southern Race Problem," "It is best for the negro; best for the South; best for the whole country. It comes as the unaided result of the unrestricted operation of economic law," A. S. Van de Graaff wrote. "It needs no other help than the maintenance of peace and tranquility, assuring the undisturbed action of natural forces." A. S. Van de Graaff, *Forum* 21 (1896): 342, 344.

51. John Burgwyne McRae diary, Jan. 2, 1890, UVA; Logan, *Negro in North Carolina*, 132; William F. Holmes, "Labor Agents and the Georgia Exodus, 1899–1900," *South Atlantic Quarterly* 79 (Autumn 1980): 445–46. Black laborers in Louisiana migrated from the cotton fields to cottonseed-oil mills to the wharves of New Orleans to the sugar plantations. See Bennetts, "Black and White Workers," 72–73.

52. Logan, "Movement of Negroes from North Carolina," 63; Holmes, "Labor Agents and the Georgia Exodus," 437; letterhead on letter from F. H. Holiday to Maj. A. J. Richardson, Aug. 10, 1894, in William E. Bibb Papers, UVA. For dramatic examples of the effects labor agents could exert, see Daniel F. Littlefield, Jr., and Lonnie E. Underhill, "Black Dreams and 'Free' Homes: The Oklahoma Territory, 1891–1894," *Phylon* (Dec. 1973): 342–57, and Alfred W. Reynolds, "The Alabama Negro Colony in Mexico, 1894–1896," *Alabama Review* 5 (1952): 243–68, and 6 (1953): 31–58.

53. This account comes from the thorough and revealing article by William F. Holmes, "Labor Agents and the Georgia Exodus," especially 440–42.

54. North Carolina *Labor Report* (1902), 74, quoted in I. A. Newby, *Plain Folk in the New South: Social Change and Cultural Persistence, 1880–1915* (Baton Rouge: LSU Press, 1989), 69.

55. Pickens, *Bursting Bonds*, 28–30.

56. William Edward Vickery, "The Economics of the Negro Migration, 1900–1960" (Ph.D. diss., Univ. of Chicago, 1969), 27–28; William Cohen, *At Freedom's Edge: Black Mobility and the Southern White Quest for Racial Control, 1861–1915* (Baton Rouge: LSU Press, 1991), a comprehensive overview; Peter Gottlieb, *Making Their Own Way: Southern Blacks' Migration to Pittsburg, 1916–1930* (Urbana: Univ. of Illinois Press, 1987), 12–33.

57. Woofter, *Negro Migration*, 149; Daniel M. Johnson and Rex R. Campbell, *Black Migration in America: A Social Demographic History* (Durham: Duke Univ. Press, 1981); 69–70. In the coal mining counties of West Virginia, Virginia, and Kentucky, the number of black females per 100 black males fell as low as 26 and averaged only about 50; in those same counties, the number of white women per 100 white males averaged about 85. See Randall G. Lawrence, "Appalachian Metamorphosis: Industrializing Society on the Central Appalachian Plateau, 1860–1913" (Ph.D. diss., Duke Univ., 1983), 125. The standard deviations for women as percentage of population among a state's counties show a range for blacks as high as 10.8 and 10.5 for Georgia and West Virginia; the regional average standard deviation for blacks was 4.8, but only 3.0 for whites; quote from *Raleigh News and Observer*, Jan. 30, 1883, in Logan, *Negro in North Carolina*, 128.

Percentage of Females in White Population, 1890

Atlantic Plain	47.6
Piedmont	49.4
Mountains	48.1
Black Belt	49.2
Central plateau	47.0
Gulf Plain	44.4
River counties	46.0
Cotton uplands	45.0
Western prairies	43.7

Percentage of Females in Black Population, 1900

Atlantic Plain	50.2
Piedmont	51.7
Mountains	51.9
Black Belt	51.0
Central plateau	49.5
Gulf Plain	49.7
River counties	49.7
Cotton uplands	49.9
Western prairies	50.0

58. W.E.B. Du Bois ed. *The Negro American Family* (Atlanta: Atlanta Univ. Press, 1908), 129.

59. Crandall A. Shifflett, *Patronage and Poverty in the Tobacco South: Louisa County, Virginia, 1860–1900* (Knoxville: Univ. of Tennessee Press, 1982), 84–95, 98; Jacqueline Jones, *Labor of Love, Labor of Sorrow: Black Women, Work, and the Family from Slavery to the Present* (New York: Basic Books, 1985), 84–85, 91–92; JoAnn Manfra and Robert R. Dykstra, "Serial Marriage and the Origins of the Black Stepfamily: The Rowanty Experience," *JAH* 71 (June 1985): 18–44; Elizabeth Ruth Bethel, *Promiseland: A Century of Life in a Negro Community* (Philadelphia: Temple Univ. Press, 1981). These kind of relationships had flourished, too, under slavery. See Herbert Gutman, *The Black Family in Slavery and Freedom, 1750–1925* (New York: Pantheon, 1975).

60. Joel Williamson, *New People: Miscegenation and Mulattoes in the United States* (New York: Free Press, 1980), 88–91; Lawrence J. Friedman, *The White Savage: Racial Fantasies in the Postbellum South* (Englewood Cliffs, N.J.: Prentice-Hall, 1970), 123–24; John W. Eldridge, *Industrial Commission*, 514.

61. Philip Alexander Bruce, "The American Negro of To-day," *Contemporary Review* 77 (Jan.–June 1900): 287; Dr. H. B. Frissell quoted in Clarence H. Poe, "Lynching : A Southern View," *Atlantic Monthly* 93 (1904): 164; A. N. Jackson to Albion Tourgée, March 23, 1892, in Otto H. Olsen, "Albion W. Tourgée and Negro Militants of the 1890s: A Documentary Selection," *Science and Society* 28 (Spring 1964): 195.

62. Alice Thrasher to Arthur P. Thrasher, Sept. 28, 1896, Thrasher Papers, LSU; unnamed informant in Archer H. Mayor, *Southern Timberman: The Legacy of William Buchanan* (Athens: Univ. of Georgia Press, 1988), 73–74.

63. C. Meriwether, "The Southern Farm Since the Civil War," *Nation* 57 (1893): 265; *Industrial Commission*, 66; also see Mark V. Wetherington, "The New South Comes to Wiregrass Georgia, 1865–1910" (Ph.D. diss., Univ. of Tennessee, 1985), 434–35.

64. See Edward L. Ayers, *Vengeance and Justice: Crime and Punishment in the Nineteenth-Century American South* (New York: Oxford Univ. Press, 1984), 223–65; Cohen, *Freedom's Edge*, 222–24; Samuel N. Pincus, *The Virginia Supreme Court, Blacks and the Law, 1870–1902* (New York: Garland, 1990).

65. Ayers, *Vengeance and Justice*, 185–222.

66. *Ibid.*, 223–65; Williamson, *Crucible of Race*, 58–59.

67. *St. Landry Clarion*, Sept. 26, 1896; Anne Simon Deas Diary, Sept. 19, 24, 1893, SCa.

68. Ayers, *Vengeance and Justice*, 266–76; Thomas D. Clark, *Pills, Petticoats, and Plows: The Southern Country Store* (Indianapolis: Bobbs-Merrill, 1944), 130; Mell Marshall Barrett, "Recollections of My Boyhood: The Picnic at Pitman's Mill," 15–16; memoir at GDAH; W. T. Sears to John A. Pugh, Sept. 11, 1896, in Pugh Papers, UNC-SHC.

69. Beginning in 1882, the *Chicago Tribune* compiled a list of all the lynchings of which the paper knew. In 1905, James Elbert Cutler used this compilation and augmented it with his own research in his *Lynch-Law: An Investigation into the History of Lynchings in the United States* (New York: Longmans, Green). The records on lynchings have been based on the resulting book: *Thirty Years of Lynching in the United States* (New York: National Association for the Advancement of Colored People, 1919). There can be no doubt that these numbers are a bare minimum, but they can help give us some sense of where and why black people were killed in such barbaric ways. The tables below are based on the NAACP's numbers.

In recent years, historians have tried to build more substantial data bases by close readings of newspapers from individual Southern states for longer periods of time. See William Fitzhugh Brundage, "Lynching in the New South: Georgia and Virginia, 1880–1930" (Ph.D. diss., Harvard Univ., 1988). In his *Racial Violence in Kentucky, 1865–1940: Lynchings, Mob Rule, and "Legal Lynchings"*

(Baton Rouge: LSU Press, 1990): 70–71, George C. Wright has discovered that the decade immediately following the Civil War accounted for the greatest number of lynchings in Kentucky, though there was indeed another upsurge in the 1890s. E. M. Beck and Stewart Tolnay, "The Killing Fields of the Deep South: The Markets for Cotton and the Lynching of Blacks, 1882–1930," *American Sociological Review* 55 (Aug. 1990): 526–39, explore economic sources for the brutality and offer a convenient review of the statistical literature.

Number of Black Southerners Lynched Between 1889 and 1909 by Region
(number of incidents)

	1889–94	1895–99	1900–1904	1905–9	TOTAL
Atlantic Plain	48 (43)	36 (25)	34 (31)	28 (22)	146 (121)
Piedmont	58 (51)	44 (35)	38 (36)	26 (17)	166 (139)
Mountains	81 (71)	28 (27)	29 (29)	13 (11)	151 (138)
Black Belt	48 (31)	47 (36)	24 (17)	22 (18)	141 (102)
Central plateau	83 (74)	52 (41)	30 (24)	25 (19)	190 (158)
Gulf Plain	95 (60)	70 (49)	59 (44)	46 (38)	270 (191)
River counties	85 (63)	61 (50)	65 (50)	48 (41)	259 (204)
Cotton uplands	129 (103)	87 (63)	64 (49)	70 (55)	350 (270)
Western prairies	11 (9)	7 (5)	3 (0)	9 (0)	30 (14)
TOTAL	638 (505)	432 (331)	346 (280)	287 (221)	1,703 (1,337)

Lynchings per 1,000 Black Men Over 21 Years of Age, 1889–1909

	LYNCHING RATE	% BLACK 1890	% BLACK POPULATION CHANGE, 1880–1910	POPULATION PER SQUARE MILE, 1900	NON-DEMOCRATIC VOTE, 1894
ALABAMA					
Piedmont	.20	43	41	41	56
Mountains	1.35	24	29	35	52
Black Belt	.58	78	21	42	14
Central plateau	1.38	29	101	27	53
Gulf Plain	1.90	39	101	23	36
ARKANSAS					
Mountains	.99	4	37	27	32
River counties	1.01	67	143	21	1
Cotton uplands	1.71	40	94	24	13
FLORIDA					
Atlantic Plain	1.49	44	130	14	19
Gulf Plain	1.44	51	132	18	15
Georgia					
Atlantic Plain	1.23	47	182	26	34
Piedmont	.81	53	29	53	31
Mountains	1.53	17	54	44	26
Black Belt	.93	62	171	36	34
KENTUCKY					

	LYNCHING RATE	% BLACK 1890	% BLACK POPULATION CHANGE, 1880–1910	POPULATION PER SQUARE MILE, 1900	NON-DEMOCRATIC VOTE, 1894
Mountains	2.15	6	36	39	59
Central plateau	1.35	17	–3	49	51
River counties	3.90	14	24	46	48
LOUISIANA					
Gulf Plain	1.26	42	59	29	38
River counties	1.21	65	28	38	22
Cotton uplands	2.00	58	46	23	37
MISSISSIPPI					
Black Belt	1.00	60	9	40	23
Central plateau	6.12 *	9	8	25	30
Gulf Plain	2.16	39	147	26	36
River counties	1.00	73	59	38	20
Cotton uplands	1.37	47	39	36	31
NORTH CAROLINA					
Atlantic Plain	.17	46	19	30	55
Piedmont	.24	35	23	45	52
Mountains	1.92	9	67	36	52
SOUTH CAROLINA					
Atlantic Plain	.27	65	12	36	34
Piedmont	.51	53	27	48	25
Mountains	.45	26	36	36	14
Black Belt	1.13	68	28	38	16
TENNESSEE					
Mountains	2.07	12	27	50	66
Black Belt	.98	15	1	32	–
Central plateau	1.17	21	14	40	47
River counties	1.13	37	17	48	39
TEXAS					
Gulf Plain	1.48	39	117	14	48
Cotton uplands	1.27	35	65	29	48
Western prairies	.45	13	98	33	49
VIRGINIA					
Atlantic Plain	.22	52	19	66	44
Piedmont	.58	46	–11	38	50
Mountains	1.12	14	76	36	52
WEST VIRGINIA					
Mountains	1.22	4	4,136	44	55

* This figure represents 3 lynchings among a black male population of 490 in 1890.

71. Lynching rates by region: Atlantic Plain, .68; Piedmont, .53; Mountains, 1.58; Black Belt, 0.90; Central plateau, 1.47; Gulf Plain, 1.86; River counties, 1.28; Cotton uplands, 1.76; Western prairies, 1.21. The major exception to this generalization is the Atlantic Plain of Georgia, which had the highest rate of black population growth and one of the lowest population densities in the South, yet saw a lynching rate slightly below the regional average. While Governor William J. Northen denounced lynching in the 1890s, it is not apparent why that region should prove such an exception to the general trends.

72. In the woods around Valdosta, Georgia, the local paper admitted, "many murders are committed on the turpentine farms and at the saw mills . . . where the negroes are numerous and perhaps only recently and temporarily imported." *Valdosta Times*, July 6, 1889, quoted in Thomas F. Armstrong, "Georgia Lumber Laborers, 1880–1917: The Social Implications of Work," *Georgia Historical Quarterly* 67 (Winter 1983): 449; W. H. Council, quoted in Sheldon Hackney, *From Populism to Progressivism in Alabama* (Princeton: Princeton Univ. Press, 1969), 185.

73. *Savannah Morning News*, March 29, 1897, quoted in Ayers, *Vengeance and Justice*, 244.

74. Wright, *Racial Violence in Kentucky*, 78; interview of Mrs. Sam Orr by Mrs. Herbert Weaver, March 4, 1952, Waller Project Collection, Vanderbilt.

75. For fear among young blacks, see James R. McGovern, *Anatomy of a Lynching: The Killing of Claude Neal* (Baton Rouge: LSU Press, 1982), 6.

76. Barrett, "Reminiscences," 49–50.

UNIT 2

AFRICAN AMERICAN THOUGHT AND OPPOSITION TO SEGREGATION

INTRODUCTION 48

2-1 • WASHINGTON CARTOON 49

2-2 • ATLANTA EXPOSITION ADDRESS 50
Booker T. Washington

2-3 • OF MR. BOOKER T. WASHINGTON AND OTHERS 53
W.E.B. Du Bois

2-4 • THE NIAGARA MOVEMENT DECLARATION OF PRINCIPLES 61

2-5 • THE NAACP AS A REFORM MOVEMENT, 1909–1965 65
"TO REACH THE CONSCIENCE OF AMERICA"
August Meier and John H. Bracey, Jr.

2-6 • MARCUS GARVEY AND THE POLITICS OF REVITALIZATION 83
Lawrence W. Levine

2-7 • THE OBJECTIVES OF THE UNIVERSAL NEGRO IMPROVEMENT ASSOCIATION 104
Marcus Garvey

2-8 • MARCUS GARVEY AND THE NAACP 106
W.E.B. Du Bois

2-9 • A FRENCH DIRECTIVE 108
ON THE TREATMENT OF BLACK AMERICAN TROOPS

2-10 • NAACP ADVERTISEMENT, 1933 110

INTRODUCTION

African Americans responded to the challenge of segregation with a variety of political, economic and social strategies. Three major African-American figures during the first decades of the twentieth century were Booker T. Washington, W.E.B. Du Bois, and Marcus Garvey. Though much divided the three men, their writings demonstrate that they also have much in common.

By the turn of the century, most whites and many blacks recognized Booker T. Washington (1856–1915) as the most important African-American leader in the country. Born into slavery, Washington's most enduring accomplishment was founding the Tuskegee Institute in Alabama, a school devoted to moral and industrial education for African Americans. Although he worked behind the scenes to halt Jim Crow's progress, in his public statements Washington appeared to accept segregation. He believed African Americans should concentrate on attaining economic self-reliance rather than pushing for political or social equality. The *Atlanta Exposition Address* (2-2) delivered at the Cotton States Exposition in 1895 is the most famous articulation of Washington's philosophy.

W.E.B. Du Bois, a Harvard and European educated historian, sociologist, and social activist, was among the best known of Washington's critics. In addition to his criticism of Booker T. Washington (2-3)—his first public break with Washington—and of Marcus Garvey (2-8), Du Bois was a principal organizer of the Niagara Movement and the National Association for the Advancement of Colored People (NAACP). In 1905, a number of prominent African Americans gathered on the Canadian side of Niagara Falls, where they drafted the Niagara Movement Declaration of Principles (2-4). When the NAACP was organized four years later, the founders incorporated many of the Declaration's principles into the NAACP's goals. Du Bois also served as the NAACP's first publicity director.

Marcus Garvey's Universal Negro Improvement Association (UNIA), founded in his home nation of Jamaica in 1914, was the first and largest mass-based black organization in the twentieth century. Garvey (1887–1940) emigrated to the United States in 1916, bringing with him his goal of combining black economic self-reliance with pan-Africanism through attempts to unite economically blacks in the United States, the Caribbean, and Africa (2-7). The UNIA rose and fell very quickly; the organization had many thousands of members within just a few years of its founding, but collapsed rapidly after Garvey's 1925 imprisonment for mail fraud.

KEYS TO THE SITUATION

See Who Holds Them, for What and Where the Race Is

UNIT 2-2

Atlanta Exposition Address

Booker T. Washington

Mr. President and Gentlemen of the Board of Directors and Citizens:

One third of the population of the South is of the Negro race. No enterprise seeking the material, civil, or moral welfare of this section can disregard this element of our population and reach the highest success. I but convey to you, Mr. President and Directors, the sentiment of the masses of my race when I say that in no way have the value and manhood of the American Negro been more fittingly and generously recognized than by the managers of this magnificent exposition at every stage of its progress. It is a recognition that will do more to cement the friendship of the two races than any occurrence since the dawn of our freedom.

Not only this, but the opportunity here afforded will awaken among us a new era of industrial progress. Ignorant and inexperienced, it is not strange that in the first years of our new life we began at the top instead of at the bottom; that a seat in Congress or the State Legislature was more sought than real estate or industrial skill; that the political convention or stump-speaking had more attraction than starting a dairy farm or truck garden.

A ship lost at sea for many days suddenly sighted a friendly vessel. From the mast of the unfortunate vessel was seen a signal: "Water, water; we die of thirst!" The answer from the friendly vessel at once came back: "Cast down your bucket where you are." A second time the signal, "Water, water; send us water!" ran up from the distressed vessel, and was answered: "Cast down your bucket where you are." And a third and fourth signal for water was answered, "Cast down your bucket where you are." The captain of the distressed vessel, at last heeding the injunction, cast down his bucket, and it came up full of fresh, sparkling water from the mouth of the Amazon River. To those of my race who depend upon bettering their condition in a foreign land, or who underestimate the importance of cultivating friendly relations with the Southern white man who is their next-door neighbor, I would say: "Cast down your bucket where you are"—cast it down in making friends, in every manly way, of the people of all races by whom we are surrounded.

Cast it down in agriculture, mechanics, in commerce, in domestic service, and in the professions. And in this connection it is well to bear in mind that whatever other sins the South may be called to bear, when it comes to business, pure and simple, it is in the South that the Negro is given a man's chance in the commercial world, and in nothing is this

Delivered at the Opening of the Cotton States' Exposition in Atlanta, Georgia, September, 1895.

Exposition more eloquent than in emphasizing this chance. Our greatest danger is that in the great leap from slavery to freedom we may overlook the fact that the masses of us are to live by the productions of our hands, and fail to keep in mind that we shall prosper in proportion as we learn to dignify and glorify common labor, and put brains and skill into the common occupations of life; shall prosper in proportion as we learn to draw the line between the superficial and the substantial, the ornamental gew-gaws of life and the useful. No race can prosper till it learns that there is as much dignity in tilling a field as in writing a poem. It is at the bottom of life we must begin, and not at the top. Nor should we permit our grievances to overshadow our opportunities.

To those of the white race who look to the incoming of those of foreign birth and strange tongue and habits for the prosperity of the South, were I permitted, I would repeat what I say to my own race, "Cast down your bucket where you are." Cast it down among the eight million Negroes whose habits you know, whose fidelity and love you have tested in days when to have proved treacherous meant the ruin of your firesides. Cast down your bucket among these people who have without strikes and labor wars tilled your fields, cleared your forests, builded your railroads and cities, brought forth treasures from the bowels of the earth, and helped make possible this magnificent representation of the progress of the South. Casting down your bucket among my people, helping and encouraging them as you are doing on these grounds, and, with education of head, hand, and heart, you will find that they will buy your surplus land, make blossom the waste places in your fields, and run your factories. While doing this, you can be sure in the future, as in the past, that you and your families will be surrounded by the most patient, faithful, law-abiding, and unresentful people that the world has seen. As we have proved our loyalty to you in the past, in nursing your children, watching by the sick bed of your mothers and fathers, and often following them with tear-dimmed eyes to their graves, so in the future, in our humble way, we shall stand by you with a devotion that no foreigner can approach, ready to lay down our lives, if need be, in defense of yours, interlacing our industrial, commercial, civil, and religious life with yours in a way that shall make the interests of both races one. In all things that are purely social we can be as separate as the fingers, yet one as the hand in all things essential to mutual progress.

There is no defense or security for any of us except in the highest intelligence and development of all. If anywhere there are efforts tending to curtail the fullest growth of the Negro, let these efforts be turned into stimulating, encouraging, and making him the most useful and intelligent citizen. Effort or means so invested will pay a thousand per cent interest. These efforts will be twice blessed—"Blessing him that gives and him that takes."

There is no escape through law of man or God from the inevitable:

The laws of changeless justice bind
Oppressor with oppressed;
And close as sin and suffering joined
We march to fare abreast.

Nearly sixteen millions of hands will aid you in pulling the load upward, or they will pull, against you, the load downward. We shall constitute one third and more of the ignorance and crime of the South, or one third its intelligence and progress; we shall contribute one third to the business and industrial prosperity of the South, or we shall prove a veritable body of death, stagnating, depressing, retarding every effort to advance the body politic.

Gentlemen of the Exposition, as we present to you our humble effort at an exhibition of our progress, you must not expect overmuch. Starting thirty years ago with ownership here and there in a few quilts and pumpkins and chickens (gathered from miscellaneous sources), remember, the path that has led from these to the inventions and production of agricultural implements, buggies, steam engines, newspapers, books, statuary carving, paintings, the management of drugstores and banks, has not been trodden without contact with thorns and thistles. While we take pride in what we exhibit as a result of our independent efforts, we do not for a moment forget that our part in this exhibition would fall far short of your expectations but for the constant help that has come to our educational life, not only from the Southern states, but especially from Northern philanthropists, who have made their gifts a constant stream of blessing and encouragement.

The wisest among my race understand that the agitation of questions of social equality is the extremest folly, and that progress in the enjoyment of all the privileges that will come to us must be the result of severe and constant struggle rather than of artificial forcing. No race that has anything to contribute to the markets of the world is long, in any degree, ostracized. It is important and right that all privileges of the law be ours, but it is vastly more important that we be prepared for the exercise of those privileges. The opportunity to earn a dollar in a factory just now is worth infinitely more than the opportunity to spend a dollar in an opera house.

In conclusion, may I repeat that nothing in thirty years has given us more hope and encouragement, and drawn us so near to you of the white race, as this opportunity offered by the Exposition; and here bending, as it were, over the altar that represents the results of the struggles of your race and mine, both starting practically empty-handed three decades ago, I pledge that, in your effort to work out the great and intricate problem which God has laid at the doors of the South, you shall have at all times the patient, sympathetic help of my race; only let this be constantly in mind, that while, from representations in these buildings of the product of field, of forest, of mine, of factory, letters, and art, much good will come, yet far above and beyond material benefits will be that higher good, that, let us pray God, will come in a blotting out of sectional differences and racial animosities and suspicions, in a determination to administer absolute justice, in a willing obedience among all classes to the mandates of law. This, coupled with our material prosperity, will bring into our beloved South a new heaven and a new earth.

UNIT 2-3

Of Mr. Booker T. Washington and Others

W.E.B. Du Bois

From birth till death enslaved; in word, in deed, unmanned!

* * *

Hereditary bondsmen! Know ye not
Who would be free themselves must strike the blow?

—*Byron*

Easily the most striking thing in the history of the American Negro since 1876 is the ascendancy of Mr. Booker T. Washington. It began at the time when war memories and ideals were rapidly passing; a day of astonishing commercial development was dawning; a sense of doubt and hesitation overtook the freedmen's sons,—then it was that his leading began. Mr. Washington came, with a simple definite programme, at the psychological moment when the nation was a little ashamed of having bestowed so much sentiment on Negroes, and was concentrating its energies on Dollars. His programme of industrial education, conciliation of the South, and submission and silence as to civil and political rights, was not wholly original; the Free Negroes from up to war-time had striven to build industrial schools, and the American Missionary Association had from the first taught various trades; and Price and others had sought a way of honorable alliance with the best of the Southerners. But Mr. Washington first indissolubly linked these things; he put enthusiasm, unlimited energy, and perfect faith into this programme, and changed it from a by-path into a veritable Way of Life. And the tale of the methods by which he did this is a fascinating study of human life.

It startled the nation to hear a Negro advocating such a programme after many decades of bitter complaint; it startled and won the applause of the South, it interested and won the admiration of the North; and after a confused murmur of protest, it silenced if it did not convert the Negroes themselves.

To gain the sympathy and coöperation of the various elements comprising the white South was Mr. Washington's first task; and this, at the time Tuskegee was founded, seemed, for a black man, well-nigh impossible. And yet ten years later it was done in the word spoken at Atlanta: "In all things purely social we can be as separate as the five fingers, and yet one as the hand in all things essential to mutual progress." This "Atlanta

Compromise" is by all odds the most notable thing in Mr. Washington's career. The South interpreted it in different ways: the radicals received it as a complete surrender of the demand for civil and political equality; the conservatives, as a generously conceived working basis for mutual understanding. So both approved it, and to-day its author is certainly the most distinguished Southerner since Jefferson Davis, and the one with the largest personal following.

Next to this achievement comes Mr. Washington's work in gaining place and consideration in the North. Others less shrewd and tactful had formerly essayed to sit on these two stools and had fallen between them; but as Mr. Washington knew the heart of the South from birth and training, so by singular insight he intuitively grasped the spirit of the age which was dominating the North. And so thoroughly did he learn the speech and thought of triumphant commercialism, and the ideals of material prosperity, that the picture of a lone black boy poring over a French grammar amid the weeds and dirt of a neglected home soon seemed to him the acme of absurdities. One wonders what Socrates and St. Francis of Assisi would say to this.

And yet this very singleness of vision and thorough oneness with his age is a mark of the successful man. It is as though Nature must needs make men narrow in order to give them force. So Mr. Washington's cult has gained unquestioning followers, his work has wonderfully prospered, his friends are legion, and his enemies are confounded. To-day he stands as the one recognized spokesman of his ten million fellows, and one of the most notable figures in a nation of seventy millions. One hesitates, therefore, to criticise a life which, beginning with so little, has done so much. And yet the time is come when one may speak in all sincerity and utter courtesy of the mistakes and shortcomings of Mr. Washington's career, as well as of his triumphs, without being thought captious or envious, and without forgetting that it is easier to do ill than well in the world.

The criticism that has hitherto met Mr. Washington has not always been of this broad character. In the South especially has he had to walk warily to avoid the harshest judgments,—and naturally so, for he is dealing with the one subject of deepest sensitiveness to that section. Twice—once when at the Chicago celebration of the Spanish-American War he alluded to the color-prejudice that is "eating away the vitals of the South," and once when he dined with President Roosevelt—has the resulting Southern criticism been violent enough to threaten seriously his popularity. In the North the feeling has several times forced itself into words, that Mr. Washington's counsels of submission overlooked certain elements of true manhood, and that his educational programme was unnecessarily narrow. Usually, however, such criticism has not found open expression, although, too, the spiritual sons of the Abolitionists have not been prepared to acknowledge that the schools founded before Tuskegee, by men of broad ideals and self-sacrificing spirit, were wholly failures or worthy of ridicule. While, then, criticism has not failed to follow Mr. Washington, yet the prevailing public opinion of the land has been but too willing to deliver the solution of a wearisome problem into his hands, and say, "If that is all you and your race ask, take it."

Among his own people, however, Mr. Washington has encountered the strongest and most lasting opposition, amounting at times to bitterness, and even to-day continuing strong and insistent even though largely silenced in outward expression by the public opinion of the nation. Some of this opposition is, of course, mere envy; the disappointment of displaced demagogues and the spite of narrow minds. But aside from this, there is among educated and thoughtful colored men in all parts of the land a feeling of deep regret, sorrow, and apprehension at the wide currency and ascendancy which some of Mr. Washington's theories have gained. These same men admire his sincerity of purpose, and are willing to forgive much to honest endeavor which is doing something worth the doing. They coöperate with Mr. Washington as far as they conscientiously can; and, indeed, it is no ordinary tribute to this man's tact and power that, steering as he must between so many diverse interests and opinions, he so largely retains the respect of all.

But the hushing of the criticism of honest opponents is a dangerous thing. It leads some of the best of the critics to unfortunate silence and paralysis of effort, and others to burst into speech so passionately and intemperately as to lose listeners. Honest and earnest criticism from those whose interests are most nearly touched,—criticism of writers by readers, of government by those governed, of leaders by those led,—this is the soul of democracy and the safeguard of modern society. If the best of the American Negroes receive by outer pressure a leader whom they had not recognized before, manifestly there is here a certain palpable gain. Yet there is also irreparable loss,—a loss of that peculiarly valuable education which a group receives when by search and criticism it finds and commissions its own leaders. The way in which this is done is at once the most elementary and the nicest problem of social growth. History is but the record of such group-leadership; and yet how infinitely changeful is its type and character! And of all types and kinds, what can be more instructive than the leadership of a group within a group?—that curious double movement where real progress may be negative and actual advance be relative retrogression. All this is the social student's inspiration and despair.

Now in the past the American Negro has had instructive experience in the choosing of group leaders, founding thus a peculiar dynasty which in the light of present conditions is worth while studying. When sticks and stones and beasts form the sole environment of a people, their attitude is largely one of determined opposition to and conquest of natural forces. But when to earth and brute is added an environment of men and ideas, then the attitude of the imprisoned group may take three main forms,—a feeling of revolt and revenge; an attempt to adjust all thought and action to the will of the greater group; or, finally, a determined effort at self-realization and self-development despite environing opinion. The influence of all of these attitudes at various times can be traced in the history of the American Negro, and in the evolution of his successive leaders.

Before 1750, while the fire of African freedom still burned in the veins of the slaves, there was in all leadership or attempted leadership but the one motive of revolt and revenge,—typified in the terrible Maroons, the Danish blacks, and Cato of Stono, and veiling all the Americas in fear of insurrection. The liberalizing tendencies of the latter half of the eighteenth century brought, along with kindlier relations between black and white, thoughts of ultimate adjustment and assimilation. Such aspiration was especially voiced in the earnest songs of Phyllis, in the martyrdom of Attucks, the fighting of Salem and Poor, the intellectual accomplishments of Banneker and Derham, and the political demands of the Cuffes.

Stern financial and social stress after the war cooled much of the previous humanitarian ardor. The disappointment and impatience of the Negroes at the persistence of slavery and serfdom voiced itself in two movements. The slaves in the South, aroused undoubtedly by vague rumors of the Haytian revolt, made three fierce attempts at insurrection,—in 1800 under Gabriel in Virginia, in 1822 under Vesey in Carolina, and in 1831 again in Virginia under the terrible Nat Turner. In the Free States, on the other hand, a new and curious attempt at self-development was made. In Philadelphia and New York color-prescription led to a withdrawal of Negro communicants from white churches and the formation of a peculiar socio-religious institution among the Negroes known as the African Church,—an organization still living and controlling in its various branches over a million of men.

Walker's wild appeal against the trend of the times showed how the world was changing after the coming of the cotton-gin. By slavery seemed hopelessly fastened on the South, and the slaves thoroughly cowed into submission. The free Negroes of the North, inspired by the mulatto immigrants from the West Indies, began to change the basis of their demands; they recognized the slavery of slaves, but insisted that they themselves were freemen, and sought assimilation and amalgamation with the nation on the same terms with other men. Thus, Forten and Purvis of Philadelphia, Shad of Wilmington, Du Bois of New Haven, Barbadoes of Boston, and others, strove singly and together as men, they said, not as slaves; as "people of color," not as "Negroes." The trend of the times, however, refused them recognition save in individual and exceptional cases, considered them as one with all the despised blacks, and they soon found themselves striving to keep even the rights they formerly had of voting and working and moving as freemen. Schemes of migration and colonization arose among them; but these they refused to entertain, and they eventually turned to the Abolition movement as a final refuge.

Here, led by Remond, Nell, Wells-Brown, and Douglass, a new period of self-assertion and self-development dawned. To be sure, ultimate freedom and assimilation was the ideal before the leaders, but the assertion of the manhood rights of the Negro by himself was the main reliance, and John Brown's raid was the extreme of its logic. After the war and emancipation, the great form of Frederick Douglass, the greatest of American Negro leaders, still led the host. Self-assertion, especially in political lines, was the main programme, and behind Douglass came Elliot, Bruce, and Langston, and the Reconstruction politicians, and, less conspicuous but of greater social significance Alexander Crummell and Bishop Daniel Payne.

Then came the Revolution of 1876, the suppression of the Negro votes, the changing and shifting of ideals, and the seeking of new lights in the great night. Douglass, in his old age, still bravely stood for the ideals of his early manhood,—ultimate assimilation *through* self-assertion, and on no other terms. For a time Price arose as a new leader, destined, it seemed, not to give up, but to re-state the old ideals in a form less repugnant to the white South. But he passed away in his prime. Then came the new leader. Nearly all the former ones had become leaders by the silent suffrage of their fellows, had sought to lead their own people alone, and were usually, save Douglass, little known outside their race. But Booker T. Washington arose as essentially the leader not of one race but of two,—a compromiser between the South, the North, and the Negro. Naturally the Negroes resented, at first bitterly, signs of compromise which surrendered their civil and political rights, even though this was to be exchanged for larger chances of economic development. The rich and dominating North, however, was not only weary of the race problem, but was investing largely in Southern enterprises, and welcomed any method of peaceful coöperation. Thus, by national opinion, the Negroes began to recognize Mr. Washington's leadership; and the voice of criticism was hushed.

Mr. Washington represents in Negro thought the old attitude of adjustment and submission; but adjustment at such a peculiar time as to make his programme unique. This is an age of unusual economic development, and Mr. Washington's programme naturally takes an economic cast, becoming a gospel of Work and Money to such an extent as apparently almost completely to overshadow the higher aims of life. Moreover, this is an age when the more advanced races are coming in closer contact with the less developed races, and the race- feeling is therefore intensified; and Mr. Washington's programme practically accepts the alleged inferiority of the Negro races. Again, in our own land, the reaction from the sentiment of war time has given impetus to race-prejudice against Negroes, and Mr. Washington withdraws many of the high demands of Negroes as men and American citizens. In other periods of intensified prejudice all the Negro's tendency to self-assertion has been called forth; at this period a policy of submission is advocated. In the history of nearly all other races and peoples the doctrine preached at such crises has been that manly self-respect is worth more than lands and houses, and that a people who voluntarily surrender such respect, or cease striving for it, are not worth civilizing.

In answer to this, it has been claimed that the Negro can survive only through submission. Mr. Washington distinctly asks that black people give up, at least for the present, three things,—

First, political power,

Second, insistence on civil rights,

Third, higher education of Negro youth,—

and concentrate all their energies on industrial education, the accumulation of wealth, and the conciliation of the South. This policy has been courageously and insistently advocated for over fifteen years, and has been triumphant for perhaps ten years. As a result of this tender of the palm-branch, what has been the return? In these years there have occurred:

1. The disfranchisement of the Negro.
2. The legal creation of a distinct status of civil inferiority for the Negro.
3. The steady withdrawal of aid from institutions for the higher training of the Negro.

These movements are not, to be sure, direct results of Mr. Washington's teachings; but his propaganda has, without a shadow of doubt, helped their speedier accomplishment. The question then comes: Is it possible, and probable, that nine millions of men can make effective progress in economic lines if they are deprived of political rights, made a servile caste, and allowed only the most meagre chance for developing their exceptional men? If history and reason give any distinct answer to these questions, it is an emphatic *No.* And Mr. Washington thus faces the triple paradox of his career:

1. He is striving nobly to make Negro artisans business men and property-owners; but it is utterly impossible, under modern competitive methods, for workingmen and propertyowners to defend their rights and exist without the right of suffrage.
2. He insists on thrift and self-respect, but at the same time counsels a silent submission to civic inferiority such as is bound to sap the manhood of any race in the long run.
3. He advocates common-school and industrial training, and depreciates institutions of higher learning; but neither the Negro common-schools, nor Tuskegee itself, could remain open a day were it not for teachers trained in Negro colleges, or trained by their graduates.

This triple paradox in Mr. Washington's position is the object of criticism by two classes of colored Americans. One class is spiritually descended from Toussaint the Savior, through Gabriel, Vesey, and Turner, and they represent the attitude of revolt and revenge; they hate the white South blindly and distrust the white race generally, and so far as they agree on definite action, think that the Negro's only hope lies in emigration beyond the borders of the United States. And yet, by the irony of fate, nothing has more effectually made this programme seem hopeless than the recent course of the United States toward weaker and darker peoples in the West Indies, Hawaii, and the Philippines,—for where in the world may we go and be safe from lying and brute force?

The other class of Negroes who cannot agree with Mr. Washington has hitherto said little aloud. They deprecate the sight of scattered counsels, of internal disagreement; and especially they dislike making their just criticism of a useful and earnest man an excuse for a general discharge of venom from small-minded opponents. Nevertheless, the questions involved are so fundamental and serious that it is difficult to see how men like the Grimkes, Kelly Miller, J. W. E. Bowen, and other representatives of this group, can much longer be silent. Such men feel in conscience bound to ask of this nation three things:

1. The right to vote.
2. Civic equality.
3. The education of youth according to ability.

They acknowledge Mr. Washington's invaluable service in counselling patience and courtesy in such demands; they do not ask that ignorant black men vote when ignorant whites are debarred, or that any reasonable restrictions in the suffrage should not be applied; they know that the low social level of the mass of the race is responsible for much discrimination against it, but they also know, and the nation knows, that relentless color-prejudice is more often a cause than a result of the Negro's degradation; they seek the abatement of this relic of barbarism, and not its systematic encouragement and pampering by all agencies of social power from the Associated Press to the Church of Christ. They advocate, with Mr. Washington, a broad system of Negro common schools supplemented by thorough industrial training; but they are surprised that a man of Mr. Washington's insight cannot see that no such educational system ever has rested or can rest on any other basis than that of the well-equipped college and university, and they insist that there is a demand for a few such institutions throughout the South to train the best of the Negro youth as teachers, professional men, and leaders.

This group of men honor Mr. Washington for his attitude of conciliation toward the white South; they accept the "Atlanta Compromise" in its broadest interpretation; they recognize, with him, many signs of promise, many men of high purpose and fair judgment, in this section; they know that no easy task has been laid upon a region already tottering under heavy burdens. But, nevertheless, they insist that the way to truth and right lies in straightforward honesty, not in indiscriminate flattery; in praising those of the South who do well and criticising uncompromisingly those who do ill; in taking advantage of the opportunities at hand and urging their fellows to do the same, but at the same time in remembering that only a firm adherence to their higher ideals and aspirations will ever keep those ideals within the realm of possibility. They do not expect that the free right to vote, to enjoy civic rights, and to be educated, will come in a moment; they do not expect to see the bias and prejudices of years disappear at the blast of a trumpet; but they are absolutely certain that the way for a people to gain their reasonable rights is not by voluntarily throwing them away and insisting that they do not want them; that the way for a people to gain respect is not by continually belittling and ridiculing themselves; that, on the contrary, Negroes must insist continually, in season and out of season, that voting is necessary to modern manhood, that color discrimination is barbarism, and that black boys need education as well as white boys.

In failing thus to state plainly and unequivocally the legitimate demands of their people, even at the cost of opposing an honored leader, the thinking classes of American Negroes would shirk a heavy responsibility,—a responsibility to themselves, a responsibility to the struggling masses, a responsibility to the darker races of men whose future depends so largely on this American experiment, but especially a responsibility to this nation,—this common Fatherland. It is wrong to encourage a man or a people in evil-doing; it is wrong to aid and abet a national crime simply because it is unpopular not to do so. The growing spirit of kindliness and reconciliation between the North and South after the frightful differences of a generation ago ought to be a source of deep congratulation to all, and especially to those whose mistreatment caused the war; but if that reconciliation is to be marked by the industrial slavery and civic death of those same black men, with permanent legislation into a position of inferiority, then those black men, if they are really men, are called upon by every consideration of patriotism and loyalty to oppose such a course by all civilized methods, even though such opposition involves disagreement with Mr. Booker T. Washington. We have no right to sit silently by while the inevitable seeds are sown for a harvest of disaster to our children, black and white.

First, it is the duty of black men to judge the South discriminatingly. The present generation of Southerners are not responsible for the past, and they should not be blindly hated or blamed for it. Furthermore, to no class is the indiscriminate endorsement of the recent course of the South toward Negroes more nauseating than to the best thought of the South. The South is not "solid"; it is a land in the ferment of social change, wherein forces of all kinds are fighting for supremacy; and to praise the ill the South is to-day perpetrating is just as wrong as to condemn the good. Discriminating and broad-minded criticism is what the South needs,—needs it for the sake of her own white sons and daughters, and for the insurance of robust, healthy mental and moral development.

To-day even the attitude of the Southern whites toward the blacks is not, as so many assume, in all cases the same; the ignorant Southerner hates the Negro, the workingmen fear his competition, the money-makers wish to use him as a laborer, some of the educated see a menace in his upward development, while others—usually the sons of the masters—wish to help him to rise. National opinion has enabled this last class to maintain the Negro common schools, and to protect the Negro partially in property, life, and limb. Through the pressure of the money-makers, the Negro is in danger of being reduced to semi-slavery, especially in the country districts; the workingmen, and those of the educated who fear the Negro, have united to disfranchise him, and some have urged his deportation; while the passions of the ignorant are easily aroused to lynch and abuse any black man. To praise this intricate whirl of thought and prejudice is nonsense; to inveigh indiscriminately against "the South" is unjust; but to use the same breath in praising Governor Aycock, exposing Senator Morgan, arguing with Mr. Thomas Nelson Page, and denouncing Senator Ben Tillman, is not only sane, but the imperative duty of thinking black men.

It would be unjust to Mr. Washington not to acknowledge that in several instances he has opposed movements in the South which were unjust to the Negro; he sent memorials to the Louisiana and Alabama constitutional conventions, he has spoken against lynching, and in other ways has openly or silently set his influence against sinister schemes and unfortunate happenings. Notwithstanding this, it is equally true to assert that on the whole the distinct impression left by Mr. Washington's propaganda is, first, that the South is justified in its present attitude toward the Negro because of the Negro's degradation; secondly, that the prime cause of the Negro's failure to rise more quickly is his wrong education in the past; and, thirdly, that his future rise depends primarily on his own efforts. Each of these propositions is a dangerous half-truth. The supplementary truths must never be lost sight of: first, slavery and race-prejudice are potent if not sufficient causes of the Negro's position; second, industrial and common-school training were necessarily slow in planting because they had to await the black teachers trained by higher institutions,—it being extremely doubtful if any essentially different development was possible, and certainly a Tuskegee was unthinkable before; and, third, while it is a great truth to say that the Negro must strive and strive mightily to help himself, it is equally true that unless his striving be not simply seconded, but rather aroused and encouraged, by the initiative of the richer and wiser environing group, he cannot hope for great success.

In his failure to realize and impress this last point, Mr. Washington is especially to be criticised. His doctrine has tended to make the whites, North and South, shift the burden of the Negro problem to the Negro's shoulders and stand aside as critical and rather pessimistic spectators; when in fact the burden belongs to the nation, and the hands of none of us are clean if we bend not our energies to righting these great wrongs.

The South ought to be led, by candid and honest criticism, to assert her better self and do her full duty to the race she has cruelly wronged and is still wronging. The North—her co-partner in guilt—cannot salve her conscience by plastering it with gold. We cannot settle this problem by diplomacy and suaveness, by "policy" alone. If worse come to worst, can the moral fibre of this country survive the slow throttling and murder of nine millions of men?

The black men of America have a duty to perform, a duty stern and delicate,—a forward movement to oppose a part of the work of their greatest leader. So far as Mr. Washington preaches Thrift, Patience, and Industrial Training for the masses, we must hold up his hands and strive with him, rejoicing in his honors and glorying in the strength of this Joshua called of God and of man to lead the headless host. But so far as Mr. Washington apologizes for injustice, North or South, does not rightly value the privilege and duty of voting, belittles the emasculating effects of caste distinctions, and opposes the higher training and ambition of our brighter minds,—so far as he, the South, or the Nation, does this,—we must unceasingly and firmly oppose them. By every civilized and peaceful method we must strive for the rights which the world accords to men, clinging unwaveringly to those great words which the sons of the Fathers would fain forget: "We hold these truths to be self-evident: That all men are created equal; that they are endowed by their Creator with certain unalienable rights; that among these are life, liberty, and the pursuit of happiness."

UNIT 2-4

THE NIAGARA MOVEMENT DECLARATION OF PRINCIPLES

Any discrimination based simply on race or color is barbarous, we care not how hallowed it be by custom, expediency or prejudice.

W.E.B. Du Bois was the moving force in the creation of the Niagara Movement, an organization of prominent African American leaders that first convened in the summer of 1905 at Niagara Falls. The purpose of the organization was to establish an assertive alternative to the accommodationist politics of Booker T. Washington. The group, however, was unable to develop enough funding to establish a permanent staff or headquarters and appeared to be heading for the same fate as previous efforts to organize a black protest organization.

But in 1908, race riots in Springfield, Illinois, the hometown of Abraham Lincoln, prompted a group of whites to plan an organization that would revive the abolitionist spirit on behalf of black rights. Mary White Ovington, a social worker; William English Walling, a journalist; and Oswald Garrison Villard, publisher of the New York Post, convened a national conference to renew "the struggle for political and civil liberty." The white leaders joined forces with the black leaders of the Niagara Movement to create the National Association for the Advancement of Colored People. The principles of the Niagara Movement became the principles of the new NAACP.

PROGRESS

The members of the conference, known as the Niagara Movement, assembled in annual meeting at Buffalo, July 11th, 12th and 13th, 1905, congratulate the Negro-Americans on certain undoubted evidences of progress in the last decade, particularly the increase of intelligence, the buying of property, the checking of crime, the uplift in home life, the advance in literature and art, and the demonstration of constructive and executive ability in the conduct of great religious, economic and educational institutions.

SUFFRAGE

At the same time, we believe that this class of American citizens should protest emphatically and continually against the curtailment of their political rights. We believe in manhood suffrage; we believe that no man is so good, intelligent or wealthy as to be entrusted wholly with the welfare of his neighbor.

CIVIL LIBERTY

We believe also in protest against the curtailment of our civil rights. All American citizens have the right to equal treatment in places of public entertainment according to their behavior and deserts.

ECONOMIC OPPORTUNITY

We especially complain against the denial of equal opportunities to us in economic life; in the rural districts of the South this amounts to peonage and virtual slavery; all over the South it tends to crush labor and small business enterprises; and everywhere American prejudice, helped often by iniquitous laws, is making it more difficult for Negro-Americans to earn a decent living.

EDUCATION

Common school education should be free to all American children and compulsory. High school training should be adequately provided for all, and college training should be the monopoly of no class or race in any section of our common country. We believe that, in defense of our own institutions, the United States should aid common school education, particularly in the South, and we especially recommend concerted agitation to this end. We urge an increase in public high school facilities in the South, where the Negro-Americans are almost wholly without such provisions. We favor well-equipped trade and technical schools for the training of artisans, and the need of adequate and liberal endowment for a few institutions of higher education must be patent to sincere well-wishers of the race.

COURTS

We demand upright judges in courts, juries selected without discrimination on account of color and the same measure of punishment and the same efforts at reformation for black as for white offenders. We need orphanages and farm schools for dependent children, juvenile reformatories for delinquents, and the abolition of the dehumanizing convict-lease system.

PUBLIC OPINION

We note with alarm the evident retrogression in this land of sound public opinion on the subject of manhood rights, republican government and human brotherhood, and we pray God that this nation will not degenerate into a mob of boasters and oppressors, but rather will return to the faith of the fathers, that all men were created free and equal, with certain unalienable rights.

HEALTH

We plead for health—for an opportunity to live in decent houses and localities, for a chance to rear our children in physical and moral cleanliness.

EMPLOYERS AND LABOR UNIONS

We hold up for public execration the conduct of two opposite classes of men: The practice among employers of importing ignorant Negro-American laborers in emergencies, and then affording them neither protection nor permanent employment; and the practice of labor unions in proscribing and boycotting and oppressing thousands of their fellow-toilers, simply because they are black. These methods have accentuated and will accentuate the war of labor and capital, and they are disgraceful to both sides.

PROTEST

We refuse to allow the impression to remain that the Negro-American assents to inferiority, is submissive under oppression and apologetic before insults. Through helplessness we may submit, but the voice of protest of ten million Americans must never cease to assail the ears of their fellows, so long as America is unjust.

COLOR-LINE

Any discrimination based simply on race or color is barbarous, we care not how hallowed it be by custom, expediency or prejudice. Differences made on account of ignorance, immorality, or disease are legitimate methods of fighting evil, and against them we have no word of protest; but discriminations based simply and solely on physical peculiarities, place of birth, color of skin, are relics of that unreasoning human savagery of which the world is and ought to be thoroughly ashamed.

"JIM CROW" CARS

We protest against the "Jim Crow" car, since its effect is and must be to make us pay first-class fare for third-class accommodations, render us open to insults and discomfort and to crucify wantonly our manhood, womanhood and self-respect.

SOLDIERS

We regret that this nation has never seen fit adequately to reward the black soldiers who, in its five wars, have defended their country with their blood, and yet have been systematically denied the promotions which their abilities deserve. And we regard as unjust, the exclusion of black boys from the military and naval training schools.

WAR AMENDMENTS

We urge upon Congress the enactment of appropriate legislation for securing the proper enforcement of those articles of freedom, the thirteenth, fourteenth and fifteenth amendments of the Constitution of the United States.

OPPRESSION

We repudiate the monstrous doctrine that the oppressor should be the sole authority as to the rights of the oppressed. The Negro race in America stolen, ravished and degraded, struggling up through difficulties and oppression, needs sympathy and receives criticism; needs help and is given hindrance, needs protection and is given mob-violence, needs justice and is given charity, needs leadership and is given cowardice and apology, needs bread and is given a stone. This nation will never stand justified before God until these things are changed.

THE CHURCH

Especially are we surprised and astonished at the recent attitude of the church of Christ—of an increase of a desire to bow to racial prejudice, to narrow the bounds of human brotherhood, and to segregate black men to some outer sanctuary. This is wrong, unchristian and disgraceful to the twentieth century civilization.

AGITATION

Of the above grievances we do not hesitate to complain, and to complain, loudly and insistently. To ignore, overlook, or apologize for these wrongs is to prove ourselves unworthy of freedom. Persistent manly agitation is the way to liberty, and toward this goal the Niagara Movement has started and asks the cooperation of all men of all races.

HELP

At the same time we want to acknowledge with deep thankfulness the help of our fellowmen from the Abolitionist down to those who today still stand for equal opportunity and who have given and still give of their wealth and of their poverty for our advancement.

DUTIES

And while we are demanding and ought to demand, and will continue to demand the rights enumerated above, God forbid that we should ever forget to urge corresponding duties upon our people:

The duty to vote.
The duty to respect the rights of others.
The duty to work.
The duty to obey the laws.
The duty to be clean and orderly.
The duty to send our children to school.
The duty to respect ourselves, even as we respect others.

This statement, complaint and prayer we submit to the American people, and Almighty God.

UNIT 2-5

THE NAACP AS A REFORM MOVEMENT, 1909–1965

"TO REACH THE CONSCIENCE OF AMERICA"

August Meier and John H. Bracey, Jr.

The history of the National Association For The Advancement of Colored People (NAACP) from its origin in the Progressive movement to the victories achieved in the passage of the Civil Rights Act of 1964 and the Voting Rights Act of 1965 illuminates the history of American reform in the twentieth century.[1] The focus of this essay will be on the development of the NAACP and its programs and the dynamics of their interrelationships with the changing social milieu in which the Association operated. Involved on the one hand are both the political and economic transformations that were taking place in U.S. society and the long-range shifts that were taking place in white attitudes toward racial minorities. On the other hand are the NAACP's responses to rivals and critics from within the black community. As in any organization there were also internal conflicts over program and strategy and intense rivalries between leading personalities. In contrast to the situation in many social movement organizations, however, these internal conflicts had scant impact on the basic direction of the NAACP's programs and goals.

The authors' interest in these particular issues stemmed from our attempts to address two broad questions. One was that posed some years ago by historians who were investigating the fate of the Progressive movement and the possible relationship of the Progressive movement to the New Deal. The other was the sociological one of how a reform organization interacts over time with its changing environment. Using this conceptual framework we have carried our analysis of the NAACP's history through to the climax of American liberalism and civil rights reform in the 1960s.

Born in 1909 on the fringes of Progressive Era reform, the Association single-mindedly kept to its original goal of securing the basic citizenship rights guaranteed by the Fourteenth and Fifteenth Amendments of the Constitution. However, the NAACP also proved to be a flexible organization, modifying its tactics and strategies to meet the challenges of the changing economic and political environment in which it operated. For example, beginning with the Great Depression and the New Deal, the NAACP was able to incorporate into its program new economic concerns without altering its basic goal. Amid the reform impulses unleashed during the depression and World War II, the

NAACP flourished. The membership and staff grew to unprecedented size. Its legal arm, the NAACP Legal Defense and Educational Fund Inc., won a series of stunning victories before the Supreme Court in the space of ten years: from *Smith v. Allwright*, which outlawed the white primary in 1944, to the *Brown* decision of 1954.[2] There then followed a decade of legislative successes culminating in the passage of the Civil Rights Act of 1964 and the Voting Rights Act of 1965, which together brought to a conclusion the struggle to achieve the original goals enunciated by the NAACP in 1909.

Given this long history and its relationship to American reform, it is interesting to note that the NAACP and its achievements are given scant attention in virtually all of the general studies of Progressivism and liberal reform. The early influential study of the Progressive movement, John Chamberlain's *Farewell to Reform: Being a History of the Rise, Life and Decay of the Progressive Mind in America* (1932), has no references to Negroes or to the NAACP. Twenty years later, another influential study, Richard Hofstadter's *The Age of Reform: From Bryan to FDR,* (1956) has only seven incidental references. Scholars such as Eric F. Goldman in *Rendezvous with Destiny* (1952) and Allen F. Davis in *Spearheads for Reform: The Social Settlements and the Progressive Movement, 1890–1914* (1967) do pay significant attention to racial matters. In *An Encore for Reform: The Old Progressives and the New Deal* (1967), Otis L. Graham, Jr., exhibits an awareness that support for the NAACP was a significant indicator of Progressive sentiments but otherwise ignores the question. And in his later volume, *Toward a Planned Society: From Roosevelt to Nixon* (1976), there is no reference at all to racial matters.

It is indeed surprising that even after the shift in racial consciousness brought about in the late 1950s and 1960s, most of the books on liberal reform either have omitted or have given only passing attention to the NAACP. Thus for example a symposium published by the Lyndon B. Johnson School of Public Affairs and edited by Wilbur J. Cohen, entitled *The Roosevelt New Deal: A Program Assessment Fifty Years After* (1986), has chapters on the New Deal and Jews, the New Deal and women, and the New Deal and labor, but none on the New Deal and blacks![3]

A survey that does pay attention to race and to the NAACP is Arthur S. Link and Richard L. McCormick, *Progressivism* (1983). This is in sharp contrast to Link's seminal 1959 article, "What Happened to the Progressive Movement in the 1920s?" in which race is not mentioned at all. On the other hand, Alonzo L. Hamby's *Liberalism and Its Challengers: FDR to Reagan* (1985), while uneven, does devote a full chapter to Martin Luther King, Jr., and the civil rights movement of the 1960s, but its references to the NAACP are generally inaccurate. Significant exceptions are two studies of Americans for Democratic Action (ADA), the leading predominantly white liberal reform organization of the post-World War II era, which made civil rights one of its central concerns. Thus Clifton Brock in *Americans for Democratic Action: Its Role in National Politics* (1962) does address this matter. Oddly enough, while devoting much attention to the ADA's civil rights activities, Steven M. Gillon's more recent study, *Politics and Vision: The ADA and American Liberalism, 1947–1985* (1987), does not use the NAACP papers nor does it contain any mention of the NAACP's interactions with the ADA. Moreover, the index contains no references to such prominent NAACP leaders as Clarence Mitchell, Jr., Walter Francis White, or Roy Wilkins. From the NAACP's point of view, Denton L. Watson's *Lion in the Lobby: Clarence Mitchell, Jr.'s Struggle for the Passage of Civil Rights Laws* (1990) contains numerous references to the ADA and to Joseph L. Rauh, the ADA's most notable civil rights advocate.[4]

Given the extreme racism of the Progressive period, the discriminatory impact of some important Progressive reforms (*e.g.*, the way in which the new primary system served to disenfranchise black voters in the South) and the racist attitudes of many Progressive leaders and intellectuals from John R. Commons to Theodore Roosevelt, it is paradoxical that among the highly varied reform organizations originating at that time was one like the NAACP. Although some of its leaders were prominent in other reform activities (most notable perhaps was Oswald Garrison Villard, publisher of the New York *Evening Post* and editor of the Nation, whose interests ranged from pacifism to women's suffrage), the NAACP itself was marginal to the Progressive movement as a whole. But this is especially ironical in view of the NAACP's attempt to extend Progressive values, goals, and methods into the area of race relations. The Association's belief in investigation and exposure and in the importance of laws and of the state as a guarantor of social order, its faith in the assimilability of minority groups, its belief in progress and the essential rationality of human behavior, all reflect the ideas of mainstream Progressivism. But unlike most other Progressives who either ignored the race problem or considered blacks and Asians to be inferior, the NAACP was willing to carry the implications of Progressivism to their logical conclusions and in this regard was more progressive than most of the Progressives themselves. Above all the appeal of the NAACP like that of the Progressives was fundamentally a moral one, or as the NAACP said in its tenth annual report its goal was "to reach the conscience of America."

Like many of the organizations formed during the Progressive Era, the NAACP had links back to nineteenth-century reformism through the descendants of white abolitionists and a few veterans of the older black self-help organizations such as the Afro-American League.[5] The leading founders among both the whites and the blacks ranged ideologically from socialist intellectuals like W.E.B. Du Bois to politically conservative Republicans like Moorfield Storey of Boston (a past president of the American Bar Association), who were united by their intense dislike of imperialism and racism and their skepticism as to the efficacy of the strategies of Booker T. Washington. This group, resolutely interracial in its outlook, virtually adopted the program of Du Bois's Niagara Movement (1905–1910) as its own. Both the Niagara Movement and the NAACP were united in their opposition to Booker T. Washington's policies and in their program of militant protest and litigation against the denial of constitutional rights guaranteed to black Americans by the Fourteenth and Fifteenth Amendments. Like the Afro-American League, the Niagara Movement was all black. Given conditions at the turn of the century this mode of organizing appeared at least to its adherents to be the only viable option. Du Bois and most of his colleagues in the Niagara Movement acted with little hesitation when given the opportunity to forge effective alliances with sympathetic whites. In fact, it was largely through Du Bois's efforts that people like Villard became convinced of the bankruptcy of Washington's approach and were willing to ally with blacks in posing an alternative.[6]

This of course was a period of disfranchisement legislation, Jim Crow laws, sharecropping and debt peonage, lynchings and racial pogroms. Given these extreme manifestations of white racism, the indifference of even most enlightened northern opinion, and the reluctance of most black intellectuals to challenge the leadership of Booker T. Washington, the NAACP began as a frail organization. Except for Du Bois, the principal figures in the early years were leading white Progressives such as Villard and Joel Elias Spingarn, and for the first decade the executive secretaries of the NAACP were white reformers. Du Bois edited the *Crisis*, which served as an effective vehicle for keeping the organization's programs and activities before the black public. With its limited resources, the NAACP began its long-term strategy of undermining the legal foundations of the American race system by involving itself in court cases dealing with disfranchisement and residential segregation. In 1915 the Supreme Court declared Oklahoma's "grandfather clause" unconstitutional and two years later overturned the Louisville, Kentucky, municipal residential segregation ordinance. The Association also initiated public protests against Jim Crow arrangements being instituted in federal offices in Washington, D.C., and against showing D. W. Griffith's 1915 racist movie, *The Birth of a Nation*. In both the legal cases and the protests the NAACP achieved only limited results. Much more successful was its vigorous opposition to the rash of anti-Negro legislation that came before Congress and a number of northern state legislatures during Woodrow Wilson's presidency.[7]

From its founding until past the middle of the century what highlighted the NAACP's activities and dramatized its work were its efforts to secure the protection for black Americans of the basic rights to life and liberty. Both rights were threatened by mob violence (lynchings and race riots) and by gross mistreatment in the area of criminal justice on the part of law enforcement authorities and the courts. This mistreatment took place in the South and in the North. In addition to its intrinsic importance, the attention to lynchings and criminal justice was sound strategy that enabled the Association to rally the broadest possible range of support and garner maximum publicity for its programs.

For nearly thirty years the NAACP devoted immeasurable amounts of energy and large amounts of money in the ultimately futile effort to achieve the passage of a federal antilynching bill, although lynchings did almost come to a halt by 1940. Similarly the NAACP devoted considerable efforts to cases involving injustice before the courts, especially in the South. The NAACP was involved in attempts to protect the lives of individual blacks and/or to bring to justice whites guilty of mob violence in such cases as the Coatesville, Pennsylvania, lynching of 1912; the railroading of soldiers in the all-black Twenty-fourth Infantry Regiment of the U.S. Army to death sentences and long prison terms because of their alleged involvement in the Houston riot of 1917; the East St. Louis riot of the same year; the Elaine, Arkansas, and Chicago riots of 1919; the Tulsa, Oklahoma, riot of 1921; the Ossian Sweet case in Detroit in 1925; the Scottsboro case, which began in 1930; the Detroit riot of 1943; the blinding of World War II veteran Isaac Woodward by two white South Carolina policemen in 1946; the assassination of Harry T. Moore, NAACP state coordinator of branches for Florida, and his wife in 1951; and the Emmett Till and Mack Charles Parker lynchings in 1955 and 1959, respectively.[8]

A striking and unusual case that illustrates the strengths and limitations of the NAACP's approach to mob violence was the Aiken, South Carolina, lynchings in October 1926. What we know about the lynchings is due to the efforts of Walter White, the NAACP's assistant secretary who, able to pass for white, undertook an investigation that included interviews with members of the mob and the compilation of vivid eyewitness accounts. White, using his contacts with the press, persuaded the New York *World* to do a lengthy series of articles spotlighting these South Carolina lynchings. The gist of this case was that in April 1925 a family of sharecroppers named Lowman was accused of making and selling illegal liquor. During the attempt to arrest Sam Lowman, the father and head of the family, who was away at the time, a gunfight occurred in which the white sheriff and Mrs. Annie Lowman were killed. The three children, the oldest of whom was thirteen, were seriously wounded. The Lowman children were arrested, charged, tried hastily, and convicted of murder. The two males were sentenced to death, and the female received a life sentence. The father was subsequently charged with possession of liquor and given a two-year sentence on a chain gang.

The injustice of these proceedings outraged N. J. Frederick of Columbia, South Carolina, the only black lawyer in the state who took civil rights cases and had previously handled NAACP cases. Frederick initiated an appeal of his own, retaining at his own expense a white lawyer who was willing to assist him. They were successful in securing from the South Carolina Supreme Court a reversal of the convictions, resulting in a directed verdict of "not guilty" for one defendant and jury trials for the remaining two. The youth who had been acquitted was immediately rearrested on new charges and sent back to jail. Late that same night a mob of two thousand people stormed the jail where the three black children were being held, took them away, told them to run, and then shot them from behind until they were dead. Despite a quite vigorous publicity campaign that caused some South Carolina newspapers to condemn the lynchings, no members of the mob were ever brought to justice. The NAACP's annual report for 1926 seized upon this situation to make yet another appeal for a federal antilynching law.[9]

Despite the unsatisfactory resolutions of many of the NAACP's legal cases, there were enough victories to warrant the observation by Ralph J. Bunche, a NAACP critic from Howard University, that in the first three decades of the NAACP's history "the most important of the tactics employed by the NAACP is that of legal redress. The outstanding victories of the Association have been in court."[10]

Meanwhile during and following World War I there were major changes in race relations that affected the workings—both internal and external—of the NAACP. These tumultuous years witnessed extensive migration of blacks to northern cities, antiblack riots, the revival of the Ku Klux Klan, the rise of Marcus Garvey, the onset of the Harlem Renaissance, the introduction of varieties of Marxist thought among black intellectuals, and the emergence of a new breed of black politician in northern cities (that would in 1928 lead to the election of Oscar De Priest of Chicago as the first black congressman from a northern district and the first black in Congress since 1901). In short, the general atmosphere was one of heightened racial consciousness on all fronts, epitomized by the widespread usage among blacks of the term "the New Negro."

In this context the NAACP, while holding on to its basic program of seeking legal redress and legislative reform, underwent important changes in internal organization. Due in large part to wartime prosperity and the shift in black population to northern cities where it was safer to join the organization, NAACP membership grew among blacks so rapidly that by 1920 membership fees from blacks were supplying most of the organization's income. This development masked the failure of the deliberate attempt to attract large numbers of white members. But perhaps the most important internal consequence was the transfer of administrative power to the black secretariat. In 1916 James Weldon Johnson was employed as field secretary. This was followed in 1918 by the appointment of Walter White as assistant executive secretary. In 1921 Johnson was promoted to executive secretary on a permanent basis, a post he held for the next decade. The same rise in race consciousness that led to the success of Marcus Garvey's nationalist appeal also had an impact on the NAACP. This consciousness coupled with the hiring of black staff led to the increase in black membership, which in turn reaffirmed the strategy of hiring black staff. The stature and talent of these new staff members were further affirmations; both Johnson and White as well as Robert W. Bagnall, the director of branches, were men of considerable organizational skills with extensive contacts among black fraternal orders, churches, and business and civic leaders.

As editor of the *Crisis*, W.E.B. Du Bois was at the center of much of the ideological controversy that characterized the postwar period. Even though Du Bois had been fostering his own version of Pan-Africanism since the beginning of the century, that did not prevent Marcus Garvey from attacking Du Bois from Garvey's own nationalist point of view. The NAACP's interracial makeup, its politics of integration and assimilation, and even Du Bois's light skin color were anathema to Garvey who, in his speeches and in his newspaper the *Negro World*, ridiculed the NAACP and called Du Bois "purely and simply a white man's nigger." Although Du Bois had considered himself a socialist for some time, he was also attacked from the left by socialists such as A. Philip Randolph, the militant editor of the *Messenger*. In Randolph's view Du Bois and the NAACP had sold out to bourgeois interests and were not at all concerned with the problems facing the black working class. Despite all the attention that these polemics received, there was no discernible effect on the NAACP's programs or direction. At the end of the decade the *Crisis* was still the preeminent black journal while Randolph's *Messenger* was defunct and Garvey's *Negro World* had lost most of its influence.[11]

The NAACP's relationship with the Harlem Renaissance can be best understood as "the politics of art," to use David Levering Lewis's phrase.[12] Characteristic of this renaissance was the intricate interaction of racial advancement organizations with art and artists. From the point of view of NAACP strategy there was a widespread assumption that the work of black artists was an aspect of the struggle to advance the status of black Americans. The positive images flowing from their art were widely recognized as a cultural force capable of both undermining notions of white supremacy and encouraging self-esteem among Negroes.

From its founding the NAACP had among its leaders creative writers and literary critics. The writings of Du Bois of course are well known. Less known are the writings of Du Bois's closest NAACP associates during this period, Joel Spingarn and Mary White Ovington, both white liberals. Spingarn, a poet, leading literary critic, and a founder of the "new criticism," served for many years as treasurer or chairman of the board of directors of the NAACP. Mary White Ovington, a founder who was active in the NAACP for almost four decades, was a novelist and playwright.[13]

When the NAACP began to expand the number of its black staff, the most prominent of its additions, James Weldon Johnson, had extensive literary and cultural interests and was appointed to the staff at Spingarn's insistence. It is easy to infer that one of the reasons that Spingarn found the multitalented Johnson so attractive was the quality of his literary work. Walter White, who came from an insurance background, did not begin to write until well after he joined the NAACP staff. Perhaps influenced by the number of writers around him, White wrote both novels and nonfiction. Beginning in the late 1910s and 1920s the *Crisis*, like the Urban League's *Opportunity* magazine later on, encouraged young writers to publish in its pages and to compete for a literary prize named for Amy Spingam, Joel's wife. Also joining the staff during this period were the novelist Jessie Redmon Fauset, literary editor of the *Crisis*, and William Pickens, field secretary from 1919 to 1938.[14]

Given this unparalleled collection of literary talent in one organization the NAACP was in an ideal position to exercise a major role in the creative flowering of the 1920s and to undertake a program of cultural advancement in conjunction with its legal and protest activities. The NAACP, in providing an outlet for some of the early writers of the Harlem Renaissance, both stimulated the cultural outpouring and benefited from this newly awakened consciousness.

During the 1920s, a period when Republicans dominated the White House and black voters remained overwhelmingly Republican, the black vote, such as it was, was essentially taken for granted. Conditions in the South were not improving for blacks, and conditions in the North in many respects were growing worse. The NAACP continued the fight for an antilynching bill and chipped away with minor successes against the white Democratic primaries in the South. The NAACP had less success opposing the restrictive covenants that hemmed the growing urban black populations into overcrowded ghettos.[15]

The 1920s was neatly bracketed by two important legal battles: the Arkansas riot case that arose in 1919 and the opposition to the nomination to the U.S. Supreme Court of Judge John J. Parker of North Carolina, who had endorsed black disfranchisement. The Arkansas riot case had arisen from an incident in 1919 when, as a result of a racial altercation, eighty-nine blacks were convicted for their alleged involvement; twelve were sentenced to death. The NAACP took the case all the way to the Supreme Court, and after five years of litigation the defendants were freed on the grounds that an impartial trial had not been possible because of mob intimidation of the community and court. Then in 1930, emboldened by the increasing black voting power in the North, the NAACP made significant contributions to mobilizing senators to vote against the confirmation of Judge Parker. This political effort challenged President Herbert C. Hoover's "lily-white" policies and his indifference to the black electorate. After campaigning vigorously against the reelection of four of the senators who had voted for Parker, the Association could take considerable credit for the defeat of two of them.[16]

Although the anti-Parker campaign was dramatic, it had no lasting impact on the NAACP. However, a tentative decision taken about the same time initiated a series of legal steps that would have an enormous impact on the NAACP's future course of litigation. By the end of the 1920s the Association was exploring the utility of exposing the blatant inequities between black and white schools in the South as an opening wedge in the long-range effort to overturn *Plessy v. Ferguson*, the 1896 court decision that based segregation on the doctrine of separate but equal facilities.[17]

Building on the legal work of the 1920s the NAACP program of litigation continued to expand, even during the Great Depression. The deaths in 1929 of both Louis Marshall and Moorfield Storey, two whites who were among the country's leading constitutional lawyers and who had worked for the NAACP for years on a pro bono basis, compelled the Association to consider whether to develop its own paid legal staff and what role black lawyers would play. After discussing these issues for several years and weighing pressures from the black bar association, the NAACP by mid-1935 had employed Charles Hamilton Houston as its full-time special counsel. This decision would prove to be the beginning of the development of a black legal staff.

Houston played a critical role in this process. First, the move to hire a black counsel was facilitated by the emergence of a small group of black lawyers who had studied constitutional law under Felix Frankfurter of the Harvard Law School. Two of the most prominent of them were Houston himself and his close friend William H. Hastie, both of whom were destined to play important roles in the future of the NAACP. Second, in its effort to improve black higher education in general, the Rockefeller Foundation's General Education Board decided to develop a first-rate law school at Howard University under Houston's leadership. Houston was committed to creating a cadre of skilled black lawyers who would be experts in civil rights law, and he firmly believed that such a cadre would then be able to undertake the litigation requited to overturn discrimination in the South.

Houston was optimistic about what could be done through the use of the law, which he saw as a tool for social engineering. In this regard Houston's ideas undoubtedly reflected the more general ethos of New Deal social planning and anticipated Gunnar Myrdal's later application of this approach to the solution of the race problem.[18] Although Houston resigned the post of special counsel in mid-1936, he was succeeded by his most brilliant law student, Thurgood Marshall.

During the 1930s the NAACP's litigation maintained a remarkable continuity with that of the 1920s. Much effort was still devoted to legal redress on behalf of individuals, with the NAACP selecting cases from the many received on the basis of two criteria: 1) an issue of citizenship rights had to be involved, and 2) the racial discrimination had to be clear. By 1940 the volume of this kind of litigation, most of it originating in the local branches, had grown to the point that the legal staff now decided to limit itself to cases that had the potential of establishing a new precedent of constitutional significance. NAACP lawyers also continued the earlier campaigns against restrictive covenants and white primaries. They won three Supreme Court victories against the Texas white primary system, although the Texas Democrats continued to find ways to circumvent the decisions.[19] But legal victories in the restrictive covenant cases proved elusive.

The major new legal initiative, underwritten in part by the American Fund for Public Service, a philanthropy more commonly known as the Garland Fund, was the inauguration of the fight against educational discrimination in the South. A two-pronged strategy was involved: directly attacking the exclusion of blacks from the professional and graduate schools at state universities and indirectly attacking segregation in the primary and secondary grades with litigation calling for full equalization of salaries, length of school term, and physical facilities in the public schools. The rationale for this indirect approach was to make segregated public schooling so expensive that the choice would be desegregation or economic ruin. The plan adopted was to begin with the border states, then move into the upper South, and finally challenge the Deep South. A latent function of this strategy was to use these local cases as opportunities to raise funds for the NAACP and increase its membership.

While the legal program and the campaign for an antilynching law were characterized by significant continuity and were shaped independently of the Great Depression, it would be difficult to overestimate the impact of the economic collapse and the New Deal on other aspects of the NAACP's programs and activities. The NAACP was operating in a radically new environment, and a series of mutually reinforcing developments caused a number of changes. At the initiative of a strengthened executive branch led by Franklin D. Roosevelt, there was a proliferation of federal programs addressing the nation's economic problems. By the end of the 1930s the majority of black voters had shifted from the Republican to the Democratic party. The importance of this shift was heightened by the continued migration of blacks into urban centers generally controlled by Democratic political machines. There was also a general shift to the left on the part of substantial numbers of Americans. One manifestation of this leftward shift was a relatively large and extremely active Communist party that continually criticized the NAACP for its lack of radicalism. Another response to both the depression and government initiatives was the rise of the Congress of Industrial Organizations (CIO), which, while not free of discrimination, had made serious efforts to implement its official policy of organizing all workers. Finally, from within the black community itself came a range of challenges to the NAACP's traditional assumptions and programs.

In response to these circumstances and the accompanying pressures, the NAACP as early as 1930–1931 began to make economic issues more important to its agenda. Blacks were faced with obvious inequities in the implementation of New Deal programs: for example, wage differentials sanctioned by the National Recovery Administration; virtual exclusion of black sharecroppers from the benefits of the Agricultural Adjustment Act; the exclusion of certain occupations in which blacks were heavily represented, such as sharecropping and domestic work, from coverage by Social Security. Even those agencies that were most helpful to blacks—the Works Progress Administration, the National Youth Administration, and the United States Housing Authority—and did the most to attract blacks to the Democratic party also exhibited discriminatory practices. The NAACP monitored the patterns of such discrimination and lodged protests with the appropriate federal agencies. The Association established personal contacts with leaders in the New Deal administration, most notably with Eleanor Roosevelt, who in contrast to her husband was openly supportive of the NAACP. Her warm relationship with Walter White and sincere interest in the NAACP's goals epitomized the growing sensitivity of some left-wing New Dealers to racial discrimination.

Blacks suffered disproportionately from the economic devastation of the Great Depression, and one result was that NAACP members and other segments of the black community put increased pressure on the Association for assistance. Local branches began to entreat the national office for help as the full effects of the depression began to be felt. The majority of the protests that the NAACP filed with New Deal agencies resulted from such complaints. The NAACP had responded as best it could to economic discrimination since its 1909 origin, when at its founding convention it was presented with a petition from a group of black firemen on the Georgia railroads being forced out of their jobs by racist white workers. In the absence of relevant federal law or a favorable legislative consensus, there was almost nothing the NAACP could do. However, after 1930 not only did the urgency and volume of the complaints escalate but the national government was committed to some sort of response.

The Association's most painful internal conflict, although it had negligible long-range consequences, was between Du Bois and Walter White. The contention was rooted in a long-simmering hostility between the two men. Among other reasons, the economic downturn of the 1930s had exacerbated their disagreement over the allocation of funds for the *Crisis*, an issue that had bedeviled Du Bois and other leaders of the Association for two decades. The particular confrontation that led to Du Bois's resignation in 1934 was his proposal, published in the Crisis, to solve the economic problems of the black masses by creating all-black cooperative enterprises while downplaying the struggle for integration. In fact Du Bois's willingness to accept a large degree of voluntary separation seemed to represent a repudiation of the founding principles and goals of the NAACP. To White and his colleagues, such a distinction between forced segregation and voluntary separation (a distinction made with much more success under different circumstances by Malcolm X thirty years later) was unacceptable. In the ensuing debate and struggle Du Bois was forced to resign from the organization that he had helped to found and played a leading role,in for a quarter of a century.[20]

At the same time a small group of radical intellectuals centered primarily at Howard University urged the NAACP to reorient its programs and approaches toward an alliance with the white working class. The most prominent of these radicals were economist Abram L. Harris, sociologist E. Franklin Frazier, and political scientist Ralph J. Bunche.

Charles H. Houston, who in his own law practice represented southern black railway workers, also thought that the NAACP needed to pay greater attention to economic problems and privately nudged White in that direction. After some resistance, the NAACP leadership responded by commissioning Harris to head a committee for making specific recommendations. The so-called Harris Report in 1935 advocated such sweeping changes to the Association's organization that it foreclosed any possibility of being adopted. The report did, however, sensitize the NAACP leadership to the importance of the relationship between black and white workers. As a result, the Harris Report had long-range consequences for the organization.

Relations with the Communist party were predictably quite stormy, even during the period of the Popular Front (1935–1940). In addition to fundamental ideological differences, there was a bitter struggle over which of the two organizations would benefit from the increased militancy of black people. This discord became clear in the conflict between the NAACP and the Communist party over defense of the so-called Scottsboro Boys. Thus, long before the Cold War and McCarthyism, the resolutely liberal NAACP had its own reasons for opposing American Communists. That the NAACP saw fit to interact with American Communists at all was due to the Communist party's success among the black population with such militant tactics as picketing, holding marches, organizing unemployment councils, and fighting with landlords over evictions.

The National Negro Congress (NNC) emerged as a result of the intersecting concerns of the Howard radicals (especially Bunche) and the Communist party. The NNC was the outgrowth of a conference on the economic problems of blacks held at Howard University in 1935, underwritten by the Julius Rosenwald Fund and arranged by John P. Davis, a black Harvard graduate who was very close to the Communists. Projected as a broad coalition of racial advancement organizations, the NNC adopted a program quite similar to that of the NAACP but with the promise of more militant action and closer ties to white workers in the new industrial unions. Roy Wilkins, then assistant secretary to Walter White, attended the 1936 founding convention in Chicago as an observer and reported with obvious distaste on the number of Communists he saw active in the proceedings. But the following year black support for the NNC had grown to such an extent that even Walter White agreed to appear as one of the convention speakers. From the NAACP's point of view it was quite fortunate that the NNC and the Popular Front began to fall apart in 1939 over disagreements on Soviet foreign policy.

In contrast, the NAACP formed a lasting relationship with the CIO. The road to cooperation was complicated by mixed motives on both sides. The CIO policy of organizing black workers contrasted greatly with that of the craft unions in the American Federation of Labor (AFL), most of which had herded blacks into impotent Jim Crow locals, excluded them altogether from jobs under AFL control, and even driven black workers from jobs they had already held. Many of the NAACP leaders were impressed by the positions taken by the CIO but were constrained from readily embracing the new union by two factors: the extent of Communist leadership among some unions and the justifiable skepticism many NAACP branch leaders and rank-and-file members felt about unions in general. This distrust was not confirmed only to the black elite but was widely shared by working-class blacks who had a long history of bad experiences with racist white workers and their unions. The CIO unions themselves were anxious to capitalize on the militancy of black workers but had earlier turned to the NNC because it had a stronger and more consistently pro-CIO stance than the NAACP did. The collapse of the NNC and the successful collaboration of the United Automobile Workers with the NAACP in the Ford strike of 1941 prompted the NAACP to form an alliance with the CIO, a coalition with labor that continued even after the merger of the AFL and the CIO in 1955.

At the end of the 1930s like the end of the 1920s the NAACP had weathered the storms of both internal and external challenges and emerged as the strongest of all the race advancement organizations. In fact, the membership of the NAACP, although not equal to its earlier peak in 1918, doubled between 1929 and 1939. Surprisingly, membership figures during the Great Depression in the early 1930s held up remarkably well, and numerous branches were revitalized and others founded. The Association was now firmly under black control and direction, and effective power had passed from the board to the executive secretary. Thus the organization was prepared to shape actively the future of the black struggle for equal rights. in the crisis of the depression, blacks, especially those in urban areas outside the South, could be mobilized as never before, and the organization that they chose to join was the NAACP.

Much of the credit for building membership in the local branches should go to countless black women, whose activities have yet to be carefully examined. Women also served in a variety of leadership capacities in the branches, particularly as secretaries and treasurers, some as vice presidents, and, on occasion, as branch presidents or chairs of the executive board. More visible than local women officers were the unusual succession of talented black women on the national staff whose achievements have thus far been overlooked by most historians. In the aftermath of the elevation of James Weldon Johnson to executive secretary, Mary B. Talbert of Buffalo, a past president of the National Association of Colored Women's Clubs, was appointed field secretary. She was followed by Addie W. Hunton of Brooklyn and by Daisy Lampkin of Pittsburgh, who worked with extraordinary success even during the depths of the depression. In the mid-1930s the Association appointed Juanita E. Jackson of the powerful Baltimore branch to increase the involvement of black youth. Ella J. Baker, better known for her later work with the Southern Christian Leadership Conference (SCLC) and Student Nonviolent Coordinating Committee (SNCC), served both as a field secretary and during the 1940s a brief but vigorous term as director of branches. After the war came the appointment of individuals like Lucille Black and Ruby Hurley who served long terms as membership secretary and southeast regional secretary, respectively.

The outbreak of World War II in Europe, the subsequent mobilization of the American economy for war, and the creation of millions of new jobs solidified the NAACP's concern with economic matters. At first white workers were the main beneficiaries of the expanding economy, while black workers still found themselves in the depths of the depression. Protestations to Washington were decidedly unproductive. In this context A. Philip Randolph proposed a march of 100,000 blacks on Washington to take place in June 1941.

Randolph was no stranger to the NAACP. Although he had been one of its most outspoken critics early in his career, the Association had supported his efforts to organize the Pullman porters in the 1920s. Following the recognition of the Brotherhood of Sleeping Car Porters by the AFL in 1935 and the collective bargaining agreement with the Pullman Company in 1937, Randolph was widely hailed as the leading spokesman for black workers. He served as president of the National Negro Congress from 1936 until forced out by the Communists in 1939. Influenced by the success of mass action demonstrations to achieve economic goals, even the NAACP mounted a picket line outside the 1934 AFL convention in San Francisco while inside Randolph was giving a speech that addressed the practice of discrimination by the craft unions. It therefore is not surprising that the NAACP welcomed Randolph's call for a March on Washington and played a key role in helping him use this tactic to force President Roosevelt to establish a Fair Employment Practices Committee (FEPC) in 1941.[21] An important factor in the calculations of both Roosevelt and the NAACP was the growing political strength of northern black voters as part of the Democratic coalition.[22]

In short, the depression and the New Deal proved to be a watershed in the NAACP's history. Unlike many other reform organizations of the Progressive Era, the NAACP had been able to adapt successfully, taking on economic concerns without abandoning its traditional agenda.

World War II provided a more favorable environment for NAACP activism. The goal to defeat Nazi Germany, which expressed an openly racist ideology, promoted concern for domestic racial problems among some white Americans. Although there was much racial tension, even rioting, in wartime America, both official and popular attitudes were significantly different from those of the World War I period. Race riots no longer took the exclusive form of pogroms, for blacks were now better able to defend themselves, inflict casualties on whites, and even attack white property in predominantly black areas.

A telling indicator of the differences between the eras was the soaring NAACP membership, which for the first time surpassed the heights it had reached during World War I. As during the preceding decades, economic and demographic factors loomed large. Continuing job discrimination notwithstanding, wartime labor needs had encouraged a massive increase in black migration to cities in the North and West, which continued at the rate of one million per decade through the 1960s. Although there was some economic reversal following the war, basically blacks had been able to establish firm footholds in semiskilled positions outside southern agriculture.[23]

The wartime gains in employment had stemmed in part from the embarrassing testimony at public hearings conducted by the FEPC, and also from the quiet work of regional FEPC and War Manpower Commission staff members negotiating with industry officials in the North and West. However, the FEPC lacked enforcement powers, was constantly attacked by southern congressmen, and ceased operations at the end of the war. In 1943 A. Philip Randolph created a coalition of organizations known as the National Council for a Permanent FEPC with which the NAACP at first cooperated on an ad hoc basis and eventually joined after the end of the war. For the next two decades the enactment of fair employment legislation would prove to be an elusive goal. But largely through the adroit machinations of Roy Wilkins the National Council evolved by 1952 into an influential lobby for civil rights legislation, the Leadership Conference on Civil Rights (LCCR). This coalition, however, was led not by Randolph but by the NAACP.

This particular development, which has escaped the notice of historians, marked a radical transformation of the NAACP's lobbying strategy from one based on personal contacts by a few top officers of the Association to one that mobilized the resources of scores of civic, labor, and religious organizations. This change was made possible by a significant shift in white public opinion toward accepting the necessity to confront the issue of racial inequality. This influx of support and the new climate of public opinion that it indicated in turn raised the expectations of the NAACP and encouraged it to press its agenda even more forcefully.

The nine years between the end of World War II and the *Brown* decision of 1954 coincided with the onset of the Cold War and the climax of McCarthyism. Although generally unrecognized by scholars, the anti-Communist atmosphere actually had a contradictory impact on the NAACP and the struggle for equal rights. On the one hand, for many white southerners and right-wing conservatives, civil rights for blacks was perceived to be part of an international Communist conspiracy, and the NAACP was attacked repeatedly as being Communist-inspired, -led, and -dominated. On the other hand, the NAACP, which like some other liberal organizations maintained its vigorous opposition to Communist influence, employed the threat posed by the Cold War and the influence of the Soviet Union among nonwhite peoples of the world to press its own agenda. The gist of the argument was that American racial practices played into the Soviet argument about the nature of capitalism, imperialism, and racism.[24] In fact, as an organization, the NAACP entered its most prosperous period during the heyday of the Cold War. Through expanded and effective fundraising mechanisms such as the Life Membership campaigns and the "Freedom Fund" banquets, it established a firm financial footing. This permitted an expansion of the NAACP staff, including maintaining a Washington bureau headed by a full-time lobbyist and the employment of a specialist to deal with organized labor on questions of discrimination.

Late in the war (1944–1945) and in the postwar era, labor and lobbying activities revolved around an alliance between the NAACP and the CIO. The NAACP lobbied in behalf of labor-sponsored social welfare legislation such as minimum wages, public housing, and expansion of unemployment compensation and campaigned against right-to-work laws and the Taft-Hartley Act. From the NAACP's perspective, labor's legislative agenda, if enacted, would also benefit blacks. For its part the CIO not only supported antilynching legislation but was also a vigorous proponent of bills for a permanent FEPC. In part this was a marriage of convenience because, as was frequently said, "both blacks and labor are facing identical enemies in Congress: Southern Democrats and conservative northern and western Republicans." With migration from the South continuing at a high level, blacks were more than ever an essential part of the New Deal-Fair Deal coalition. In 1948 civil rights policy became an important national political issue for the first time since Reconstruction, and black votes in the North and West were key to Harry S Truman's victory in 1948.[25]

During this period the NAACP also forged alliances with certain leading Jewish secular organizations including the Anti-Defamation League, the American Jewish Committee, and the American Jewish Congress. There has been a mythological tone about what has been called the "Black-Jewish Alliance."[26] For more than three decades after the NAACP was founded, Jewish involvement was limited to the contributions of a handful of individuals. Among the few people of Jewish ancestry connected with the NAACP in the early years were Joel Spingarn and his brother Arthur Spingarn, a lawyer, who as chair of the legal committee played a major role in NAACP litigation until Houston and Thurgood Marshall were hired in the 1930s. Louis Marshall, a constitutional lawyer, was a founder and president of the American Jewish Committee, which played no role in the affairs of the NAACP during this period. Marshall's son-in-law Jacob Billikopf was active in Jewish philanthropic circles during the Great Depression. He arranged for substantial contributions from a few wealthy Jews like Lessing Rosenwald (whose father Julius Rosenwald had given some fairly large contributions to the NAACP during its early years), Joseph Fels of the Fels-Naptha Soap Company, and Herbert Lehman, the prominent Democratic politician. After mid-century, individuals of Jewish ancestry held important positions on the NAACP staff, including Herbert Hill as labor secretary and June Shagaloff as education secretary. However, cooperation between Jewish organizations and the NAACP began only with the campaign to establish a permanent FEPC. This particular alliance played a decisive role in the LCCR legislative coalition that lobbied for the passage of the civil rights acts in 1964 and 1965. In fact, Arnold Aronson, the executive secretary of the LCCR who had a career in Jewish advancement organizations, became executive secretary Roy Wilkins's most trusted ally. Like most political alliances this one was based on a combination of self-interest, shared goals, and idealism.

President Truman's support for equal rights was not entirely consistent, and he had to be prodded. In 1946 he did appoint a Committee on Civil Rights that issued a report the following year entitled *To Secure These Rights*. Among other recommendations was "the elimination of segregation, based on race, color, creed, or national origin, from American life."[27] In the aftermath Truman issued an order integrating the armed forces. This action illustrates something of the complex maneuvering required for even limited changes. A. Philip Randolph had dramatized the issue by calling for a civil disobedience campaign against the draft; the NAACP, like other race advancement organizations, disavowed the strategy but used the threat posed by Randolph to underline its own concern with the issue. Receiving private assurances that the president would act to integrate the armed forces, Randolph then withdrew his call, and after some delay Truman issued the appropriate executive order.

The NAACP abandoned the seemingly hopeless fight for an antilynching bill. The struggle for a permanent FEPC, which, after early 1949, became the NAACP's top legislative priority, also proved frustrating. The NAACP—unhappy with Randolph's direction of the National Council—had created the LCCR. Probably the most important gains made by the NAACP itself during the period from 1944 to 1954 came through its long-standing program of litigation in the federal courts. Not only had the Supreme Court overturned the system of white primary elections in 1944, but four years later it declared restrictive covenants unenforceable. In the early 1950s came a series of decisions banning the exclusion or segregation of blacks in publicly owned recreation facilities. The NAACP's campaign against Jim Crow schools was coming to a climax. In a series of decisions the Supreme Court required southern states to admit blacks to graduate and professional schools in public universities.

In 1948, possibly capitalizing on the recommendations in *To Secure These Rights*, the NAACP officially undertook a series of suits aimed directly at overthrowing the *Plessy* doctrine of separate but equal. Finally in 1954 in the combination of cases subsumed under *Brown v. Board of Education*, the Supreme Court accepted unanimously the NAACP argument that separate schools were inherently unequal.[28] At the local level coalitions led chiefly by the NAACP and Jewish organizations succeeded in obtaining FEPC laws in a number of states and cities and, in a few places, fair housing laws as well.

During the years following the *Brown* decision, though the pace of change seemed to accelerate, federal court decisions were not self-enforcing and the NAACP had plenty of work to do. In fact, there was a notable expansion of NAACP activity on all fronts. In the southern states white resistance intensified, manifest in a resurgence of the Ku Klux Klan, the formation of white Citizens' Councils, and massive resistance to school desegregation (most notably in the violence at Little Rock that was quelled only when President Dwight D. Eisenhower reluctantly sent in federal troops). Three southern states, Texas, Louisiana, and Alabama, passed laws making it illegal for the NAACP to operate within their boundaries, and across the South violence and intimidation against the NAACP increased. For its part the Association continued to win victories before the courts. The LCCR, backed by a growing array of organizations and sympathetic figures in the Eisenhower administration, was able to secure passage of the civil rights acts of 1957 and 1960. Modest though their provisions were, having been diluted by the compromises of Senate majority leader Lyndon B. Johnson, they were nevertheless significant as the first national civil rights laws passed since 1875.

In retrospect, the policies of the Eisenhower administration could be characterized as moderate Republican.[29] For example, the NAACP labor secretary Herbert Hill utilized well the machinery of the President's Committee on Government Contracts, which was charged with resolving incidents of discrimination practiced by both management and labor in cases involving contracts with the federal government. This sort of mechanism had first been put into place by Truman after the continued failure of the Congress to pass fair employment legislation. Headed by Vice President Richard M. Nixon, Eisenhower's committee performed with surprising efficacy. Acting on complaints from the NAACP and other groups, it resolved a number of the most egregious individual cases.

All of this was taking place against the background of the rise of anticolonial movements in Asia and Africa. Ghana's independence in 1957 prompted the view among black Americans that their brothers and sisters in Africa were achieving freedom at a more rapid pace than blacks in America.

Domestically the pace of events also quickened but at a slower rate. State FEPC laws, Supreme Court decisions, and congressional legislation seemed to promise so much but made only relatively small dents in basic patterns of discrimination. An example of the difficulties faced can be seen in the Supreme Court ruling in 1955, which blunted the thrust of the Brown decision by sanctioning "all deliberate speed" and thereby afforded the white South the encouragement and time to mobilize against the movement toward equal rights. Another example was the situation with regard to the franchise. By 1954, a decade after the white primary decision, black voter registration in the South had risen from 250,000 to 1,250,000, with increases chiefly in the upper South but also in repressive areas of the Deep South such as some of the Louisiana parishes. But an important aspect of the development of southern resistance to black advances was the increased use of intimidation and of technicalities such as literacy tests that actually reduced the number of blacks registered.[30]

In this context there was what we may call a "revolution in expectations" among American blacks, a new sense of urgency to speed the dismantling of barriers to racial equality. The result was an outpouring of nonviolent direct action that by the early 1960s came to characterize this most recent phase of the civil rights movement. Tens of thousands of people-black and white-were mobilized for the first time, and the rise of new organizations such as SCLC, SNCC, and many local organizations ended the NAACP's hegemony over the civil rights movement. Ironically the NAACP's successful work in the courts and legislatures had created the impatience and dissatisfaction with its tactics and strategies.

The first organizational challenge to the NAACP came from the Montgomery bus boycott, which led to the rise of Martin Luther King, Jr., and the founding of SCLC in 1957. Unlike the situation with Randolph, the NAACP had no knowledge of or working relationship with King before his appearance as a leader; King, for his part, did not need the NAACP. Therefore the NAACP leadership was unable to exert substantial influence over his activities. In this changing climate, and given King's personal magnetism, the founding of SCLC posed the most serious threat to the NAACP's leadership that it had faced since the founding of the National Negro Congress in 1936. Even though the Supreme Court case resulting from the Montgomery bus boycott was won by NAACP lawyers, King's charisma was such that this achievement—which effectively clinched the victory—went virtually unnoticed.

During the early 1960s, though vastly overshadowed in the mass media by King, by the southern student revolt and the rise of SNCC, by the resurgence of the Congress of Racial Equality (CORE) under James Farmer's leadership, and by the appearance of Malcolm X, the NAACP was more active and successful than ever before. The sixties was a period of especially intense conflict and competition among civil rights organizations partly over questions of strategy, tactics, and the pace of change but largely over organizational credit. The NAACP was criticized from both within and without the Association's ranks as being a conservative, bureaucratic organization that was out of touch with the new militancy. In the context of the early 1960s this lack of unity was actually quite helpful as civil rights organizations at both the national and local levels competed with one another in their quest for victories in the struggle for equality. Oddly enough its long-established structure enabled the NAACP to reap the benefits from the new racial consciousness, and by 1963 its membership crested at over 400,000, making it by far the largest civil rights organization. Moreover, it was the only civil rights organization that was funded primarily by the black community.

As could be expected in an organization of its age and size, there was an enormous range of attitudes and responses in the branches to the new wave of demonstrations. Some branches figuratively sat on their hands, while others embraced the new activism with enthusiasm. In fact, the NAACP branches were probably the major source of legal aid to the youthful activists of 1960 and 1961, and the Association's own youth councils and college chapters did much to make this phase of the movement effective. In South Carolina, for example, in 1963 and 1964 the NAACP State Conference of Branches led the direct action struggle. As Roy Wilkins said with some justice, "the NAACP branches put up the money and others get the credit." The NAACP was also deeply involved in litigation against de facto school segregation in northern cities and provided support for school boycotts in Boston, New York, and other cities in 1963 and 1964. Numerous NAACP members were also among the demonstrators at construction sites in northeastern cities protesting discrimination in the building trades and among the masses of protestors against job discrimination in such places as the cities in the San Francisco Bay area.

With regard to the issue of racial bias by many labor unions, beginning in the late 1950s the NAACP labor secretary Herbert Hill had adopted an innovative approach to job discrimination. Using a combination of litigation and publicity, Hill kept constant pressure on government, corporations, and labor unions to do their part in opening up more job opportunities for blacks. At the same time Hill was carrying out this aspect of the NAACP program, Clarence Mitchell, head of the Washington bureau, and the whole LCCR strategy were heavily dependent on the AFL-CIO legislative lobby for stronger civil rights legislation. In effect NAACP executive secretary Roy Wilkins was pursuing a skillful two-pronged strategy of confronting labor with specific examples of discrimination while continuing to maintain an alliance with labor on matters of joint legislative interest. This whole strategy depended upon the need for the AFL-CIO's leadership to maintain the liberal image of the labor movement and labor's role and influence in the New Deal coalition. Moreover, the AFL-CIO leadership admitted that on the question of union discrimination it could not clean its own house without the assistance of federal fair employment legislation.

The culmination of direct action North and South came during the year following the Birmingham demonstrations of spring 1963. The August 1963 March on Washington symbolized unprecedented national support for some form of civil rights legislation. In this context of dramatic confrontations displaying both racist repression and individual courage, the NAACP mobilized the LCCR for the successful lobbying for the passage of the Civil Rights Act of 1964 and the Voting Rights Act of 1965. The support of both the large AFL-CIO lobby in Washington and the representatives of the major religious faiths was vital as was the political pressure applied by President Johnson, but it was the NAACP's executive secretary who made the important decisions, including the one to incorporate a strong employment antidiscrimination clause that became Section 7 of the 1964 Act. One should not discount the role of the direct action organizations in awakening public opinion and exerting tremendous moral and political pressures. But it is important to emphasize the development of a symbiotic relationship between the campaigns led by new waves of demonstrators and the NAACP's skillful translation of their joint concerns into lasting legislative victories.

The civil rights legislation came during the apex of New Deal-style reformism that characterized the war on poverty. This legislation finally removed the legal barriers that had prevented blacks from exercising their basic rights under the Fourteenth and Fifteenth Amendments, which the NAACP had sought since its founding. This legislation also brought into being the legal sanctions against employment discrimination that the NAACP had first included in its national agenda during the Roosevelt era.

The enactment of the civil rights laws of 1964 and 1965 produced what A. Philip Randolph called a crisis of victory. It soon became apparent that the mere passage of legislation and the recognition of constitutional rights were not sufficient to redress three hundred years of racial oppression. The issues associated with economic inequality—widespread poverty, poor and inadequate housing, inferior schools, police brutality, and other inequities in the criminal justice system proved to be virtually intractable. Much of the black power response consisted of attempts to deal with the difficulties and frustrations of this situation. Ideologically the NAACP resisted this tendency toward separatism, and the national leadership's success in this matter was probably due to the commitment, especially in the South, of its largely middle-aged membership to the struggle for integration. Yet at this point the national board for the first time became all black, and it has remained that way ever since.

Just as the New Deal-style economic and social programs of the Great Society were on the verge of decline, so also the NAACP, from an organizational point of view, was looking at a bleaker future. Finding that its traditional strategies of legal redress and legislative reform were not adequate to deal with problems of this magnitude and that there was no national consensus on how to deal with these matters, the Association began to drift and decline. The NAACP began to lose its membership and its leadership role.

The Voting Rights Act opened up the possibility of significant gains in the political system; consequently much of black leadership has gravitated toward electoral politics. Leadership began to develop from the local level through the Congressional Black Caucus. The irony is that it was the NAACP's success in lobbying for black voting rights that helped lay the groundwork for the drift away from the organization and toward political activism. However, the increase in black voting power caused many white southerners and northern white ethnics to shift to the Republican party, reinforcing the decline in liberalism associated with the Republican ascendancy since the end of the 1960s.

In short, the NAACP, which outlived many of the Progressive and New Deal organizations and had a successful post-World War II career, now appears to have suffered the general fate of liberal reform in the 1970s and 1980s.

ENDNOTES

1. This essay is a synthesis based principally upon years of research in the National Association for the Advancement of Colored People (NAACP) Papers in the Manuscript Division of the Library of Congress, selective research in other manuscript and archival collections, extensive reading in all the major black newspapers, interviews with NAACP officials, and insights gained from participation in NAACP branches and in the larger black protest movement. Earlier publications based on this research are August Meier and Elliott Rudwick, "Attorneys Black and White: A Case Study of Race Relations with the NAACP," *Journal of American History,* LXII (March 1976), 913–46; Rudwick and Meier, "The Rise of the Black Secretariat in the NAACP, 1909–35" in Meier and Rudwick, *Along the Color Line: Explorations in the Black Experience* (Urbana, Chicago, and London, 1976), 94–127; Meier and Rudwick, *Black Detroit and the Rise of the UAW* (New York and Oxford, 1979); and John H. Bracey, Jr., and Meier, "Allies or Adversaries?: The NAACP, A. Philip Randolph and the 1941 March on Washington," *Georgia Historical Quarterly,* LXXV (Spring 1991), 1–17. We wish to thank David Katzman for suggesting to Professor Meier this topic as an appropriate one for a presidential address.

2. The "Inc." Fund was established in 1940 as a tax-exempt mechanism that carried out the organization's legal strategies. In 1957 changes in Internal Revenue regulations forced its complete separation from the parent body.

3. John Chamberlain, *Farewell to Reform: Being a History of the Rise, Life and Decay of the Progressive Mind in America* (New York, 1932); Richard Hofstadter, *The Age of Reform: From Bryan to FDR* (New York, 1956); Eric F. Goldman, *Rendezvous with Destiny* (New York, 1952); Allen F. Davis, *Spearheads for Reform: The Social Settlements and the Progressive Movement, 1890–1914* (New York, 1967); Otis L. Graham, Jr., *An Encore for Reform: The Old Progressives and the New Deal* (New York, 1967), and Graham, *Toward a Planned Society: From Roosevelt to Nixon* (New York, 1976); Wilbur J. Cohen, ed., *The Roosevelt New Deal: A Program Assessment Fifty Years After* ([Austin, Texas], 1986). Other relevant volumes that omit or pay scant attention to blacks and the NAACP include Clarke A. Chambers, *Seedtime of Reform: American Social Service and Social Action, 1918-1933* (Minneapolis, 1963); Robert Higgs, *Crisis and Leviathan: Critical Episodes in the Growth of American Government* (New York and Oxford, 1987); Steve Fraser and Gary Gerstle, eds., *The Rise and Fall of the New Deal Order, 1930–1980* (Princeton, 1989); Alan Dawley, *Struggles for Justice: Social Responsibility and the Liberal State* (Cambridge, Mass., 1991); and James T. Kloppenberg, *Uncertain Victory: Social Democracy and Progressivism in European and American Thought, 1870–1920* (New York and Oxford, 1986).

4. Arthur S. Link and Richard L. McCormick, *Progressivism* (Arlington Heights, Ill., 1983); Link, "What Happened to the Progressive Movement in the 1920s?" *American Historical Review,* LXIV (July 1959), 833–51; Alonzo L. Hamby, *Liberalism and Its Challenges: FDR to Reagan* (New York and Oxford, 1985). The ADA studies are Clifton Brock, *Americans for Democratic Action: Its Role in National Politics* (Washington, D.C., 1962) and Steven M. Gillon, *Politics and Vision: The ADA and American Liberalism, 1947–1985* (New York and Oxford, 1987). The ADA and the NAACP are discussed in Denton L. Watson, *Lion in the Lobby: Clarence Mitchell, Jr.'s Struggle for the Passage of Civil Rights Laws* (New York, 1990).

5. See James M. McPherson, *The Abolitionist Legacy: From Reconstruction to the NAACP* (Princeton, 1975) and Emma Lou Thornbrough, "The National Afro-American League, 1887–1908," *Journal of Southern History,* XXVII (November 1961), 494–512.

6. For a somewhat different version of these matters see Nancy J. Weiss, "From Black Separatism to Interracial Cooperation: The Origins of Organized Efforts for Racial Advancement, 1890-1920," in Barton J. Bernstein and Allen J. Matusow, eds., *Twentieth-Century America: Recent Interpretations* (2d. ed.; New York and other cities, 1972), 58–67.

7. On the early years see for example B.Joyce Ross, *J. E. Spingarn and the Rise of the NAACP, 1911–1939* (New York, 1972). *On The Birth of a Nation* see Thomas R. Cripps, "The Reaction of the Negro to the Motion Picture Birth of a Nation," *Historian,* XXV (May 1963), 344–62.

8. Robert L. Zangrando, *The NAACP Crusade Against Lynching, 1909–1950* (Philadelphia, 1980). All of the cases mentioned are discussed in the NAACP annual reports, and most have been the subject of scholarly monographs. See Dennis B. Downey and Raymond M. Hyser, *No Crooked Death: Coatesville, Pennsylvania, and the Lynching of Zachariah Walker* (Urbana and Chicago, 1991); Elliott M. Rudwick, *Race Riot at East St. Louis, July 2, 1917* (Carbondale, Ill., 1964); Robert V. Haynes, *A Night of Violence: The Houston Riot of 1917* (Baton Rouge, 1976); William M. Tuttle, Jr., *Race Riot: Chicago in the Red Summer of 1919* (New York, 1970); Richard C. Cortner, *A Mob Intent on Death: The NAACP and the Arkansas Riot Cases* (Middletown, Conn., 1998); Scott Ellsworth, *Death in a Promised Land: The Tulsa Race Riot of 1921* (Baton Rouge and London, 1982); Dan T. Carter, *Scottsboro: A Tragedy of the American South* (Baton Rouge, 1969); Stephen J. Whitfield, *A Death in the Delta: The Story of Emmett Till* (New York and London, 1988); and Howard Smead, *Blood Justice: The Lynching of Mack Charles Parker* (New York and Oxford, 1986).

9. See files on Aiken, South Carolina, lynchings, Containers 365 and 366, Group 1, Series C, in NAACP Papers, Library of Congress.

10. Ralph J. Bunche, "The Programs, Ideologies, Tactics and Achievements of Negro Betterment and Interracial Organizations," p. 48 (Unpublished Memorandum for the Carnegie-Myrdal Study, 1940); copy at the Schomburg Center for Research in Black Culture, New York Public Library).

11. For the documentary record of these debates see Theodore G. Vincent, ed., *Voices of a Black Nation: Political Journalism in the Harlem Renaissance* (San Francisco, 1973), Chapters 3 and 4.

12. David Levering Lewis, "The Politics of Art: The New Negro, 1920–1935," *Prospects: An Annual of American Cultural Studies*, III (1977), 237–61.

13. In addition to chapter 1 in the biography by B. Joyce Ross cited above, Joel E. Spingarn's literary activities are given more extensive treatment in Marshall Van Deusen, *J. E. Spingarn* (New York, 1971). Mary White Ovington wrote in a variety of genres. The most relevant works for our purposes include *The Shadow* (New York, 1920), a novel; *Hazel* (New York, 1913) and *Zeke* (New York, 1931), novels written for black youth; *The Awakening* (New York, 1923) and *Phyllis Wheatley* (New York, 1932), plays about black life; *The Upward Path; A Reader for Colored Children . . .* (New York, 1920); and *Portraits in Color* (New York, 1927), a collection of biographical sketches of twenty prominent black men and women living at that time.

14. James Weldon Johnson was a prolific writer in a variety of genres both fictional and nonfictional. His most significant works during this period include *The Autobiography of an Ex-Colored Man* (Boston, 1912; 2d ed., 1927), a novel; *The Book of American Negro Poetry . . .* (New York, 1922; rev. ed., 193 1); *God's Trombones: Seven Negro Sermons in Verse* (New York, 1927); *Black Manhattan* (New York, 1930), a social and cultural history of blacks in New York City; and *Along This Way: The Autobiography of James Weldon Johnson* (New York, 1933). The standard biography of Johnson is Eugene Levy's *James Weldon Johnson: Black Leader, Black Voice* (Chicago and London, 1973). White wrote two novels during this period: *The Fire in the Flint* (New York, 1924) and *Flight* (New York, 1926). His relationship to the Renaissance has been discussed in Edward E. Waldron, *Walter White and the Harlem Renaissance* (Port Washington, N.Y., 1978). Jessie Redmon Fauset's novels include *There is Confusion* (New York, 1924); *Plum Bun* (New York, 1929); *The Chinaberry Tree* (New York, 1931); and *Comedy, American Style* (New York, 1933). William Pickens was the author of *The New Negro: His Political, Civil, and Mental Status; and Related Essays* (New York, 1916); an autobiography, *Bursting Bonds: Enlarged Edition, The Heir of Slaves* (Boston, 1923); a collection of short stories, *The Vengeance of the Gods* (Philadelphia, 1922); and an anthology entitled *American ÆSOP: Negro and Other Humor* (Boston, 1926). The best overall study of the relation of art to politics in the Harlem Renaissance is David Lovering Lewis, *When Harlem Was in Vogue* (New York, 1981).

15. Clement E. Vose, *Caucasians Only: The Supreme Court, the NAACP, and the Restrictive Covenant Cases* (Berkeley and Los Angeles, 1959).

16. Richard L. Watson, Jr., "The Defeat of Judge Parker: A study in Pressure Groups and Politics," *Mississippi Valley Historical Review*, L (September 1963), 213–34. See also Kenneth W. Goings, *"The NAACP Comes of Age": The Defeat of Judge John J. Parker* (Bloomington and Indianapolis, 1990).

17. See Richard Kluger, *Simple Justice: The History of Brown v. Board of Education and Black America's Struggle for Equality* (New York, 1975)and especially *Mark V. Tushnet, The NAACP's Legal Strategy Against Segregated Education, 1925–1950* (Chapel Hill and London, 1987).

18. Gunnar Myrdal, *An American Dilemma: The Negro Problem and Modern Democracy* (New York and London, 1944). See also Walter A. Jackson, *Gunnar Myrdal and America's Conscience: Social Engineering and Racial Liberalism, 1938–1987* (Chapel Hill and London, 1990). For a biography of Houston see Genna Rae McNeil, *Groundwork: Charles Hamilton Houston and the Struggle for Civil Rights* (Philadelphia, 1983); for Hastie see Gilbert Ware, *William Hastie: Grace Under Pressure* (New York and Oxford, 1984).

19. Darlene Clark Hine, *Black Victory: The Rise and Fall of the White Primary in Texas* (Millwood, N.Y., 1979).

20. For a more complete presentation of Du Bois's argument than is found in the *Crisis* or in the NAACP Papers, see his 1936 essay, "The Negro and Social Reconstruction," in W.E.B. Du Bois, *Against Racism: Unpublished Essays, Papers, Addresses, 1887–1961*, edited by Herbert Aptheker (Amherst, Mass., 1985), 103–58.

21. On Randolph's career see Jervis Anderson, *A. Philip Randolph: A Biographical Portrait* (New York, 1973); Paula F. Pfeffer, *A. Philip Randolph, Pioneer of the Civil Rights Movement* (Baton Rouge and London, 1990); William H. Harris, *Keeping the Faith: A. Philip Randolph, Milion P. Webster, and the Brotherhood of Sleeping Car Porters, 1925–37* (Urbana, Chicago, and London, 1977); and Herbert Garfinkel, *When Negroes March: The March on Washington Movement in the Organizational Politics for FEPC* (Glencoe, Ill., 1959). For our understanding of the NAACP's role in the 1941 March on Washington see Bracey and Meier, "Allies or Adversaries?" For general studies of the relationship between blacks and organized labor see especially Sterling D. Spero and Abram L. Harris, *The Black Worker: The Negro and the Labor Movement* (New York, 1931) and Horace R. Cayton and George S. Mitchell, *Black Workers and the New Unions* (Chapel Hill, 1939).

22. For the shift to the democratic party see especially Harvard Sitkoff's *A New Deal for Blacks: The Emergence of Civil Rights as a National Issue* (New York, 1978) and Nancy J. Weiss, *Farewell to the Party of Lincoln: Black Polities in the Age of FDR* (Princeton, 1983).

23. For general conditions of blacks in industry during the 1940s see Herbert R. Northrup, *Organized Labor and the Negro* (New York and London, 1944) and Robert C. Weaver, *Negro Labor: A National Problem* (New York, 1946).

24. The juxtaposition of these issues was graphically demonstrated on the front page of the *New York Times* of May 18, 1954, the day after the Brown decision. A two-line banner headline across the top of the page announced: "HIGH COURT BANS SCHOOL SEGREGATION; 9-TO-0 DECISION GRANTS TIME TO COMPLY." There followed an across-the-page headline in smaller letters, "McCarthy Hearing Off a Week as Eisenhower Bars Report." And in the lower right-hand corner was an article about the Voice of America flashing the court ruling to the world in thirty-four different languages.

25. On the new importance of the black vote in national elections see Henry Lee Moon, *Balance of Power: The Negro Vote* (Garden City, N.Y., 1948).

26. On black-Jewish relations see for example Robert G. Weisbord and Arthur Stein, *Bittersweet Encounter: The Afro-American and the American Jew* (Westport, Conn., 1970); Hasia R. Diner, *In the Almost Promised Land: American Jews and Blacks, 1915–1935* (Westport, Conn., and London, 1977); and David Levering Lewis, "Parallels and Divergences: Assimilationist Strategies of Afro-American and Jewish Elites from 1910 to the Early 1930s," *Journal of American History*, LXXI (December 1984), 543–64.

27. *To Secure These Rights: The Report of the President's Committee on Civil Rights* (Washington, 1947), 166. On Truman's civil rights policies see especially William C. Berman, *The Politics of Civil Rights in the Truman Administration* (Columbus, Ohio, 1970).

28. For a complete list of these cases see Jack Greenberg, *Race Relations and American Law* (New York and London, 1959), 401–2, entitled "Appendix B: NAACP Legal Defense Cases Before the Supreme Court."

29. For differing views see Eisenhower, see Robert Fredrick Burk, *The Eisenhower Administration and Black Civil Rights* (Knoxville, 1984) and Stephen E. Ambrose, *Eisenhower* (2 vols.; New York, 1983–1984), Volume II: *The President*.

30. For a comprehensive treatment of the struggle against disfranchisement see Steven F. Lawson, *Black Ballots: Voting Rights in the South, 1944–1969* (New York, 1976).

UNIT 2-6

MARCUS GARVEY AND THE POLITICS OF REVITALIZATION

Lawrence W. Levine

The legal and legislative drive of the National Association for the Advancement of Colored People for fulfillment of the Negro's constitutional rights and the integration of blacks into American society did not go uncriticized in the Afro-American community. Among the leading critics of the association and its integrationist policy was the West Indian black nationalist, Marcus Garvey. Arriving in the United States at the height of the flood of black migration to northern cities during World War I, Garvey capitalized upon the disillusionment of the hundreds of thousands of new black city dwellers, who bore the brunt of economic discrimination and the wave of racial violence that followed the war. Garvey was a charismatic leader who offered his followers a sense of pride and self-esteem by celebrating the glories of the African past. He proposed a twofold nationalist solution for the problems of America's black citizens: one, the achievement of economic security by banding together to build their own enterprises if they stayed in the United States; and two, the creation of a glorious new empire on an African continent that was, at the time, controlled by the European imperialist powers.

The world has made being black a crime, I hope to make it a virtue.

—*Marcus Garvey*

In 1916, Marcus Garvey, a West Indian black without funds, influence, or substantial contacts, arrived in the United States for the first time. By the early 1920s he had built the largest and most influential Afro-American mass movement in American history. Before the decade ended, the movement he created and led, though it continued to exist both in the United States and abroad, was a weakened shadow of itself-internally divided and bereft of mass support. To understand the brief, dramatic, and profoundly significant career of Garvey and his Universal Negro Improvement Association (UNIA), one needs to understand the dynamic mix of personality and historical situation. Accordingly, this essay focuses upon the formative experiences of Garvey, the situation of American blacks when Garvey first arrived on American soil, and the interaction between the leader and the people he wanted to lead.

Marcus Mosiah Garvey, the eleventh child of Marcus and Sarah Garvey, was born in 1887 in St. Ann's Bay, a rural town on the north coast of Jamaica in the British West Indies. In a 1923 magazine article, Garvey shared his memories of his parents:

> My parents were black negroes. My father was a man of brilliant intellect and dashing courage. He was unafraid of consequences. He took human chances in the course of life, as most bold men do, and he failed at the close of his career. He once had a fortune;—he died poor. My mother was a sober and conscientious Christian, too soft and good for the time in which she lived. She was the direct opposite of my father. He was severe, firm, determined, bold and strong, refusing to yield even to superior forces if he believed he was right. My mother, on the other hand, was always willing to return a smile for a blow, and ever ready to bestow charity upon her enemy. Of this strange combination I was born.

Garvey's account was corroborated by a white neighbor who testified that the elder Garvey, a master stonemason who took jobs only sporadically, preferring to lock himself in his room and read, "always acted as if he did not belong among the villagers; he was well read, and gave advice as a local lawyer. He was silent, stern. . . . He was 'Mr. Garvey' to every one, even to Sarah—his wife and children." Mrs. Garvey "was just the opposite to him in every way. She was one of the most beautiful black women I have ever seen. . . . Her voice was gentle and caressing, her figure well shaped and erect. She was a regular Church-goer at the Wesleyan Methodist Church.

Because nine of his siblings died in childhood, Garvey seems to have grown up close only to his older sister, Indiana. Among his other daily playmates were the nine children of the two white families that lived on the adjoining land. "To me, at home in my early days," Garvey recalled, "there was no difference between white and black." His closest friend, a white girl, "knew no better than I did myself. We were two innocent fools who never dreamed of a race feeling and problem." Their innocence ended abruptly when Garvey's friend informed him that she was being sent away to school in Scotland and that she was instructed by her parents "never to write or try to get in touch with me, for I was a 'nigger.'" His friendship with white boys lasted a bit longer: "We played cricket and baseball, ran races and rode bicycles together, took each other to the river and to the sea beach to learn to swim." At maturity, these associations, too, ended. "I grew up then to see the difference between the races more and more. My schoolmates as young men did not know or remember me any more. Then I realized that I had to make a fight for a place in the world."

The young Garvey's fight was complicated by his father's growing stubbornness and reclusiveness, which damaged the family's financial position. At fourteen, Garvey left school to be apprenticed to his godfather, Mr. Burrowes, a printer. Though Garvey always felt insecure about his lack of formal education, this development was in many ways a happy one. At this small country printing establishment, Garvey was able to learn all facets of a trade that was to constitute one of his main means of communicating with those he wanted to influence. An added bonus was Burrowes's large library in which Garvey could continue to develop his interest in books. This experience only seems to have increased Garvey's resolve to succeed. As a schoolboy he had rebelled against those teachers who wanted to punish him physically: "I simply refused to be whipped. I was not made to be whipped. It annoys me to be defeated." In the printing trade he learned that he had sufficient intelligence and experience to manage men: "I was strong and manly, and I made them respect me. I developed a strong and forceful character."

At the age of sixteen Garvey made the first of a series of moves that were to take him from the periphery to the center of events: he left his rural apprenticeship to take a position as a printer with his uncle in the city of Kingston. Here Garvey furthered his knowledge of the newspaper business. It was in Kingston, too, that Garvey became impressed with the power of oratory. Struck by the skill of the speakers he heard at barbershop forums and debates in local parks, Garvey set about learning the art with his characteristic energy. He went from church to church, absorbing the oratorical and platform styles of a variety of preachers. He would spend long hours alone in his room reciting poetry and passages from school readers and experimenting with different gestures. As his confidence grew, Garvey took an increasingly active role in the Saturday night discussion groups at Victoria Pier, where speakers debated and explored subjects of every sort. His acquaintances during these years were impressed by Garvey's enormous zeal. "He carried a pocket dictionary with him," one of them recalled, "and said he studied three or four words daily, and in his room he would write a paragraph or two using these words." Such energy led this teenager to rise to the position of foreman at one of Jamaica's largest printing establishments. But his ambitions extended beyond his own career. He helped to train black youth in elocution and arranged concerts and elocution contests for their edification. "He was always busy, planning and doing something for the underprivileged youth. Uplift work we called it," another early companion remembered. "I started to take an interest in the politics of my country," Garvey himself wrote of these years, "and then I saw the injustice done to my race because it was black, and I became dissatisfied on that account."

Garvey's dissatisfaction disrupted the orderly progress of his career. During the printers' strike of 1907, Garvey was the only foreman who took the side of the workers. Becoming a leading spokesman for their cause, Garvey found himself blacklisted once the strike failed. Though he was able to secure employment with the Government Printing Office, Garvey's mind was clearly on politics and the need for organization rather than on his vocation. In 1910 Garvey helped to found a political organization—the National Club—and created the *Watchman,* the first of his many newspapers. The failure of both ventures made evident the need for money to fund his political activities, and Garvey joined the stream of West Indian workers migrating to Central and South America in search of better opportunities. Thus, at the age of twenty-three, Garvey began a restless journey that was to keep him out of his native Jamaica for much of the remainder of his life.

In Costa Rica Garvey's uncle helped him secure a job as timekeeper on one of the United Fruit Company's banana plantations. Appalled at the conditions under which the West Indian migrants were forced to live and work, Garvey soon left the plantation and journeyed to Limón to protest to the British consult the treatment accorded those black British subjects. Met by an indifference that convinced him that black lives were simply of no consequence to white officials, Garvey tried more direct action by founding a paper, *La Nacionale,* which soon failed for lack of funds. Going next to Panama, Garvey was similarly disturbed by the condition of the West Indian workers on the Panama Canal. Again he protested, again he tried to establish a newspaper, *La Prensa,* and again he failed. In Ecuador, Nicaragua, Spanish Honduras, Colombia, and Venezuela the story was the same. Everywhere he traveled, Garvey was sickened by the exploitation of his people in the fields, mines, and cities. Returning to Jamaica in 1911, Garvey demanded that the governor take steps to protect overseas Jamaicans and was told—in a modern version of "Let them eat cake"—that if the Jamaicans disliked their treatment abroad they could always return home. If His Majesty's representatives proved indifferent, Garvey decided to see what might be done in England itself. Aided by his sister Indiana, who was working in England as a child's nurse, Garvey set out for London in 1912.

Garvey's two-year sojourn in England proved to be of great importance in shaping his future. Arriving in England with his plans still fluid and uncertain, he departed with a much clearer notion of what he wanted to accomplish. His own version of how this happened is a model of simplicity: "I read 'Up From Slavery,' by Booker T. Washington, and then my doom—if I may so call it—of being a race leader dawned upon me in London. . . . I asked, 'Where is the black man's Government?' 'Where is his King and his kingdom?' 'Where is his President, his country, and his ambassador, his army, his navy, his men of big affairs?' I could not find them, and then I declared, 'I will help to make them.'" Garvey's poetic rendition of his conversion to race leadership should not be taken literally. His decision was neither so simple nor so sudden; it had been in the making for years. A man of Garvey's temperament and upbringing had long chafed under Jamaica's tripartite racial system, which placed the island's 630,000 blacks under the 168,000 coloreds or mixed-bloods, with the 15,000 whites at the top of the racial pyramid. His years in London were important not merely for his reading of Washington—as crucial as this proved to be—but even more so for the blacks from all over the world he met and with whom he exchanged ideas. A British Consul General Report notes that "when in London, Garvey met a number of his own race from Africa and the West Indies . . . he heard form the lips of his countrymen and other coloured people about the sufferings of the darker races, and of their desire to unite for mutual understanding and protection."

Garvey and his movement have become so closely identified with the United States, where indeed they enjoyed their greatest success, that it is sometimes forgotten that Garvey grew up as a colonial in the British Empire and thus had most in common with the Africans and other West Indians who like himself had been living as part of a colonized majority in their own lands. Though he does not mention them in his scant autobiographical writings, there can be no doubt that Garvey was privy to the ideas and dreams of that group of black colonial writers and intellectuals who coalesced in London around the *African Times and Orient Review* for which Garvey himself wrote. Within this circle, the young Garvey was exposed to ideas concerning race conservation, the preservation of group identity, anticolonialism, and African unity. It is not surprising, then, that when Garvey came to espouse the philosophy of Washington, it was with such significant additions as an emphasis on blackness and the glories of the black past and a determination to work for the redemption of Africa from foreign rule.

Before leaving England, Garvey articulated a new mission that coupled his sense of himself as a Jamaican with his growing identification with the entire black race. There would soon be a turning point in the history of the West Indies, he prophesied in the fall of 1913: "The people who inhabit that portion of the Western Hemisphere will be the instruments of uniting a scattered race who, before the close of many centuries, will found an Empire on which the sun shall shine as ceaselessly as it shines on the Empire of the North today." With this vision of himself and his fellow West Indians as the mechanism through which "the beloved and scattered millions" of the black diaspora would be united, Garvey found it impossible to remain any longer in London. "My brain was afire. There was a world of thought to conquer."

Garvey arrived home in Jamaica on July 15, 1914, and on the first of August—the anniversary of emancipation in the British West Indies—he established the Universal Negro Improvement and Conservation Association and African Communities' League, later shortened to the UNIA. The association's aims were stated in two parts. Those having to do with local conditions in Jamaica, which stressed the establishment of educational and industrial colleges, the elevation of the degraded to a "state of good citizenship," the promotion of commerce and industry, and the strengthening of "the bonds of brotherhood and unity among the races," could have been endorsed fully by Washington. The association's "General Objects" went a bit further and included such aims as the following: "To establish a Universal Confraternity among the race," "to promote the spirit of race pride and love," "to establish Commissionaries or Agencies in the principal countries of the world for the protection of all Negroes irrespective of nationality," "to conduct a world-wide commercial and industrial intercourse," and the vaguely worded "to strengthen the imperialism of independent African States."

If the goals of Garvey's new organization—with its bold motto: "ONE GOD! ONE AIM! ONE DESTINY!"—indicated the ways in which Garvey would supplement the goals of his mentor, Garvey's language in this period often remained pure Washingtonian. In his address to the first annual meeting of the UNIA in August 1915, Garvey stated that "the bulk of our people are in darkness and are really unfit for good society." Six months later he advised his fellow Jamaicans that Europeans were "longing to see the Negro do something for himself." Once the Negro raised himself to a higher state of civilization, "all the other races would be glad to meet him on the plane of equality and comradeship. It is indeed unfair to demand equality when one of himself has done nothing to establish the right to equality."

Garvey found it easier to proclaim the existence and aims of the UNIA than to get others, especially Jamaica's powerful middle class of coloreds, to share his vision of the destiny of West Indians and of the black race. Indeed, he found white government officials and clergy frequently more willing to help than were the affluent members of his own race. "I was openly hated and persecuted by some of these colored men of the island who did not want to be classified as negroes, but as white. They hated me worse than poison. They opposed me at every step," Garvey recalled. It was not only his organization, but his very pretensions to leadership they opposed: "I was a black man and therefore had absolutely no right to lead; in the opinion of the 'colored' element, leadership should have been in the hands of a yellow or a very light man." It was while he was suffering these shattering blows to his dreams that Garvey began, perhaps unconsciously, to explore other alternatives. If the Negro population of Jamaica was too divided and myopic to provide the leadership necessary to unite the world's blacks, Garvey would have to search elsewhere. Whether he came to this determination before or only after arriving in the United States is not clear. Nevertheless, it was during this crisis that Garvey wrote to Washington of his desire to travel to the United States to acquaint himself with America's black people. Washington's death in November 1915 deprived Garvey of the chance to meet the man who had influenced him so profoundly, but it did not alter his determination, or his need, to visit the United States. Before leaving Jamaica, Garvey wrote a final appeal to his fellow "Afro-West Indians":

> For God's sake, you men and women who have been keeping yourselves away from the people of your own African race, cease the ignorance; unite your hands and hearts with the people Afric, . . . Sons and daughters of Africa, I say to you arise, take on the toga of race pride, and throw off the brand of ignominy which has kept you back for so many centuries. Dash asunder the petty prejudices within your own fold; set at defiance the scornful designation of "nigger" uttered even by yourselves, and be a Negro in the light of the Pharaohs of Egypt, Simons of Cyrene, Hannibals of Carthage, L'Ouvertures and Dessalines of Haiti, Blydens, Barclays and Johnsons of Liberia, Lewises of Sierra Leone, and Douglasses and Du Boises of America, who have made, and are making history for the race.

In this mood, Garvey made his way to America.

Garvey had chosen precisely the right time for his American journey. The black population of the United States was in the midst of an experience that was to make it an ideal constituency for a man with Garvey's mission, energies, and oratorical abilities. To understand the ethos characterizing black America in the years following Garvey's arrival in March 1916, it is necessary to comprehend the impact of World War I on the dreams and expectations of many black Americans. Fifty years earlier blacks had emerged from the Civil War with hope in the American political process that, in the immediate aftermath of the war, produced three constitutional amendments and a host of Reconstruction reforms positively affecting the position of blacks within the system. "The Republican party is the deck," Frederick Douglass declared, "all else is the sea." The abandonment of the freedmen by the Republican party in the 1870s and 1880s abruptly ended the dream that Negro rights could be secured through conventional political behavior and gave rise to the view, advanced by some teachers and leaders, that no one had to be poor, that there was no need to fail, that the individual was the architect of his own fortune. Thus it is not surprising that with the blocking of political channels by federal indifference and southern disfranchisement, the new Negro leadership, epitomized by Washington, preached the possibilities of advancement through moral and economic development. Blacks must prove themselves worthy of freedom by developing their own capabilities. Tact, good manners, a resolute will, a tireless capacity for hard work ensured success for the individual and for the race, Washington insisted.

Although variations of this philosophy persisted long after 1918, World War I dealt it a blow from which it never fully recovered. With few exceptions, black Americans entered the armed forces with alacrity and served with enthusiasm and hope. Here was a perfect opportunity to prove their worth; a situation made to order for the Horatio Alger philosophy whose heroes had always proved themselves through inspired acts of heroism and devotion. The Texas Grand Master of the Negro Masons articulated the expectations of many when he announced: "We believe that our second emancipation will be the outcome of this war." This loyalty and hope were rewarded by segregating black troops; by subjecting them to untold indignities in training camps; by assigning them to labor battalions far out of proportion to their skills and intelligence; by warning the French not to fraternize with them lest they rape French women; by cautioning black troops at the end of the war not to expect in their homeland the kind of latitude they had enjoyed abroad.

Indeed, the America to which black troops returned was frighteningly familiar. Black soldiers were greeted not with gratitude but with fear. Ten returned soldiers were among the more than seventy blacks lynched in 1919; a far larger number were among those blacks assaulted in the year's twenty-five race riots. One veteran, returning from work during the Chicago race riot, was set upon by a white mob shouting, "There's a nigger! Let's get him!" "The injustice of the whole thing overwhelmed me," he later testified. "Had the ten months I spent in France been all in vain? Were those little white crosses over the dead bodies of those dark-skinned boys lying in Flanders field for naught? Was democracy merely a hollow sentiment?"

His question and his anger were reflected throughout black America. Blacks had played the game by the rules and discovered that the rules simply did not apply to them. "We have been fighting the wrong fellow," a Negro Masonic leader in California insisted. "The low American, and not the German, is the brute who has ravished our women, lynched, flayed, burned and massacred our men and women." Black people should practice the Christian virtues, Bishop John Hurst maintained. "If while exercising these virtues, however, his assailants . . . persist in molesting him, let him do what self respecting people should do—namely use his gun with effect and impose respect." "Let every Negro arm himself," the black New York *Commoner* advised, "and swear to die fighting in defense of his home, his rights and his person."

Implicit in all of these reactions was a heightened tendency to look inward, to reach within the community for protection, understanding, and sustenance. Not the least of the results of the great tension produced by the demonstrated failure of the American success ethos for black Americans was the impetus it gave to internal development and to searching within Afro-American culture and looking to the black people themselves for those things necessary to survival and the building of a meaningful dream. The anthropologist Anthony F. C. Wallace has argued that when a perceptible gap arises between the images and expectations a culture has created within its citizens and the realities of the culture, the resulting anxiety can often be relieved only through the agency of what he has called a *revitalization movement*: "a deliberate, organized conscious effort by members of a society to construct a more satisfying culture," one that comes closer to their longstanding dreams and expectations. The forms such movements take vary from culture to culture. In the United States they have tended to stress the revival of central cultural beliefs and values and the elimination of alien influences. While the importance of such movements in the 1920s has been emphasized for some time now, there has been less recognition of the extent to which black America was characterized by them as well.

Garvey came to the United States prepared to preach the message of revitalization to a people ready, often eager, to hear it. The time had come, Garvey insisted, for blacks to stop emulating heroes of other races: "We must canonize our own saints, create our own martyrs, and elevate to positions of fame and honor black men and women who have made their distinct contributions to our racial history." When Europe was inhabited by savages, heathens, and pagans, he reminded his listeners, "Africa was peopled with a race of cultured black men, who were masters in art, science and literature; men who were cultured and refined; men, who, it was said, were like the gods. . . . Black men, you were once great; you shall be great again." He enjoined his audiences to "take down the pictures of white women from your walls. Elevate your own women to that place of honour. . . . Mothers! give your children dolls that look like them to play with and cuddle." God, he insisted, "made no mistake when he made us black with kinky hair. . . . We have outgrown slavery, but our minds are still enslaved to the thinking of the Master Race. Now take these kinks out of your mind, instead of out of your hair. You are capable of all that is common to men of other Races." "We have a beautiful history," he thundered, "and we shall create another one in the future." Over and over he insisted, "The faith we have is a faith that will ultimately take us back to that ancient place, that ancient position that we once occupied, when Ethiopia was in her glory."

In all of this Garvey articulated—more brilliantly than any other Afro-American spokesman of the time—the doctrine of revitalization. In 1933 one of his supporters wrote that "Garvey sold the Negro to himself." This theme has been picked up by a number of scholars so that one author writes that "Garvey tried to restore to the black man the masculinity stolen from him during the centuries of slavery," another that "Garvey put steel in the spine of many Negroes . . . [and] helped to destroy their inferiority complex," and still another that "he stirred some two million Negroes to a fierce race-consciousness which is still a compelling force in Negro life." While there is validity in such observations, their total effect is to obscure the substantial reservoir of pride, strength, and sense of history that existed in the black folk throughout slavery and the years that followed. Blacks certainly had hoped and worked to become part of the nation's economic and political fabric, but they continued to retain a vivid sense of who and what they were. Garvey did not create "race consciousness." How could black men and women living in the racial situation that prevailed in the United States in the early decades of the twentieth century not have been race conscious? Indeed, Garvey was able to rise so suddenly and attract a following so dramatically precisely because blacks retained a healthy consciousness of identity and community. What Garvey did was to provide a political channel and a global perspective for that consciousness.

Before exploring the movement Garvey built, it is important to remember that he was not the only force for black revitalization in the 1920s. The black writers of the Harlem Renaissance expressed revitalization in their search for their African past. "I was a black man," lamented Langston Hughes:

> But the white men came.
> And they drove me out of the forest.
> They took me away from the jungles.
> I lost my trees.
> I lost my silver moons.
> Now they've caged me
> In the circus of civilization.

They expressed it in their search for themselves. "What she needed to do now," Wallace Thurman wrote of one of his characters whose complexion ostracized her within the middle class, "was to accept her black skin as being real and unchangeable, to realize that certain things were, and would be, and with this in mind begin life new, always fighting, not so much for acceptance by other people, but for acceptance of herself." And, finally, they expressed it in their rediscovery of the black folk and their culture. Only among "the working girls and boys of the country," one of Claude McKay's characters in *Banjo* concludes, could one find cultural integrity: "that raw unconscious and the-devil-with-them-pride in being Negro that was his own natural birthright. . . . Down there the ideal skin was brown skin. Boys and girls were proud of their brown, sealskin brown, teasing brown, tantalizing brown, high-brown, low-brown, velvet brown, chocolate brown."

Among the black folk themselves one can see revitalization in a number of ways: in the continued revival of traditional black religious practices and their spread from the Holiness churches to the larger denominations; in the inclusion of traditional Afro-American musical forms in jazz and gospel music; and in the rise of the blues—an inward-looking music that insisted upon the meaningfulness of the daily yearnings, problems, and dreams of everyday black people. Garvey, then, for all of his uniqueness, was not an isolated force in the 1920s. His power and influence proceeded from his superb articulation of what many of his followers had long believed and acted upon in quiet dignity and strength: that blackness was nothing to apologize for; that black men and women shared a common proud heritage; and that the future was by no means hostage to white people. From the days of slavery, this had been the message of black Christianity in various forms, and it had been reiterated in myriad ways by the black folk in their songs, tales, proverbs, and anecdotes. The disillusioning difficult postwar years gave it added impetus. Like so many leaders, Garvey's influence was based upon not how far he was from, but how close he was to, the mass of the people to whom and for whom he tried to speak.

Garvey's initial activities in the United States were less those of organizing and politicking than of traveling and observing. He did deliver speeches in Harlem and elsewhere, but his main energies were devoted to learning about the conditions of American blacks. Washington was dead, but there was still much to be gained from trips to Tuskeegee Institute and other Afro-American institutions in the thirty-eight states Garvey visited. Everywhere he went Garvey endeavored to meet black leaders, and with few exceptions he perceived in them the same qualities that characterized their Jamaican counterparts. What passed for race leadership in the United States, Garvey asserted, was little more than "treachery and treason of the worst kind," since anyone who wanted to lead had to first find some wealthy white benefactor "who will dictate to him what he should do in the leadership of the Negro race." Worse yet, Garvey was certain that the identical pettiness and self-hatred that plagued his race in Jamaica existed in the United States as well. Visiting W.E.B. Du Bois in the offices of the National Association for the Advancement of Colored People Garvey was "dumbfounded" to find that it was impossible to tell whether one was in a white office or that of a black protest organization. "There was no representation of the race there that any one could recognize. . . . you had to be as near white as possible, otherwise there was no place for you as stenographer, clerk or attendant in the office of the National Association for the Advancement of 'Colored' People." In America as in Jamaica, Garvey concluded, the race's leaders "had no program, but were mere opportunists who were living off their so-called leadership while the poor people were groping in the dark."

Convinced that he had found a leadership vacuum, Garvey in 1917 established the New York Division of the UNIA. Garvey later claimed that he had had no intention of shifting his center of operations to the United States and that he remained only when it became necessary for him to defeat the aims of local politicians who threatened to take over and pervert the purposes of the new organization. It is doubtful that Garvey needed this kind of inducement to stay in the United States. A man so perceptive and ambitious must have realized at once that Jamaica simply could not match the potential of America's large, diverse black population. Indeed, Garvey himself made this point just eight months after he arrived in the United States, calling the American Negro "the most progressive and the foremost unit in the expansive chain of scattered Ethiopia." Industrially, financially, educationally, and socially "the Negroes of both hemispheres have to defer to the American brother." Most crucially, he concluded, American blacks were far ahead of West Indians in "the spirit of self-consciousness and reliance." Garvey could not have failed to arrive at the corollary conclusion that the ideal place to build a movement for the unification of the world's blacks was not his native island, where he had recently failed so badly, but the United States. His "brief" visit was to last eleven years.

Garvey's ultimate intentions may be revealed as well by the fact that almost from the moment of his arrival he spoke as an integral part of the American black community. During the 1917 race riot in East St. Louis, Illinois, he denounced America's "continuous round of oppression" of black people who for three hundred years had "given their life blood" to help build the republic. His refusal to act or to speak like an alien visitor continued with his repeated opposition to black participation in World War I. Shortly after the armistice, as disillusioned black troops returned to America, Garvey warned that his people would not allow themselves to be exploited in this way again. "The first dying that is to be done by the black man in the future will be done to make himself free. And then when we are finished, if we have any charity to bestow, we may die for the white man. But as for me, I think I have stopped dying for him."

Statements like these, of course, matched the mood of many American blacks in those difficult postwar years and were responsible for increasing Garvey's popularity and his audience. "I am the equal of any white man; I want you to feel the same way," Garvey told his listeners. "No more fear," he thundered, "no more cringing, no more sycophantic begging and pleading." Blacks were demanding "that freedom that Victoria of England never gave; that liberty that Lincoln never meant; that freedom, that liberty that will see us men among men, that will make us a great and powerful people." Garvey's appeal was based not only upon his militance but also upon his sense of destiny and hope. "There is much to live for," he declared. "I see before me a picture of a redeemed Africa, with her dotted cities, with her beautiful civilization, with her millions of happy children, going to and fro. Why should I lose hope? . . . Lift up yourselves, men, take yourselves out of the mire and hitch your hopes to the stars; yes, rise as high as the very stars themselves. Let no man pull you down, let no man destroy your ambition, because . . . man is your brother; he is not your lord."

Words like these make it evident that if Garvey's rhetoric was revolutionary as racial doctrine, it was also appealingly familiar, steeped as it was in traditional nineteenth-century American ideology. Many of Garvey's widely circulated aphorisms could have been inserted into any American primer for schoolchildren: "Whatsoever man has done, man can do." "A man's bread and butter is only insured when he works for it." "If you have no confidence in self, you are twice defeated in the race of life." "[Man is] master of his own destiny, and architect of his own fate." No prophet of the American success ethos could have put these things better. Thus Garvey won an immediate audience not only because he preached the doctrine of revitalization at precisely the right time, but because he preached it in the right syllables. He used a tone and an ideological context that were instantly recognizable to those to whom traditional American ideology was still familiar. He was able to show his followers that the ideas they were raised on could lead to their own liberation.

When Garvey shouted out to his audiences, "Up, you mighty race!" he was not reciting totally new doctrine. Blacks had been enjoined to rise since they were emancipated. Garvey was appealing to a set of dreams and ideals that had long existed among American blacks. He was able to take Washington's philosophy and transform it from a doctrine geared to help one up the ladder of American mobility into a mechanism designed to increase the worldwide consciousness, unity, power, and autonomy of the race. He took a philosophy suffused with overtones of individualism and bent it to serve the purposes of the group.

Much of Garvey's labors were geared to instill a sense of responsibility in blacks for their place in the world. "Blame not God," he told his listeners, "blame not the white man for physical conditions for which we ourselves are responsible." The Creator intended humanity to be free. "That the Negro race became a race of slaves was not the fault of God

Almighty . . . it was the fault of the race." "Sloth, neglect, indifference caused us to be slaves," he insisted. "Confidence, conviction, action will cause us to be free men to-day." He told the UNIA's Second International Convention in 1921: "If you want liberty you yourselves must strike the blow. if you must be free you must become so through your own effort, through your own initiative." Garvey was able to aim the Social Darwinist arguments that were so intertwined in his thought against the whites as well. If the latter really were convinced that the Negro was inferior, why did they find it necessary to hedge him in with laws enforcing his inferior state? The answer was obvious: whites feared black capabilities and talents, were afraid that blacks would outshine them. Give blacks a chance, Garvey taunted, and in fifty years "I will show you a nation of proud, refined and cultured black men and women, whose comeliness will outshine that of the age of Solomon." It was because Garvey did not expect whites to accept his challenge that he worked so hard to convince blacks they had to rise on their own.

The Negro, Garvey taught, was not at the bottom because he was held in contempt, he was held in contempt because he was at the bottom. Only when the race lifted itself up through its own initiative would it be in a position to demand respect. Many of his aphorisms were designed to illustrate that: "A race without authority and power, is a race without respect." "Don't be deceived; there is no justice but strength." "A race that is solely dependent upon another for its economic existence sooner or later dies." If power and autonomy were the goals, organization was the only viable means. One of the fundamental messages of Garvey's speeches, editorials, and articles was: organize as a race or perish as a race! He was convinced that "the greatest weapon used against the Negro is DISORGANIZATION." If Washington had lived, Garvey maintained, he would have had to change his program, for the New Negro needed a political voice as well as industrial opportunity. In the short run, political organization meant the creation of a strong and effective UNIA; ultimately, it entailed building an independent African nation powerful enough to protect black people everywhere.

Unlike most other black American political leaders of the period, Garvey understood the need to reach out with his message and his organization to the black people in general and not just the more educated classes. "The masses," he was convinced, "make the nation and the race." Certainly no other black spokesman was better equipped to affect the masses. Not only the content of Garvey's message, but the eloquence with which he propounded it, the skillful use he made of his weekly newspaper, and the spectacular pageantry that soon became characteristic of UNIA events were all designed to reach a maximum audience. In 1919 Garvey purchased an auditorium on 138th Street in Harlem, renamed it Liberty Hall, and held nightly meetings to bring his message to as many as 6,000 listeners at a time. In the next few years liberty halls appeared in such UNIA centers as Philadelphia, Pittsburgh, Cleveland, Detroit, Cincinnati, Chicago, and Los Angeles. On the platforms of these meeting halls, Garvey, whose wife described him as "calm, almost phlegmatic in conversation," was transformed into a charismatic speaker whose rich voice and dramatic gestures converted many of his listeners into followers. For all of his criticisms, Du Bois conceded that Garvey's "singular eloquence" made him "an extraordinary leader of men."

Those not within the reach of Garvey's voice were exposed to his message through the *Negro World*, which Garvey began in 1918 and which by the early 1920s had a weekly circulation of from 50,000 to 200,000. In order to communicate with blacks throughout the world, it carried columns in Spanish and French. That its readership did go beyond the United States is attested to by those colonial administrators who held it partially responsible for anti-white riots in 1919 in Jamaica, Trinidad, and British Honduras, by other authorities who banned it from their jurisdictions in the New World and Africa, and by Jomo Kenyatta, the future president of Kenya, who testified that "in 1921 Kenya nationalists, unable to read, would gather round a reader of Garvey's newspaper, the *Negro*

World, and listen to an article two or three times. Then they would run various ways through the forest, carefully to repeat the whole, which they had memorised, to Africans hungry for some doctrine which lifted them from the servile consciousness in which Africans lived."

Garvey did not base his appeal exclusively upon his impressive oratorical and journalistic skills. Organization depended upon more than an audience; it required participants. To ensure the maximum number of participants, Garvey created a host of groups: an African Legion clad in blue military garb, Black Cross Nurses, uniformed marching bands, choristers, and various auxiliaries. The pageantry implicit in all of this was revealed during the UNIA's First International Convention in 1920. Spectators lined the streets of Harlem for miles to watch Garvey in military uniform and plumed hat lead his impressively arrayed followers marching under such banners as: "We Want a Black Civilization," "God and the Negro Shall Triumph," "Uncle Tom's Dead and Buried," "Africa Must be Free," and, at the head of the Woman's Auxiliary, "God Give Us Real Men!" The onlookers, according to Mrs. Garvey, "could not help but catch the spirit of the occasion; they clapped, waved flags and cheered themselves hoarse." Garvey, who was elected president general of the UNIA and provisional president of Africa, and who created numerous titles for his associates, seemed to have an insatiable appetite for ceremony. His wife described the court reception held during the convention of 1921:

> The Hall was transformed into a magnificent tropical setting, with lighting effects, appropriate music being played. Each Dignitary was timed to arrive according to his rank, and an anthem or appropriate music played until he was seated. . . . Young ladies were presented, and honours conferred on persons who had served the Race faithfully and well. Titles were: Knight Commander of the Nile, Distinguished Service Order of Ethiopia, and the Star of African Redemption. After the ceremonies, supper was served; guests were seated according to rank. Then followed the Grand Ball, with all the courtliness of training, natural gift for dancing and love of music.

Garvey's need to garb himself and his associates in the anachronistic trappings of aristocracy brought him enormous ridicule, especially from whites and the black middle class. He was "a clown strutting around in gaudy uniforms," a charlatan "who led big parades of ignorant people down the street selling pie in the sky." But there were other reactions as well, particularly from those groups Garvey was attempting to reach: "I remember as a lad in Cleveland, Ohio, during the hungry days of 1921, standing on Central Avenue, watching a parade one Sunday afternoon when thousands of Garvey Legionnaires, resplendent in their uniforms marched by. When Garvey rode by in his plumed hat, I got an emotional lift, which swept me up above the poverty and the prejudice by which my life was limited."

It seems to be indisputable that Garvey attracted millions of followers. It is more difficult to determine how many of them joined the UNIA. By the end of 1919, Garvey claimed two million members. Two years later he counted twice that number, and in June 1923 he announced that six million blacks were members of the UNIA. These figures reflected Garvey's hope and pride more than they did reality. Still, Garvey had much to be proud of. He had built not only the largest but the broadest mass movement in Afro-American history. The Communist party, surely no friend of Garvey's, was impressed by his success with the very elements the party itself had failed to enlist in substantial numbers: black workers and farmers. While it is not certain just how successful Garvey was outside the large northern cities, the organizational records of the UNIA indicate that the movement was not confined to these urban centers. By the mid-1920s the UNIA had established more than 700 branches in thirty-eight states in every section of the country including the Deep South. In addition, it had established more than 200 branches outside the United States, with the bulk of these clustering in the West Indies, Central America, and northern South America.

A clue to Garvey's unprecedented success in building a mass movement can be found in William L. Sherril's description of how he came to join the UNIA in Baltimore:

> One night on my way to a Show, I saw a huge crowd outside a Church, I went up and said, "what's going on in there?" A lady turned to me and said, "man alive, don't you know that Marcus Garvey is in there talking, yes, indeed, Garvey in person." "Shucks," I said, "I may as well see what he looks like." . . . I squeezed in, until I could get a good look at him; then suddenly he turned in my direction, and in a voice like thunder from Heaven he said, "men and women, what are you here for? To live unto yourself, until your body manures the earth, or to live God's Purpose to the fullest?" He continued to complete his thought in that compelling, yet pleading voice for nearly an hour. I stood there like one in a trance, every sentence ringing in my ears, and finding an echo in my heart. When I walked out of that Church, I was a different man—I knew my sacred obligations to my Creator, and my responsibilities to my fellow men, and so help me! I am still on the Garvey train.

Sherril, of course, was describing a conversion experience. For him, and presumably for many other members of the UNIA, Garvey's movement had deep religious overtones and significance.

Throughout the years of bondage American slaves had continued the African practice of drawing no clear line between the sacred and the secular, between the spiritual and the temporal world. This tendency remained strong in Afro-American culture in the years of freedom as well. Certainly it came to characterize the movement Garvey built and the style of leadership he created. One of Garvey's greatest assets was his comprehension of the importance of religion in black culture and his ability to incorporate so many of its elements in his movement.

It was not uncommon for Garvey's followers to refer to him as a Black Moses, a John the Baptist. Nor was it surprising, since Garvey himself invited such comparisons. He regularly employed a religious vocabulary, as in this speech he delivered in Liberty Hall in February 1921: "I wish I could convert the world of Negroes overnight to the tremendous possibilities of the Universal Negro Improvement Association. Let all the world know that this is the hour; this is the time for our salvation. Prayer alone will not save us; sentiment alone will not save us. We have to work and work and work if we are to be saved. . . . the time is now to preach the beatitude of bread and butter. I have contributed my bit to preaching this doctrine." More than this, Garvey dwelt endlessly on the suffering and betrayal of Jesus Christ, frequently casting himself in the role of Jesus. "If Garvey dies," he told his followers, "Garvey lives." "Christ died to make men free," he wrote in 1923; "I shall die to give courage and inspiration to my race." In his first message from Atlanta Prison in 1925, Garvey assumed the mantle of a full-fledged prophet assuring his fellow blacks: "Would I not die a million deaths for you? Then why be sad? . . . I tell you the world shall hear from my principles even two thousand years hence. . . . Look for me in the whirlwind or the storm, look for me all around you, for with God's grace, I shall come."

The religious quality of the UNIA was not confined to its leader's messianic style and rhetoric. Garvey utilized religion not merely to strengthen his own leadership, but to bolster the will and determination of those he wanted to lead. One of Garvey's favorite biblical texts was Psalms 68:31, which promised that "princes shall come forth from Egypt; Ethiopia shall soon stretch forth her hand to God." But before Africa could be redeemed, black men and women had to redeem themselves from the errors they had learned through the white people's religion. In his 1922 Easter Sunday sermon Garvey called for a new resurrection: "A resurrection from the lethargy of the past—the sleep of the past—from that feeling that made us accept the idea and opinion that God intended that we should occupy an inferior place in the world." No God, he insisted a year later, "would create me a black man, to be a hewer of wood and a drawer of water. It is a lie! It is a damned lie." The God that blacks worshiped and adored created them the equals of all humanity and expected them to take control of their own destiny. God, Garvey taught, gave humans the gift of life and sovereignty over the earth, but He did not run an employment bureau; He did not dispense jobs to His children. He gave people the opportunities, the accomplishment was up to them.

Though Garvey taught of an impartial God who created all as equals, his anger at the way blacks had been treated led him at times to imply that suffering had rendered blacks more noble, more Christ-like than other races. "The Cross," he wrote, "is the property of the Negro in his religion because it was he who bore it." Although this dualism between universalism and particularism existed in Garvey's thought, he fell short of committing the error for which he condemned whites: advocating that God had a chosen race. In essence Garvey followed the spirit of the Old Testament itself and urged his fellow blacks to act not as a chosen but as a *choosing* people, a people with the same opportunities, the same possibilities, the same potential control over their destiny as every other people. Thus for Garvey religion was not an otherworldly affair; it taught ethical and practical principles that needed to be acted upon in this world: "I trust that you will so live to-day as to realize that you are masters of your own destiny, masters of your fate; if there is anything you want in this world it is for you to strike out with confidence and faith in self and reach for it, because God has created it for your happiness wheresoever you may find it in nature."

Garvey was often ridiculed for picturing God as black. What he actually taught was more subtle and interesting. God, Garvey repeated over and over, had no color. However, since human beings were able to think of Him only in human terms, it was natural for them to conceive of God in their own physical shape. Whites, who had long done this themselves, had been successful in denying blacks the same privilege. It was now time "to see God through our own spectacles. . . . we shall worship Him through the spectacles of Ethiopia." "God is not white or black," he told a Cincinnati audience in 1921, "angels have no color, and they are not white peaches from Georgia. But if [whites] say that God is white, this organization says that God is black; if they are going to make the angels beautiful white peaches from Georgia, we are going to make them beautiful black peaches from Africa." Accordingly, the 1924 convention canonized Jesus Christ as a "Black Man of Sorrows," the Virgin Mary as a "Black Madonna," and resolved to idealize "God as a Holy Spirit, without physical form, but a Creature of imaginary semblance of the black race, being of like image and likeness."

James Weldon Johnson, who attended a number of UNIA meetings in New York's Liberty Hall, noted the elaborate liturgy and religious zeal he found there. Johnson's perceptions were quite accurate. The weekly meetings—generally held Sunday evenings—in liberty halls in New York and elsewhere closely resembled religious services. They were filled with the pomp and ceremony Garvey so loved and often featured processions of uniformed African Legionnaires or Black Cross Nurses. Hymns were sung, prayers recited, offerings received, just as in church. When Garvey was present, he delivered the major talk in his emotional, sermonizing style. When he was not, there would be a public reading of his front-page editorial in the week's *Negro World*. In addition, there would be talks by other UNIA leaders and sermons by clergy in attendance. And generally there were members of the clergy present, since a substantial number of black clergymen—Professor Randall Burkett has painstakingly identified more than 250—were active in the UNIA and helped to intensify the religious character already prominent in the movement.

Garvey worked hard to recruit clergy, hoping through them to reach their congregations. On occasion the strategy was more successful than Garvey could have hoped. At the 1924 convention, the Reverend R. H. Cosgrove of Natchez, Mississippi, reported that every one of the 500 members of his church was a member of the UNIA. Not surprisingly, those clergymen who became prominent in the UNIA tended to share Garvey's views and his militance. In 1923 the Reverend Thomas W. Anderson of the Second Baptist Church of Adrian, Michigan, told his Christmas Day audience that "the black man . . . must learn to fight; he must believe that God almighty . . . believes also in fighting." Blacks had to take charge of their own destiny. "If you don't have a bit of heaven here," he assured his audience, "don't worry, you won't have any hereafter.

The most important and influential of these ministers was the Episcopal priest George Alexander McGuire, who electrified the UNIA's first annual convention in 1920 by insisting that "the Uncle Tom nigger has got to go and his place must be taken . . . by a black man with a black heart." The element of revitalization was central to McGuire's appeal: "You must forget the white gods. Erase the white gods from your hearts. We must go back to the native church, to our own true God." The 1920 convention elected McGuire chaplain-general of the UNIA, and he quickly set about creating a *Universal Negro Ritual* and a *Universal Negro Catechism* intended to help reshape black religion. "O blessed Lord Jesus," read one of his suggested prayers, "Redeem Africa from the hands of those who exploit and ravish her. Renew her ancient glory, and grant that her oppressed and downtrodden children . . . may shortly be restored to their divine inheritance." In 1921 McGuire founded the African Orthodox Church and became its first bishop. Though there were many ties between the African Orthodox Church and the UNIA, Garvey neither endorsed nor joined McGuire's church for fear of alienating the many ministers and congregants of other denominations who were active in his movement, including such eclectic bands of non-Christian followers as black Jews and black Muslims. Whatever tensions existed between the two leaders, Garvey completely agreed with, and always acted upon, a principle McGuire enunciated at the 1924 convention: "Let it be understood, once and for all, that no constructive program for the Negro can be effective which underestimates the hold his religious institutions have upon him."

Garvey never made the mistake of underestimating the significance of religion. Nor did he commit the opposite error of focusing upon the spiritual to the neglect of the material needs of his people. From the beginning, fraternal sickness and death benefits were one of the features for which members were urged to pay their monthly 35-cent dues. Liberty halls served not only as scenes of inspirational public rituals but also as community centers sponsoring such social events as concerts, dances, and classes of various kinds. Notice boards held news of rooms or jobs. Liberty halls were sometimes converted into soup kitchens to feed the unemployed or into temporary dormitories for those without housing. "In the freezing winter days," Amy Jacques Garvey remembered, "stoves had to be kept going to accommodate the cold and homeless until they 'got on their feet' again."

Important as they were, Garvey considered such activities mere stopgaps. His organization was to function not as a welfare agency administering aid to the indigent, but as the center of a vast series of enterprises that would finally end black economic dependence. The Negro had for too long been a consumer, not a producer. "Let Edison turn off his electric light and we are in darkness in Liberty Hall in two minutes. The Negro is living on borrowed goods." In order to reverse this situation, Garvey established the Negro Factories Corporation in 1919 and offered "200,000 shares of common stock to the Negro race at par value of $5.00 per share." The ultimate object was to operate factories throughout the Western Hemisphere and Africa "to manufacture every marketable commodity." In New York City the corporation operated three grocery stores, two restaurants, a printing plant, a steam laundry, and a men's and women's manufacturing department that made the uniforms, hats, and shirts worn by members along with other items of clothing. In addition, the New York division owned several buildings, trucks, and the *Negro World*. Similar enterprises were operated or planned in other parts of the United States as well as in Central America and the West Indies. During the early 1920s, there were times when the UNIA and its allied corporations employed more than 1,000 blacks in the United States alone. The UNIA, Garvey pointed out to the white world, "employs thousands of black girls and black boys. Girls who could only be washer women in your homes, we made clerks and stenographers. . . . You will see from the start we tried to dignify our race." Here was a step toward Garvey's dream of a self-contained world of Negro producers, distributors, and consumers who could deal with or be independent of the rest of the world as necessity and circumstances dictated.

Garvey's attempts to lift the black world up economically were bedeviled by the very forces that Garvey decried: the difficulties of raising sufficient capital from an economically depressed and dependent group and the problems of dealing with white businessmen who were all too willing to exploit the economic disadvantages of blacks. Nothing demonstrated this more graphically than the failure of Garvey's most spectacular and significant economic activity: the Black Star Line that he created in June 1919 to operate a worldwide network of steamships. Within three months the Black Star Line had raised enough money through the sale of $5 stock certificates to purchase its first ship. Within a year the line had raised $610,000 and owned three ships. In spite of these initial successes, Garvey's dream of creating a great fleet of ships manned by black officers and men, so that "our race, too, would be respected in the mercantile and commercial world," was not to be. By the beginning of 1922, the Black Star Line was forced to suspend its operations, a victim of white businessmen who sold it decrepit vessels at inflated prices, of the inexperience and carelessness of Garvey and his chief associates, and of the dishonesty of some of its officers.

Economically, Garvey's venture into the maritime world left much to be desired. Its political capital, however, was considerable. Garvey pointed to the line as "the great attraction that brought to the Universal Negro Improvement Association millions of supporters." That attraction was manifest in the widespread sale of Black Star Line stock, which was limited to members of the Negro race. "I have sent twice to buy shares amounting to $125," one supporter wrote. "Now I am gaining $35 for seven more shares. You might think I have money, but the truth, as I stated before, is that I have no money now. But if I'm to die of hunger it will be all right because I'm determined to do all that's in my power to better the conditions of my race." The child of another supporter recalled: "My mother was an intense Garveyite. She bought stock in it. . . . She lost money in its ventures and was disillusioned, but not in the principles involved. . . . The Back-to-Africa part was not important. Pride was. Negroes should have something of their own." The Black Star Line, the lawyer Henry Lincoln Johnson asserted, "was a loss in money but it was a gain in soul."

That gain was felt throughout the Western Hemisphere. Hugh Mulzac, a black ship's officer who sailed for Garvey on the *Yarmouth* in 1920, recorded the reception the ship received everywhere it docked. When it entered the harbor at Havana, "sympathizers flocked from all parts of the island toward the docks to greet the first ship they had ever seen entirely owned and operated by colored men. They came out in boats when we arrived, showering us with flowers and fruit . . . [we] were overrun with visitors from dawn until sunset." When the ship docked at Colon, "literally thousands of Panamanians swarmed the docks with baskets of fruit, vegetables and gifts. I was amazed that the *Yarmouth* had become a symbol for colored people of every land." In Costa Rica "we were accorded the welcome of conquering heroes. At Bocas del Toro thousands of peasants came down from the hills on horses, donkeys, and in makeshift carts . . . In the tumult that followed dancing broke out on the deck, great piles of fruit and flowers mounted on the hatch covers, and UNIA agents signed up hundreds of new members." In Philadelphia, Boston, and New York as well, there were spectacular receptions for the ship "with thousands joining the parades. Garvey made impassioned speeches, whipping the people into frenzied support of the association." The problem, Mulzac discovered, was that little or no distinction was being made between the commercial and symbolic functions of the voyage. There was no economic reason to be in many of these ports, and while the demonstrations were going on, hundreds of passengers aboard had to be fed and cared for, and hundreds of tons of coconuts were rotting in the hold. "It was," Mulzac concluded, "a helluva way to run a steamship."

The tension between the pragmatic and the symbolic was evident in other aspects of the Garvey movement as well. Garvey employed no symbol more frequently or more effectively than that of the African homeland. "Hail! United States of Africa!" he entitled a poem:

> The treason of the centuries is dead,
> All alien whites are forever gone;
> The glad home of Sheba is once more free.

Garvey embroidered this portrait of a free, independent African continent endlessly and argued for its necessity incessantly. "Show me the race or the nation without a flag, and I will show you a race of people without any pride," he proclaimed. Consequently, the convention of 1920 added to the "objects" of the UNIA the establishment of "a central nation for the race," created a red, black, and green flag for the African republic, and adopted a national anthem that began: "Ethiopia, thou land of our fathers, / Thou land where the gods loved to be."

The "brilliant, noble and grand" African past was a constant theme for Garvey in speech after speech, but he reminded his followers in 1923, "WE CANNOT LIVE BY THE PAST." The only "salvation for the Negro" was "through a free and independent Africa." Without that, blacks would be forever the exploited wards of other races, eternally incapable of demonstrating what they could accomplish. If the race remained a scattered, drifting remnant, "it will be only a question of time when the Negro will be as completely and complacently dead as the North American Indian, or the Australian Bushman." The question of independence was too crucial for Garvey to contemplate failure. African redemption, he prophesied, "is in the wind. It is coming. One day, like a storm, it will be here." He warned the white world: "We are coming 400,000,000 strong and we mean to retake every square inch of the 12,000,000 square miles of African territory belonging to us by right Divine."

Garvey utilized the idea of Africa to touch deeply many of the yearnings and needs of his people. He was preaching more than the redemption of Africa; he was preaching the redemption of the entire Negro people, the revitalization of the entire black race. Nevertheless, when Garvey cried out, "Wake up Ethiopia! Wake up Africa! Let us work towards the one glorious end of a free, redeemed and mighty nation," he was not being merely allegorical. He really did want to end white hegemony and substitute a black republic stretching, as he put it in one of his poems, "From Liberia's peaceful western coast / To the foaming Cape at the southern end. " He did believe that so long as blacks lacked an autonomous, powerful nation of their own they would never be accorded their rights anywhere in the world. The diplomatic pressure an independent Africa could exert, for example, would be far more effective in protecting American Negroes than any anti-lynching Pill.

Consequently, Garvey worked in every way he could for African independence, insisting that his goal was the exact counterpart of the Jewish yearning for a homeland in Palestine or the Irish desire for an independent Eire. He supported Senator Joseph France's plan to have the United States liquidate its allies' war debts in return for enough of their African territory to establish an independent nation for American Negroes. He petitioned the League of Nations to deliver the ex-German colonies in Africa to the custody of the UNIA. He negotiated with Liberia for a UNIA immigrant settlement on the Cavalla River in southern Liberia. This latter arrangement, scheduled to begin with 500 American families in 1924, failed on the eve of its birth due to a combination of British and French pressure to keep the deeply anticolonial Garveyites out of Africa and the growing fear of the elite Liberian governing class that an influx of American immigrants would ultimately threaten the Liberian status quo.

Garvey was deeply disappointed at his failure to win a settlement in Liberia, which he had envisioned as a beachhead from which Western Negroes could spread modern technical, scientific, and humanistic knowledge throughout the continent. There is no indication that Garvey ever worried about what effects the accelerated imposition of the body of Western knowledge would have upon indigenous African cultures. It is important to remember that Garvey's opposition to the West was political; he did not disdain Western culture, which he was, after all, part of. "Those of us who lead are well versed in Western civilization and are determined that the black man shall not be a creature of the past, but a full-fledged man of the present." In this respect, Garvey was never a cultural nationalist. He looked back to the glories of the African past, but even there he was proudest of those attributes that had contributed directly to the store of Western culture. He had little, if anything, to say about the glories of African religion or expressive art or social mores and patterns. These were not concerns of his, and he seems to have been willing to see them replaced as expeditiously as possible with their Western counterparts. It is not surprising, then, that one of the consistent "objects" of the UNIA was "to assist in civilizing the backward tribes of Africa."

In spite of Garvey's many activities concerning Africa, his widow insisted that "the term, back-to-Africa, was used and promoted by newspapers, Negro newspapers mostly, to ridicule Garvey. There was no back-to-Africa movement except in a spiritual sense." Mrs. Garvey was essentially correct. Garvey envisioned African independence as a gradual, long-term process and never seems to have advocated the massive return of blacks from the diaspora. Nevertheless, Garvey's vagueness and perhaps confusion about his plans, coupled with his tendency toward rhetorical excess, often gave a different impression. Thus, in 1921 he insisted that "we are not preaching any doctrine to ask all the negroes of Harlem and of the United States to leave for Africa. The majority of us may remain here." But he also declared that when the pioneer mechanics and artisans had built the necessary railroads and institutions, "The time will come for the command to be given, 'Come home!'" The vision of the biblical exodus often informed his speeches: "We shall gather together our children, our treasures and our loved ones, and, as the children of Israel, by the command of God, faced the promised land, so in time we shall also."

Above all, it was his pessimism about the possibility of whites and blacks living in harmony that made him appear a champion of total repatriation. One of the salient messages emerging from his speeches and writings was his conviction that American blacks would never be accorded true equality. As the white population grew, blacks would be pushed out of the marketplace and become increasingly redundant economically. Nor could they look for protection to a government controlled by a white majority. He reminded those who believed that the black minority would win a share of the white majority's economic and political power that "nothing of the kind has happened in all human history." So long as whites feared black competition, so long would there be "not only prejudice, but riots, lynchings, burnings." The only solution was to provide an outlet for black energy and ambition where it would not threaten whites. The conclusion was obvious: "The future of the Negro therefore, outside of Africa, spells ruin and disaster."

If Garvey's distrust of whites and his desire to build a sense of black solidarity produced ambiguities in his attitudes regarding emigration to Africa, they created a consistent set of racial policies—too consistent, perhaps, for Garvey's own good. Garvey wanted to unite his people not only politically and economically but racially. "I believe in a pure black race," he announced and argued that it was time to end "the curse of many colors within the Negro race" that slavery had produced; it was time to stop this "wholesale bastardy" and to create "a race type and standard of our own." The UNIA, Garvey announced, "is against miscegenation and race suicide. . . . It believes in the social and political physical separation of all peoples to the extent that they promote their own ideals and civilization." He assured the whites that blacks did not want racial amalgamation, and he pleaded with his people to be true to themselves: "The Anglo-Saxon doesn't want to be a Japanese; the Japanese doesn't want to be a Negro. Then, in the name of God and all that is holy, why should we want to be somebody else?" Garvey insisted that he was not attempting to exclude anyone. "For once we will agree with the American white man, that one drop of Negro blood makes a man a Negro." In the UNIA "100 percent Negroes and even 1 percent Negroes will stand together as one mighty whole."

Garvey's zeal on the race issue led him to promote blackness wherever he could. He banned ads for skin lighteners and hair straighteners from his papers; he urged that children be given black dolls to play with and black role models to admire; he wrote odes to the beauty of black women: "Black Queen of beauty, thou has given colour to the world,/ Among other women thou art royal and the fairest." His zeal led him also into more dangerous waters. In the postwar years the black urge to revitalization clashed with such white revitalization movements as the Klu Klux Klan. These separate movements looked back with nostalgia on different heritages and forward with longing to distinct futures. Garvey, however, saw race policy as a means of bridging the gap. In 1922 Garvey met with leaders of the Klan in Atlanta to explain how close the UNIA and the KKK were on such matters as miscegenation and social equality. No other act of Garvey's brought him more criticism or cost him more support. Yet he refused to apologize for it. Compared with the "farce, hypocrisy and lie" typical of most whites, he welcomed the "honesty of purpose" of the Klan. "They are better friends to my race, for telling us what they are, and what they mean, thereby giving us a chance to stir for ourselves." Potentially, he warned, "every whiteman is a Klansman . . . and there is no use lying about it."

It would be a mistake to see Garvey's attitudes toward the Klan as an aberration. They were deeply representative of Garvey's racial views and his abiding pessimism concerning the future of blacks in the United States. When President Warren G. Harding spoke out in 1921 "against every suggestion of social equality," Garvey sent him a telegram of congratulations. Speaking in North Carolina in 1922, Garvey thanked southern whites for having "lynched race pride into the Negro." In 1925 he forged an alliance with the Anglo-Saxon Clubs, invited their leader, John Powell, to speak in Liberty Hall, and announced: "I unhesitatingly endorse the race purity idea of Mr. Powell and his organization." A year and a half before he died, Garvey endorsed the bill of the racist Mississippi Senator Theodore Bilbo for the repatriation of American Negroes to Africa and instructed all divisions of the UNIA to give it their "undivided and wholehearted support."

Garvey's racial ideology helped to determine his response to politics in general. In 1924 he answered a friendly overture from the Worker's party by stating: "We belong to the Negro party, first, last and all the time." His fear of the racism of the white working class, combined with his lingering affection for Washingtonian self-help, gave his domestic politics a conservative cast. He was a consistent foe of the Communists, whom he branded "a group of lazy men and women who desire to level all initiative and intelligence and set a premium on stagnation." Communists and trade unionists, he warned, were "more dangerous to the Negro's welfare than any other group at present." He attributed the failure of modern government to individual selfishness and greed, which could be remedied by paying government officials enough to remove them from temptation and punishing them by death should they succumb anyway. He proposed to reform capitalism by limiting individual fortunes to one million dollars and preventing any corporation from controlling more than five million dollars. While reforms were necessary, Garvey hailed capitalism as "necessary to the progress of the world" and branded its opponents "enemies to human advancement." "The only convenient friend the Negro worker or laborer has, in America, at the present time, is the white capitalist," Garvey announced, since the capitalist's desire to maximize profits made him willing to use the cheapest available labor. Garvey urged the black worker to "keep his scale of wage a little lower than the whites until he is able to become, through proper leadership, his own employer."

One of Garvey's most remarkable achievements was the ease with which he bridged the cultural and political gulf between Jamaica and the United States and learned to comprehend and speak to the needs and aspirations of millions of American blacks. The areas in which he failed to make this transition sufficiently were ones in which he committed his most serious errors. Among these were those aspects of his racial ideology that led him to attempt to form a common front with white racists and that affected his relations with his fellow black leaders. Given the nature of many of his programs, it was inevitable that Garvey would make a number of potent enemies within the ranks of black intellectuals, editors, civil rights leaders, and political activists. His very attempt to articulate the feelings of the masses was bound to create some animus among a significant number of the educated and affluent. However inevitable some of this might have been, it cannot be attributed—as Garvey liked to do—wholly to his opponents. Not only Garvey's programs but his style and temperament helped to create the impossibly poor relations with other black leaders that constituted one of Garvey's greatest weaknesses and hampered his cause significantly.

Certainly Garvey was provoked. To give but two examples, Du Bois described him as "a little, fat black man, ugly, but with intelligent eyes and big head," who was "the most dangerous enemy of the Negro race in America and the world . . . either a lunatic or a traitor," and A. Philip Randolph's *Messenger* referred to him as "the supreme Negro Jamaican Jackass," a "monumental monkey," and an "unquestioned fool and ignoramus." Garvey bore more than a little responsibility for determining the tone of this debate and surely for setting its racial dimensions. He brought with him from Jamaica an abiding distrust of the light-skinned, middle-class Negroes who constituted so many of the leaders in America. The basis of his distrust was not only, or even primarily, their program but their class and color. He attacked Cyril Briggs, the light-complexioned leader of the militant African Blood Brotherhood, with which Garvey certainly might have forged an alliance, as a "white man." He criticized the "near-white" leaders of the NAACP, which Garvey delighted in calling the "National Association for the Advancement of Certain People." His favorite target was Du Bois, whom he branded a "lazy dependent mulatto" whose mixed Dutch, French, and Negro ancestry made him "a monstrosity" who "bewails every day the drop of Negro blood in his veins." The Negro press, "controlled by crafty and unscrupulous persons who have no love of race," was "the most venal, ignorant and corrupt of our time." Du Bois and his allies were planning the extinction of the black race through miscegenation and were thus "the greatest enemies the black people have in the world."

This unhappy, unproductive debate not only drained the energies of all involved and rendered impossible the kind of unified black community Garvey claimed he wanted, but also it ultimately undermined Garvey's leadership and the effectiveness of his organization. A number of black leaders and journalists with whom Garvey had been feuding mounted a campaign against Garvey's operation of the Black Star Line, alerting government officials to alleged illegalities. In January 1922 Garvey and three of his associates were arrested and in February indicted on twelve counts of fraudulent use of the mails to sell Black Star stocks. A prolonged delay in beginning the trial, during which Garvey was released on bail, annoyed his opponents and on January 15, 1923, eight prominent black men and women, including three editors, two NAACP officials, and three business people, wrote to the attorney general of the United States, denouncing Garvey as a demagogue who preached "distrust and hatred of all white people," and demanded that the attorney general "disband and extirpate" Garvey's "vicious movement" and speedily push the government's case against him. The trial began within four months. Though there was no evidence that Garvey was guilty of anything more than poor management, inexperience, and bad judgment in choosing some of his associates, he alone of the four defendants was found guilty and sentenced to five years in prison.

From New York City's Tombs Prison, which Garvey entered in the middle of June 1923, he asserted, "I am not here because I committed any crime against society or defrauded anyone, but because I have led the way to Africa's redemption." In September he was released on bail pending his appeal and enjoyed his last seventeen months of freedom in America. On February 2, 1925, Garvey's appeal was denied, and six days later he entered Atlanta Penitentiary. In his many prison messages and editorials, Garvey was at his most prophetic and messianic: "If I die in Atlanta my work shall then only begin." Garvey was not destined to die in Atlanta. On November 18, 1927, President Calvin Coolidge commuted Garvey's sentence, which still had slightly more than two years to run. Early the next month, Garvey was deported as an undesirable alien. Hundreds of Garvey's followers gathered at the New Orleans pier to bid him farewell. "Be not dismayed," he told them. "Africa's sun is steadily and surely rising, and soon shall shed its rays around the world. I live and shall die for Africa redeemed. Steady yourselves and go forward!"

Despite Garvey's optimistic rhetoric and the considerable personal courage he exhibited during his prosecution and imprisonment, his incarceration and deportation separated him from the most powerful constituency he had and effectively destroyed his movement in the United States. Certainly it is true, as Amy Jacques Garvey has pointed out, that though Garvey was forced to leave America, "Garveyism remained." But it remained in severely diminished circumstances. In Garvey's absence its following declined drastically, and its leadership became hopelessly divided. At the time of Garvey's deportation, the UNIA was bankrupt with liabilities of over $200,000. The final ship in its fleet had been auctioned off for payment of debts; it had lost its liberty halls in New York and Pittsburgh as well as its New York office buildings and publishing plant. The UNIA continued to function, but its days of power and glory were behind it.

Garvey was to live more than twelve years in forced exile from the United States. They were years of characteristic energy and activity and of uncharacteristic isolation and futility. Making Jamaica his base of operations, Garvey edited several newspapers, hosted international conventions of the UNIA in 1929 and 1934, served three months in prison for contempt of court, was elected to the governing body of Kingston and its parish but was defeated in his bid for the Jamaican legislature, made an abortive attempt to organize a Jamaican People's party, and spent much time and energy feuding with his former UNIA colleagues in America and seeking financial support for his movement. Once again, Garvey was to find his native island too confining. On his way down, no less than on his way up, Garvey needed to be near the center of events.

In March 1935 Garvey took his magazine, the *Black Man*, which he had begun the year before, and moved permanently to London. When the colonial secretary in Jamaica warned British Military Intelligence that Garvey might relocate in London, the reply was: "he can do very little harm over here." That judgment proved to be correct. Garvey continued the patterns of the past: he edited his impressive magazine, he spoke in Hyde Park whenever the weather was fair and indoors wherever he could find a hall and an audience, but he seems not to have had meaningful interaction with London's black population, which had grown somewhat larger and more diverse since Garvey had lived there before World War I. Throughout these final years the major outlines of his philosophy remained familiar. He continued to be a proponent of racial separation, of success through individual and group initiative, and of African redemption. Nevertheless, he was no more predictable at the end of his life than he had been in the beginning. Even as he denounced Benito Mussolini for his rape of Ethiopia, he openly admired aspects of his regime and complained: "Mussolini copied fascism from me. . . . Mussolini and Hitler copied the program of the UNIA." Even as he championed the principles of liberty and the rights of oppressed peoples, he proved strangely indifferent to the plight of the Jews in

Germany, charging that their troubles had "been brought on by themselves," because—of all reasons—"their particular method of living is inconsistent with the broader human principles that go to make all people homogeneous."

Garvey longed to return to the United States, if only for a visit, but was denied permission. He came as close as he could, spending three summers, from 1936 to 1938, in Toronto, where he held two regional UNIA conferences and his last international convention. Though the days of his own leadership were behind him, one of his final gestures was to establish a School of African Philosophy in Toronto to recruit and train prospective new leaders for the UNIA. In June 1939 his precarious financial situation forced him to suspend publication of the *Black Man*. For almost the first time since his youth, Garvey was without a journalistic voice. The last year of his life in London was lived in silent penury. In January 1940 he suffered a stroke that left him partially paralyzed, and on June 10, nine weeks short of his fifty-third birthday, he died.

Though he died in isolation, Garvey was not to be forgotten. Decades after his death, his name was still invoked, his ideas still discussed, his influence still felt. Garvey would not have been surprised; it was always his conviction that this would be so. Throughout his stormy, difficult life, Garvey had nurtured his vision of a proud, united black race and an independent Africa. He may not have always worked for it wisely or effectively, but he never ceased working for it and believing in it. In his "Appeal to Racial Pride," printed in the penultimate issue of the *Black Man*, Garvey closed with words that might well serve as his epitaph: "The end is not in our day but in our time we can make certain contribution toward it. . . . Let us not turn back, let us hold on, so that when the final history of man is to be written, there will not only be glory for others but there will be glory for us."

NOTE ON SOURCES

Those interested in Garvey should begin with his own writings, especially *Philosophy and Opinions of Marcus Garvey*, ed. Amy Jacques Garvey (New York: Atheneum, 1969), and *More Philosophy and Opinions of Marcus Garvey*, ed. E.U. Essien-Udom and Amy Jacques Garvey (London: Frank Cass, 1977). Garvey's final magazine, *The Black Man*, has been reprinted in full in an edition edited by Robert A. Hill (Millwood, N.Y.: Kraus-Thomson, 1975). Garvey's revealing autobiographical article, "The Negro's Greatest Enemy," *Current History*, 18 (Sept. 1923), has been reprinted in John Henrik Clarke, ed., *Marcus Garvey and the Vision of Africa* (New York: Random House, 1974), which also contains other important pieces by Garvey. Garvey's long narrative poem, *The Tragedy of White Injustice* (1927), has also been reprinted (New York: Haskell House, 1972).

The most useful biographical overview is Edmund David Cronon, *Black Moses: The Story of Marcus Garvey and the Universal Negro Improvement Association* (Madison: University of Wisconsin Press, 1955). It should be supplemented by Theodore G. Vincent, *Black Power and the Garvey Movement* (Berkeley, Calif.: Ramparts Press [1971]), and Tony Martin, *Race First: The Ideological and Organizational Struggles of Marcus Garvey and the Universal Negro Improvement Association* (Westport, Conn.: Greenwood Press, 1976). Amy Jacques Garvey's biography of her husband, *Garvey and Garveyism* (Kingston: A. Jacques Garvey, 1963), is especially interesting on Garvey's final years in the West Indies and London. For her article, "The Early Years of Marcus Garvey," and Robert A. Hill's important article, "The First England Years and After, 1912–1916," see the Clarke volume cited above. Robert A. Hill's introduction to *The Black Man*, also cited above, contains an excellent detailed discussion of Garvey's years in exile. Hugh Mulzac's autobiography, *A Star to Steer By* (New York: International Publishers, 1963), provides a fascinating inside picture of the Black Star Line. Finally, the most indispensable recent study of Garvey and his followers is Randall K. Burkett, *Garveyism as a Religious Movement: The Institutionalization of a Black Civil Religion* (Metuchen, N.J.: Scarecrow Press, 1978).

UNIT 2-7

THE OBJECTIVES OF THE UNIVERSAL NEGRO IMPROVEMENT ASSOCIATION

Marcus Garvey

The declared objects of the association are:

"To establish a Universal Confraternity among the race; to promote the spirit of pride and love; to reclaim the fallen; to administer to and assist the needy; to assist in civilizing the backward tribes of Africa; to assist in the development of Independent Negro Nations and Communities; to establish a central nation for the race, to establish Commissaries or Agencies in the principal countries and cities of the world for the representation of all Negroes; to promote a conscientious Spiritual worship among the natives tribes of Africa; to establish Universities, Colleges, Academies and Schools for the racial education and culture of the people; to work for better conditions among Negroes everywhere."

SUPPLYING A LONG FELT WANT

The organization of the Universal Negro Improvement Association has supplied among Negroes a long-felt want. Hitherto the other Negro movements in America, with the exception of the Tuskegee effort of Booker T. Washington, sought to teach the Negro to aspire to social equality with the whites, meaning thereby the right to intermarry and fraternize in every social way. This has been the source of much trouble and still some Negro organizations continue to preach this dangerous "race destroying doctrine" added to a program of political agitation and aggression. The Universal Negro Improvement Association on the other hand believes in and teaches the pride and purity of race. We believe that the white race should uphold its racial pride and perpetuate itself, and that the black

---

Amy Jacques-Garvey, ed., *Philosophy and Opinions of Marcus Garvey* (New York: Universal Publishing House, 1925), pp. 38–39. Reprinted by permission.

race should do likewise. We believe that there is room enough in the world for the various race groups to grow and develop by themselves without seeking to destroy the Creator's plan by the constant introduction of mongrel types.

The unfortunate condition of slavery, as imposed upon the Negro, and which caused the mongrelization of the race, should not be legalized and continued now to the harm and detriment of both races.

The time has really come to give the Negro a chance to develop himself to a moral-standard-man, and it is for such an opportunity that the Universal Negro Improvement Association seeks in the creation of an African nation for Negroes, where the greatest latitude would be given to work out this racial ideal.

There are hundreds of thousands of colored people in America who desire race amalgamation and miscegenation as a solution of the race problem. These people are, therefore, opposed to the race pride ideas of black and white; but the thoughtful of both races will naturally ignore the ravings of such persons and honestly work for the solution of a problem that has been forced upon us.

Liberal white America and race loving Negroes are bound to think at this time and thus evolve a program or plan by which there can be a fair and amicable settlement of the question.

We cannot put off the consideration of the matter, for time is pressing on our hands. The educated Negro is making rightful constitutional demands. The great white majority will never grant them, and thus we march on to danger if we do not now stop and adjust the matter.

The time is opportune to regulate the relationship between both races. Let the Negro have a country of his own. Help him to return to his original home, Africa, and there give him the opportunity to climb from the lowest to the highest positions in a state of his own. If not, then the nation will have to hearken to the demand of the aggressive, "social equality" organization, known as the National Association for the Advancement of Colored People, of which W.E.B. Du Bois is leader, which declares vehemently for social and political equality, *viz.*: Negroes and whites in the same hotels, homes, residential districts, public and private places, a Negro as president, members of the Cabinet, Governors of States, Mayors of cities, and leaders of society in the United States. In this agitation, Du Bois is ably supported by the "Chicago Defender," a colored newspaper published in Chicago. This paper advocates Negroes in the Cabinet and Senate. All these, as everybody knows, are the Negroes' constitutional rights, but reason dictates that the masses of the white race will never stand by the ascendancy of an opposite minority group to the favored positions in a government, society and industry that exist by the will of the majority, hence the demand of the Du Bois group of colored leaders will only lead, ultimately, to further disturbances in riots, lynching and mob rule. The only logical solution therefore, is to supply the Negro with opportunities and environments of his own, and there point him to the fullness of his ambition.

UNIT **2-8**

MARCUS GARVEY AND THE NAACP

W.E.B. Du Bois

A brief but illuminating summary of Du Bois' relationship with and attitude toward Garvey and his movement was published in The Crisis soon after President Coolidge (whose election Garvey had favored) released him from prison in 1927 and ordered his deportation.

Many persons are under the impression that the NAACP has been the persistent enemy of Marcus Garvey. This is due to repeated accusations published in the *Negro World* without the slightest basis of fact. For the sake of the truth, it may be well to recall certain matters of clear record.

The Crisis has published five articles on Marcus Garvey. The first articles, March 1920 and January 1921 ended with this summary:

> To sum up: Garvey is a sincere, hard-working idealist; he is also a stubborn, domineering leader of the mass; he has worthy industrial commercial schemes but he is an inexperienced business man. His dreams of Negro industry, commerce and the ultimate freedom of Africa are feasible, but his methods are bombastic, wasteful, illogical and ineffective, and almost illegal. If he learns by experience, attracts strong and capable friends and helpers instead of making needless enemies; if he gives up secrecy and suspicion and substitutes open and frank reports as to his income and expenses, and above all if he is willing to be a co-worker and not a czar, he may yet in time succeed in at least starting some of his schemes toward accomplishment. But unless he does these things and does them quickly he cannot escape failure.

No more prophetic word was ever written about Marcus Garvey!

The third and fourth articles dealt with the Black Star Line and the Universal Negro Improvement Association and were based on published documents with little comment.

It was not until September, 1922, that *The Crisis* had a sharp word of criticism. This was based on Garvey's threats against his critics, his connection with the Ku Klux Klan and his distribution of pamphlet propaganda against American Negroes. We quoted, among other things, this:

"The white race can best help the Negro by telling him the truth, and not by flattering him into believing that he is as good as any white man."

Concerning this we said:

"Not even Tom Dixon or Ben Tillman or the hatefullest enemies of the Negro have ever stooped to a more vicious campaign than Marcus Garvey, sane or insane, is carrying on. He is not attacking white prejudice, he is grovelling before it and applauding it; his only attack is on men of his own race who are striving for freedom; his only contempt is for Negroes; his only threats are for black blood."

On the other hand Garvey's attacks on the NAACP have been continuous, preposterous and false. He has claimed:

1. That we kept his representative from activity in Paris in 1919.
2. That Moorfield Storey came from Boston to secure his conviction in 1924.
3. That the collapse of the Black Star Line came about "because men were paid to make this trouble by certain organizations calling themselves Negro Advancement Associations. They paid men to dismantle our machinery and otherwise damage it so as to bring about the downfall of the movement."
4. That the NAACP was responsible for his incarceration and deportation.

Every single statement in these and dozens of similar charges are absolutely false and without any basis of fact whatsoever. As *The Crisis* said in May, 1924:

> No Negro in America ever had a fairer and more patient trial than Marcus Garvey. He convicted himself by his own admissions, his swaggering monkey-shines in the court room with monocle and long tailed coat and his insults to the judge and prosecuting attorney.
>
> Marcus Garvey was long refused bail, not because of his color, but because of the repeated threats and cold blooded assaults charged against his organization. He himself openly threatened to "get" the District Attorney. His followers had repeatedly to be warned from intimidating witnesses and one was sent to jail therefor. One of his former trusted officials after being put out of the Garvey organization brought the long concealed cash account of the organization to this office and we published it. Within two weeks the man was shot in the back in New Orleans and killed.
>
> Everybody, including the writer, who has dared to make the slightest criticism of Garvey has been intimidated by threats and threatened with libel suits. Over fifty court cases have been brought by Garvey in ten years.

We are reminding our readers of all this not to revive forgotten rancor but for the sake of historical accuracy. When Garvey was sent to Atlanta, no word or action of ours accomplished the result. His release and deportation was a matter of law which no deed or wish of ours influenced in the slightest degree. We have today, no enmity against Marcus Garvey. He has a great and worthy dream. We wish him well. He is free; has a following; he still has a chance to carry on his work in his own home and among his own people and to accomplish some of his ideals. Let him do it. We will be the first to applaud any success that he may have.

Unsigned, but written by W.E.B. Du Bois, in *The Crisis*, February, 1928; XXXV, 51.

UNIT 2-9

A French Directive
On the Treatment of Black American Troops

[*To the*] *French Military Mission stationed with the American Army. August 7, 1918. Secret information concerning the Black American Troops.*

It is important for French officers who have been called upon to exercise command over black American troops, or to live in close contact with them, to have an exact idea of the position occupied by Negroes in the United States. The information set forth in the following communication ought to be given to these officers and it is to their interest to have these matters known and widely disseminated. It will devolve likewise on the French Military Authorities, through the medium of the Civil Authorities, to give information on this subject to the French population residing in the cantonments occupied by American colored troops.

1. The American attitude upon the Negro question may seem a matter for discussion to many French minds. But we French are not in our province if we undertake to discuss what some call "prejudice." [*recognize that*] *American opinion is unanimous on the "color question," and does not admit of any discussion.*

The increasing number of Negroes in the United States (about 15,000,000) would create for the white race in the Republic a menace of degeneracy were it not that an impassable gulf has been made between them.

As this danger does not exist for the French race, *the French public has become accustomed to treating the Negro with familiarity and indulgence.*

This indulgence and this familiarity [*These*] *are matters of grievous concern to the Americans. They consider them an affront to their national policy.* They are afraid that contact with the French will inspire in black Americans aspirations which to them (the whites) appear intolerable. *It is of the utmost importance that every effort be made to avoid profoundly estranging American opinion.*

Although a citizen of the United States, the black man is regarded by the white American as an inferior being with whom relations of business or service only are possible. The black is constantly being censured for his want of intelligence and

---

The Crisis, XVIII (May, 1919), pp. 16–18. Reprinted by permission.

discretion, his lack of civic and professional conscience, and for his tendency toward undue familiarity.

The vices of the Negro are a constant menace to the American who has to repress them sternly. For instance, the black American troops in France have, by themselves, given rise to as many complaints for attempted rape as all the rest of the army. And yet the (black American) soldiers sent us have been the choicest with respect to physique and morals, for the number disqualified at the time of mobilization was enormous.

Conclusion

1. We must prevent the rise of any pronounced degree of intimacy between French officers and black officers. We may be courteous and amiable with these last, but we cannot deal with them on the same plane as with the white American officers without deeply wounding the latter. We *must not eat with [the blacks] them, must not shake hands or seek to talk or meet with them outside of the requirements of military service.*

2. We must not commend too highly the black American troops, particularly in the presence of (white) Americans. It is all right to recognize their good qualities and their services, but only in moderate terms strictly in keeping with the truth.

3. Make a point of keeping the native cantonment population from spoiling the Negroes. (White) *Americans become greatly incensed at any public expression of intimacy between white women with black men.* They have recently uttered violent protests against a picture in the "Vie Parisienne" entitled "The Child of the Desert" which shows a (white) woman in a "cabinet particulier" with a Negro. Familiarity on the part of white women with black men is furthermore a source of profound regret to our experienced colonials who see in it an overweening menace to the prestige of the white race.

Military authority cannot intervene directly in this question, but it can through the civil authorities exercise some influence on the population.

[*Signed*] Linard

HELP THE

N. A. A. C. P.

To Fight for You—

1. To secure for Negro workers equal wages and decent hours under the various codes being adopted by the National Recovery Administration and to check violations of these codes after they are in effect.

2. To bring the 30,000 levee camp workers along the lower Mississippi river under a code to raise their wages and shorten their hours.

3. To put Negroes on juries in the South in accordance with the U. S. Constitution. (The George Crawford extradition case which the N.A.A.C.P. fought in Boston, Mass., and has now taken to the U. S. Supreme Court, is responsible for Negroes being called for jury service in Alexandria, Va., and Richmond, Va., for the first time in thirty years. In Richmond a white farmer was fined $10 for refusing to serve on a grand jury with a Negro.)

4. To get a proportionate share of jobs for Negro workers on construction and relief projects financed by federal, state, county and municipal funds, for which Negro citizens are taxed at the same rate as others.

5. To fight against the rising tide of lynchings, posse killings, legal lynchings, court injustices, horse-whippings and mob terrorism during the period of crisis.

6. To fight for equal teachers' salaries, equal school equipment and equal educational opportunities throughout the south. A legal campaign has been launched in North Carolina against the proposed state maximum salary for Negro teachers of $560 a year as against a maximum salary for white teachers of $720 a year.

7. To continue the fight against all forms of segregation and discrimination.

8. To procure the full use of the ballot as a weapon for freedom.

NOVEMBER, 1933

N. A. A. C. P., 69 Fifth Avenue, New York, N. Y.

Enclosed is $......for the work of the National Association for the Advancement of Colored People. (Memberships of $2.50 and up carry with them a subscription to the CRISIS.)

Name ....Street ....

City ....State ....

UNIT 3

NEW DEAL AND WORLD WAR II

INTRODUCTION 112

3-1 • THE IMPACT OF THE NEW DEAL ON BLACK SOUTHERNERS 113
Harvard Sitkoff

3-2 • A. PHILIP RANDOLPH: LABOR LEADER AT LARGE 125
Benjamin Quarles

3-3 • A. PHILIP RANDOLPH'S MARCH ON WASHINGTON: 1941 142
THE BLACK MAN DEMANDS A SHARE IN WORLD WAR II
A. Philip Randolph

3-4 • PRESIDENT ROOSEVELT'S FAIR EMPLOYMENT PRACTICES COMMITTEE 145
EXECUTIVE ORDER 8802, JUNE 25, 1941

3-5 • A BASIS FOR INTERRACIAL COOPERATION AND DEVELOPMENT IN THE SOUTH 147
A STATEMENT BY SOUTHERN NEGROES

3-6 • STATEMENT OF CONFERENCE OF WHITE SOUTHERNERS ON RACE RELATIONS 154

3-7 • RESOLUTIONS OF THE COLLABORATION COMMITTEE 156

3-8 • RESOLUTION LAUNCHING THE SOUTHERN REGIONAL COUNCIL 159

3-9 • ADDRESSED TO WHITE LIBERALS 161
Lillian Smith

3-10 • WHAT THE NEGRO WANTS 164

INTRODUCTION

During the 1930s and 1940s there were many marked changes in Southern race relations. Harvard Sitkoff's essay (3-1) is an overview of the impact of the New Deal on black Southerners, explaining how many black Southerners began to see the federal government in a more positive light. One of the most well known African Americans of the 1940s was the labor leader A. Philip Randolph whose life is chronicled in 3-2. His pressure tactics (3-3) brought about Executive Order 8802 (3-4), one of most important civil rights advances of the decade.

The 1940s also witnessed the birth of the one of the foremost interracial organizations in the South—the Southern Regional Council (SRC). Born from the failure of the Commission on Interracial Cooperation (1919–1943), the SRC emerged from an exchange of written statements between black (3-5) and white (3-6) Southerners. Document 3-7 is the result of a collaboration between those two groups, and document 3-8 is the SRC's founding resolution. From the beginning the SRC had many critics on the right and on the left; Lillian Smith, the author of *Strange Fruit* and other novels about the South, roundly criticized the new organization for not directly confronting segregation (3-9).

New South was the SRC's monthly journal. It served as a forum by which the SRC sought to shape the opinion of Southern leaders and moderate whites. The organization sponsored fact-finding missions and statistical surveys which were published in *New South*. SRC leaders believed that, when presented with the "facts" of Southern life, white Southerners would conclude segregation was wrong. Southern activists and the national media considered the *New South* the best source for accurate, up-to-date information on the movement.

The last item in this unit is a long excerpt from *What the Negro Wants*, a 1944 collection of essays by twelve prominent African Americans speculating on black hopes for the post-World War II era.

UNIT 3-1

The Impact of the New Deal on Black Southerners

Harvard Sitkoff

We did not dare to breathe a prayer,
Or to give our anguish scope;
Something was dead in each of us,
And what was dead was Hope.

—*Oscar Wilde*
The Ballad of Reading Gaol

The New Deal brought to black southerners both the change of hopefulness and the continuation of suffering and misery. More potent in promise than in performance, the New Deal significantly conditioned the future of Afro-Americans but could not escape the black past. President Franklin Delano Roosevelt, whatever his own racial inclinations or ideology, had no *tabula rasa* upon which to work. The heritage of racism shaped the circumstances in which the New Deal operated. It set the limits on possibilities for racial reform in the 1930s. And because the hand of history weighed more heavily on certain regions, the New Deal positively affected blacks less in the South than in the North, and rural southern blacks least of all.[1]

Past politics severely circumscribed the potential of a new deal for black southerners. Because of an entrenched one-party system in Dixie, Democratic weakness above the Mason-Dixon line in the 1920s, and the continuation of the seniority rule to determine congressional power, Roosevelt had little alternative to seeking the support of, and capitulating to the racism of, the white southerners who controlled Congress. He needed their votes for New Deal legislation and appropriations, and the president would take no action on the racial front that would estrange the white southern politicians who commanded over half the committee chairmanships and a majority of leadership positions in every congressional session during the 1930s. "I did not choose the tools with which I must work," Roosevelt explained when declining to press for anti-lynching legislation:

> Had I been permitted to choose them I would have selected quite different ones. But I've got to get legislation passed by Congress to save America. The Southerners by reason of the seniority rule in Congress are chairman or occupy strategic places on most of the Senate and House committees. If I come out for the anti-lynching bill now, they will block every bill I ask Congress to pass to keep America from collapsing. I just can't take that risk.

Powerful traditions of decentralization and states' rights also undermined the quest of Afro-Americans for equitable treatment in the Great Depression. The local administration of relief and recovery projects, despite numerous executive orders and legislative clauses prohibiting racial discrimination in the New Deal, left southern blacks at the mercy of those planters, industrialists, union chieftains and political officeholders who stood to profit the most by continuing to oppress Afro-Americans. Those who made the decisions at the local level made sure black southerners never shared fully or fairly in the material benefits of the New Deal.[2]

The deficiencies of broker state leadership for the least influential, moreover, prevented blacks from receiving the kind and amount of governmental assistance they desperately needed. A political system dispensing aid on the basis of the strength of the groups demanding it necessarily worked to the disadvantage of the largely poor and unorganized black community. As Henry Lee Moon of the National Association for the Advancement of Colored People wrote:

> The public interest, democratic principles, justice, ethics, or even the law are seldom the bases upon which conflicts are resolved. Faced with the necessity of resolving a conflict, administration invariably yields to that group which can bring the greatest pressure to bear, illustrating anew that government in a democracy is government by compromise. Too frequently this compromise is characterized by the forced yielding on the part of the weaker to the stronger of two contending groups. . . . It is obvious that under such conditions, the claims of the Negro, however sound, just and legal, are seldom granted when they appear to conflict with the claims of a white group.

Southern blacks could not get a new deal when their oppressors held all the power cards and could stack the deck against Afro-Americans.

In addition, the very ubiquity of the worst depression in American history determined the limited parameters of the New Deal's efforts to remedy the plight of blacks. Hard times defined Roosevelt's mandate and kept the pressure on the New Deal to promote economic recovery at the expense of other needed changes. All else had to wait. "First things come first," the President repeated again and again, "and I can't alienate certain votes I need for measures that are more important at the moment by pushing any measures that would entail a fight." Roosevelt would not permit New Deal solicitude for blacks to jeopardize the economic reconstruction that he and the vast majority of the American people considered their immediate and preeminent priority. Therefore caution, often timidity, governed the New Deal's fundamental approach to racial matters in the South.[3]

Most importantly, three centuries of southern history prior to the New Deal had trapped the mass of blacks in what Oscar Lewis would later call the "culture of Poverty." The wrongs of the past continued to injure blacks who sought to survive the depression. Millions of blacks in the 1930s remained enslaved by disease and disfranchisement, by a dearth of opportunity for employment and education, by social disorganization and dormancy, by isolation and intimidation. Fear, weakness, and resignation bred a crippling paralysis of will to struggle. Those most likely to resist oppression went north when they could, convinced that migration was the surest path to advancement. Those that stayed lacked the wherewithal to overcome those insisting that they remain the mudsill. Their debilitated status left black southerners without the weapons to fight for the rights of citizenship or a rightful share of New Deal largess. The heritage of black poverty and powerlessness underlay the constraints on Roosevelt, and the New Deal's failure to attack Jim Crow or to succor southern blacks to the extent warranted by their distress.[4]

The early New Deal efforts at economic recovery starkly revealed the institutional and structural determinants inhibiting salutary change for black southerners. Afro-Americans played no role in the planning or implementation of the programs handled by the National Recovery Administration (NRA), the Agricultural Adjustment Administration (AAA), and the Tennessee Valley Authority (TVA). They had no influence with the officials who managed these matters. And they could hardly gain from policies which callously neglected those at the bottom rungs of the economic ladder.

Quickly following its inception, Afro-Americans jibed that NRA meant "Negro Run Around," "Negro Removal Administration," or "Negroes Ruined Again." The NRA primarily affected black southerners by increasing the prices they had to pay as consumers and by inducing employees to replace black labor with white workers. The NRA's effort to raise labor standards largely bypassed southern blacks since the wage codes excluded those who toiled in agriculture and domestic service. Less than one in four employed blacks worked in industry or commerce. In addition, the manufacturing and retail codes of the NRA were heavily weighted in favor of large-scale, efficient, modernized enterprises, and against those firms operating at the margins of the economy, which included the bulk of southern black businesses. Consequently, the NRA hastened black bankruptcies and forced disadvantaged black entrepreneurs to close shop and join the ranks of the unemployed.

The NRA's requirement that labor receive higher wages, moreover, led to thousands of black workers being displaced by white employees. The NRA certainly did not initiate this process. Given the surplus of available white labor, precious few southern industrialists saw any reason to hire blacks. But, ironically, the NRA hastened the mass firing of Afro-Americans by not acquiescing to the white southern demand for a racial differential, a lower wage scale for blacks. Few southern bosses could stomach the notion of nonracist equal pay for equal work; and when the NRA increased the average wage in tobacco manufacturing from 19¢ to 32¢ an hour, and the Fair Labor Standards Act later raised it to 65¢ an hour, the upshot was a halving of black employment and a simultaneous gain in the number of white workers by more than 40 percent. For most southern black laborers, the only alternative to displacement was acceptance of spurious occupational classifications. These meant either lower wages than whites received for the same work, as happened in the southern foundries, or exclusion from NRA coverage, which transpired for the thousands of blacks employed in southern cotton oil and textile mills. Few blacks dissented when the *Norfolk Journal and Guide* categorized the Blue Eagle as "a predatory bird instead of a feathered messenger of happiness."[5]

The administration of the Agricultural Adjustment Act proved even more harmful for southern blacks. The AAA aimed to raise farm prices by creating scarcity; it provided subsidies for farmers who restricted acreage and crop production. But, never intending to reform landlord-tenant relationships, the AAA eschewed safeguards to protect the exploited landless peasantry that constituted a quarter of the southern population. The result for more than 5.5 million southern whites and nearly 3 million southern blacks was either the forced exodus from the lands they toiled or the worsening of a miserably poor existence marked by chronic squalor and servility.

The AAA cotton program did little for southern tenant farmers that a plague of boll weevils could not have done. It reduced cotton acreage, and acquiesced in the massive cheating of croppers out of their share of the subsidy and in the eviction of tenants whose labor was no longer needed. This callous indifference to the plight of the South's "forgotten farmers" by the large landowners who dominated the county committees, abetted by the Farm Bureau—Extension Service—land grant college axis which set agricultural policies in Washington, undoubtedly reflected as much class as racial bias. But because more than three out of every four black farmers worked land they did not own, compared to slightly less than half the white farmers in the South, and because black agricultural operators constituted some 40 percent of all employed black southerners, the tragic harm perpetuated by the AAA wreaked epidemic affliction on Afro-Americans. Instead of higher incomes, the AAA brought greater indigence to the black tenantry.[6]

The economic boom promised by the Tennessee Valley Authority proved similarly illusory. The TVA's vaunted rhetoric of "grassroots democracy" once again meant local control by those southern whites most determined to prevent Afro-Americans from getting a new deal. Those who had traditionally oppressed blacks in the Valley stayed "in the saddle," and white racism rode high. White southerners excluded blacks from living in the new model town of Norris; segregated work crews relegated blacks to the least skilled, lowest paying jobs; refused to admit blacks to TVA vocational schools or to training sessions in foremanship; denied blacks clerical positions; established racially separate employment offices and drinking fountains; and Jim-Crowed blacks in housing and recreational facilities. Although TVA's employment situation gradually changed for the better for blacks, so that by the end of the decade the number of blacks in the work force and their percentage of the total payroll constituted a higher proportion than their population in the area, TVA continued to conform to the racist byways of the region. Segregation and white supremacy remained inviolate.[7]

The recovery program simply did not take the needs of black southerners into account. It sought to restore the morale and jobs of middle-class America. It never contemplated reforming the structural bases of black impoverishment and infirmity. NRA administrator Hugh Johnson would not permit his subordinates even to consider the special plight of blacks in the South. TVA chairman Arthur Morgan, ever-fearful of provoking local white hostility to the Authority, would offer Afro-Americans nothing more than the admonition that they continue "inching along." And Cully Cobb, the head of the Cotton Section, implanted into AAA policies all the prejudices acquired from a lifetime of work with the white southern agricultural establishment.[8]

The relief and welfare operations of the New Deal, on the other hand, did assist black southerners to a significant extent. At the least, they enabled Afro-Americans to survive the depression. More sensitively administered, overall, these New Deal programs took some real strides toward ameliorating black distress. In the face of strident southern white opposition, such New Dealers as Will Alexander, Harold Ickes and Aubrey Williams battled for a fair share of relief for blacks. Although their commitment proved salutary, their accomplishments remained limited. Black southerners endured, but did not advance in the 1930s. The New Deal could neither aid Afro-Americans to the extent their privation required nor vanquish Jim Crow in the South.

Robert Fechner never tried. The director of the Civilian Conservation Corps (CCC), a southerner and former head of a white-only labor union, Fechner even sought to impose segregation in northern locales that opposed Jim Crow. Throughout the South, Fechner cooperated with state directors of selection like John de la Perriere of Georgia who desired to see black youth only chopping cotton, and who argued that "there are few negro families who . . . need an income as great as $25 a month." Despite an unemployment rate for young black males twice that of white youth, the southern local officials who picked the CCC enrollees consistently gave preferences to whites. Blacks constituted less than 3 percent of the first 250,000 in the CCC. Counties with black majorities in Georgia had no blacks in the CCC, and Mississippi, over half-black, permitted but 1.7 percent of its CCC allotment to go to Afro-Americans.

Gradually, protests from Negro organizations and pressure from New Dealers sympathetic to the plight of blacks forced Fechner to relent, somewhat. Although blacks in the

South stayed in segregated CCC units, were kept out of training programs that would lead to their advancement, were generally excluded from educational and supervisory positions, and continued to remain numerically underrepresented, their numbers and opportunities slowly increased. By late 1936, they made up some 6 percent of the youths in the Corps, nearly ten percent a year later, and 11 percent in 1938. That year about 40,000 young blacks were sending $700,000 a month home to their parents and dependents. By the start of 1939, almost 200,000 blacks had served in the CCC, and, because the defense boom caused a drop in white enrollments, when the Corps ended in 1942 the number of blacks who had joined the CCC totaled 350,000. Over 40,000 Afro-Americans who had entered the CCC as illiterates had learned to read and write.[9]

Despite the perpetuation of Jim Crow, it is obvious how much such assistance meant to blacks. And a hint of a new deal did appear in many relief and welfare operations. The Unemployment Relief Act of 1933, setting up the Federal Emergency Relief Administration, specifically banned racial discrimination, and Harry Hopkins, FDR's choice to head the relief program, conscientiously worked toward that goal. Both FERA and the Civil Works Administration, the work-relief effort of the winter of 1933–34, sought to provide adequate allotments without regard to race. But resistance from southern whites came swiftly. They found CWA's uniform wage scale and FERA's equal relief grants bitter pills to swallow. Complaints poured in of blacks spoiled by relief, no longer beholden to local landlords, no longer hungry and a willing source of cheap labor, earning more on work-relief than white laborers in private enterprise.

Relief thus jeopardized dearly held class and racial arrangements, and Hopkins's resolve slackened. New regulations prohibited relief payments from exceeding prevailing salaries in a region, lowered the hourly minimum wages on work-relief, permitted the closing of relief projects during the cotton-picking season to provide the labor planters desired, and gave great discretion to state and local relief officials in the administration of their programs. Consequently, the Negro's chance for obtaining relief, and the amount of relief, was greatest in the urban North, less in the cities of the South, and least of all in the rural South, where the majority of Afro-Americans still lived in the 1930s. Discrimination was rife and blacks remained at the mercy of the lily-white personnel in local relief offices. Yet, federal relief enabled southern blacks to survive the depression. Although they never received assistance commensurate with their need, blacks comprised a higher proportion of the work relief rolls than their percentage of the population almost everywhere in the South throughout most of the decade.[10]

Much the same pattern of assistance with discrimination in the South prevailed in the Works Progress Administration. Executive orders prohibiting discrimination notwithstanding, local relief officials made it more difficult for blacks than whites to get on the WPA rolls and paid blacks less for the work-relief they performed than they did whites. By mid-1940, the fourteen southern and border states still had only eleven blacks among its more than ten thousand supervisors. Yet, the millions of dollars spent by the WPA for southern blacks meant survival, when even that had been in doubt. In 1938, some 140,000 black southerners worked on WPA projects. The following year, nearly three-quarters of a million black families in the South lived primarily on their WPA earnings. Indeed, the Works Progress Administration by the end of the 1930s rivaled both agriculture and domestic service as the chief source of black income in the South.[11]

The Public Works Administration also provided work-relief for the unemployed. Tightly run by Harold Ickes, a former president of the NAACP in Chicago, who insisted "that Congress intended this program to be carried out without discrimination," the PWA stipulated that all its construction contracts specify that the number of blacks hired and their percentage of the project payroll be equal to the proportion of blacks in the 1930 occupational census. Although sometimes disregarded by local officials and contractors, this quota resulted in unprecedented wages for southern black laborers and led to the admission of hundreds of blacks into previously all-white southern construction trade unions. It later led to similar quotas by the United States Housing Authority, the Federal Works Agency, and the President's Committee on Fair Employment Practices.

Due primarily to Ickes's vigilance, moreover, blacks received 59 percent of the federally subsidized PWA and USHA housing in the South, and some $40 million in PWA funds went into the construction or renovation of over eight hundred hospitals, school buildings and libraries for southern blacks. This was a sum far, far greater than the federal government had spent for blacks during the seven decades after Emancipation.[12]

Following Ickes's lead, Aubrey Williams, the head of the National Youth Administration until its end in 1943, also made assistance to blacks one of his top priorities. Although the NYA accepted segregated projects in the South and employed a disproportionate number of southern blacks in servile work, Williams was attacked by white supremacists as a "nigger lover" and traitor to his native Alabama because he hired black administrative assistants to supervise Negro work in every southern state, forbade either geographical or racial differentials in wages, and insisted that Afro-American secondary and college students in every southern state receive aid at least in proportion to their numbers in the population. Still, the NYA helped only a minority of southern black youth who needed assistance. Despite Williams's fervor and the presence of more Afro-Americans in administrative posts in the NYA than in any other New Deal program, ably led by Mary McLeod Bethune, who headed the Office of Negro Affairs, the presence of proportionally far fewer black students than white in the South and the extremely limited scope of the out-of-school work program minimized the impact of the National Youth Administration.[13]

Similarly, despite the best of intentions toward Afro-Americans, the Resettlement Administration and the Farm Security Administration also barely scratched the surface of the needs of impoverished rural blacks in the South. The federal government's first "war on poverty" was simply overwhelmed by problems beyond its resources. Both Rexford Tugwell, chief of the RA, and Dr. Will Alexander, head of the FSA, showed real concern for southern blacks. Against determined opposition by the southern agricultural establishment and its spokesmen in Congress, even against the wishes of their own local committees in the South that administered RA and FSA programs, Tugwell and especially Alexander managed to insure benefits for black farmers roughly proportionate to their percentage of southern farm operators. But they could not prevent local committees from discriminating against blacks in the amount of loans awarded. And they could not force appropriations out of Congress to provide for more than a mere 1,393 black families on FSA resettlement communities by 1940. Even this minimal effort, however, earned the FSA a reputation as a "disturber of the peace," and a top place on the southern conservative's "death list" of New Deal agencies.[14]

Whether the New Deal could have done more to aid black southerners economically is problematic; the shortcomings of what it did are obvious. It never spent the kind of truly massive sums for relief that might have provided a new deal for those on the bottom rungs of the economic ladder. And, except for the small minority of New Deal projects actually controlled by officials in Washington, like the contracts for PWA construction, it largely capitulated to local prejudice against blacks and allowed racial discrimination in the administration of relief. The great mass of black southerners remained in 1941, as they had been in 1933, victims of a brutally inequitable caste system. They continued to be mired in the ranks of menials, sharecroppers, unskilled laborers and domestics, twice as likely to be unemployed as southern whites and earning only half the income of them when they could find work.

Nevertheless, in no small part because of the economic assistance that Afro-Americans did receive, blacks supported the New Deal enthusiastically. They expressed their gratitude for New Deal efforts to relieve black distress in letters to the White House, in responses to interviewers, in lofty proclamations and in earthy blues music, in how they voted and struggled to vote. Black southerners who had never before received more than crumbs eagerly accepted half a loaf. Despite receiving less aid than they needed, the New Deal exceeded their expectations. Hence, for the vast majority of southern blacks, the continuity of discrimination seemed secondary to the significance of work–relief, access to better housing, a government-sponsored health clinic or infant care program, a federal program of part-time employment so youths could stay in school, a FSA loan to purchase a farm, new recreational or educational facilities in the neighborhood, a chance for vocational training or the opportunity to learn to read and write in WPA literacy classes.[15]

Black southerners responded to the New Deal record on race relations comparably, glorifying Roosevelt on the basis of what they believed could be and has been rather than damning him on a standard of what might be. They expected the leadership of civil rights groups to criticize the president's failings yet, overall, blacks judged FDR as far superior to past presidents on racial matters. They credited him for taking political risks for blacks and for defying white supremacists, however deficient his actual effort to insure racial justice. Southern blacks well understood the stiff resistance encountered by even racial moderation and gradualism. Their expectations did not yet demand a frontal assault on Jim Crow, and the New Deal's limited immediate consequences seemed of less import than the implied promise of change.[16]

In this spirit, blacks lauded the growing roster of Afro-Americans working for the government. The number of blacks on the federal payroll more than tripled during the depression decade, doubling the proportion of blacks in government jobs in the 1920s. Although most of the 150,000 black federal employees in 1941 worked in unskilled and semiskilled positions, New Dealers unprecedently hired blacks as economists and engineers, as lawyers and librarians, as scientists and office managers. Gunnar Myrdal termed this novel development "the first significant step toward the participation of Negroes in federal government activity." And to prepare the way for future steps, the Roosevelt Administration abolished the Civil Service regulations that had required job-seekers to designate their race and to attach a photograph to their application forms. Numerous New Deal officials, moreover, desegregated the cafeterias, restrooms, and secretarial pools in their agencies and departments, further signifying that black interests counted, that the Democratic constituency included blacks, and that the New Deal sought—in Ralph Bunche's words—"the full integration of the Negro into administrative government."[17]

The appointment of over a hundred blacks to administrative posts in the New Deal proved an even more visible reminder of a concern for Afro-American needs shown by no previous administration. Reversing two decades of diminishing black patronage, Roosevelt elicited howls from his white southern supporters that "Negroes were taking over the White House" by his selection of a far larger number than ever before of race relations advisers in formal government positions and his placement of them in positions of public importance so that both other government officials and blacks regarded their presence as significant. Popularly referred to as the Black Cabinet or Black Brain Trust, these black officials pushed for more equity in the relief and recovery programs and for greater concern by the Roosevelt Administration on all issues of civil rights. They rarely succeeded. They never possessed real power. But the very fact of such a large number of black government officials, Roy Wilkins of the NAACP emphasized, "had never existed before." Their presence and prominence symbolized a New Deal effort to break with prevailing customs of racial conservatism, as did Roosevelt's selection of William Hastie as the first Afro-American federal judge in American history. In political language, such appointments meant that blacks now mattered.[18]

So did the rhetoric and gestures of the Democratic party in election years. To garner black votes, Roosevelt orchestrated a series of precedent-shattering "firsts." Thirty black delegates attended the 1936 Democratic national convention. Never before had the Democrats accredited an Afro-American as a delegate. For the first time, moreover, the Democrats in 1936 invited black reporters into the regular press box, chose a black minister to offer the convention invocation, selected black politicians to deliver the welcoming address and one of the speeches seconding Roosevelt's renomination, and even placed a

Negro on the delegation to notify Vice-President John Nance Garner of Texas of his renomination. During the campaign, Roosevelt pointedly promised that in his administration there would be "no forgotten races" as well as no forgotten men. In 1940, the President publicly affirmed his administration's intention to include blacks fully and fairly in defense training and employment, promoted the first black to the army rank of brigadier general, and, for the first time, included a specific Negro plank in the party platform, pledging "to strive for complete legislative safeguards against discrimination in government service and benefits in the national defense forces." Such political tokens promised more than they delivered; but in the context of the times they had significant impact in their future implications and in whetting the appetites of blacks for truly decisive government action. One consequence was the very significant increase in the size of the black electorate in the north during the Roosevelt era, and the mobilization of a large number of black southern organizations to promote voter registration and to arouse an interest in political participation among the masses of apathetic or apolitical blacks.[19]

The civil rights activities of members of Roosevelt's official family also implied change, gave hope, and raised racial expectations and consciousness. However much the president often remained outside the racial fray, he generally allowed those around him to plunge in. No previous administration had ever had so many prominent officials regularly conferring with black leaders, addressing the conventions of civil rights organizations, and declaring publicly for racial justice and equality. The racial statements and actions of Will Alexander, Harold Ickes, and Aubrey Williams repeatedly gained the plaudits of the Negro press and civil rights groups, as did those of W. Frank Persons of the Labor Department, Hallie Flanagan of the Federal Theatre Project, John M. Carmody of the Rural Electrification Administration, and Nathan Straus of the United States Housing Authority. Their outspoken advocacy of black rights helped make that issue a part of the liberal agenda and gave unprecedented official recognition to the plight of blacks. No administration had ever before devoted as much public attention to black needs, or expressed its sympathies so openly.[20]

The president's appointments to the Supreme Court, moreover, immediately and vitally affected the progress of black southerners toward full citizenship. With the exception of James Byrnes, Roosevelt's eight appointees proved to be true partisans of the civil rights cause. They began the dismantling of a century of law discriminating against blacks in their decisions involving the exclusion of blacks from juries, the right to picket against discrimination in employment, racial restrictive covenants, segregation in interstate transportation, peonage, disfranchisement, and discrimination in payment of black teachers and in graduate education. Their federalizing of the Bill of Rights left blacks less at the mercy of states' rights. Their expansion of the concept of state action severely circumscribed the permissible boundaries of private discrimination. And their insistence on inquiring into the facts of "separate but equal," rather than just the theory, diminished the possibility of segregation meeting the test of constitutionality. Accordingly, when the Supreme Court struck down the white primary of 1944, the only dissenter was the single justice then sitting whom Roosevelt had not appointed.[21]

Certainly no individual did more to encourage the hopefulness of black southerners than Mrs. Franklin Delano Roosevelt. She played the role of unofficial ombudsman for blacks, influenced her husband and other New Dealers to pay greater heed to the concerns of blacks, and prominently championed the civil rights cause. Repeatedly breaking with tradition, Eleanor Roosevelt openly hosted black receptions at the White House, posed for pictures with blacks, and associated herself with the major Negro and interracial groups of the decade. She supported the campaigns for antilynching and antipoll-tax legislation, and regularly promoted racial justice in public addresses, in her syndicated newspaper column, and in many published articles. At the opening session of the Southern Conference for Human Welfare in Birmingham, Alabama, in 1938, Mrs. Roosevelt defied the local segregation ordinance by conspicuously taking a seat on the

"Colored" side of the auditorium. And when the Daughters of the American Revolution in 1939 would not permit its Constitution Hall to be used for a concert by a famous black contralto, Marian Anderson, Eleanor Roosevelt publicly decried the DAR's bigotry and resigned her membership, and then assisted the NAACP in arranging to hold the concert in front of the Lincoln Memorial. Throughout the Roosevelt era, the First Lady's actions stirred the wrath of the white South and emboldened southern blacks.[22]

While Franklin Roosevelt encouraged his wife to take certain public positions that he felt constrained to do, the president himself gradually assumed an egalitarian posture. With increasing frequency he invited blacks to the White House as guests and performers, appeared before black audiences, and conferred with civil rights leaders. He backed the movement to end all poll-tax requirements for voting, declaring that such taxes "are inevitably contrary to fundamental democracy and its representative form of government in which we believe." More cautiously, he condemned lynching and indicated his support for federal antilynching legislation. But he would never press for such a bill or try to thwart the filibusters by southern Democrats that kept the proposals from coming to a vote in the Senate. Most likely, nothing that FDR could have done would have secured antilynching legislation in the 1930s. The civil rights leadership understood this and acted accordingly. The president's pronouncements counted for more to them than his refusal to battle behind the scene. They recognized Roosevelt's need to mollify southern congressional leaders and the insurmountable barriers to cloture being voted. And they took heart from his establishment of a special Civil Rights Section of the Justice Department with power to investigate all lynchings that might involve some denial of a federal right.[23]

Perhaps most importantly, the reform spirit of the New Deal helped create a psychological climate in which black southerners and their allies could struggle with expectations of success. Real racial change began to seem a possibility. Often with presidential blessing, almost always with New Dealers playing a leading role, new reform movements in the South battled for racial justice. Southern liberals, nourished by Roosevelt and the New Deal, challenged the local power structures and forced the defenders of white supremacy on the defense. The "Silent South" grew vocal in its condemnation of racial discrimination and encouragement of black political consciousness. And black southerners responded with direct action campaigns against Jim Crow far greater in number than in any decade since Emancipation and which would not be surpassed until the 1960s. In boycotts and picket lines, marches and "sit-ins," southern blacks dramatically lobbied for civil rights legislation and protested against police brutality, cutbacks in relief appropriations, discrimination in employment and Jim Crow public facilities.[24]

"It is true that the millennium in race relations did not arrive under Roosevelt," the *Crisis* summed, "but cynics and scoffers to the contrary, the great body of Negro citizens made progress." Blacks did not expect miracles in the Great Depression. They dared to hope for progress not perfection; and the intermixture of symbolic and substantive assistance, of rhetoric and recognition, swelled further hope in the formerly disheartened. Despite the fact that little had changed for the better in the concrete aspects of life for most black southerners, a belief that "we are on our way" took root. A new faith emerged. Blacks associated the New Deal with it, and idolized Franklin D. Roosevelt for it. A quarter of a century after his death, southern blacks would still be naming their children after FDR, and hanging his picture on the wall, more than that of any other public figure, white or black. Given the heritage of racism that shaped the political circumstances of the 1930s, they credited the New Deal with establishing government precedents favorable to blacks, with helping to end the "invisibility" of the race problem and make civil rights a part of the national liberal agenda, with generating reform and, as never before in our nation's history, propounding the federal government's responsibility in race relations. These changes did little to ameliorate the continuity of racism staining the New Deal, but they would help transform the despair, the discouragement, the dreadful apathy of black southerners into a fighting conviction of a better world that could soon and surely be achieved.[25]

ENDNOTES

1. This essay is in part a revision of, and in part a restatement of, some of the themes treated at length in Harvard Sitkoff, *A New Deal For Blacks, The Emergence of Civil Rights as a National Issue, Volume 1: The Depression Decade* (New York, 1978). It has been greatly aided by a critique by Professor John B. Kirby, as well as by the ideas he expressed in his *Black Americans in the Roosevelt Era, Liberalism and Race* (Knoxville: University of Tennessee Press, 1980). My work is also much indebted to Professor Raymond Wolters for his extensively researched *Negroes and the Great Depression: The Problem of Economic Recovery* (Westport, Conn.: Greenwood Press, 1970), and incisive "The New Deal and the Negro," in John Braeman, *et al.*, eds., *The New Deal, The National Level* (Columbus, Ohio, 1975), 170–217.

2. Roosevelt is quoted in Walter White, *A Man Called White* (New York, 1948), 169–70. Also see Walter White to Charles Houston, March 9, 1935 and Edwin R. Embree to Walter White, April 16, 1935, NAACP Papers, Library of Congress, Washington, D.C.; Allan Morrison, "The Secret Papers of FDR," *Negro Digest*, 9 (January 1951), 9; Rayford Logan, "The Negro and the National Recovery Program," Sphiinx, March 1934, p. 10; Donald H. Grubbs, *Cry From the Cotton, The Southern Tenant Farmers' Union and the New Deal* (Chapel Hill: University of North Carolina Press, 1971), 107, 147–157; Lester C. Lamon, *Blacks in Tennessee, 1791–1970* (Knoxville: University of Tennessee Press, 1981), 91; and Anthony P. Dunbar, *Against the Grain, Southern Radicals and Prophets, 1929–1959* (Charlottesville: University Press of Virginia, 1981), 187.

3. Henry Lee Moon, "Racial Aspects of the Federal Public Relations Programs," *Phylon, 4* (First Quarter, 1943), 69; Eleanor Roosevelt, *This I Remember* (New York, 1949), 162; and Roy Wilkins, *Oral History Collection*, Butler Library, Columbia Library (hereafter cited "COHC"), 98–99. Also see Wolters, *Negroes and the Great Depression*, xi–xiii.

4. Wolters, *ibid.*, 110–112; Robert C. Weaver, "Federal Aid, Local Control, and Negro Participation, *Journal of Negro Education*, 11 (Jan. 1942), 47–59; Lamon, *Blacks in Tennessee*, 88–89; and Ralph J. Bunche, "The Political Status of the Negro" (unpublished manuscript prepared for the Carnegie-Myrdal Study, 1940, Schomburg Branch, New York Public Library), 1414–15. Also see John Dollard, *Caste and Class in a Southern Town* (New Haven: Yale University Press, 1937) and *Children of Bondage: The Personality Development of Negro Youth in the Urban South* (Washington, D.C.: American Council on Education, 1940).

5. John P. Davis, "Blue Eagles and Black Workers," *New Republic*, 91 (Nov. 14, 1934), 7–9; Negro Complaints Against Codes," *Christian Century*, LI (March 28, 1934), 434; Donald Richberg to Eleanor Roosevelt, Oct. 23, 1934, and Walter White to Franklin Roosevelt, May 21, 1935, NAACP papers; and *Journal and Guide* quote in Leslie H. Fishel, Jr., "The Negro in the New Deal Era," *Wisconsin Magazine of History*, 48 (Winter 1964), 114. Also see Michael S. Holmes, "The Blue Eagle as 'Jim Crow Bird': The NRA and Georgia's Black Workers," *Journal of Negro History*, 67 (July 1972), 276–83; and Allan A. Banks, Jr., "Wage Differentials and the Negro Under the NRA" (M.A. thesis, Howard University, 1938).

6. Thomas J. Woofter, "The Negro and the Agricultural Policy" (unpublished memorandum prepared for the Carnegie-Myrdal Study, 1940, Schomburg Branch, New York Public Library), 53–59; E. E. Lewis, "Black Cotton Farmers and the AAA," *Opportunity*, 13 (March 1935) 72–74; Harold Hoffsommer, "The AAA and the Sharecropper," *Social Forces*, 13 (May 1935), 494–502; and Roy Wilkins to Henry Wallace, March 8, 1935 and Walter White to Franklin Roosevelt, Feb. 16, 18, 1935, NAACP Papers. Also see David Eugene Conrad, *The Forgotten Farmers: The Story of Sharecroppers in the New Deal* (Urbana, Ill.: University of Illinois Press, 1965); and Arthur F. Raper, *Preface to Peasantry* (Chapel Hill: University of North Carolina Press, 1936).

7. Cranston Clayton, "The TVA and the Race Problem," *Opportunity*, 12 (April 1934), 111–12: Arthur E. Morgan to Eleanor Roosevelt, Oct. 19, 1934, Eleanor Roosevelt Papers, Franklin D. Roosevelt Library, Hyde Park, New York; J. Max Bond to Walter White, June 4, 1935, and Robert C. Weaver to Arthur E. Morgan, Nov. 12, 1935, NAACP Papers; Charles H. Houston and John P. Davis, "TVA: Lily-White Reconstruction" *Crisis*, 41 (Oct. 1934), 290–91; and John P. Davis, "The Plight of the Negro in the Tennessee Valley," *ibid.*, 42 (Oct. 1935), 294, 315. Also see R.G. Tugwell and E. C. Banfield, "Grass Roots Democracy—Myth or Reality?" *Public Administration Review*, 10 (1950), 47–55.

8. William Pickens, "NRA—'Negro Removal Act'?" *World Tomorrow*, 16 (Sept. 28, 1933), 539–40; Arthur Morgan, *The Making of the TVA* (Buffalo: Prometheus Books, 1974), 74–75; Will Alexander, COHC, 606–08; and Rexford G. Tugwell, *Roosevelt's Revolution: The First Year—A Personal Perspective* (New York: MacMillan, 1977), 218. Also see Jesse O. Thomas, "The Negro Looks at the Alphabet,"

Opportunity, 12 (Jan. 1934), 11–12; and John G. Van Deusen, "The Negro in Politics," *Journal of Negro History*, 21 (July 1936), 273–74.

9. Walter White to Franklin Roosevelt, July 30, 1935, NAACP Papers: John A. Salmond, "The Civilian Conservation Corps and the Negro," *Journal of American History*, 52 (June 1965), 75–88; and Luther C. Wandall, "A Negro in the CCC," *Crisis*, 42 (Sept. 1934), 254.

10. W. J. Trent, Jr., "Federal Sanctions Directed Against Racial Discrimination," *Phylon*, 3 (Second Quarter, 1942), 171–82; Lorena Hickock to Harry Hopkins, Jan. 14, 16, Feb. 8, 14, 18, April 13, 17, 1934 in Lorena Hickock Papers, Roosevelt Library; Gardner Jackson to Harry Hopkins, Sept. 12, 1936, Franklin Roosevelt Papers, OF 444-C, Roosevelt Library; Esther Morris Douty, "FERA and the Rural Negro," *Survey*, 70 (1934), 215–16; and Forrester B. Washington, "The Negro and Relief," *Proceedings of the National Conference of Social Work* (Washington, D.C., 1934), 188–90. Also see Richard Sterner, *The Negro's Share* (New York: Harper, 1943), 218–38.

11. Sterner, *ibid.*, 239–53; Ruth Durant, "Home Rule in the WPA," *Survey*, 75 (Sept. 1939), 274–75; and Donald S. Howard, *The WPA and Federal Relief Policy* (New York: Russell Sage, 1943), 285–90.

12. Harold Ickes to Walter White, March 1, July 11, 1933, NAACP Papers; Robert C. Weaver, "An Experiment in Negro Labor," *Opportunity*, 14 (Oct. 1936), 295–98; Marc W. Kruman, "Quotas for Blacks: The Public Works Administration and the Black Construction Worker," *Labor History*, 16 (Winter 1975), 37–49; Robert C. Weaver, "Racial Policy in Public Housing," *Phylon*, 1 (Second Quarter, 1940), 153–54; and Robert C. Weaver, "The Public Works Administration School Building—Aid Program and Separate Negro Schools," *Journal of Negro Education*, 7 (July 1938), 366–74.

13. Walter Daniel and Carroll Miller, "The Participation of the Negro in the National Youth Administration," *ibid.*, 361; Marian Thompson Wright, "Negro Youth and Federal Emergency Programs: CCC and NYA," *ibid.*, IX (July 1940), 402–05; and Allen F. Kifer, "The Negro Under the New Deal" (Ph.D. diss., University of Wisconsin, 1961), 82–83, 127–28.

14. Donald Holley, "The Negro in the New Deal Resettlement Program," *Agricultural History*, 45 (1971), 179–93; Paul E. Mertz, *New Deal Policy and Southern Rural Poverty* (Baton Rouge: Louisiana State University Press, 1978), 193–95; Sidney Baldwin, *Poverty and Politics: The Rise and Decline of the Farm Security Administration* (Chapel Hill: University of North Carolina Press, 1968), 193–97, 279; Grubbs, *Cry From the Cotton*, 158; and Dunbar, *Against the Grain*, 184.

15. James T. Patterson, *America's Struggle Against Poverty*, 1900–1980 (Cambridge, Mass.: Harvard University Press, 1981), 75–77; John L. Robinson, ed., *Living Hard: Southern Americans in the Great Depression* (Washington, D.C.: University Press of America, 1981), 103; Mary McLeod Bethune to Franklin Roosevelt, Oct. 17, 1939, Roosevelt Papers, OF 93, Roosevelt Library; Mary McLeod Bethune, "I'll Never Turn Back No More!" *Opportunity*, 26 (Nov. 1938), 324–26; W.E.B. Du Bois, "Race Relations in the United States, 1917–1947," *Phylon*, 9 (Third Quarter, 1948), 240–41; and Washington, "The Negro and Relief," 190. Also see Andrew Buni, *The Negro in Virginia Politics*, 1902–1965 (Charlottesville: University Press of Virginia), 1967), 113–14; and John Solomon Otto, "Hard Times Blues" (1929–1940): Downhome Blues Recordings as Oral Documents," *Oral History Review* (1980), 73–80.

16. Editorials in Baltimore *Afro-American*, April 7, 1934, April 27, 1935, and Norfolk *Journal and Guide*, Oct. 31, 1936; Bunche, "The Political Status of the Negro," 106, 418–19, 427–29; William Brink and Louis Harris, *The Negro Revolution in America* (New York: Simon and Schuster, 1964), 90; Rayford W. Logan, ed., *The Attitude of the Southern White Press Toward Negro Suffrage*, 1932–1940 (Washington, D.C.: The Foundation Publishers, 1940), 62–66; Howard W. Odum, *Race and Rumors of Race: Challenge to American Crisis* (Chapel Hill: University of North Carolina Press, 1943), 81; and Walter White to William Pickens, Nov. 9, 1932, and Walter White to Claude A. Barnett, Nov. 11, 1932, NAACP Papers.

17. Laurence J. W. Hayes, *The Negro Federal Government Worker: A Study of His Classification Status in the District of Columbia: 1883–1938* (Washington, D.C.: The Graduate School, Howard University, 1941), 73, 153; Gunnar Myrdal, *An American Dilemma: The Negro Problem and Modern Democracy* (New York: Harper, 1944), 503; Roy Wilkins, COHC, 68–69; Jane R. Motz, "The Black Cabinet: Negroes in the Administration of Franklin D. Roosevelt" (Master's Thesis, U. of Delaware, 1964), 34–36; and Bunche, "Political Status of the Negro," 1359–78, quote at 1361.

18. William Birnie, "Black Brain Trust," *American Magazine*, 135 (Jan. 1943), 36–37, 94–95; Will Alexander, COHC, 369; Motz, "The Black Cabinet," *op. cit.*; Wilkins, COHC, 68; *Opportunity*, 15 (March 1937), 69; and B. Joyce Ross, "Mary McLeod Bethune and the National Youth Administration: A Case Study of Power Relationships in the Black Cabinet of Franklin D. Roosevelt," *Journal of Negro History*, 60 (Jan. 1975), 28.

19. "Blacks on Blacks," *Time*, 27 (April 27, 1936), 10–11, and "Black Game," *ibid.*, XXVIII (Aug. 17, 1936), 10–11; Heywood Broun, "Roosevelt Comes Up Swinging," *Nation*, 143 (July 4, 1936), 9;

New York Times, Oct. 27, 1936; "The Democratic Convention," *Opportunity*, 14 (July 1936), 197; Pittsburgh *Courier*, July 13, 20, 27, 1940; Chicago *Defender*, Oct. 19, 26, Nov. 2, 1940; editorial, Norfolk *Journal and Guide*, Nov. 2, 1940; Myrdal, *An American Dilemma*, 488; Lee Collier, "The Solid South Cracks," *New Republic*, 92 (March 23, 1938), 185–86; Larry W. Dunn, "Knoxville Negro Voting and the Roosevelt Revolution, 1928–1936," *East Tennessee Historical Society's Publications*, 43 (1971), 87; Angus Campbell, et al., *The American Voter* (New York: Wiley, 1960), 153–54; Kristi Anderson, *The Creation of a Democratic Majority, 1928–1936* (Chicago: University of Chicago Press, 1979), xii; and Bunche, "Political Status of the Negro," 307–317, 325–326, 422–24, 444–46.

20. Frank Freidel, *F.D.R. and the South* (Baton Rouge: Louisiana State University Press, 1965), 97; editorial, Pittsburgh *Courier*, April 20, 1935; editorial, Chicago *Defender*, Oct. 13, 1934; column by David W. Howe, *ibid.*, Feb. 3, 1940; and Walter White to Rexford Tugwell, July 26, 1935, and William Hastie to Walter White, Jan. 4, 1939, NAACP Papers.

21. Will Alexander, COHC, 258; Bernard Nelson, "The Negro Before the Supreme Court," *Phylon*, 8 (First Quarter 1947), 34–38; Milton R. Knovitz, "A Nation Within a Nation—the Negro and the Supreme Court," *American Scholar*, 11 (Jan. 1941), 69–78; and Raymond Pace Alexander, "The Upgrading of the Negro's Status by Supreme Court Decisions," *Journal of Negro History*, 30 (April 1945), 137.

22. Roy Wilkins with Tom Mathews, *Standing Fast: The Autobiography of Roy Wilkins* (New York: Viking Press, 1982), 130–31; *Opportunity*, 12 (June 1934), 167, and XIV (Jan. 1936), 5; Joseph Lash, *Eleanor Roosevelt: A Friend's Memoir* (Garden City, N.Y.: Doubleday, 1964), 168–69; *Crisis*, 46 (Feb. 1939), 54, and (Sept. 1939), 265; Odum, *Race and Rumors of Race*, 81; and editorials in Baltimore *Afro-American*, April 7, 1934, April 27, 1935, May 23, 1936, Philadelphia *Independent*, Feb. 20, 1938, Pittsburgh *Courier*, Dec. 3, 1938, and Chicago *Defender*, March 4, 1939.

23. Eleanor Roosevelt, "Some of My Best Friends Are Negro," *Ebony*, 8 (Feb. 1953), 26; Joseph P. Lash, *Eleanor and Franklin* (New York: Signet Books, 1971), 671–77; Eli Ginzberg and Alfred S. Eichner, *The Troublesome Presence, American Democracy and the Negro* (Glencoe, Ill.: The Free Press of Glencoe, 1964), 293; Freidel, *F.D.R. and the South*, 98; *New York Times*, Sept. 10, 1938; W.E.B. Du Bois, "Roosevelt," *Crisis*, 41 (Jan. 1934), 20; Baltimore *Afro-American*, April 16, 1938; L.C. Dyer to Walter White, Jan. 28, 1935, "Memorandum on Interview of the Secretary of the N.A.A.C.P. with the President at the White House on January 2, 1936," and Walter White to William Hastie, April 15, 1938, NAACP Papers; Wolters, *Negroes and the Great Depression*, 302–52, 365–66; Roy Wilkins, COHC, 70–71, 75–76; Walter White to Eleanor Roosevelt, Dec. 23, 1938, Eleanor Roosevelt Papers; and Henry A. Schweinhaut, "The Civil Liberties Section of the Department of Justice," *Bill of Rights Review*, 1 (1940–41), 206–07.

24. Editorial in Philadelphia *Tribune*, Oct. 27, 1938; Mary McLeod Bethune, "I'll Never Turn Back No More!" *Opportunity*, 16 (Nov. 1938), 324–26; William Hastie to Franklin Roosevelt, Feb. 11, 1939, NAACP Papers; Dewey W. Grantham, *The Democratic South* (Athens: University of Georgia Press, 1963), 74, 96; Morton Sosna, *In Search of the Silent South, Southern Liberals and the Race Issue* (New York: Columbia University Press, 1977), chs. 4–5; and August Meier and Elliot Rudwick, "The Origins of Nonviolent Direct Action in Afro-American Protest: A Note on Historical Discontinuities," in their *Along the Color Line, Explorations in the Black Experience* (Urbana, Ill.: University of Illinois Press, 1976), esp. 314–344. Also see Clark Foreman, "The Decade of Hope." *Phylon*, 12 (Second Quarter, 1951), 137–50; H.C. Nixon, "The New Deal and the South," *Virginia Quarterly Review*, 19 (Summer 1943), 321–33; and Charles S. Johnson, "More Southerners Discover the South," *Crisis*, 41 (Jan. 1939), 14–15.

25. "Franklin D. Roosevelt," *ibid.*, LII (May 1945), 129; Adam Clayton Powell, Jr., *Marching Blacks* (New York, 1945), 116–18; editorial in Norfolk *Journal and Guide*, April 21, 1945; Myrdal, *An American Dilemma*, 74, 1022; Rackham Holt, *Mary McLeod Bethune* (Garden City: Doubleday, 1964), 182; Walter White to Daisy Lampkin, June 23, 1938, NAACP Papers; and Lerone Bennett, Jr., *Confrontation: Black and White* (New York: Johnson Publishing Co., 1965), 142. Also see "Conclusion" in Richard Wright, *12 Million Black Voices* (New York, 1941); E. Franklin Frazier, "Sociological Theory and Race Relations," *American Sociological Review*, 12 (June 1947), 265–71; Charles S. Johnson, *et al.*, *Into the Mainstream, A Survey of Best Practices in Race Relations in the South* (Chapel Hill: University of North Carolina Press, 1947) *passim*; and Lyonel Florant, "Youth Exhibits a New Spirit," *Crisis*, 43 (Aug. 1936), 237–38, 253–54.

UNIT 3-2

A. PHILIP RANDOLPH: LABOR LEADER AT LARGE

Benjamin Quarles

In addition to the nationalist critique of the legal struggle for constitutional rights that was advocated by most northern race spokesmen during and after World War I, a radical Socialist critique also appeared. The most important representative of this school of thought was the militant black orator and editor, A. Philip Randolph, who saw the solution to the race's problems in an alliance with the white working class. His magazine, the Messenger, *not only demonstrated Randolph's radicalism, but beginning in the mid-1920s, it became the organ through which Randolph promoted his work in forming and winning recognition for the Brotherhood of Sleeping Car Porters. From his base in this union Randolph moved into larger arenas, attacking discrimination in white dominated trade unions. At critical junctures he emerged as a magnetic, electrifying leader of national importance who temporarily welded the diverse protest organizations into grand coalitions that battled successfully for greater federal action against economic and other forms of discrimination.*

At the time of his death in 1979, at the age of ninety, A. Philip Randolph had a reputation as the first national labor leader to emerge among black Americans and as a figure of major force in the mid-twentieth century civil rights movement. Randolph had become a dominant figure in black circles in 1937, when the Pullman Company grudgingly gave official recognition to the union that he organized and led, the Brotherhood of Sleeping Car Porters. Randolph's leadership image had been foreshadowed the preceding year, when he had prodded the American Federation of Labor (AFL) to grant an international charter to the Brotherhood, thereby making it equal to the other unions in the federation. From this double-barreled labor base Randolph had not only pressed insistently for further racial reforms in labor and industry but had joined in the battle against color discrimination on a broad-based front, whether in the armed services and the public schools or in government and politics.

Randolph's leadership was characterized by its receptive attitude toward new strategies in combating racial discrimination. In black circles he was a pioneer in the use of mass protest, a trail-blazing technique that he brought into play in the summer of 1941 on the eve of America's entry into World War II. Deeply concerned because black workers were denied an equal share in the newly created jobs in the production of defense and military equipment and supplies, Randolph called for a "March on Washington." Not caring to run the risk of a mass of protesters converging on the nation's capital, President Franklin D. Roosevelt issued an executive order establishing a committee to ensure fair employment practices. A breakthrough in enlisting the support of the federal government in striking at job discrimination, Roosevelt's decree was "the most significant executive action in the field of race relations since President Lincoln issued the Emancipation Proclamation."

Randolph's role as a black leader resulted from the pattern of race relations that prevailed during his formative years and, in equal measure, from his own qualities of mind and spirit. Born in 1889 in Crescent City, Florida, his father a struggling African Methodist minister, his mother a hard-working helpmate, Asa Philip Randolph grew up in a family marked by its respect for learning. Working at a variety of unskilled or semi-skilled jobs during his teens, Randolph was graduated from the high school at Cookman Institute in Jacksonville.

In 1911, at age twenty-two, he left Florida, coming to New York City, his first and last migration. Taking odd jobs during the day, he attended City College during the evenings, his wide-ranging choice of courses embracing political science, philosophy, economics, and history. During the summer of 1914, Randolph married beautician Lucille Campbell Green, a most compatible union that lasted until her death in 1963.

The wedding of the Randolphs took place a few months after the outbreak of World War I, a development that brought a flood of southern blacks to northern cities like New York. Totaling nearly one-third of a million blacks during the decade 1910 to 1920, these migrations tended to raise the aspirations of urban northern blacks, old inhabitants as well as newcomers, leading them to press for equal rights in general and better job opportunities in particular. It was in the wake of this "northern fever" that swept the South that Randolph would seek his way, in the social and economic ferment of the war years and their aftermath that he would launch his career.

It was inevitable that Randolph would view the black working class as offering the greatest potential for an aspiring leader. Neither of the two existing major black betterment organizations, the National Association for the Advancement of Colored People nor the Urban League, had worked directly with laborers, nor had the black leadership in these organizations come from the working class. Considering the marked influx of blacks in the industrial labor market during World War I, there was much to be done in stimulating a labor consciousness among them, particularly in promoting labor unionism. To Randolph the trade union movement was the major remedy for the ills that beset blacks. In the labor movement lay the power to challenge the oppressors of the people.

Young Randolph's formulations of programs and strategies for blacks was typical of the analytical approach that would characterize his career. Unlike some black leaders, Randolph was not antitheoretical. A wide reader with a meditative turn of mind, he was at home in the world of ideas. Reflecting this somewhat scholarly temperament, his speeches and writings bore a steady note of high seriousness with few light or humorous touches. His rich vocabulary sometimes took on scriptural accents; a word like "verily" would not come unnaturally to one who had been a Bible reader since boyhood.

Randolph's readiness in diagnosis was matched by an equal penchant for prescription. To him theory and application were inseparable; vision must be linked to reality. As he pointed out in 1926, a reformer must go further than calling attention to social evils-he must also "indicate the cause and prescribe a remedy." A born organizer, Randolph would perpetually be trying to form unions of working people and coalitions of reformers to carry out the strategies he had conceived and publicized.

To the tasks he set for himself Randolph brought an array of leadership qualities. To begin with, he was never daunted by the thought of failure, never dismayed by the enormity of the odds against him. His struggle against the Pullman Company pitted him, as a contemporary put it, against "Pullman's millions of dollars when half the time he didn't have a dime in his pocket." According to George S. Schuyler, a staff worker on a monthly edited by Randolph in the 1920s, his employer was a man of unshakable aplomb "whether the rent was due and he did not have it, whether an unexpected donation failed to materialize, or whether the long-suffering printer in Brooklyn was demanding money." Of a silver-lining temperament, Randolph maintained an air of confidence however adverse the circumstances.

Another facet of Randolph's leadership was his integrity, a trait that endowed him with an air of moral authority. He could not be bought or bribed, easy money having no allure for him. His private life was likewise unassailable; a private, nonbusiness letter coming to his office from a woman trying to make his acquaintance would be routinely filed away and forgotten. Scandal-lovers and gossip columnists knew better than to waste their time on him.

Randolph's leadership qualities owed something to his bearing and manner, even though he conveyed more of an air of aloofness than any other twentieth-century black leader, including W.E.B. Du Bois. Never folksy or "down home," Randolph kept his distance. In a tête-à-tête he tended to speak as if addressing a public meeting. A visitor to his office would find, as in the case of Edwin R. Embree, president of the Julius Rosenwald Fund, that although Randolph kept his eyes on his caller's face, they "seem focussed on far-distant places."

Randolph's formality, however, was mitigated by his innate graciousness and by a courtesy bordering on politeness. After forty years as his close friend and associate, Bayard Rustin said that he had never "once seen Mr. Randolph treat any human being with anything less than complete dignity and respect." Hence if Randolph seemed preoccupied, even remote, in his contacts with others, he certainly did not give them the impression that he looked down on them.

Randolph's leadership, however, did not rest in person-to-person negotiations behind closed doors. His strength rested more in addressing himself to the public. Bent on becoming a leader, he had schooled himself in the forms of public address. His deep bass voice had been trained by his courses in oratory at the College of the City of New York, by his study with a private tutor, and by his membership in "Ye Friends of Shakespeare," an amateur group of thespians-when he first came to New York he had thought of becoming a stage actor. During these early years of leadership preparation Randolph acquired the so-called "Harvard accent," which his followers regarded not as an affection but as another manifestation of his inherent dignity. And finally as to his image as a public figure, Randolph made an appeal to the eye as well as to the ear. His good looks and well-built physique were put to their best advantage by a carefully selected wardrobe.

Endowed with a combination of leadership qualities and confident he could acquire those he initially lacked, Randolph was ready by 1915 to take his first steps toward the making of a career that, he hoped, would give new meanings to the whole concept of black leadership in action. As it turned out, he did not underestimate himself. His impressive record as a mover and shaker for half a century might be illustrated by reviewing his activities as a Socialist, a labor organizer, a proponent of mass action along a united front, a disciple of nonviolent protest, a shaper of black thought, and, however paradoxical it might appear, a consciously black leader whose outlook was not circumscribed by the color line.

Accepting an award at Carnegie Hall in 1944 from the Workers' Defense League, a Socialist-oriented group that raised money for the legal defense of union workers, Randolph said that one of the fundamental forces that shaped his life was his study and reading in Socialist philosophy and literature and his participation in the Socialist movement. To this movement, he added, he owed his understanding of social forces, his awareness of the mission of the working class, and his world perspective.

Randolph's introduction to the tenets of Socialism came from his courses at City College in 1912 and 1914 and from his contacts with campus activist groups. By 1917 when the United States entered World War I, Randolph had become a Socialist, and his attitude toward this conflict and America's participation in it reflected the standard Socialist theory that wars were brought about by the machinations of contending groups of capitalists and hence were of little concern to the workers of the world. After the United States entered the war, Randolph advised blacks to resist the draft and confine their fighting to the home front.

Fortunately for Randolph, his views about the war and on other issues could be expressed not only in personal appearances on tours to northern cities but also through the pages of the *Messenger*, a monthly magazine he edited in partnership with Chandler Owen, another black Socialist. The duo worked well together, although Randolph was much the more influential of the two, his the more dominant voice. Moreover, Owen's participation would come to an end in 1923, when he left amicably to begin a new career in Chicago.

The *Messenger* drew much of its financial support from the predominantly white Socialist-oriented needle trades and clothing unions, and it, in turn, favorably reported their activities and carried their advertisements. Asserting that blacks had been lulled into a false sense of security by the Booker T. Washington type of leader and by the gradualist approaches of the National Association for the Advancement of Colored People and the National Urban League, the *Messenger* called for a bold, black Socialist leadership. Proudly announcing the magazine's radical orientation, its editors defined radicals as those who had the courage of their convictions, who sought "to get at the root of our social problems," in essence, seekers after truth.

Radicalism as interpreted by Randolph and Owen embraced the use of the strongest language and the open advocacy of the most controversial of causes. The *Messenger* did not hesitate to denounce those in the highest places, President Woodrow Wilson among them. In an article summarizing his two terms in the White House up to September 1919 the *Messenger* stated that "the chief beneficiaries of his public career are the combined manufacturers and capitalists and himself." Others, such as liberals, radicals, and Negroes, "would willingly witness the setting of his sun in public without grief. Unhonored, he will go down to the narrow, bigoted grave of private life from whence he sprang."

The *Messenger's* boldness reached its peak in its support of the new regime in Russia. Coming at a time when the country was in the grip of a "red scare," the *Messenger's* support of a government run by Communists inevitably drew fire. In a speech in the House of Representatives on August 15, 1919, James F. Byrnes charged that Randolph and Owen were "Bolsheviks." In a lengthy "Reply to Congressman James F. Byrnes of South Carolina," the accused editors stated that "they would be glad to see a Bolshevik government substituted in the South in place of your Bourbon, reactionary, vote-stolen, misrepresentative Democratic regime." Not to be silenced in the matter, the *Messenger's* December 1919 issue, a so-called "Thanksgiving" issue, reported that among the things for which it was thankful was "the Russian Revolution, the greatest achievement of the twentieth century."

The pro-revolutionary stance of the magazine had not escaped the attention of the Department of Justice, Randolph and Owen falling under its surveillance. While addressing a mass meeting in Cleveland on August 4, 1919, the two black Socialists were arrested by an agent of the Department of Justice and spent two days in jail. Three months later the department submitted to the Senate Judiciary Committee a lengthy report dealing with radicalism in general and with due attention to its incidence among blacks. J. Edgar Hoover drafted this report, which characterized the *Messenger* as "the exponent of open defiance and sedition" and as "by long odds the most able and most dangerous of all the Negro publications." Almost half of the section of the report that concentrated on blacks was devoted to a reprinting of articles, editorials, and poems that had appeared in the *Messenger*. Additional censure and condemnation were visited upon the magazine by the New York state legislature through its Joint Committee Investigating Seditious Activities.

Although hailing the violent overthrow of the czarist regime in Russia, Randolph and Owen had in mind a more orderly Socialist revolution for the United States. Their method was to unionize the workers and then get them to support the Socialist party. To this end Randolph and Owen formed a short-lived union of blacks who worked in hotels and apartments, the United Brotherhood of Elevator and Switchboard Operators. For a few months in 1917 the duo edited a trade journal published by the Headwaiters and Sidewaiters Society of New York, a monthly that went out of existence a few weeks before the birth of the *Messenger*. In 1919 Randolph and Owen served on the board of directors of the National Brotherhood Workers of America, an umbrella organization that tried to establish a national federation of labor but without success.

Undaunted by this succession of initial failures, Randolph and Owen in 1920 launched the Friends of Negro Freedom, an interracial but black-controlled organization whose overly ambitious program included the organizing of black laborers on an international scale. Almost simultaneously, however, the Randolph-Owen duo diluted the strength of the Friends by creating an overlapping organization, the National Association for the Promotion of Labor Unionism among Negroes. In 1923, after these two groups had become moribund, Randolph and Owen announced the formation of a United Negro Trades. Its objectives—to unionize and upgrade the black workers—were similar to those of its predecessors, and so was its fate.

Supplementing their efforts to unionize blacks, Randolph and Chandler, particularly the former, were active in Socialist party activities. Noting the Republican party's hold on Negroes, the *Messenger* asserted that inasmuch as blacks were workers they had nothing in common with a party dominated by capitalists and employers. "The Negro was a Republican and had been a Republican for fifty years because his father was a Republican and Abraham Lincoln was a Republican. But awake, old black brother Republican." As far as Negroes were concerned there was, said Randolph, no difference between the Republicans and the Democrats because "whichever wins, the people lose."

In 1917 Randolph and Chandler campaigned for the Socialist party candidate for mayor of New York, Morris Hillquit. In 1920, having served his apprenticeship, Randolph was nominated by the Socialists as their candidate for the state comptroller of New York, and two years later the party nominated him for the office of secretary of state of New York. (He would never run for public office again, graciously declining "because of union duties"—an invitation in 1944 to become the Socialist party candidate for vice-president of the United States.)

For all his dedication to the Socialist cause Randolph could hardly have been surprised that he was able to make few converts among his fellow blacks. He may not have given sufficient weight to the class lines within the black community, but he was well aware of the strength of the Republican party therein. He knew, too, that most blacks and their leaders saw little point in voting for Socialist and other third-party candidates not likely to be elected.

In seeking to win blacks to Socialism, however, Randolph tended to give insufficient consideration to certain race-related conditions. Holding that the black people needed allies, Randolph advocated working class solidarity across the line. Randolph himself worked smoothly with white Socialists, never seeking to establish a black wing of the group.

Interracial cooperation and harmony among Socialists, however, were not as simple as they might sound. Most white Socialists regarded race and color as incidental to the larger problem of race conflict. They did not sense that the black American was the victim not only of class oppression but also of race oppression. Hence, they did not think of the Negro question as one that required special approaches and remedies. It did not escape the notice of blacks that some white Socialists were prejudiced against them, and that in deference to its southern wing the party tended to gloss over the disfranchisement and lynching of Negroes in southern states. Hence, although the Socialists began a campaign to woo blacks during the years that Randolph was an active party member, the obstacles against them were formidable, the fruits were few.

Despite the Socialist party's lack of success in recruiting blacks, Randolph found much to be pleased with as a result of their work. The Socialists had, he claimed, succeeded in forcing black organizations to examine anew their programs and their leadership and in forcing the two major political parties to become more liberal in matters of race and color. The *Messenger* had broken new ground in organizing "the Radical Movement among Negroes in America" and in presenting "the Negro workers' question to the European workers, radicals and liberals." In an article published in *Opportunity* in January 1926 touching on Negro Radicals, Randolph credited them with having shaped "a working class economic perspective in Negro thought." If any of his readers were ignorant of Randolph's own role in shaping this perspective, they certainly must have surmised it.

But by the time he wrote this article Randolph himself had become much less doctrinaire, having learned that blacks, even among the working masses, would not easily be converted to Socialism. By the mid-1920s the *Messenger* had dropped its tone of ridicule as to black business and the black bourgeoisie and had begun to pay more attention to predominantly black issues and programs. During this period Randolph began to channel his energies into the practical and time consuming work of trade-union organizing, with fewer precious moments to spare in holding forth on Socialist theory and reformist doctrine.

The event that signaled Randolph's newer orientation and gave a whole new thrust was a mass meeting held in the Elks auditorium in Harlem on August 25, 1925, at which time Randolph accepted an offer to become the "general organizer" of the Brotherhood of Sleeping Car Porters. A newly formed organization, the Brotherhood sought to induce other porters to join them and to induce the Pullman Company to recognize it as the bargaining agent for the porters.

If the Brotherhood viewed the appointment of Randolph as advantageous, so did he. Its leaders had selected him because he had made a reputation as a forceful and well-informed public speaker; because he was not inexperienced as a labor organizer (although admittedly with little success thus far); and because he was not a porter and thus he was not subject to reprisals by the Pullman Company. Randolph, moreover, was editor of the *Messenger*, which, as he pointed out, "could be used to spread the propaganda of the organization," and which indeed became the Brotherhood's official organ, exchanging its more revolutionary accents for the less exciting tones of a trade journal.

Randolph, in turn, was pleased with the appointment, viewing it as an opportunity to test himself as a leader. Having schooled himself well in the theory of labor reform, he was now ready to tackle a job that would require more than a skill in dialectics. He must now face a more practical challenge, demonstrating the ability to cope with a formidable array of concrete problems, including the task of working cooperatively with a variety of other leaders and organizations. And nobody was more aware than he that blacks who attempted to form labor unions encountered peculiar difficulties, their color and marginal status making reprisals easier, not to mention their inequality before the law and their relative lack of personal security.

The most obvious and immediate problem confronting the new union and its general organizer was the economic plight of the Pullman porters. Their wages were low, making it necessary for them to depend upon tips, and out of their earnings they had to pay for their uniforms for the first ten years of service, for shoe polish, and for meals during runs. Porters averaged 400 hours a month on the job as contrasted with 240 hours for other train-service employees. Porters also wanted pay for preparatory time—the time from which a porter reported for work rather than from the time the train pulled out of the station.

The Pullman Company's attitude toward the new union was predictably hostile. In 1920, in order to forestall an earlier effort at union organization by the porters and maids, Pullman had formed a company union, the Employees Representation Plan. To combat the Brotherhood the Pullman Company hired detectives to identify porters who were union members, and it threatened to replace Negro porters with Asians, particularly Filipinos. In its opposition to the union the company sought to enlist the support of blacks in all walks of life.

Such anti-Brotherhood blacks were not hard to find. Reflecting their middle-class orientation, most black professionals and intellectuals were cool toward organized labor. Some Pullman porters, too, according to Sterling D. Spero and Abraham Harris, contemporary authorities on black labor, "had all of the familiar middle-class prejudices of the white-collar worker and the upper servant," thus tending to identify with the rich and influential passengers who rode their cars.

With some notable exceptions, a majority of the black newspapers were against the Brotherhood. At its meeting in Atlanta in 1924 the National Negro Press Association went on record as "condemning all forms of Unionism and economic radicalism." Perry Howard, Republican national committeeman from Mississippi, charged that the Brotherhood was Communist-supported, but his criticism lost some of its force when it became known that he was a paid consultant to the Pullman Company. Opposition also came from the black clergy, particularly from those black congregations that depended upon white financial support. Reflecting their religious traditionalism, the more evangelical denominations were either anti-union or indifferent ("the greater the religiosity, the less the militancy," writes Preston Valien).

Randolph was quick to strike back at the Brotherhood's black critics. In January 1926 he charged two Chicago weeklies, the *Whip* and the *Defender*, with having surrendered to "gold and power." A month later, in a more sweeping indictment, he accused "hypocritical and corrupt Negro leaders" with having been "bought and paid with Pullman money. Like the dog before the gramophone, they are listening to their master's voice, the Pullman Company."

Not able to count on the black church, Randolph sought assistance in other black quarters, soon enlisting the support of the NAACP and the Urban League. In early 1926 James Weldon Johnson, executive secretary of the NAACP, wrote public letters endorsing the Brotherhood, and in its April 1926 issue the *Crisis*, organ of the NAACP, carried an editorial by Du Bois condemning the Pullman Company for its machinations in trying "to block the belated effort of the Pullman porters to form a real and effective labor union." Randolph successfully wooed the influential black fraternal organization, the Improved and Benevolent Order of Elks of the World, winning its endorsement in 1928, not an inconsiderable feat inasmuch as the fraternity at its convention in 1925 had unanimously condemned organized labor. To no one's surprise, at its first national convention in 1929 in Chicago, the Brotherhood elected Randolph as president.

Whether coming in contact with him through the Brotherhood releases or from listening to him in public address, the porters were favorably impressed by their leader, viewing him as one who was wholeheartedly and single-mindedly devoted to their welfare. Warming to their high appraisal, Randolph exerted his spell, stirring them with words of hope and exhortation interspersed with snatches of fatherly advice. "A new Pullman porter is born," he informed them in the April 1926 issue of the *Messenger*. "He has caught a new vision. His creed is independence without insolence; courtesy without fawning; service without servility."

Randolph urged the porters to do their best on the job despite their multiple grievances. "The Brotherhood will not injure the Pullman Company," he wrote. "It does not counsel insubordination, but efficient discipline." Sounding like a latter-day Washington, Randolph preached the gospel of work and habits of industry. (In 1940, in the *Black Worker*, a Brotherhood periodical, Randolph would present to the porters a list of ten "Don'ts," beginning with "Don't drink on the job," and ending with "Don't annoy women.")

Viewing Randolph in terms of his external relationships to them and in the light of the public image he cast, the Brotherhood rank and file could hardly be aware of any leadership flaws with which his closer associates, the second echelon administrators, had to cope. On them fell the real task of organizing and operating the Brotherhood, Randolph showing little interest in administrative work or grasp of its content and perhaps not fully sensing its importance. At home in reading a treatise on theoretical economics on a global scale, Randolph found less satisfaction in scanning a Brotherhood balance sheet placed on his desk.

Fortunately for Randolph, throughout his long leadership of the Brotherhood he was able to develop a cordial relationship with one or another able subordinate who was willing to assume the major responsibilities for administrative operations. In the early years this role was admirably filled by Milton P. Webster, a former Pullman porter himself, who had come from Chicago, where he had been influential in black political and labor circles. Holding the rank of first vice president of the Brotherhood, Webster was second only to Randolph in command. No "yes-man," Webster never hesitated to differ with "the Chief," vigorously defending his viewpoints but winning or losing with equal grace. Early in their relationships the two leaders had learned to respect and trust each other.

During the early years of the Brotherhood Randolph was equally successful in winning the strong personal loyalty of a countrywide network of dedicated lieutenants, whether in Oakland, Detroit, Pittsburgh, or St. Louis. Their dual devotion to Randolph and the Brotherhood was one of the major causes of the union's ultimate success.

After a twelve-year fight the persistence of Randolph and the patience of his followers was rewarded. The Railway Labor Act of 1934 outlawed company unions and granted railroad employees the right to organize without interference by the employer. Such legislative sanction of collective bargaining, a long-sought Randolph goal, was a significant victory for organized labor as a whole. The following year the Brotherhood, in an election contest with a union loyal to the Pullman Company (the Pullman Porters and Maids Protective Association), decisively won the right to represent the porters in collective bargaining. The Pullman Company held out for two more years, finally capitulating in August 1937 when it recognized the Brotherhood as the bargaining agent for the porters and maids, negotiating a contract covering wages, hours, and working rules.

The Randolph-led union had won an important victory. In a letter to Du Bois two years earlier (May 24, 1935) Randolph asserted that "when the Brotherhood wins this fight, it will probably be the most significant economic victory and stride of substantial and constructive progress the Negro has made in history." Randolph's evaluation was not without substance, if we grant that leaders as a class are entitled to a touch of hyperbole.

For indeed, the victory over the Pullman Company was a demonstration of the ability of blacks to organize and run a union despite a "sea of troubles." It made blacks more union-aware, decreasing their anti-labor sentiment; it provided an organized group whose resources and leadership could be enlisted for service in other black causes, and it marked the beginning of black influence on national labor policy and in national labor circles.

The capitulation of the Pullman Company came at a propitious juncture in Randolph's fortunes, coming just when AFL, growing weary of his continuous strictures, had considered ejecting the Brotherhood from the federation. In 1929 the Brotherhood had joined the AFL, although it had not received the kind of charter it sought. Randolph and his followers wanted an international charter that would make the Brotherhood equal with the other member unions, thereby wielding more influence in national labor circles and enabling it to operate independently in negotiating its own working conditions. Instead of receiving such autonomy the Brotherhood was placed under the direct jurisdiction of the president of the AFL, William Green, and its Executive Council. Randolph accepted this more limited "federal" charter because he deemed such a step as a temporary expedient, "establishing a beach-head," as he phrased it.

Randolph proceeded to use the annual conventions of the AFL as a forum, pressing for an international charter for the Brotherhood and sharply condemning the racial practices and policies of the member unions. He called for the elimination of the color clauses in their constitutions and the color pledges in their rituals, demanding the expulsion of "any union maintaining the color bar." In light of the deeply rooted patterns of racial exclusion and job discrimination so typical of its craft-union membership, the AFL could hardly deny Randolph's charges. At the annual meetings, however, Randolph's resolutions were generally referred to a committee which either pigeonholed them, recommended nonconcurrence, counseled patience, or expressed hopes for a more friendly spirit in the house of labor.

In 1936, however, upon the heels of the Brotherhood's decisive victory over the union sponsored by the Pullman Company, the AFL decided to grant Randolph's application for an international charter. The first predominantly black union to receive such a charter, the Brotherhood now became an autonomous unit, equal to other international units.

The organized labor movement would continue to discriminate against Negroes, and for more than one-third of a century Randolph would be a leader in the fight against such practices. But this recalcitrance on the part of white labor did not diminish the importance of the Brotherhood's feat in obtaining an international charter. However slow the organized labor movement might be in erasing the color line, its membership from top to bottom now became much more conscious of the Negro workers, their problems and possibilities.

Strengthened by its international union status and by its victory over the Pullman Company, the Brotherhood had become a dominant force in Negro circles by the late 1930s. Its cohesiveness and power enabled it to exert a major influence both in coming to the aid of other black unions and in assisting other black betterment movements and efforts. And, as a concomitant factor, Randolph himself now became a figure of consequence in black life. Girded by the power and prestige of the Brotherhood, and by the accolades his leadership of the Brotherhood had brought him, he bore a new confidence and authority as he moved onto a wider stage.

Grounded in theory, Randolph knew something of black leadership as a type. In black life so little power was available that the competitive struggle for its exercise was bound to be intense, often ruthless. Randolph knew, too, that there was a multiplicity of black leaders and organizations, varying in strategy and tactics, and that no one of them spoke for all blacks. But if there were no universal leader, Randolph, by the late 1930s, was prepared to speak to and for an ever widening constituency, having already indicated his own broad social concerns and having already demonstrated his ability to work with other black leaders and other black protest and improvement organizations. In black leadership he aspired to exemplify the principle of collective action.

However inclusive his leadership outreach, Randolph spurned the overtures of one group, the Communists. Randolph had hailed the Russian revolution of World War I years, but when the American Socialists divided into right and left shortly after the war Randolph remained with the former. Hence, when the American Communist party was organized in 1921, he did not become a member.

To Randolph, the Communists imperiled all efforts toward joint action and interorganizational unity. From the year of its founding in 1925 Randolph denounced the American Negro Labor Congress, charging in September of that year that it was "not representative of the American Negro worker because its seat of control is Moscow." During the long struggle between the Pullman porters and the Pullman Company Randolph reiterated the point that the Brotherhood of Sleeping Car Porters was "not backed by Moscow, nor has it any Communistic connections." In a letter written in June 1928 he referred to the Communists as a "sinister and destructive crowd."

Randolph's highly critical appraisal of the Communists was heightened in the late 1930s as a result of his experience as president of the National Negro Congress. Organized in 1930, this was an umbrella-like combination of about twenty organizations, white and black, whose goal was racial advancement in general with emphasis on the problems of the black worker. To Randolph this seemed to be the kind of a "united front of all Negro organizations," which had become the dominant goal in his life. In his presidential address of 1936 (read in his absence) he opened by invoking "the spirit of Frederick Douglass and Nat Turner, of Gabriel and Denmark Vesey, of Harriet Tubman and Sojourner Truth—those noble rebels who struck out in the dark days of slavery that Negro men and women might be free." Randolph closed this initial presidential address by reminding the delegates that the ambitious program envisioned by the Congress would require the cooperation of various Negro organizations—"church, fraternal, civil, trade-union, farmer, professional, college and what not—into a framework of a united front, together with white groups of workers, lovers of liberty and those whose liberties are similarly menaced."

During its first four years, nearly half of its brief existence, the National Negro Congress did much to improve the lot of blacks, locally and nationally. But its significant accomplishments were obscured by the rising role and influence of the Communists within the organization. They had stayed in the background at first, but within two years it had become obvious that theirs was the dominant voice, theirs the source of funding. During these first years Randolph took little time in the operation of the Congress, his energies devoted to the Brotherhood's culminating struggles with the Pullman Company on one hand and the AFL on the other. Moreover, as in his leadership of the porters, Randolph showed little interest in administrative work. In the Brotherhood this shortcoming had been covered up by able and loyal subordinates, but in the Congress it emerged for all to see, thus diminishing his effectiveness.

The Congress did not convene in 1938 and 1939, and hence it was not until 1940 that the issue of Communist control reached its denouement. At that meeting Randolph resigned, charging the Congress was Communist-dominated. "I quit the Congress because it was not truly a Negro Congress," he wrote in an article in the *Black Worker*, "Why I Would Not Stand for Re-election for President of the National Negro Congress." During his speech of resignation the Communists staged a demonstration, followed by a walk-out.

The Communist party would not enroll many blacks. Not ideology oriented, Negro Americans sought to improve the capitalist system rather than to liquidate it. Nonetheless the Communists had some success, in America and abroad, in dramatizing the grievances of black Americans, particularly of the black workers. Moreover, Randolph's own exposure to Marxist theory and practice had contributed to the tone and militance of his vocabulary and to his convictions as to the use of mass direct action techniques. But whatever their contribution to black advancement or to his own outlook or approaches, the Communists could only count Randolph as one of their most bitter black critics. In 1944 in proposing a "non-partisan political bloc," he called for their exclusion, asserting that "the Communist Party seeks only to rule or ruin a movement." In 1946, at the twenty-first anniversary celebration of the Brotherhood of Sleeping Car Porters, he characterized the Communists as "one of the greatest menaces to labor, the Negro, and other minorities."

Randolph's mindset about Communists was a factor in his decision to exclude all whites from participation in the "March on Washington" he scheduled for the summer of 1941. The possibility of Communist infiltration into this projected demonstration was, however, but one reason, and not the major reason, for Randolph's announced policy of racial exclusion. To white liberal groups and associates, such as the Fellowship of Reconciliation and its leader, A. J. Muste, who questioned this policy, Randolph had a ready answer. The proposed march, he explained, was "pro-Negro, not anti-white." Such an all black movement would "create faith by Negroes in Negroes," developing "a sense of self-reliance with Negroes depending upon Negroes in vital matters."

Destined to be of major importance for its accomplishments and for its trail-blazing techniques in direct mass black pressure and action, the March on Washington Movement was a cooperative venture, with Randolph as its operating head. The movement grew out of the plight of the urban Negro worker on the eve of America's entry into World War II, black unemployment having reached 25 percent in 1940. The long-existent discriminatory practices in hiring, in on-the-job training, and in upgrading were more aggravating than ever to the Negro workers as they noted their country's eagerness to contrast the American creed of liberty and equality with the suppressions that characterized the Fascist nations, Hitler's Germany in particular. And although American industry was increasing its production to meet the needs of the national defense program, blacks were being turned away at the defense-plant gates.

On September 27, 1940, Randolph and two other black spokesmen, Walter White of the NAACP and T. Arnold Hill of the National Urban League, conferred with Roosevelt, but this White House meeting accomplished little, thus convincing Randolph that nothing short of mass action by blacks would suffice. Hence through the Negro newspapers (see, for example, the *Pittsburgh Courier*, January 25, 1941) he issued a call. Negro Americans, ran his summons, must bring their "power and pressure to bear upon the agencies and representatives of the Federal Government to exact their rights in National Defense employment and the armed forces of the country." He suggested that 10,000 Negroes march on Washington, their slogan, "We Loyal Negro American Citizens Demand the Right to Work and Fight for our Country."

Randolph's appeal exceeded even his characteristically optimistic expectations, drawing enthusiastic support throughout the black community, including the clergy, the press, and the rank and file. The leaders of other black organizations, including the Urban League and the NAACP, found themselves swept into the fold. However much Randolph's growing popularity might threaten their own leadership standing in black uplift, these spokesmen and spokeswomen could hardly stay on the sidelines, even though direct mass action of a marching kind took on a somewhat more confrontational style than some of them preferred. Their choice was predictable. "No Negro leader could risk the Uncle Tom label," explains Herbert Garfinkel in analyzing their uniformly affirmative response.

It would not be the last time that Randolph would put other black leaders in a position in which they felt themselves to be somewhat coerced into supporting a strategy he espoused. But it is to be noted that if Randolph made constant use of other organizations and their leaders, he in turn reciprocated in full measure. He was, for example, a longtime supporter of the NAACP's crusade against lynching.

Their groundwork laid, Randolph and seven other black leaders formed a March on Washington Committee, scheduling the march for July 1, 1941, and multiplying their projections as to the number of marchers. "Dear fellow Negro Americans," exhorted Randoph, with growing confidence, "be not dismayed in these terrible times. You possess power, great power. Our problem is to harness and hitch it up for action on the broadest, daring and most gigantic scale."

In early June the mushrooming march movement forced itself upon Roosevelt. Exercising his political skills, he tried to have the march called off, enlisting the services of his wife Eleanor, whose popularity among blacks was already legendary, and of New York's mayor, Fiorello H. La Guardia, also a favorite in black circles. The failure of such emissaries made it necessary to arrange a White House conference on June 18 with four black leaders, including Randolph. Calling the idea of a march "bad and unintelligent," Roosevelt strongly urged the leaders to cancel it. When it became evident that his plea was unacceptable without a quid pro quo, Roosevelt brought the thirty-minute conference to a close by appointing a committee of five high-ranking whites to meet with the black leaders in order to reach an agreement.

Following a quickly arranged series of meetings and telephone conversations, the two groups resolved their differences, and on June 25, one week after the White House conference, Roosevelt issued Executive Order 8802, decreeing that "there shall be no discrimination in the employment of workers in defense industries or government because of race, creed, color or national origin" and establishing a Committee on Fair Employment Practices (FEPC). Appointed on July 19, 1941, this six-member committee included Webster, vice-president of the Brotherhood, Randolph having declined an invitation to serve. In the meantime, in exchange for Roosevelt's order, Randolph called off the scheduled march, proceeding instead to form a new organization, the March on Washington Movement, to act as a watchdog over the FEPC, among other activities.

Randolph's success in persuading Roosevelt to issue Executive Order 8802 illustrated a technique familiar in black leadership circles for over a hundred years. This was the practice of operating from a relatively weak power base, but of making demands nonetheless, hoping to achieve the group's goal by the use of strong rhetoric along with the threat of a disruptive physical confrontation that would certainly reach the public eye, even if it failed to touch the public conscience. Bearing some semblance to the game of bluff, this technique sometimes failed, as in the Brotherhood's threat to strike against the Pullman Company in 1928. Keenly aware of the riskiness of this technique, Randolph also knew full well that a black leader does not enjoy a wide range of weapons.

A group, or coalition of groups, whose power was problematic faced another disheartening possibility, *i.e.*, the victory they won might turn out to be less fruitful than they had expected. The aftermath of Randolph's march was a case in point. Despite its leader's vigorous efforts, the campaign for a permanent FEPC was unsuccessful, the wartime committee quietly expiring in the spring of 1946. Inadequately financed by the Congress and with little power to enforce its findings, the committee encountered bitter and unrelenting attacks. Malcolm Ross, its chairman beginning in October 1943, described it as the most hated agency in Washington, southern Congressmen and their constituents regarding it as an attempt to impose social equality upon their states.

The National Council for a Permanent FEPC, established in 1943, had been unable to halt its demise, running completely out of funds in 1946 and facing internal dissension with a rift between co-chairman Randolph and executive secretary Anna Arnold Hedgeman. Nonetheless, the FEPC was important for its pioneering role-for "making the issue part of the national consciousness," as Hedgeman said later. In the some 10,000 cases it handled during its five-year existence it met with some success in changing the discriminatory policies of employers and trade unions. Rather than face charges by the commission, some employers erased their color line, and others broadened their hiring policies.

Moreover, the existence of the FEPC meant that the federal government had now assumed a role in the elimination of Jim Crow practices in employment, that a precedent had been established for considering job discrimination a denial of one's civil rights. In addition the FEPC had its influence on the issuing of court decrees against job discrimination and on the establishment of state FEPC laws and of federal government contract compliance committees, the last-named capped by a committee on equal employment opportunity. And to Randolph, as to other black opinion-makers, no movement could be counted a failure that had succeeded in establishing among Negroes a greater sense of collective self-reliance.

Along with mass action and public demonstrations, Randolph made use of another technique that would foreshadow the civil rights revolution of the 1950s and 1960s, *i.e.*, the Gandhian approach of nonviolent civil disobedience. During his *Messenger* days Randolph had been an exponent of retaliatory violence, but an older Randolph, under the influence of such pacifists as Rustin, then on the threshold of a long career in reformist causes, modified his views. At its founding in 1942 the Congress of Racial Equality named Randolph to its National Advisory Committee, well aware that he shared its philosophy of nonviolent direct action. At the annual meeting of the March on Washington Movement in 1943 in Detroit, Randolph challenged the 1,200 delegates "to adopt nonviolent, goodwill, direct action as organizational policy." Such an approach, as Randolph pointed out later that year, would require persons "who had undergone a rigid training and discipline to develop self-control and the requisite moral and spiritual resources to meet the most trying ordeal."

Randolph himself put this technique to the test in his campaign against segregation in the armed forces during the 1940s. During World War I Randolph had spoken out against discrimination in the armed forces, and he sounded a similar note on the eve of World War II. The White House meeting on September 14, 1940, between Roosevelt and the three black leaders, Randolph included, discussed the participation of Negroes not only in defense industries but in the military. The call to the March on Washington, issued in the spring of 1941, included a petition "for the integration of Negroes in the armed forces, such as the Air Corps, Navy, Army and Marine Corps of the Nation." To Randolph's disappointment, however, Roosevelt's Executive Order 8802 was confined to defense industries. Hence the abolition of Jim Crow policies in the armed services, including the Women's Auxiliary Army Corps and the Waves, became one of the major objectives of the March on Washington Movement.

The war ended but not the issue, the latter taking a new momentum in 1947 when a Universal Military Training bill came before the Congress. A peacetime draft, it contained no anti-discrimination proviso. Responding to this omission, Randolph and Grant Reynolds, the black New York State Commissioner of Correction, established in November 1947 a Committee Against Jim Crow in Military Service and Training, a step that was hailed by blacks throughout the country.

The effort of this committee to persuade Congress to enact an antisegregation law for the armed services, or to persuade President Harry Truman to establish such a policy by executive decree, met with opposition from southern Congressmen and from high army officials. Reflecting the mood of their constituents, a group of black leaders met with Truman late in March 1948, urging him to insist that the proposed draft law include an antisegregation amendment. Not mincing his words, Randolph reported that in his travels around the country he "found Negroes not wanting to shoulder a gun to fight for democracy abroad unless they get democracy at home." Following a further exchange of views between Truman and the black delegation, the meeting came to an inconclusive end.

In his testimony before the Senate Armed Services Committee nine days later, Randolph was just as frank as he had been at the White House. If Congress passed a "jimcrow draft," he warned, he would advise blacks to resort to "mass civil disobedience" along the line of Gandhi's struggles against the British in India. Randolph openly pledged himself to counsel and assist young people, white and black, to "quarantine" a segregated "conscript system." When one senator raised the question of treason, Randolph replied that "we are serving a higher law than the law which applies to the act of treason."

When Congress, on June 22, 1948, passed a draft law that did not ban Jim Crow practices, Randolph announced the formation of a League for Non-Violent Civil Disobedience Against Military Segregation, which proposed to concentrate its efforts on persuading the president to alter the situation by executive order. The league called upon Truman to issue such an anti-discrimination order, stating that if such a step were not taken by August 16 (when the new draft law became operative), the league would conduct a campaign of noncompliance. Again making use of a technique that bore the earmarks of bluff, Randolph operated from no substantial base of power, and his willingness to go to jail in such a cause is open to question.

Truman, however, needed little further convincing. During his presidency he had grown more liberal on race issues, more concerned about civil rights. Moreover, in the presidential election to be held later that year, he needed the black vote, which had become increasingly important as the black population shifted from the South, where blacks could not vote, to the North, where they could. On July 26 Truman issued Executive Order 9981 declaring, as presidential policy, "that there shall be equality of treatment and opportunity for all persons in the armed services." A month later Randolph and Reynolds announced the termination of the league, the latter pointing out that the league had accomplished its mission "not in familiar legal or Constitutional terms" but in a program of noncompliance that had gone outside the traditionally accepted boundaries.

Randolph's crowning experience as an advocate of direct mass action by a coalition of reform-minded groups and agencies came in the summer of 1963 with the "march on Washington for Jobs and Freedom." Publicly announced from Randolph's office in Harlem in February of that year, the idea for such a demonstration grew out of a conversation between Randolph and Rustin, his assistant, a few weeks earlier. Originally concentrating on black unemployment, the march soon broadened its scope to include the whole range of civil rights in response to the cry "Freedom Now!"—the slogan of blacks during the hundredth anniversary of the Emancipation Proclamation. Sponsors of the march sought to bring pressure on Congress to enact a civil rights bill, then dormant in the House Rules Committee. "Politicians," said Randolph, "don't move unless you move them."

A labor leader himself, it was natural for Randolph to have originally thought of the proposed march as primarily a demonstration for jobs. But he had no quarrel with the slogan, "March on Washington for Jobs and Freedom," inasmuch as he held that economic freedom was the base of other freedoms, for, as he said, "Freedom requires a material foundation." But Randolph also knew that freedom had a protean quality, taking on a myriad of guises and fulfilling itself in many ways. Indeed, it was in quest of such an indivisible freedom that Randolph, now in his mid-seventies at the time of the march in 1963, had devoted his long career, as a moment of reflection would tend to indicate.

As to his sensitivity in the matter of jobs for blacks, Randolph stood above all other black leaders. During the twenty-five years between the granting of an international charter to the Brotherhood of Sleeping Car Porters and the proposed march on Washington in 1963, Randolph's devotion to the cause of the black workers had been unflagging and these workers needed such dedication. From his position as international president of the Brotherhood, Randolph raised an insistent voice for racial justice in the councils of the AFL. At its annual meetings in the 1940s and 1950s he proposed a series of resolutions, including those calling for the appointment of committees to investigate discriminatory practices among the member unions. As a rule the AFL reaffirmed its policy of opposition to Jim Crow practices but confessed itself without sufficient power to influence the autonomous individual unions. Randolph's own union, he noted, did not practice racial discrimination; of its 12,000 members in 1947 approximately 20 percent were whites, including Filipinos and Mexicans.

Randolph was hardly popular at the annual meetings of the AFL. Boos were not uncommon when he arose to speak, some delegates walking out and milling around in the halls until he took his seat. But Randolph was not to be silenced, winning the title, "the conscience of the AFL," and forcing the leaders to address themselves to the touchy questions of race and color.

In 1955 when the AFL merged with the Congress of Industrial Organizations (CIO) to form the AFL-CIO, the new federation named two blacks as vice-presidents, Randolph and Willard S. Townsend of the United Transport Service Employees. Founded in 1935, the CIO had made a strong effort to win the support of blacks. Organized along industry-wide lines rather than the more restrictive craft lines, and forming new unions unburdened by a history of racial discrimination, the CIO's racial and social policies were broader than those of the AFL, even though Randolph had preferred to keep the Brotherhood in the latter. By the time of the merger, however, the CIO had become less vigorous in pressing for racial equality.

To Randolph's gratification the constitution of the new federation provided for a Civil Rights Committee, one pledged to "the effective implementation of the principle of non-discrimination." Randolph became disenchanted, however, at the union's failure to expel locals that were guilty of discriminatory racial practices. Randolph's insistent charges that the AFL-CIO's attack on color barriers was half-hearted became increasingly galling to George Meany, its president. Meany had grown impatient with Randolph, charging that his indictments were overdrawn and that he failed to give the federation any credit for its successes against segregation. The Meany-Randolph imbroglio came to a head in 1959 at the annual convention of the union. In a sharp exchange between the two, Meany gave way to his ire, saying to Randolph, "Who in hell appointed you as guardian of the Negro members in America?"

Bent on exerting pressure on the AFL-CIO, Randolph in 1960 founded the Negro American Labor Council, made up of black officials of existing unions. Representing the council as its president, Randolph presented to the AFL-CIO a list of grievances accompanied by suggested remedies. The federation leadership responded by denying the charges and sharply criticizing Randolph himself for causing "the gap that has been developed between organized labor and the Negro community." This rift in the Negro-labor alliance, however, was relatively short-lived, with Meany a featured speaker at the annual meeting of the Negro American Labor Council in 1962.

If the black worker and the organized labor movement were indebted to Randolph, the same was true, if to a lesser extent, of the civil rights movement as a whole. Randolph's social vision was broad. As president of the Brotherhood of Sleeping Car Porters, he reminded its membership of the necessity of supporting "progressive forces for the securing and maintaining of democratic institutions for the Negro." In 1957, at the request of Martin Luther King, Jr., Randolph became one of the sponsors of the Prayer Pilgrimage to Washington, an effort to prod the federal government to take further action on "the unresolved civil-rights issue." Randolph delivered a moving address to the some 20,000 gathered at the Lincoln Memorial on May 17, the third anniversary of the Supreme Court decree against segregation in the public schools.

To the seventy-four-year-old Randolph, therefore, a march was nothing new; "Mr. Randolph is a march man," observed Whitney M. Young, Jr., in 1963. "He's been marching since 1941." A march focusing on jobs and freedom was a fitting climax to a career such as his. It was Randolph, wrote King, who "proposed a March on Washington to unite in one luminous action all the forces along the far-flung front." It was Randolph who headed the march's organizing committee of six blacks and four whites, and it was Randolph's deputy director, Rustin, who planned and coordinated the operations, handled the complex details, and recruited the volunteers. Joining forces with Randolph in 1950, Rustin had soon become a trusted and efficient lieutenant, skilled as a troubleshooter.

To Randolph the 1963 march was the high point of his public life. Over 200,000 marchers took the mile-long walk from the Washington Monument to the Lincoln Memorial. At the more formal proceedings, held at the foot of the memorial, Randolph presided and also delivered the keynote address. The march "is not the climax of our struggle but a new beginning, not only for the Negro but for all Americans, for personal freedoms and a better life," he said. "The civil rights revolution is not confined to Negroes; nor is it confined to civil rights."

Randolph introduced the other nine speakers in turn, ending with King, whose address, "I Have a Dream Today," marked the high water mark in twentieth-century civil rights oratory. Orderly and inspiring, the march was characterized by a note of high seriousness from beginning to end. "The imposing dignity and patience of A. Philip Randolph toned the whole affair," observed *Newsweek* columnist Kenneth Crawford.

Randolph counted the 1963 march as the most memorable day of his life, the crowning event associated with his leadership. And indeed the march was notable both as a symbol of past struggles and aspirations and, as Randolph had said, the herald of a new beginning.

There were, however, two aspects of the emergent black protest and activism of the 1960s that the aging Randolph found questionable, *i.e.*, the cry of "black power" and the call for black separatism. Randolph held that although "black power" could be construed as "a valid and poetic 'cry for deliverance,'" its advocates had not succeeded in formulating a concrete program that was "applicable to the needs of practical political action." To Randolph, "black power was a slogan and slogans solve no problems."

Randolph did not believe that blacks should "go it alone," and thus he was out of tune with the position paper adopted in August 1966 by the Student Nonviolent Coordinating Committee: "If we are to proceed toward true liberation, we must cut ourselves off from whites." Forty years earlier Randolph had condemned the racially separatist tenets of the Marcus Garvey movement. Holding that anti-white doctrines are dangerous and false, Randolph charged that Garveyism broadened the chasm between white workers and black workers and "engenders and fosters a virulent race prejudice." As for Garvey's cry that Negro Americans must establish an independent nation in Africa, Randolph replied that the liberation of Africa could come only "by allying the Negro liberation movement with the movements for the liberation of all the world's enslaved of all races, creeds and colors."

Randolph's attitude toward the black power militants of the 1960s was thus a reaffirmation of his essential ecumenism. Except for a brief spell while launching the 1941 March on Washington, Randolph's long leadership had consistently reflected a coalitionist bent. Randolph's concerns were global; for example, while most black leaders viewed World War II as an opportunity to win victory on the home front as well as victory over the Axis powers, Randolph viewed the conflict as an opportunity for a "Peoples' Revolution" that would "possess the fighting faith and crusading confidence of the masses of all colors and race," as he wrote in 1944. "The people can cause this war to usher in the Century of the Common Man."

Randolph's outlook embraced the generality of mankind. He strove to "win a decent place in America" for blacks, but he sought to win it without "destroying the possibilities for mutual goodwill." Within black circles he stressed the commonalities that transcended the lines of class and occupation, among other dividers. Beyond the color line he sought the universals in the human experience.

It might be noted that Randolph's faith in the power of reason and his belief in people's common destiny led him at times to underestimate the tenacity of race and color prejudice in his native land. Devoid of such feelings himself, he did not gauge fully the status advantages to be derived from racial discrimination—that whites in labor unions, for example, were fearful not only of losing their economic benefits but also of jeopardizing their social standing if blacks were accorded job equality. Randolph does not seem to have fully weighed the social uses of racism, its role as a form of cultural taboo, its service as an ego-prop.

To the end Randolph believed that self-interest balanced by a concern for the common good would ultimately prevail, and that the enlightened, particularly those who were the victims of oppression, would make common cause. Working toward this goal was Randolph's essential contribution, and it received its most cogent expression from Rustin, his close friend and associate. Shortly after Randolph's death in 1979, Rustin listed what he had learned from his mentor, including nonviolent protest and the economic roots of racism. "But, above all," wrote Rustin, "I learned that the struggle for the freedom of black people is intertwined with the struggle to free all mankind."

Rustin was fortunate in having had the opportunity to learn such things firsthand. Others, however, would not go unendowed, the Randolph legacy having an outreaching quality, embracing in particular the seekers of social insight.

NOTE ON SOURCES

The important manuscript source on Randolph is the papers of the Brotherhood of Sleeping Car Porters in the Manuscript Division of the Library of Congress and in the Manuscript Division of the Chicago Historical Society.

In the periodical literature, the most valuable single source is the *Messenger,* which was published in New York City from 1917 until its cessation in 1928. It is indispensable for Randolph's early career as a labor organizer and a Socialist, and it describes his activities in laying the foundations for the Brotherhood and setting its course.

The secondary sources include one full-length study, Jervis B. Anderson's *A. Philip Randolph: A Biographical Portrait* (New York: Harcourt Brace, and Jovanovich, 1973), in style, content, and insight an admirable introduction to the man. This work may be supplemented by a body of specialized studies of high caliber in which Randolph is the central figure. Listed according to their chronological coverage, the first is Theodore Kornweibel, Jr.'s *No Crystal Stair: Black Life and the Messenger, 1919–1928* (Westport, Conn.: Greenwood Press, 1975), a scholarly exposition and analysis of that journal's viewpoints. A similarly thorough volume, William H. Harris's *Keeping the Faith: A. Philip Randolph, Milton P. Webster, and the Brotherhood of Sleeping Car Porters, 1925–1937* (Urbana: University of Illinois Press, 1977), traces in detail the long battle between the Brotherhood and the Pullman Company, pointedly analyzing Randolph's leadership characteristics throughout. Harris holds that even though Randolph and his Brotherhood associates viewed themselves as path-breakers and innovators, "they functioned much in the tradition of other black leaders. " The pioneer study of the Randolph-led union is Brailsford R. Brazeal's *The Brotherhood of Sleeping Car Porters: Its Origin and Development* (New York: Harper and Brothers, 1946), a solid work with an interpretive touch.

Works that deal with issues about which Randolph was concerned and his role therein including the following. Herbert Garfinkel's *When Negroes March: The March on Washington Movement in the Organizational Politics for FEPC* (Glencoe Ill.: The Free Press, 1959) is skillfully organized and copiously documented, its conclusions soundly reasoned. Garfinkel may be supplemented by two additional studies that add to our understanding of that agency: Louis C. Kesselman's *The Social Politics of FEPC: A Study in Reform Pressure Movements* (Chapel Hill: University of North Carolina Press, 1948) and Louis Ruchames's *Race, Jobs and Politics: The Story of FEPC* (New York: Columbia University Press, 1953). The fight against Jim Crow practices in the services, with due attention to Randolph's role, is recounted in Richard M. Dalfiume's *Fighting on Two Fronts: Desegregation of the U.S. Armed Forces, 1939–1953* (Columbia: University of Missouri Press, 1969). Histories of black labor union movement of the twentieth century include Sterling D. Spero and Abram L. Harris's *The Black Worker: The Negro and the Labor Movement* (New York: Columbia University Press, 1931), which is somewhat critical of Randolph's leadership during the early years of the Brotherhood. One of the best of the studies that broadly and comprehensively covers the black worker is Philip S. Foner's *Organized Labor and the Black Worker, 1619–1973* (New York: Praeger Publishers, 1974), its index listing over forty references to Randolph.

UNIT 3-3

A. PHILIP RANDOLPH'S MARCH ON WASHINGTON: 1941

THE BLACK MAN DEMANDS A SHARE IN WORLD WAR II

A. Philip Randolph

ABOUT THE DOCUMENT

In the late 1930s, when American involvement in the war already raging in Europe seemed inevitable, black men resented bitterly their exclusion from the nation's defense industries. Of the thirty thousand defense workers in New York City, for example, only 142 were black, and even these few were restricted to such jobs as sweepers, janitors, and elevator operators. Many plants with government contracts refused to hire black labor at all.

In the armed forces, segregation was still the official government policy, a carry-over from the Civil War. Black newspapers reported race riots at Fort Oswego; discrimination at Fort Devens; Jim Crow conditions at Camps Blanding and Lee; and the edict "not to shake a nigger's hand at Camp Upton." The Baltimore *Afro-American* called for thousands of black men to desert rather than serve in army camps in the South.

Increasingly, black men began asking questions like these:

> Just how far removed is this brand of democracy that we practice from Fascism, Nazism and barbarism?

and

> If you haven't got democracy yourself, how can you carry it to somebody else?

Black leaders pleaded with, and petitioned, the federal government, the largest employer of civilian and military labor in the country, to meet its responsibilities.

A. Philip Randolph, head of the Brotherhood of Sleeping Car Porters union, said in January 1941 that the government would not act on behalf of blacks until it saw "Ten, twenty, fifty thousand Negroes on the White House lawn." Leaders of all the major black organizations offered to join Randolph, and the March-on-Washington Movement was formed.

In June 1941 it was announced that the March-on-Washington Movement, led by Randolph, with Walter White, Adam Clayton Powell, Jr., and Frank Crosswaith, would rally fifty thousand black men in Washington on July 1, to demand that the federal government take action to stop discrimination in the defense industries and the armed forces.

The idea of a black revolt in a time of crisis threw Washington into a panic. President Roosevelt called the march leaders to Washington and tried to persuade them to call it off. They refused. On June 25, 1941, Roosevelt capitulated and signed the famous Executive Order. No. 8802—the Fair Employment Practices Act—banning discrimination in defense plants and government offices and services "because of race, creed, color, or national origin." The march never did take place, since it had achieved its objective.

It was the first time since Lincoln had signed the Emancipation Proclamation that a President had acted to protect the civil rights of black men. The March-on-Washington threat had shown the value, in Randolph's words, of a "non-violent demonstration of Negro man power" as a tactic of protest.

THE DOCUMENT

From the article titled "Why Should We March," in the *Survey Graphic*, November 1942.

PROGRAM OF THE MARCH ON WASHINGTON MOVEMENT

1. We demand, in the interest of national unity, the abrogation of every law which makes a distinction in treatment between citizens based on religion, creed, color, or national origin. This means an end to Jim Crow in education, in housing, in transportation and in every other social, economic, and political privilege; and especially, we demand, in the capital of the nation, an end to all segregation in public places and in public institutions.
2. We demand legislation to enforce the Fifth and Fourteenth Amendments guaranteeing that no person shall be deprived of life, liberty or property without due process of law, so that the full weight of the national government may be used for the protection of life and thereby may end the disgrace of lynching.
3. We demand the enforcement of the Fourteenth and Fifteenth Amendments and the enactment of the Pepper Poll Tax bill so that all barriers in the exercise of the suffrage are eliminated.
4. We demand the abolition of segregation and discrimination in the army, navy, marine corps, air corps, and all other branches of national defense.
5. We demand an end to discrimination in jobs and job training. Further, we demand that the FEPC be made a permanent administrative agency of the U.S. Government and that it be given power to enforce its decisions based on its findings.
6. We demand that federal funds be withheld from any agency which practices discrimination in the use of such funds.

7. We demand colored and minority group representation on all administrative agencies so that these groups may have recognition of their democratic rights to participate in formulating policies.
8. We demand representation for the colored and minority racial groups on all missions, political and technical, which will be sent to the peace conference so that the interests of all people everywhere may be fully recognized and justly provided for in the postwar settlement.

UNIT 3-4

PRESIDENT ROOSEVELT'S FAIR EMPLOYMENT PRACTICES COMMITTEE

EXECUTIVE ORDER 8802, JUNE 25, 1941

Reaffirming Policy of Full Participation in the Defense Program by All Persons, Regardless of Race, Creed, Color, or National Origin, and Directing Certain Action in Furtherance of Said Policy

Whereas it is the policy of the United States to encourage full participation in the national defense program by all citizens of the United States, regardless of race, creed, color, or national origin, in the firm belief that the democratic way of life within the Nation can be defended successfully only with the help and support of all groups within its borders; and

Whereas there is evidence that available and needed workers have been barred from employment in industries engaged in defense production solely because of considerations of race, creed, color, or national origin, to the detriment of workers' morale and of national unity:

Now, therefore, by virtue of the authority vested in me by the Constitution and the statutes, and as a prerequisite to the successful conduct of our national defense production effort, I do hereby reaffirm the policy of the United States that there shall be no discrimination in the employment of workers in defense industries or government because of race, creed, color, or national origin, and I do hereby declare that it be the duty of employers and of labor organizations, in furtherance of said policy and of this order, to provide for the full and equitable participation of all workers in defense industries, without discrimination because of race, creed, color, or national origin;

And it is hereby ordered as follows:

1. All departments and agencies of the Government of the United States concerned with vocational and training programs for defense production shall take special measures

6 Fed. Reg. 3109 (1941).

appropriate to assure that such programs are administered without discrimination because of race, creed, color, or national origin;

2. All contracting agencies of the Government of the United States shall include in all defense contracts hereafter negotiated by them a provision obligating the contractor not to discriminate against any worker because of race, creed, color, or national origin;

3. There is established in the Office of Production Management a Committee on Fair Employment Practice, which shall consist of a chairman and four other members to be appointed by the President. The Chairman and members of the Committee shall serve as such without compensation but shall be entitled to act and necessary transportation, subsistence and other expenses incidental to performance of their duties. The Committee shall receive and investigate complaints of discrimination in violation of the provisions of this order and shall take appropriate steps to redress grievances which it finds to be valid. The Committee shall also recommend to the several departments and agencies of the Government of the United States and to the President all measures which may be deemed by it necessary or proper to effectuate the provisions of this order.

FRANKLIN D. ROOSEVELT
THE WHITE HOUSE
June 25, 1941

UNIT 3-5

A Basis for Interracial Cooperation and Development in the South

A Statement by Southern Negroes

Durham, North Carolina—October 1942

The war has sharpened the issue of Negro-white relations in the United States, and particularly in the South. A result has been increased racial tension, fears, and aggressions, and an opening up of the basic questions of racial segregation and discrimination, Negro minority rights, and democratic freedom, as they apply practically in Negro-white relations in the South. These issues are acute, and threaten to become even more serious as they increasingly block, through the deeper fears aroused, common sense consideration for even elementary improvement in Negro status, and the welfare of the country as a whole.

With these problems in mind, we, a group of southern Negroes, realizing that the situation calls for both candor and wisdom, and in the belief that we voice the sentiments of many of the Negroes of the Nation as well as the South, take this means of recording our considered views of the issues before us.

1. Our Nation is engaged in a world-wide struggle, the success of which, both in arms and ideals, is paramount and demands our first loyalty.
2. Our loyalty does not, in our view, preclude consideration now of problems and situations that handicap the working out of internal improvements in race relations essential to our full contribution to the war effort, and of the inevitable problems of post-war reconstruction, especially in the South where we reside.
3. The South, with its twenty-five million people, one-third of whom are Negroes, presents a unique situation, not only because of the patterns of race relations which are invariably and universally associated with racial discriminations. We recognize the strength and age of these patterns.

We are fundamentally opposed to the principle and practice of compulsory segregation in our American society, whether of races or classes or creeds, however, we regard it as both sensible and timely to address ourselves now to the current problems of racial discrimination and neglect, and to ways in which we may cooperate in the advancement of programs aimed at the sound improvement of race relations within the democratic framework.

4. We regard it as unfortunate that the simple efforts to correct obvious social and economic injustices continue, with such considerable popular support, to be interpreted as the predatory ambition of irresponsible Negroes to invade the privacy of family life.
5. We have the courage and faith to believe, however, that it is possible to evolve in the South a way of life, consistent with the principles for which we as a Nation are fighting throughout the world, that will free us all, white and Negro alike, from want, and from throttling fears.

POLITICAL AND CIVIL RIGHTS

1. We regard the ballot as a safeguard of democracy. Any discrimination against citizens in the exercise of the voting privilege, on account of race or poverty, is detrimental to the freedom of these citizens and to the integrity of the State. We therefore record ourselves as urging now:
   a. The abolition of the poll tax as a prerequisite to voting.
   b. The abolition of the white primary.
   c. The abolition of all form of discriminatory practices, evasion of the law, and intimidations of citizens seeking to exercise their right of franchise.
2. Exclusion of Negroes from jury service because of race has been repeatedly declared unconstitutional. This practice we believe can and should be discontinued now.
3. a. Civil rights include personal security against abuses of police power by white officers of the law. These abuses, which include wanton killings, and almost routine beatings of Negroes, whether they be guilty or innocent of an offense, should be stopped now, not only out of regard for the safety of Negroes, but of common respect for the dignity and fundamental purpose of the law.
   b. It is the opinion of this group that the employment of Negro police will enlist the full support of Negro citizens in control of lawless elements of their own group.
4. In the public carriers and terminals, where segregation of the races is currently made mandatory by law as well as by established custom, it is the duty of Negro and white citizens to insist that these provisions be equal in kind and quality and in character of maintenance.
5. Although there has been, over the years, a decline in lynchings, the practice is still current in some areas of the South, and substantially, even if indirectly, defended by resistance to Federal legislation designed to discourage the practice. We ask that.the States discourage this fascistic expression by effective enforcement of present or of new laws against this crime by apprehending and punishing parties participating in this lawlessness.
   If the States are unable, or unwilling to do this, we urge the support of all American citizens who believe in law and order in securing Federal legislation against lynching.
6. The interests and securities of Negroes are involved directly in many programs of social planning and administration; in the emergency rationing, wage and rent control

programs. We urge the use of qualified Negroes on these boards, both as a means of intelligent representation and a realistic aid to the functioning of these bodies.

Industry and Labor

Continuing opposition to the employment of Negroes in certain industries appears to proceed from (1) the outdated notions of an economy of scarcity, inherited from an industrial age when participation in the productive enterprises was a highly competitive privilege; (2) the effects of enemy propaganda designed to immobilize a large number of potentially productive workers in the American war effort; (3) the age-old prejudices from an era when the economic system required a labor surplus which competed bitterly within its own ranks for the privilege of work; (4) the established custom of reserving technical process to certain racial groups; and (5) craft monopolies which have restricted many technical skills to a few workers.

Our collective judgment regarding industrial opportunities for Negroes may be summarized as follows:

1. The only tenable basis of economic survival and development for Negroes is inclusion in unskilled, semiskilled and skilled branches of work in the industries or occupations of the region to the extent that they are equally capable. Circumstances will vary so as to make impossible and impracticable any exact numerical balance, but the principles annunciated by the President's Fair Employment Practices Committee are regarded by us as sound and economically essential.
2. There should be the same pay for the same work.
3. Negro workers should seek opportunities for collective bargaining and security through membership in labor organizations. Since there can be no security for white workers if Negroes are unorganized and vice versa, labor unions of white workers should seek the organization of Negro workers, on a fair and equal basis.
4. We deplore the practice of those labor unions which bar Negroes from membership, or otherwise discriminate against them, since such unions are working against the best interest of the labor movement. We hold that only those labor unions which admit Negroes to membership and participation on a fair and democratic basis should be eligible for the benefits of the National Labor Relations Board, Railway Labor Act, State Labor Relations Acts and other protective labor legislation.
5. It is the duty of local, state and federal agencies to insist upon and enforce provisions for the industrial training of Negroes equal in quality and kind with that of other citizens. We believe, further, that Negroes should have equal opportunity in training programs carried on by industries and by labor organizations.
6. We urge Negro representation on regional organizations concerned with the welfare of workers.
7. We regard the wage-and-job-freezing order of the War Manpower Commission as holding the seeds of a distinct disadvantage to Negroes and other marginal workers. Most of these workers are now employed in the lowest-income job brackets. The "freeze" order can remove the opportunity for economic advancement. There is as yet no assurance that under existing circumstances the War Manpower Commission can deal more equitably with the Negro in the future than it has in the past.

8. We are convinced that the South's economic and cultural development can be accelerated by increasing the purchasing power and skills of Negro workers.

SERVICE OCCUPATIONS

Any realistic estimate of the occupational situation of Negroes supports the view that Negroes will be employed in greatest proportions for a long time in service occupations. We see, however, possibilities of making of these fields scientifically guided areas in which training and organization will play a greater part in bringing about results mutually beneficial to employer and employee. We believe that greater service will be rendered and greater good will be engendered in the service fields if the following principles are observed.

1. More thorough training should be provided workers who plan to enter the service field, but the reward of the job and treatment on the job should be such as to make the workers feel that their training is justified. Opportunity should be given the service worker to advance through the opening up of additional opportunities.
2. A wholesome environment, living accommodations, food, uniforms and rest rooms, all of an approved standard, should be provided service workers.
3. Opportunity should be given the service worker to live, after his stipulated hours of work, as an individual undisturbed in his private life by the whims and caprices of his employers.
4. In view of the strides made by labor in general, while the service worker's lot has remained about the same, service workers should be organized into unions with recognized affiliations.[1]
5. Service workers should be included in the provisions for old age insurance, unemployment compensation, workman's compensation, the wage and hour act, and other benefits of Social Security legally provided to workers of other categories.

We believe that these provision will help to insure some intelligent service and wholesome loyalty (which will improve both the quality of labor and personal relations) in service occupations.

EDUCATION

As equal opportunity for all citizens is the very foundation of the democratic faith, and of the Christian ethic which gave birth to the ideal of democratic living, it is imperative that every measure possible be taken to insure an equality of education to Negroes, and indeed to all underprivileged peoples.

1. Basic to improvement in Negro education is better schools, which involves expenditures by States of considerably more funds for the Negro schools. This group believes that a minimum requirement now is (**a**) equalization of salaries of white and Negro teachers on the basis of equal preparation and experience; (**b**) an expanded school building program for Negro schools designed to overcome the present racial disparity in physical facilities; this program to begin as soon as building materials are available; (**c**) revision of the school program in terms of the social setting, voca-

tional needs and marginal cultural characteristics of the Negro children; and (**d**) the same length of school term for all children in local communities. Our growing knowledge of the effect of environment upon the intelligence and social adjustment of children, in fact leads us to believe that to insure equality of educational opportunity it is not enough to provide for the underprivileged child, of whatever race, the same opportunities provided for those on superior levels of familial, social and economic life. We feel it a function of Government to assure equalization far beyond the mere expenditure of equivalent funds for salaries and the like.

2. The education of Negroes in the South has reached the point at which there is increased demand for graduate and professional training. This group believes that this training should be made available equally for white and Negro eligible student in terms defined by the United States Supreme Court in the decision on the case of *Gaines v. The University of Missouri.*
3. Where it is established that States cannot sustain the added cost of equalization, Federal funds should be made available to overcome the differentials between white and Negro facilities and between southern and national standards.
4. It is the belief of this group that the special problems of Negro education make demands for intelligent and sympathetic representation of these problems on school boards by qualified persons of the Negro race.
5. The education of Negro youth can be measurably aided by the use of Negro enforcement officers of truancy and compulsory education laws.

AGRICULTURE

The South is the most rural section of the Nation, and Negroes, who constitute 33 percent of its population, are responsible for an important share of the agricultural production on southern farms.

We recognize that the South is economically handicapped and that many of its disabilities are deeply rooted in agricultural maladjustments. To win the war, there is need for increased production of food, fibre and fats. In the present organization of agriculture, Negroes are a large part of the sharecropper and tenant group and a great majority of the rural Negro workers are in this class. Circumstances deny the Negro farmer sufficient opportunity to make his full contribution as a citizen. We suggest the following measures as means of increasing the production of the area, raising the status and spirits of Negro farmers, and of improving the region's contribution to the total war effort.

1. Establishment of sufficient safeguards in the system of tenancy to promote the development of land and home ownership and more security on the land, by:
   - **a.** Written contracts
   - **b.** Longer lease terms
   - **c.** Higher farm wages for day laborers
   - **d.** Balanced farm programs, including food and feed crops for present tenants and day laborers.
2. Adequate Federal assistance to Negro farmers should be provided on equitable basis. The war effort can be materially aided if adequate provisions are made now for the interpretation of governmental policies to rural Negroes.
3. The equitable distribution of funds for teaching agriculture in the Negro land grant colleges to provide agricultural research and experimentation for Negro farmers.

4. The appointment of qualified Negroes to governmental planning and policy making bodies concerned with the common farmer, and the membership of Negro farmers in general farmers' organizations and economic cooperatives, to provide appropriate representation and to secure maximum benefits to our common wealth.

MILITARY SERVICE

We recognize and welcome the obligation of every citizen to share in the military defense of the nation and we seek, along with the privilege of offering our lives, the opportunity of other citizens of full participation in all branches of the military service, and of advancement in responsibility and rank according to ability.

Negro soldiers, in line of military duty and in training in the South, encounter particularly acute racial problems in transportation and in recreation and leave areas. They are frequently mistreated by the police. We regard these problems as unnecessary and destructive to morale.

SOCIAL WELFARE AND HEALTH

1. We believe that some of the more acute problems of Negro Health, family and personal disorganization are a reflection of deficiencies in economic opportunity, but that social and health services for Negroes will continue to be necessary in considerable amounts even with improvement of their economic status. As a means of reducing the mortality and public contagion resulting from inadequacies of medical attention and health knowledge, this group believes that minimum health measures for Negroes would include the following:
   a. Mandatory provisions that a proportion of the facilities in all public hospitals be available for Negro patients;
   b. That Negro doctors be either included on the staff for services to Negro patients, according to their special qualifications, or permitted as practitioners the same privileges and courtesy as other practitioners in the public hospitals;
   c. That Negro public health nurses and social workers be more extensively used in both public and private organizations.
2. We advocate the extension of slum clearance and erection low-cost housing as a general as well as a special group advantage The Federal government has set an excellent precedent here with results that offer much promise for the future.

It is a wicked notion that the struggle of the Negro for citizenship is a struggle against the best interests of the Nation. To urge such a doctrine, as many are doing, is to preach disunity and to deny the most elementary principles of American life and government.

The effect of the war has been to make the Negro, in a sense, the symbol and protagonist of every other minority in America and in the world at large. Local issues in the South, while admittedly holding many practical difficulties, must be met wisely and courageously if this Nation is to become a significant political entity in a new international world. The correction of these problems in not only a moral matter, but a practical necessity in winning the war and in winning the peace. Herein rests the chance to reveal our greatest weakness or our greatest strength.

[SIGNED]

Gordon B. Hancock
F. D. Patterson
Benjamin E. Mays
Ernest Delpit
Rufus E. Clement
Horace Mann Bond

James E. Jackson
WM. M. Cooper
P. B. Young
Chas. S. Johnson
Chairman Sub-Editorial Committee

ENDNOTES

1. In the present hysteria of many housewives who are losing poorly paid servants to better paying war industries, its seems desirable to emphasize that this proposal bears no relation to the fantastic and probably Axis inspired rumors of so-called "Eleanor Clubs."

UNIT 3-6

STATEMENT OF CONFERENCE OF WHITE SOUTHERNERS ON RACE RELATIONS

ATLANTA, GEORGIA—APRIL 8, 1943

In October, 1942, a representative group of Southern Negro leaders met in Durham, N.C., and issued a statement in which they addressed themselves "to the current problems of racial discrimination and neglect, and to ways in which we may cooperate in the advancement of programs aimed at the sound improvement of race relations, within the democratic framework."

Their statement is so frank and courageous, so free from any suggestion of threat and ultimatum, and at the same time shows such good will, that we gladly agree to cooperate.

We do not attempt to make here anything like a complete reply to the questions raised nor to offer solutions for all the vexing problems. We hope, however, to point the pathway for future cooperative efforts and to give assurance of our sincere good will and desire to cooperate in any sound program aimed at the improvement of race relations.

These Negro leaders rightly placed emphasis in their statement on discrimination in the administration of our laws on purely racial grounds. We are sensitive to this charge and admit that it is essentially just. From the Potomac to the Rio Grande, there are some ten million Negroes. While all citizens are governed by the same laws, it is recognized that Negroes have little voice in the making and enforcement of the laws under which they must live. They are largely dependent upon the will of the majority group for the safety of life and property, education and health, and their general economic condition. This is a violation of the spirit of democracy. No Southerner can logically dispute the fact that the Negro, as an American citizen, is entitled to his civil rights and economic opportunity.

The race problem in any Southern community is complicated by our economic limitations. The factors which have kept the South a tributary section have also kept it poor and lacking in sufficient industry to develop and provide enough jobs and enough public funds for every public need. Yet, the only justification offered for those laws which have for their purpose the separation of the races is that they are intended to minister to the welfare and integrity of both races. There has been widespread and inexcusable discrimination in the administration of these laws. The white Southerner has an obligation to interest himself in the legitimate aspirations of the Negro. This means correcting the discrimination between the races in the allocation of school funds, in the number and quality of schools, and in the salaries of teachers. In public travel where the law demands a separation of the races, primary justice and a simple sense of fair play demand the facilities for safety, comfort, and health should be equal. The distribution of public utilities and public benefits, such as sewers, water, housing, street and sidewalk paving, playgrounds, public health and hospital facilities should come to the Negro upon the basis of population and need.

It is recognized that there is often practical discrimination by some peace officers and in some courts in the treatment of Negro prisoners and in the abrogation of their civil rights. There is no such discrimination incorporated in the laws of any of the Southern states. False arrests, brutal-beatings, and other evils must be stopped.

In the economic field, unquestionably procedures should be undertaken to establish fully the right to receive equal pay for equal work. To do otherwise, works a wrong to our entire economic life and to our self respect. With so large a proportion of our wage-earning population belonging to the minority race, if we cannot plan for a well-trained, well-employed and prosperous Negro population, the economic future of the South is hopeless.

Most of the Negroes in the South are on farms and in rural communities. Failure to provide for them all the facilities for improving agricultural practices through schools, county agents, and supervision holds back all of the South. Fair wages, longer tenures of leases, and increased opportunities for farm ownership are also necessary.

All men who believe in justice, who love peace, and who believe in the meaning of this country are under the necessity of working together to draw off from the body of human society the poison of racial antagonism. This is one of the disruptive forces which unless checked will ultimately disturb and threaten the stability of the nation. Either to deny or to ignore the increased tension between the white and the colored races would be a gesture of insincerity.

That there are acute and intricate problems associated with two races living side by side in the South cannot be denied. But these problems can be solved and will ultimately disappear if they are brought out into an atmosphere of justice and good will. If we approach them with contempt in one group and resentment in the other group, then we work on hopeless terms. The solution of these problems can be found only in men of both races who are known to be men of determined good will. The ultimate solution will be found in evolutionary methods and not in ill-founded revolutionary movements which promise immediate solutions.

We agree with the Durham Conference that it is "unfortunate that the simple efforts to correct obvious social and economic injustices continue, with such considerable popular support to be interpreted as the predatory ambition of irresponsible Negroes to invade the privacy of family life." We agree also that "it is a wicked notion that the struggle by the Negro for citizenship is a struggle against the best interests of the nation. To urge such a doctrine, as many are doing, is to preach disunity, and to deny the most elementary principles of American life and government."

It is futile to imagine or to assert that the problem will solve itself. The need is for a positive program arrived at in an atmosphere of understanding, cooperation and mutual respect.

UNIT 3-7

RESOLUTIONS OF THE COLLABORATION COMMITTEE

RICHMOND, VIRGINIA—JUNE 16, 1943

This is a day of great differences, strong feelings, and epochal conflicts throughout the world. Yet, the world's greatest need and hope is to find common ground for universal action and balanced harmony among all peoples. Manifestly, such a goal must be reached through cooperative approximation to the largest measure of agreement in line with the largest number of values and the largest number of people.

We face, therefore, the double crisis of standing firm for the conservation and preservation of human rights; yet to seek these ends by the way of peace and planning rather than by conflict and revolution.

In America, and particularly in the South, we face the problem of readjustments to meet the demands of present and post-war conditions with reference to the Negro and the future development of a great region of the Nation. This, exclusive of the war, is the great crisis of the South and the Nation.

This is the problem of two great peoples caught up in the midst of transition between the powerful heritage of the past and the mighty pull of the future. For here is the white South, a great people often doing little things and good people often doing bad things. And here is the Negro South, caught as always between the upper and nether millstones of conflicting forces and also paying the price of extraordinary transition from level to level of cultural achievement, and needing plenty of understanding and cooperation. And here is the white South inexorably conditioned by cultural complexes, suffering terribly too, and needing sympathy and help as few peoples have ever needed in the annals of man. And even more important, the two, white South and black South, are part and parcel of the Nation, whose people need scarcely less than the two regional peoples the sense of time and wisdom.

The war has sharpened the issue of Negro-white relations in the United States, and particularly in the South. A result has been increased racial tensions, fears, and aggressions, and an opening up of the basic questions of racial segregation and discrimination, Negro minority rights, and democratic freedom, as they apply practically in Negro-white relations in the South. These issues are acute and threaten to become even more serious as they increasingly block, through the deeper fears aroused, common sense consideration for even elementary improvements in Negro status and the welfare of the country as a whole.

This is a rare challenge to the leadership of the South; to the white leadership to find new ways of cooperation and to justify increased confidence of the Negro leadership in the white South; to the Negro leadership, to sense the difficulties involved and to meet increasing demands, without slowing down.

As evidence of the promise of this leadership, two recent Southern conferences on race relations, one at Durham, under the auspices of Negro leadership, and one in Atlanta under the auspices of white leadership, have blazed new trails. As a follow-up of these and with the above problems and backgrounds in mind, we, a group of Southern whites and Negroes, representing both the Durham and Atlanta groups, meeting as a collaboration committee at Richmond, Virginia, June 16, 1943, and following the general trend of the Atlanta group, urge the general adaptation of the Durham statement entitled "A Basis For Interracial Cooperation and Development in the South," which has had extraordinary nation-wide endorsement.

The framers of this covenant, realizing that the situation calls for both candor and wisdom, have included adequate and searching analysis of the principal issues involved, duly interpreted in their proper perspective. The problems so featured include political and civil rights, industry and labor, service occupations, education, agriculture, military service, social welfare, and health.

In the area of political and civil rights: the essential problems featured were those of franchise and the ballot, jury service, personal-security, services in public carriers, the elimination of violence, within and without the law, the elimination of lynching, and the employment of an increasingly larger number of Negroes in the public service.

In the area of work opportunities: the increased training for all skilled, semi-skilled, and unskilled labor, and opportunity for employment; the readoption of labor union policies both for the best interests of Negroes and labor union; the problems of dual standards of pay; support of, but guarding against discrimination in, local, state, and federal procedures; special problems of service workers and standards of living.

In the area of education: equalized opportunities in all aspects but especially including institutions of higher learning, professional training, and equal salaries.

In the area of agriculture: adequate opportunity for the Negro farmer, including a sound system of tenancy, adequate state and federal assistance, increased opportunity for farm ownership, fair farm wages, and the wider employment of Negro farm and home agents.

In the area of military service: along with the obligation to serve, the opportunity for full participation and advancement in the war activities and a continuing better adjustment of unsatisfactory situations.

In the area of social welfare and health: adequate provisions for safeguarding the public health, for training physicians and nurses, and for their employment. Also, the erection of low-cost housing and other facilities for improving community life.

We recognize now the importance of affirmative action, without which we shall fall far short of our hopes and possibilities. To this end, we direct that the continuing committee, as appointed by the two groups now consolidated in this larger collaboration committee, be charged with the responsibility for working out methods and practical means of approach. We urge especially that efforts be begun to prepare the post-war world for a wise and successful reception of our returning soldiers and to prepare both the soldiers and the people for attitudes and procedures adequate to a new sense of the meaning of these needs as they accord with our professed principles of Christianity and democracy.

Signed: Charlotte Hawkins Brown
Virginius Dabney
A. W. Dent
William G. Gehri
Archdeacon B. W. Harris
S. S. Morris
Josephine Wilkins
Howard Odum, Chairman

UNIT 3-8

RESOLUTION LAUNCHING THE SOUTHERN REGIONAL COUNCIL

ATLANTA, GEORGIA—AUGUST 4, 1943

We are gathered together here in solemn assembly, conscious of our heritage and opportunity. In the name and spirit of America and all her resources and institutions, we covenant together in harmony and unanimity to make this day, or what this day should bring to pass, epochal in a new purpose, a new understanding, and a new fellowship.

In the name and spirit of America's science and education, we seek to find and tell the truth. In the name and spirit of America's democracy, we seek the way of equal opportunity. In the name of America's patriotism, we strive for loyalty to the American dream, for leadership to guide, and for statesmanship adequate to carry the burden of the new America. In the name and spirit of America's Christianity, we search for the new faith of fellowship. In the name of humanity, we propose to substitute the measures of the good society for the old biological struggle for physical survival. In the name and spirit of all these and the living reality of a complex world, we dedicate ourselves to the task of doing the most and the best that can be done here and now.

Four ways there are, and perhaps more, of approaching these laudable and attainable ends. First, we agree upon a new declaration of American principles and a new dedication of ourselves to the task of covenanting together with all regions and all races for the continued better ordering of our society. We recognize fully that in the present crisis this covenant is as important as the earlier compacts of the forefathers, and that the framework within which we covenant together must comprehend a concept and a charter which guarantees equality of opportunity for all peoples. This means more specifically as bearing upon the burden of our present counseling that the Negro in the United States and in every region is entitled to and should have every guarantee of equal opportunity that every other citizen of the United States has within the framework of the American-democratic system of government.

Second, we dedicate ourselves unswervingly to the successful achievement of this talk. Since in the order of all nature and creations and of the growth and development of the people and society there are always certain features peculiar to each society; since in the order of democracy there are certain elemental principles of self-government that are inherent in each folk and regional society; and since in both the physical and cultural heritage of the South there are certain cumulative and tragic handicaps that represent powerful factors in the situation, we appeal to the Nation, in covenant with the South, to exercise a wisdom and maturity through which methods, procedures, and rates of change may be worked out in the spirit of, and in conformity with, the principles of our American democracy.

Third, to the end that there will be actual realistic accomplishments, rather than mere words and that there may be possible ways and means of actually insuring progress in all approaches to these goals of equal opportunity, we urge the South to pool its efforts and set up a strong, unified, Southern Regional Council, constituted of representatives of both races and of private and public groups. Such a Council, in subscribing to the new declaration of principles, would work with and utilize all other available agencies and individuals in private and in public life and especially with a similar national group when established.

Fourth, since the crisis is not only southern but national, not only for whites but for Negroes and other races as well, and since the central purpose of the new council is cooperation and the building of active good will, we urge the formation of a National Committee on race and regional development, constituted of representative of all races and of public and private groups. Such a committee, subscribing to the declaration of principles, would work with and utilize all available agencies and individuals in private and public life.

We recognize the sweep and power of the emotions in time of war and crisis and the rights and tendencies in the democratic way of life for thousands of individuals and groups to agitate, organize, and promote their own peculiar programs. This is and must be the essence of a democracy to focus upon fundamentals and to give opportunity to responsible leadership through the orderly agencies of government and of private citizens. To this end, no greater service can be rendered to the Nation than to covenant together in responsible organizations, to provide leadership and clearinghouse, and to avoid conflicts, waste and overlapping, on the one hand, and, on the other, to minimize the harmful influence of irresponsible forces in this great hour of need for good will and for effective ways of doing what is needed. We feel that in these councils may be approximated needs more nearly than in any other ways that now appear.

The Nation is committed now to what is generally called, both in private business and public life, post-war planning to the end that we may be ready for the demobilization and reintegration of our millions of returning soldiers into the best possible American way of life. Recognizing that the problems of the folk and of race constitute a more difficult problem than that of physical planning, by the same token we urge all the more obligation to apply to this great area of our democracy the best the sciences, social sciences, the humanities, and religion can do in the realistic working out of next steps.

To this end, the present membership of the Continuation Committees of the Durham and Atlanta Conferences is hereby constituted the nucleus of the new Council; and the officers are authorized (1) to take immediate steps for the legal incorporation of the Council; (2) to appoint immediately the necessary staff personnel to implement this program; and (3) to enlarge the present membership in order to make it fully representative of all the interests encompassed by this program.

It is also respectfully urged that the President of the United States appoint a National Committee such as is suggested above.

UNIT 3-9

ADDRESSED TO WHITE LIBERALS

Lillian Smith

We are facing a serious racial crisis in our American life today, a crisis that cannot be met in the old way or with the old answers if we are to avoid tragedy. The hopeless believe this tragedy is unavoidable. But those of us who believe in the power of the creative mind, cannot accept such defeatism. We know there is a way out if we can but find it. Many of us are searching for that way, though some still refuse to leave the old path, retracing their steps again and again in circles, as all lost men tend to do.

I believe we can find the way if we are willing to look in a new direction for the source of our trouble. We have looked at the "Negro problem" long enough. Now the time has come for us to right-about-face and study the problem of the white man: the deep-rooted needs that have caused him to seek those strange, regressive satisfactions that are derived from worshiping his own skin-color. The white man himself is one of the world's most urgent problems today; not the Negro, not other colored races. We whites must learn to confess this.

There are many among us who think of segregation as merely a Southern tradition, a Southern "custom" that grew out of poverty, out of certain economic patterns, out of certain racial dilemmas, when in reality segregation is an ancient psychological mechanism used by men the world over whenever they want to shut themselves away from problems which they fear and do not feel they have the strength to solve. When men get into trouble they tend to put barriers between themselves and their difficulties. We white people got into deep trouble long ago when we attempted to enslave other human beings. A trouble we have never faced and never tried with all our strength to solve. Instead, to shut our troubles from us, we have used a mechanism so destructive that it, in itself, has become a menace to the health of our culture and our individual souls. For segregation as a way of life—or shall we say *a way of death*—is cultural schizophrenia, bearing a curious resemblance to the schizophrenia of individual personality. It is chilling to note the paranoid symptoms of those among us who cling to segregation: their violence, their sensitiveness to criticism, their stereotyped defenses, their inability to identify their over-esteem of themselves with the emotional needs of others, their reluctance to reach out and accept new ideas, their profound desire to withdraw from everything hard to face, everything that requires of their personalities further growth.

TNR, September 18, 1944.

Those who believe in this philosophy of segregation have chosen the schizophrenic way: withdrawing from reality; and this withdrawal has profoundly affected their minds and emotions.

It is the *effect of segregation* upon the human beings who segregate as well as upon those who are segregated that should concern us all. For we cannot consider racial segregation (and its counterparts, political and economic isolationism) apart from man's whole personality, apart from his whole culture. We cannot separate men's specific needs from the destructive effects of a *way of life* that attempts to withdraw from reality; nor can we meet these specific ends, one by one, first, and then hope that somehow in the shuffle this schizophrenic philosophy of death will change into a philosophy of creative living.

Hard as it is to acknowledge, the simple truth is that the South's and the nation's racial problems cannot be solved by putting a loaf of bread, a book and a ballot in everyone's hand. I am not unsympathetic to those among us who are trying to believe that the loaf, the book, the ballot are all the Negro needs—or wants. I understand the desperate fear that causes certain Negroes to deny their hunger for things that make men human. I understand also the fear in the white man's heart that makes him more willing to work for specific, short-range goals such as the vote, better schools, better jobs for Negroes, than to change his own attitude about himself and his white race.

These fears, these emotional hungers, need to be faced and understood by all of us, though it will not be easy for white or black to face them.

A first step is to acknowledge that man is not an economic or political unit. To pretend that he is, is to ignore personality and cheapen the human spirit. And by ignoring man's psychological needs, by pretending to ourselves that his economic or political status is more important than his personality status, we oversimplify a complex, subtle, tragically profound problem and fail miserably in our efforts to solve it. As we have been failing for almost a century.

We whites cling desperately to the belief that the problem of race relations is the "Negro problem," that it is a matter of economics, that it will take a long time to "educate the Negro." Why? Because we dare not face the fact that race prejudice and the cultural and psychological patterns of segregation which have grown out of the white man's complex feelings about skin color profoundly affect us and our children on every level of our life and culture. We dare not acknowledge and meet in a creative way those emotional needs within our own families that, in a white-supremacy culture, we have been permitted to project upon the Negro, making him our scapegoat, using him as our psychological safety valve. Upon whom can we turn our hate if we no longer can turn it upon him? To whom can we feel superior, if we bring the Negro up to us on a level of human equality? We say it will "take a long time" for the Negro to "get to the place where he is worthy of democracy." Some of us, I fear, hope it will take a long time—*because we do not know what we shall do* with our own fears and hates when we can no longer take them out on the Negro or on some other scapegoat. We hope "it will be a long time" before we have to change our own selves, our attitudes toward sex, our family patterns; before we have to find new outlets for old frustrations, not only economic frustrations but those deeper hungers of our emotional lives that in our culture are too often left unsatisfied. These are complex, difficult problems which must be probed more deeply before we shall fully understand them, and before we can confess their implications for our personal lives.

It is easier, however, to see the immediate effects of racial segregation upon children. We know a child's personality cannot grow and mature without self-esteem, without feelings of security, without faith in the world's willingness to make room for him to live as a human being. Self-esteem and emotional security are to character what vitamins are to the body. No colored child in our country, however protected within the family, is being given today what his personality needs in order to grow and mature fully and richly. No white child, under the segregation pattern, North or South, can be free of arrogance, hardness of heart, blindness to human needs. The bitter and inescapable fact is that our children, white and colored, are growing distorted, twisted personalities within the crippling frame of segregation which we have imposed upon them.

I personally would prefer that my own child do without shoes than that he do without the esteem of his fellows, and I would prefer that he never look into a book than that he look down upon another human being. Of course, I want him to know what is in books, but I want him much more to know what is in men's hearts. This he can never learn unless he looks at them with level eyes. Shoes are important for both white and colored feet—who would deny this! But a child can go barefooted without great harm; he cannot go one day unesteemed by his fellows without deep injury to his personality. Our children, Negro and white, need all of these things, but will probably have little of them as long as we refuse to acknowledge them as human beings in *need of that which makes men human.*

Believing this, I cannot endure the idea so many liberals hold that segregation must change slowly. I believe it can change as rapidly as each of us can change his own heart. I believe it will never change until we look at what it is doing to the personality and character of every child, every grown-up, white and colored, in the South today—and to a less bitter degree throughout the country. Segregation is spiritual lynching. The lynched and the lynchers are our own people, ourselves, *our children.*

These are grave matters, troubling matters, which I feel must be faced, analyzed. For problems must be enunciated before we can know clearly what they are. We who do not believe in segregation as a way of life, must say so. We must break the conspiracy of silence which has held us in a grip so strong that it has become a taboo. We must say why segregation is unendurable to the human spirit. We must somehow find the courage to say it aloud. For, however we rationalize our silence, it is fear that is holding our tongues today. A widespread denial of a belief in segregation and all that it implies will shake this way of life to its roots. Each of us in his heart knows this. In the beginning was the Word and today the Word is powerful. To remain silent while the demagogues, the Negro haters, the racists, the mentally ill, loudly reaffirm their faith in segregation and the spiritual lynching which their way of life inflicts, is to be traitorous to everything that is good and creative and sane in human values. I believe the time has come when we must take our stand.

Clayton, Ga.

UNIT 3-10

WHAT THE NEGRO WANTS [1944]

WHAT THE NEGRO WANTS AND HOW TO GET IT: THE INWARD POWER OF THE MASSES

Leslie Pinckney Hill

WHAT THE NEGRO WANTS

There is little doubt now as to what the American Negro wants. Never, perhaps, has the Negro himself been more vocal or emphatic in his appeal, and never have so many helpfully approving, influential voices been raised in the surrounding white world. We have heard Mrs. Roosevelt, Sumner Welles, Pearl Buck, and Wendell Willkie sounding forth the warning that all the legitimate aims of the war and of the peace may be lost if America fails to accord to its Negro minority freedom, justice and fundamental equality. Negroes want to be accepted by our American society as citizens who in reality belong, who have the respect of their fellow man and equality of opportunity for life, liberty and the pursuit of happiness. Negroes want what good men want in every democratic society. If they wanted less they would not deserve the status of citizens.

These desires, harmonized with those four great freedoms which the Allied Nations have proclaimed as universal war objectives, are widely published by press and radio. They are now carefully documented. Negro and white leaders in many parts of the nation, and inter-racial committees North and South have been at pains to set out, in language which Negroes themselves have formulated, most of the specifics of the social political and economic aims of Negro striving. When Negroes meet in Durham, North Carolina, to develop a platform of agreements, it is significant that white leaders in Atlanta, Georgia, are sitting down very soon afterwards to make known to the world the attitude of the white South. Both groups, fortunately, are at last making the attempt to find acceptable bases for agreement.

The National Broadcasting System made history recently by presenting for the first time its own attitude on the highly controversial race question. Then it was that Wendell Willkie announced, and emphatically endorsed, at least six of the immediate aims of Negro effort:

1. Protection under the law and no discrimination in the administration of the law
2. Equality of education
3. Equality of expenditure for health and hospitalization
4. Elimination of all inhibiting restrictions in voting—through taxes or otherwise
5. Equal work opportunity and equal pay
6. The right to fight in any branch of the services

He might have included freedom from a generalizing press and from the usual moving picture presentation of the Negro as a scaramouch. These are minimum specifics. They are all however, only items in the total urge of Negro life, under the impact of vast world forces, towards that status, precious now and consciously desired by all the peoples of the earth, in which equal recognition and full freedom will be accorded to the dignity and sanctity of all human personality in all human relations. The question is: How can the Negro achieve that status?

How Can the Negro Get What He Wants—Leadership?

In attempting any answer to that question we have no lamp for our footing but the lamp of experience. Our light must shine from history, from the findings of all the sciences, and from the deathless words and example of those illumined spirits of every age and race in whom mankind has found inspiration and guidance. These all speak together of effort rooted in vision and long-enduring patience. No race or nation mushrooms up *en masse* into full-blown social accomplishment. No Rome was ever built in a day. There is no such thing as getting anywhere without going there. Time and the content we give it are always the final determinants.

And inasmuch as every people of whom we have record has been obliged to look to leaders through whose heart and mind they could express their hopes and define their directives—there is nowhere in history a single record to the contrary—it is clear that Negroes, whether in the disordered perspective—warping present time of tension and crisis, or in the outwardly calmer days of peace, will move forward only as the leaders whom they follow can effectively point the way. Of all the forces operating now towards the reaching of our aims and the molding of our future none is more potent for good or for evil than the force of this leadership.

Therefore I submit this fundamental thesis: The Negro will get the things he legitimately wants and strives for only if during the world crisis, and after it, he will follow leaders who have a known, articulate and unifying philosophy of life adequate to the exactions both of the crisis and to the still more difficult peace-time of reconstruction and rehabilitation. "The hungry sheep look up and are not fed." That was Milton's indictment of leaders whom he described as "blind mouths." But of another Leader it is written that the people heard Him gladly, that He spoke as one having authority because He brought the bread of life, the truth and a way. Who now will feed the discontented, disillusioned but willing masses of Negro people, and show them a path? What kind of leader must we magnify for a hindered but potentially great race?

We do not single out today any one all-dominating personality. There was a kind of social economy in the general uses made of the leadership of Frederick Douglass and Booker T. Washington. We have never had their equal in the responsibility these two men carried as referees in all the vexed issues confronting their people. They dispensed a vast patronage, made nominations to the government for all kinds of services available to Negroes, were called into conference in all parts of the nation where dangers threatened, spoke with authority to both races and by both were gladly heard. Neither was a university man, and the scholar often raised the old question of the source of their authority. But they possessed high elemental powers which they wielded unwearyingly and unselfishly for the common good. Negro aspiration in America for generations was to be typified by the vigor and achievement of these two spokesmen.

Today the scene has changed. Not even in George Washington Carver were Negroes generally aware of a consciously accepted influence. He was for long years rather a self-effacing prophet representative of new inter-racial values which only the future of our culture will explore. Today there are many leaders, and their development in Negro life is deeply significant and heartening. These are men and women who have strong influence and loyal following in all those areas of action and interest in which Negroes struggle. They are teachers and preachers, business men and women, journalists, authors and artists, social workers, labor organizers, politicians, parents, farmers and soldiers. They are spread over the land, North, South, East and West. Each, in his community, has some positive effect upon the social, moral, political and economic life of both races. Their compounded power is immeasurable. A thousand men and women with self-possession, informed outlook and active energy must, in the nature of things, promise more that is desirable in a democratic society than one compelling figure, however gifted or potent.

The most impressive single fact in this wide dispersion of leaders is the unanimity of their convictions. What can be said or attempted or done differs, of course, with the geographical locus. Atlanta and New Orleans cannot duplicate the precise procedures of Philadelphia or New York. Nevertheless, Negro leaders in all these places want the same thing. They want in Georgia and Pennsylvania, here at home, the same freedom for which the democracies say they are fighting on the other side of the Pacific in Burina or Munda. They want that sense of being acceptable and belonging which can be realized only when there is ungrudging respect for all human personality, whatever the accident of color. And the legitimacy and the necessity of these inspirations are now progressively acknowledged not only by our comparatively liberal North but even by brave and democratic spirits emerging in our South.

Now this manifold leadership can be wrought into effective power if it can be inspired and harmonized by a conscious philosophy that will constitute an unfailing frame of reference for leaders in every field. Not always can that philosophy be translated easily into the language of the masses but to those masses it will invariably be consecrated. Gradually the people will feel its power. The leader's philosophy must look before and after. It must be the sanctuary of his spirit, the repository of his social and moral values, must keep him calm and resourceful under every challenge or provocation, and strengthen him to survive the strain of mental and physical exertion. It must be the power of that grace which in the old world, as Plutarch reports, kept the face of Phocion serene and unperturbed, and in our century, made Gandhi a figure of world concern.

Long ago I formulated for myself as a teacher, and thus perilously and inescapably a leader of youth, a brief but comprehensive personal philosophy of human relations, which time and experience have seemed to confirm. When I think or speak in detail of the racial scene here at home it is always against this universal background. I submit this philosophy to my responsible brethren in the United States or elsewhere who find themselves swept by the sudden but temporary alarms of tension and conflict, or challenged by the perduring blind pressures of prejudice.

A Personal Philosophy of Human Relations

The human family is one. The geographical or social factors that bind human beings together serve chiefly as conditioning settings from which proceed all those widely varying contributions, racial or national, that make up the culture of the world. Science continually proves the interdependency of all the races of man. Religion, education, politics and all the arts reinforce that proof. Race and nation are only terms by which we distinguish in this one human family vast aggregates of its members who have similar or identical characteristics.

* * *

No race or nation—as long as we think and behave under these concepts—can depend upon any other race or nation for its own advancement. Interdependence—now acknowledged everywhere—means fundamentally that each of the races must bear its own peculiar burden and, by working out its own salvation, help all the others.

* * *

Every race worthy of survival must make some definite and continuous contribution to the general welfare. Each in good faith, must give as well as take. Rights must be balanced by obligations. Education must search out and develop every creative potentiality, large or small, and the whole group must magnify all the manifestations of genius.

* * *

No race can long survive or advance in full freedom if it fails to utilize its available resources and opportunities. These, left undeveloped, will be taken over and utilized, soon or late, by some other race.

* * *

Mandatory social objectives for the American Negro in his multi-racial environment must be adaptation and adjustment by cooperation. That indispensable cooperation will be powerfully assisted by strong personal self-control, good manners, intelligent tolerance, faith in the proved leaders and spokesmen of both races, and a reverent regard for the meaning and power of words. These are control factors directly related to the opening of opportunity for all kinds of participation and upgrading in the national service and elsewhere.

* * *

The greatest positive contribution the race can make to a deranged and demoralized civilization will be disciplined parents in upright, democratic homes wherein children are wanted and secure, and wherein they shall be taught respect for the laws of God and man, obedience to rightful authority, the universal need of self-sacrifice, responsibility for some worthy service to the family group, and the value of all work well done. Second only to the parent in all of this is the Negro teacher. Close to the school is the church. If these fail the street will thwart home, school and church alike.

* * *

The race must keep all the friends it has in the dominant white world and work unceasingly to multiply them. Potent will be that discriminating intelligence by which Negroes will acknowledge the blessings they enjoy, as well as the wrongs they suffer. Praise must not be sacrificed to protest, nor protest to praise. No philosophy or procedure that produces racial hatred and antagonism can advance the common good.

* * *

World experience teaches that Negroes will make headway best by taking thought of one another and of their white friends in working out their common problems. Isolated individual is impotent in an age whose genius is organization. By collective thinking every good mind, every skilled hand, every gift or grace of the spirit, every agency and every office is strengthened. In it there is room for all. It is the only guarantee of that effective group action required by the ordeal of war or the exigencies of peace.

* * *

The common foe of the whole human race is war, because war is a heinous and blasphemous negation of all right human relations. Nevertheless, a nation is often drawn into this disaster, and then every citizen becomes a guardian of his country's life. Then loyalty demands every sacrifice save that of honor.

* * *

In every emergency, the Negro race in America must give to the nation its unreserved allegiance. Wrongs will remain, but increasing opportunities and obligations will surpass them. Our democracy is not yet a satisfying reality, but Negroes are still free to live, strive and die to make it come in God's unhurried time. All else by comparison is trivial.

SUMMARY

What does the American Negro want? Full citizen status in our American democracy. How shall he reach that goal? By the inward power of the masses. And how shall that power be acquired? Fundamentally, on the highest plane and on the humblest, by a leadership motivated by a world-encompassing philosophy which is rooted in the will of God—a leadership which, itself a vital part of the force of events, is consecrated in humility to the immediate and practical education of the people.

About the Author

Leslie Pinckney Hill was born on May 14, 1880, in Lynchburg, Virginia. He was graduated from Harvard University A.B. (Phi Beta Kappa), 1903, and A.M., 1904. He taught at Tuskegee Institute from 1904 to 1907, and was Principal of Manassas Industrial Institute (Virginia) from 1907 to 1913. In 1913 he became Principal of the Institute for Colored Youth and its President when its name was changed to State Teachers College, Cheyney, Pennsylvania. Lincoln University conferred the degree of Litt. D. upon him in 1929 and Morgan an LL. D. in 1939. He is the founder and President of the Pennsylvania State Negro Council; a member of the Committee of National Council of Student Christian Associations of Work among Negro Colleges; of the National YMCA Committee of Colored Work; of the Peace Section of the American Friends Service Committee; and of many other boards and committees. Dr. Hill has contributed articles to a number of educational magazines and is the author of the lyric poems, *The Wings of Oppression* (1927); a dramatic history, *Toussaint L'Ouvenure* (1928); an idyl *Marc Anders* (1933), and occasional poems.

THE NEGRO HAS ALWAYS WANTED THE FOUR FREEDOMS

Charles H. Wesley

. . . There will be a vast gulf between what the Negro wants and what he can get in present social situations, even with the abnormal changes brought about by the war. This result has led and will continue to lead to frustration and outbreak. Suppressed wrath has finally found expression in inter-racial rioting and in-group violence. Nevertheless the Negro is now moving from "his place" in the social structure in all avenues of life. White liberalism, weakened by realistic examinations of its lack of democratic practices, may have enough life to meet this rising tide and continue to advance with it.

What then are the wants which must be faced in the future by our democracy? In answering this question it is difficult for one to endeavor to speak for the Negro. He must speak mainly from his own point of view, his faith, his hopes and his experiences.

1. *The Negro wants a revision of the concept of race and of racism.* Discriminations in industry, labor unions, education, the Jim Crow pattern for the Army and Navy are based upon fascist racism. The white people of the United States have strong and positive ideas about racial equality. They use these justifications for discriminations. Before the latter can be removed, there must be some change in the former. The Negro is pressing forward against these barriers but the assumption of racial equality is being resisted. The war, with its emphasis upon democracy and its apparent opposition to racial superiority, is continuing to raise the issue, and will have to be met with sincerity. Speeches and well-meaning committees cannot solve it by themselves. There will have to be education on the subject of race. We shall have to learn that the doctrine of racism has no scientific foundation. It is, however, one of the most dangerous of dogmas. It was almost unknown prior to the period of the French Revolution. The first complete expression of racism was made by Count Arthur de Gobineau in his *Essay on the Inequality of Human Races* published between 1853 and 1857. The successors of Gobineau expanded these doctrines with pseudo-scientific investigations, which soon associated racist dogma with nationalism. Houston Chamberlain in 1899 with his *Foundations of the Nineteenth Century* developed the doctrine so that the Germans became a type of superior "chosen race." By 1914, race was closely associated with the national spirit in other countries, and here in the United States, we interpreted it to mean "white" people. This absurd scientific dogma became an instrument of justification for antagonism against a minority group. Actually the cause of racial antagonism goes deeper than the surface evidences of race. Competition for employment, poverty and the apparent need to guard a group's possessions from others who are unlike lead them to seek a scapegoat in the minority. The unequal rights of citizens based upon racial claims are so intermingled with racism that the exploitation and inequality from which the minority suffers are diverted into racial attitudes, which, passed from generation to generation, tend to become fixed. The schools can undertake to give their pupils instruction in the basic issues of race, rather than to continue the present hands-off program. Such instruments can be related directly to the welfare of democracy. The church, the movies, the library, the stage and radio can use their powerful influences in this endeavor. The newspapers of both white and black editorships can be employed as effective materials.

2. *The Negro wants a realistic interpretation of religion in terms of brotherhood.* The church is seen consistently to practice segregation and division, although its theory is universal. If it were not for the Negro Church, it is probable that there would be thousands of enemies of Christianity among Negroes. If the church does not desire to be known as a hypocrite in history and in fact, it must cleanse itself of segregation, discrimination and exclusion and begin to minister to all groups without the long-handled spoon. If the church would save itself, it must develop a crusading ardor for Christianity in relation to all men. The church can give the people the will to do, for facts will not suffice in this situation.

3. *The Negro wants ultimately the abolition of segregation in education and the equalization of educational opportunity as an immediate step.* The segregated Negro school is usually an inferior school and a disparity in the bi-racial system continues to develop. This is due largely to the fact that such a school is a reflection of the inferior economic and social status of the Negro. This inferiority is represented by inequalities in school terms, training of teachers, buildings and equipment. The inequalities extend from the elementary schools through the graduate school. Although the laws of some states prohibit educational segregation, it is not infrequently found, and these separate schools for Negroes are usually unequal evidences of the separation which reflects deeper maladjustments of the peoples, white and black.

It may be argued that the Negro in his present situation needs the separate school in order that his faith, pride and enthusiasm may be inspired and that the truth of history and social science may be made known to him. Nevertheless, if we abolish the racial causation for the school namely, race prejudice and discrimination, this type of school is no longer an expedient but rather a fosterer of segregation. Ultimately, this segregated school should and will be abolished, and we shall have American youth educated in schools for Americans who will not be separated from one another by either class or race.

4. *The Negro wants to be considered a citizen of the nation under whose allegiance he was born.* His citizenship and presence in the states are as old as any other Americans. He regards himself as an American among Americans. He was here in the United States when its fundamental documents of citizenship rights were adopted. He voted in at least five of the original thirteen states. There were nearly a half million free Negro citizens in 1860. Of 12,865,500 Negroes listed in the 1940 census, 99.4 percent were native born and about 97 percent were entirely of native born parents. The Negro is not an alien. This is his country and he knows it. He has developed with this nation and has been molded by its patterns of democratic life. He therefore feels himself entitled to all of its privileges—the ballot with the abolition of restrictions including the poll tax, the white primary and similar barriers; representation in political bodies and such community agencies as the jury, the school board, teaching staffs, hospital staffs and all civilian agencies; the best home that can be afforded without residential or other restriction; the privilege of association with or of forming a legal marriage with the person who is willing to marry him, and to take the consequences as in all such cases, and not to be compelled to live a life of lies and deceits because of what is known as social policy, to which neither nature nor science give any measure of support; the right to work for equal wages wherever he is qualified and with whoever is equally qualified whether in government office, industry, agriculture or other activity; the right to be considered just as other applicants for any appointment in state, school, university or research organization either public or private; the right to serve as other citizens in the armed forces without discrimination in either camp or field, on the sea or in the air; and the right to enjoy all citizenship privileges and to accept all obligations and perform all duties expected by the nation of its citizens.

5. *The Negro wants democracy to begin at home.* As one was heard to say during the Detroit riots, "I would rather die for democracy here than in Germany." This attitude is typical of many Negroes. They want to secure freedom and democracy for the rest of the world but they also want these here at home. Some are already beginning to doubt that this war is for freedom or democracy. They are beginning to believe that it is a war to save an outworn civilization and to continue an old system of life represented in a nineteenth-century order. They are beginning to be disillusioned when they think of the result of the first world war to save the world for democracy. They want democracy to save itself for the world. The argument from silence in our democracy should give way, to active participation in the extension of its practice. The future of our democratic life is insecure so long as the hatred, disdain and disparagement of Americans of African ancestry exist. The disappearance between the censuses of thousands of Americans of color through absorbing on into the "white" population group is an aspect of flight from this situation as well as the pursuit of other advantages which the change seems to provide. The unmolested ignorance of our democratic public mind about the Negro is one of the barriers to racial understanding. The Negro wants the education which is received by Americans to be one which includes not only information in the sciences, the arts and languages but also in democratic life as a whole, so that the citizen will adjust more rapidly to his environment and to his fellowmen with an adequate and correct knowledge of them.

6. *The Negro wants not only to win the war but also to win the peace.* He desires that reality shall be given to the democratic faith for which he and others are fighting and giving their substance and their lives. He wants the peace to be free of race and color restrictions, of imperialism and exploitation, and inclusive of the participation of minorities all over the world in their own governments. When it is said that we are fighting for freedom, the Negro asks, "Whose freedom? Is it the freedom of a peace to exploit, suppress, exclude, debase and restrict colored peoples in India, China, Africa, Malaya in the usual ways? Is it to be a freedom of racial arrogance, economic lordships, and social differentiation in the post-war era? Will Great Britain and the United States specifically omit from the Four Freedoms their minorities and subject peoples? The Negro does not want such a peace.

7. *The Negro wants freedom to work and to maintain, with others, the accepted American standard of living.* He is realizing that there are those who have themselves profited by race prejudice and have been motivating its increase among white workers. The owners of land and industry have often forged tighter the chains of poverty and caste upon white and black workers alike. They have used the old technique of "divide and rule" and have sought to encourage labor union strife as well as to inflate the pride of poor whites in regard to their former jobs and to debase wages and jobs by designating them for Negroes only. They have abandoned their Christian professions and bartered their souls in the long, bitter struggle to keep their profits and their White Supremacy. White and black workers need to realize that they must cooperate in order to achieve a higher living standard. Black workers seem to be living to accept this challenge.

CONCLUSION

In all of these wants, there are ultimate, long-run proposals and more immediately approximate ones. Unless we begin the march now towards the long-run objectives, we shall never make the journey. These wants are not utopian and impractical in any other sense than that democracy is also. Unless we take these into consideration, we shall not be able to preserve freedom for other Americans, for it cannot be preserved by restricting its benefits to some and extending it to others.

The Negro's wants are not entirely selfish and do not affect his group economy alone. The settlement of his problem will lead to a realistic interpretation of democracy's faith. These wants are the tests of democracy. They are not necessarily new, although their expressions have taken different forms through the years. As a matter of fact, the Negro wants what he has always wanted, and yet he has had different ways of saying it.

And now, the colored peoples throughout the world wait for the answer to the question whether or not the struggle of World War II is one of freedom everywhere in the world or of freedom limited only to white people in the world and measured in broken doses to colored peoples. The answer to this question determines, on the one hand, the future status of the Negro, but on the other hand, it may sound the tocsin of another of civilization's advances or the death knell of democratic western civilization.

About the Author

Charles H. Wesley was born December 2, 1891, in Louisville, Kentucky. He received his bachelor's degree from Fisk University in 1911; his master's degree from Yale University in 1913; and his doctor's degree (history) from Harvard University in 1925. During 1930-1931 he was a Guggenheim Fellow in London. From 1913 to 1942 he served as Instructor, Assistant Professor, Associate Professor, Professor and Head of the Department of History at Howard University. From 1938 to 1942 he was also Dean of the Graduate School. Since September, 1942, he has been President of Wilberforce University, Wilberforce, Ohio. Dr. Wesley served in the Army Y.M.C.A. during World War I and was a Pastor and Presiding Elder in the A.M.E. Church from 1918 to 1938. He is a Trustee of Fisk University and a member of many local and national boards and committees. Dr. Wesley has contributed articles and reviews to many scholarly journals and is the author of *Negro Labor in the United States, 1850–1925* (1927); *The History of Alpha Phi Alpha* (four editions, 1930, 1934, 1939, 1942); *Richard Allen* (1935); *The Collapse of the Confederacy* (1938); and a *Manual of Research and Thesis for Graduate Students* (1941).

THE NEGRO PEOPLE IN THE NATIONAL FRONT FOR VICTORY

Doxey A. Wilkerson

To assert that the progressive nature of this war "requires" the further extension of Negro freedom is not to immunize the importance of continued struggle. The changes now in process are not automatic, nor will they be in the future. The inherent liberating character of the war will not "solve" the problems of the Negro or of the nation as a whole; it but creates highly favorable conditions for the achievement of progressive solutions. Their realization will come only through deliberate and persistent struggle.

Quite the opposite point of view is advanced by important circles in our country. Curiously enough, it is embraced by both the Martin Dies type of reactionary and the John Temple Graves type of Southern liberal. Both find common ground in the proposition that, "for the sake of national unity," there must be a wartime moratorium on agitation for Negro democratic rights.

One of the clearest and most forthright answers to this specious argument is that given by the General Secretary of the Communist party:

> There is another field of problems in which national unity demands a much more strict interpretation of equality. Typical . . . is the problem of our thirteen million Negro citizens. Here it would be dangerously destructive of national unity to try to make our peace with the status quo, which is a status of a shameful heritage from chattel slavery based on Hitler-like racial conceptions; and it would further undermine the United Nations, destroy confidence between the United States on the one side, and our allies and potential allies of the colored races on the other. We dare not, on pain of humiliating defeat in this war, rest complacently on the present status of the Negro citizens of the United States. *We must, as a war necessity, proceed to the systematic and relentless wiping out of every law, custom, and habit of thought, which in flagrant violation of our Constitution enforce an unequal status between Negro and white citizens of the United States.*[1]

Whoever now attempts to differentiate between the victory-goal of the nation and the freedom-goal of the Negro, setting one against the other, either fails to grasp or deliberately ignores the fundamental unity of the two. The nation's struggles toward victory now necessarily advance the cause of Negro freedom, and the Negro's struggles toward freedom likewise advance the cause of victory for the nation as a whole.

This wartime mutuality between the wartime interests of the Negro people and the rest of the nation serves to emphasize the necessity for ever more vigorous struggles for Negro democratic rights. It does more. It also suggests the direction and form which such struggles must assume if maximum results are to be achieved.

There are some Negro leaders who now propose to "bargain" with their embattled country, offering Negro support of the war "in return for" the correction of existing injustices. Their approach is fundamentally unsound in principle and stupid as a tactic of minority group struggle.

This is not a war which the Negro *may* support if; rather, it is a war which the Negro *must* support-regardless. The lives and property of the Negro people, too, are at stake in this war. Moreover, all the social gains the Negro has made since slavery, and all he may hope to achieve in the future, are utterly dependent upon victory over the Axis forces of fascist enslavement. Nothing could more surely alienate the Negro people from the very progressive forces who they must win as allies, nothing could more surley defeat their present and future goals of freedom than for the Negro now to stand aloof from the developing national front for victory-petulant, impotent, and absurd. The Negro's support of this war is, and must be, unconditional. On no other basis can he now find solution for his problem.

There are also Negro leaders whose main stock in trade now is to denounce "the Government" and "white people" for still existing racial injustices, and to organize mass struggles of the Negro people, *as Negroes*, against both. They too are following a path which weakens the victory program of the nation and leads to the ultimate defeat of their adherents.

In the first place, the Roosevelt Administration has given convincing evidence of its sincere desire to advance the cause of Negro freedom. Indeed, it has fought hard and achieved substantial results toward this end. For the Negro people now to join forces with the Poll-tax Democrats and the reactionary Republicans in further undermining the strength of the progressive Roosevelt Administration would serve the interests neither of victory nor of Negro freedom. It would effectively retard the achievement of both. Again to quote Earl Browder:

> There is a loud-mouthed cult in our country which is willing to admit every weakness and error so long as they can blame it on the President. These are the demagogues of reaction. But there are too many honest democrats, progressives, and even labor men, who weaken the President's position by leaving all problems for him to settle, by failing to take energetic action themselves to help solve these problems. . . . No one has any right to criticize the President who is not himself in the midst of the hottest and most uncompromising fight to halt the mob of reaction now controlling the majority of Congress and threatening the whole country and its war effort.[2]

* * *

Second, although there is some justification for "all-Negro" liberation movements, the crying need of this period is for ever broader unity between progressive white and Negro Americans to promote their common and mutual ends of victory and a democratic peace. Such Negro-white unity is not only more possible because of conditions created by the war; it is also more necessary.

Just as our nation would be in mortal peril if separated from her British, Soviet and Chinese allies, so would the Negro people face certain defeat if they allowed themselves to become separated from and placed in opposition to the other democratic forces of our country. Moreover, the strength of the whole progressive camp would thereby be weakened, and the goals for which this war is being fought would be placed in jeopardy.

The Negro freedom movement derives its main wartime strength from its integral relations with the victory program of the country as a whole. It necessarily follows, therefore, that conscious struggles for Negro freedom during this period will achieve maximum results to the extent that they are carried on within the framework of the nation's struggle for victory. This premise is fundamental. From it there flow several practical implications for the wartime movement to extend the freedom of the Negro people.

First, organized struggles for Negro freedom must declare their unconditional support of the war effort of our nation. They must declare their full support of the win-the-war policies of our Commander-in-Chief. There must never be the slightest doubt about their genuinely patriotic character.

Second, demands for the correction of specific injustices must be raised as essential war measures to promote victory. Thus, racial bars to employment, abridgments of civil rights, denials of the franchise, discrimination in the armed forces, and the whole array of obstacles to Negro freedom should be challenged as obstacles to victory-which, in very truth, they are. Their removal should be demanded, not solely on the grounds of democratic justice, but especially also on the broader and even more urgent grounds of national security.

Third, organized movements for Negro freedom must direct their attention not only to specific issues of "Negro rights," but also to those larger wartime issues of the nation which profoundly affect the solution of the Negro's problems. They should fight implacably against the defeatist foes of our war effort. They should give aggressive support to such essential win-the-war measures as price and rent control subsidies, a realistic tax program, an honest and democratic soldier vote bill, poll tax repeal, and the fullest use of war manpower. They should combat all defeatist efforts to disrupt the unity of our nation and of the United Nations. They should struggle to strengthen the program of the Anglo-Soviet-American coalition—for the quickest possible defeat and thorough destruction of fascism, for the organization of a just and enduring peace. Especially should they rally to the support of President Roosevelt and the election of a win-the-war Congress in the 1944 elections. In short, they must throw their full resources into the fight for all measures essential for wining the war in the shortest possible time. In the triumph of the cause of victory will the cause of Negro freedom achieve maximum realization of its goals.

Fourth, the Negro freedom movement must forge the closest possible unity among the Negro people themselves, and between the Negro people and their natural allies in the progressive white population and the organized labor movement. Petty organizational rivalries and factionalism should now be put aside. There should be uncompromising opposition to all reactionary attempts to use the "menace of communism" bogey as a tactic to divide, and thus defeat, the progressive organizations of the people. The growing virus of anti-Semitism must be fought. Above all, the Negro people must enter the labor movement in ever increasing hundreds of thousands, joining actively with their white fellow-workers in the solution of their common trade union problems, and turning the power of their unions increasingly to the related tasks of victory and Negro freedom.

Unequivocal support of this people's war of national liberation and survival. Demands for Negro liberation as a means of winning the war. Vigorous support of the win-the-war policies of our Commander-in-Chief. Solid unity of the Negro people with all other progressive, win-the-war forces of the nation. These are the basic essentials of a wartime program for the Negro people. Herein lie the correct strategy and tactics which will best advance the cause of Negro freedom. It is as an integral and struggling sector of the developing national front for victory that the Negro people can now make their most substantial progress toward attainment of "What the Negro Wants."

POST-WAR PROSPECTS FOR THE NEGRO AND THE NATION

And once the war is won, what then of Negro freedom? Will not the Negro's wartime gains very shortly disappear? What, if any, basis is there for the prospect of continued progress toward freedom in the post-war world? The essential answers to these questions are largely implied in the preceding discussion. It is well to make them explicit.

There are those who see nothing durable in the wartime extensions of freedom for the Negro people. They believe these gains will vanish once the emergency from which they arose has passed. To them these advances "must" be transitory because they were yielded under duress; they did not arise out of the chastened hearts of men. There are several considerations which suggest that this pessimism is quite unwarranted.

In the *first* place, the fact that wartime extensions of Negro freedom arise out of historic necessity, far from suggesting their weakness, is in reality their greatest strength. The history of human progress is a record of social gains which were impelled by the inherent logic of events and the struggles of mankind for freedom. "Humanitarianism" and "good will," noble sentiments that they are, have proved to be among the most unstable forces of history. They readily accommodate themselves to the necessities of time and place. It is well for Negro Americans to recall that the Emancipation Proclamation was not dedicated by noble sentiments, but rather by the stern requirements of military necessity.

Second, the events of this period are forging new relationships between the Negro people and the rest of the nation, relationships which, in themselves, are a substantial guarantee of permanence for the wartime extensions of Negro freedom. By way of illustration, consider the position of the new hundreds of thousands of Negro industrial workers, especially in comparison with the last war. After World War I, many—by no means all—Negro workers were ousted from their new-found jobs in the industries of the North. Not only were they members of a subordinate minority race, but they were also recent migrants to their communities, and many had been brought in as "scabs" and "strike-breakers." In the increased post-war competition for jobs, they found themselves in direct conflict with organized white workers into whose unions they had made but little headway. They were replaced.

After World War II, an entirely different situation will obtain. The pre-war influx of Negro workers into the trade union movement will have been enormously increased, especially in the great democratic unions of the CIO in basic industries. In the course of common wartime struggles on the industrial and political fronts, hundreds of thousands of Negro workers will have established firm relations of comradeship with their white fellow-workers. Their unions will have come more and more to take up the struggle for economic security and full democratic rights for the Negro people. Their jobs will be far more secure.

As in the industrial world, so in many other areas of our national life, the wartime experiences of the Negro people are fundamentally altering their relationship with their countrymen. New and different social structures are being built, and in their wake different attitudes emerge. In the development of these new wartime relationships, there lies a substantial basis for confidence that the wartime gains of the Negro people will abide.

Third, the future of the Negro's freedom in America will be decisively influenced by the quality of the peace which issues from this war, and here the prospect is far from discouraging. World War II cannot end in another Versailles, precisely because of the nature of the forces in combat, the inherent liberating character which the war has been forced to assume, and the power of the masses of freedom loving peoples which it has set into motion the world over.

Contrast the anti-Soviet Pact of Munich, which unleashed the fascist military right upon the world, with the Anglo-Soviet American Declaration of Teheran, which opens up an entirely new perspective for mankind. The capitalist and socialist worlds, once in serious conflict, are now firmly united in "complete agreement," on measures for the military destruction of fascism and the establishment of a just and enduring "peace which will command good will from the overwhelming masses of the peoples of the world." Precisely those three nations which represent the greatest concentrations of military, economic, and political power in the world have now agreed to "work together in the war and in the peace which will follow."

They reached this agreement because of historic necessity—the necessity to collaborate in order to survive. They have the determination and the strength to carry it out. And they will carry it out, for there is no other way to victory, and to peace "for many generations."

In a world bathed in blood by the reactionary policies of Munich, this historic Declaration of Teheran represents an enormous achievement. It opens up the perspective of enduring peace and prosperity for all peoples. It inspires new hope and confidence in all progressive mankind. It lays the basis for the building of a truly progressive peace. It is, by far, the greatest possible guarantee of that kind of post-war world in which the Negro people can continue their march toward complete freedom.

Finally, a word should be said about the tremendous concern in certain quarters over "post-war plans" for the Negro's freedom. The position of the Negro people in the post-war world will not be determined by the blue-prints now formed in the heads of "planners." Rather, it will be determined by the relative strength of the pro-Teheran forces of progress and the anti-Teheran forces of reaction which now struggle for dominance in the world and in our nation. Especially will it be determined by the relations of the Negro people to these forces. Now to draft idealistic post-war plans for the Negro is not necessarily a harmful pastime—except that it tends to divert much needed energy from the really urgent task of today: to win the war at the earliest possible moment. It would be naïve to assume, however, that such "plans" will constitute an important factor in shaping the future of the Negro people.

The Negro's future is being decisively shaped by the struggles for victory and freedom today. Let the Negro people now exert their maximum strength toward winning the war. Let them fight for their own freedom within the framework of the nation's fight for survival. Let them do all in their power to hasten the unconditional surrender of the Axis and the complete destruction of fascism. Let them establish the firmest possible unity with the developing coalition of all other progressive win-the-war forces of our nation—fighting for the triumph of the Roosevelt Administration in the 1944 elections, for that speedy victory in war and that just and enduring peace which are the promise of Teheran.

Let the Negro people do these things *now.* This is their best possible guarantee of freedom in the post-war world. Along this path alone lies the ultimate attainment of "What the Negro Wants."

About the Author

Doxey A. Wilkerson was born in Excelsior Springs, Missouri, April 24, 1905. He attended the public schools of Kansas City, Missouri and completed his high school work in Kansas City, Kansas. He was graduated from the University of Kansas, B.A., 1926, and M.A., 1927. After teaching English and Education at Virginia State College, he served on the faculty of Howard University from 1935 to 1943. For a year he was Education Specialist with the OPA, a position which he resigned on June 15, 1943, to join the Communist Party and become its educational director for Maryland and the District of Columbia. He was National Vice-President of the American Federation of Teachers from 1937 to 1940 and later an active member of the United Federal Workers of America, CIO. In 1943 he was elected Vice-President of the International Labor Defense. He is now Executive Editor of *People's Voice* and a member of the National Committee of the newly organized Communist Political Association. Mr. Wilkerson has contributed articles to many journals, is the author of *Special Problems of Negro Education* (1939), and contributed a chapter to J. S. Roucek's *Sociological Foundations of Education* (1941).

SUMMARY

Frederick D. Patterson

An attempt has been made to set forth the peculiar position in which American Negroes find themselves as citizens who are without their full privileges. They are at times confused, embarrassed and mistreated. They recognize that they have been permitted to make substantial progress and many of their relationships are normal. They find the special restrictions which are imposed upon them out of keeping with professed national ideals. Negro youth particularly and the present generation of adults, having experienced no status except that of free men, fail to understand much of the treatment they receive which can be explained only in terms of the inferiority associated with a status of slavery.

Negroes, having no ideology other than that of democracy, cannot consistently behave in any pattern except that which seeks complete freedom of expression and assures them the same rights, privileges and responsibilities as are possessed by other Americans. They ask not for special privilege, but for the opportunity to achieve in accordance with their individual abilities as human beings.

To bring about the full participating status desired, the writer believes there must be organized, simultaneously, efforts, as thoroughly coordinated as possible, in several directions. This will consist in part of a vigorous and sustained combat against injustices. This effort should be constituted in the main by sound, practical and realistic programs which recognize clearly the limitations which exist and attempt to overcome them by the most feasible methods. A few such methods have been suggested, many more are necessary and possible. As these are applied with increasing effectiveness the problem of race with its manifold aspects will move steadily toward a solution that win be consistent with our national ideals in their economic, social, and Christian principles.

About the Author

Frederick Douglass Patterson was born in Washington, D.C., October 10, 1901. He received the degree of D.V.M. from Iowa State College in 1923; M.S. from Iowa State College in 1927; Ph. D. from Cornell University, 1932. He has been awarded an LL. D. by Virginia State College; D. Humanities, Wilberforce University; and D. Sc., Lincoln University. He is a trustee of Tuskegee Institute, Fisk University, Hampton Institute, Booker T. Washington Agricultural and Industrial Institute of Liberia, Palmer Memorial College and Bethune-Cookman College. He taught at Virginia State

College and Tuskegee and since 1935 has been President of Tuskegee. Dr. Patterson is a member of the Southern Education Foundation, the Executive Board of the National Urban League, the Southern Conference for Human Welfare, President Roosevelt's Commission on Farm Tenancy, the Southern Regional Council and other boards. He is also serving as a Special Assistant to the Secretary of Agriculture. President Patterson has contributed articles to a number of journals.

COUNT US IN

Sterling A. Brown

Negroes want to be counted in. They want to belong. They want what other men have wanted deeply enough to fight and suffer for it. They want democracy. Wanting it so much, they disregard more and more the warnings: "This is not the time." "The time isn't ripe." "Take your time, take your time." Nearly a hundred years ago, in desperation at the plight of the slaves, Herman Melville wrote, "Time must befriend these thralls." And in crucial moments since, time has been pointed to as the solvent. Patience, urges David Cohn, rule out the emotional and irrational and then the burden will rest "upon the whites to do for the Negro what they have not done at all, or only in part." But the Negro has difficulty in finding the guarantees of this hope that so many Negro and white spokesmen have promised to him. Southern Negroes are not of one mind with Southern whites that "outside interference is hateful and incompetent." They do not see democracy as a commodity to be quarantined at the Potomac and Ohio Rivers; as a sort of a Japanese beetle to be hunted for in the luggage before travelers are allowed to go on. Negroes are glad whenever democratic ideas circulate through the South, whether by means of liberal weeklies, *PM*, the speeches of labor organizers, pamphlets, sermons, radio forums, books, Negro newspapers and magazines, or letters from the boys in service. They know, of course, that if democracy is to be achieved in the South, where it is least found, the greatest work must be done by Southerners, whites and Negroes together. But they welcome whatever help they can get from any sources.

And they know, furthermore, that the agencies working for democracy are not necessarily "outside agitators." The National Association for the Advancement of Colored People may have its headquarters in New York, but, as its name suggests, it is a *national* association. Many of its leaders are Southerners by birth and training. Many of its courageous workers are living in the South. The Negro teachers who risk their jobs and even worse in the struggle for equalization of salaries are Southern born and bred. Negro journalists in the deep South generally speak out uncompromisingly for justice. Southern Negroes have not needed Northern agitators to stir up dissatisfaction with discrimination and abuse. As pointed out earlier, they have learned the hard way, and the lessons have sunk in deeply.

They have heard the threats. Against their democratic aspirations they see a concerted line-up: college professors as well as hoodlums; congressmen as well as vigilantes; Rotarians as well as manual laborers; cotton planters as well as cotton hands. Negroes expect that some of them are going to get hurt before they get what they want. This is no new experience for them; they have been getting hurt in this country since 1619. But getting hurt in a stand-up struggle for justice is one thing; getting hurt merely because of the color of your skin, while lying down, is quite another.

On trips through the South, I have talked with several who had been hurt. With Roland Hayes, for example, shortly after he had been savagely beaten by the policemen of Rome, Georgia. With Hugh Gloster, a young colleg professor, who had been thrown off a train in Tupelo, Mississippi, because he asked the conductor to let Negroes who were standing in the aisles of the Jim Crow coach overflow into a white coach, only partly filled. With Clinton Clark, who had been beaten, arrested, jailed and threatened with the rope time and time again for organizing the cane-cutters and cotton hands of Louisiana into a union. Roland Hayes talked broodingly; Hugh Gloster, sardonically; Clinton Clark, stoically, without any surprise: "You try to organize people to get out of slavery, may as well expect the big planters and their boys—the sheriffs and deputies—to get tough." But all of these, and others who told me their stories of abuse, knew the shock of the sudden oath, the blow, the murderous look in the eye.

They had been hurt, no doubt of that. But it is unlikely that they, or many other Negroes, merely because of the violence, will become reconciled to what caused it. Many Negroes are still going to protest rough language to their wives, as Roland Hayes did; or unfair travel accommodations, as Hugh Gloster did; or exploitation in the cane and cotton fields, as Clinton Clark did. "Get out and stay out of this parish," the jailer in Natchitoches told Clark, "I'll be back," said Clark, "I'll have a stronger organization behind me the next time."

Some of the victims do not forget the lessons that the rubber hose, the fist, the long black hours in the smelly cell fix so deeply. But from as many other victims comes this: "And if I had it to do all over, I'd do the same thing again."

Negroes who profess faith, whether real or not, in passive waiting for decent whites to take up their burden, are losing that faith. Negroes who feared that asking for democracy would lead to some Negroes' getting hurt, are losing that fear. But losing the passive faith is not defeatism, and losing the fear is not bravado.

There are many Negroes who are not convinced, as some forlorn liberals are, that democracy is a doomed hope in the South. They see heart-warming signs. They see the opponents of the poll tax gathering strength. The filibusters may rant so long or maneuver so craftily that the repeal may not pass this year, but the struggle against the poll tax will continue. Negroes applaud the Supreme Court decisions outlawing the white primary as a private club's election. They see the FEPC holding on, a symbol of the hope to abolish discrimination in industry, though challenged on many sides, flouted occasionally, and hard beset. They hear native white South Carolinians disclaim "white supremacy" resolution of their House of Representatives in humiliation "because it is white people who have thus held up the state to scorn. . . . The only white supremacy which is worthy of the name is that which exists because of virtue, not power." White supremacy is not the issue, they say, but that Negroes should serve on juries, that they should be allowed representation on boards which administer affairs involving Negro citizens and their property; that Negro policemen should be provided in Negro residential districts; that the disfranchisement of all Negroes in South Carolina cannot endure indefinitely; these are some of the pressing issues. Negroes are aware of the importance of such words from representative citizens, neither inter-racialists nor "radicals," in Cotton Ed Smith's bailiwick.

Of course, many Negroes keep their fingers crossed. They expected Congressman Rankin's blast at the Supreme Court vote, which ran true to form: "I see that the parlor pinks in the Department of Justice are already starting to harass the Southern states as a result of the blunder of the Supreme Court. The Negroes of the South are having their hope of peace and harmony with their white neighbors destroyed by these pinks." Canny through long experience with the politicos, Negroes realize that the road from outlawing white primaries and the poll tax to widespread voting may be long and rocky. "Let 'em try it," said the *Jackson Daily News*, "There are other ways of preserving southern tradition," the *Birmingham Post* said "We will maintain white supremacy, let the chips fall where they may," said the Governor of South Carolina.

It may be a long and rocky road. But it is the right road. Some Negroes may remain lethargic about their rights and duties as citizens. Some Negroes may get hurt; some may be timorous; the overpraised "harmony" may go off-key. As a sign that they are being "counted in" Negroes see several Southern editors applauding the decision. One called it "a much-needed political safety valve" instead of a threat. Virginius Dabney writes that

Tennessee, Kentucky, North Carolina, and Virginia, all of them without the white supremacy, have never seen white supremacy endangered. More significantly, he writes: "No society . . . is truly democratic . . . which shuts out anywhere from a quarter to a half of its people from all part in the choice of the officials under whom they must live and work."

Another cheering signpost, indicating that some mileage has been covered on the long journey, is the work of certain Southern white liberals. Virginius Dabney performed a historic act in advocating the abolition of Jim Crow on Virginia street cars and buses. It is true that he had to surrender his proposal; though numerous white Virginians applauded it, Mr. Dabney became convinced that the time was not right. But it was a first step that may count, and the proof that Virginia white opinion was not unanimous for Jim Crow is worth recording. Hoping that Negro leadership will rest in Atlanta (not so coincidentally Walter White's native city) rather than in New York, Mr. Dabney realizes that steps toward democracy must be taken *in the South.* This realization is quite as honest as his fear of trouble.

Southern white liberals deplore the demands of outsiders, and then come out themselves for many of the same reforms. The Atlanta Conference of representative white Southerners praised the Southern Negro Conference at Durham for frankness and courage. Among so much else the Atlanta Conference conclusions stated: "No Southerner can logically dispute the fact that the Negro, as an American citizen, is entitled to his civil rights and economic opportunities"; and "we agree . . . that it is 'unfortunate that the simple efforts to correct obvious soical and economic injustices continue, with such considerable popular support, to be interpreted as the predatory ambition of irresponsible Negroes to invade the privacy of family life. . . . ' We agree also that 'it is a wicked notion that the struggle by the Negro for citizenship is a struggle against the best interest of the nation.'"[3]

Negroes look with hope to the continuing conference, composed of several Southern Negro leaders who met in Durham and Southern whites who met in Atlanta. The conference is "to convenant together for better co-operation, more positive and specific action, and for enduring ways and means for carrying out the recommendations." They have reason for confidence in the two co-chairmen, Guy Johnson of the University of North Carolina and Ira Reid of Atlanta University. Many Negroes deplore the isolation of the problem as a Southern regional affair, but they want the results that such a conference may achieve. They notice the stress on good manners and good will and on the absence of "any suggestion of threat and ultimatum," and may wonder just how these terms are defined; but they suspect that this forward step would not have been taken without the activity of organizations like the NAACP. "We want those fellows to keep the heat on," a quiet Southern Negro preacher said to me.

On the national scene, wherever significant work is done to integrate the Negro into the war effort: in industry, in agriculture, in community planning, in the armed services, Negroes are cheered, and their morale rises accordingly. Sometimes discounted as drops in the bucket, these instances of integration might also be considered leaks in the levee, straws in the wind, or as the signposts I have frequently called them. If signposts, Negroes know that the longer, perhaps rougher journey lies ahead. They are therefore not in the mood for stopping, for laying over, for slowing up, or for detouring. And they do not want to be mere passengers, a sort of super-cargo, hitch-hikers being given a lift, guests being sped along. They want to do some of the map-reading and some of the driving. Thomas Sancton, a white Southerner who recognizes this truth, writes: "The real liberal knows that the Negro is never going to win any right he doesn't win for himself, by his own organization, courage, and articulation."[4]

The sticking point in the co-operation of Negro and Southern white liberals is segregation. The Atlanta Conference stepped gingerly about it: "We do not attempt to make here anything like a complete reply to the questions raised. . . . The only justification offered for [segregation] laws . . . is that they are "intended to minister to the welfare and integrity of both races."[5]

However segregation may be rationalized, it is essentially the denial of belonging. I believe that Negroes want segregation abolished. I realize that here, as so often elsewhere, it is presumptuous to talk of what *the* Negro wants. I understand that Negroes differ in their viewpoints toward segregation: the half-hand on a back county farm, the lost people on Arkansas plantations, the stevedore on Savannah docks, the coal miner in Birmingham, the cook-waitress-nurse in Charleston, the man-on-the-street in Waco, Los Angeles, New York, Boston, the government workers, the newspaper editors, the professional men, the spokesmen for pressure groups—all see segregation from different angles. An illiterate couple on Red River may differ greatly in attitude from their children on River Rouge. On the part of many there has been a long accommodation to segregation; but I believe that satisfaction with it has always been short.

An old railroad man in Birmingham, directing me to the FEPC hearings in the Federal Building, told me that whites and Negroes entered the court room by the same door (there was only one), but that they did not sit together. "No," he said. "They sits separate; whites on one side, the colored on the yother." Then he added, "And that's the way I'd ruther have it, too, ef'n I had my druthers. Of course I don't believe in scorning nobody, but—." He might have had memories of whites and Negroes "mixing socially," where the gains had all fallen to the whites, or where insult or violence had followed. But he knew, in spite of his "druthers," that segregation and scorn were bedfellows.

During Mr. Talmadge's campaign against the co-education of the races, one Georgia Negro college president gave white folks the assurance that "Negroes didn't want to attend the University of Georgia; all they wanted was a little school of their own." I found a young Negro Army doctor who sharply opposed the setting up of mixed military units, especially a mixed hospital. Only in an all Negro hospital according to his experience, could a Negro physician function to the best of his ability, realize his full development, and be free from insult. He was nevertheless violently opposed to Jim Crow in transportation and public services.

I heard varying defenses of segregation, but I still did not find many supporters of it, even in the South. Of the many who had gained from it in safety, comfort, wealth and prestige, I found some who were candid enough to admit that in segregated schools, churches, lodges, banks, and business they had risen higher than they might have risen in competition with whites. Many were fighting to improve their side of the bi-racial fence, to equalize teachers' salaries, to obtain buses for students, and for similar ends. But the fighting was not to buttress bi-racialism but to make the most of a bad thing, to lessen the inferiority that segregation always seemed to mean. The young flyers at the segregated Tuskegee base trained rigorously to become first-rate fighting men, to prove that Negroes should be piloting planes; but their most fervent admirers, however proud of their achievement, would not say that they would have made a poorer record at an unsegregated base. And they would not deny that there were indignities at the segregated base.

A sign in Atlanta read: "This line marks the separation of the races which were [*sic*] mutually agreed to by both." My friend, certainly no hot-head but long "accommodated," interpreted it: "Mutual agreement. You know: a man puts his gun in your ribs and you put your pocketbook in his hands."

When the conference in Durham excluded Northern Negroes, many white Southerners (and Negroes, for that matter) were led to expect a conservative set of principles. As Benjamin Mays, an important member of the conference, states: "They were Negroes the whites of the South knew. They were not radicals. They were Negroes the South says it believes in and can trust." Yet the Durham charter went on record as fundamentally opposed to segregation, and Walter White considered the recommendations to be almost identical in language and spirit with those of the NAACP and the March-on-Washington movement.

A chief difference between Southern and Northern Negro spokesmen is not that one group defends and the other condemns segregation, but that Southern leaders, in daily contact with it, see it as deeply rooted; Northern leaders, not seeing it to be so widespread and knowing that occasionally it can be ripped out, do not see the long, sturdy tentacles. The dangers are that Southern Negroes will believe it ineradicable and that Northern Negroes will believe it can be easily uprooted by speeches and governmental decree.

At Negro mass meetings in the North, demands that racial segregation should be abolished, "that the Negro and the white must be placed on a plane of absolute political and social equality," have been roundly applauded. It is doubtful if even the orators themselves envisaged that their demands would be immediately or even soon forthcoming. Delegates from the South knew that on the return trip home, at St. Louis or Cincinnati or Washington, they would be herded into the inferior Jim Crow coach; that if they wished to travel by bus they would be lucky even to get on, into the rear seats; that once home, Jim Crow would be all about them wherever they turned. Even Northern delegates knew where Jim Crow had caught hold in their communities.

Negroes know that more than stirring speeches will be needed to remove Jim Crow. But they also know another thing, on all levels—and in all callings—whether an illiterate sharecropper comparing the one-room ramshackle school for his children with the brick consolidated school for the white children, or a college president who knows, in spite of the new brick buildings, how unequal a proportion of state funds has come to his school—Negroes recognize that Jim Crow, even under such high-sounding names as "bi-racial parallelism," means inferiority for Negroes. And most American whites know this too, and that is the way that many prefer it. As the beginning of one kind of wisdom, Negroes recognize that the phrase "equal but separate accommodations" is a myth. They have known Jim Crow a long time, and they know Jim Crow means scorn and not belonging.

What Negroes applauded from their orators, many recognized as a vision, the vision of a good thing. Though a dream, and difficult of achieving, it still was not wild and illogical. It made more sense than the reality: that in the world's leading democracy, democratic rights were withheld from one man out of every ten, not because he had forfeited his right to them, but because his skin was darker and his hair of a different texture from those of the other nine. The reality was that—in a war against an enemy whose greatest crimes are based on spurious race thinking, this democracy indulged in injustice based on race thinking just as spurious.

This war is the Negro's war as much as it is anybody's. If the Axis were victorious, Negroes would be forced from the present second-class citizenship to slavery. Hitler's contempt for Negroes as apes and his sadistic treatment of Jews and all the conquered peoples, and Japan's brown Aryanism, similarly ruthless and arrogant, offer far less hope than America's system of democracy, bumbling though it may be, but still offering opportunity for protest and change. Even at the cost of the preservation of the *status quo*, this is still the Negro's war.

These are truisms. But they do not incite high morale. Indeed, they are somewhat like telling a man with a toothache that he should consider himself fortunate, since he might have a broken back. True, but his tooth still aches, and he wants something done for it.

This is even more the Negro's war, if it is truly a people's war, a war of liberation, aimed at establishing the Four Freedoms, ushering in the century of the common man, as the fine slogans have it. The Negro could do well with the Four Freedoms, especially the Freedoms from want and fear, for these two Freedoms have long been strangers to him. This is all the more the Negro's war if, as Michael Straight hopes, the peace will "guarantee to all of its citizens the right to constructive work at fair wages; to good low-cost housing; to minimum standards of nutrition, clothing, and medical care; to full opportunity for training and adult education; to real social security."

There is more cleverness than wisdom in the remark of John Temple Graves that asking for complete democracy at home is as logical as saying "that because America's house was on fire America must take the occasion for renovating the kitchen or putting Venetian blinds in the parlor." The trouble with the house is more serious than that; it really has much to do with the foundations. Wendell Willkie warns that:

> We cannot fight the forces and ideas of imperialism abroad and maintain any form of imperialism at home. . . . We must mean freedom for others as well as ourselves, and we must mean freedom for everyone inside our frontiers as well as outside.[6]

Pearl Buck points out.

> Our democracy does not allow for the present division between a white ruler race and a subject colored race. If the United States is to include subject and ruler peoples, then let us be honest about it and change the Constitution and make it plain that Negroes cannot share the privileges of the white people. True, we would then be totalitarian rather than democratic.[7]

Daily reports of the violations of democracy crowd upon the Negro, breeding cynicism. Nevertheless, while denouncing them, he does so in the framework of democracy. He continually relies on America's professions of democracy as having some validity; he has not yet descended to the hopeless view that America prefers totalitarianism.

As has been so often stated: If America is to indoctrinate the rest of the world with democracy, it is logical to expect that the American Negro will share it at home. It may take a long time, but segregation must be abolished before there will be true democracy at home. True democracy will mean the right and opportunity to win respect for human worth. It can have no truck with Nazi concepts of race-supremacy, with Nazi contempt for people because of race. Democracy will mean equal pay for equal labor, equal employment opportunities, opportunities to learn and use technical skills and to advance according to mastery of them, and the right to join and participate fully in trade unions. The tentative beginning made by FEPC must be developed. Democracy will mean equal educational opportunities, equalized salaries for teachers, equalized facilities in the schools. The spread of the segregated system of education must be checked and eventually abolished as wasteful and unjust. Democracy will mean that the Federal Government will go on record against mob violence, for, in spite of the decline in lynching, threats of mob-violence are still powerfully coercive. Democracy will mean the discouraging of police brutality, will mean justice in the courts rather than patronizing clemency or cruel intolerance. Negroes will serve on the police force, at the lawyers' bar, in the jury docks, and on the judges' bench. Democracy will mean the franchise, with elimination of the poll tax and the subterfuges and intimidations that keep qualified Negroes from the polls. It will mean training Negroes to fulfill the duties of free citizens. Democracy will mean the strengthening and extension of the social legislation begun by the New Deal in such agencies as the Farm Security Administration and the Federal Housing Authority; and the opportunity not only to share in the benefits of such agencies but also in their planning and operation. Democracy will mean the opportunity to qualify for service in the armed forces in all its branches; the opportunity for whites and Negroes to fight side by side in mixed commands. Democracy will mean simply the opportunities for all Americans to share to the full extent of their capacities in the defense of America in war and the development of America in peace.

This is not much to ask for, since it is essentially what America guarantees to every white citizen. Only when viewed from the angle that these opportunities are to be extended to Negro citizens, does the list seem staggering, outrageous to some, foolishly idealistic and unattainable to many.

I think that most Negroes are not so optimistic that they foresee the overnight arrival of these opportunities. No group should know better that perfectly functioning democracy in the United States has always been a hope, rather than an actuality. Even in those sections where one undemocratic practice—legal segregation—has been missing, democracy—to whites as well as to Negroes—has not been simon-pure. The poverty of the South would be oppressive on both whites and Negroes even if segregation laws were stricken from the books, and discrimination from the practices, tomorrow. The Negro's plight in the South will be lightened substantially only when the plight of the poor white is enlightened; when these cannot be pitted against each other in contempt and hatred; when genuine democracy replaces the fictitious (and fictitious not only in the matter of race relations). Nevertheless, however Herculean the task, Negroes are not so defeatist that they think democracy to be unattainable. They are good Americans in nothing more than in their faith that "democracy *can* happen here." Worth fighting for in Europe, it is worth working for here. But since time does not stand still, all America—black and white—had better start to work for it. President Roosevelt, speaking of the Four Freedoms, has said: "Magna Carta, the Declaration of Independence, the Constitution of the United States, the Emancipation Proclamation and every other milestone in human progress—all were ideals which seemed impossible of attainment—yet they were attained."[8]

Negroes should not want fundamental rights of citizenship donated to them as largesse, and should not consider them as barter for loyalty, or service. American whites should not consider Negroes as beneficiaries, being accorded gifts that to men of different complexion are rights. Nor should they think of Negroes as passive objects of humanitarianism, since Negroes can really be allies in a common struggle for democracy. Even after Hitler and Tojo are defeated, democracy is going to need all of its strength to solve grave problems. The strength of the Negro will be as much needed and as useful in the coming economic and political crises as it is needed and should be useful now.

I believe that many Negroes realize this, and wish to be allowed to share in the sacrifice and travail and danger necessary to attain genuine democracy. Wendell Willkie's world trip excited him with "fresh proof of the enormous power within human beings to change their environment, to fight for freedom with an instinctive awakened confidence that with freedom they can achieve anything."[9] In times of frustration, Negroes would do well to recognize that power, and to understand that it fights on their side.

Negroes know they have allies. There are the numerous colored peoples of the world, the millions of yellow, brown, and black men in China, India, the Philippines, Malaysia, Africa, South America, the Caribbean, all over the globe, where hope for democracy is stirring a mighty ferment. Almost all are concerned with their own perplexities, but they agree in their fight against color prejudice. The success of the Soviet Union in destroying race prejudice gives hope and courage. And there are other allies abroad, in the smaller as well as the larger, the conquered as well as the unconquered nations, who are tied, not by a common urge to abolish race prejudice, but by the determination to be free. And in America there are allies too. It does not seem over-optimistic to believe them on the increase, although still outnumbered by the indifferent or the hostile. Negroes must join with these American allies, in the North and in the South, in a truly interracial program, or better, a democratic program. The minority must work with the men of good will in the majority. Negroes recognize their allies here without difficulty, and their affection for them runs strong and deep.

Americans, Negroes and whites, may believe that to achieve full democracy is arduous. It may well take a slow pull for a long haul. But it can no longer be postponed. American dreams have been realized before this, however difficult they seemed to the faint-hearted and skeptical. Americans, Negro and white, have mustered the doggedness and courage and intelligence needed. I have confidence in my own people that they will help achieve and preserve democracy, and will prove worthy of sharing it. But we must be counted in.

About the Author

Sterling A. Brown was born in Washington, D.C., May 1, 1901. Educated in the Washington schools, Williams College (A.B., Phi Beta Kappa, 1922) and Harvard University (A.M., 1923), he has taught at Virginia Seminary (Lynchburg), Fisk University, Lincoln University (Missouri), as visiting lecturer at Atlanta University and at New York University, and at Howard University where he is now Professor of English. From 1936 to 1939 he served as Editor on Negro Affairs for the Federal Writers' Project; in 1939 he was a staff member of the Carnegie Myrdal Study of the Negro. He was a Guggenheim Fellow 1937–1938. He has contributed poetry, reviews, and essays to numerous publications. His books are *Southern Road* (1932), *The Negro in American Fiction* (1938), *Negro Poetry and Drama* (1938), and *The Negro Caravan* (1941) which he edited in collaboration with Arthur P. Davis and Ulysses G. Lee. He is now completing work on *A Negro Looks at the South.*

ENDNOTES

1. Browdor, *op. cit.*, pp. 90–91. (Italics not in the original)
2. *Policy for Victory* (New York, 1943), p. 66.
3. Odum, *op. cit.*, p. 199.
4. Sancton, *op. cit.*, p.15.
5. Odum, *op. cit.*, p. 197.
6. Wendell Willkie, *One World* (New York, 1943), P.190 ff.
7. Pearl Buck, *American Unity and Asia* (New York, 1942), p.15.
8. Franklin D. Roosevelt, "The Four Freedoms" in Clayton Wheat, ed., *The Democratic Tradition in America* (Boston, 1943), p. 291.
9. Willkie, *op. cit.*, p. 163.

UNIT 4

BROWN, LITTLE ROCK AND CHARLOTTESVILLE

INTRODUCTION 187

4-1 • NAACP ADVERTISEMENT, 1955 188

4-2 • SEGREGATION MAP, MAY 1954 189

4-3 • BROWN V. BOARD OF EDUCATION 190

4-4 • A RANDOM THOUGHT ON THE SEGREGATION CASES 200
William H. Rehnquist

4-5 • THE OPINION OF MANKIND 202
THE U.S. SECRETARY OF STATE ON SEGREGATION AND WORLD RELATIONS
Dean Acheson

4-6 • AFRO-AMERICAN CARTOONS 204

4-7 • EXCERPTS FROM INFORMAL MEMORANDUM FROM HARRY ASHMORE 209
Dred Scott Ashmore

4-8 • EDITORIAL 211
SEGREGATION DECISON

4-9 • SRC REACTS TO THE BROWN DECISION 216
A STATEMENT BY THE EXECUTIVE COMMITTEE
OF THE SOUTHERN REGIONAL COUNCIL

4-10 • INTERPRETATION OF SUPREME COURT DECISION
AND THE NAACP PROGRAM 223
Thurgood Marshall and Roy Wilkins

4-11 • OPPORTUNITY FOR THE SOUTH 229
Marion A. Wright

4-12 • LETTER TO NAACP FROM ATHENS COLLEGE 233

4-13 • DECLARATION OF CONSTITUTIONAL PRINCIPLES 234

4-14 • Public Opinion and the School Decision 237

4-15 • Charlottesville School Closing Letter 240

4-16 • Public School Desegregation 242
Charlottesville, Virginia, 1955–62
Paul M. Gaston and Thomas T. Hammond

4-17 • Charlottesville Daily Progress 255
Editorial and Letters to the Editor

4-18 • A Box Lunch, A Chair and A Drinking Cup 258

4-19 • Little Rock 260
Anthony Lewis

INTRODUCTION

Unit 4 examines *Brown v. Board of Education*, the immediate reaction of black and white Southerners to the decision, and two early attempts at school desegregation. Document 4-3 reproduces both *Brown v. Board of Education*, where the Supreme Court declared segregated schooling inherently unequal, and the implementation decree—usually referred to as *Brown* II— issued one year later, when the Court stated segregated schools must be integrated with "all deliberate speed." The next two documents include an argument in support of *Brown* by the Secretary of State (4-5), and William Rehnquist's argument against desegregation when he served as a clerk for the Supreme Court in 1954 against the decision (4-4).

The middle of this unit (4-7 to 4-11) studies the immediate reaction to *Brown* I and II. The initial optimism of many liberal white Southerners is eloquently seen in Harry Ashmore's informal memo (4-7). Ashmore, an editor of the *Arkansas Gazette* and Southern Regional Council member, wrote these words less than 24 hours after the Court announced the first decision. Document 4-8 reproduces the NAACP's reaction to the first *Brown* decision as found in *The Crisis,* its official magazine. The NAACP sought to shape opinion not only in its editorials, but also through the use of newspaper excerpts culled from around the country. As calls of defiance were just beginning to be heard across the South, the SRC devoted a substantial portion of the March 1955 issue of *New South* to an argument for a peaceful acceptance of the Court's ruling. Documents 4-10 and 4-11 reveal how the NAACP and the SRC revised their positions in light of *Brown* II. Officially titled a "Declaration of Constitutional Principles," the "Southern Manifesto" (4-13) was a denunciation of *Brown* signed by 101 of the 128 Southern congressmen and senators and inserted into the official *Congressional Record.*

The third section of the unit focuses closely on the first efforts at desegregation in Charlottesville, Virginia, and in Little Rock, Arkansas. The report on Charlottesville (4-16) was written contemporaneously by Paul Gaston and Thomas Hammond, two history professors at the University of Virginia in Charlottesville; the authors were assisted by the women who organized the Parents Committee for Emergency Schooling (PCES), which is mentioned in the pamphlet. Document 4-17 is an editorial and several letters-to-the-editor from a 1958 issue of the Charlottesville (Va) *Daily Progress* concerning the school closings. Document 4-18 demonstrates how the Defenders of State Sovereignty and Individual Liberties (DSSI), a popular organization in Virginia founded after *Brown* to oppose desegregation, viewed the school closings. More information on the DSSI can be found in Unit 6: "Segregation and Its Adherents."

Charlottesville's story can be contrasted with the better known events in Little Rock. The selection on Little Rock is taken from *Portrait of a Decade* (1964) a contemporary account of the Civil Rights Movement by *New York Times* reporter Anthony Lewis. Both accounts highlight the ability of segregationists to seize the initiative in school desegregation and the role of moderates in forging a compromise.

CAN YOU SPARE A FEW MINUTES

In order that NAACP's Fight for Freedom Crusade achieve its goal: the full emancipation of the Negro by January 1, 1963, nation-wide assistance is needed by individuals who can organize groups of solicitors or act as solicitors themselves. Men and women are needed at once to organize the promotion of NAACP Life Memberships in their social groups, clubs, churches, employee groups, fraternal and political organizations. The spare minutes you spend at this important work can insure the success of this most vital of causes.

for the most vital cause in the modern history of the Negro?

Wanted: hundreds of solicitors to assist the life membership committee

If you can organize a group of solicitors for NAACP Life Memberships or act as a solicitor yourself, please send us your name at once and we will send you full details with our grateful thanks.

LIFE MEMBERSHIP COMMITTEE

KIVIE KAPLAN DR. BENJAMIN MAYS

CO-CHAIRMEN

Kelly Alexander	Dr. Mordecai Johnson
Bishop W. Y. Bell	Robert H. Johnson
*Mrs. Mary McLeod Bethune	Mrs. Daisy E. Lampkin
Dr. Allan Knight Chalmers	Hon. Herbert H. Lehman
Dr. W. Montague Cobb	Dr. James J. McClendon
Earl B. Dickerson	A. Philip Randolph
Dr. Harry Emerson Fosdick	Walter Reuther
Morton S. Grossman	Mrs. Eleanor Roosevelt
Dr. Ralph Harlow	Ike Smalls
Carl Johnson	A. Maceo Smith
Dr. Channing H. Tobias	

*Deceased

N.A.A.C.P.
West 40th Street
w York 18, N. Y.

☐ I wish to volunteer as an organizer of a group of solicitors for NAACP Life Memberships.

☐ I wish to volunteer as an individual solicitor for NAACP Life Membership.

Name ....

Address ....

City and State ....

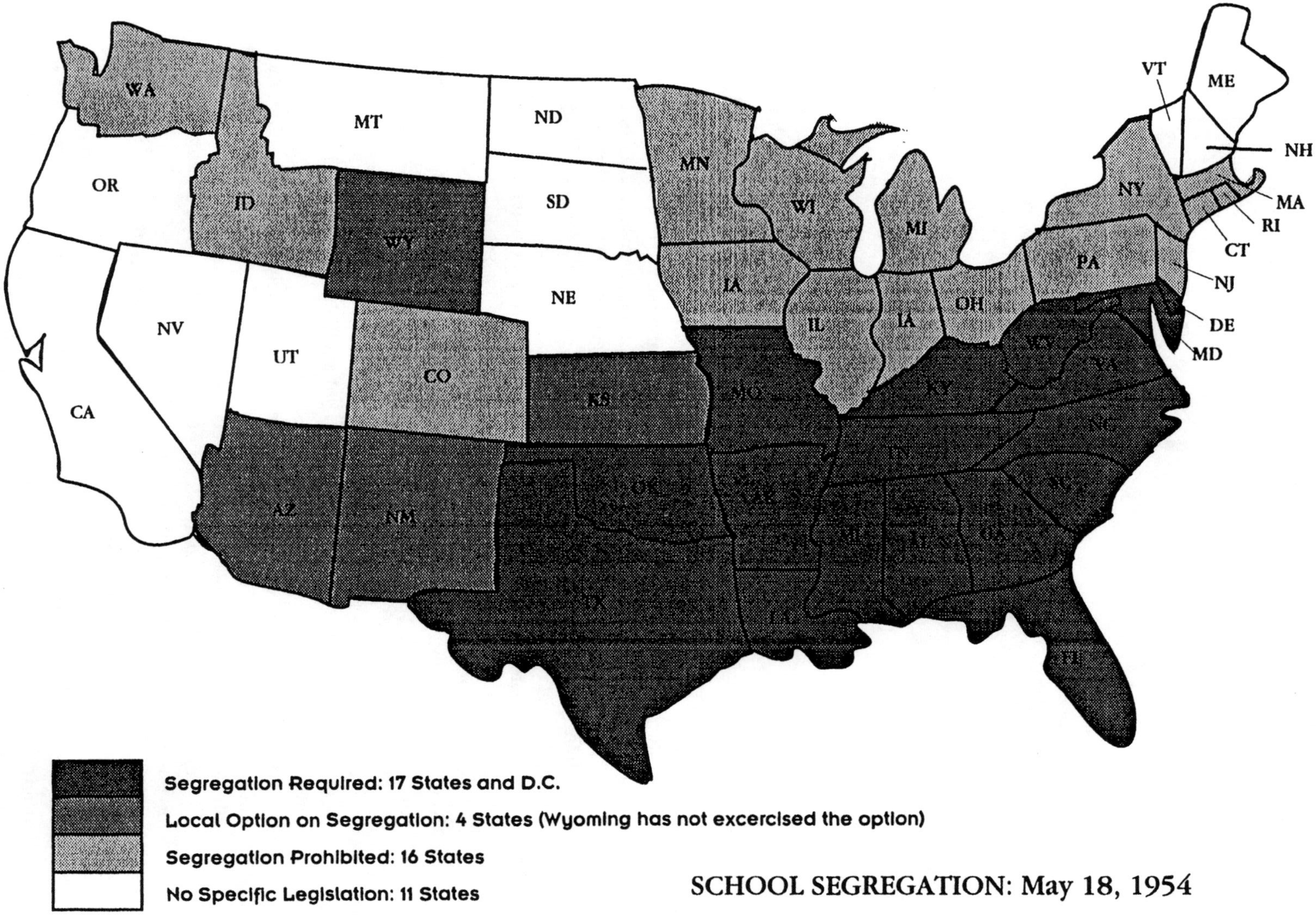

SCHOOL SEGREGATION: May 18, 1954

UNIT 4-3

BROWN V. BOARD OF EDUCATION

Syllabus

BROWN Et Al. v. BOARD OF EDUCATION OF TOPEKA Et Al.

NO. 1. APPEAL FROM THE UNITED STATES DISTRICT COURT FOR THE DISTRICT OF KANSAS.[1]

Argued December 9, 1952—Reargued December 8, 1953—Decided May 17, 1954

Segregation of white and Negro children in the public schools of a State solely on the basis of race, pursuant to state laws permitting or requiring such segregation, denies to Negro children the equal protection of the laws guaranteed by the Fourteenth Amendment even though the physical facilities and other "tangible" factors of white and Negro schools may be equal. Pp. 486–496.

(**a**) The history of the Fourteenth Amendment is inconclusive as to its intended effect on public education. Pp. 489–490.

(**b**) The question presented in these cases must be determined, not on the basis of conditions existing when the Fourteenth Amendment was adopted, but in the light of the full development of public education and its present place in American life throughout the Nation. Pp. 492–493.

(**c**) Where a State has undertaken to provide an opportunity for an education in its public schools, such an opportunity is a right which must be made available to all on equal terms. P. 493.

(**d**) Segregation of children in public schools solely on the basis of race deprives children of the minority group of equal educational opportunities, even though the physical facilities and other "tangible" factors may be equal. Pp. 493–494.

(**e**) The "separate but equal" doctrine adopted in *Plessy v. Ferguson*, 163 U.S. 537, has no place in the field of public education. P. 495.

(**f**) The cases are restored to the docket for further argument on specified questions relating to the forms of the decrees. Pp. 495–496.

Robert L. Carter argued the cause for appellants in No. 1 on the original argument and on the reargument. *Thurgood Marshall* argued the cause for appellants in No. 2 on the original argument and *Spottswood W. Robinson, III*, for appellants in No. 4 on the original argument, and both argued the causes for appellants in Nos. 2 and 4 on the reargument.

Louis L. Redding and *Jack Greenberg* argued the cause for respondents in No. 10 on the orginal argument and *Jack Greenberg* and *Thurgood Marshall* on the reargument.

On the briefs were *Robert L. Carter, Thurgood Marshall, Spottswood W. Robinson, III, Louis L. Redding, Jack Greenberg, George E. C. Hayes, William R. Ming, Jr., Constance Baker Motley, James M. Nabrit, Jr., Charles S. Scott, Frank D. Reeves, Harold R. Boulware* and *Oliver W. Hill* for appellants in Nos. 1, 2, and 4 and respondents in No. 10; *George M. Johnson* for appellants in Nos. 2 and 4. *Arthur D. Shores* and *A. T. Walden* were on the Statement as to Jurisdiction and a brief opposing a Motion to Dismiss or Affirm in No. 2.

Paul E. Wilson, Assistant Attorney General of Kansas, argued the cause for appellees in No. 1 on the original argument and on the reargument. With him on the briefs was *Harold R. Fatzer*, Attorney General.

John W. Davis argued the cause for appellees in No. 2 on the orginal argument and for appellees in Nos. 2 and 4 on the reargument. With him on the briefs in No. 2 were *T. C. Callison*, Attorney General of South Carolina, *Robert McC. Figg, Jr., S. E. Rogers, William R. Meagher* and *Taggart Whipple*.

J. Lindsay Almond, Jr., Attorney General of Virginia, and *T. Justin Moore* argued the cause for appellees in Nos. 2 and 4 on the original argument and for appellees in Nos. 2 and 4 on the reargument. On the briefs in No. 4 were *J. Lindsay Almond, Jr.*, Attorney General, and *Henry T. Wickham*, Special Assistant Attorney General, for the State of Virginia, and *T. Justin Moore, Archibald G. Robertson, John W. Riely* and *T. Justin Moore, Jr.* for the Prince Edward County School Authorities, appellees.

H. Albert Young, Attorney General of Delaware, argued the cause for petitioners in No. 10 on the original argument and on the reargument. With him on the briefs was *Louis J. Finger*, Special Deputy Attorney General.

By special leave of Court, *Assistant Attorney General Rankin* argued the cause for the United States on the reargument, as *amicus curiae*, urguing reversal in Nos. 1, 2 and 4 and affirmance in No. 10. With him on the brief were *Attorney General Brownell, Philip Elman, Leon Ulman, William J. Lamont* and *M. Magdelena Schoch. James P. McGranery*, then Attorney General, and *Philip Elman* filed a brief for the United States on the original argument, as *amicus curiae*, urging reversal in Nos. 1, 2 and 4 and affirmance in No. 10.

Briefs of *amici curiae* supporting appellants in No. 1 were filed by *Shad Polier, Will Maslow* and *Joseph B. Robison* for the American Jewish Congress, by *Edwin J. Lukas, Arnold Forster, Arthur Garfield Hays, Frank E. Karelsen, Leonard Haas, Saburo Kido* and *Theodore Leskes* for the American Civil Liberties Union, *et al.*; and by *John Lightenberg* and *Selma M. Borchardt* for the American Federation of Teachers. Briefs of *amici curiae* supporting appellants in No. 1 and respondents in No. 10 were filed by *Arthur J. Goldberg* and *Thomas E. Harris* for the Congress of Industrial Organizations and by *Phineas Indritz* for the American Veterans Committee, Inc.

MR. CHIEF JUSTICE WARREN delivered the opinion of the Court.

These cases come to us from the States of Kansas, South Carolina, Virginia, and Delaware. They are premised on different facts and different local conditions, but a common legal question justifies their consideration together in this consolidated opinion.[2]

In each of the cases, minors of the Negro race, through their legal representatives, seek the aid of the courts in obtaining admission to the public schools of their community on a nonsegregated basis. In each instance, they had been denied admission to schools attended by white children under laws requiring or permitting segregation according to race. This segregation was alleged to deprive the plaintiffs of the equal protection of the laws under the Fourteenth Amendment. In each of the cases other than the Delaware case, a three-judge federal district court denied relief to the plaintiffs on the so-called "separate but equal" doctrine announced by this Court in *Plessy v. Ferguson*, 163 U.S. 537. Under that doctrine, equality of treatment is accorded when the races are provided substantially equal facilities, even though these facilities be separate. In the Delaware case, the Supreme Court of Delaware adhered to that doctrine, but ordered that the plaintiffs be admitted to the white schools because of their superiority to the Negro schools.

The plaintiffs contend that segregated public schools are not "equal" and cannot be made "equal," and that hence they are deprived of the equal protection of the laws. Because of the obvious importance of the question presented, the Court took jurisdiction.[3] Argument was heard in the 1952 Term, and reargument was heard this Term on certain questions propounded by the Court.[4]

Reargument was largely devoted to the circumstances surrounding the adoption of the Fourteenth Amendment in 1868. It covered exhaustively consideration of the Amendment in Congress, ratification by the states, then existing practices in racial segregation, and the views of proponents and opponents of the Amendment. This discussion and our own investigation convince us that, although these sources cast some light, it is not enough to resolve the problem with which we are faced. At best, they are inconclusive. The most avid proponents of the post-War Amendments undoubtedly intended them to remove all legal distinctions among all persons born or naturalized in the United States. Their opponents, just as certainly, were antagonistic to both the letter and the spirit of the Amendments and wished them to have the most limited effect. What others in Congress and the state legislatures had in mind cannot be determined with any degree of certainty.

An additional reason for the inconclusive nature of the Amendment's history, with respect to segregated schools, is the status of public education at that time.[5] In the South, the movement toward free common schools, supported by general taxation, had not yet taken hold. Education of white children was largely in the hands of private groups. Education of Negroes was almost nonexistent, and practically all of the race were illiterate. In fact, any education of Negroes was forbidden by law in some states. Today, in contrast, many Negroes have achieved outstanding success in the arts and sciences as well as in the business and professional world. It is true that public school education at the time of the Amendment had advanced further in the North, but the effect of the Amendment on Northern States was generally ignored in the congressional debates. Even in the North, the conditions of public education did not approximate those existing today. The curriculum was usually rudimentary; ungraded schools were common in rural areas; the school term was but three months a year in many states; and compulsory school attendance was virtually unknown. As a consequence, it is not surprising that there should be so little in the history of the Fourteenth Amendment relating to its intended effect on public education.

In the first cases in this Court construing the Fourteenth Amendment, decided shortly after its adoption, the Court interpreted it as proscribing all state-imposed discriminations against the Negro race.[6] The doctrine of "separate but equal" did not make its appearance in this Court until 1896 in the case of *Plessy v. Ferguson, supra*, involving not education but transportation.[7] American courts have since labored with the doctrine for over half a century. In this Court, there have been six cases involving the "separate but equal" doctrine in the field of public education.[8] In *Cumming v. County Board of Education*, 175 U.S. 528, and *Gong Lum v. Rice*, 275 U.S. 78, the validity of the doctrine itself was not challenged.[9] In more recent cases, all on the graduate school level, inequality was found in that specific benefits enjoyed by white students were denied to Negro students of the same educational qualifications. *Missouri ex rel. Gaines v. Canada*, 305 U.S. 337; *Sipuel v. Oklahoma*, 332 U.S. 631; *Sweatt v. Painter*, 339 U.S. 629; *McLaurin v. Oklahoma State Regents*, 339 U.S. 637. In none of these cases was it necessary to re-examine the doctrine to grant relief to the Negro plaintiff. And in *Sweatt v. Painter, supra*, the Court expressly reserved decision on the question whether *Plessy v. Ferguson* should be held inapplicable to public education.

In the instant cases, that question is directly presented. Here, unlike *Sweatt v. Painter*, there are findings below that the Negro and white schools involved have been equalized, or are being equalized, with respect to build curricula, qualifications and salaries of teachers, and other "tangible" factors.[10] Our decision, therefore, cannot turn on merely a comparison of these tangible factors in the Negro and white schools involved in each of the cases. We must look instead to the effect of segregation itself on public education.

In approaching this problem, we cannot turn the clock back to 1868 when the Amendment was adopted, or even to 1896 when *Plessy v. Ferguson* was written. We must consider public education in the light of its full development and its present place in American life throughout the Nation. Only in this way can it be determined if segregation in public schools deprives these plaintiffs of the equal protection of the laws.

Today, education is perhaps the most important function of state and local governments. Compulsory school attendance laws and the great expenditures for education both demonstrate our recognition of the importance of education to our democratic society. It is required in the performance of our most basic public responsibilities, even service in the armed forces. It is the very foundation of good citizenship. Today it is a principal instrument in awakening the child to cultural values, in preparing him for later professional training, and in helping him to adjust normally to his environment. In these days, it is doubtful that any child may reasonably be expected to succeed in life if he is denied the opportunity of an education. Such an opportunity, where the state has undertaken to provide it, is a right which must be made available to all on equal terms.

We come then to the question presented: Does segregation of children in public schools solely on the basis of race, even though the physical facilities and other "tangible" factors may be equal, deprive the children of the minority group of equal educational opportunities? We believe that it does.

In *Sweatt v. Painter, supra,* in finding that a segregated law school for Negroes could not provide them equal educational opportunities, this Court relied in large part on "those qualities which are incapable of objective measurement but which make for greatness in a law school." In *McLaurin v. Oklahoma State Regents, supra,* the Court, in requiring that a Negro admitted to a white graduate school be treated like all other students, again resorted to intangible considerations: "... his ability to study, to engage in discussions and exchange views with other students, and, in general, to learn his profession." Such considerations apply with added force to children in grade and high schools. To separate them from others of similar age and qualifications solely because of their race generates a feeling of inferiority as to their status in the community that may affect their hearts and minds in a way unlikely ever to be undone. The effect of this separation on their educational opportunities was well stated by a finding in the Kansas case by a court which nevertheless felt compelled to rule against the Negro plaintiffs:

> Segregation of white and colored children in public schools has a detrimental effect upon the colored children. The impact is greater when it has the sanction of the law; for the policy of separating the races is usually interpreted as denoting the inferiority of the negro group. A sense of inferiority affects the motivation of a child to learn. Segregation with the sanction of law, therefore, has a tendency to [retard] the educational and mental development of negro children and to deprive them of some of the benefits they would receive in a racial[ly] integrated school system.[11]

Whatever may have been the extent of psychological knowledge at the time of *Plessy v. Ferguson,* this finding is amply supported by modern authority.[12] Any language in *Plessy v. Ferguson* contrary to this finding is rejected.

We conclude that in the field of public education the doctrine of "separate but equal" has no place. Separate educational facilities are inherently unequal. Therefore, we hold that the plaintiffs and others similarly situated for whom the actions have been brought are, by reason of the segregation complained of, deprived of the equal protection of the laws guaranteed by the Fourteenth Amendment. This disposition makes unnecessary any discussion whether such segregation also violates the Due Process Clause of the Fourteenth Amendment.[13]

Because these are class actions, because of the wide applicability of this decision, and because of the great variety of local conditions, the formulation of decrees in these cases presents problems of considerable complexity. On reargument, the consideration of appropriate relief was necessarily subordinated to the primary question the constitutionality of segregation in public education. We have now announced that such segregation is a denial of the equal protection of the laws. In order that we may have the full assistance of the parties in formulating decrees, the cases will be restored to the docket, and the parties are requested to present further argument on Questions 4 and 5 previously propounded by the Court for the reargument this Term.[14] The Attorney General of the United States is again invited to participate. The Attorneys General of the states requiring or permitting segregation in public education will also be permitted to appear as *amici curiae* upon request to do so by September 15, 1954, and submission of briefs by October 1, 1954.[15]

It is so ordered.

OCTOBER TERM, 1954

Syllabus

BROWN Et Al. v. BOARD OF EDUCATION OF TOPEKA Et Al.

NO 1. Appeal from the United States District Court for the District of Kansas.[16]

Reargued on the question of relief April 11–14, 1955—Opinion and judgments announced May 31, 1955.

1. Racial discrimination in public education is unconstitutional, 347 U.S. 483, 497, and all provisions of federal, state or local law requiring or permitting such discrimination must yield to this principle. P. 298.
2. The judgments below (except that in the Delaware case) are reversed and the cases are remanded to the District Courts to take such proceedings and enter such orders and decrees consistent with this opinion as are necessary and proper to admit the parties to these cases to public schools on a racially nondiscriminatory basis with all deliberate speed. P. 301.
   - **(a)** School authorities have the primary responsibility for elucidating, assessing and solving the varied local school problems which may require solution in fully implementing the governing constitutional principles. P. 299.
   - **(b)** Courts will have to consider whether the action of school authorities constitutes good faith implementation of the governing constitutional principles. P. 299.
   - **(c)** Because of their proximity to local conditions and the possible need for further hearings, the courts which originally heard these cases can best perform this judicial appraisal. P. 299.
   - **(d)** In fashioning and effectuating the decrees, the courts will be guided by equitable principles-characterized by a practical flexibility in shaping remedies and a facility for adjusting and reconciling public and private needs. P. 300.
   - **(e)** At stake is the personal interest of the plaintiffs in admission to public schools as soon as practicable on a nondiscriminatory basis. P. 300.
   - **(f)** Courts of equity may properly take into account the public interest in the elimination in a systematic and effective manner of a variety of obstacles in making the transition to school systems operated in accordance with the constitutional principles enunciated in 347 U.S. 483, 497; but the vitality of these constitutional principles cannot be allowed to yield simply because of disagreement with them. P. 300.

(g) While giving weight to these public and private considerations, the courts will require that the defendants make a prompt and reasonable start toward full compliance with the ruling of this Court. P. 300.

(h) Once such a start has been made, the courts may find that additional time is necessary to carry out the ruling in an effective manner. P. 300.

(i) The burden rests on the defendants to establish that additional time is necessary in the public interest and is consistent with good faith compliance at the earliest practicable date. P. 300.

(j) The courts may consider problems related to administration, arising from the physical condition of the school plant, the school transportation system, personnel, revision of school districts and attendance areas into compact units to achieve a system of determining admission to the public schools on a nonracial basis, and revision of local laws and regulations which may be necessary in solving the foregoing problems. Pp. 300–301.

(k) The courts will also consider the adequacy of any plans the defendants may propose to meet these problems and to effectuate a transition to a racially nondiscriminatory school system. P. 301.

(l) During the period of transition, the courts will retain jurisdiction of these cases. P. 301.

3. The judgment in the Delaware case, ordering the immediate admission of the plaintiffs to schools previously attended only by white children, is affirmed on the basis of the principles stated by this Court in its opinion, 347 U.S. 483; but the case is remanded to the Supreme Court of Delaware for such further proceedings as that Court may deem necessary in the light of this opinion. P. 301. 98 F. Supp. 797, 103 F. Supp. 920, 103 F. Supp. 337 and judgment in No. 4, reversed and remanded. 91 A. 2d 137, affirmed and remanded.

MR. CHIEF JUSTICE WARREN delivered the opinion of the Court.

These cases were decided on May 17, 1954. The opinions of that date,[17] declaring the fundamental principle that racial discrimination in public education is unconstitutional, are incorporated herein by reference. All provisions of federal, state, or local law requiring or permitting such discrimination must yield to this principle. There remains for consideration the manner in which relief is to be accorded.

Because these cases arose under different local conditions and their disposition will involve a variety of local problems, we requested further argument on the question of relief.[18] In view of the nationwide importance of the decision, we invited the Attorney General of the United States and the Attorneys General of all states requiring or permitting racial discrimination in public education to present their views on that question. The parties, the United States, and the States of Florida, North Carolina, Arkansas, Oklahoma, Maryland, and Texas filed briefs and participated in the oral argument.

These presentations were informative and helpful to the Court in its consideration of the complexities arising from the transition to a system of public education freed of racial discrimination. The presentations also demonstrated that substantial steps to eliminate racial discrimination in public schools have already been taken, not only in some of the communities in which these cases arose, but in some of the states appearing as *amici curiae*, and in other states as well. Substantial progress has been made in the District of Columbia and in the communities in Kansas and Delaware involved in this litigation. The defendants in the cases coming to us from South Carolina and Virginia are awaiting the decision of this Court concerning relief.

Full implementation of these constitutional principles may require solution of varied local school problems. School authorities have the primary responsibility for elucidating, assessing, and solving these problems; courts will have to consider whether the action of school authorities constitutes good faith implementation of the governing constitutional principles. Because of their proximity to local conditions and the possible need for further hearings, the courts which originally heard these cases can best perform this judicial appraisal. Accordingly, we believe it appropriate to remand the cases to those courts.[19]

In fashioning and effectuating the decrees, the courts will be guided by equitable principles. Traditionally, equity has been characterized by a practical flexibility in shaping its remedies[20] and by a facility for adjusting and reconciling public and private needs.[21] These cases call for the exercise of these traditional attributes of equity power. At stake is the personal interest of the plaintiffs in admission to public schools as soon as practicable on a nondiscriminatory basis. To effectuate this interest may call for elimination of a variety of obstacles in making the transition to school systems operated in accordance with the constitutional principles set forth in our May 17, 1954, decision. Courts of equity may properly take into account the public interest in the elimination of such obstacles in a systematic and effective manner. But it should go without saying that the vitality of these constitutional principles cannot be allowed to yield simply because of disagreement with them.

While giving weight to these public and private considerations, the courts will require that the defendants make a prompt and reasonable start toward full compliance with our May 17, 1954, ruling. Once such a start has been made, the courts may find that additional time is necessary to carry out the ruling in an effective manner. The burden rests upon the defendants to establish that such time is necessary in the public interest and is consistent with good faith compliance at the earliest practicable date. To that end, the courts may consider problems related to administration, arising from the physical condition of the school plant, the school transportation system, personnel, revision of school districts and attendance areas into compact units to achieve a system of determining admission to the public schools on a nonracial basis, and revision of local laws and regulations which may be necessary in solving the foregoing problems. They will also consider the adequacy of any plans the defendants may propose to meet these problems and to effectuate a transition to a racially nondiscriminatory school system. During this period of transition, the courts will retain jurisdiction of these cases.

The judgments below, except that in the Delaware case, are accordingly reversed and the cases and remanded to the District Courts to take such proceedings and enter such orders and decrees consistent with this opinion as are necessary and proper to admit to public schools on a racially nondiscriminatory basis with all deliberate speed the parties to these cases. The judgment in the Delaware case—ordering the immediate admission of the plaintiffs to schools previously attended only by white children—is affirmed on the basis of the principles stated in our May 17, 1954, opinion, but the case is remanded to the Supreme Court of Delaware for such further proceedings as that Court may deem necessary in light of this opinion.

It is so ordered.

ENDNOTES

1. Together with No. 2, *Briggs et al. v. Elliott et al.*, on appeal from the United States District Court for the Eastern District of South Carolina, argued December 9–10, 1952, reargued December 7–8, 1953; No. 4, *Davis et al. v. County School Board of Prince Edward County, Virginia, et. al.*, on appeal from the United States District Court for the Eastern District of Virginia, argued December 10, 1952, reargued December 7–8, 1953; and No. 10, *Gebhart et al. v. Belton et al.*, on certiorari to the Supreme Court of Delaware, argued December 11, 1952, reargued December 9, 1953.

2. In the Kansas case *Brown v. Board of Education*, the plaintiffs are Negro children of elementary school age residing in Topeka. They brought this action in the United States District Court for the District of Kansas to enjoin enforcement of a Kansas statute which permits, but does not require, cities of more than 15,000 population to maintain separate school facilities for Negro and white students. Kan. Gen. Stat. § 72–1724 (1949). Pursuant to that authority, the Topeka Board of Education elected to establish separated elementary schools. Other public schools in the community, however, are operated on a nonsegregated basis. The three-judge District Court, convened under 28 U.S.C. §§ 2281 and 2284, found that segregation in public education has a detrimental effect upon Negro children, but denied relief on the ground that the Negro and white schools were substantially equal with respect to buildings, transportation, curricula, and educational qualifications of teachers. 98 F. Supp. 797. The case is here on direct appeal under 28 U.S.C. § 1253.

In the South Carolina case, *Briggs v. Elliott*, the plaintiffs are Negro children of both elementary and high school age residing in Clarendon County. They brought this action in the United States District Court for the Eastern District of South Carolina to enjoin enforcement of provisions in the State constitution and statutory code which require the segregation of Negroes and whites in public schools. S.C. Const., Art. XI, § 7; S.C. Code § 5377 (1942). The three-judge District Court, convened under 28 U.S.C. §§ 2281 and 2284, denied the requested relief. The court found that the Negro schools were inferior to the white schools and ordered the defendants to begin immediately to equalize the facilities. But the court sustained the validity of the contested provisions and denied the plaintiffs admission to the white schools during the equalization program. 98 F. Supp. 529. This Court vacated the District Court's judgment and remanded the case for the purpose of obtaining the court's views on a report filed by the defendants concerning the progress made in the equalization program. 342 U.S. 350. On remand, the District Court found that substantial equality had been achieved except for buildings and that the defendants were proceeding to rectify this inequality as well. 103 F. Supp. 920. The case is again here on direct appeal under 28 U.S.C. § 1253.

In the Virginia case, *Davis v. County School Board*, the plaintiffs are Negro children of high school age residing in Prince Edward County. They brought this action in the United States District Court for the Eastern District of Virginia to enjoin enforcement of provisions in the state constitution and statutory code which require the segregation of Negroes and whites in public schools. Va. Const., § 140; Va. Code § 22–221 (1950). The three–judge District Court, convened under 28 U.S.C. §§ 2281 and 2284, denied the requested relief. The court found the Negro school inferior in physical plant, curricula, and transportation, and ordered the defendants forthwith to provide substantially equal curricula and transportation and to "proceed with all reasonable diligence and dispatch to remove" the inequality in physical plant. But, as in the South Carolina case, the court sustained the validity of the contested provisions and denied the plaintiffs admission to the white schools during the equalization program. 103 F. Supp. 337. The case is here on direct appeal under 28 U.S.C. § 1253.

In the Delaware case, *Gebhart v. Belton*, the plaintiffs are Negro children of both elementary and high school age residing in New Castle County. They brought this action in the Delaware Court of Chancery to enjoin enforcement of provisions in the state constitution and statutory code which require the segregation of Negroes and whites in public schools. Del. Const., Art. X, § 2; Del. Rev. Code § 2631 (1935). The Chancellor gave judgment for the plaintiffs and ordered their immediate admission to schools previously attended only by white children, on the ground that the Negro schools were inferior with respect to teacher training, pupil-teacher ratio, extracurricular activities, physical plant, and time and distance involved in travel. 87 A. 2d 862. The Chancellor also found that segregation itself results in an inferior education for Negro children (see note 10, infra), but did not rest his decision on that ground. Id., at 865. The Chancellor's decree was affirmed by the Supreme Court of Delaware, which intimated, however, that the defendants might be able to obtain a modification of the decree after equalization of the Negro and white schools had been accomplished. 91 A. 2d 137, 152. The defendants, contending only that the Delaware courts had erred in ordering the immediate admission of the Negro plaintiffs to the white schools, applied to this Court for certiorari. The writ was granted, 344 U.S. 891. The plaintiffs, who were successful below, did not submit a cross-petition.

3. 344 U.S. 1, 141, 891.

4. 345 U.S. 972. The Attorney General of the United States participated both Terms as *amicus curiae*.

5. For a general study of the development of public education prior to the Amendment, see Butts and Cremin, A History of Education in American Culture (1953), Pts. I, II; Cubberley, Public Education in the United States (1934 ed.), ce. II–XII. School practices current at the time of the adoption of the Fourteenth Amendment are described in Butts and Cremin, supra, at 269–275; Cubberley, supra, at 288–339, 408–431; Knight, Public Education in the South (1922), cc. VIII, IX. See also H. Ex. Doc. No. 315, 41st Cong., 2d Sess. (1871). Although the demand for free public schools followed substantially the same pattern in both the North and the South, the development in the South did not begin to gain momentum until about 1850, some twenty years after that in the North. The reasons for the somewhat slower development in the South (*e. g.*, the rural character of the South and the different regional attitudes toward state assistance) are well explained in Cubberley, *supra*, at 408–423. In the country as a whole, but particularly in the South, the War virtually stopped all progress in public education. *Id.*, at 427–428 The low status of Negro education in all sections of this country, both before and immediately after the War, is described in Beale, A History of Freedom of Teaching in American Schools (1941), 112–132, 175–195. Compulsory school attendance laws were not generally adopted until after the ratification of the Fourteenth Amendment, and it was not until 1918 that such laws were in force on all the states. Cubberly, *supra*, at 563–565.

6. *Slaughter-House Cases*, 16 Wall. 36, 67–72 (1873); *Strauder v. West Virginia*, 100 U.S. 303, 307–308 (1880):

"It ordains that no State shall deprive any person of life liberty, or property, without due process of law, or deny to any person within its jurisdiction the equal protection of the laws. What is this but declaring that the law in the States shall be the same for the black as for the white; that all persons, whether colored or white, shall stand equal before the laws of the States, and, in regard to the colored race, for whose protection the amendment was primarily designed, that no discrimination shall be made against them by law because of their color? The words of the amendment, it is true, are prohibitory, but they contain a necessary implication of a positive immunity, or right, most valuable to the colored race, the right to exemption from unfriendly legislation against them distinctively as colored, exemption from legal discriminations, implying inferiority in civil society, lessening the security of their enjoyment of the rights which others enjoy, and discriminations which are steps towards reducing them to the condition of a subject race."

See also *Virginia v. Rives*, 100 U.S. 313, 318 (1880); *Ex parte Virginia*, 100 U.S. 339, 344–345 (1880).

7. The doctrine apparently originated in *Roberts v. City of Boston*, 59 Mass. 198, 206 (1850), upholding school segregation against attack as being violative of a state constitutional guarantee of equality. Segregation in Boston public schools was eliminated in 1855. Mass. Acts 1855, c. 256. But elsewhere in the North segregation in public education has persisted in some communities until recent years. It is apparent that such segregation has long been a nationwide problem, not merely one of sectional concern.

8. See also *Berea College v. Kentucky*, 211 U.S. 45 (1908).

9. In the Cumming case, Negro taxpayers sought an injunction requiring the defendant school board to discontinue the operation of a high school for white children until the board resumed operation of a high school for Negro children. Similarly, in the Gong Lum case, the plaintiff, a child of Chinese descent, contended only that state authorities had misapplied the doctrine by classifying him with Negro children and requiring him to attend a Negro school.

10. In the Kansas case, the court below found substantial equality as to all such factors. 98 F. Supp. 797, 798. In the South Carolina case, the court below found that the defendants were proceeding "promptly and in good faith to comply with the court's decree." 103 F. Supp. 920, 921. In the Virginia case, the court below noted that the equalization program was already "afoot and progressing" (103 F. Supp. 337, 341); since then, we have been advised, in the Virginia Attorney General's brief on reargument, that the program has now been completed. In the Delaware case, the court below similarly noted that the state's equalization program was well under way. 91 A. 2d 137, 149.

11. A similar finding was made in the Delaware case: "I conclude from the testimony that in our Delaware society, State-imposed segregation in education itself results in the Negro children, as a class, receiving educational opportunities which are substantially inferior to those available to white children otherwise similarly situated." 87 A. 2d 862, 865.

12. K. B. Clark, Effect of Prejudice and Discrimination on Personality Development (Midcentury White House Conference on Children and Youth, 1950); Witmer and Kotinsky, Personality in the Making (1952), c. VI; Deutscher and Chein, The Psychological Effects of Enforced Segregation: A Survey of Social Science Opinion, 26 J. Psychol. 259 (1948); Chein, What are the Psychological Effects of Segregation Under Conditions of Equal Facilities?, 3 Int. J. Opinion and Attitude Res. 229 (1949); Brameld, Education Costs, in Discrimination and Welfare (MacIver, ed. 1949), 44–48; Fraizier, The Negro in the United States (1949), 674-681. And see generally Myrdal, An American Dilemma (1944).

13. See *Bolling v. Sharpe*, *post*, p. 497, concerning the Due Process Clause of the Fifth Amendment.

14. "4. Assuming it is decided that segregation in public schools violates the Fourteenth Amendment

"(a) would a decree necessarily follow providing that, within the limits set by normal geographic school districting, Negro children should forthwith be admitted to schools of their choice, or

"(b) may this Court, in the exercise of its equity powers, permit an effective gradual adjustment to be brought about from existing segregated systems to a system not based on color distinctions?

"5. On the assumption on which questions 4 (a) and (b) are based, and assuming further that this Court will exercise its equity powers to the end described in question 4 (b),

"(a) should this Court formulate detailed decrees in these cases;

"(b) if so, what specific issues should the decrees reach;

"(c) should this Court appoint a special master to hear evidence with a view to recommending specific terms for such decrees;

"(d) should this Court remand to the courts of first instance with directions to frame decrees in these cases, and if so what general directions should the decrees of this Court include and what procedures should the courts of first instance follow in arriving at the specific terms of more detailed decrees?"

15. See Rule 42, Revised Rules of this Court (effective July 1, 1954).

16. Together with No. 2, *Briggs et al. v. Elliott et al.*, on appeal from the United States District Court for the Eastern District of South Carolina; No. 3, *Davis et al. v. County School Board of Prince Edward County, Virginia, et al.*, on appeal from the United States District Court for the Eastern District of Virginia; No. 4, *Bolling et al. v. Sharpe et al.*, on certiorari to the United States Court of Appeals for the District of Columbia Circuit; and No. 5, *Gebhart et al. v. Belton et al.*, on certiorari to the Supreme Court of Delaware.

17. 347 U.S. 483; 347 U.S. 497.

18. Further argument was requested on the following questions, 347 U.S. 483, 495–496, n. 13, previously propounded by the Court:

"4. Assuming it is decided that segregation in public schools violates the Fourteenth Amendment

"(a) would a decree necessarily follow providing that, within the limits set by normal geographic school districting, Negro children should forthwith be admitted to schools of their choice, or

"(b) may this Court, in the exercise of its equity powers, permit an effective gradual adjustment to be brought about from existing segregated systems to a system not based on color distinctions?

"5. On the assumption on which questions 4 (a) and (b) are based, and assuming further that this Court will exercise its equity powers to the end described in question 4 (b),

"(a) should this Court formulate detailed decrees in these cases;

"(b) if so, what specific issues should the decrees reach;

"(c) should this Court appoint a special master to hear evidence with a view to recommending specific terms for such decrees;

"(d) should this Court remand to the courts of first instance with directions to frame decrees in these cases, and if so what general directions should the decrees of this Court include and what procedures should the courts of first instance follow in arriving at the specific terms of more detailed decrees?"

19. The cases coming to us from Kansas, South Carolina, and Virginia were originally heard by three-judge District Courts convened under 28 U.S.C. §§ 2281 and 2284. These cases will accordingly be remanded to those three-judge courts. See *Briggs v. Elliott*, 342 U.S. 350.

20. See *Alexander v. Hillman*, 296 U.S. 222, 239.

21. See *Hecht Co. v. Bowles*, 321 U.S. 321, 329–330.

UNIT 4-4

A Random Thought on the Segregation Cases

William H. Rehnquist

Inside The Court

William H. Rehnquist's Memorandum to Justice Robert Jackson
on *Brown v. Board of Education*

As a law clerk to Justice Robert Jackson in 1952–53, William Rehnquist wrote a memorandum to the justice on Brown v. Board of Education. *Later, at his confirmation hearings on his nomination to the Supreme Court in 1971, Rehnquist claimed that the memo was written at Jackson's request and reflected the justice's views rather than his own. But the content and style of the memo (as well as the fact that Justice Jackson's private papers contain several other memos written by Rehnquist) indicate that the memo reflected Rehnquist's views on the case and the role of the Court.*

One-hundred fifty years ago this Court held that it was the ultimate judge of the restrictions which the Constitution imposed on the various branches of the national and state government. *Marbury v. Madison.* This was presumably on the basis that there are standards to be applied other than the personal predilections of the Justices.

As applied to questions of inter-state or state-federal relations, as well as to inter-departmental disputes within the federal government, this doctrine of Judicial review has worked well. Where theoretically co-ordinate bodies are disputing, the Court is well suited to its role as arbiter. This is because these problems involve much less emotionally charged subject matter than do those discussed below. In effect, they determine the skeletal relations of the governments to each other without influencing the substantive business of those governments.

As applied to relations between the individual and the state, the system has worked much less well. The Constitution, of course, deals with individual rights, particularly in the First Ten and the Fourteenth Amendments. But as I read the history of this Court, it has seldom been out of hot water when attempting to interpret these individual rights.

Source: Robert H. Jackson Papers, Library of Congress.

Fletcher v. Peck, in 1810, represented an attempt by Chief Justice Marshall to extend the protection of the contract clause to infant business. *Scott v. Sanford* was the result of Taney's effort to protect slaveholders from legislative interference.

After the Civil War, business interest came to dominate the Court, and they in turn ventured into the deep water of protecting certain types of individuals against legislative interference. Championed first by Field, then by Peckham and Brewer, the high water mark of the trend in protecting corporations against legislative influence was probably *Lochner v. NY.* To the majority opinion in that case, Holmes replied that the Fourteenth Amendment did not enact Herbert Spencer's Social Statics. Other cases coming later in a similar vein were *Adkins v. Children's Hospital*, *Hammer v. Dagenhart*, *Tyson v. Banton*, *Ribnik v. McBride*. But eventually the Court called a halt to this reading of its own economic views into the Constitution. Apparently it recognized that where a legislature was dealing with its own citizens, it was not part of the Judicial function to thwart public opinion except in extreme cases.

In these cases now before the Court, the Court is, as Davis suggested, being asked to read its own sociological views into the Constitution. Urging a view palpably at variance with precedent and probably with legislative history, appellants seek to convince the Court of the moral wrongness of the treatment they are receiving. I would suggest that this is a question the Court need never reach; for regardless of the Justice's individual views on the merits of segregation, it quite clearly is not one of those extreme cases which commands intervention from one of any conviction. If this Court, because its members individually are "liberal" and dislike segregation, now chooses to strike it down, it differs from the McReynolds court only in the kinds of litigants it favors and the kinds of special claims it protects. To those who would argue that "personal" rights are more sacrosanct than "property" rights, the short answer is that the Constitution makes no such distinction. To the argument made by Thurgood Marshall that a majority may not deprive a minority of its constitutional right, the answer must be made that while this is sound in theory, in the long run it is the majority who will determine what the constitutional rights of the minority are. One hundred and fifty years of attempts on the part of this Court to protect minority rights of any kind—whether those of business, slaveholders, of Jehovah's Witnesses—have all met the same fate. One by one the cases establishing such rights have been sloughed off, and crept silently to rest. If the present Court is unable to profit by this example, it must be prepared to see its work fade in time, too, as embodying only the sentiments of a transient majority of nine men.

I realize that it is an unpopular and unhumanitarian position, for which I have been excoriated by "liberal" colleagues, but I think *Plessy v. Ferguson* was right and should be re-affirmed. If the Fourteenth Amendment did not enact Spencer's *Social Statics*, it just as surely did not enact Myrdahl's *American Dilemma*.

UNIT 4-5

THE OPINION OF MANKIND

THE U.S. SECRETARY OF STATE ON SEGREGATION AND WORLD RELATIONS

Dean Acheson

January 1953

I wrote the Chairman of the Fair Employment Practices Committee on May 8, 1946, that the existence of discrimination against minority groups was having an adverse effect upon our relations with other countries. At that time I pointed out that discrimination against such groups in the United States created suspicion and resentment in other countries, and that we would have better international relations were these reasons for suspicion and resentment to be removed.

During the past six years, the damage to our foreign relations attributable to this source has become progressively greater. The United States is under constant attack in the foreign press, over the foreign radio, and in such international bodies as the United Nations because of various practices of discrimination against minority groups in this country. As might be expected, Soviet spokesmen regularly exploit this situation in propaganda against the United States, both within the United Nations and through radio broadcasts and the press, which reaches all corners of the world. Some of these attacks against us are based on falsehood or distortion; but the undeniable existence of racial discrimination gives unfriendly governments the most effective kind of ammunition for their propaganda warfare.

The hostile reaction among normally friendly peoples, many of whom are particularly sensitive in regard to the status of non-European races, is growing in alarming proportions. In such countries the view is expressed more and more vocally that the United States is hypocritical in claiming to be the champion of democracy while permitting practices of racial discrimination here in this country.

The segregation of school children on a racial basis is one of the practices in the United States that has been singled out for hostile foreign comment in the United

---

From a statement by the Secretary of State as quoted in the United States Government's brief before the Supreme Court, December 1952.

Nations and elsewhere. Other peoples cannot understand how such a practice can exist in a country which professes to be a staunch supporter of freedom, justice, and democracy. The sincerity of the United States in this respect will be judged by its deeds as well as by its words.

Although progress is being made, the continuance of racial discrimination in the United States remains a source of constant embarrassment to this Government in the day-to-day conduct of its foreign relations; and it jeopardizes the effective maintenance of our moral leadership of the free and democratic nations of the world.

He'll Need Help to Pry Him Loose

NEWS ITEM—The Legal Defense and Education Fund needs money to complete the job. Send your tax deductible contribution to 107 W. 43rd St., New York 18, N. Y.

The Bridge to Complete Equality

Not too much protection there, boys!

Saboteur at Work

. . . When they saw the Star they rejoiced!

UNIT 4-7

EXCERPTS FROM INFORMAL MEMORANDUM FROM HARRY ASHMORE

"Dred Scott" Ashmore

Looking out over the debris this morning (the day after the Court's decision) I'm right proud of the South. Herman Talmadge exploded on schedule, but virtually every other politician of standing took to the high ground. And the Southern press, as I have had a chance to check it so far, seems to have acted with complete responsibility.

Put this down to undue immodesty if you will, but I am convinced that the project had a lot to do with it. The book was in the hands of all the key editors and most of the politicians by the time the blow fell, and it can only have had a soothing influence. Furthermore, I am convinced they will be turning to it in the critical days ahead. I believe we can already assure Justice Roberts that the Fund's risk capital investment is paying dividends.

Incidentally, while I have by no means seen all the Southern reviews of the book I have looked over a couple of dozen. All are favorable, and most important of all, everywhere we are being credited with objectivity. Remarkably enough, at this reading at least, we haven't been blasted anywhere.

Since the decision came down yesterday I have talked to dozens of people all over Arkansas, many of them educators. A few are distressed, but all are calm. Actually, if I had to define the prevailing feeling here—and I believe this is generally true over the South except in the really hot spots—I would say it is one of relief that the other shoe has finally dropped. There is a great difference in brooding over an abstraction and wrestling with a concrete problem that has edges you can get hold of. I think I can see the beginning of that time I have always dreamed of—when you can conduct a conversation in the South without having it degenerate into an argument over where a man should sit in a street car.

Informal Memo from Harry Ashmore, Editor, *Arkansas Gazette*, to George Mitchell, Executive Director SRC, May 18, 1954.

The manner in which the Court handed down the decision was magnificent—so much so that I am thinking about writing a fan letter to the Chief Justice if I can only figure out the protocol in the matter. The unanimous opinion spiked many a gun, and the setting of the new precedent well in advance of handing down the specific decrees was a master-stroke. It gives everybody time to get used to the idea, and opens the possibility of intelligent and specific argument on ways and means before the Court which was impossible while the advocates felt they would have to concede their major point if they discussed anything less than Armageddon.

UNIT 4-8

EDITORIAL
SEGREGATION DECISION

The United States Supreme Court handed down a historic decision on May 17. By declaring racial segregation in the public schools to be unconstitutional, the Court took a step which will inevitably destroy present forms of segregation wherever practiced. The "separate but equal" fiction as legal doctrine now joins the horsecar, the bustle, and the five-cent cigar. While the NAACP and *The Crisis* hail this decision as marking a turning point in American race relations, we also feel it necessary to temper our exultation with the warning that this is a major battle won, not a campaign concluded. In fact, implementation of the decision remains to be argued this fall before the Court issues its decrees.

We are at that point in our fight against segregation where unintelligent optimism and childish faith in a court decision can blind us to the fact that legal abolition of segregation is not the final solution for the social cancer of racism.

While the South as a whole has taken the Supreme Court decision in its stride, and there is more than a little evidence that many white Southerners are willing to comply with the decision, opponents of unified white and Negro public schools are trying to sow disunity by greeting the impression that our highest tribunal has asked the South to do something that neither its white nor Negro citizens really want. A liberal southerner like Dr. Howard W. Odum has already been quoted (*Tarboro Southerner*, N.C.) as fearing that the South might lose its gains by reacting to the segregation ruling:

> Talmadge and his cohorts, on the one hand, and the NAACP extremists on the other, by openly fanning the fires of physical conflict must surely be playing into the Communist strategy of divide and conquer as well as strengthening the demagoguery of McCarthy in the South.

Dr. Odum must know that he is talking nonsense when he halters us with Talmadge and suggests that the NAACP is an extremist organization. The Association has always worked within the law without appeals to violence; actually its goal is enforcement of basic constitutional law, because we want America to maintain her spiritual solvency by practicing her democratic principles.

Crisis, June–July 1954.

On the other hand, there are those in the South who are arguing against immediate integration in the schools on the ground that "the change-over may require decades." This group is much more dangerous than the one that accuses us of extremism. They are the fellows who are inviting *local Negro leaders* to sit around the conference table to work out amicable solutions which will be "fair to both races." What this group wants is continued segregation. And they are stressing the achievements of southern Negroes in the segregated South.

We shall, therefore, have to be on our guard against those who would stir up dissension by pinning hobgoblin whiskers on integrationists as well as those peddlers of soda-fountain syrup who are suddenly fearful of souring "friendly race relations in the South."

What should we Negroes do to facilitate integration? For what we do or fail to do will determine both the character and the speed with which we unify the bi-racial public school system of the South. First, the NAACP is absolutely opposed to any compromise of principle in the integration of white and Negro pupils in the public schools of the South. The Atlanta Declaration (P. 358) is emphatic on this point. Secondly, the NAACP is aware of the administrative problems involved in the changeover, but we are not going to coddle school boards and superintendents who may attempt to use these problems as an excuse for unnecessary delay or to avoid desegregation. The Association's credo is that the quicker the integration the better it will be for Negroes, the South, and America. And remember that we have other battles ahead of us.

NATION'S PRESS ON SEGREGATION RULING—

SOME EDITORIAL EXCERPTS

"FOUL BLOW"

The Register, Danville, Va.

Our own opinion is that a turn-coat Court his misinterpreted a Force Amendment to strike a foul blow at Public education in the South and at a way of life in the South which no court ruling can end by dictum.

"TERRIFIC BLOW"

Tuscaloosa News, Ala.

Action by the United States Supreme Court in ruling that segregation in public schools is unconstitutional is a terrific blow to Southern custom and sentiment.

"NO ADVANCEMENT"

Mobile Press, Ala.

The National Association for the Advancement of Colored People fought for the ruling that segregation in public schools is unconstitutional and naturally, is cheering the decision.... But there is no advancement for colored teachers in this ruling.

"SLAVES OF LAW"

Jacksonville News, N.C.

It is hoped that this breaking down of custom and tradition can be bridged without too much friction....

Crisis, June–July 1954.

"WHAT WAS EXPECTED"
Mobile Register, Ala.

The United States Supreme Court has done precisely that which was expected—it has nullified state laws and held segregation unlawful. . . . The ultimate effect of this decision is something that only time can tell.

"NOT ENTIRELY POPULAR"
New Orleans State, La.

To say that its decision in this matter was not entirely popular with many Southern elected officials is to state the obvious.

"LAW OF LAND"
New Orleans Item, La.

The court's decision, however unpopular, is the law of the land and must be complied with.

"COOL HEADS"
Opelika News, Ala.

The vital need at this moment in our nation is for cool heads and great minds. Possible fuel for a disastrous explosion has been released.

"GREAT SHOCK"
Huntsville Times, Ala.

. . . A great shock . . . a crushing blow to all the customs, traditions and modes, extending over more than 200 years, that have been built or grown up around the principle and practice of segregation.

"DECISION INEVITABLE"
Columbia Tribune, Mo.

Most thinking Americans will, we believe, agree that yesterday's decision of the United States Supreme Court was inevitable. . . .

"VICTORY AGAINST REDS"
Post-Dispatch, Mo.

Nine men in Washington have given us a victory that no number of divisions, arms and bombs could ever have won [in our struggle against Communism].

"STRIFE FORECAST"
Jackson Daily News, Miss.

It means racial strife of the bitterest sort. Mississippi cannot and will not try to abide by such a decision.

"APPLY INTELLIGENCE"
Charlotte News, N.C.

The South must apply its intelligence coolly and dispassionately and must find the resources for giving all its children equality of education.

"BALANCE UPSET"
Charleston News & Courier, S.C.

The court decision drove another nail into the coffin of states rights. In the past, the Constitution was a balance wheel. Now that balance has been upset and a new one must be established.

"ERA ENDS"
Dallas News, Texas

When unanimously the United States Supreme Court ruled school segregation unconstitutional, a long era came to an end. Whether we are better off for that, time alone will tell. . . . The effect will reach all interracial relations.

"TIME FOR CALM"
Richmond Times-Dispatch, Va.

This is a time for calm and unhysterical appraisal of the situation by the officials and people of Virginia and the other sixteen states affected.

"THINK CLEARLY"
Atlanta Constitution, Ga.

It is a time for Georgia to think clearly. Our best minds must be put to work, not to destroy, but to arrive at constructive conclusions. . . .

"HISTORIC DECISION"
Trenton Times, N. J.

What is especially encouraging about the Supreme Court decision is its frank and unqualified insistence that this country has no room for second-rate citizenship of the type implicit in a system of segregation.

"HISTORIC DECISION"
Newark Star-Ledger, N. J.

The historic decision yesterday by the Supreme Court—declaring unconstitutional race segregation in the public schools—is one of the most important developments in the touchy problem of race relations since the emancipation of the slaves during the Civil War.

"NEW GLORY"
New York City Post

The Supreme Court has given new glory to the idea of American democracy by the simple but majestic announcement that segregated schools deprive Negroes of "the equal protection of the laws guaranteed by the 14th Amendment."

"JOIN APPLAUSE"
New York City Daily News

We'll join in the applause for the U. S. Supreme Court's unanimous decision that race segregation in the nation's public schools must start getting out.

"TRUE EQUALITY"
New York Herald-Tribune

In yesterday's historic decision the Supreme Court of the United States squared the country's basic law with its conscience and its deepest conviction.

"DECISION INEVITABLE"
New York Times

. . . The decision reached was inevitable in the year 1954 regardless of what may have been the case in 1868, when the Fourteenth Amendment was adopted or in 1896, when the "separate but equal" doctrine was laid down in the case of *Plessy v. Ferguson*.

"MIGHTY BLOW"

Minneapolis Tribune, Minn.

The Supreme Court of the United States has now said with unmistakable clarity and emphasis that racial segregation in the public schools must come to an end. With this pronouncement it has also struck a mighty blow at racial intolerance in every other phase of our national life as well.

DID YOU KNOW—

That the Freedmen's Bureau, set up by Congress in 1865, launched more than 4,000 elementary schools in the South? These were all segregated schools.

* * *

That the southern segregated school operates under the same administrative structure as the white?

* * *

That the gap between white and Negro public schools in the South is greater in rural than in urban areas?

UNIT 4-9

SRC Reacts to the Brown Decision

A Statement by the Executive Committee of the Southern Regional Council

Nine months have passed since the Supreme Court held segregation in the public schools unconstitutional. Although the Court has not yet handed down its implementation decrees, school segregation is already disappearing in four of the 17 states chiefly affected, as well as in the District of Columbia and in states where segregation has been permissive. How quickly and harmoniously the remaining states bring their practices into accord with the law of the land will depend on the quality of leadership, public and private, displayed by the South in the months ahead.

We believe that this is a time for Southerners to take stock, to look realistically at the challenge confronting the region and at our resources for meeting it wisely and well. As one effort in this direction, we here summarize our collective view of the impact to date of the Supreme Court's decision.

* * *

School desegregation is proceeding successfully in some 80 out of 129 border-state counties where separate schools were formerly required by law. The significance of this fact-indeed, the fact itself—has been obscured by the widespread publicity given disturbances in a few localities. It is less sensational, but far more important, that this many counties have adjusted successfully in so short a time to the principle of the school decision. Their experience currently demonstrates to the world that American democracy has the vigor and capacity to solve its thorny racial problems. The entire country owes a heavy debt of gratitude to the hundreds of private citizens and public officials whose allegiance to the law of the land made this progress possible.

Although these communities are in border states, they are nonetheless places where segregation has been embedded in law and custom for generations. What can be done in Missouri, Delaware, Maryland, and West Virginia can be and ultimately will be done in those states where political stratagems now deny Southerners of good will the opportunity to work similarly toward compliance with the Supreme Court decision.

New South, March 1955.

* * *

In the upper South and the Southwest, several states are preparing soundly for early compliance. But others pursue a policy of "wait and see" that might better be described as "look the other way." Planning and even consideration of the desegregation process is discouraged on the ground that no action is now required and none may be required for a long time. Such an attitude promotes paralysis of public thought, and thereby forfeits a valuable opportunity for advance discussion and planning to insure smooth transition to integrated schools.

The Court has said unequivocally that legal segregation in the public schools is unconstitutional. Its implementation decrees will hardly fail to make this ruling effective. Nor is it reasonable to expect the Court to allow an indefinite period of delay. This interim period is precisely the time for joint fact-finding and planning by all elements of the community.

* * *

In four of the deep South states South Carolina, Georgia, Mississippi, and Louisiana—the official leadership is busily creating dangerous illusions and enacting defiant measures. Some political leaders in these states are assuring the people that the schools will remain segregated indefinitely, if not forever, even though public education may be abolished in the process. These threats and the legal stratagems devised to carry them out are better adapted to hoodwink the people than to preserve segregation.

Most of these measures impose heavy penalties on any local authorities or school systems that choose voluntarily to comply with the Supreme Court ruling. Ironically, the proponents of these measures are the same spokesmen who repeat over and over that most Negroes and virtually all white persons will defend segregation at any cost. Obviously they do not believe their own words.

Moreover, leading Southern authorities on constitutional law who have examined these circumventing measures have agreed that they are dodges and will not stand in court.

There are truths that need saying in the deep South. There is a wide range of information that should be made known through every medium. Views of every kind need to be freely and fully aired. Instead, there is presently a concerted attempt by official leadership to stamp out independent thought and stifle all dissent with respect to school segregation. Consequently, it is imperative that responsible Southerners confirm the fact that vast numbers of us will not defy the United States Constitution, the teachings of our religion, and the prevailing opinions of the free world.

Despite all the bluster of the demagogues, most Southerners recognize that segregation is on the way out. Not all of them are happy about it, but they see it as an evident reality. Few would actually be willing to jettison their public schools and throw their educational systems into a dark age of confusion and chaos.

Those who advocate such a course do irreparable harm to the progress of the South and to the cause of freedom throughout the world. But, fortunately, they will not have the last word. In the end, the people of the region will reject those who would lead them down the blind alley of rebellion. There are thousands of Southerners, white and Negro, for whom the demagogues do not speak, and whose voices have been little heard above the din of controversy. Ultimately, these responsible Southern voices will repudiate fraudulent leadership on the school segregation issue. Speaking together, they can give the region a new confidence in its capacity for democratic growth.

* * *

We in the Southern Regional Council reaffirm our belief that the vast majority of Southerners accept what is now the law of the land, want to have done with bitterness and obstruction, and are willing to meet on equal terms with their fellow citizens and find the best ways to move ahead. The Council strongly recommends local planning by citizens of the two races as the soundest means of preparing for compliance with the Supreme Court decision.

How to Implement the Supreme Court Decision

Marion A. Wright

Marion A. Wright, president of the Southern Regional Council, is a native of South Carolina, where he played a prominent part in legal and civic affairs. He now lives in Linville Falls, N.C. This article is based on a recent speech before the New Orleans Committee on Race Relations.

Of course, the Supreme Court itself will, so far as lies within its power implement its decision of May 17 by later decision. This later decision will give the South either a time-table or formula to bring about the integration of the public school systems. The decision will either spell out in exact terms just when certain things must be done or it will delegate authority to lower courts, or other instruments of its choosing, to establish the rate and method of integration.

The complete answer, however, cannot be found in a few words or a few paragraphs written upon paper and signed by members of the Supreme Court. There is an area of activity apart from the merely judicial or merely legal in which every good citizen may function.

Men begin to come to maturity when they think of government not as "they" but "we." Thus, we recognize the sacred partnership which exists between the individual and his government. Upon every citizen there rests the obligation to exert himself in an effort to bring about the widest acceptance of the law of the land. The acceptance which the decree shall receive rests, I firmly believe, as much upon non-official, as upon official, action.

Indeed, the talk of evasion, where it is found, seems to come largely from official or political sources.

I think we should know that all of these schemes, in addition to the dark evils which would follow in their train, are doomed to frustration. Space does not here permit an analysis of these devices. But I may point out that within recent weeks they have been condemned upon the ground of naked unconstitutionality by three Southern law journals—possibly by others. Journals of the University of Virginia, the University of South Carolina, and the University of North Carolina have carried full briefs by law professors, in which the various schemes were analyzed and all found to be completely vulnerable upon constitutional grounds. These briefs were not by outsiders meddling in Southern affairs but were by the most competent Southern legal writers analyzing the problems of their own region.

The Varied South

It is quite evident that the problem of implementation is not a general one having the same degree of solubility in all areas of the South. It will vary by states and even within states. That fact was made perfectly clear in a recent talk by Mr. C. A. McKnight, editor of *Southern School News*, before the North Carolina Press Association. He pointed out that, even without awaiting the court's final decree, Delaware, West Virginia, Missouri and the District of Columbia began or completed desegregation in the current school year. States which are in the "wait and see" class are Maryland, Florida, Kentucky, Oklahoma,

New South, May 1955.

Tennessee, North Carolina, Virginia, Texas, Arkansas, and Alabama. "The unyielding resistance" states include Georgia, Mississippi, South Carolina, and Louisiana.

And I think it entirely safe to assume that the core of resistance will be found much harder in certain areas of a given state than in others.

If that fact means anything it means that local leadership has its great obligation and its great opportunity. No one in Atlanta, for example, may with the slightest degree of authority tell Louisiana what it should do. No one in New Orleans with the slightest degree of authority may tell the hinterlands of Louisiana what they should do. But the hinterlands must decide for themselves, with all the help which we may give, what they should do. Having thus admitted the localized nature of the problem and the particularized problems which must be met by the several communities, there seem to be words of advice which we as friends may utter with applicability to every section of the South. We have available now the experiences of various communities, from which experiences certain practical lessons may be drawn.

First of all, integration will not be made less difficult by white action or by Negro action. It will be made less difficult only by joint action. And the first prerequisite to joint action is joint discussion and planning.

Until members of the two races, without the slightest restraint, may sit around a table in some church or school building and talk in friendly man-to-man fashion, they will get nowhere. As I visualize it, there may be a half dozen meetings in a community which may not crystallize into a resolution or other formal expression of joint opinion. Such meetings will not be wasted. The greatest hurdle will be passed in the mere fact that such meetings have been held.

Communication

The greatest obstacle to solution of all of our racial problems lies in the lack of communication between the races. If the channels of communication are created so that the whites may know what the Negroes are thinking and the Negroes may know what the whites are thinking, their positions will not be found to be poles apart.

Men instinctively wish to be heard, to register their views. Evil concoctions are brewed in minds which are denied the legitimate opportunity for self-expression. So in every community in the South, there should be these discussion groups for the ventilation of opinion.

The second thing which seems obviously to be needed is the inclusion of Negroes in parent-teacher associations. So long as there were white schools and Negro schools, there might have been a semblance of justification for racially divided parent-teacher groups. But from this point on there will be no such thing as white education and Negro education. It will be education for all of the children. The parents and teachers of these children will for the first time be dealing with the sacred subject of education in its wider aspects. They should deal with it, not as white or Negro parents or teachers, but simply as parents and teachers of school children.

In a sense, this lowering of the barriers of parent-teacher groups may be thought to be a fairly small thing to do. But it is a most symbolic thing. It symbolizes a broadening of the minds of citizens to the point that racial distinctions have lost significance. It would be an important token of the advance of our people, a long forward step in civilization.

Teachers Groups

Collateral to the consolidation of parent-teacher groups, is the consolidation of teacher associations upon all levels. I suppose that universally throughout the South there exist white teacher associations and Negro teacher associations. They were the fairly logical accompaniment of segregated schools. Each group conceivably could have had problems peculiar to itself. Until the courts took a hand, the salary schedules and the qualifications of the two groups were different. White teachers were concerned with legislative action affecting their own salaries and qualifications; likewise the Negro teachers. Now, however, following judicial decrees, at least in theory and certainly in legal principle, salaries and qualifications are identical.

Whatever reasons may have heretofore existed for the creation and maintenance of separate groups, such reasons no longer exist. On the contrary, there now exists the compelling reason that the teachers themselves should be thoroughly integrated in preparation for integration of the schools. The time is already overdue for white and Negro teachers to come to know each other and to share with each other in friendly association all that experience and training have taught them. The transition will be not nearly so difficult if those who teach have developed professional and personal contact with each other.

BOARD REPRESENTATION

Another step is to see that Negroes have representation on local, county and state boards of education. The step has been taken in many southern states with gratifying results. Governor Scott of North Carolina some years ago appointed Dr. Harold Trigg, able and distinguished president of a Negro college, to the state board of education. I am sure that such calmness and wisdom as North Carolina is exhibiting in its attitude toward integration stem in part from this appointment.

The most important asset which may be possessed by any government is the justified faith of all of its citizens in the fairness of government. When all of the policy is fashioned by one group, all of the funds distributed by that group, and all of the employment made by that group, we are asking a great deal of the other group to assume the complete fairness and impartiality of government.

It is a part of our tradition to go along as cheerfully as we can with any decisions which have been made if we have been represented and our voice has been heard in the making of such decisions. If a state wishes to secure for itself this priceless asset of the confidence of its citizens, it must give them all a voice in fashioning its policy. Taxation without representation is unjust; but the framing of policy which affects a citizen's life while denying him a voice is tyranny.

THE SCHOOL ADMINISTRATOR

We must all realize that the key man in the school system is the local administrator. Integration will be accomplished with relative difficulty or relative ease depending upon the resolution and strength of conviction of the administrator—and of the school board which often fashions the policies under which he must operate. Integration will place upon his shoulders no small burden in the early years. He will need all of the strength of character which he may muster and all of the stiffening support which the community may supply.

The administrator is probably unaware of the existence in his community of any considerable opinion favorable to integration. It is significant that most of the discussion of the impact on education of the decision of the Supreme Court has taken place in the political, rather than the educational, arena. Hence, the administrator has been pretty well informed by the views of politicians that integration is a bad thing and must be evaded by any means possible.

The time has now come for those of us who disagree with certain of our politicians to stick our necks out and make our voices heard. The chief result of that action would be to acquaint the school administrator and the school board with the fact that statesmanship and firmness on their part will have some measure of moral backing and support.

Another key figure in the picture is the police official, be he city policeman, sheriff, or what not. After all, the disagreeable truth must be met. There may be evilly disposed persons who will seek to disrupt the orderly transition. They deal with inflammatory material. Their methods are illegal or extra-legal—incitement to riot or rebellion, and intimidation. When their action constitutes a violation of law, there should be no wavering or vacillation on the part of the police. The police are an arm of government. Merely to suggest is not to govern. The right to attend school as permitted under law is a right fully as sacred as any other right and as much entitled to protection in its exercise. The public has a right to expect of its law enforcement officers prompt evidence of a lack of toleration for incitement to violence.

Many factors contributed to the decline of lynching in the South. None was more effective than the action of a group of women in each county seat in advising their sheriff that they fastened upon him responsibility for protecting his prisoner. The same technique may be wisely employed in the school situation. Better still would be insuring that, wherever possible, police officials would be brought to approve in their hearts the laws they are seeking to enforce.

Integration Experience

The local communities have at hand a valuable asset which should not be overlooked. That is, they have, in nearly every instance, people, usually young, who have had experience with integration. Few indeed are the towns or cross roads which do not include in their citizenship a sprinkling of white people who have attended in other states or in private or parochial schools classes also attended by Negroes. Some of these are Southerners who have received a part of their education in the North. Others are Northerners who have moved South upon the tide of industrial migration or in response to other less practical lures.

Certainly, too, there must be nearly everywhere white veterans who have learned of democracy in the hard school of war. Such veterans do not willingly strangle the fraternity which had its birth in Europe, in the Pacific, in Korea. In one Southern state, in 22 counties the veterans' administrator left to the veterans themselves to decide whether they would receive their GI training under segregated or integrated conditions. Their unanimous vote was for integration. One dose of democracy in action lasts a long time.

Surely the local communities will not fail to use to the fullest extent the talents and capacities of students and veterans of good will who have savored elsewhere of the very condition we seek to create here.

Information

What we all need is information, information on what other communities are doing and the plans that they are making. Fortunately for all of us *Southern School News*, established by a grant from the Fund for the Advancement of Education, and completely controlled, managed, and edited by Southerners, gives that information month by month. The delightful thing about *Southern School News* is that, like salvation, it is free. While being entirely objective and impartial, its presentation of the record shows a most encouraging acceptance of the idea of integration in large areas of the South. Conversely, it establishes the isolation of those Southern states and communities which are toying with their evasive schemes. Through this medium a citizen may learn what other communities are doing. That knowledge may not merely prod him to action but insure the wisdom of such action as he may take.

We will not be well served by paternalists from the one group or Uncle Toms from the other. There was a time in this cause when one acquired a reputation for wisdom merely by stating, "You can't change human nature by law." One acquired a reputation for goodness merely by stating, "There are wrongs in discrimination and some day we must attack them." Those were the meanly wise, the feebly good.

The men and women now needed are of a more robust school, cast in a more heroic mold.

THE POSITIVE VIEW

I think that in all that we say and do we must stress the positive, the affirmative. We should take no short range view of history. Through integration ultimately we will gain escape from delusions of superiority or inferiority which are a hangover from the old master and servant days. The community and the state will be able to utilize in governmental and social planning and operation all the brains, talents, and skills of the community—not just half. They will escape the financial drain entailed by duplicating schools, libraries, parks, playgrounds, and the like. Integration will eliminate the day to day causes of irritation and friction which go with enforcing arbitrary and wholly foolish rules of conduct.

Perhaps it may all be summed up by saying that, for the first time in their lives, white Southerners may use without flinching and sense of guilt such ancient phrases as "equality before the law. . . . equality of opportunity," "brotherhood of man," and "Fatherhood of God."

UNIT 4-10

INTERPRETATION OF SUPREME COURT DECISION & THE NAACP PROGRAM

Thurgood Marshall and Roy Wilkins

An interpretative analysis of the Supreme Court Decision of May 31, 1955, and an indication of the NAACP program by Thurgood Marshall and Roy Wilkins, special counsel and executive secretary, respectively, of the NAACP.

The May 31 decision combined with the May 17 decision of last year must be viewed as the latest in a series of steps toward full integration of Negroes into American life. When the NAACP began this campaign it was met with state statutes requiring or permitting segregation in public education. These statutory provisions were a complete block to all voluntary efforts to end segregation.

The first cases destroyed the validity of out-of-state scholarships as an excuse for the exclusion of Negroes from professional schools. This was followed by the cases which declared unconstitutional provisions for jim-crow graduate and professional schools. And then the May 17, 1954, decision declared that segregation in public education was unconstitutional. This was followed by the May 31 decision that "all provisions of federal, state or local law requiring or permitting" segregation in public education "must yield to" the principle announced in the 1954 decision.

This determination by the Supreme Court clears the way for school boards to desegregate their systems voluntarily. This is being done in many parts of the South. The opinion also gives us the necessary legal weapons to bring about compliance in areas of the South which openly flout the mandate of the Supreme Court.

The question now before us is: under what conditions and with what directives were the school cases remanded to lower courts? We know that the highest court did not (**a**) set a deadline date for either the beginning or the completion of desegregation in the public schools; and (**b**) outline a definite plan by which desegregation must proceed and by

---

All selections in 4-10 from *Crisis*, June–July 1955.

which lower courts might judge the efforts of local school boards toward compliance with the May 17 and May 31 rulings. Not having done this, what did the Court do? What language did it use?

RE-AFFIRMATION OF PRINCIPLE

May 17, 1954 decision re-affirmed. "These cases were decided on May 17, 1954. The opinions of that date, declaring the fundamental principle that racial discrimination in public education is unconstitutional, are incorporated herein by reference."

Last year's opinion, as we all know, declared: "We conclude that in the field of public education the doctrine of 'separate but equal' has no place. Separate educational facilities are inherently unequal." On May 31 the Court said simply, as an introduction to its opinion, that this principle stands and that everything in the May 31 opinion hangs upon it; that the items in the May 31 opinion must be considered at all times and under all circumstances in the light of the clear principle in the 1954 opinion. The Court refers to the 1954 "constitutional principles" a total of six times in its May 31 opinion, once as "governing constitutional principles."

All school segregation laws are invalid: "All provisions of Federal, state or local law requiring or permitting such discrimination must yield to this principle."

This means that all laws, local state and federal, requiring or permitting racial segregation in the public schools are now null and void and that no school or other public official or body is bound by such laws.

GOOD FAITH REQUIRED

Local school authorities responsible: "School authorities have the primary responsibility for elucidating, assessing, and solving these problems" of ("full implementation of these constitutional principles").

This means just what it says. It means further that it is right and proper for citizens and community groups to begin the campaign for desegregation with the local school authorities.

Good faith required: "... courts will have to consider whether the action of school authorities constitutes good-faith implementation of the governing constitutional principles."

The Court is saying here that alleged good faith in carrying out the "governing" constitutional principle of non-segregation can be brought before a court for determination and need not rest upon mere assertion by school authorities or newspapers or politicians or others.

Interest of the plaintiffs: "At stake is the personal interest of the plaintiffs in admission to public schools as soon as practicable on a non-discriminatory basis."

Plaintiffs have a right (as set forth in the May 17, 1954, decision) to admission to public schools on a nondiscriminatory basis "as soon as practicable." The latter phrase must be taken to mean with only such delay as may be permitted by the lower courts in the context of language elsewhere in the May 31 opinion.

MUST START PROMPTLY

Obstacles to be eliminated: "To effectuate this interest may call for elimination of a variety of obstacles in making the transition to school systems operated in accordance with the constitutional principles set forth in the May 17, 1954, decision."

When the Court says, as it does here, that to protect the right of the plaintiffs "may call for elimination of a variety of obstacles" it must he taken to mean that the Court in effect is ordering that such obstacles be removed. By the strongest inference it means that pleas of the existence of such obstacles cannot be considered valid reasons for denying plaintiffs their rights. The defendants are duty bound, if such obstacles exist, to remove them, whatever their nature.

Must start promptly: "While giving weight to these public and private considerations, the courts will require that the defendants make a prompt and reasonable start toward full compliance with our May 17, 1954, ruling."

Here the Court says that even while the lower courts may give due weight to the public interest (of the community at large) and to private considerations (the rights of the plaintiffs) the courts "will require" a "prompt and reasonable start toward full compliance with our May 17, 1954 ruling." "Will require" is strong, definite, positive language in legal terms, a directive which no lawyer or judge misunderstands or underestimates.

Burden Upon Defendants

Disagreement no basis for failure to comply: "Courts of equity may properly take into account the public interest in the elimination of such obstacles in a systematic and effective manner. But it should go without saying that the vitality of these constitutional principles cannot be allowed to yield simply because of disagreement with them."

Very simply this means that just because individual citizens, officials, or groups do not like or do not agree with the May 17, 1954, opinion they may not ignore, evade or defy it. That is, they may not do so in court in a final determination, no matter how much they talk or write about it in disagreement outside of a courtroom showdown.

Burden upon the defendants: "Once such a start has been made, the courts may find that additional time may be necessary to carry out the ruling in an effective manner. The burden rests upon the defendants to establish that such time is necessary in the public interest and is consistent with good-faith compliance at the earliest possible date."

It should be noted that only *after* a start has been made will a request for additional time be considered. Here, as in other phases under the jurisdiction of the courts, we have the privilege of challenging such requests for time in the courts, forcing a hearing and a determination. We need not depend upon the mere assertion of a school official that more time is necessary.

Administrative Problems

Problems to be considered by courts: "To that end, the courts may consider problems related to administration, arising from the physical condition of the school plant, the school transportation system, personnel. . . . "

Non-Racial school districts: " . . . Revision of school districts and attendance areas into compact units to achieve a system of determining admission to the public schools on a non-racial basis. . . . "

Revision of local laws: " . . . and revision of local laws and regulations which may be necessary in solving the foregoing problems."

In all its pleadings before the courts, the NAACP has granted that allowance should be made for the solving of administrative problems, but it has insisted that diligent attention to solving these would not require a prolonged period. In its section on administrative problems the Court enumerates those which the courts may consider. The time alleged to be required is subject to the burden-of-proof stipulation in the opinion. The nature of the solution of each problem is subject to the "good faith" and "constitutional principles" stipulations. All proposals are subject to challenges in the courts.

It is significant that whereas the Court merely enumerates other administrative problems, it deals in some detail with the possible revision of school districts and attendance areas, in effect saying these should be made "into compact units to achieve a system of determining admission to the public schools on a non-racial basis." This would seem to mean that both school officials and the lower courts are warned against attempting the gerrymandering of school districts through use of wandering boundary lines for the purpose of insuring racial schools.

In referring specifically to the revision of local laws and regulations hitherto requiring racial segregation in the schools, it would appear that the Court, not content with repeated citations of the "constitutional principles" involved, or with its declaration that all laws must yield to these principles, has pressed the point once more upon school officials and the lower courts. It says plainly that in solving administrative problems no local law or regulation may bar the transition to a non-segregated school system.

ADEQUACY OF PLANS

Adequacy of plans: "They (the courts) will also consider the adequacy of any plans the defendants may propose to meet the problems and to effectuate a transition to a racially non-discriminatory school system."

After listing administrative problems that may be considered by the courts, the Court includes these and every other item in any plan for transition in this one sentence on adequacy. The test is whether a plan of a given school district satisfies the principle laid down in the May 17, 1954, decision. Here again all such plans are subject to challenge in the courts and the school authorities have the burden of proving adequacy.

Courts retain jurisdiction: "During this period transition, the courts will retain jurisdiction of these cases."

Until the transition is complete the cases remain in the courts, subject at all times to its hearings and judgments on matters raised. No new actions need be commenced and no old ground re-covered in fresh proceedings.

The May 31 opinion, technically, applies only to the cases before the Court, but as a matter of fact the ruling rendered will be the pattern for all such cases as may be brought in the future.

In the overwhelming majority of instances it can be expected that compliance without legal action will be the rule, perhaps grudgingly and reluctantly in some areas, but compliance, nevertheless.

LEGAL WEAPONS IN HAND

Armed with the powers embodied in the language of the Court's opinion, we look confidently toward the future. We stand ready with qualified experts in public education and community organization to cooperate with any and all school boards willing to work toward desegregation.

We always realized that there are those who would defy the ruling and others who would drag their feet no matter what language the Supreme Court used. We now have the weapons to make them accept the highest court's affirmation of true American principles. This we shall do. We shall not rest until we have ended second-class education for all Americans.

STATEMENT OF THE EMERGENCY SOUTH-WIDE NAACP CONFERENCE

Atlanta, Georgia, June 4, 1955

We the State Conference officials of the NAACP, representing 16 southern states and the District of Columbia have met here today, on June 4, 1955, to map a program of action to make full use of the two historic decisions of the Supreme Court desegregating public schools.

We adopt and approve the staff memorandum interpreting the May 31 decision and we authorize our branches in every state to act to secure desegregation beginning next September, by filing petitions with their school boards requesting the "prompt" beginning set forth in the May 31 opinion. In the absence of any affirmative actions by school boards by the opening of schools in September, 1955, our branches will take whatever action is necessary to get the school board to initiate the process of desegregation. To this end, we are sending the following eight-point directive to all of our branches.

To the recalcitrant states determined to flout the Constitution we say: maintenance of segregated schools is unconstitutional and all state laws and practices to the contrary "must yield" to this principle of desegregation. This is the law of the land which applies to every state, county, city and hamlet. There will be no local option on this. Whenever and wherever a state or county refuses to recognize this principle, our answer will be the same as the legal action begun here in Atlanta on June 3, 1955.

Armed with the powers embodied in the language of the Court's opinion, we look confidently toward the future. We stand ready with qualified experts in public education and community organization to cooperate with any and all school boards willing to work toward desegregation.

We always realized that there are those who would defy the ruling and others who would drag their feet no matter what language the Supreme Court used. We now have the means to assure enforcement of the highest court's affirmation of true American principles. This we shall do. We shall not rest until we have ended second-class education for all Americans.

Directives to the Branches Adopted by Emergency South-Wide NAACP Conference

On May 17, 1954, the United States Supreme Court in a historic decision outlawed racial segregation in public schools. On May 31, 1955, in another unanimous decision, the Court ordered "good faith compliance" with this decision "at the earliest practicable date" and made the lower federal courts guardians in the enforcement of this order and arbiters as to whether good faith is being practiced by school authorities.

A sampling of sentiment throughout the country indicates a generally favorable reaction to the May 31 decision, with Kentucky, Oklahoma, Maryland, Missouri, Delaware and West Virginia promising full compliance. There will be resistance in the rest of the South in varying degrees, but make no mistake about it, this decision in no way cuts back on the May 17 pronouncement. Indeed, the May 31 decision merely affords to law-abiding public officials an easy method to conform to the Constitution of the United States. The decision places a challenge on the good faith of the public officials, on the militancy of Negroes and on the integrity of the federal courts.

For our part, we must be prepared to meet the challenge in a forthright manner. Our branches must seek to determine in each community whether the school board is prepared to make a prompt and reasonable start towards integration of the public schools and whether it will proceed with good faith towards full compliance with the May 31 decision at the earliest practicable date. Promises unaccompanied by concrete action are meaningless; nor can there be concern with the attitudes of individuals towards a change in the school system. Segregated schools are illegal, and the Court is merely allowing school boards time to get their houses in order. It does not allow time to procrastinate, stall or evade. It is the job of our branches to see to it that each school board begins to deal with the problem of providing non-discriminatory education. To that end we suggest that each of our branches take the following steps:

1. File at once a petition with each school board, calling attention to the May 31 decision, requesting that the school board act in accordance with that decision and offering the services of the branch to help the board in solving this problem.
2. Follow up the petition with periodic inquiries of the board seeking to determine what steps it is making to comply with the Supreme Court decision.
3. All during June, July, August and September, and thereafter, through meetings, forums, debates, conferences, etc., use every opportunity to explain what the May 31 decision means, and be sure to emphasize that the ultimate determination as to the length of time it will take for desegregation to become a fact in the community is not in the hands of the politicians or the school board officials but in the hands of the federal courts.
4. Organize the parents in the community so that as many as possible will be familiar with the procedure when and if law suits are begun in behalf of plaintiffs and parents.
5. Seek the support of individuals and community groups, particularly in the white community, through churches, labor organizations, civic organizations and personal contact.
6. When announcement is made of the plans adopted by your school board, get the exact text of the school board's pronouncements and notify the State Conference and the National Office at once so that you will have the benefit of their views as to whether the plan is one which will provide for effective desegregation. It is very important that branches not proceed at this stage without consultation with State offices and the National office.
7. If no plans are announced or no steps towards desegregation taken by the time school begins this fall, 1955, the time for a law suit has arrived. At this stage court action is essential because only in this way does the mandate of the Supreme Court that a prompt and reasonable start towards full compliance become fully operative on the school boards in question.
8. At this stage the matter will be turned over to the Legal Department and it will proceed with the matter in court.

SAMPLE PETITION

We, the undersigned, are the parents of children of school age entitled to attend and attending the public elementary and secondary high schools under your jurisdiction. As you undoubtedly know, the United States Supreme Court on May 17, 1954, ruled that the maintenance of racially segregated public schools is a violation of the Constitution of the United States and on May 31, 1955, reaffirmed that principle and requires "good faith compliance at the earliest practicable date," with the federal courts authorized to determine whether local officials are proceeding in good faith.

We, therefore, call upon you to take immediate steps to reorganize the public schools under your jurisdiction on a non-discriminatory basis. As we understand it, you have the responsibility to reorganize the school systems under your control so that the children of public school age attending and entitled to attend public schools cannot be denied admission to any school or be required to attend any school solely because of race and color.

The May 31 decision of the Supreme Court, to us, means that the time for delay, evasion or procrastination is past. Whatever the difficulties in according our children their constitutional rights, it is clear that the school board must meet and seek a solution to that question in accordance with the law of the land. As we interpret the decision you are duty bound to take immediate concrete steps leading to early elimination of segregation in the public schools. Please rest assured of our willingness to serve in any way we can to aid you in dealing with this question.

UNIT 4-11

OPPORTUNITY FOR THE SOUTH

Marion A. Wright,
President of the Southern Regional Council

The Supreme Court's implementation decrees in the school segregation cases are wise, moderate, and workable. Generous allowance has been made for the wide variety of conditions found in Southern communities; opportunity has been provided for every community to work out plans and preparations for orderly compliance.

The choices now to be made by the Southern states are too important to our region, the nation, and the world to be left solely to the judgment of political leaders. It is the obligation of every citizen to study the decrees carefully, to explore their practical implications, and to make his independent judgment known to those in authority.

If thoughtful Southerners adopt this course, we can make the required transition in a way that will command the respect of the civilized world. For we Southerners, no less than other Americans, recognize our duty as citizens to abide by the law of the land. Under our system of government, the Supreme Court is the final arbiter of the law. There is no honorable alternative to observing the law, so defined, in letter and in spirit.

Compliance with this ruling is not, however, merely a moral obligation. If we choose to make it so, it can be a great opportunity to enrich and benefit Southern life. By working together, white and Negro, for orderly transition to integrated schools, we can demonstrate the vigor of the democratic process to our own countrymen and to doubting millions throughout the world. We can realize, at home, resources of skill and public service in the Negro segment of our population that have had little chance for expression in the past.

Those who claim that our prejudices as a people are too strong to permit such changes, are blind to the great strides already made. There are literally hundreds of examples, drawn from every Southern state, of voluntary desegregation. Church schools and colleges, as well as other private institutions of learning, have opened their doors to students of both races. Professional associations have extended unqualified membership to Negro doctors, lawyers, nurses, ministers, social workers, and other professionals. Many private organizations and agencies have taken the same step in the interest of their own operations.

All selections in 4-11 from *New South,* June 1955.

These and a host of other changes have not been imposed upon the South; they have been made by the free choice of Southerners who recognized that they were in the public interest. They represent the growing conviction in the South that we will have a stronger, healthier, more productive society if we admit every citizen to unqualified participation in public life. We must now bring this growing insight to bear on the field of public education. The only real obstacles are our own fears and uncertainties. Once these obstacles are overcome, white and Negro Southerners working in full partnership are more than equal to the task.

EDITORIAL COMMENT

NEWSPAPERS AND THE SCHOOL DECISION

Charlotte, N.C., *Observer*

The law, as we see it, is clear. The forcible segregation of races in the public school is now prohibited. . . . How the order will be met is a local responsibility. In some communities, voluntary desegregation will be accomplished with little confusion. In others, voluntary segregation may supplant the compulsory type. Official resistance, through evasion or otherwise, can only result in law suits to compel compliance. In any event, each community should draw its plan for a course of action. The time is too late for emotional debate.

Norfolk, Va., *Journal and Guide*

Despite the solid front of Virginia *officialdom* against compliance with the highest court's decision and implementing decrees, the Norfolk (Va.) board formally asserts:

"We intend without mental reservation, to uphold and abide by the laws of the land."

That is a simple, statesmanlike, democratic, and sensible declaration.

It says in just fifteen words what anyone has to say who pretends to fulfill his citizenship duties as an American citizen.

San Antonio, Texas, *Express*

. . . All in all, those (district) judges are a group of citizens of ability, integrity and moral courage. They will enforce the orders of the nation's highest court to the letter, without fear of or favor to local politicians or rabble rousers of any category. . . .

Then why not, in the name of common sense, get down now—right away to the integration task, and quit the silliness of attempting to invoke state laws or local regulations to the contrary which are now as though they never have been? . . .

The only issue properly before the citizens of communities maintaining separate schools for white and Negro pupils is to "keep the law in calmness made"—and to keep it in calmness. . . .

For economic considerations, as well as those of justice and decency, dictate that local school authorities fritter away no further time in devising schemes to thwart, or even unduly delay, the integration process. . . .

The federal courts are going to see to it that the Constitution and laws of the nation are upheld in Texas, as in every state in the Union, and its people, as citizens of the United States, are minded to see that the law is upheld here. It should be done calmly, reasonably, sensibly—but upheld it shall be.

Birmingham, Ala., *News*

In essence, the Supreme Court's decision on public school segregation held that students must not be barred from school on racial grounds. Any plan for dealing with the problems growing out of the decision, if it is to be sound, must take adequate account of that sound, basic fact.

Raleigh, N.C., *News and Observer*

. . . Anyone who gives fuel to the fires of extremities at this time does no private or official or mixed service to the people who are trying to work out reasonable solutions to difficult problems. . . .

There may be those who agree with (a) program which would result in the destruction of the public school system in North Carolina. Most citizens, however, will look to school leadership for school plans. No citizens of North Carolina should be confused by a private campaign by a public official which disregards the care, the caution and the considered good sense which North Carolina officialdom in its official capacity has been applying to this problem. It is one which involves the long standing good relations of all people of both races in North Carolina. And no official has any greater private or public duty than to work to maintain those good relations while efforts to secure a good solution go forward.

Columbus, Ga., *Ledger-Enquirer*

It is time to speak out against some of the pusillanimous and dangerous foolishness to which the public now is being submitted by Atty. Gen. Eugene Cook and the Georgia Board of Education. . . .

As an attorney, Mr. Cook surely is familiar with the democratic judicial concept of freedom even for the thought that is hated in the United States, and as an education administrator Mr. Whitman (chairman of the board) must place some value on liberty of thought, else he is grotesquely misplaced.

Whether one likes the aims and objectives of the National Association for the Advancement of Colored People is of no moment here. It is a legitimate organization. It is not subversive or illegal grouping. Before the law and the Constitution it suffers no lower status and is denied rights of being no more than the Rotary Club or the National Association of Manufacturers.

If the Attorney-General of any State can seduce—of all organizations—a State Board of Education to limit the affiliation of teachers with any legitimate or legal organization, woe to the people of the state. Such a precedent warns the public that there could be a penalty against joining or contributing to any group.

As for a penalty of dismissal against any teacher who might be "in sympathy" with the purposes of a legitimate organization, in this case the NAACP, this is such a broad and indefinitely described transgression as to make even thinking dangerous. It could include any teacher who is a Democrat or a Republican, since both parties for years have carried platform planks similar to NAACP purposes.

It could include teachers who are Presbyterians, since the 67th General Assembly of the Presbyterian Church in the United States has voted in favor of desegregating the public schools, which surely was a move "sympathetic" to the NAACP. It could include Baptists, in view of the Southern Baptist Convention resolution in St. Louis last year, and members of other denominations. . . .

The situation is one calling for more common sense than now is being demonstrated, and . . . it is a duty and the personal responsibility of right-thinking citizens, in their own defense to protest to the Attorney General and the State Board of Education this rape of constitutionality and democracy.

Tampa, Fla., *Morning Tribune*

Southern states, including Florida, can take any legal measures they wish to avoid integrated schools. They can even abolish their public school systems arid subsidize public school systems instead. That is their privilege. If, however, the South permits its segregated schoolhouses to be spotted with the blood of mob victims, the stains will remain to shame generations of Southerners yet unborn. We like to think of Florida as one of the more enlightened states, not only in the South but in the entire nation. As such, its people should condemn every act of racial abuse . . . and its elected officials should be vigilant in seeing that justice is done.

Florence, S.C., ***Morning News***

. . . It is also to be noted that the National Association for the Advancement of Colored People declared their intention to cooperate with school authorities—not to press them with needless legal action, so long as they could see action toward desegregation. The alternative is clear—constant legal harassment of public school authorities who don't act.

These are the facts, plain for all to see. And closing our eyes to them won't make them go away.

The sands of time are fast running out for segregated school systems supported by public funds.

Winston-Salem, N.C., ***Journal***

The question whether a district or a county is to have segregated or integrated schools is largely a problem to be worked out cooperatively between the white and Negro leaders and citizens of each district or county. In some areas population ratios and other circumstances probably will make the problem rather easy to solve. In others the solutions will be more difficult. But in due time satisfactory adjustments can be made everywhere if a reasonable, cooperative spirit prevails on both sides.

Norfolk, Va., ***Journal and Guide***

The Fourth Circuit Court of Appeals decided recently that segregation on local buses is unconstitutional. The Circuit Court followed closely the U.S. Supreme Court ruling in the school cases. . . .

The day after . . . subordinate bus officials in Norfolk, Newport News and one or two other Virginia cities stated that no serious problem was involved because the companies had practically abandoned the enforcement of jim crow state laws on bus segregation.

In another few days, however, all of this was changed. There came out in the papers formal statements to the effect that until the law in Virginia was repealed by the state legislature, or declared unconstitutional by the "Supreme Court of Virginia," or by the Supreme Court of the United States, the bus segregation laws would be enforced in all intrastate transportation.

The apparent willingness on the part of the bus company management to let Jim Crow on buses expire, was quickly checked by the unseen but well known powers who said: "We will not retreat one inch until a court in a case carried up from our city compels us to do so."

There we have a lack of moral consciousness that is amazing.

Athens College

Athens, Alabama

DEAN-REGISTRAR OFFICE

FOUNDED 1842

June 2, 1954

HLW

Herbert L. Wright
Youth Secretary, NAACP
20 W. 40th Street,
New York 18, N. Y.

Dear Sir:

We thank you for the list of negro teachers who aspire to teach in white colleges. The same is being returned to you with our compliments.

You are most presumptious in believing that so soon after the Supreme Court ruling, that private white colleges are ready to hire "nigger" teachers. We will probably never hire any of them. Your northers "Yankee" friends will employ them. Not us.

Don't insult us any more with such expectations.

Yours truly

F S Ward

F. S. Ward, Registrar

EDITOR'S NOTE - THIS LETTER SPEAKS FOR ITSELF. NO COMMENT NEEDED.

UNIT 4-13

DECLARATION OF CONSTITUTIONAL PRINCIPLES

The unwarranted decision of the Supreme Court in the public school cases is now bearing the fruit always produced when men substitute naked power for established law.

The Founding Fathers gave us a Constitution of checks and balances because they realized the inescapable lesson of history that no man or group of men can be safely entrusted with unlimited power. They framed this Constitution with its provisions for change by amendment in order to secure the fundamentals of government against the dangers of temporary popular passion or the personal predilections of public officeholders.

We regard the decision of the Supreme Court in the school cases as a clear abuse of judicial power. It climaxes a trend in the Federal Judiciary undertaking to legislate, in derogation of the authority and to encroach upon the reserved rights of the States and the people.

The original Constitution does not mention education. Neither does the 14th amendment nor any other amendments. Debates preceding the submission of the 14th amendment clearly show that there was no intent that it should affect the system of education maintained by the States.

The very Congress which proposed the amendment subsequently provided for segregated schools in the District of Columbia.

When the amendment was adopted in 1868, there were 37 States of the Union. Every one of the 26 States that had any substantial racial differences among its people, either approved the operation of segregated schools already in existence or subsequently established such schools by action of the same law-making body which considered the 14th amendment.

As admitted by the Supreme Court in the public school case (*Brown v. Board of Education*), the doctrine of separate but equal schools "apparently originated in *Roberts v. City of Boston* (1949), upholding school segregation against attack as being violative of a State constitutional guarantee of equality." This constitutional doctrine began in the North, not in the South, and it was followed not only in Massachusetts, but in Connecticut, New York, Illinois, Indiana, Michigan, Minnesota, New Jersey, Ohio, Pennsylvania and other

---

March 11, 1956.

northern States until they, exercising their rights as States through the constitutional processes of local self-government, changed their school systems.

In the case of *Plessy v. Ferguson* in 1896 the Supreme Court expressly declared that under the 14th amendment no person was denied any of his rights if the States provided separate but equal public facilities. This decision has been followed in many other cases. It is notable that the Supreme Court, speaking through Chief Justice Taft, a former President of the United States, unanimously declared in 1927 in *Lum v. Rice* that the "separate but equal" principle is "within the discretion of the State in regulating its public schools and does not conflict with the 14th amendment."

This interpretation, restated time and again, became a part of the life of the people of many of the States and confirmed their habits, customs, traditions, and way of life. It is founded on elemental humanity and common sense, for parents should not be deprived by Government of the right to direct the lives and education of their own children.

Though there has been no constitutional amendment or act of Congress changing this established legal principle almost a century old, the Supreme Court of the United States, with no legal basis for such action, undertook to exercise their naked judicial power and substituted their personal political and social ideas for the established law of the land.

This unwarranted exercise of power by the Court, contrary to the Constitution, is creating chaos and confusion in the States principally affected. It is destroying the amicable relations between the white and Negro races that have been created through 90 years of patient effort by the good people of both races. It has planted hatred and suspicion where there has been heretofore friendship and understanding.

Without respect to the consent of the government, outside agitators are threatening immediate and revolutionary changes in our public schools system. If done, this is certain to destroy the system of public education in some of the States.

With the gravest concern for the explosive and dangerous condition created by this decision and inflamed by outside meddlers:

We reaffirm our reliance on the Constitution as the fundamental law of the land.

We decry the Supreme Court's encroachments on rights reserved to the States and to the people, contrary to established law, and to the Constitution.

We commend the motives of those States which have declared the intention to resist forced integration by any lawful means.

We appeal to the States and people who are not directly affected by these decisions to consider the constitutional principles involved against the time when they too, on issues vital to them, may be the victims of judicial encroachment.

Even though we constitute a minority in the present Congress, we have full faith that a majority of the American people believe in the dual system of government which has enabled us to achieve our greatness and will in time demand that the reserved rights of the States and of the people be made secure against judicial usurpation.

We pledge ourselves to use all lawful means to bring about a reversal of this decision which is contrary to the Constitution and to prevent the use of force in its implementation.

In this trying period, as we all seek to right this wrong, we appeal to our people not to be provoked by the agitators and troublemakers invading our States and to scrupulously refrain from disorder and lawless acts.

Signed by:

MEMBERS OF THE UNITED STATES SENATE

Walter P. George, Richard B. Russell, John Stennis, Sam J. Ervin, Jr., Strom Thurmond, Harry F. Byrd, A. Willis Robertson, John L. McClellan, Allen J. Ellender, Russell B. Long, Lister Hill, James O. Eastland, W. Kerr Scott, John Sparkman, Olin D. Johnston, Price Daniel, J. W. Fulbright, George A. Smathers, Spessard L. Holland.

MEMBERS OF THE UNITED STATES HOUSE OF REPRESENTATIVES

ALABAMA: Frank W. Boykin, George M. Grant, George W. Andrews, Kenneth A. Roberts, Albert Rains, Armistead I. Selden, Jr., Carl Elliott, Robert E. Jones, George Huddleston, Jr.

ARKANSAS: E. C. Gathings, Wilber D. Mills, James W. Trimble, Oren Harris, Brooks Hays, W. F. Norrell.

FLORIDA: Charles E. Bennett, Robert L. F. Sikes, A. S. Herlong, Jr., Paul G. Rogers, James A. Haley, D. R. Matthews.

GEORGIA: Prince H. Preston, John L. Pilcher, E. L. Forrester, John James Flynt, Jr., James C. Davis, Carl Vinson, Henderson Lanham, Iris F. Blitch, Phil M. Landrum, Paul Brown.

LOUISIANA: F. Edward Hébert, Hale Boggs, Edwin E. Willis, Overton Brooks, Otto E. Passman, James H. Morrison, T. Ashton Thompson, George S. Long.

MISSISSIPPI: Thomas G. Abernethy, Jamie L. Whitten, Frank E. Smith, John Bell Williams, Arthur Winstead, William M. Colmer.

NORTH CAROLINA: Herbert C. Bonner, L. H. Fountain, Graham A. Barden, Carl T. Durham, F. Ertel Carlyle, Hugh Q. Alexander, Woodrow W. Jones, George A. Shuford.

SOUTH CAROLINA: L. Mendel Rivers, John J. Riley, W. J. Bryan Dorn, Robert T. Ashmore, James P. Richards, John L. McMillan.

TENNESSEE: James B. Frazier, Jr., Tom Murray, Jere Cooper, Clifford Davis.

TEXAS: Wright Patman, John Dowdy, Walter Rogers, O. C. Fisher.

VIRGINIA: Edward J. Robeson, Jr., Porter Hardy, Jr., J. Vaughan Gary, Watkins M. Abbitt, William M. Tuck, Richard H. Poff, Burr P. Harrison, Howard W. Smith, W. Pat Jennings, Joel T. Broyhill.

UNIT 4-14

Public Opinion and the School Decision

A Norfolk Sampling

Evidence that Southern opinion on desegregation isn't solidly of the "we won't do it" variety is growing daily. One of the latest groups to burst the "solid South" bubble on the subject is The Women's Council for Interracial Cooperation of Norfolk, Virginia. The council's March 1955, news sheet carries an analysis of 132 letters to the editor of the Norfolk *Virginian Pilot*, and the study adds significantly to the proof that Southern opinion is far from being completely against the Supreme Court decision in the school segregation cases.

News Lively

The letters analyzed were printed between May 17, 1954, and October 31, 1954, "a period during which racial news sparked a lively exchange of opinion." Events in the newspaper, as listed by the Women's Council, included "the U.S. Supreme Court's May 17th decision that separation of the races in public schools contradicts the 14th Amendment to the Constitution; declarations of opposition to the decision by Virginia's Governor and State Attorney General; appointment of an all-white, all-Legislator, Governor's Commission 'to hear and study public opinion,' with an admittedly prosegregation chairman; refusal by the Governor and many Virginia officials to attend the 200th anniversary celebration of John Marshall's birth, when Chief Justice Warren was principal speaker; trouble locally when Negroes purchased houses in the previously all-white subdivision of Coronado; opposition stirred up by agitators when the first Negro pupils were admitted to white schools in Delaware."

The *Virginian Pilot* is a white daily with a large circulation in Norfolk and neighboring areas and, in the words of the Women's Council, it "tries to present both sides of controversial subjects on its editorial page."

Of the 132 letters studied, 77 express "a rational, calm attitude toward desegregation and/or a strong disapproval of the public stand of Virginia officials." Thirty-nine of the

---

All selections in 4-14 from *New South*, May 1955.

letters "oppose desegregation and/or applaud state officials," and 16 of the letters do not present a definite stand. "Repeat" writers on both sides of the question place the number at 72 persons "pro" desegregation and 33 "anti." The council reports that many of the letter writers favoring desegregation describe themselves "as to profession, geographical origin, age, experience and race, often stating or implying that they are white." Of the anonymous letters, the percentage is larger among the "antis" the study shows.

CONFERENCE

The news sheet reports that a conference with editors of the newspaper revealed that while many letters were cut for lack of space, the basic arguments, were kept intact and that no letters were suppressed except a few so "scurrilous or so incoherent that they were considered unfit to print."

Results from the study show that among "anti" desegregation writers there is a wide variation in the degree of opposition to the Supreme Court decision. Opposition ranges from being in favor of abandoning the public school system to declaring that if the final decrees still hold for desegregation the writer will accept it. On the "pro" desegregation side, specific suggestions are presented such as putting a Negro on the Norfolk School Board "to help in this crucial period" and that Virginia, as a border state, should take the lead in desegregating as peacefully as possible.

MODERATE OPINION

In concluding the survey report, the Women's Council declared:

"From this analysis emerges the salient fact that there exists in this area of the South a body of moderate, informed, thoughtful, educated and earnest public opinion which would accept desegregation easily. Extremist opinion is always noisy and people who are against anything shout louder than those who are simply acquiescent.

"In addition to the evidence in the letters studied, there is the almost complete silence of 'writing readers' after the admission of Negro doctors to the Norfolk County Medical Association, the admission of Negro ministers to the Norfolk Ministerial Union, and the desegregating of the annual Norfolk Preaching Mission. These three milestones in race relations were passed with apparent equanimity by the news-reading public.

"It is obvious that nobody has yet found out the whole of public opinion in Virginia. It is time that someone does."

FAULKNER ON SCHOOLS

The following letter published by the Memphis Commercial Appeal was written by William Faulkner, Mississippi's distinguished novelist and recipient of the 1947 Nobel Prize for Literature.

OXFORD, Miss.—We Mississippians already know that our present schools are not good enough. Our young men and women themselves prove that to us every year by the fact that, when the best of them want the best of education which they are entitled to and are competent for, not only in the humanities but in the professions and crafts—law and medicine and engineering—too, they have to go out of the state to get it. And quite often, too often, they don't come back.

So our present schools are not even good enough for white people; our present state reservoir of education is not of high enough quality to assuage the thirst of even our white young men and women. In which case, how can it possibly assuage the thirst and need of the Negro, who obviously is thirstier, needs it worse, else the Federal Government would not have had to pass a law compelling Mississippi (among others, of course) to make the best of our education available to him.

That is, our present schools are not even good enough for white folks. So what do we do? Make them good enough, improve them to the best possible? No. We beat the bushes, rake and scrape to raise additional taxes to establish another system at best only equal to that one which is already not good enough, which therefore won't be good enough for Negroes either; we will have two identical systems neither of which is good enough for anybody. The question is not how foolish can people get, because apparently there is no limit to that. The question is, how foolish in simple dollars and cents, let alone in wasted men and women, can we afford to be?

—*William Faulkner*

Copy

COMMONWEALTH OF VIRGINIA
GOVERNOR'S OFFICE
RICHMOND

J. LINDSAY ALMOND, JR.
GOVERNOR

September 18, 1958

FROM: The Governor of Virginia

TO: Mr. Fendall R. Ellis, Superintendent

Mr. R. Stanley Goodman, Chairman
2411 Jefferson Park Avenue

Mr. Harry A. Wright
1320 East Market Street

Mr. Roscoe S. Adams
Evergreen Avenue

Mr. J. Harry Michael, Jr.
P. O. Box 895

Mr. Earl V. Thacker, Jr.
628 Druid Avenue

Dr. John G. Wall
1821 Edgewood Lane

Mr. P. A. Wallenborn
1330 Rugby Road

Members of the School Board of the City of Charlottesville

Under compulsion of an order issued by the United States District Court for the Western District of Virginia, both white and colored children have been enrolled effective September 22, 1958, in Lane High School and Venable Elementary School located in the City of Charlottesville.

-2-

Pursuant to the provisions of Chapter 9.1, Title 22, of the Code of Virginia, the above-named schools are closed and are removed from the public school system, effective September 22, 1958, and all authority, power and control over such schools, principals, teachers, other employees and all pupils now enrolled or ordered to be enrolled, will thereupon be vested in the Commonwealth of Virginia, to be exercised by the Governor.

Accordingly, by virtue of the authority vested in me as chief executive of the Commonwealth of Virginia, I will thereupon assume all power and control over such schools and hereby request all local officials and all citizens to cooperate with the Department of State Police and local law enforcement officers in the protection of public property and the security of public peace and order.

You are requested to forthwith notify all teachers, and other personnel connected with such schools, and all parents and other persons having the custody and care of all pupils enrolled in such schools, of this action.

Given under my hand, this, the 18th day of September, 1958.

Governor

UNIT 4-16

PUBLIC SCHOOL DESEGREGATION

CHARLOTTESVILLE, VIRGINIA, 1955–62

Paul M. Gaston and Thomas T. Hammond

PREFACE

This study could not have been written without the assistance of a number of local citizens who have special competence in one area or another. Altogether, some fifteen persons or more (of both races)—many of whom were intimately involved in the history we describe—gathered material and contributed ideas. Needless to say, we take responsibility for the facts and the interpretations that are presented, except as indicated.

Before beginning, we should point out that Charlottesville had a population in 1950 of 29,391 of whom 23,830 were white and 5,561 colored. The city operates seven elementary schools.[1] One of them, Jefferson, is exclusively for Negroes; Venable School was desegregated in 1959 and remained the only desegregated elementary school until early October, 1962, when four Negroes entered Johnson School. The other elementary schools remain segregated. There are two high schools in the city. Burley High School is operated jointly by the city and county and has Negro students only. Lane High School, predominantly white, was desegregated in 1959.

I. BEFORE THE STORM: THE PRELUDE TO DESEGREGATION

The immediate origins of the school desegregation issue go back to 1955, when forty-three Negro parents of school-age children, urged by the local branch of the

A report presented to the Nashville Conference on "The South: The Ethical Demands of Integration," a consultation sponsored by the Southern Regional Council and the Fellowship of Southern Churchmen. December 28, 1962.

NAACP, petitioned the School Board to desegregate its city schools. The Board agreed to study the request but no desegregation plan was forthcoming. The failure of the city to respond positively led the Negroes to turn to the staff of the NAACP. Suit was entered in 1956 requesting a court order to compel school desegregation. Thus began the litigation that led to the inevitable demise of segregation in Charlottesville. Thus began, also, the basic pattern which has characterized school desegregation history to the present time: Negro demands for an end to unlawful discrimination; School Board refusal to act voluntarily toward ending the discrimination; and court orders compelling the School Board to act.

The events that followed cannot be fully appreciated without some knowledge of the city's history in race relations. In comparison with many other Southern cities, Charlottesville was a reasonably good town in this field in the years before the Supreme Court decision of May 17, 1954. The Interracial Commission (now superseded by the Council on Human Relations) was making slow progress in the area of private employment; Negroes had played a major role in winning better working conditions for white and Negro alike at the University Hospital; Negroes had been admitted to the University graduate and professional schools since 1950; occasional Negro candidates, one of whom was successful, had made no bones about seeking Negro votes with a sincere promise to improve conditions for Negroes. There were no Negro policemen as there were in some other towns (and there still are none) but there was a movement on to appoint a Negro to the School Board.

Negro housing had been the principal concern of groups which launched an effort to eradicate slums. Five years before the Supreme Court decision, city and county voters had approved a $1,000,000 bond issue to build a joint city-county high school for Negroes—something which was influenced by ominous court decisions but which came in many other Southern communities only after the ax had fallen. At the time, school bond issues usually met resistance on non-racial grounds.

The first local activity on the political front came in the winter of 1953–54 when an influential member of the Albemarle County Board of Supervisors began calling for local and state authorities to prepare a plan of action should the court outlaw segregation. He got little response. It was still inconceivable to most local politicians, apparently, that the court would make such a decision.

On the day of the decision—May 17, 1954—reactions varied, but most local politicians' comments were far short of the flaming oratory some used a year or so later when Massive Resistance became the accepted line. A school official commented that the decision was "morally right" but gave Southern schoolmen an impossible task to achieve.

The state response to the Supreme Court decision is told in detail in Benjamin Muse's *Virginia's Massive Resistance*. The Governor appointed a State Commission on Public School Education, known as the Gray Commission, which proposed a tuition grant program that implied minimum compliance with the court's decision. Before the Gray Plan could be put into effect, however, Senator Byrd called a switch and jettisoned the Gray Plan for the program of Massive Resistance, which provided that any public school ordered to desegregate would be closed by the Governor.

In Charlottesville, neither the city nor the county member of the House of Delegates was an enthusiastic Massive Resistance man, but neither felt that the program could be fought. While the City Council felt that local option was preferable to school closing, very few Charlottesville citizens protested against Massive Resistance and cocktail conversation on schools and race became unpopular. Vocal segregationists virtually pre-empted the field of opinion making. Up to this point city politics had been relatively free of the race issue, but if a pro-integration candidate had arisen, there is little doubt he would have been shouted down. In the county, political leaders were almost unanimously behind resistance of any form.

By the spring of 1958 a crisis atmosphere was developing. It has been almost two years since Federal District Judge John Paul had first heard arguments in the school case and by this time the last appeal against integration had failed; Judge Paul had said "September." In an interview later, Johan Galtung, a Norwegian sociologist studying the Charlottesville school situation, observed that the spring and summer of 1958 was the time of greatest tension in the community. Ministers became aware of the possibility of violence. Judge Paul's order was inevitably going to take effect the following fall; the General Assembly had adopted a new round of Massive Resistance legislation which promised school closing as the response to court-ordered desegregation. Good friends had fallen out over the school issue; communications between those of opposing viewpoints was virtually nil. One meeting tool place between city officials, a few leading citizens, and members of the local branch of the NAACP. The NAACP was asked to abandon its support of Negro admissions to Lane High School on the grounds that the school would be closed. The NAACP refused to grant this request. This is the only occasion on which city official have requested conversations with the NAACP.

City Council elections that spring centered on the school question for the first time, but in a reserved manner. A Massive Resistance advocate lost, but the winners supported continued legal opposition to integration. An impasse had been reached. Overwhelmingly, the powers of the state demanded loyalty to the Massive Resistance stance. Locally, leadership was in general divided between massive resisters and local-option segregationists. And as September approached it became increasingly clear that there could be no further delay in granting the Negro plaintiffs their constitutional rights—unless, of course, the schools were closed altogether.

II. CITY IN CRISIS: 1958–59

The vast majority of Charlottesville's citizens, hard to stir decisive action, had remained pretty much on the sidelines from 1955 to 1958 as the crisis slowly approached. If there were those who sensed the impending troubles, and there must have been more than a few, they remained relatively quiet. The local chapter of the Council of Human Relations had sponsored a constructive meeting on the subject, "When School Desegregation Comes to Charlottesville," but no white organization, and no city official or group, offered a plan to make desegregation a reality. Some may have been lulled by the Governor's rhetoric in the campaign of 1957 when he promised that public schools would not be closed. By late spring of 1958 his promises seemed hollow and the community began to awaken.

In May the PTA Board of Venable Elementary School, the only one of the five white elementary schools to which Negroes were to be assigned, sent out a questionnaire to parents of Venable children. The questionnaire put the issue realistically, asking parents whether they preferred a public school with some measure of integration, or a closed public school. Of those responding, 58% preferred the former. Following this poll, another group of Venable parents, with predominantly segregationist sympathies, sent out their own questionnaire, including in their choice of preferences segregated private schools, *with tuition grants provided* (although tuition grants were not available at the time). About 90% of those responding checked this preference.

From these two polls stemmed the organization of two groups, each proposing a different approach to the school crisis. One group, made up principally of housewives who later jokingly referred to themselves as the "basement mothers," or the "emergency mothers," became the Parents Committee for Emergency Schooling (PCES). They decided that if Governor Almond closed the schools they would organize *temporary* classes until the public schools should be reopened. The other group became the Charlottesville Educational Foundation (CEF). Dominated by segregationists, the CEF looked toward private segregated schools as a *permanent* thing. Both groups began to plan elementary and high school classes. . . .

On September 13, Judge Paul signed the court order requiring the admission of ten Negroes to Venable and two to Lane. On September 16, the Court of Appeals refused to stay the effective date of the injunction. Three days later, on the 19th, the Governor invoked the Massive Resistance program, took control of the two affected schools out of the hands of the city and ordered them not to be opened. This action, as it later turned out, was in violation of provisions of the constitutions of both the United States and the Commonwealth of Virginia. At the time, however, citizens and officials of Charlottesville were powerless to reverse the Governor's action.

More than 1700 Venable and Lane students, as well as the twelve Negroes whose rights were not yet to be honored, were affected by the Governor's action. At this point the two emergency groups moved into action. The CEF began classes for elementary school children in a large house, instructing 182 displaced Venable students. The majority of the former Venable students—340—attended classes launched by the PCES in various homes. Former Venable teachers, for the most part, taught in the two schools, splitting between the two groups more on the basis of need than of ideology.

A crucial development at this stage was the decision of the Lane High faculty to teach in a single body or not at all. This forced the adoption of a cooperative high school program, presided over by the Lane principal and supervised by an equal number of representatives from the PCES and the CEF. Thus the Lane teachers prevented the segregationist group (the CEF) from leading the Lane students into a private segregated high school which could have become a permanent replacement for the public high school. Of the 1,080 students who had been expected to enroll in Lane, 862 enrolled in the emergency program. These students met their classes in various churches and other buildings across the city.

Throughout the period of the emergency schools, the public school teachers who staffed them continued to receive their salaries. Because of this fact, Judge Paul ruled that the twelve Negro plaintiffs could not be refused admission to the emergency schools. The Negroes, however, elected to receive private tutoring, cautiously awaiting the time when they should be enrolled in desegregated public schools.

A lack of violence in these tense weeks can be attributed in large measure to the fact that the man who took office as mayor in the midst of the excitement was a person of independent spirit who was not afraid of political retaliation from the state political machine. Mayor Thomas J. Michie stated unequivocally that violence would be punished, regardless of its source. He made it plain that no citizens, including community leaders, would be immune if they dropped a match in this sea of gasoline. Mayor Michie was one of the few Virginians freely to label himself a "liberal Democrat" in a state where such men are a scarce commodity. He was also one of the few elected officials in the community to declare that desegregation was inevitable.

The first significant citizen reaction to the school closing, after the inauguration of the emergency school program, was the organization of a Committee for Public Education (CPE). The chairman and most of the members of the CPE were persons who had never before taken an active part in local political affairs. Prominent among the CPE leaders, however, were several professional educators who called community attention to the threat to public education. Declaring that it was concerned "neither with encouraging integration nor perpetuating segregation," the CPE announced its determination to "pursue every legal means to keep public schools open," and stated its objection to "any permanent arrangement which entrusts public education to private hands having no responsibility or accountability to the general public."

After two organizational meetings, the CPE held a mass meeting, attended by 450 persons, and adopted a resolution urging City Council to petition the Governor for return of the schools to local control. City Council, at its next meeting, declined to act on the petition. The Council, as well as state officials in Richmond, had apparently expected much more vocal opposition to the school closings than actually developed. There were, moreover, opposite political pressures on the Council urging that no action be taken. Part of the explanation for the failure of more citizens to protest probably lies in the fact that Mayor Michie called for a temperate approach, and many persons placed their faith in him. He and others were confident that the Massive Resistance legislation would be struck down by the courts before too much time had passed.

This belief was well founded. In January key provisions of the Massive Resistance legislation were declared unconstitutional by the Virginia Supreme Court of Appeals. The way was now open for the Charlottesville School Board to comply with Judge Paul's order. For the first time since litigation had begun in 1956, the School Board undertook to draft a plan for desegregation. On the basis of this plan, and giving assurance that special tutoring would be arranged for the twelve Negro plaintiffs, the School Board attorney, John S. Battle, Jr., was able to persuade the Circuit Court to stay Judge Paul's injunction until the following September. Declaring that "the School Board's present attitude deserves commendation," Chief Judge Simon Sobeloff expressed the court's "full confidence in Mr. Battle."

With the requirement to desegregate postponed until the fall, the School Board ordered the re-opening of Lane and Venable in February, 1959. Advocates of public education—the "moderates" who had guided the city through its crisis period—heaved a sigh of relief and received congratulations for a job well done. Leaders in the Negro community and white advocates of desegregation were well aware that the real job had hardly begun. Meanwhile, the CEF announced that when integration came to the community in the fall, segregated "private" schools would be available for those who would not accept integration.

Two sociologists studying community attitudes in the spring of 1958 found that 88% of Charlottesville's "influentials" believed that the schools would be desegregated in the fall, despite the fact that 73% of these people preferred segregation. This study, based on a rather small sample, reached conclusions which veteran observers would validate. By the time, then, that Charlottesville had finally faced up to the reality of desegregation—albeit on a small scale—the majority of the community had adjusted to the idea and had accepted it as inevitable, if not desirable. This development augured well for further small gains.

III. DESEGREGATION: THE FIRST THREE YEARS

In September, 1959, nine Negro children entered Venable Elementary School and three enrolled in Lane High. Almost four years had passed since the Negroes first requested the School Board to comply with the Supreme Court's desegregation requirement. The city and the state had gone through the turmoil of Massive Resistance and closed schools. By the time desegregation finally came, most responsible citizens recognized that it was unavoidable and, on the day school opened, there was no violence and little tension in the city.

For the next three years the pattern was much the same. There were twelve Negroes in desegregated schools that first year, eighteen the following year, and thirty-five the next. A clear pattern of tokenism emerged that the white community found acceptable. In fact, a University of Virginia Law professor, reporting to the Civil Rights Commission in mid-1962, declared that Charlottesville's "temperament is such that it can accept more desegregation. . . . " Commenting on this study in December, the editor of the Charlottesville *Daily Progress* (who is also a member of the School Board and an advocate of "freedom of choice") concurred in this view but asserted that any large increase in the number of Negroes entering formerly all-white schools would endanger popular support for public schools.

Token desegregation in these three years was largely, although not exclusively, the result of the school assignment plan approved by Judge Paul in 1959. The relative ease with which desegregation proceeded was due, in part at least, to the existence of the tuition-grant supported "private" schools (discussed below in Part IV) which siphoned off from the public schools those who objected most vigorously to desegregation.

Under the court-approved plan, students were assigned to elementary and high schools by the Superintendent. To determine assignments at the elementary school level, the city was divided into six districts. Students were normally to attend the school in their zone. However, white students living in the Jefferson (Negro) district were in fact assigned (technically, "transferred") to one of the other schools.

Negro students living in one of the "white" zones were normally assigned to Jefferson. If they wished to attend the school in their district they were required to make a written request. The procedure was altered slightly in 1961 (see Section V). In 1961–62, some 50 Negroes were "transferred" to Jefferson, while 149 whites were "transferred" out of the Jefferson district.

The Jefferson district was by far the most populous of the six zones (last year, the Jefferson School had 40% more students than the next largest school). The district also contained within it the great majority of the city Negroes. Moreover, Negroes living in the Jefferson district—unlike the whites similarly situated—were not allowed to transfer out of their zone. Thus, by the manner in which the district lines were drawn, and by placing restrictions on the right of transfer, the Charlottesville plan was a blueprint for containment, with a almost built-in guarantee of token desegregation at the elementary school level.

At the high school level, there were no district lines, since there was but one Negro and one white high school, but all whites were assigned to Lane and all Negroes to Burley. To attend Lane, a Negro was required to apply for transfer and to satisfy certain residence and academic requirements not applied to whites. The residence criterion required that the Negro live closer to Lane than to Burley, and the academic criterion required that the Negro should demonstrate on tests that his academic aptitude and scholastic achievement equipped him to perform adequately in the grade to which he was applying. These obstacles, not placed in the way of the whites, plus the reticence of Negroes long accustomed to segregated schools, largely account for tokenism at the high school level.

Within this restricted framework, Charlottesville's experience with desegregation has been highly successful. Before any Negro students were admitted, a majority of the white parents probably looked upon desegregation with either disapproval or fear. Some of the Negro applicants were worried that they might be beaten, humiliated, or ostracized by the white students. Arch segregationists warned that there would be fights, knifings, and riots. Many predicted educational standards would decline. But when desegregation became a reality the world did not come to an end and these fears proved groundless. In the three years since desegregation began, not a single serious incident has been reported. In no significant way has the situation in the desegregated schools worsened.

On the contrary, in many ways desegregation has turned out to be something of value to students of both races. No study has been made of the white student or parent attitudes toward the desegregation experience, but it is commonly agreed by many who are involved in the schools that white children frequently go out of their way to welcome new Negroes to the schools; not so much because they are Negroes as because they are new students. Such events occur more frequently in the elementary school than in the high school. In addition, some white parents have gone beyond "accepting" desegregation to welcoming it as a valuable experience in democracy for their children.

As far as the Negroes are concerned, there is little doubt that the experience has been rewarding for most of them. It is probably true that the process of integration has proceeded further in the elementary school than in the high school, but, on the other hand, only two high school students have elected to transfer from Lane back to Burley. . . .

No violence whatever has been encountered. Roughly half have met some unpleasant treatment, usually name-calling, but only one Negro said that an attempt was made to throw something at him. Furthermore, the situation seems to be improving, for only one instance of name-calling was reported in 1962.

All of the students found the teachers friendly and helpful. None of the Negroes found the white students as a whole hostile; 45% said they were neutral, while 55% said they were friendly. When asked whether school officials or students offered moral support during the first days at school, 63% of the Negro students answered in the affirmative. This reply was particularly frequent among the earliest entrants. Examples given included: (**1**) shaking hands, (**2**) sharing tables in the library and cafeteria, and (**3**) walking together to and from classes.

Two-thirds of the Negroes said they had made friends among the white students. Half studied together, including 2% who studied at each other's homes. On the other hand, 27% said that they did not completely feel like "one of the bunch."

While 67% of the Negro students felt that participation is extracurricular activities was allowed, only one student actually takes part in the concert band, 3 in preparatory band, none in the concert choir, 4 in the "treble choir," and none in athletics. The students' opinions were equally divided as to whether school officials encourage or disapprove their participation. there was general agreement that the Negro students in desegregated schools were more highly motivated to learn and that the educational standards are higher than those in the Negro schools, a major fact which underlies the quest for a desegregated education.

IV. "SAFETY VALVE": PUBLIC MONEY AND PRIVATE SCHOOLS

When Negro children entered Venable and Lane in the fall of 1959, the CEF kept its promise to offer "private" segregated schools for those who would not accept desegregation. Earlier in the year the General Assembly had made this escape mechanism possible by providing tuition grants for children attending non-sectarian schools other than those to which they would normally be assigned.

The economics of tuition grants, a subject of debate in the community, is discussed below. Here it should be noted that, from the beginning, many advocates of the tuition-grant program preferred to avoid the racial argument that underlay it. They chose, instead, the somewhat more appealing principle of "freedom of choice." Leon Dure, a retired newspaper man living near Charlottesville, is Virginia's major "freedom of choice" spokesman. Here, as well as in other parts of the South, Mr. Dure has argued that the "freedom of choice" program has brought to view a new human right: the freedom to associate or not to associate with whom one pleases. Despite the fact that the tuition-grant program was born of segregationist demands to escape enforced desegregation, his effort has been to project a non-racial, human rights image of it. In Charlottesville, Mr. Dure has been strongly supported by Chester Babcock, editor of the *Daily Progress*, and their combined efforts have doubtless influenced large numbers in the community, especially the "moderate" segregationists who would be uncomfortable in basing their support of the program on racial grounds alone.

It is difficult to say how strong the anti-tuition-grant sentiment is within the community. There has been little sustained criticism of "freedom of choice" on educational and philosophical grounds and it has not yet become an immediate constitutional issue. Among local critics of "freedom of choice," Professor Hardy Dillard, of the University of Virginia School of Law, has engaged in public debate with Mr. Dure and the two men elaborated their arguments recently in the *Virginia Quarterly Review* (Summer, 1962, pp. 400–435). In addition to finding serious constitutional shortcomings in the "freedom of choice" program, Professor Dillard concludes that the "right" it claims to secure is illusory and that, in the last analysis, the program is inconsistent with democratic values.

The practical effect of tuition grants locally was to make possible the relatively easy operation of the two CEF schools, Robert E. Lee Elementary School and Rock Hill Academy. When the two schools opened in 1959, about 30% of the students who normally would have attended Venable and Lane were enrolled. This year, the two schools have a combined enrollment of about 700. Of these, 488 are city students, as compared with over 1700 city students in Venable and Lane.

When the schools opened, they were widely regarded as "safety valves," making unlikely an explosion in the public, desegregated schools. They are still so regarded today. Political leaders, and many others, look upon them as providing a necessary alternative for those who find desegregation repugnant and unacceptable. Most observers agree that public school desegregation has gone smoothly in part because of the existence of the CEF schools. The pupils from homes where the atmosphere might encourage them to participate in "incidents" in desegregated schools are the ones most inclined to go to the private schools.

When the private schools began, there was some doubt that they could survive for very long. It appears now, in their fourth year of operation, that their future is relatively secure, provided tuition grants continue to be available. On the other hand, the schools must be assured of a solid base for enrollment and there are indications that the gradual acceptance of desegregation in the city may have a tendency to erode that base. Desegregation of county schools would probably broaden it considerably. The recent growth in enrollment in the CEF schools has come from county students.

Financially, the schools have been troubled by the need for capital construction funds. Two new buildings were erected in a residential area to serve as the elementary school, while for the high school a large dwelling with spacious grounds was purchased from one of the supporters of the program. Several classroom buildings were erected and more construction has followed. An assembly hall is planned. Tuition grants have covered most, although not all, of actual operating expenses. Fund drives as well as loans have helped to meet financial needs, but needs have generally kept a few paces ahead of funds. How long tuition grants will remain available is, of course, one of the great imponderables. Their constitutionality has not yet been determined, but many constitutional lawyers believe that federal courts would find that schools supported substantially by public funds are, in fact, public schools and subject to the requirements of the Fourteenth Amendment.

Another aspect of the private school development has been the ambiguity over the central purpose and role of the schools. Probably more out of necessity than out of choice, the authorities of the Foundation have continued to play on the idea of the schools as a strong hold of segregationist and state rights views. This stand is apparently necessary in order to attract enough students to keep enrollments high enough for economical operation. On the other hand, a number of teachers and patrons of the schools are more interested in them at this point for a variety of educational reasons than as a symbol of resistance. Some families have children in both private schools and public desegregated schools; and while some CEF patrons have strong segregationist views, other have moderate views, or no strong feelings one way or another.

While many—perhaps most—citizens look upon the private schools as a valuable safety valve, far fewer are happy with the price that must be paid for them. The analysis of the economics of tuition grants that follows makes it clear that "freedom of choice," contrary to the claims of its advocates, is not free.

Charlottesville issued 630 tuition grants in 1961–62.[2] Albemarle County, with no public school integration, issued 436 grants. In Charlottesville tuition grants are used largely to avoid sending children to desegregated schools. Of the 630 grants, 495 were used to send children to the CEF schools. Almost all of the other grants were used to send children to other local private schools that were in existence prior to desegregation.

In Albemarle County, only 124 of the 436 grants were for children attending the new private schools; 225 were used for children attending other local private schools; 79 were used for sending children to other *public* schools, *57 of them going to the two desegregated schools.*

Under Virginia's tuition-grant program, a locality is required to pay each student no less than the lowest of three figures: the per pupil cost of public education, the actual tuition of the school to be attended, or an arbitrary figure of $275 for high school students and $250 for elementary school students. The locality is reimbursed by the state in the amount of $150 for each high school grant and $125 for each elementary grant. The difference is borne by the locality.

From the start of the tuition-grant program, City Council has voluntarily set the amount of all tuition grants at the per pupil cost of public school education. The CEF waits each year until the amount of the tuition grant is announced before setting its tuition for the year. It has then always set its tuition $15 above the amount of the tuition grant.

Charlottesville's 630 grants cost a total of $196,805.70. Of this, $84,850 was reimbursed by the state and $111,955.70 was borne by the city. If City Council had set the tuition grants at the minimum of $275 for high school students and $250 for elementary school students, the total cost would have been $167,510.00, or $29,655.70 less than they actually cost. The state's portion would have remained the same, so this cost of nearly $30,000 was borne entirely by the locality. In terms of the local real and personal property tax rate, the higher tuition grant cost the taxpayer 5-1/2 cents for each $100 of assessed value. The same $30,000 would give each public school teacher a raise of $150, or would finance public school kindergartens for 200 children, or would provide five badly needed guidance counselors for the city's high schools.

Because of their easy availability, tuition grants are used freely by parents who would send their children to a private school regardless of the integration question. Although the number in this category is impossible to determine, it is reasonable to assume that the 135 Charlottesville grants to children attending already established private schools fall mostly into this category. These grants cost a total of $42,172.65, of which $23,122.65 was paid from local funds. In Albemarle County, without desegregation, the 436 grants cost $111,918.48, of which $54,243.56 was paid from local tax money.

The division of public funds into private schooling caused by the voluntary overpayment of Charlottesville's tuition grants and the use of tuition grants for purposes other than to avoid integration amounted to $52,778.35 for Charlottesville and $54,243.46 for Albemarle County. The total drain for the Charlottesville-Albermarle community was $107,021.81.

The cost of private schooling has been a subject of continuous argument since the inception of the tuition-grant program. The proponents of tuition grants argue that the grants actually save the locality money because the city pays only the per pupil cost of operating the public school to a tuition-grant student and does not have to pay the cost of buildings, grounds, and furnishings for him. Furthermore, they argue, the state pays 48% of the tuition grant for each high school student and 40% of the grant for each elementary school student, while contributing approximately 30% of the cost of Charlottesville public education.

This argument, while having some elements of truth in it, ignores many considerations. Administrative and maintenance costs, for example, would not increase appreciably if all children attended public schools. Classroom space has been available for all the tuition-grant children until last year although it was disproportionately located in the elementary schools. To educate the 495 city children at the CEF schools in the public school system would probably cost between $100,000 and $125,000 for teachers and supplies, rather than the $154,000 it costs for tuition grants. Of this, about $45,000 would be received from the state aid for teachers salaries alone. Thus, the city of Charlottesville would pay from local funds only $55,000 to $80,000 for the education of these children in public schools. The tuition grants for these students costs the city $84,308.05 from local funds. Until this year, no building space would have been needed, so the city might have saved $4,000 to $29,000 by educating these children in public schools. The cost of tuition grants for children attending already established private schools was shown to be over $23,000 in local funds. Thus, the tuition grant program probably costs local taxpayers from $27,000 to $52,000 a year.

Tuition-grant costs are but a small part of the price Charlottesville is paying to adjust to the new order of things. A far more staggering sum—one that has not yet been disclosed to the public—has gone to pay lawyers' fees and court costs for six years of almost continuous litigation. There are indications that the School Board, at least, is tired of this form of expenditure. But tuition grants, despite considerable opposition, will doubtless continue to be a drain on public resources for many years to come—unless, or until, the tuition-grant program is found to be unlawful.

V. From Crisis to Crossroad

The crisis out of which Charlottesville came in 1958–59 was followed by a three-year period of tokenism, a School Board policy of containment, and a gradual acceptance in the community of the new situation. That period has come to an end and Charlottesville finds itself at a crossroad again. There is no crisis atmosphere and probably none will develop, but the time has arrived when new and crucial decisions must be made.

Two recent and related developments make the new departure imminent. First, the fourth Circuit Court of Appeals on September 17, 1962, invalidated key features of the school assignment plan. Second, the crowded condition of Lane High School has led to mounting pressure form all sides to expand the school system. How the community—and particularly the School Board—will respond to these new developments is difficult to predict.

To begin with, the Superintendent can no longer operate under the old assignment plan. Prior to this year it was possible to contain nearly all the Negro elementary school pupils in the large Jefferson district. As early as April 14, 1961, the Circuit Court warned the School Board that its assignment procedures were discriminatory, but refrained from invalidating them on the Board's assurance that these procedures would be changed. In the wake of this warning, the Board made a slight alteration in the assignment system, but retained its substance. *Prior* to the warning, Negro students living outside the Jefferson district were initially assigned to Jefferson and had to make application to attend the school in the district where they lived. *After* the warning, the students were assigned initially to the school in their district and, if they wished to transfer to Jefferson, they had to sign a form supplied them by mail and return it to the Superintendent. Left unchanged was the practice—which the court was now to condemn—of routinely granting whites in the Jefferson district free transfers to one of the other schools, but routinely denying such transfers to Negroes. The rationale for this procedure was that Negroes living in one of the "white" zones were granted free transfer to Jefferson; or to put it another way, any child was allowed to transfer if he found himself assigned to a school in which his race was in the minority.

In finally upsetting this arrangement, the majority of the Circuit Court on September 17, 1962, declared that "little progress in the integration of the schools may be expected if the Board is permitted to pursue the policy which, after mature consideration, it has deliberately adopted." The Court found no fault with the desire to allow students to transfer out of a school in which their race was in a minority, but pointed out that this could be achieved by a system which freely permitted transfers to both races, rather than one which restricted transfers in a discriminatory way.

The full effect of the Court's ruling is not yet clear.[3] The Board has not announced what assignment procedure will be used for the next academic year. All that is certain is that the Board may not routinely grant whites in the Jefferson district transfers and routinely deny transfers to Negroes in the same district. It also seems fairly obvious that Negroes in the Jefferson area will be required to take the initiative, by applying for transfer, in order to attend a desegregated school.

At the high school level, the Court issued a warning in April, 1961, that the assignment procedure, in applying academic and residence criteria to Negroes alone, was discriminatory. Again, however, it refrained from outlawing these procedures in the hope that the Board would act of its own accord. The Board did abandon the residence criterion, but is refused to grant transfers to Negroes who failed to meet the special academic requirements set only for them. In September, 1962 the Court declared this procedure unconstitutional, stating that the "discrimination involved is too clear to require discussion." It conceded that academic considerations may form valid criteria for school assignment, but reminded the Board of the obvious constitutional requirement that such criteria, if used, must be applied to whites as well as Negroes.

For the next academic year, the import of the Court's decision for high school enrollment appears fairly clear: any Negro who wishes may be granted a transfer to Lane. Undoubtedly, all but a few Negroes will be assigned to Burley, but their right to transfer to Lane seems established. However, the present overcrowded condition of Lane may have some effect on the assignment of Negroes to it.

The immediate effect of the Court's September decision was to increase the number of Negroes in desegregated schools. Although classes had already begun, the Court would not delay further the admission of the plaintiff children. Nineteen additional Negroes were assigned to Venable and Lane, bringing the total in those two schools to sixty-three.

More important, four Negroes were assigned to Johnson Elementary School, ending desegregation there. Highly significant is the fact that no white children dropped out of Johnson. This underscores the extent to which the whites have come to accept the fact of desegregation. Moreover, no incidents have been reported at Johnson and the Negroes have received a friendly reception from both teachers and fellow pupils.

The future is complicated by the growing size of the school population and the overcrowding of Lane High School. With a "comfortable" operating capacity of 1,035, Lane's enrollment has grown to 1,200, and an increase to 1,400 is expected for next year. Aware of the need to expand school facilities, the city authorities began last year to plan for the future.

Last spring a special committee recommended to the School Board that a new high school be constructed in the northwestern part of the city. Had the Board adopted this policy, it would have been an indication of a desire to hew closely to the "containment" policy, for the new high school would have been in a section where no Negroes live. It would have become the "white" high school. Lane, the desegregated high school, would have served the southeastern section of the city, where segregationist sentiment is strong. The new high school could have been financed only by a bond issue, and it became clear to city officials (though of course never publicly stated) that a bond referendum would probably be defeated by an "unholy alliance" of Negroes and white segregationists in the Lane area.

Some members of the special committee favored a junior high school system for the city, but they had been requested not to include such a recommendation in their original report. Over the summer, however, sentiment changed and informed persons realized that the proposal to build a new high school was dead. In December the special committee made a second report, this time calling for the construction of three junior high schools.

The committee's report calls for enlarging Burley (the Negro high school) and converting it into a junior-senior high school. It recommends that two additional junior high schools be built "on sites located as strategically as possible." Precisely what assignment procedure would be used for the junior high schools is, of course, unknown, but the report contemplates the continuation of a dual educational system, with most of the Negro graduates of Jefferson going to Burley junior high and then to Burley senior high.

Negro leadership in the community is disappointed in the report. To enlarge and convert Burley into a junior-senior high school is regarded by the NAACP as a means of perpetuating segregation. The branch president has informed the School Board that the NAACP will object in court should this part of the proposal be adopted. He expressed the NAACP's approval of the idea of junior high schools as a solution to the city's educational problems, but requested the School Board to consult "Negro experts in the field of education and local Negro citizens...on plans which so vitally affect Negroes. . . . "

The situation is in such flux at this writing that it would be foolish to speculate on the precise nature of decisions to be made in the next few weeks and months. Instead, we may conclude with some general observations which we hope will shed light on the direction of events in the future.

Nearly all signs point to a continued and slow steady advance of desegregation. In the first place, recent School Board actions give some cause for encouragement. Before the decision had been reached to appeal the latest decision of the Fourth Circuit Court (a political decision in which Richmond played a part), the School Board chairman indicated his feeling that it would be a waste of money and effort to appeal. The Board also requested—and City Council enacted—a compulsory school attendance ordinance, even though the assignment plan had been upset. The apparent switch of the Board away from the new high school to the junior-high school idea was made despite the fact that the latter plan will involve more desegregation considerations.

In the past, the School Board has been accustomed to receiving criticism primarily from segregationists. This situation has changed markedly as educational matters have come to the forefront. Many parents, no longer fearful of desegregation, criticize the Board for what they consider to be lack of Board leadership in school problems. They maintain that school decisions based primarily on racial considerations frequently interfere with constructive planning. Continued desegregation, they point out, is inevitable, and greater educational gains will be made by accepting it rather than by seeking further useless means of resisting it.

The shifting attitudes of the PTA is another indication of the general change in viewpoint now being expressed to the Board. When the public schools were closed in 1958, a resolution protesting school closing died in one PTA meeting for lack of a second. The subject was considered too controversial to discuss at PTA meetings. Today, the PTAs have lost their hesitancy and, under active leadership, play an important role in leading community acceptance of desegregation. For example, last year the School Board banned all school dances when they heard that Negroes were to attend a high school dance. The high school PTA Executive Committee protested to the Board, and the PTA members overwhelmingly supported the protest.

The firmness of Negro leadership, backed by an NAACP branch with over 1400 members, is another factor which indicates continued expansion of desegregation. To date, the NAACP's principal role has been in keeping the Charlottesville case in federal court, where the School Board's containment policy has been subjected to continuous scrutiny. A possible step in the future (although not now apparently under serious consideration) would be to request rezoning of the elementary school districts on the grounds that the present lines have the effect of containing nearly all of the Negroes in one school—a school which has 40% more students than any other city elementary school. The size of the Jefferson district might be reduced, with the result that more Negroes would be assigned to desegregated schools.

In conclusion, then, shifting sentiments within the white community and continued firmness in the Negro community indicate a steady and continued growth in desegregation. For many years to come, however, there is likely to be a considerable amount of voluntary segregation, especially among those who have had several years of segregated school experience. True integration—defined as the glad welcoming and full participation of Negroes in the public schools—is not just around the corner.[4] Progress toward that end is apparent, but its achievement will depend heavily upon strong support for public schools and upon the extent to which those who understand the goal are willing to work for it.

ENDNOTES

1. The seventh elementary school opened in September, 1962. It serves pupils in an area recently annexed by the city and is not treated in the study.

2. Tuition-grant figures for 1962–63 were released too late to be analyzed for this study. They alter in no important way the conclusions reached below.

3. The decision has been appealed to the U.S. Supreme Court, but a stay of the Circuit Court's order was not granted.

4. It should be noted that, so long as public schools are supported, there is little reason to expect that complete integration would result in what some segregationists refer to as "engulfment." Only about 25% of the city school children are colored and Negroes will, therefore, always be a distinct minority in the school system.

UNIT 4-17

Charlottesville Daily Progress

Editorial and Letters to the Editor

Legislative Action Is Needed

Richmond News Leader, which has been the most eloquent newspaper advocate of Virginia's "massive resistance" laws, made editorial acknowledgement Tuesday of the failure of these laws as instruments for preserving segregated public schools.

"This city's (Richmond's) racially separate system of public schools has only a year to live," it said. "Next year at this time we will have two alternatives: Integrated schools, under the compulsion of federal forces, or closed schools, under the requirements of state law."

The unhappy situation which the *News Leader* sees in prospect for Richmond is precisely the one in which Warren County and Charlottesville already find themselves and which court orders make imminent for Arlington and Norfolk. Court actions which have already been instituted make it likely that Alexandria and Newport News, along with Richmond, will be in the same boat within a year. No locality in Virginia can regard itself as safe. All are vulnerable under the rules laid down by the federal courts and under the laws adopted by the General Assembly of Virginia.

The *News Leader* isn't happy about the outlook, but instead of urging legislative action to open a road of escape from the dilemma it merely calls for private action to ameliorate the consequences.

". . . Some relief," it says, "may be available in a third form: *Bona fide* private schools."

So it may. In fact it is only through private schools or perhaps rather through an assurance of their availability if needed, that many and probably most Virginia localities can solve the problem created by the Supreme Court's decision.

But the unpleasant truth is that the very laws that were adopted to resist that decision stand in the way of an escape from it through private schools.

Charlottesville Daily Progress, September 28, 1958.

The *News Leader* properly calls for responsible leadership to come forward to begin "prudent and resourceful planning" for the private schools it believes Richmond will need within a year. There is need, no doubt, for leadership and planning. But the best leadership and the best planning can't do an adequate job without adequate funds. It is idle dreaming to suppose that funds sufficient for the proper and continuing education of all of the children of Richmond or any other locality can be raised privately. Tax support must be provided if even a reasonably good job is to be done. It won't be and can't be provided under the present laws which make a pretense of providing it.

It is hardly necessary to tell the people of Charlottesville that a community without schools is in a socially and economically intolerable position. Something has to be done about it and something will be done about it. The question so far as the people of this city are concerned, is whether the state will provide us with a way out or whether we must seek our own way out by going to the courts for relief from laws preventing the operation of our schools. Governor Almond spoke yesterday as if he would regard the latter step as sedition against the state. That is poppycock, as the Governor must know. It is nevertheless a step which the people of Charlottesville would be reluctant to take and which we believe they would take only as a last resort.

There should be no need of it. The massive resistance laws aren't working. Nobody knows better than Governor Almond how vulnerable they are to legal attack. It is past time now, from the standpoint of Charlottesville and a few other localities, to turn to something that is workable and that will stand up in the courts. It will soon be late from the standpoint of Richmond and numerous other localities.

Have we not the right to expect from our Governor and from others in places of political power the kind of leadership by which this mean can be cleaned up before irreparable damage is done?

"YOUR RIGHT TO SAY IT"

COURAGE OF CONVICTIONS

(To the editor)

The formation of the Committee for Public Education with its plan for schools at any cost has aroused my dander. I'm amazed to hear of the number of people who are just blindly following a man who doesn't even come from here. Who is doing your thinking? Not you as individuals, for if you were you would face the facts:

1. We are here in Virginia and in America because we were opposed to tyranny. Remember why we left England? Why do we have so many immigrants?
2. Where were you when you were given an opportunity to vote for or against massive resistance? Were you at the polls?
3. These idiotic statements of "my child's education is suffering." What in two weeks? Or even two months? Except for Lane High's seniors who have college entry exams to face, can you honestly say their education is suffering? Or are you tired of your children under foot, or resentful because of other schools being open? (My child goes to Venable.) Suppose you were on a late vacation or your child was ill or there was a serious epidemic. Would you then worry about their education?

Aren't you being a biddy-brain when you don't realize that "school at any cost" means just that—any cost. To whom? All of us. That means not only school integration. It eventually comprises integration in your parks, all forms of recreation and, most important, in housing. Think again of what happened in Washington, D.C., and many other cities because of housing integration. Do a little soul-searching and a little thinking of your own and then have the courage of your convictions. Ignore those who have moved into Virginia and would lead you down the garden path to get what they desire.

I am not rabid on the subject of integration vs. segregation. I just honestly don't believe it would work. There are great number of the Negro race that I like and respect and consider as friends. But no one will make me believe that the majority of the Negroes want to integrate. There couldn't be anything but misery for each race. The real point is democracy. Let those who prefer integration move on. We can and did get along very nicely without them. But you, the people who are Virginia born and bred, exercise your own brain cells and help to preserve our democracy.

—Anne R. North
1442 Rugby Ave.

PREDICTS EASIER SAILING

(To the editor:)

Too much fuss is being made over the integration of our schools, so please let us try to do something very soon before our taxes are raised again in order to keep on fighting this thing.

Just a few miles from Charlottesville on R.F.D. 1, where there is a Negro population of about 200, a white family has moved into a former colored school and is living there very peacefully. Besides, several white people are now living in our homes out in that section and I don't think anyone of us is going to try to stop the whites or anyone else from living where they can get shelter and food. So why pay more taxes to keep children from going to schools where they want to go?

When I went to school 50 years ago, my brother and I had to walk five miles. We lived on a farm. He and I were the oldest of five children there, three of them being of another race (white). So we five left home together for school five days a week and for four years we walked these three white children to their school, which was only a mile from home. Then we had to take off four more miles before we reached our schoolhouse. Now that was not right, was it?

Anyhow, this has been going on much too long. So please let's stop trying to take everything and give a little. I have a feeling that it won't be so bad after the sailing gets good. And it will you know.

—Paul E. Pollard
301 10 1/2 St.

EDUCATION BY TELEVISION

(To the editor:)

When Thomas A. Edison was asked what he himself considered the most important of his inventions for the use of man, he said, without hesitation, "The coming of visual education." Why are we so long about it?

Little Rock is to some extent using TV to take up the public school classes to avoid integration. It may be the beginning of a revolution in teaching, carrying on into college, medical schools, research. Everybody gets the best at a minimum cost. At present TV hardly justifies itself as a practical or cultural factor. It is concerned chiefly with advertising while ignoring its potential as a great cultural agent.

—Elizabeth W. Steptoe
17th St., NW.

UNIT 4-18

A Box Lunch, A Chair and A Drinking Cup

Pupils in Charlottesville's private schools are expected to bring such things as a chair, a box lunch and a drinking cup to Mrs. O'Hanlon's basement room where education is being dispensed as though the children were in Venable or Lane.

To those faint of heart and weak of knee who said it wouldn't be done; that parents would knuckle under when the blue chips were down—this is their answer. This is Virginia's answer to the Warrens, the Pauls, the Oliver Hills.

No, Mrs. O'Hanlon's basement room doesn't have all the frills and conveniences and comforts offered at Venable and Lane, but it's cosy and it's comfortable, and what's more it's livable for Virginians who would suffer infinitely worse before they would surrender to the gang of cut-throats oppressing them at every turn.

The Charlottesville experiment in noble and courageous living will be repeated elsewhere in Virginia, and perhaps the day may come when private schools will replace all public schools. The NAACP and the Supreme Court are in ascendancy now and the moves are up to them.

As the state and its localities await the next bolts of lightning it is time for all of us to do a little re-thinking, a little serious and sober thinking about some grave realities of life.

First off, it must be realized that no institution, not even the church has been so cloaked in holy raiment as have the public schools, and this is largely due to the mistaken idea that a public education is a panacea for all the ills that beset us—from catching up with Russia in the field of space travel, to eliminating all the social evils plaguing society. We are living in the age of the educationist, an age that has permitted the professional educator to take over the responsibility of the parent and the parson. Allowed this responsibility, and taking other liberties not delegated, the educators have built up in the schools a sort of untouchable system that the outside world can do little about. Criticize the schools today, and one is branded as ignorant, reactionary and heretical.

It is in character that a few of the dedicated educationists, such as the principal at Norfolk, accept integration—accept anything but the closing of a public school. Happily all educationists are not so dedicated, and fortunate, too, that most teachers are willing to

---

Defenders' News and Views, 1958 (reprinted from the *Halifax Gazette*, October 2, 1958).

teach even if it means dispensing the 3 R's under an oak tree, as our good Congressman Tuck so aptly phrased it.

Secondly, it must occur to many of us that the tail has been wagging the dog rather lustily. This generation of school children is coddled, sugar-coated and pampered to such a degree that some parents would surrender to every whim and caprice of their offspring.

If Johnny laments audibly (and so the national TV networks can hear) that football will go with the closing of the public school, if Mary weeps on CBS that the sorority will be broken up (just terrible, sob) then mamas and papas will agree that these are catastrophic things that must be prevented at all costs. So, mama and papa join a committee that isn't interested in segregation or integration at all, but interested only in saving Siwash and the sorority. Bosh! Pure Bosh!

It's only human that parents want something better for their children than they had for themselves. That's a warmly human instinct, and it sells more autos, sweaters and hi-fi sets. But in buying the better life for the children, parents sometime barter away more than they bargained for. And, these would be the priceless traits of industry, incentive, initiative and the battle-tested child who has wrestled with adversity and won the scuffle.

How many of the older generation truly regret the experience of childhood when lunches were taken to school in tin pails, when water was brought to the poorly heated schoolroom from a well or spring, when the likes of Mrs. O'Hanlon's basement would appear as a castle by comparison to the shabbiness of a one-room school? Such primitive facilities as were offered conditioned the child of yesterday and prepared him for manhood and responsibilities. Furthermore, it inculcated a deep sense of appreciation for books and the great world found within their covers.

Society cannot and will not turn back the clock, but the fact that many present day leaders in all walks of life endured these hardships and came out of them the better for it should tell us not to despair if the schools close and we have to all fall back on our own resources to educate our children. Surely the educational processes will continue and continue efficiently if a thousand such basements have to be renovated for school purposes.

Virginians should take heart and proceed to plan for an eventual wholesale close down of the public schools. It would be completely out of character for the state and its people to cower and run in the face of such an attack as we now face. Let us lick our wounds and retire to the basements and churches and Elks halls and Moose lodges, but let us never surrender our priceless heritage of freedom and independence.

Let us get back to the real essentials of education, and these after all are confined to a teacher, a child and a book. Wherever these three can be brought together, the educational processes will continue. Let us not fret, either, about the bugaboo of accreditation—a fancy word but positively meaningless in these days and times when crowded colleges require that a student pass a college entrance test.

Let us then go our determined, stubborn way. Let us dedicate ourselves to a system of education second to none. If what we have doesn't have all the frills and folly of public education, let us be content just to turn out more Jeffersons and Henrys and Robert E. Lees as products of Mrs. O'Hanlon's basement experiment in democratic education.

UNIT 4-19

LITTLE ROCK

Anthony Lewis

As the 1957–58 school year began, southern resistance to the Supreme Court decision was proving highly effective. Voluntary desegregation, which had occurred in hundreds of school districts in the first three years after the decision, had come to an almost complete stop. Legally, southern devices to delay integration were proliferating. Politically, a unified southern voice was speaking out against the Court and its ruling, while President Eisenhower and his Administration said nothing in their support.

The South's effort, putting aside the merits of racial segregation, was within an American tradition of resistance to disliked judicial decisions. More than once in the past, criticism of a Supreme Court decision had eventually persuaded the country or the Court itself that the position was unsound; only a generation before, a Court that had held New Deal measures unconstitutional changed its mind within a few years. The South was following a beaten path in attempting, as the Southern Manifesto said, "all lawful means to bring about a reversal of this decision."

But now the South changed tactics. As Professor Alexander M. Bickel of the Yale Law School put it: "Having scented victory, the southern leaders, or at least a sufficient number of them, sought to assure it by turning from litigation and agitation to direct action by the use of mobs. Thus they abandoned the tradition in which they had been acting."

Few would have expected Little Rock, Arkansas, to be the testing ground for the new course of violence. Little Rock was a city of the New South, a middle-class, moderate town with an enlightened mayor (Woodrow Wilson Mann), congressman (Brooks Hays) and newspaper (the Arkansas *Gazette*, edited by Harry Ashmore). Arkansas had had some integration at the university level for years, and Governor Orval Faubus had never been a race-baiter; indeed, his election had been considered a liberal victory. The federal courts had approved a desegregation plan proposed by the Little Rock School Board and fought by the NAACP. A most gradual plan, it was to begin with the senior high schools in the fall of 1957—specifically, with the admission of a few Negro children to Central High School on Tuesday, September 3, 1957.

On Monday night, September 2nd, Governor Faubus made an unexpected television address to the state. He said it would "not be possible to restore or to maintain order if

---

Chapter from *Portrait of a Decade, The Second American Revolution,* by Anthony Lewis and the *New York Times*, 1964.

forcible integration is carried out tomorrow" at Little Rock. He announced that he was therefore posting National Guardsmen outside Central High, to act "not as segregationists or integrationists but as soldiers."

The Guardsmen acted as soldiers on the side of segregation. They were there the next morning, two hundred and seventy of them, and on the advice of the School Board no Negro child appeared. The Board went before Federal District Judge Ronald N. Davies—serving in Little Rock temporarily on assignment from North Dakota—and asked what to do. He said he would take the Governor's word about the neutrality of the troops "at its face value," and he ordered the desegregation plan into effect "forthwith."

The next morning, Wednesday, September 4th, nine Negro children tried to exercise their legal right to attend Central High along with nearly two thousand white students. A crowd waited along with the soldiers. Suddenly the cry went up:

"A nigger! They're coming! Here they come!"

It was fifteen-year-old Elizabeth Ann Eckford, first of the nine that morning. She walked quietly up toward a school door, but a National Guardsman barred her way. Then, to leave the tense scene, she had to walk a hundred-yard gauntlet of ugly gestures and jeers from the crowd. She finally reached a bench at a bus stop and sat down. A white woman went over to comfort her. "What are you doing, you nigger-lover?" someone yelled from the mob. The woman answered: "She's scared. She's just a little girl." The two finally got on a bus and left.

Just why Orval Faubus chose this path of physical defiance to federal law may never be known. Some militant segregationist leaders from Georgia had lately been in town and talked to him. The Governor himself never gave a straightforward explanation; he only repeated that he had acted to prevent violence. The result of his action was the mob.

The events in Little Rock were immediately recognized by almost everyone as a direct challenge to the Federal Government. President Eisenhower's first comment missed the point. At a press conference on September 3rd, the day the Guard was posted at Central High, he was asked about the news. He repeated his familiar contention that "you cannot change people's hearts merely by laws" and added the unfortunate remark that people in the South "see a picture of mongrelization of the race, they call it." But by the next day the Federal Bureau of Investigation had agents in Little Rock looking into the situation. Faubus telegraphed the President, who had gone to Newport, Rhode Island, for a vacation, to stop the "unwarranted interference of federal agents." He received a reply that marked by far the strongest position yet taken by Mr. Eisenhower on the school-segregation issue: "The only assurance I can give you is that the federal Constitution will be upheld by me by every legal means at my command."

Outside Central High School the mob stood watch. The *Times*'s education editor, Benjamin Fine, who was covering the story, more than once found himself the object of taunts.

"You got a nigger wife?" a woman asked the reporter. She was identified later as a waitress in a Little Rock tavern.

Mr. Fine did not answer.

"Are you a Jew?" the woman shouted.

"Yes," Mr. Fine said.

On Monday, September 9th, the FBI delivered a four-hundred-page report to Judge Davies on the causes for obstruction of the school-integration order. He asked the United States to enter the case—which was formally a lawsuit by the Negro school children and their parents against the School Board—as a friend of the court. The Government promptly asked the judge to enjoin Governor Faubus from interfering with the integration plan. A hearing on that request was set for ten days later.

At this point the use of force by the Federal Government did not seem a likely course. A Washington dispatch to the *Times* accurately reflected the mood when it said:

"It is all very well to discover a statute that would allow the President to send an army into Little Rock. But no responsible person in or out of government thinks this would advance peaceful acceptance of the Supreme Court decision in the South. The one certainty about the Administration's plans is that there is no desire for an open test of strength."

Instead, the theory went, the Administration would rally moderate opinion in the South and persuade Governor Faubus to climb down. But this was only a theory. President Eisenhower made no great effort to arouse the South, or the country, to the issues at Little Rock in those early days of the episode. Nor did he undertake any dramatic gesture such as going down to Little Rock and taking the Negro children into Central High School himself, as some had suggested. He did talk to Governor Faubus, in a meeting at Newport, and they both issued complimentary statements afterward. But the Governor did not remove the Guardsmen; he said later that he thought he was making some headway in arguing his case to Eisenhower until Attorney General Herbert Brownell intervened.

On September 20th Judge Davies granted the injunction against Governor Faubus. When school opened the following Monday, September 23rd, the Guardsmen were gone. The nine Negro children went into the school. What happened next was described by Benjamin Fine in a dispatch from Little Rock that evening:

> A mob of belligerent, shrieking and hysterical demonstrators forced the withdrawal today of nine Negro students from Central High School here.
>
> Despite a heavy turnout of local and state police to see that the Negroes were not molested in Little Rock's newest attempt to integrate the high school, city authorities bowed to the fury of about one thousand white supremacists. They ordered the Negro students to leave the school about noon. The integration attempt had lasted three hours thirteen minutes.
>
> While fringe fights broke out and several persons were roughed up by irate segregationists, the mob shouted insults and obscenities against the "niggers" and "nigger-lovers." Groups of white students who had walked out of the school after the nine Negroes entered chanted: 'Two, four, six, eight, we ain't gonna integrate."
>
> Mayor Woodrow Wilson Mann charged that the violence outside the school had been stirred up by plan and "bore all the marks of the professional agitator." He said that detailed information on the events of the day would be turned over to the Department of Justice for whatever action the Federal Government considered warranted.
>
> Many of those who milled in front of the school today were from out of town, some from communities two hundred miles distant. It was noted that one of those in the crowd of demonstrators was Jimmy Karam, Athletic Commissioner for the state and a close friend of the Governor.
>
> Mrs. Daisy Bates, president of the Arkansas NAACP branch, said the Negro students "will not be out there again until they have the assurance of the President of the United States that they will be protected from the mob."
>
> For a time this morning it appeared as though integration would take place smoothly in this city of 102,213 population. A few persons had arrived at the high school by six o'clock. By seven, with the sun just beginning to break through the clouds, only one hundred or so had gathered at both ends of the street leading to the two-block-long school. Wooden barricades, placed at either end of the street, stopped them at those points.
>
> Eighty members of the local police force, some on motorcycles and in squad cars, but most on foot, were on the school grounds or in the vicinity. Fifty state troopers were in the area, ready to help if needed.
>
> At eight o'clock it was evident that the violence that Governor Faubus had predicted would take place. By this time some five hundred persons had gathered. They appeared in a fighting mood.

"The niggers won't get in," members of the crowd said, time and again.

At eight forty-five the school buzzer could be dimly heard. School was in session.

"Where are the niggers?" one person asked another. "Let them try to get in . . . "

"We'll lynch them all," several yelled.

"Sure, and all you Yankee newspapermen with them: a gravel-voiced man shouted. This was met with a howl of approval.

The police tried to keep the crowd off the street. The surging angry mob kept pushing forward. "Please keep back, step back," the police said politely at first, then with more authority.

"Don't you dare lay your hands on me," one woman screamed as a police officer asked her to move away.

"Lady," he pleaded, "I'm not going to touch you. I'm just doing my duty."

Suddenly a yell went up: "There they are, they're coming."

The crowd rushed after four men who turned out to be Negro newspapermen. They were manhandled by the crowd, but managed to escape.

A man yelled: "Look, they're going into our school."

Six girls and three boys crossed over into the schoolyard. They had arrived in two automobiles and had driven to the side of the school. Mrs. Bates accompanied them.

Slowly, almost as though they were entering a normal classroom on a normal school day, the students walked toward the side door of the school. The boys, in open shirts, and the girls, in bobby-socks, joked and chatted among themselves. They carried armfuls of textbooks.

The crowd now let out a roar of rage. "They've gone in," a man shouted.

"Oh, God," said a woman, "the niggers are in school."

A group of six girls, dressed in skirts and sweaters, hair in pony-tails, started to shriek and wail.

"The niggers are in our school," they howled hysterically.

One of them jumped up and down on the sidewalk, waving her arms toward her classmates in the school who were looking out of the windows, and screamed over and over again: "Come on out, come on out."

Tears flowed down her face, her body shook in uncontrollable spasms.

Three of her classmates grew hysterical and threw their arms around each other. They began dancing up and down.

"The niggers are in," they shrieked, "come on out of the school. Don't stay there with the niggers. Come on out. Come on . . . "

Hysteria swept from the shrieking girls to members of the crowd. Women cried hysterically, tears running down their faces.

"I'm going to get the niggers out," said Mrs. Clyde Thomason, recording secretary of the Mothers League of Central High, a segregationist group.

She started toward the school. Two policemen blocked her way.

"Please go back on the sidewalk," one begged quietly.

"Go on and hit me, just go and hit me," Mrs. Thomason, who had been enjoined by Judge Davies not to interfere with the integration program, said. She became hysterical.

A man walked over to the policemen who were struggling to restrain Mrs. Thomason. "This is my wife, officer," he said. "I'll take her with me."

An elderly man jumped upon the barricade. "Let's go over the top," he shouted. "Who's going over with me?"

"We'll all go," the crowd yelled.

Over the wooden barricade they went. A dozen policemen stood in the way. Slowly the crowd gave way.

The police were taunted by the mob, well out of hand by now. Instead of tapering off, as it had at previous morning demonstrations, the crowd grew in numbers. By ten o'clock it had grown to about one thousand.

"Turn in your badge," the crowd yelled at the police.

One of the policemen said, apologetically: "I'm only doing my duty. If I didn't I'd lose my job."

Another one, Thomas Dunaway, took off his badge and walked away.

"Hurray! Hurray!" the crowd cheered.

"He's the only white man on the force," a young man in a plaid shirt shouted.

"Let's pass the hat around," someone suggested.

In a moment several persons went through the crowd, collecting money. Dollar bills were tossed into the hat. It was estimated that about two hundred dollars had been collected for the policeman who gave up his badge.

The men and women, augmented by students, surged over the "off limits" line and spread into the street facing the school grounds. For a time it appeared as though the local police would be completely overwhelmed by the angry crowd.

"Come on out of school, come on out, the niggers are in there," the crowd yelled.

Four girls slowly walked down the side steps of the high school.

A tremendous cheer echoed through the crowd.

"They're coming out," was shouted time and again.

Soon a group of six left. The students began to leave the school at more frequent intervals. At first the police did not permit adults to enter the school. They were acting under order of Virgil T. Blossom, Superintendent of Schools.

"I'm going to get my child," one parent said defiantly.

"Sorry, you'll stay right here," the policeman answered.

Quickly this order changed. One by one, mothers and fathers walked up the school steps, and then returned with their children. Each time a student walked out of the school the cheers increased.

"Mother, come and get me," a girl telephoned. "They're fighting something awful here inside the school."

By twelve o'clock the mob had reached its greatest strength, and by now completely ignored the local police. The crowd remained behind the barricade, but it did not maintain order there. Several newsmen were attacked and beaten. A Negro reporter was kicked and manhandled.

Threats, jeers, and insults became more ominous.

"Let's rush the police," a ringleader shouted. "They can't stop us.

At noon the police received this message on their short-wave radios: "This is the Mayor. Tell Principal Jeff Matthews [of Central High] that the Negroes have been withdrawn. Tell Mr. Matthews to announce that to the student body. I've talked with Virgil Blossom and Negroes have been withdrawn."

At twelve-fourteen Lieutenant Carl Jackson of the Little Rock police force stood on the school grounds facing the crowd. Over a loudspeaker set up on the sidewalk in front of the school the officer said, "The Negroes have been withdrawn from school."

"We don't believe you," the crowd yelled back. "That's just a pack of lies."

"Is there anyone whom you would believe?" he asked.

"I saw a nigger standing in the doorway just now," a woman yelled.

"Let's go in and see," another shouted.

"If you have any one person in the crowd you believe, he can go in and see, then report to you," Lieutenant Jackson said.

Mrs. Allen Thevenet, of the Mothers League of Central High School, stepped forward across the street.

> "Will you accept Mrs. Thevenet's word?" the Lieutenant asked. The crowd gave a reluctant approval.
>
> Accompanied by a policeman, Mrs. Thevenet went into the. school. On her return she came to the loudspeaker and said: "We went through every room in the school and there was no niggers there."
>
> The Negro students, meantime, had been taken out through a side door and escorted in two police cars to their homes. Despite the rumors that had been flying through the crowd that the students "had been beat up," they were not molested while in school.
>
> "They were surprised when they were told to leave at noontime," Mrs. Bates said later.
>
> "Nothing much happened at all," Thelma Mothershed, one of the nine Negro students, said.
>
> Nothing really happened," agreed Terrance Roberts, age sixteen. "We went to classes as scheduled. After the third period we were taken out and driven home. Some school officials came in to see us." He added: "I was pushed once but I wasn't hit. It was quiet after we got into our classes. A few white students walked out."
>
> Another of the girls, Elizabeth Eckford, said: "I was the only Negro girl in my class."
>
> Would they want to come back?
>
> "Yes," they agreed, "if we can come here without causing any trouble. The students will accept us once we go with them for a while."

That evening President Eisenhower denounced what he called the "disgraceful occurrence" at Little Rock and said a federal court's orders "cannot be flouted with impunity by any individual or mob of extremists." Invoking a statute with deep roots in United States history, he issued a proclamation directing those who had obstructed federal law "to cease and desist therefrom and to disperse forthwith." But on Tuesday morning a crowd still milled about Central High School. No attempt was made to bring the Negro children in.

The President then took the ultimate action—one that on July 17th he had called unthinkable, one that only three weeks earlier few had considered a real possibility. For the first time since Reconstruction, federal troops were sent into the South to protect the rights of Negroes. Eisenhower ordered one thousand paratroopers to Little Rock and placed ten thousand members of the Arkansas National Guard on federal service to put down the mob. The soldiers were under the command of Major General Edwin A. Walker—the same General Walker who was removed from his command in Germany in 1961 for spreading right-wing extremist propaganda and who was to fulminate against federal forces sent to the University of Mississippi by President Kennedy in 1962.

The dispatch of troops brought the expected outcry from the South and its friends. Senator Richard B. Russell of Georgia, ordinarily a wise and cultivated man, sent the President a telegram comparing the soldiers in Little Rock to "Hitler's storm troopers." One of the main charges was that the use of troops was illegal, an unconstitutional invasion of states' rights. Except for the agitated political atmosphere, this claim would doubtless have been laughed off as frivolous. For an explicit statute on the books since 1792 permitted the use of federal forces whenever federal law was obstructed. George Washington had invoked the statute to put down the Whiskey Rebellion. Even in the absence of such specific authority, many would have considered it the constitutional duty of the President to use all necessary force to protect the federal rights of American citizens against mob violence condoned or encouraged by state officials.

The nine Negro children re-entered Central High School on Wednesday morning, September 25th. The mob was dispersed, and twenty-four Paratroopers patrolled inside the school to prevent incidents. Desegregation had been achieved—but at what anyone would admit was a heavy price. Some non-segregationist critics thought the Administration had jumped too quickly from no force to too much; they said federal marshals might have been tried first, for example. The Justice Department said that would have been ineffectual temporizing, and in any event the argument by hindsight could get nowhere. The troops were there, and now the problem was to get them out. That was a problem primarily in the assumption of responsibility by the moderates of Little Rock. The terrible dilemma they faced—one to be repeated in so many other southern communities—was described by Cabell Phillips of the *Times* in the *Times Magazine* of October 20, 1957:

> Central High School here was in its fourth week of continuous operation under military occupation when I went to keep an appointment, one evening recently, at the home of one of the city's top education officials. His handsome suburban house was dark when I arrived by taxi and a hall light came on only after I had rung the bell. He admitted me, grim and unsmiling, turned off the hall light and led me to his study at the back of the house.
>
> "I hope you won't mind," he said, "if we have our talk in a hotel downtown. We are all packed and I am moving my family down there for the time being.
>
> "We have put up with quite a lot of threats and anonymous telephone calls. Of course, nothing serious has happened so far. But I have to be away from the house so much of the time, and there's talk of another flare-up at the school tomorrow, that—well, I'll just feel safer if they are not here by themselves."
>
> Why did one of the most respected citizens of this normally civilized community fear for the physical safety of his family? How is it that a fractional defiant minority in a community of one hundred and fifty thousand, backed by a few scores of hoodlums and agitators, could obliterate the instinct for decency and public order of an overwhelming majority?
>
> To understand, one has to recognize the fact that school integration is so uniformly unpopular in the South that even men of the most generous good will cannot conscientiously be its advocates. And when, as in Little Rock and Nashville, Tennessee, and Charlotte, North Carolina, there comes the ultimate, dreaded dilemma of either accepting Negroes in the white schools or condoning defiance of civil authority, the responsible citizen makes his choice for law and order reluctantly, and often fearfully. Even then, wholly a concern for the integrity of civil authority; it may contain such subjective factors as "face" for his town or state, or awareness of the political or economic consequences of defiance.
>
> There are, I believe, no whole-hearted, all-out Pro-integrationists among the generality of white citizens of the South and none at all of substantial influence. The awareness of racial "difference"—*not* racial animosity, necessarily—strikes deeply into the subconscious mind, beyond the reach of introspection or reason or prayer. It is a fundamental coloration, an ineradicable trace element in the chemistry of the southern white's mind. One may tell himself that he has cast it out, but the mere fact that he reminds himself of his cleansing is a clue that its debris remains.
>
> Thus, however right a southerner may believe the rule of integration to be in terms of legality or justice or inevitable social change, it cannot be a cause that arouses his fervor and devotion. If he nevertheless takes a stand for it, reason compels him, not his heart. This is the melancholy burden of the moderate.
>
> Segregationists, on the other hand, have invested their cause with a searing emotional impact. It has been made to appeal to the most susceptible tribal impulses: patriotism, racial purity, religious dogmas, group solidarity, status and personal pride. At the top, it has been given an intellectual and political gloss by introducing questions of constitutionality and states' rights. What is more important, the segregationist has a tangible, human symbol for his fears—the Negro. In the volatile, undisciplined lower echelons of the movement these impulses fuse unpredictably and explosively into hatred and mob violence.

Thus, the temperate southerner who would weigh justice and respect for the law against his native customs and sensibilities is trapped between the cold sea of indecision and the zealot's fire. Not being quite sure what he is *for,* he cannot effectively oppose what he is *against.* So it is that there has emerged throughout the South the pattern of silent assent among those who would be moderates in this superheated struggle. Bogged by irresolution and taking a prudent heed of their own best interests, they melt into the faceless anonymity of the sidelines and let him who will carry the flag.

There are among them, of course, courageous ones who are willing to stand up and be counted. But often the articulate moderate can make himself heard only by singing less stridently in the same key as the segregationist.

And so it is that we have had the spectacle, time after time, where the segregation controversy has fared, of the "good" citizens seemingly being cowed into impotence while others defied the law or even resorted to violence.

In Little Rock, as mobs faced troops across the barricades around the school, and the city ached with tension, Governor Orval Faubus, the benignly ambiguous leader of the insurrection, was showered daily with praise and messages of encouragement from states' righters, segregationists and the lunatic fringe of "nigger haters" all over the South.

From the other side there was little but stunned silence. Little Rock's two newspapers, it is true, opened up their editorial artillery, Mayor Woodrow Wilson Mann made a future grab to wrest control of the situation from the Governor's hands; the Ministerial Alliance called resolutely for observance of the Golden Rule. But the great mass of the "good" people of Little Rock—and their spokesmen and leaders—played it safe.

A break in this wall of apathy came only after a month. Twenty-four of the city's outstanding business and professional leaders got together in the first week of October on a statement of principles that called for an end to violence and submission to legal authority. The following day forty ministers and rabbis adopted a similar resolution and launched a "ministry of reconciliation." Late in the same week, Winthrop Rockefeller, the state's most distinguished adopted citizen, said on a national television program that the whole episode was having a disastrous effect on efforts to rehabilitate Arkansas' sagging industrial economy. It began to appear at last that a counterforce of public opinion was being thrown against the defiant minority.

The tardiness with which Little Rock faced up to its crisis can be attributed to a number of factors.

One was the conviction that "it can't happen here." This is not a Deep South city and its record of race relations for the last quarter of a century is quite good. Furthermore, the general acceptance which seemed to have been accorded token integration allayed the fears of most people that there would be violent opposition at the last moment.

Another factor was the lack of rapport and communication between the city government and community leaders. For many reasons, Mayor Mann does not enjoy widespread confidence either among the public or within his own administration (eight of his ten aldermen aligned themselves with Governor Faubus). City Hall did not offer a rallying point for community action.

Little Rock has no bi-racial organization equipped to deal with abrasive community problems of this kind. The one possible exception is a chapter of the Urban League, which this year was frozen out of the Community Chest because it is "controversial."

And while Little Rock is not Deep South, it still is southern enough to be acutely attuned to southern Democratic mores. It is the trading center of the most intensely conservative region of the state, the rich farming counties of the Mississippi Delta. Eastern Arkansas is as Confederate—and pro-segregation—as Mississippi or Georgia, and it controls the legislature and the Democratic party in Arkansas. When Little Rock's merchants, bankers, brokers and other business leaders said (as many of them did) that they didn't want to stick out their necks to oppose Governor Faubus and the Citizens Council, they undoubtedly were thinking of the customers they do business with in the eastern counties.

Finally, there was the risk—or the fear—of reprisal. Mothers of carrier boys for the Arkansas *Gazette*, whose outspokenness has made it a prime target of the militant segregationists, were warned by telephone that their boys might be hurt in some way if they continued delivering the paper.

School Superintendent Virgil T. Blossom and other school officials were subjected to anonymous threats and harassment. Some merchants and professional men were threatened with boycotts. The father of a student leader at Central High refused to let this reporter interview the boy on sentiment in the school. "I do business with people on both sides of this issue," the father said, "and I can't afford to take any chances."

Such is the pattern of silent assent; it is true not only in Little Rock but wherever in the South the question of segregation plagues the conscientious citizen.

But in the wake of Little Rock the moderate well may wonder if silent assent is enough. Had he rallied sooner, marshaled public opinion, demanded with a voice as loud and insistent as the mob leaders' that solutions be found in law and not in violence—had he done these things in Little Rock, might not the catastrophe have been averted?

A good many responsible people in this town think so. They point to the example of Nashville, where an almost simultaneous eruption was put down in less than a week.

There are differences, of course. The mayor and the Governor of Tennessee made it plain at the outset that they would tolerate no disorders over integration of the city schools. That gave the moderates solid political and legal backing. Furthermore, there had been for many years in Nashville an effective and realistic bi-racial community organization to prepare the citizens at all levels for the impact of social change. So, when violence flared on that first day of integration—Negro children were heckled, a school was dynamited—there was an explosive response of outraged public opinion backed up by a determined police force.

The race issue is an agonizing one wherever it exists, in Philadelphia and Detroit as well as in Birmingham and Little Rock. But in the South it has an extra dimension, for many of the root causes of this tension are imbedded in the laws and customs of the states.

There should be no doubt in anyone's mind any longer that wherever segregation is sanctioned, the might and majesty of the United States Government is now committed to its eradication—not today or this year necessarily, but ultimately, and with bayonets if need be. Little Rock is more than an incident; it is a precedent.

There is no likely turning back from this course, and intelligent leaders of the South admit it, however privately and ruefully. If this reality is to be lived with, and with a minimum of bitterness and shock, the moderate will have to contribute something more to the effort than his silent assent.

The soldiers never did leave Central High during that school year. Four moderate southern governors—Luther H. Hodges of North Carolina, Frank G. Clement of Tennessee, LeRoy Collins of Florida and Theodore R. McKeldin of Maryland—tried to persuade Governor Faubus to take over responsibility for maintaining order with the

Negro children in the schools so the federal force could be withdrawn. But this effort collapsed when Faubus reneged on a promise to issue an agreed statement. The troops were gradually thinned out; the paratroopers left by the end of November, and a reduced force of Guardsmen on federal duty patrolled the school.

Inside Central High, school went on under difficult circumstances, described on October 12th by Homer Bigart of the *Times*:

> Subjected to tensions and pressures inconceivable to most Americans, the students have had to concentrate on a tough and exacting academic routine while the cries of adult white mobs and the tread of paratroopers' boots intruded from the streets outside.
>
> Against this tumultuous background, teenagers tried to concentrate on algebra, or Latin, or perhaps on one of the "frill" courses of which Central is proud: music, water-color painting, costume designing, photography, commercial law, printing.
>
> There was some trouble inside the school, too. Jeers, rebel yells and muttered threats were directed at the Negroes. The troublemakers were of a group of perhaps one hundred to one hundred and fifty students who came from "disturbed" homes. They had absorbed the racial hatred of segregationist parents who felt that their whole way of life was being threatened by "race mixing."
>
> Some of the troublemakers boycotted school when the paratroopers came. They hung around near the street-corner barricades, taunting the soldiers: "Join the paratroopers and see Central High."
>
> So long as the chief troublemakers stayed out of school, peace reigned in the classrooms. Not one of the student leaders, not one of Central's championship football team, joined the rebels. A fierce pride in their school helped them resist the slurs of "chicken" (coward) heaped on them by young agitators when they refused to join a walkout.
>
> Even the most ardent segregationists could not stomach the end of Central High. "I'm not going to let nine Negroes keep my daughter from getting an education," said one mother. Common sense began to prevail as soon as passions cooled.
>
> Fewer than sixty students participated in a planned walkout October 3rd. Attendance rose slowly from a minimum of 1,400 to nearly 1,800 at the close of this week. After the walkout failed, Governor Faubus tried to keep the parents in turmoil. He charged last week that paratroopers had committed "very grave indiscretions" by invading girls' dressing rooms. He refused to reveal any evidence to prove it. His charge was promptly denied by army officers and school officials. Students laughed at it.
>
> Meanwhile students were getting a better understanding of the federal troops guarding their school. In a smart public-relations gesture, paratroopers and their officers attended school football games and cheered for the Central High "Tigers." There was plenty to cheer about—Central's big team has won twenty-six games in a row.
>
> There have been no clashes between students and troops. The student paper, the *Tiger*, carried in its latest issue a page-one article deploring the taunting of soldiers. "They're somebody's husband, somebody's son, somebody's boy friend, and they want to be friendly with the students of Central High," said the paper. "They were sent here to do a job with a minimum of force and as quickly as possible." The paper urged a "sensible, peaceful neutrality," and that students should "accept the situation without demonstration."
>
> As for relations between the majority of white students and the nine Negroes, they are cautious and correct. A small minority of troublemakers has tried to jostle

and insult the Negroes, and one Negro boy was kicked and pummeled, but the Negroes, well prepared in advance for this ordeal, have behaved with poise and dignity. Not one of the nine has "chickened out" by requesting transfer back to all-Negro Horace Mann High School.

The self-control of one of the Negro children did finally crack. Minnijean Brown, sixteen years old, was unable to go on enduring the segregationist students' taunts—and worse—without replying in kind. She was suspended briefly in December and then again in February for getting into a fray. Persons in the North then got up a fund to send Minnijean to a private school in New York, the New Lincoln School, and she graduated from there the following year. Before she left Central High, Minnijean participated in a remarkable interview conducted for the National Broadcasting Company by a Norwegian correspondent, Mrs. Jorunn Ricketts. Five other Central students were on the program: three white girls—Sammy Dean Parker, Kay Bacon and Robin Woods—one white boy, Joseph Fox, and one Negro boy, Ernest Green. These excerpts from the transcript were printed in the *Times* on October 14, 1957:

MRS. RICKETTS: Do you think it is possible to start working this out on a more sensible basis than violent demonstration?

SAMMY: No, I don't because the South has always been against racial mixing and I think they will fight this thing to the end. . . . We fight for our freedom—that's one thing. And we don't have any freedom any more.

ERNEST: Sammy, you said that you don't have freedom. I wonder what do you mean by it—that you don't have freedom? You are guaranteed your freedoms in the Bill of Rights and your Constitution. You have the freedom of speech—I noticed that has been exercised a whole lot in Little Rock. The freedom of petition, the freedom of religion and the other freedoms are guaranteed to you. As far as freedom, I think that if anybody should kick about freedoms, it should be us. Because I think we have been given a pretty bad side on this thing as far as freedoms.

SAMMY: Do you call those troops freedom? I don't. And I also do not call free when you are being escorted into the school every morning.

ERNEST: You say why did the troops come here? It is because our government—our state government—went against the federal law. . . . Our country is set up so that we have forty-eight states and no one state has the ability to overrule our nation's government. I thought that was what our country was built around. I mean, that is why we fight. We fought in World War II together—the fellows that I know died in World War II, they died in the Korean War. I mean, why should my friends get out there and die for a cause called "democracy" when I can't exercise my rights—tell me that.

ROBIN: I agree with Ernest.

JOE: Well, Sammy, I don't know what freedom has been taken away from you because the truth there—I know as a senior myself—the troops haven't kept me from going to my classes or participating in any school activity. I mean, they're there just to keep order in case—I might use the term "hotheads"—get riled up. But I think as long as—if parents would just stay out of it and let the children of the school at Central High figure it out for themselves, I think it would be a whole lot better. I think the students are mature enough to figure it out for themselves. . . . As far as I'm concerned, I'll lay the whole blame of this trouble in Governor Faubus's lap.

SAMMY: I think we knew before this ever started that some day we were going to have to integrate the schools. And I think that our Governor was trying to protect all of us when he called out the National Guard—and he was trying to prepare us, I think.

Ernest: . . . Well, I have to disagree. . . . I know a student that's over there with us, Elizabeth, and that young lady, she walked two blocks, I guess—as you all know—and the mob was behind her. Did the troops break up the mob?

Robin: . . . And when Elizabeth had to walk down in front of the school I was there and I saw that. And may I say, I was very ashamed—I felt like crying—because she was so brave when she did that. And we just weren't behaving ourselves—just jeering her. I think if we had had any sort of decency, we wouldn't have acted that way. But I think if everybody would just obey the Golden Rule—do unto others as you would have others do unto you—might be the solution. How would you like to have to . . . walk down the street with everybody yelling behind you like they yelled behind Elizabeth?

Mrs. Ricketts: Sammy, why do these children not want to go to school with Negroes?

Sammy: Well, I think it is mostly race mixing.

Mrs. Ricketts: Race mixing? What do you mean?

Sammy: Well, marrying each other.

Minnijean: Hold your hand up. I'm brown, You are white. What's the difference? We are all of the same thoughts. You're thinking about your boy—he's going to the Navy. I'm thinking about mine—he's in the Air Force. We think about the same thing.

Sammy: Ill have to agree with you.

Ernest: Well, getting back to this intermarriage and all that. I don't know [where] people get all that. Why do I want to go to school? To marry with someone? I mean, school's not a marriage bureau. . . . I'm going there for an education. Really, if I'm going there to socialize, I don't need to be going to school. I can stand out on the corner and socialize, as far as that.

Minnijean: Kay, Joe and Robin—do you know anything about me, or is it just that your mother has told you about Negroes? . . .

Mrs. Ricketts: . . . Have you ever really made an effort to try to find out what they're like?

Kay: Not until today.

Sammy: Not until today.

Mrs. Ricketts: And what do you think about it after today?

Kay: Well, you know that my parents and a lot of the other students and their parents think that the Negroes aren't equal to us. But—I don't know. It seems like they are, to me.

Sammy: These people are—we'll have to admit that.

Ernest: I think, like we're doing today, discussing our different views . . . if the people of Little Rock . . . would get together I believe they would find out a different story—and try to discuss the thing instead of getting out in the street and kicking people around and calling names—and all that sort of thing. If . . . people got together it would be smoothed over.

Kay: I think that if . . . our friends had been getting in this discussion today, I think that maybe some of them—not all of them—in time, they would change their mind. But probably some of them would change their mind today.

Sammy: I know now that it isn't as bad as I thought it was—after we got together and discussed it.

Kay: [Sammy and I] We both came down here today with our mind set on it [that] we weren't going to change our mind that we were fully against integration. But I know now that we're going to change our mind.

MRS. RICKETTS: What do your parents say to that?
KAY: I think I'm going to have a long talk with my parents.

The episode exposed the error in President Eisenhower's view that "you cannot change people's hearts merely by laws." It may be true that law cannot at once alter emotions. But by forcing a change in objective circumstances, law does alter patterns of conduct in ways that may, in time, change a human being's outlook. Had the law not brought Sammy Dean Parker and Kay Bacon into contact with Negro children, the racist preconceptions imbibed from their parents would have gone undisturbed. The law, in short, can change one's experience—and experience changes hearts.

But it was not the time, in the 1957-58 school year, for this lesson to be learned in Little Rock. Federal force had not lessened the determination of the segregationists, from Governor Faubus down, to bring implementation of the Supreme Court decision to a stop there and then. In the face of the pressures, the School Board late in the school year asked the federal judge then on duty there, Harry J. Lemley of Arkansas, to suspend the integration plan for two and one-half years because of the "unfavorable community attitude."

On June 27, 1958, Judge Lemley granted the request of the School Board. The tensions in Central High, he said, were "intolerable," and enforcement of the principle of desegregation would have to wait.

The Lemley decision brought a second constitutional crisis to Little Rock. The first had been one of force—a physical clash of federal and state sovereignties. The second was one of law. The question was whether the Constitution had to give way when faced with community resistance.

Inevitably, that question had to be settled in the place where the law of the Constitution had originally been decided, in the Supreme Court of the United States. After some indecisive intermediate appellate proceedings, the Court met in special session on August 28, 1958, to hear argument of the Little Rock case, *Cooper v. Aaron*. (William G. Cooper was a School Board member, John Aaron one of the Negro pupils.) In the lofty marble courtroom that afternoon there was the air of a great occasion in that court different from all other courts, given final authority to distribute sovereign power in this country. At the end of the day James Reston wrote in the *Times*:

> It was the Court, in all its majesty, that was in command today, dominating the proceedings, bringing the lawyers back to root questions, even managing to hush the normally noisy Washington crowds that rush after all great battles in the Capital.
>
> The Court may not tame the South, but at least it does something no other branch of the government manages to do. It concentrates on great rather than small issues and it provides a calm and orderly forum for their disposition.
>
> This is one of the great gaps elsewhere in the Capital. Both the executive and the legislative branches spend much of their time in trivial things that are debated in an untidy uproar. But not the Court.
>
> It was appealing again today to "the universal constituency of reason and justice." It was dealing with the momentous issues of law, and education, and human reason and at least commanding unanimous respect, if not consent.

The Court did not decide the case that day; it asked for further argument two weeks later, on September 11th. But the questions from the bench gave ample clues to the justices' frame of mind. Their questions were directed most sharply at the lawyer for the Little Rock School Board, Richard C. Butler, who argued that the people of Arkansas were confused by Governor Faubus's attacks on the School Segregation decision as unlawful and that desegregation should be postponed until a clearer "national policy could be established."

"Why aren't the two decisions of this Court a national policy?" Justice Frankfurter asked.

Chief Justice Warren intervened. "Suppose every other school board in the South," he asked, "said the same thing: 'We'll postpone this thing until the law is clarified.' How would it ever be clarified? . . .

"Can we defer a program of this kind merely because there are elements in a community that will commit violence to prevent it from going into effect?"

The Chief Justice's question was answered by the Court itself on September 12th, the day after the second argument of the case. The answer was No: The law will not give way to violent resistance. The Court unanimously rejected Judge Lemley's order for suspension of the Little Rock desegregation plan. Its opinion, filed September 29th, said: "Law and order are not here to be preserved by depriving the Negro children of their constitutional rights."

Governor Faubus had one more string to his bow. He ordered all the high schools in Little Rock closed to prevent "impending violence and disorder." They stayed closed through the 1958-59 school term. White students went to private schools, moved away, took correspondence courses—or gave up school altogether. Most of the Negroes enrolled in segregated county public schools just outside Little Rock.

At first, events seemed to be moving with the Governor. In the fall of 1958 voters ended the House career of Congressman Brooks Hays, a moderate man who had tried to bring order out of the school chaos; a write-in campaign chose in his place a militant segregationist, Dr. T. Dale Alford. The legislature armed Faubus with new weapons, such as the school-closing laws. Three members of the Little Rock School Board took a pro-Faubus view. But then the mood seemed to shift. Those three School Board members were removed by Little Rock voters in a recall election. A federal court found the school-closing laws unconstitutional. During the summer of 1959 the School Board decided to reopen the city's high schools, assigning three Negro children to Central and three to Hall, another white school.

On August 12, 1959, Elizabeth Ann Eckford, who had walked so bravely through the mob toward Central High School two years earlier, made the trip again. Again there was a mob—but this time the Little Rock police sternly maintained order. The mob and the tension gradually faded, and token desegregation of the schools was peacefully accomplished. The battle of Little Rock was over.

UNIT 5

THE MONTGOMERY BUS BOYCOTT

INTRODUCTION 276

5-1 • ARREST RECORD, ROSA PARKS, DECEMBER 1, 1955 277

5-2 • CHALLENGE AND RESPONSE IN THE MONTGOMERY BUS BOYCOTT OF 1955–1956 278
J. Mills Thornton III

5-3 • A LETTER FROM THE WOMEN'S POLITICAL COUNCIL TO THE MAYOR OF MONTGOMERY, ALABAMA 312

5-4 • SPEECH BY MARTIN LUTHER KING, JR., AT HOLT STREET BAPTIST CHURCH 314
Martin Luther King, Jr.

5-5 • "KEEP YOUR EYES ON THE PRIZE," SONG 316

INTRODUCTION

Unit 5 examines the Montgomery Bus Boycott in detail. "Challenge and Response" (1980) (5-2) by J. Mills Thornton, a native Alabaman and Professor of History at the University of Michigan, is one of the most important scholarly articles written about the Civil Rights Movement. Thornton was among the first historians to study the movement by focusing intensively on a single community. This approach, the community study, is now considered the pre-eminent method of studying the movement. The article furthers our understanding of the period by effectively connecting World War II with the 1950s, white politics with black activism, and the initial demands for an amelioration of segregation with the eventual demand for a complete end to bus segregation. Thornton's success lies, in part, in his ability to question the assumptions of scholars and then to reconstruct the chronology in surprising detail.Documents 5-3 and 5-4 provide a glimpse into the goals and tactics of African Americans around the time of the boycott. The first is a 1954 letter from the black Women's Political Council (5-3) requesting that the City Council relax segregation on the busses, foreshadowing the boycott by a year and a half. Martin Luther King's Holt Street Baptist Church speech (5-4), given just days after the arrest of Rosa Parks, was the young minister's first important speech on civil rights.

POLICE DEPARTMENT
CITY OF MONTGOMERY

Date 12-1-55 19

Complainant J.F.Blake (wm)

Address 27 No. Lewis St. Phone No.

Offense Misc. Reported By Same as above

Address Phone No.

Date and Time Offense Committed 12-1-55 6:06 pm

Place of Occurrence In Front of Empire Theatre (On Montgomery Street)

Person or Property Attacked

How Attacked

Person Wanted

Value of Property Stolen Value Recovered

Details of Complaint (list, describe and give value of property stolen)

We received a call upon arrival the bus operator said he had a colored female sitting in the white section of the bus, and would not move back.

We (Day & Mixon) also saw her.

The bus operator signed a warrant for her. Rosa Parks, (cf) 634 Cleveland Court.

Rosa Parks (cf) was charged with chapter 6 section 11 of the Montgomery City Code.

Warrant #14254

THIS OFFENSE IS DECLARED:
UNFOUNDED ☐
CLEARED BY ARREST ☐
EXCEPTIONALLY CLEARED ☐
INACTIVE (NOT CLEARED) ☐

Officers F. B. Day
D. W. Mixon

Division Patrol Time 7:00 pm
12-1-55

UNIT 5-2

Challenge and Response in the Montgomery Bus Boycott of 1955–1956

J. Mills Thornton III

Shortly after five o'clock on the evening of December 1, 1955 Mrs. Raymond A. Parks boarded the Cleveland Avenue bus of the Montgomery City Lines at Court Square in Montgomery, Alabama. She sat next to the window on the side opposite the driver, in the first row of seats in the black section of the bus. The bus driver, James F. Blake, wrenched the yellow bus into gear and headed it up Montgomery Street towards its stop in front of the Empire Theater—towards that moment when Mrs. Raymond A. Parks and James F. Blake would change the course of American history.[1] In order to understand how their disagreement could have had such an effect, one must understand the context of past experiences and relationships that shaped the reactions of Montgomerians to it.

At the end of 1955 municipal politics in Montgomery was in the midst of a fundamental transformation. For essentially the preceding half century Montgomery had been ruled by the Gunter Machine, headed for most of that time by William A. Gunter, Jr., the city's mayor from 1910 to 1915 and from 1919 to his death in 1940. Mayor Gunter had come to power after more than a dozen years of bitter factional warfare between two groups of the city's wealthy older families. Thereafter, he turned back all challenges to his rule. He could always rely upon the unwavering support of the city's morning newspaper, the Montgomery Advertiser, whose editor, Grover C. Hall, Sr., was one of his closest advisers, and upon the allegiance of the majority of Montgomery's older families. In the final two decades of his life he also had the unanimous support of city employees, whom—as a result of an act which he pushed through the state legislature—he could in effect hire and fire at will.[2]

If there were no successful challenges to the Machine after 1919, however, the unsuccessful challenges were many. During the 1920s Gunter's uncompromising opposition to the Ku Klux Klan made him a special object of Klan hatred. His repeated expressions of

Alabama Review, 1980.

disapproval for the prohibition experiment placed the Anti-Saloon League in the ranks of his enemies, and fundamentalists condemned him for his generally lax enforcement of public morality. During the 1930s he turned the city government into a relief operation, putting hundreds on the public payroll and earning the bitter hostility of fiscal conservatives for unbalancing the city budgets. At the time of his death in 1940 he was admired by much of Montgomery's upper class and by large numbers of the city's unemployed. But he was also detested by many owners of small businesses and conservative citizens, strict Baptists and Methodists, and others to whom his values—rooted in the easygoing tolerance and aristocratic paternalism of his planter and Episcopalian background—were anathema.

After Gunter's death the Machine spent the next decade searching for a leader. The mayor was immediately succeeded by Cyrus B. Brown, who had long been one of Gunter's most powerful lieutenants and was at the time president of the Montgomery County governing body, the Board of Revenue. But Brown, an elderly man, died in 1944. David Dunn, who had earlier been a political protégé of former Governor Bibb Graves, obtained Machine endorsement to succeed Brown but resigned in 1946 to go into private business.

The mayoralty then passed to City Attorney John L. Goodwyn, a cousin of Gunter's wife, whom Gunter had appointed city attorney in 1930. Goodwyn resigned in 1951 to accept a position in the state government; this position led eventually to his being appointed to the state Supreme Court. Goodwyn was succeeded by William A. "Tacky" Gayle, a Machine stalwart who had been a member of the City Commission since 1935.[3]

During this decade of rapid changes in leadership the Machine grew steadily weaker. The rapidity of these changes itself contributed to the process. Another factor in the Machine's decline was Gunter's penchant for surrounding himself with colorless, if often quite competent, administrators. Early in the century the Gunter forces had secured the abolition of the mayor-council form of government for the more easily controlled three-man commission.

In addition to the mayor there was a commissioner of public affairs, who administered the police and fire departments, and a commissioner of public works, who had charge of parks, libraries, street maintenance, and garbage collection. During the 1930s Gunter turned to two retired military men to fill these posts. Gayle, a veteran of World War I, had subsequently served as Alabama's adjutant general and had returned to active duty in World War II. In 1943 while serving in Britain as an air force colonel, Gayle was elected to his third term on the City Commission in absentia. The other commissioner, General William P. Screws, had been the commander of the Alabama contingent in the famed Rainbow Division during World War I. This tradition continued when George L. Cleere, another former state adjutant general, was selected to succeed Gayle as commissioner of public works when Gayle became mayor in 1951. These men, for all their efficiency, were by no means Gunter's equals as politicians, and without him they had trouble in holding the voters' affection.

By far the most important reason for the Machine's decline, however, was the changing character of the city's population and residence patterns. During the first half of the twentieth century Montgomery grew rapidly, at an average of 30 percent a decade. This steady growth concealed after 1940 an important change in the city's racial composition. In 1910, as Gunter was first taking office as mayor, Montgomery's white population for the first time achieved parity in numbers with blacks. During the remainder of the Gunter years the relative proportion of the two races remained stable at 55 percent white and 45 percent black. But after Mayor Gunter's death the proportions began to change, under the impact both of increased black emigration to the North and of increased rural white movement into the city. In 1950 Montgomery was 60 percent white and 40 percent black; the white population grew by 47 percent during the 1940s and the black by only 23 percent. This trend continued during the 1950s. By 1955 Montgomery contained about 120,000 people, of whom some 63 percent were white and 37 percent were black.

The increasing white population meant that the number of residents in the city who could vote was growing even faster than was the population at large. The Machine had no hold upon either the gratitude or the affection of many of these new voters. Moreover, changing residence patterns reinforced this development. Resentments of Gunter's policies on the part of the lower middle class had existed in the 1920s and 1930s, but the resentment had found little institutional support. The town was small and could sustain few institutions alternative to the ones controlled by the well-to-do. During the 1940s and early 1950s the development of housing subdivisions on the edges of the city with small homes intended for the white lower middle class, effectively separated that group from the institutional control of the upper class and the upper middle class. In the eastern section of Montgomery—Capitol Heights, Dalraida, and Chisholm—there developed churches whose congregations did not contain a mix of classes and within which leadership could therefore fall to the lower middle class. In 1931, for instance, there were only seven white Baptist churches in the city, and in 1940 there were still only eleven, but by 1952 there were twenty. The number of white churches belonging to the Pentecostal sects, always a refuge for poorer elements of the population, also advanced rapidly. In 1931 white Pentecostal congregations constituted less than a fourth of the city's white churches, but by 1940 they were a third of the total, and by 1952 almost 40 percent of it.[4]

Similarly, East Montgomery developed alternative men's clubs; the Lions Club and the Exchange Club, for instance, both established separate East Montgomery units, leaving the downtown clubs in the hands of the businessmen who had dominated them. The growth to the east also demanded new schools, and with them came PTAs to be run by men and women unlikely to be leaders in a PTA in which the various classes were commingled—as had been the case with the PTAs of the few schools in the earlier, smaller city. Power in these earlier organizations had gravitated toward social leaders. East Montgomery also developed separate shopping and entertainment areas. In these and countless other ways the simple growth of the city gave the white lower middle class a separate community life and allowed it some measure of self-consciousness as a unit.

Meanwhile, this institutional "de-intermixture" of white classes was proceeding from the other side as well when subdivisions for wealthier residents were developed in South Montgomery, particularly in the Cloverdale section. Between 1951 and 1954 no less than sixty new subdivisions were completed in East and in South Montgomery, and in 1955 another thirty-three were reported to be in the planning stages.[5]

The first hint of what these developments portended for the Machine came in the city elections of 1947, when General William P. Screws, a member of the City Commission since 1931, was challenged by a young East Montgomery schoolteacher and football coach, Earl D. James. James's connection with physical education at Capitol Heights Junior High School placed him in an excellent position to capitalize upon the emerging sense of community in that section of the city. Screws beat James in Cloverdale, while James swamped all of his opponents in Capitol Heights and also ran well in an older, lower middle class ward, Oak Park. James thus erected a majority upon a basis not previously seen in Montgomery politics. The division between South Montgomery and East Montgomery that was demonstrated in these returns was to become characteristic of municipal elections for the next thirty years.[6]

Nevertheless, the Machine did not yet foresee its doom. It still controlled two of the Commission's three seats. James proved an able and relatively tractable official. He was elected to a second term in 1951 but resigned in 1953 to enter business. In the special election to choose James's successor the newly emerging shape of city politics first became completely clear. State Representative Joe M. Dawkins gathered endorsements for his candidacy from Montgomery's most prominent citizens. In the first primary Dawkins carried every precinct in the city and missed winning without a run-off by only 523 votes. In the second primary Dawkins faced Dave Birmingham, a man whose candidacy was regarded by the city's upper class as a bad joke. Birmingham had been an early and zealous supporter of former Governor James E. Folsom, and he shared much of Folsom's aggressive hostility to the wealthy. Birmingham was a classic demagogue. During his campaign he suggested that the chlorination of the city's drinking water had caused the preceding summer's devastating polio epidemic. He charged—contrary to well-documented fact—that the red color that sometimes appeared in the water was not iron but mud. The burden of Birmingham's appeal was an attack on the Machine. Dawkins was, Birmingham said, "hogtied to the old ring masters. . . . It is never good for a city to let one 'click' [*sic*] completely dominate it. Progress would stagnate." He opposed appointive municipal boards: "The ring masters through the board masters are strangling you to death with taxes without any responsibility to you as to how they will spend this tax money." He unremittingly attacked "that cesspool of gangsters at City Hall" and particularly decried the taxes that had been levied in order to finance the extension of services to new areas of the rapidly growing city.

Birmingham beat Dawkins in the run-off by a margin of 53 percent to 47 percent. Dawkins carried the wealthier precincts; his best ward was Cloverdale. Birmingham swept the lower middle class and lower class white precincts; he ran best in Capitol Heights and did well in precincts in which a substantial minority of the voters was black. The meaning of this election for the fortunes of the disintegrating Machine was unmistakable. Advertiser editor Grover C. Hall, Jr., commented that, with Birmingham a member of the Commission, "The City Hall is going to be notably different for the foreseeable future." Doubtless, Hall had no real conception of just how right he was.[7]

The principal reason for the Machine's demise was the growing independence of the white lower middle class. Politicians called this phenomenon "the silent vote." In a 1955 article the *Advertiser's* city editor, Joe Azbell, explained the meaning of the term. In the 1920s and 1930s, in a city dominated by personal acquaintance, family alliances and personal favors rather than issues really decided the outcome of elections. But the growth of the city had added many voters to the rolls who were not members of the family alliances. The abolition of the city spoils system in favor of appointment by civil service examination had deprived the Machine of much of its power to bind voters to it by favors. By 1955, Azbell noted, voters lacked personal knowledge of the candidates and had thus begun to make voting decisions on the basis of issues, as filtered through the mass media. Politicians therefore lacked any real sense of where the voters were moving until the election returns were counted. In 1953, 1954, and 1955 knowledgeable observers had repeatedly guessed wrong about the election outcome because the voters no longer were members of cousinries or other blocs whose behavior could be predicted. Of the 1955 municipal elections Azbell commented, "No one seemed to care how the Hills were moving. No one seemed concerned about the political blocs. But twenty years ago a political observer would not dare comment on an election without first determining how the blocs were going. For the first time in city political history, ring politics played no important part in the local election, because the old ring politics has been overshadowed by a growing city where there is no control or method of determining how the voters will cast their ballot." As a result, city administrators feared their new constituents.[8]

If the growing independence of the white lower middle class was the principal factor that had altered the structure of municipal politics, another factor of almost equal significance was the newly important black vote. The white lower middle class might be unfamiliar to the politicians, but the black community was virtual *terra incognita*. The state Democratic primary of 1946 represented the first primary in which blacks could legally vote; earlier such elections had been conducted under the white primary rule, which the Supreme Court had forbidden in 1944. Because they could now participate in the only elections that mattered in Alabama, blacks sought to register in increasing numbers during the late 1940s and early 1950s, particularly in the cities. The number of blacks registered in Montgomery grew slowly but steadily, and by 1955, 7.55 percent of the city's 22,210 registered voters were black. This percentage was well above the 5 percent ratio statewide. Moreover, in some wards black voters represented a substantial proportion of the total: 31 percent in Beat 7W, almost 25 percent in Beat 2, and 20 percent in Beat 6. Seven and a half percent is quite a small figure, but given the near equiponderance in the rivalry between South Montgomery and East Montgomery during these years, blacks could easily represent a balance of power.[9]

The returns in the special election of November 1953 appeared to black leaders to demonstrate that Birmingham owed his margin of victory over Dawkins to blacks, and they prepared to press the new commissioner for interest on this debt. Moreover, Birmingham stood ready to respond, both because he needed to hold the political allegiance of the blacks and because his racial views appear to have been genuinely, remarkably liberal.[10] The inauguration of Dave Birmingham as a city commissioner, therefore, marked the beginning of a heady period for the black leadership in which it found itself with genuine access to the city government for the first time.

The most important black spokesman in making demands upon the newly constituted City Commission was Edgar D. Nixon, a sleeping-car porter who was also president of the Montgomery local of the International Brotherhood of Sleeping Car Porters. Moving beyond his union power base, Nixon in the late 1940s and early 1950s had become more and more publicly active in demanding amelioration of conditions for members of his race. Throughout these years he was the dominant figure in the Montgomery chapter of the NAACP and was state president of that organization in 1948–49. He was also president of the Montgomery chapter of the Alabama Progressive Democratic Association, which had been organized during the 1940s as a black alternative to the regular party apparatus. In 1954 he created a great stir in Montgomery as a candidate for the County Democratic Executive Committee, the first black in living memory to seek public office. Though he lost to a white candidate, Joseph W. Carroll, he won more than 42 percent of the vote in the precinct, only a fourth of whose voters were black. In 1955 Nixon sought unsuccessfully to purchase a ticket to a Jefferson-Jackson Day dinner in Birmingham; the evening's principal speaker, Governor G. Mennen Williams of Michigan, abruptly cancelled his appearance in protest against Nixon's exclusion. Such highly visible efforts made Nixon the best known "activist" in Montgomery and gave him a considerable following in the black community.[11]

Equally as prominent in the dealings with the City Commission were two other blacks, Rufus A. Lewis and Mrs. Jo Ann Robinson. A former football coach at Alabama State College, Lewis was at the time a successful businessman and the chairman of the Citizens' Steering Committee, a group that had been formed in the fall of 1952 to press for better treatment for blacks. Mrs. Robinson, an English teacher at Alabama State College, was the moving spirit behind the black Women's Political Council, a group organized in 1949 to urge black women to register to vote; thereafter, the Council became the most militant and uncompromising organ of the black community. Led by Mrs. Robinson, Mrs. Mary Fair Burks, and Mrs. Thelma Glass, all of the Alabama State College faculty, and Mrs. A. Wayman West, Jr., the wife of a dentist, and sometimes aided by the more moderate Federation of Negro Women's Clubs, the Council repeatedly protested to the City Commission against discrimination and injustice in Montgomery. Indeed, with exceptions such as Nixon and Lewis, the blacks who addressed complaints to the City Commission in this period usually were women.[12]

The election of Dave Birmingham encouraged these groups for the first time to seek redress from the city government for long-standing grievances: the lack of black policemen, the inadequacy of parks and playgrounds in black sections of the city, and the conditions on the city buses. Immediately after Birmingham's election the Montgomery County Grand jury and the Montgomery *Advertiser* had both urged the city to join Dothan, Anniston, and Talladega in hiring black policemen. Possibly supporters of the Machine saw this action as a way to cope with Birmingham's popularity in the black community. But the two Machine commissioners apparently remained dubious. After

Birmingham's inauguration a delegation of black leaders met with the Commission; at this meeting Birmingham extracted from his colleagues a promise to hire black officers if funds could be found to pay their salaries. Birmingham continued to press the proposal and finally, in early May 1954, succeeded in obtaining the addition of four blacks to the force. Their hiring caused consternation among the city's extreme segregationists, whose resentment expressed itself two years later, during the boycott, when the home of one of the four, Patrolman Arthur G. Worthy, became a target for bombers. In the summer of 1955 Police Chief Goodwyn J. Ruppenthal sought to placate still hostile citizens by reassuring them that the new policemen were "just niggers doing a nigger's job."[13] But the doubts of many Montgomerians were not so easily assuaged, and the controversy rendered Birmingham's two colleagues increasingly unwilling to join him in taking other similar actions. The Machine could not afford to alienate either black or white segregationist voters. This difficulty virtually immobilized the two Machine commissioners on every racial issue from late 1953 through early 1955, as the city prepared for the crucial municipal elections of late March 1955. In addition, their position was rendered even more awkward by the considerable heightening of white fears and black hopes that followed the Supreme Court's school integration decision in mid-May 1954.

Meanwhile, no such hesitation bound Birmingham or the black leadership. The question of parks in black areas escalated to a new level of public controversy in January 1955, when a delegation from the Women's Political Council appeared at a City Commission meeting to urge the appointment of a black to the city Parks and Recreation Board and to suggest Council member Mrs. A. Wayman West, Jr., for the position. Commissioner Birmingham immediately moved that the next vacancy go to a black, but Mayor Gayle persuaded him to withdraw the motion until a vacancy actually occurred. The mayor, who had actively supported a city program under which three new playgrounds for blacks had been recently built, assured the delegation that its request would be given every consideration when there was a vacancy. He continued his effort to define a medial position later in the same week when he appeared before a large group of blacks gathered to celebrate the inauguration of Governor James E. Folsom and there praised the work of the city's black policemen. But the question of black representation on the Parks and Recreation Board could not be dismissed so easily. It was to become a principal issue in the city elections in March. In August, Commissioner Birmingham, now a lame duck, offered a motion to expand the Parks and Recreation Board from five to seven members and to designate the two new places for blacks, but Gayle and Cleere voted the resolution down. However, the mayor in July and the Parks and Recreation Board in September assured angry black delegations that if the city's voters would approve the proposed issuance of a million dollars in parks bonds, significant improvements in Negro parks would immediately be forthcoming.[14]

While the public was concerned with the issues of black policemen and black membership on the Parks and Recreation Board, tension over racial relations on the city's buses had quietly been mounting. At the end of 1953, encouraged by Birmingham's recent election, the Women's Political Council met with the city Commission to lodge three complaints: that blacks sometimes had to stand beside empty seats, in cases where the black section was filled but the white section was not; that black passengers were compelled to get on at the front door to pay their fare and then to get off and to reboard at the back door to take a seat, rather than being permitted simply to walk down the aisle of the bus; and that buses stopped at every corner in white neighborhoods but only at every other corner in black neighborhoods. Allegations of discourtesy by drivers and of buses' passing by waiting black passengers were also made. The meeting was inconclusive, but representatives of the bus lines, who were present, evidently offered to investigate specific charges of discourtesy. Several months later, in the spring of 1954, the Women's Political Council again met with the Commission and representatives of the bus company to reiterate its three complaints and to offer a list of specific instances of abuse by bus drivers. At this meeting the delegation from the Political Council was accompanied by Rufus Lewis representing the Citizens' Steering Committee, by a delegation from the Federation of Negro Women's Clubs, and by a large group representing black trade union locals. At this meeting as at the earlier one the principal spokesman for the blacks was Jo Ann Robinson of the Political Council.

As a result of this meeting the problem of buses' stopping only at every other corner in black areas was remedied. Addressing the issue of seating, the Commission, on the advice of City Attorney Walter Knabe and bus company attorney Jack Crenshaw, informed the blacks that it was legally powerless to do anything about the problem of black passengers' being compelled to stand beside empty seats. The city ordinance and the state statute on the subject were both read aloud to the petitioners. The meeting was evidently a stormy one. Subsequently, Mayor Gayle testified that several days later Mrs. Robinson called him angrily "and said they would just show me, they were going in the front door and sitting wherever they pleased." In April 1954 the Reverend Uriah J. Fields, a militant young black minister who was later to break spectacularly with Martin King, brought the seating complaints before the public with a letter to the Montgomery Advertiser demanding that the policy be altered. There the matter rested until the following spring.[15]

Meantime, the elections that could kill the already moribund Machine were approaching. Gayle and Cleere both sought re-election. Gayle's only opponent was Harold McGlynn, a candy wholesaler who was a political associate of Commissioner Birmingham. Cleere's principal opposition came from Frank Parks, an East Montgomery interior decorator who was a former Grand Master of Alabama's Masons. Parks set out to create an electoral coalition like that which had enabled Birmingham to upset Dawkins a year and a half earlier. Though Gayle and Cleere supported each other, and Birmingham supported McGlynn and Parks, it is unclear whether or not Gayle and Cleere supported one of the candidates opposing Birmingham; at any rate, they did not do so publicly. Birmingham drew two principal opponents. Sam B. Stearns, the owner of a downtown parking garage and a nephew of a former Montgomery County sheriff, ran a vigorous and well-financed campaign, but the returns showed him much less popular than observers had thought. The real threat to the incumbent was former State Representative Clyde C. Sellers, a resident of South Montgomery and the owner of an exterminating business. Sellers effectively emphasized his extensive experience in law enforcement; he had joined the state Highway Patrol shortly after its formation, had worked his way up through its ranks, and in 1945 had been appointed director of the department by Governor Chauncey Sparks. His four years in the state legislature also strengthened his credentials. That he had been a star football player for Auburn University in the 1920s gave him additional popularity. But the issue that was to carry him to victory was provided by the events of the canvass.

Birmingham launched a typically demagogic campaign. His two colleagues on the Commission had voted to increase the city sewerage fee in order to finance the extension of sewer mains into the Allendale-Wildwood section, a South Montgomery area. Birmingham denounced this decision as class legislation and demanded that the wealthy homeowners in the section pay for the sewers themselves. Frank Parks loudly echoed this argument. Birmingham revived his accusation that chlorination of the water supply was dangerous; he alleged as proof that city water would kill camellia bushes. He also charged that Gayle and Cleere might have favored the construction of a city sewage treatment plant only in order to make a private profit by selling the plant's effluent for fertilizer. With such allegations Birmingham hoped to hold, and Parks to build, constituencies of whites of the lower class and the lower middle class. McGlynn refused to stoop to this level, and perhaps for that reason his campaign against Gayle never really gained momentum. McGlynn did join Birmingham and Parks in a strong effort to gain the allegiance of the black vote.[16]

As the campaign of 1955 began, black leaders hoped to use the black balance of power between South Montgomery and East Montgomery to extract real concessions from the candidates. They had just passed through a year in which the city government had shown unprecedented willingness to listen to their proposals. Birmingham, Parks, and McGlynn were eager for black support. One of Birmingham's opponents, Stearns, was equally as willing to seek black votes. Nor, indeed, were Gayle and Cleere hostile. Though more reticent than were their opponents about openly campaigning for black ballots, still both men were racial moderates. The remnants of the Machine that they represented could command a certain residue of good will in the black community. Mayor Gunter's actions in the 1920s and 1930s had endeared him to many blacks, and after World War II the Machine-dominated city government had constructed a number of low-rent public housing projects for poor blacks. By 1955 the Montgomery Housing Authority, which was headed by the late Mayor Gunter's son-in-law Charles P. Rogers, administered four such developments and had a fifth in the planning stages. Its public housing record was not an unmixed asset for the Machine, however, because many blacks resented the demolition of their homes and their removal into crowded apartments, however modern.[17]

All of these circumstances so emboldened the leaders that they decided in February to hold a public meeting in order to question the various Commission candidates about their stands on racial issues. The candidates subsequently also appeared before organized labor and the Junior Chamber of Commerce.[18] But the spectacle of office seekers appearing before blacks to submit to interrogation was a sight for which the electorate was unprepared.

The meeting, held under the auspices of Nixon's Progressive Democratic Association, convened in the Ben Moore Hotel, the city's only black hotel, on the evening of February 23. All of the candidates were present. The session commenced with Nixon's distributing to them a questionnaire asking their position on a number of specific black grievances. The first area of complaint on the list was "the present bus situation. Negroes have to stand over empty seats of city buses, because the first ten seats are reserved for whites who sometime never ride. We wish to fill the bus from the back toward the front until all seats are taken. This is done in Atlanta, Georgia, Mobile, Alabama and in most of our larger southern cities." Next came requests that a black be appointed to the Parks and Recreation Board and that blacks be considered for all municipal boards. The third subject mentioned was the lack of middle-class housing subdivisions for relatively well-to-do blacks. The authors of the questionnaire had been upset by the city's decision a week earlier to forbid the development of such an area because of the protests of neighboring whites. The fourth plea was that qualified black applicants be considered for civil service jobs with the city. "Everybody cannot teach," the questionnaire noted, in reference to the limited professional opportunities available to Montgomery's middle-class blacks. The document concluded with three complaints about the inadequacy of city services in black neighborhoods. It asked for the installation of more fireplugs in these sections, the extension of sewer mains to eliminate outdoor privies, and the widening and paving of streets and the addition of curbing.

In their responses Birmingham, McGlynn, and Parks all agreed to appoint a black member of the Parks and Recreation Board. Stearns, who had adopted the strategy of attempting to defeat Birmingham by outbidding him for the allegiance of the city's various groups, also agreed, and added a proposal for a sixteen-member all-black advisory board as an adjunct of the Parks Board. The press reported that black leaders were as a result closely divided as to whether they should endorse Birmingham or Stearns. Gayle and Cleere remained noncommittal on the Parks Board issue. Sellers gave a general talk that did not speak to any of the points in the questionnaire; he said later that he did not see the document until the end of the meeting. Accounts of the session do not indicate any reply by any of the candidates to the questionnaire's proposal on bus seating.[19]

After the candidates had completed their presentations, the meeting adjourned, but its repercussions were still being felt years later. Clyde Sellers quickly saw that the black proposals and their deferential handling by his two opponents presented him with the issue that would allow him to win a majority. It appeared that Stearns and Birmingham were going to divide the black vote. Sellers, as a South Montgomerian, could count on a large vote from that section in response to Birmingham's vociferous attacks on its residents. Previously, though, there had seemed to be no way to cut into Birmingham's solid following in East Montgomery. Now, demagogic exploitation of racial tensions promised to counter Birmingham's exploitation of class tensions and thus to capture support in the eastern wards. During March, before the election on the 21st, Sellers made the most blatantly and insistently racist addresses heard in Montgomery since the days of J. Johnston Moore, the Ku Klux Klan's candidate against Mayor Gunter in the 1920s. Sellers converted the Ben Moore Hotel meeting into the principal issue of the canvass. He answered the questionnaire point by point in his speeches and advertisements. He asserted flatly that the blacks' bus seating proposal would violate state law-not bothering to explain how, in that case, the system could be used in Mobile. He pledged himself to oppose the appointment of blacks to city boards. To the request that qualified blacks be allowed to apply for civil service jobs, he said, "If the commission were to comply with this request, it would be only a short time before negroes would be working along side of whites and whites along side of negroes . . . I have always felt that if a man wanted a job bad enough, he could go where the job, for which he is qualified, is available. There are places in this nation where civil service jobs for negroes in cities are available but not in Montgomery. I will expend every effort to keep it that way."[20] Sellers's campaign was aided by the first of the bus incidents, the arrest on March 2 and the trial on March 18 of Claudette Colvin for violation of the segregation ordinance.

Sellers had been correct about the effect of his racial appeal upon the electorate. In the returns he took 43 percent of the poll, to 37 percent for Birmingham, 16 percent for Stearns, and 4 percent for a minor candidate, John T. Weaver. Birmingham carried the wards with substantial black registration and also took the poorest white wards. But the white lower middle class areas of East Montgomery that he had swept in 1953 now went to Sellers. Capitol Heights, which had given Birmingham 62 percent of its vote in 1953, making it his banner precinct, now gave him only 31 percent, to 44 percent for Sellers. At the same time South Montgomery voted heavily against Birmingham; Sellers took 60 percent of the poll in Cloverdale. Despite Sellers's solid lead over Birmingham, a run-off between the two men would have been necessary. However, two days after the election Birmingham collapsed while preparing to give a television speech; his doctor diagnosed his condition as "overexertion and exhaustion" and advised him to withdraw from the race. Birmingham did so, and Sellers was declared elected. We can never know whether Birmingham could have defeated Sellers. Birmingham had come back from an even more substantial deficit to defeat Dawkins in 1953, but Birmingham's chances of repeating this accomplishment in 1955 were poor. Sam B. Stearns, the third important candidate in the race, had made shrill personal attacks on Birmingham. It is unlikely that a white voter who had cast his ballot for Stearns in the first round would thereafter have moved to the support of Birmingham.

In the mayoral election McGlynn had seldom indulged in the demagogic appeals of Birmingham and Parks. He may have been hurt by the fact that he was a Roman Catholic, but on that point evidence is lacking. Although McGlynn received 40 percent of the vote and carried the wards with substantial black registration and also the city's poorest white ward, West End, nevertheless Mayor Gayle won easily.

In the election for commissioner of public works the incumbent, George Cleere, had refused to follow Sellers in exploiting the racial issue. Instead, he had attempted to answer with reason the strident class-oriented accusations of Parks, particularly with reference to the sewerage fee. The result was that Parks was elected on returns whose geographical distribution was virtually identical to the distribution of the support for Birmingham in his race against Dawkins in 1953. Cleere swept the South Montgomery wards, taking more than 75 percent of the vote in Cloverdale, but Parks carried the substantially black precincts and those of the white lower class and lower middle class.[21]

The election's outcome puzzled Grover C. Hall, Jr.; why should the voters have elected Parks, Birmingham's ally, over Cleere, Gayle's ally, but then have repudiated Birmingham himself and returned Gayle?[22] The meaning of the election was probably much clearer to Gayle, now the sole Machine survivor in municipal politics, seated between an uncompromising segregationist on his right and an adversary of Montgomery's wealthy on his left. The Machine's traditional policies of moderate, paternalistic racial attitudes, and a firm alliance with the city's upper class had failed to sustain it, and they held little likelihood of endearing Gayle to the constituencies that had elevated either of his two colleagues. Clearly, Gayle needed a new strategy immediately. The lesson of Parks's victory appeared to be that, given the new social realities produced by the city's rapid postwar growth, an East Montgomerian would always defeat a South Montgomerian when the issues remained class oriented. The lesson of Sellers's victory appeared to be that the vigorous exploitation of racial antipathies could give a South Montgomerian at least a fighting chance of defeating an East Montgomerian. Gayle was, of course, a South Montgomerian. But Gayle's dilemma was much more complicated than this analysis would imply. First, he was unlikely to abandon a set of beliefs that he had held sincerely for many decades merely because political strategy seemed to dictate this course. Second, developments within the business community rendered it less than certain that a sound strategy actually dictated this course. To understand this factor, we must briefly explore the attitude of Montgomery's businessmen towards their city government.

The business community believed that the source of all genuine social ills was the lack of industrialization. Montgomery's economy rested primarily on the presence of the state government and of two air force bases, Maxwell and Gunter. One in every seven families in the city was an air force family in 1955. Aside from income generated by federal and state governmental expenditures, Montgomery relied almost exclusively on its role as a marketing center for the surrounding agricultural area.[23] By 1955 businessmen were armed with legislation passed during the preceding decade providing Alabama municipalities with powerful tools for attracting industry to the state, particularly in the form of tax advantages and of public financing of plant construction. Business leaders therefore had high hopes of broadening Montgomery's economic base.

This zealous commitment to industrialization was the source of the tension between businessmen and the city government. Business leaders believed that the city's politicians had been inept in attracting industry. Near the end of October 1953 the *Advertiser* had broken the story that DuPont had purchased 850 acres near Montgomery "as a prospective site for an industrial plant." The article had concluded excitedly, "Announcement is expected soon on the type of plant to be constructed." Months passed, and no such announcement was forthcoming. Reportedly, four other "very large companies" that had considered building factories in Montgomery had been lost to other cities during 1954 and 1955. Worried businessmen sought to discover what they were doing wrong. The Chamber of Commerce desperately debated ways to attract favorable national publicity for the city. Chamber of Commerce President James G. Pruett ominously warned the Rotary Club that "industry will come to Montgomery and Alabama only when there is a healthy climate for it and when government on all levels is not hostile to it." In this atmosphere of frustration at the repeated recent failure in the drive for industrialization, forty of the city's most important businessmen met in mid-October 1955 to organize the Men of Montgomery. Adopting the frank motto "We Mean Business," they chose as their first project a campaign to compel the City Commission to act on a proposal that had languished in the City Hall bureaucracy for years: to construct a new terminal for the municipal airport to give visitors to the city a more favorable first impression.[24]

Mayor Gayle had always counted on business support. The Gunter Machine had been closely allied with business interests. Gayle himself was a brother-in-law of one of the most influential businessmen in Alabama, Birmingham industrialist Donald Comer of Avondale Mills.[25] Now the mayor faced a business community organized with a new efficiency and motivated by a new hostility. By the fall of 1955 his dilemma was acute. His colleagues on the Commission each represented constituencies only recently defined, and Gayle had no real access to either. The black leadership was making militant demands upon the city for the first time and was asking for public responses. The business community was suddenly dubious of his competence and disposed to press him for positive action. If he moved towards one of the newly emerging constituencies, he risked permanently alienating the elements in the city politics which he had relied ever since he had first entered politics. Against this background the city moved towards the events of early December.

At the Ben Moore Hotel meeting on February 23 bus seating had headed the list of grievances. On the afternoon of March 2 came the arrest of Claudette Colvin, a fifteen-year-old black girl who refused to vacate her seat when ordered to do so by a bus driver, Robert W. Cleere. Miss Colvin, who was returning from school, was seated far back in the bus, just forward of the rear door, on a seat with an older black woman, a Mrs. Hamilton. The bus was entirely filled, and Cleere ordered the two blacks to stand in order to give their seats to boarding whites. Mrs. Hamilton refused, and Cleere summoned police. When the police arrived, a black man got up, gave his seat to Mrs. Hamilton, and left the bus. Miss Colvin, who apparently was led into her resistance by the actions of Mrs. Hamilton, now found herself deserted to face the music alone. She became hysterical, kicked and scratched the arresting officers, and had to be carried bodily from the bus.[26]

Because of her age Miss Colvin was brought to trial before Juvenile Court Judge Wiley C. Hill, Jr., a first cousin of U.S. Senator J. Lister Hill. She was not the first person to be arrested for violation of the bus seating ordinance, but according to Commissioner Birmingham she was the first person ever to enter a plea of not guilty to such a charge. Her twenty-four-year-old attorney, Fred D. Gray, one of two black lawyers in Montgomery, interposed two defenses. The first, that segregated seating violated the U.S. Constitution, was overruled in short order by Judge Hill. The second defense was more troublesome. When the city ordinance requiring segregation on public conveyances had first been adopted in 1900, it had provoked a black boycott of the city trolley lines. This boycott had lasted throughout the summer of 1900 and had ended only when the City Council agreed to amend the new ordinance to forbid compelling anyone to vacate his seat unless there was another seat to which he could move. This proviso remained a part of the city code. Because both sides in the Colvin case agreed that the bus had been entirely filled, the bus driver, rather than Miss Colvin, had violated the segregation ordinance.

State laws supersede city ordinances, however. In 1945 the state legislature had enacted a statute requiring the Alabama Public Service Commission to see that all bus companies under its jurisdiction enforced racially segregated seating. This statute, unlike the city ordinance, gave bus drivers absolute power to seat passengers. It was unclear whether or not the Public Service Commission had jurisdiction over municipal bus lines. A year later the state was to contend in federal court that the state law was inapplicable in such situations in order to avoid having it at issue in the suit seeking to declare the segregation of Montgomery buses unconstitutional. Now Circuit Solicitor William F. Thetford moved to meet Gray's defense by amending the complaint so as to allege a violation of the state law rather than of the city ordinance. Judge Hill overruled Gray's objection that the state law did not apply, found Miss Colvin guilty both of violating the state bus segregation statute and of assault and battery on the arresting officer, declared her a juvenile delinquent, and ordered her placed on probation. Gray filed an appeal to Circuit Court, but on the appeal the state pressed only the charge of assault and battery, and on that ground Miss Colvin's sentence of probation was affirmed. As a result Gray was deprived of any way to use this case as a means to contest the various questions that had been raised with regard to the segregation laws.[27]

Meanwhile, Miss Colvin's arrest had moved the city's black leaders to make one more effort to deal with the bus problem through the political mechanism. In mid-March, as the municipal election campaign climaxed, blacks arranged two meetings with white officials. At the first one Commissioner Birmingham and the bus company's manager James H. Bagley met in Bagley's office with a delegation that included the Reverend Martin L. King, Jr., a twenty-six-year-old Baptist minister who had moved to Montgomery the preceding September to take up his first pastorate, and who in the intervening six months had become quite active in the city's NAACP chapter. It appears that, at this meeting as at earlier ones, the principal spokesman for the blacks was a conspicuous member of King's new congregation, Jo Ann Robinson.

This encounter was relatively amicable. Birmingham was eager to conciliate the blacks, and Bagley did not wisk to offend his customers gratuitously. The black delegation pointed out that forcing a passenger to stand in order to seat another passenger violated both company policy and the provisions of the city code. Bagley acknowledged that the policy did forbid such action; he promised to investigate and to reprimand the bus driver in the Colvin case if it was warranted. The blacks evidently brought up the seating plan proposed in the questionnaire presented at the Ben Moore Hotel meeting; Birmingham promised to secure a formal opinion from City Attorney Walter Knabe on what seating arrangements were legally permissible. Unfortunately, nothing came of either of these promises.[28]

Birmingham's failure to act is understandable; within two weeks he was a lame duck, his influence greatly diminished and his health precarious. Bagley's inattention to the matter was simply shortsighted. A principal source of friction on the buses was the company's loosely defined seating policy. In practice the policy varied enormously from route to route and from driver to driver. Even under the company's official policy, the middle sixteen seats of the bus had no fixed racial designation; it was the responsibility of the driver to shift the racial line forward or back in order to provide a number of seats roughly proportionate to the racial composition of the group of riders at any given moment. Under these circumstances the drivers had to reseat passengers rather frequently. The embarrassment and humiliation to blacks of being thus publicly forced to acknowledge and accept legal discrimination was exacerbated by the fact that the harried drivers usually adjusted the seating simply by shouting peremptory commands over their shoulders. If Bagley had attempted to specify the seating policy more fully and had sought more vigorously to enforce company rules requiring courtesy from drivers, he could have eliminated much of the ill will between the bus line and the black community. If he had emphasized to the drivers the company policy against unseating passengers when other seats were unavailable, he would have forestalled both the Claudette Colvin and the Rosa Parks incidents.[29]

The second meeting in response to Miss Colvin's arrest appears to have been much stormier than that with Bagley and Birmingham. Bagley arranged this meeting for the blacks. The black delegation included, as usual, members of the black Women's Political Council and the Federation Negro Women's Clubs. It also included Rufus A. Lewis of the Citizens' Steering Committee and attorney Fred Gray. Mayor Gayle and City Attorney Knabe represented the city. The bus company was represented by its attorney, Jack Crenshaw. The blacks apparently pressed the seating proposal contained in the questionnaire distributed at the Ben Moore Hotel meeting. Gray believed that the proposal violated no existing law. Crenshaw adamantly maintained that the proposal flouted both the city ordinance and the state statute, an opinion in which Knabe concurred.

The importance of Crenshaw's intransigence both in producing and in sustaining the bus boycott can hardly be overstated. He was an excellent lawyer, educated at Harvard. He was a political ally of the racially moderate Governor Folsom. Despite this background, however, he proved incapable of understanding the strategic advantage of accepting a modest compromise in order to forestall a full-scale assault on segregation. He dismissed Gray's arguments out of hand and informed Bagley that the law left the bus company absolutely no room for compromise. The meeting adjourned with the complaints of the blacks still unanswered.[30]

Through the summer and fall of 1955 a series of events kept the bus question before the public. Early in the year a black woman, Sarah Mae Flemming, had sued the city bus line of Columbia, South Carolina, for damages for its having enforced the segregation laws against her. In mid-July the U.S. Court of Appeals for the Fourth Circuit ruled in this case that segregated seating on buses was unconstitutional—a decision that received headline treatment in the Montgomery *Advertiser.* Later in July a young black, James M. Ritter, had defied the order of a bus driver in Richmond, Virginia, to move to the rear and had been fined ten dollars for his action. In Montgomery itself another black teenager, Mary Louise Smith, was arrested on October 21 for refusing to yield her seat to a white woman. This case did not create the furor which the Colvin incident had, however, because Miss Smith chose to plead guilty; she was fined five dollars.[31]

Equally important in focusing attention on the bus company was the fact that its franchise was about to expire. National City Lines, Inc., of Chicago, owned the Montgomery bus company. That firm had been granted a twenty-year city franchise in 1936; the franchise would come up for renewal in March of 1956. In late October an official of the company came to Montgomery to open negotiations. He and the city commissioners surveyed the city from the air in order to plan revisions in the bus routes, and delegations from a number of the new subdivisions on the city's outskirts appeared before the Commission to seek the extension of bus service to their areas. At the same time the bus company was bargaining with the bus drivers' union for a new two-year contract. Montgomerians who recalled that all bus service had been suspended during a brief strike in December 1953 watched the progress of the negotiations apprehensively.[32]

In the fall of 1955 the press was filled with accounts of events in Selma. There a group of twenty-nine blacks in September petitioned the city board of education urging the integration of the schools. In mid-September the head of the recently organized Dallas County White Citizens Council, attorney M. Alston Keith, reported that the efforts of the Council had resulted in the firing of sixteen of the twenty-nine petitioners from their jobs. Blacks retaliated by refusing to buy the milk of a dairy that had agreed to discharge a petitioner. Next came incidents of arson and kidnapping, both directed against a black grocer who had been a participant in the boycott of the dairy. Finally, in late October six young white men, two of them members of the Selma police force, were arrested and indicted for the actions directed at the grocer, and one of the accused policemen thereupon committed suicide.[33]

In early November black Congressman Adam Clayton Powell visited Montgomery to speak to the Progressive Democratic Association. Congressman Powell spent the night at the home of Edgar D. Nixon. In his speech Powell warned the Citizens Councils that their economic pressure "can be counter met with our own [black] economic pressure." The example of the events in Selma and the force of Powell's remark doubtless made an impact upon Nixon, who because of his background in the labor movement and because of his long association with and intense admiration for his union's president, A. Philip Randolph, was predisposed in any case to believe in the efficacy of economic action.[34]

The arrest of Rosa Parks struck a spark to this tinder. When Mrs. Parks boarded the bus, it was divided into twenty-six seats for blacks and ten for whites. Two blocks farther on, when the bus stopped in front of the Empire Theater, it was completely filled, and both whites and blacks were standing; all white standing room was taken. Driver James F. Blake undertook to readjust the seating to a more equitable ratio by clearing one row of seats, altering the racial division to fourteen white and twenty-two black. Since the four unseated blacks would have to stand, Blake's action violated both company policy and the city code. At the same time, inasmuch as company policy forbade allowing whites to stand in the black section, if Blake had not taken his action, none of the whites waiting to board could have been accommodated, although standing room was available in the rear of the bus.

Rosa Parks had been for most of the preceding decade the secretary of the Montgomery chapter of the NAACP. She had grown up on a farm in southern Montgomery County. Against great odds she obtained a high school diploma in 1933. Montgomery then provided no public high school for blacks. But Mrs. Parks's family, ambitious for her advancement, had arranged to send her to the laboratory school of Alabama State College. Although she thus became one of a very small number of black high school graduates in the city, she found herself unable to obtain employment commensurate with her educational level. She worked at a number of relatively menial jobs; in 1955 she was a seamstress altering ready-to-wear clothes in the city's principal department store, the Montgomery Fair. This situation very probably produced a certain bitterness in her and contributed to her decision during World War II to become an active member of the NAACP. She was elected the chapter secretary in 1943 and later also became the adviser to the chapter's youth auxiliary. She had therefore been particularly concerned with the arrest of Claudette Colvin. In the summer of 1955 she had attended an integrated seminar on race relations at the Highlander Folk School, an invitation she had received at the suggestion of Mrs. Clifford J. Durr, the wife of a liberal white attorney. Mrs. Parks worked for Mrs. Durr on a part-time basis as a seamstress. All of these circumstances had made Mrs. Parks peculiarly sensitive to the importance of the series of meetings, petitions, and remonstrances in relation to the bus situation during the years before 1955. We may well suppose that, had she not been so intimately connected with the controversy, she might have been inclined to join the other three blacks on the row of seats in obeying Blake's instruction. But she, alone of the four, did not move. Blake summoned the police, who took her to the city jail. From the jail she contacted her colleague in the NAACP chapter, Edgar D. Nixon. Nixon made bond for her.[35]

If Mrs. Parks had not been a close friend of Nixon's and a prominent figure in the black community, Nixon might not have been moved to such decisive action, and the people whom he contacted might not have responded so readily. But Mrs. Parks and her husband, a barber at Maxwell Air Force Base who had resided in the city for more than a quarter of a century, were distinctly civic leaders and, at least socially, members of the middle class. Nixon returned from the jail and began calling the city's most prominent blacks to suggest that blacks stage a strike of the buses. Those called phoned others. One of those calls took the matter out of Nixon's hands. Attorney Fred Gray called Jo Ann Robinson.

Mrs. Robinson and her associates in the Women's Political Council saw Rosa Parks as one of their own, a woman of similar social status and community standing. The Council did not await the outcome of Nixon's consultations; it acted. Early the next morning, December 2, Mrs. Robinson mimeographed at her office at Alabama State College a call for a boycott of city buses on December 5, the day of Mrs. Parks's trial: "Another Negro woman has been arrested and thrown into jail because she refused to get up out of her seat on the bus and give it to a white person. It is the second time since the Claudette Colbert [*sic*] case that a Negro has been arrested for the same thing. This must be stopped. . . . Until we do something to stop these arrests, they will continue. The next time it may be you or you or you." Council members busied themselves throughout the afternoon and evening of December 2 distributing these handbills in the black sections of the City.[36]

Meanwhile, Nixon's calls to black civic leaders during the night of December 1 and the morning of December 2 had produced sufficient support for a boycott to set up a meeting for the night of December 2 at the Dexter Avenue Baptist Church. But when the forty or so leaders convened, they found themselves faced with a *fait accompli* because of the action of the Women's Political Council during the afternoon. The meeting was reduced to attempting to assure that the boycott that had been called by the handbills would be successful. Committees were appointed to attend to various organizational details, and a mass meeting was scheduled for the night of December 5 to consider future action in the light of how successful the boycott that day might prove.[37]

When sixteen black leaders met on the afternoon of December 5 to plan the evening's mass meeting, they considered two new pieces of information. The boycott had been brilliantly successful, far more so than leaders had permitted themselves to hope. And Rosa Parks had been convicted and fined ten dollars. At the trial City Prosecutor D. Eugene Loe had faced the problem of the city code's prohibition of unseating a passenger unless another seat was available and had met it as had Solicitor Thetford in the Colvin case, by moving to amend the complaint so as to allege a violation of the state law rather than of the city ordinance. Mrs. Parks's attorney, Fred Gray, had again contended that the state law did not apply to municipal bus lines, but his argument had been overruled by Recorder's Court Judge John B. Scott, a nephew and appointee of the late Mayor Gunter.[38]

The success of the boycott's first day and the conviction of Mrs. Parks made it clear that the boycott would continue, at least until the blacks received conciliatory overtures from the city. The sixteen persons present at the afternoon meeting decided to create a formal organization to run the boycott. At the suggestion of the Reverend Ralph D. Abernathy, twenty-nine-year-old pastor of the First Baptist Church (black), they adopted the name Montgomery Improvement Association. They constituted themselves the Association's Executive Board and proceeded to choose officers. Presiding at this meeting, as at the meeting on December 2, was the Reverend L. Roy Bennett, a Methodist who was the president of the black Interdenominational Ministerial Alliance. Bennett's gavel had been wielded in an extremely high-handed fashion at the December 2 session, thus provoking much resentment. When Bennett opened the floor for nominations for president of the new organization, Rufus A. Lewis of the Citizens' Steering Committee saw an opportunity to depose Bennett gracefully. He suggested Martin L. King. Lewis, as a member of King's church, had some knowledge of King's talents; King had recently submitted a dissertation to Boston University for the S.T.D. degree, which marked him as considerably better educated than most of Montgomery's black ministers. The selection of King did not proceed, however, from any clear recognition of his potential for leadership but rather from general hostility to Bennett. Lewis chose King largely because King was Lewis's pastor. King was quickly and unanimously elected, and Bennett was then made vice-president. King's election determined the element within the MIA that would become dominant in shaping its policy. Bennett was an older man and a Methodist. King's advisers were almost uniformly Baptists and were usually young, often not out of their twenties. It is also interesting to note that, in February, Bennett was to become the sole member of the black leadership to urge the acceptance of the business community's proffered compromise.[39]

The Board next named a committee to draft a resolution for the consideration of the mass meeting that evening. The resolution explicitly attributed the boycott to the failure of the bus company to clarify its seating policy following the two March meetings and to the resultant misunderstandings that had produced the Smith and Parks arrests. It called on "every citizen in Montgomery, regardless of race, color or creed" to participate in the boycott, and urged employers voluntarily to afford transportation to their employees.[40]

The Montgomery chapter of the Alabama Council on Human Relations, the Alabama branch of the Southern Regional Council, arranged a meeting with the MIA, the City Commission, and the bus company on December 8—a success due primarily to the ironic circumstance that the ACHR's most prominent white member in the city, the Reverend Thomas Thrasher, an Episcopalian, was the rector of Mayor Gayle's church. The task before the meeting was large. Both the bus company's manager James H. Bagley and its attorney Jack Crenshaw had emphasized in their public statements their belief that the company could not legally alter bus seating arrangements. Crenshaw had maintained that blacks "have no quarrel with our company. If they don't like the law we have to operate under, then they should try to get the law changed, not engage in an attack on our company." To this position King had replied, "We are not asking an end to segregation. That's a matter for the Legislature and the courts. We feel that we have a plan within the law." Thus a principal question before the December 8 meeting, as before all the earlier ones, was whether the law allowed its enforcers any discretion.[41]

The meeting began with Martin King's reading a list of three demands, satisfaction of which was a prerequisite to the end of the boycott: more courtesy from bus drivers; the hiring of black drivers on the four predominantly black routes; and the seating of blacks from the back towards the front and of whites from the front towards the back without insisting that a section always be kept clear for each race. The demands appear to reflect the thinking of Edgar D. Nixon; the seating proposal was lifted from the questionnaire of the Ben Moore Hotel meeting, and the request for black drivers was consistent with Nixon's long-standing commitment as a labor leader to opening additional occupations to blacks.

Crenshaw replied by denying that drivers were discourteous, except in the rarest instances; by flatly rejecting the idea of black drivers, at least for the coming decade; and by declaring the seating proposal illegal. On this last point he joined battle with Gray. Gray offered a full-scale legal brief attempting to demonstrate that the 1945 state statute did not apply to Montgomery City Lines and urged the City Commission to seek a formal opinion from the state attorney general on the question. In any case, he noted, both city code and state statute simply required separate but equal accommodations; they made no attempt to specify the precise arrangements by which this goal was to be accomplished. As King put it in a statement issued two days later, presumably written in consultation with Gray, "The Legislature, it seems clear, wisely left it up to the transportation companies to work out the seating problem in a reasonable and practical way . . . We feel that there is no issue between the Negro citizens and the Montgomery City Lines that cannot be solved by negotiations between people of good will. And we submit that there is no legal barrier to such negotiations." At the meeting King emphasized that the suggested seating plan was in use in Mobile and other Southern cities. Crenshaw did offer to have every other bus on the heavily black Washington Park route designated exclusively for blacks, but beyond this concession he simply reiterated that the company could not "change the law."

After some hours of these exchanges, Mayor Gayle suggested that it might be useful if a smaller group conferred in private. He then withdrew, taking the press, television cameramen, spectators, and peripheral participants with him. King, Gray, and perhaps other blacks remained to talk with Bagley and Crenshaw and the two new commissioners, Sellers and Parks. According to King's account of this session, as soon as the reporters had gone, Parks—who had defeated Cleere with black votes—ventured, "I don't see why we can't arrange to accept this seating proposal. We can work it within our segregation laws." At once Crenshaw replied, "But Frank, I don't see how we can do it within the law. If it were legal I would be the first to go along with it, but it just isn't legal. The only way that it can be done is to change your segregation laws." Then he added, "If we granted the Negroes these demands, they would go about boasting of a victory that they had won over the white people, and this we will not stand for." Facing this determined opposition from Crenshaw and knowing that Sellers could not be brought to compromise, Parks crumbled, and the next day resignedly informed the press that he regretted that the conference had produced no settlement but that "We cannot break the law."[42]

This sequence of events had been most peculiar. Although all the blacks were integrationists, the thrust of their efforts was so to reform the actual practice of segregation as to make it acceptable and thus to remove the impetus for its elimination. Crenshaw, a firm segregationist, was by implication urging the blacks to seek the complete abolition of segregation in the courts.

Since March the blacks had repeatedly pointed out that their plan was in effect in many Southern cities, including Mobile. King had reiterated this point at the meeting on December 8. Yet, Bagley subsequently testified that he had been unaware of this fact on December 8 and found it out later. When the *Advertiser* printed on December 31 an article confirming the accuracy of the blacks' statements, the article was thought worthy of prominent treatment and seems to have caused surprise among whites. Nevertheless, the illogic of maintaining that the state law permitted in Mobile what it forbade in Montgomery escaped the white citizenry; when Bagley was asked about the inconsistency, he replied merely, "I cannot testify what they would do in Mobile, or what they can do, but I know what we can do in Montgomery." True, the Mobile City Code specifically required the seating plan in use in that city. But it is also true that the Montgomery City Code prescribed no specific seating plan.[43]

Similarly, Gray had argued at length at both the Colvin and the Parks hearings that the state statute did not apply to municipal bus lines and had submitted a brief to the Commission and the bus company expounding this position. No one in authority, except possibly Frank Parks, appears to have paid any attention. Gray had suggested that the Commission seek a ruling from the attorney general; the Commission toyed with the idea of doing so but in the end took no action. The following spring, however, when Gray joined the Public Service Commission as a defendant in his federal court suit to void bus segregation, in order to have the state law as well as the city ordinance declared unconstitutional the state suddenly took up Gray's earlier argument in its entirety. At the trial the president of the Public Service Commission, C. C. "Jack" Owen, flatly denied that his agency had any jurisdiction over municipal bus systems. The Court read the state statute of 1945 to Owen and asked him if his construction of the act was that it "does not include common carriers such as busses in the City of Montgomery?" Owen, evidently nonplussed by the question, stammered in reply, "I had never thought of it in that particular line of thinking. This is the first time that point has ever been brought up. It seems to me like that means segregation as far as segregation is concerned."[44]

Whites simply did not reflect carefully on the legal points which the blacks raised. Indeed, President Owen—a Montgomerian whose position ought to have made him more than ordinarily concerned with this aspect of the controversy—did not even know that the question of the applicability of the 1945 act had been at issue throughout the preceding year. These attitudes appear particularly puzzling because what Gray and his associates were actually trying to do was to rationalize the segregation system. Why did segregationists find it so difficult to accept the modest reforms which the blacks suggested—reforms whose acceptance would clearly have strengthened segregation itself, by diminishing opposition to it? Consideration of three efforts to reach a compromise will help provide an answer to this question.

Mayor Gayle's copy of the resolution adopted by the black mass meeting on December 5, which Fred Gray had handed to the mayor at the December 8 meeting, was offered in evidence at King's trial for violation of the anti-boycott law. On its back someone, presumably the mayor, had jotted in pencil, "How about *again* appointing [a] com[mittee of] Retailer[s] *etc.* to meet with [K. E.] Totten [vice-president of National City Lines of Chicago] to bring some recommendations to [the] City Com[mission]?" The reference was to the course which the commissioners had successfully followed in the bus drivers' strike of December 1953. At that time the Commission had named a committee of six—the presidents of the Chamber of Commerce, the Retail Merchants Association, the white Ministerial Association, and the PTA, an attorney, and a prominent black—to mediate the conflict. When the December 8 meeting produced no settlement, the Commission evidently decided to make use of this precedent.

Totten returned to Montgomery on December 15 to continue negotiations for the renewal of the company's expiring franchise. After conferring with him the Commission called a meeting of all parties to the controversy on the morning of December 17, and there the mayor suggested the appointment of a ten-member committee—eight whites and two blacks—to act as mediators between the MIA and the bus company. Jo Ann Robinson at once insisted that the number of whites and blacks on the committee be equal. Apparently, the commissioners conceived of the dispute as being between the bus company and the MIA, and of the committee as a neutral mediator, while the MIA thought of the dispute as being between Montgomery's whites and blacks, and of the committee as a sort of collective bargaining arrangement. After some discussion the mayor agreed to add six MIA members to his original ten. These sixteen people met on the afternoon of December 17 and again on December 19 but reached no agreement.[45]

The blacks included King, Abernathy, Robinson, attorneys Fred Gray and Charles D. Langford, the Reverend Hillman H. Hubbard, pastor of one of the city's largest black congregations and one of the few older black preachers prominent in the MIA's leadership, and the two well-to-do black businessmen who were Gayle's choices, Pluie M. Blair, who owned a dry-cleaners and who was called the "Negro Mayor of Montgomery," and Dungee Caffey, a realtor with diverse interests. The white delegation, balancing the black one, included also three ministers: Dr. Henry Allen Parker of the First Baptist Church (white), the Reverend G. Stanley Frazer of St. James Methodist Church, and the Reverend Henry Edward Russell of Trinity Presbyterian Church, brother of U.S. Senator Richard Russell of Georgia. There were two businessmen: James J. Bailey, the manager of a furniture store and president of the Furniture Dealers Association, and William H. Fields, the manager of a local J. C. Penney store and president of the Retail Merchants Association. Mrs. Earnest R. Moore was the wife of a dental technician and the president of the city-county PTA. Mrs. Logan A. Hipp, Jr., the wife of an insurance adjuster, worked as a secretary in the office of the city Chamber of Commerce. The final white member was William G. Welch, a bus driver for the Montgomery City Lines and president of the bus drivers' local union.[46]

King charged that the mayor had "not appointed a representative committee of whites." At first glance the allegation would appear unfounded. But an investigation of the committee's deliberations casts the notion into a different light. The blacks advanced their seating proposal, and Gray argued that it could be effected within existing law. At the initial session the white delegation, unlike the black, contained no lawyers. The whites relied for legal advice upon City Attorney Walter Knabe, who attended the meetings. Knabe had been involved in the negotiations stretching back to the preceding spring and was committed to the position that the seating proposal was illegal. He informed the whites that Gray was simply wrong, and the whites adopted this position in their final report, issued on January 18. King states that K. E. Totten acknowledged to him privately that the black proposal was used by National City Lines' Mobile affiliate; Totten, King reports, said that he could not see why what worked in Mobile could not work in Montgomery. If Totten made this admission privately, he refused to do so publicly. Instead, he declined to become involved in the local negotiations, saying only that National City Lines would abide by any arrangement accepted by Montgomerians. Understandably, a national firm that dealt with cities across the country would wish to avoid becoming entangled in heated municipal controversies. This motive must have been particularly strong in the Montgomery situation because Totten was at this very time attempting to secure a new franchise from the city government. However, Totten's refusal to intervene, coupled with the whites' reliance upon Knabe's advice, left the committee within the limits of the controversy that had previously been defined, unable to approach the problem from a new perspective.

Of course, the whites on the committee were segregationists; had they not been, they would not have reflected accurately the sentiment of the community which they represented. Yet segregationist attitudes in themselves were no real barrier to a settlement, because the black delegation emphasized that it had no desire to disestablish segregation. Ill will between the two sides on the committee was exacerbated by the inability of Frazer and Russell to resist the urge to lecture the blacks on the morality of segregation and the immorality of ministerial involvement in politics. The black clergymen responded with lectures of their own. Still, the white committee members were not opposed to compromise. Frazer presented what he took to be a compromise: that fixed lines of racial division be marked on every bus, determined by the proportion of the races on each route, but that riders be permitted to sit forward or back of the line until the seats were needed by the other race. The proposal, as Charles Langford noted, ignored the principal black complaint, the unseating of passengers already seated. At least Frazier's proposal demonstrated a willingness to try to find a solution. Bailey even stated to the committee, "I came here prepared to vote for liberalization of interpretation of the city's laws with certain conditions."[47]

The failure of the committee to discover a compromise was not entirely attributable to the racial attitudes of the committee members, though such attitudes doubtless contributed to the impasse. None of the whites on the committee was a member of Montgomery's upper class; Bailey, the member of the white delegation who seems to have been most favorable to compromise, was the one member who was at all prominent in the city's business community. This fact is significant. When King called the whites unrepresentative, what he evidently meant was that they were all too representative. The situation demanded men and women who were sufficiently confident of their social position to allow them to be original in their approach to the problem. The committee contained no such members, and it is primarily for that reason that its deliberations proved sterile.

The mayor had not appointed any of the city's social and economic leaders to the committee because of his weak political position. The March elections had emphasized that Gayle could no longer permit himself to seem a front man for Montgomery's upper class. Rather, he needed to seek the support of other social elements among the whites. He certainly could not permit himself the luxury of an action that flew in the face of white community sentiment. A compromise suggested by the committee he did appoint would give some promise of generating community consensus. Precisely because the committee was representative, its deliberations were doomed without the intervention of some outside figure like Totten. Gayle may initially have hoped that Totten would help, but when Totten refused, the committee became an exercise in futility.[48]

The encounter between the city and its black citizens entered a new stage in late January, when attitudes in both camps had hardened considerably. After the December 19 meeting the biracial committee held no further sessions. On January 6 Clyde Sellers appeared at a meeting of the White Citizens Council and dramatically announced that he was joining the organization. On January 9 the City Commission met with an MIA delegation for two hours at King's request, but neither side would modify its position. On January 18 the white members of the biracial committee issued a final report publicly acknowledging the failure of their efforts and urging all parties to accept Frazer's compromise proposal. At least by the same time in mid-January some MIA leaders were concluding that further negotiations would be fruitless and were beginning to discuss the possibility of a federal court suit to have bus segregation declared unconstitutional.[49]

During this period discontent had been growing among those black ministers who were not a part of the MIA's leadership. The boycott had so captured the imagination and the loyalties of the city's blacks that the failure of a black minister to be included occasionally as a speaker at the frequent mass meetings which were the movement's backbone demeaned him in the eyes of his congregation. Probably, jealousies thus generated lay behind the decision of three black ministers to contact white officials with the offer to negotiate a settlement. The Reverend Benjamin F. Mosely, pastor of the First Presbyterian Church (black), Bishop Doc C. Rice, pastor of the Oak Street Holiness

Church, and the Reverend William K. Kind, pastor of the Jackson Street Baptist Church, one of the few prominent black preachers in the city who had not been chosen a member of the MIA's executive board, perhaps expected that, if they were able to engineer the creation of a compromise acceptable to the black community, they might gain for themselves a portion of the public attention being focused upon King, Abernathy, Gray, and their associates.

On January 21 the City Commission met with the three ministers, together with Paul B. Fuller, the executive secretary of the Chamber of Commerce, and the Reverend Thomas Thrasher of the Alabama Council on Human Relations. The meeting produced a compromise under which ten seats in the front would always be reserved for whites, ten seats in the rear for blacks, and the remaining sixteen seats would be filled as the MIA proposed, blacks sitting from the rear and whites from the front; in addition, all-black buses would be provided during rush hours on three predominantly black routes. The proposal did not specify whether passengers seated in the middle sixteen seats could be unseated. It stated that the City Commission had no authority to alter the bus company's hiring policies; the company had repeatedly refused to hire blacks, so this statement implied the rejection of the request for black drivers.

The MIA promptly denounced this agreement and stated that the three ministers did not speak for the city's blacks. It soon became apparent, moreover, that virtually the entire black community supported the MIA's position in this regard. The three ministers thereupon repudiated the compromise; they told King that they had not understood the proposal and had attended the meeting under the impression that it was to discuss the city's insurance. The commissioners were livid with rage at this turn of events. Mayor Gayle subsequently swore that both Fuller and Thrasher had read the agreement carefully to the ministers who had fully understood and approved of it. On this basis the commissioners had publicly committed themselves to the compromise. All three commissioners were increasingly in awe of Montgomery's rapidly growing White Citizens Council, whose membership local newspapers reported to be 6,000 at the beginning of February and 12,000 by the end of that month. By that time it had become the largest single organization in Montgomery County. Sellers, in a speech to the council on January 6, had pledged to continue fighting the blacks' demands and had repeated the promise in even stronger terms on January 17. Gayle and Parks had been somewhat less vocal but naturally wished to avoid offending council members unnecessarily. Now all three commissioners found themselves revealed to the voters as willing to compromise but deprived at the same time of any compromise to show for their pains. They felt betrayed.[50]

On January 23 Mayor Gayle announced, "The Negro leaders have proved they will say one thing to a white man and another thing to a Negro." He said, "The City Commission has attempted with sincerity and honesty to end the bus boycott in a businesslike fashion. We have held meetings with the Negroes at which proposals were made that would have been accepted by any fair-minded group of people. But there seems to be a belief on the part of the Negroes that they have the white people hemmed up in a corner and they are not going to give an inch until they can force the white people of our community to submit to their demands—in fact, swallow all of them. . . . We attempted to resolve their reasonable complaints but they proved by their refusal to resolve the reasonable ones that they were not interested in whether the bus service was good or not. What they are after is the destruction of our social fabric." He called the black leadership "a group of Negro radicals" whose only real goal was to "stir up racial strife." He stated, "The white people are firm in their convictions that they do not care whether the Negroes ever ride a city bus again . . . " He concluded, "When and if the Negro people desire to end the boycott, my door is open to them. But until they are ready to end it, there will be no more discussions."

This statement appears to have been the product of a moment of anger, but the astonishing approbation with which whites greeted it transformed it into fixed policy.

Appreciative calls swamped the City Hall switchboard; hundreds of congratulatory telegrams flooded in, and voters eager for the opportunity to shake Gayle's hand crowded the mayor's office. Commissioner Parks reported himself "amazed with the avalanche" of approval. He concluded, "There is no need for us to straddle the fence any longer. I am taking a stand and so are the other commissioners." Both Gayle and Sellers moved at once to identify themselves even more firmly with the "get tough" stand. Gayle called for whites to refuse to drive their domestics to and from work or to pay their taxi fare; "the Negroes are laughing at white people behind their backs" because of the whites' willingness to do so, he warned. Sellers instructed the police to arrest blacks waiting to catch a ride and to charge them with loitering. "A person has a perfect right to wait for a ride," he noted, "but the practice of six or eight Negroes huddling together for an hour or more, trampling lawns and making loud noises in white residential districts must cease." On January 24 Mayor Gayle and Commissioner Parks announced that they, too, had joined the White Citizens Council. Within weeks all members of the County Board of Revenue also had joined. The council's attorney proclaimed that the group was now so large that blacks would never again be able to influence candidates for local office by "dangling their bloc votes" before aspirants.[51]

Stronger and stronger statements followed, as politicians rushed to associate themselves with the City Commission's popular stand. The pronouncements soon bore fruit. On the night of January 30 a stick of dynamite was thrown onto the porch of Martin L. King's home; his wife and a visitor narrowly escaped injury. The MIA leadership had been discussing the advisability of a federal court suit for at least two weeks, as a political settlement seemed increasingly illusory. However, the bombing of King's home convinced the MIA that simply to continue pressure on the city through the boycott to force agreement to the blacks' demands was no longer a reasonable strategy. If negotiations ever could produce an agreement, it would be in the far future. Meantime, the boycott would be fraught with excessive risk. On February 1 Fred Gray filed suit challenging the constitutionality of bus segregation.[52] Mayor Gayle denounced the suit as "proof beyond any doubt that Negroes never wanted better bus service as they were claiming, but complete integration." The blacks, he said, stood convicted of double-dealing.[53]

These events strikingly illuminate the commission's ignorance of sentiment among both blacks and extremist whites. First, the events emphasize how tenaciously the commissioners and their advisers believed that the MIA did not actually speak for the city's blacks. The commissioners had repeatedly urged the masses of blacks to repudiate King and other spurious leaders who owed their apparent positions as spokesmen for the black community only to the apathy of many blacks and to the intimidation of the remainder by MIA goon squads. Commissioner Sellers estimated that 85 to 90 percent of the city's blacks would immediately resume riding the buses if there were no danger of physical reprisal. "The innocent Negroes should wake up," Commissioner Parks warned. "They don't know what they are doing, but I'm afraid they're going to find out. The white people have been their friends, and still want to be, but we can't sit here and watch them destroy our transportation system." Mayor Gayle accepted both Parks's emphasis on ignorance and Sellers's emphasis on fear, although there is relatively little evidence of intimidation and none linking the intimidation to the MIA. Unfortunately, one of the few instances in which intimidation was alleged involved Mayor Gayle's father-in-law's cook. The mayor's closeness to this particular incident perhaps increased his sense of the violence surrounding the boycott. Whether because of Sellers's dark, conspiratorial explanation or because of Parks's more benign one, the city's political leaders were convinced that the MIA's claims to represent Montgomery's blacks were false.

This attitude accounts for the commissioners' otherwise inexplicable notion that the three non-MIA black ministers constituted, as the statement of January 21 claimed, a "group representing the Negroes of Montgomery." At the time of the appointment of the biracial committee on December 17 Gayle had insisted on appointing two prominent blacks, Blair and Caffey, who had not been nominated by the MIA, perhaps partly in the hope that he would tap the reservoir of anti-MIA feeling which he thought to exist. This expectation failed; Blair and Caffey proved to be completely committed to the MIA's demands. When the three ministers approached white leaders in late January, the commissioners evidently felt that they had at last forced from hiding a leadership alternative to King. Of course, the commissioners knew that no organized group had appointed the three ministers. On the other hand, the commissioners regarded the views of the three ministers as more fully consonant with those of the black masses. If the commissioners had been correct in their analysis, it would have been reasonable to have supposed that the conclusion of a settlement with the ministers would give most blacks sufficient encouragement to return to the buses. The compromise produced no such result simply because the Commission was wrong; Montgomery's blacks were dedicated to the achievement of the MIA's program. Unfortunately, the repudiation of the settlement by the three ministers obscured this fact for city political leaders.[54]

The Commission betrayed similar ignorance in failing to gauge the effect upon the city's racist extremists of the intemperate statements issued in late January. The extremist element evidently took the "get tough" policy and the resulting public ovation as a license for violence. In addition to the bombing of King's home on January 30 the home of Edgar D. Nixon was bombed on February 1, though the latter explosion caused no damage. In later months, incidentally, the belief became general in Citizens Council circles that blacks themselves had staged both of these bombings to gain sympathy and contributions from Northerners.[55] The absence of any sense of the state of sentiment among blacks and among white racial extremists is a complementary phenomenon with a single culprit: these segments of the population were essentially excluded from political life, and the Commission had such limited contact with them that it lacked any mechanism for understanding their motives and assumptions.

Contemporary with the events of January, the third and last effort to formulate a compromise acceptable to the MIA emerged from the business community. The Men of Montgomery, already dubious of city politicians, were persuaded by January that the Commission's mismanagement of the crisis had prevented a settlement and that businessmen might well succeed where politicians had failed. Moreover, the organization had three good reasons to try. The boycott had intensified racial hatred in the city, damaged trade, and directed such unfavorable publicity to the city as to complicate any effort to attract industry to the area. Mayor Gayle's announcement on January 23 that the Commission would not negotiate further made the politicians' inability to secure an agreement explicit. The bombing of Dr. King's home clearly announced that the entire affair had gotten out of hand and that unless a compromise could be found quickly, seriously unfavorable reports in the national press would be inevitable.[56] These two events moved the Men of Montgomery to intervene in the boycott. Thus, rather ironically, the same set of circumstances convincing the black leadership that additional negotiation would be fruitless, finally moved the city's economic powers to undertake the mediation of the controversy.

During the first three weeks of February a committee of the Men of Montgomery held two full-scale negotiating sessions with MIA leaders and at least one with the City Commission. It was also in almost constant informal contact with the two groups in an effort to locate tenable middle ground. The Men of Montgomery members advanced no proposals of their own; they apparently saw themselves as brokers rather than as parties to the conflict. King later wrote of them that they had proved themselves "open-minded enough to listen to another point of view and discuss the problem of race intelligently," and in reference to their arbitration he concluded, "I have no doubt that we would have come to a solution had it not been for the recalcitrance of the city commission." However, the obstacles to any such happy outcome appear genuinely insuperable. The commissioners' statements during the last week of January had made it virtually impossible for them to agree to any substantial concessions; and their receptiveness to compromise was not increased by the fact that on February 10, at a White Citizens Council rally which filled the state coliseum, a crowd of some 12,000 gave both Mayor Gayle and Commissioner Sellers sustained, emotional standing ovations.[57]

For its part the MIA was no longer in a position to negotiate. At no time would it have been easy for the MIA to have made concessions; as King had noted in mid-January, "We began with a compromise when we didn't ask for complete integration. Now we're asked to compromise on the compromise."

The filing of the federal court suit on February 1, however, had eliminated even the small basis for an accord that had been present. The MIA's initial requests had sought only a reform of specific practice within the general framework of segregation; the MIA had repeatedly and strenuously affirmed its view that its proposals were in keeping with city and state law. But the suit sought the elimination of segregation. It so changed the MIA's position that King had evidently given serious consideration to recommending that the boycott be called off. The boycott had been intended to move the City Commission and the bus company to action. If the MIA were going to rely on a court order to produce the action, there was no longer a reason for a boycott. Indeed, the only difficulty with this logic was that the MIA could not be certain that the federal courts would declare bus segregation unconstitutional. Despite the decision of the MIA to continue with the boycott, the organization could hardly be expected to agree to a compromise perpetuating segregation while it was at the same time asking the courts to compel full integration. The Men of Montgomery's efforts would appear therefore to have been doomed from the outset.[58]

Nevertheless, the Men of Montgomery pressed mediation because the city's good reputation could be restored only if Montgomerians solved the boycott themselves. Their task was made especially urgent when some prominent Montgomery lawyers began to advocate a course that would almost certainly destroy whatever respect for the city remained among national opinion leaders: the mass indictment of virtually all the city's most prominent blacks for violation of the Alabama anti-boycott law.

The anti-boycott law had been passed in 1921 as a part of a series of statutes provoked by a bloody strike of Birmingham coal miners in that year. From the beginning of the bus boycott the applicability of this act to the situation had been discussed, but the question was not taken very seriously because, as the *Advertiser* noted editorially on December 8, "As a practical matter, we doubt that either the bus company or the solicitor will attempt to jail 5,000 Negroes." As the hatreds generated by the dispute deepened, some Montgomerians considered prosecution as a realistic weapon. On January 9 Frederick S. Ball, an important figure in both legal and social circles in the city, dispatched a letter to the *Advertiser* demanding the boycotters' indictment. "An individual has the right to ride a bus or not as he or she sees fit and that right should not be interfered with and should be protected by the police," he wrote, "but when certain so-called leaders call a group together and organize a boycott, they are taking the law into their own hands and should be prosecuted. Whether the bus company or its drivers have or have not always themselves obeyed the law and given colored passengers their rights is not the question at all, because two wrongs do not make a right and there is always legal redress against the bus company for anything it does wrong. The question is whether the officials whose duty it is to enforce the law are going to sit idly by and permit the illegal destruction of a transportation system which is most certainly needed by both races." He added pointedly, "A copy of this letter goes to the county solicitor with the suggestion that he give consideration to presenting this matter to the grand jury . . . "

Grover C. Hall, Jr., clearly shared the view of the business leaders that this course would be sheer folly. Hall attempted to dispose of Ball's argument with gentle ridicule. "Atty. Ball . . . is against lawlessness. So he has asked Solicitor Thetford to prosecute. What leaves us confused is the question whether Atty. Ball is also opposed to the lawlessness of defying the U.S. Supreme Court, the supreme law.... We ask then, is Atty. Ball for law-abiding at the local level and lawlessness at the Supreme Court level? And, as we asked Dec. 8, what if Atty. Ball got some bus boycotters convicted in a Montgomery court? Would not the Supreme Court automatically reverse the convictions? Another perplexity left by Atty. Ball's brief letter is whether he is against all persons who have entered an 'arrangement' to boycott? For example, Police Commissioner Clyde Sellers is a card-carrying member of the White Citizens Council, an organization dedicated to boycott and economic sanctions against Negroes. Does Atty. Ball want White Councilman Sellers indicted also?"

But Ball was not so easily dissuaded. On January 12 he replied, "The question is not, as put in your [editorial], how far to 'cast the net' of law enforcement, or whether we should abide by our own state laws or the most recent ruling of the federal Supreme Court on segregation in public schools. The question is not what the White Citizens Council stands for.... The law against boycotting is not a segregation law. It applies to all instances where people organize to prevent the operation of a lawful business. The single question here is whether certain religious and other misguided leaders who are openly and publicly violating the law against boycotting should be permitted to do so at the expense of the risk of our city losing a much-needed bus system, or whether the law against boycotting should be enforced. I think it should be enforced, and soon, before it is too late."

Hall continued to believe that sensible officials would not pursue Ball's suggestion. On January 15 Hall referred to "the contradictions and impracticality of Lawyer Ball's vexed demand that the solicitor jug the bus boycott leaders for violation of the anti-boycott law," and noted, "The polite silence of the solicitor substantiates our reservations about the Ball formula." On January 17 an *Advertiser* reader, George C. Poulos, wrote the paper, "If an organized boycott is against the law, as Mr. Fred Ball states..., then why should anyone have to present his letter to the Circuit Solicitor? Doesn't the Solicitor know his job? Why does he have to be reminded of his duty? Maybe he is worried about the Negro vote. He had better start worrying about the white vote."[59]

Hall's confidence and Poulos's fear were both misplaced. On January 10, the day after Ball's initial letter appeared, Circuit Solicitor Thetford contacted Commissioner Sellers and asked that two detectives be assigned to the solicitor's office to investigate the boycott. Sellers agreed at once, and the investigation was launched on January 11. That it was being conducted did not become public knowledge during January, but by February 13 it had become clear that officials had determined to seek indictments; on that day Circuit Judge Eugene W. Carter charged the new county grand jury to determine whether the bus boycott violated the anti-boycott law.[60]

The negotiating efforts of the Men of Montgomery now became a race against time to find a settlement before the forces seeking prosecution could obtain the adoption of their strategy. On February 8 the Men of Montgomery published in the newspapers the name and telephone number of their executive secretary, William R. Lynn, and urged anyone having a suggestion for a compromise formula to contact him. In the end the City Commission was not in a position politically to offer much more than it had previously conceded to the three non-MIA black ministers: the reservation of ten seats at front and rear, with blacks seating from the rear and whites from the front in an unreserved middle section of sixteen seats. The Men of Montgomery sought to make this proposal more palatable to blacks by adding other reforms, such as mechanisms for more effectively institutionalizing the right of blacks to enter complaints against drivers. After a two-hour meeting on the morning of February 20 the Men of Montgomery succeeded in extracting from the commissioners a public promise "that there will be no retaliation whatsoever resulting from the bus boycott" almost certainly a reference to the grand jury investigation then entering its final stages. The concessions, which might well have satisfied the black leadership a year earlier, came far too late. At an MIA mass meeting on the evening of

February 20 the audience shouted the proposals down; only the Reverend L. Roy Bennett and his assistant pastor openly supported the compromise. On February 21 the grand jury returned indictments of eighty-nine blacks, twenty-four of whom were ministers, for the misdemeanor of conspiring to boycott.[61]

The collision between the business community and the bar over the correct tactics to pursue in the crisis is worth some comment. The Men of Montgomery contained but a single lawyer among its forty founding members; it was composed of merchants, realtors, land developers, contractors, insurance men, bankers, brokers, and other men of similar occupations.[62] From the outset the most inflexible of the whites were lawyers. The differences in attitude which the differing vocations produced is one of the most puzzling aspects of the episode. We may in part explain the attitudes of Judge Carter and Circuit Solicitor Thetford by pointing to the pressures of an elective position; though Judge Carter was quite strong politically, Solicitor Thetford was a young man just beginning his second term in office. That explanation does not account for the stance of such men as Crenshaw, Knabe, and Ball. One might think that they would have seized upon the black proposals as a way to preserve segregation. In fact, however, they repeatedly displayed an absolutist predisposition that precluded compromise.

Nor is their temperament to be explained as a narrow devotion to the letter of the law. Gray's reading of the text of the acts was at least as reasonable as Crenshaw's and Knabe's—a fact proved when the contending parties actually later switched sides, as a result of the federal court suit, on the question of the applicability of the state statute. Ball's construction of the anti-boycott law involved considerable legal difficulties as well. The constitutionality of the law had been specifically considered and affirmed by the Alabama Supreme Court in 1943. However, in that opinion Justice William H. Thomas, writing for the court, had saved the act by interpreting it very strictly. The statute prohibited conspiring to boycott "without a just cause or legal excuse." Such a law could be upheld, Justice Thomas said, when regarded as an effort by the legislature to prohibit the use of force, violence, or other unlawful activities to prevent someone from engaging in business. If the statute were so construed as to permit the state to interfere with protest carried out by lawful means, it would be unconstitutional. But when limited in its scope and application simply to conspiracies to hinder a lawful occupation by actions otherwise illegal, the statute was within the state's police power. The U.S. Supreme Court had indicated its satisfaction with this decision by denying certiorari in the case. When Martin King was brought to trial in March—the first and only one of the boycotters to be tried—the prosecution was clearly aware of Justice Thomas's opinion and sought to prove that the boycott had indeed been accompanied and maintained by violence: shots had been fired at buses and a number of blacks had been forcibly restrained from riding, the testimony alleged. There was, however, no evidence connecting the MIA to these actions. In fact, at the conclusion of the trial Judge Carter, though convicting King, refused to sentence him to prison on the grounds, explicitly stated, that King had worked to prevent violence. At the very least the applicability of the anti-boycott law to the Montgomery situation was debatable.[63]

One might, of course, attribute the lawyers' maladroit handling of the boycott situation to ignorance or to poor legal training. But Crenshaw and Knabe had both received their legal education at Harvard. Knabe had been an undergraduate at Yale. Ball had been graduated from Princeton and had attended law school at Columbia and Emory. If these men desired to preserve segregation, as they certainly did, it was surely not a lack of mental acuity that prevented their seeing that acceding to the blacks' modest demands would strengthen, rather than weaken, the system.

Racism is no adequate explanation for the phenomenon; Montgomery's attorneys were no more nor less racist than were her business leaders, who were eager to compromise. Neither a literalist reading of the law nor a defective legal education provides an explanation; indeed, the facts contradict both contentions. Perhaps the answer lies in the role demanded of a lawyer as a representative of his client. Lawyers are poorly prepared to participate in the give-and-take of negotiations because they are trained to think of themselves as defending their clients' interests from the assaults of hostile adversaries. Such an attitude does not lend itself easily to the search for common ground. Rather, it almost inevitably conceives of the parties to a negotiation as enemies and tends to emphasize the elements in each position that are irreconcilable. In the boycott this tendency was exacerbated by racial prejudice and by the threat which the black effort seemed to pose to the white attorneys' own social position. But prejudice and social position could as readily have become motives to seek some settlement that would have preserved segregation in an ameliorated form, as the example of the business community shows. The key to the puzzle must be the legal turn of mind upon which the prejudice and the fear of social disintegration were acting, not merely the racial and class positions themselves.

However that may be, by the end of February 1956 both black and white leaders had abandoned the search for compromise and with it the political process and had determined to trust their respective causes to the rigid and unconditional judgment of the courts. The pressures leading to this decision among the whites have already been explained. Equally perplexing is why the blacks had not reached this decision much earlier. As logic would indicate that the whites should have been willing to compromise to preserve segregation, so logic would appear to dictate that blacks should have turned to the courts at once to attack the system which they despised. Indeed, as the *Advertiser* noted editorially at the conclusion of the boycott, the boycott itself accomplished absolutely nothing; only a decision of the courts ended the encounter, and that decision could have been obtained at any time, without the necessity for a boycott, simply by entering suit.

This riddle is solved in part by the observation that Montgomery's blacks had not yet developed the faith in the federal court which future years would generate. The city's federal judge, Frank M. Johnson, Jr., was still an unknown quantity, not a legend. He had held his position for just three months and had received Senate confirmation only the day before Gray filed the suit seeking to enjoin bus segregation. Southern federal judges certainly had not proved particular enemies of segregation in previous years. In fact, in the Montgomery bus suit itself, one of the three federal judges who heard it, Seybourn H. Lynne of Birmingham, dissented strongly from his colleagues' holding that the school integration decision of 1954 was applicable to bus seating.[64]

Yet lack of faith in the courts is not the most important explanation for the initial willingness of the black leadership to settle for a compromise within the framework of segregation. The real reason is that the bus boycott in its origins was much less a social than a political movement. During the year and a half that Dave Birmingham served on the City Commission black leaders developed a strengthened sense of the malleability of the system. The size of the black vote grew every year, and the city government paid new attention to black complaints. The decision to hold a public session to interview candidates for commissioner in 1955 and to release a list of endorsements reflected this growing confidence that politics could be made to subserve the needs of blacks. However, the outcome of the election dealt a considerable blow to this optimism. Black leaders had been permitted a brief experience of a happier relationship with their rulers, only to have it snatched away.

Bus seating had been one of the areas in which blacks had genuinely expected that they would be able to make progress. In the conferences that had followed the arrest of Claudette Colvin they had been promised public clarifications, which would have represented a clear acknowledgment of their ability to compel the city to respond to their concerns. No clarifications were forthcoming; the Commission formally rejected Birmingham's motion to add black members to the Parks and Recreation Board; the segregationist Sellers was inaugurated; and Mrs. Parks was arrested under the same circumstances as Miss Colvin. The MIA's statements at the beginning of the boycott emphasize unmistakably the connection between the city's failure to define the precise requirements of the segregation ordinance following the Colvin incident and the decision to boycott. The city elections, which had seemed in the spring so likely to produce an amelioration of the blacks' lot, had produced instead a situation that if anything was the worse for having earlier seemed so hopeful.

If government was ever really to benefit blacks, it now seemed, black leaders would have to discover some mechanism other than the electoral process by which to influence politicians. The boycott was intended to be such a mechanism. In the minds of its organizers, at least, it appears to have been analogous to a strike—a way for persons individually weak to bring collective pressure to bear upon the powerful once negotiations have failed. The boycott was not a revolution; it was merely an extension of the negotiations. The black leaders persisted in offering in December their seating proposal advanced in March precisely because they initially conceived their movement not so much as a direct action against bus segregation itself as rather a search for a means to manipulate the political process. They genuinely believed that, faced with this proof of how seriously blacks took the grievance, the City Commission would be compelled to seek a remedy.[65] For this device to work successfully, the blacks could only ask for something which the commissioners could legally grant—an amelioration of segregation.

Both the Ben Moore Hotel meeting and the boycott were politically naïve. Under other circumstances the black leaders surely would have known that public endorsement of a candidate by blacks was likely to be counterproductive. They would similarly have known that for the commissioners to respond to pressure applied openly through a boycott—to knuckle under to blackmail, as it would have seemed to segregationists—would have infuriated a large part of the electorate. One cannot condemn the black leadership for its naïveté in these matters; inasmuch as blacks had been almost entirely excluded from political life in Alabama for two generations, it could hardly have been otherwise. Yet, the political process was clearly not analogous to an industrial dispute precisely because the interests involved were so many and varied and the conflicting pressures upon the Commission were so manifold. Surely, there was never any real likelihood of achieving a negotiated settlement of the boycott.

At the outset of the boycott the *Advertiser* had stated editorially, "The boycott makes an innocent sufferer of bus company. Had the company defied city and state laws, its franchise would have been canceled. The quarrel of the Negroes is with the *law.* It is wrong to hold the company a hostage."[66] The blacks replied over and over again—though the whites never seemed to listen—that their quarrel was not at all with the law, that they had no intention of asking the company to abandon segregation, that they merely wished to have the company apply the law in Montgomery as it did in Mobile. In a peculiar sense, however, the *Advertiser* was right, and the blacks wrong. What the boycott taught the city's black leaders as it dragged on was that their quarrel was—had to be—with the law. Compromise with segregation was impossible because segregation so forged and underlay social relationships that even the most modest reform of its requirements threatened—just as the white politicians claimed—the entire social fabric. In such a situation reform was impossible; only "revolution" would do. The white response to the boycott revealed this truth forcefully to the blacks; that revelation is the boycott's supreme achievement, and it is something which no court suit could ever have accomplished.

Perhaps the most interesting single aspect of the boycott is that the inflexibility of segregation was something which black leaders had to learn. It was so much the fundamental presumption of the civil rights movement in later years that we find it difficult to believe that there could have been a time when a black—when anyone—was unaware of this characteristic of the system. Indeed, it is this difficulty that makes the MIA's position in the initial stages of the boycott seem so peculiar. But segregation revealed the true extent of its inflexibility only under the pressure of the civil rights movement itself. For those who had lived inside the segregation system, black and white, the pervasiveness of its impact was not so readily apparent. It is not the author's intention to maintain that blacks were not acutely aware of the constant humiliation that segregation entailed. Yet, the enormous variety of interracial associations even under segregation made the institution seem less fundamental to the shaping of attitudes than in fact it was. Particularly in a city like Montgomery, in which the Gunter Machine had defeated the Ku Klux Klan and ruled with relative benevolence, it was easy not to know how exceedingly far, into how many unrelated organs, the infection had spread. Black leaders had been too ready to believe that the brief thaw that Dave Birmingham's tenure had represented for them marked the beginning of spring. The writer believes that they made this mistake because they, in common with most white Southerners, had conceived of their world, though suffused with segregation, as fictile. Only after segregation came under assault and its supporters roused themselves to fight back were blacks, and later whites, able to discover the omni-presence and rigidity of the system.

In a sense Martin King, having learned these lessons during the bus boycott, spent the rest of his career arranging demonstrations of them for others. Blacks, especially older blacks, in other Southern cities had to be shown that they were more fully imprisoned than they had believed. Moderate whites had to be shown that, whatever the extent of their good will, segregation had the power to render their best efforts vain. In these demonstrations the medium was the message; the immediate goals in a given city were less important than the process of placing segregation under stress in order to reveal the nature of its hold upon society. Iconoclasts sometimes note that King did not create the boycott, as a way of questioning his greatness. But King's greatness actually lies in the fact that during the boycott, by observing what was happening, he grew. He, far more than any of his contemporaries, white or black, learned the truths which the events of the boycott contained about the nature of the Southern dilemma.

In the end, the bus boycott teaches that segregation could have been disestablished only in the way in which it was disestablished: by internal pressure sufficient to compel intervention from outside the South. For all its diversity and complexity—in large part because of its diversity and complexity, since any fundamental reform would affect an infinite variety of interests—the South did not possess within itself the capacity to save itself. The strength of segregation was bound up with the pluralism of Southern society. As no man could untie the Gordian knot, so segregation would not—could not—yield to negotiation. Thus the boycott, because it failed to achieve its initial goals, succeeded for that reason in changing the course of American history.

ENDNOTES

1. Montgomery *Advertiser*, December 2, 1955; *Montgomery Alabama Journal*, December 5, 1955; Trial Transcript, *Rosa Parks v. City of Montgomery* (Records of the Alabama Court of Criminal Appeals, Office of the Clerk, Supreme Court Building, Montgomery), 9. This article has greatly benefited from interviews conducted with the following people on the dates noted: Ralph D. Abernathy, February 28, 1979; Joe F. Bear, March 1979; Eugene W. Carter, October 16, 1978; Jack Crenshaw, July 15, 1977; Virginia F. Durr, May 2, 1979; C.T. Fitzpatrick, January 11, 1979; Fred D. Gray, October 17, 1978; Mark W. Johnston, July 19, 1977; Walter J. Knabe, August 5, 1977; Rufus A. Lewis, July 27, 1977; William V. Lyerly, September 2, 1976; William R. Lynn, December 29, 1976; Edgar D. Nixon, August 2, 1977; Rosa L. Parks, May 22, 1978; James G. Pruett, Sr., January 2, 1977; Jo Ann Robinson, January 27, 1978; William F. Thetford, September 4, 1976. At the request of Mr. Pruett, I have regarded his interview as confidential.

2. Thomas M. Owen, *History of Alabama and Dictionary of Alabama Biography* (4 vols. Chicago, 1921), III, 716; Montgomery *Advertiser*, April 1, 2, 1911, May 18, 20, 1919. *Acts of Alabama*, 1911, pp. 289–315, 1915, pp. 52–76, 1919, pp. 97–102; *House Journal*, 1915, pp. 1461–66; *Senate Journal*, 1915, pp. 1144–49, 1170–71, 1173–75.

3. Montgomery *Advertiser*, March 15, 16, 1943, August 9, 12, September 5, 6, 1944, March 8, May 5, 9, 1946, March 18, 1947, March 19, 20, 1951; Montgomery *Alabama Journal*, May 9, 1946, March 18,

1947. Dunn had resigned in order to permit returning soldiers to participate in the choice of their mayor—one of his campaign pledges in 1944—but had declined himself to become a candidate in the special election "as I am entering private business here in Montgomery."

4. The figures as to churches were developed from Montgomery city directories. After 1952 city directories ceased to designate their entries by race. Dalraida and Chisholm were not within the city limits at this period.

5. Montgomery *Advertiser,* February 20, March 15, 1955.

6. Montgomery *Alabama Journal,* March 18, 1947; Montgomery *Advertiser,* August 28, 1953, October 28, 1955.

7. Montgomery *Advertiser,* September 15, October 3, 4, 18, 24, 27, November 1, 3, 4, 1953.

8. *Ibid.,* March 27, 1955; cf. May 12, 1954.

9. *Ibid.,* May 8, 1946, November 9, 1953, March 25, 1955; *Smith v. Allwright,* 321 U.S. 649.

10. *E.g.,* Dave Birmingham to James E. Folsom, October 28, 1955, James E. Folsom Papers, Manuscripts Division, Alabama State Department of Archives and History, Montgomery.

11. Montgomery *Advertiser,* February 6, March 21, April 20, May 6, 1954, September 23, 30, 1955; Montgomery *Alabama Tribune,* September 30, October 14, 1955; Montgomery *Alabama Journal,* February 2, 1956; Clifford J. Durr to Hubert T. Delany, September 4, 1955, Durr to Herbert H. Lehman, March 25, 1957, both in Clifford J. Durr Papers, Alabama State Department of Archives and History, Montgomery; Thomas J. Gilliam, "The Montgomery Bus Boycott of 1955–1956" (M.A. thesis, Auburn University, 1968), 12–13. Nixon today believes that he may have been counted out in the executive committee race (interview, August 2, 1977).

12. Trial Transcript, *M. L. King Jr. v. State of Alabama* (Records of the Alabama Court of Criminal Appeals, Office of the Clerk, Supreme Court Building, Montgomery), 256–57, 349–59; Martin Luther King, Jr., *Stride Toward Freedom: The Montgomery Story* (New York, 1958), 34, 73; Montgomery Alabama Tribune, December 23, 1955. Mrs. Burks and Mrs. Robinson organized the Council when they were refused membership in the League of Women Voters. Mrs. Robinson suggests that black women were able to be more aggressive in dealing with whites than were black men because in the environment created by segregation, women were under somewhat fewer strictures (interview, January 27, 1978). Lewis had been employed by the Montgomery Board of Education at the end of World War II to organize classes under the GI Bill for returning black veterans, and the veterans whom he taught became the backbone of his organization (interview, July 27, 1977).

13. Montgomery *Advertiser,* November 7, December 17, 1953, April 15, 17, 23, June 20, 1954; Juliette Morgan to William A. Gayle, July 13, 1955, Juliette Morgan Scrapbook, Alabama State Department of Archives and History, Montgomery.

14. Montgomery *Advertiser,* December 20, 1953, January 19, July 20, August 10, September 14, 1955; Montgomery *Alabama Tribune,* January 28, August 19, 1955. The *Advertiser* alleged editorially that Birmingham's August resolution was merely the opening gun in his rumored race for a seat on the County Board of Revenue. At the July meeting with the blacks Cleere and Birmingham almost came to blows and had to be separated by the mayor. The land that was promised as the site of a large new Negro park at the September meeting ultimately became a parking lot for a white football stadium.

15. Trial Transcript, *King v. State,* 141, 256–57, 349–59; Montgomery *Advertiser,* April 6, 1954.

16. Montgomery *Advertiser,* February 1, 6, 9, 13, 16, 20, 27, 28, March 10, 13, 16, 20, 23, 24, 27, 1955.

17. 1956 Montgomery City Directory; Montgomery *Advertiser,* May 9, 1954, February 1, 9, 1955. An additional highly visible alteration in race relations, though one unconnected with politics, was the hiring in the winter of 1953-54 of black players for the city's professional baseball team.

18. Montgomery *Advertiser,* February 9, 16, March 16, 1955, January 13, 1956.

19. *Ibid.,* February 18, 24, 25, March 1, 16, 20, 1955. Abernathy gives the membership of the committee that drafted the questionnaire as including himself, Nixon, Lewis, Robinson, Mrs. A. Wayman West, and James E. Pierce, a professor of political science at Alabama State (interview, February 28, 1979). Nixon, who presided at the meeting, says that all of the candidates chose to duck the bus-seating question (interview, August 2, 1977).

20. *Ibid.,* March 16, 20, 1955.

21. *Ibid.,* February 9, 13, March 16, 20, 22, 24, 25, 29, 1955. Because of the presence on the ballot of a minor candidate, George J. Rivers, the race between Parks and Cleere was forced into a run-off, but the geographical distribution of the vote was identical in both elections.

22. *Ibid.,* March 30, 1955.

23. Montgomery *Alabama Journal,* January 13, 1956.

24. Montgomery *Advertiser,* October 28, 1953, January 15, 1954, February 20, 24, March 7, 10, October 19, December 11, 1955, March 4, 1956; Montgomery *Alabama Journal,* November 3, December 9, 1955, March 4, 1956; Montgomery *Alabama Journal,* November 3, December 9, 1955, January 10, 1956.

25. Montgomery *Advertiser,* December 11, 1955.

26. *Ibid.,* March 6, 1955; Trial Transcript, *Aurelia S. Browder v. William A. Gayle,* Civil Action 1147-N, U.S. District Court, Middle District of Alabama (Federal Records Center, Atlanta, Georgia, FRC Box Number 426114), 17–20, and Colvin arrest warrant and complaint contained in case file.

27. Montgomery *Alabama Journal,* March 18, 19, 1955; Montgomery City Code of 1952, Chapter 6, Sections 10-11; Code of Alabama, 1940, Recompiled, Title 48, Section 301 (31 a); Gilliam, "Bus Boycott," 17. Gray had only returned to Montgomery six months earlier, after attending law school in Cleveland, Ohio. The Colvin case was his first joust with the segregation laws (interview, October 17, 1978). But he quickly became a leader of the black community; that summer found him serving as a spokesman for the black delegation in the meetings with the city concerning the parks.

28. King, *Stride,* 41–42; Trial Transcript, *King v. State,* 240, 344–46; Gilliam, "By Boycott," 18–19; Montgomery *Alabama Tribune,* March 16, 1956.

29. Trial Transcript, *King v. State,* 360–486, 510–47; Trial Transcript, *Browder v. Gayle,* 58–69.

30. Trial Transcript, *King v. State,* 256–57, 344–46, 357–59, 539–40. On Crenshaw's and Knabe's opinions of the legality of the Negro proposal, see below, notes 43, 47. Crenshaw and his brother had handled Governor Folsom's suit to compel the Dixiecrat presidential electors to vote for Harry Truman: *Folsom v. Albritton,* 335 U.S. 882; *State v. Albritton,* 251 Ala. 422.

31. *Flemming v. South Carolina Electric and Gas Co.,* 128 F. Supp. 469, 224 F. 2d 752; Montgomery *Advertiser,* July 15, 1955; Montgomery *Alabama Tribune,* July 22, 29, 1955; Trial Transcript, *Browder v. Gayle,* 10–12.

32. Montgomery *Advertiser,* December 12–16, 1953, October 25, 27, December 7, 20, 1955, January 25, February 16, 1956.

33. *Ibid.,* September 8, October 22, 23, 26, 1955; Montgomery *Alabama Tribune,* September 16, October 28, 1955. A petition seeking the integration of Montgomery's schools was also presented to the local board of education in August, and similar petitions were submitted throughout Alabama, evidently at the instance of the national NAACP. These petitions appear to have been the trigger for the establishment of a great many of the Alabama chapters of the White Citizens Council.

34. Montgomery *Advertiser,* November 6, 1955; interview with Nixon, August 27, 1–7 In the 1930s both Powell and Randolph had organized black boycotts of Northern merchants who refused to hire blacks.

35. Interview with Rosa L. Parks, May 22, 1978; interview with Virginia F. Durr, May 2. 1979; Trial Transcript, *Parks v. City of Montgomery,* 7–9; Montgomery *Advertiser,* December 2, 6, 1955; Montgomery *Alabama Journal,* December 5, 1955. From the jail Mrs. Parks telephoned her mother, who located Nixon. Nixon called his close friend Durr, a former member of the Federal Communications Commission during World War II, and together they arranged the bond.

36. Gilliam, "Bus Boycott," 22–23; B.S. Thompson, Sr., ed., *A Century of Negro Progress in Montgomery City and County, 1863–1963* (Montgomery, 1963), 2; interview with Jo Ann Robinson, January 27, 1978. Furious, Alabama State's president H. Councill Trenholm threatened to dismiss Mrs. Robinson for having placed the college in danger of white retaliation by her actions. She retained her job only by swearing to keep her role secret. In this she was eminently successful; Solicitor Thetford stated that despite his most diligent efforts, he was never able to discover the origin of the handbills (interview, September 4, 1976). Rufus Lewis believes today that the real source of the boycott was the prominence and popularity of Mrs. Parks, which moved the city's black women to take action (interview, July 27, 1977).

37. King, *Stride,* 43–49; Trial Transcript, *King v. State,* 446–48; Montgomery *Alabama Tribune,* December 9, 16, 1955. Additional copies of Mrs. Robinson's handbill were run off by King and Abernathy in the church office after the meeting that night and were distributed on December 3 and 4. The text of the handbill also was reprinted on the front page of the Montgomery Advertiser on December 4 and was read from the pulpits of many black churches that day, a Sunday. The persons whom Nixon called after the arrest were largely people who had been active in the NAACP and thus had known Mrs. Parks. But Nixon evidently recognized that this group of activists—many of whom were Alabama State faculty members—was unlikely to be successful in involving the black masses without the support of the clergy. Nixon had very little contact with the black clergy, but he did know Abernathy well. Abernathy was one of the few ministers who was also a leader of the NAACP. He was therefore the ideal bridge between the two groups. Nixon requested Abernathy to arrange for the attendance of the leading black ministers, and Abernathy did so. Abernathy states that King offered his church as the site of the meeting in the hope that he would not be asked to do anything further for the cause. But because the church was King's, he necessarily was appointed along with Abernathy to prepare the additional copies of the handbills that night, thus involving him reluctantly in organizing the boycott (interview, February 28, 1979).

38. Montgomery *Alabama Journal*, December 5, 1955, Montgomery Advertiser, December 6, 1955. On Judge Scott, see Montgomery Advertiser, September 25, 1955. Gray states today that whether the prosecution was carried out under the state law or the city ordinance seemed a matter of no real importance to him (interview, October 17, 1978). Abernathy states that none of the boycott's leaders had ever dreamed that the boycott could last longer than four days (interview, February 28, 1979).

39. King, *Stride*, 30, 46–58, 72–74; Montgomery *Advertiser*, January 19, 1956; Trial Transcript, *King v. State*, 106–28, 334. Abernathy reports that at the outset of the December 2 meeting there were perhaps 125 people present, but that Bennett's conduct of the meeting had reduced the attendance to 40 by the time that the vote was taken on the resolution endorsing the boycott. Lewis states that in suggesting King, he was merely searching for another name as an alternative to Bennett; he calls the nomination the luckiest accident of his life. Nixon claims that he had early recognized King's talents and was planning to nominate King if Lewis had not done so. But Abernathy says that Nixon barely knew King at the outbreak of the boycott; he says that when Nixon telephoned him on December 2, he himself suggested King's name to Nixon as a minister who might be cooperative. I am inclined to believe that Nixon's memory of his early appreciation of King's talents is influenced by the bitter struggle for King's mantle of leadership in which Nixon and Lewis engaged between 1961 and 1968—a struggle that culminated in Lewis's victory and that has left Nixon rather embittered. Indeed, Abernathy believes that Lewis suggested King's name as a way of preventing Nixon's own election as president, but I think that Abernathy is reading the later fierce rivalry back into an earlier time (interviews with Abernathy, February 28. 1979, Lewis, July 27, 1977, Nixon, August 2, 1977).

Nixon says that when he called the president of the Montgomery NAACP chapter. Robert L. Matthews, to report Mrs. Parks's arrest, Matthews refused to allow the chapter to become involved in a boycott without the approval of the NAACP national headquarters. Nixon states that it was this attitude of Matthews which forced the creation of a separate organization to run the boycott. But Abernathy reports that he and King had been discussing for months the need for an umbrella organization to bind Montgomery's blacks together, and that he seized the opportunity afforded by the boycott to suggest the creation of one.

40. Trial Transcript, *King v. State*, 59–61, 344-46; Montgomery *Alabama Tribune*, December 16, 1955.

41. Montgomery *Advertiser*, February 1, December 7, 1955; Montgomery *Alabama Journal*, December 7, 1955.

42. King, *Stride*, 108–13; Trial Transcript, *King v. State*, 239, 248–50, 336, 346–47; Montgomery *Advertiser*, December 9–11, 1955; Montgomery *Alabama Journal*, December 8, 9, 1955; *Browder v. Gayle* case file, Exhibit A: "Legal Requirements Concerning the Segregation of Races on City Buses." Abernathy states that the three demands were composed at a meeting at noon on December 5 consisting of Abernathy himself, Nixon, and Edgar N. French, director of the pensions office of the A.M.E. Zion churches in Montgomery, and were subsequently accepted by the MIA Executive Board (interview, February 28, 1979). He may, however, be confusing the demands with the resolution of December 5 mass meeting. King's statement that the demands were adopted by the meeting (*Stride*, 63–64, 108–09) is erroneous. Gray cannot today recall whether he helped King prepare the statement issued on December 10 (interview, October 17, 8), but its argument clearly is derived from Gray's brief. Crenshaw does not recall interchange with Parks which King reports, but he does confirm that Parks was more amenable to accepting the MIA's demands than were the other two commissioners—particularly Sellers. As Gayle and the reporters left the meeting, Gayle told those remaining that he wanted them to find a settlement as quickly as possible. Crenshaw even today rather resents that remark, feeling that it was an effort on the mayor's part to pass the buck to the bus company, which Crenshaw still regards as an innocent third party in the dispute (interview, July 15, 1977).

43. Trial Transcript, *King v. State*, 539–41; Montgomery *Advertiser*, March 20, December 31, 1955; King, *Stride*, 110; Mobile City Code of 1947, Chapter 20, Article 1. Crenshaw continues to believe today that the Montgomery Code required in detail the bus company's specific seating arrangement; when I told him that the Code merely required that the seating be separate and equal, he replied that he was positive that I was wrong. He is also under the impression that Mobile had adopted its seating plan only a few months before the outbreak of the boycott. He states that the Montgomery company had always been willing to accept the Mobile plan if the City Commission would amend the ordinance to permit the arrangement, but that the Commission adamantly refused to do so (interview, July 15, 1977).

44. Trial Transcript, *Browder v. Gayle*, 46–48; Motion of Public Service Commission for Dismissal of Complaint, in *Browder v. Gayle* case file. This reversal of positions was so complete that it has left Crenshaw confused about what his position had been on the issue earlier in the boycott. He believes that he had argued to the City Commission that the state statute was not applicable and that Gray had maintained that it was (interview, July 15, 1977).

45. Trial Transcript, *King v. State*, 346; Montgomery *Advertiser*, December 13, 1953; Montgomery *Alabama Journal*, December 16, 1955; King, *Stride*, 117–18. Just as the Commission apparently thought of the MIA and the bus company as the principal disputants, so the bus company thought of the MIA and the Commission as the principal disputants. This odd situation tended to inhibit both the company and the city in the negotiations with the blacks.

46. At the second meeting Luther Ingalls, an attorney prominent in the Montgomery White Citizens Council, was added to the white delegation, and Mrs. Hipp became a non-voting secretary of the committee—an alteration that provoked an outraged protest by King.

47. King, *Stride*, 114–21; Montgomery *Advertiser*, December 18, 20, 1955; Montgomery *Alabama Journal*, December 17, 19, 20, 1955, January 18, 1956; Trial Transcript, *King v. State*, 233–36, 248-50, 336, 539–41. Knabe states today that he never doubted the legality of the MIA's seating proposal. He says that he opposed granting the concession only because he was convinced that doing so would not really produce an end to the boycott (interview, August 5, 1977). But if he held such an opinion at the time, he certainly never gave any public hint of it. Crenshaw believes that Knabe supported his position (interview, July 15, 1977).

48. Crenshaw states that National City Lines hoped that by refusing to get involved, it could avoid making anyone mad (interview, July 15, 1977). The national company's determinedly noncommittal position is well illustrated by B. W. Franklin [executive vice-president] to Wilhelmina D. Long, March 20, 1956, enclosed in Wilhelmina D. Long to James E. Folsom, May 9, 1956, in Governors' Correspondence: Folsom II, Civil Archives Division, Alabama State Department of Archives and History, Montgomery.

49. Montgomery *Advertiser*, January 7, 10, 1956; Montgomery *Alabama Journal*, January 18, 1956; Montgomery *Alabama Tribune*, January 20, 1956; Gilliam, "Bus Boycott," 114–16. The origins of the idea for a federal suit are disputed. Gray states that he had favored filing a federal suit from the outset but had been unable to convince the MIA Executive Board to authorize the action, both because the strategy was new and untried for Montgomery blacks and because many MIA leaders had high hopes for negotiations in the early weeks (interview, October 17, 1978). Abernathy states that the idea of a federal court suit was first suggested to him near the end of December, he believes by Gray (interview, February 28, 1979). Nixon states that the idea of a federal court suit was suggested to him by his friend Clifford J. Durr. Nixon says that he passed the suggestion along to King and Abernathy; he dates this exchange to mid-February, however, which is impossible (interview, August 2, 1977). Mrs. Durr says that her husband originally suggested the idea to Gray after Ball's letter of January 9. She also states that Durr helped Gray with all the briefs and submissions in the boycott suit and that she personally typed them (interview, May 2, 1979). Lewis states that no one opposed a suit until shortly before it was actually filed, after the negotiations had proved unsuccessful (interview, July 27, 1977). Despite these differing accounts, it would appear certain that MIA leaders were discussing filing suit at least by mid-January, and it seems highly unlikely that the idea was much considered before late December.

50. Trial Transcript, *King v. State*, 252–53; Montgomery *Alabama Tribune*, January 27, 1956; Montgomery *Advertiser*, January 7, 18, 19, 22, 24, February 5, 28, 1956; Montgomery *Alabama Journal*, January 23, 24, 1956. My account of this episode differs considerably from that in King, *Stride*, 124–26. King accepted the three ministers' explanation at face value. I am led to reject it and to credit Gayle's testimony at King's trial on the point for two reasons. Most important, King's version does not adequately account for the nature and content of Gayle's statement of January 23. Secondly, an attempt by the city to perpetrate a hoax is inconsistent with the presence of Thrasher at the meeting. The Montgomery chapter of the White Citizens Council had been organized at a meeting on October 3, 1955 with about 300 persons in attendance. It was the tenth chapter to be organized in Alabama (Montgomery *Advertiser*, October 3, 4, 1955).

51. Montgomery *Advertiser*, January 24–26, February 14, 1956; Montgomery *Alabama Journal*, January 24, 1956.

52. Montgomery *Advertiser*, January 31, February 2, 1956; Montgomery *Alabama Journal*, January 31, 1956. Between January 26 and January 29, with the situation obviously deteriorating rapidly, Governor James E. Folsom attempted a secret mediation. Abernathy states that Folsom intervened after a delegation of blacks requested him to do so. But the governor's efforts proved fruitless (interview with Abernathy, February 28, 1979; interview with William V. Lyerly, September 2, 1976; Trial Transcript, *King v. State*, 254–55, 496–97). Gray confirms that the bombing was the trigger for the filing of the federal suit. He states that many in the MIA leadership remained hopeful even through January that the boycott would produce concessions and so, though he had begun preparing the suit, the MIA Executive Board had continued to hesitate about filing it. But the bombing, he says, clearly made it necessary for the MIA to appear to be taking firm retaliatory action, and therefore the Executive Board, at a meeting the morning after the bombing, instructed him to file, which he did later the same day (interview, October 17, 1978).

53. Montgomery *Advertiser*, February 3, 1956.

54. *Ibid.*, December 5, 1955, January 18, 26, 1956; Montgomery *Alabama Journal*, January 24, 27, 1956; Trial Transcript, *King v. State*, 213–27; Trial Transcript, *Browder v. Gayle*, 32–36; King, *Stride*, 115, 118, 120. White Montgomery leaders repeatedly told me that they knew there had been intimidation of many blacks to keep them off the buses because they had been told so by their servants or other employees. I am inclined to believe that these stories were usually told employers in an effort to offer acceptable explanations for cooperation with the boycott. But the tales, while protecting the individual black from reprisal, had the harmful effect of preventing whites from recognizing the extent of black support for the MIA. Abernathy reports that the commissioners made repeated efforts to divide King from the remainder of the MIA leadership as well (interview, February 28, 1979).

55. Montgomery *Advertiser*, February 2, August 26, 1956; Gilliam, "Bus Boycott," 114, 137; Clifford J. Durr to Corliss Lamont, February 7, 1957, Durr Papers. Jack Crenshaw believes even today that rivalries among various factions within the MIA leadership produced the bombings (interview, July 15, 1977). At the other extreme, Fred Gray still suspects the City Commission of having ordered the bombings (interview, October 17, 1978). Many of the whites whom I interviewed believe that the boycott was prolonged unnecessarily as a sort of confidence game through which sympathetic Northerners were being rooked for contributions.

56. It is worth noting in this regard that stories about the boycott had not yet reached the front page of the *New York Times* and did not do so until the indictment of MIA leaders for violation of the anti-boycott law, except for one article on the White Citizens Council rally at the state coliseum on February 10.

57. King, *Stride*, 121–22; Montgomery *Advertiser*, February 11, 1956. A considerable number of businessmen participated in the negotiations at one stage or another, but the principal business negotiators appear to have been Joe F. Bear, owner of a lumber and construction firm, C. T. Fitzpatrick, owner of a laundry and dry-cleaning business, James G. Pruett, president of the local division of the Trailways bus system, and Mark W. Johnston, vice-president of a bank. Bear was the Men of Montgomery chairman for February; the organization's chairmanship rotated monthly, on an alphabetical basis. Fitzpatrick, Pruett, and Johnston were the presidents of the Chamber of Commerce for, respectively, 1954, 1955, and 1956.

58. Montgomery *Advertiser*, January 19, February 8, 9, 1956. Despite King's statement most of the surviving black leaders agree with my assessment (interviews with Abernathy, February 28, 1979, Gray, October 17, 1978, Robinson, January 27, 1978). Rufus Lewis adds the interesting point that because white leaders, after years of ignoring blacks, were at last taking them seriously, the MIA was rendered quite reluctant to end the boycott that had finally given them access to power (interview, July 27, 1977). The business negotiators are unanimous in stating that, though they approached the negotiations with high hopes, convinced that a settlement could be found, they quickly came to see that the blacks were unwilling to make any concessions. I should also note Gray's statement that after February 1, all elements of the white community expressed to him privately a willingness to accept the MIA's original proposals if he would withdraw the federal suit and even offered him bribes to secure his agreement (interview, October 17, 1978). The sequence of events during February and early March makes this assertion seem implausible to me.

59. Montgomery *Advertiser*, December 8, 1955, January 11, 12, 15, 17, 19, February 15, 1956; Code of Alabama, 1940, Recompiled, Title 14, Section 54.

60. Trial Transcript, *King v. State*, 161–62, 186–87, 190; Montgomery *Alabama Journal*, February 13, 1956; Montgomery *Advertiser*, February 14, 1956. Thetford states that he was deeply dubious of indictments under the anti-boycott law as a tactic; he felt that, after a series of lengthy and emotional trials, the prosecution would result only in small fines for the boycotters or at most brief jail terms, without doing any real damage to the boycott itself. His own preference was for the bus company to seek a broad injunction against the MIA on the ground that its carpool operation was violating the company's exclusive franchise. If the MIA then disobeyed the injunction, its leaders could be jailed indefinitely for contempt. This strategy, he believes, would have broken the boycott. But he was unable to convince Crenshaw to adopt it. Crenshaw states that he was equally dubious of prosecuting under the anti-boycott law, but that he was unwilling to sue for an injunction because doing so would have involved abandoning the company's position as an innocent, neutral third party and was not, he thought, likely to end the boycott in any case. Thetford says that his hand was finally forced on the anti-boycott law when, as a result of the Ball letter, Judge Carter became convinced of the necessity to enforce the statute and came to him with the information that he intended to charge the next grand jury on the subject. Judge Carter does not recall the Ball letter, but he confirms that he decided to charge the grand jury about the act and thereupon informed Thetford of his intention (interviews with Thetford, September 4, 1976, Crenshaw, July 15, 1977, Carter, October 16, 1978).

61. Montgomery *Advertiser,* February 6, 21, 22, 28, 1956; Montgomery *Alabama Journal,* February 8, 20, 21, 1956. The MIA Executive Board's only white member, the Reverend Robert Graetz, also favored the compromise but did not support it publicly (Trial Transcript, *King v. State,* 486–92). There may have been unpublished elements in the compromise; rejection, Abernathy refers to the "proposals submitted by your organization approved by the City Commission and City Bus Line and with the fare conveyed to me by telephone . . . " Abernathy no longer recalls what he meant by the latter phrase (Abernathy to Men of Montgomery, February 20, 1956, in File 2279, Records of the Solicitor's Office, Fifteenth Circuit, Montgomery County Courthouse, Montgomery interview, February 28, 1979). Lynn reports that the Men of Montgomery did not receive a single suggestion as a result of its appeal (interview, December 29, 1976). Thetford says that he was convinced that the Men of Montgomery mediation would fail, but that if the blacks had accepted the compromise, he would have entered a *nolle prosequi* as to the indictments (interview, September 4, 1976).

62. Montgomery *Advertiser,* October 19, 1955; Montgomery City Directories for and 1956.

63. Montgomery *Advertiser,* March 23, 1956; Trial Transcript, *King v. State,* 193–227; *Lash v. State,* 244 Ala. 48; *Lash v. Alabama,* 320 U.S. 784, 814.

64. *Browder v. Gayle,* 142 F. Supp. 707; Montgomery *Advertiser,* October 23, 25, November 6, 1955, February 4, December 9, 1956, June 6, 1959; Montgomery *Alabama Journal,* October 24, 1955, January 31, 1956.

65. Montgomery *Alabama Tribune,* December 30, 1955. The purpose of the boycott is a matter of some dispute among surviving MIA leaders. Mrs. Robinson states that, because of the progress which the Women's Political Council had already been able to secure, she was initially quite optimistic about the prospects for negotiations. Gray says that he never had any hopes for the negotiations and favored a federal suit from the beginning, but he also says that most of the members of the MIA Executive Board believed that the negotiations would produce a settlement. Abernathy says that because the city and bus company officials had seemed willing to listen at earlier meetings and because the black proposals seemed to him so modest, he expected the whites to accept the MIA's position. Lewis states that at the outset no one really thought about whether or not the boycott was likely to produce concessions; he says that the boycott was born in the anger over Mrs. Parks's arrest and that its initial purpose was not to gain alterations in the bus seating policy but to demonstrate forcefully the extent of black resentment. Nixon says that the exchanges at the time of the Colvin arrest had convinced him of the futility of negotiating, and that he supported the boycott not because he thought it likely to produce concessions but because he thought that by making Mrs. Parks's case a *cause célèbre,* blacks would be able to prevent the white courts from shunting her case aside. He feared, he says, that white judges would never consider a test of the segregation laws seriously unless the test was so surrounded with publicity that they were compelled to do so (interviews, January 27, October 17, 1978, February 28, 1979, July 27, August 2, 1977). Each of these positions is entirely plausible, and very probably each reflects some aspect of the historical reality. At the same time the memory of each participant has necessarily been shaped to some extent by his knowledge of and reaction to subsequent events. In the final analysis the historian must ground his judgement in the sense which he has derived from the contemporary documents.

66. Montgomery *Advertiser,* December 8, 1955.

UNIT 5-3

A LETTER FROM THE WOMEN'S POLITICAL COUNCIL TO THE MAYOR OF MONTGOMERY, ALABAMA

The Montgomery bus boycott of 1955–1956 marks a watershed in the modern era of America's civil rights years. For twelve and a half months, black residents of Alabama's state capital walked, carpooled, and rode in taxis and hearses temporarily converted into buses rather than ride in the back of segregated "Jim Crow" buses. Jo Ann Robinson's May 21, 1954, letter (written on behalf of the Women's Political Council, of which she was president) to the mayor of Montgomery presaged the great nonviolent boycott by eighteen months.

Dear Sir:

The Women's Political Council is very grateful to you and the City Commissioners for the hearing you allowed our representatives during the month of March, 1954, when the "city-bus-fare-increase case" was being reviewed. There were several things the Council asked for:

1. A city law that would make it possible for Negroes to sit from back toward front, and whites from front toward back until all the seats are taken;
2. That Negroes not be asked or forced to pay fare at front and go to the rear of the bus to enter;
3. That busses stop at every corner in residential sections occupied by Negroes as they do in communities where whites reside.

We are happy to report that busses have been stopping at more corners now in some sections where Negroes live than previously. However, the same practices in seating and boarding the bus continue.

Mayor [W. A.] Gayle, three-fourths of the riders of these public conveyances are Negroes. If Negroes did not patronize them, they could not possibly operate.

More and more of our people are already arranging with neighbors and friends to ride to keep from being insulted and humiliated by bus drivers.

There has been talk from twenty-five or more local organizations of planning a city-wide boycott of bussing. We sir, do not feel that forceful measures are necessary in bargaining for a convenience which is right for all bus passengers. We, the Council, believe that when this matter has been put before you and the Commissioners, that agreeable terms can be met in a quiet and unostensible manner to the satisfaction of all concerned.

Many of our Southern cities in neighboring states have practiced the policies we seek without incident whatsoever. Atlanta, Macon and Savannah in Georgia have done this for years. Even Mobile, in our own state, does this and all the passengers are satisfied.

Please consider this plea, and if possible, act favorably upon it, for even now plans are being made to ride less, or not at all, on our busses. We do not want this.

Respectfully yours,
The Women's Political Council
Jo Ann Robinson, President

UNIT 5-4

SPEECH BY MARTIN LUTHER KING, JR., AT HOLT STREET BAPTIST CHURCH

Martin Luther King, Jr.

This is a substantial portion of the speech delivered by Martin Luther King, Jr., on the evening of December 5, 1955, at Holt Street Baptist Church, Montgomery, Alabama.

We are here this evening for serious business. We are here in a general sense because first and foremost we are American citizens, and we are determined to apply our citizenship to the fullness of its means. We are here because of our love for democracy, because of our deep-seated belief that democracy transformed from thin paper to thick action is the greatest form of government on earth. But we are here in a specific sense, because of the bus situation in Montgomery. We are here because we are determined to get the situation corrected.

This situation is not at all new. The problem has existed over endless years. For many years now Negroes in Montgomery and so many other areas have been inflicted with the paralysis of crippling fear on buses in our community. On so many occasions, Negroes have been intimidated and humiliated and oppressed because of the sheer fact that they were Negroes. I don't have time this evening to go into the history of these numerous cases. . . . But at least one stands before us now, with glaring dimensions. Just the other day, just last Thursday to be exact, one of the finest citizens in Montgomery—not one of the finest Negro citizens but one of the finest citizens in Montgomery—was taken from a bus and carried to jail and arrested because she refused to get up to give her seat to a white person. . . . Mrs. Rosa Parks is a fine person. And since it had to happen I'm happy it happened to a person like Mrs. Parks, for nobody can doubt the boundless outreach of her integrity. Nobody can doubt the height of her character, nobody can doubt the depth of her Christian commitment and devotion to the teachings of Jesus. . . .

And just because she refused to get up, she was arrested. . . . You know my friends there comes a time when people get tired of being trampled over by the iron feet of oppression. There comes a time my friends when people get tired of being flung across the abyss of humiliation where they experience the bleakness of nagging despair. There comes a time when people get tired of being pushed out of the glittering sunlight of life's July and left standing amidst the piercing chill of an Alpine November.

We are here, we are here this evening because we're tired now. Now let us say that we are not here advocating violence. We have overcome that. I want it to be known throughout Montgomery and throughout this nation that we are Christian people. We believe in the Christian religion. We believe in the teachings of Jesus. The only weapon that we have in our hands this evening is the weapon of protest. And secondly, this is the glory of America, with all of its faults. This is the glory of our democracy. If we were incarcerated behind the iron curtains of a Communistic nation we couldn't do this. If we were trapped in the dungeon of a totalitarian regime we couldn't do this. But the great glory of American democracy is the right to protest for right.

My friends, don't let anybody make us feel that we ought to be compared in our actions with the Ku Klux Klan or with the White Citizens' Councils. There will be no crosses burned at any bus stops in Montgomery. There will be no white persons pulled out of their homes and taken out to some distant road and murdered. There will be nobody among us who will stand up and defy the Constitution of this nation. We only assemble here because of our desire to see right exist.

My friends, I want it to be known that we're going to work with grim and firm determination to gain justice on the buses in this city. And we are not wrong, we are not wrong in what we are doing. If we are wrong, then the Supreme Court of this Nation is wrong. If we are wrong, the Constitution of the United States is wrong. If we are wrong, God Almighty is wrong. If we are wrong, Jesus of Nazareth was merely a utopian dreamer and never came down to earth. If we are wrong, justice is a lie. And we are determined here in Montgomery to work and fight until justice runs down like water and righteousness like a mighty stream.

I want to say that with all of our actions we must stick together. Unity is the great need of the hour. And if we are united, we can get many of the things that we not only desire but which we justly deserve. And don't let anybody frighten you. We are not afraid of what we are doing, because we are doing it within the law. There is never a time in our American democracy that we must ever think we're wrong when we protest. We reserve that right. . . .

We, the disinherited of this land, we who have been oppressed so long are tired of going through the long night of captivity. And we are reaching out for the daybreak of freedom and justice and equality. . . . In all of our doings, in all of our deliberations . . . whatever we do, we must keep God in the forefront. Let us be Christian in all of our action. And I want to tell you this evening that it is not enough for us to talk about love. Love is one of the pinnacle parts of the Christian faith. There is another side called justice. And justice is really love in [application]. Justice is love correcting that which would work against love. . . . Standing beside love is always justice. And we are only using the tools of justice. Not only are we using the tools of persuasion but we've got to use the tools of coercion. Not only is this thing a process of education but it is also a process of legislation.

And as we stand and sit here this evening, and as we prepare ourselves for what lies ahead, let us go out with a grim and bold determination that we are going to stick together. We are going to work together. Right here in Montgomery when the history books are written in the future, somebody will have to say "There lived a race of people, black people, fleecy locks and black complexion, of people who had the moral courage to stand up for their rights." And thereby they injected into the veins of history and of civilization. And we're gonna do that. God grant that we will do it before it's too late.

Keep Your Eyes on the Prize

Music: traditional ("Keep Your Hand on the Plow")
Words Adapted by Alice Wine & the Civil Rights Movement

This is a song that has been through every chapter of the movement. The words "keep your eyes on the prize" (replacing the more common "keep your hand on the plow") came from Alice Wine, one of the first proud products of voter education schools — on Johns Island, South Carolina in 1956. The song had meaning for the sit-in students who were the first to be 'bound in jail' for long periods of time. It went with the Freedom Riders to Jackson and into Parchman, and then on to Albany and all of the many other areas of struggle.

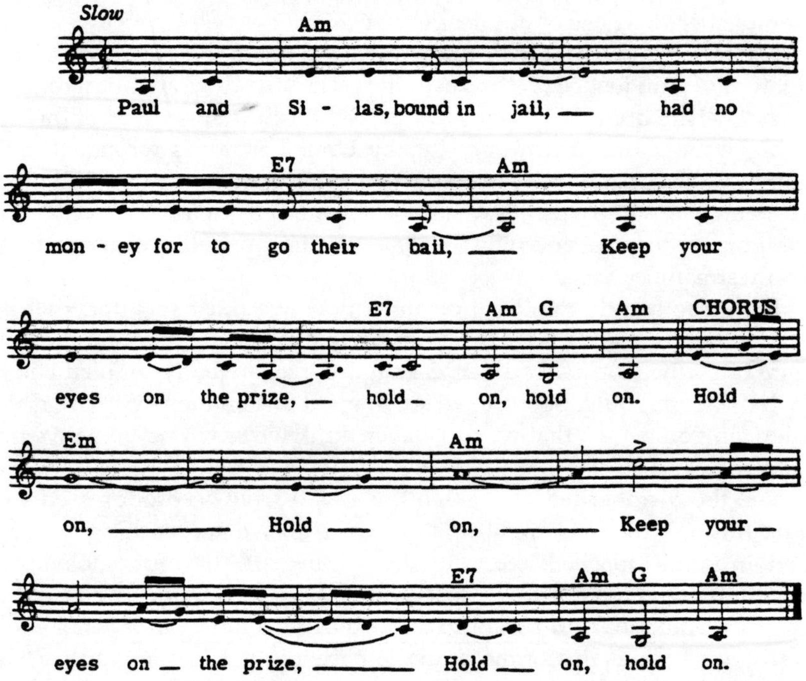

Paul and Silas begin to shout, the jail door opened and they walked on out.
Keep your eyes on the prize, hold on.

Freedom's name is mighty sweet, soon one day we're gonna meet.

Got my hand on the Gospel plow, I wouldn't take nothing for my journey now.

The only chain that a man can stand, is that chain of hand in hand.

The only thing we did wrong, stayed in the wilderness a day too long.

But the one thing we did right, was the day we started to fight.

We're gonna board that big Greyhound, carryin' love from town to town.

We're gonna ride for civil rights, we're gonna ride both black and white.

We've met jail and violence too, but God's love has seen us through.

Haven't been to heaven but I've been told, streets up there are paved with gold.

UNIT 6

SEGREGATION AND ITS ADHERENTS

INTRODUCTION 318

6-1 • ASK YOURSELF THIS IMPORTANT QUESTION 319

6-2 • THE CITIZENS' COUNCIL 320
ORGANIZED RESISTANCE TO THE SECOND RECONSTRUCTION, 1954–64
Neil R. McMillen

6-3 • DEFENDERS' NEWS AND VIEWS 338
SELECTIONS, 1955–59

6-4 • RICHMOND TIMES DISPATCH EDITORIAL, OCTOBER 1961 349

6-5 • RICHMOND NEWS LEADER 350
INTERPOSITION EDITORIALS, 1956

6-6 • AN ARGUMENT THAT THE NEGRO IS INHERENTLY INFERIOR 370
Carleton Putnam

6-7 • THE WHITE CITIZENS' COUNCIL 376
POWER FOR THE STATUS QUO

6-8 • YOU CAN HELP . . . 380

INTRODUCTION

Segregation and its Adherents charts the range of arguments offered by defenders of the old order, and attempts to understand the values of segregationists. The chapter from Neil McMillen's 1971 book *The Citizens' Council: Organized Resistance to the Second Reconstruction* (6-2), the single best account of the White Citizens' Council movement in the deep South, provides an overview of the many arguments offered by segregationists.

Defenders' News and Views (6-3) was the official publication of the Defenders of State Sovereignty and Individual Liberties (DSSI), Virginia's more genteel version of the White Citizens' Councils. Founded in Prince Edward County soon after *Brown* was announced, the Defenders grew within two years to number more than 12,000 members. While presenting a variety of arguments, these articles highlight the relationship that segregationists believed existed between communism and civil rights. Note also how the language in *Defenders' News and Views* and the advertisement in 6-1 parallels the language of movement activists in portraying themselves as the underdog in the struggle over Jim Crow; both groups believed victory rested on the ability to sway a largely indifferent moderate majority to their side.

James Kilpatrick, the editor of the Richmond *News Leader,* authored the famous interposition editorials (6-5). Kilpatrick tried to revive John C. Calhoun's antebellum idea that a state could 'interpose' its laws between the federal government and the people. Though popular among whites throughout the region, Kilpatrick's ideas were never effectively applied in the South; federal courts rejected any attempt by Virginia and other states to employ this doctrine as policy.

From the North, however, Carleton Putnam offered the most comprehensive and widely read biological and anthropological defense of segregation. A 1959 letter from Putnam to Attorney General William Rogers is reproduced here (6-6); he later expanded these arguments in a 1961 book called *Race and Reason: A Yankee View.*

ASK YOURSELF THIS IMPORTANT QUESTION:

What have I personally done to Maintain Segregation?

If the answer disturbs you, probe deeper and decide what you are willing to do to preserve racial harmony in Selma and Dallas County.

Is it worth four dollars to prevent a "Birmingham" here? That's what it costs to be a member of your Citizens Council, whose efforts are not thwarted by courts which give sit-in demonstrators legal immunity, prevent school boards from expelling students who participate in mob activities and would place federal referees at the board of voter registrars.

Law enforcement can be called only after these things occur, but your Citizens Council prevents them from happening.

Why else did only 350 Negroes attend a so-called mass voter registration meeting that outside agitators worked 60 days to organize in Selma?

Gov. Wallace told a state meeting of the council three weeks ago: "You are doing a wonderful job, but you should speak with the united voice of 100,000 persons. Go back home and get more members."

Gov. Wallace stands in the University doorway next Tuesday facing possible ten years imprisonment for violating a federal injunction.

Is it worth four dollars to you to prevent sit-ins, mob marches and wholesale Negro voter registration efforts in Selma?

If so, prove your dedication by joining and supporting the work of the Dallas County Citizens Council today. Six dollars will make both you and your wife members of an organization which has already given Selma nine years of Racial Harmony since "Black Monday."

Send Your Check To THE DALLAS COUNTY Citizens Council

SELMA, ALABAMA

UNIT 6-2

The Citizens' Council

Organized Resistance to the Second Reconstruction, 1954–64

Neil R. McMillen

The Prosegregation Argument

"Seldom have so few been accepted by so many as the voice of all," declared Wilma Dykeman and James Stokely. After traveling through thirteen southern and border states to sample the region's mood, this husband and wife team from Tennessee concluded in their award-winning book *Neither Black nor White* (1957) that "North and South, the W[hite] C[itizens'] C[ouncil]'s defiant pronouncements have been heeded as 'the' voice of 'the' South."[1] Indeed, although always a numerical minority, the organization did become the mouthpiece of southern defiance. Its affirmations on race and states' rights were quoted in the nation's congressional chambers and in state legislative halls. From pulpits, editorial columns, political hustings, and schoolhouse lecterns, the assumptions of the movement were approvingly reiterated. Its propaganda films and tape recordings were used weekly by sympathetic television and radio stations in many parts of the region, and its pamphlets, many of which were superbly printed, were distributed either free or at a nominal fee to defiant whites across the South.

Yet despite the wide exposure of its views on race and government, the Council movement as a whole did not develop a systematic intellectual framework in which to operate. For Council attitudes, like the subregions in which they evolved, frequently varied from one locality to the next. The Citizens' Councils of Florida differed from the Citizens' Councils of Mississippi, just as the peripheral South differed from the Deep South. Nor was the regional organization, the Citizens' Councils of America, able to overcome this intra-organization heterogeneity. Although seldom hesitating to speak for state and local Councils on matters of general policy, CCA headquarters in Jackson never managed to dominate fully the entire movement. Unlike such authoritarian-structured organizations as the John Birch Society and the Nation of Islam, there emerged within the Council movement no authority figure—no Robert Welch, no Elijah Muhammad—

possessed of sufficient power to dictate policy. The CCA's president, Roy V. Harris, was little more than a figurehead whose frequently embarrassing extremist utterances were endured but not always adhered to. Even William J. Simmons, the most powerful member of the Council's professional staff, never presumed to speak in anything but general terms for the organization's rank and file. True to the original design, the Council associations of the various states remained largely autonomous. Although the several state Councils, through their publications and public professions, exercised considerable influence over local Council organizations, ultimate authority over a wide range of actions rested with the local leadership itself.

The results of this decentralization were confusing, as the status of the Jew within the movement's racial construct well illustrated. Although the CCA from the outset endeavored to dissociate the Council from the onus of anti-Semitism, an anti-Jewish undercurrent persisted within the ranks of the movement. Despite its repeated disavowals, the organization's headquarters never managed to refute effectively the charge that it was anti-Jew as well as anti-Negro.[2] Periodic professions of innocence by William J. Simmons and other CCA professionals were not sufficient to offset the blatant Jew-baiting of state and local Councils in Louisiana and Arkansas,[3] for example, nor to obscure the occasional anti-Semitic outbursts of the organization's own president, Roy Harris.[4] But though much of Citizens' Council thought may have been fraught with contradictions and incongruities, there was a common body of assumptions generally acceptable to the entire movement. Though disagreement existed on many issues, all Councilors could agree with the CCA's executive director, Louis W. Hollis, when he declared the United States to be "a white man's government, conceived by white men and maintained by them through every year of its history." Like Hollis, they were united in their determination that "by the God of our fathers, it shall be ruled by the white man until the end of time."[5]

Primarily the ideology of the Citizens' Council was the ideology of white supremacy. Like Negrophobes of an earlier age the Councilors rested their case for white dominance on the postulate that Negroes were inherently different from Caucasians and that this difference, this hereditary inferiority, rendered them unsuitable for free association with white society.[6] In the Council's view the black man's presence could be tolerated only so long as the range of his economic, political, and social interaction with the white man's world could be systematically defined. In the Council's syllogism of white supremacy, then, segregation was the conclusion that necessarily followed the premise that human worth is calculable in terms of apparent physical characteristics.

The color-caste notion of social structure in mid-twentieth century America, as in earlier periods, thrived on the expression of racial differences. Councilors, like white supremacists before them, indulged their most imaginative fancies in delineating these differences. In order to demonstrate to southern school children that the black was not simply "a sun-burned white man," the CCA enumerated in an official handbook for fifth- and sixth-graders what it believed to be the eleven most essential differences between the two races:

1. The Negro's arm is about two inches longer than the white man's.
2. The jaw is shaped differently.
3. The weight of the brains differ.
4. The eyes are different.
5. The noses are different.
6. The lips are different.
7. The cheek bones are different.
8. The skulls are different.

9. The ears are different.
10. The hair is different.
11. The voices are different.[7]

Many of the Council's publications for adult consumption were hardly more sophisticated. Typical of this genre of propaganda was a Mississippi association brochure, *Racial Facts,* which listed such standard racist "facts" as "the Negro IQ is from 15 to 20 points below the average white IQ" and the "characteristic odor of the Negro's skin . . . is inherent and not caused by uncleanliness."[8]

One of the most intemperate expressions of racial differences may be found in Judge Brady's *Black Monday.* Throughout the movement's first decade, this hastily written, unabashedly racist manifesto of white southern resistance was widely regarded as the most systematic expression of Council thought. A spiritual descendant of such best-selling historical romances of an earlier generation as Thomas Dixon's *The Leopard's Spots* (1902) and *The Clansman* (1905), *Black Monday* contained a portrait of the Negro which recalled a description given by one of Dixon's characters.[9] Speaking through a Clansman, the novelist had described a "creature, half-child, half-animal . . . a being who left to his will, roams at night (and sleeps in the day, whose speech knows no word of love, whose passions, once aroused, are the fury of the tiger . . . "[10] In faithful paraphrase, Brady echoed: "You can dress a chimpanzee, housebreak him, and teach him to use a knife and fork, but it will take countless generations of evolutionary development, if ever, before you can convince him that a caterpillar or a cockroach is not a delicacy. Likewise the social, political, economic, and religious preferences of the Negro remain close to the caterpillar and the cockroach. . . . "[11]

But the venomous Negro-baiting that served Thomas Dixon so well early in the twentieth century could have little appeal to more sophisticated modern Americans. Since the days of the silent cinema when Dixon's glorification of white supremacy in its film version, *The Birth of a Nation,* had been seen by an estimated one hundred million people,[12] the burden of proof of Negro inferiority had gradually shifted from the black man to the white racists themselves. Well before World War I, new-school social scientists, led by anthropologist Franz Boas, began to challenge not only misguided popular notions on race but the ill-founded theories of older generations of sociologists, anthropologists, and psychologists, whose speculations about innate racial traits had long dignified the illogic of prejudice.[13] Indeed, by 1944 scientific thought in the United States had progressed to a point where Gunnar Myrdal could approvingly observe that "*it is now difficult for even popular writers to express other views than the ones of racial equalitarianism and still retain intellectual respect.*"[14]

Yet the race theories so prominent in an earlier age had not capitulated; they were merely in retreat. On May 17, 1954, when the Supreme Court at last guaranteed equal educational opportunities, scientists of the old school began dusting off their outmoded conceptions in preparation for the campaign against what William J. Simmons liked to call "the equalitarian dogma" of modern science.[15] Once again the authority of science, that perennial handmaiden of race bigotry, was invoked by those who sought to negate the Negro's constitutional right to full citizenship. But the "new racism," as Oscar Handlin has called it,[16] differed markedly in several respects from the old. Most noticeably, it abandoned the widely inclusive discriminatory pattern of the past and identified only one inferior human type. An older generation of scientific racists, including Anglo-Saxon nativists like Madison Grant and Theodore Lothrop Stoddard, had created a veritable pyramid of human worth with "Nordics" representing the apex, other members of the "races" of Europe—the "Alpines" and the "Mediterraneans"—enjoying lesser though still exalted status, and the "dregs" of humanity, the Negro among them, situated at the base.

The white supremacists of the new racist persuasion, however, resorted to the shibboleths of Anglo-Saxonism only infrequently; rather, their focus was the black man. Second, and far more important, neoracism could not hide beneath the protective canopy of intellectual respectability. Although an earlier age had seldom questioned biological interpretations of history and civilization, the newly refurbished scientific racism had limited appeal to the American public of the mid-twentieth century.

Not remarkably, then, Carleton Putnam, the most influential spokesman of the new racism, was not a scientist at all, but a retired airline executive. When he turned to ethnology in 1958, Putnam had a baccalaureate degree in history and politics from Princeton and a degree in law from Columbia; he had pioneered in commercial aviation and been chairman of the board of Delta Air Lines;[17] he had written an interesting and highly readable memoir about his career, and he was the author of an impressive history of Theodore Roosevelt's early years.[18] By any standard, this was a commendable record; but it could hardly qualify him as an authority on cultural anthropology. Yet despite his lack of formal credentials in the biological and natural sciences, Putnam had qualities that would well serve the cause of segregation. Possessed of an impeccable pedigree stretching back in American history to the French and Indian Wars, he was clearly of Yankee stock and therefore not subject to accusations of regional bias. An impassioned social and economic conservative who viewed race as the key to civilization, this descendent of a Revolutionary War hero[19] fancied himself a kind of latter-day ethnological Paul Revere riding to alarm a sleeping people of the perils of racial miscegenations.

Setting forth his ethnological assumption in an influential and widely circulated book, *Race and Reason* (1961), Putnam asserted that one need not have advanced scientific training to dispute theories of racial equalitarianism: "Any man with two eyes in his head can observe a Negro settlement in the Congo . . . can compare this settlement with London or Paris, and can draw his own conclusions regarding relative levels of character and intelligence. . . . " That so few informed Americans saw things so clearly was compelling proof to Putnam that the nation had been victimized by a "pseudo-scientific hoax" popularized by such early exponents of racial equipotentiality as Franz Boas and several subsequent generations of like-minded anthropologists more devoted to "the demi-Goddess of Equalitarianism" than to "the Goddess of Truth."[20]

A veritable white supremacist's catechism consisting largely of refutations of desegregation arguments, *Race and Reason* reportedly sold 60,000 copies in its first six months; by 1969 its publisher indicated that sales totaled 150,000.[21] Taking early note of this reception, the Council of the American Anthropological Association denounced Putnam's position. Similarly critical were the Committee on Science in the Promotion of Human Welfare (an affiliate of the American Association for the Advancement of Science), the American Association of Physical Anthropologists, and a host of leading scientists, including the geneticist Theodosius Dobzhansky, all of whom issued statements condemning the work as unscientific.[22] But the disapprobation of distinguished scholars and learned societies had little effect, either on Putnam or the prosegregation South.

Senators J. Strom Thurmond of South Carolina, Harry Flood Byrd of Virginia, Richard B. Russell of Georgia, and a host of lesser southern statesmen gave *Race and Reason* their unqualified endorsement. So too did leading southern journalists like Thomas R. Waring, editor of the Charleston *News and Courier,* Virginius Dabney, editor of the Richmond *Times-Dispatch,* and John Temple Graves, regionally syndicated columnist.[23] The Louisiana State Board of Education purchased 5,000 copies for distribution to public schools. The Virginia House of Delegates entertained a resolution calling upon the board of education to consider the book as required reading in the commonwealth's schools.[24] By concurrent resolution, both houses of the Mississippi legislature urged the creation of a special course so that the state's school children might study *Race and Reason,* "a book that exposes the flagrant distortion and perversion of scientific truth by so-called social anthropologists and socialistically oriented sociologists." Governor Ross Barnett declared October 26, 1961, to be "Race and Reason Day in Mississippi," and called upon Magnolia State citizens to observe the occasion by reading and discussing Putnam's volume.[25]

Leading the Putnam bandwagon, of course, was the Citizens' Councils of America from its offices adjacent to the governor's mansion in Jackson. The Council's chief executive, William J. Simmons, one of Governor Barnett's close advisers, had been largely instrumental in the declaration of Race and Reason Day. One of Simmons's lieutenants, Louis W. Hollis, executive director of the Jackson Citizens' Council and business manager of the Council's official journal, played a key role in the planning of the Race and Reason Day Dinner.[26] The lead editorial of the November, 1961, issue of *The Citizen*—an issue devoted entirely to Carleton Putnam and his book—hailed Putnam's Race and Reason Day address as "the turning point" in the region's struggle to preserve segregation.[27] Through *The Citizen*, the CCA offered the paperback edition of *Race and Reason* to subscribers at half price and announced the release of a fifty-minute long-playing record album of "highlights" of the festivities. In order to exploit fully the entire range of the communications media, the Citizens' Council Forum produced and distributed to sympathetic radio and television stations a thirty-minute documentary film and a sixty-minute tape recording of the occasion.[28]

Plaudits for Putnam were not exclusively confined to the segregationist laity of the South. Treading the perimeter of academic respectability were a few elder scientists who certified the "inescapable scientific validity" of *Race and Reason*. Among them, one of the most notable of the American scholars was Wesley Critz George (born 1888), professor emeritus of histology and embryology and former head of the department of anatomy at the University of North Carolina Medical School, who would soon become a Citizens' Council hero in his own right. Indeed, even before endorsing the Putnam study, Dr. George emerged from retirement to write his own tract on innate racial characteristics. Entitled *The Biology of the Race Problem*, it resembled, in both content and motivation, a work by Thomas R. Dew, the antebellum professor of history and metaphysics at the College of William and Mary who was asked in 1831 by the Virginia legislature to produce a summary of the controversy over the abolition of slavery. Like Dew's *Review of the Debate* in the Virginia legislature of 1831–32, George contended that as an inferior being the Negro's subjugation to the white man was morally justifiable. Like Dew again, George was retained by a southern state expressly to arrive at these conclusions. Paid $3,000 by the Alabama Governor's Emergency Fund, George surveyed the findings of "the most credible scientists"[29] and concluded that desegregation and its inevitable result, intermarriage, could result only in evil. And "doing evil," he concluded, "is not Christian."

justification

Not remarkably, the impresarios of massive resistance delighted in the George Report. With the desegregation crisis at the University of Mississippi raging about them, Council leaders in Jackson jubilantly proclaimed that "another major scientific report has shattered the equalitarian myth."[30] The October, 1962, issue of *The Citizen* offered it in booklet form at fifty cents a copy, and in lots of ten for $3.50. Council administrator William J. Simmons, lecturing on "the scientific aspect of race differences," recommended it to university audiences at Yale, Notre Dame, and Virginia as an antidote to the "false science" and "equalitarian dogma" which "has been disseminated so widely in academic circles during recent years. . . ."[31]

Similarly well regarded were the controversial works of Carleton S. Coon. The president of the American Association of Physical Anthropologists and curator of ethnology and professor of anthropology at the University Museum in Philadelphia, Coon speculated—largely on the basis of fossil skulls and fire remains—that the evolutionary development of the Negroid was some 200,000 years behind that of the Caucasoid race.[32] But, unlike George and Putnam, he did not attempt to relate his theories to the debate over segregation. Moreover, the anthropologist pointed out that although the use of fire in Europe could be traced back 250,000 years as compared to a mere 40,000 in Africa, its first use in China occurred fully 360,000 years ago. Untroubled by such details, *The Citizen* proclaimed Coon's work to be "a major breakthrough in anthropology" which "should put an end once and for all to the bogus equalitarian propaganda now parading as 'science.'"[33] In a later issue of the same journal, Carleton Putnam offered further interpretations of Coon's findings as "new evidence" of Negroid inferiority.[34] Understandably, he failed to apply a similar kind of logic to the Caucasoids' sluggish 110,000-year lag behind precocious Mongoloid fire-builders.

Psychology, too, could be employed in the defense of Jim Crow customs. In Henry E. Garrett (born 1894), professor emeritus of psychology at Columbia and past president of the American Psychological Association, segregationists found an old-style devotee of the World War I Army's alpha intelligence test unhesitatingly willing to attribute intelligence quotients of "average" Negro children and "average" white children to inborn racial differences.[35] For sociological justification they invoked the name of Harvard's late Pitirim Sorokin, in whose *Contemporary Sociological Theories* (1928) Councilors found compelling evidence that heredity, not environment, explained why "American negroes have not up to this time produced a single genius of great caliber."[36]

The prosegregation argument invoked God as readily as it did science. "The races of man are the handiwork of God, as is everything in nature," a Mississippi Citizens' Council tract declared. "If He had wanted only one type of man, He would have created only one."[37] It was, then, the duty of the godly to keep the races as He had made them—distinct.

There was ample precedent for the Council's use of providential judgment as justification for its racial attitudes. Indeed, a most pervasive theme in the history of white supremacy in America has been the readiness of its advocates to swaddle their beliefs in the holy writ. The scriptural defense of bondage was a mainstay of the antebellum proslavery argument. Nor did the theological defense of human subordination atrophy with the advent of abolition. To be sure, the language of subjugation shifted during the postbellum period in recognition of the Negro's free status, but the tenets of religion were still used to defend his inferior position in society. Both the original Klan and its twentieth-century successors, as well as turn-of-the-century Anglo-Saxon expansionists, practiced their own peculiar version of the Ten Commandments, secure in the knowledge of divine approval. Against such a backdrop, it is not remarkable that the Citizens' Council, which drew the bulk of its membership from Bible-belt fundamentalists, should have enlisted providence in the campaign to keep the Negro in his place. But the Council's effort to preempt the religious argument for the prosegregation position was greatly complicated by the readiness with which the South's major denominational bodies embraced the Court's decision.[38]

Scarcely a month after the rendering of the school desegregation decree of May 17, 1954, the Southern Baptist Convention met in St. Louis to approve overwhelmingly the report of its Christian Life Commission: "the Supreme Court decision is in harmony with the constitutional guarantee of equal freedom to all citizens, and with the Christian principles of equal justice and love for all men." After expressing confidence in the nation's public schools, the Convention called upon political and religious leaders of the South to act responsibly in order that "this crisis in our national history shall not be made the occasion for new and bitter prejudices, but a movement toward a united nation."[39]

Following the example of the Baptists, the region's largest and perhaps most conservative church, the general convocations of the other major denominations of the Protestant South issued similarly positive affirmations of Christian brotherhood.[40] Thus, at least in terms of official policy, the overwhelming majority of southern church members belonged to denominations which had endorsed the school desegregation decision. But all too frequently the policies adopted by church hierarchies did not reflect the attitudes of the local congregations from which came the rank and file of the organized resistance movement. The readiness with which individual Baptists, Methodists, Presbyterians, and Episcopalians rallied to defend traditional southern racial customs was one very valid index to the growing cleavage between denominational leaders in the South and their communicants.[41] This estrangement from high church councils became increasingly apparent during the first decade of desegregation. But it was not indicative of diminishing piety among southern churchgoers. Indeed, prosegregation gatherings frequently exhibited all of the religiosity of old-fashioned revival meetings. Typical was a Jackson Citizens' Council rally of June, 1958, commemorating the third anniversary of the movement's birth. Following the invocation ("Thou didst keep men apart in their differences and their habitations"), the pastor of the Highland Baptist Church of Montgomery, Dr. Henry L. Lyon, who had twice served as state president of Alabama's more than 600,000 Baptists, spoke on the topic "Why Integration is Un-Christian." Using as his text Matthew 7:12 ("Whatsoever ye would that men should do to you, do ye even so to them . . . "), Dr. Lyon advised Council members that "separation of the races is the commandment and the law of God." With appropriate Sunday morning responsiveness, a portion of the crowd was moved to say, "Amen."[42]

Not every Council rally ended with a chorus of amens, but virtually every Council had its chaplain and most meetings did begin with a prayer for God's blessings.[43] Moreover, a sizable portion of the movement's leadership came from the Protestant clergy. On the twelve-member editorial board of *The Citizens' Council* and its successor, *The Citizen,* official organs of the Citizens' Councils of America, there were three clergymen—the Reverend Henry J. Davis, of Dundas, Virginia; the Reverend James P. Dees, rector of Trinity Episcopal Church, Statesville, North Carolina; and the Reverend L. B. McCord, an ordained Presbyterian minister who loved the unenviable responsibility of serving as superintendent of schools in Clarendon County, South Carolina, in 1954. In addition to his ministerial and editorial duties, Dees was president of the statewide Council movement in North Carolina, the Defenders of States' Rights. Similarly, Davis headed the Association of Citizens' Councils of Virginia, and McCord served as executive secretary of the statewide Council association in South Carolina.[44] William T. Bodenhamer, the executive secretary of the Georgia States' Rights Council, was also the pastor of the Baptist Church in Ty Ty.[45] In Arkansas, the Reverend Wesley Pruden, who rose from the post of chaplain to become president of Little Rock's Capital Citizens' Council, was one of the most powerful Council spokesmen in the state.[46] The first executive secretary of the Council's statewide association in Florida was the Reverend George H. Downs, a Baptist minister.[47]

Like its leadership, much of the Council's literature bore an ecclesiastical impress that possessed remarkable appeal to religious Southerners, torn in the seemingly irreconcilable conflict between their WWII deep-seated racial attitudes and the liberal statements of their churches. Among the most widely circulated of the Council's many propaganda pieces were those that sought to establish the moral justice of segregation by reference to divine revelation. In format these materials varied from crudely mimeographed throwaways to more sophisticated pamphlet-length expositions, but in substance they differed very little. Bearing such titles as *Christianity and Segregation, God the Original Segregationist, Is Segregation Un-Christian?, The Church and Segregation,* and *Christian Love and Segregation,* the great bulk of this propaganda had but a single theme: "segregation—God's own plan for the races."[48] Typical of this genre of literature was a tract by a Presbyterian minister, the Reverend G. T. Gillespie, president emeritus of Belhaven College,

Jackson. Published by the Mississippi Association of Citizens' Councils, and given regional distribution by the Citizens' Councils of America, Gillespie's *A Christian View on Segregation* was remarkably similar to works published by proslavery advocates during the decade before the Civil War. In the spirit of the *Pro-Slavery Argument* (1853), that massive collaboration in propaganda by Thomas R. Dew, Chancellor William Harper, Governor James H. Hammond, and William Gilmore Simms, Gillespie's defense of segregation invoked historical and scriptural justifications, focused on the ruinous effects of abolishing the institution, and ultimately concluded that it was not merely a social necessity but a positive good.[49]

Less dogmatic than proslavery militants, Gillespie would admit that the scriptures contained no precise mandate for or against segregation. Nevertheless, he argued, they do contain considerable evidence from which "valid inferences" may be derived in support of segregation as a development of divine purpose. Supporting his exegesis on providential will, Gillespie cited passages in Genesis, Leviticus, Ezra, the Gospels, Acts, Epistles, and Revelation to demonstrate that segregation was sanctioned by divine authority during the patriarchal age, vested with legal status in the Mosaic period, and wholly in harmony with the spirit and the teachings of Christ and the Apostles.[50] In effect, Gillespie's study of the Bible brought him in 1954 to the same conclusions reached in 1845 by the eminent Baptist divine, Dr. Richard Fuller: "WHAT GOD SANCTIONED IN THE OLD TESTAMENT AND PERMITTED IN THE NEW, CANNOT BE SIN."

Willing to concede that Jesus had taught not only the love of God for all mankind but the essential oneness of all Christian believers, Gillespie proved more hesitant in stamping Jim Crow with the unqualified endorsement of Christ than were many writers of subsequent Citizens' Council tracts. For example, the Reverend T. Robert Ingram, rector of St. Thomas Episcopal Church of Houston and one of the foremost exponents of the morality of compulsory social separation,[52] believed that race discrimination was simply applied Christianity: "The most complete and devastating discriminatory practices that can ever be exercised," he asserted in the Council journal, "are those of Jesus Christ." To embrace human equality, the minister warned, was to judge Jesus, the great discriminator, accursed." Had not He damned some and saved others?[53]

Biblical interpretations such as these reinforced the Council's view, as expressed by Judge Brady at a New Orleans segregation rally in 1955, that "segregation is a holy thing."[54] If segregation had the sanction of the providentially inspired writings and the approval of the Son of God, then integration could only be sinful, the work of either Satan or (as Council propaganda came increasingly to assert) his blood brother, Karl Marx. Indeed, the whole "myth of equality" could be traced to those nefarious "-isms"—socialism, communism, and one-worldism—which threatened the ultimate annihilation of all Christendom. By accepting this myth, and declaring segregation un-Christian, the general assemblies of the region's major denominations became the dupes of "false prophets."[55] Moreover, Council spokesmen believed that the organization which represented most of American Protestantism, the National Council of Churches of Christ in America, had become so infused by "multi-racial, collectivist theorists" and "ecclesiastical bureaucrats" that it had been reduced to a "propaganda tool" for "left wing movement of every kind."[56]

Believing as it did that the proper role of the church was to teach racial harmony through separation, the Council focused the brunt of its attack on liberal theology, upon the "pinkos in the pulpit." Having decided that "racial preference" is un-Christian, these ministers of "socialized Christianity" had also declared that "private enterprise, rugged individualism, and conservatism in politics are equally un-Christian." This "pharisaical concern" with social reform, this meddling in race relations and other purely social, economic, and political affairs, Council literature asserted, so preoccupied the "Social Gospel left winger" that he had neglected individual religious experience—the church's only legitimate sphere of interest.[57]

The Council's offensive against liberal clergy was in some ways reminiscent of Bible-belt attitudes during the Scopes trial. Yet it was less a reflection of the suspicions of Deep South fundamentalism toward intellectually oriented theology than it was of Deep South racial mores. The "Social Gospelers," as the Councils were wont to call all but the most ardently prosegregation clergymen, embodied a threat to the white supremacists' resolute conviction that the Negro, by the will of God and the testimony of science, occupied a status considerably lower than the white man.

The corollary to the Citizens' Council contention that segregation was the law of God is the assertion that it was also the law of nature. In the Reverend Gillespie's view racial separation was not only commanded by nature, but it was "one of nature's universal laws."[58] Conversely, the Reverend James P. Dees affirmed that racial mixing was a "violation of God's natural law in creation," a "crime against nature." "Do black birds," he inquired, "intermingle with blue birds? Does the redwing fly with the crows? Would it make sense for my Senior Warden to mix Black Angus cattle with his pure-bred Herefords?" Such would be "abhorrent to the natural created order."[59]

Thus the elementary laws of the universe taught that black-skinned people, like Black Angus cattle, could be crossed with white-faced creatures, Caucasian or Hereford, only by violating one of nature's most fundamental precepts. History taught that segregation was not simply natural, it was beneficial. Much more than a social necessity, it was an unqualified good. For where else, ran the Council's argument, had the Negro progressed so rapidly in so few years as he had in the segregated South?[60] Had he not, as Judge Brady insisted, been "saved from savagery," been "compelled to lay aside cannibalism, [and] his barbaric savage customs," and had he not been transported from aboriginal ignorance and superstition and been "introduced to God?"[61]

Believing that Negroes had failed to develop even the rudiments of civilization in their "natural habitat," Councilors could only conclude that whatever culture blacks had acquired they owed to the white society in which it had been their good fortune to dwell.[62] Recurring throughout segregation literature, this view was given characteristic expression in CCA president Roy V. Harris's weekly tabloid, the Augusta *Courier*: "in the land of the Nile both the Negro and the white man started. No race of people in antiquity. developed and made progress as did the Egyptians. . . . Yet during all this development, the Negro contributed two things to the history of mankind: 1. Human slavery. 2. Cannibalism."[63] Brady, too, juxtaposed the pyramids against the cannibals in order to demonstrate the Negro's innate incapacity for civilization. While Caucasoid man in Egypt, Greece, and Rome was creating the intellectual and technological foundations of western civilization, while Mongoloid man during the Chow and Ming dynasties formulate the art, literature, and high standards of eastern morality, Negroid man, Brady averred, "like the modern lizard," had not evolved. While the culture of the modern world had found its matrix in the white and the yellow races, the black race had spawned no elemental idea, given birth to no fundamental innovation. Instead, "although both the other races of mankind had for some time tabooed it, cannibalism was an expected risk in the life of the Negro of this period."[64]

From the Council's historical perspective, the presence of the Negro was a threat to more than just the flesh of his neighboring tribesman. For despite the white man's superior capacity for civilization, he could not withstand the infusion of the black man's blood. The "facts" of history, Council spokesmen believed, revealed that whenever and wherever the white man drank "the cup of black hemlock," whenever and wherever he infused his blood with that of the Negro, white intellect and white culture perished. This was the tragic story of Egypt and Babylon, Greece and Rome; and it was the story of India, Spain, and Portugal—"negroid blood like the jungle, steadily and completely swallowing up everything."[65]

A careful study of the past, then, revealed that the Negro carried in his very blood a destructive force that could pull down the mightiest of civilizations. But history had other lessons from which its modern students could profit. In the papers of the nation's most revered heroes, segregationists discovered some of their most effective parries for the thrusts of the desegregationists. "If we are bigoted, prejudiced, un-American . . . " Councilors argued, "so were George Washington, Thomas Jefferson, Abraham Lincoln, and our other illustrious forebears who believed in segregation."[66]

Theodore G. Bilbo, the Magnolia State's loquacious Negro-baiting progressive, was an obvious choice as a source of authority on racial questions for the Mississippi-dominated Citizens' Councils of America. His speeches were colorful, quotable, and virtually always couched in the argot of white supremacy. Particularly useful was his statement on miscegenation. If all of the tangible evidence of American civilization—its buildings, its highways, its cities, and even its army—were destroyed, he had said, the nation could survive and would ultimately recover. "But if the blood of our white race should become corrupted and mingled with the blood of Africa, then the present greatness of the United States of America would be destroyed and all hope for the future would be forever gone."[67]

This quotation was repeated in Council speeches, cited in its pamphlets, and distributed by it on ink blotters and leaflets.[68] But a statement by Bilbo had only limited value for the prosegregation argument. Although his memory was much revered by a broad segment of Deep South society, particularly by poor whites of the rural, red clay hills, his popular reputation outside the region was scarcely that of wisdom.

The same could hardly be said of Thomas Jefferson. His writings, too, when submitted to the selective mining of the organized resistance movement, bore a rich ore capable of being hammered into a flimsy armor for white supremacy. In his autobiography, the third president alluded to certain unbridgeable racial differences which required the colonization of the Negro, once emancipated, in another land: "Nothing is more certainly written in the book of fate, than that these people are to be free; nor is it less certain that the two races, equally free, cannot live in the same government. Nature, habit, opinion have drawn indelible lines of distinction between them."[69] Lifted from the context of Jefferson's voluminous papers, this statement made effective propaganda for the segregationists cause. Like the one from Bilbo, it too became a part of the CCA's "Famous Quotations" series of blotters and leaflets. It too, was cited in speech and pamphlet as evidence of the "fact" of Negro inferiority.[70]

Even more useful to the prosegregation argument were Abraham Lincoln's numerous statements on race.[71] Claimed as he has been by the advocates of Negro rights, the Great Emancipator's darker side was not universally recognized. Lamenting what he termed "the big lie about Lincoln," William J. Simmons charged that "dishonest integrationists in a brazen historical theft" had appropriated the prestigious name and memory of the sixteenth president for their own "devious ends." If Lincoln were alive today, Simmons assured his fellow Councilors, "his position would be regarded not merely as that of a segregationist, but of an out-and-out white supremacist."[72] In order to rescue the Illinois president's reputation from "such disgrace," the Citizens' Councils of America launched a national advertising campaign to acquaint the American people with the "real" Abraham Lincoln. A special Lincoln's birthday issue of *The Citizen* for February, 1964, was entirely devoted to quotations from his debates with Douglas, his first inaugural, and his speeches at Peoria (1854), Springfield (1857), and Chicago (1858)—all in an effort to equate the ideas of the Civil War statesman with those of massive resistance. Emerging from these carefully chosen excerpts was Lincoln, the impassioned critic of the high Court, who had warned that "if the policy of the government . . . is to be irrevocably fixed by the decisions of the Supreme Court . . . the people will have ceased to be their own rulers. . . . " An intractable champion of states' rights, the sixteenth president had denied that he possessed the constitutional authority to interfere with the institutions of the sovereign southern states. So fearful of miscegenation was he that he wished to carry racial disassociation to the point of deporting the Negro.[73]

Concomitant with the Lincoln issue of *The Citizen*, the CCA's information minister, Richard Morphew, announced a newspaper advertising scheme also designed "to save Lincoln's good name" by canonizing him as the patron saint of segregation. The objective was to blanket the North with a quarter-page publicity release, featuring "Lincoln's hopes for the Negro": "What I would most desire would be the separation of the white and black races." According to the organization's own calculations, the advertisement ran in more than six hundred "major" newspapers on February 10 and 11, and before the month had passed it had been printed in more than one thousand.[74]

Patently transparent though it was, the argument from history (like that from science and nature) did lend authority to the assumptions of the segregationists. However, the movement resorted to levels of defense which lacked even that support. That oft-repeated affirmation that segregation's antonym, integration, would lead inexorably to miscegenation, that "horrifying byproduct" of racial coexistence, was perhaps the most compelling of these defenses. Council leaders tirelessly reiterated their Manichean conviction that segregation was the essence of all things good—"the freedom to choose one's associates, Americanism, state sovereignty, and the survival of the white race." Its alternative was an unqualified evil, representing only "darkness, regimentation, totalitarianism, communism, and destruction."[75] Integration always meant miscegenation, for by lowering the racial barriers in the public schools, the Supreme Court had opened the floodgates of "*amalgamation*."[76] Amalgamation, Council spokesmen declared, was precisely what the integrationists wanted. According to the "Manual for Southerners," the CCA's official handbook for the fifth and sixth grades: "The Race-Mixers even want Negroes and whites to date each other. They know that if the boys and girls share the school room, lunch room, dances, sports, rest rooms, and playgrounds, then the boys and girls will want to date each other."[77] "To integrate the races means to have them live with each other and marry each other. It is the Race-Mixers who want to integrate the races. Integration always leads the races to marry one another."[78] Certainly the Council had not created the segregationist's maxim that mixed schools meant mixed blood, but it seldom missed an opportunity to exploit the fears inspired by such a notion.

On its most dignified plane the case for segregation as the most effective means of preventing intermarriage took the form of a refurbishment of the cult of southern womanhood, that romantic adulation of femininity which Wilbur J. Cash has called "gyneolatry."[79] Writing in *Black Monday*, Judge Brady expressed this chivalric mood in appropriately turgid prose: "the loveliest and purest of God's creatures, the nearest thing to an angelic being that treads this terrestrial ball is a well-bred, cultured white woman or her blue-eyed, golden-haired little girl."[80]

On a related but less lofty plane, Councilors sought to rout the enemies of separate-but-equal schools by drawing upon the white's darkest fears about integration. This approach focused on the popularly held conviction that the way to the bedroom was through the schoolhouse door.[81] Thus Council spokesmen like state Senator Walter C. Givhan of Alabama unhesitatingly exploited sexual anxieties by revealing that when the NAACP petitioned the courts for desegregation, it did so in order "to open the bedroom doors of our white women to Negro men."[82] Similarly, a pamphlet used by the movement in both Louisiana and Arkansas presented a cause-and-effect series of photographs under the caption: "Is this YOUR little girl's future?" The pictorial sequence began with a preschool-age girl in a party dress dancing with a Negro boy, and progressed to the denouement—Negro men passionately embracing provocatively attired white women.[83] Almost every issue of *The Citizens' Council* carried inflammatory headlines such as "White and Negro Marriage Is Goal," "Mixed Marriage Will Become Commonplace," "Mixed Love for Negroes and Whites," "Sex Atrocity in Massachusetts: Blacks Rape White Girl Repeatedly," "Mixed Love in Kentucky," and "Sex Orgies in Iowa." Apologizing for printing such "sordid bit[s] of news," editor William J. Simmons explained that honest journalism required it; they are "becoming increasingly typical of stories filtering back from areas where racial integration is proceeding 'with all deliberate speed. . . .'"[84] Always there was the insinuation that at the root of the problem lay the Negro's own atavistic lusts. Or, as one Council spokesman explained it to the Commonwealth Club of California, "the Negro, in so far as sex is concerned is not immoral, he is simply nonmoral. He surely follows his natural instincts."[85]

Mounting sexual offenses were not the only effects of desegregation against which the white resistance group warned. Crime, disease, and violence, according to Council statisticians, also followed in the wake of racial mingling. In one statistical summary published by the Mississippi Association of Citizens' Councils entitled *Crime Report Reveals Menace of Integration,* the Negroid 10 percent of the population of the United States was credited with 63 percent of the arrests for murder, 62 percent for prostitution, and 40 percent for rape. The same single-sheet handout cited aggregate figures on the prison population in thirty-two states to "prove" that Negroes not only committed more crimes per capita than did whites, but that they ran afoul of the law far more frequently when segregation was not practiced.[86] Statistics such as these, Councilors believed, demonstrated what perceptive southern white men—and intellectually honest scientists—had known all along: the Negro possessed genetically determined "criminal tendencies" which rendered him unfit for free association in white society.[87]

In addition to their greater proclivity for crimes of violence, Councilors believed that blacks were more prone to disease, especially social disease, than whites.[88] In this vein, the Capital Citizens' Council of Little Rock cautioned against the "diabolical venereal phase of integration." Releasing figures purporting to show that in Arkansas fifteen Negroes were syphiloid for every white who carried the disease, it warned that "uncontested" medical data demonstrated that little girls were "highly susceptible" to contracting the dreaded affliction from contact with drinking fountains, books, towels, and gym clothes.[89] Some Councilors believed that the very blood of the Negro was a carrier for disease and demanded that the American Red Cross label plasma and whole blood by race so that Caucasians would not contract sickle cell anemia and other diseases frequently found in "negroid blood."[90] With disease among Negroes, as with crime, Council statisticians demonstrated that the rates were much higher in such "integrated" states as Illinois, Massachusetts, New Jersey, and Ohio than in Alabama, Georgia, Louisiana, and Mississippi. "The moral restrictions inherent in segregation," hypothesized one anonymous Council pamphleteer, accounted for the relatively low incidence of disease, illegitimacy, and crime among the states of the Deep South.[91]

Segregation, then, was right. It was right not simply because of history, nor even because of science and religion. It was right because integration—the very quintessence of ignorance, evil, and unholiness—was so utterly wrong.

ENDNOTES

1. Wilma Dykeman and James Stokely, *Neither Black nor White* (New York: Rinehart, 1957), 109.

2. See esp. Southern Regional Council, "Partial Description of Anti-Semitic Activities, and of Literature Recommended and Distributed by White Citizens' Councils and Other Groups in the South" (unpublished manuscript, Southern Regional Council, February 27, 1956); interoffice memoranda, 1960–62, Southern Office, A-DL.

3. The newspapers published by both the Citizens' Councils of Arkansas and the Citizens' Councils of Louisiana are replete with anti-Semitic suggestions.

4. Harris's latent anti-Semitism emerged occasionally, as it did in the *Augusta Courier*, December 7, 1959. Although insisting that he was not "prejudiced against the Jews, or the members of any other race," Harris, the arch-Negrophobe, stated that "Jewish money and Jewish influence" must be directed away from "race-mixing" or the Jewish "race" may suffer "the wrath of the Anglo-Saxon people in this nation."

5. Louis W. Hollis, *Integrity: An Address to the Annual Conference of the Citizens' Councils of America, Montgomery, Alabama, January 16, 1965* (Jackson: Citizens' Councils of America, n.d.), 5.

6. See Guion Griffis Johnson, "The Ideology of White Supremacy, 1876–1910," *Essays in Southern History*, ed. Fletcher Melvin Green (Chapel Hill: University of North Carolina Press, 1949), 124–56; and James W. Vander Zanden, "The Ideology of White Supremacy," *Journal of the History of Ideas*, 20 (June–September, 1959), 385–402.

7. "A Manual for Southerners," *The Citizens Council*, June, 1957, 3.

8. Association of Citizens' Councils of Mississippi, *Racial Facts* (n.p., n.d.), 5.

9. Despite his ties with the Ku Klux Klan, which the more respectable Citizens' Councils held in contempt, Councilors often felt a kinship with Dixon. See untitled, undated citizens' Councils of America broadside, Southern Education Reporting service, which contains excerpts from *The Leopard's Spots* and *The Clansman*. See also *The Councilor*, March 6, 1967, and the Kansas City, Missouri, Citizens' Council, *The Greater Citizen*, August 15, 69.

10. Quoted in Muse, *Ten Years of Prelude*, 41–42. Muse suggests "one might suspect that Judge Brady had just put down an old copy of *The Leopard's* Spots."

11. Brady, *Black Monday*, 12. In retrospect, Brady informed the author that this passage of his book was "unfortunate," the "product of too much haste." Nevertheless, he insisted that the analogy was valid. "It's all true. I wouldn't change a word of it."

12. *Variety*, January 8, 1958, as cited by Muse, *Ten Years of Prelude*, 41.

13. Standard studies of scientific racism in the United States include: William Stanton, *The Leopard's Spots: Scientific Attitudes Towards Race in America, 1815–1859* (Chicago: University of Chicago Press, 1960); William Sumner Jenkins, *Pro-Slavery Thought in the Old South* (Chapel Hill: University of North Carolina Press, 1935), Thomas F. Gossett, *Race: The History of an Idea in America* (New York: Schocken Books, 1965); John Higham, *Strangers in the Land: Patterns of American Nativism*, 1866–1925 (New Brunswick: Rutgers University Press, 1955); Oscar Handlin, *Race and Nationality in American Life* (Boston: Little, Brown, 1957); Idus A. Newby, *Jim Crow's Defense: Anti-Negro Thought in America*, 1900–1930 (Baton Rouge: Louisiana State University Press, 1965).

14. Gunnar Myrdal, *An American Dilemma: The Negro Problem and Modern Democracy* (New York: Harper and Brothers, 1944), Vol. 1, 96. See also Newby, *Jim Crow's Defense*, viii.

15. Simmons's fondness for this expression can be seen in much of his writing and speech-making. For example, see the following addresses: *Race Relations and Civil Rights: An Address to the Yale Political Union, New Haven, Connecticut, February 28*, 1963 (n.p., n.d.); *Why Segregation Is Right: An Address Presented at Notre Dame University, South Bend, March* 7, 1963 (n.p., n.d.); *Civil Rights and the Second Reconstruction: An Address to the Jefferson Society, University of Virginia, Charlottesville, March 22, 1963* (n.p., n.d.).

16. For a brief but suggestive analysis of the post-*Brown* genre of scientific racism, see Handlin, *Fire Bell in the Night: The Crisis in Civil Rights* (Boston: Little, Brown, 1964), 73–85. A much fuller statement on the same subject is Idus A. Newby, *Challenge to the Court: Social Scientists and the Defense of Segregation, 1954–1966* (Baton Rouge: Louisiana State University Press, 1967).

17. William D. McCain, "Who Is Carleton Putnam?" *The Citizen*, 6 (November, 1961), 9–11.

18. Carleton Putnam, *High Journey: A Decade in the Pilgrimage of an Air Lines Pioneer* (New York: Charles Scribner's Sons, 1945); *Theodore Roosevelt: A Biography, Vol. 1: The Formative Years, 1858–1886* (New York: Scribner's, 1958). Although only the first of a projected four-volume effort has appeared, Putnam's life of Roosevelt has been well received. In the words of Howard K. Beale, "Putnam has written an interesting and important book that any professionally trained historian could he proud of." See *American Historical Review, 64* (October, 1958), 124–26.

19. William D. McCain observes that Putnam is directly descended from the grandfather of Israel Putnam . . . and from the brother of General Rufus Putnam. . . . " ("Who Is Carleton Putnam?" *The Citizen, 6* [November, 1961], 9.)

20. *Race and Reason: A Yankee View* (Washington: Public Affairs Press, 1961). Putnam's more recent *Race and Reality* is a similar, though enlarged, treatment of the same subject. For Putnam's defense of his "scientific" views on race, see his *These Are the Guilty: Address Delivered before the Washington Putnam Letters Club, February 12, 1963* (Richmond: National Putnam Letters Committee, n.d.).

21. M. B. Schnapper, editor, Public Affairs Press, to the author, March 24, 1970.

22. See *American Anthropologist,* 64 (June, 1962), 616–17, and Newby, *Challenge to the Court,* 167–69. For Putnam's view of the "pseudo-scientists" who attacked *Race and Reason,* see his *The Road to Reversal: An Address Delivered before the Fifth Annual Attorney General's Conference for District Attorneys, State of Louisiana, New Orleans, February 16, 1962* (Washington: National Putnam Letters Committee, n.d.).

23. See the *Washington Post,* December 2, 1969; C. Lawson crowe, "Race and Reason: A Study in Frustration," *Christianity and Crisis,* July 9, 1962, 122; and Putnam, *Race and Reason,* iii–v, 1–14. In the foreword to Putnam's book, Waring called it "a succinct reply to every sophistry advanced by the propagandists."

24. Crowe, "Race and Reason: A Study in Frustration," 122; Baton Rouge *State Times,* July 26, 1961; *New York Times,* February 18; Norfolk *Journal and Guide,* February 24; *Washington Post,* March 2, 1962. The Virginia resolution died in committee after the Virginia Teachers' Association testified against it.

25. *Southern School News,* May, 1962, 9, 12; Jackson *Daily News,* October 26, 1961. Barnett's proclamation was reprinted in *The Citizen,* 6 (November, 1961), 4.

26. Louis W. Hollis, "Here's How We Did It," *The Citizen,* 6 (November 1961), 39–41. For a list of civic leaders, headed by U.S. Representative John Bell Williams, serving on the Carleton Putnam Dinner Committee, see "Distinguished Community Leaders," *The Citizen,* 6 (November, 1961), 42–45.

27. "The Turning Point," ibid., 2. A subsequent issue of *The Citizen* was also devoted wholly to Putnam's work. This issue Simmons entitled "A Southern Survival Kit," *The Citizen, 7* (March, 1963), 2.

28. *The Citizen,* 6 (November, 1961), 11, 38, 47.

29. *Southern School News,* December, 1961, 3; *New York Times,* March 13, 1956; and Wesley Critz George, *The Biology of the Race Problem* (Richmond: Patrick Henry Press, [1962]), 1–2. George's list of "the most credible scientists" differed not at all from Putnam's. George cites R. Ruggles Gates, Robert Gayre, Henry E. Garrett, Henry Pratt Fairchild, Carleton S. Coon, and R. M. Yerkes, among others, as his "authorities." (See iv–vii.)

30. William J. Simmons, "The Truth about Racial Differences," *The Citizen,* 7 (October, 1962), 7. For an example of the coverage the George Report got among Councils on the local level, see a tract by Herbert C. Sanborn, professor emeritus and former chairman of the department of philosophy and psychology, Vanderbilt University: *Dr. W. C. George's* The Biology of the Race Problem: A *Review* (Nashville: Nashville Citizens' Councils, [1962]).

31. William J. Simmons, *Race Relations and Civil Rights and the Second Reconstruction.* The great faith which the Council possessed in the intellectual appeal of George's work can also be seen in the example of the state association of South Carolina, which distributed his *Race, Heredity and Civilization: Human Progress and the Race Problem* (New York: Alliance, 1963) to students at Clemson University.

32. See his *The Story of Man* (New York: Alfred A. Knopf, 1954) and *The Origin of Races* (New York: Alfred A. Knopf, 1962). Representative attitudes of American scientists on Coon's research are: F. S. Hulse, *American Anthropologist,* 65 (June, 1963), 685; Margaret Mead, *Saturday Review,* 46 (June 22, 1963), 41; and Theodosius Dobzhansky, *The Scientific American,* 208 (February, 1963), 172. Dobzhansky noted that, in *The Origin of Races,* Coon committed "some unfortunate misstatements that are susceptible to such misinterpretation." "[But] there are absolutely no findings in Coon's book that even suggest that some human races are superior or inferior to others in their capacity for culture or civilization."

33. "A Meeting of the Minds," *The Citizen,* 6 (June, 1962), 2. See also William J. Simmons's endorsement of "the most eminent of living American physical anthropologists" in *Why California Is Organizing,* 8–9.

34. Carleton Putnam, "Evolution and Race: New Evidence," *The Citizen,* 6 (July-August, 1962), 7–11.

35. For a summary of Garrett's views on the results of intelligence testing, see John J. Synon, "White IQ vs. Negro IQ," *The Citizen,* 10 (September, 1966), 11–12. See also the following examples of Garrett's work: *Race: 11 Questions and 11 Answers* (Washington: National Putnam Letters Committee, n.d.); *The South and the Second Reconstruction* (n.p., n.d.); and *How Classroom Desegregation Will Work* (Richmond: Patrick Henry Press, n.d.). The last was first published in *The Citizen,* 9 (October, 1965). All of these pamphlets have been distributed by the Council through *The Citizen.* A more detailed account of Dr. Garrett's contribution to scientific racism may be found in Newby, *Challenge to the Court,* 99–105.

36. *The Citizens' Council,* January, 1957, 2. See also William J. Simmons, "Race in America: The Conservative Stand," *The Search for America,* ed. Huston Smith (Englewood Cliffs, N.J.: Prentice-Hall, 1959), 54–64.

37. *Racial Facts,* 6.

38. For insightful overviews of the three dominant Protestant sects during this period, see Kenneth K. Bailey, *Southern White Protestantism in the Twentieth Century* (New York: Harper and Row, 1964), 130–59, and David M. Reimers, *White Protestantism and the Negro* (New York: Oxford University Press, 1965), 109–33. See also C. Vann Woodward, "The 'New Reconstruction' in the South: Desegregation in Historical Perspective," *Commentary,* 21 (June, 1956), 507. In this article Woodward compares the post-*Brown* period, the "New Reconstruction," with the "Old Reconstruction" and notes that one of the striking ways in which the new differed from the old has been the unanimity of organizational policy of the major churches North and South on the race question.

39. Quoted in "The Churches Speak," *New South,* 9 (August, 1954), 1–6.

40. See ibid. and "Answers for Action: Schools in the South," *New South,* 9 (June-July, 1954), 6ff.; Bailey, *Southern White Protestantism,* 142ff. Ernest Campbell and Thomas Pettigrew, *Christians in Racial Crisis: A Study of Little Rock's Ministers* (Washington: Public Affairs Press, 1959), 157ff.; Thomas D. Clark, *The Emerging South* (New York: Oxford University Press, 1961), 261–62; Reimers, *White Protestantism and the Negro,* 116ff.

41. State conferences of the upper South generally found it more expedient to endorse the positions adopted by general denominational convocations than did those of the lower South. When conferences in the states of the Deep South did endorse the high court ruling, they very often encountered opposition from ministers and laymen at the local level. The Methodist Men's Club of Asbury Memorial Methodist Church in Charleston, for example, repudiated the liberal position adopted by the Annual Conference of the Methodist Church in South Carolina in 1955 and urged "all Christians to actively engage in these [Citizens'] councils." Similarly, the Florence Methodist Church went on record as "being 100 per cent in accord with the Citizens' Council" following the statement by the Annual Conference in South Carolina. (Charleston *News and Courier,* October 21, 23, 1955.) See also Bailey, *Southern White Protestantism,* 144–45; Quint, *Profile in Black and White,* 55–70.

42. Quoted in *Jackson Daily News,* June 11, 1958.

43. To quote an editorial in *The Citizens Council,* May, 1956, 2, "The Citizens' Council not only believes that God is on its side . . . but it also believes it is on God's side. Every session is opened with fervent prayer to God for guidance, leadership, and protection in these times when the devil is shaking the very foundations of our land."

44. See *The Citizens' Council,* March, 1961, 2, and *The Citizen,* 6 (October, 1961), p. 14.

45. *Atlanta Journal,* November 6, 1955; "Biography of William T. Bodenhamer" (unpublished manuscript, Southern Education Reporting Service, 1958).

46. *The Citizens' Council,* January, 1958, 3. In announcing Pruden's election as the successor to Robert Ewing Brown as president of the Little Rock Council, *The Citizens' Council* said: "A Southern Baptist Convention minister, Reverend Pruden is symbolic of the churches of the South who are standing firm on America's traditional ways of life and freedom."

47. Miami *Herald,* June 26, 1956; St. Petersburg *Times,* January 1, 1957.

48. Quotation from J. Paul Barrett, *The Church and Segregation.* See also W. A. Criswell, *Christianity and Segregation: An Address by Dr. W. A. Criswell, Pastor, First Baptist Church, Dallas, Texas, to the Sovereign State of South Carolina* (n.p., n.d.); Carey Daniel, *God the Original Segregationist* (Dallas: By the Author, [1957]); *Is Segregation Un-Christian?* (Montgomery: Citizens' Councils of Alabama, n.d.); and S. Emory Rogers, *Christian Love and Segregation* (Summerton: Association of Citizens' Councils of South Carolina, n.d.).

49. G. T. Gillespie, A *Christian View on Segregation* For a critical analysis of Gillespie's biblical defense of segregation, see Everett Tilson, *Segregation and the Bible* (New York: Abingdon Press,

1958). For the moral aspects of the proslavery argument, see especially studies by Jenkins, *Pro-Slavery Thought in the Old South,* 200–241, and Arthur Young Lloyd, *The Slavery Controversy,* 1831–1860 (Chapel Hill: University of North Carolina Press, 1939), 162–93, as well as William Harper et al., *The Pro-Slavery Argument as Maintained by the Most Distinguished Writers of the Southern States* (Philadelphia: Lippincott, Grambo, and Co., 1853).

50. Gillespie, *A Christian View on Segregation,* 1–13.

51. Richard Fuller and Francis Wayland, *Domestic Slavery Considered as a Scriptural Institution* (*New* York, 1845), as quoted in Lloyd, *The Slavery Controversy,* 188.

52. See T. Roger Ingram, ed., *Essays on Segregation* (Houston: St. Thomas Press, 1960).

53. T. Robert Ingram, "'Civil Rights' Proposals Are Anti-Christian." *The Citizen,* 8 (November, 1963), 4–5. See also "Courage, Christian Soldiers!" *The Citizen,* 6 (December, 1961), 20–23, and "Why Integration Is Un-Christian," *The Citizen,* 6 (June, 1962), 6–16. Ingram also appeared on the Citizens' Council "Forum" television and radio series.

54. *Jackson Daily News,* November 2, 1955.

55. "The Myth of 'Equality,'" *The Citizen,* 8 (November, 1963), 2, 15. See also Rogers, *Christian Love and Segregation,* 1–4, and Ingram, *Essays on Segregation,* 1–14.

56. Council literature is replete with attacks on the National Council of Churches. For some of the more representative examples, see Thomas R. Waring, "Aroused Churchmen Are Studying Leftist Trends," *The Citizen,* 6 (April 1962), 11–12; "Pinkos in the Pulpit," *The Citizens' Council,* December, 1956, 2; "Church Council is Propaganda Tool," *The Citizens' Council,* November, 1957, 1; "Church Group Names Left President Again," *The Citizens' Council,* January, 1958, 1. Similar in tone is John R. Leatherbury, *The National Council of Churches of Christ—Activities Revealed,* which suggests that the N.C.C. is pro-Communist. See also a news bulletin published by the Citizens' Council of Atmore, Alabama, *The Southern Defender,* July, 1965.

57. See the literature listed in the endnote above as well as the cartoons in *The Citizens' Council,* June, 1957, 1, 4; August, 1957, 2; September 1957, 4.

58. Gillespie, *A Christian View of Segregation,* 2.

59. *The Citizens' Council,* April–May, 1961, 1, 4; James P. Dees, "Should Christians Support Integration?" *Essays on Segregation,* 35–51.

60. See, for example, James O. Eastland, *We've Reached Era of Judicial Tyranny, an Address before the State-Wide Convention of the Association of Citizens' Councils of Mississippi, Jackson, December 1, 1955,* 9.

61. Brady, *Black Monday,* 11.

62. In an editorial ("Lesson from the Congo," *The Citizens' Council,* July, 1960, 1–2), William Simmons pointed to the Congo as evidence that the Negro remains even today a "howling savage": "Once the discipline of white control was removed, the innate savagery of Congolese Negroes burst through the thin veneer acquired by several generations of exposure to Caucasian civilizations." For additional examples of the Council's equation of the American Negro with African savagery, see *The Citizens' Council,* December, 1958, January, 1959, February, 1959 and *The Citizen,* 8 (March, 1964), 2.

63. *Augusta Courier,* January 9, 1956. See also Amos R. Koontz, "'Uhuru' Does Not Confer 'Equality,'" *The Citizen,* 8 (November, 1963), 6–10; and Louis W. Hollis, *A Five Point Action Program: An Address to the Reorganization Rally, Savannah Citizens' Council, Savannah, Georgia* [*July 22, 1963*] (n.p., n.d.), 15.

64. Brady, *Black Monday,* 2.

65. *Ibid.*, 5, 7; *Racial Facts,* 4.

66. *The Citizens' Council: The South's Only Answer* (Montgomery: Citizens' Council of Alabama, n.d.).

67. Typical of the Council's pamphlets in which this Bilbo statement appears are: Louis W. Hollis, *Integrity, 5,* and *Racial Facts, 7.*

68. Southern Education Reporting Service, Citizens' Council materials.

69. Thomas Jefferson, *Autobiography,* Vol. 1 of *The Writings of Thomas Jefferson,* Andrew A. Lipscomb and Albert Ellery Bergh, eds. (Washington: Thomas Jefferson Memorial Association, 1903–4), 72–73.

70. *Racial Facts,* 7; Southern Education Reporting Service, Miscellaneous Files. See also Workman, *The Case for the South,* 142, and Herman Talmadge, *You and Segregation* (Birmingham: Vulcan Press, 1955), 48–49. Other Jeffersonian quotations on Negro-white relations were overlooked by segregationists—particularly those demonstrating the Sage of Monticello's misgivings about his own views on innate racial characteristics. For Jefferson's views on environment as a possible explanation for apparent racial differences, see Thomas Jefferson to General Chevalier de Chastellux, June 7, 1785, and Jefferson to M. Henri Gregoire, February 25, 1809, *Writings of Thomas Jefferson,* Lipscomb and Bergh, eds., Vol. 5, 6; Vol. 12, 254–55.

71. For analyses of the uses to which the segregationists have put Lincoln, see Paul Anthony, "An Analysis of the Hate Literature of Resistance Groups of the South" (unpublished manuscript, Southern Regional Council, 1956), and Shepherd Raymond, "Lincoln and the White Supremacists," *Fact* (May–June, 1964, 49–52. For other examples of the Council's uses of Lincoln quotations, see "Abe Said: More Words of Lincoln That the Race-Mixers Never Quote," *The Citizens' Council,* May, 1956, 3; December, 1957, 3, 4; March, 1958, 3, and Robert B. Patterson, *The Truth Cries Out: Speech to Annual Leadership Conference, Chattanooga, Tennessee, January 8, 1966* (Greenwood: Association of Citizens Councils of Mississippi, [1966]), 6.

72. The Big Lie about Lincoln," *The Citizen,* 8 (February, 1964), 1, 15.

73. Lincoln's Real Views on Race," ibid., 4–14. see also Richard D. Morphew, *The Citizens' Councils and the Negro Revolution: An Address to a Convocation at Beloit College, Beloit, Wisconsin [February 25, 1964]* (n.p., n.d.).

74. Greensboro (N.C.) *Daily News,* September 1; *Jackson Daily News,* February 12, 25; Columbia (S.C.) *State,* March 2; *San Francisco Chronicle,* February 14; *Los Angeles Times,* February 13; *New York Times,* February 11, 1964.

75. *2nd Annual Report, August, 1956,* 2; Robert B. Patterson, *The Citizens' Council: A History* (Jackson: Citizens' Councils of America, [1963]), 5; Louis W. Hollis, *Integrity,* 5.

76. For example, see a pamphlet by Herbert R. Sass, *Mixed Schools and Mixed Blood* (Greenwood: Association of Citizens' Councils, [1956]). This pamphlet was also published by the States' Rights Council of Georgia, Inc. The subtitle of Brady's *Black Monday: Segregation or Amalgamation, America Has Its Choice* also reflects the Councils penchant for the either-or dichotomy.

77. "Manual for Southerners," *The Citizens' Council,* July, *1957,* 3.

78. "Manual for Southerners," *The Citizens' Council,* August, 1957, 3.

79. Wilbur J. Cash, *The Mind of the South* (New York: Vintage Books, 1941), 89.

80. Brady, *Black Monday, 45.*

81. See Calvin C. Hernton, *Sex and Racism in America* (Garden City: Doubleday, 1965).

82. From an address at Linden, Alabama, in 1954, quoted in "How White Citizens' Councils Came to Alabama," *New South,* 10 (December, 1955), 11.

83. Capital Citizens' Councils, *The Little Rock School Board's Plans for Your Child* (Little Rock: Capital Citizens' Council, n.d.); Greater New Orleans Citizens' Council, *Integration Today Means Racial and National Suicide Tomorrow* (New Orleans: Greater New Orleans Citizens' Council, n.d.). For other examples of the Council's exploitation of sex anxieties through pictures, see *The Arkansas Faith,* November, 1955; March, 1956; and the following broadsides: Tarrant Educational Citizens' Council, "Destroying the White Woman Destroys the White Race" (Birmingham: Tarrant Educational Citizens' Council, n.d.), and miscellaneous untitled broadsides, Southern Education Reporting Service, Miscellaneous Files. The latter, not bearing the Council's imprint, were enclosed in regular mailings by the Association of Citizens' Councils of Mississippi.

84. See *The Citizens' Council,* October, 1956, 3; November, 1956, 4; February, 1956, 1–2; August, 1957, 2; February, 1957, 3. Occasionally the Council focused on jazz music as a symbol of the sexual threats implicit in desegregation. In an early issue of *The Citizens' Council* it was pointed out that the word jazz "is a slang word which originally meant illicit sexual intercourse"; that jazz "originated in an atmosphere of illicit sex; and that the "same [jazz] rhythms were known and used in Africa . . . for sexual orgies. . . . "(William Stephenson, "From Bawdy Houses to Parlor," *The Citizens' Council,* January, 1956, 4.)

85. Tom P. Brady, *Segregation and the South: An Address to the Commonwealth Club of California, October 4, 1957,* 8.

86. Association of Citizens' Councils of Mississippi, *Crime Report Reveals Menace of Integration* (Greenwood, n.d.). This one-page flier was offered for mass distribution by the Council's Greenwood office at a price of $1.00 for twenty copies.

87. "Army Covering up Negro Crime Rate with Double Talk," *The Citizens' Council,* October, 1956, *2;* George, *The Biology of the Race Problem,* 23; "Savages Stalk Corridors of Northern 'Blackboard Jungles,'" *The Citizens' Council,* November, 1960, 4.

88. Association of Citizens' Councils of Mississippi, *The St. Louis Story: Integrated Schools Hurting Both White, Colored Pupils* (Greenwood, n.d.). This single-sheet, legal-size flier contains tables on crime and disease based on statistics provided by the American States' Rights Association.

89. Capital Citizens' Council, *The Little Rock School Board's Plans for Your Child*, 14.

90. For example, see the anonymous pamphlet, *Sickle Cell Anemia* (n.p., n.d.), probably published by the Association of Citizens' Councils of Arkansas in its 1959 campaign on behalf of Arkansas House Bill 385, which would have required labeling of blood by race. See also Arkansas *Democrat*, February 16, 1959, for numerous Capital Citizens' Council-sponsored advertisements calling for labeled blood, and a letter to the editor by L. D. Poynter, president of the Association of Citizens' Councils of Arkansas, in the *Arkansas Gazette*, February 28, 1958, outlining the organization's case for blood labeling.

91. Association of Citizens' Councils, *The St. Louis Story*.

the Defenders' NEWS and VIEWS

Published by Defenders of State Sovereignty and Individual Liberties
405-A East Franklin Street **Richmond, Virginia**

JK 325 D4

Vol. 3, No. 11 August-September, 1959

DEAR FELLOW VIRGINIAN AND FELLOW AMERICAN:

You know what has happened in Virginia. Do you know why? You have heard it said that integration is a part of the Communist program, but do you know how true this is? Do you know that it is a fact that the official publication of the Communist Party, U.S.A., salutes the National Association for the Advancement of Colored People in practically every issue?

Your organization feels that the Communist program has advanced to the point now that THERE IS VERY LITTLE TIME LEFT if our grass roots are going to do anything about saving the United States of America. Patriots have been sleeping while the enemies of our form of government have been working overtime. For this reason this issue of the *News & Views* carries the first of a series of articles contributed by member Defenders who have made a study of the international conspiracy. We are indebted to these loyal Virginians for the enormous amount of research they have done, and everything appearing in this and subsequent issues can be documented. You are invited to request from this office documentation of any statement or report that you might question.

The NAACP's membership is large, their financial status sound; but remember this: IT IS NOT THE SIZE OF THE DOG IN THE FIGHT, BUT THE SIZE OF THE FIGHT IN THE DOG. If you do not think it necessary to read this now, then we suggest that you put it aside in a safe place. Then, when it is too late—take this out and read it, and say, "Somebody did tell me. Why didn't I listen?"

Sincerely,

BOB CRAWFORD,
President.

UNIT 6-3

DEFENDERS' NEWS AND VIEWS
SELECTIONS, 1955–1959

"I am glad to have been one of the first to join the Defenders of State Sovereignty and Individual Liberties. I consider this a fine organization.

"The tides of executive, legislative and judicial invasion and control of state and individual conduct will never cease until the people, goaded beyond endurance, turn upon their reforming tormentors, demand a halt, and then enforce it. The fundamental principles laid down in our Constitution and Bill of Rights are the definitions and axioms of a free society, and are cherished by all good Virginians and Americans. These principles should serve as a rebuke and a stumbling-block to those who tear at us, both from within and from without. I hope that our Virginia people may now see the dangers confronting them and unite in this or some other similar organization to overcome the forces of evil, which apparently are determined to destroy our American way of life, and substitute in its place a totalitarian form of government."

September 12, 1955

(signed) Wm. M. Tuck
5th District, Virginia
Congress of the United States

"SEGREGATION, BUT—"

Collins Denny, Jr., Counsel for the Defenders

There appears still to be among us those who believe that there must be some simple easy legal procedure that will permit us without any confusion, stress or strain to maintain racially segregated secondary education in Virginia. I think that in one way or another I have been in contact with or had access to the general thought of most of those that work on this subject. I know of no person who has worked in this field who believes there is any such smooth and easy road.

The fact of the matter is that the school session of 1955–1956 will be the last session of the public schools as we have known them. Our schools have been segregated by law—the State has forbidden racial intermixture. The Supreme Court has held that racial segregation enforced by law in the public schools is unconstitutional. Accordingly, whatever schools we may have in the future will not be the public school system we have known in the past. That system, under which education has flourished in Virginia, is now dying and with the end of this year will be dead.

This is not to say that segregation in secondary education cannot be preserved. It is to say that the system and the method by which we heretofore established segregated education and maintained it is no longer available to us.

We have a great many people who say: "I believe in the segregated school, BUT . . . " With them the "But" is the important consideration. They believe in segregation, but only to the extent that the present system for public schools is not affected or so long as no confusion in the school system can possibly occur. Always people have desired to eat their cake and also to keep it. That is just as possible as it is to maintain segregation without some possibility of confusion in public education. Virginia must choose between the one or the other. Indeed, as I have talked to men and women from all over the State, I find roughly three groups of thought: first, there are sincere people who believe that any racial distinctions are wrong and who hail the thought of the integrated school as a thing desirable in itself—fortunately there are not many such; second, there are those of us who believe that racial separateness is sufficiently advisable, indeed, so necessary as to warrant whatever honorable and legal steps may be taken to preserve it, even though as in Prince Edward County it may be necessary for a season even to go so far as to terminate the public schools; and third, there are those who claim to be with us in their desire for segregation, but whose desire is so weak that it is immediately surrendered when confronted with the possibility that the public school may be affected. It is this last group that unwittingly will be responsible for breaking down our way of life, if it be broken.

Schools are a service organization. As such the people have established them. If public confidence in them be lost they cannot be supported, and they cannot render the service expected. Large elements of our population, constantly growing as the seriousness of the situation sinks in upon the consciousness of the people will not support the integrated public school. In final analysis people generally get in this life what they really want. If we have sufficient determination solemnly to resolve that we will not have integrated public education in Virginia and to stand by the resolution, I have no doubt that in the analysis the determined voice of the people of Virginia will prevail and we will have a system of education in which we have confidence. If we do not have that determination and are not ready to live by it, then we will see only such publicly supported schools as are not worthy of our confidence and to which we will not be willing to send our children.

Why is this amendment so important? Seventeen of our forty-eight states make up the South; thirty-one comprise the North and West. Of the seventeen Southern states six are states with an average negro population of only 9.27% (Oklahoma, Missouri, Kentucky, West Virginia, Delaware, Maryland). Texas might easily be classed as a border state having a negro population of 12.7% of the total. Thus, the states most affected and concerned number only ten. The simplest arithmetic shows that we in the "Black Belt" stand little chance of avoiding integration on the basis of the race issue alone. But in the other thirty-eight states as well as the ten states fighting integration, there is strong feeling that education belongs to the states and local communities. This has always been the feeling. It is so much a part of the people who support the schools that no nine men in black robes can ever change it, in any of the forty-eight states. It is on the basis of this issue of school control that the decision of the Supreme Court may be overruled by the people. For the white people of all states have a tradition of states rights based on the 10th Amendment to the Constitution which serves the forty-eight states. On this tradition they would vote to restore the schools to the state and local communities.

September 17, which is Constitution Day. Here is a prayer for Americans which might be used on any day of the year!

Strengthen Us, O God, in Our Resolve
To Uphold—Protect—and Preserve
American Independence
Our Flag

Our Constitution and Its Bill of Rights
And the Freedom for which They Stand
Teach Us to Value Our Blessings
And Keep Us Free
From Entanglements in Alien Ideologies

LITTLE ROCK—
HERE ARE ITS ORIGIN AND ITS AFTERMATH

(Reprinted from the *New Bedford, Massachusetts Standard Times*)

No domestic problem is more important to the people of this country than relations between white and Negro Americans.

An issue in which the extremist views are so widely separated is a natural for exploitation by the Communist Party.

In this series of articles, *The Standard-Times* comments and reviews the Communist campaign to promote racial unrest in the South and the influence of that campaign in the origin of, and the aftermath to, the impasse at Little Rock.

This series was written by Edward B. Simmons of *The Standard-Times* staff. Mr. Simmons received the award of Sigma Delta Chi, national professional journalism fraternity in 1951 for outstanding general reporting.

He gathered material for these articles in trips along the Eastern Seaboard, to the Midwest, in discussions with members of Congress and from study of U.S. Senate and House committee files.

Based on experience in New Bedford, where diversity lives in the highest harmony, the Editors believe that the material in these articles will make for better understanding of a most difficult and trying issue.

THE EDITORS
New Bedford, Mass. Standard-Times

FORCED INTEGRATION FAILS TO PROMOTE HARMONY

WASHINGTON, July 21—The luster is wearing thin at Little Rock, Ark., where bayonets were used last Fall to enforce integration in a public school. Some of the trail-blazers appear to have washed their hands of the cause of Negro "rights." Others have been seen in roles considerably less flattering than those they played last Fall.

Ernest Green's observation, "I'm glad that's all over," is perhaps not untypical. Ernest, 18, was one of the nine Negro youths admitted to Little Rock's Central High School under the guns of federalized National Guardsmen and U.S. paratroopers.

Last month Ernest was graduated. One of the nine was expelled; the other seven may never return to Central.

If the experiment continues at Central, it will have to do so without the assistance of many persons who were instrumental in launching it.

Mayor Woodrow Wilson Mann of Little Rock, who made the telephone calls to the White House that led to Federal intervention has left town.

He is now a resident of Denver, Colo., working in an investment banking firm.

Max Rabb, the presidential assistant who was at the White House end of the Mayor Mann calls and was a key man in the decision to send Federal troops, has left Washington.

He is now a partner in a big New York law firm.

Despite apparent "success" in its part in obtaining the Little Rock test, the National Association for the Advancement of Colored People has experienced a "sharp drop" in membership.

Federal Judge Ronald Davies, whose ruling that integration must begin "forthwith" in Little Rock was the foundation for what followed, has long since left Little Rock.

He is now back in his court in North Dakota where there are but 257 Negroes in the entire State. Arkansas has 462,000.

Harry Ashmore, the Little Rock editor whose editorials in behalf of integration stirred the controversy and brought him a Pulitzer prize, has conceded he will not employ a Negro on his newspaper.

Mrs. Grace Lorch, the Little Rock "housewife" who attracted national attention by "befriending" one of the nine students, has since refused to declare whether she is a Communist.

Herbert Brownell, whose U.S. Justice Department gave the orders for dispatch of troops, is no longer attorney general.

He has taken up the more lucrative private practice of law.

The Justice Department, itself, has had a change of heart. Under its new chief, William P. Rogers the word is "never again" on the use of Federal troops to enforce integration.

The Little Rock School Board, which had worked out a gradual integration program that Judge Davies' ruling nullified, has thrown in the sponge on any integration in the near future.

Central High School has claimed that the educational program for its 2,000 students was so badly dislocated by the one-year experiment the school could not survive another year without complete disintegration of morale.

This was a major consideration in Federal Judge Harry J. Lemley's approval of a 2 1/2 year stay of integration for the Little Rock high school, a decision that may have made the best of a very unfortunate situation.

MAJORITY NEEDS CONSIDERATION

Judge Lemley, while acknowledging the interest of Negroes in obtaining equal rights, said the "public interest" of the majority rated consideration, too. The burden placed on other Central High students and the "racial tension and unrest" created in Little Rock itself demanded a delay in integration, he said.

The ruling led to another example of apparent change in viewpoint among those who had been insistent on an immediate end of segregation.

When Judge Lemley's decision was taken to the U.S. Supreme Court, whose 1954 "sociological" and subsequent decrees had started the ferment in the South, that body declined to break up its Summer vacation for a special sitting.

The court, in effect, passed the buck to a lower court with an admonition to act fast.

Little Rock, the morning after, appears to have been a venture that has not served racial harmony or promoted integration. As such, its origin, its leaders and its original objectives invited inquiry.

COMMUNISTS' BASIC GOAL: TO INCITE RACIAL STRIFE

WASHINGTON, July 22—To incite racial strife is one of the oldest objectives in the Communist program for getting world domination. "We must realize that our party's most powerful weapon is tension," states a Communist Party handbook of 1912, well before a few hundred Bolsheviks seized control of Russia.

"By propounding into the consciousness of the dark races that for centuries they have been oppressed by the whites, we can mold them to the program of the Communist Party," the handbook continues.

"In America, we will aim for subtle victory. While inflaming the Negro minority against whites, we will endeavor to instill in the whites a guilt complex for their exploitation of the Negroes. Thus will begin a process which will deliver America to our cause."

Coincidence or Strategy?

Is it coincidence or the result of strategy that, some 45 years later, racial unrest in an outstanding Southern city, Little Rock, Ark., has increased so sharply that a Federal judge called for a 2 1/2 year delay in any integration?

Again, is it coincidence or the result of Communist strategy that one of the most influential of Southern Negro leaders, the Rev. Martin King, exhorts his followers with these words:

"It (the Montgomery, Ala., bus boycott) is a part of something that is happening all over the world. The oppressed people are rising up. They are revolting against colonialism and imperialism and all other systems of oppression."

When Mr. King draws a parallel between the situation of the American Negro and "oppressed peoples" rising against "colonialism" and "imperialism" he is following exactly, to the word, the Communist line.

Direct Approach Failed

At first, the Communist drive for creation of strife called for a direct approach to Negroes, using labor unions and Communist fronts like the American Negro Labor Congress and the League for Struggle for Negro Rights. Former Communist Joseph Kornfelder, one of the party founders in the United States and its first director of Southern operations, has described what happened:

"The South to the Communists was always one of the most vexing problems," Kornfelder told a joint legislative committee of the State of Louisiana in March 1957. "Moscow could never understand it . . . according to Marx' theory, the South should be leading the United States in Communist development.

"It just didn't work out that way.

"It was just to the contrary. The South proved to be a hard nut and it didn't conform to the doctrine.

Blocked by Religion

"They decided that the big block against penetration of the South is religion. The Negroes believed in religion; the hillbillies believed in religion; nearly everybody is religious. The South is more religious than the North.

"Therefore, they decided maybe they should get at them under the auspices of the Cross."

Kornfelder and two Negro former Communist leaders, Manning Johnson and Leonard Patterson, told the Louisiana committee that the new tactics included, besides use of the church, penetration of reputable Negro organizations and the founding, but not obvious control, of others.

World War II, with its migrations and general dislocation of living habits, produced what Kornfelder described as a "sort of honeymoon situation" between the Communist organizers and Negro organizations.

FOUR AGENCIES INFILTRATED

"It seems the intellectuals during that time had shown a remarkable weakness," he testified. "They were bigger suckers for the Communist propaganda than many others were, apparently because they sort of led a life apart from the daily troubles and toil of the population."

"They were the ivory tower boys who picked up the theories of the Communists, not looking at what is behind the theories."

The results of this "honeymoon" were vital Communist infiltration of the most important agencies in the South dealing in Negro issues. The Communists infiltrated four of these organizations and actually helped found three of them.

They are the Southern Conference Educational Fund, the Southern Regional Council, the Highlander Folk School in Tennessee and the National Association for the Advancement of Colored People.

An almost incredible maze of interlocking officials, agencies with the Communist Party.

COUNCIL GOT FORD GRANT

The Regional Council and the Educational Fund were both off-shoots of the old Southern Conference for Human Welfare, which was dissolved in 1943 after twice being described by the Federal Government as "a Communist front serving the Soviet Union and its subservient Communist Party."

Former directors and officers of the Conference for Human Welfare became directors and officers of the Regional Council and the Educational Fund and of the Highlander School. The Communist Daily Worker openly boasted that James E. Jackson, chief of the Southern branch of the U.S. Communist Party, was a co-founder of the Regional Council.

Although the Regional Council is not widely known in the North, its influence in the South is attested by its receiving a $497,000 grant from the Ford Foundation's Fund for the Republic.

Likewise, the Highlander School plays an important role in Southern civil rights developments, although it is scarcely known in the North. The school, according to testimony before the Senate Internal Security Subcommittee, was co-founded by a Communist and by a man who refused to testify on his beliefs.

NAACP INFILTRATED

During these "organizing" years by the Communist Party, the NAACP was extensively infiltrated, although not dominated by Communist sympathizers. Many of its leading officials were members of Communist fronts.

In fact, by 1954 and the crucial Supreme Court decision, the Communist Party was so confident it had set the stage for developments in its favor that the party's national convention in the Winter of 1953 declared, "The next period ahead will witness momentous struggles of the Negroes ... given the vanguard leadership of the Communist Party, we may be confident that the Negro liberation movement will ally itself more fully with the camp of peace and democracy."

The Communist Party was in a position to follow its long-proved doctrine:

To get a "sociological" or pro-Communist book on the reading list of influential persons, like a Supreme Court justice;

To persuade a Negro to violate a civil rights statute, in the cause of "civil disobedience;"

To inject a fellow-traveler in the forefront of a civil rights dispute;

To support the program of the NAACP.

These objectives were attained in the year to come.

REDS GOAD NAACP TO END MODERATION

WASHINGTON, July 23—The success of Communist efforts to exploit the Southern Negro under the guise of "democratization" became fully evident in 1954 and the three subsequent years. The Supreme Court's historic 1954 ruling on school segregation was in judgment on four cases brought before it by the National Association of Advancement for Colored People, which for years had been a priority objective of Communist infiltration.

The NAACP charged that Negro children in Delaware, Kansas, South Carolina and Virginia were being denied their rights under the 14th Amendment.

The court did not rule on this aspect. Instead, Chief Justice Earl Warren in the written opinion, declared that the court found for the NAACP because segregated schools induced a feeling of inferiority among Negro children.

SIX BOOKS CITED

This sociological view, the justice stated, is "amply supported by modern authority." He cited six books by such "modern authority."

Two of the six authorities were Theodore Brameld and E. Franklin Frazier. Between them they have been members of or identified with 28 organizations listed as Communist, Communist-fronts or Communist-dominated.

A third "authority" was K. B. Clark. While arguments were being heard by the court on the four cases, Clark was on the payroll of the NAACP as a "social science expert."

A fourth authority cited by Justice Warren was the book, "An American Dilemma," edited by Gunnar Myrdal, a Swedish Socialist. The chief justice emphasized the importance of this book in the court's deliberations by saying it was depended on "generally," that is from cover to cover.

RECORDS NOTED

Sixteen of the contributors to Myrdal's book have long records of pro-Communist affiliation and activity. One, W.E.B. Du Bois, identified by the Communist Party as the "honorary chairman" of the NAACP, had a hand in 82 parts of the book. Dubois has been identified with 80 Communist fronts, reportedly more than any other American citizen.

Dubois intervened in behalf of executed Communist spies Julius and Ethel Rosenberg and sent the Kremlin a message of condolence on the death of Stalin.

Myrdal, himself, has written that the U. S. Constitution is "impractical and unsuited to modern conditions." Its adoption was "nearly a plot against the common people," said this foreign authority on American Negro problems.

The court's decision gave new influence to the NAACP. Its officers hailed the decision but indicated that it would not change the organization's plan for calm and orderly progress in race relations.

"We accept the decision quietly, unless there is deliberately fomented trouble," said the late Walter White, then executive secretary of NAACP.

WANTED STRUGGLES

Thurgood Marshall, chief NAACP counsel, had argued the school cases before the court, "The people will get together and work this thing out."

The Communist Party, however, wanted no part of moderation. It wanted the "big sharp struggles" its leaders had forecast, and racial unrest. Communist publications and officials shrilled for "immediate implementation of the Supreme Court decision, immediate abolition of segregation and discrimination from every facet of American life, immediate enforcement. . . . "

The record from the Supreme Court decision until the climax at Little Rock makes it plain which philosophy was the dominant one.

Moderation was forgotten.

The next three years brought unprecedented civil disobedience and violence in the South's racial affairs. There were all-out "incidents" of long duration in Tuskegee, Ala., Charleston, S.C., Tallahassee, Montgomery, Ala., Americus, Ga., and Clinton, Tenn., to name only the major ones.

COMMUNISTS BLAMED

The NAACP played a prominent role in each, but the atmosphere was not the moderate one ostensibly espoused by the NAACP.

"In my opinion, every major racial disturbance in the South since 1954 has been incited and directed by the Communist Party," Mrs. Paul Crouch, widow of a former Communist leader, told *The Standard Times*. Her husband was a top Communist functionary in the South for 13 years, and she was his aid [sic] throughout the period.

Communist exploitation of the Negro through the NAACP is attested by the Proceedings of the national convention of the Communist Party. The convention adopted as its main resolution, "the question of Negro freedom . . . the crucial domestic issue of the day . . . requiring support of the program of the National Association for the Advancement of Colored People."

Communist penetration of the NAACP in these important years is conceded by the NAACP itself.

ALL CHAPTERS WARNED

On Feb. 14, 1956, Roy Wilkins, who succeeded White as NAACP executive secretary, warned all chapters to guard against the "intensive efforts" of Communists to infiltrate.

At that very time, however, the NAACP's official publication, "The Crisis," was recommending as MUST background reading for Negroes, books by Claude Lightfoot, chairman of the Illinois Communist Party, and Doxey E. Wilkerson, member of the party's National Committee. Both have written extensively in behalf of racial unrest.

Communist dominance of Negro civil rights developments after the Supreme Court decision is illustrated, also, in the activities of the Highlander School, influential "sociological" workshop in the South. Highlander, according to testimony before a congressional committee, was founded by a Communist and by a man who refused to state his beliefs.

IS PROGRAM SINCERE?

Since 1954, Highlander has held a series of "workshops to develop plans for an orderly transition from segregated to integrated schools." At the last workshop, held over the Labor Day weekend just before the trouble at Little Rock, the leaders of every important racial strife incident in the South since 1954 were present.

How sincere is the Highlander program for "orderly transition" in desegregation?

The actual curriculum at Highlander, its pamphlet statement in behalf of "orderly transition" notwithstanding, preached that "desegregation is more effectively accomplished in a single step than in a series of steps with delays in between."

This is fellow-traveler vernacular for the straightout Communist program of "immediate desegregation."

Among those attending the important Highlander workshop was the Rev. Martin Luther King, leader of the Montgomery, Ala., bus boycott. King was to be at Little Rock, and, in 1958, at the White House, protesting integration delay.

By the time Central High School in Little Rock was to open for its 1957–58 school year, the Communist Party was marching step by step with the NAACP, whether the good element in the NAACP liked it or not.

DAILY WORKER LED THE CRY FOR FEDERAL INTERVENTION

WASHINGTON, July 24—"The honor of our country requires Federal intervention now, to end the organized defiance of decency and justice in the South." These words were not spoken by Mayor Mann of Little Rock. Nor by Maxwell Rabb, White House assistant to whom the mayor talked daily by telephone in the hectic days preceding intervention by the National Guard and Paratroopers.

They were not spoken by an official of the National Association for the Advancement of Colored People, the dominant U.S. Negro organization.

The words were an official pronouncement of the Communist Party of the United States, issued two years before Little Rock, and printed in the party's official political guide, Political Affairs, issue of October 1955.

UTTERED BY COMMUNIST

"The Federal Government has the power and the duty to use troops and whatever other constitutional means are available to enforce the law of the land."

Use of the word "constitutional" in the above might lead someone to think a good American had said those words.

They were uttered 18 months before Little Rock's Federal troop intervention by Benjamin J. Davis, chairman of the Negro Commission of the U.S. Communist Party.

"The Federal Government hasn't hesitated to use the force of jail and seizures in trying to destroy the Communists and other foes of Jim Crow," said Davis, who, like other Communists, has been able to predict the future in civil rights matters.

PRESSED FOR TROOPS

"It should not hesitate to use whatever force—troops if necessary—to put down violent defiance of the law of the land, and murderous terror against peaceful citizens seeking to exercise their constitutional rights."

From the very beginning of the Little Rock incident, the Communists pressed for "dispatch of Federal troops to keep order in the South."

The Communist Daily Worker shrilled a demand for "action," on Sept. 5, the day after Governor Faubus stationed National Guardsmen around Central High School.

"The insurrection in Arkansas" must be put down, strummed the *Worker* the next day.

"G-men must be sent," said another edition, blasting FBI director Hoover for refusing to do so.

THE FACE OF THE NAACP

NAACP LIFE MEMBER — Thurgood Marshall (center), NAACP special counsel, receives plaque denoting his life membership in the NAACP from Kivie Kaplan, Boston, Massachusetts, co-chairman of the Association's Life Membership Committee. Looking on is Arthu. ipingarn, NAACP President. The NAACP IS NOT A NEGRO ORGANIZATION and never has been. There is not a single Negro led and Negro directed organization fighting for integration in the country today.

* * *

COMMUNIST PARTY PLATFORM
YEAR 1928

1. Abolition of whole system of racial separation. Full racial integration.
2. Integration in housing.
3. Registration of Negro voters.
4. Abolition of laws forbidding intermarriage of persons of different races.
5. Integration in schools and universities.
6. Integration in hotels, theatres, restaurants, and waiting rooms.
7. Integration in the Armed Forces.
8. Integration in trade unions.
9. Integration in employment.

ALL GOD'S CHILLUN is the title of a 43-page booklet written by a Virginia surgeon, Dr. Franklin Adam Tyler. Dr. Tyler depicts Southern interracial problems in a lighter vein, with illustrations by Fred O. Seibel. We recommend this book to our members. Copies may be secured by addressing Box 455, Chester, Virginia. Price is $1.00.

* * *

COMMITTEE HEARINGS ON JENNER BILL

At the request of the Defenders, Judge William Old appeared before the Internal Security Subcommittee on February 26th to testify on behalf of S. 2646 to limit the appellate jurisdiction of the Supreme Court in certain cases. Judge Old told the committee that "the Congress is clothed with full power to make exceptions to the appellate jurisdiction of the Supreme Court and to regulate the exercise of such jurisdiction . . . It is now clearly apparent, from a long list of revolutionary decisions by the Supreme Court, headed by Chief Justice Warren, that the Court is determined to destroy our dual system of government under the Constitution and create, by usurpation and encroachment, judicial oligarchy of unparalleled proportions."

* * *

WHAT'S THIS?

On the recently appointed Civil Rights Commission is one Reverend Theodore M. Hesburgh of Indiana. The Reverend is also listed on the letterhead of the Institute of International Education, Inc. The Institute of International Education, Inc., is listed by the House Un-American Activities Committee, Union Calendar 833, pages 4 and 6 issued May 26, 1956, as an "American Branch of the Communist International." AND, in a folder titled "The Aims and Program of the Institute of International Education" is this:

> "The administration budget for 1956–1957 is approximately $1,473,000. About half of this was received in fees from programs that HE administered for other private and public organizations. These fees came CHIEFLY FROM THE U.S. GOVERNMENT AND FROM FOUNDATIONS . . . "

10 Richmond Times-Dispatch

DAVID TENNANT BRYAN, *President and Publisher*
VIRGINIUS DABNEY, *Editor*

Tuesday, October 16, 1956

Tragedy of the Negro Teacher

One of the major tragedies growing out of the Supreme Court's decision against segregation in the public schools is seen in the plight of many worthy and well-trained Negro school teachers, whose jobs are endangered.

With some 79,000 colored teachers in the Southern and border states at the time of the court's anti-segregation ruling, the question is how many of them would be able to retain their teaching positions, if the schools were mixed. This is a phase of the problem which disturbed many persons of both races before the Supreme Court's decision was handed down.

Already "between 450 and 500 Negro teachers in the South have lost their jobs as a result of integration," it has just been reported by BENJAMIN FINE of the New York *Times*.

Most of these dismissals were in rural areas, and 295, or more than half of the total, took place in Oklahoma. The Oklahoma dismissals occurred, it is explained by STATE SUPERINTENDENT OLIVER HODGE, because the all-Negro schools in which these teachers had taught, have been closed. Other dismissals, by states, include Kentucky, 60; West Virginia, 52; Texas, 35, and Missouri, variously estimated at from 10 to 40. In South Carolina, where there has been no integration, 24 teachers were dropped when they did not satisfactorily complete questionnaires explaining any connections with the NAACP.

The foregoing Negro teachers in Southern and border states who have lost their jobs (some of whom have found re-employment in other states) are the victims of an unsound and idealistic court ruling, handed down before the country was ready for it.

Apparently the North and West aren't ready for the employment of many Negro teachers either. There is only the merest handful of such teachers, even in such cities as New York, Chicago and Detroit, with their immense colored populations. Furthermore, such an episode as occurred recently in Gloucester, Mass., points up the attitude of the North.

The Gloucester school board employed a Eugene, Ore., teacher by mail. When he arrived, he turned out to be a Negro—a fact which could not be ascertained in advance, since Massachusetts law forbids any inquiry into race or religion on application forms. The man went back to Oregon the next day, with a check for $1,000 to cover his two transcontinental trips and the time involved.

If Gloucester, Mass., is unwilling to employ this colored teacher in its public schools, what would be the fate of Negro teachers throughout the South, if it ever got to the point where the Southern schools were mixed?

THE DEFENDERS OF STATE SOVEREIGNTY AND INDIVIDUAL LIBERTIES

405-A East Franklin Street - Richmond, Virginia

Reprinted in *Defenders' News and Views,* 1961.

UNIT 6-5

RICHMOND NEWS LEADER

INTERPOSITION EDITORIALS, 1956

INTRODUCTION

On November 21, 1956, The *Richmond News Leader* launched an editorial campaign that brought an old Constitutional doctrine out of American history and gave it new meaning for this generation.

It is the doctrine of Interposition.

In other days, the right of the States to interpose their sovereign powers against encroachment by the Federal Government was expounded by such great men as Jefferson, Madison, Calhoun, and the brilliant but neglected John Taylor of Caroline. In bygone years, right was assorted not only in the South, but in New England and the Midwest also.

The assertion of this right pre-supposes that ours is a Union of co-equal sovereign States, and together under a compact, called the Constitution, by which the member States delegate certain of their sovereign powers to a common Federal Government, and reserve all other powers to themselves respectively, or to the people. The doctrine of Interposition protects the right of each State to judge for itself an infraction of the compact; and depending upon the seriousness of the violation, to interpose its sovereign powers in such honorable constitutional manner as it deems best in order to arrest the progress of the evil.

The *News Leader* took the position editorially that the United States Supreme Court, on May 17, 1964, violated the Constitution by encroaching upon the amendatory powers of the States, guaranteed to them under Article V of the Constitution. In an intensive series of editorial page presentations, it reproduced documents, speeches and letters supporting the right of the States to interpose.

The campaign succeeded phenomenally. Across the South, one State after another took up the doctrine. In cities remote from problems of school segregation, editors and columnists discussed it. Some assailed it; some defended it. A national news magazine commented that interposition "had become a household word." Members of Congress debated the same Constitutional issues Webster and Hayne had debated more than 100 years ago.

The following pages offer some of the editorials from this campaign as they appeared in the *Richmond News Leader*, together with a selection of supporting documents, a bibliography, and the text of Virginia's Resolution of Interposition of February 1, 1956.

In Virginia, a Resolution of interposition was seen as a supplement to the legislative amendations of a State Commission on Public Education (known as the Gray Commission).

By overwhelming vote, Virginia's General Assembly adopted the resolution urged by advocates of interposition. Alabama, South Carolina, Georgia and Mississippi joined in the movement. It is the newspaper's hope that other States may be persuaded to ponder soberly the grave Constitutional problem here reviewed.

THE TRANSCENDENT ISSUE

Section 15—That no free government, or the blessings of liberty can be preserved by any people, but by a firm adherence to justice, moderation, temperance, frugality and virtue, and by frequent recurrence to fundamental principles.

—Constitution of Virginia.

In commenting upon the report of the Gray Commission a week ago, this newspaper extended its support generally to the commission's program, but we directed our comments first to what the report termed the "transcendent" issue.

This was the grave action taken by the Supreme Court, when, irrespective of precedent, long acquiesced in, it asserted the right to change its interpretation of the Constitution at its pleasure, disregarding the orderly processes for its amendment set out in Article V thereof.

"It means," said the commission, "that the most fundamental of the rights of the States and of their citizens exist by the court's sufferance, and that the law of the land is whatever the court may determine it to be by the process of judicial legislation."

Can it be right, we have inquired, that binding "law of the land" can be fashioned in this cavalier way? Was it ever intended by the founding fathers that such authority should be vested in the court? If the commission correctly states the degeneracy of constitutional process, does not Virginia have a right and a duty to interpose its sovereignty in a valiant effort to halt the evil?

An examination of these profound questions of constitutional rights and powers has prompted us, even as the Constitution of Virginia suggests, to recur to fundamental principles for guidance. Over the next several days, we propose to offer on the editorial page certain historic documents that shed light upon evil of today that were prophetically seen long ago. The first of these documents appear at right.[page 3].

THE RIGHT OF INTERPOSITION

From the very day of the Supreme Court opinion in the school segregation cases, the South, in searching for a wise course of action, has been handicapped by a fault that in ordinary times is among our highest virtues: It is our reverence for law, and our obedience to constituted authority.

Thus, when the Supreme Court handed down its decision, there was everywhere an agonizing, but automatic acceptance of the court's authority. The decision was wrong, we said; it was directly contrary to a long line of accepted judicial interpretations; it was violative of the Fourteenth Amendment as the amendment had been universally understood for more than 80 years. Yet the Supreme Court had declared that the right to operate racially separate schools was, as of May 17, 1954, a right now "prohibited to the States." And a people too long accustomed to submissiveness agreed that the court, indeed, was "supreme."

The Gray Commission, in a single great and simple paragraph, has explained to us what this agreement implies. "It means," said the commission, "that the most fundamental of the rights of the States and of their citizens exist by the court's sufferance." It means further, "that the law of the land is whatever the court may determine it to be by the process of judicial legislation."

This is the third time in 10 days that we have quoted these few lines from the report of the Gray Commission. They go to the very heart of the gravest issue to confront not merely Virginia and the South, but rather the entire nation, in nearly a century.

This is, as the Gray Commission said, *the transcendent issue*. Measured against its solemn implications, problems of local school segregation, serious as they are, seem almost petty.

What we must ask ourselves as Virginians, as heirs to the philosophical inheritance of Jefferson and Madison, whether any means exist by which the "process of judicial legislation" may be brought to a pause. If the "most fundamental of the rights of the States and their citizens" are not to be swept away by judicial encroachment, and the states reduced to the status of mere counties must we not exert every possible effort to halt the courts in their usurpation of our sovereign powers?

Surely, it would appear, such an effort is imperative; and perhaps Governor Stanley and his Gray Commission, even at this desperately late hour, could explore fundamental principles as enunciated by Jefferson and Madison. Virginians of today may yet inquire if these great men long ago, did not foresee the constitutional crisis before us in 1955 and point a way toward its peaceful solution.

The commission would find, we believe, that Jefferson and Madison did prophesize a time when the Federal government might usurp powers not granted it. And in such an emergency, these great men asserted, the States may declare their inherent right—inherent in the nature of our Union—to judge for themselves, not merely of the infractions, but "of the mode and measure of redress."

This is the *right of interposition*.

WHAT IS THIS RIGHT?

If the Gray Commission, which includes some of the finest minds in Virginia, undertakes to explore this transcendent problem, it will wish first to inquire into the nature of the right of interposition. Does it exist? What are the conditions that must arise before so solemn and drastic a remedy may be proposed? Under what circumstances has it been in the past? Do such circumstances obtain today?

Careful reasoning, we believe, would lead the Gray Commission to conclude that the right does indeed exist. Ours is a Union formed of sovereign States who voluntarily have surrendered certain of their powers to a central government, and voluntarily have prohibited the exercise of certain powers to themselves. By solemn compact, they have agreed the rights not delegated to the United States by the Constitution, nor prohibited by it to the States are reserved to the States *respectively*, or to the people. Thus each of the respective States stands coequal in the compact with every other States; theirs is a joint venture, an agreement among principals; it was only by the individual States that the Union came into being at all.

If one of the *principals* has no right to agreement, who then has the right? If the central government created by the States should usurp powers that might destroy the states, can it be contended that the principals have no right of protest, no right of appeal to their coequals, to resolve an issue of contested powers? Is it reasonable to believe that the States, like Frankenstein, have created an agency superior to themselves, and that they are utterly powerless to contest their own destruction?

The briefest statement of the hypothesis suggests its absurdity. The right of interposition, as Jefferson and Madison termed it, exists because it has to exist. Without such a right, the Constitution is a hollow shell; and the "perfect Union" it was intended to insure is disclosed as no Union at all, no joining of respective parts, but rather a single mass, monolithic, a creature more powerful than its creator.

If the existence of the right of interposition be admitted (and this is to admit no more than a right of survival, a right of compact), the Gray Commission might next inquire into the nature of the right. What are the conditions precedent to asserting the right of interposition? In what way may the people of a State interpose the shield of State sovereignty between the Federal government and the object of the Federal government's encroachments?

"DELIBERATE . . . PALPABLE . . . DANGEROUS"

The right of interposition, as Jefferson and Madison saw it, is a right of last resort. Ordinarily, the Congress could be expected to take no action so grossly violative of the compact among the States that satisfactory redress could not be found in the words of the Constitution—by judicial relief, by executive veto, by the election of a new Congress. And ordinarily the executive would assert no drastic powers that could not be curbed by well-established procedures. The greatest danger lay in the possibility of judicial usurpation, but here, it was thought, some confidence would have to be reposed in the restraint and moderation of men or our highest bench. The Federal government, it was anticipated, would recognize its limited authority and operate therein; the States, for their part, would recognize the surrender of certain of their powers, and would restrict their activities to the fields reserved for them.

"In cases of little urgency or importance," said Jefferson, "the prudence of both parties will keep them aloof from the questionable ground.

What, then, are the characteristics by which we may recognize the "great and extraordinary cases," as Jefferson termed them, in which the right of interposition may be asserted? Madison explored this very question in his thoughtful report to the General Assembly in 1799, an excerpt from which appears on (page 8).

A State, he said, must be confronted with a usurpation of power that "deeply and essentially" affects its vital principles. The right is not to be exercised "either in a hasty manner or on doubtful or inferior occasions." The conditions expressly required for such an interposition are that the offense must constitute "a deliberate, palpable, and dangerous breach of the Constitution by the exercise of powers not granted by it."

His exposition of this requirement merits our most careful study. *Deliberate . . . palpable . . . dangerous*: These are the characteristics that must be present.

Has such a breach of the compact occurred in the Supreme Court's mandates under its school decision? Does the court's opinion "deeply and essentially" affect vital principles of our political system? Is this a "great and extraordinary case," and not a "doubtful or inferior occasion"?

These questions we most respectably commend to the Gray Commission as the group best qualified, by reason of its enunciation of the transcendent issue, to explore them.

If the commission should conclude that such a grave breach of the constitutional compact has been committed; that an issue of contested powers has developed, so serious that it can be put to rest only by constitutional amendment, the commission may wish to consider recommendations to the Governor—late as the hour may be—by which Virginia would appeal to her sister States as the final umpire in a controversy of towering importance to the people of the South.

LATE HOUR FOR LIBERTIES

We have come this far in an editorial consideration of what Jefferson and Madison long ago termed a State's "right of interposition":

First, that the right exists; it was by the most illustrious of America's great men in the earliest days of the republic; it was described by Calhoun in the great address reprinted on this page today, as "the fundamental principle of our system, resting on facts historically as certain as our revolution itself, and deductions as simple and demonstrative as that of any political or moral truth whatever."

Secondly, that the nature of the right lies in the inherent power of American sovereign parties to a joint compact, to protest a breach of that compact by the Federal government they have jointly created. It is the right of a State, when it believes such a breach has been committed, to appeal to its sister States for adoption or rejection of a constitutional amendment, in order that a question of contested power may be set at rest.

Thirdly, that the exercise of the right is limited to certain grave and extraordinary cases. The breach of understood powers must be, in Madison's phrase, "deliberate, palpable and dangerous." The encroachment of the Federal government must "deeply and essentially affect vital principles of a State's political system." The right is not to be invoked "in cases of little urgency or importance."

ONCE GEORGIA INTERPOSED

We would now submit that Governor Stanley and the Gray Commission may wish to explore the forms in which this right has been exercised in the past. On Monday, attention was directed to the historic Kentucky and Virginia Resolutions of 1798, in which interposition took the form of a ringing protest, avowing the unconstitutionality of the Alien and Sedition Acts. We may recall Madison's clear statement that "farther measures" could have been taken by the General Assembly.

It is of keen interest to reflect upon a still earlier exercise of the right of interposition, with a contemporary analogy too clear to be overlooked.

When the Constitution originally was ratified, it was with the plain understanding of the ratifying States that the judicial power of the Federal Courts would not extend to claims brought against a sovereign State. This was nowhere spelled out in the compact. It was simply understood, as men in their daily life rely in every field upon understandings not put in words.

Yet the Federalist Supreme Court, in the teeth of this understanding, undertook to hear a claim against Georgia and entered an order compelling Georgia to pay. Georgia flatly refused. (The Georgia House of Representatives even passed a bill, which never became law, providing that any Federal marshal who attempted to enforce the mandate would be hanged). It was Georgia's position that this power had *not* been granted to the Federal government. It was the court's position that it *had* been granted. So Georgia, in effect, invoked in 1792 the right of interposition: Georgia called upon all of the States to decide the issue. And in 1795, the States ratified the Eleventh Amendment by which Georgia was declared right, and the court wrong.

While this appeal to the primary sovereignty of the people was pending, Georgia naturally withheld payment of the claim.

It is a late hour, we confess, to suggest that Governor Stanley and the Gray Commission ponder the interposition of Georgia 160 years ago, in terms of its possible application to Virginia's problem today.

It is a late hour to submit that Virginia may learn something from the defiance of Northern States, in the 1850s; through their Personal Liberty Laws. The enforcement of these State enactments, in the very teeth of the Supreme Court's opinion in the Dred Scott case, may indicate that States are not quite so helpless before the court as we have assumed. In the history of the enforcement of the Personal Liberty Laws may be found, also, a precedent on this point: That a State, or a group of States, may defy the court on one question and remain wholly obedient to its orders on every other, the whole remaining in the Union.

WHAT DID THE WAR CHANGE?

Now, it will be objected that all of this was settled by the Civil War; that the North's victory over the South established the supremacy of the Federal government not only militarily but constitutionally also. That the war established a certain military supremacy, Virginia would be the last to deny: the war, if it proved anything, proved that when one group of States is determined by force to contest the effort of another group of States to withdraw from the Union, law and sovereign rights are blown to the four winds and the issue is resolved on naked force alone.

But if the war also established the constitutional supremacy of the Federal government over the member States of the Union, then this fact surely would have been spelled out for us to read in the Constitution today. This nowhere appears. The three Reconstruction Amendments provided, first, that slavery shall not exist "within the United States, or any place subject to *their* [not *its*] jurisdiction"; secondly, that the right to vote shall not be abridged on account of race; and thirdly, in the vague and uncertain language of the Fourteenth Amendment, that

> No State shall make or enforce any law which shall abridge the privileges or immunities of citizens of the United States, nor shall any State deprive any person of life, liberty or property without due process of law, nor deny to any person within its jurisdiction the equal protection of the laws.

These were all the amendments to the Constitution that were made in the period immediately following the war. The Thirteenth Amendment was declared ratified in 1865, the Fourteenth in 1868, the Fifteenth in 1870. A period of 43 years then elapsed before the Constitution was modified again. The significant point is that the Reconstruction Amendments in no way altered the basic structure of the compact. Ours is still a Union *of States*, each State retaining certain sovereign rights that it never has surrendered to the general government, each State still entitled to make its own decisions except where a power has been prohibited to the States by the Constitution.

THE CLEAR UNDERSTANDING

Let us come down, then, to the specific issue of public schools and other public facilities.

We will note, first, that the very Congress—the Thirty-ninth Congress—that proposed the Fourteenth Amendment for ratification itself established separate schools in the District of Columbia.

There was implicit understanding among the States that the amendment in no way prohibited the operation of separate schools. This understanding was expressly confirmed by the Supreme Court in 1896, and again expressly confirmed by a unanimous Supreme Court in 1927.

For a period of more than 80 years, the States acquiesced in this understanding. It was agreed that what was prohibited to the States in this field was the right to operate separate but *unequal* schools. And pursuant to this agreement and understanding, the South, struggling from the poverty and ruins of Reconstruction, painfully began to build up a school system that would provide some education for her children.

NINE MEN, OR 36 STATES

On May 17, 1954, *not* by action of three fourths of the States *but on the naked and arrogant declaration of nine men*, the Supreme Court itself undertook to wipe out this long understanding and *by its own act*, in effect to amend the Constitution. In that moment, nine men arrogated unto themselves powers vested by the Constitution in the people of no fewer than 36 states.

We would submit most earnestly to Governor Stanley, and to the Gray Commission, that they consider whether Virginia, summoning to her aid the great voices of Madison and Jefferson, should not protest this rape of the Constitution with all the power and eloquence at our command.

Can we not ask of our sister States, in honor and in dignity, that if the court's opinion actually be the people's will, then the people should spell it out so that all uncertainty will be ended? If the power to operate separate schools and other public facilities is to be prohibited to the States, should not this grave and drastic change in public powers be nailed into the Constitution by appropriate amendment?

Let us ponder this transcendent issue. Already the Supreme Court, bent upon destroying the constitutional understandings of more than 80 years, has ordered an end to separate school and parks. The next wind that blows from the court will take with it a State's power to prohibit interracial marriage. One by one, the reserved powers of sovereign States will be swept away. Unless interposition is made now, in a desperate effort to halt this process of judicial amendment of the Constitution, the States inevitably will lie reduced to nonentities and the whole structure of our Union will be radically altered.

Think upon these things, Virginians!

Whether one opposes racial integration, as we do, or supports integration, as many do, is beside the point. All Virginians, liberal and conservative, from the Tidewater or the Valley, are united in a devotion to the Constitution and a reverence for its proper administration. If we fail now to make at least the effort to preserve the Constitution from the greedy hands of the Supreme Court, bent upon shaping it as a thing of wax, we shall have failed as Americans and Virginians in an hour of solemn crisis.

AN OLD DOCTRINE STILL NEW

With our readers' indulgence, we would return now to the editorial discussion launched last week of the "right of interposition." The longer we have examined this principle of government, the more strongly we are persuaded that the right existed when the Union was formed; that nothing has occurred since then that has abolished the right; that it still exists and that its assertion by the Virginia General Assembly might well serve to check the United States Supreme Court in its usurpation of power. At the very least, a fresh enunciation of this cardinal principle of our Union would serve to provoke widespread reflection upon this nation's drift from historic moorings.

The right of interposition, as enunciated by Jefferson, Madison, Calhoun, Hayne, Randolph and many others, is seen historically as the States' right to interpose their sovereignty between the Federal Government and the object of its encroachments upon powers reserved to the States. This right rests in the incontrovertible theory that ours is a Union of sovereign States; that the Federal Government exists only by reason of solemn compact among the States; that each respective State is a coequal party to this compact; that if the compact is violated by the Federal government every State has a right to judge of the infraction; and that when an issue of contested power arises, *only the States themselves*, by constitutional process, may finally decide the issue.

In last week's presentation we dwelled especially upon the enunciation of this right in Southern States from time to time. It is well to recall that Southerners have been by no means alone in declaring that in grave and extraordinary cases, the States may challenge an action taken by the Federal government.

NEW ENGLAND PROCLAIMED THE RIGHT

In December of 1814, at a time of intense opposition in the New England States to the War of 1812, a convention met at Hartford to consider a number of constitutional questions. Delegates were elected to this convention from Connecticut, Massachusetts, Rhode Island, New Hampshire and Vermont; and except for the last two States, where delegates were chosen by local conventions, the delegates were named by State Legislatures. The Hartford convention has often been ridiculed, but there is no question of the seriousness of its purpose or the validity of the delegates' credentials.

Out of the Hartford convention, among other resolutions, came this declaration:

"In case of deliberate, dangerous and palpable infractions of the Constitution, affecting the sovereignty of a State and the liberties of the people, it is not only the right, but the duty of such State to interpose its authority for their protection, *in the manner best calculated to secure that end*. When emergencies occur which are either beyond the reach of Judicial tribunals, or too pressing to admit of the delay incident to their forms, States which have no common umpire must be their own judges and execute their own decisions." (Our italics.)

As events turned out, Jackson's victory at New Orleans in January of 1815, and the following month's Peace of Ghent, put at rest the peculiar problems that had aroused a desire for interposition. Yet the declaration remains as a solemn expression from New England, echoing the very position Virginia and Kentucky had asserted 16 years earlier.

WISCONSIN PROCLAIMED THE RIGHT

For a second example of the assertion of this right, outside the South, we may look at events in Wisconsin in 1858 and 1859. We may recall that Congress, in 1850, had enacted the Fugitive Slave Law, and the Supreme Court, in 1857, had followed this with the Dred Scott decision upholding slavery as a practice reserved to the States to regulate.

The abolition movement was especially strong in Wisconsin; and when a United States marshal at Racine attempted to arrest and return a fugitive slave named Joshua Glover, a mob of irate citizens, led by an editor named Sherman M. Booth, broke into jail, rescued Glover and prevented his return. Booth was arrested in violation of the Federal Act, but the Wisconsin State Supreme Court intervened with a writ of habeas corpus, and for a period of several years—until the onset of war—the Wisconsin court waged a defiant battle with the United States Supreme Court.

In this battle, the Wisconsin court had the support of the Wisconsin General Assembly. Let us look at Joint Resolution No. 4 of the Wisconsin Legislature, adopted March 19, 1859. After declaring that the United States Supreme Court had acted "without process, or any of the forms recognized by law," the Legislature denounced the court's "assumption of power" and said the court's effort "to become the final arbiter" was in direct conflict with the Constitution. The resolution continued:

"Resolved, that this assumption of jurisdiction in the said case, and without process, is an act of undelegated power, and therefore without authority, void and of no force.

"Resolved, that the government formed by the Constitution of the United States was not made the exclusive or final judge of the extent of the powers delegated to itself, but that, as in all other cases of compact among parties having no common judge, each party has an equal right to judge for itself, as well of infractions as of the mode and measure of redress.

"Resolved, that the principle and construction contended for . . . that the general government is the exclusive judge of the extent of powers delegated to it, stops nothing short of despotism, since the discretion of those who administer the government, and not the Constitution, would be the measure of their powers; that the several States which formed that instrument have the unquestionable right to judge of its infraction; and that a positive defiance by those sovereignties, of all unauthorized acts done or attempted to be done under color of that instrument is the rightful remedy."

Again, the voice of Jefferson and Madison, this time after 61 years; and this powerful statement of "positive defiance" came not from the South, but from Wisconsin. And again, may we suggest that the issue of contested power asserted by Wisconsin was ultimately to be resolved, so far as the Constitution is concerned, by constitutional amendment? Just as Georgia in 1792 compelled adoption of the Eleventh Amendment, prohibiting Federal courts from hearing claims against a State, so the Northern States finally were to nail into the Constitution the Thirteenth Amendment, prohibiting slavery.

IOWA SUCCESSFULLY CHALLENGED

One further instance of successful challenge of the court's authority, from outside the South, may be noted. In the period immediately after the Civil War, an Iowa legislature undertook to give large favors and grants to the expanding railroads. The Iowa Supreme Court at first held these grants lawful. Then a subsequent Iowa court held the grants unlawful. The United States Supreme Court which then was exceedingly pro-railroad, attempted to reverse the second position of the Iowa court.

Professor Fred Rodell of Yale University has described what happened, in his recent book, *Nine Men*: "[The justices] saw their orders disobeyed and flouted. . . . The Iowa Supreme Court did indeed disregard the U.S. Supreme Court's orders in three consecutive cases until it forced the high tribunal, devoid at that time of the prestige that underlies its power, to ignominiously back down."

THE ULTIMATE APPEAL

We may note, in concluding this brief sketch of challenges to the Supreme Court's authority, this aspect of the story: Georgia defied the court in the 1790s, refused to obey its orders, and remained in the Union as a loyal and obedient State in every other regard. So, too, did Wisconsin 60 years later defy the court, refuse to obey its orders, and remain in the Union as a loyal and obedient State in every other regard. So, too, did Iowa, in the 1870s and 1880s, defy the court, refuse to obey its orders, and remain in the Union as a loyal and obedient State in every other regard.

The point is simply that to contest an assertion of authority by a Federal agency, through solemn reliance on the reserved powers of the States, is not rebellion, anarchy or revolution, It is a process of ultimate appeal; and the Southern States, we firmly believe, have every right: First, to interpose their sovereignty in order that such an appeal may be taken in so flagrant a case as the Supreme Court's reversal of a long established construction of the Constitution; and secondly, to submit that while the appeal is pending—while the States are considering a constitutional amendment which, by ratification, would sustain the court, or by rejection, would rebuke the court—such great and irrevocable damage would be done to our public education that further efforts to compel racial integration, as a condition of maintaining public schools, should properly be stayed.

We can imagine the scorn and ridicule with which such an approach may be greeted by the NAACP, and by centralists who believe in the absolute supremacy of the Federal government. Beyond doubt, there are many who believe—and sincerely believe—that the Supreme Court has only to usurp a power for the power to be effectively seized from the States; and that as many as 35 States are powerless to resist so long as merely 13 States are agreeable to the encroachment.

We cannot believe this is a fair or reasonable interpretation of the clear intent of the Founding Fathers, who prudently—and prophetically—placed such great emphasis upon the sovereignty of the perspective States. The great men who erected our Union, erected it upon the foundation of States rights and reserved powers. Surely there can be no argument with the proposition that if this foundation is now to be destroyed, it should be by constitutional process, not by judicial legislation.

INTERPOSITION, NOW!

The General Assembly of Virginia was to meet in special session on Wednesday, November 30, 1955. On the evening of Tuesday, November 29 the following editorial appeared.

With the publication on today's editorial page of Virginia's Resolution of 1829, this newspaper concludes its presentation of the historical background of the Right of Interposition. In the past week, we have offered excerpts from the Kentucky and Virginia Resolutions of 1798, the Madison Report of 1799, the Hartford Convention of 1814, Calhoun's address of 1831, the resolutions of the Wisconsin Legislature in 1859, and other material touching upon the right of sovereign States to challenge a usurpation of power by the General Government they have created.

These examples could be multiplied, for the amazing thing as one delves into the subject—is not how seldom the States have resisted encroachment upon their powers, but how frequently they have arisen in their sovereign capacities and asserted the solemn powers so clearly inherent in the nature of our Union.

The resolution that occupies our page today is offered as one more assertion of this right, one more eloquent exposition of the fundamental principles upon which our Union was formed. It is not as moving, perhaps, as Madison's beautifully phrased Report of 1799, yet it merits a reading upon this eve of a union of the General Assembly of Virginia. For here is enunciated, in wonderfully clear terms, the tradition of Virginia's Assembly in the face of Federal encroachments: Whenever an attempt has been made to pervert the Constitution, said the Assembly in 1829, "Virginia has even been prompt to avow her unqualified disapprobation, and manifest her undisguised discontent."

More than this: "To subject our local or domestic affairs to any other authority than our own Legislature would be to expose to certain destruction the happiness and prosperity of the people of Virginia."

RESPONSIBILITY LIES UPON THE LEGISLATURE

And beyond this lies the comment that the founders of our Nation apprehended that "the sacred liberty of the American citizen should be invaded by the arbitrary acts of the General Government." How could these apprehensions be allayed? Only by the assurance and conviction "that the State Governments were adequate to the resistance of Federal encroachments." It is the Legislatures of the several States, said Virginia's General Assembly in 1829, which are "the guardians of our political institutions," and it is their sacred duty to preserve these institutions unimpaired.

That brings our discussion, then, at long last, to tomorrow's session of the General Assembly.

The question we would submit to the Assembly—the "transcendent issue" that surpasses any questions of racial segregation—is whether the compact among States has been violated by the Supreme Court; and if the compact has been violated, whether Virginia's General Assembly will meet the infraction with the same high courage, and the same eloquent reliance upon fundamental principles that Jefferson and Madison relied upon in years gone by.

That the Supreme Court acted unconstitutionally in its decision of May 17, 1954 this newspaper now asserts with all the earnestness at its command. Under the guise of "interpretation," the court so drastically cast aside the long established construction of the Fourteenth Amendment as in effect to amend the amendment.

If that proposition be accepted, the remaining question, in the language of the resolution on this page today, is whether our State Government is "adequate to the resistance of Federal encroachments." If the Assembly fails to interpose now—if it fails to challenge this deliberate, palpable and dangerous encroachment of the Federal Government upon the amendatory rights of the States—our opportunity for effective action will have passed. It should be remembered that Virginia's Assembly has not met since the opinion of May, 1954. Ours is the challenging opportunity to speak now, to assert the existence of a contested power, to demand that our sister States—who alone have authority to decide such a contest—resolve the issue through constitutional process.

This newspaper has done everything within its power to suggest that such interposition is an age-old right of the Virginia Assembly. We would not be so presumptuous as to suggest that it is also a "sacred duty," but that is the term the Virginia Assembly itself employed in 1829.

Let us move, now, to the immediate present. Let us examine the benefits and advantages to be found in a legislative Resolution of Interposition, and ask ourselves if this is not the right, sound, and most eminently desirable course for Virginia to take.

FOUR ADVANTAGES SEEN IN RESOLUTION

In the view of this newspaper, four prime considerations suggest the wisdom of the Assembly's adoption of a Resolution of Interposition.

The first of these (and if there were no more, this in itself would be sufficient) is simply that it is the course of right conduct. Whether or not such a resolution may be expedient, whether or not we win or lose, whether or not we are derided by centralists and scorned by the advocates of Federal supremacy, Virginia once more should enunciate the sovereignty of States; we should recur to fundamental principles. This is our heritage. This is our tradition. This was the philosophy of the great men who walked in the halls of our own Capitol; in the rights of States are the very guideposts of American Government, as the Resolution of 1829 made clear, that our fathers "happily pointed out to future generations." We ought not to repudiate them now. We ought, more properly, to express again our devotion to their high ideals of this Union, and by such an expression hope to awaken those States which have been so woefully apathetic to the Federal Governments encroachments upon their powers.

Secondly (and here we approach more immediate considerations), the General Assembly may well recognize that in defending racial segregation, we are defending a practice that to much of the Nation seems indefensible. We who live in the South know clearly the sound reasons that support the wisdom of a dual society; we know, vividly and by first-hand experience, the gulf that divides the mores of two disparate races.

We know these things, but others do not know. And the second advantage of the proposed resolution is that Virginia, by the adoption of such a resolution, might succeed in elevating this controversy from the regional field of segregation to the transcendent, national field of State sovereignty. There is a tactical advantage in higher ground, and we would do well to seek it.

"THE MEASURE OF REDRESS"

On January 19, 35 members of the Virginia State Senate joined in sponsoring a Resolution of Interposition. Only minor amendments were made in the measure as introduced. It appears hereafter. The following editorial accompanied the text of their resolution.

At right appears the text of a Resolution of Interposition that will be introduced in the Senate of Virginia today, under the sponsorship of a majority of the members of that body. We hope that in its present form every advocate of State's rights and every foe of compulsory integration will support the measure.

Several comments may be made on the final text here advanced, but a few general observations on the nature of interposition, as we conceive that doctrine, may well be offered first.

It has seemed to us, the longer we have explored this absorbing subject, that by "interposition" is meant the basic right of a State to assert its sovereignty against Federal encroachments. Assertion of this right may take many forms—mild, moderate, and strong; and the right may be asserted, as we see it, by any of the branches of a State government. Yesterday the Virginia Supreme Court of Appeals, in an admirable action, interposed against the Supreme Court of the United States in a miscegenation case. Governors, in times past, have asserted their executive powers against Federal bureaus. Several years ago, Indiana exercised its powers of interposition in the matter of welfare grants, by insisting upon her right, as a sovereign state, to open welfare rolls for public inspection if she wished.

Interposition should not be confused with nullification; the former is the genus, the latter a species thereof. Nullification is an act of interposition, but interposition is by no means confined to nullification. All blows are not knockout blows; all motor vehicles are not 30-ton trucks; all aircraft are not jet bombers. Similarly, assertions of the right to interpose may range from temperate protest at the one extreme to flat nullification at the other.

The resolution at right falls midway between the extremes. It reflects the spirit of the Virginia Resolution of 1798, in which our Legislature announced that it "doth particularly protest against the palpable and alarming infractions of the Constitution in the two late cases of the 'Alien and Sedition Acts.'" Madison himself, construing the Resolution of 1798 in his report the following year, emphasized that the action was intended only as a protest, "to excite reflection."

But Madison went on to point out that "farther measures"—something more than a protest could have been taken if necessary, and the resolution offered in Virginia today does, in fact, go a bowshot beyond mere protest.

This resolution would declare, unequivocally, that Virginia has *never* surrendered her right to operate racially separate public schools; it would charge the Supreme Court with unconstitutional encroachment upon the State's exclusive power to amend the Constitution; it would pledge the Assembly's "firm intention" to resist this encroachment by all honorable and constitutional means.

This language, to be sure, stops short of a measure with the bared "teeth in it" that might have been offered. It is not so strong as the resolution Alabama is now pursuing, but it is stronger than the resolution adopted by North Carolina last year. Thus it embodies Jefferson's concept that each State "has an equal right to judge for itself, as well of infractions as of the mode and measure of redress."

The "mode and measure of redress" here suggested represents an effort by the sponsoring legislators to accomplish two aims.

The first is an appeal to all the States in this Union to awaken to encroachments by the Federal government upon their sovereign powers. Virginia would ask them especially to join in settling a question of contested power involving a State's right to operate separate public institutions.

The second aim is to do what the Assembly can—*and no one knows exactly what Virginia can do*—to prevent enforced integration of our schools until the constitutional question of the court's decree is put to rest.

Now, some earlier drafts of the resolution were stronger than the fifth version which appears on this page today; and because the court's action in the school cases seems to us so powerful a usurpation of authority, we might have preferred a more powerful assertion of Virginia's rights. But we are persuaded by such first rate Senators as Culpeper's Robert Button and Brunswick's Albertis Harrison that a moderate declaration will satisfactorily serve the aims in view. Their feeling is that the suggested resolution (**1**) will have a greater chance of eliciting sympathetic support outside the South, and (**2**) will leave the Virginia Assembly in a more flexible position to proceed with a legislative program if we are driven by sheer force to swallow Federal decrees so grievously objectionable to us.

Let us conclude with a comment from John C. Calhoun that seems worth repeating: In 1831, discussing the general doctrine of interposition, he emphasized that its most solemn exercise should be limited to those cases of "dangerous infraction" of the Constitution when, "if the right to interpose did not exist, the alternative would be submission and oppression on one hand, or resistance by force on the other." And he continued:

"That our system should afford, in such extreme cases, an intermediate point between these dire alternatives, *by which the government may be brought to a pause*, and thereby an interval obtained to compromise differences, or, if impracticable, be compelled to submit the question to a constitutional adjustment, *through an appeal to the States themselves*, is an evidence of its high wisdom: An element not, as is supposed by some, of weakness, but of strength; not of anarchy and revolution, but of peace and safety."

CERTAINLY WE THINK IT "ILLEGAL"

One word in the pending resolution seemed to be causing most objection: Should the Assembly term the court's decision flatly an "illegal" encroachment? This editorial discussed the point on January 27.

Much of yesterday's discussion of interposition dealt with the word "illegal," as it appears in the fourteenth and final resolve of the pending measure. Here the Assembly would pledge its firm intention

> to take all appropriate measures honorably, legally and constitutionally available to us, to resist this illegal encroachment upon our sovereign powers . . .

It evidently was the feeling of Senators Breeden and Spong, and of Delegate Robert Whitehead, that the word is susceptible to some misconstruction at the bar. Said Mr. Whitehead: "If the decision is 'illegal' it is unlawful; and if unlawful it is not law; if it's not law, no one's bound by it."

The wonderfully heartening action that developed in the House yesterday, when upwards of 70 members endorsed a resolution containing the phrase just quoted, probably makes extended comment unnecessary. It is evidently the will of the Assembly to adopt the strongest possible measure, short of flat nullification, that can be devised. Needless to say, this will suit us perfectly.

But a few observations may be made on the point that concerns our critics. The resolution now before the Senate was designed to echo the spirit and intention of the Virginia Resolution of 1798. This was Madison's Resolution, offered in the House by the brilliant John Taylor of Caroline. Their measure termed the Alien and Sedition Acts a "most palpable violation" of constitutional rights, and went on to express Virginia's scrupulous fidelity to the Constitution. The resolution continued:

> The General Assembly doth solemnly appeal to the like dispositions of the other States, in confidence that they will concur with this Commonwealth in declaring, as it does hereby declare, that the acts aforesaid are unconstitutional, and that the necessary and proper measures will be taken by each, for co-operating with this

> State in maintaining unimpaired the authorities, rights and liberties reserved to the States, respectively, or to the people.

Thus it will be seen that the Assembly did not hesitate in 1798 to declare unequivocally "that the acts aforesaid are unconstitutional." And following Mr. Whitehead's reasoning, it may be said that if an act is unconstitutional, it is void; and if void, it is not law; and if not law, no one's bound by it.

But Madison did not regard the declaration as any legally binding pronouncement. This is what he said on the point in his Report of 1799:

It has been said that it belongs to the judiciary of the United States, and not the State Legislatures, to declare the meaning of the Federal Constitution.

But a declaration that proceedings of the Federal government are not warranted by the Constitution, is a novelty neither among the citizens, nor among the Legislatures of the States; nor are the citizens or the Legislature of Virginia singular in the example of it.

> Nor can the declarations of either, whether affirming or denying the constitutionality of measures of the Federal government, or whether made before or after judicial decisions thereon, be deemed, in any point of view, an assumption of the office of the judge. The declarations, in such cases, are expressions of opinion, unaccompanied with any other effect than what they may produce on opinion, by exciting reflection. The expositions of the judiciary, on the other hand, are carried into immediate effect by force. The former may lead to a change in the legislative expression of the general will; possibly to a change in the opinion of the judiciary; the latter enforces the general will, whilst that will and that opinion continue unchanged.

This same exposition was advanced by Senator Harry C. Stuart in the letter to Mr. Whitehead which is published in full on this page today. No expression by this Assembly on the Supreme Court's decree can, in itself, undo that decree, render it void, or bind lower Federal courts to ignore it. Until the Constitution is amended or the court reverses itself, the court's decrees are the law, because, in Mr. Madison's phrase, the judiciary can carry them into effect "by force."

But that consideration surely does not gag the General Assembly of Virginia, or prevent it from interposing the sovereignty of this State in an effort to arrest the progress of the evil done to the Constitution by the court. This Assembly may express itself in any way it pleases—the stronger the better!—In the hope (it can be nothing more) that solemn legislative declarations will have a persuasive effect upon the courts and upon public opinion.

It has been complained that this is not only "not nullification" but "not even interposition." Our response is that Madison, Jefferson, Taylor and Calhoun, who certainly were more astute thinkers upon the Constitution than any of us today, many times described Virginia's Resolution of 1798 as "interposition." Governor John Floyd, in the message we republished on Wednesday, described it thus. So did Littleton Waller Tazewell. So did Abel Parker Upshur.

If one wants to get at the meaning of nullification, it may be suggested that South Carolina's ordinance—not resolution, but *ordinance*—of 1832 is the model for proper reference. This was designed "to nullify certain Acts of Congress." It declared the Tariffs of 1828 and 1932 "null, void, and no law, nor binding upon this State, its officers or citizens." It declared that all judicial proceedings affirming the acts "are and shall be utterly null and void." It declared that "from and after the first day of February next [1833], all persons resident or being within the limits of this State . . . are hereby required and enjoined to obey and give effect to this Ordinance." It wound up with a declaration that should the Federal Government employ force to collect its customs, the people of

South Carolina will thenceforth hold themselves absolved from an further obligation to maintain or preserve their political connection with the people of the other States, and will forthwith proceed to organize a separate government, and do all other things which sovereign and independent States may of right do.

That, gentle reader, was nullification, vintage of 1832. To suggest that the Stuart Resolution of 1956 in any way adopts that pattern is to suggest an absurdity.

No. The resolution before the Senate is one of interposition solely—yet as such, it remains a strong and hopefully effective declaration. It pledges the Assembly's intention firmly to resist illegal encroachment—the line might well read, "illegal and unconstitutional encroachment"—by whatever honorable legal and constitutional measures may prove open to us. These would include litigation, legislation, appeals to sisters States for Constitutional amendment, proceedings within our State courts, and every other tactic, in Senator Stuart's phrase, calculated "to impede" enforcement of the court's decrees.

To the best of our ability—*whatever this "best of our ability" may prove to be*—we would seek "to arrest the progress of the evil." That is our aim; that is our purpose; and it is not to be defeated by legalistic lint picking or haggling over the juridical effect of a word here or a word there.

SEN. STUART TO DELEGATE WHITEHEAD

The letter from State Senator Harry C. Stuart, chief patron of the Virginia Resolution, to Delegate Robert Whitehead, leading opponent, accompanied the editorial of January 27. The letter follows.

January 24, 1956

Honorable Robert Whitehead
House of Delegates
State Capitol
Richmond, Virginia

Dear Robert:

I am in receipt of yours of the twentieth, in which you propound nine legalistic questions relating to the Joint Resolution introduced on the nineteenth by 35 members of the Senate, myself among them. You are of course aware that I am not a lawyer; but I have discussed your questions with certain of my colleagues, who have joined in sponsoring this resolution, and would now respond to them.

First, let me say this of the resolution. I perceive its intention to be this: It warns our people against the encroaching spirit of the Federal government; it argues the unconstitutionality of the Supreme Court's decision in the school cases; it points to other instances in which the constitutional limits have been overleaped; it dwells upon the dangerous usurpation of amendatory powers; and in general presses the necessity of watching over the consolidating tendency of the Federal government. Beyond this, it declares the opinion of this Assembly as to the power reserved to the States to maintain certain racially separate public schools, and asserts that Virginia, at least, has never surrendered such power, however, it acknowledges the contrary opinion of the Supreme Court, and suggests that a question of whether the court has violated the Constitution ought not to be decided by the court itself, but should be taken to the one tribunal that Jefferson and Madison regarded as superior to the court's authority—the tribunal of the States themselves. Hence an earnest appeal is made to the sister States to settle the question by clear constitutional process, pursuant to Article V of the Constitution. And until the appeal is settled, it is proposed that the Assembly take whatever proper measures may be honorably, legally, and constitutionally available to us, firmly to resist what we believe is an illegal encroachment upon our powers.

This is a resolution of interposition. The word seems to frighten you. It does not frighten me. It is a good word. It was employed in this context by the author of the Declaration of Independence and by the "father of the Constitution." In the sense in which they used it, and in which it is used in the resolution, I understand it to mean an action taken on behalf of a State by one of its departments, seeking to protect the State and its people from invasion of the reserved power of the State by some department of the Federal government. That right I believe we have. That right the resolution would invoke.

My own reasons, as a layman, for believing that this right exists are derived from my own understanding of the nature of our government and our novel system of "dual sovereignty." As I comprehend this system, the people of the States, acting not as any mass of people, but rather as States, created a Federal government and delegated to it certain enumerated powers. All other attributes of sovereignty they specifically reserved to themselves.

In order to preserve this admirable system, they established certain checks and balances. Some of the "checks" on the executive and legislative branches are specifically contained in the Constitution itself, for example, the veto power of the President, and the Senate's power to confirm certain presidential appointments. In addition, the people themselves, through exercise of their suffrage, retain an immediate and direct check upon these departments.

But the one most familiar "check" upon the executive and legislative branches—the power asserted by the judiciary to declare their acts unconstitutional—is nowhere spelled out specifically in the Constitution. The brilliant mind of John Marshall perceived that such a check existed because it had to exist, as a matter of necessity, in order that our form of government may survive.

Not until comparatively recent years has it appeared vitally necessary for us to reappraise this system of checks and balances, to determine if something is missing. The problem of judicial encroachment seems not to have been fully perceived by the founding fathers. Mr. Hamilton, in the *Federalist*, terms the Supreme Court the "weakest" of all departments; he thought the people "could never fear oppression from that quarter."

Now the question is before the country and demands an answer: *What is the check upon the judiciary?* What recourse have we if the Supreme Court commits gross error in a decision on a constitutional question?

Mr. Madison, to whom both of us have a fondness for adverting, suggested "remonstrances," but surely mere remonstrance is a flimsy shield for a free people. He suggested "impeachment," but impeachment lies only for "treason, bribery, or other high crimes and misdemeanors," and it is not to be supposed that even gross error falls within this purview. He did not suggest packing of the court, which was done in the 1860s and again attempted in 1937, but to me, at least, that is a dishonorable remedy. Neither did he suggest an act of Congress to deprive the court of jurisdiction to hear a particular kind of case, though this, too, was done in the 1860s. It evidently was Mr. Madison's view that this would be but a temporary expedient that affords no solutions. Is a check to be found in Congress' power over the purse, in its right to control appropriations for the judiciary? Surely this would be a contemptible remedy, kin to bribery and extortion. Is the missing check to be found, then, in the death of members of the court and the appointment of new members? To ask the question is to answer it.

Mr. Madison did suggest "amendment to the Constitution," and because that approach figures in our resolution, it should be examined carefully. But if amendment be the "check" and if by its action the court has amended the Constitution, and amendment by the States be now required to restore the Constitution to its purity, you will at once recognize that 13 States can defeat that restoration. I, for one, emphatically deny that amendment can be accomplished by a majority of nine judges supported by 13 States. Certainly no word in the Constitution would give support to such a claim.

I know of no other "checks" set forth in the Constitution. It has seemed to me, the longer I have thought on this issue, that we must do today precisely what Marshall did long ago: We are compelled to look beyond the Constitution, even as he did, to find the "check" that must exist, as a matter of necessity, in order that our form of government may survive.

I find this power in the States themselves. It was they who ordained the Constitution; they are the parties to the compact; they alone can alter its terms. By entering into this compact, the States did not surrender the right and the power to preserve it from destruction by a court which owes its existence to it.

I turn to your specific questions. The first of these reads:

1. The original Kilpatrick resolution recognizes that "the jurisdiction of the court (Supreme Court) encompassed the issue submitted to it in the school cases decided by it on May 17. 1954." Does your resolution recognize that jurisdiction and the power of the court to render a decision in those cases?

My answer is this: The resolution, in its present form, no longer contains the phrase to which you refer. It is not the intention of the resolution to deny in any respect the jurisdiction of the Supreme Court to hear any case in which a constitutional right is claimed, and one was claimed in the school cases. But I would make two points: The first is that I do not believe the court's authority to try cases in law and equity arising under the Constitution vests the court with any right in effect to amend the Constitution. I do not believe that five judges equal 36 States. Secondly, I would draw a clear distinction between "right" and "power." The court had the power: the resolution emphatically denies that it had the right to exercise this power in such a way as to stultify the Constitution.

Your second question reads:

2. Is that decision now the law of the land, and is it now law in Virginia? If not, why?

My answer is: The Constitution is the supreme law of the land and supreme in Virginia. For the moment its provisions, as they were understood for 80 years, have been supplanted by an act of judicial legislation which has brought about a situation, binding by force of Federal power, but not binding in right. Because this resolution cannot by itself restore the situation as it existed prior to the decision, and we must take other steps to protect our people, we will shortly amend our State Constitution and, I doubt not, adopt protective legislation of the sort recommended by the Gray Commission. I would emphasize that our resolution is in no sense intended as a substitute for such protective legislation.

Your third question is:

3. If your resolution is adopted, will the said decision be the law of the land. and will it be binding on the Federal courts in Virginia?

The answer to the preceding question answers this also. This resolution cannot "bind" Federal courts. We would hope, however, that it would have a highly persuasive effect upon them.

Your fourth question reads:

4. If your resolution is adopted, will it have the effect of legally suspending the enforcement of the decision in Virginia? It so, why, and for what period?

The resolution in itself will not legally suspend the enforcement of the decision in Virginia. However, I hope the resolution will set in motion a chain of actions that will not only impede the enforcement of it in Virginia, but will entirely obliterate the decision in Virginia and elsewhere.

Next you ask:

5. Do you concede or deny that a decision of the Supreme Court of the United States construing the Constitution of the United States is the law of the land and binding in every State in the Union unless and until there is an amendment to the Constitution approved by three-fourths of the States overriding the decision? In this connection, I call your attention to the adoption of the fifteenth amendment overriding the decision in the Chisholm case, and the sixteenth amendment overriding the decision in the income tax case.

First, let me observe that it was not the fifteenth amendment that overturned the Chisholm case, but the eleventh. And, let me observe also that in the interim of more than one year between the court's opinion in the Chisholm case and the ratification of the eleventh amendment, Georgia flatly refused to abide by the court's decision. It seems to me an admirable example.

Secondly, the decisions of the court are binding unless and until there is an amendment, or unless and until the court changes its mind. This last contingency has manifested itself 36 times in the past 20 years, a fact that might be called to the attention of those who fear such "disorder" and "chaos" if the States undertake to express their views on constitutional matters.

Subject to this qualification, I agree that the court's opinions are binding. But I submit that in the case of "deliberate, palpable and dangerous" errors by the court, to borrow the language of Jefferson and Madison, such erroneous opinions are binding not as a matter of right, because they are palpably wrong; and not binding because they are constitutional, because they are unconstitutional. They are binding as a matter of superior force.

Next you ask:

6. If your resolution is adopted, do you maintain that the decision of the court can be permanently overridden or vetoed by the action of one-fourth of the States? If so, is this not the Calhoun (of South Carolina) doctrine of State veto or nullification?

I maintain this: That under Article V of the Constitution, it is clearly intended that substantive changes should not be made in the Constitution except by the approval of not fewer than three-fourths of the States. This protective clause was placed in the Constitution expressly to assure the rights and interests of a numerical minority of the States from oppression by a numerical majority.

In the case immediately under consideration, the fourteenth amendment was adopted with the explicit and demonstrable understanding that it did not prohibit to the States the power to operate racially separate public schools. This was the fourteenth amendment as three-fourths of the States consented to it. Now the court has undertaken to changed this understanding, and in effect to change the amendment. Again, I believe that the consent of three-fourths of the States should be required.

If it can be shown that three-fourths of the States do *not* consent to this substantive change in their Constitution, I believe that such a showing would be a powerful rebuke to the court. It might not be sufficient permanently to override the decision, for nothing is permanent in this world, and especially the opinions of the Supreme Court seem not to be permanent. But such action might cause the country seriously to consider whether it wishes to let a majority of a nine-man court amend the Constitution, or whether it intends to preserve this amendatory power to the States.

This is not nullification, in the manner of Mr. Calhoun or otherwise.

Your next question reads:

7. In your resolution reference is made to the "issue of contested power" as between the Federal government and the State government. Is not this but a reaffirmation of the basic concept of the Calhoun (or South Carolina) doctrine of State veto or nullification, and a modern recognition of that doctrine?

My answer is No. The recognition of an "issue of contested power" is the recognition that the fact of that issue exists. The experience of the issue, and the recognition thereof does not demand that a particular course of action be pursued.

Your next question is:

8. I assume that you are well aware of the views of James Madison on the subject of State interposition, veto or nullification. In this connection, I refer you to his letter of December, 1831, in which he expressly repudiated the theory that a resolution of interposition would make it possible for one-fourth of the States to abrogate the Federal law. Do you agree or disagree with Mr. Madison?

My answer is this: I believe I am fairly familiar with the views of Mr. Madison on the subject, but I must confess I am puzzled to know precisely what Mr. Madison's views were. You refer me to his letter of December, 1831 (and here I assume you have in mind Mr. Madison's letter to N.P. Trist), in which he repudiated the theory you describe. But you assuredly are aware that this was by no means the only letter in which Mr. Madison expressed these opinions. On the contrary, he appears to have spent most of his time in 1829, 1830, and 1931, in earnest endeavors to explain away the opinions he had expressed so unequivocally in 1800, when he was a good deal closer to the Constitution than he was 30 years later.

But it is difficult for me, at least, to recognize the position Mr. Madison expressed so fervently at this late period in his life, when he was "in the very crippled and feeble state of my health," with that which he expressed with such vigor and positiveness at the time of the Virginia Resolution of 1798. That he gave the most profound thought to his Report of 1799 is not to be doubted; I would submit that this formal, public expression is of more meaning than the personal letters he wrote much later, and it is not amiss to call particular attention to what he said in the Report referred to. Among other things, he said:

> It appears to your committee to be a plain principle, founded in common sense, illustrated by common practice, and essential to the nature of compacts, that, where resort can be had to no tribunal, superior to the authority of the parties, the parties themselves must be the rightful judges in the last resort, whether the bargain made has been pursued or violated. The Constitution of the United States was formed by the sanction of the States, given by each in its sovereign capacity. It adds to the stability and dignity, as well as to the authority of the Constitution, that it rests on this legitimate and solid foundation.

The States, then, being the parties to the constitutional compact, and in their sovereign capacity, it follows of necessity, that there can be no tribunal above their authority, to decide in the last resort, whether the compact made by them be violated: and, consequently, that as the parties to it, they must themselves decide, in the last resort, such questions as may be of sufficient magnitude to require their interposition.

Permit me to quote one more paragraph, immediately following the paragraphs just quoted, because certain language from our own proposed resolution of 1956 has been drawn directly from it.

> It does not follow, however, that because the States, as sovereign parties to their constitutional compact, must ultimately decide whether it has been violated, that such a decision ought to be interposed, either in a hasty manner, or on doubtful and inferior occasions.
>
> . . . In the case of an intimate and constitutional union, like that of the United States, it is evident that the interposition of the parties, in their sovereign capacity, can be called for by occasions only deeply and essentially affecting the vital principles of their political system.

You inquire whether I agree or disagree with Mr. Madison in the matter of interposition. Alluding to the sentence just quoted, I would reply that I most certainly agree with the Mr. Madison of 1799, in believing that the court's decision of May 17, 1954, is of a character so "deeply and essentially affecting the vital principles of (our) political system" as to justify Virginia in the most strenuous measures of interposition we can put forth.

Finally, you inquire:

9. Would the adoption of your resolution challenge and impair the settled doctrine of judicial review by the Federal courts of State law?

I recognize the jurisdiction of the Supreme Court where a provision of the Federal Constitution is involved. But I repeat what was said in responding to your first question: The resolution does not deny that jurisdiction. Hence it does not challenge the authority of the court to hear and decide a case in which it is alleged that a State law violates the United States Constitution.

In closing, let me revert to the fundamental issue here at stake, far transcending the immediate problem of school segregation. It seems to me that if the Supreme Court may fasten upon us entirely what it will, our Constitution is but a "scrap of paper," and ours is no longer a government of laws, but a government by five out of nine men who are entrenched in impregnable position. The Constitution is no longer the supreme law of the land; the court's unchecked discretion is the supreme law of the land. We are no longer the masters and government no longer our servant; the positions are reversed, and the bulwark of our liberties has crumbled. The powers of the States, so carefully reserved in the tenth amendment, in this view were reserved merely until such time as a majority of the court might choose to snatch them from us.

I cannot believe this is the true meaning of the Constitution.

The remedy of interposition here proposed is, admittedly, a drastic and unfamiliar one. But the circumstances are drastic and unfamiliar also. I could not predict with certainty what success, if any, the action may have. If we were sure of success, the amendment of the Virginia Constitution shortly to be adopted, and the revision of our statutes to protect us against some of the evils of the recent school decision, would be unnecessary. But that we may not succeed is no reason why open, dignified and manly effort should not be made.

If it is your feeling that the powers of the States should be extinguished by judicial decree, it is of course your privilege to hold that view; and if you feel that gross and palpable abuse of the Constitution should be docilely accepted by our people, you are wholly at liberty to advance that counsel to Virginia. But I do not believe the people will follow you in it. Rather, I cherish the great hope that Virginians, once again looking upon the face of tyranny, will once again stand squarely in opposition to it. There are, thank God, free men left who will not surrender their convictions and principles, their rights and their liberties, before the hollow idol of judicial supremacy.

This response has been longer than I had intended it to be, but that is ever the misfortune of one who may be put to the answering of complex questions, as distinguished from the easy advantage of one whose only function is the propounding of them.

Recalling that you inadvertently released your letter of January 20th to the press before I had so much as seen a copy of it, I would emphasize that I have taken particular pains to deliver the original of this response into your hands before exercising, myself, the liberty of making it public.

Most faithfully yours,
HARRY C. STUART

UNIT 6-6

An Argument That the Negro Is Inherently Inferior

Carleton Putnam

EDITORIAL NOTE: *The strongest and most elaborate argument against the desegregation decision came from Carleton Putnam, businessman, lawyer, and historian. Born in New York City and educated at Princeton and Columbia Universities, Putnam adopted, almost in toto, the traditional Southern view of the proper relations between the white and the Negro races. In 1959 he sent the following letter to Attorney-General William P. Rogers—with copies to the President and members of the Supreme Court. The following year he elaborated his argument in a book,* Race and Reason: A Yankee View, *which was received with immense enthusiasm throughout the South. Mr. Putnam's anthropolitical arguments, though generally rejected by scientists, received some support from the respected Professor Carleton Coon of the University of Pennsylvania.*

Letter to the Attorney-General of the United States, March 16, 1959

Following my correspondence with your Department in December, I have had a chance to review your briefs in the school desegregation cases and also to scan, as carefully as time permitted, the nine relevant volumes of the *Supreme Court's Records and Briefs*. I hesitate to impose further upon your kindness, but my survey has left one question in my mind upon which the record does not appear to touch, and which you may be able to answer.

I turn to you for the reason that, as a non-adversary party to these proceedings, I understand you to have represented the people of the United States. Since a majority of the population of the South are obviously against integration, and since the Gallup Poll for September 24, 1958, indicates that 58% of the white population of the North would not put their children in schools where more than half the enrollment is Negro, it becomes a close question whether the decision of the Supreme Court in these cases was not in fact contrary

Carleton Putnam, *Race and Reason: A Yankee View*, 1961.

to the wishes of a national majority. While I recognize that this would in no way affect the validity of the decision, it would seem to have placed a peculiar responsibility upon you.

The matter which I find curious is the omission in your briefs of any challenge to the authorities cited by the Court in Footnote 11 to their opinion of May 17, 1954. I assume there must have been some indication, in argument or elsewhere, that these authorities were to be used. They appear, in large measure, to form the foundation of the decision. They reflect a point of view rooted in what I may call modern equalitarian anthropology—a school which holds that all races are currently equal in their capacity for culture, and that existing inequalities of status are due solely to inequalities of opportunity. While the briefs for the State of Virginia touch upon the qualifications of some of the individual psychologists who testified in the lower courts, they contain no examination of the underlying anthropological theory. It seems to me that such an examination should have been made. I have a science degree, I have read with some diligence in the field of anthropology and I have discussed the subject with competent anthropologists. It is my considered opinion that two generations of Americans have been victimized by a pseudoscientific hoax in this field, that this hoax is part of an equalitarian propaganda typical of the left-wing overdrift of our times, and that it will not stand an informed judicial test. I do not believe that ever before has science been more warped by a self-serving few to the deception and injury of so many. On this subject there may be disagreement. But it is clear to me the Court should have been invited to examine the question.

Allow me to give my reasons for this opinion. The Court says in Footnote 11 "See generally Myrdal, *An American Dilemma*," and I start with this book. I need hardly dwell upon the highly socialistic bias of its foreign author, and the startling remarks with which his text is peppered, such as his comment that the American Constitution "is in many respects impractical and ill-suited for modern conditions," that the Constitutional Convention of 1787 "was nearly a plot against the common people" and that in the conflict between liberty and equality in the United States "equality is slowly winning." A foreign socialist could not, perhaps, have realized that Jefferson's statement "all men are created equal" was a corruption from the Virginia Declaration of Rights, where the original wording read "all men are created equally free," nor that if equality (in any sense other than equality of opportunity and equality before the law) is defeating liberty in the United States, then everything America has stood for is in jeopardy, but certainly it was essential that these matters be called to the Court's attention in evaluating Myrdal's book.

I hasten, however, to the basic hypothesis underlying Myrdal's 1,400 pages. On pages 90–91 he introduces the doctrines of Franz Boas, a foreign-born Columbia University professor who arrived in the United States in 1886, who was himself a member of a racial minority group, and who may be called the father of equalitarian anthropology in America. From these pages forward, Myrdal's *Dilemma* is founded upon the philosophy of Boas and his disciples. Thereafter, one constantly finds in Myrdal such sentences as these:

> The last two or three decades have seen a veritable revolution in scientific thought on the racial characteristics of the Negro. . . . By inventing and applying ingenious specialized research methods, the popular race dogma [that races are not by nature equal in their capacity for culture] is being victoriously pursued into every corner and effectively exposed as fallacious or at least unsubstantiated. . . . It is now becoming difficult for even popular writers to express other views than the ones of racial equalitarianism and still retain intellectual respect.

If you have not already read him, I invite you to a thorough and impartial study of Boas. I am confident you will find his views wholly unconvincing, his doctrines more "unsubstantiated" than those he attacks, and his approach so saturated with wishful thinking as to be pathetic. In even the most superficial analysis of the subject, Boas should have been challenged and his more obvious errors exposed. Boas, for example, may have been convinced that the average African's improvident indifference to "tomorrow" is just a healthy "optimism," but I dare say the proverbial reasonable man on a jury would think of it less charitably.

If the deceptions of the Boas school were unconscious, they were nevertheless serious. People, for instance, were induced to believe that because early anthropologists put emphasis on brain pan size in their studies of race, and brain pan size later proved to be an invalid criterion, this automatically made all races equal. No one took the time to point out that not only is brain pan size not a final test of intelligence, but that, even if it were, equal brain size would not prove equal capacity for civilization. The character-intelligence index—the combination of intelligence with all of the qualities that go under the name of character, including especially the willingness to resist rather than to appease evil—forms the only possible index of the capacity for civilization as Western Europeans know it, and there is no test for this index save in observing the native culture in which it results. Such observation does not sustain the doctrine of equality.

Indeed, the entire foundation of the Boas theory rests on sand. It is based on the assumption that present day cultural differences between the Negro and other races are due not to any natural limitations, but to isolation and historical accident. This theme has been taken up again and again by later anthropologists such as Kluckhohn of Harvard, and repeated as established scientific fact. I may illustrate the argument by comparing the condition of the white tribes of Northern Europe just before the fall of Rome with the Negro tribes in the Congo. Both were primitive and barbaric, both were isolated from civilization. With the conquest of Rome by the white barbarians, the northern tribes were brought in contact with the ancient Greco-Roman civilization and gradually absorbed its culture. The Negro, on the other hand, lacked such a contact and therefore remained in *statu quo*.

This was Boas' historical accident, and his explanation of the Negro's present level of civilization in Africa. Boas had various additional points and refinements of his thesis, such as the advantage the white barbarians enjoyed in contiguity of habitat and the more moderate differences in modes of manufacture in earlier times, which made it easier for backward peoples in those days to compete commercially with more advanced cultures than was the case in later centuries when our white civilization invaded Africa, but these arguments hang on the first point. In other words, had the Negroes shown the enterprise and initiative of the white barbarians, the Negroes themselves would have established a continuity of habitat and had the advantage of more moderate differences in modes of manufacture.

As far as isolation is concerned, it hardly seems necessary to point out that the Alps did not keep the white barbarians out of Italy, and that the Nile Valley was open to the Negroes into Egypt. One observer, recently returned from an intensive tour of Africa and himself apparently a racial equalitarian, nevertheless feels compelled to include these sentences in his report:

> Why, when in China, India, Mesopotamia and on the Mediterranean coasts and islands, men isolated almost completely from one another, during some 5,000 years independently developed writing and metal tools, invented compasses, built temples and bridges, formulated philosophies, wrote books and poems—why, then, did similar progress not occur in Africa?
>
> I posed the question to many Africans. Their answer: the desert, the heat, disease, isolation—and always these words: "For centuries our most vigorous young men were taken off as slaves."
>
> The answer falls short. China has a desert; India's climate is as hot and as unhealthy; Mesopotamia indeed is hotter—and was surrounded by deserts. As for the slave trade, why were the Africans not making slaves of the Portuguese and the Arabs?

This report, prepared by the assistant to the publisher of *Time* magazine, goes on to seek justification for the equalitarian viewpoint in the modern intelligence test and the modern performance of the exceptional Negro, answers which fall as far short as the others. The field of the intelligence test, like the field of Boas' anthropology, is filled with wishful thinking, with comparisons of the better Negroes and the poorer whites, with studies of mulattoes whose successes are largely proportionate to the admixture of white genes, and with similar avoidance of the essential point, namely, that in matters of race either the average of one must be compared with the average of the other, or the best of one must be compared with the best of the other.

If we are to compare averages, there is probably no better laboratory than the rural area around Chatham, Ontario, Canada. Chatham is a town at the northern end of the pre-Civil War "underground railroad" where a community of the descendants of escaped slaves has existed for 100 years. The social and economic situation of Negroes and whites in the rural area around Chatham is approximately equal. The schools have always been integrated, yet the tests of Negroes in these rural schools show them, after 100 years, to be as far below the whites in the same schools as the Negroes in the schools of the South are below the whites in the schools of the South. Dr. H. A. Tanser, now Superintendent of Schools at Chatham, published a study of this matter in 1939. The study is never mentioned by the modern school of equalitarian anthropology, but you will find it in the Library of Congress. Did your Department give it consideration?

In this connection, you are perhaps aware that Dr. Audrey M. Shuey, Chairman of the Department of Psychology at Randolph-Macon Woman's College, published a report in 1958 surveying and summarizing the results of 40 years of intelligence tests involving whites and Negroes. Dr. Shuey took her B.A. at the University of Illinois, her M.A. at Wellesley, and her Ph.D. at Columbia. Her book contains a foreword by Dr. Henry E. Garrett, former president of the American Psychological Association, the Eastern Psychological Association, the New York State Association of Applied Psychology and the Psychometric Society. In his foreword, Dr. Garrett says:

> Dr. Shuey finds that at several age levels and under a variety of conditions, Negroes regularly score below whites. There is, to be sure, an overlapping of scores, a number of Negroes scoring above the white medians. This overlap means that many individual Negroes achieve high scores on the tests. But the mean differences persist. Dr. Shuey concludes that the regularity and consistency of the results strongly implies a racial basis for these differences. I believe that the weight of evidence supports her conclusion.

Dr. Shuey states that "the remarkable consistency of test results . . . all point to the presence of some native differences between Negroes and whites determined by intelligence tests," and she adds the significant comment: "The tendency for the IQ's of colored children to become progressively lower with increase in age has been reported by a number of investigators who tested Negro children. . . . One is confronted with the probability of a continuance during adolescence of what seems to be a widening gap between the races." I recognize that Dr. Shuey's report was not extant at the time of the Brown decision, but a large part of her material was available, and in my opinion should have been submitted to the Court. I repeat that I do not consider the intelligence test decisive, as I believe character to be more important than intelligence, but in answer to those who use the intelligence test to support theories of racial equality, surely Tanser's and Shuey's material belonged in the record.

If, on the other hand, we compare the best with the best, the discrepancies are even clearer. I had occasion to ask Kluckhohn a question with respect to a statement in his *Mirror for Man* at page 126. This statement reads: "It is true that the total richness of Negro civilizations is *at least quantitatively* less impressive than that of Western or Chinese civilization."

(Emphasis mine). [I asked Kluckhohn if he would mind defining in what respects he found it *qualitatively* as impressive. I told him I was curious as to one poem equal to Milton's *Paradise Lost*, one history equal to Gibbon's *Decline and Fall*, one novel equal to Dickens' *David Copperfield*, one playwright equal to Shakespeare, one philosopher equal to Aristotle, one medical discovery equal to Salk's polio vaccine, one military leader equal to Napoleon, one inventor equal to Edison, one physicist equal to Einstein, one pioneer equal to Columbus, one statesman equal to Abraham Lincoln, one composer equal to Beethoven, one painter equal to Rembrandt. I have received no reply, but Kluckhohn's "at least quantitatively" seems to me typical of the deceptive words used by our modern equalitarian anthropology.] The Court should not have been left in the dark on this tendency. Although they do not specifically cite Kluckhohn, he is one of the leaders of the modern school on which Myrdal rests his case.

I have found that a favorite method used by Boas and Kluckhohn for throwing dust in the eyes of the public is to create an impression that there is really no such thing as race. Although Kluckhohn begins the third paragraph of the fifth chapter of his *Mirror for Man* with the sentence "There are undoubtedly human races," he nevertheless entitles this chapter "Race: A Modern Myth." His thesis is that culture, not race, is what makes human beings what they are. Yet nowhere is the obvious fact examined that culture is absorbed, refined and advanced in proportion to racial capacity. There are, of course, certain modifying variables, among the chief of which are climate and economic conditions. The white culture of New England differs from the white culture of the Deep South, but not as much as the white culture of southern Florida differs from the black culture of Haiti, where the climate is approximately the same. That is to say, the effect of the variables is clearly less decisive than the fundamental difference in race.

Undoubtedly an individual or group, taken out of the cultural environment of their own race and brought up in that of another, will sometimes absorb some features of the culture of the new environment, but in such instances they become parasites upon the culture of the second race. They are carried up, or carried down, as the case may be, by the overwhelming impact of the environment of the second race. Their own capacity to contribute to, and to sustain, a culture can only be judged by the performance of their own race in its native habitat. And if that capacity is low, then too many of them, too freely integrated, must inevitably in the long run lower the culture of the second race.

There have, not unnaturally, been situations in which a race has captured the spark of culture in one habitat but not in another. In the case of the fall of the Roman Empire, the barbarians were, broadly speaking, members of the same race as the conquered. Here we find two branches of the white race, one of which had produced a culture while the other had not, and here the Boas theory of historical accident is tenable. Similarity of tinder permitted passage of the spark. It was still the white race that absorbed, and eventually carried forward, the Roman culture.

The essential question in this whole controversy is whether the Negro, given every conceivable help regardless of cost to the whites, is capable of full adaptation to our white civilization within a matter of a few generations, or whether the record indicates such adaptation cannot be expected save in terms of many hundreds, if not thousands, of years, and that complete integration of these races, especially in the heavy black belts of the South, can result only in a parasitic deterioration of white culture, with or without genocide. I am certain neither you nor the Court, nor any significant number of Northerners would knowingly shackle their racial brothers in the South against their will with a system which would produce either of the latter results. The sin of Cain would pale by comparison.

Yet to my mind it seems obvious that all the facts, and a preponderance of theory, are against Myrdal and his authorities. I would go so far as to say that in the last fifty years anthropology has been drafted to serve the demi-Goddess of Equalitarianism instead of the Goddess of Truth, and that the modern school in this field has a stern judgment to face, both at the bar of American public opinion and at the hands of two generations of youth whose thinking has been corrupted by it. One does not build a healthy society on error. One faces the truth, and deals with it as best one can.

I pass now from Myrdal, and the sources upon which his more general assumptions rest, to the remaining authorities cited in Footnote 11. All of these deal primarily with the adverse psychological effect of segregation upon Negroes and only secondarily with its alleged adverse effect upon white children. Nowhere is any study cited of a third question, namely, of the quite possible adverse effect of *integration* upon whites in schools with large percentages of Negroes. Was any such study made and presented to the Court?

The third question was well put by William Polk in his book *Southern Accent*: "If the Negro is entitled to lift himself up by enforced association with the white man, why should not the white man be entitled to prevent himself from being pulled down by enforced association with the Negro?" This question seems particularly important in view of the patent partiality of the authorities cited in favor of integration. The majority of these appear either to belong to Negro or other minority groups, or to have prepared their studies under the auspices of such groups. To expect these groups to present impartial reports on the subject of racial discrimination is like expecting a saloon keeper to prepare an impartial study on prohibition, or a meat packer to pass an unbiased judgment on the Humane Slaughter Bill. Their point of view is important and deserves consideration. Many of them are brilliant and consecrated men. But to permit them to provide the overwhelming preponderance of the evidence is manifestly not justice. If this is compounded by an absence of any consideration of the damaging effects of integration upon white children, it becomes doubly serious. While the brief for the State of Virginia touches upon the subject, it seems to me that the people of the United States, whom you represented, had a particular interest in seeing it more fully developed. I would appreciate your directing me to such a study, if one was made, and also your providing me with some explanation as to why the evidence on damage to the Negro was from such partisan sources.

Any American worthy of the name feels an obligation of kindness and justice toward his fellow man. He is willing to give every individual his chance, whatever his race, but in those circumstances where a race must be dealt with as a race, he realizes that the level of the average must be controlling, and that the relatively minor handicap upon the superior individual of the segregated race, if it be a handicap at all, must be accepted until the average has reached the point where desire for association is mutual.

This leads me to my final query. I will be frank to say that I was startled at the uncritical manner in which the Supreme Court was allowed to accept one phrase in the language of the lower court, to wit: "A sense of inferiority [produced by segregation] affects the motivation of a child to learn." Did neither you nor counsel for any of the appellees take occasion to point out that if a child is by nature inferior, enforced association with his superiors will increase his realization of his inferiority, while if he is by nature not inferior, any implication of inferiority in segregation, if such there be, will only serve as a spur to greater effort? Throughout history, challenges of this sort, acting upon individuals, groups and races of natural capacity, have proved a whip to achievement, times without number. The point was one of the legal hinges on which the case turned. In fact without it the decision falls apart, for there is no other even remotely arguable excuse why separate facilities cannot be made equal within any possible stretch of the meaning of the Fourteenth Amendment. Consequently, I would have thought it imperative that you raise it.

UNIT 6-7

THE WHITE CITIZENS' COUNCIL
POWER FOR THE STATUS QUO

The National Guard Armory was full of 1500 white citizens in their Sunday best eating barbecue chicken at $1.50 a person. By their looks the audience was made up of middle class business people, professionals and well to do farmers, with their wives and children. It could have been a Monday night church dinner anywhere in the United States. But this dinner wasn't just anywhere; it was in Selma, Ala., and the people were there to hear Ross Barnett.

"Thank God that I am an American, a Southerner, a Mississippian and a charter member of the Mississippi White Citizens' Council." yelled Barnett. The former Mississippi governor was the main attraction at the Dallas County White Citizens' Council annual membership dinner and rally.

Barnett told them that, "The secret purpose of our enemies is to diffuse our blood, confuse our minds and degrade our character, that we may not be able to stand against the wiles of the devil."

While he was speaking an equal number of Negroes were meeting across town in two churches listening to John Lewis, chairman of the Student Nonviolent Coordinating Committee (SNCC) and Dr. Martin Luther King of the Southern Christian Leadership Conference (SCLC). King told the crowd, "Nothing will turn us back now."

The SNCC and SCLC voter registration drive had, on that Feb. 22, gone into its sixth week with over 3,500 people seeing the jails of Selma and Marion, in nearby Perry County.

Barnett's speech called for the maintenance of racial purity and the Anglo-Saxon Protestant heritage, and continuing the fight against the communist conspiracy. He seemed unaware of recent happenings in the county. Barnett talked in generalities. The people were looking for answers to their problems; they wanted specifics; Barnett talked of "Americanism."

The former governor did not once mention Negro voter registration which was in the minds of the crowd in a county where Negroes make up 57% of the population.

Dallas County, population 57,000, is located in the heart of Black Belt Alabama. Selma is its county seat. It is a county where 87% of all Negro families make less than 43,000 [sic] and where 67% of the Negroes have less than a high school education.

Student Voice, March 26, 1965.

It is a county that boasts that it has the first, largest and most active chapters of Alabama's Association of Citizens Councils.

The announced program of the Dallas County White Citizens' Council is "to maintain states rights, segregation and racial integrity." The Council states that it is "leading the resistance movement against race mixers, and keeping advocates of racial strife out of many communities." It says that, "It is preserving our social and economic order by acting quietly and without fanfare. . . . to prevent racial strife."

The Council's definition of "racial strife" was brought out in an ad in the *Selma Times-Journal*, June 2, 1963. It asked, "Is it worth four dollars (membership) to you to prevent sit-ins, mob marches and wholesale Negro voter registration efforts in Selma?"

In order to "prevent" Negro activity the Council must maintain control over the whole community. This means not only keeping Negroes "in line" but also whites who do not follow its program.

The white group maintains this control through two means: organization and infiltration. It organizes the white leadership of the community to effect its program, because in order to be effective the Council must eliminate all dissent from whites.

Most whites in the community are members, but not all by choice. "There is great social and economic pressure to join. Not to join would be socially lowering and economically damaging," a local white woman said.

The Council has many means to pressure those who do not join. In May, 1959, the Dallas Council dealt with uncooperative whites by publishing a list of all business and professional people who were not members.

With the whites organized, the Council "infiltrates" the community, or as Robert Patterson, Executive Secretary of the Citizens' Councils of Mississippi puts it:

> The Citizens' Councils think and plan as a group and then are able to act as individuals within their various churches, schools or any other organization to which they may belong. This has already proved effective in many, many instances.

The Council most effectively works through individual members who are in important business and government positions. It uses these people to put its program into practice.

Thus the Council's power lies not in the organization but through its individual members who wield an enormous amount of personal power by virtue of their positions in the community.

The Dallas County Council is a prime example of the group's power; its leadership reads like a who's who of the community.

The president of the Dallas Council is former mayor Chris Heinz. Heinz is a member of the board of directors of the Chamber of Commerce and a leading insurance and real estate man. He is also a good friend of Col. Richard Ault, commandant of Craig Air Force Base, one of the major "industries" of Selma. Ault has, on numerous occasions, refused requests by SNCC to declare Selma off limits to air force personnel.

It was Heinz who introduced Barnett at the rally. He told the group. "We can no longer afford the luxury of the attitude of 'Let George (Wallace) do it.'"

"We have arrived at a point when all white people must stand up and be counted," the former mayor said. "We must lay aside personal differences and stand united as one unbreakable unit."

The Citizens' Council has its legislative leader in State Senator Walt Givhan of the 30th district which includes Dallas and adjoining Lowndes County. The senator is past president of the Alabama Association of Citizens' Councils and a member of the executive committee of the Dallas Council.

An even more potentially powerful man than Senator Givhan is Earl Goodwin. Goodwin is owner of two large firms that hire over 300 people. He is former vice-president of the Chamber of Commerce, "Manufacturer of the Year," and a member of the white group's executive committee. Much of his power lies in the fact that he is a member of the State Democratic Executive Committee. Through this office Goodwin controls much of the patronage in the area. "Earl Goodwin is being talked about as the next candidate for governor," a local white reported.

(One of the heads of the Democratic Committee is the infamous Eugene "Bull" Connor of Birmingham. Connor, who is originally from Selma, is Democratic National Committeeman from Alabama. He appeared at the Barnett rally and was heard to comment, "I've belonged to this county [Citizens' Council] since it's been organized.")

The Dallas unit, which might be called a model Council, has an executive committee that includes president and past president of the Real Estate Association, the past president of the Exchange Club, members of the board of directors of the Chamber of Commerce, the County Engineer, the Clerk in charge of issuing county licenses, a member of Dallas County Court of Revenues (the governing body of the county), the director of recreation for city of Selma, and a member of the State Agriculture Department.

The Council must keep control of the white community in order to control the Negro community. And control of the Negro community means holding down registration. Although it was organized in November 1954 as a reaction to the Supreme Court school decision, the Council has concentrated its activities on the prevention of Negro registration.

The Council's method of controlling Negro registration is reported by Hodding Carter in THE SOUTH STRIKES BACK. The Mississippi editor says,

> During an organizational meeting of the Citizens' Council . . . in Dallas County . . . one speaker said: 'We intend to make it difficult, if not impossible for any Negro who advocates desegregation to find and hold a job, get credit or renew a mortgage.'

Economic control is established by having officers of the four major banks on the executive committee. This group is headed by H. P. Hansell, Associate Vice-President of the City National Bank and Treasurer of the Citizens' Council. A SNCC worker reported, "Businessmen who do not support the White Citizens' Council cannot make loans at the local banks."

That the Council has been effective can be seen from a Justice Department report that states: "From June 1954 . . . through 1960, the Board of Registrars of Dallas County registered more than 200 white persons and only 14 Negroes."

An example of the way the Council and its members "prevent" Negro registration is an incident involving Charlie Dunn, a reported Citizens' Council member and owner of Dunn's Rest Home: In the summer of 1964, workers for SNCC sponsored a "Freedom Day" in which local Negroes line up at the courthouse to attempt to register. On that day Dunn went to the courthouse to check if any of "his Negroes" were on the registration line. He saw one; and the next day when the Negro woman appeared for work, Dunn also assaulted her, which led to the rest of his 40 Negro employees walking off their jobs.

The unemployed negroes found it impossible to find new jobs. A local white woman explained "Dunn and/or the Citizens' Council had circulated a 'blacklist' of the names of the people who had left."

Distressed local white women got together and attempted to get jobs for the Negroes. They contacted whites who needed maids, but the white women were afraid to hire them. They called the management of the newly-opened Holiday Inn, who told them that he had been given a list of Negroes who had tried to register or who were "agitators" and that he couldn't buck Dunn and the Council.

A restaurant owner attempted to employ one of the fired women. A white man told the reporter that "Dunn threatened to have his supplies cut off and institute a boycott." He fired the lady.

Finally, Negro registration is effectively stifled by an alliance of Council members with law enforcement officials who, if they are not dues-paying members of the organization, work very closely with it.

The sheriff of Dallas County, Jim Clark, is the final link in the conspiracy to restrict Negro citizenship. Clark, who appeared on the podium with Connor and Barnett at the Citizens' Council rally, has a 300-man posse behind him. He is now a defendant in three Justice Department suits charging him with voter intimidation and interference.

Also defendants under the same charges are Blanchard McCleod, Circuit Solicitor and a "proud member" of the adjoining Wilcox County Citizens' Council; the county solicitor; the circuit judge; his clerk; Robert O. Wilkinson, Jr., Foreman of the Grand Jury and member of the Executive Committee of the Dallas County Council; and the Dallas County Citizens' Council.

The suit charges the Council and its members with "Adopting and attempting to carry out a program:

- "to use economic sanctions against Negro citizens of Dallas County;
- "to frustrate federal court orders designed to eliminate discrimination of race in registering to vote;
- "of deterring Negro citizens . . . from attending voter registration meetings;
- "of preventing wholesale Negro voter registration;
- "of resisting efforts of the United States government in enforcing the Civil Rights Acts of 1957 and 1960."

The case, now before Federal District Judge Daniel Thomas, is yet to be decided.

In order for the Negro citizens to register to vote, they must face the combined forces of the above-mentioned powers. Someone suggested that the Negroes be given a medal. "After facing all that," SNCC Chairman John Lewis replied, "they should be given the vote."

UNIT 6-8

YOU CAN HELP . . .

WHITE CITIZENS LEGAL FUND IS STARTED TODAY

Local citizens today started a legal fund for use in defending white people involved in civil rights cases.

A spokesman for the group said: "For many years the NAACP has operated a legal defense fund. They have raised and spent millions of dollars on the prosecution of civil court actions involving civil rights and in the defense of individual negroes charged with various crimes, all this in addition to having the avowed comfort, aid and support of the United States Justice Department. Their success is apparent. This fund has enjoyed a tax exempt status for many years."

"Today we see the lives of white citizens both as individuals and in groups swept into the current racial chaos. Many white citizens are unable or hesitant to secure prompt and competent legal assistance."

"We believe the time has come to establish a white citizens legal fund for counter action against various civil rights suits and to provide legal advice and counsel for white citizens who are threatened with or involved in civil rights litigation at the earliest possible moment in all cases where it is deemed necessary and advisable."

"Byron DeLa Beckwith, an ex Marine wounded in combat, has been charged with the murder of NAACP Field Secretary Medgar Evers. Mr. Beckwith is a 32nd Degree Mason, a Shriner, a Communicant of Episcopal Church, and is a member of the Sons of the American Revolution. We do not condone the murder of Medgar Evers, and of course, we have no idea of the guilt or innocence of the accused but we feel that he is entitled to competent legal counsel and to a fair trial.

"Monies collected for this fund initially will be used to provide legal counsel for Mr. Beckwith if he is found to be in need of funds. The fund will be administered by a committee of prominent Greenwood citizens who will make any decision necessary as to disbursements from the fund. It is intended to incorporate the fund.

"An attempt will be made to acquire a tax exempt status! A spokesman for the fund said anyone who is interested in contributing to mail his check, cash, or money order to the White Citizens Legal Fund, P.O. Box 738, Greenwood, Mississippi. "

Greenwood Commonwealth, Greenwood, Mississippi. June 24, 1963.

Directors Chosen for Citizens Fund

Greenwood Group to Defend Whites in Lawsuits

Greenwood, Miss., July 8.—A board of directors has been named to handle the White Citizens Legal Fund recently organized here for use in defending white persons involved in civil rights cases. The fund was started two weeks ago after a Greenwood man, Byron De La Beckwith was charged with the murder of NAACP Field Secretary Medgar Evers.

Named to the board were T. A. Barrentine, J. T. Thomas Sr., Sam Williams, J. J. Ferguson Ellett Lawrence II, Frank K. Odom, Hugh Critz, J. H. Stanton, A. H. Bell, Robert Wingate, Charles D. Saunders, Noll Davis, G. Hite McLean and Howard Stanton.

The presidents of Greenwood's three banks, R. P. Parish Jr., W. C. Neill, and J. H. Peebles, are serving as financial advisers.

A spokesman for the fund said, "We do not condone the murder of Medgar Evers and, of course, we have no idea of the guilt or innocence of the accused but we feel that he is entitled to competent legal counsel and to a fair trial."

He added, "It is certainly hoped that the area of activity of the fund will be much broader than in assisting in financing this one man's defense. When you consider the awesome spectacle of one man standing alone against the preponderous power, authority, wealth and ingenuity of the Federal Government, special agents of the Federal Bureau of Investigation, Federal marshals, the Jackson Police Department and all other police authorities of the State of Mississippi, not to mention $27,000 in reward money, it staggers the imagination."

It was pointed out that the NAACP has operated a legal defense fund for many years and has spent millions of dollars on the prosecution of civil court actions involving civil rights and in defense of individual Negroes.

The Commercial Appeal, Memphis. July 9, 1963.

YOU CAN HELP!

CONTRIBUTE

TO THE

WHITE CITIZENS

LEGAL FUND

P. O. BOX 738

GREENWOOD, MISSISSIPPI

GREENWOOD'S THREE BANK PRESIDENTS ARE ACTING FINANCIAL ADVISORS FOR THE FUND.

UNIT 7

SIT-INS AND THE ESTABLISHMENT OF SNCC

INTRODUCTION 385

7-1 • "BALLAD OF THE STUDENT SIT-INS," SONG 386

7-2 • SIT-IN, VOTING MAP, 1960 387

7-3 • THE SIT-IN MOVEMENT,1960–61 388

7-4 • SIT-INS—THE STUDENTS REPORT 392

7-5 • FIRST OCCURRENCE OF SIT-INS IN A LOCALITY 401
Martin Oppenheimer

7-6 • SCLC NEWS ALERT 403

7-7 • BIGGER THAN A HAMBURGER 406
Ella J. Baker

7-8 • STATEMENT TO THE PRESS 408
Dr. Martin Luther King, Jr.

7-9 • PERSONAL NOTES FROM FOUNDING CONFERENCE 410
Charles Jones

7-10 • RECOMMENDATIONS 412
OF THE FINDINGS AND RECOMMENDATIONS COMMITTEE ARE AS FOLLOWS

7-11 • SNCC: FOUNDING STATEMENT 414

7-12 • NAACP MEMO ON SHAW STUDENT CONFERENCE 415

7-13 • ROY WILKINS TO MARTIN LUTHER KING 417
Roy Wilkins

7-14 • ROY WILKINS TO JAMES LAWSON 419
Roy Wilkins

7-15 • ROY WILKINS TO BENJAMIN MAYS 422
Roy Wilkins

7-16 • DEMOCRATIC CONVENTION STATEMENT, JULY 1960 425
Marion Barry

7-17 • SNCC FUND APPEAL, 1961 430

7-18 • "I'M GONNA SIT AT THE WELCOME TABLE," SONG 434

INTRODUCTION

The student sit-ins and the establishment of the Student Nonviolent Coordinating Committee (SNCC) in 1960 represented an acceleration in the Civil Rights Movement. In many ways, the mass action of the Montgomery Bus Boycott appeared to have fizzled out in the intervening years from 1956 to 1960. The important milestones in civil rights occurred in school desegregation, and those mainly by court order. The sit-ins not only revitalized mass action, they took the concept to a completely new level.

The first five documents in this unit chart the outbreak and the spread of the sit-ins through maps (7-2), eyewitness accounts (7-4), and charts (7-5). A 1961 SRC report published in *New South* (7-3) provides a brief overview of the events and also illustrates the perspective of Southern white liberals towards the sit-ins.

Documents 7-6 through 7-11 present a contemporary look at the establishment of SNCC. The students' next step, their goals, even whether to form an independent civil rights organization, were unsettled questions on the eve of the Shaw Conference. Both the Southern Christian Leadership Conference (SCLC) and the NAACP sought to enlist the students as a youth branch; Ella Baker's speech (7-7) ultimately convinced the students to follow their instincts and form an independent organization. The first SNCC Chairman, Marion Barry, summed up the goals of the new organization in a statement to the Democratic Convention less than four months after the Shaw Conference (7-15).

As the movement grew, more organizations surfaced that re-inforced old tensions and created new ones. The rivalry between civil rights organizations is evident in King's statement to the press (7-8), the NAACP Memo (7-12), and the correspondence of Roy Wilkins (7-13 to 7-15).

Ballad of the Student Sit-Ins

Words and music by Guy Carawan, Eve Merriam and Norman Curtis

Since February 1, 1960, sit-in demonstrations have occurred in over three hundred cities in the USA. They have been mainly in the South and have involved Negro students accompanied by a small number of white sympathizers. Over 5,000 students have been to jail and many have suffered violence from hoodlums and police. Following the first sit-in in Greensboro, N.C., they spontaneously mushroomed all over the South where Negro student communities existed. After a year-and-a-half they had already brought about the desegregation of lunch counters in close to 150 Southern cities. In the North and in other parts of the country many people held demonstrations supporting the students in the South. In the last year-and-a-half, the emphasis has shifted to other forms of demonstrations such as Freedom Rides, the mass walks and praying at the City Hall in Albany, Georgia, voter registration work in deep South, Freedom Walks and mass demonstrations in Birmingham, Ala. At the same time, however, sit-ins have been popping up in new places, both North and South: Talladega, Huntsville, Gadsden, Ala.; Little Rock, Arkansas; Englewood, N. J.; Baltimore, or Route 40, etc...

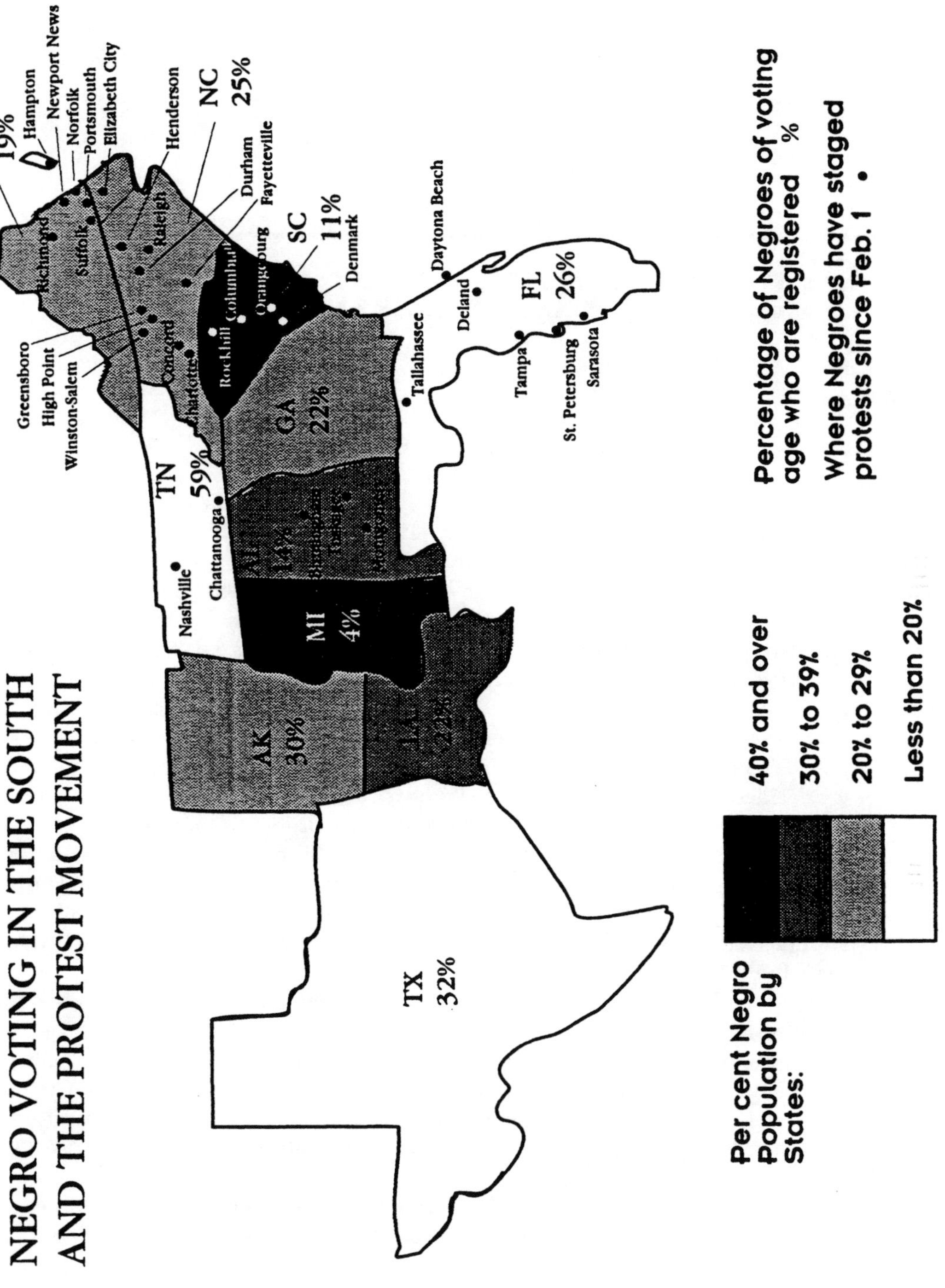
NEGRO VOTING IN THE SOUTH
AND THE PROTEST MOVEMENT
VA
19%
Hampton
Newport News
Norfolk
Portsmouth
Elizabeth City
Henderson
NC
25%
Durham
Fayetteville
Richmond
Suffolk
Raleigh
Greensboro
High Point
Winston-Salem
Concord
Charlotte
Rockhill
Columbia
Orangeburg
SC
11%
Denmark
Daytona Beach
Deland
FL
26%
Tallahassee
Tampa
St. Petersburg
Sarasota
GA
22%
TN
59%
Nashville
Chattanooga
AL
14%
MI
4%
AK
30%
LA
TX
32%
Per cent Negro
Population by
States:
40% and over
30% to 39%
20% to 29%
Less than 20%
Percentage of Negroes of voting
age who are registered %
Where Negroes have staged
protests since Feb. 1 •

UNIT 7-3

THE SIT-IN MOVEMENT, 1960–61

A new epoch in the Negro revolution in America began February 1, 1960, at 4:30 P.M. in Greensboro (N.C.), a small (population 119,574), upper South city named after American Revolutionary War hero Nathaniel Greene.

On that winter afternoon, four Negro students, freshmen at Greensboro's North Carolina A&T College, sat down at the lunch counter of a Woolworth five and ten cent store, where Negroes were forbidden, and tried in vain to get served. Thus began the sit-ins.

Later, the four said their action was on "impulse," and expressed surprise at what and how much it started. Recalling the event three years later, David Richmond, one of the four, now graduated from the college, said: "For about a week, we four fellows sat around the A&T campus where we were in school, talking about the integration movement. And we decided we ought to go down to Woolworth's and see what would happen."

Apparently, a lot of other students had been sitting around talking at Negro college campuses of the South. Within a week, the "impulse" which moved the four in Greensboro had moved others all over North Carolina (in Winston-Salem, Durham, Charlotte, Fayetteville, Raleigh, Elizabeth City, and High Point). Within six weeks, the demonstrations had spread to every southern state except Mississippi. (They reached Mississippi in early 1961.)

"We had been ready to do something like this for a long time," the students told reporters.

The spread of the sit-ins was largely spontaneous and imitative: Students (including some white ones) were the participants, and lunch counters the targets. The protest was easily understood. It was against the refusal to serve food to Negroes by stores only too glad to sell them anything else. The spirit (and in all but the rarest of cases, the performance) was in the tradition of non-violence.

Demonstrations were also, at this early stage, despite impulsiveness and spontaneity, guided by careful rules of decorum (neat dress, polite behavior), and elaborate training (how to be non-violent in the face of physical and emotional punishment). Sophisticated methods of subtle pressure were applied behind the raw act of demonstration on nearly all levels of the white community. These included boycotts.

New South, October 1963.

All unplanned, the sit-ins seemed designed to destroy a series of white southern myths and stereotypes. Just by their presence, the demonstrators were saying: (**1**) that not all Negro Southerners were content with their lot; (**2**) that agitation for change was not from outside, but burst from within the local Negro community; (**3**) that there were polite, educated, well-dressed Negro Southerners; and (**4**) that moreover there were ones brave enough and dedicated enough to conduct the demonstrations.

Against such a barrage, the white South had to invent new rationalizations. A chief one, more or less beside the point, was that the sit-ins were the acts of irresponsible kids, out of control, unsupported by their elders. Indeed, in many cases adult Negro Southerners were probably as surprised and aghast as their white contemporaries at the audacity of the younger generation—not just in the way the their demonstrations threatened the old social structure, but also in how they impinged upon the old and established Negro leadership.

But as the demonstrations gained momentum through the spring of 1960, and as they broadened their goals to include a variety of other types of segregation not immediately threatened by court actions (churches, libraries, movie theaters, even bathing beaches), it was possible for this kind of appraisal (by Nashville newspaperman Wallace Westfeldt) to appear in a report prepared for the Nashville Community Relations Conference:

> This boycott was not started by outsiders nor was it maintained by outsiders. It was executed by the Nashville Negro, for the Nashville Negro, and any attempt to charge anyone else for its responsibility is indulging in wishful thinking.
>
> This boycott, incidentally, also destroyed another concept about the sit-ins widely held by Southerners, the concept that the sit-in was purely a student movement, unsupported and unrecognized by responsible adults in the Negro community.

There were of course many other reactions. In Chattanooga, demonstrators and white persons openly clashed until police controlled the situation. In Montgomery, where students from Alabama State College sat in at the Montgomery County Court House on February 25, 1960, the police later crushed a Negro demonstration in the name of preventing "trouble," in effect doing the bidding of a white mob.

The demonstrators during the waves of sit-ins went out realizing that they faced possible beatings, imprisonment, even death. (The only fatality recorded was indirectly connected with demonstrations. A Negro man who was not a demonstrator, was, in fact, a former convict, ran a road-block set up by police in Jacksonville (Fla.), during a night of rioting on August 27, 1960, and was shot by a white service station attendant.)

Many demonstrators were beaten and arrested. Disciplinary action from their own colleges became another risk faced. The Southern Regional Council, in a special report of September 29, 1961, *The Student Protest Movement: A Recapitulation*, gave this summary of sit-in statistics:

- At least 70,000 Negroes and whites actively participated in sit-in activities affecting each southern and border state, as well as Nevada, Illinois, and Ohio—20 states in all.
- An estimated 3,600 students and supporters in southern and border states were arrested.
- At least 141 students and 58 faculty members were dismissed by southern colleges and universities.

In many other southern cities, however, genuine attempts were made to offer more justice to Negroes as a result of sit-ins.

The first large southern city to desegregate its lunch counters was San Antonio, on March 16, 1960. (The first breakthrough had come a week earlier, March 7, at three drugstores in Salisbury (N.C.), a smaller city where there was precedent for lunch counter desegregation at other downtown stores.)

By June, target eating facilities in 18 cities had desegregated. By August 10, officials of national variety chain stores reported to U.S. Attorney General William Rogers that lunch counters in their stores in 69 southern cities had opened to all. And by late September of the following year, 1961, the Southern Regional Council estimated that one or more eating establishments in 108 southern or border states cities had desegregated as a result of sit-ins.

This was the most spectacular thing. "They work, they work," demonstrators told reporters and themselves and other Negroes, partly in surprise, partly in self-congratulation, mainly in a pragmatic rallying cry that helps explain the quick spread of the sit-ins and the birth of an era of direct action.

For the first time in history, large numbers of Negroes across the South had expressed more or less simultaneous discontent with the status quo of segregation—and what was more important, had succeeded in forcing many communities to remove some segregation without legal compulsion.

It is no wonder that for participants and for the watching millions of Negroes of the nation, there came a new sense of pride and power, and a new determination to have done with discrimination. The psychological effect upon Negroes probably cannot be overestimated.

The psychological effect on white southerners was also big, but less easy to describe. If some felt a new necessity to concede, reluctantly or otherwise, that discontent was prevalent, and not just from outside agitators, many also surely suffered a hardening of prejudice, and a new version of the old haunting fear of slave rebellion. There was also genuine anguish on the part of some people of both races who saw in the sit-ins the doom of whatever good in an evil situation they had been able to establish in their own interracial relationships.

But practically, the sit-ins meant most of all a convincing of white Southerners that desegregation, in degrees not previously conceded, was inevitable. The most compelling, persuasive force was the dollar loss incurred or feared in racial disorders by the white business communities.

It is important to note, however, that most of this convincing occurred in the border states and upper South. A state by state summary of cities where sit-ins produced desegregation, released in late 1961 by the Southern Regional Council. shows this:

> Arkansas, 1 city; Florida, 15; Georgia, 3; Kentucky, 9; Maryland, 3; North Carolina, 17; Oklahoma, 5; Tennessee, 7; Texas, 10; Virginia, 23. No desegregation in Alabama, Louisiana, Mississippi, or South Carolina.

The sit-ins did not crack the deep South. Not until mid-1961 did they make some changes in Georgia.

Where they did succeed, one of the good achievements was the process of negotiation involved. For out of the sometimes torturous and almost always time-consuming sessions of negotiation came candid talk and more understanding, between the races, a quality of communication that had not occurred in the South before. White Southerners faced Negro Southerners across the bargaining table man-to-man, as equals. This experience came in a number of cases through the formal creation of biracial committees, most merely for the duration of the particular sit-in crisis, but some permanent, community agencies of communication in the general problems of race relations.

In these cases, communication and mutual respect were continued and strengthened. And these municipalities were able to keep their racial problems locally controlled, out of the storms of state politics. Studies made two points about such committees: they were formed by initiative of white leaders under pressure; but they were not successful unless the Negro leaders named to them had the trust of the Negro community.

Out of the sit-ins also came the youngest and most militant of the Negro civil rights organizations, the Student Nonviolent Coordinating Committee. SNCC was set up by southern Negro students at the close of an April, 1960, meeting at Shaw University in Raleigh (N.C.), sponsored by Dr. Martin Luther King, Jr.'s Southern Christian Leadership Conference. Initially, it was a loose alliance of local student groups. But after a second conference, October 14–16, 1960, in Atlanta, they established permanent headquarters and a separate identity as a full-time civil rights organization.

With bold invasion of field workers into the deepest strongholds of segregation, in southwest Georgia and the Mississippi Delta, and sometimes with tactics and timing that made older civil rights leaders shudder, SNCC has been in the vanguard of virtually all direct action since the sit-ins, gradually forcing the respect and confidence of older hands. Its members are often in the vanguard, also, of introspective enunciation of goals and philosophical meanings of the Negro revolution.

Two factors in retrospect stand out for being missing during the sit-ins. One was the absence of any overt action of the federal government. Efforts to help national store chains work out local problems of desegregation by Attorney General Rogers were reported at the time, but these were largely behind the scenes. The second missing factor was a sophisticated model of resistance by southern communities. Local police forces (and chambers of commerce) coped with the sit-ins individually by ear and as best they could.

But by the end of the next phase of direct action in the Negro revolution, the federal government was deeply involved, and a tough southern pattern of resistance had emerged. These came during the saga of the Freedom Rides.

UNIT 7-4

SIT-INS—THE STUDENTS REPORT

On February 1, 1960, a student sit-in at Woolworth's in Greensboro, North Carolina, set off a South-wide movement of student sit-ins which became the most significant nonviolent action since Montgomery.

The technique in which CORE had pioneered without publicity for eighteen years had finally become daily nationwide news copy. As a result, CORE for the first time became widely know throughout the United States.

The CORE office became unrecognizable to me. Although it had expanded into adjacent rooms, it was as jammed as the New York subway at rush hour. Volunteers worked on mailings. Paid staff members—now four—answered endless long-distance phone calls, many from Southern student leaders wanting CORE to send down a field secretary, to bail out arrested students, or simply to give strategy advice on sit-ins, picketing, and so on. Reporters frequented the office daily, seeking interviews with Southern students whom CORE would bring North to tell their stories on radio and TV and at big public meetings.

Some of the students told their stories more vividly than could the best author or reporter writing from the sidelines; they made me feel as though I were on the scene. I decided that a written account of the sit-ins must be done by the students themselves. Here are their stories, written at the peak of the sit-in movement—not by me—but by them. Only the compiling and editing are mine.

TALLAHASSEE: THROUGH JAIL TO FREEDOM

Patricia Stephens, Florida Agricultural and Mechanical University

I am writing this in Leon County Jail. My sister Priscilla and I, five other A & M students, and one high school student are serving sixty-day sentences for our participation in the sit-ins. We could be out on appeal but we all strongly believe that Martin Luther King was right when he said, "We've got to fill the jails in order to win our equal rights." Priscilla

Freedom Ride, by James Peck, 1962.

and I both explained this to our parents when they visited us the other day. Priscilla is supposed to be on a special diet and mother was worried about her. We did our best to dispel her worries. We made it clear that we want to serve out our full time.

Students who saw the inside of the county jail before I did, and were released on bond, reported that conditions were miserable. They did not exaggerate. It is dank and cold. We are in what is called a "bull tank" with four cells. Each cell has four bunks, a commode, and a small sink. Some of the cells have running water, but ours does not. Breakfast, if you can call it that, is served at six-thirty. Another meal is served at twelve-thirty and in the evening, "sweet" bread and watery coffee. At first I found it difficult to eat this food. Two ministers visit us every day. Sundays and Wednesdays are regular visiting days, but our white visitors who came at first are no longer permitted by the authorities.

There is plenty of time to think in jail and I sometimes review in my mind the events which brought me here. It is almost six months since Priscilla and I were first introduced to CORE at a workshop in Miami. Upon our return we helped to establish a Tallahassee CORE group, whose initial meeting took place last October. Among our first projects was a test sit-in at Sears' and McCrory's. So, we were not totally unprepared when the Southwide protest movement started in early February.

Our first action in Tallahassee was on February 13. At eleven A.M. we sat down at the Woolworth lunch counter. When the waitress approached, Charles Steele, who was next to me, ordered a slice of cake for each of us. She said, "I'm sorry. I can't serve you," and moved on down the counter, repeating this to the other participants. We all said we would wait, took out our books, and started reading—or at least, we tried.

The regular customers continued to eat. When one man finished, the waitress said, "Thank you for staying and eating in all this indecency." The man replied, "What did you expect me to do? I paid for it."

One man stopped behind Bill Carpenter briefly and said, "I think you're doing a fine job. Just sit right there." A young white hoodlum then came up behind Bill and tried to bait him into an argument. Unsuccessful, he boasted to his friends, "I bet if I disjoint him, he'll talk." When Bill didn't respond, he moved on. A number of tough-looking characters wandered into the store. In most instances the waitress spotted them and had them leave. When a few of them started making derisive comments, the waitress said about us, "You can see they aren't here to start anything." Although the counters were closed twenty minutes after our arrival, we stayed until two P.M.

The second sit-in at Woolworth's occurred a week later. The waitress saw us sitting down and said, "Oh Lord, here they come again!" This time a few white persons were participating secretly. They simply sat and continued eating without comment. The idea was to demonstrate the reality of eating together without coercion, contamination, or cohabitation. Everything was peaceful. We read. I was reading the *Blue Book of Crime* and Barbara Broxton, *How to Tell the Different Kinds of Fingerprints*—which gave us a laugh in light of the arrests which followed.

At about three-thirty P.M. a squad of policemen led by a man in civilian clothes entered the store. Someone directed him to Priscilla, who had been chosen our spokesman for this sit-in. "As Mayor of Tallahassee, I am asking you to leave," said the man in civilian clothes.

"If we don't leave, would we be committing a crime?" Priscilia asked. The mayor simply repeated his original statement. Then he came over to me, pointed to the "closed" sign, and asked, "Can you read?" I advised him to direct all his comments to our elected spokesman. He looked as though his official vanity was wounded but turned to Priscilla. We did too, reiterating our determination to stay. He ordered our arrest.

Two policemen "escorted" each of the eleven of us to the station. I use quotes because their handling of us was not exactly gentle nor were their remarks courteous. At four forty-five we entered the police station. Until recently the building had housed a savings and loan company, so I was not surprised to observe that our cell was a renovated bank vault. One by one, we were fingerprinted.

After about two hours, the charges against us were read and one of us was allowed to make a phone call. I started to call Reverend C. K. Steele, a leader of nonviolent action in Tallahassee whose two sons were involved in the sit-ins. A policeman stopped me on the grounds that Reverend Steele is not a bondsman. I heard a number of policemen refer to us as "niggers" and say we should stay on the campus.

Shortly, the police captain came into our cell and announced that someone was coming to get us out. An hour later we were released-through the back door, so that the waiting reporters and TV men would not see us and give us publicity. However, the reporters were quick to catch on and they circled the building to meet us.

We were arraigned February 22 and charged with disturbing the peace by riotous conduct and unlawful assembly. We all pleaded not guilty. The trial was set for March 3. A week prior to the date the entire A & M student body met and decided to suspend classes on March 3 and attend the trial. The prospect of having three thousand students converge on the small courtroom was a factor, we believe, in causing a two-week postponement.

Our biggest single demonstration took place on March 12 at nine A.M. The plan was for Florida State University students, who are white, to enter the two stores first and order food. A & M students would arrive later and, if refused service, would share the food which the white students had ordered. It was decided that I should be an observer this time rather than a participant because of my previous arrest.

The white and Negro students were sitting peacefully at the counter when the mayor and his corps arrived. As on the previous occasion, he asked the group to leave, but when a few rose to comply, he immediately arrested them. As a symbolic gesture of contempt, they were marched to the station in interracial pairs.

After the arrests many of us stood in a park opposite the station. We were refused permission to visit those arrested. I rushed back to report this on campus. When I returned to the station, some two hundred students were with me. Barbara Cooper and I, again, asked to visit those arrested. Again, we were refused.

Thereupon, we formed two groups and headed for the variety stores. The seventeen who went to McCrory's were promptly arrested. The group headed for Woolworth's was met by a band of white hoodlums armed with bats, sticks, knives, and other weapons. They were followed by police. To avoid what seemed certain violence, the group called off the sit-in at Woolworth's and returned to the campus in an orderly manner.

We asked the president of the student body to mobilize the students for a peaceful march downtown. He agreed but first tried, without success, to arrange a conference with the mayor.

However, the mayor was not too busy to direct the city, county, and state police who met us as we neared the downtown area. There were one thousand of us, in groups of seventy-five-each with two leaders. Our hastily printed posters said: "Give Us Our Students Back," "We Will Not Fight Mobs," "No Violence," "We Want Our Rights: We are Americans, Too."

As we reached the police line-up, the mayor stepped forward and ordered us to disperse within three minutes. But the police did not wait. They started shooting teargas bombs at once. One policeman, turning on me, exclaimed, "I want you!" and thereupon aimed one of the bombs directly at me.

The students moved back toward campus. Several girls were taken to the university hospital to be treated for burns. Six students were arrested, bringing the total arrests for the day to thirty-five. Bond was set at five hundred dollars each and within two days all were out.

The eleven of us arrested on February 20 were tried on March 17. There was no second postponement. The trial started promptly at nine-thirty. Five additional charges had been made against us, but were subsequently dropped. During the trial, Judge Rudd tried to keep race out of the case. He said it was not a factor in our arrest. But we realized it was the sole factor. The mayor in his testimony used the word "nigger" freely. We were convicted and sentenced to sixty days in jail or a three-hundred-dollar fine. All eleven had agreed to go to jail but three paid fines upon advice of our attorneys.

So, here I am serving a sixty-day sentence along with seven other CORE members. When I get out, I plan to carry on this struggle. I feel I shall be ready to go to jail again if necessary.

Portsmouth: A Lesson in Nonviolence

Edward Rodman, Norcom High School

Our story here in Portsmouth, Virginia, begins on February 12, Lincoln's Birthday. Several girls decided to observe the occasion by staging a sit-in, in sympathy with the students of North Carolina. So after school, the first sit-in of Portsmouth's history took place. There was no violence, but no one was served. We sat until the lunch counter at Rose's Variety Store closed.

Our group was a loosely knit collection of high school students, each with the same ideal: equality for all. Frankly speaking, that is about all we had in common. We were lacking organization, leadership, and planning.

By February 15, our numbers had increased considerably. We demonstrated at two stores at the Shopping Center. Again we met no obstruction-only a few hecklers, whose worst insults we passed off with a smile. Things were looking good. The newspaper and radio reporters were there getting our story.

Our spontaneous movement was gaining momentum quickly. We were without organization; we had no leader and no rules for conduct other than a vague understanding that we were not to fight back. We should have known the consequences, but we didn't.

I was late getting to the stores the following day, because of a meeting. It was almost four P.M. when I arrived. What I saw will stay in my memory for a long time. Instead of the peaceful, nonviolent sit-ins of the past few days, I saw before me a swelling, pushing mob of white and Negro students, news photographers, TV cameras, and only two policemen. Immediately, I tried to take the situation in hand. I did not know it at the time, but this day I became the sit-in leader.

I didn't waste time asking the obvious questions, "Who were these other Negro boys from the corner?" "Where did all the white hoods come from?" It was obvious. Something was going to break loose, and I wanted to stop it. First I asked all the girls to leave, then the hoods. But before I could finish, trouble started. A white boy shoved a Negro boy. The manager then grabbed the white boy to push him out and was shoved by the white boy. The crowd followed. Outside the boy stood in the middle of the street, daring any Negro to cross a certain line. He then pulled a car chain and claw hammer from his pocket and started swinging the chain in the air.

He stepped up his taunting with the encouragement of others. When we did not respond, he became so infuriated that he struck a Negro boy in the face with the chain. The boy kept walking. Then, in utter frustration, the white boy picked up a street sign and threw it at a Negro girl. It hit her and the fight began. The white boys, armed with chains, pipes, and hammers, cut off an escape through the street. Negro boys grabbed the chains and beat the white boys. The hammers they threw away. The white boys went running back to their hot rods. I tried to order a retreat.

During the fight I had been talking to the store manager and to some newspapermen. I did not apologize for our sit-in-only for unwanted fighters of both races and for their conduct. Going home, I was very dejected. I felt that this outbreak had killed our movement. I was not surprised the following day when a mob of three thousand people formed. The fire department, all of the police force, and police dogs were mobilized. The police turned the dogs loose on the Negroes—but not on the whites. Peaceful victory for us seemed distant.

Next day was rainy and I was thankful that at least no mob would form. At ten A.M. I received a telephone call that was to change our whole course of action. Mr. Hamilton, director of the YMCA, urged me to bring a few students from the original sit-in group to a meeting that afternoon. I did. That meeting was with Gordon Carey, a field secretary of CORE. We had seen his picture in the paper in connection with our recent campaign for integrated library facilities and we knew he was on our side. He had just left North Carolina where he had helped the student sit-ins. He told us about CORE and what CORE had done in similar situations elsewhere. I decided, along with the others, that Carey should help us organize a nonviolent, direct action group to continue our peaceful protests in Portsmouth. He suggested that an all-day workshop on nonviolence be held February 20.

Reverend Chambers organized an adult committee to support our efforts. At the workshop we first oriented ourselves to CORE and its nonviolent methods. I spoke on "Why Nonviolent Action?" exploring Gandhi's principles of passive resistance and Martin Luther King's methods in Alabama. We then staged a sociodrama acting out the right and wrong ways to handle various demonstration situations. During the lunch recess, we had a real-life demonstration downtown-the first since the fighting. With our new methods and disciplined organization, we were successful in deterring violence. The store manager closed the counter early. We returned to the workshop, evaluated the day's sit-in, and decided to continue in this manner. We established ourselves officially as the Student Movement for Racial Equality.

Since then, we have had no real trouble. Our struggle is not an easy one, but we know we are not alone and we plan to continue in accordance with our common ideal: equality for all through nonviolent action.

NASHVILLE: A COMMUNITY STRUGGLE

Paul Laprad, Fisk University

There were about thirty of us in the first group of sit-inners arrested in Nashville. It was approximately one-thirty p.m. on February 27. We were escorted from the store by police—not too gently. There were cheers from hundreds of people along the sidewalks. The cheers, I fear, were for the police, not for us.

During the few minutes it took the paddy wagon to get from the store to the city jail, I reflected on what a long way we had come since the idea of sit-ins first hit Nashville. The present action climaxes nearly two years of work by Jim Lawson of the Fellowship of Reconciliation, the Reverend Kefly Miller Smith of the Nashville Christian Leadership Conference, and Nashville CORE.

Back in 1958, following the opening of the new Cain-Sloan store with its segregated eating facilities, desegregation of restaurants became a prime objective. Starting last fall, Jim Lawson, as projects director of the NCLC, began holding training sessions on nonviolence, which were attended by Fisk and Tennessee A & I students. Although Nashville was almost completely unaware of it, test sit-ins were held at Harvey's department store on November 28, 1959, and at Cain-Sloan's on December 5. Hence, the movement which spread from Greensboro did not strike a vacuum when it hit Nashville.

The morning of February 10, Jim Lawson called me to say that CORE's field secretary Gordon Carey and the Reverend Douglas Moore had called him from Durham asking Nashville to help the North Carolina sit-ins. I told him I would talk with some of the students on campus. They were already quite excited over the North Carolina developments.

The next evening we were able to get together about fifty students from Fisk, A & I, and American Baptist Theological Seminary. We decided to go into action and the first sit-in took place February 13. About one hundred students participated at three stores: Woolworth's, McLellan's, and Kress's. We were refused service and remained seated until the stores closed. There was no hostility. Five days later, we tried again. This time two hundred students took part and we were able to cover a fourth store, Grant's.

First sign of possible violence came on February 20, a Saturday, with school out and the white teen-agers downtown. Some of them jeered at the demonstrators. At Walgreen's, the fifth store to be covered, a boy got into a violent argument with a white co-ed from Fisk.

Police were present during all of these sit-ins, but did not make arrests or attempt to interfere with the demonstrators. Between February 20 and 27, however, a merchants' committee called upon Mayor Ben West to halt the sit-ins. He said city attorneys had advised him that anyone has the right to sit at a lunch counter and request service. However, he expressed the viewpoint that it is a violation of law to remain at a lunch counter after it has been closed to the public.

This set the stage for February 27, again a Saturday. Every available man on the police force had been ordered into the downtown area at the time of our demonstration. I was with the student group which went to Woolworth's. Curiously, no police were inside the store when white teen-agers and others stood in the aisles insulting us, blowing smoke in our faces, grinding out cigarette butts on our backs and, finally, pulling us off our stools and beating us. Those of us pulled off our seats tried to regain them as soon as possible. But none of us attempted to fight back in any way.

Failing to disrupt the sit-in, the white teen-agers filed out. Two or three minutes later, the police entered and told us we were under arrest. To date, none of the whites who attacked us have been arrested, although Police Chief D. E. Hosse has ordered an investigation to find out why.

As might be expected, even the jail cells in Nashville are segregated. Two other white students and I were isolated from the others in a fairly large room, but we managed to join in the singing which came from the horribly crowded cells where the Negro students were confined.

There were eighty-one of us, in all, arrested that day. We hadn't been in jail more than a half hour before food was sent in to us by the Negro merchants. A call for bail was issued to the Negro community and within a couple of hours there was twice the amount needed.

Our trials were February 29. The regular city judge refused on a technicality to handle the cases and appointed a special judge whose bias was so flagrant that Negro lawyers defending us were shocked. At one point, Z. Alexander Looby, a well-known NAACP attorney and city council member, threw up his hands and commented, "What's the use!" During the two days I sat in court, every policeman who testified under oath stated that we had been sitting quietly at the lunch counters and doing nothing else.

The judge's verdict on disorderly conduct charges was guilty. Most of us were fined fifty dollars and costs. A few of the cases are being appealed as test cases. Next, we were all rearrested on state charges of conspiracy to obstruct trade and commerce, but the district attorney has expressed doubts as to the validity of this charge and to date no indictments have been returned by the grand jury.

On March 2 another sixty-three students were arrested at Nashville's two bus stations—Greyhound and Trailways. They too were charged with disorderly conduct and then conspiracy. It began to look as though we might well fill the jails. The next day, however, a new development occurred. At the urging of the Friends Meeting, the Community Relations Conference, the Ministerial Association and other groups, Mayor West appointed a seven-man biracial committee to try to work out a solution.

Although some Negroes expressed doubts about whether the committee was truly representative, we decided to discontinue the sit-ins temporarily to give it a chance to deliberate. However, a boycott of the stores by the Negro community was started at this time. By March 25, we felt the committee had had sufficient time to answer what is essentially a moral problem and we took action again. This time we covered an additional drugstore, Harvey's, and Cain & Sloan's. Only four students were arrested—all at the drugstore. Police appeared to have received orders not to molest us.

This sit-in provoked a violent reaction from Governor Buford Ellington, who charged that it was "instigated and planned by and staged for the convenience of Columbia Broadcasting System." The charge stemmed from the fact that two CBS documentary teams had been with us for a week, filming our meetings and getting material for "Anatomy of a Demonstration." Of course, the idea that we would stage a sit-in purely for the convenience of cameramen is ridiculous.

Meanwhile, the first breaks in the pattern had occurred. On March 16, four Negro students were served at the Greyhound bus station.

The Mayor's committee announced it had been ready to report but, because of the March 25 sit-in, was unable to do so. On April 5 the committee recommended that for a ninety-day trial period the stores "make available to all customers a portion of restaurant facilities now operated exclusively for white customers," and that pending cases against the sit-in participants be dropped.

The plan of the Mayor's committee was rejected by the store management and by the student leaders. The students said "The suggestion of a restricted area involves the same stigma of which we are earnestly trying to rid the community. The plan presented by the Mayor's committee ignores the moral issues involved in the struggle for human rights." We were not prepared to accept "integrated facilities" while "whites only" counters were maintained.

Demonstrations were resumed April 11. A month later, on May 10, under a city-wide agreement, Nashville's lunch counters desegregated.

One final note should be added about the effects of the sit-ins here. They unified the Negro community in an unprecedented manner. The boycott proved effective in sharply curtailing seasonal Easter business in the variety stores. On April 19, within only a few hours after the bombing of Looby's home, over twenty-five hundred demonstrators marched on City Hall. Adult leaders assured us that, even if the students suddenly vanished from the seene, the action campaign would continue unabated. In Nashville, this is *not* a "students only" struggle.

I can not close without reference to the academic freedom fight involving Jim Lawson, one of three Negro students at Vanderbilt's divinity school. He was expelled March 3 because of his "strong commitment to a planned campaign of civil disobedience." He did not actually participate in the sit-ins, but he was our adviser and counselor throughout. His expulsion touched off a storm of protest not only in Nashville but in academic and ministerial circles from coast to coast.

BATON ROUGE: HIGHER EDUCATION—SOUTHERN STYLE

Major Johns, Southern University
(until March 30, when he was expelled for his role in the student protest)

Some Negro University and college administrations have supported their students' lunch counter sit-ins or, at least, have remained neutral. Others have taken a stand in opposition to the students. Southern University in Baton Rouge and its president, Dr. Felton G. Clark, fall in this latter category.

Dr. Clark had the opportunity of taking a courageous position and becoming one of the world's most respected educational leaders. Instead, he choose to buckle under to the all-white State Board of Education, which administers the university.

Early in March the Board issued a warning that any student participating in a sit-in would be subject to "stern disciplinary action." The sit-in movement had not yet spread to Baton Rouge but, as one law student expressed it, "When the Board spoke, it became a challenge to us and we could not ignore it." A representative student committee then met with Dr. Clark and asked, specifically, what would happen to students who sat-in. He replied that the Board had left him no alterative but to expel them.

On March 28, seven students sat-in at the Kress lunch counter. In less than twenty minutes they were arrested. Bond was set at the astronomical figure of fifteen hundred dollars each. However, the money was promptly raised by the Negro community and the students were released. A mass meeting was held on campus at which students pledged support of the jailed sit-inners. The following day, nine more students engaged in sit-ins at Sitman's drugstore and at the Greyhound bus station. They remained in jail six days pending a court hearing, and were released on bond April 4. These cases eventually reached the Supreme Court and resulted in its key decision of December 11, 1961, outlawing "disorderly conduct" statutes as a device for arresting Negroes seeking equal service. The same issue is involved in the mass arrests of Freedom Riders in Jackson, Mississippi.

The day after the second arrests, thirty-five hundred students marched through the center of town to the State Capitol, where we held an hour-long prayer meeting. As chief speaker, I attacked segregation and discrimination not only here in Baton Rouge but in other parts of the country.

I was unaware that this speech would sever my connections with the university before the day was over. That afternoon Dr. Clark retumed from a conference in Washington and immediately cast his lot against the students. He summoned faculty members who were known to oppose the sit-ins and were furthest removed from really knowing the students. Immediately following this meeting, he announced the expulsion of seventeen students, the sixteen who had participated in the two sit-ins and myself.

This suddenly shifted the focus of the Baton Rouge student protest from lunch counters to the university administration. As Marvin Robinson, participant in the first sit-in and president of the senior class, expressed it, we had a choice, "Which is the more important, human dignity or the university? We felt it was human dignity."

The students voted to boycott all classes until the seventeen of us were reinstated. Lines were tightly drawn: the students on one side; the administration, faculty, State Board of Education, and a group of hand-picked alumni on the other. We seventeen were no longer permitted on campus. But twice daily, in the morning and afternoon, we would address the students from the balcony of a two-story house across a railroad track from the campus. By using a loudspeaker we were able to make ourselves heard by the large groups of students assembled on the campus side of the track. This went on for two days.

Unable to get the students back to class, administration officials started calling their parents and telling them that the student leaders were inciting to riot. This move boomeranged. It caused many parents to fear for their sons' and daughters' safety to the extent of summoning them home. The administration countered by announcing that any student who wanted to withdraw from the university and go home could do so. Such a sizable number of students applied at the registrar's office for withdrawal slips that the administration amended its ruling to the effect that these slips would have to be cosigned by parents.

Meanwhile certain persons in the community and on campus moved to negotiate a settlement. They initiated several meetings with administration officials. Dr. Clark admitted to friends that he had acted in haste, but remained adamant in refusing to readmit the seventeen expelled students. Finally, he agreed to meet with eight of the student leaders. The meeting started at five P.M. on April 2 and lasted until eleven-thirty. Throughout the six and one-half hour meeting over three thousand students sat in front of the building where the meeting was held. When the eight emerged, announced their decision to leave the university, but urged the other students to stay on and return to classes, there was an outcry. Some burst into tears, others shouted that they wanted to quit also. The student leaders reaffirmed their decision and gave assurance that they had reached it on their own after the administration had agreed not to dismiss anyone else.

The following morning, however, the administration broke its part of the agreement and expelled another student. The leaders thereupon called a meeting and urged that the students stay out of class. A local citizens' committee, which had raised bail-bond money and had agreed to use some of it to help home-going students pay their transportation, requested a meeting with Dr. Clark. The upshot was that the committee reversed itself and decided that money raised could be used only for bail bond and not for students' bus or rail fares home.

Jim McCain, CORE field secretary who had come to Baton Rouge to help us, tried to dissuade the committee from this decision, but without success.

"I tried my best to show them that helping the students to leave Southern, even if the university should close as a result, would strike a real blow at segregation," McCain said.

Withdrawal of the transportation funds was responsible for reducing considerably the total number of students who withdrew in protest. Nevertheless, the number who left on the weekend of April 2 was in the thousands. Of those, between one thousand and fifteen hundred have not yet returned. As I write this, I do not know the exact number of students who permanently withdrew to protest an administration which serves segregation and discounts human dignity.

The protest movement by students at Southern will be remembered in Baton Rouge. One instructor died, another had a heart attack, and we are told that Dr. Clark is under medical care. It is reported by persons close to Dr. Clark that he has received several hundred letters and wires from all over the world—not one of them complimentary. Dr. Clark, I am sure, has lost many friends because of the position he has taken against his students. Until this protest, Southern University was an island unto itself. Dr. Clark has been its president since 1938, and his father was its president from 1914 until 1938. Southern University will not be able to live by itself any longer. How far the community will proceed in continuing the movement which the students have started, only time will tell. But segregation in Baton Rouge has received a severe jolt.

UNIT 7-5

FIRST OCCURRENCE OF SIT-INS IN A LOCALITY

Martin Oppenheimer

DATE	CITY
Feb. 1, 1960	Greensboro, N.C.
Feb. 5	Chevy Chase, Md. (not a sit-in)
Feb. 8	Durham, N.C.; Winston-Salem, N.C.
Feb. 9	Charlotte, N.C.
Feb. 10	Raleigh, N.C.
Feb. 11	High Point, N.C.; Hampton, Va.
Feb. 12	Concord, Norfolk, Portsmouth, Va.; Rock Hill, S.C.
Feb. 13	Nashville, Tenn.; Tallahassee, Fla.
Feb. 14	Sumter, S.C.
Feb. 16	Salisbury, N.C.
Feb. 17	Chapel Hill, N.C.
Feb. 18	Charleston, S.C.; Shelby, N.C.
Feb. 19	Chattanooga, Tenn.
Feb. 20	Richmond, Va.
Feb. 22	Baltimore, Md.; Frankfort, Ky.
Feb. 25	Montgomery, Ala.; Orangeburg, S.C.; Henderson, N.C.
Feb. 27	Lexington, Ky.; Petersburg, Va.; Tuskegee, Ala.
Feb. 29	Tampa, Fla.

Others initiated during February: Newport News, Suffolk, Whaleyville, Va.

March 2	St. Petersburg, Daytona Beach, Fla.; Columbia, S.C.
March 3	Atlanta, Ga.
March 4	Miami, Fla.; Houston, Tex.
March 7	Knoxville, Tenn.
March 8	New Orleans, La.
March 10	Little Rock, Ark.
March 11	Austin, Galveston, Tex.

March 12	Jacksonville, Fla.
March 13	San Antonia, Tex.
March 15	St. Augustine, Fla.; Statesville, N.C.; Corpus Christi, Tex.
March 16	Savannah, Ga.
March 17	New Bern, N.C.
March 19	Memphis, Tenn.; Wilmington, N.C.; Arlington, Va.
March 26	Lynchburg, Va.
March 28	Baton Rouge, La.
March 29	Marshall, Tex.
March 31	Birmingham, Ala.

Others initiated during March: Annapolis, Md.; Bluefield, W. Va.; Columbus, Ga.; Douglasville, Ga.; Deland, Fla.; Denmark, S.C.; Elizabeth City, N.C.; Fayetteville, N.C.; Florence, S.C.; Huntsville, Ala.; Lenoir, N.C.; Monroe, N.C.; Orlando, Fla.; Rutherford, N.C.; Sarasota, Fla.; Shreveport, La.; Xenia, Ohio; Charleston, W. Va.; Greenville, S.C.; Oklahoma City, Okla.

April 2	Danville, Va.
April 4	Darlington, S.C.
April 9	Augusta, Ga.
April 17	Biloxi, Miss.
April 28	Dallas, Tex.

Others initiated during April: Jackson, Miss. (boycott, no sit-ins); Pensacola, Fla.

Initiated During May: Columbia, Mo.; Starkville, Miss.
Initiated During June: Kansas City, Kansas and Missouri
Initiated During July: Killeen, Tex.; Rockville, Md.; Spartanburg, S.C.; Fredericksburg, Va.
Initiated During August: Hopewell, Va.; Jefferson City, Mo. (concluded that month; initial date not known); Murphysboro, Ill.; Myrtle Beach, S.C.; Glen Echo, Md. (not known precisely).
Initiated During September: Huntington, W. Va.; Jackson, Tenn.; St. Louis, Mo.
Initiated During December: Covington, Ky.

(*Note:* From February through April, "others initiated" indicates communities concerning which precise dates are not known, or those in which the sit-ins were not sustained, or concerning which there is inadequate information upon which to base any real discussion.)

Crusade For Citizenship

TO DOUBLE THE NUMBER OF QUALIFIED NEGRO VOTERS IN THE SOUTH

SPONSORED BY

The Southern Christian Leadership Conference, Inc.

208 AUBURN AVENUE, N. E., ATLANTA 3, GEORGIA
Room 203 — Telephone: JAckson 5-1763

MISS ELLA J. BAKER
Executive Director

OFFICERS

President
REV. M. L. KING, JR.
Montgomery, Ala.
First Vice-President
REV. C. K. STEELE
Tallahassee, Fla.
Second Vice-President
REV. J. E. LOWERY
Mobile, Ala.
Third Vice-President
REV. SAMUEL W. WILLIAMS
Atlanta, Ga.
Fourth Vice-President
REV. T. J. JEMISON
Baton Rouge, La.
Secretary
REV. F. L. SHUTTLESWORTH
Birmingham, Ala.
Assistant Secretary
MRS. KATIE E. WHICKAM
New Orleans, La.
Financial Secretary-Treasurer
REV. RALPH D. ABERNATHY
Montgomery, Ala.
Chaplain
REV. KELLEY M. SMITH
Nashville, Tenn.
Historian
L. D. REDDICK, Ph.D.
Montgomery, Ala.

EXECUTIVE BOARD
(All officers are members of the Executive Board)

ATTY. I. M. AUGUSTINE
New Orleans, La.
MRS. DAISY BATES
Little Rock, Ark.
REV. WILLIAM H. BORDERS
Atlanta, Ga.
REV. HENRY C. BUNTON
Memphis, Tenn.
REV. A. L. DAVIS
New Orleans, La.
REV. W. A. DENNIS
Chattanooga, Tenn.
REV. EDWARD T. GRAHAM
Miami, Fla.
REV. WALTER L. HAMILTON
Norfolk, Va.
REV. W. H. HALL
Hattiesburg, Miss.
DR. AARON E. HENRY
Clarksdale, Miss.
CLARENCE HENRY
New Orleans, La.
REV. D. E. KING
Louisville, Ky.
REV. M. L. KING, SR.
Atlanta, Ga.
I. S. LEEVY
Columbia, S. C.
REV. MATTHEW D. MCCOLLOM
Orangeburg, S. C.
REV. DOUGLAS MOORE
Durham, N. C.
ROBERT D. ROBERTSON
Norfolk, Va.
REV. S. S. SEAY, SR.
Montgomery, Ala.
REV. R. B. SHORTS
Atlanta, Ga.
W. E. SHORTRIDGE
Birmingham, Ala.
C. O. SIMPKINS, D.D.S.
Shreveport, La.
REV. DANIEL B. SPEED
Tallahassee, Fla.
REV. WYATT TEE WALKER
Petersburg, Va.

April 11, 1960

NEWS - ALERT

JET [illegible]

TO: Press, Radio and Televison Media

RE: Southwide Youth Leadership Conference on Nonviolence

April 15 - 17, 1960

SHAW UNIVERSITY (West Campus), Raleigh, N.C.

PRESS CONFERENCE

Friday, April 15 .... 4:00 P.M.
Sunday, April 17 ....12:30 P.M.

PUBLIC MASS MEETING

Saturday, April 16 .... 8:00 P.M.
MEMORIAL (City) AUDITORIUM

Conference Participants

Youth Leaders from forty (40) communities in ten (10) Southern states will meet to evaluate recent Sit-Ins and other student demonstrations, and to chart future goals.

SPONSORED BY - The Southern Christian Leadership Conference with cooperation from the Congress of Racial Equality, American Friends Service Committee, National Student Association, and the Fellowship of Reconciliation.

ADULT ADVISORS - will include Dr. Martin L. King, Jr., Atlanta, Ga. Rev. Ralph D. Abernathy, Montgomery, Ala., Rev. Wyatt T. Walker, Petersburg, Va., Attorney Len Holt, Norfolk, Va., and Rev. James Lawson, Nashville, Tenn. Information may be secured from director, Miss E. J. Baker

SIGNED:

Ella J. Baker, Director

THE FRANCHISE IS A CITIZEN'S RIGHT . . . NOT A PRIVILEGE

YOUTH LEADERSHIP MEETING
SHAW UNIVERSITY
RALEIGH, N. C. - APRIL 15-17, 1960

WHY THIS MEETING?

Recent lunchcounter Sit-ins and other nonviolent protests by students of the South are tremendously significant developments in the drive for Freedom and Human Dignity in America.

The courageous, dedicated and thoughtful leadership manifested by hundreds of Negro students on college campuses, in large cities and small towns, and the overwhelming support by thousands of others, present new challenges for the future. This great potential for social change now calls for evaluation in terms of where do we go from here. The Easter week-end conference is convened to help find the answers. Together, we can chart new goals and achieve a more unified sense of direction for training and action in Nonviolent Resistance.

WHO WILL ATTEND?

Representation is invited from all areas of recent protest. However, to be effective, a leadership conference should not be too large. For this reason, each community is being asked to send a specified number of youth leaders. Adult Freedom Fighters will be present for counsel and guidance, but the meeting will be youth centered.

SCHEDULE:

The opening session will be Friday, April 15 at 7:30 o'clock. Saturday will be devoted to workshops, buzz-sessions and committee work. There will be a public meeting Saturday night, and the conference will close at lunchtime Sunday.

EXPENSES:

We believe that your community will want to help share your travel expenses; and the Southern Christian Leadership Conference hopes that housing and meals will be underwritten. The total cost for six (6) meals and housing for two (2) nights will be $6.30 per person.

FOR FURTHER INFORMATION, Contact the Southern Christian Leadership Conference, 208 Auburn Avenue, N. E., Atlanta, Ga..

Dr. Martin L. King, Jr.
President

Ella J. Baker
Executive Director

- 2 -

8:45 - 10:00 A.M.	Committee Hour
10:00 - 12:30	Plenary Session - Findings and Recommendations.
12:30 - 1:00 P.M.	PRESS CONFERENCE
1:00 P.M.	LUNCHEON

AREAS OF DISCUSSION

The student Sit-In movement holds great potential for social change. The Easter weekend meeting is designed to evaluate what has happened, why it happened, and what the next steps are, in the drive for human dignity. Many questions have been raised, and the following are suggestive of the points to be explored by the Student Leadership Conference:

1. Advantages and Disadvantages: of Mass Demonstrations of Small Sit-Ins.
2. "Jail vs Bail" ..... Going to Jail with a Purpose
3. Where Picketing and Economic Pressure are Useful
4. Dangers, Limitations, and Potentials of the Legal Approach.
5. Philosophy and Techniques of Nonviolence.

COMMITTEES:

The following committees seem desirable, and we hope that all students will come prepared to serve where needed:

1. Steering Committee
2. Reporting Committee (To cover workshop discussions)
3. Committee on Findings and Recommendations.
4. Press Committee
5. Devotions Committee

ARRIVAL - IMPORTANT!

Please try to arrive Friday, in time for the 4:00 P.M. Press Conference; but by all means, in time for the opening meeting.

UNIT 7-7

BIGGER THAN A HAMBURGER

Ella J. Baker

RALEIGH, N.C.—The Student Leadership Conference made it crystal clear that current sit-ins and other demonstrations are concerned with something much bigger than a hamburger or even a giant-sized coke.

Whatever may be the differences in approach to their goal, the Negro and white students, North and South, are seeking to rid America of the scourge of racial segregation and discrimination not only at lunch counters, but in every aspect of life.

In reports, casual conversations, discussion groups, and speeches, the sense and the spirit of the following statement that appeared in the initial newsletter of the students at Barber-Scotia College, Concord, N.C., were re-echoed time and again:

> We want the world to know that we no longer accept the inferior position of second-class citizenship. We are willing to go to jail, be ridiculed, spat upon and even suffer physical violence to obtain First Class Citizenship.

By and large, this feeling that they have a destined date with freedom, was not limited to a drive for personal freedom, or even freedom for the Negro in the South. Repeatedly it was emphasized that the movement was concerned with the moral implications of racial discrimination for the "whole world" and the "Human Race."

This universality of approach was linked with a perceptive recognition that "it is important to keep the movement democratic and to avoid struggles for personal leadership."

> It was further evident that desire for supportive cooperation from adult leaders and the adult community was also tempered by apprehension that adults might try to "capture" the student movement. The students showed willingness to be met on the basis of equality, but were intolerant of anything that smacked of manipulation or domination.

Southern Patriot, May 1960.

This inclination toward *group-centered leadership*, rather than toward a *leader-centered group pattern of organization* was refreshing indeed to those of the older group who bear the scars of the battle, the frustrations and the disillusionment that come when the prophetic leader turns out to have heavy feet of clay.

However hopeful might be the signs in the direction of group-centeredness, the fact that many schools and communities, especially in the South, have not provided adequate experience for young Negroes to assume initiative and think and act independently accentuated the need for guarding the student movement against well-meaning, but nevertheless unhealthy, over-protectiveness.

Here is an opportunity for adult and youth to work together and provide genuine leadership—the development of the individual to his highest potential for the benefit of the group.

> Many adults and youth characterized the Raleigh meeting as the greatest or most significant conference of our period.

Whether it lives up to this high evaluation or not will, in a large measure, be determined by the extent to which there is more effective training in and understanding of non-violent principles and practices, in group dynamics, and in the re-direction into creative channels of the normal frustrations and hostilities that result from second-class citizenship.

Miss Baker is executive director of the Southern Christian Leadership Conference, which issued the call for the Student Leadership Conference on Non-violent Resistance to Segregation. This was held at Shaw University, Raleigh, N.C., on Easter weekend with 142 students from the South and 30 from the North in attendance. A sizeable delegation of white students joined the young Negro leaders for the conference.

UNIT 7-8

STATEMENT TO THE PRESS

Dr. Martin Luther King, Jr.

This is an era of offensive on the part of oppressed people. All peoples deprived of dignity and freedom are on the march on every continent throughout the world. The student sit-in movement represents just such an offensive in the history of the Negro peoples' struggle for freedom. The students have taken the struggle for justice into their own strong hands. In less than two months more Negro freedom fighters have revealed to the nation and the world their determination and courage than has occurred in many years. They have embraced a philosophy of mass direct nonviolent action. They are moving away from tactics which are suitable merely for gradual and long term change.

Today the leaders of the sit-in movement are assembled here from ten states and some forty communities to evaluate these recent sit-ins and to chart future goals. They realize that they must now evolve a strategy for victory. Some elements which suggest themselves for discussion are:

1. The need for some type of continuing organization. Those who oppose justice are well organized. To win out the student movement must be organized.
2. The students must consider calling for a nation-wide campaign of "selective buying." Such a program is a moral act. It is a moral necessity to select, to buy from these agencies, these stores, and businesses where one can buy with dignity and self respect. It is immoral to spend one's money where one cannot be treated with respect.
3. The students must seriously consider training a group of volunteers who will willingly go to jail rather than pay bail or fines. This courageous willingness to go to jail may well be the thing to awaken the dozing conscience of many of our white brothers. We are in an era in which a prison term for a freedom struggle is a badge of honor.
4. The youth must take the freedom struggle into every community in the south without exception. The struggle must be spread into every nook and cranny. Inevitably this broadening of the struggle and the determination which it represents will arouse vocal and vigorous support and place pressures on the federal government that will compel its intervention.

Statement to the press by Dr. Martin Luther King, Jr. at the beginning of the Youth Leadership Conference. Friday, April 15, 1960 in Raleigh, N.C.

5. The students will certainly want to delve deeper into the philosophy of nonviolence. It must be made palpably clear that resistance and nonviolence are not in themselves good. There is another element that must be present in our struggle that then makes our resistance and nonviolence truly meaningful. That element is reconciliation. Our ultimate end must be the creation of the beloved community. The tactics of nonviolence without the spirit of nonviolence may indeed become a new kind of violence.

UNIT 7-9

PERSONAL NOTES FROM FOUNDING CONFERENCE

Charles Jones

Group IV

Leader: Charles Jones

Counselor: Mark Harris

We discussed the following points:

I. What kind of help do we desire from white supporters?

- **a.** White participation in direct action would depend upon the temper of the community.
- **b.** Statement of support. Public identity.
- **c.** Interpretation by people of what they are doing in the area
- **d.** Financial Assistance.
- **e.** We should attempt to work quietly with groups and merchants ourselves.

II. The interracial thrust as it makes contact within the community. Some ways of making this contact effective are:

- **a.** By use of the person to person contact.
- **b.** Use of mediation (liaisons) to establish contact.

One fundamental problem is whether or not we accept others after we have won this battle.

. . . Should we educate the white community at large as well as the Negro? Should students be educated first? How can we support those whites who support us?

RECOMMENDATIONS

1. This movement should not be considered one for Negroes but one for people who consider this a movement against injustice. This would include members of all races.

   This movement will affect other areas beyond "services" such as politics and economics.

2. Our basis and method of communication should work not for us but with us, for the principle of empathy.

UNIT 7-10

RECOMMENDATIONS

OF THE FINDINGS AND RECOMMENDATIONS COMMITTEE ARE AS FOLLOWS

I. a. That there be established a Temporary Coordinating Committee;

b. Whose headquarters shall be in Atlanta Georgia. The Committee should consist of one representative, the states of Florida, Georgia, Alabama Mississippi, Louisiana, South Carolina, Tennessee, Arkansas, Texas, Kentucky, Maryland, Virginia, North Carolina; organizations such as an the National Student Association, National Student Christian Federations and any region that is interested, and this committee should come together at the earliest possible time during the coming month in Atlanta. The purpose of the Temporary Committee would be to deal particularly in the areas of finance and communication.

The Reverend Martin Luther King Jr. as president of the Southern Christian Leadership Conference, and the Reverend James M. Lawson, as coordinator of this present student leadership conference should be present in an advisory capacity.

The address of the Coordinating Committee is:

The Student Nonviolent Coordination Committee
c/o Southern Christian Leadership Conference
208 Auburn Avenues. N.E.
Atlanta 3, Georgia

II. a. Suggestions from anyone will be welcomed and should be sent to this address. The representatives from designated states must be elected today, and this committee must hold its first meeting this afternoon at which time it must elect a chairman; additional advisors, if necessary; plan for its Atlanta meeting, and make arrangements in any further areas necessary for expediting this recommendation.

b. That we recommend those attorneys who have contributed their services to the movement to date, and appeal to attorney in general to refrain from charging exorbitant prices for defense of participants in the movement.

c. That *nonviolence* is our creed, and the coordinating committee shall work out a definite statement.

d. That this conference recognizes the virtue of the movement and endorses the practice of *going to jail rather than accepting bail.*

e. That a booklet which will be a report on the discussions finding and recommendations of this conference shall be printed and mailed to a volume of colleges and organizations. This responsibility shall belong to the Coordinating committee.

f. That we identify ourselves with the African struggle as a concern of all mankind.

We understand there is a possibility that President Eisenhower will make a visit to Africa this fall, and agree that this is a desirable step-up. We feel that before going to Africa, the president should lend this prestige of his office to the solution of the racial problems of this country, and this he shall be even better prepared for his visit to Africa.

g. That this conference approves and endorses movements on all campuses, in sympathy with expulsion of any student who is expelled from school for standing up for human rights.

SOUTHWIDE YOUTH LEADERSHIP CONFERENCE
SHAW UNIVERSITY, RALEIGH, N.C.
April 15–15, 1960

UNIT 7-11

SNCC: Founding Statement

We affirm the philosophical or religious ideal of nonviolence as the foundation of our purpose, the presupposition of our belief, and the manner of our action.

Nonviolence, as it grows from the Judeo-Christian tradition, seeks a social order of justice permeated by love. Integration of human endeavor represents the crucial first step towards such a society.

Through nonviolence, courage displaces fear. Love transcends hate. Acceptance dissipates prejudice; hope ends despair. Faith reconciles doubt. Peace dominates war. Mutual regards cancel enmity. Justice for all overthrows injustice. The redemptive community supersedes immoral social systems.

By appealing to conscience and standing on the moral nature of human existence, nonviolence nurtures the atmosphere in which reconciliation and justice become actual possibilities.

Although each local group in this movement must diligently work out the clear meaning of this statement of purpose, each act or phase of our corporate effort must reflect a genuine spirit of love and good-will.

UNIT 7-12

NAACP MEMO ON SHAW STUDENT CONFERENCE

MEMORANDUM

TO: Mr. Roy Wilkins

FROM: John M. Brooks

RE: A discussion with Mr. Chester Hampton, reporter for the Afro-American Newspaper, after his return from the Youth Leadership Conference in Raleigh, North Carolina held on April 17, 1960.

Mr. Hampton stated that Rev. James Lawson from Nashville, Tennessee made a statement similar to this in one of the secret workshops during the Raleigh Conference to a group of high school students: The Crisis magazine of the NAACP is a magazine for the black bourgeoisie. This statement and the tone of Rev. Lawson's speech produced an anti-NAACP atmosphere.

After the meeting the reporters present in Raleigh very skillfully questioned the students and gained knowledge of Rev. Lawson's speech. Later in the day when Rev. Lawson was questioned, he is alleged to have made this type of statement: The top leadership of the Southern Christian leaders is not in harmony with the NAACP.

True or not true, Rev. Lawson's alleged statements certainly reflect the attitude of some of the Southern Christian leadership groups in the south, in spite of the fact that the whole movement is using the foundation built by the NAACP. Even though we have to be diplomatic in dealing with these opportunists, I think we should hit them in their weakest spot . . . legal defense.

Regardless of how much shouting there is about sitting down and going to jail, there is always a pause first to find out if the NAACP will give legal aid. Without the assurance of this aid from the local branches, there would be a decrease in sit-down efforts. Yet we have NAACP branches that don't recognize this important factor and we have Southern Christian leadership officials who place our legal aid and a picket sign committee in the same category.

I think it would be good strategy to:

1. Publicize not only our offer to give legal aid to the students, but publicize the current work of the NAACP lawyers with the protest movement.
2. Let the word get around to the effect that unless local branches are an integral part of the protest movement, it will be difficult and awkward for the NAACP to offer legal aid.

I realize it is easier to write suggestions than it is to put them into action. My suggestions may be out of order, but the overall picture is very cloudy.

In conclusion I will say it is getting harder and harder to be nice when you know your organization is being used for the promotion of a few people.

UNIT 7-13

ROY WILKINS TO MARTIN LUTHER KING

Roy Wilkins

April 27, 1960

Dear Martin:

We were puzzled and greatly distressed at the criticism of the NAACP voiced by the Rev. James Lawson at the Raleigh meeting April 16–17 called by the Southern Christian Leadership Conference.

This has caused considerable discussion among our members. In one way or another they have stated that since they understood that the NAACP had cooperated with the SCLC how did the Lawson blast come about and how was it that Lawson claimed his views were shared by other leaders in the SCLC?

This last brings you into the matter, of course. Miss Baker evidently thought the situation serious enough to volunteer to newspapermen that Mr. Lawson was voicing a personal opinion.

I know that you join me in the determination not to have a break between our groups. We seek the same goals and we have the same enemies. Those enemies would be happier than they have been for forty years if a split should develop.

At the same time we feel aggrieved over this unwarranted attack. The SCLC did not initiate the sit-downs. That we know. CORE did not initiate them. That we know. The NAACP did not initiate the wave that began February l, but the NAACP staged the only successful sit-down at lunch counters in Oklahoma City and in Wichita, Kansas in 1958. That we do know.

But in the present case we did what SCLC and CORE did. We rushed in to help the youngsters. Upon what basis does Mr. Lawson speak so bitterly? If the NAACP had condemned the sit-down tactic and had refused to permit its youth units to participate or if the NAACP had remained outside, we could understand Mr. Lawson.

The Memphis NAACP Branch alone put up $3,400 in bail; the whole Orangeburg operation was an NAACP operation with bail money being furnished by us; we arranged for bail of the last students in Baton Rouge; it was the NAACP legal defense fund which called the lawyers conference in Washington and coordinated the complicated and varied strategy of defense; it,was the NAACP youth group in San Antonio who won the battle without firing a shot, just by announcing their intention to sit down. I am hopeful that you can help clarify the situation. I know you will want to.

There are some other disturbing elements in the picture which I would not care to go into here, but which I feel you and I should discuss privately as soon as possible.

Very sincerely yours,

Roy Wilkins,
Executive Secretary

Dr. Martin Luther King
Southern Christian Leadership Conference
407 Auburn Avenue, N.E.
Atlanta, Georgia

RW/emb

UNIT 7-14

ROY WILKINS TO JAMES LAWSON

Roy Wilkins

May 13, 1960

Dear Mr. Lawson:

I appreciate having your letter of May 9.

Enclosed you will find a reproduction of the news story carried here April 17 by The New York Times. It is not calculated to win friends and influence people among followers of the NAACP or its officials. It is one which has caused rejoicing in the camps of the opponent of Negro aspirations.

A reading of your text tends to sustain the account in The New York Times. The assertions on page 7, "middle-class conventional half-way efforts" and "specifically a judgment upon contemporary civil rights attempts" certainly constitutes a sharp reflection upon NAACP. The language in the paragraph near the bottom of page 7 certainly says (**a**) that *The Crisis* magazine is an organ of a "black bourgeois club" and (**b**) that the NAACP puts its emphasis on fund-raising and court action.

It is difficult for one to imagine any more devastating indictments. With *The Crisis* as an example you say, in effect, that the NAACP, whose official organ the magazine is, is concerned primarily with bourgeois society and with fund-raising. The former allegation is an emotional one which throughout the history of its employment has been a sure method of splitting the Negro community on a mean level difficult to repair. The latter allegation is a twin of the former, a charge also on a low level, calculated to arouse suspicion among individuals and groups that the funds they send to the NAACP are not used truly to advance the cause.

These charges were repeated in essence by Mr. Bernard Lee, described as an assistant to Rev. Martin Luther King in the Southern Christian Leadership Conference, at a gathering of students at the University of Michigan on April 30. Not having the ability to wrap an idea in the delicate but meaningful language of your April 16 speech, Mr. Lee said baldly that anyone who wanted to help, the Southern situation should not send money to the NAACP, since the NAACP was not functioning in the South,

Mr. Lee added a touch of his own, although not an original one: CORE and the NAACP cannot further the aspirations of Negro Americans because both include white persons in their membership; therefore the Southern Christian Leadership conference is the only organization which can serve the cause of the Negro effectively.

Thus, within a space of two weeks a group of Negro students in the South and a group of students, predominantly white, in the North were given false impressions of the NAACP by persons speaking in the name of, or at conferences sponsored by the Southern Christian Leadership Conference. In the light of my knowledge of Dr. King's personal attitude of cooperation and mutual respect, I suspect that these pronouncements have done no disservice to the SCLC.

Your letter states: "while I do not believe in unanimity at the sacrifice of principle neither do I believe family differences should become public matter, but should be talked over with the family. I thought the Raleigh Conference was within the family.

We are unable to accept the assertion that the Raleigh Conference was "within the family." The NAACP as such was not invited to Raleigh, although some members might have been. There was no intimation, even to those invited, that a discussion of "differences within the family" would take place. No NAACP official suspected that the Conference would be one in which ideological and procedural approaches to the continuing overall problem would be debated. It was to be, we heard, a conference to coordinate student activity in the sit-in crusade.

Instead there was a keynote address which included a castigation of an organized group whose chief representatives, competent to defend its position in any debate were uninvited.

We feel that if an evaluation of the various approaches to the race problem was to be attempted, then all the exponents and spokesmen should have been invited. The president of the SCLC was present and addressed the conference and the national executive director of CORE was present, but no comparable national officer of the NAACP was asked to attended. We feel that such a session should have been a thing apart (both in time and site) from a student coordinating gathering.

The young people at Raleigh were there because of the immediate sit-in campaign. The vast Majority was not prepared to discuss, CORE, the NAACP, SCLC, ACLU, FOR, or any one of a dozen other organizations. Yet these youngsters were subjected to "orientation" which included sharp criticism of an absent organization.

Who created the climate in which the sit-in efforts could take place? The late Scipio A. Jones of Arkansas walked into a courtroom bristling with guns in Elaine county in 1919 and heard his clients condemned in less than two minutes. Yet despite guns and the pall of fear and hate, Jones (and the NAACP) secured the freedom of every one of his 79 defendants in a space of four years. Twenty years ago Thurgood Marshall went into an Oklahoma town which declared an ominous business and school holiday because no one there had ever seen a Negro lawyer, and this one had come to defend a Negro accused of murdering a white family! But Marshall was laying the groundwork for the subsequent outlawing of "torture confessions" as evidence by the U.S. Supreme Court. These men and the accompanying drumbeat of publicity and the building of Negro political influence in national politics and a host of other pressures and developments made the happenings of the past few months possible.

Indeed, as your keynote speech is examined in detail, one wonders if the purpose of the Raleigh Conference was to coordinate activation of students in a specific campaign, or to use that campaign to turn their minds from any other philosophy or technique or leadership into an embryonic organization based exclusively upon moral imperatives.

There is not anywhere a hint that the present activity may be a supplementary one, or that it is tentatively advancing its claims to efficacy in an admittedly difficult field, one that has been cluttered with trial and error, progress and retrogression, ever since men of different colors, backgrounds and customs first touched each other here on earth.

Here instead is bland assumption, ready condemnation, facile use of smear-words, disdainful dismissal of others who have not brought back the Holy Grail, and shameless resort to the dubious appeal of class.

" . . . the critique of all efforts to bring creative social change," your letter says. Why does a speech to young college students, active in a particular project, have to contain a critique of anything except segregation? Why cannot it be an informative, inspirational stimulant to the completion of their chosen project? Why not let time and the degree of success either in themselves constitute a clear evolution, or force, by their sturdy emergence, a later full-scale evaluation of "all efforts" to achieve social change? Why does a college student coordinating conferences have to be keynoted by an attack on all other efforts?

There has been some embarrassment here, but it has been, I think, embarrassment *for* the spokesmen who have so quickly assumed all wisdom and so glibly (and brashly in Mr. Lee's case) laid about upon other earnest workers in the vineyard. There has been irritation at the "trick" of the Raleigh meeting for we of the NAACP know so well that the travail of the past has made possible the further steps forward of today, and we stand ready to demonstrate that on any occasion. We were not given that occasion at Raleigh.

Frankly, I do not know what you can do at this date to correct the impression that has been created. With the kind of text you had in Raleigh, it must be obvious by now that you cannot plead that you were misquoted, or that your words did not constitute an attack on the NAACP. The words are too plain and the meaning too clear. Perhaps in future speeches and writing you can clarify the situation.

I appreciate your membership in the NAACP and the past history of your family and yourself in support of it.

Impatience in young people, Negro and white, I can understand. The pace toward racial justice has been slow. I can also understand the constant probing to discover whether this or that *other* method will not accomplish more permanent gains at a faster rate than the methods traditionally in use.

What I have difficulty understanding is that in a situation as charged with hurts as ours is, as beset with infinite complexities, some doctrinaires in each generation blithely dismiss the past as having been completely impotent. In their book, *now* begins progress, with us.

That all efforts by many groups and individuals to end segregation have not accomplished the task does not mean, necessarily, that an entirely new method must be adopted and the other "useless" ones discarded. It could mean (**a**) that current efforts have not been given the support (even though they had the acclaim) or (**b**) that supplementary methods should be employed.

I understand you have spent several years in India. No one should know better than you, then, how intricately difficult a social problem is. No one should know better that no single formula can solve the manifold troubles of a people in this modern world, even though that people re-discover and re-activate the necessary ingredients of soul strength.

Because you must know this, the tone, wording and course of your Raleigh speech are cause for as much disappointment as irritation.

Very sincerely yours,

Roy Wilkins,
Executive Secretary

Mr. J. M. Lawson, Jr.
3708 Clare Avenue, Apt. D
Nashville 8, Tennessee

UNIT 7-15

Roy Wilkins to Benjamin Mays

Roy Wilkins

May 19, 1960

Dear Dr. Mays:

Thank you for your letter of May 18. I am happy to know that you felt that we had an effective meeting in Atlanta on May 7. We thought it was very helpful and the one held the following day in Chicago was equally good.

I share your belief that there ought not to be any derogatory remarks made by staff members of the NAACP and the Southern Christian Leadership Conference. Dr. King and I have discussed this on several occasions and we made public statements designed to emphasize our positions.

I would be less than frank, however, if I did not say to you that a number of our state presidents, our staff members and some of our general membership have been increasingly irritated by reported remarks and by the tactics of some persons connected with the Southern Christian Leadership Conference.

I am sure that Dr. King did not have and does not now have any idea of setting up an organization to duplicate the work of the NAACP, yet the very items that he announces are traditional NAACP items and it is natural that many of his followers would assume not that he is attempting to help the NAACP or supplement its efforts, but that he is supplanting the organization.

He himself has never said anything like this; but on the other hand he has never said that he regards his activities as one more effort to secure freedom in addition to those already in being. He has extolled the non-violent passive resistance movement and has implied that the legal approach, while good, is slow and less effective than the kind of pressure he envisages.

The best indication that this is the impression that has been received by the general public is to be found in the repeated questions that are asked us by newspapermen, radio and television interviewers, special writers, and by other organizations. In fact they say to us "What do you think of the *other* method of passive resistance and non-violence?" or "Do you believe non-violence to be a better approach than the NAACP's traditional legal action?" or "Does the NAACP plan to adopt the passive resistance technique and drop its legal action?"

Sometimes the questions are framed in directly competitive language such as "Do you believe that the legal approach has seen its best days and that Dr. King's method will have to be the one used from now on if the Negro is to secure his full rights?"

As I say, these questions indicate the type of emphasis that has been given by spokesman for the SCLC. This is natural and we are not complaining because the public always grasps something that sounds new whether it's new or not.

The disturbing developments to us are that under the stimulus of the college sit-in campaigns certain spokesmen of SCLC have come right out with direct attacks on the NAACP. I enclose a copy of our letter written to Dr. James Lawson in response to a letter he wrote me. Apparently his letter was stimulated by Dr. King following a conference I had with Dr. King on the afternoon of May 7 in Atlanta. There is no other way to explain Mr. Lawson's writing to me as late as May 9 expressing his astonishment at the report in a Nashville daily paper April 16 of an attack he had made on the NAACP. If Mr. Lawson was astonished on April 16 at the report in his home town newspaper and was concerned about possible embarrassment to the NAACP, it seems reasonable to suppose that he would have written at once and sent us a copy of his speech so that we would understand what he had said. However, he did not write until May 9 after I had spoken in very plain fashion to Dr. King. This suggests that Mr. Lawson was not and is not particularly concerned about embarrassing the NAACP and that he has taken this stop only at the request of Dr. King. The fact that he does not conceive that certain passages in his Raleigh speech were undeniably attacks on the NAACP and its methods indicates, I think, his state of mind.

In my letter to Mr. Lawson I referred, also, to the remarks of Mr. Bernard Lee at a student meeting at the University of Michigan on April 30, These remarks were heard by a member of my own staff who was there to participate in the conference. Subsequently, another member of my staff met Mr. Lee along with SCLC's leader and Mr. Lee seemed in no wise abashed over his very hostile remarks at Ann Arbor.

In addition to all this the man in charge of the New York office of the SCLC which is collecting money for the defenses of Dr. King has been reported to us by several persons as having said in their presence in a very private conference that he intended to drive CORE and the NAACP out of the Southern picture altogether and to "wrap up the territory" for Martin Luther King.

It is true that the NAACP is the oldest and the strongest. It does not have to stoop to name-calling or petty attacks and it should (and does) welcome all groups and individuals to work in the vineyard of civil rights. However, the people who work for the NAACP not only have great pride in their organization, but they are human beings and they react when the organization to which they have given so much is subjected to snide attacks.

Mr. Bernard Lee by himself is an upstart, a recent student at Alabama State College. He was probably born since the Great Depression. He was a little boy when the NAACP was battling tooth and toenail before and during World War II to knock out Jim Crow in the armed forces and to knock out segregation in education.

The irritating aspect to us is that these youngsters and many adults who don't know the facts assume that the NAACP has done nothing all these years and that now they come along with a fresh new and only effective method of attacking the problem. We just don't believe that other people have to get ahead by kicking the NAACP in the teeth and our people are getting pretty tired of acting like a good-natured St. Bernard dog while other people snap at us and disseminate sentiment that washes away our public support as we remain dignified, cooperative and calm.

We are getting reports from many, many areas indicating that sentiment has been slyly spread that the NAACP has no connection with the sit-ins, that the sit-ins are a "revolt" against the NAACP, that the NAACP's legal approach is too clumsy and too slow and that the young people under the direction of CORE and Dr. King have taken matters into their own hands, repudiating the effective NAACP. In the midst of dictation of this letter I received a telephone call relating information from a meeting held at Cornell University and another from a meeting held by a private school in Poughkeepsie. The students had been told that the NAACP was outmoded and that Dr.King's organization was the "wave of the future." I don't feel good about it and there isn't much use pretending that I do.

I will be happy to hear from you further and you may be assured that in the meantime we will not countenance any overt pronouncements on our part.

Very sincerely yours,

Roy Wilkins,
Executive Secretary

Dr. Benjamin E. Mays, President
Moorehouse College
Atlanta University
Atlanta, Georgia

UNIT 7-16

Democratic Convention Statement, July 1960

Marion Barry

Statement Submitted by the Student Nonviolent Coordinating Committee to the Platform Committee of the National Democratic Convention. Thursday Morning, July 7, 1960, Los Angeles, California

Mr. Chairman and members of the 1960 democratic platform committee:

I am Marion S. Barry, Jr. of Nashville, Tennessee and with me are Mr. Bernard Lee of Montgomery, Alabama and Mr. John Mack of Darlington, South Carolina. We appear before you as elected representatives of the STUDENT NON-VIOLENT COORDINATING COMMITTEE, which is composed of students from eleven (11) Southern states, Maryland, and the District of Columbia.

We also represent the thinking of thousands of Negro and white Americans who have participated in, and supported student efforts that have been characterized, generally, as Sit-Ins., but which in truth were peaceful petitions to the conscience of our fellow citizens for redress of the old grievances that stem from racial segregation and discrimination. In a larger sense, we represent hundreds of thousands of freedom loving people, for whom our limited efforts have revitalized the great American dream of "liberty and justice for all."

What the Student Movement Is

On February 1, 1960, four freshmen left the campus of A & T College in Greensboro, North Carolina, went to the heart of that city, and took their seats in forbidden territory—the lunch counter of Woolworth, Inc. In a sense, this was the beginning of the student protest movement. But the threads of the quest for freedom and human dignity reach much farther—back into the days of 1955 when thousands of Negroes walked and the buses of Montgomery, Alabama were under boycott.

The threads of freedom form the basic pattern in man's struggle to know himself and to live in the assurance that other men will recognize this self. The ache of every man to touch his potential is the throb that beats out the truth of the American Declaration of Independence and the Constitution. America was founded because men were seeking room to become.

We again are seeking that room. We want room to recognize our potential. We want to walk into the sun and through the front door. For three hundred and fifty years, the American Negro has been sent to the back door in education, housing, employment, and the rights of citizenship at the polls. We grew weary. Our impatience with the token efforts of responsible adult leaders was manifest in the spontaneous protest demonstrations which, after February 1; spread rapidly across the entire South and into the North as sympathetic students sought to display their own dissatisfaction with race relations in the United States.

The movement is a protest and it is an affirmation. We protest and take direct action against conditions of discrimination. We affirm equality and brotherhood of all men, the tenets of American democracy as set forth in the Constitution, and the traditions of social justice which permeate our Judaic-Christian heritage.

WHAT THE STUDENT MOVEMENT IS NOT

The student movement, despite the accusations of some public figures, is neither Communist-controlled or inspired. Such charges are unfounded and merely serve to heighten the tensions which must come in any social change. To label our goals, methods, and presuppositions "communistic" is to credit Communism with an attempt to remove tyranny and to create an atmosphere where genuine communication can occur. Communism seeks power, ignores people; and thrives on social conflict. We seek a community in which man can realize the full meaning of the self which demands open relationship with others. What we, the participants in the movement, have in *common* are our beliefs in the dignity of the individual, our hope in the democratic form of government, and our devotion to our homeland.

WHY WE ARE HERE

We appreciate the opportunity to appear before this Committee, but we are conscious that we cannot adequately bespeak the hearts and minds of those whom we represent in the allotted ten (10) minutes.

We must also state frankly that we are interested in something more than a strong civil rights plank in the platform to be adopted by this convention. Many of us are old enough to remember, and others have observed through studying the records, that all too often, such planks seem devised mainly to woo election votes, and then, for all practical purposes, are forgotten.

We are here today to urge the leaders and candidates of the Democratic Party to stop playing political football with the civil rights of eighteen million Negro Americans and to take forthright and definitive action to make American citizenship a vital and living reality to all, regardless of race or creed.

We are here to ask leaders of our nation to face up to the reality that racial discrimination is America's number one social issue, and that, our national government must assume responsibility to guarantee the fundamental rights of all citizens without discrimination.

We have come to urge that this convention not only *speak* to these issues but *pledge* itself to see that the full weight of the Federal government is used to eradicate our national shame, Jim Crow, and second-class citizenship.

WHAT DO NEGRO STUDENTS WANT?

The question has been asked, "What do Negro students want?" Our answer is firm and clear: we want all the rights, opportunities, and responsibilities enjoyed by any other American, no more, no less; and we want these things now! Because of this, thousands of young Negroes have faced abuse and mob action; more than 1600 have been arrested; some have spent as much as sixty days in jail, and all have faced charges from disorderly conduct to conspiracy to restraint of trade.

As citizens we are interested in the total civil rights issue; but as students we have special interest in four (4) considerations. They are:

I. *Education*—that the legislative and executive branches of government act firmly and immediately to implement the 1954 Supreme Court decision against segregated public schools,

II. *Employment*—that the Federal government set the pace for equal employment opportunities by using the existing statutes and executive orders to see that Negroes are hired without discrimination on federal jobs, and jobs where federal contracts are held.

III. *Voting*—the unhampered exercise of the franchise for all citizens.

IV. *Legal Protection*—against violation of the constitutional rights of freedom of assembly and freedom to petition peaceably for redress of grievances.

I. EDUCATION

In 1956, the Democratic Platform on Civil Rights said very little in the way of direct endorsement of the May 17, 1954 Supreme Court ruling against segregation in the public schools. Instead, the platform stated that the court ruling "brought consequences of vast importance" and that such court decisions were "a part of the law of the land."

In six years since the Supreme Court ruling, states have executed programs whereby the law could be circumvented through token and nominal integration. Today, 94% of the Negro children of school age have not been integrated into public schools. The 6% who have fought their way through courts have been subjected to public humiliation, mob violence, and Klan action. America cannot continue to let such illegality go unchecked.

RECOMMENDATION ONE

- We urge that the members of this Committee endorse a plan to with-hold Federal funds from any school system which has not and will not begin integration now.
- By the same principle, we urge that the Federal government offer full technical assistance and financial aid to those areas in which honest efforts are being made to end segregation in education.
- Further, we urge you to insist that the Federal government require areas where discrimination in education continues to submit concrete plans to end this discrimination.

We cannot continue to accept second-class schools and inferior material. It is extremely important to us as future leaders and heads of families that we receive the best possible education in the public schools of America.

In all justice, we urge the adoption and implementation of a plan of action which will give meaning to the words "with all deliberate speed." Integration of 6% of the school children in six years is a denial of these words and a mockery of the Supreme Court. Aside from the fact that it is law, school integration is the beginning of encounter between persons; consequently, the beginning of communication which is essential to the practice of social justice.

II. EMPLOYMENT

Equal chance for individual economic advancement is one of America's proud boasts. Negro youth, like other youth, dream of jobs and "making a living"; but for them the dream is too often fraught with disillusionment and despair. Discrimination in employment is not limited to the South, but there it is accentuated and defended by local custom. Trained and skilled Negroes have almost no hope for professional employment, except the limited number of jobs in segregated facilities. Thus, many college trained Negroes are offered the "mop and broom" when seeking employment in private industry.

State and municipal governments offer not too much more. Even in Federal facilities, jobs are limited by local administration. Yet, there are statutes and executive processes through which the Federal government could start immediately to guarantee:

- Equal opportunities on Federal jobs
- Non-discriminatory employment by firms holding government contracts

Making a good living is basic to making a good life. Negro youth cannot make its fullest possible contribution to the future welfare and security of America if job discrimination continues. At a time when despotism and nuclear power threaten both the existence of a free world and that of any world at all, it is essential that America utilize her full human potential.

RECOMMENDATION TWO

- We, therefore, call upon this convention to accept responsibility for decisive action towards a Federal fair employment law, with adequate enforcement machinery.

III. VOTING

The right to vote is basic to a democratic governments ". . . Governments are instituted among men", the Declaration of Independence stated, "deriving their just powers from the consent of the governed". Yet today, ninety (90) years after the passage of the Fifteenth Amendment, many Americans are denied the franchise because of race. This is being accomplished largely through the arbitrary interpretation and application of complex voter-qualification laws, literacy and education tests, that frequently have been enacted for the express purpose of thwarting the Negro voter.

But even more shameful than the legal blockade are the extra-legal harassments to which potential Negro voters have been and still are subjected. Economic reprisals, threats, physical violence, even death are part of the pattern; Presently, in Haywood and Fayette Counties Tennessee persons are denied the right to buy gasoline, farm supplies, and even medical aid because they are Negroes and are trying to register for voting. To such conditions there is but one answer—*the right to vote must be assured and protected by the Federal government.*

RECOMMENDATION THREE

- Hence, we call upon all political candidates to pledge themselves to work to strengthen and implement the 1957 and 1960 voting legislation and to work toward a

Constitutional amendment that will encourage rather than discourage every qualified citizen to register and vote.

- Further, we urge immediate action to provide self-government to the voteless residents of our nation's capital, the District of Columbia.

IV. LEGAL PROTECTION

It has been amply demonstrated that the white South is not averse to subjecting the Negro to law; it only objects to including him under a common law.

Nothing is more frustrating to a young Negro than to be barred from spending his money in public places. But it adds insult to injury to be invited, even urged, to shop at a store, buy at all counters . . . EXCEPT the lunch counter, because of the color of your skin.

We have been falsely told that the law forbids white and Negro eating together, or that the law forbids giving service to Negroes in "white" eating establishments and department store lunch counters. Often, it is not the law, but it is "local custom" which is being used to prevent the Negro from receiving his rights.

In the peaceful attempt to demonstrate our dissatisfaction with special laws for Negroes; we have been arrested, convicted and jailed. Then new laws have suddenly been enacted, denying the right to assemble and petition for redress of grievances, the right to be secure in our homes, and the right to be free of excessive bail and excessive fines.

We have been met with the "Protection" of the police . . . fire hoses, clubs and tear gas. In many places, local officials have sanctioned the policies of rabid white supremacists and have actually deputized members of such groups.

Of the so-called Reconstruction Amendments, only the Thirteenth (XIII) has been carried out. Enforcement of state laws of segregation and disfranchisement have negated the others. Time is far overdue for making real the citizenship rights guaranteed by the Fourteenth (XIV) Amendment.

RECOMMENDATION FOUR

We, therefore, urge the leaders and candidates of this convention to pledge that the basic provisions of the Part III of the 1957 Civil Rights Act will be enacted into a law that makes clear that Negroes are citizens of the UNITED States and that "No state shall make or enforce any law which shall abridge the privileges and immunities of citizens of the United States."

Surely, the American government is not powerless to make good this promise of more than ninety years ago.

CONCLUSION

On July 4, 1776, the Continental Congress, adopting the Declaration of Independence of the United States of America; created a new potential for life and liberty. On July 16, 1945, the explosion of the first atomic bomb at Alamogordo, New Mexico created the possibility of death and enslavement. We stand today between these great turning points in human history, saying that America cannot fail in its responsibility to the free world. We must be strong. Civil defense and economic power alone will not assure the continuation of democracy. This democracy itself demands the great intangible strength of a people able to unite in a common endeavor because they are granted a common dignity. This challenge cannot be met unless and until all Americans, Negro and white, enjoy the full promise of our democratic heritage—first class citizenship. Dedicated to this end, we, the students of America, must continue our movement.

Student Nonviolent Coordinating Committee

135 Auburn Avenue, N.E.
Atlanta 3, Georgia

MUrray 8-0331

The Right To Vote...100 Years Later

One hundred years after the Emancipation Proclamation and ninety-eight years after the passage of the Fifteenth Amendment to the Constitution of the United States, less than 13.8 percent of the Negroes of voting age in Louisiana, Mississippi, and Alabama are allowed to vote. In Mississippi, less than 6.1 percent of the qualified Negroes are allowed to vote.

Think what this means. These American Negroes are ruled—without benefit of representation—by white men in the United States today. The machinery of legislation, of judicial process, of the simplest justice, is closed to one segment of American society. No offense has been committed by these disenfranchised men and women—except the worst offense of all: they were born of a different color.

That so few Negroes are allowed to vote in the deep South is one of the world's greatest injustices. Besides the broken promise to our own citizens, think what this simple fact means to our country's status in the world today. How does American democracy look—how can it look—to our allies (and to our enemies) when so large a proportion of our population is not allowed to vote?

The Non-violent Approach

The Student Non-violent Coordinating Committee is devoted to helping qualified colored voters to vote in the states where they are now disenfranchised.

One of its main functions is to advise potential colored voters as to their rights and help them to register. To do this, it must coordinate the work of many individuals and many groups.

An organized effort of students who understand their rights as Americans is mandatory to bring true democracy to the deep South. The original credo of purpose adopted by the SNCC stated:

> "We affirm the philosophical or religious ideal of non-violence as the foundation of our purpose, and the manner of our action. . . . By appealing to the conscience and standing on the moral nature of human existence, non-violence nurtures the atmosphere in which reconciliation and juctice become actual possibilities."

Benefits of SNCC Action

The work of the Student Non-Violent Coordinating Committee is carried on by student protest groups and twenty field representatives throughout the South. The staff, a small band of dedicated men goes about its work quietly and systematically, telling Negroes of voting age about their rights under the Constitution. The requirements for registration in the various areas are explained. Frightened people are accompanied to the polls. All of this work is done according to the principle of non-violence which characterizes all of SNCC's work.

SNCC's main purpose is to co-ordinate the activities of student protest groups across the entire deep South. Today, this relatively new organization has expanded its program and has taken its place among the forerunners of the civil rights organizations. It has captured the imagination of students in colleges all over the nation because of its grass roots work in the vital area of voter registration.

Student protest groups have sprung up across the nation as a response to the courageous actions of the SNCC in the South. Some of these groups supply much needed financial assistance to the SNCC. As they continue to aid the struggle in the South, they are paying increasing attention to the housing, employment, and education discrimination problems existing in the North.

The work of the SNCC is bringing to both white and colored students all over the United States the realization that democracy really means equality—and if one group suffers because of its color, we, as Americans all suffer. As long as these injustices prevail, we are all guilty.

The twenty dedicated field secretaries of SNCC are on leave from their respective colleges and universities. They left to go into an untouched area of the struggle: the rural community. Field secretaries have gone into the farm areas of Mississippi, Georgia, Alabama, and Louisiana in order to establish voter registration schools. The schools have been the main stimulus in getting the people of these communities to register and vote.

Unfortunately, these schools have also been the chief cause of the staunch segregationists' threats, attacks, and murders perpetrated against persons affililiated with these schools.. Though these students may be in the vanguard in the South, they also give inspiration and leadership to some Northern Communities.

The immense uproar in the South against a relatively small organization illustrates better than any words possibly could, how effective SNCC really is. The following page lists just a few of the "incidents" that have characterized the work of SNCC representatives during their ordinary day's work in the deep South. This is perhaps only the beginning — as this is being written, some field representatives are out on bail. They must go again to the courts to stand trial. If convicted, these dedicated men must appeal until justice is attained.

Pattern of Harassment

SNCC's field representatives are being opposed by white supremecists all over the South. White diehards know that voter registration is the first valid step toward true integration. They realize that as the education of the colored people proceeds, Negroes will learn their Constitutional rights. White supremacy will have lost. Therefore, SNCC's field representatives are fighting continuously against southerners who still won't accept the Fifteenth Amendment.

White extremists retaliate against the field representatives of SNCC by threats, beating, or even throwing them into jail. For example, on February 17, 1962, two staff members of the SNCC were arrested in Baton Rouge, Louisiana and charged with "criminal anarchy." This charge carries a maximum sentence of ten years at Angola State Prison in Louisiana. Bail was set at $7,000 each.

SNCC Chairman Charles McDew and white SNCC Field Secretary, Robert Zellner, a native of Alabama, visited the East Baton Rouge jail in an attempt to see a fellow staff member who was in jail on charges of vagrancy, criminal anarchy, and two counts of disorderly conduct. At the jail McDew and Zellner were arrested and charged with being vagrants, too, though they had over $100 between them. Criminal anarchy charges against them followed shortly thereafter, even though they had only been in town for a total of three hours.

Bail for Dion Diamond was raised to $12,000 and then to $13,000 and he was subsequently placed in solitary confinement. On September 7, John Hardy, an SNCC staff member, accompanied two persons to the registrar's office in Walthall county, Mississippi. The registrar ordered him out, and as he turned to leave struck him aside his head with pistol. John was then arrested in the street by the sheriff for disturbing the peace!

This case was so clearly a violation of civil rights that the Justice Department filed a suit in Federal courts asking for a court order stopping the trial. The fifth circuit court granted the request, and the State of Mississippi has appealed to the Supreme Court of the United States.

Other SNCC staff members have been beaten. Bob Moses, who has a Master's Degree from Harvard, was beaten by a relative of the Sheriff in Amite County, Mississippi. Charles Sherrod, a divinity student, has been threatened by the Ku Klux Klan in Southwestern Georgia and has been intimidated by the Sheriff of Terrell County, Georgia. Cordell Regon and Charles Jones have been arrested by public officials in Albany, Georgia. Dion Diamond had a shotgun blast pass less than a foot over his body as he lay in bed in McComb, Mississippi.

This is the pattern of harassment that SNCC representatives undergo daily. These harassments are so frequent, the SNCC members are used to them. They believe that this pattern will persist until democracy becomes a reality.

SNCC Needs Your Help...Desperately!

Since many obstacles are put in the way of Negro registration by the white registrars in the deep South, the course is difficult. Every contingency must be foreseen and every eventuality prepared for. But the work goes on—quietly and systematically. Those who do learn to vote in turn teach others so that in time all will reach their rightful stature as truly franchised Americans. But SNCC needs money to carry on. The pay of its field representatives is low—only $40 per week for the unmarried men and $60 for the married men. But because of lack of funds, sometimes even these small payrolls have been missed.

Please send whatever you can to further the work of SNCC. Any amount that you can afford will be sincerely appreciated. And every cent of every dollar you send will be used intelligently to radiate the work of educating Negroes into their rights as American citizens.

$800 *will cover the total cost of a voting school for one month in a typical Southern town.*

$100 *will purchase stamps for 2,500 informative letters to students across the country who work under coordinated SNCC efforts.*

$ 60 *will pay subsistence wages for one week for one married field representative.*

$ 40 *will pay subsistence wages for one week for one unmarried field representative.*

$ 5 *will aid in purchase of much needed office supplies.*

Any amount will be of assistance in our fight.

Please Send In Your Contribution Now!

The entire cost of printing this letter has been defrayed by a friend. Won't you please help also?

Send a check, money order, or cash for whatever you can afford. We gratefully welcome any contribution that will help us carry on this work. Please fill in your name and address if you wish to be kept informed of the Student Non-violent Coordinating Committee's activities.

STUDENT NON-VIOLENT COORDINATING COMMITTEE
135 Auburn Avenue N. E., Atlanta 3, Georgia

Gentlemen:

I am happy to send you a contribution of $__________ to help SNCC in the South.

NAME ____________________

ADDRESS ____________________

CITY ____________________

ZONE __________ STATE __________

I'm Gonna Sit at the Welcome Table

Adaptation of traditional song by members of SNCC

"When I first came to Nashville, I learned that there was only one movie theatre in that city, the capital of Tennessee, to which Negroes could go without having to enter through a back door or an alley entrance and climbing up to the ceiling or the balcony. I noticed that the lives of the Negro students in Nashville were, for the most part, spent on campus . . . simply because there was no place to go. They didn't have the right to sit at a lunch counter or do anything else any other citizen of Nashville could do. I couldn't believe that the children of my classmates would have to be born into a society where they had to believe that they were inferior."

— Diane Nash

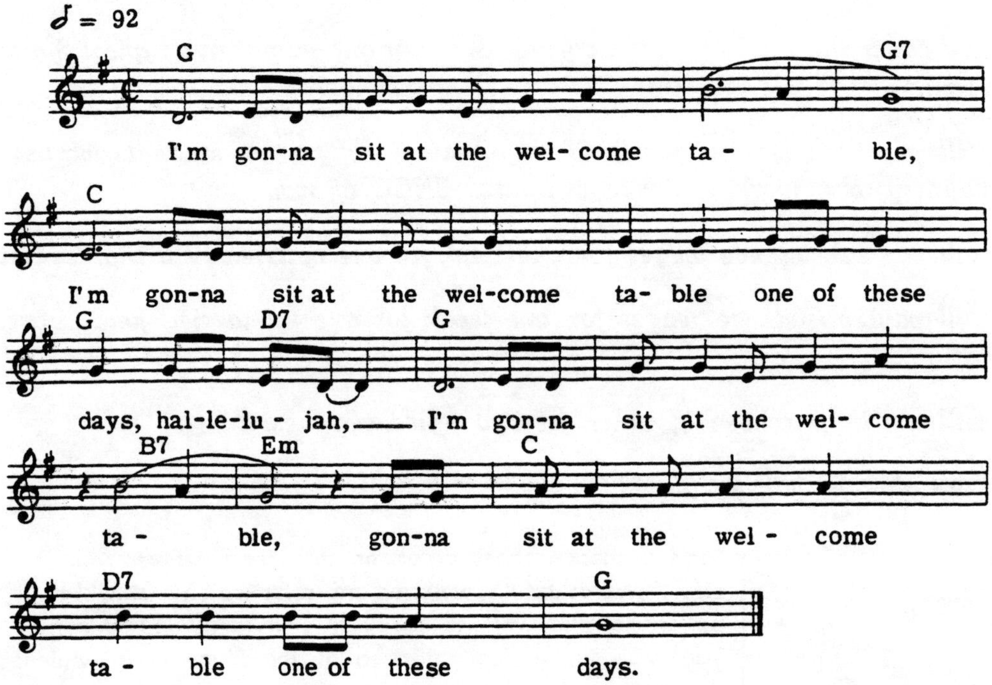

I'm gonna walk the streets of glory,
I'm gonna walk the streets of glory
one of these days, hallelujah,
I'm gonna walk the streets of glory,
I'm gonna walk the streets of glory
one of these days.

I'm gonna tell God how you treat me...

I'm gonna get my civil rights ...

I'm gonna sit at Woolworth's lunch
counter ...

UNIT 8

ATLANTA: PROTEST TO POLITICS

	INTRODUCTION	436
8-1 •	A SECOND LOOK THE NEGRO CITIZEN IN ATLANTA	437
8-2 •	AN APPEAL FOR HUMAN RIGHTS	447
8-3 •	ATLANTA STUDENT MOVEMENT	448
8-4 •	TABLE OF ORGANIZATION: ATLANTA STUDENT MOVEMENT FROM FEBRUARY 4TH TO THE PRESENT	450
8-5 •	STUDENT-ADULT LIAISON COMMITTEE	453
8-6 •	"STUDENT MOVEMENT AND YOU," #1, #5, #6, AND "FREEDOM AND YOU"	455
8-7 •	CHRISTMAS BOYCOTT CALLED!	462
8-8 •	3,000 MARCH IN ATLANTA	464
8-9 •	"OPEN CITY" DRIVE BEGINS	467
8-10 •	JAILS FILL AS PROTESTS RISE	468
8-11 •	IN STRUGGLE: SNCC AND THE BLACK AWAKENING OF THE 1960S *Clayborne Carson*	470
8-12 •	BOND ATTEMPTS TO HEAR VOICE OF PEOPLE	473
8-13 •	BOND CAMPAIGN LITERATURE	475
8-14 •	GEORGIA'S NEW ERA THE YOUNG POLITICIANS	478
8-15 •	THE JULIAN BOND CAMPAIGN	481
8-16 •	BOND/MARTIN LUTHER KING MARCH	483
8-17 •	THE BOND CASE: ITS MEANING TO AMERICA	484

INTRODUCTION

Unit 8 covers the transition from protest to politics in SNCC and Atlanta, Georgia. The unit is divided into three sections: the establishment in 1960 of the Atlanta student sit-in organization, Atlanta's protests, and Julian Bond's first campaign for the Georgia House of Representatives in 1965.

The first document is a pamphlet—*A Second Look at Atlanta*—produced by a group of young Atlanta black professionals, detailing the inadequacies of black life in the "city too busy to hate." "An Appeal for Human Rights" (8-2) is the first public declaration of the Atlanta sit-in organization, drawn largely from *A Second Look*. Both documents strongly imply criticism of established black leadership and the conduct of race relations in Atlanta.

Documents 8-3, 8-4, and 8-5 show the development of the Atlanta student movement from sit-ins to campaigns for black employment; the evolving organizational structure reveals how adults tried to influence the movement's strategy and tactics (pay careful attention to how the organizational charts keeps changing). "The Student Movement and You" leaflets (8-6) reveal the movement's propaganda efforts and its attempts to build community support and to counter opposition.

Documents 8-7 through 8-10—pages from SNCC's newsletter, *Student Voice*—pick up the Atlanta story in 1963 and 1964 where the movement is on-going, even as the Southwide protest movement widened and intensified and national attention was focused elsewhere.

Documents 8-11 through 8-17 are Julian Bond campaign literature, a SNCC memo, and a *Southern Patriot* article that place the Bond Campaign and his expulsion from the legislature in a movement context. SNCC's skill at community organization eases the group into urban politics where the organization's radicalism challenges and threatens Georgia's political culture.

UNIT 8-1

A SECOND LOOK
THE NEGRO CITIZEN IN ATLANTA

FOREWORD

Most Atlantans take pride in their city—whether because of its dogwoods, maypoles and graceful homes, or out of appreciation for the music of its cash registers and the giant shovels and bulldozers making way for the latest skyscraper, expressway or subdivision. Nothing in the pages that follow is intended to deny the obvious fact that Atlanta is a dynamic and generally forward-looking city—potentially a great city.

But for a city, as for an individual, nothing can be more harmful in the long run than complacency and self-delusion. As Atlantans committed to doing whatever they can to help their city realize her fullest potential, the members of the Atlanta Committee for Cooperative Action have chosen this means of asking their fellow citizens to take a second look at Atlanta: specifically, to take a long, hard, honest look at some problems which will not simply go away if we wink at them or ignore them long enough.

Most of these problems keenly and directly affect the Negro citizens of Atlanta, but by the same token they threaten the civic health of the entire Atlanta community. Whether we look at them in cold dollar and cents terms, in terms of social progress, or in terms of basic Christian justice, they are inescapable reminders that Atlanta will become a truly great American metropolis only as it increasingly makes the fullest and wisest use of all its human resources.

We are not interested merely in fault-finding, nor in propagandizing others to think as we do. But we hope that our fellow Atlantans will read and ponder the contents of the pages that follow. It does not matter so much that all of us will not see a given situation in precisely the same way. It may matter a great deal that enough of us should at least take the trouble to look.

THE ATLANTA COMMITTEE FOR COOPERATIVE ACTION
January 1960

EDUCATION: CITY OF ATLANTA

If education is one of the major sources of the strengths that make men free, then what American city has a higher potential for freedom than metropolitan Atlanta—with a dozen colleges and institutions of higher learning, over 180 elementary schools, over 30 high schools, two vocational schools, two special schools, four night schools? Education—the kind, the amount, its availability—affects every Negro citizen in the Atlanta area. For it has bearing not only on the problems of literacy, but on employment, justice and law enforcement, housing and health as well.

- Despite repeated queries, there are no ROTC units in Negro high schools.
- Students in Negro schools have been known to attend classes for weeks without being able to secure the textbooks required for their courses; meanwhile, the practice continues of supplying Negro students with used or out-dated texts discarded by Atlanta's white students.
- Double sessions continue in about half of the Negro public schools, and many Negro children travel ten miles a day to reach a school that will admit them.
- The following are among the fields of advanced training available locally only to white students: Medicine, Dentistry, Law, Nursing, Architecture, Aeronautical Engineering, Civil Engineering, Electrical Engineering, Industrial Management, Mechanical Engineering, and Textile Engineering.
- Without the added expense and inconvenience of leaving the city, white Atlantans may study for many advanced degrees which are not offered locally to Negroes, Among these are the Ph.D. and B.B.A.
- Though free cultural exchange is so basic to our civilization that Russia and the United States have met on this common ground, there is disturbingly little mutually helpful exchange between the educational communities of white and Negro Atlanta.
- It is a fact that, as the Atlanta Chamber of Commerce states: "There are more institutions of higher learning for Negroes in Atlanta than in any other city in the world."

  These, too, are facts:

  . . . Atlanta is the southeastern capital of commerce, industry, the arts and professions;

  . . . Over 3,300 of the nation's leading business concerns have thriving branches in Atlanta;

  . . . Some 55 departments and agencies of the U. S. Government are located here.

  Yet it remains a fact that most of the graduates of our Negro institutions of higher learning must leave Atlanta if they hope to find positions on a par with their qualifications.
- While teaching as a job market for Negroes in this region has reached the saturation point, hundreds of able young Negroes continue to enroll in teacher-training programs because of the rigid racial barriers blocking careers in other fields.
- Meanwhile, it is still nearly impossible for Negro youth to secure first-class modern vocational training in the city of Atlanta. The vocational program of Carver Vocational School is suffering because a rising high school population has made necessary the use of Carver's facilities for academic curricula; the city's white vocational school (Smith-Hughes) remains what it was intended to be—a vocational school.

- And finally, enlightened Atlantans look in vain for the kind of responsible leadership which did so much to solve educational problems with a minimum of friction and lost motion in Louisville, Nashville, St. Louis, and Washington.

Education: State of Georgia

The Negro citizen of Atlanta may sometimes allow himself to forget momentarily that he is also a citizen of the State of Georgia. Such forgetfulness is a luxury he can ill afford, especially as it relates to the all-important issue of education. The three exhibits which follow provide their own graphic commentary.

Exhibit C: Research

As stated in one university catalogue, "A university serves the three-fold purpose of the expansion, the preservation, and the dissemination of knowledge, and the graduate school is the division of the university organization that is most intimately concerned with the first of these three functions. Creative scholarship, largely in the form of research in the humanities, the social sciences, the natural sciences and the several fields of their application, constitutes the central endeavor around which graduate work must be developed."

1958 Expenditures for Research in the University of Georgia System

Research Expenditures at Institutions for Whites	$6,147,782.66
Research Expenditures at Institutions for Negroes	13,097.24

Health

The health of one-third of a city's population is important not only to the people who make up that one-third, but to the remaining two-thirds as well. There may be disagreement as to the causes of the often poor health conditions of Atlanta's Negro citizens. No one, we believe, would deny that the situation is a concern of the whole city.

- Death rate for white Atlantans, 8.3 per 1,000; death rate for Negro Atlantans, 11.7 per 1,000.
- Atlanta's 14 general hospitals and 9 related institutions provide some 4,000 available beds (exclusive of VA and Army facilities). Except for some 430 beds at Grady Hospital, Negroes are limited to the 250 beds in three private Negro hospitals. Some of the hospitals barring Negroes were built with federal funds.
- There are 2,500 graduate nurses in Atlanta; only 157 are Negro. There is no post-graduate training program available for Negro nurses in Atlanta.
- The Fulton County Medical Society has some 900 members; racial restrictions bar all of Atlanta's 38 Negro physicians from membership—a situation not duplicated in some Southern cities which make fewer claims to "progressiveness."

- A surgical training program for Negro physicians has been instituted at the Hughes Spaulding Pavilion, but at Grady Memorial Hospital Negro doctors are still denied visiting staff privileges.
- Records list 328 white medical technologists in Atlanta. with 75 of them in training; there are currently three Negro medical technologists in Atlanta. No training program for technologists in Atlanta hospitals is open to Negroes.

EXHIBIT A: EDUCATION IN THE STATE OF GEORGIA

Higher Education: University of Georgia System.

The University of Georgia Is Controlled by a Twenty (20) Member Board of Regents. Number Whites on Board of Regents (20). Number Negroes on Board of Regents (0).

Education and General Expenditures
Fiscal Year 1958

Institutions for White Youths Only	*Total Expenditures*
University of Georgia	$14,390,448.77
Georgia Institute of Technology	7,956,175.51
Georgia State College of Business Administration	1,889,710.90
Medical College of Georgia	
(Eugene Talmadge Memorial Hospital)	5,261,327.32
Plus Other Small Colleges	2,134,394.68
Total White Only Senior Units	$31,632,057.18
Institutions for Negro Students	*Total Expenditures*
Albany State College	$450,564.81
Fort Valley State College	822,763.89
Savannah State College	727,798.36
No Medical School Counterpart	—0—
(Regents paid $22,500 to Meharry Medical	
College for Georgia Negro Students)	
Total Negro Senior Units	$2,001,127.06
Junior Colleges for White Youth	
Georgia Southwestern College	$183,996.34
Middle Georgia College	189,911.54
South Georgia College	198,035.49
Abraham Baldwin Agricultural College	247,995.96
Total White Junior College Units	$819,939.33
Junior Colleges for Negro Youths	
NONE	
Total Negro Junior College Units	—0—

Total of $34,453,123.57 Spent for All Senior and Junior Units, White and Negro.
94% of the Amount Was Spent for White Youths.
6% Was Spent for Negro Youths.

Exhibit B: Area Trade Schools of the State

Expenditures For Fiscal Year 1958

Area Trade Schools for White
North Georgia Trade $314,198.03
South Georgia Trade.................................... 228,307.86

Total Amount Spent for White $542,505.89

Area Trade Schools for Negroes

NONE

—0— *

* Under the Trade Division Program at Savannah State College, $45,718.31 is listed as paid for Personal Services.

Housing

By now it is fairly well established that housing for Negroes in Atlanta is better in many respects than will be found in many northern communities. Certain facts, however, would suggest that this state of affairs is more nearly an indictment of the rest of the country than a vindication of Atlanta's policies and practices in regard to housing for its Negro citizens.

- The bulk of the Negro population in Atlanta is still:
  ... locked into the more undesirable and overcrowded areas of the city;
  ... paying a proportionally higher percentage of income for rental and purchase of generally lower quality property;
  ... blocked and hamstrung in its effort to secure better housing by political maneuvers and direct or indirect racial restrictions.
- The Metropolitan Planning Commission's report of April 2, 1959, shows that the non-white population, which constitutes 35.7 percent of Atlanta's total population, is occupying only 16.4 percent of the "total developed residential land."
- The 221 program to provide low-cost housing has been crippled by new zoning restrictions approved by the Board of Aldermen which rezoned large tracts of land which might have been used for minority group occupancy.
- 70% of the dwelling units occupied by whites in Atlanta are owner-occupied; only 29% of the non-white dwelling units are owner-occupied.
- In the renter-occupied category, over 80% of the white dwellings have both private toilet and bath and hot running water; only 45% of the non-white renters enjoy these same facilities.
- As indicated by the Greater Atlanta Council on Human Relations in its report of March, 1959:

  > "Racial segregation is much more complete in new housing developments than in established neighborhoods. Public housing developments have extended and strengthened patterns of segregation in some localities." (A case in point is the Joel Chandler Harris Homes in southwest Atlanta.)

- Only two Negroes are employed in the regional Federal Housing Administration, in segregated offices; only two Negroes are employed in the regional Public Housing Administration—in segregated offices. To date, no Negroes are employed in the regional Urban Renewal Administration.

EMPLOYMENT

In a modern city such as Atlanta, any group which is economically handicapped is strait-jacketed as it attempts to achieve its full potential in education, in health, and in creative citizenship. Every third man in Atlanta's million is a Negro—though it would be difficult for a visitor to believe this if he surveyed the offices, the labs, the mechanized production lines, and the counters from behind which the goods which help make Atlanta's wealth are sold. Often a porter—seldom if ever a production assistant; often a handler of bundles or crates—seldom if ever a driver; a taxpayer supporting his city, his county, his state, his country—but seldom on their payrolls above the janitorial rank—the Atlanta Negro as a job—holder is indeed a "marginal" man.

- Policies and practices of governmental agencies, private employers, and labor unions in Atlanta are reflected in such white-to-Negro employment ratios as these: social welfare and recreational workers, 9 to 1; bookkeepers, 200 to 1; electricians, more than 20 to 1; overall professional, technical and kindred workers, 13 to 1.
- In addition to locally owned and operated concerns, over 3,300 of the country's leading business organizations have business in Atlanta for manufacturing, warehousing, and distributing. Many of these provide on-the-job training. Again, the prevailing pattern is to adopt discriminatory employment patterns and to exclude Negroes partially or wholly from the training programs.
- The following are but a few of the 55 Atlanta-based federal offices and agencies employing over 18,000 people, whose clerical and white-collar staffs either contain no Negroes or provide token employment *related to "advisory" or "consultant" positions*: Department of Health, Education and Welfare; Housing and Home Finance Agency; Department of Labor; Veterans Administration; National Labor Relations Board; Small Business Administration; Department of Agriculture; Civil Service Commission.
- As thousands of Negro householders pay their light, gas, electricity, and water bills they find little comfort in the fact that there are no Negro meter readers, technicians, or white collar workers employed by Atlanta's public utilities agencies.
- Although Negroes provide a sizable proportion of the dollar income which sparks the growth and expansion of Atlanta's department stores, food chains, factories, etc., the typical employment pattern is one of little or no adequate job opportunities for the graduates of Atlanta's Negro high schools and colleges.

JUSTICE AND LAW ENFORCEMENT

The chairman of Atlanta's Citizens' Crime Committee indicated recently the interrelationship between housing, economics, and Atlanta's crime and delinquency rate. The Committee also noted the influence on crime rates of family life, supervised recreation, guidance, and the attitude-forming roles of the church and the community. These findings of the Citizens' Crime Committee should be remembered in considering the following facts:

- Atlanta's Police Department has done much to merit its present reputation as ranking well above most Southern police forces in its treatment of Negro citizens. However, during the past year several Negro organizations and individuals publicly expressed their view that the Perry Homes incident represented a serious blight on the record of the police Department and the other agencies of justice involved.
- Of 803 members of the Atlanta Police Department, only 31 are Negroes. (Figure excludes 36 school-crossing policewomen.)
- Of 76 detectives, four are Negroes.
- To date no Negroes are included among the 29 sergeants, 27 lieutenants, 14 captains, four superintendents, and five regular-duty policewomen.
- Only six of 19 Juvenile Court Probation officers are Negroes. There are no Negro adult Probation Officers.
- Though it is standard procedure in many modern police departments, no program providing basic training in race relations has been instituted by the Atlanta Police Department.
- There are no Negro attorneys employed by the City of Atlanta—nor has there been any move to consider appointment of a Negro magistrate in any court. There are 26 attorneys on the Fulton County Solicitor General's staff and only one is Negro.
- Though official statistics have not been compiled, qualified observers have commented on the survival of the old "double standard" of justice for Negroes and whites in the local (non-Federal) courts. Judge Luther Alverson and others have specifically called attention to the tendency of juries to deal lightly with crimes of violence in which all the parties involved are Negroes. Negro leaders, meanwhile, continue to note instances of uneven justice in cases in which the accused is white and the injured party Negro.

TRANSPORTATION

As with many modern cities, Atlanta's transportation problems are basically traffic problems which—particularly at the rush hour —affect everybody in about the same way. To Atlanta's credit is the fact that desegregation of public transportation has proceeded without undue incident. Perhaps it is not too much to hope that progress may now be made in related areas.

- Studies by a committee of the Georgia State Senate and others have shown that, in dollars and cents, the highest income-producing lines for the Atlanta Transit Company are Numbers 3 (Irwin-West Hunter), 5 (Decatur Street-Magnolia), 24 (McDaniel Street), and 13 (West Fair). These lines are used mostly by Negroes and help to support the less-lucrative lines. To date the Atlanta Transit Company has shown no disposition to hire Negro operators even on those lines which serve predominantly Negro neighborhoods.
- Over 100,000 air passengers fly in and out of Atlanta each month, and according to plan, this number will continue to rise sharply as Atlanta moves toward becoming a truly international airport. It is ironic to compare this projected future with present

anachronistic policies, by which skin color determines restaurant service, taxi-rides into town, and the use of rest-room facilities.

- While there is a degree of compliance with the Supreme Court decisions outlawing segregation in interstate travel, Negro passengers seeking train reservations out of Atlanta still report assignment to special cars and special spaces when they can be identified as Negro. Though there are exceptions, local railroad employees continue to share with certain transit operators and police officers a marked tendency to be abrupt, rude, and offensive in their dealings with Negroes. Atlanta's dual taxicab system, which blights any illusions about Atlanta held by the dark-skinned visitor who gets off at Peachtree (Brookwood) Station by mistake, is outmoded, by the standards of some of our smallest and most "backward" Southern communities—where Negro and white drivers compete freely in providing service to passengers without regard to race.

RECREATION

A gentleman who has labored long and hard for improvement in the recreational facilities available to Atlanta's Negroes recently summarized the situation in these words: "Better than it was; worse than it ought to be." Parents, teachers, and citizens concerned with crime and juvenile delinquency rates in our community understandably feel that the situation is a whole lot worse than it ought to be. The public golf courses are open. Negroes who wish to read for pleasure may now enter Atlanta's Main Library without being ushered out onto the street again. But Negro Atlantans can't help smiling wryly when the Chamber of Commerce says: "Atlantans and their visitors have amusement facilities in abundance."

What does the City of Atlanta actually provide?

- 42 major parks for white Atlantans; three for Negroes.
- 92 small parkways for whites; none for Negroes.
- 20 football fields for whites; none for Negroes.
- 16 recreation centers for whites; three for Negroes.
- 12 swimming pools for whites; three for Negroes.
- 22 baseball diamonds for whites; three for Negroes.
- 119 tennis courts for whites; no more than eight for Negroes.
- Not only are some of the facilities listed above for Negroes substandard, but the tensions and frustrations brought on by overcrowding tend to convert some of these recreation centers into potential trouble spots.
- Though some of the programs and activities for whites sponsored or co-sponsored by the City are duplicated for Negroes, there are others for which no parallel program or activity for Negroes exists.
- Except for the necessarily-limited fare provided by the modest budgets of the local Negro educational institutions, Negro Atlantans who are interested in first-run movies, opera, concerts, live theater, and the dance are either excluded altogether or restricted to participation on a segregated basis.
- Except for the YMCA and YWCA, only a few agencies in the Negro community have been able to provide facilities and personnel for supervised recreation and guidance on a continuing basis; the Citizens' Crime Committee has said that such guidance is an important deterrent to juvenile delinquency and crime.

POLICY-MAKING

Long before the American colonists made a burning issue of it, men had come to realize that those who are not represented when policies are being made run the risk of having their needs and problems minimized or ignored. As a modem metropolis, Atlanta depends on certain elected officials, boards, committees, authorities, and agencies to make the basic decisions for its citizenry. Whenever one of these top-level groups sits down around a table in Atlanta to discuss or make plans, the odds are overwhelming that some 300,000 Negro Atlantans simply are not represented at all.

- There are no Negroes on the 16-member Atlanta Board of Aldermen.
- There are no Negroes on such boards and committees as the Library Board, the Recreation Board, and the Public Welfare Board (whose clientele is 70% Negro).
- Two Negroes are members of the 16-member City Executive Committee which oversees city elections; two Negroes are on the 96-member Fulton County Democratic Executive Committee. These members have nothing to do with voter registration, are elected from a predominantly Negro ward, and, as Negroes, are barred from official membership in the Democratic party of Georgia.
- There is one Negro serving on Atlanta's nine-member Board of Education, but the top official role in public health filled by a Negro is that of the physician employed (part-time) as one of the "Principal Staff Members" of the Fulton County Health Department.
- Positions held by Negroes in the Republican Party of Georgia include the following: Vice-chairman of the State Central Committee; Secretary of the State Central Committee; Assistant Secretary of the State Central Committee; 33 memberships on the 132-member State Central Committee; seven County chairmen. Corresponding representation by Negroes in the official councils of the Democratic Party of Georgia: none.
- The "freeze-out" of Negroes at the level of influence and decision in municipal, state, and federal agencies is compounded by the strictly segregated pattern in such private or voluntary groups as the Atlanta Chamber of Commerce, the Atlanta Real Estate Board, the Fulton County Medical Society, and the executive bodies of the Georgia Educational Association and most of the larger trade unions.

The publication of this booklet was made possible, in part, through the kindness of the Atlanta Life Insurance Company. The company has in excess of one thousand life insurance sales representatives serving families and communities in Georgia, Alabama, Florida, Tennessee, Texas, Kentucky, Kansas, Missouri, Ohio, Michigan and Illinois.

The Atlanta Life Insurance Company believes it to be the American way to air all sides of vital public issues confronting our time. However, the responsibility for the information, views and opinions expressed in this booklet rests solely with the ATLANTA COMMITTEE FOR COOPERATIVE ACTION.

A FINAL WORD

The Atlanta Committee for Cooperative Action is an organization of young business and professional men who share a concern for the future of the city in which they and their children live, a belief that all Atlantans have a right to a full citizen's role in that future, and a desire to work earnestly and patiently with individuals and groups willing to plan and act unselfishly toward just, reasonable, and clearly defined objectives in bringing that future to pass.

When you or your group has read this booklet we should appreciate having your candid reaction.

The Atlanta Committee for Cooperative Action—
Box 9055, Atlanta

J. T. Bickers
Clarence D. Coleman
James Hayley
Jesse Hill, Jr.
M.Carl Holman
Leroy R. Johnson, Atty.
L. H. Pitts
M. T. Puryear
Herman Russell
Albert Saddler
Clinton Warner, M.D.
Samuel Z. Westerfield
Q. V. Williamson
Whitney Young
(John G. Gloster and Mozell Hill were members of the Committee until they moved from the city.)

AN APPEAL FOR HUMAN RIGHTS

We, the students of the six affiliated institutions forming the Atlanta University Center — Clark, Morehouse, Morris Brown, and Spelman Colleges, Atlanta University, and the Interdenominational Theological Center—have joined our hearts, minds, and bodies in the cause of gaining those rights which are inherently ours as members of the human race and as citizens of these United States.

We pledge our unqualified support to those students in this nation who have recently been engaged in the significant movement to secure certain long-awaited rights and privileges. This protest, like the bus boycott in Montgomery, has shocked many people throughout the world. Why? Because they had not quite realized the unanimity of spirit and purpose which motivates the thinking and action of the great majority of the Negro people. The students who instigate and participate in these sit-down protests are dissatisfied, not only with the existing conditions, but with the snail-like speed at which they are being ameliorated. Every normal human being wants to walk the earth with dignity and abhors any and all proscriptions placed upon him because of race or color. In essence, this is the meaning of the sit-down protests that are sweeping this nation today.

We do not intend to wait placidly for those rights which are already legally and morally ours to be meted out to us one at a time. Today's youth will not sit by submissively, while being denied all of the rights, privileges, and joys of life. We want to state clearly and unequivocally that we cannot tolerate, in a nation professing democracy and among people professing Christianity, the discriminatory conditions under which the Negro is living today in Atlanta, Georgia—supposedly one of the most progressive cities in the South.

Among the inequalities and injustices in Atlanta and in Georgia against which we protest, the following are outstanding examples:

(1) Education:

In the Public School System, facilities for Negroes and whites are separate and unequal. Double sessions continue in about half of the Negro Public Schools, and many Negro children travel ten miles a day in order to reach a school that will admit them.
On the university level, the state will pay a Negro to attend a school out of state rather than admit him to the University of Georgia, Georgia Tech, the Georgia Medical School, and other tax-supported public institutions.

According to a recent publication, in the fiscal year 1958 a total of $31,632,057.18 was spent in the State institutions of higher education for white only. In the Negro State Colleges only $2,001,177.06 was spent.
The publicly supported institutions of higher education are inter-racial now, except that they deny admission to Negro Americans.

(2) Jobs:

Negroes are denied employment in the majority of city, state, and federal governmental jobs, except in the most menial capacities.

(3) Housing:

While Negroes constitute 32% of the population of Atlanta, they are forced to live within 16% of the area of the city.

Statistics also show that the bulk of the Negro population is still:

a. locked into the more undesirable and overcrowded areas of the city;

b. paying a proportionally higher percentage of income for rental and purchase of generally lower quality property;

c. blocked by political and direct or indirect racial restrictions in its efforts to secure better housing.

(4) Voting:

Contrary to statements made in Congress recently by several Southern Senators, we know that in many counties in Georgia and other southern states, Negro college graduates are declared unqualified to vote and are not permitted to register.

(5) Hospitals:

Compared with facilities for other people in Atlanta and Georgia, those for Negroes are unequal and totally inadequate.

Reports show that Atlanta's 14 general hospitals and 9 related institutions provide some 4,000 beds. Except for some 430 beds at Grady Hospital, Negroes are limited to the 250 beds in three private Negro hospitals. Some of the hospitals barring Negroes were built with federal funds.

(6) Movies, Concerts, Restaurants:

Negroes are barred from most downtown movies and segregated in the rest.
Negroes must even sit in a segregated section of the Municipal Auditorium.
If a Negro is hungry, his hunger must wait until he comes to a "colored" restaurant, and even his thirst must await its quenching at a "colored" water fountain.

(7) Law Enforcement:

There are grave inequalities in the area of law enforcement. Too often, Negroes are maltreated by officers, of the law. An insufficient number of Negroes is employed in the law-enforcing agencies. They are seldom, if ever promoted. Of 830 policemen in Atlanta only 35 are Negroes.

We have briefly mentioned only a few situations in which we are discriminated against. We have understated rather than overstated the problems. These social evils are seriously plaguing Georgia, the South, the nation, and the world.

We hold that:

(1) The practice of racial segregation is not in keeping with the ideals of Democracy and Christianity.
(2) Racial segregation is robbing not only the segregated but the segregator of his human dignity. Furthermore, the propagation of racial prejudice is unfair to the generations yet unborn.
(3) In times of war, the Negro has fought and died for his country; yet he still has not been accorded first-class citizenship.
(4) In spite of the fact that the Negro pays his share of taxes, he does not enjoy participation in city, county and state government at the level where laws are enacted.
(5) The social, economic, and political progress of Georgia is retarded by segregation and prejudices.
(6) America is fast losing the respect of other nations by the poor example which she sets in the area of race relations.

It is unfortunate that the Negro is being forced to fight, in any way, for what is due him and is freely accorded other Americans. It is unfortunate that even today some people should hold to the erroneous idea of racial superiority, despite the fact that the world is fast moving toward an integrated humanity.

The time has come for the people of Atlanta and Georgia to take a good look at what is really happening in this country, and to stop believing those who tell us that everything is fine and equal, and that the Negro is happy and satisfied.

It is to be regretted that there are those who still refuse to recognize the over-riding supremacy of the Federal Law.

Our churches which are ordained by God and claim to be the houses of all people, foster segregation of the races to the point of making Sunday the most segregated day of the week.

We, the students of the Atlanta University Center, are driven by past and present events to assert our feelings to the citizens of Atlanta and to the world.

We, therefore, call upon all people in authority—State, County, and City officials; all leaders in civic life—ministers, teachers, and business men; and all people of good will to assert themselves and abolish these injustices. We must say in all candor that we plan to use every legal and non-violent means at our disposal to secure full citizenship rights as members of this great Democracy of ours.

Willie Mays
President of Dormitory Council For the Students of Atlanta University

Don Clarke
President of Student Body For the Students of Morehouse College

James Felder
President of Student Government Association For the Students of Clark College

Mary Ann Smith
Secretary of Student Government Association For the Students of Morris Brown College

Marion D. Bennett
President of Student Association For the Students of Interdenominational Theological Center

Roslyn Pope
President of Student Government Association For the Students of Spelman College

UNIT 8-3

ATLANTA STUDENT MOVEMENT

Following the demonstrations in other southern cities and as a result of the widespread unrest among the student bodies of the various institutions forming the Atlanta University Center, a meeting of student leaders was called in an attempt to organize and coordinate the many groups then existing on the several campuses.

It was the opinion of many persons attending that initial meeting that a "statement of purpose and intent" would definitely be in order to express our support of the student movement, our dissatisfaction with the existing scheme of affairs in the nation, the South, and Atlanta, and to state we intend "to use every legal and non-violent means at our disposal to secure full citizenship rights as members of this great Democracy of ours." This document, composed entirely by students, was read to and approved by all of the 4,000 students in the Atlanta University Center, signed by the presidents of the various student bodies and published in the three daily papers as a full page advertisement under the title, "An Appeal for Human Rights."

The "Appeal" first appeared on March 9. Since that time it has been entered into the *Congressional Record* and published in the *Nation*. Copies were sent to all the Georgia legislators, both state and national, and all persons whom we considered to be in positions of influence.

On March 15, 200 students from the Atlanta University Center schools and the Blayton School of Accounting entered nine cafeterias located in down-town Atlanta in public, tax-supported buildings. As a result of this request for service, 77 students were arrested. One of these students, a minor, has been banished from the state of Georgia for a year. The remaining 76 have been released from jail on bails of $300 and $600. Since this action, the signers of the "Appeal" have also been indicted and charged with conspiracy. If convicted, these students face six years on the public works, three years in the county jail, and/or $6,000 fines.

Although the request for service was spontaneous in origin and application, a committee was formed on March 26 to serve as a steering council for future student action. This committee, composed of three representatives from each of the Atlanta University Center schools and representatives from the Blayton School of Accounting, Georgia Tech., Agnes Scott, Emory, and Oglethorpe Universities, is called Committee on the Appeal for Human Rights.

Georgia College Student News and Views, June 1, 1960.

The reaction of the various student bodies to the "Appeal" might well be described as overwhelming. The presidents of the institutions pledged their full support and individual faculty members have done the same.

Governor Vandiver declared that the "Appeal" was a "left-wing statement, calculated to breed dissatisfaction (not) prepared in any Georgia school or college . . . anti-American." Mayor Hartsfield of Atlanta had this to say about the "Appeal": "(It) performs the constructive service of letting the white community know what others are thinking . . . the legitimate aspiration of young people throughout the nation . . . "

Reaction from the white community was sparse but gratifying, Many letters of an encouraging nature have been received. A group of Atlanta ministers, the signers of the "Atlanta Ministers Manifesto" supported the "Appeal." Students from the eleven Atlanta institutions of higher learning, Agnes Scott, Clark, Morehouse, Morris Brown, Spelman, and Georgia State Colleges, Atlanta, Emory, and Oglethorpe Universities, The Georgia Institute of Technology and the Interdenominational Theological Center signed a statement reaffirming the "Appeal."

The student committee has held meetings with Atlanta ministers, members of the Chamber of Commerce and the Association of Retail Merchants, Mayor Hartsfield and Chief of Police Jenkins. Members of the committee attended conferences in Raleigh, North Carolina and Washington D.C. dealing directly with the student movement, and have spoken at Emory University, Georgia State College, Agnes Scott College and Oglethorpe University.

It is regrettable that no commercial establishment officially changed its discriminatory policies. Integrated groups have been granted service at a few "white" establishments.

The committee has been conducting a selective buying campaign aimed primarily at the A&P food chain. After being refused any sort of negotiations, picketing was begun and is being continued with much success.

For the future, the committee's plans revolve upon continuing and initiating such action as will end all discrimination and secure full human rights for all citizens.

UNIT 8-4

TABLE OF ORGANIZATION: ATLANTA STUDENT MOVEMENT

FROM FEBRUARY 4TH TO PRESENT

PHASE 1: FEBRUARY 4 TO MARCH 16, 1960

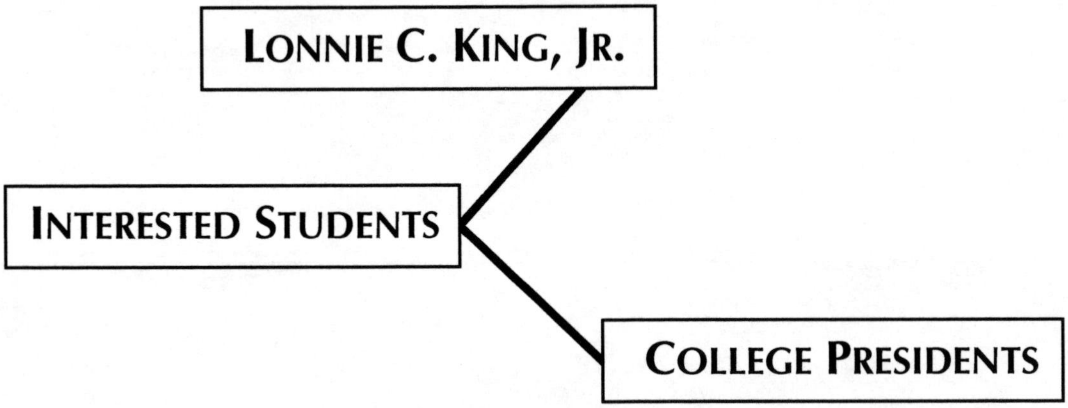

Meeting at Yates & Milton Drug Store #2 and M'house Campus.

PHASE 2: MARCH 16 TO MAY 30, 1960

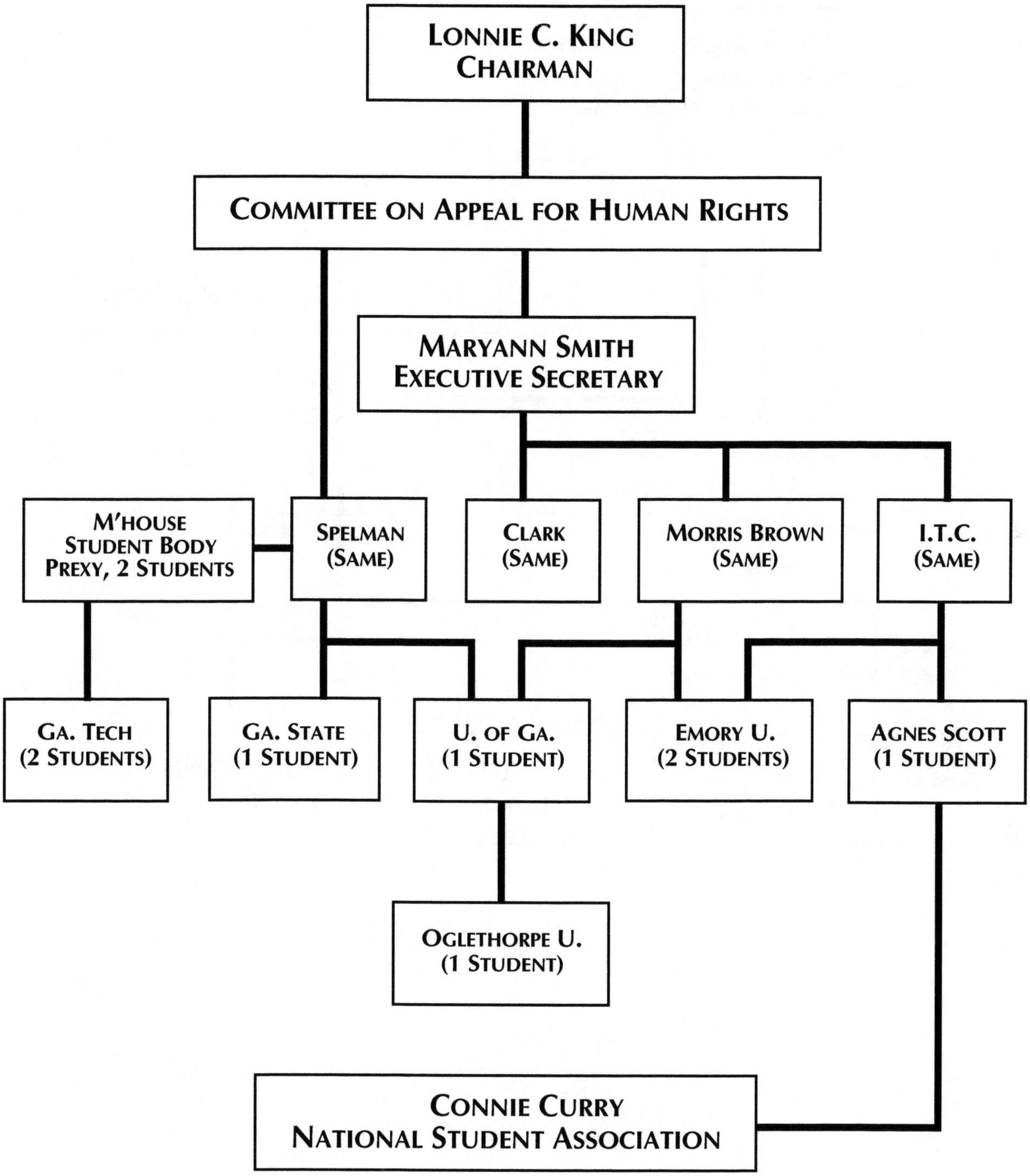

Meeting at Atlanta University until white students join at which time President Clement refuses to allow the group to meet on A.U. property. Meeting at Morehouse.

PHASE 3: MAY 30 TO SEPTEMBER 20

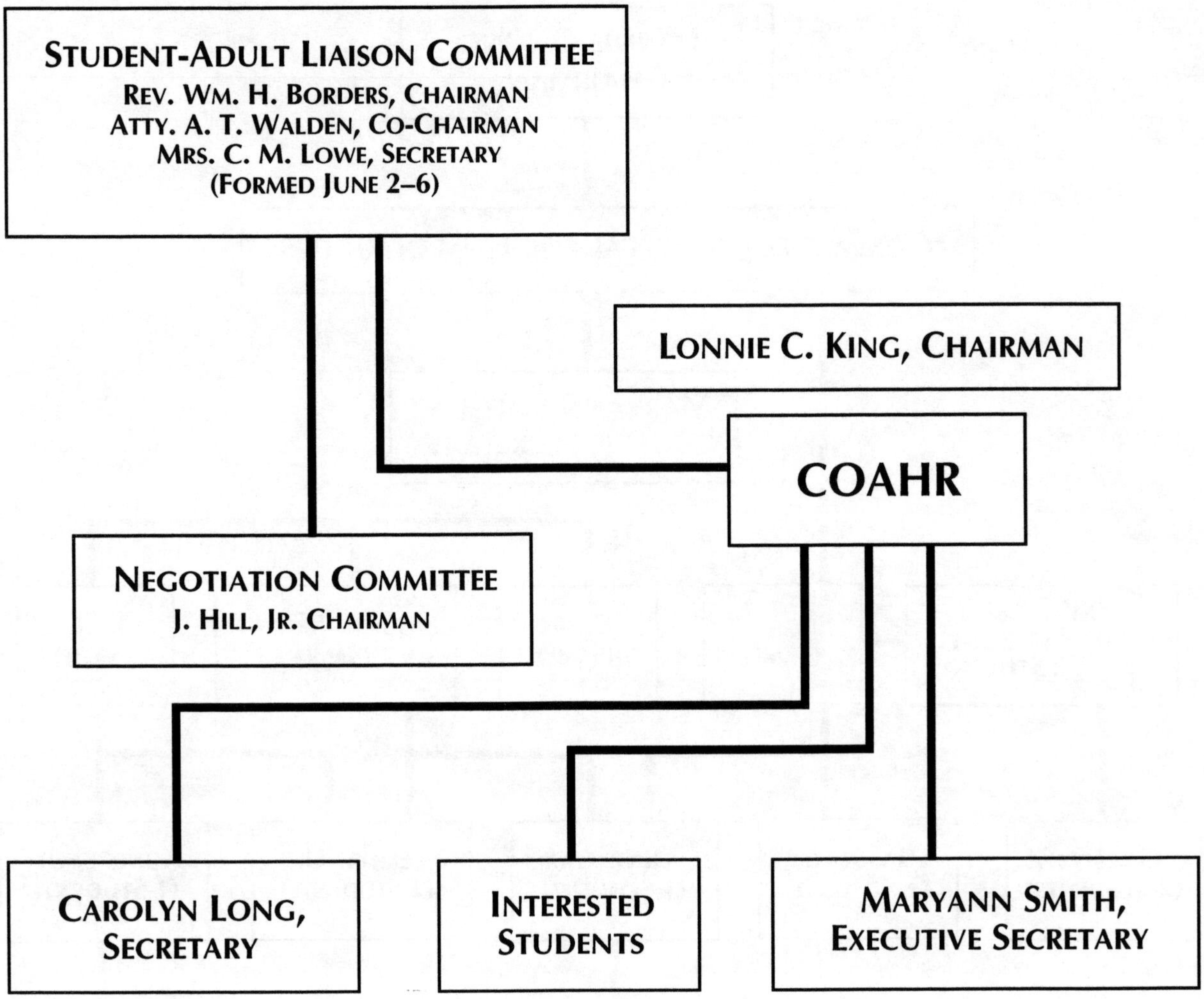

Meeting in NAACP office and Southeastern Fidelity Building.

UNIT 8-5

STUDENT-ADULT LIAISON COMMITTEE

ATLANTA STUDENT MOVEMENT

Following an earlier forum called by the citizens of Comm. on Employment & Economic Opportunity at which representatives of the Student Movement and the adult community were present it was decided that the students might profit from the assistance and support of some organized representative group of adults. On May 26, 1960, Rev. Wm. Holmes Borders, at the request of the students, convened a meeting of students and adults at Wheat St. Baptist Church. On June 2 an organizational meeting was held, with a cross section of the community present. An organizational statement was drawn up, officers were nominated—Rev. Borders was chosen as Chairman, Atty. A. T. Walden, Co–Chairman and Mrs. Charlie Mae Lowe as Secretary.

Organization was completed by June 6 and the group sponsored advertisements in the *World*, the *Journal* and the *Constitution*, announcing adult support of the student government (scheduled to appear Sunday, May 29 in the *World*, Monday May 30 in the two white papers.)

Weekly meetings followed, except for a period toward the end of the summer. Labor meetings occurred on the call of the Chairman. A Negotiations Committee, headed by Jesse Hill, Jr. was added as a subcommittee; other subcommittees on Picketing, Eunice Cooper; Publicity, M. C. Holman, etc., were added. strategy Committee has been headed by Co-Chairmen Jesse Hill, Jr. and Q. V. Williamson.

Within the past two months the subcommittee designated as the Negotiations–Strategy Committee has been headed by Co-Chairmen Jesse Hill, Jr. and Q. V. Williamson.

The statement issued in June by the Secretary follows:

ORGANIZATIONAL STATEMENT— ATLANTA STUDENT-ADULT LIASON COMMITTEE

We, as adult citizens and organizational leaders of the Atlanta community, have come together for the following purposes:

1. To Establish a medium for advising and counseling with students who are seeking to obtain basic justice and human rights through non-violent means.
2. To interpret, recommend or refer to other community organizations, as well as, the community at large, phases of the student movement and program.
3. To carry on this liaison only as long as it is deemed necessary and advisable, with the understanding that we will take such steps as will be required to carry out the objectives outlined above.

* * *

In order to pursue these objectives through city-wide leadership, each affiliated organization may have at least three representatives in this body, with one a member of the steering committee, which shall have the authority to select its own chairmen and appoint sub-committees. Officers, including a chairman, vice-chairmen, secretary, assistant secretary, treasurer and parliamentarian, shall also be members of the steering committee, all of whom are responsible to this parent body.

It is expected that the city-wide organization shall meet at least once each month and the steering committee as often as necessary. Either group may, at its discretion, arrange conferences with student loaders for the purpose of discussion, counseling or interpretation, in regard to mutual problems and programs.

Adopted this second day of June, 1960.

Atlanta Student-Adult Liaison Committee
(Rev.) Wm. Holmes Borders, Chairman
(Mrs.) Charlie Mae Lowe, Secretary

The following officers were elected:

Chairman	Rev. Wm. Holmes Borders
Vice-Chairmen	Rev. T. P. Grissum
	Mr. C. V. Williamson
	Mrs. Johnnie Yancoy
	Mr. M. Carl Holman
Secretary	Mrs. Charlie Mac Lowe
Assistant Secretary	Mr. J. H. Calhoun
Treasurer	Mrs. Nina K. Miller
Parliamentarian	Rev. J. A. Middleton

These officers, plus one representative from each affiliated organization, will form the steering committee.

THE STUDENT MOVEMENT AND YOU

Except for a few publicized events, THE COMMUNITY HAS NOT KNOWN WHAT THE MOVEMENT IS DOING. This is because the white newspapers, radio stations and television stations do not want to help the movement in any way, and because our only Negro newspaper for some reason has not thought IT WORTHWHILE to give coverage to the movement.

The result is that YOU have no way of knowing what is going on unless you know some of the students whom you can ask about it.

The STUDENTS NEED YOU. This is a good way that we can let you know what is going on. We hope that this handbill proves to be a good way to get in touch with you.

The students (and some housewives, too) have been picketing two A & P stores, one at Edgewood and Bell, and one at Boulevard and Forrest. They have been picketing these stores which receive most of their money from Negroes yet refuse to hire Negro managers, cashiers, food checkers, and butchers. All the decent jobs in these stores are for white only, while our boys and girls who graduate from high schools must take jobs as porters, janitors, curb boys and sackers. They cannot make a decent salary.

Negroes should not buy in any A & P Stores until the management respects the money of Negroes as much as they do the money of whites.

The picketing students (and the housewives) have caused these two A & P Stores to lose most of their business. If they do not change their unfair practices, they will have to close those stores. But they think that if they wait a little while longer, the students will stop picketing and Negroes will start buying again and they continue giving all good jobs to whites and the poor-paying jobs to Negroes.

BUT WE WILL NOT STOP

The students will keep picketing, and if you STOP BUYING from all A & P Stores, they will have to meet our requests if they want our money. The students have taken on another big job - RICH'S DEPARTMENT STORE. BECAUSE OF THIS, WE NEED YOU. DON'T BUY IN RICH'S. As you know students were refused service in Rich's Thursday, June 23. Rich's gets most of the money spent by Negroes downtown, but they won't let Negroes eat in their cafeterias and lunch counters (except for the one in the SUB-BASEMENT) and they don't hire Negro salesmen and saleswomen.

Since Rich's is a leader in this city, other stores have to follow their example.

They are "nicer" to Negroes than some other stores because they want

---

Student Movement and You, March 1960.

THE STUDENT MOVEMENT AND YOU (CON'T) 2.

our money. They will change as much as they have to because they don't want to lose our money.

We ask you -- stop buying in Rich's, keep on paying your bills there, but don't buy anything new.

If only one-half of the Negroes stop buying in Rich's, the store will lose millions of dollars. No business can afford that. MONEY IS POWER.

It will take almost ONE THOUSAND PEOPLE A WEEK TO PICKET RICH'S. The students can not keep a picket line at Rich's during the summer, as most of them are out of town or working to make money for school next year. But we can all stop buying at Rich's. Several of the students must wear old shoes, trousers, dresses, and shirts because their parents have accounts only at Rich's. Let's all wear our old clothes for dignity.

Look for a Mass Meeting with the Committee On Appeal for Human Rights SOON in the Northwest Area.

PASS THIS ON TO A FRIEND

REMARKS AND SUGGESTIONS MAY BE SENT TO: Atlanta Student Movement
236 Auburn Avenue, N. E.
Atlanta, Georgia

THE STUDENT MOVEMENT AND YOU

Vol. 1, # 5

STRENGTH IN UNITY! Negroes in other Southern cities have brought an end to segregation in services and employment, by working together. The boycott has proved to be the Negro's most effective weapon in the struggle for immediate recognition of his rights.

SUCCESS IN NASHVILLE

Nashville, Tenn. ----------------- Desegregation of downtown lunch counters and the hiring of Negro white collar workers in Nashville was brought about through a Negro boycott of the downtown area.

STUDENTS STAGE SIT-INS

Demands for the end of discrimination began with sit-in demonstrations staged by Negro students from colleges here. The student's requests for service at segregated lunch counters led to massive arrests of the demonstrators. Owners and managers of the stores involved in the sit-ins met the student's charges regarding the immorality of segregation by denying leadership responsibility. One spokesman for the merchants described the nature of their business as such that it was "most impractical for a small group of stores to assume the role of leading such a social change." "This is a student affair," the merchants said, "led and organized by outsiders. Our customers are not student types."

DON'T SHOP AT RICHS

NEGROES BOYCOTT DOWNTOWN

Nashville Negroes countered by boycotting all stores in the downtown shopping area, including those without lunch counters. The boycott was maintained for nearly seven weeks at about 98% effeciency, according to merchant's estimates. The boycott was kept alive and strong within the Negro community through "maximum use" of the telephone, ac-

(continued in second column)

cording to one Negro spokesman. Mass meetings and churches also helped, this source reports. "We would ask for all those present who had not spent any money downtown since the beginning of the boycott to stand up. In most cases, the entire audience or congregation would rise."

The Reverend Kelly Miller Smith, chairman of the Christian Leadership Council stated, "Our ground for the boycott is simply that it is morally indefensible for Negroes to cooperate with a system we consider evil and which we are trying to change."

DOWNTOWN SUFFERS

Nashville's businessmen began to discover what a Negro boycott meant. Customers from within a distance of 75 miles of Nashville were staying away because of the sit-ins. The absence of Negro customers meant the loss of up to 15 or more percent of business for most stores. Transit company volume fell off sharply, along with newspaper advertising and downtown parking. Finally, a large number of whites joined the Negroes in their boycott. Merchants were alarmed. They appealed to the city's white leadership and to the Chamber of Commerce. "But they didn't do a - - - - thing," said one merchant, "even though they knew we were having the economic - - - being beat out of the downtown area." Said another merchant, "We had to change whether we wanted to or not."

MERCHANTS REQUEST NEGOTIATIONS

When it became clear that there was no other way out, Nashville's bus-

(continued on other side)

Student Movement and You, July 1960.

iness men requested negotiations with Negro student and adult leaders. The businessmen asked that the Negro leaders be "truly representative" of the Negro community's thinking, and not just Negroes of prestige. Negotiations began after some informal sessions, during which merchants stated that they were agreed "to cooperate with the inevitable." It was found that the white community was not so opposed to desegregation as the merchants had at first believed. And, as one merchant expressed it, "we discovered the deep feelings of the Negro men and women who live and work here. This wasn't just a student thing."

NEGRO DEMANDS MET

A plan for desegregation was drawn up making use of the police department, sympathetic news coverage and church groups from the white community. At 3:15 PM on Tuesday, May 10, 1960, small groups of Negroes calmly walked up to the lunch counters in six downtown stores and sat down to an historical afternoon snack.

PEACE, PROSPERITY RETURN TO NASHVILLE

Since that time, cases against 63 of the students involved in the original sit-ins have been retired and it is reliably reported that the remaining cases will be disposed of in a similar fashion. Another result of the sit-ins has been the hiring of Negroes as white collar workers in some downtown stores. Businessmen report that merchandise sales are booming. Merchants admit to having been wrong in predicting dire consequences to integration. "It has all ended, " said one, "with the pleasing sound of cash registers ringing up sales."

The Nashville story is simple. It is the story of Negro determination and Negro unity ..... WHEN WILL THE ATLANTA STORY BE WRITTEN?????????????????

WHY FEED JIM CROW?

DON'T SHOP AT A&P

PANEL DISCUSSION: The Student Movement and You
July 24, 1960
7:30 PM
Zion Hill Baptist Church
McDaniel and Georgia Avenue

RADIO PROGRAM: What You Should Know
July 24, 1960
3:05 PM
WERD

All clubs and individuals who wish to help by picketing, typing or making telephone calls are urged to contact us at: Room 105
197½ Auburn Avenue, N. E.
Atlanta, Georgia
Jackson 4 0314

When you have read your handbill, please hand it on to a neighbor or friend!

Issued by: COMMITTEE ON APPEAL DOR HUMAN RIGHTS

THE STUDENT MOVEMENT AND YOU

Vol. 1, # 6

SEGREGATION HURTS!

DEPARTMENT STORE SALES RISE!
An article in the Atlanta Journal-Constitution of Sunday, July 24, reported that department store sales in central Atlanta showed a 22% drop for the week ended July 16 as compared with a year ago. A report issued by the Federal Reserve Bank of Atlanta disclosed the Atlanta department store slump, despite a general rise in sales for other cities in the southeast. The decrease in sales caused by a Negro boycott of Rich's Inc., largest department store in the southeast, was felt by some to have been the chief reason for sales lags in the Atlanta area.

BOYCOTT BRINGS INTEGRATION
Negro demonstrations and boycotts brought desegregation of lunch counters to three more southern cities this week. Integration of lunch counters in Norfolk, Portsmouth and Greensboro raised the total number of southern cities where desegregation of eating facilities has taken place since February to 30. According to one store official in Norfolk, a Negro boycott could have meant the loss of 40% of business.

*** *** *** *** *** ***

DON'T SHOP AT RICH'S

It is difficult to understand how certain brides and brides-to-be can thoughtlessly force their friends into positions of having to choose between loyalty to them and loyalty to the Negro's struggle. Yet, this is exactly the situation which is created when silverware is registered at Rich's and when gowns and gifts are ordered from Rich's

*** *** *** *** *** *** *** ***

1. Are you completely against all forms of segregation?
2. Are those whom you consider your leaders against all forms of segregation?
3. How much will you sacrifice to end segregation?

*** *** *** *** *** *** *** ***

CLOSE YOUR ACCOUNT WITH SEGREGATION !!

Student Movement and You, August 1960.

FREEDOM AND YOU

CALLING ALL ATLANTANS!!! CALLING ALL ATLANTANS!!!

On Monday March 6, 1961 an agreement was signed by Negro leaders which stated in part that complete lunch-counter desegregation of most of the downtown stores would come no later than a specified date in the early fall. This agreement was and is not contingent on the DESEGREGATION OF THE PUBLIC SCHOOLS!!!

A part of the agreement asked that Negroes call off the boycott "as soon as possible." We feel that "as soon as possible" is only when those COUNTERS HAVE BEEN OPENED TO ALL PERSONS WITHOUT REGARD TO COLOR AND NOT BEFORE.

DON'T

SHOP

DOWN

TOWN

Student Movement and You, March 1961.

We are not preaching hatred and violence. The students started the movement on the principle of non-violence and replacing hate with love. No thinking Negro can afford to even entertain the idea of violence. Our strength lies in our ability to suffer creatively. Remember, it is not our aim to put the merchants out of business but to put justice in business. We have stayed out of town this long so let's all stay out a little while longer. Easter is coming and we must not let the merchants get all of our money and not accord us the same privileges that all customers enjoy.

SPECIAL EDITION

THE STUDENT VOICE

Vol. 4, No. 6 The Student Nonviolent Coordinating Committee, 6 Raymond St., N.W. Atlanta, Ga. 30314 November 21, 1963

XMAS BOYCOTT CALLED

STUDENTS PROTEST JOB DISCRIMINATION AT RICH'S

RICH'S SAYS NO TO JOB DEMANDS

Page 2 November 2., 1963 STUDENT VOIC:

'Don't Buy At Rich's,' Say Civil Rights Groups

ATLANTA, GEORGIA - Operation Breadbasket, the Committee on Appeal for Human Rights, and the Student Nonviolent Coordinating Committee united today in a massive downtown march to obtain more jobs for Negroes at Rich's.

The leaders of the three groups called for a Christmas boycott until a settlement is reached.

COAHR leaders and leading Negroes here - who formed a community-wide "Summit Leadership Conference" several weeks ago - have been trying to get Rich's and other stores here to upgrade Negro employees and hire additional Negro workers in higher paying positions.

"Last year, Rich's agreed to hire 12 Negroes and only hired 6", COAHR Chairman Larry Fox said. "This year they proposed hiring 41 Negro saleswomen by Christmas and up to 100 others by June 1, 1964. When they were asked to put this agreement in writing, they rudely refused," Fox said.

The student leader said that only 6 of 740 sales people at the store are Negroes.

Fox asked all Atlanta citizens interested in participating in further protests and in the selective buying campaign to call the COAHR office at 524-0207. The office is located in Rush Congregational Church.

Student leaders here said they requested written copies of the agreement because of broken promises made by Atlanta businessmen several times in the past.

In the spring of 1961, 77 Atlanta stores agreed to integrate their lunch counters and to upgrade Negroes. The counters now serve all comers, but Negroes still hold only menial jobs in most stores.

Last summer, 50 private restaurants agreed to integrate after continued protests from COAHR-led demonstrations. Most "re-segregated" however, as have some hotels that formerly agreed to integrate.

Although Atlanta has made some progress toward integration, several other Southern cities have moved ahead of Georgia's capital.

Both Knoxville and Nashville, Tennessee are now considered "open cities" after continued student protests there.

Other Southern cities such as Houston, Texas and Greensboro, N. C., have moved far ahead of Atlanta in offering jobs and public and private facilities to all their citizens.

James Forman, SNCC Executive Secretary who participated in today's march, said Rich's refusal to hire Negroes is "a deliberate slap in the face of every Negro who ever spent a dollar there."

COAHR leaders have called on the Atlanta community to "support equal opportunity by joining the selective buying campaign." They have also asked for volunteers for office work and picketing to report to the COAHR office daily. Fox said that COAHR leaders hope to arrange picketing schedules so that no student would miss classes, and also made a plea for adult support, both financial and on the picket line. He said cars were needed badly.

Fox said students from each of the 6 Negro schools here, in addition to Turner, Washington, Howard and Archer high schools, Emory University and Georgia Tech participated in the massive march.

Ministers from "Operation Breadbasket" and representatives from other groups also participated.

Student leaders said the march was "the beginning of an all-out drive to make Atlanta a truly integrated city."

ATLANTA, GA., Nov. 21 --- Four hundred singing and clapping students marched here at Rich's Department Store for more than an hour today to kick off a Christmas boycott.

The students, mostly from the Atlanta University Center, high schools and some from Emory University and Georgia Tech, (predominantly white colleges here) carried signs and distributed leaflets calling for equal job rights.

The march was led by the Rev. Ralph Abernathy, Secretary-Treasurer of the Southern Christian Leadership Conference, and Larry Fox, head of the Atlanta University Committee on Appeal for Human Rights.

Police Captain R. E. Little told leaders twice that unless marchers spaced themselves 15 feet apart, "I'm gonna start cleaning up." There were no arrests although marchers did not strictly adhere to the order.

The marchers carried signs reading "6 out of 740 - Equal Job Rights?" and "Does Rich's Condone Segregation?"

They chanted "Don't Buy at Rich's," "We Want Jobs," and "We Want Freedom Now," and sang "We Shall Overcome."

Leaflets urging the selective buying campaign were given out to bystanders and were thrust to riders in passing buses and cars by the students.

The march, which took place at the rush hour, drew attention from motorists and pedestrians, as well as Rich's employees who watched from the store windows.

The Rev. Ralph Abernathy addressed the marchers at Morehouse College where the demonstration originated. He told them that Atlanta's image as a progressive city did not measure up to the facts.

HOW YOU CAN HELP

If you want to see Atlanta's Negroes get better jobs, you can help by:

giving your time as a volunteer worker to the Committee On Appeal For Human Rights; asking your friends and neighbors to respect the selective buying campaign; helping COAHR with transportation and expenses; remember: "don't pay to be segregated!"

High School Students

The battle will continue for Jobs and Civil Rights. You can help!

1. Join the picket lines.
2. Speak to your friends.
3. Come to the office.

Contact Larry Fox at the COAHR office at Rush Memorial Church on Chestnut.

THE STUDENT VOICE

VOL. 4, NO 8. The Student Voice, Inc. 6 Raymond Street, N.W., Atlanta 14, Ga. DECEMBER 16, 1963

Negro Testifies Later Arrested

WINONA, MISSISSIPPI — A young Negro who told a federal jury last week that policemen "paid" him a pint and a half of corn whiskey to beat two civil rights workers was arrested in nearby Kilmachael for an offense supposedly committed while he was behind bars.

23-year-old Roosevelt Knox was one of two Negroes who were prisoners in the Winona jail when five Negro civil rights workers were beaten by police. Knox and another prisoner testified they had been ordered to assist in two beatings.

Knox's parents told SNCC workers in Greenwood the youth was charged with passing a bad check during the period he was held in the Winona jail.

His trial on the bad check charge, scheduled for December 10, was not held when charges against him were dropped.

CONTINUED ON PAGE 4

3000 MARCH IN ATLANTA

Marchers Brave Cold In Atlanta Demonstration

ATLANTA, GA., Dec. 15 — More than 3,000 Atlantans, Negro and white, braved below freezing weather today to hear speakers from a variety of groups declare that some action must be taken soon to implement an integration plan presented by this city's Summit Leadership Conference.

Each speaker echoed the same theme: Atlanta, once a showcase city for the South and a model of "smooth" race relations, is lagging behind other Southern cities and even other Georgia cities.

While some encouraged a continuation of negotiations carried on by the Summit group, others called for direct action if Negro demands are not met soon.

James Forman, Executive Secretary of SNCC, told the crowd that overflowed Atlanta's Hurt Park here: "No one leader, no group of leaders can get your rights. You have to get them for yourselves."

Forman said, "We have two powerful weapons, the dollar and the vote."

The SNCC leader reminded the crowd of the up-coming presidential race in 1964. He called for consideration of an Easter Boycott here, and for a possible school boycott aimed at eliminating segregation and triple sessions in Negro schools. He called for a program to ease slum conditions in Negro neighborhoods, telling Atlanta Vice-Mayor Sam Massell, representing the city on the speakers' platform, "people are swimming in Buttermilk Bottom" (a slum section of the city.)

Martin Luther King, Jr., featured speaker at the junior March on Washington demonstration, told the audience "time is run-

CONTINUED ON PAGE 2

DEMONSTRATIONS BEGIN

FIVE ARRESTED IN DANVILLE

Danville Demonstration-Summer, 1963

DANVILLE, VA., Dec. 15 — Anti-segregation protests resumed in this Southside Virginia city as five students were arrested at a Howard Johnson's restaurant December 10.

Sit-ins at Howard Johnson's, other restaurants and movie theaters are being conducted by students, most of them from Danville, as part of a drive to open the public facilities of this city.

A 22-year-old white SNCC worker from Chapel Hill, N.C., J.V. Henry, reported that hot ammonia had been thrown on the floor of one restaurant where a sit-in took place — Staley's Restaurant — "to get rid of us."

Henry stated that Danville students and SNCC workers were

CONTINUED ON PAGE 4

MISS. RIGHTS GROUPS MEET

JACKSON, MISS., Dec. 15 — Close to 300 representatives of civil rights groups and civic organizations met here today at a state-wide meeting of the Council of Federated Organizations (COFO.)

The meeting was called to discuss the organizational structure of COFO, and to plan the direction of civil rights activities in Mississippi for the coming year.

COFO is a federation of representatives from voting leagues and NAACP chapters, and staff members from the Student Nonviolent Coordinating Committee, Southern Christian Leadership Conference and Congress of Racial Equality, who are working in Mississippi.

One item of business was the adoption of by-laws, in which the purpose of COFO is outlined as working for "total democracy, racial equality and economic justice" in Mississippi.

"The program of COFO consists of voter registration and citizenship education projects, political action — both mock and official, the implementation of government programs and general civil rights work," according to the newly amended by-laws.

"Mock" political action refers to the recent Freedom Ballot Campaign in which Aaron Henry, President of COFO, ran for governor and polled 85,000 Freedom Ballots from officially disenfranchised Negroes.

Robert Moses, Director of SNCC's Mississippi vote drive since July 1961, was re-elected Project Director for COFO. CORE staff member Dave Dennis was elected Assistant Project Director.

"SNCC's wholehearted participation in COFO is part of our South-wide ONE MAN — ONE VOTE campaign aimed at breaking down all barriers to Negro voter registration except residence and age," stated John Lewis, Chairman of SNCC.

THE STUDENT VOICE

Published Once A Week
On Mondays at Atlanta,
Fulton County, Georgia.

BY STUDENT VOICE, INC.
8 1/2 Raymond Street, N.W.
Atlanta, Georgia 30314

ATLANTA

CONTINUED FROM PAGE 1

ning out for Atlanta."

The SCLC head said, "If our words fail to move them (the power structure) then our actions must show them."

Other speakers were Larry Fox, Chairman of the Committee on Appeal For Human Rights; Dr. C.M. Smith, for the Atlanta NAACP; Rev. Ralph D. Abernathy, for Operation Breadbasket; and the Rev. William Holmes Borders.

Two members of the National States Rights party, attired in Nazi storm trooper uniforms, picketed the gathering with signs reading: "Negro, your future is not here but in Africa."

The theme of the meeting was that Atlanta, despite its image as a city "too busy to hate," is still as segregated as many deep South towns.

Public schools are integrated tokenly; only lunch counters and a few restaurants downtown admit all comers. All movie theatres are integrated, as are the colleges in the area. But Atlanta Negroes are still shunted into slums and ghettoes in the city.

Today's "Pilgrimage for Democracy" was the first demonstration held here since President Kennedy's assassination.

The day before the large march, 275 Atlanta area clergymen — Protestant and Jewish, Negro and white — signed a petition supporting the aims of the Pilgrimage.

Leaders of the Summit Conference reported to the crowd on the progress of negotiations to implement their plan for total integration of Atlanta.

The Atlanta Summit Leadership Conference is composed of representatives from 10 civil rights organizations and representatives from "at least 75" other community groups, according to Summit Co-chairman Attorney A.T. Walden.

The group called a city-wide conference on October 19, 1963, where over 300 people, from a cross-section of Atlanta life, discussed and recommended action in the following areas: public accomodations, employment, education, registration and voting, health and social services, housing, political issues and law enforcement.

Since then, members of the group's steering committee have

CONTINUED ON PAGE 3

They Came......

They Heard.....

James Forman Say "You Must Get Your Rights Yourself"

Henry Suit Appealed

Dr. Aaron Henry

CLARKSDALE, MISS., - Dec. 3, A libel suit filed against Aaron Henry, recent gubernatorial candidate on the Mississippi Freedom Ballot, was appealed to the United States Supreme Court.

The defamation suit, filed by the Chief of Police and the District Attorney, resulted from a press conference following Henry's conviction on a morals charge in 1962.

Henry, state president of the NAACP, was convicted in Justice of Peace Court, in Shelby, Miss. on March 15, 1962 on charges of making perverse advances on a white teen-ager hitchhiker. Henry stated that the charges were a complete fabrication, and presented an alibi supported by sworn witnesses.

When Henry later stated in a press conference that the prosecutor and the police chief, who figured in the trial, had conspired to frame him, Henry was sued by them for defamation.

The Mississippi State Supreme Court upheld the libel suit in a December 2 ruling, and awarded $15,000 to the police thereby reversing an earlier decision.

Has No Authority Says Justice Dept.

ATLANTA, GEORGIA - A spokesman for the Department of Justice has told a California senator the government "has no authority" to intercede in the case of a 67-year-old white minister held in jail here since August 28.

The senator, Thomas Kuchel (R-Cal.), forwarded the letter to the SNCC office here.

The letter was written by Burke Marshall, Assistant Attorney General.

The elderly minister, the Reverend Ashton Bryant Jones, a native Georgian now residing in San Gabriel, California, is being held under $20,000 bail on charges growing out of a protest demonstration at an all-white church here this summer.

Since Jones' conviction is being appealed, his time behind bars is "dead time" and does not count against his sentence.

Protest March

CONTINUED FROM PAGE 2

met with city, county, state and private groups in an attempt to negotiate increased integration here.

Cooperating groups include SCLC, NAACP, SNCC, Operation Breadbasket, the Committee on Appeal For Human Rights, the Gandhi Youth Society, the All Citizens Registration Committee and the Atlanta Negro Voters League.

WE SHALL OVERCOME is a new book of "songs of the Southern Freedom Movement." It is available from SNCC, 6 Raymond Street, Atlanta, for $1.95.

BLIND CASHIER NIXES BIAS

TALLAHASSEE, FLA. — The cafeteria of the Florida State Capitol Building was desegregated recently because its cashier is blind.

Several Florida A&M University students, along with SNCC field secretary Sam Shirah, went to the end of the line to pay, the cashier could not see to refuse their money.

This is the first time that a SNCC staff member has worked in Florida. A militant student action group here, which Shirah helped organize, has requested affiliation with SNCC.

"Most people don't realize that northern Florida is as rigidly segregated as Alabama in many places," Shirah stated. The 20 year old SNCC worker, from Atlanta, is a white native of Alabama.

SCEF Case In Federal Court

NEW ORLEANS, LA. — A case challenging the constitutionality of Louisiana's communist control laws was taken under advisement by a three-judge federal court on December 9.

The Southern Conference Educational Fund and its executive director, James A. Dombrowski, original plaintiffs in the case, were joined by attorneys Benjamin E. Smith and Bruce C. Waltzer whose request for intervention was granted by the court.

Smith, who is the Fund's treasurer, and his law partner, Waltzer, were arrested along with Dombrowski on October 4th for allegedly violating the state anti-communist statutes — as managers of a "subversive" organization and for distributing "communist" literature, -- and all SCEF records were seized. Conspiracy charges against the three men were dismissed by a Criminal District Court, but the records were not returned to SCEF.

The plaintiffs are now asking for a temporary injunction against state and city officials preventing them from enforcing the statutes, and prohibiting the Louisiana Joint Legislative Committee on Un-American Activities (LUAC) from turning over the seized SCEF records to the Orleans Parish Grand Jury.

CORE Worker Stricken

ATLANTA, GEORGIA — CORE field secretary Zev Aleony was hospitalized here last weekend with a heart attack.

Aleony was one of the Americus Five held in that Southwest Georgia city for two months on charges of attempting to incite insurrection.

Aleony is 25 years old, and a native of Minneapolis, Minnesota.

"We Shall Overcome," the official recording of the August 28, 1963 March On Washington may be purchased by using the coupon on this page. Money collected from the sale of this record will be used to further civil rights acitvities.

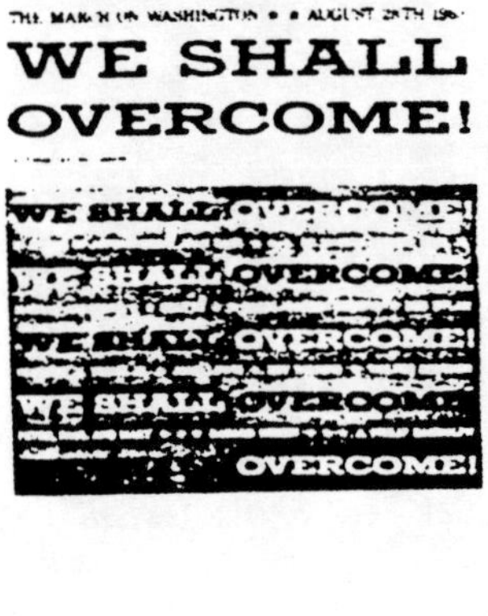

COUNCIL FOR UNITED CIVIL RIGHTS LEADERSHIP
10 East 44th Street
New York 17, New York.

Please send me ______ copies of the authorized recording(s) of the March on Washington at the special Council price. I understand the proceeds from the sale of this record will benefit the civil rights movement throughout the country. I enclose $3.00 for each record ordered.

NAME ______________________

ADDRESS ______________________

CITY ______________ ZONE ______ STATE ______

Please make check or money order payable to Council for Unity.

S.N.C.C. Branch ______________________

KENYA CONGRATULATED

ATLANTA, GEORGIA — The Student Nonviolent Coordinating Committee extended "heartiest congratulations" to Kenya Prime Minister Jomo Kenyatta on the evening that country achieved independence, December 12.

The SNCC cablegram from Chairman John Lewis and Executive Secretary James Forman called Kenya's struggle for independence "an inspiration for all freedom struggles."

STUDENT VOICE January 14, 1964 Page 3

ATLANTA ROUNDUP

'Open City' Drive Begins

ATLANTA, GEORGIA - High school and college students here are beginning an all-out drive to make Atlanta an "open city."

The drive began here two days after the Student Nonviolent Coordinating Committee (SNCC) announced an end to demonstrations at the Dobbs House outlets in Atlanta. SNCC workers and members of the Committee On Appeal for Human Rights (COAHR) with the help of comedian Dick Gregory successfully integrated more than 15 Dobbs and Toddle Houses locally.

The new demonstrations - some led by John Lewis, SNCC Chairman, and Gloria Richardson, Chairman of the Cambridge (Maryland) Nonviolent Action Committee - are aimed at integrating public and private eating places and hotels and securing more jobs for Negroes.

Several local civil rights groups met last Monday night, January 6, to adopt a battle plan for integration of Atlanta. A coalition of Negro groups - the Atlanta Summit Leadership Conference, has attempted to negotiate some integration but several members of the Negro community are dissatisfied with the slow pace.

Schools and busses integrated after Negroes filed suits. Lunch counters opened only after prolonged demonstrations and a boycott of downtown stores. Negroes have picketed some stores to win jobs for Negroes.

Mayor Allen told the city's Board of Aldermen this week he will seek a public accommodations ordinance if "voluntary desegregation" does not occur soon.

DICK GREGORY sits-in at a Toddle House restaurant. Gregory and SNCC workers ended protest here after management agreed to integrate Dobbs House outlets in Atlanta and other Southern cities.

Agreement Reached With Dobbs Houses

ATLANTA, GEORGIA - "A satisfactory agreement" has been reached between the management of Dobbs House, Inc. and the Student Nonviolent Coordinating Committee (SNCC), suspending demonstrations that had closed 12 restaurants in the chain.

Richard Yates, Dobbs House vice president, confirmed that an agreement had been reached.

"We've reached a satisfactory agreement," John Lewis, SNCC Chairman said. Lewis was arrested at a Toddle House restaurant here Sunday, December 22, and spent Christmas in jail with 23 others.

Mrs. Lillian Gregory, 26, wife of comedian Dick Gregory, and two other demonstrators held in jail since Christmas Eve were also released on Thursday, January 2.

Gregory had come to Atlanta

SNCC WORKERS PROTEST Atlanta's false image before the home of Mayor Ivan Allen, Jr. SNCC protest here against Dobbs House sparked a new drive to make Atlanta an "open city."

Lewis, Walker 11 More Jailed

CONTINUED FROM PAGE 1

Summit Leadership Conference - a coalition of national and local civil rights groups here. They had met to consider direct action attempts to integrate public places in Atlanta, but the four hour summit meeting was nearly split on tactics to be followed.

Those arrested Saturday night were: SNCC workers Joyce Barrett and Prathia Hall, SNCC Chairman John Lewis, Rev. Wyatt Tee Walker, Rev. John Morris, state NAACP field secretary Leon Cox, Mrs. Eunice Cooper, Rev. Joseph Boone Dr. Clinton Warner, Harry Boyle, John Gibson and Albert Dunn of SCLC, and Gary Robinson.

All the demonstrators were released on $1000 bail late Saturday night. The girls arrested at the Krystal's sit-in were released also.

Police refused to arrest the Heart of Atlanta demonstrators until a county judge signed warrants for them.

Leaders of the more active groups here planned a Sunday meeting to plot continued protests.

The Holiday Inn sit-in was led by James Forman, SNCC Executive Secretary, who, with his wife, tried to get a room at the segregated hotel. They were refused and with a group of 15 other protestors, remained inside the hotel for several hours.

SNCC worker Judy Richardson, a participant in the Heart of Atlanta sit-in, had to get emergency treatment at a white hospital after being dragged for 50 feet by a hotel employee. The hospital at first refused to treat her, Forman said, but finally gave her emergency treatment. Another SNCC worker was beaten by three hotel employees, and another had a tear gas pistol fired point blank at his face.

The tear gas missed.

Several Krystals here - including the one where the eight girls were arrested - are now closed. One has a sign reading "Closed because of Niggers" on its front door.

On Sunday afternoon, student demonstrators integrated the cafeteria at the Georgia Baptist Hospital.

Others tried unsuccessfully to get into the Heart of Atlanta Motel again. The group finally settled in the segregated Holiday Inn, where they closed down a restaurant.

STUDENTS SUSPENDED FOR DEMONSTRATING

ATLANTA, GEORGIA - At least 79 Negro students have been suspended from high school here after they had participated in two days of anti-segregation protests.

The day of the suspensions, an official at Washington High School told a delegation from the Student Nonviolent Coordinating Committee (SNCC), Committee On Appeal For Human Rights (COAHR), and the Southern

CONTINUED ON PAGE 4

THE STUDENT VOICE

VOL. 5, NO. 3 The Student Voice, Inc. 6 Raymond Street, N.W., Atlanta 14, Ga. JANUARY 27, 1964

CANTON CRACKS DOWN ON RIGHTS ACTIVITY

CANTON, MISS. — Sixteen civil rights workers have been arrested here in a three day period in what appears to be the first sign of a forthcoming crackdown on integration activity in this central Mississippi city.

Between January 22 and 24, 16 workers for the Council of Federated Organizations - a coalition of civil rights organizations in this state - were arrested while either inside or in the vicinity of the community center-voter registration office of COFO.

Among the arrested was Carole Merritt, a 23-year-old worker for SNCC from Cincinnati, Ohio. Miss Merritt was arrested January 24 on a charge of "contributing to the delinquency of a minor" and allegedly causing a juvenile to distribute "leaflets of a libelous nature." Bond was set at $500.

Eight persons were arrested January 23 under a newly-passed

CONTINUED ON PAGE 3

12 Convicted In Greenwood

GREENWOOD, MISSISSIPPI - Forty-five Negroes arrested and convicted here last June after they were smoke bombed from a voter registration meeting face sentencing Monday, January 27.

Twelve were found "guilty as charged" by a jury last week. Attorney Carsie Hall, acting for the group, said the remaining 33 will plead not guilty and will waive their right to a jury trial, since evidence in all cases is the same.

The case has been complicated with Federal litigation.

On December 26, the United States Department of Justice asked a Federal judge to dismiss its appeal of a suit against Leflore County officials.

The Department had been appealing Federal Judge Claude Clayton's denial of a temporary

CONTINUED ON PAGE 4

In Atlanta

JAILS FILL AS PROTESTS RISE

GETTING CARRIED AWAY is SNCC Executive Secretary James Forman, jailed during a Sunday night demonstration at a segregated eating place. Seventy-nine demonstrators arrested Sunday night were released later on their own recognizance.

Eighty-Six Arrested

ATLANTA, GEORGIA - Eighty-six anti-segregation demonstrators were arrested, held on two sets of different charges and under two bonds, and finally released here under their own recognizance on Sunday night.

The 86 were arrested during full day demonstrations at segregated restaurants here.

Among those jailed were comedian Dick Gregory and SNCC Executive Secretary James Forman.

All were originally charged with "disorderly conduct" and "inciting to riot," and bond was set at $1000 each.

Later, the charge was changed to "disorderly conduct" and bail reduced to $15 cash and $50 property.

Still later, all were released on their own recognizance and allowed to sign their own bonds.

SNCC's James Forman, Attorney Donald L. Hollowell and Atlanta Police Chief Herbert Jenkins signed a statement saying all would be released and that SNCC would make "every effort" to comply with Atlanta picketing regulations.

Demonstrators were critical of police handling of the protests. Four girls were hospitalized - two knocked unconscious - after the protests.

Negro demonstrators and robed and hooded (but not masked) members of the Ku Klux Klan met for the second time in downtown Atlanta Saturday night, January 25.

The demonstrators, numbering as many as 500 at some points, had met on the Atlanta University Center campus and marched into the downtown area.

On Friday night, SNCC workers and members of the Committee On Appeal For Human Rights

CONTINUED ON PAGE 3

CANTON ,MISS.

CONTINUED FROM PAGE 1

city ordinance for "distributing leaflets without a permit." The law had been passed by the city council two days prior to the arrests. Bond was set at $800 each - an unusually high bond for that offense.

Other charges included "intimidating an officer," "breach of the peace" and burning trash without a permit."

Two rights workers, Clarence Chinn and James Collier, were charged with "violation of the building code," and were arrested while making repairs on the COFO office. Their bond was set at $350 each.

SNCC workers in Jackson report that simultaneous to the passage of the new city law, two constables and another police cruiser were added to law enforcement agencies in Canton. A bill recently passed by the state legislature will aid cities in making exchange of jail space.

The leaflets, which pressed for continuation of an effective boycott already underway here, asked Negroes to withhold patronage from merchants who address Negro customers as "boy" or "nigger."

SNCC spokesmen have labeled the anti-circular law as "a clear violation of First Amendment rights guaranteed by the Constitution."

WE SHALL OVERCOME is a new book of "songs of the Southern Freedom Movement." It is available from SNCC, 6 Raymond Street, Atlanta, for $1.95.

YOUNG FREEDOM FIGHTERS march away from the White House after picketing there. The group had tried to see President Johnson, and when they failed, sent him a letter saying they want "equal rights today, not tomorrow, not next year, but today!"

NEGRO CHILDREN PICKET WHITE HOUSE

WASHINGTON, D.C. - A group of Negro fifth grade students picketed the White House here January 18 with signs demanding an end to "Rats, Roaches and Rent-robbers."

The group told newsmen they had consulted the Washington SNCC office and asked the SNCC workers to get them an appointment with President Johnson.

The group's leader, 10-year-old Lawrence Dunbar Twyman III, admitted the notice was short, but said, "It seemed to me that although the President is busy with a lot of things, he has a lot of assistants."

Ten-year-old Jackie Scott said, "I'll bet the President is not too busy to see white folks."

Before leaving the White House the fifth graders sang "We Shall Overcome" and "Ain't Gonna Let Nobody Turn Me Round."

RENT STRIKE ORGANIZED

WASHINGTON, D.C. - Tenants at a Girard Street tenement, assisted by SNCC workers, have organized a rent strike against property realtor David E. Barry because of poor conditions in their building.

All seven household heads in the building signed an agreement saying living conditions in the house are "unhealthy and not safe."

"When we paid our rent," the tenants said, "we expected services which the landlord has chosen to deny us. Before we resume payment of rent to the landlord at the present level, this apartment must be made sanitary and safe," the tenants said.

SNCC worker Bill Mahoney said "This is the first in the strides toward freedom of Washington Negroes. As long as slumlords don't supply services and repairs, and as long as they overcharge tenants, the tenants should assert their right not to pay rent."

The rent strike began when the landlord tried to evict a family of six. Fifteen members of the Nonviolent Action Group (NAG), the local SNCC affiliate, entered the apartment and prevented the eviction.

Mahoney said the landlord denied he was delinquent in making repairs, but was struck by water dripping from a ceiling when he left the building.

He collects $600 a month rent from the building.

DEMONSTRATOR FACES KLANSMAN in downtown Atlanta. Over 500 protesters confronted the Klu Klux Klan during the 11 hour demonstration Saturday.

Atlanta

CONTINUED FROM PAGE 1

(COAHR) had demonstrated before the Riviera Motel where members of the United Nations Subcommission of the Prevention of Discrimination and the Protection of Minorities were meeting. The group carried signs reading "Welcome To Atlanta, a Segregated City." Other protesters Friday night staged a four hour sit-in at the Segregated Travel Lodge Motel. There were no arrests.

During Saturday's demonstration, which ended after midnight, the Klan and protesters often picketed a few inches apart.

Two fist fights occurred, one involving Klansmen and police.

The protesters were joined by comedian Dick Gregory who flew into Atlanta from Chicago to join the demonstrations.

A special target of the sit-ins is Leb's Restaurant, where several demonstrators were jailed during last summer's demonstrations.

While marching, the demonstrators chanted "The old KK. she ain't what she used to be" while Klansmen yelled "We want a white Mayor."

THE STUDENT VOICE

Published Once A Week
On Mondays at Atlanta,
Fulton County, Georgia.

BY STUDENT VOICE, INC.
8 1/2 Raymond Street, N.W.
Atlanta , Georgia 30314

UNIT 8-11

IN STRUGGLE: SNCC AND THE BLACK AWAKENING OF THE 1960S

Clayborne Carson

The Lowndes County project was an important aspect of SNCC's transformation, yet so were its efforts to apply in urban black communities the ideas culled from its work in the rural deep South. SNCC was afforded an unexpected opportunity to mobilize a political force of urban blacks when a Supreme Court decision required the reapportionment of Georgia's legislature. This resulted in the creation of a predominantly black district near SNCC's Atlanta headquarters. Ivanhoe Donaldson urged Julian Bond, SNCC's communications director, to run for the new seat in the House of Representatives.

Bond, the son of noted scholar Horace Mann Bond, was an atypical SNCC worker, although he had been associated with SNCC since the founding conference in Raleigh. He had not participated in protest activity since 1960, and his position in the Atlanta headquarters, coupled with the responsibility of providing for a wife and children, had isolated him from SNCC's field operations. Nonetheless, he was greatly respected within the organization for his dedication and intelligence. Donaldson doubtless believed that the slightly-built, softspoken writer-activist was the staff member most likely to attract moderate black support. Although Bond disliked making public appearances, he had long urged SNCC to establish a project in Atlanta and recognized that a political campaign would stimulate SNCC's organizing efforts in the city.

Rather than run as an independent candidate, Bond entered the Democratic primary. But his campaign was a demonstration of SNCC's distinctive approach to electoral politics. Deciding that poor black voters in the district could not be reached through traditional candidates' rallies, Bond emphasized personal contacts. "We would go around to people, knock on their doors, and ask them what they wanted their state representative to do," he recalled. "And it was at first confusing for a great many people, because they had never had a real state representative. . . . We had to try to explain to people what it was that a state representative did, and after we explained it, people began to tell us their problems were largely economic." Based on these conversations, Bond drew up a platform that called for a two dollar minimum wage, improved urban renewal programs, repeal of the right to work law, and an end to the literacy test for voters.[1]

Entry into conventional polities prompted criticism from SNCC workers who objected to working within the Democratic party and believed that SNCC should not "play the political game." Cobb, who became Bond's campaign manager, was told by other SNCC workers that those in the campaign must have "sold out," since many were wearing ironed shirts, ties, and slacks instead of overalls. Defending the campaign workers, Cobb argued that their conformity to this middle-class standard avoided "the irrelevant question of dress" and allowed them to focus on the important issues. Cobb admitted that he "approached the campaign with some misgivings and ambivalence." He seriously questioned whether one could "function effectively in the state legislature without the support of the 'establishment.'" Nonetheless, he defended the campaign as an attempt "to explore American politics and the ways it can be shaped (if it can at all) to meet our needs." He hoped that the campaign could "mesh and hook up with the radical forms of our own (like FDP)." Although a few members objected, a majority of SNCC's Executive Committee agreed to loan Bond the money to pay his qualifying fees and to provide funds to establish a campaign headquarters.[2]

Black residents were enthusiastic about the Bond campaign. Cobb noted that many were impressed by the willingness of Bond to come into their homes and listen to them. "I think that literally 100% of the people I canvassed had never had anyone come to their house, sit down and seriously talk to them about their community." Bond easily won the primary election in May, defeating a black minister, and received eighty-two percent of the vote in the June election, running against a black Republican who was dean of men at Atlanta University.

Unaware of the obstacles that still awaited Bond in his attempt to represent the blacks in his district, the campaign encouraged SNCC workers who were intent on mobilizing blacks to achieve political power. "Imagine, ten SNCC guys in the Georgia House committed to . . . using the seats in the House to meet community needs defined by the community," Cobb wrote. Fascinated with the idea of using traditional political forms on behalf of "people whose needs are not being and probably will not be met by these forms anyway," Cobb concluded that organizing in the urban areas was the same as rural organizing. "What people need—all over!—is something they can grab hold to, to build; that is their own."[3]

Bond's successful campaign encouraged several veteran SNCC workers who had grown up in the cities to launch organizing efforts in other urban communities. Donaldson left the Bond campaign to begin work in Columbus, Ohio; Bill Hall went to Harlem; Marion Barry moved to Washington, D.C. Within a year SNCC had also established footholds in Newark, Philadelphia, Chicago, and Los Angeles.

These urban efforts strained SNCC's capabilities and made the staff painfully aware of their meager resources and lack of long-range programs to confront urban problems. For some staff members, organizing among urban blacks was a way of escaping the responsibilities they had faced in the deep South or, in some northern cities, of abandoning fund-raising obligations. Most of the urban offices floundered during 1965, although Donaldson had some success in helping to establish a "community foundation" in Columbus that made small grants for local projects approved by a democratically-elected community board.

Once they began working in cities, SNCC organizers found that their rural experiences had not prepared them to deal with the problems of urban black residents who were more varied than rural blacks in their class and educational backgrounds, institutional ties, and political experiences. There were no black institutions in cities comparable to the rural black church which served as a cohesive force in the deep South capable of reaching large segments of the black populace. Urban organizers were forced to discover new issues around which to mobilize blacks, since many of the civil rights reforms of the rural

South were available to urban blacks. They found that the poorest urban blacks, who were the focus of their efforts, were more alienated, anti-social, and angrier than their counterparts in the rural South. Lacking the sharply defined target of southern racism, SNCC workers in urban areas began the formidable task of building a social movement among blacks filled with undirected hostility and generalized distrust. They soon realized that their previous victories in the deep South had exaggerated their sense of power to confront the entrenched, resilient institutions responsible for the social problems of urban, industrial society.

ENDNOTES

1. Gwen Gillan interview, July 6, 1967, tape 497, SHSW. See also John Neary, *Julian Bond: Black Rebel* (New York: William Morrow, 1971), pp. 77–79.

2. Charles Cobb, "A Reflective Look," May 7, 1965, mimeograph. Reprinted as "Atlanta: The Bond Campaign," *Studies on the Left* 5 (Spring 1965): 79–82.

3. *Ibid.*, pp. 80, 81, 82.

UNIT 8-12

BOND ATTEMPTS TO HEAR VOICE OF PEOPLE

ATLANTA, Ga.—The successful campaign of a young SNCC worker for the Georgia House of Representatives has begun a new phase of political organizing for SNCC.

The worker, Julian Bond, defeated a Negro Republican 5 to 1 in the General Election called this spring to fill seats in Georgia's newly apportioned House.

"The campaign was a new one for Atlanta for several reasons," Bond said. "For one, we tried to run on issues and not labels, on people's concerns and not their prejudices. Atlanta has never had a house-to-house, block meeting campaign like this one, where people knew the candidate and got a chance to question him."

"The next step," a campaign worker said, "is to put people inside Julian's District in touch with each other, so they can use each other to get things for themselves."

"People don't 'use' politics because they don't know how. They know politicians take money, and some of them steal, and a few of them do things to help people, but people don't know how to 'use' politics to help themselves."

Already, a group living in substandard housing have [sic] begun to talk about rent strikers here.

"But more important," Bond says, "they've begun to talk about including in the strike others acrose the city who live in the same kind of houses. They want to organize everyone who wants a better house through their actions."

The campaign was unique because Bond and his campaign workers asked residents of the District—voters and non-voters alike—what it was they expected from a State Representative and what they were prepared to do for themselves.

"I'd like to see people organized acrose the District," SNCC worker Judy Richardson said. "I'd like to see a community advisory board that would tell their representative what to do in the Georgia House and would give them opportunity to plan what they can do for themselves in the community."

The campaign gave some workers doubts about partisan elections. "We'll never know how many people voted for/or against Julian because of his party label," one said. Bond is a Democrat.

Student Voice, July 1965

Bond is a college dropout, and rebelled against other candidates who stressed their education and formal training, jobs or civic organization memberships as "qualifications" for the Georgia House.

"The state of Georgia says anyone who is 21 years old and who has $500 is 'qualified' and can run for the office," Bond said, "and I agree with them completely. The real qualification is interest and a willingness to work."

The campaign workers expressed disappointment at the responses they received from the few whites in Bond's District. "It was impossible to get past race," one worker explained, "although only Negroes offered for that seat, most whites felt they could not be represented by any Negro."

The workers did discover that whites were willing to discus issues of jobs, housing and schooling, and were surprised to learn that Negro canvassers had more success in white areas than whites did.

You will vote at the following locations:

3 S Egan Homes
821 Play Lane, N. W.

3 H The A. U. Reading Clinic
179 Chestnut Street, S. W.

3 A Walker Street School
165 Walker Street, S. W.

7 R Fire Station # 7
535 West Whitehall, S. W.

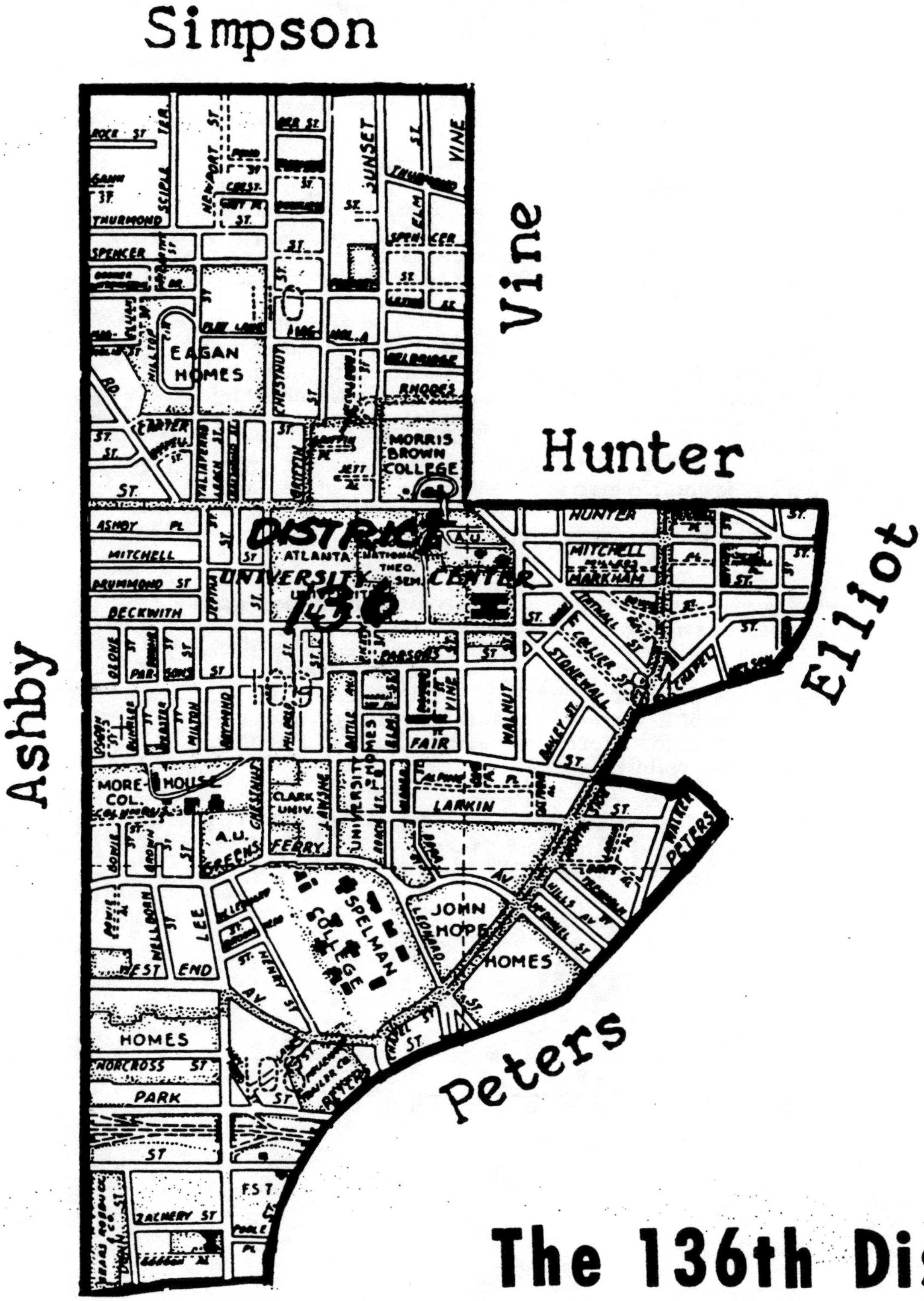

The 136th District

Vote For Julian Bond

Julian Bond, a national civil rights leader and former Atlanta newspaper editor is a candidate for the House of Representatives from the 136th District of Georgia.

Bond has gained national eminence as Communications Director of the Atlanta-based Student Nonviolent Coordinating Committee (SNCC).

While he was a Morehouse student, Bond was one of the organizers and became Executive Secretary of the Committee on Appeal For Human Rights, the Atlanta University student movement group that helped integrate this city's lunch counters, restaurants and movie theaters and won many job opportunities for Atlanta's Negroes. The group also sparked voter registration drives throughout the city's Negro neighborhoods which added thousands of Negroes to city and county voter lists.

His work at SNCC has taken him to the scene of voter registration and anti-segregation drives in South Georgia, Alabama, Mississippi and Arkansas. He is editor of the SNCC bi-monthly newsletter, the STUDENT VOICE.

He is the son of Dr. and Mrs. Horace Mann Bond. Dr. Bond is Dean of Education at Atlanta University. The candidate is married to the former Miss Alice Clopton of Atlanta. They have two children. He is 25 years old.

"Vote For A Man You're Sure Will Vote For You"

JULIAN BOND

Democratic Candidate

Georgia House of Representatives

136th District

June 8, 1965

Dear Friend:

I am writing to you once again to ask for your vote and support on Wednesday, June 16, in the General Election.

One of the ways you have a chance to choose who will make decisions for you is by voting; if you don't vote, someone else makes that decision for you.

I want to give you that chance, not only on election day, but on every day after that. My job in the State House of Representatives is to represent you; to me, that means that I do what each of you wants me to do.

I have tried to talk to as many people who live in the 136th District as possible; some of you are interested in housing, some in getting better jobs, some in getting better pay, some in improving schools, some in helping our young people have a future. All of us are interested in making the 136th District, the city of Atlanta and the state of Georgia a better place to live.

If we win the election on June 16, we will have a chance to work together, to make decisions about our own lives.

I pledge myself to continue working with people in the 136th District. I'd like to see the people of this area set up community groups that would meet and make decisions about what to do, and then take action to improve their lives.

If you want to have something to say about what happens to your life, your home, your job, your children, vote June 16 for Julian Bond.

And remember, after you vote, your responsibility is just beginning. I want to hear from each of you, to speak with each of you, and to work with each of you to solve the problems that all of us have.

Vote the straight Democratic ticket on June 16, and make yourself and your neighbor a committee to keep on voting every day of the year for the things you need.

Sincerely,

Julian Bond

Julian Bond

Julian Bond Campaign Headquarters

862 Hunter Street, SW **Atlanta, Georgia 30314** **Phone: 524-2638**

UNIT 8-14

GEORGIA'S NEW ERA
THE YOUNG POLITICIANS

ATLANTA, Ga.—When the Georgia legislature convenes in January, Southern history will pass an important milestone.

For one thing, there will be 10 Negroes in this legislature—whereas four years ago there were none, and even last year only two. That's few enough in a state where Negroes make up 28 percent of the population, but it's more than in any other state except Michigan.

Even more important, however, is the fact that these 10 will include two very young men, representatives of a new generation of Southerners.

They are Ben Brown and Julian Bond, both 25, both products of the Southern student upsurge of 1960. With the exception of Clarence Mitchell, III, who was elected to the Maryland legislature in 1962, they are the first leaders of the Southern sit-in movement to win political office.

What has made all this possible is reapportionment of the Georgia legislature last year. Previously Fulton County (Atlanta) had three representatives; now it has 24, three elected at large, but 21 by districts. This meant inevitably that some Negroes would be elected. The ghetto is a fact of life in southern cities as in Northern—and becoming more so.

(Prior to this year's elections, there were two Negro senators in the Georgia legislature, Leroy Johnson and Horace Ward, but no members of the House.)

Ben Brown is executive secretary of the Atlanta branch of NAACP, native of Georgia and a product of Fulton County public schools. He was student body president at Clark College in Atlanta at the height of the sit-in movement when that campus produced mass student participation in the early Atlanta demonstrations. Brown became a leader of the Atlanta Committee on Appeal for Human Rights, which coordinated the sit-ins. He had his share of arrests.

"Five times, I believe it was," he says. It's the mark of distinction of a new generation.

After Brown and Bond were elected this year, some newspapers made much of a story that both of them would, in January, be returning to the legislative hall where they were thrown out of the gallery just two years ago for challenging segregated seating.

The story is not quite accurate. This happened to Bond, but not to Brown. By 1963, he had gone to Howard University to study law.

Southern Patriot, September 1965.

"But I was once with a group that was turned back by police at the state capitol," he recalls. "This was in the spring of 1961 when 3,000 students marched to protest segregation."

Brown returned to Atlanta in June, 1964, after getting his law degree. Last year he cut his political teeth by managing Horace Ward's campaign for state senator.

Brown says one of his main objectives in the legislature will be to help elevate the educational system of Georgia—which means more resourceful people and more money.

"That's the reason for what I guess is one of my most revolutionary proposals," he says. He wants to legalize gambling and tax it so the state can derive revenue from it.

"It isn't that I want to promote gambling," he explains. "The gambling is going on now. I want the state to get some money out of it. We must have money if we are going to lift this state economically."

He also favors abolition of the death penalty, legislation to give the people a voice in condemnation proceedings and urban renewal, and a state anti-discrimination law.

For Ben Brown, his entry into the state legislature will be the culmination of a long dream.

"I remember telling my ninth grade teacher that I wanted to be the first Negro senator in Georgia," he says. "Well, I didn't quite make that, but I've been convinced for a long time that it is through politics that I can make my greatest contribution to life."

With Julian Bond, it is different. Even a year ago if someone had told him he would be is the legislature, he would not have believed it.

Bond was one of the earliest full-time staff members of SNCC and serves as its communications director. Like many SNCC people, he has considered traditional politics corrupt and decadent and has maintained that the freedom movement must create a new kind of world, new relationships, and new politics—and must avoid, at all costs, getting sucked into the structure of the old.

Neither his campaign nor his election really changed these doubts and opinions.

"The problem is that politics and people are too far apart," he says. "Maybe it is not possible for people to use the political machinery instead of it using them—but I want to find out."

Bond is the son of Dr. Horace Mann Bond, well-known educator, now dean of education at Atlanta University. The younger Bond was born in Nashville, lived at Ft. Valley State College in Georgia and from 1945 until 1957 near Lincoln University in Pennsylvania, where his father was president—and where he also fought segregation in public schools through the first such suit filed in Pennsylvania. Young Bond attended both public and Quaker schools.

When he was 17, the family moved back to Georgia, and he entered Morehouse College in 1957.

In 1960, a fellow student came to him and suggested that the two of them organize sit-ins like those just started in North Carolina. "Why us?" asked Bond, but he joined in. That other student was Lonnie King, who became leader of the Atlanta movement, and this started the sit-ins here.

Then Bond helped start a new newspaper covering the Negro community, The *Atlanta Inquirer*, and left school to work full-time. From there, he went to SNCC. When he later became SNCC's first married staff member and had his first child (he now has two), the traditional $10-to-$40 a week SNCC pay went up to $60 for married people to enable him to stay.

Bond has not been as much in the public eye as some frequently jailed SNCC workers. He was especially equipped to do the crucial behind-the-lines drudgery—and he did it. He is a poet and talented creative writer, and also a topnotch reporter with a special talent for organizing facts so that they are clear and understandable.

Many were the days he spent on the telephone patiently explaining to newspaper reporters the historic events that were occurring scarcely noticed under their noses. It was a long and often discouraging task—but when the real story of the unsung heroes of the South began to reach the nation and the world, Bond was one of those who had done it. He's still at it.

He decided to run for office last spring because people kept urging him to—and because, he says, he got tired of listening to other candidates talking "about the same old generalities of good government and better education they've been talking about for the past 20 years without saying anything."

He launched a unique campaign. Most of the people in his district are poor; the average income, he found, is $1,800 a year. His program called for a $2-an-hour state minimum wage law with coverage of low-paid workers like domestic and restaurant employees; reform of urban renewal procedures; abolition of capital punishment and removal of all voter registration requirements except age and residence.

Then he and his SNCC co-workers set out to visit people at home and find out what they wanted. They visited hundreds. (The effects of a campaign of this kind are described in the article below.)

The most important thing that came out of the campaign, he feels, is that he built a relationship with people and they now have a relationship with their legislator and—even more important—with their neighbors.

"I didn't promise anyone instant freedom," he emphasizes. "People would ask me if I thought the $2 minimum wage was possible. I said I didn't know but people needed it and we should fight for it. I told people that they themselves have political power if they organize."

What if he finds that present political machinery, after all, is not the way people can gain control over their own lives?

Then he'll get out, Bond says, and fast.

"That is, of course, unless I become corrupt too," he says, his eyes twinkling.

Asked what kind of pressures arise to lure the office-holder to corruption, Bond replied:

"Well, one thing that disturbed me: I found that many people voted for me not because they were familiar with my program but just because I was a Democrat. Now in this situation, a successful candidate could begin to wonder how much he owes the Democrats, how free is he to criticize them."

Furthermore, he says, he has found that if a Southern Negro office-holder wants to go on the speaking circuit under party sponsorship and say the right things it can be very lucrative—"at least $400 an engagement," he says.

It might be tempting to some people. But Bond has worked in the movement too long not to hear a different drummer. The possibility of his "corruption" seems about the most unlikely prospect in Georgia polities at the moment.

UNIT 8-15

THE JULIAN BOND CAMPAIGN

The Julian Bond Issue created by the SNCC statement on Vietnam made the staff who were in Atlanta for the executive committee meeting very concerned about one glaring weakness in the Julian Bond election. The weakness was that no tightly knit organization had been built in his district. Therefore it was going to be difficult to mobilize those people around Julian's ouster. We discussed what action SNCC was going to take to back Julian up in his fight for his seat. The first major problem was who do we have to give full time to the campaign. The people of the Atlanta Staff were tied to their office work and could only be counted on for marginal support. Worth, Charlie and Ivanhoe (the three who ran his first campaign) were working elsewhere. (Later both Charlie and Ivanhoe were able to give a few days to the issue). A few people, John Baptisto, Jessie Harrison, Frank Holloway, Mike Simmons, Jim Forman, and Gwen Robinson volunteered to stick it out. Later, Mendy Samstien and Bill Ware joined the crew.

We decided to ask SCLC if they would give us a hand. They immediately replied that they would do all that they could. The offered us the use of their print shop; helped us set up mass meetings at various churches in Julian's district (providing named SCLC spokesman), offered us the use of their sound equipment. Of course, Dr. King sent several telegrams denouncing the actions of the Georgia State Legislature and also became one of the plaintiffs in a suit filed by the 136th District against the Georgia State Legislature.

The small group worked tirelessly, without much moral or physical support from Atlanta office personnel. Some of us felt that this was because of the heated dispute in the executive committee meeting between persons working on Julian's campaign and Jack Minnis and other members of the finance committee.

Because Julian had no organization behind him in the district, all the work had to be done by those who had volunteered. There were mass meeting help practically every night. Of course for each mass meeting, there was the leafleting, the canvassing with aid of sound truck, etc. In collaboration with SCLC, there was a 2,500 man march onto the State Capitol. We held house meetings in many homes in Julain's district. During the day, we went to the State Legislature with as many community people as we could muster to watch the activities of the Georgia Legislature. The last week of the campaign began the intensive canvassing. We would begin the day by getting up every morning at 6am to go to bus-stops downtown, where hundreds of black people pass on their way to the white suburbs. We would canvass from 6 A.M. to 9 A.M. Producing leaflets on a day to day basis

---

SNCC internal memo, circa February 1966.

meant that some of us were up to 4 in the morning, running off the leaflets which had to be put out hours later by these same persons. Let us mention, that if it had not been for the untiring efforts of Wilson Brown, through many a night, many a person would not have been reached.

Julian's being put on the national stage by the SNCC statement and involved in fund raising for SNCC, he wasn't able to devote much time to the campaign until the very last days.

On the eve of the campaign, we had everything set up for the big day. We had lined up baby sitters for voting mothers; knocked on the doors to inform them of free rides to the polling place; lined up students from the AU center to call Julian's constituents all day to remind them to go to the polls. Because we planned to carry people to the polls, we saw this as an excellent opportunity to meet people from the 136th on a personal level and begin the task of setting up a political machine that works for the people in that district. Therefore the taking of people to the polls was a very crucial part of any future plans for the district. We had spoken to Forman a couple of days before about the necessity of renting three or four cars to carry out our plans. He had assured us that some way or another we would have the cars.

SUPPORT JULIAN BOND!

JOIN Martin Luther King Jr.

March to the State Capitol!

Friday, Jan. 14, 1:00 P. M.

STARTING POINTS

ATLANTA UNIVERSITY LIBRARY
CORNER OF CHESNUT STREET
AND GREENFERRY ROAD
1:00 P.M.

EBENEEZER BAPTIST CHURCH
CORNER OF AUBURN AVE.
AND JACKSON BLVD.
1:00 P.M.

DISTRIBUTED BY SNCC-SCLC

UNIT 8-17

The Bond Case: Its Meaning to America

ATLANTA, Ga.—The Georgia Legislature adjourned its 1966 special session still minus its now-most-famous member-elect, Julian Bond. It was a defeat not so much for young Bond as for the democratic processes in America.

No more important case has arisen in the Southern freedom movement than the Bond case. When the Georgia legislators voted 184 to 12 to deny Bond his seat because he supported a statement by the Student Nonviolent Coordinating Committee (SNCC) against the war in Vietnam, at least three basic questions were involved:

1. Is opposition to war going to be considered treason? That's what Georgia legislators said Bond's position was.

At this level, the Bond case is a simple free speech fight. In other words, will mass hysteria rise to such a level that dissent is stamped out?

2. But because Bond is a Negro and a militant civil rights advocate, there is another dimension: Is the Negro's right to vote in the South going to be simply the right to vote for positions and people approved by those in power, or will people have the right to choose their own representatives and to take the stands on important issues that *they* want to take?

Eliza Heard, a writer and long-time observer of the Southern scene, commented after watching the proceedings in Atlanta:

"The lesson was plain. A Negro can now become a part of the 'Consensus' if he does not dispute its premises and its objectives. But a Negro cannot disagree with the direction of foreign policy of the U.S. Government and still be accepted. . . . If this policy holds, no Negro who is elected to office in the South, or in the country, can be sure he is not going to be rejected."

3. And finally, because Julian Bond is not only a Negro but a young man who is part of a new generation with new ideas, what is the chance for a new politics in the South—one geared not to old ideas of "the possible" but to the needs of the people?

Herbert Shapiro, professor at Morehouse College and one of Bond's constituents, summed up this aspect of the case in a report to *The Patriot*:

"To a great extent this fight had the usual cast of characters in Southern politics. There are the business-minded white moderates who speak of integration but become livid

---

Southern Patriot, 1966.

whenever Negroes take a position that deviates from their gradualist orthodoxy . . . There are the open segregationists in the Legislature who have forgotten nothing and learned nothing and who took their revenge. . . .

"But there are also some new factors. There is Julian Bond himself, 26 years old. . . . it is difficult to fit him into any stereotype. Bond is a politician, but he is also a poet who has published in several major anthologies.

"Julian Bond is a spokesman for a new politics and much of the heat in the present situation comes from those who abhor his challenge to the usual politics of expediency.

"The standard political pattern is to present a platform of promises to constituents after consultation with party leaders. If elected the politician is governed not by what his constituents need but by what is possible in the legislature as currently constituted. . . .

"Bond is of another sort. His campaign was based on extensive sounding out of the needs of his community and of what his prospective constituents wanted their representative to do. In the course of the campaign he discussed issues personally with hundreds of voters.

"Other Negro legislators in Georgia have introduced or supported worthwhile legislation, but in the main they have operate on the assumption that politics is the art of the possible.

"There is much to indicate that Julian Bond is committed to a politics of meeting the necessities of the community. He seems ready to associate himself with the legislative tradition exemplified by such members as Norris and LaFollette. . . .

"Julian Bond desires a politics of true service to the community; those who deny him his seat seek to impose a politics of conformity and silence. Their dream is an America of 'know nothings.' Bond's exclusion is a challenge to Americans of decency and good will everywhere."

These questions raised by the Bond case still remain to be answered; it is far from over. When the legislature refused to seat him, Bond took the issue to the federal courts and a three-judge panel split 2 to 1 to decide that the legislature's action was legal. Bond will now carry that question to the U.S. Supreme Court.

Meantime, he also took the case back to the people of his 136th legislative district in Atlanta—a virtually all-Negro district, where average income is $1,800 a year.

These people had elected him last summer by 82 percent of the vote, the largest percentage won by any Georgia legislator; it also represented the largest turn-out of eligible voters of any legislative district in the state.

When a special election was called to fill his seat in February, he qualified to run again and no one dared to run against him. On the day of the election, despite protests, voters were required to go all the way to the Fulton County Courthouse to vote—a real hardship for people who are poor. It was a cold day with rain and sleet. He was running unopposed—a circumstance that keeps many voters at home in any election.

Despite all these factors, he received one-third as many votes this time as he did last summer. Station WSB, the NBC outlet in Atlanta, called it a "spectacular" showing.

The legislative session was over before the special election was held, and of course it had taken steps to deny him the seat again anyway. The original election was only for a special one-year term, and regular elections are scheduled for the fall. Bond has already indicated he'll run again, and next time there will be opposing candidates.

There will be high-powered efforts to destroy his support, both inside his district and out. No one can say for sure that it won't work.

Support for his right to be seated was strong among Georgians working for civil rights and civil liberties in the early days of the legislature. Some of this has since probably been weakened by persistent attacks on Bond and on SNCC, especially in the Atlanta press. Steady barrages can cloud even the clearest issues.

Because facts have been grossly distorted in some press reports, it is important to clarify two points:

1. *What the SNCC statement on Vietnam said:* The statement opposed the war with strong words—calling the U.S. policy in Vietnam one of "murder" and "aggression." SNCC has always been a group that said what it thought in plain language; in the past many people now denouncing it admired its courage for doing so.

But the statement did not suggest that anyone "dodge the draft" or burn draft cards—as many press reports have indicated. SNCC Chairman John Lewis suggested in an interview—and Bond supported the idea—that Congress add work for civil rights to the list of acceptable forms of alternative service open to young men who oppose war.

2. *Why SNCC issued the statement when it did:* The most fantastic reasons have been suggested by the press. One SNCC staff member said: "They seem unable to understand that we just wanted to issue a statement and we did."

The most common distorted explanation by SNCC's opponents is that the organization was broke and wanted to create a "cause celebre" to raise money—and thus deliberately timed the statement to coincide with the opening of the legislature, counting on the Georgia lawmakers to create an issue by doing just what they did.

Actually the truth is the exact opposite. The timing of the statement the week before the legislature opened was a complete coincidence with no one in SNCC foreseeing the effect it would have on Bond's seat.

The statement had been drawn up in draft form at a SNCC meeting in the fall and circulated among SNCC staff throughout the South for discussion. Rather than seeing it as a money-raiser, most SNCC people felt it might destroy the organization financially—costing them the contributions of many people who disagreed.

The decision to go on and issue it was one of high courage—a decision that this was something that was right and that they must do even if it did destroy them.

As it turned out, with the interest in the Bond case, it did bring in many new contributions, but this was temporary. SNCC still has serious financial problems—not, it is generally believed, because of the Vietnam position but because of the slump all civil rights groups are feeling because too many people have the grossly mistaken notion that the civil rights battle is won.

But the support they got in response to the Vietnam statement was a pleasant surprise for most SNCC people. "I think," said one long-time SNCC worker, "that it showed a lot of us how important it is to take positions of principle, and that these would not necessarily be our death toll."

It is an interesting sidelight on the case that while SNCC and Bond were grappling with high principle and conscience, the Georgia legislators who rejected him were dabbling in trivia. The Birmingham News, no supporter of Bond, commented under a heading "Bond Not Missing Much":

"Little in the way of general legislation has been approved while the august body (the Georgia Legislature) has wrestled with such items as a bill to ban liquor advertising, to prohibit nudist camps in the state, and to memorialize a coon dog." (The dog, it seems, was killed two years ago by a state Game and Fish Department employee, and the legislators passed a resolution to erect a monument to its memory in a state park.)

It was obviously Bond and not his attackers who emerged from the fray with the stature of the heroic. He comes from a long tradition of the pioneer and the dissenter.

His father, Horace Mann Bond, is one of America's most noted Negro educators who has blazed his own trails; he in turn was named for Horace Mann, who pioneered the beginning of free public education in America and was an ardent Abolitionist in the early 19th Century. Young Bond upheld the tradition well.

Describing the attack on him as a "witch-burning," Eliza Heard wrote: "But in spite of the odor of burning, Julian Bond did not burn. He stayed calm, cool, collected and in perfect command of himself. . . . He did not give in an inch in his opposition to the war, he maintained his position and did so with the most perfect composure. The anger, wrath, denunciation was all on the other side. . . . "

In its September, 1965, issue *The Southern Patriot* described Julian Bond's election campaign, his victory, and his belief in a new politics where people use the political machinery instead of it using them. The article concluded with these paragraphs:

What if he finds that present political machinery, after all, is not the way people can gain control over their own lives?

Then he'll get out, Bond says, and fast.

"That is, of course unless I become corrupt too," he says, his eyes twinkling. . . .

. . . But Bond has worked in the movement too long not to hear a different drummer. The responsibility of his "corruption" seems about the most unlikely prospect in Georgia politics at the moment.

Rarely is a journalistic assessment put to the test of life so quickly—and it proved valid.

UNIT 9

THE MOVEMENT EXPANDS

	INTRODUCTION	490
9-1 •	FREEDOM RIDE MAP	491
9-2 •	THE FREEDOM RIDES	492
9-3 •	FREEDOM RIDE—1961 *James Peck*	495
9-4 •	BRINKLEY TAKES STAND AGAINST "FREEDOM RIDERS"	503
9-5 •	THE AGONY OF ALBANY	504
9-6 •	THE BLOODY BATTLEGROUND OF ALBANY *Slater King*	509
9-7 •	THE NEW BLACK RADICALS *Charles McLaurin and Randy Battle*	515
9-8 •	REFLECTIONS ON THE DEATH OF A CHILD *Marion King*	519
9-9 •	ALBANY, FAILURE OR FIRST STEP? *Wyatt Tee Walker*	521
9-10 •	ALBANY POLICE DEPARTMENT *Laurie Pritchett*	526
9-11 •	HOMEGROWN MOVEMENT IN MACON *George A. Doss, Jr.*	528
9-12 •	"AIN'T GONNA LET NOBODY TURN ME ROUND," SONG	535

INTRODUCTION

Unit 9 examines two major milestones in the Southern Civil Rights Movement: the Freedom Rides and the Albany, Georgia, demonstrations.

As the map (9-1) demonstrates, the Freedom Rides lasted only twenty days, but they cut through the South literally and metaphorically. The violence that the Freedom Rides elicted caught the nation's attention. Opinion throughout the country was often divided between those that thought the Freedom Rides advanced the movement (9-2) and those that believed it retarded racial progress (9-4).

The rest of the unit discusses the important demonstrations in Albany and the process of community organizing in the movement. Albany was an early attempt by SNCC to mobilize an entire community of blacks in the struggle to end racial discrimination in the South; the appearance of Martin Luther King after the demonstrations began brought intense media scrutiny to that small Georgia town. Though many observers deemed Albany a setback, many movement activists considered the efforts there a success. Wyatt Tee Walker, a King confidant, confronts this question directly in 9-9. Three of the documents that precede Walker's essay (9-5, 9-6 and 9-8) reprint the coverage of the demonstrations in *New South.* Slater and Marion King were important local black leaders who participated in the demonstrations. Another *New South* article (9-11) juxtaposes a little known local movement in nearby Macon, Georgia, with the events in Albany. Drawn from the Albany city records, 9-5 highlights the city's effective efforts to stifle civil rights protests.

In 9-7, Charles McLaurin and Randy Battle describe the strategies employed by SNCC to organize a community in the struggle for civil rights.

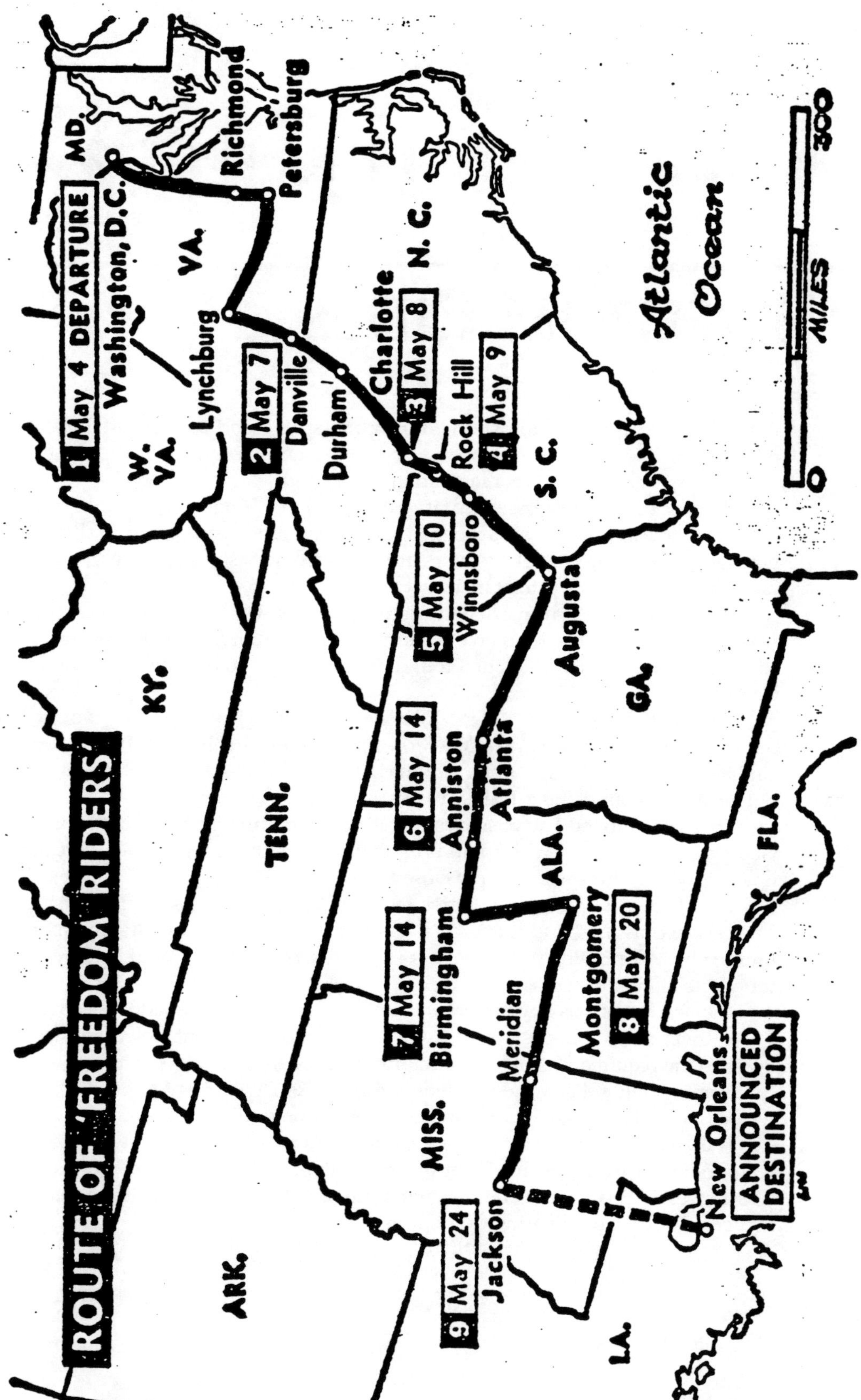
ROUTE OF 'FREEDOM RIDERS'
1 May 4 DEPARTURE
Washington, D.C.
MD.
VA.
W. VA.
Lynchburg
Richmond
Petersburg
2 May 7
Danville
Durham
Charlotte
3 May 8
N. C.
Rock Hill
4 May 9
S. C.
5 May 10
Winnsboro
Augusta
GA.
6 May 14
Anniston
Atlanta
ALA.
7 May 14
Birmingham
Meridian
Montgomery
8 May 20
MISS.
9 May 24
Jackson
New Orleans
ANNOUNCED DESTINATION
KY.
TENN.
ARK.
LA.
FLA.
Atlantic Ocean
0
MILES
300

UNIT 9-2

THE FREEDOM RIDES

After the main thrust of the sit-ins during the spring and summer of 1961, a period of relative lull in direct action occurred. It seemed to be a time of recuperation, of taking stock, of organization and reorganization.

The first indication of new activity came from the Congress of Racial Equality. A little more than a year after the sit-ins began, CORE announced on March 13, 1961 that a small biracial group would travel on interstate buses from Washington to New Orleans to test racial discrimination in interstate travel terminals.

It was no secret that many had segregated waiting rooms and lunch counters. This was despite Interstate Commerce Commission and Supreme Court rulings, including a Richmond case in 1960 which had found discrimination to be in violation of the Interstate Commerce Act.

After first advising President John F. Kennedy when the rides would begin and requesting federal protection, CORE on May 4 sent out the first 1961 (there had been similar rides in previous years) freedom riders—six whites and six Negroes 18 to 61 years old, on a Greyhound and a Trailways bus.

They encountered few obstacles traveling down through Virginia, the Carolinas, and Georgia. Some facilities which had until that moment been segregated were among those open to them. Others were simply closed.

Trouble began in Alabama. A mob met the Greyhound bus six miles outside Anniston. They slashed its tires, and it fled on flats for six miles. Then the pursuing mob threw fire into the bus, destroying it. Passengers escaped serious injury, though some were treated for effects of inhaling smoke.

The Trailways bus encountered a mob at Anniston, but made it into Birmingham. There, the freedom riders stepped from the bus into the violent crowd and were savagely beaten. One required 50 stitches for injuries to the head.

Birmingham police were warned by the Justice Department to expect violence when the bus came. Police did not arrive at the bus station until ten minutes after the bus did.

Thus received, the original 13 freedom riders took a plane to New Orleans. But they were followed by many more. In all, more than 1,000 persons made Freedom Rides. CORE, SCLC, SNCC, and the Nashville Student Movement sent riders, and formed a Freedom Riders Coordinating Committee.

New South, October–November 1963.

From jeers to beatings, the subsequent waves of freedom riders ran into trouble—again mostly in Alabama. Mobs and tension built so high in Montgomery on May 20, 21, 22, that President Kennedy ordered some 600 federal marshals into the city for its own protection and that of the riders.

For the lap of the journey from Montgomery to Jackson (Miss.), a new pattern developed. The riders were heavily guarded enroute, and then, when they stepped off the bus in Jackson, they were arrested. As fast as they might arrive during the ensuing weeks, they were taken to jail.

This finally stopped the Freedom Rides short of the destination of New Orleans, but not before they had accomplished their overt purpose—federal action that would end virtually all discrimination in carriers and terminals used by interstate travelers.

A series of government actions accomplished this: a petition by Attorney General Robert Kennedy asking that the Interstate Commerce Commission issue rules prohibiting racial discrimination in the interstate facilities; action by the ICC on September 22; subsequent posting of signs in interstate carriers on November 1 that seating "is without regard to race, color, creed or national origin"; and an ICC order that interstate carriers could not use terminals where travelers were segregated by race.

Thus, although as late as July 20, 1961, the Justice Department had reported "open racial segregation" in 97 of 294 bus terminals throughout 12 of 17 states surveyed, there was nearly none after the November 1 order.

This, on the face of it, was a clearcut victory. Unlike the delay and compromise which block many goals, here was swift action by the federal government moved by direct action protest against the violation of federal law. Here, also, was the first federal intervention to keep the peace in a direct action situation.

Moreover, the rides took the fight effectively into the deep South. Alabama, where governmental power was used the previous year to wreck the sit-ins, and Mississippi, the only state where there had been no 1960 sit-ins, ultimately lost to the freedom riders. And the face of Alabama mobs, officially tolerated, was shown to the nation.

The positive effect on Negro morale again was strong. But the victory was not without cost. In actual money, this amounted to upwards of half a million dollars, largely in legal expenses. Much of this money is still tied up as jail bond in cases not yet brought to trial.

The cost in good public opinion may have been even greater. Like the sit-ins, the Freedom Rides showed the nation and the world a just cause and a courageous determination, and inspired in Negroes more feeling of solidarity and of solid power. They also revealed to an amazed nation and world the crudity of Alabama and Mississippi injustice.

But the Freedom Rides reinforced the old rationalization of white Southerners that race trouble is always caused by outside agitators. Not very successful were sophisticated explanations that local Negroes would not normally use local bus terminals, and that therefore outsiders had to come to do so. Thus, the rebuttal made by the sit-ins against the outside agitator theory had been undermined.

For another thing, the Freedom Rides seemed to many to go beyond the needs of the moment in order to antagonize white Southerners. Even people sympathetic to the goals of the riders became critical of their tactics, particularly the continuation of the rides after the Attorney General had commenced the government's action.

This brought the South, and indeed the nation, up against the question of the moral and legal validity of non-violence that provokes violence. A June 1961 Gallup Poll showed that while a majority of Americans approved of ending segregation in interstate travel, 64% disapproved of the freedom riders' methods, largely on grounds they "were causing too much trouble."

Thus the almost solid sympathy for sit-ins outside the South, and a certain grudging admiration from even die-hard southern segregationists, was reduced.

An even more portentous development (though probably inevitable eventually), was the use in Jackson of a new weapon which would be imitated and refined over the South against direct action. This was the concept of quick arrest of demonstrators, filling the jails as fast as they came.

Beyond these gains and losses, there were in the Freedom Rides other factors that were new.

Emotional and tone coloring changed from the sit-in days. The anger and violence the rides attracted seemed deeper, stronger, uglier. And the previous emphasis of demonstrators on good manners and neat dress declined notably.

The very nature of the rides, simple and concentrated in one kind of action, made it easier for the rest of the nation to follow what was happening in the South.

And there were political ramifications because of the involvement of the federal government. What the Kennedy Administration did was weighed by voters. This was slightly different from the one political ramification of the sit-ins—the Negro votes that a campaigning Kennedy may have picked up with his telephone call of solicitation to Mrs. Martin Luther King, Jr. when her husband was jailed in connection with a Georgia sit-in. Now white votes were involved, also, on both sides.

So direct action in the second big campaign in the second year of its emergence was becoming more complex in the national consciousness.

And, beginning in Jackson, there was a need for the nation to make a new distinction about the role of police power in direct action. Was the nation, standing back startled at the implications of the Freedom Rides, coming to the point where just the absence of violence was all that it asked in the handling of demonstrations? Something close to that is suggested by what happened in the next great crisis. It occurred in a small place in Georgia called by its Chamber of Commerce, "the tenth fastest booming city in the USA." The place was Albany.

UNIT 9-3

FREEDOM RIDE—1961

James Peck

Little did I realize that my second interracial bus trip through the South would end in a mob beating which almost cost me my life. Such a trip had been contemplated even before the 1947 Journey of Reconciliation was over. Several years thereafter, Billie Ames of the St. Louis CORE group started to organize one, but it never materialized. In the winter of 1961, riding aboard a bus together, Thomas Gaither, whose story is told in Chapter 7, and Gordon Carey, CORE field director, broached the subject in earnest and devised the term Freedom Ride. The idea was accepted enthusiastically by the next national CORE council meeting. The Ride would take place in the spring.

What made the timing particularly opportune was that in December the U.S. Supreme Court had issued a decision in the Bruce Boynton case extending the Irene Morgan ruling which had been the basis for the 1947 Journey. The Morgan decision had outlawed segregation of interstate passengers only aboard the vehicles on which they traveled. The Boynton decision extended that ruling to cover facilities used by interstate passengers outside the actual vehicles. This meant waiting rooms, rest rooms, terminal restaurants, rest stops, and so on. The Freedom Ride would test all these facilities, not merely the seating aboard buses.

Also, the Freedom Ride would penetrate the Deep South, not merely the upper South as had the 1947 Journey. The route decided upon was Washington to New Orleans. The starting date was May 4. Gaither traveled the entire route, as Houser had traveled the Journey's route, setting up meetings and arranging housing for the overnight stops.

Applications for participants went out from the CORE office. It was made clear that the policy in event of arrest was to remain in jail rather than pay fines or bail out. The first two volunteers were Jim Farmer, one of CORE's founders who had become national director, and myself. The group which assembled May I at Fellowship House in Washington for training, totaled thirteen. It was a very different type of group from the one which had gathered in Washington fourteen years previously for the same type of project. It included a number of what has become known as "the new Negro"—Southern students who took part in the sit-in movement and for whom arrest or the threat thereof had become commonplace. Most of the group were young people in their twenties. Very few of them were pacifists. I was the only participant who had been on the 1947 Journey, and was therefore in a good position to make contrasts or comparisons with the trip fourteen years before. The outstanding contrast, and most heartening to me, was that, aboard the buses, desegregation had become a reality. On the Journey, members of our group had been the only passengers to sit unsegregated. On the Freedom Ride, even in the Deep South, ordinary Negro passengers no longer confined themselves to the rear seats.

The outstanding comparison was that, in the terminals and at the rest stops—even in Virginia's larger cities where the white and colored signs had been removed—segregation still prevailed as it had aboard the buses in 1947. Our Freedom Riders were about the only persons to wait, wash, and eat unsegregated in these terminals.

It was disheartening to me, that in a city such as Richmond, which is not far from the nation's capital and where the color signs had been removed, Negroes were sticking to the formerly separate and grossly unequal colored waiting rooms and restaurants. This was true both in the Greyhound and Trailways terminals.

The first white and colored signs encountered were only fifty miles south of Washington—atop the restroom doors at the Greyhound stop in Fredericksburg. Charles Person, a Negro student from Atlanta, went into the white rest room and I went into the colored rest room without incident.

In Farmville, center of Prince Edward County, where school closing had left Negro children schoolless since 1959, the white and colored signs were painted over but still visible. Freedom Riders were served without incident.

While there were no color signs in the Lynchburg Trailways terminal, there was a divider in the middle of the counter, making persons on one side virtually invisible to those on the other.

Danville, Virginia, was the first place where testers were refused service. At the colored counter, Ed Blankenheim, a white, sat for ten minutes until his bus was ready for departure. Genevieve Hughes, a white, and I, aboard a later bus, were at first refused service but we—and Walter Bergman—finally got refreshments after a brief discussion with the manager.

Greensboro, though reputed for its liberalism, was the first city where the color signs started to become the rule. The first greetings to arriving bus passengers are oversized signs all around the building with arrows pointing to the colored waiting room. On the other hand, the colored lunch room, which was no bigger than a goodsized closet and equally gloomy, had been closed permanently a week before our arrival. A Negro in the colored waiting room told me he was amazed when upon entering the colored lunch room one day, he was advised to walk around to the formerly white restaurant.

Our meeting in Greensboro was at the Shiloh Baptist Church, the same church where fourteen years ago our Journey group had gotten such a moving welcome following the incident of violence in Chapel Hill. The church looked exactly the same. But now Greensboro had become famous, civil-rights-wise, as being the birthplace of the sit-in movement. Chairman of our meeting was Dr. George Simkins, Jr., head of the local NAACP, who the day the first sit-in started, phoned CORE to get the benefit of its long experience in this technique. The local NAACP was sponsoring our meeting, although the Freedom Ride, like the 1947 Joumey, got no backing from the national NAACP office. The NAACP rallied to support the Freedom Rides only after they had gained national momentum.

From Greensboro on, we were venturing into territory not covered by the 1947 Journey. In Salisbury, the color signs were on every terminal facility. However, two Negro women passengers from our bus, after watching our testers, sat down and ate at the white lunch counter.

Charlotte was the scene of the trip's first arrest—and the birth of a new "in," the shoe-in. Charles Person climbed onto a shoeshine chair and, after being refused service, remained seated until a cop with handcuffs arrived. Person then left, since no policy regarding shoeshines had yet been decided by the group and, as on the Joumey, each step and who was to take it would be decided at group meetings before every lap of the Ride. When Person went for the shine, he didn't even think of it as a test. He simply looked at his shoes and thought he needed a shine. It was then hastily decided by the group that Joe

Perkins should make a test and stay in the shoeshine chair until arrested. The trip's first arrest came within minutes. Attorney Thomas Wyche won an acquittal on the basis of the Supreme Court's Boynton decision, and Perkins rejoined us a day later.

Violence against the Freedom Riders erupted for the first time in Rock Hill, South Carolina, where the press had headlined our arrival and where hoodlums had recently attacked lunch-counter pickets. In fact several of the hoodlums waiting at the Greyhound station were recognized as the same individuals who had assaulted the local student pickets.

As the Greyhound contingent of Riders arrived, some twenty of these ruffians were waiting. When John Lewis, who is Negro, approached the entrance of the white waiting room, he was assaulted by two of them. Three started slugging Albert Bigelow, a white, who was next in line.

Aside from their commitment to nonviolence, these two Freedom Riders were as dissimilar as any two individuals could possibly be. Lewis is a short, muscular divinity student. Bigelow is a tall, grey-haired, ex-naval commander. Lewis is taciturn. Bigelow is articulate. Lewis is one of ten children born on a southern Alabama farm—the only one to finish high school. Bigelow's family background is blueblood, New England. Lewis got his extensive nonviolent training during the lunch counter sit-ins in Nashville, where he was studying for the ministry. Bigelow became a pacifist in revulsion over his World War II experiences as a naval commander and had, like me, participated in protest actions against nuclear tests and war. Had it not been for the Freedom Rides, these two never would have met. Yet, here they were together, being slugged in front of the Greyhound terminal in Rock Hill, South Carolina, and remaining completely nonviolent.

In the course of the slugging, Genevieve Hughes, who was behind Lewis and Bigelow, was pushed to the ground. At that point the police, who had been standing by but taking time in performance of their duty, arrived. The police captain asked Lewis and Bigelow whether they wanted to press charges against any of their assailants. They declined. Thereupon, the Riders entered the white waiting room unmolested.

When the group with which I was riding arrived at the Trailways terminal a few hours later, some of the hoodlums were waiting in cars. However, they did not attack, but only drove after us a few blocks toward Friendship Junior College. The Trailways terminal building was completely locked up. Its eating facilities had been closed since Friendship students had conducted sit-ins there.

It was a memorable experience to meet and talk with the nine jailed-in students and with Reverend C. A. Ivory, the courageous, crippled minister, whose stories are related in Chapter 7. (He died six months later.) When Reverend Ivory met us at the bus station, he stared right back at the hoodlums in the other cars. Later, at his home, he told us of the continuous telephone threats he received. He went on to explain that none of them materialize and that they don't frighten him. "The other night the person on the other end threatened to plant a bomb under my house," he related. "'Why don't you plant two, while you're at it?' I asked. Nothing ever came of it." Reverend Ivory was chairman of our meeting that night, and the nine jailed-in students sang along with our group's chief singer, Jimmi McDonald.

When we left the next day, the Trailways white waiting room was open and a test team sat there unmolested. The same was true at the Greyhound station. The hoodlums did not stage a repeat performance.

Our Trailways group left Rock Hill about lunchtime. At what was supposed to be the lunch stop in Chester, "closed" signs had been hastily put on the doors.

The lunch stop turned out to be Winnsboro, an ultrasegregationist little town. Here occurred the Freedom Ride's first arrest of lunch-counter sit-inners. It all happened so quickly it seemed like a film being reeled too fast.

Henry Thomas, a lanky Negro student, and I entered the white lunch room and sat at the counter. The restaurant owner dashed away from the counter to phone the police.

Within two minutes a police officer who was a stereotype for such a role in Hollywood, stepped over and drawled to Thomas, "Come with me, boy!"

I stepped over to ask about my team mate and was also promptly arrested. We were driven away in a police car before the bus had left the rest stop. Aboard the bus, there was no outspoken reaction, as we learned later from others in the group. Mrs. Bergman, an elderly woman, who had been designated as our observer, got off the bus and braved the hate-filled town alone, trying to find out what the authorities intended to do with us.

We were segregated in the jail and unable to communicate with each other. It was several hours before we were told what the charges against us were. The officer who booked us had been overanxious to fill in that section but the cop who drove us had kept insisting, "Don't write anything down before we talk with the chief." The charge against Thomas turned out to be "trespass," and that against me, "interfering with arrest." However, after eight to ten hours in jail, we were released and the charges dropped. Local officials apparently concluded that our cases would not hold in view of the Supreme Court's Boynton decision.

Thomas was released in the middle of the night, as carloads of hate-filled segregationists still roamed around town. One of them had parked directly in front of the jail with his car's headlights glaring into my cell. I didn't know that Thomas had been released. By the time I was set free, it was dawn. Jim McCain had driven over from his home in Sumter to give me a ride. I learned for the first time that Thomas had gotten out.

After his release, Thomas went to the bus station. A cluster of segregationists were there and it was too late for a bus. "Go in the nigger waiting room," one of them ordered. Thomas entered the white waiting room, bought a candy bar and walked out past the gaping segregationists. Such is his boldness. Some call it foolhardiness. An aunt in Georgia, whom he sometimes visits, prays that God guide him to cease these hazardous activities. But Thomas is determined to make the world better than the one he knew as a youth. He was raised along with nine other children by a drunken stepfather in an overcrowded Georgia shack. While still attending the separate and very unequal school, he worked as road laborer and cotton chopper. He finally managed to win a scholarship at Howard, where he was studying when he joined our Freedom Ride.

Although it was well past midnight and he had been threatened with arrest for "vagrancy," he finally found refuge in the home of a Negro minister who got him a ride to Columbia. From there he took a bus to Sumter. Just as I hadn't known that he had been let loose, he didn't know that I had. When he entered McCain's home and saw me, he came over and shook hands. I crossed the room to meet him. It was a meaningful handshake.

At Sumter, both on arrival and on departure, the white waiting room was tested without incident. There is no restaurant in the Sumter terminal.

In Augusta, Georgia, at both the Trailways and Greyhound terminals, Freedom Riders used all facilities without incident. It marked the first time that Negroes had ever eaten at the terminal restaurants. In fact, only a few months before, a Negro serviceman had been arrested for trying to eat there. Yet our presence at the tables drew little attention. Neither racist hoodlums nor mere curiosity seekers gathered.

To make sure that the policy change was not solely for our arrival and departure, a test team—Herman Harris and Walter Bergman—went back to both terminal restaurants during the evening of our overnight stop and were served courteously.

The rest stop on the way from Augusta to Atlanta was Athens, scene, the previous fall, of mob action against admission of two Negro students to college. Freedom Riders were served at the lunch counter without question. Again, there were no gapers. A person viewing the Athens desegregated lunch counter and waiting room during our fifteen-minute rest stop might have imagined himself at a rest stop up North rather than deep in Georgia.

In Atlanta we were welcomed at the Greyhound terminal by a large group of students, many of whom had participated in the local lunch-counter picketing and sit-ins.

The terminal restaurant was closed but we used the waiting room and rest rooms. The Trailways terminal restaurant was open and two of our teams tested it on departure without incident. During our evening in Atlanta, Martin Luther King, who lives there, stopped by to talk with us and express his support. So did Lonnie King and Ed King, local student leaders. (Neither is related to Martin Luther King.)

Our experiences in traveling through Georgia were clear proof of how desegregation can come peacefully in a Deep South state, providing there is no deliberate incitement to hatred and violence by local or state political leaders. In Alabama, it was the flagrant incitement on the part of Governor Patterson, Eugene "Bull" Connor, Birmingham's notorious police chief, and other high-placed politicians which built up the mob violence which we were to face.

The most nightmarish day of our Freedom Ride was Sunday, May 14, Mother's Day. I identify the date with Mother's Day because when Police Chief Connor was asked why there was not a single policeman at the Birmingham Trailways terminal to avert mob violence, he explained that since it was Mother's Day, most of the police were off duty visiting their mothers. That there was going to be a mob to meet us had been well known around Birmingham for several days. Reverend Fred Shuttlesworth told me so when I phoned to give him the scheduled arrival times of our two buses.

However, we did not know in advance that a similar mob was waiting in Anniston, a rest stop on the way. Our first contingent, aboard Greyhound, learned of this when their bus stopped just outside of Anniston and their driver conferred briefly with the driver of a bus going the other way.

When the Greyhound bus pulled into Anniston, it was immediately surrounded by an angry mob armed with iron bars. They set upon the vehicle, denting the sides, breaking windows, and slashing tires. Finally, police arrived and the bus managed to depart. But the mob pursued it in cars. One car got ahead of the bus and prevented it from gathering speed. About six miles out, one of the tires went flat and the bus was forced to pull over to a gas station.

Within minutes, the pursuing mob was again hitting the bus with iron bars. The rear window was broken and a bomb was hurled inside. Suddenly the vehicle became filled with thick smoke. The passengers, including the Freedom Riders, ducked toward the floor in order to breathe. A few climbed out of a window. Some tried to get out the door, but it was being held shut from the outside.

As Henry Thomas tells it, he shortly succeeded in pushing the door open. As he stepped out, he walked toward a man who looked friendly. Suddenly the man wielded a club from behind his back and struck him over the head.

All the passengers managed to escape before the bus burst into flames and was totally destroyed. The extent of the destruction was shown in the grim newspaper photos of its charred interior and exterior. Policemen, who had been standing by, belatedly came on the scene. A couple of them fired shots in the air. The mob dispersed and the injured were taken to a local hospital. The Freedom Riders were finally transported to Birmingham in cars dispatched by Reverend Shuttlesworth.

When the Trailways bus carrying our contingent arrived in Anniston an hour later, the other passengers learned of what had happened to the Greyhound bus and discontinued their trip. While waiting for the bus to proceed, we heard the sirens of ambulances taking the injured to the hospital, but we didn't know what had happened.

We learned of it only when eight hoodlums climbed aboard and stood by the driver as he made a brief announcement. He concluded by stating that he would refuse to drive on unless the Negroes in our group moved to the formerly segregated rear seats. They remained quietly in their front seats. The hoodlums cursed and started to move them bodily to the rear, kicking and hitting them at the same time.

Walter Bergman, who is a retired professor, and I were seated toward the rear. We moved forward and tried to persuade the hoodlums to desist. We, too, were pushed, punched, and kicked. I found myself face downward on the floor of the bus. Someone was on top of me. I was bleeding. Bergman's jaw was cut and swollen. None of us realized that he also had received a crushing blow on the head which would bring him close to death four months later. Following an appendicitis operation, he suffered an almost fatal stroke which attending doctors attributed to a "pre-existent condition of brain damage" resulting from the Anniston assault. They notified police, because had Bergman died, it would have been a case of murder. Fortunately he recovered.

Mrs. Bergman, who observed the beating, commented later, "I had never before heard the sound of human flesh being hit; it was terrible!"

Finally, all of our group—whites and Negroes—and one Negro passenger who had not gotten off, had been forced to the back of the bus. The hoodlums—together with a pregnant woman whom they had brought aboard—sat in the very front. The seats in between remained empty. At that point the driver agreed to proceed to Birmingham. Some of us doubted whether he would really head there or turn up some obscure side road for another mob scene. For the entire two-hour ride to Birmingham, the hoodlums craned their necks to make sure we didn't move into any of the empty rows of front seats.

Upon arrival in Birmingham, I could see a mob lined up on the sidewalk only a few feet from the loading platform. Most of them were young—in their twenties. Some were carrying ill-concealed iron bars. A few were older men. All had hate showing on their faces.

I looked at them and then I looked at Charles Person, who had been designated as my team mate to test the lunch counter. Person, a slim youth, quiet and determined, had been jailed-in for sixteen days during the campaign to desegrate Atlanta lunch counters. On our overnight stop in Atlanta he visited his parents—reluctantly, he said, because he knew they would try to dissuade him from continuing the Freedom Ride. At departure time, one of us wondered whether the parents had prevailed. Most of us were confident that they hadn't and sure enough, just as we were leaving for the bus station, Person appeared.

Now we stood on the Birmingham unloading platform with the segregationist mob only a few feet away. I did not want to put Person in a position of being forced to proceed if he thought the situation too dangerous. When I looked at him, he responded by saying simply, "Let's go."

As we entered the white waiting room and approached the lunch counter, we were grabbed bodily and pushed toward the alleyway leading to the loading platform. As soon as we got into the alleyway and out of sight of onlookers in the waiting room, six of them started swinging at me with fists and pipes. Five others attacked Person a few feet ahead. Within seconds, I was unconscious on the ground.

I learned only later that the mob went on to assault Tom Langston of the Birmingham *Post-Herald* and smashed his camera. Langston had been sufficiently quick-witted to remove his film, and the photo of my beating, clearly showing the hate-filled expression of my assailants, appeared in next morning's *Post-Herald* and in many newspapers throughout the country. Then, Clancy Lake, a radio newsman, was attacked as he sat in his car, broadcasting an account of the onslaught.

When I regained consciousness, the alleyway was empty. Blood was flowing down my face. I tried to stop the flow with a handkerchief but it soon became soaked. A white soldier came out of the waiting room to see whether I needed help. I declined, because I suddenly saw Bergman coming from the loading platform. He helped me to get a cab. The first two refused to take me, but a third agreed. I told the driver to go to the home of Reverend Shuttlesworth, which was our Birmingham headquarters.

The first thing Reverend Shuttlesworth said to me as I got out of the cab was, "You need to go to a hospital." He called an ambulance. While waiting for it to arrive, I looked for Person among the assembled Negro onlookers. I finally found him and we shook hands. He had a gash in the back of his head and his face was swollen, but he did not require hospitalization. I did not realize how seriously I had been hurt. My head required fifty-three stitches. X rays were taken to determine whether my skull had been fractured and whether my ribs were intact.

I was on an operating table for hours. The doctor who was sewing my stitches had to leave periodically to attend to other emergency cases. During one of these interruptions, reporters arrived. Hospital regulations required that I sign a paper permitting them to interview me and snap photos. I did. Although I was feeling weak and nauseous, I answered their questions to the best of my ability.

Finally, after eight hours in the hospital, I was discharged, my face and head half hidden by bandages. It was two A.M. I had missed the meeting at Reverend Shuttlesworth's church, which I later heard had been packed to capacity. The first thing I did was phone my home in New York to make sure my wife and children wouldn't be frightened by what would appear in the morning papers. Next, I phoned Reverend Shuttlesworth to say that I was ready to leave the hospital. He drove down himself to get me.

I went outside the hospital door to watch for him, but soon a cruising police car drove up and I was warned that if I didn't get off the street, I'd be arrested for vagrancy. I went inside, only to be told by a hospital guard that discharged patients were not permitted in the hospital. I went out again and soon Reverend Shuttlesworth's car arrived. Apparently, the police had been watching, for they followed us and stopped the car after it had gone only a few blocks.

A policeman started harassing the driver until Reverend Shuttlesworth, who was sitting next to him, spoke up. We were then allowed to proceed. "They don't want to get into another tangle with me," Reverend Shuttlesworth explained. The most militant civil rights leader in Birmingham, Reverend Shuttlesworth had been arrested many times. His church had been bombed and his children had been assaulted. Yet he remains undaunted.

We reached his house and I lay down on the living room couch. I felt too tired and sick to sleep. I must have looked sick for, next morning, some of the group insisted that I should fly home immediately. I said that for the most severely beaten rider to quit could be interpreted as meaning that violence had triumphed over nonviolence. It might convince the ultrasegregationists that by violence they could stop the Freedom Riders. My point was accepted and we started our meeting to plan the next lap, from Birmingham to Montgomery. We decided to travel in a single contingent on a Greyhound bus leaving at three in the afternoon.

Reverend Shuttlesworth and two members of his church drove us to the terminal, but the bus never left. Drivers of both Greyhound and Trailways had determined to refuse to drive the Freedom Riders. We waited more than an hour on the loading platform as the mob started to gather. We recognized some of their faces. We sat down in the white waiting room. As evening approached, it became clear that we would not get out of Birmingham in time to make our scheduled meeting in Montgomery and that in fact we might not get a bus out of Birmingham for several days. We decided to fly to New Orleans to make sure of being at the mass rally there marking the end of the Freedom Ride on May 17, anniversary of the Supreme Court's key antisegregation decision.

In cars supplied by Reverend Shuttlesworth, we rode from the bus terminal to the airport and got reservations on an Eastern Air Lines plane leaving about an hour later. No sooner had we boarded it than an announcement came over the loudspeaker that a bomb threat had been received, and all passengers would have to debark while luggage was inspected. Time dragged on and eventually the flight was canceled. The mob started to gather in the airport. Dressed in T shirts and dungarees and clustered in groups, they were obviously not airline passengers. Near the doorway to the loading gates, I heard a youth tell his girl friend, "We're going to get them as they come through this way." What deterred the ever-growing mob from staging a repeat performance of the previous day's assault was that, this time, police were present in sizable numbers.

One heartening incident occurred. A white man approached us and introduced himself as a resident of Birmingham. He said he was sorry about what had happened to us there and wanted us to know that there were some whites in the city who thoroughly disapproved.

We got reservations aboard a Capital Airlines plane, which was the next flight to New Orleans. That flight was canceled also, though no public announcement was made of a bomb scare.

By about ten P.M., police cleared the mob out of the airport and set up a roadblock nearby to prevent them from returning. We finally took off on an Eastern Air Lines plane at eleven, after six tense hours in the airport. An hour later we landed in New Orleans. A deputation of the New Orleans CORE group was at the airport to welcome us. A battery of newspaper photographers snapped photos as we walked from the plane into the waiting room. The first Freedom Ride had ended.

30 THE ATLANTA CONSTITUTION, Friday, May 26, 1961

As I See It

Brinkley Takes Stand Against 'Freedom Riders'

By PAUL JONES

I always thought David Brinkley was the best newsman on television—and now I know it.

Brinkley's keen judgment, his sardonic humor and his devotion to his job and to the welfare of the country are at once evident.

Throughout the 1960 presidential conventions, Brinkley separated fiction from fact, put people, places and things in their proper perspective.

Jones

His reports on the Washton scene which comprise the most important part of the Huntley-Brinkley Report are concise, newsy, spiced with the Brinkley pepper of wit which has helped make him one of the most respected men in TV journalism.

Brinkley said something during a Wednesday news program which heightened my esteem of the man.

"What follows," he said, in reporting on the "Freedom Riders" excursion through Alabama and Mississippi, "is opinion, clearly labeled:

"It is time for those so-called 'Freedom Riders' to stop this. They are accomplishing nothing whatsoever and, on the contrary, are doing possible harm.

"Aside from physical injuries done to dozens of people, all this is humiliating the United States around the world. There is no doubt the Negro in the South needs and deserves better schools, better jobs and a better deal in many respects. But this kind of exhibition now in progress is not going to get this for them.

"On the contrary, it is more likely to inflame Southern opinion still further and make these advances even more difficult than they already were.

"And we can't help believing that schools, jobs and the right to vote are a lot more important than who should swear at the bus station. That particular aspect of segregation certainly could wait until last.

"The bus riders are, of course, within their legal rights in riding buses where they like, but the result of these expeditions are of no benefit to anyone, white or Negro, the North or the South, nor the United States in general. We think they should stop it."

David Brinkley

BRINKLEY'S comments were in sharp contrast to those made the other day by Dave Garroway, who allowed anger to overshadow good judgment when the audio portion of a report on the "Freedom Riders," which originated at WSB-TV, failed because of technical difficulty.

Garroway muttered something to the effect that news was being "censored" by the South before being released for consumption in the North.

Garroway's statement was not only incorrect—it was inflammatory.

WSB-TV informed both Garroway and NBC-TV. An apology was made on the Today show on the following morning by Frank Blair, Today newsman. Garroway should have made it.

Dave Garroway

The most significant thing about Brinkley's comments was the statement, in the beginning, that "What follows is opinion, clearly stated."

MRS. C. F. WYSONG of Atlanta writes: "Congratulations on your excellent column about (Dave) Garroway et al. I agree with you wholeheartedly."

UNIT 9-5

THE AGONY OF ALBANY

There had been an undercurrent of unrest in Albany. Negro leaders early in 1961 had presented fairly modest proposals to the City Commission, which were ignored. But it was not until November of that year that, out of entirely avoidable friction over the ICC terminal ruling, the energies of discontent were set off in Albany so furiously that it was to become notorious worldwide as a site and symbol of Negro protest and white resistance.

Various attempts were made at Albany in November to test the ICC ruling, beginning the first day it went into effect. In some cases police ordered Negroes out of the Trailways bus terminal, and in others made arrests on charges of breach of the peace. Protests of these arrests with mass marches began. For the protests, there was a loose organization composed of ministerial alliances and an outpost of SNCC field workers engaged in voter registration activity, with some support of the local NAACP. This later came to be called the Albany Movement.

Out of the at-first unclear focus of protest of the Albany Movement there gradually emerged a frontal assault on all forms of segregation in the small city—bus and train station, library, park, hospital, municipal transit, jury, public and private employment—and against police brutality. It was the first such attack on all segregation by direct action, although there were smaller-scale precedents in other cities. And it was the most ambitious undertaking so deep in the heart of the segregationist deep South, in the Black-Belt country of the old plantations where the social sense of segregation had been instilled in both races as deeply as law and custom could do it.

The bus station protests began a pattern—of crowded church meetings, singing and praying, marches into the business district, arrests, and protest marches against the arrests. This chain reaction built up to an explosive night meeting in mid-December when Dr. Martin Luther King, Jr., head of SCLC, the Rev. Ralph Abernathy, and other nationally known leaders spoke as guests of the movement.

The next day was a Saturday in the county-seat town, with shoppers from the surrounding area on the broad downtown streets festooned with Christmas decorations. Hundreds of Negroes marched behind King and Abernathy and Dr. W. G. Anderson, leader of the movement, toward those streets, silently at first, singing their hymns of defiance when trouble came. Trouble, as in previous demonstrations, met them in the form of beautifully disciplined and efficiently deployed forces of Police Chief Laurie

---

New South, October–November 1963.

Pritchett. They quickly arrested the demonstrators, and as swiftly marched them safely, singing their songs, to jail.

To keep the city jail from overflowing, to keep its threat potent, police had all along been taking the demonstrators to prisons of surrounding counties made available to Albany in its emergency. Including Dr. King, and those who followed him on that Saturday, arrests stood at 737 since demonstrations began.

At this point, City Hall began negotiations with leaders of the Albany Movement. These were conducted by Chief Pritchett rather than the City Commission which had adamantly refused all along all approaches for negotiation. These talks resulted in release of all demonstrators on bond (including King and Abernathy), some indications that discussion on other points would continue, and the end of the mass demonstrations.

Albany Negroes were told by their leaders they had won. But the congratulations pouring in from all over the country, including one from Attorney General Robert Kennedy, were not so much to the Albany Movement for what it had tried to achieve for Albany Negroes, as to the city for having avoided violence.

The police force unquestionably had achieved this in a trying situation. Superb police work broke up anything that had the potential of a white mob; it controlled streets and alleys; it moved marchers out of harm's way straight into jail. Only in the aftermath, and from only those especially concerned with civil rights, came suggestions of a further function and duty of police power—protection of the rights of citizens, including those of the Negro demonstrators of Albany to petition and protest.

Constantly in the background of this first siege of demonstrations in Albany was the U.S. Justice Department, To what end? "The department," said the Southern Regional Council afterward, "apparently decided not to exercise any enforcing power in Albany; it confined its efforts to attempted persuasion and mediation... By its nature, as an enforcing agency, the Department is not a good instrument of mediation and persuasion... "

Evident from the beginning in Albany was something of importance true in most other mass movements—the role of the Negro church in the Negro revolution. Some courageous ministers, ever in Negro society more influential than most of their white contemporaries, showed their great value in the deeds of the hour and, probably more importantly, in the effect of their words about freedom uttered through the years from their pulpits. Precepts of the Judeo-Christian tradition in support of Negro aspirations wound through mass meetings in songs, in prayers, in the reading of the Bible, and in the awesome spirit that moved many individuals to acts of courage and selflessness far beyond normal demands of American life.

The uneasy truce won by these acts disintegrated during the first six months of 1962. White leaders refused to make any concessions, attempt any compromises; what had seemed to be promises evaporated; the frail lines of biracial communication snapped.

Then surprisingly, with a hot Georgia governor's race underway, the Recorders Court of the City of Albany called Dr. King and the Rev. Mr. Abernathy back to the city to stand trial on charges incurred in the pre-Christmas demonstration—parading without a permit, obstructing the sidewalk, and disorderly conduct. They were found guilty on July 10, and chose to go to jail for 45 days rather than pay $178 fines.

The Albany Movement, already stirring with boycotts and sit-ins, began to march again.

There were more mass meetings, more fervent even than those six months before; more demonstrations and mass arrests; an injunction against demonstrations issued by a newly appointed federal judge, J. Robert Elliott; a night march in violation of the injunction; a setting aside of the injunction by Judge Elbert P. Tuttle of the U.S. Court of Appeals; release and re-arrest of Dr. King; a federal court suit filed by Negro plaintiffs against all segregation in Albany, and continued demonstrations.

But insurgents against segregation were not so eager to march during July and August as they had been in November and December when success seemed certain. The only thing certain during that summer campaign was jail at the end of the march. Nevertheless by Labor Day, when the thrust of the campaign more or less gently collapsed, to continue sporadically the rest of the year in minor sorties of picketing and boycotts, total arrests, including the 700 during the winter and others in between, stood at 1,500.

Some of the summer marches were at night, and they moved their emotion through a row of Negro beer joints and honkey-tonks, bringing occupants, in various degrees of intoxication, into the streets in near-mob mood. From such crowds, rocks and bricks were thrown toward police. The violence was not from demonstrators or Movement regulars (indeed leaders of the Movement performed bravely and effectively to calm the crowds attracted to the demonstrations), but such distinctions were not made by Albany white people, including police, hostile to the Movement. "Look what those non-violent bricks did," police called to reporters as one of their number was helped away with an injured jaw.

Violence came from other sources during that muggy-hot time of tension. C. B. King (no relation to Dr. M. L. King, Jr.), first and only Negro lawyer in Albany and a Movement leader, entered the office of Dougherty County Sheriff D. C. (Cull) Campbell on July 28, to inquire about a prisoner. A few moments later he staggered out of the office bleeding from head wounds. A witness said Sheriff Campbell had caned him. Sheriff Campbell told the *New York Times*: "He didn't get out so Goddamit I put him out."

Mrs. Slater King, wife of the Movement vice-president (and sister-in-law of C. B. King), on July 23 was kicked and knocked to the ground by deputies at the Mitchell County jail in Camilla, where she was visiting prisoners transferred there from Albany. Mitchell County Sheriff John W. Maples, who denied that she was struck or kicked, said that she attacked deputies, and that her injuries came from a fall when she swung at one of them. Mrs. King was pregnant at the time. (She later lost the child.) Her three children were with her, a three-year old in her arms. The Federal Bureau of Investigation was reported at the time to be investigating.

To date there has been no Justice Department action in either of these cases, nor federal action on whether the police violated in November 1961 the ICC ruling at the bus terminal. (Sheriff Campbell has since died.)

Justice did act in another case—against Albany Movement leaders. A federal grand jury brought indictments on August 9, 1963 against the president and two other members of the Movement on charges of obstructing justice. It indicted six others for perjury before the grand jury. The indictments grew out of a boycott campaign in April 1963. They alleged that the Movement boycotted and drove a supermarket out of business because its owner, while serving on a federal trial jury, voted against a Negro plaintiff in a civil rights suit. (The plaintiff had unsuccessfully sought $125,000 damages on grounds that Sheriff L. Warren Johnson of Baker County had shot him after he had been placed under arrest.) One of the defendants on the obstruction of justice charge entered a guilty plea from his new home in New York state. Dr. W. G. Anderson, former president of the Albany Movement, who has since moved to Detroit, was tried in Albany during October 1963, and a deadlocked jury resulted. The case was expected to be retried.

The contrast between Justice Department diligence in this case, and its failure to act on the others was noted in an editorial in the *Atlanta Journal*:

> The Justice Department in the past usually has acted as if it could forget Albany. Although the federal government has clear authority in cases involving conspiracy to deny constitutional rights, the department has never moved against any such denials in Albany.

After the end of the second phase of the big Albany campaigns, national magazines and most observers appraised the efforts of the Negro people there as having lost much, gained little. The gains: transportation terminals had been used on a desegregated basis; the city library, after first removing its chairs, removed barriers to Negroes.

Perhaps the most positive achievement was the effect on some other small Georgia cities. "We don't want another Albany here," said their white leaders, and sat down to work out desegregation problems. This happened most successfully in Brunswick and Macon.

Albany in 1963 dropped all its segregation ordinances, but this was generally viewed as a technical move to aid in legal action defending segregation. "Albany is just as segregated as ever," said Chief Pritchett. In 1963 also, the city sold its large Tift Park swimming pool and tennis courts to a private owner—the former New Englander who publishes the segregationist Albany *Herald* and dabbles in segregationist state politics, James C. Gray. These facilities, which had been built by taxpayers, would be for whites only, said their new owner.

Albany represents "at once the triumph of sophisticated segregation and the low point for the mass demonstration . . . " said Atlanta newsman Reese Cleghorn writing in *The New Republic*. Said Charles F. Wittenstein, Southeast Director of the American Jewish Committee:

> We have seen an enormous amount of time, effort, money and sacrifice expended in an effort which has, to this day, failed to desegregate anything whatsoever. All it has succeeded in doing is to create bitterness locally and embarrassment for the United States internationally. The explanation for the failure is the lack of clear thinking about tactics . . .

His argument was that direct action was the wrong tactic to use in a situation like Albany's, where it had little chance of changing minds or prevailing against a police-state apparatus of resistance. He urged court action.

The blanket suit seeking desegregation of all public facilities, filed by the Albany Movement in the heat of the summer campaign, was thrown out by Judge Elliott. Subsequently, Judge Elliott, in a suit brought by Albany Negroes, ordered the Dougherty County Board of Education to submit a proposal to begin desegregating public schools on a grade-a-year basis, beginning with the first grade. The board submitted such a plan, to go into effect in 1964.

Thus the dismal dragging on of the Albany story seems to do nothing but point up failures of direct action—a thing undreamed of during the early heady days when "it works!" was the rallying cry.

(One further aspect of failure that showed plainly in Albany was dissension and open competition between the civil rights organizations. This was mostly behind-the-scenes, but apparent enough to be noted in newspaper stories.)

In defense of what happened in Albany, in claiming for it a certain kind of victory, officials of the Southern Christian Leadership Conference and others have stressed intangible gains, in the individual attainments of dignity and the group attainment of cohesiveness among Albany Negroes.

No one who saw and felt the spirit of the Albany Movement, knew the moments of truth and of individual courage and strength which quite ordinary Negro people came to in their fight against all the fears and furies of segregation can question that there was an extraordinary intangible quality to it all. Once he had felt what was there, an individual would never again be the same.

But America tends to watch public events like baseball. Winning is important. Also, despite the heavy press and television coverage, it is doubtful if much of the intangible quality of Albany was communicated effectively to the nation. Maybe the nation wasn't ready for anything quite this powerful. Certainly it was not ready to admit that police action "to keep the peace" could be an instrument of oppression.

And this was the key. If Albany were a failure, it was a failure of the American people and their national government, who gave tacit and frequently outspoken approval to the use of the police in behalf of the interest of one race of people, to the theory that preservation of order requires the repression of individual rights. Over the country, people forgot who had caused the Albany demonstrations, and applauded, now quietly and now decisively, those same people for repressing what their own defiance of federal authority in November 1961 had caused. If Albany were a failure, it was because the forces ranged against the Albany Movement were too powerful.

But by the next big phase of direct action, the nation was better prepared to understand and even act on the implications of Albany. All of these implications, for good, for evil, were present on a larger, clearer canvass in Birmingham—and after Birmingham, over the nation.

UNIT 9-6

The Bloody Battleground of Albany

Slater King

Around 1903, Dr. W.E.B. Du Bois came to Albany, Dougherty County, Georgia, the heart of the black belt, to do a study on the lives of the Blacks who inhabited the fertile black land. He viewed this study symbolically as applying to Blacks across the whole of America. He further stated, "In these chapters I have studied the struggles of the massed millions of the Black Peasantry."

Since this time, very little has been heard of Albany except that it was the home of a few Negro notables, such as Congressman William Dawson, Ray Charles and Dr. Jeanne Noble. Repeatedly, for seven or eight years, it was also heard of as being one of the ten fastest growing cities in the United States.

Most people were amazed to read in December, 1961 of 700 Albany residents going to jail in protest demonstrations. What made people look at the Albany situation a little closer was that past civil rights demonstrations, such as the sit-ins and freedom rides, had involved mainly college youth, but here the total community was involved, both young and old. Let us look at Albany and see what factors led to the demonstrations. Its population is now approximately 60,000, approximately 40 per cent Negro, or about 24,000. Albany lies in the center of a vast sea of blackness; excluding the northern metropolitan areas, it is estimated that only in Mississippi is there a heavier concentration of Negroes than is found within a 50-mile radius of Albany. This was a vast slave breeding area in the heart of the cotton kingdom. Whenever whites were heavily outnumbered, the severity of the repressive measures used against Negroes increased inversely.

Albany sits in the heart of an area that has a long history of lynchings and horrible police brutality. There is Leesburg, Lee County; Newton, Baker County; Dawson, Terrell County; and Camilla, Mitchell County.

There is no record of any Negro ever having been "officially" lynched in Dougherty County. It has been thought of as a "relatively" good town for Negroes, in comparison to the surrounding towns. Dr. Du Bois stated the following in *The Souls of Black Folk*, in 1903:

New South, 1964.

> The Black Belt was not, as many assumed, a movement towards fields of labor under more genial climatic conditions; it was primarily a huddling for self-protection, a massing of the black population for mutual defense in order to secure the peace and tranquillity necessary to economic advance. In Dougherty County, Georgia, one can see easily the results of this experiment in huddling for protection. Only 10 percent of the adult population was born in the county, yet the blacks outnumber the whites four or five to one. There is undoubtedly a security to the blacks in their very number, of personal freedom from arbitrary treatment which make hundreds of laborers cling to Dougherty in spite of low wages and economic distress.

So Albany has been a little more lenient than the surrounding areas and the following factors may have contributed to it.

There has always been a strong Jewish influence, both economic and political.

Early in the history of Albany there was founded an American Missionary Association School which helped to lift the educational and cultural horizon in the community.

There has been relatively a little more wealth in Albany among Negroes than you would find in comparative southern towns; i.e., ten Negro families whose wealth exceeds a quarter of a million dollars each. Another instance: one downtown bank which has six million dollars in Negro deposits out of a total deposit of 22 million dollars; a larger number of Negro businesses than would be found in a comparative southern town of similar size.

Approximately one per cent of the Negro population live exceedingly well; ten per cent who exist on a median income—such as teachers, civil service employees at the post office, local marine base and Turner Air Force Base; while the other 89 per cent of the masses live on a bare subsistence level. The persons in the above average and median income groups usually act as a buffer zone to keep the discontent of the masses quiescent.

Other factors were that there had been a strong Negro voters league in Albany after suffrage was granted to Negroes in Georgia. The league was later split by a leadership conflict in Albany. In the meantime, a staunch segregationist who was a native New Englander and a graduate of Dartmouth College purchased the only daily newspaper, a radio station, and put up the only television station in Albany, which gave him a complete monopoly of the news media. Another factor was the conservative leadership that went underground after the 1954 decision. Many of the officers of the local NAACP were even afraid to accept membership after 1954.

THE BIRTH OF THE ALBANY MOVEMENT

The City Commission had a policy of denying all Negro requests. There was also the continuation of white men constantly invading the privacy of Albany State College, while the President of the College would not allow any action to be taken by the more militant faculty members and students against the guilty parties; the continued affronts and approaches made to Negro women attending Albany State College by whites bred discontent. There were windows broken out of ministers' homes because they dared request the only local daily, the Albany Herald, to discontinue its abusive treatment of Negroes in the news. The catalytic agents who helped to channel this discontent were two student field directors from the Student Nonviolent Coordinating Committee, Atlanta Office; these were Charles Sherrod and Cordell Reagon. They held mass meetings with the youth and finally some of this feeling of great discontent under the repressive system channeled over into the older people. The Albany Movement was founded because of the rivalry between some of the existing civil rights organizations, and it was a feeling that if all of the activities were put under the aegis of one head then the program could be carried on much more effectively.

Therefore, on November 17, 1961, The Albany Movement was founded. Dr. W. G. Anderson was elected president, M. S. Paige, secretary, and I, Slater King, vice president.

The aim of the organization is to totally desegregate all city facilities and secure equal educational and economic opportunities for every citizen. In an attempt to effect the aims of the organization, the Albany Movement has petitioned, attempted to negotiate and protested.

These protest demonstrations involved the whole of the Negro community and in the summer of 1962, they began anew, and approximately 2,000 people had been jailed.

After the dust had settled, many people began evaluating the situation. The whites said that nothing had been gained and that the Negroes were now further behind than they had ever been. I think that the immediate reaction of most Negroes, right after the demonstrations, was the feeling of being let down. For most expected out of the great emotionalism and drama that was a part of the first stage of the demonstrations—that these few days of jailing would act as penance to force the whites to accord to Negroes the privileges that they had withheld so long. There are very few visible gains; the municipal buses agreed to desegregate after the Negroes refused to ride, but the city stubbornly refused to give any written assurances to the Albany Movement that it would not harass and intimidate Negro passengers, so the bus line withdrew and Albany now has no municipal transit system.

The library has been integrated. The city has struck down all of its statutes involving segregation (this was done to give the individual businesses a stronger legal basis for the maintenance of segregation). The public schools have been ordered to desegregate, by a court order, in September of 1964. Negroes gained the right to use the interstate bus station waiting rooms and restaurants without being harassed and intimidated by the local police.

These tangible gains (if they can be called gains) are negligible and hardly worth mentioning. The main gains that I see are those that have internally shaken the Negro community.

There is more of a sense of community and identity in the Negro community than ever before. Crime among Negroes has dropped considerably.

There has been a tremendous number of self-help organizations arising in the Negro community—such as, the teachers volunteering to teach night classes to the old and to those who were not able to receive education in the past; the Albany Movement has acted as the organization to see that to those Negroes who are without, charity is extended in the form of clothes and food. It has also attempted to see that for those Negroes who have good minds and have been unable, because of economic reasons, to secure an education, some way be found to help them scholastically to further their education. This has been done in attempting to propagate many of the policies of Dr. Du Bois, who felt that the Negro could never advance as long as he allowed his best minds to wither and atrophy.

Another gain is the breaking down of the snobbishness with which professional Negroes formerly looked at the Negro masses. Out of the downtown boycott, the existing Negro businesses have been strengthened and new ones have been added.

THE MOVEMENT EDUCATES THE MASSES

For two years the Movement has been the place where the Negroes have come for inspiration, to learn Negro history, and to further the strong feeling of identity, to know that they are not alone, to learn how politics work, and how they have been taken advantage of. They have heard speakers with opinions ranging from Dr. Lonnie X. Cross, representative of the Black Muslims to Dr. Martin Luther King, Jr., representing the integrationist. This has been a tremendous educative process for the masses.

In the liability ledger, I would state the following items:

In the Albany area, there are so many areas where Negroes need help and yet there are so few trained people to work.

I feel that we have not brought a wide enough spectrum of speakers before the people in our meetings; I feel that the socialist should have been represented by speakers such as Norman Thomas, the Communist by speakers such as Benjamin Davis, the Black Muslims by such speakers as Malcolm X and others.

I feel that the masses should be educated by being exposed to all of the political ideologies and let them decide what assets they wish to accept or reject in making a new and more workable system.

We have aroused emotions of the people and whetted their desire for freedom but we have not done the thorough organizational work which I think is essential to the success of any movement. You have to have emotion, but you also have to have discipline, well-thought-out plans that our best minds must help draft, and army-like discipline. Most civil rights movements, including ours, have lacked these.

In my opinion, we have attacked segregation too broadly. We have really attacked too many areas to do an effective job on any one of them. We must now put all of our energies behind one project at one time, and then move on to another; *e.g.*, in Savannah, Birmingham, and Albany, all three cities have had tremendous demonstrations. Savannah has desegregated its hotels, motels, and movie theaters. Birmingham and Albany desegregated little or none. The difference is that in Savannah, before beginning demonstrations, Mr. Hosea Williams, the chairman of the Chatham County Crusade for Voters, had thoroughly organized the Negroes in his total Congressional District and had a large disciplined political machine that moved instantaneously and with unity. Because of this concentration on the political area in Savannah, the Negroes had been the balance of power which had elected the sheriff and mayor.

This is no attempt to state a panacea, but to really be effective in our Movements across the country, we must unite these three ingredients: Protest, Political Mobilization, and Economic Unity.

I recently ran for mayor of the city of Albany. The masses of the Negroes were very enthusiastic towards the candidacy of a Negro for mayor. It was only among some of the older and professional Negroes that it was felt that we were moving too rapidly, that a Negro should not run for the highest office in the city. However, the candidacy accomplished the following:

It consolidated the Negro vote and formed one bloc unit where Negroes voted 90 per cent together on all of the candidates.

It brought an end to a few Negro ministers and businessmen being able to sell out the Negro vote for money.

The racists have a monopoly of the news, but through paid television appearances, we were able to tell the other half of the story. I stated the Negro demands unequivocally, which opened many eyes and gained some white supporters.

We created a new image for Negro boys and girls, a quickening interest in the political, and a desire to take part in the political sphere.

My candidacy further served as a vehicle to teach Negroes how politics work. Heretofore, the candidates have come into the Negro community to pay the Negroes to vote for them. Negroes must learn that they must support financially the candidate most interested in their welfare. *All expenses for my campaign were paid for out of the Albany Negro community.*

One of the items that we spoke against in the campaign was the lack of a Negro truant officer in Albany. Now, a trained truant officer, a college graduate, has been hired.

The massed and unified black voting power frightens many of the white politicians and will make them grant concessions according to the number and unanimity of that vote.

It has greatly increased voter registration among Negroes, and many are continuing to register.

THE FEDERAL GOVERNMENT INDICTS THE VICTIMS!

At the beginning of the Movement, we felt that we were not alone and that the power of the federal government was with us in our efforts. Though this feeling was rapidly washed away, as many Negroes began to feel that the FBI was as prejudiced as the local police, we still were shocked by the series of events that took place.

On April 8th, there was a trial in Albany, Georgia, of Ware vs. Johnson, involving a Negro, Charlie Ware, who charged that Baker County sheriff L. Warren Johnson shot and beat him.

On April 12th, a federal jury decided in favor of the sheriff. Carl Smith, a white grocer, whose store received 99 per cent Negro patronage, was a juror.

It is alleged by the Justice Department that at the Monday night meeting on April 15th, Dr. W. G. Anderson, President of the Albany Movement, mentioned Carl Smith in the course of his remarks.

Saturday, April 20th, some high school students set up a picket line at the Smith store. They demanded that Smith upgrade Negro employees to responsible positions, such as cashiers. All Negro employees at the store held menial jobs. Similar campaigns had been started against employers throughout Albany during the previous eighteen months.

No picket sign made reference to Smith's service on the jury. The line lasted about an hour, during which time, several pickets were arrested, effectively breaking the picket line. The line was never renewed.

Monday, April 22nd, Smith began to move out of the store, contending that he had been driven out of business by the boycott. It is alleged that his attorney, B. C. Gardner, member of the legal firm of Smith, Gardner, Kelley, and Wiggins (Asa Kelley is Albany's mayor), requested immediate investigation. The Justice Department conducted the most vigorous prosecution yet seen in the history of the civil rights movement.

On August 9th, nine Albany leaders were indicted. Anderson, Luther Woodall, and Robert Colbert were charged with conspiracy to injure a juror because of his assent to a verdict in clearing the sheriff in a federal case.

Mrs. Goldie Jackson, Rev. Samuel Wells, Thomas Chatmon, and Robert Thomas and I were charged with perjury before the grand jury. The charges state that they either denied having been at a lawyer's meeting during the week of July 29th or denied remembering having been there.

Joni Rabinowitz, a white field worker with the Student Nonviolent Coordinating Committee, working in the area of voter registration in Albany was charged with perjury because she said that she was not at the scene of the picketing.

I am now acting president of the Albany Movement. Mrs. Jackson is recording secretary and full time employee of the Movement. Rev. Wells is one of the most active voter registration workers and led a protest march last July. Chatmon works in the area of voter registration and was a recent candidate for city commissioner of the city of Albany. The youth, Robert Colbert, pleaded guilty in New York and was sentenced to 18 months on a suspended sentence. Dr. Anderson and Luther Woodall were tried in Albany. There was a mistrial, and it is alleged that three jurors on the all-white jury voted for acquittal. *The Justice Department has announced that they will try the Anderson and Woodall cases again in Albany in April.*

In the other charges, all defendants were held guilty of perjury except Mrs. Elza (Goldie) Jackson, whose trial will come up the second Monday in January. The five of us who had been found guilty are Rev. Samuel B. Wells, Joni Rabinowitz, Robert Thomas, Thomas Chatmon and myself.

As I write this, John L. S. Barnum, treasurer of the Sumter County Movement in neighboring Americus, Georgia, has also been charged on two counts of perjury by the grand jury there.

DISILLUSIONMENT WITH THE FEDERAL ROLE

As one observes this, one wonders if these perjury cases are precedents that may be used to stifle civil rights leaders throughout the south.

This is very hard for us to understand, since the government has never taken any affirmative action resulting in relief in Albany where there have been clear violations of Negroes' civil rights. Examples of such cases are: *Walter Harris was shot down in cold blood on the streets of Albany by the police; Attorney C. B. King was caned over the head by Dougherty County Sheriff D. C. Campbell, and required many stitches; William (Bill) Hansen's jaw was broken and several ribs cracked; my wife, Marion, of Albany, was beaten and kicked by police, causing the death of our unborn child; over 100 cases of police brutality have been reported to the Justice Department. Out of all these cases reported, there have been no indictments.*

From my observation the majority of the black people of Albany are disillusioned, frightened, and bitter. The faith that they had in the mighty white federal government has dwindled. They now seem to feel that they are on their own.

It is reported that the sales of guns and rifles among whites and blacks is at an all-time high.

There are two growing forces. There is a white opposition that says, "never" and the ever-growing number of Negroes who say "NOW!"

When two determined forces meet, there can only be a great conflagration. If the government continues its policy of evasiveness and its constant attempts to appease the segregationists who are in high places all over the country, these two forces will meet in what I am afraid will be a bloody battleground. I surely do not want to see this, because I feel that it may spell more loss for the Negroes than for the whites, but unless the government takes decisive action, all of America can be hurt.

When Du Bois wrote *The Souls of Black Folk,* in reference to this area and Dougherty County, Georgia, he stated that it had implications for millions of black people. We, too, in Albany, sixty years later, feel that what has taken place here in the past, and what takes place in the future will have heavy implications for twenty million blacks in America.

HEAVY LADEN

Doris Derby

The soul of my people bleeds,
Gushing with sadness
Just as Mother Earth's does
When, after a heavy rainstorm
She, laden with water
Is stepped upon
By heavy, sharp-heeled boots
And the water within
Is forced out in spurts.

UNIT 9-7

THE NEW BLACK RADICALS

Charles McLaurin and Randy Battle

LETTER FROM AN AMERICUS JAIL

Randy Battle

ABOUT ORGANIZING

I have found that it's better to go into a community if you are planning on staying for a while, and first getting to know people and letting people get to know you. Now you can become known and get to know people in many ways. You can first start by going to the churches, cafés, school dances, community club meetings, if there are such. And at all of these, whatever you go to, you should talk to people, and try to get them to either let you come around to their homes or you ask them to yours.

If you are young, like most of us are, then you must be careful about how you go about talking to older people. The best way to get to the older people is to have something to offer. If you have ever been in the field, often it is found that older people like to talk about jobs, bad streets, no street lights, bad housing, and how the white school is so much better than their own. People talk about these because most of the time they don't know enough about any of the other things that affect them to talk about them. So the thing for you to do is to kind of ask questions and answer them at the same time. To do this will, or would, give people other things to think about.

After you have made yourself known you are then able to ask things of the people. You can ask them why they are living in such a bad house and get an answer without offending the person whom you are talking to. But without being known you just can't talk truthfully with a man or woman who only makes $10 a week in Miss Ann's kitchen, or who toms for Mr. Charles for $25 or $30 a week, and look for an answer. I have found that now they will tell why they don't do anything or go along with the things The Movement does. I find mostly people will say that M. L. King won't give me a job when I lose the one I have, nor will he give me any food for my hungry children. So I am going to keep away from them Movement people like my boss told me, because she is the one who is going to help me.

What I will say is that the first thing you do when you go into a community is to get to know as many people as you can, not as a leader or anything of that kind, but as a person tired of living in bad houses on bad streets without lights, no place for your child to go after school, and not a very good school.

I don't think you should worry about making contact when you go into a community, because if you do the things I have stated heretofore then you have made your contacts. Also, by this time you should know who the key people are, whatever that means. Maybe I should ask what kind of people are considered as key people. Then maybe I could speak to that. I don't know how to get people into a leadership position. But there are ways, I know. Sometimes you just kind of force them one way or another by asking them to do little things, whatever may be the situation where you are or maybe where he's working. All people are not the same; it takes more to get some people going than others.

But to me there is something in your letter of which I have read, that has some real meaning to me. And that is how do you overcome fear, apathy, and suspicion—not only in the hard-core areas, but everywhere there is a movement under way. I don't believe anyone knows how to overcome these. One can only say what he or she feels is the best way to overcome apathy, fear, and suspicion.

Before I say what I feel, I would like to go back to what Sherrod would say when he asked people to go down in a march or sit-in. He would look at you a while, then slowly he would say, "If you can free a person's mind, then he or she is able to think." In so many words he would say if you can give a blind man 20–20 vision, then he will be able to see when he comes to a corner. How do you free one mind? In my own mind I would say somewhat in the same way you overcome apathy, fear, and suspicion.

But there is just one thing that I worry about most; and that is fear; for I believe if you can overcome fear then all of the others you can easily overcome. There are many ways to overcome fear, and for some people a few or one of the ways will help them to overcome fear. And for others it may take all of them. The way to overcome fear could be for some people registering to vote, or going downtown in a march or sit-in, or going to the police station to go someone's bond.

NOTES ON ORGANIZING

Charles McLaurin

Since I am under the impression that SNCC workers are organizers, I think that this is what they should do.

A SNCC worker should never take a leadership role in the community unless he is in his own community. A SNCC worker should give the responsibility of leadership to the community person or persons whom he has or is building. The SNCC worker should give form and guidance to the people's organization, and/or their programs.

I think that in each area one faces different kinds of problems. I've attempted to state some of the problems found in small communities such as Ruleville and Indianola, Miss.

The larger, more middle-class communities will be somewhat different.

I think you at first meet the people on their own terms, or you lose.

ENTERING THE COMMUNITY

There are two ways to enter a community: the *invited* and the *uninvited* way.

The *invited* is the easiest, because you know that somebody wants you. Somebody will put you up for a while, and through this person or persons, you will meet others.

An invited person goes to live with X person in Y community, Mr. X carries the person to church on Sunday. He introduces him to his friends and neighbors. You are there to do a job which at this time is undefined; so you act friendly, smiling and greeting the ladies as they approach you. Then, with your warm, kindly face you say to the people: "I want to do something for this community." That afternoon you are asked out to someone's home for dinner. Go, because this is one time you will be able to talk with a family, or maybe several families. Remember, try to answer all questions asked of you at this point, because you are on trial. You must impress, as well as express.

An *uninvited* worker faces many difficulties; first, he is unexpected and in many cases unwanted by the do-nothing leaders of the community. He is a stranger to the people, and therefore, he is alone in a strange place. If he is to be successful, he must become a part of the community.

How One Becomes Part of the Community

First, get a place to stay. It is best to get a place in the community, with a well-known family. Once you have a place to stay, you have made the first contact in the community; however, in many cases it will not be as easy as writing words on paper.

It may just happen that you are not able to find a place for weeks; but do not give up. You may have to get a room in a rooming house; but try to stay as close to the community as possible. This will enable you to spend long hours in the community without worrying about a way home afterwards.

Making Contact

Since you have found a place to stay, say with a family, then the work starts, and it starts just as do most things, in the home.

You should spend as much time as the family has talking to them, because they have information about the people—both white and black. They have been there all of their lives; they know the community; they know the people who will help. Take time and talk to them; ask questions, for it is here that you get real *community education*.

Now you know the key people in the community, from this talk with the family. But some of them work out; do not get discouraged. Keep on pushing.

Canvass the whole community one afternoon. Talk with the people, laugh with them, joke with them; do most anything that gets some attention on you, or on some kind of conversation. It is very important to learn what bugs them. It may happen that they are thinking about trying to get the vote. You'll know when they talk.

The most important thing is to move the community by action; the community will move when the people move. The people will move when they are *motivated*.

Some Ways of Motivating People

Canvass two or three days the first week. Do not worry too much about what you hear from the people. If you just talk and ask questions, some of them may talk about Chicago or Welfare checks; this is good, this is what is on their minds presently.

During canvassing, be sure to take down the names and addresses of the people who talked, who seemed to you that there is hope in them. This could be only two people; or it could be ten. No matter what the number is, these are contacts. You have a small group of people. Now you need a *place to meet* with them. Try to get a church or an empty building; if you cannot get either, use one of the person's homes for a meeting place. Again, start with the people where you live; ask to hold the meeting there.

Building Leaders

The reason for using this home is that you have now found that dependable leadership does not exist. You must, from this little group, find and build a leader or leaders. How?

In this meeting, plan some kind of action. You put suggestions before the group. Let them talk over the suggestions, about paved streets, stop signs, street lights, or recreational facilities, and how the vote can get these and more.

You may need to hold ten or more of these kinds of meetings; at the same time, trying to get a church, getting the word out about the house meeting by leafletting or word of mouth. But let it get out! Elect a chairman to chair the meetings; you should not do this after the first meeting. Each meeting, give more and more of the responsibilities to this group, and as the group grows, form committees so as to involve more of the people.

To overcome the fear, many of the things above mentioned will apply. By getting the people together, they will see that they are not alone. By stopping by each one's home as much as possible, you will let them know you are sincere, in what you say and do—that you not only care about the meetings but you are interested in continued progress in their community and family life. The feeling of being close together will help overcome the fear.

Apathy will disappear when you give the people some responsibility. When you subject them to association with each other, through the conversations of personal and community problems, the apathy will disappear. At first the family educated you; now together they are educating each other.

Suspicion comes from mistrust. So many have led us wrong, that it is hard to trust people we don't know. You must be friendly, reliable, and most of all trustworthy. With this, suspicion will disappear. When the people trust you and trust your judgment, suspicion will be a thing of the past.

UNIT 9-8

Reflections on the Death of a Child

Marion King

My husband has said that he cannot always buy non-violence and that had he been present when the incident occurred at Camilla, he would have had to die trying to protect me. But let me say that we have both learned many lessons in non-violence during the past year, and we are still learning.

As I stand here now and look into your faces I feel that we are attending a home-coming, for I see so many people whom we have had the pleasure of having in our home at some time or other during the last critical year in Albany. And I know the names of others of you who have visited in our home, although we didn't know you were there at the time, because we were in jail and you were out, and later you were in and we were out, and we didn't have the chance to meet!

I would like to take this opportunity to thank you of the Nonviolent Coordinating Committee for what your coming to Albany has meant to us, and for what it will mean to the world. You may feel discouraged because things are not happening as fast as you thought they would, because you think you don't see any change in a place where they are still excluding Negroes from the dignity, opportunity and liberties of life in Albany, and where Negro citizens are still put in jail for peacefully petitioning for redress of our grievances, for asking for a share in our government and public places and for walking in orderly non-violent demonstration on our own wide streets.

But I would thank you young people of SNCC for starting something that will not die and that cannot be stopped. You have given my children something that cannot be taken away from them. Even my little three-year-old knows many of the Freedom songs we have sung in Albany and that you have sung here tonight—word for word. Many, many other children have seen the struggle for freedom in the marches on the streets of Albany. Thousands of children have seen pictures of it on television and have heard about it on the radio. And they will not forget. This vision cannot be taken from them and I know that the fight you have started will go on and on.

New South, 1963.

There has been much publicity for the Peace Corps, but let me re-emphasize a statement of Bill Weatherby, correspondent for the *Manchester Guardian*: you are the real Peace Corps, the unsung heroes who will be the salvation of America.

So, may I say that I am happy that Charles Sherrod and Cordell Reagan of SNCC saw fit to come down to the "bushes" of Albany, 170 miles southwest of Atlanta, to help us start this movement, this struggle, this vision and this faith in freedom that will not die and cannot be stopped.

As to the loss in our family, I cannot say that I have received any "divine revelation" out of the whole ordeal. There are a few things, though, that stand out in my mind and feelings.

First, I cannot forget the pure, unadulterated hatred of the two persons who attacked me and my children. I say they attacked my children because I was holding one child in my arms and had the others right there with me. I really feel that in the eyes of those policemen we were much lower than human beings, not to mention fellow men. I have asked myself and my God "why" a few thousand times. It would be easy to give a ready-made answer, such as that they are products of an evil system which has brutalized them, and that we must forgive them and get rid of the system. But I cannot be completely satisfied with this, and I wonder again and again what is the matter with the white people of Albany.

Second, I have been amazed at the strength that has come pouring into me from some source outside myself. Despite the many days and the sleepless nights of labor, even when I knew for sure that the baby would not make it, I felt literally physically strong. I could hoe a few rows in my yard in the bright autumn sunshine and I gradually grew spiritually stronger, too.

Third, the love which we now share with our little children seems newer and stronger than ever and compensates more than enough for any loss that we might have sustained. It is probably natural that we should be more dear to each other.

So, even though we don't understand why the incident happened or all of its implications, and even though I have had some moments of real despair, I do feel that there is some master plan, some purpose for it all. I have had more moments of real hope than of despair. I see in some white Southerners of just and generous spirit "Signs of the coming of the Lord," and I know that "His truth is marching on."

The author is Mrs. Slater King of Albany, the mother of three young children. Mr. and Mrs. King are frequently jailed leaders of the Albany Movement. Last July in the sixth month of her pregnancy, Mrs. King was slapped, struck down and kicked by two Mitchell County policemen when, with her three small children, she went to the jail at Camilla to take food and clothes to imprisoned demonstrators. Shortly after, the Kings lost their fourth child in a miscarriage. Mrs. King here recalls her remarks to a recent conference of Student Nonviolent Coordinating Committee members in Nashville and further appraises her experience for *New South*.

UNIT 9-9

ALBANY, FAILURE OR FIRST STEP?

Wyatt Tee Walker

"ALBANY, Ga., has become one of the most critical cities in the nation in regard to the desegregation struggle. Here one of the largest of desegregation struggles was effectively broken and the entire desegregation movement faltered."

Last March I read this appraisal of the Albany Movement, printed on the program of a Conference on Civil Disobedience and The American Police Executive, in New York. It is an evaluation with which I could not disagree more, and one which is, unfortunately, shared by many Southerners and Americans who look, regretfully or gratefully, at the temporary triumph of white Albany politicians and police over a long, heroic uprising of Negroes seeking their rights.

It is true that Albany, despite repeal of all local segregation laws, is still segregated, in schools, public places, lunch counters, theaters, parks, stores and to an appalling extent in travel facilities. Only the public libraries are open, and that on a standup basis, with reserve and research rooms closed, lest whites and Negroes sit down to read or study together. The city has sold a tennis court and one swimming pool for private operation, and closed others.

So, the present facts of life in this southwest Georgia city somewhat support the opinions that Albany Movement has "failed," that its "back is broken," and even that the two-year struggle and sacrifice of Albany Negroes has not only been in vain, but has retarded Negro liberation generally.

But this, I feel, is a superficial interpretation of facts, and an ignorance of Negro intent and resolution, of the course of history and of the power of the nonviolent movement.

In Albany Negroes have pending a suit to desegregate public schools; the Negro vote nearly defeated a bond issue for new segregated public buildings; the Albany Movement is publicly planning new pushes for equality and an estimated 450 Negroes have been arrested this year for peaceful demonstration, picketing, sit-ins and passing out of handbills urging defeat of the bond issue for more segregated facilities.

New South, 1963.

The truth is that we have a social revolution on our hands, in which the ordeal and effort of Albany is an historic high point. I thank God that our revolution, our Negro push, is still, with few provoked exceptions, nonviolent, and I hope and believe its future progress will be similarly passive and bravely persistent.

The reality of Negro history in this country impels me to admit, in the broad view of the Negro's dilemma, even in 1963, 100 years removed from "Emancipation," that we are just now digging in the beaches in the fight for our rights. Albany is a milepost in the early stage of the nonviolent revolution. Our nonviolent revolution is not yet full-grown. I do not know if it will ever come to adulthood, but I pray that it will; our nation needs this revolution to freedom and equality far worse than the people who are its soldiers.

The Albany Movement has been criticized for mistakes, losses and setbacks by worried arm-chair strategists and by active participants looking back on our campaign. I'm sure we made mistakes, tactically and perhaps emotionally, and suffered disagreements which may have temporarily retarded us. We made sacrifices and radical efforts which yielded no immediate results. But this Movement is young. Albany was an inspired, honest and united nonviolent Negro uprising without previous tactical experience. I think the Albany Movement blazed a trail in pragmatic experience and endured an ordeal which was, and is, a big beginning in the Deep South. I also believe that this Movement lit a fire which cannot be extinguished, though it has stages of temporary defeat and frustration. But the beat and high aspiration are unquenched.

We can never escape the truth that Albany's dilemma was not created by students "who came in from the outside," or by Martin Luther King or a thousand other "devils" and "agitators" upon whom the blame has been placed. Albany's dilemma was sprung from the holy unrest of Albany Negroes bravely resolved to fight and sacrifice for rights, freedom and dignity. The "outsiders," mostly southern Negro leaders born in Georgia, Alabama, Virginia and other Deep South states, were summoned to Albany by native Negroes ready for change. The "outsiders" did not create the dilemma or subvert Albany Negroes, nor yet rouse them to demands and demonstrations. They came, on invitation, to show the nonviolent way, to preach the techniques of the creative, conscience-attacking demonstration, to persuade to the loving philosophy of Negro sacrifice for white and black redemption and reconciliation.

Everything would *not* have been "all right" had not these catalytic agents, the "outsiders," been present, because everything was basically all wrong. If "Albany" had not happened last summer or last winter, it would have happened this summer or this winter or some summer before too long, because the human spirit always inevitably rebels against oppression.

In 1962 Albany's time had come, whether it was convenient for the Governor's race in Georgia, the Kennedy Administration programs or our foreign policy concerns.

There is no need for me to catalogue all the ills of Albany for any person socially identified as "a Negro." Housing, education, recreation, libraries, public accommodations, economic exploitation—you name it; Albany has it, as had as any southern city its size. Albany is but the notorious reflection of what the South is like for Negroes.

The Albany Movement is unique in our history, and in the course of the Negro's nonviolent uprising, for two factors. First, the Albany Negroes assaulted the entire system of segregation, an attack unprecedented in the Negro push. Second, they united—Negro janitors, domestics, ditch-diggers, cultivated educators and prosperous business and professional people in legal, peaceful demonstrations, jail sentences, boycott and other perilous techniques. Thus the Albany Movement, for the first time, represented a *whole* Negro community, including children, who were jailed demanding equality and democratic opportunity. (The Montgomery bus boycott involved a united Negro community, another historic victory; but the Montgomery Negroes attacked only their city transportation.)

There has been no comparable blanket protest and sacrifice in the Negro movement. But, other communities, like Albany, may emerge very soon in unified and persistent protest. We can only hope that Negro impatience and frustration with white intransigence will appear in another Albany, rather than in a race riot.

For many Negroes, lunch counters one year, libraries another year, schools a grade or two at a time, hotels and restaurants a little later, have become too slow. So, it would very well be that in a month or a year, we could have a hundred Albanys on our hands.

I have already stressed the complete segregation and isolation in this typical southern town imposed on its Negroes. And the nonviolent, protesting response of our people deserves consideration. Nonviolent direct action is the best, most effective and perhaps the only revolutionary instrument for the minority Negro in America. I use the word revolutionary advisedly, as a good word in sad disrepute; this nation, with all its promise to each of us, could never have been born without revolution. If the Negro dilemma—or, the American dilemma—is to be resolved, we must have nothing short of a revolution. The structure of our nation, our society, our prejudices, is such that the Negro doesn't have a chance without social revolution. He has only marginal power politically and economically. Against this marginal power is the behemoth of the social illness of exclusion and discrimination, a giant which casts his shadow and flexes his muscles to distort and destroy the fabric of our nation.

We apparently have neither the will nor the intent to grapple voluntarily with the task of healing this crippling wound of Negro discrimination. So, the Negro needs a revolution nonviolent but forcefully harnessed to the economic political and conscience-arousing power which we can wield.

This revolution will be hastened by the commitment of the Negro's very life to the nonviolent protest which is at his command. This, indeed heroic and revolutionary action, can generate moral force which may stir our country to get our house in order.

The very character of nonviolent direct action includes tension and crisis, creative tension and creative crisis which forces a resolution of the dilemma. Of course, the tension and crisis are not really created by the nonviolent resisters, but rather by the injustice which invokes the dramatic protest.

The general inability to grasp this fact makes for much misunderstanding of the true role of the militant civil rights organizations. Some critics say the actionists "do not finish the job." Actually, the very role they must play in severe social change makes it impossible for them fully to "finish the job." In the mind of the opposition, who inevitably must yield their position of extreme advantage, the Negro actionists are the enemy, and understandably so. It is at the point of maximum crisis and tension when the opposition relents, that the militant forces must withdraw in favor of reconciliation affected by persons and agencies who in the public mind are not so revolutionary. The actionists in a social revolution will never win popularity contests because they represent change, and any society resists change of any sort, and those who fight for change. Where this change displaces a community from its extreme advantage, the resistance is intense.

The nonviolent resister uses civil disobedience to express his moral objections to injustice, to refuse to acquiesce in injustice. The foes of segregation direct their disobedience against the subtle and not-so-subtle law that foster and perpetuate these evils. The nonviolent resister cannot, in good conscience, obey a law which is immoral and unjust. So, he protests by deliberately breaking that law and accepting the penalty willingly as his witness against its immorality and in order, by his punishment, to stir the public conscience to change the law.

In Albany, and other scenes of Negro nonviolent resistance, we need to distinguish between civil disobedience and *uncivil* disobedience. Segregationists may choose to violate a law which they consider unjust or immoral (although in the context of Constitutional guarantees their logic is at best tortuous), but they are unwilling to accept the penalty for violation of that law. Also, they do not recognize that an unjust law is one out of harmony with the laws of God and mankind as established in our Judeo-Christian tradition, or a law immoral for its cruel and discriminating hardships. Nor do they realize that an unjust law is one imposed on the minority and which does not apply to the majority which enacted and enforces it, and that it is further unjust because the minority on whom it is imposed could not participate in the making of the law. The nonviolent resister, as in Albany, must also practice civil disobedience to protest a just law when it is falsely applied to discriminate, so that its enforcement is unjust, as in breach of the peace statutes and anti-trespass ordinances invoked against Negroes breaching no peace and "trespassing" peacefully on premises to which they have a public right.

The apparent "failure" of Albany involved not only unjust use of just laws by police victimized by an unjust system but the do-nothing posture of the federal government. No one can sensibly argue that in July and August of 1962—a time of mass arrests of Negroes exercising their rights of peaceful assembly, petition for redress of grievances and other civil rights—the Albany Negroes' constitutional rights were repeatedly violated in the name of "law and order," and in reality to punish them for exercising these rights. The Federal Bureau of Investigation officers, notified of nearly every move of the protestors, on hand at most of the arrests, crammed their notebooks full of details and presumably reported to Washington, D.C.; yet not once did the federal government raise a finger to protect the rights of these Negro citizens, to assert and show that the laws of the nation supersede the laws of any state. And then, of course, there was the *coup de grace*: a federal judge threw out their appeal for an injunction against segregated public facilities on the grounds that the Negroes had not proved that they were denied access because of race.

Sharp social change, the process of which is inexorably launched in Albany, is painfully slow. So, the lack of clear and dramatic gains, were interpreted as failure of the Movement. Many observers, particularly those distant from the scene concluded (and still do) that stubborn resistance to the Negro effort had carried the day. These somber and superficial appraisals are deeply in error.

We must remember that the Albany story began with a city commission which adamantly declared it would not talk to leaders of the Movement, nor consider any change in the laws and customs of their community. They reiterated publicly and privately an uncompromising "No" to Negro aspirations to freedom and justice.

Their first compromise was the closing of parks and libraries to avoid demonstrations and Negro use of these services. In the fact of repeated frontal assaults, they gave up important municipal facilities.

The Albany Movement shifted its offensive to the courts, and the same city commission which had declared "Never!" now gallantly proclaimed that the battle should have been waged in the courts and not in the streets. They announced, with pious compromise of previous intransigence, that when the Court of Appeals directed integration, they would lawfully comply. Anyone who knows the Deep South knows that official agreement of avowed segregationists to comply with a desegregating court order is a retreat from defiance of the law of the land.

The recent repeal of Albany's segregation laws indicates clearly that the city fathers are, at last, realistically facing the legal death of segregation. Thus, they compromised their position again, showing that the city dares not battle in court, since the outcome, with all its cost, is a foregone conclusion.

In the wake of the legal retreat of Albany's white officialdom, the public library was opened on a 30-day "trial basis," integrated without chairs and a closed reference room; but this "vertical" integration is always a prelude to full integration, as demonstrated in a dozen cities over the South.

Unquestionably, the adamant stance of the power structure in Albany has been altered and softened under the pressure of the Negro Albany Movement.

The shift in drive to voter registration of Negroes brought an increase of a third in Negro registration. When the gubernatorial election came, and a bitter segregationist contended with a malleable moderate, the pundits conceded that Albany's Dougherty County would vote solidly for the flamboyant segregationist, Marvin Griffin. But, the increased Negro vote united with white voters who, in the secrecy of the polling booths, voted for justice and sanity. To the chagrin of former Governor Griffin and other segregationists and cynical political experts over the state, Dougherty County went solidly for Carl Sanders, the moderate lesser of the anti-Negro evils. And, the segregationist-controlled press in south Georgia acknowledged in angry humiliation that "the Negro bloc vote" had lost Albany and the county for Griffin.

More important than these changes, gains and surprise upsets in the segregated status quo is that the nonviolent direct action thrust of Albany Negroes aroused the Negro to the injustice and immorality of his segregation. Certainly, the full demands and proper aspirations of the Albany Movement are not yet realized; but the Negroes have gained much difficult and hard-fought ground. And they are by no means defeated and quiescent, as 1963 arrests—several hundred of them—in punishment for peaceful and lawful demonstrations and protests prove.

This Negro community will never again return willingly and despairingly to segregation. And their sacrificial summer of 1962 will influence the fight on segregation wherever it exists.

It is, I believe, no "failure" when a united Negro community drives and sacrifices for nearly two years to assert and demand its rights. People who make such assertions and endure such persecution are by no means defeated or broken. They will never succumb and their sacrifice is an offering to the inevitable new order of justice in the South and all the United States.

The "defeat" of Albany is, then, a protest and penalty in necessary demonstration and suffering which has obviously changed Albany and inspired other Negro communities, as it has warned and cautioned white authorities elsewhere in the South.

In the words of Marion King, an Albany mother who has given and lost a great deal to the Movement, the community has now "this vision and this faith in freedom that will not die and cannot be stopped."

Rev. Mr. Walker is executive assistant to Dr. Martin Luther King, Jr., of the Southern Christian Leadership Conference, and an SCLC leader who preached, led, demonstrated and was jailed in the Albany Movement. *New South* presents his sanguine appraisal of the Albany Movement as a perspective on the sense of that apparently stalemated community, and as an insight into recent defensive Negro violence in Birmingham, Jackson, Cambridge, Danville, Savannah, and other southern centers of Negro impatience and aggression on their rights.

UNIT 9-10

ALBANY POLICE DEPARTMENT

Laurie Pritchett

During the fiscal year 1961–62, the Albany Police Department has faced many problems concerning the civil rights struggle in Albany, Georgia and the South. The Albany Police Department was first confronted with this problem in the month of October, 1961. During this month the Student Non-Violent Coordinating Committee combined of both white and negro students first appeared on the scene in Albany, Georgia. This mixed group infiltrated into the negro community of Albany and Dougherty County and began the voter registration drive which was used to unite the negro community.

On October 26, 1961, the situation was agitated by the shooting of Officer T. W. Dunbar at the Trailway bus station, located at the edge of Harlem. Five days after this unfortunate killing, the Interstate Commerce Commission ruling was put into effect at the Trailway bus station, railroad terminal and McAfee air terminal.

During the month of November, 1961, the indirect action of the Student Non-Violent Coordinating Committee together with the Albany Movement and the NAACP began a drive to integrate all public facilities in the City of Albany. On December 10, 1961, a group of mixed freedom riders from the Student Non-Violent Coordinating Committee, headquarters in Atlanta, Georgia, attempted to integrate the train facilities form Atlanta to Albany. Upon arriving in Albany, this group of mixed people was arrested at Roosevelt Avenue for disorderly conduct, failing to obey an officer's command and blocking the flow of traffic. This group was brought before the Recorder's Court on December 12th and found guilty. On this date the Police Department and the City of Albany experienced the first mass demonstration in which 267 people were arrested and placed in jail. During the month of December there was approximately 735 negroes and whites arrested for mass demonstrations in the City of Albany.

On December 18th mass demonstrations were halted pending the outcome of the trial of Dr. Martin Luther King for a period of 60 days. During this 60-day period there were no mass demonstrations by the negro people in Albany, or Dougherty County, but numerous arrests were made by this department for violations of the city ordinances and state laws.

On July 10, 1962, Dr. Martin Luther King, Jr., Rev. Ralph Abernathy, Soloman Walker and Eddie Jackson were arraigned and sentenced by Judge A. N. Durden, Sr., Recorders Court Judge. On this date mass demonstrations by the negroes of Albany and Doughtery

---

Albany, Georgia City Records, 1962.

County began again. During the month of July the Albany Police Department arrested a total of 500 negroes and whites in mass demonstrations.

During the fiscal year 1961–62 the total arrests of negroes and whites for violations of our city ordinances and state laws were approximately 1,300 people. These people are now out of jail on either cash bonds or security bonds and are being brought to trial at the convenience of the Recorders Court of Albany, Georgia.

Prior to this civil rights struggle in Albany, the Police Committee, along with the Chief of Police, visited and talked with police officials in other cities concerning their operation plan and from these cities we gained valuable information. This information was studied and for the first time in any civil rights struggle a non-violent operation was put into effect. For a period of four to five months members of the Albany Police Department were indoctrinated to this plan of non-violence by the staff officers of the Police Department. At each roll call the members of the Albany Police Department were lectured and shown films on how to conduct themselves in this non-violent operation.

I, along with the staff officers of the Albany Police Department, credit our success in handling all racial disturbances to the operation of non-violence and this credit goes to each individual member of the Albany Police Department who so successfully carried out this plan. The non-violent movement by the Albany Police Department could not have been carried out without the full cooperation of each member of this department and I feel that the City of Albany, the citizens of Albany and Dougherty County owe a deep gratitude to each member of this department who has stood firmly and enforced the laws of our city and state, regardless of race, color or creed.

Amount of Fines Assessed	$229,795.00
Less Fines Worked Out	$40,934.50
Cash to Treasurer	$188,860.50
Number of Individual Arrests	5,976
Number of Companion Arrests	2,877
Total Arrests	8,853
Number of Cases Tried by Recorder	2,546
Bond Forfeitures	6,113
Dismissed Cases	194
Days Served on Street in Lieu of Fines	6,134
State Cases Made by Department	637
Complaints Answered	5,094

Without your cooperation I feel sure that the Albany Police Department could not have complied the outstanding report which I am submitting to each of you for the fiscal year 1961–62.

The far-coming year of 1962–63, we, of the Albany Police Department, wish to pledge to you, the City Manager, Police Committee and entire City Commission and the citizens of Albany and we will continue to do our best to make Albany a safer and more desirable place in which to live and work. We know also that we will be confronted with many complex problems concerning the civil rights struggle in the coming year. To this end, we pledge to continue to enforce our laws to the fullest extent, regardless of race, color or creed, and with the full cooperation and support of the City Manager, the Mayor, City Commission, we will reach this goal.

Respectfully submitted,
Laurie Pritchett
Chief of Police

UNIT 9-11

HOMEGROWN MOVEMENT IN MACON

George A. Doss, Jr.

Since early 1961 when the State of Georgia gave up its effort to buck federal authority on the integration question, probably no other community in the state has moved further than Macon to grant its Negro citizens free use of both public and privately-operated facilities and equality of opportunity.

In these two years the city government has dropped racial bars at its libraries and golf course. Even earlier the city opened a new airport terminal without any segregation. Macon also dropped, entirely without fanfare, its few segregation ordinances when a new city code was adopted in 1962. And the city voluntarily quit segregation in its elections even as the Bibb County government and Democratic committee refused to do so without a court order, which promptly was issued when the Department of Justice filed a suit.

Even more important changes have come in the private sector. Lunch counters in principal drug and variety stores downtown and at the big new Westgate Shopping Center began, without incident, serving Negroes along with whites on October 31, 1961. Then, in March, 1962, after a three week boycott and a court suit, the city bus line, operated by Bibb Transit Company, dropped segregation. The bus boycott was followed by an intensive Negro voter registration drive and a "selective buying" campaign when negotiations broke down, and this led to the most important break-through of all—a new policy of Macon merchants to hire qualified Negroes in "white" jobs.

And, trustees of Mercer University, 130-year-old Baptist school, voted in April to admit a Ghanian student in the fall and, as Mercer's liberal president, Rufus C. Harris, has long advocated, any other qualified applicant, thus opening the university doors to southern Negroes.

How did it happen? Why in Macon, surrounded as it is by rural, typically Black Belt counties?

As recently as June, 1960, racial harmony in Macon had been shaken by Superior Court Judge Oscar L. Long's charge to a grand jury to investigate "Negro bloc voting" in city and county elections. The charge brought critical reaction, which obviously startled its

New South, 1963.

author, from Bibb County Sheriff James I. Wood and Macon Mayor Ed Wilson. Long's charge cited several laws, including one which made it a misdemeanor to hire workers qualified to vote to canvass for or influence votes in behalf of any candidate, and called for its enforcement. "Some may say," the judge's charge said, "that the hiring of people for the purpose of canvassing and influencing voters to vote for one candidate rather than another is a common practice in elections and therefore should be overlooked. It is obvious that the situation we face today demonstrates the wisdom of this law."

Sheriff Wood issued a statement the following day calling the charge "one of the most deplorable examples of race agitation to come out of Middle Georgia in recent years."

"At a time when all thinking people want to preserve the good will and cooperation between the races in Bibb County, this action appears either as a crude attempt at judicial intimidation, or, at best, as agitation for a 'Negro vote' issue in local politics," Wood said.

"It is shocking to find a judge charging a grand jury in the style and language of a race baiting candidate for political office. It further seems the height of hypocrisy to dust off an old blue law that has been ignored for 50 years and suddenly order its rigid enforcement against a minority group of voters."

A week later, Mayor Wilson called Judge Long's charge "the worst blow to race relations in Bibb County in recent years." He said the charge was "political in its content" and "an insult to all public officers who have received a large Negro vote." Both Wilson and Wood more than once had received lopsided Negro majorities, spotlighted by the local system of segregated ballot boxes which ends June 1 by federal court order. Wilson called attention to a statement filed by Long in the Superior Court clerk's office in 1934 showing that as a candidate for solicitor of City Court of Macon he had paid for campaign workers. Of the judge's charge asking for enforcement of the old law, the mayor said Long seemed to be saying that "here is a law which has never been enforced, but it is a good weapon to use against the Negro voters."

A month after his statement, and less than two weeks before a primary to nominate his successor, Sheriff Wood was cited for contempt of court. He was sentenced to pay $600 in fines and serve 20 days in jail on August 13, 1960, by Judge A. M. Anderson, who with Judge Hal Bell had sanctioned Long's charge to the grand jury. But the U.S. Supreme Court on June 25, 1962, upheld the right of Sheriff Wood, now out of office and practicing law, to freedom of speech and relieved him of the sentence. No charge was made against Wilson.

The grand jury which heard Judge Long's charge in 1960 came back with a report praising the judge and condemning the very Negro leadership which since has achieved so much; it said most candidates had violated the law cited by the judge; but it returned no indictments. The General Assembly passed in 1962 a bill sponsored by Bibb Rep. J. Taylor Phillips, now a state senator, repealing the 1890 law prohibiting the hiring of election workers which Long had sought to have enforced against "bloc voting."

Macon has its share of die-hard segregationists in authority, including the police department, and its Ku Kluxish "white citizens" organization, but it has also the distinction of never having elected a candidate for public office on an open racist appeal.

Up to the beginning of 1961, Negro citizens had limited their influence in the community largely to election days and had exacted few commitments for their support of candidates. They had, in 1954 and 1955, asked school authorities to follow the 1954 Supreme Court ruling, but they had failed to follow up their requests. The white community, however, had begun to stir against the possibility of closing the schools and the "open schools" legislation adopted by the General Assembly in January, 1961, seemed to open the way for action in Macon.

In February, 1961, the Macon Council on Human Relations sent a statement to city and county officials asking them to re-examine their policies in the light of the "new realism in Georgia's official approach to the constitutional prohibition against racial discrimination by action of state and local governments" and advising that Negro citizens soon would be making new demands for local compliance. "The question in Macon, as in all of Georgia, no longer is whether we can continue as in the past," the Council said. "It is whether change will come under community planning and control, or whether it shall come under the explicit direction of a federal court."

The Macon Council is the successor to an interracial council which has existed in Macon for more than 40 years. It has continued to hold monthly meetings attended by both white and Negro ministers, usually in the parish house of Christ Episcopal Church, throughout the racial tension of recent years. Faculty members and students of Mercer University and Wesleyan College have made up a large part of its white membership lately, but there have always been others, including ministers, business and professional men and women. Many of the Negro members, including ministers and leaders of the integration movement, have belonged to the Council for years. When the Council issued its 1961 statement, Joseph M. Hendricks, now dean of men at Mercer University, and the late Rev. E. B. Paschal, Negro pastor of Tremont Temple Baptist Church, were co-chairmen of the Council. Mr. Paschal later led the bus boycott after his arrest in a test of bus segregation. Shortly before his death, he won an award from the National Association for the Advancement of Colored People for his work last year. The Rev. James A. Holman succeeded Mr. Paschal as co-chairman of the Council and now serves jointly with Mr. Hendricks.

In the 1961 statement, the Macon Council said it had succeeded an organization which had existed in the community for many years—"long before the present crises and controversies arose—and it has been essentially conservative in the best sense of that often-abused term. During the past years when defiance and resistance-at-all-cost were the official policy of Georgia, we made no public effort to reverse a trend which was quite apparently beyond our power of influence. We spoke out only occasionally and then only in specific instances of injustice which we felt demanded a voice against the tide."

The Council has, nevertheless, lent important support to the fight for Negro equality. It has furnished white observers of the lunch counter sit-in demonstrations and at court hearings involving Negro rights, and has conducted surveys of employment opportunities, housing conditions and other racially-related problems. Council committees have met with officials to discuss injustices. The organization gets monthly reports on the campaign to end all racial bars.

The Bibb Board of Public Education acknowledged receipt of the Macon Council statement in 1961 and appointed a special study committee headed by one of its bitter-end segregationists, Attorney Wallace Miller, Jr.

The Board committee never reported on its study of the issues raised by the Council's statement. There was no other direct response to the statement, but the argument it contained seemed nevertheless to make its impact on the community. When Negro golfers petitioned to mayor and council for use of the golf course, there was a delay until annexation, which nearly doubled the population and more than doubled the land area of Macon, had been approved in a referendum with the full support of the Negro leadership and voters; but in June, 1961, the golf course request was granted with the explanation that there never had been any legal prohibition against Negroes using the course. Despite dire predictions, the course has continued to operate without strife for the benefit of all golfers, regardless of race. Even earlier, library desegregation had been achieved with order, although there had been no public request or notice of that action. The same was true of the airport terminal, well before federal authorities achieved airport desegregation in at least one other Georgia city through special persuasion.

Bus and train stations also have been opened fully to Negroes without resistance to federal orders, although in one incident three Negro students were detained briefly after eating in the Greyhound cafeteria formerly reserved for white persons on December 11, 1960. Benjamin Brown of Atlanta, Betty Williamson of Atlanta, and Norma Wilson of Jacksonville, Fla., were served in the cafeteria during a regular meal stop of their interstate bus from Atlanta to Jacksonville. As they were finishing their meal, two detectives of the City of Macon, summoned by the policeman on the beat, arrived and asked the cafeteria manager to request the Negroes to leave. (The manager stressed later that he had not called the police and that he was caught between state and federal authority. "They could arrest me for serving them," he said.) So the manager made the request, and when the Negroes refused to leave, they were arrested and taken to the city jail. The Monday before, the U.S. Supreme Court had ruled that Negroes on interstate travel could not be refused service in restaurants operated in stations. After a conference of Mayor Wilson, Police Chief L. B. McCallum and City Attorney Buckner F. Melton, police released the Negroes without placing any charges against them and arranged for them to continue to Jacksonville on a later bus. No Negro has been disturbed by city authorities since in the full use of bus and train station facilities in Macon.

On February 25, 1961, 18 Negro students sought to ride up front in Bibb Transit Company buses, after efforts of Negro leaders to negotiate with the bus company had been rebuffed. Drivers stopped these buses and, called police, who arrested all 18. Top city and county officials had met quietly the day before to consider the impending test, of which they had advance knowledge. Company Attorney Wallace Miller, Jr., cited a state law already declared unconstitutional by federal Judge Frank Hooper in an Atlanta case, and insisted that it be enforced against the expected Negro demonstrators. Some of the youngsters arrested were sent to Juvenile Court, but cases against 12 of them were sent to City Court of Macon. A pilot case against John Elijah Glover had resulted in conviction and was on appeal when the bus issue was settled once and for all in federal court in Macon in 1962.

Macon police, in one of their frequent bobbles where race is concerned, suspected the worst on March 8, 1961, when several white women, officials of the Veterans of Foreign Wars Auxiliary, drove to a Negro neighborhood to inspect the records of a Negro unit. While the visitors were in the home of a Negro VFW official, a swarm of policemen and detectives converged on the scene, searched the white women's car and broke the lock on the door of a house across the street, where they suspected them to be, in an attempted search. City authorities backed off sheepishly when the facts were revealed.

Macon's first lunch counter sit-ins occurred on June 2, 1961, and resulted in one minor instance of violence. Floyd E. Prince, a 67-year-old white man, struck a 17-year-old Negro high school student, Benjamin Snead, as the boy sat on a stool at Woolworth's lunch counter. Both were arrested by policemen who did not see the incident, and charged with disorderly conduct. The cases against both were dismissed a month later by Macon Recorder W.W. Hemingway, who said the city had the responsibility to prosecute and had failed to produce evidence against either of the defendants. Mayor Wilson ordered an investigation of the police failure, but nothing ever came of it. None of the other sit-in demonstrators was arrested, but all lunch counters were closed on this occasion when they sat down.

Negro leaders and white merchants began negotiations soon after the June demonstrations, and most of the lunch counters were desegregated on October 31, with adults testing the effectiveness of the agreement. Only two of the stores refused them service. The names—even the existence—of the committee of white negotiators have never been revealed publicly, but the effectiveness of the program is the best evidence of the influence and good faith of the negotiators.

The bus boycott of February, 1962, cemented the Negro community into an effective unit. Out of it grew the Bibb County Coordinating Committee, it group representing all local Negro organizations of any size, including the Macon Branch of the National Association for the Advancement of Colored People. William P. Randall, a "building contractor and long-time political leader, is chairman of the committee and the recognized spokesman for the Negro community in the unity which grew out of the boycott. The group since has increased its influence Macon.

Negro leaders were somewhat surprised that a boycott was required to end segregation on the buses. A valuable communication with the white leadership of the community had grown up through the quiet dealings which brought lunch counter desegregation, and earlier approaches to the bus company had suggested a willingness of its officials to work something out. There was no city ordinance requiring bus segregation and the state law already had been declared unconstitutional.

But when the issue was pressed, Bibb Transit President Linton D. Baggs, personal and political friend and appointee to the State Board of Regents of former Gov. Marvin Griffin, balked. When they got no reply to a request for a conference with Baggs, four Negro ministers, including the late Mr. Pischal, decided to test the buses on February 9, 1962. All four were arrested after the driver stopped the bus and called police. The next day the Negro organization, still emphasizing a willingness to talk, announced their boycott of the buses would begin on the following Monday, February 12, and continue "until we can ride in dignity and without risk of arrest." The bus company, which earlier had not answered a communication from Negro leaders, now offered to talk, but when William P. Randall reached Miller, the company attorney, Miller said a meeting could not be set up before Monday. Told that would be too late to forestall the boycott, Miller said, according to Randall's report, "Well, let her rip."

Rip she did on Monday, February 12, 1962. There were a few, but very few, Negro riders on the buses on the first day. Thereafter, the boycott was almost 100% effective. Negroes got to school and to their jobs by use of a highly effective city-wide car pool operated by the organization. Baggs ran an ad in the local newspapers on February 13, charging that "Certain colored leaders now desire to defy the courts, take the law into their own hands and force economic pressure by boycott on Bibb Transit Company so that [the company] will ignore and violate the very law that at this juncture has been held valid in their own test case." This was a reference to the year-old Glover case, still on appeal. Baggs added significantly, "If in the test case the courts hold the law invalid, that will be the end of it."

On February 16, Judge W.A. Bootle in U.S. District Court refused to grant an immediate restraining order against the bus company because Attorney Miller refused to consent to it, although he told reporters he didn't oppose it. The judge set a hearing on the petition of the Negro leaders for a preliminary injunction for February 28. Mayor Wilson immediately called Negro leaders and bus company representatives to a meeting the next day to which he invited Chairman Kenneth W. Dunwody of Bibb County commissioners and Bibb Sheriff Jimmy E. Bloodworth. Bloodworth, who had been elected the previous September without Negro support, sent a telegram declining the invitation. "I am a law enforcement officer and until the courts order otherwise I will recognize the state laws on the books as being valid," the sheriff said. "This boycott has promoted violence on the part of those people who say they want peace and it has been enforced by intimidation of those who do not want to participate." The night before, two Negro men had been wounded when a car full of white men fired into a dance hall and two white persons had been injured by a brick thrown into a bus on which they were passengers.

But the mayor's negotiations broke down and the boycott dragged on. On February 26, Baggs ran another ad in the newspapers saying not enough white persons were riding the buses and that unless they gave the company more support operations would have to be suspended. The hearing finally was held before Judge Bootle, who, on March 1, issued a sweeping order declaring state segregation laws and the bus segregation policy of Bibb Transit Company illegal and ordering the company to end segregation on its buses. At the same time, he flatly turned down a company proposal of separate buses for whites and Negroes.

Next day, a hearing was held before Judge Long in Bibb Superior Court on a bus company suit to enjoin Negro leaders from encouraging others to boycott the buses or to engage in intimidation or violence. Judge Long said he had hoped that Judge Bootle's ruling would make the question before him moot, but because Miller and Attorney

Donald L. Hollowell, representing the Negro defendants, could not agree on a settlement, he issued the sweeping injunction sought by the bus company. This almost stalled the end of the boycott which had seemed assured by Judge Bootle's ruling and the company's earlier statement that it would abide by such a ruling. An appeal from Judge Long's ruling would not be possible, however, if there were a full settlement, and some of the defendants felt that the ruling clearly violated their constitutional freedoms and should be appealed. But after an exchange of bitter statements by Miller and Hollowell, the boycott was ended and Bibb Transit Company buses have operated without segregation for more than a year. There have been few racial incidents and no apparent drop in bus patronage by white riders.

Thousands of Negroes held mass meetings in churches in various parts of the city during the boycott. These meetings have continued once weekly ever since. The unity created by the boycott led to nearly doubling Negro voter registration in Bibb County before the deadline for the 1962 elections last May. Another registration campaign now is in progress. During last summer, while a Negro boycott was threatening professional baseball in Savannah, Macon Negroes successfully integrated the Macon Peaches' grandstand without incident.

The bus boycott also spawned the "White Citizens National Organization for the Betterment of America, Inc.," which since has shortened its title unofficially to Macon Citizens Council. This group became involved in the "Reverse Freedom Rides," during the summer of 1962. Its first rider was "Bullfrog Millhouse," a town character who got a five-day round trip to Detroit with his return fare paid by a local white jeweler who was shocked by the cruelty of the scheme. The Negro victim of this ride has since been committed to the state mental hospital at Milledgeville. All of the candidates endorsed by the "White Citizens Organization" lost in the 1962 elections and it now is reduced to an occasional rally and a counter petition calling for full segregation every time Negro citizens file one for more integration.

Negotiations between the Bibb County Coordinating Committee and representatives of the white merchants continued after the lunch counter success and removal of racial signs on restrooms and water fountains. Employment of Negroes in all types of jobs was now the issue. When no results had been achieved on this score as the Christmas shopping season approached, a "selective buying" campaign was begun the day after Thanksgiving, with pickets on most downtown stores, except Woolworth's which already had hired a Negro clerk. After two days many of the merchants began calling the Negro negotiators asking for job applicants. A week later, pickets were withdrawn and since that time at least 150 Negroes have been employed as clerks, cashiers or office help in stores of all types. The Piggly Wiggly grocery chain and several large independent supermarkets were among the early ones to hire Negroes, as were most large department and variety stores, clothing stores and many smaller shops. The white and Negro negotiating committees continue to hold regular meetings to iron out problems such as reluctance of any merchants to carry out agreements made during negotiation; training and qualifications of applicants, and other grievances on either side, as well as to discuss extension of the equal employment program. Some merchants have reported unofficially that their new Negro clerks are selling more than any of their others.

The Bibb County Coordinating Committee has filed a new petition for school integration, with signatures of about 250 adult Negroes. The board now shows signs of some urgency in handling the petition and reportedly is about evenly divided on the question of working it out locally or awaiting a court order. As one member remarked informally before the meeting at which the petition was presented, "It no longer is a question of whether we'll do it, but how we'll do it."

Petitions have been filed with the city and county asking for an end to segregation in all other public facilities, such as courtrooms, the city auditorium and city parks where separation of the races has continued by custom. These petitions were referred to committees. Macon Hospital, owned by the city but with its public functions financed largely by the county, has bowed to some minor requests of the Negro committee but continues most of its segregation policies. The hospital is expected to be the target of a court suit as soon as the school question is settled.

Negro children began using playground facilities in two public parks at the end of March and the city said it had no policy to segregate these parks. But the playground supervisor at Tattnall Square Park refused to issue balls and other equipment to the Negro children. For several days there were interracial baseball games in the park, however, with no suggestion of trouble. Older whites moved into the park early in April, throwing rocks, bottles and even shoes, and one Negro man was stabbed and three of his white attackers arrested. City council authorized Mayor Wilson, in a resolution which put the blame for the trouble on the Negroes, to close the parks to keep peace, but the mayor declined to do so, saying it would be "a terrible reflection on our city if it becomes necessary to deny our children the use of the playgrounds in order to keep the peace."

On April 6 a pipe bomb exploded in Mayor Wilson's home mailbox. Four days later fathers of two teen-age boys turned them in to police as perpetrators of the bombing, with three other white boys, because "they didn't like the mayor's policies about integrating Tattnall Square Park."

Disorders at Tattnall Square and Baconsfield Park, across the river, where a few Negroes were driven away by a park employee brandishing a pistol, followed inadequate preparation of police and city employees and an appearance of official uncertainty which usually invites defiance and violence. (Park employees who resisted desegregation were fired or moved to other jobs.)

The mayor's overruling of the council vote to close parks, a firmly announced policy of open parks and populace protection and other signs of city resolve prevailed, however, and Negroes and whites now use both parks in peace.

As the park desegregation began, promoters of a touring ice show turned 13 Negro adults away from a performance in the municipal auditorium, with police standing by to keep order but the city insisting the promoters who leased the building were free to segregate or not to segregate as they saw fit. The Negroes, leaders of the Coordinating Committee, threatened to take everybody involved to federal court.

The Negro committee is seeking equality of employment in various businesses and industries and reports that one large baking company already has hired Negroes on its production line for the first time. Other targets of subcommittees already set up are theaters, hotels and motels. Nearly everybody agrees that integration of swimming pools will present the thorniest problem of all. There is no indication that the Negro leadership will try to push that one this summer.

The city is to elect a new mayor and council later this year, with Mayor Wilson ineligible to succeed himself. The future progress of the community in race relations may well hinge on the outcome of the election, although there is no indication so far that the racial issue will be raised openly by any candidate.

Mr. Doss is political and race relations reporter for *The Macon News*.

Ain't Gonna Let Nobody Turn Me Round

Adaptation of traditional song by members of the Albany Movement

This old spiritual was first introduced in Albany by Reverend Ralph Abernathy during the summer of 1962 when mass arrests and demonstrations erupted for the second time. He taught it one night to a mass meeting of the Negro community at Mount Zion Baptist Church. It immediately caught on and became widely used in the demonstrations. A nationally televised CBS documentary showed spirited students rhythmically clapping and singing "ain't gonna let Chief Pritchett turn me 'round" while the policemen picked them up, two to a student, and carried them into the paddy wagons.

". . . anybody who thinks this town is going to settle back and be the same as it was, has got to be deaf, blind, and dumb."
— A Negro woman in Albany, Ga.

Ain't gonna let nobody turn me 'round,
turn me 'round, turn me 'round,
Ain't gonna let nobody turn me 'round,
I'm gonna keep on a walkin', keep on a talkin'
Marching up to freedom land.

Ain't gonna let Nervous Nelly turn me 'round . . . (term applied to typical segregationist)

Ain't gonna let Chief Pritchett . . .

Ain't gonna let Mayor Kelly . . .

Ain't gonna let segregation . . .

Ain't gonna let Z. T. . . .
(Z. T. Mathews, sheriff of Terrell County, Georgia)

Ain't gonna let no jail house . . .

Ain't gonna let no injunction . . .
(after a federal injunction prohibiting further demonstrations)

UNIT 10

BIRMINGHAM, SELMA, VIOLENCE AND NONVIOLENCE

	INTRODUCTION	538
10-1 •	SOUTHERN BOMBINGS	539
10-2 •	FEAR AND HATRED GRIP BIRMINGHAM RACIAL TENSION SMOLDERING AFTER BELATED SITDOWNS *Harrison E. Salisbury*	540
10-3 •	BIRMINGHAM AND BEYOND	544
10-4 •	THE SOUTHERN CHRISTIAN LEADERSHIP CONFERENCE AND THE SECOND RECONSTRUCTION, 1957–1973 *Adam Fairclough*	550
10-5 •	RETROSPECT AND PROSPECT	562
10-6 •	CIVIL DISOBEDIENCE AND THE LAW	566
10-7 •	REPORTS FROM SELMA'S "BLOODY SUNDAY"	570
10-8 •	DALLAS COUNTY CHRISTIAN MINISTERS UNION	573
10-9 •	THE BLACK MAN AND SELF-DEFENSE: 1962 THE CASE FOR ANSWERING VIOLENCE WITH VIOLENCE *Robert F. Williams*	574
10-10 •	LETTER FROM BIRMINGHAM CITY JAIL *Martin Luther King, Jr.*	582
10-11 •	IS VIOLENCE NECESSARY TO COMBAT INJUSTICE? *Robert F. Williams and Martin Luther King, Jr.*	592

INTRODUCTION

The central theme of Unit 10 is the debate in the movement over nonviolence. The unit opens with two stark reminders of the brutality and fear evident throughout the Deep South. The first selection (10-1) comes from a June 1963 issue of *New South*. The second (10-2), a famous *New York Times* article by Harrison Salisbury, demonstrates the power that the print media had in shaping national perceptions of the South and civil rights activism in the region.

10-3, taken from a 1964 *New South,* is a brief overview of Birmingham and an assessment of the national Movement's prospects at the time. In the immediate aftermath of the demonstrations, how did informed sympathetic observers view the impact of Birmingham? Adam Fairclough's essay (10-4), on the other hand, places Birmingham and the SCLC in the broader context of the events of the 1950s, 60s, and 70s.

Two pieces taken from *New South* highlight the nature and uses of civil disobedience and direct action tactics in the Civil Rights Movement. The first article (10-5) charts the legal efforts by state and local officials throughout the region to limit nonviolent demonstrations. The second (10-6) is a meditation on direct action from the perspective of a Movement sympathizer.

The reader takes a quick glimpse at the Selma demonstrations in (10-7,8). It contrasts hospital reports from Selma with the attitude of the town's ministers towards civil rights demonstrations.

10-9 and 10-10 reconstruct the "debate" within the movement between self-defense and nonviolence, using King's "Letter from Birmingham City Jail" (10-10) and an excerpt from Robert Williams's *Negroes with Guns* (10-9). In 1960, The *Southern Patriot* explicitly contrasted King's and Williams's views (10-11). The *Patriot* was the official organ of the Southern Conference Educational Fund, Inc., a group dedicated to "ending discrimination based on race, creed, color, national origin, or economic condition." SCEF was among the most liberal groups in the South; it was often accused of being a communist front organization. The *Patriot* and SCEF were extremely supportive of the student movement and SNCC.

DATE	ALABAMA	ARKANSAS	FLORIDA	GEORGIA	LOUISIANA	MISSISSIPPI	NORTH CAROLINA	SOUTH CAROLINA	TENNESSEE	TEXAS	VIRGINIA
1956 JANUARY	Montgomery—home of Martin Luther King										
MARCH				Atlanta—Negro home in a mixed neighborhood							
JULY				Atlanta—Negro home in predominantly white neighborhood							
AUGUST	Montgomery—home of Negro minister								Clinton—5 different dynamite blasts in Negro section		
1957 JANUARY	Montgomery—4 churches, 3 houses			Americus—Koincnia Farm						Beaumont—2 Negro homes	
FEBRUARY									Knoxville—auditorium		
MARCH	Mobile—home in mixed neighborhood									Beaumont—3—truck, home, church of white "moderates"	
APRIL	Bessemer—2—Negro church and home										
MAY									Chattanooga—Negro home in white neighborhood		
JULY	Birmingham—Negro home										
AUGUST									Jersey—Negro home		
SEPTEMBER									Nashville—integrated school		
OCTOBER							Greensboro—Negro home		Chattanooga—2 Negro homes		
NOVEMBER	Bessemer—Negro home			Ringgold—Negro home			Charlotte—synagogue (attempted)	Gaffney—home of white "moderate"	Chattanooga—Negro home		
DECEMBER	Birmingham—5 Negro homes							Cowpens—Negro home			
1958 JANUARY		Little Rock—home of NAACP official							Chattanooga—YWCA		
FEBRUARY							Gastonia—synagogue (attempted)		Chattanooga—school		
MARCH			Miami—synagogue						Nashville—synagogue		
APRIL	Birmingham—synagogue (attempted)		Jacksonville—2—Negro school and synagogue								
MAY	Bessemer—Negro home										
JUNE	Birmingham—Negro church									Beaumont—white home	
JULY	Birmingham—Negro home			Columbus—Negro home							
AUGUST									Memphis—Negro church		
OCTOBER				Atlanta—synagogue					Clinton—school		
1959 AUGUST				Ringgold—3 homes, 2 Negro, 1 white Roscoe—Negro church							
SEPTEMBER		Little Rock—3—school board office, fire chief's car, business office of mayor									
DECEMBER										Houston—playground	
1960 FEBRUARY		Little Rock—Negro home							Chattanooga—Negro home		
MARCH	Gadsden—synagogue										Chesterfield County—2 Negro homes
APRIL				Atlanta—Negro home					Nashville—Negro home		
MAY				Ringgold—Negro home					Nashville—Negro home		

UNIT 10-2

FEAR AND HATRED GRIP BIRMINGHAM

RACIAL TENSION SMOLDERING AFTER BELATED SITDOWNS

Harrison E. Salisbury

BIRMINGHAM, Ala., April 8—From Red Mountain, where a cast-iron Vulcan looks down 500 feet to the sprawling city, Birmingham seems veiled in the poisonous fumes of distant battles.

On a fine April day, however, it is only the haze of acid fog belched from the stacks of the Tennessee Coal and Iron Company's Fairfield and Ensley works that lies over the city.

But more than a few citizens, both white and Negro, harbor growing fear that the hour will strike when the smoke of civil strife will mingle with that of the hearths and forges.

It is not accidental that the Negro sit-in movement protesting lunch-counter segregation has only lightly touched brooding Birmingham. But even those light touches have sent convulsive tremors through the delicately balanced power structure of the community.

The reaction has been new manifestations of fear, force and terror punctuated by striking acts of courage.

No New Yorker can readily measure the climate of Birmingham today.

Whites and blacks still walk the same streets. But the streets, the water supply and the sewer system are about the only public facilities they share. Ball parks and taxicabs are segregated. So are libraries. A book featuring black rabbits and white rabbits was banned. A drive is on to forbid "Negro music" on "white" stations.

Every channel of communication, every medium of mutual interest, every reasoned approach, every inch of middle ground has been fragmented by the emotional dynamite of racism, reinforced by the whip, the razor, the gun, the bomb, the torch, the club, the knife, the mob, the police and many branches of the state's apparatus.

From the *New York Times*, April 12, 1960.

In Birmingham neither blacks nor whites talk freely. A pastor carefully closes the door before he speaks. A Negro keeps an eye on the sidewalk outside his house. A lawyer talks in the language of conspiracy.

Telephones are tapped, or there is fear of tapping. Mail has been intercepted and opened. Sometimes it does not reach its destination. The eavesdropper, the informer, the spy have become a fact of life.

Volunteer watchmen stand guard twenty-four hours a day over some Negro churches. Jewish synagogues have floodlights for the night and caretakers. Dynamite attempts have been made against the two principal Jewish temples in the last eighteen months. In eleven years there have been twenty-two reported bombings of Negro churches and homes. A number were never reported officially.

Community of Fear

Birmingham's whites and blacks share a community of fear. Some Negroes have nicknamed Birmingham the Johannesburg of America.

"The difference between Johannesburg and Birmingham," said a Negro who came South recently from the Middle West, "is that here they have not yet opened fire with the tanks and big guns."

"I have lived in Alabama all my life," said a newspaperman. "Birmingham is going to blow one of these days. And when that happens that's one story I don't want to be around to cover."

"Remember," a business man said, "Birmingham is not place for irresponsible reporting. Be careful of what you say and who you mention. Lives are at stake."

"I'm ashamed to have to talk to you off the record," said an educator. "It is not for myself. But these are not ordinary times. The dangers are very real and people up North must realize that."

"Excuse me," an educated Negro woman said. "But I just don't understand the white people around here. They seem to act so crazy. It doesn't make any sense. Don't they know there is a limit to what people will stand?"

"If you sow hate, you reap hate," said a Negro pastor.

The Birmingham of another era, that of the happy-go-lucky, ignorant Negro, the serio-comic dramas of Eighteenth Street (the Harlem of Birmingham), and the setting of Octavius Roy Cohen and his Florian Slippery stories, has vanished. Gone with it is Birmingham's fabulous Judge Abernathy, who let Negro prisoners determine the length of their stay in the Birmingham jail with a roll of the dice.

Quiet in Early Phases

When the Negro student sit-in movement reached Birmingham ten days ago, it set in motion a sequence of events almost reflexive in character.

Birmingham had not been quiet during the early phases of the student protests. Two months ago a dozen Negro students went to a public park and began a brief "prayer for freedom." It was curtailed when the police arrested the students on a charge of public disorder.

Then on Thursday, April 2, ten Negro students went two by two into five downtown Birmingham stores. They made small purchases and sat at the lunch counters. All were held eighteen hours before being able to make bond.

The next seventy-two hours were busy ones for the Birmingham police. They arrested three Negro ministers, the Rev. F. L. Shuttlesworth, the Rev. Charles Billlups and the Rev. C. Herbert Oliver. Mr. Shuttlesworth was arrested twice on successive days.

The police also arrested Thomas Reeves, a 21-year-old white student at Birmingham-Southern College and part-time preacher, and Jessie Walker, a Negro student from Daniel Payne University.

Each of those arrested was charged with "vagrancy." In addition, Mr. Reeves and Mr. Oliver, who was hauled barefooted and in his bathrobe from his home, were charged with "intimidating a witness."

By Birmingham custom, persons charged with vagrancy are not admitted to bail. They are held incommunicado for three days. In actual practice, such a prisoner is sometimes permitted to make one telephone call. But not always. A person arrested on a vagrancy warrant simply disappears for three days. His friends and family may not know what has happened to him.

A Favorite Technique

This is a favorite technique of Birmingham's Police Commissioner, Eugene Connor. Mr. Connor is a former sports broadcaster known as "Bull" because of the timbre of his voice. He served as Birmingham Police Commissioner for sixteen years in the late Nineteen Thirties and Nineteen Forties. His administration was a stormy one.

He went into eclipse for several years but made a comeback in 1958, running on a platform of race hate.

"Bull is the law in Birmingham, like it or not," a business man said.

Mr. Connor is the author of many widely quoted aphorisms. He once said:

"Damn the law—down here we make our own law."

On another occasion he declared:

"White and Negro are not to segregate together."

"Only legitimate hold-ups will be investigated," he announced after evidence had been uncovered that some Birmingham robberies were inside jobs.

Mr. Shuttlesworth has been a frequent target of Mr. Connor's men. He has three cases on appeal. His church has been bombed twice. In one bombing his home was destroyed. Both he and his wife were injured and a white pastor was badly manhandled by a Birmingham mob when the three of them sought to use the white waiting room of the local bus depot.

A test of the forces symbolized by Mr. Connor is now in the making—a product of the seismic Birmingham reaction to the Negro student sit-ins.

It centers on young Reeves. He is a slight youngster weighing about 137 pounds and standing five feet eight inches. He wears horn-rimmed glasses, suffers from asthma and is noticeably shy and diffident.

Centers on Student

He has been charged by the police with "intimidating a witness." The witness presumably was one of the ten Negro students arrested for sit-ins.

The parents of young Reeves have received threats of death. The youth has been restricted to the campus of Birmingham-Southern, technically on administrative probation. Actually, the step is for his physical protection.

A cross was burned on the Birmingham-Southern campus possibly because of the Reeves case, possibly because ninety-seven Birmingham-Southern students had signed a petition to Gov. John Patterson pretesting his action in forcing Alabama College to expel Negro sit-in demonstrators. The petition did not protest segregation. It protested political interference with the academic process.

Dr. Henry King Stanford, president of Birmingham-Southern, has been subjected to extraordinary pressures. But he has not buckled under. He supported the right of his students to send their petition to Governor Patterson on the ground of academic freedom. When he was confronted with threats and demands that young Reeves be expelled he again stood his ground. He declined to prejudge the case.

THE PRICE OF COURAGE

In Birmingham this kind of courage does not come cheaply. Dr. Stanford has been told that the college's position in the Reeves case will cost it a minimum of $1,500,000. This is the amount that the college had hoped to raise in a drive for badly-needed building funds this year.

But as one Birmingham citizen said, "You weigh the situation. You take the counsels of caution. You listen to the voices which say don't rock the boat. But finally the time comes when a man has to stand up and be counted."

If fear and terror are common in the streets of Birmingham, the atmosphere in Bessemer, the adjacent steel suburb, is even worse.

On the night the Birmingham police arrested Mr. Shuttlesworth, a band of floggers went to work in Bessemer.

The victim was a white woman, Barbara Espy, 19 years old, a former WAC. She was seized by four or five men, dragged into a car, beaten until she signed a confession that she had been "dating" Negroes.

She has since sworn out warrants charging that she was abducted and beaten by a sheriff's deputy, an alderman and three other persons.

The sheriff repeatedly refused to entertain charges against his deputy. The Federal Bureau of Investigation has been asked to look into the case for possible violation of civil rights.

One of the students who participated in the "prayer for freedom" lived in Bessemer. An evening or two later seven carloads of hooded men roared into the street where the youngster lived with his mother and sister.

Armed with iron pipes, clubs and leather blackjacks into which razor blades were sunk, the men attacked the boy and his mother and sister. The mother and sister protected the boy with their bodies. The men broke a leg of the mother, smashed open her scalp and crushed her hands.

Forty-five minutes after the alarm had been given, the police arrived, but the band had fled. The next day two deputies visited the mother in the hospital. She recoiled in horror. They were two of those who had beaten her, she said. No charges were lodged.

"She is afraid to say anything," a man familiar with the case declared.

A year ago a Negro girl and a white girl, both elementary pupils, quarreled on the way to school. A white man emerged from a near-by house with a bull whip and flogged the Negro girl. The police failed to respond to a call from the Negro school principal.

For weeks Negro children had to go to school an hour early and were held in school an hour late so they would not come into contact with white children.

The list of beatings, intimidations and violence could be continued almost indefinitely.

But not everything goes according to plan.

At the height of the last week's tension the Harvard debating team came to town. It met in an open and publicly announced contest with the debate squad of Miles College, a Birmingham Negro school.

Whites and blacks talked from the same platform. Whites sat with blacks in the audience in violation with one of Birmingham's most cherished ordinances. No policemen appeared. It could not have been more normal or peaceful had the contest been held in Cambridge, Mass.

UNIT 10-3

BIRMINGHAM AND BEYOND

Dr. Martin Luther King, Jr. went into Birmingham, Alabama, the most segregated big city of the South, in the spring of 1963, saying, "As Birmingham goes, so goes the whole South."

Following up on direct-action campaigning by the Alabama Christian Movement for Human Rights (an SCLC affiliate) led by the Rev. Fred Shuttlesworth, he turned loose a siege of demonstrations and sit-ins that lasted for five weeks—and in the process managed to tell the nation what Albany had never been able to express.

He was ably assisted in part of this communication by Police Commissioner Eugene (Bull) Connor, commanding the Birmingham police force in his last lameduck days in public office. Spread in graphic action photographs across newspapers and magazines and snarling out of the television screen were Birmingham police dogs used to halt the demonstrators, many of whom were teen-agers. Never to be forgotten were the shots of young women being knocked down and rolled over by Birmingham's high-pressure fire hoses. The hoses would be turned full blast on the civil rights demonstrators, then played idly against trees, tearing the bark off with a machine gun-like rattle.

Birmingham, in such scenes, erupted to national view after a year-long build-up of comment and interpretation about the Negro revolt. There was awareness of a new anger among Negroes. People were pondering James Baldwin's almost shrill, Old-Testament prophet's warning of the "fire next time" if Americans could not come to know the meaning of what Negroes were offering in non-violent action this time. Thus prepared, the nation awoke with the Birmingham campaign to a final full knowledge of the meaning of direct action.

It was the number-one topic not just in the South, but over the nation, and the best minds of government, journalism, business, and scholarship were put to its problems. All the good of goals and intentions so apparent in the sit-ins, and all the potentiality of the Freedom Rides, and all the implications of the struggle with police apparent in Albany—all of these and all the questions they raised were in focus finally.

There were local peculiarities. Dr. King's timing was criticized, mainly by those who feel no timing is right for demonstrations, but also by some proven friends of civil rights. The criticism concerned political developments. A reorganization of Birmingham city government had resulted in an election which ousted a segregationist administration typified by Police Commissioner Connor, long-time symbol of anti-Negro sentiment, accused often by Negroes of police brutality. A "moderate" mayor, Albert Boutwell, and

New South, October–November 1963.

council were to take office, and it was urged that demonstrations should wait until this new government had a chance to show what it would do. Replies to this included the familiar one that Negroes had been waiting too long. Specifically, it was pointed out that demonstrations had been postponed for months with no notable results from a series of negotiations with white leaders.

There was much evidence of local misgivings, but the Negro leadership closed in behind King and Shuttlesworth.

As the demonstrations gathered momentum, Negroes developed fully a tactic that had been used in Albany (and other cities): the use of the young—high school and grammar school children, some as young as seven—in heavy numbers, marching and singing. One estimate had all but 887 of the 7,386 pupils of Birmingham's seven Negro high schools absent during one day at the height of demonstrations. This aroused criticism; it also resulted in photographs of children in the grips of Birmingham police which hurt the conscience of the nation.

Under pressure of bad publicity and the hurtful effect on business, Birmingham's white leaders on May 4 began a series of conferences with Negroes to try to settle things. These were mediated by Burke Marshall, chief of the Justice Department's Civil Rights Division, flown in from Washington.

Out of the negotiations on May 10 came the Birmingham truce. Its terms were not the all-out capitulation of Birmingham which Dr. King had predicted would crack the remaining solidarity of the South, or even agreement to previous demands.

The terms amounted to a promise to desegregate some downtown lunch counters and public facilities within 90 days and a promise to improve job opportunities within 60 days. (By late November, lunch counters in perhaps a dozen stores or fewer had been desegregated. If there had been improvement in employment, it was slight.) Further, all demonstrators then in jail were released under nominal bail or their own recognizance.

Behind the scenes of the truce was pressure from Washington seeking an end to a situation not the least of whose embarrassments were those to the nation in its international relations, particularly with emerging nations of Africa and Asia. According to the *New York Times* (May 26, 1963), cabinet members and such important private citizens as Dean Eugene V. Rostow of Yale Law School were involved, busied with talking to Birmingham men of power. (Dean Rostow volunteered his aid. It included urging alumnus Roger Blough, president of U.S. Steel, to elicit more cooperation in resolving the crisis from officials of the corporation's subsidiary, Tennessee Coal and Iron, the city's largest industry.)

The truce had been in effect two days when, on the Sunday morning of May 12, a reporter telephoned a member of the Justice Department in Washington and told of havoc he had just witnessed on the streets of Birmingham.

Late that Saturday night, bombs had exploded a half hour apart at the Gaston Motel, headquarters for Dr. King and other civil rights leaders, and at the home of the Rev. A. D. King, brother of the SCLC leader. Spontaneously, in rage and in outrage, Negroes poured onto the streets—an estimated 2,500. They threw bricks and stones at police and firemen. A taxicab was set on fire. A policeman was stabbed.

Dogs arriving with police reinforcements further enraged the mob, but pleading by Negro leaders and police quieted the people finally to sullen muttering. Then Al Lingo, Alabama director of Public Safety, arrived on the scene. As the mob's anger began to roar again, Birmingham Police Chief Jamie Moore, according to *Newsweek*, said to the state policeman: "If you'd leave, Mr. Lingo, I'd appreciate it."

Commissioner Lingo refused, and in effect took control of the police situation. Two Negro stores had suddenly blazed up and were spreading fire. Rocks flew again, and one hit Birmingham Police Inspector Bill Haley in the face. Lingo and 35 troops went into action. Here is how *Newsweek* described it:

> Armed with shotguns, rifles, and billies . . . up and down the street they went, shoving and clubbing spectators, clomping up on front porches, swatting bystanders with billies and gun butts, ordering "Get inside, goddamit!" "I can't, I can't, the doors locked," one Negro screamed as police walloped him. The troopers bashed the door open with gun butts and shoved him inside. Then they joined a mixed party of deputies outside the motel and, 60 strong, charged a crowd gathered in the entrance, billies and guns flailing . . .

By 4:30 A.M., the last of the rioters had been dispersed in such fashion, and the area was sealed off by state police.

"What does it mean?" asked the Justice Department official who had been phoned by the reporter.

"Go back," was the answer, "and read James Baldwin again. This is the fire next time."

And so it seemed on that night of terrible provocation which drew probably the worst violence from Negroes in the growingly angry history of direct action. So it must have seemed also to the nation in the spread after Birmingham of demonstrations across the South and, for the first time on any large scale, into the North of the United States.

The catch-phrase, "new militance," thought up during the spring to describe an intellectual attitude in the civil rights movement, was coming for some to mean angry crowds of demonstrators verging on violence.

The new demonstrations in the South were heaviest in the border and upper South states which had already known sit-ins, and the degrees of desegregation they won. Now Negroes called for "all, now" in cities like Durham, Greensboro, Raleigh, and Nashville. Through the hot summer it went, the largest siege of direct action to date. And wherever there was trouble, the name of Birmingham was invoked.

Danville (Va.), became the scene of a full-scale, volatile campaign, with Dr. King and the Rev. Mr. Shuttlesworth urging the demonstrators on. (It was in Danville that police went into a church, kicked an office door in, and arrested three civil rights leaders.) For a period, Cambridge (Md.), was spotlighted on a peculiarly ugly stage, where the races of men had for weeks to be kept from each other's throats by National Guardsmen. In the still strongly resisting deep South, demonstrations and arrests wound on—in such places as Americus (Ga.); Savannah (Ga.); Jackson (Miss.), and Plaquemine (La.), among many others.

One fatality occurred during the summer's fierce demonstrations. In Lexington (N.C.) a white automobile mechanic was killed by a 22-calibre rifle bullet in a round of shots fired as whites and Negroes faced one another in crowds after a demonstration. Three Negroes were indicted on charges of murder.

Another murder occurred that was not directly connected with a demonstration. But the victim was a Negro leader who had been active in all the Mississippi ferment. He was Medgar W. Evers, NAACP Mississippi field secretary, acknowledged leader of the state's Negroes, shot to death in the carport of his home in Jackson (Miss.), on June 12. A white fertilizer salesman of Greenwood (Miss.) was subsequently charged with the murder.

A Justice Department report at the beginning of August showed 758 demonstrations in 186 cities during the ten weeks after Birmingham. Reports on accomplishments of demonstrations vary. The fact that total figures on southern desegregation are almost impossible to total up is an encouraging sign of how much activity is afoot. Often, desegregation occurs in a context where it is just no longer news.

An attempt by the Southern Regional Council to determine specific desegregation that occurred from April 1 to November 1, 1963, in the South shows change in at least 261 cities and counties of eleven states.

What it took to achieve this is indicated in arrests figures, which were at least 14,733 for the same eight months in the same number of states. This compares with an estimated 3,600 arrests between February 1 and September 1, 1960. Such press reports as have been available show that between April 3 and June 24, there were 10,420 arrests; between June 25 and July 24, 1,323; between July 25 and August 28, 2,043; between August 29 and Sept. 30, 947.

Intellectual ferment during the preceding year had clearly articulated for the first time the frustrations and terrors of life for Negroes in parts of the nation outside the South. Not by law but by custom and practice Negroes (including the many who had fled the South) found themselves shoved into inescapable ghettos and segregated de facto in schools, labor unions, and almost all other phases of life. After Birmingham, these Negroes who felt twice tricked—by a birthright of segregation in the South, by hypocrisy elsewhere which promised surcease but brought only the same old segregation all over again—expressed their rage and hopelessness in direct action, with perhaps the harshest, angriest tones of all.

In New York, Philadelphia, Chicago, Detroit, St. Louis, Los Angeles, and many other cities, the familiar forms of direct action—pickets, marchers, boycotts—and some imaginative variants-demonstrators chaining themselves to pillars of the New York City Hall—came home to non-southern populaces accustomed to seeing them on television far away, and sympathizing. The strain of having the Negro revolution so close showed. The voice of moderation spoke out in northern cities from official positions, ones which often in the past might have scorned that same voice when it was heard in the South. The voice of white resistance and of racism was also heard, without the usual southern drawl.

In the midst of all this, the wrangling and infighting for position among civil rights group came into the open—in speeches and public arguments. This did not help the Negro revolution in public opinion. Realization that it did not, along with an important move led by foundations in New York City to put strong and conventional economic security behind the Negro movement, soon put an end to the battling in public.

(With the sit-ins and increasingly afterward, these organizations in their relationship to each other had both drawn together and competed. Some of the fantasies spun by segregationists about vast wealth of the direct action organizations flew in the face of the fact of their often desperate need for funds. If the competition for these funds, and members, sometimes pushed them into actions that a coordinated thrust toward the mutual goal would not seem to justify, there were also creative qualities to the tension that brought breakthroughs probably not otherwise achievable.)

On the positive side of the summer's developments was a long-building burst of activity in support of direct action by white churches and religious leaders. Congregations were confronted more often and more brutally with the conflict in their religious belief and the American treatment of Negroes. Ministers joined in demonstrations. This rising at last of the white church (or at the least, or most, some of its hierarchy) to its responsibilities and true meaning was hailed by Dr. King in a speech at Atlanta University in the fall of 1963 as the most heartening happening of all the previous summer.

A chief outcome of the events and emotions set off by Birmingham was a polarization of racial attitudes outside the South. The overt unanimity which the non-South had developed in favor of racial equality began to crumble. Demonstrations and crises at home brought quiet prejudice into the open, latent prejudice into acknowledgment.

When the Kennedy administration suddenly in the spring sponsored strong civil rights legislation, this polarization became even more pronounced, and the issues of civil rights steadily took on the overtones of political controversy. In the South, President Kennedy's legislative proposals deepened greatly the divisions within the South's Democratic party, and measurably enhanced the southern Republicans' temptation to appeal to anti-civil rights sentiment.

The assassin's bullet which killed John F. Kennedy probably changed all of this. Saddened reassessments immediately after the tragedy included much hope for the attainment of many of the civil rights goals he sought in life. And the immediate reaction in the nation against lunatic-fringe extremism in the public life seemed likely to discourage openly racist politics.

President Kennedy's televised speech of June 11 announcing new intentions made clear how much the motivation came from the Birmingham spread of direct action.

> . . . Fires of frustration and discord are burning in every city, North and South . . . Redress is sought in the streets, in demonstrations, parades, and protests which create tensions and threaten violence and threaten lives.
>
> We face, therefore, a moral crisis as a country and as a people. It cannot be met by repressive police action. It cannot be left to increased demonstrations in the streets. It cannot be quieted by token moves or tort. It is a time to act in the Congress, in your state and local legislative body, and above all, in all of our daily lives.

This speech was the strongest ever made by a President on Negro rights. And it proposed the strongest legislative remedies ever to be taken seriously for securing those rights.

So the message that called from the beginning of direct action, but that had cried in vain from Albany, had finally reached to the top leadership of the nation.

Two more events of the fateful summer of 1963 helped to round out the meaning of Birmingham.

The first was the August 28 March on Washington by 200,000 Americans, mostly Negro, in general support of Negro rights, and specific support of civil rights legislation. This was a coordinated effort of many groups, including those of direct action. (One of its effects was to drain off energy during the late summer from demonstrations.)

It caught and held for a day, for most of the nation to see, the inspiring, spiritual qualities of direct action, its highest motivation, hope and performance.

There had been consternation—pious fear, articulated at its most soulful by southern Congressmen, that the march would set off a national capital race riot with never-ending, disastrous results. But the march was as peaceful and non-violent, even benevolent, as the all-day camp meeting that it in many ways resembled. The air had been full of predictions about its political effects—that it would ruin chances for civil rights legislation, that it would make passage certain. But when it had come and gone, it did not seem to have changed things either way.

Its effectiveness had to be considered in whatever it said to the American conscience—in the speeches of the many leaders at the formal ceremonies at the Lincoln Memorial, and in the spectacle of so much of the humanity of American protesting betrayals of the American dream, asking more for themselves, for their children.

What this said had the immediate effect, at least, of offsetting the ugly images of violence and mobism that direct action was coming to mean to some.

The second event was to show quite clearly from which side of the racial struggle violence was most to be feared. It was another bombing in Birmingham. It came this time not on Saturday night, like the previous one, to bring out Saturday night drinkers rioting.

This time it came on Sunday morning, during the Sunday school hour, and this time it killed children worshipping God in a Christian church.

Four Negro girls, two of them 14, one 11, and one 10, were killed by the blast of dynamite that ripped through the sanctuary and Sunday school of the Sixteenth Street Baptist Church on September 14. The church, at the scene of some of the past spring's most turbulent demonstrations, was badly damaged, with broken glass, fallen wood and plaster throughout. A large stain-glass window was somehow left standing among the many destroyed. On it the depiction of the body of Christ, as shepherd, was left intact, but His face and a small place at His heart were ripped out.

Dozens of worshippers in the church were injured, and, as they were carried away for hospital treatment, a crowd wailing grief was dispersed by police.

Then in shock, and a strange silence, the city waited for whatever reaction would come. Extra-duty city police and state troopers patrolled through a fear-filled day and night, expecting retaliatory violence. It did not come. The only added violence that Sunday was the shooting to death by white youths of a Negro boy on a bicycle without provocation, and the shooting to death of a Negro youth by police who said he ran when ordered to halt.

As ever after such raw outrages as the dynamiting, a shocked nation expressed sorrow and indignation. In Birmingham, the City Council passed a resolution of regret; there were prayers in segregated churches; one lawyer. Charles A. Morgan, Jr., angrily spoke the guilt of racism shared by all in the dynamiting, and 53 Birmingham lawyers issued a public statement calling for obedience to decisions of the U.S. Supreme Court and an end to violence.

In the midst of investigations, including work by the FBI, of the bombings, the Highway Patrol under Col. Lingo announced arrest of three men with Ku Klux Klan backgrounds on charges of illegal possession of dynamite. They were tried and given six months in jail and $100 fines. They posted appeal bonds of $300 each.

The church dynamiting having joined a long list of thus far unsolved ones in Birmingham, the nation waited to see if its effect would be at last to bring more reasonable, conciliatory attitudes there towards demands of Negroes—taking one appropriate form in the plea that Negro police be hired. They were not hired. When it was suggested to Mr. Blough that U.S. Steel use its influence, as the biggest employer in Birmingham, to reduce racial tension, he said he felt the corporation was meeting its responsibilities by following a non-discriminatory hiring policy, its officials were meeting theirs by private actions, and that using raw economic power for social reform would be "repugnant." Former Army Secretary Kenneth Royall and former West Point football coach Earl (Red) Blaik, sent after the bombing by President Kennedy to try to heal the racial breach, left after ten days of conferences, reporting privately back to the President. Charles Morgan moved to Virginia . . . And there were threats of demonstrations anew in Birmingham.

It had not been the fire this time, even in Birmingham, even at the dramatic, grief-filled moment of greatest provocation. It had not been, either, the hoped-for time of attainment of a clear consensus in American public opinion on the demands of direct action.

What it seemed to be was the communication of the message of direct action, and in various ways a beginning of the development of the national answer. The message demanded (no longer begged) full (no longer token or gradual) rights of American citizenship for Negroes. And once communicated, such a message had to be answered.

The forces necessary to finding the answer seemed finally set in motion, in Congress, in business, in public debate, and, most importantly, within the conscience of the individual American citizen—where ultimately decisions rest and to which direct action had been speaking all along.

UNIT 10-4

THE SOUTHERN CHRISTIAN LEADERSHIP CONFERENCE AND THE SECOND RECONSTRUCTION, 1957–1973

Adam Fairclough

By any orthodox standard, the Southern Christian Leadership Conference was an unusual organization. Run, as Andrew Young put it, by "a bunch of Baptist preachers," its tangled structure and lax discipline made confusion a way of life. Although it had ambitious long-term programs, SCLC thrived on crises and prided itself on spontaneity. "When you are called upon to witness, you . . . can't always analyze what might happen," explained Ralph Abernathy. "You just have to go." This impulsiveness led to sudden changes of plan that exasperated outsiders: mass meetings would wait hours for the appearance or nonappearance of scheduled speakers; marches, demonstrations, and even whole campaigns would be announced and then abruptly cancelled. Its members accepted, even took a perverse pride in, administrative chaos. As Hosea Williams put it, "we are a movement, not an organization."[1]

Its critics took a less charitable view, and described SCLC as a bureaucratic shambles, a giant fund raising machine, and a vehicle for the glorification of its president, Dr. Martin Luther King, Jr. They found King's fame and SCLC's wealth irksome and ill deserved, for the conference represented but a fraction of the civil rights movement. The National Association for the Advancement of Colored People, founded in 1910, had won the stunning legal victories that culminated in the Supreme Court overturning the "separate but equal" doctrine in 1954. The Congress of Racial Equality, founded in 1942, originated the 1961 Freedom Rides and spearheaded most of the direct action in North Carolina and Louisiana. The Student Nonviolent Coordinating Committee, organized in 1960, led the main voter registration drives in the rural Black Belt of the Deep South and began the protests

South Atlantic Quarterly, 80:2, Spring, 1981,

in Selma which led to the passage of the Voting Rights Act. While others did this work, critics asserted, SCLC staged "a few showy projects" that reaped all the credit.[2]

That SCLC, an organization of clergymen, could become what Bayard Rustin called "the dynamic center of the civil rights movement" was all the more remarkable because the black church had been the despair of generations of activists. Although it enjoyed unequalled prestige and, in Gunnar Myrdal's words, had "the Negro masses organized," black ministers had traditionally accommodated to the racial status quo and, with few exceptions, displayed a complete lack of militancy. Critics of black Christians, from Booker T. Washington to Martin Luther King, complained that they were too otherworldly, so "absorbed in a future good 'over yonder' that they condition their members to adjust to their present evils over here."[3]

The outbreak in the mid-1950s of bus boycotts in half a dozen southern cities, all of them led by black ministers, signalled a momentous change. In 1944 Myrdal had predicted that leadership might pass by default to other middle-class elements within the black community. Organized labor, however, had been stifled in the South after the Second World War, while teachers and other professionals were too economically vulnerable to assume a militant stand against white supremacy. Ministers, financially independent of whites, remained the primary source of leadership. Those who became protest leaders shared the heightened postwar militancy of the black community as a whole—an impatience to abolish segregation that had been fuelled by recent victories such as the outlawing of the white primary, the integration of the armed services, and the Supreme Court's ruling against segregation in the public schools. Although only a small minority of the black clergy, the militant few, came to exercise disproportionate influence. The Montgomery bus boycott of 1955–56 epitomized the new kind of leadership. In addition to its leader, Martin Luther King, Jr., some twenty ministers took part in the Montgomery Improvement Association. Its close ties with the church gave the protest coherence, moral authority. and religious fervor.[4]

In early 1957 King and other like-minded clergymen formed the Southern Christian Leadership Conference. SCLC had no members—unlike the NAACP, which had half a million—but consisted of a fluctuating number of affiliated organizations that were grouped together by state. Most of these affiliates comprised a number of ministers and their churches, although SCLC included some civic organizations, as well as northern affiliates that existed mainly to provide financial support. While this unusual structure had its problems—SCLC only became effective when it recruited a cadre of full-time organizers—it created a flexible network of popular local protest leaders.[5]

Its clerical leadership made SCLC uniquely equipped to communicate with ordinary blacks. For the most part excluded from politics, blacks had long used religion to sublimate or disguise their political aspirations. SCLC's leaders clothed political ideas in a religious phraseology that blacks readily understood and used Christian tenets to give the civil rights movement a divine sanction. As Ralph Abernathy, SCLC's vice-president, put it, "This is God's movement. There can be *no* injunction against God." Being preachers, they were adept at combining exhortation with entertainment, and provided what Bayard Rustin called "an emotional dimension to whip up the enthusiasm of the people." SCLC's identification with the church was invaluable when it came to organizing local protests, for churchgoers attended its mass meetings as they would Sunday services.[6]

SCLC's first few years, however, were disappointing and revealed important weaknesses. The fame that King had garnered from the Montgomery bus boycott gave an exaggerated impression of his leadership abilities. In fact, King had neither instigated the boycott nor sought its leadership, and the protest's success owed as much to the collective efforts of the Montgomery improvement Association as it did to King himself. As president of SCLC King lacked the same kind of organized and dedicated support: as late as 1960 the Conference had a full-time staff of only three. There was also confusion about SCLC's precise role. Founded to promote nonviolent direct action—boycotts, demonstrations, sit-ins, and so forth—it launched instead an ambitious but unrealistic scheme to double the number of registered black voters in the South. Voter registration drives, however, required an extensive local organization, something that SCLC, unlike the NAACP, did not yet possess. Its "Crusade for Citizenship" staged some enthusiastic rallies but failed to register many new voters.[7]

By 1959, SCLC's future appeared uncertain. Ella Baker, its first executive director, complained of an absence of "reflective thinking and planning" and criticized the failure to develop a distinctive program. When a student sit-in movement to protest segregated lunch counters swept the South in 1960, it did so spontaneously, with only slight assistance from the conference. The daring and imaginative "Freedom Rides" launched by CORE in 1961 pushed SCLC further from the limelight. The question of purpose still plagued the new organization. Should it assist local actions or should it instigate its own protests? Should it concentrate on voter registration or promote direct action to desegregate public accommodations?[8]

Primarily a strategist and a thinker, King was handicapped by his own ignorance of the practical techniques of nonviolent direct action, and only when he recruited knowledgeable tacticians and organizers did SCLC really come into its own. The staff members added between 1960 and 1963 provided this body of experience. James Lawson, C. T. Vivian, and James Bevel, ministers all, were veterans of the Nashville sit-ins and had taken part in the first "Freedom Ride" to leave that city in 1961. The Rev. Wyatt T. Walker was a long-time activist from Petersburg, Virginia, where he had served in the NAACP and organized the Petersburg Improvement Association. Hosea Williams, from Savannah, headed the Chatham County Crusade for Voters, probably SCLC's most successful affiliate in terms of both voter registration and direct action. Beneath these and the half-dozen other members of the executive staff, SCLC recruited a cadre of field organizers. As its full time staff grew from five in 1960 to sixty in 1964, it developed the ability, working with local leaders and other volunteers, to mount large scale protests that sent thousands to jail.[9]

Wyatt Walker, Hosea Williams, and James Bevel played especially noteworthy parts in perfecting SCLC's tactics. All three had a flair for inventive direct action and were willing to take risks when King hesitated to act. Walker's plans for the Birmingham protests, mapped out with Fred Shuttlesworth, called for gradually, escalating demonstrations calculated to engineer a potentially explosive level of tension. Williams took a similarly hard-headed approach, scorning negotiations and biracial committees. The tumultuous protests he led in Savannah brought desegregation to that city a full year before the 1964 Civil Rights Act, and one of his tactics, the dangerous night march, became a standard part of SCLC's repertoire. Bevel devised equally ingenious tactics, involving young children in the Birmingham demonstrations and originating the ploy of a fifty-mile march from Selma to Montgomery. Fred Shuttlesworth and C. T. Vivian shared the same combative approach toward direct action.[10]

The role of the Rev. Andrew J. Young, who joined SCLC in 1961, differed from that of the direct action specialists. Like King, Young realized that the sledgehammer tactics favored by Bevel and Williams could rarely force change by themselves, for a policy of mass arrests, if vigorously enforced and backed by court injunctions, could usually baffle nonviolent protests. Young believed that direct action was best used as a means of opening the door to negotiation. Well versed in the art of the possible, he proved adept at extricating the Conference from tactical quagmires. Conciliatory in manner and reasonable in argument, he became SCLC's principal negotiator, playing a key role, for example, in the talks that ended the Birmingham protests.[11]

To many outsiders, SCLC still looked like a one-man band. Unlike CORE and the NAACP, SCLC was not organized along democratic lines. Annual conventions and twice-yearly board meetings had little control over policy, and in practice merely approved King's proposals. Only once, when the 1965 convention refused to endorse his statements about Vietnam, did King fail to carry his organization with him. King's position at the apex of the SCLC hierarchy was unassailable, for nobody could rival his popularity or effectiveness as a publicist and fund raiser.

But despite its autocratic structure, King did not keep SCLC under his thumb, as some have asserted. His caution, tactical indecisiveness, and distaste for administration led him to delegate authority freely. As Willie Bolden, one of the field staff, recalled, "He never did believe in pulling rank. He did it only if it was necessary." Moreover, King did not surround himself with ciphers or sycophants but, as program director Randolph Blackwell admitted, with "egotistical, stubborn, arrogant people." Transcripts of staff meetings reveal spirited debates among, in Andrew Young's words, "driving, ambitious" individuals. Indeed, discussions often degenerated into shouting matches, with participants smashing furniture in their frustration. King did not hand down decisions from an Olympian height: after consulting trusted advisers outside SCLC, he hammered them out with his colleagues."[12]

It was true that King permitted, in journalist Paul Good's words, "godlike myth to surround him." SCLC's much-criticized "cult of personality," however, was to a large extent a deliberate policy, "a careful, methodical process of image-building." His aides, particularly Ralph Abernathy, praised King extravagantly and ascribed to him almost superhuman powers. This was partly a fund raising strategy, enabling SCLC to translate King's "unique symbolism," as Wyatt Walker put it, into dollars and cents. More important, SCLC lacked a mass membership and had no political base; its effectiveness as a pressure group depended in large part on King's personal prestige or charismatic authority. It was also much easier, especially for unlettered blacks who lived in the rural Deep South, to identify with a larger-than-life individual like King than with an amorphous organization like SCLC.[13]

While Abernathy's exaggerated encomiums should be discounted, it would be wrong to err in the opposite direction by underestimating King's influence. His intellectual gifts and powers of expression surpassed those of his colleagues. In an organization of preachers, King was a preacher par excellence, and although some found his style pompous and repetitive, few denied his ability to inspire audiences. "King brought to life . . . a tangible God," wrote one journalist, "not some metaphysical concept." And although outsiders criticized SCLC's habit of depicting him as a latter-day Moses and emphasized the multiplicity of black leaders, opinion polls consistently recorded King as the most popular black leader by far. He swelled the ranks of demonstrations and filled churches and meeting halls to overflowing. As the church secretary of the NAACP admitted, "King packs them in."[14]

Some argued that blacks admired King despite, rather than because of, his commitment to nonviolence as a philosophy. The ideas of Gandhi, wrote sociologist E. Franklin Frazier, had "nothing in common with the social heritage of the Negro." The psychologist Kenneth B. Clark went so far as to call King's philosophy "pathological," because it demanded an unnatural response to oppression. King and his aides readily admitted that blacks had trouble understanding and accepting Gandhian doctrines. "Birmingham was probably the most violent city in America," Andrew Young recalled, "and every black family had an arsenal." Many activists came to view the philosophy of nonviolence as demeaning even cowardly—and politically naive. Both SNCC and CORE would officially renounce it in 1966.[15]

In the early years of the civil rights movement, on the other hand, a small but influential minority of activists proved eagerly receptive to the Gandhian philosophy, which was propagated not only by SCLC but also by CORE and its pacifist progenitor, the Fellowship of Reconciliation. Nonviolence as a philosophy offered the stirring ideal of a "beloved community" as well as a cogent justification for the transgressions of the law that direct action involved. Moreover, King framed Gandhian ideas within traditional Christian dogmas, and, as John Lewis of SNCC has argued, was remarkably successful in attuning them to the religious beliefs of black southerners. Even those who scorned nonviolence as a philosophy accepted it as a sound method of social protest. As Stokely Carmichael admitted in 1970, "nonviolence was the only possibility."[16]

For most blacks, King's appeal was simple and direct. Involvement in the civil rights movement, especially in the Deep South, could bring economic reprisals, incarceration, physical injury, and even death. King instilled the fortitude and confidence to brave those threats. Stressing the dangers he faced himself, he urged blacks to develop "that quiet courage to die if necessary." Insisting that they had the power to mold their own futures if they replaced "pity with self respect," he exhorted them to "straighten their backs up." It was a message that most blacks wanted to hear. When King went to jail, thousands followed him. "He was a symbol of all their hopes for a better life," wrote Cleveland Sellers of SNCC. "By being there and showing that he really cared, he was helping to destroy barriers of fear and insecurity."[17]

Despite King's popularity, SCLC never lacked critics. Older, accommodationist black leaders echoed the charge of white segregationists that King and his crew were irresponsible trouble makers. The Rev. Joseph H. Jackson, president of the five-million-strong National Baptist Convention, cared little for King's version of the social gospel and did not hide his aversion to SCLC's leader. Most black clergymen probably shared Jackson's views: Wyatt Walker estimated that as many as 90 percent of the black ministers in Birmingham shunned SCLC's campaign there. Many black-owned newspapers showed a similar hostility. *The Birmingham World*, for example, denounce SCLC's protests as "wasteful and worthless," and urged King and his cohorts to go back to Atlanta.[18] Within the civil rights movement itself many regarded SCLC's tactics as ineffective. The NAACP remained convinced that the really substantial victories were won in the federal courts. SNCC was skeptical of direct action, for different reasons. Having sent organizers into the Black Belt only to see their protests crushed, it concluded that voter registration and the development of political power was the path to change. By 1965 SNCC scored direct action and regarded SCLC's use of demonstrations as irresponsible. The conference, SNCC charged, would organize dramatic but ineffectual marches, win a few minor concessions, and then "proclaim a great moral victory and leave town." It was certainly true that local leaders, in Birmingham and elsewhere felt that SCLC had exploited their protests for the sake of publicity and then abandoned them."[19]

Many believed that SCLC provoked white violence in an utterly cynical fashion. According to SNCC's James Forman, the SCLC strategists were delighted when "Bull" Connor turned police-dogs and firehoses against peaceful demonstrators in Birmingham, and in their elation jumped up and down chanting, "We've got a movement. We had some police brutality!" Journalists such as Pat Watters and Paul Good also noted such behavior. SCLC, wrote Good, "is frankly opportunistic, sometimes dissembles, and does not particularly care if innocents get hurt in the process."[20] King admitted that the success of SCLC's tactics often depended on whites unleashing violence against nonviolent demonstrators. White violence not only provided the civil rights movement with what Bayard Rustin called "an organizing dynamic," but also provoked, in extreme cases, federal intervention—it had brought paratroopers to Little Rock in 1957 and marshals to Montgomery during the 1961 Freedom Rides. After the dismal failure of its protests in Albany, Georgia, in 1961–62, King and his staff concluded that without such federal involvement direct action would be unable to effect fundamental change. Nonviolent protests had, it was true, had some success in the Upper South and the Border States, but even there the process of desegregation was slow and uneven. And in the Deep South, with few exceptions, direct action had failed completely as the police, armed with court injunctions, locked up protesters and intimidated their supporters.[21]

In its Birmingham and Selma protests SCLC exploited white violence to dramatize "before a national audience . . . the inhumanity of the Jim Crow system." Its strategy assumed that racism, at least in its most virulent form, was a southern anachronism, "an idea that is out of harmony with the basic idea of the nation." If its full depravity could be exposed, King contended, the "great decent majority" would bestir itself to demand protective legislation. SCLC therefore subordinated local demands to this larger goal, using Birmingham and Selma as arenas in which to stage what David Halberstam described as "a great televised morality play." As Samuel Lubell noted, "getting bloodied and beaten" was an essential part of the strategy.[22]

The charge that SCLC manipulated local movements clearly had substance. Yet the conference justified its tactics on both moral and practical grounds. Direct action might not bring about immediate changes, but the very act of defiance was necessary to "dissolve the stereotype of the grinning, submissive Uncle Tom." More important, SCLC contended that violence was intrinsic to the system of white supremacy and that direct action merely made it visible. As Andrew Young put it, SCLC made sheriffs like Jim Clark inflict their beatings "on Main Street, at noon, in front of CBS, NBC and ABC television cameras." If, as Pat Watters believed, SCLC adapted its tactics to "what the liberals in Washington wanted," those tactics paid off handsomely. President Johnson, in full-blown rhetoric, described Selma as "a turning-point in man's unending search for freedom"; and President Kennedy, in his more restrained prose, acknowledged that "the events in Birmingham" had "so increased the cries for equality that no city or state or legislative body can prudently choose to ignore them."[23]

As August Meier pointed out in 1965, SCLC's campaigns gave the civil rights movement a certain unity, coherence, and common focus. The tactical unity achieved by the "Big Five" civil rights organizations between 1963 and 1965 owed much to SCLC's ability to act as a bridge between the militant and conservative wings of the movement. On the one side, SCLC agreed with the NAACP and the National Urban League about the wisdom of working alongside sympathetic whites and within the national Democratic party. On the more militant side, SCLC shared with CORE an emphasis on Gandhian direct action, and the fact that they concentrated their efforts in different states made for a good working relationship.[24]

SCLC's relationship with SNCC was more complex. SNCC resented the fact that when they conducted joint protests in Albany, Selma, and elsewhere, SCLC received most of the publicity although SNCC had laid the vital organizational groundwork. In addition, many SNCC workers disliked the religiosity of SCLC's style and the authoritarianism of its structure. They regarded SCLC as too bourgeois, too compromising. As one SNCC worker said of King—perhaps unwittingly pinpointing the secret of his success—"He's got one foot in the cotton field and one in the White House."[25] Even so, although some of his lieutenants reciprocated SNCC's hostility, King himself viewed SNCC with fatherly affection and was quick to defend its often intemperate militancy. For this and other reasons he commanded the respect of critics like Cleveland Sellers and Stokely Carmichael and enjoyed a close rapport with John Lewis, SNCC's chairman. Until 1966 the two organizations kept up a fruitful collaboration, and although SNCC complained that the conference stole its glory at Selma, its work there would probably have been inconclusive had not SCLC's intervention forged a tactical coalition that included the Urban League, the NAACP, and organized labor—groups that SNCC scorned.

Unlike SNCC, SCLC believed strongly in the strategy advocated by King's unofficial political adviser, Bayard Rustin, of constructing the broadest possible alliance of "progressive" forces. King and his colleagues determinedly courted white liberals, labor unions, church organizations, and university people and did much to strengthen the "coalition of conscience" that indirectly brought about what historians now see as a "Second Reconstruction" of the South. SCLC's ability to mobilize clerical support was especially noteworthy: when King appealed to the churches from Selma, some four hundred nuns, priests, rabbis, bishops, and denominational heads converged on the Alabama town. Richard Hofstadter's description of Progressivism could be applied with even greater accuracy to the civil rights struggle: "No other major movement in American political history had ever received so much clerical sanction."[26]

As an individual, King was an enormously effective spokesman for the civil rights movement. He proved adept at adjusting his rhetorical style to suit different white audiences: and while his message evoked white guilt, it also, as King's biographer David Lewis pointed out, left "deeply pleasurable emotions." His emphasis on nonviolence helped to allay white fears and clothed the civil rights movement in what Lerone Bennett called "the comforting garb of love and forgiveness." By defining the movement's goals in terms of universal values like democracy, Christianity, and "the best in the American dream," he maximized white support and involvement. His intellectual and oratorical gifts plus SCLC's flair for publicity made him the leader who, in Meier's words, "symbolized for most whites the whole program of Negro advancement."[27]

King's failure in Chicago is often cited as evidence of SCLC's inability to adapt to the northern ghetto. The conference certainly underestimated the degree of white opposition and black anger it would encounter there. Viewing the South as the main bastion of racism and regarding discrimination in the North as a secondary, residual phenomenon. SCLC mistook the significance of the 1964 riots in New York and elsewhere, construing them as aberrations rather than portents. Only the massive riot in Watts brought home the depth of the problem in the North. Once in Chicago, conference workers soon discovered that the black preacher lacked the singular prestige he enjoyed in the South and that the church alone was an inadequate organizing tool. SCLC thrived on spontaneity and dramatic confrontations: it had little experience of the tedious job of community organizing. Many became dispirited by the apathy, cynicism, and hostility they encountered. Hosea Williams, whose voter registration drive got nowhere, complained that "here, the Negro has been so plantationized that he feels there's no hope of ever breaking the stranglehold." The sheer size of its task overwhelmed SCLC's resources—as Coretta King plaintively recalled, "Chicago is such a big city, and we were so few." The hostility of the Daley machine, which included many of the established black leaders, was equally daunting.[28]

Even so, SCLC's efforts in Chicago were far from inept. Some of the staff, notably James Bevel and Jesse Jackson, showed great aptitude for working in the ghetto and organized neighborhood associations, tenant unions, and consumer boycotts. The conference also embarked upon slum rehabilitation and adult education programs. When it finally turned to direct action, moreover, it forced Mayor Daley to the negotiating table and extracted an open housing agreement which, as David Lewis pointed out, was "considerably more comprehensive" than the settlement it had won in Birmingham in 1963. *Newsweek* even termed it a "solid vindication of Southern style nonviolent protest in a Northern city."[29]

Unfortunately, Mayor Daley never made a serious effort to implement this agreement and, after his easy reelection in April 1967, openly repudiated it. More important, SCLC's dramatization of discrimination in the housing market did not prevent Congress from rejecting fair-housing legislation in 1966 and 1967. The evidence of opinion polls, as well as the North's long history of race riots, demonstrated that most whites accepted with equanimity the exclusion of blacks from "white" residential areas. Fear of economic competition coalesced with this racism to produce an aggressive resentment against black demands that led to the rejection of fair-housing laws in California and other states, growing support for George Wallace, and a swing towards the Republican party. Democratic leaders were terrified by the prospect of a mass defection of white voters in the Northern cities and suburbs. As Lyndon Johnson recalled, "the open housing issue had become a Democratic liability." Political support for the civil rights movement melted away.[30]

The wave of urban riots that started in Watts in 1965 hastened the decline of SCLC's influence. Contrary to King's belief, most whites detested direct action, but the fear of black violence, and the confidence that King's moderate leadership would prevent it, had given many a pragmatic reason for backing SCLC's nonviolent crusade. When King proved powerless to curb urban rioting—as dramatically illustrated by the eruption that occurred in Chicago during SCLC's campaign there—much of his white support fell away. In this context, many black activists in the North agreed with Bayard Rustin that further direct action would only intensify the white backlash. The riots, moreover, cast doubt upon the very feasibility of nonviolent protest in the North: studies showed that significant numbers of blacks were inclining toward violence as a method of self-assertion and that the harsh suppression of the outbreaks was creating a backwash of sympathy for the rioters. King continued to argue that nonviolent "mass civil disobedience" in northern cities could be a "constructive and creative force," but privately he admitted that "people expect me to have answers, but I don't have any."[31]

Tactical disagreements mirrored a deepening split within the civil rights movement. The "Black Power" slogan, adopted by SNCC and CORE in 1966, made unity among the "Big Five" impossible. Although defined in many ways, "Black Power" clearly meant the rejection of nonviolence, coalitionism, and integration. It also had unmistakable anti-white overtones. SCLC tried to be positive about the slogan, but a split in the movement could not be avoided. The NAACP and the Urban League denounced "Black Power" and anathematized SNCC and CORE. Vainly struggling to keep the two sides together, King suspected that the NAACP welcomed the split "because they think they are the only civil rights organization;" but SNCC and CORE were equally obdurate.[32]

The war in Vietnam widened the divisions. Whereas SNCC and CORE denounced the American involvement, the Urban League and the NAACP stoutly defended it. King himself was appalled by the rapid escalation of the war, but fear of alienating President Johnson and lack of support from his own organization prevented him from speaking with his customary frankness. By early 1967, however, with his wife and many of his colleagues—notably James Bevel—already in the forefront of the antiwar movement, he could keep silent no longer. King's decision to denounce the war, this time with SCLC"s backing, brought a storm of criticism from erstwhile supporters. Whitney Young, publicly castigating King, replied that "the greatest freedom that exists for Negroes . . . is the freedom to die in Vietnam." The NAACP insisted that civil rights leaders should stay away from foreign policy. Bayard Rustin defended King's "ride to debate" Vietnam but advised blacks to shun the peace movement. From the *New York Times*, *Washington Post*, and *Atlanta Constitution* came excoriating editorials.[33]

King searched for an issue that might bridge these divisions. By the end of 1967 he believed he had found one. A campaign in Washington to dramatize poverty, he contended, would resurrect the civil rights coalition and, he hoped, attract the young opponents of the war in Vietnam. Moreover, whereas "Black Power" alienated whites and other minorities, the concept of "Poor People's Power" would unite the dispossessed of all races. King believed that SCLC could serve as the "radical middle" of a resurgent movement for social reform and predicted that the proposed protests would "create new alliances, wake new forces."[34] Most black leaders, however, regarded the plan as dangerously misconceived. John Morsell of the NAACP warned that protests in Washington would be "met with as an insurrection." Bayard Rustin thought they would attract "the most irresponsible and uncontrollable elements," and argued that direct action "can only lead . . . to further backlash and repression." King's top aides expressed other doubts. James Bevel contended that the war was now the most urgent issue and doubted that a campaign against poverty would excite the enthusiasm of students and young people. Then there was a tactical problem: would President Johnson "give enough opposition for us to build up steam and momentum?"—he was hardly likely to respond in the manner of "Bull" Connor. Hosea Williams and Jesse Jackson shared Bevel's skepticism and wanted SCLC to develop programs rather than pursue panaceas. Andrew Young believed that "with an asinine Congress like this,"most of the campaign's goals would be unattainable."[35]

Would the Poor People's Campaign have been more successful if King had lived? Despite King's still-considerable prestige, the campaign's stated demands seemed to doom it to failure at the outset. SCLC sought the passage of an "Economic Bill of Rights" along the lines of John Conyers' Full Opportunity Bill, which called for an expenditure of $30 billion over three years. Yet Congress had slashed the War on Poverty and only grudgingly appropriated $40 million for rat control. President Johnson regarded demands for new multi-billion dollar social programs as completely unrealistic. King admitted that "we're riding on the forces of history and not totally shaping things," but those forces—the mood of white opinion, the hostility of president and Congress, the primacy of the war issue—were working against SCLC. King probably realized this and might well have cancelled the campaign lest it endanger the presidential candidacy of Robert Kennedy. More likely, he would have been satisfied with minor concessions from the government. As Andrew Young later admitted, "we were trying to hold ground we had won. We weren't trying to win new victories."[36]

King's assassination and the fiasco of the Poor People's Campaign exacerbated fundamental weaknesses in SCLC's structure. In 1967 King had attempted to place the conference upon a firmer organizational foundation. Operation Breadbasket, the consumer boycott apparatus which had proved successful in Atlanta and Chicago, became a nationwide program under the direction of Jesse Jackson. To improve SCLC's overall efficiency and organizational discipline, King appointed a management consultant executive director, promoted Andrew Young to the new post of executive vice-president, and set up a central steering-committee comprising himself, Young, Ralph Abernathy, and two others.[37] But these reforms did not change SCLC's basic character. While Andrew Young and Hosea Williams wanted to orient the conference toward long-term political action, King took his own role as a prophetic leader increasingly seriously. A decade earlier, he had joked that "people will be expecting me to pull rabbits out of the hat for the rest of my life"; yet by 1967–68 he felt impelled to win fresh victories in order to avert what he saw as the threat of a right-wing takeover. His belated interest in developing SCLC as a permanent organization did not alter the fact that it remained King-centered. It never managed to establish its own identity. Dependent on King for leadership, publicity, and much of its financial support, it was ill equipped to carry on without him.[38]

By the end of 1968, SCLC was a demoralized organization. "The toll of some ten years of constant pressure is beginning to tell on all of us," admitted Andrew Young. Without King to enforce unity, personal antagonisms and policy differences became increasingly destructive. The tension and frustration became so acute that the senior staff underwent two lengthy sessions of group psychoanalysis. "We've never buried Dr. King," explained Young, "and we won't be able to do anything until we do." But this failed to keep the staff together. James Bevel, unable to win backing for a plan to intensify opposition to the war in Vietnam by using civil disobedience, left in 1969. Andrew Young resigned in 1970 to run, unsuccessfully at first, for Congress.[39] By that time, SCLC's activities had become too thinly spread and lacked a central focus. Since 1966, SCLC had ceased to be a purely southern organization, yet had failed to develop an adequate national structure. In practice, its move to the northern cities had meant temporarily abandoning the South, a fact which, combined with SNCC's collapse and CORE's decline, caused a dramatic slowdown in civil rights activity in that region. In 1965 the three organizations had fielded about one thousand workers in the South. Two years later fewer than fifty remained, and observers were pronouncing the civil rights movement dead or, at best, "fighting a last-ditch battle for survival." This collapse stunted black political growth and dulled the cutting edge of the recent civil rights laws. As Vernon Jordan of the Voter Education Project put it, "the trouble is, the Movement never reached most counties in the South."[40]

SCLC tried to penetrate these neglected areas after King's death, and the years 1968-1970 saw a minor revival of its activities in the South. Its successful intervention in the Charleston, South Carolina hospital workers' strike of 1969 was especially notable. Its efforts to become a viable national organization, however, foundered on the internecine leadership struggle that broke out between Ralph Abemathy, King's chosen successor, and

Jesse Jackson, the rising star of SCLC's expanding economic wing, Operation Breadbasket. Jackson's resignation in 1971 removed SCLC's ablest and most popular northern spokesman and wrecked Operation Breadbasket. With the launching of Operation PUSH, Jackson became a national civil rights leader in his own right, with an organization that appropriated SCLC's northern role.[41]

This blow rendered SCLC's attempts to mount ambitious national projects increasingly futile, and critics complained that the conference engaged in an endless round of rallies and marches that produced little save angry rhetoric. Its involvement with the antiwar movement, its alliance with the National Welfare Rights Organization, and its support for such causes as the California grape workers overextended its declining resources and diluted their impact. By taking on too much, SCLC neglected its southern base and became swallowed up among other national movements. By 1972, SCLC"s financial problems forced it to reduce its staff from sixty-one to twenty. A year later, Ralph Abernathy renounced the leadership, blasting those who "now occupy high positions made possible through our struggle . . . but will not support the SCLC financially." At the annual convention, however, he agreed to pick up King's mantle once again, and soldiered on for four more years.[42]

Waning black support paralleled a decline in white financial backing. Although SCLC argued that "marching is never outdated," faith in the ability of nonviolent direct action to bring about change had all but evaporated. By 1970 the election of Richard Nixon, the widespread white hostility to black demands, and the tendency to answer black protests with "massive police and military force" had driven down black expectations and ushered in a period of quietism and disillusionment. A 1970 opinion poll disclosed that most blacks expressed "profound cynicism about the American political system."[43]

Part of this pessimism may well have been a reaction against the extravagant optimism preached by King and SCLC in the previous decade. As late as 1964, when the prevalence of segregation in the North was a matter of common knowledge, King predicted that "race and color prejudice will have all but disappeared . . . in the next five years." A year later, deceived by the sympathy aroused by the Selma protests, he argued that the "vast majority of Americans" supported the direct-action methods of the civil rights movement—an assertion which opinion polls plainly contradicted. As Samuel DuBois Cook has written, until the Chicago campaign King overestimated the white majority's "sense of guilt and shame over the dehumanized role of black people." Moreover, his claim that suffering could change the oppressor's heart by appealing to his conscience raised unrealistic hopes that inevitably gave way to bitterness and disillusionment. In short, SCLC did little to prepare blacks for a long and difficult struggle against tenacious white resistance.[44]

Ultimately, however, SCLC's decline can be attributed to its very success. The organizers of SNCC, CORE, and SCLC had furnished the leadership in the South that a small and fearful black middle class could not provide. With the opening of new opportunities, the expansion of the black electorate, and the gradual decline of white violence and intimidation, indigenous leadership grew stronger and more independent. The local church and voters organizations which had formed the social base of the civil rights movement progressed, with an increasingly sure step, along the path of political action. But if the 1965 Voting Rights Act moved the civil rights movement "from protest to politics" (SCLC itself sent Andrew Young and Walter Fauntroy to Congress) it also removed its basic raison d'etre. As James Bevel put it, "there is no more civil rights movement. President Johnson signed it out of existence."[45]

It would be misleading to blame SCLC for the still-birth of what C. Vann Woodward termed "The Third Reconstruction"—the tackling of northern, or national, problems of tacit discrimination, de facto segregation, and economic inequality. Although admittedly slow to understand the deep historical roots of racism in the North, the movement in which SCLC played such a vital part was, as Watters and Cleghorn pointed out, a southern movement with Southern goals. "whose counterpart did not develop contemporaneously in the North." When King and his team went to Chicago in 1966, they had little chance of filling the northern leadership vacuum, or of mitigating in any real way the cumulative damage of generations of discrimination and neglect. SCLC's greatest achievements were in the South: these alone made it one of the most successful—and unusual—reform groups in recent American history.[46]

ENDNOTES

1. George Goodman. "He Lives, Man!," *Look*, April 15, 1969, p. 30; Pat Watters, *Down To Now: Reflections on the Southern Civil Rights Movement* (New York, 1971), p 175; Charles Fager, *Uncertain Resurrection: The Poor People's Washington Campaign*, (Grand Rapids, 1969), pp. 14, 20.

2. August Meier, "New Currents in the Civil Rights Movement," *New Politics*, Summer 1963, p. 14.

3. Bayard Rustin, *Strategies for Freedom: The Changing Patterns of Black Protest*, (New York, 1976), pp. 38–39; Gunnar Myrdal, *An American Dilemma*, (New York, 1944), pp. 873–874; Martin Luther King, Jr., *Where Do We Go From Here: Chaos or Community?* (Boston, 1968), p. 124.

4. Myrdal, pp. 875–78; King, *Stride Toward Freedom: The Montgomery Story*, (London, 1959), pp. 215–16.

5. David L. Lewis, *King: A Critical Biography* (Baltimore, 1970), pp. 88–89; SCLC, *This Is SCLC* (Atlanta, 1963). The Number of affiliates rose from 65 in 1962 to 270 in 1967.

6. Watters, pp 24, 203; Rustin, p. 40.

7. Lewis, pp. 48–56; Lawrence D. Reddick, *Crusader Without Violence* (New York, 1959), pp 117–27, 216.

8. Ella Baker, "Report of the Executive Director," "Memo to Administrative Committee," October 1959, King Papers, Boston University, File VI, folder 153.

9. Watters, p. 102; *SCLC Newsletter*, July, August 1963, 8 March 1964; Coretta King, *My Life With Martin Luther King, Jr.*, (New York, 1969), pp 207–8. The full-time staff reached a peak of about 150 in 1966.

10. Howell Raines, *My Soul Is Rested: Movement Days In The Deep South Remembered*, (New York, 1977), p. 435; Robert Terrell, "Discarding The Dream," *Evergreen Review*, May 1970, pp. 75–76; Charles E. Fager, Selma, 1965 (New York, 1974),p. 170; *Sunday Times* (London), 6 Feb. 1977; Lewis, pp.137–38.

11. *Norfolk Journal And Guide*, 21 Aug. 1965.

12. John A. Williams, *The King God Didn't Save: Reflections on the Life and Death of Martin Luther King, Jr.* (London, 1971),p.168; Raines, pp.426–27, 478–52; Barbara A. Reynolds. *Jesse Jackson: The Man, The Movement, The Myth*, (Chicago, 1975), p.188.

13. Paul Good, *The Trouble I've Seen: White Journalist / Black Movement*, (Washington, 1975), p. 226; Fager, *Uncertain Resurrection*, pp. 25–26; Robert Penn Warren, *Who Speaks for the Negro?*, (New York, 1966), p. 231.

14. Good, pp.18–20, 100–101; William Brink and Louis Harris, *The Negro Revolution in America*, (New York, 1964), pp.106–24.

15. E. Franklin Frazier, "The Negro Church And Assimilation," in Hart M. Nelson, ed., *The Black Church In America*, (London, 1971), p.137; Warren, p. 23; Flip Schulka, ed., *Martin Luther King, Jr.: A Documentary*, (New York, 1976), p. 66.

16. Watters, p. 245; Stokely Carmichael, *Stokely Speaks*, (New York, 1971), p. 190.

17. Watters, pp. 98, 198; King, "Our Struggle," *Liberation*, April, 1956, p. 53; Cleveland Sellers and Robert Terrell, *River of No Return* (New York, 1973), p. 165.

18. Lewis, pp. 157–58; Brink and Harris, p. 108; Birmingham World, 20 April 1963.

19. James Forman, *The Making of Black Revolutionaries*, (New York, 1972), p. 442; Sellers And Terrell, p. 117.

20. Forman, p. 312; Watters, p. 130; Good, p.87.

21. King, "Behind the Selma March," *Saturday Review*, 3 April 1965, pp. 16–17; Rustin, p. 43

22. Earl Black, *Southern Governors and Civil Rights*, (London, 1976), p. 322; Warren, p. 218; King, *Stride*, p. 205; David Halberstam, "The Second Coming of Martin Luther King," *Harper's*, August 1967, pp. 42–43; Samuel Lubell, *Black and White: Test of a Nation*, (New York, 1964), p. 103.

23. King, *Where?*, p. 18; James H. Lane, "Power, Conflict, and Social Change," in Don R. Bowen and Louis H. Masitti, eds., *Riots and Rebellions* (Beverly Hills, 1968), p. 190: Watters, pp. 124–25.

24. August Meier, "In the Role of Martin Luther King," in Melvin Drimmer, ed., *Black History: A Reappraisal*, (New York, 1968), p. 449.

25. Raines, p. 214; Forman, p.419; *Newsweek*, 15 May 1967, p. 23.

26. John Cogley, "The Clergy Heeds A New Call," *New York Times Magazine*, 2 May 1965; Falger, Selma, pp. 113–14; Richard Hofstadter, *The Age Of Reform*, (New York, 1955), p. 152.

27. Lewis, p. 394: Lerone Bennett, Jr., *The Negro Mood*, (Chicago, 1964), p. 30; Meier, p. 446.

28. *Newsweek*, 13 Feb, 1967, p. 18; Coretta King, p. 287.

29. SCLC, *Project Report*, (Atlanta, 1 March, 1967), p. 2; Lewis, p. 352; *Newsweek*, 5 Sept. 1966, p. 19

30. Ben Van Clarke, "The Summit Follow Up," undated, King Library; Mike Royko, *Boss: Mayor Richard J. Daley Of Chicago*, (London, 1972), p. 149; WIlliam Brink and Louis Harris, *Black and White: A Study of U.S. Racial Attitudes Today*, (New York, 1967), pp. 41, 105–13; Lyndon B. Johnson, *The Vantage Point: Perspectives of the Presidency, 1963–1969*, (New York, 1971), p. 178.

31. Rustin, pp.41–42; Brink and Harris, pp.260–65; King, "The Crisis in America's Cities." text of speech, 16 Aug. 1967, p. 10, King Library; Coretta King, p. 298.

32. *New York Times*, 9 July 1966, For King's critique of Black Power, see *Where?* pp.44–46.

33. *New York Times*, 7 Sept. 1967; Rustin, *Down The Line*, (Chicago, 1971), pp. 109, 167; *Current*, (May 1967, pp. 39–40.

34. Josè Yglesias, "Dr. King's March on Washington, Part II," in August Meier and Elliott Tudwick, eds., *Black Protest in the Sixties*, (Chicago, 1970), p. 274; *New York Times*, 22 Jan. 1968.

35. *New York Times*, 18 Dec. 1967; Rustin, *Down The Line*, p. 203; Transcript of executive staff committee meeting, 21 Dec. 1967, pp.7–8, King Library; *Wall Street Journal*, 29 May, 1968.

36. Yglesias, p. 274; Lewis, pp.384–85; Goodman,p. 29.

37. SCLC, North and South: Staff News (Dec, 1967). pp. 1–10.

38. Lerone Bennett, Jr., *What Manner of Man*, (Chicago, 1964), p. 64.

39. *New York Times*, 25 Dec. 1969; Goodman, p. 30.

40. *New York Times*, 1 Aug. 1965: 7 Feb.; 29 May 1967.

41. Reynolds, *Jesse Jackson*, passim.

42. *Christian Century*, Sept. 1970; *Washington Post*, 10 July 1973: SCLC, *Soul Force*, 14 Aug. 1973. pp. 12–13.

43. *Time*, 6 April 1970, pp.18–21.

44. Elliot M. Zashin. *Civil Disobedience and Democracy*, (London, 1972), pp. 209–10; Samuel DuBois Cook, "Is Martin Luther King, Jr., Irrelevant?" *New South*, (Spring 1971), p. 4.

45. August Meier and Elliott Rudwick, *CORE: A Study in the Civil Rights Movement, 1941–1968*, (New York, 1973), p. 329.

46. C. Vann Woodward, *The Burden if Souther History*, (New York, 1969), p. 128; Pat Watters and Reese Cleghorn, *Climbing Jacob's Ladder: The Arrival of Negroes in Southern Politics*, (New York, 1967), p. 312.

Adam Fairclough took his degree in history at Balliold College, Oxford, and his Ph.D. from the University of Keele. Currently he is a lecturer in Modern History at the University of Liverpool.

UNIT 10-5

RETROSPECT AND PROSPECT

The determination of Negroes to win full American citizenship had by the fall of 1963 confronted the nation with its most serious domestic crisis since the depression of the 1930s. Direct action had been the largest factor in pushing the situation to the crisis point.

So, in the process of individual confrontation of the crisis, there arises a more urgent need than ever for a weighing and understanding of direct action itself—an act of judgment.

There are various approaches to evaluation.

It is possible to see direct action in pragmatic, win or lose terms of specific goals in specific situations. The sit-ins for example caused desegregation of lunch counters across a wide sweep of the land, but failed effectively to penetrate the deep South. The Freedom Rides led to desegregated interstate travel and terminal facilities, more or less, across all the South, but created ill feeling. Mass demonstrations desegregated many private and some public facilities in many towns and cities. But again the deep South, with Albany as a symbol, Birmingham as an intransigent example, has not really been cracked. In competitive sports score terms, these specific efforts have resulted in some wins, some losses, some draws, and several more innings left to play.

Out of the experience of these specific situations, Negro leaders seem increasingly aware of the need to select the appropriate form of action (direct or otherwise) to fit the circumstances. The days when a crisis situation seemed in part a staging ground for a particular form of demonstration, or for proving demonstrations better than court action, for example, seem about over.

It is possible, also, to see direct action as a tactical operation in a large-scale war. The sit-ins unleashed full scale a new weapon, and from its first surprise onslaught, the enemy retreated in panic. But during the Freedom Rides, a counter weapon of mass arrests was thrown up. Both weapons have been improved and refined. Direct action developed the mass marches, the conscience—hurting voices of children piping freedom songs as they demonstrate, the boycott and other techniques for pressuring economic and political power sources, and the growing awareness of the power of the ballot and enlarged effort to gain it. Community power sources resisting direct action developed the mass arrests, police use of dogs, fire hoses, electric prod poles and other methods of making arrest unpleasant, new laws and old ones newly applied, the imposing of severe charges and large bonds, and economic reprisals. From the white south also came enough

---

New South, October–November 1963.

old-fashioned lawless methods of intimidation (shotgun blasts into homes, dynamitings) to be formidable.

Here, the battles go first one way, then the other. Increasing success of direct action in involving the federal government on its side is, in these tactical terms, a victory, perhaps, but only perhaps, the crucial one.

Consciously or not, direct action has tended to create situations where the law and power of the federal government has had to confront conflicting law and practice and lesser power of state governments. This occurred in the Freedom Rides. Birmingham undoubtedly led the administration to sponsor the strong civil rights bill of 1963. There are indications that direct action leaders are aware of the strategic importance of such confrontations for the future.

It remains to be seen whether the Justice Department will continue to serve as the chief federal government contact with civil rights situations in the South, often with the result that it has seemed to be mediating crises rather than enforcing federal law. And appointment of staunch segregationist judges to the federal bench in several instances remains an anomalous result of the split within the Democratic Party on civil rights.

Of all the achievements involving government, getting the civil rights question before Congress is greatest. Commentators (including Mayor Ivan Allen, Jr., of Atlanta, the only deep-South politician to testify in early hearings for the public accommodations bill) have pointed out how Congress has shirked its duty in this area—while all other parts of government, the federal judiciary and executive, and the municipal and even some southern state governments, in recent years have been desperately trying to cope with it.

Almost as important as the governmental developments has been involvement of national and local private business, the white church, and individual leaders at all levels of society—much of this activity prompted by White House conferences with various groups, conducted by the late President. Thinking and working on all levels of society in the best tradition of the nation continues to grow. The important question is whether all these forces, including governmental, will respond to the real demand of direct action (for "all, now"), or whether they will merely attempt half-way, palliative responses.

It is possible, finally, to see direct action through public opinion. Polls, past and present, show as much as anything else the discrepancy between almost full support of direct action by Negroes, and great splits among white Americans, with much ambivalence in individuals. They also show that while basic attitudes expressed toward Negroes might remain the same, or even have in some quarters deteriorated, ideas of what is acceptable or possible for Negroes are much advanced now from what they were before the sit-ins.

Such polls and statistics about what people think are of course only guides and indications. Similar are such indicators as the statements of Southerners who, while denouncing federal legislation on private business, accept desegregation of public institutions. Ten years ago, they denounced the desegregation of public institutions.

The scope and tone of demonstrations during the summer of 1963 had an adverse effect on national opinion of direct action, considered in the simple-minded terms of a popularity contest.

"This is a kind of temporary setback necessary to make the journey ahead," said Dr. King, acknowledging the summer's impact. "If it had not come now, it would have come at some other time. Our only reaction is to move steadily forward."

His comment that "we can never have meaningful integration until these prejudices [latent ones dredged up in the North by the summer's demonstrations] are realized and discarded," summed up the truth of the situation.

It implies the evolved meaning of "all, now"—that the Negro no longer seeks an accommodation with prejudice, but an end to it. This meaning precludes wily stratagems implicitly accepting prejudice, and battles those unconscious individual denials of self-worth which are among the most destructive results of prejudice.

What the Negro thinks becomes increasingly important. Polls show a conservative majority. But they also show, as do many other reports, an increase in anger and bitterness, and some hatred of whites. Increasingly, direct action leaders tell white America that the alternative to their approach is the reverse-racism of the Black Muslims. They describe a new function of direct action: to let off the steam of pent-up emotion that would otherwise go into hatred and violence. This may be true; it may also be a propagandistic threat.

Neither white nor black prejudice has a majority nationally. in the South, the effects of prejudice, while perhaps as deep as or deeper than ever in some individuals and in some states like Alabama and Mississippi, would seem to be, in sum, less frequently acted on. (How does one decide this? Society, despite the severest of pressure, the greatest of impatience, changes slowly. The guide is as much as anything the intuitive feelings about prevailing conditions by sensitive individuals comparing things now with things ten years ago.)

Hatred and bitterness and their fruits of violence and disorder have ever been a problem for the concern of rational, responsible institutions and individuals.

Never has a nation been so tragically aware of this than during the murderous weekend of the assassination of President Kennedy. And never, surely, has a nation been as determined against lawlessness and violence as in the aftermath shock of the tragedy.

There is still more to see about direct action. It cannot, for example, be viewed in a vacuum. Much of its meaning and many of its targets are parts of larger problems, other movements in current American history.

This is obvious in the case of votes. The light for the fundamental right of enfranchisement for the Negro goes on simultaneously with a growingly successful fight for the same fundamental right for urban white voters who long and with increasing weights against them have been disproportionately represented in state legislatures. Or, as with the county unit system of Georgia which was declared unconstitutional, they have been disenfranchised in electing state officials. Belief in democracy alone makes necessary the belief that out of these battles for more representative government will come more responsible, more responsive government. In the South, this alone would help solve many of the troubles which direct action assails.

It is also increasingly clear that the end of segregation and discrimination will not mean the end of Negro problems. With inferior education and inferior jobs out of the legacy of segregation's inferior environment, Negroes will need to master the knowledge and skills, and meet the competition of an organized, increasingly automatized society. But it is also clear that such needs are not confined to Negroes. They are an aggravated part of the nation's troubles with periodic economic depression, prolonged unemployment, poor schools, bad housing. The crime, the hopelessness of slums now visited upon the second and third generations dwelling there (trapped, no longer a part of a transient wive of immigration) are a rot eating away at the affluent society. Out of such deprivation comes a frightening figure whose anger transcends the racial struggle. He may be on one or the other or neither side of it. The real object of his wrath is society.

In such matters is unemployment and the deprivations of poverty, the goals of the Negro movement are obviously needed also for a large segment of the population that is not Negro. By the end of 1963, observers were pointing out the logic of broadening the base of the movement to include all those whose needs are urgent. One practical result of this would be to minimize white resentment based on economic fear—an old, potently manipulated factor in southern race relations spread now to other parts of the country.

Thus it may well be that in finding a solution for the American dilemma, the nation will find a new opportunity for greatness for all of its people. In the process of freeing themselves, Negro Americans may bring about "a new birth of freedom" for all Americans.

This gets close to the concept of direct action that seems most important, most pertinent in the crisis-pressured processes by which a whole nation reaches out for consensus against prejudice.

Witnesses have spoken of the inspiration and emotional catharsis of direct action. Some of this came through to many previously untouched by it during the Washington March. Proponents of direct action, often most eloquent when defending it, cite its spiritual overtones, its effect upon the individual being of participants and witnesses, as its real reason for existence. In this are combined, they say, powerful methods of moral renewal and persuasion from the mysticism of the East, from the Old and New Testaments, from the basic faiths of democracy, and the philosophy of civil disobedience. Lillian Smith, the noted novelist and commentator on psychic ailments and strengths of the South, speaks of direct action as an act of love by which Negroes, less culturally inhibited in the ability to love, are seeking to save not just themselves, but the nation itself—from nothing less than a fatal soul sickness.

This, on another level, involves the beginning premise of the direct action movement. It is simply a belief that the founding principles of America, as set forth in its great documents, embodied in its government and its social, religious, and economic, institutions, are right. It protests the exclusion of Negroes from benefits of these principles. It demands American citizenship. And by implication, it demands of every American an action—either with it for the best that the nation believes in, or against it in calamitous repudiation of what the nation believes in.

It speaks to the deepest and highest moral and political commitments and achievements of mankind. It is drastic; it may seem to some unnecessarily so. But its existence—it spontaneous rise, development, and refusal to die, although so much tries its existence—is evidence of necessity. This is a kind of necessity in the souls of individual human beings which makes it great, or which, opposed, destroys nations. Against it, so far in human history, nothing has been able permanently to prevail.

The grandeur of this human effort overcomes the doubt and despair, fear and pessimism which the awful implications of our time in history arouse in the heart. And perhaps beyond all the worlds, all the analyses, beyond even the conscious awareness of individual participants, it is this grandeur permeating the drive of direct action that is the key to a real understanding of what it means, and why it must in America succeed to the full.

UNIT 10-6

CIVIL DISOBEDIENCE AND THE LAW

From its beginning, the direct action movement has involved an issue as old as tragedy, as undying as human conflict—the right of an individual to disobey the law. In refusing to obey laws they considered unjust, in knowingly and openly violating trespass and other similarly intentioned laws, Negro Southerners have followed an ancient tradition—but one which has had a hard time winning success in modern American public opinion.

It is a tradition found in the Old Testament story of Shadrach, Meshach, and Abednego who refused to bow down before the golden idol of King Nebuchadnezzar. It is found in the martyrdom of the early Christians who died for their faith. It was carried on by the abolitionists in this country, who deliberately violated the Fugitive Slave Act of 1950. It runs through Gandhi's long passive resistance campaign against the British raj in India. Moreover, the Negro demonstrators are not the only Americans who engage in civil disobedience in our time. Those people who refuse to answer questions of census takers, those religious sects which in some states will not obey compulsory school attendance laws, those pacifists who boldly set sail for a prohibited atomic testing area, all engage in a form of civil disobedience.

But the Negro demonstrators—those who sat-in, paraded, and demonstrated throughout the South in recent years (and throughout the nation in recent months)—have attracted the greatest amount of attention, anger, and anxiety. On the one hand, Negro civil rights leaders call for Southerners to obey the Supreme Court's 1954 decision outlawing segregation in the public schools. On the other, they consciously urge their followers to break state laws and ordinances. How can they advocate breaking some laws and obeying others?

In his *Letter from Birmingham City Jail* Martin Luther King discusses this question. He contends that "one has not only a legal but a moral responsibility to disobey unjust laws." The difference between the two, according to Dr. King, is:

> . . . A just law is a man-made code that squares with the moral law or the law of God. An unjust law is a code that is out of harmony with the moral law. To put it in the terms of Saint Thomas Aquinas, an unjust law is a human law that is not

---

New South, October–November 1963.

> rooted in eternal and natural law. Any law that uplifts human personality is just. Any law that degrades human personality is unjust. All segregation statutes are unjust because segregation distorts the soul and damages the personality.

For almost four years now, Negro demonstrators have openly and deliberately violated laws they believe to be unjust; and they have openly and deliberately accepted the consequences of breaking such laws by peacefully submitting to arrest and imprisonment. By acting so openly, with no attempt at concealment, by fully accepting the consequences of their action, they have made their case for civil disobedience an ethical one. But they have also raised anew the basic issue of civil disobedience: the effect which it has on man's always tenuous commitment to the rule of law.

Some have argued against civil disobedience not only on the ground that it is a threat to law and order, but also on the ground that it is illegitimate in a political order like that of the United States, where political and judicial means exist to work for the change of laws. Such means do exist on a federal level but it is hard to find them in such states as Alabama and Mississippi. And it should be emphasized that Negro Southerners have remained loyal to the national system while aiming their direct action campaigns against the laws of southern states. These provoked a vigorous and vicious legal counterattack.

Throughout the South, local and state officials dissatisfied with the powers of the usual public safety statutes ransacked their legal codes and came up with dusty, long-forgotten laws to apply against civil rights demonstrators.

In America (Ga.), for instance, four young men arrested during demonstrations there in August 1963 were charged with "inciting an insurrection," a crime under an 1871 Georgia statute punishable by death, and held without bail for weeks. They were finally released on bond November I when a federal court declared the 1871 statute and the state's unlawful assembly law unconstitutional. The court ordered no further state prosecution of the youths on other charges "unless reasonable bond" was arranged.

It was the first time a federal court has used the 1957 Civil Rights Act as a basis for taking jurisdiction of a state court case because of alleged violation of constitutional rights.

In Danville (Va.), in another case of legal resurrection, 14 civil rights leaders were ordered tried under a Virginia law originally designed to prevent slave uprisings. They were charged with conspiring to incite Negroes to "acts of violence and war" against whites.

Besides applying the rusty legal weapons of a bygone day against Negro demonstrators, southern state legislators and municipal authorities rushed through new statutes and ordinances designed to bring the direct action movement to a halt. Following the outbreak of the 1960 sit-ins, every state legislature which met that year passed laws to regulate—and restrict—sit-in activities. The most elaborate and comprehensive new laws were those of Louisiana, Mississippi, and Virginia, but neither of these states appeared to have accomplished anything more than Georgia, which passed a statute as simple as it was brief. The Georgia statute (Act 497, February 18, 1960) said that a criminal trespass was committed by a person when he failed to leave the premises of another when requested; in practice, this required that the request be made in the presence of a police officer. Under Georgia law, as a misdemeanor, trespass is punishable by a maximum fine of $1,000, or six months in jail, or twelve months in a public work camp, or all three.

The first person actually to be tried and convicted under the Georgia law was Tom Taylor Tolg, a young white sit-in demonstrator who was arrested in the state capital on June 17, 1963. He was convicted in a state court on August 31 and given the maximum sentence (all three of the above). The Tolg case is but one of the latest in a long line of cases resulting from sit-in activity and involving such issues as the constitutionality of a state using police power to help a private storekeeper maintain segregation.

The first such case was decided in a state court in Raleigh (N.C.), on April 22, 1960, when trespass charges were dismissed against 43 Negro students arrested for demonstrating on the sidewalk of a privately-owned shopping center. The dismissal was based on a 1946 U.S. Supreme Court ruling in a similar case (*Marsh v. Alabama*), where the Court held that property ownership "does not always mean absolute dominion. The more an owner, for his advantage, opens up property for use by the public in general, the more do his rights become "circumscribed by the constitutional and statutory rights of those who use it."

Some southern judges have become adept at issuing sweeping injunctions which effectively bring a direct action movement grinding to a halt. In Danville—during the summer of 1963, for example, a Virginia court enjoined civil rights leaders from "participating in, financing, sponsoring, encouraging, or engaging in meetings or other activities," that could result in a violation of state or local law, or "engaging in any such act in a violent and tumultuous manner, or holding unlawful assemblies such as to unreasonably disturb or alarm the public within the city of Danville." In short, this ruling ran the gamut of restriction.

Another tactic employed against civil rights groups has been that of setting excessively high bail for arrested demonstrators, thereby depleting the treasuries of the organizations. In Savannah, for instance, a bond of $30,000 was set for Negro leader Hosea Williams following his arrest there in early July 1963.

Confronted by hostile local law enforcement officers and local judges, Negro demonstrators have turned to the federal courts for a redress of grievances. But the procedures of litigation and judicial review are costly and time-consuming.

A little more than a year after the sit-ins began, the U.S. Supreme Court handed down a decision which, though not directly related to the ever-increasing number of sit-in cases, did involve the refusal of a restaurant to serve Negroes. In this case (*Burton v. Wilmington Parking Authority*), the Court held that a privately owned restaurant on space leased from a state agency could not offer discriminatory services. The case concerned a coffee shop in a garage owned by the Wilmington (Del.) Parking Authority, a state agency. Six justices concurred in the ruling.

On December 11, 1961, in its first decision on cases directly involving the sit-in movement, the Court unanimously reversed the breach-of-the-peace convictions of 16 Negro students who had staged sit-ins in Baton Rouge. The students were arrested in March 1960 for seeking service at three white lunch counters, in a drug store, a department store, and a bus terminal.

Chief Justice Earl Warren wrote the opinion in this case (*Garner et al v. State of Louisiana*), pointing out that a Louisiana law defined disturbing the peace as acting "in such a manner as to unreasonably disturb or alarm the public." He ruled that there was "no evidence . . . that petitioners disturbed the peace, either by outwardly boisterous conduct or by passive conduct likely to cause a public disturbance."

The Court's most important decision to date on sit-in cases was rendered 17 months after the Louisiana ruling. On May 20, 1963, the Court swept aside the convictions of 31 sit-in demonstrators in four states (Alabama, Louisiana, North and South Carolina).

The Court overturned trespass and criminal mischief convictions in four lunch-counter cases (*Peterson v. Greenville*; *Gober v. Birmingham*; *Shuttlesworth v. Birmingham*; and *Avent v. North Carolina*) on the ground that local governments—not storekeepers—actually required the discrimination. The Court found that the owners were compelled to invoke the trespass laws in order not to be in violation of city ordinances and official policies which required segregation.

In a fifth case, from New Orleans (*Lombard v. Louisiana*), there was no segregation ordinance. But the Court said that statements by New Orleans' mayor and police superintendent had created, or maintained, a climate of customary segregation which amounted to the same thing.

The May 20 series of decisions indicated that many of the numerous other convictions of demonstrators were unconstitutional. Furthermore on June 17, the Court also overturned the 1961 trespass convictions of eight Negroes and whites convicted of violating the Virginia trespass laws in Alexandria, telling the Virginia Supreme Court to reconsider the case in the light of its May 20 ruling.

In essence, the May 20 decisions on the treatment of sit-in demonstrators at lunch-counters established the right of citizens to request service and said that local agencies of law enforcement may not interfere with them to enforce the policies or ordinances of the local government.

But these decisions sidestepped two key constitutional questions raised by the anti-segregation protests. These are: 1) whether a restaurant or store owner can, entirely at his own discretion, choose to discriminate; and 2) whether, if he so chooses, the state may help him.

These questions confronted the Court this fall when it heard arguments of five other sit-in cases soon after convening for the 1963–64 term. The five cases argued came from Maryland, Florida, and South Carolina. Each involved a situation in which demonstrators were arrested for trespass after they refused the owner's request that they leave. The demonstrators were convicted of trespass after refusing to leave segregated lunch counters or, in two Maryland cases, an amusement park at Glen Echo and a restaurant in Baltimore.

Attorneys for the demonstrators urged the Court to rule that no state may enforce racial discrimination by a private restaurant or other shop. Lawyers for the states asked the Court to make clear that there is a right to use business property as the owner wishes and a right to state enforcement of the owner's decision.

The issue before the Court—does the Constitution permit a state to prosecute individuals for demanding service without racial discrimination at privately owned businesses—is, of course, also being debated in Congress, where the administration's bill forbidding racial discrimination in places of public accommodation is being considered. Congressional passage of the public accommodations bill would lighten the burden of the Court. On the other hand, Congress would be relieved of much of the problem if the Court were to hold that the Constitution forbids state enforcement of segregation in public accommodations.

In the past, the Court has held that the 14th Amendment's ban on racial discrimination is applicable only to action by the states and their officials, and not to purely private discrimination. A brief filed by the NAACP Legal Defense and Education Fund in the sit-in cases heard this fall contended, however, that "a property right no longer includes a privilege in the individual owner to add substantially to the detriment of his fellow citizens." What the Court will decide remains to be seen.

UNIT 10-7

REPORTS FROM SELMA'S "BLOODY SUNDAY"

GOOD SAMARITAN HOSPITAL (SELMA) EMERGENCY ROOM LOG, MARCH 7, 1965

Sixteen-year-old Emerson Acoff was the first of 55 patients treated at the Emergency Room of Selma's Good Samaritan Hospital on the afternoon of March 7, 1965—"Bloody Sunday." Acoff suffered lacerations to his left arm and head. The second patient was Willie Williams who received an injury to his left knee when he was kicked by a trooper's horse. Argula Sanders was the fourth patient treated; she suffered "possible skull injuries." The seventh patient treated that day was SNCC Chairman John Lewis whose skull was fractured.

Date 3/7/65 Dr. Stewart
Name: Emerson Acoff Age 16
Address: 1121 Morgan Alley, Selma ER 300
Time: 4 P.M.
Complaint: Injury to head and left arm

How Happened: March

Diagnosis: Approx. 4" lac[eration] left forearm
Treatment: sutured and dressed

Medication: local anes[thesia]
Penicillin 600000, tetanus
Disposal: Admitted Room 311-D

Date: 3/7/65 Dr. Morse
Name: Mr. Willie D. Williams Age 18
Address: Rt 1 Box 92, Boykin, Ala ER 300
Time:
Complaint: Injury to left knee

How Happened: In March, running from tear gas, knocked down in crowd, trooper spurred horse, horse kicked pt [patient]

Diagnosis: Possible fracture rt. lg.
Treatment: Examined by Dr. Morse, to X ray

Medication: none
Disposal: Admitted to Rm 313-A Morse

Date: 3/7/65 Dr. Dinkins
Name: Mrs. Argula Sanders Age: 17
Address: 830 Griffin Ave, Selma
Time: 4:35 PM ER 300
Complaint: Injury to back of head—laceration

How Happened: March

Diagnosis: Poss. skull injuries, poss. fract[ured] skull
Treatment: Sutured by Dr. Steward

Medication: Penicillin 600000, tetanus
Disposal: admitted to Rm. 318-B

Date: 3/7/65 Dr. Dumont
Name: Mr. John Lewis Age: 25
Address: 8 1/2 Raymond St., Atlanta, Georgia
Time: 4 PM
Complaint: Injury to head, BP 178/120

How Happened: March

Diagnosis: Fractured Skull
Treatment: To x-ray & examination by Dr. Dumont

Medication: none
Disposal: Adm. Rm. 312-B

ate 3/7/65 7 Dr Dumont

ame Mr John Lewis age 25

ddress 8½ Raymond St., Atlanta, Georgia

ime 4 PM

mplaint Injury to head BP 178/120

w happened march 3.00

agnosis Fractured skull

atment To Xray p̄ examination by Dr Dumont

dication none

sposal Adm. Rm. 312 B Nurse

UNIT 10-8

DALLAS COUNTY CHRISTIAN MINISTERS UNION

Minutes—March 8, 1965
Perrins Cafeteria

The meeting was called to order by the President, Paul Grist.
Devotional and prayer was given by Paul Grist.

There was no reading of the mintues of the last meeting or a financial report due to the absence of the Secretary-treasurer.

There was a discussion of the Easter Sunrise Service. A Committee was named as follows:

Ray Howell
Ed Sivis
Jim Broomall
Don Bilbary
Bob Reeder

The Baccalaureate Services were discussed. T. Frank Matthews was named Chairman of this Committee. He is to choose those to serve with him.

A report was given on the radio work on WRWJ by Dewey Taylor, Radio Program Chairman.

Dr. George Kerlin gave a report on the Religious Emphasis Week at Parrish High School. Motion was made by Dr. Kerlin and seconded by E. E. Sivis, to write a letter commending the youth of Parrish High School. This motion was approved.

The current racial situation was discussed.

Following a motion to dismiss, the closing prayer was given by Bob Atkins, new Pastor of Elkdale Baptist Church.

Respectfully submitted,
Dewy Taylor
Acting Secretary

UNIT 10-9

THE BLACK MAN AND SELF-DEFENSE: 1962

THE CASE FOR ANSWERING VIOLENCE WITH VIOLENCE

Robert F. Williams

ABOUT THE DOCUMENT

When Robert F. Williams got out of the Marine Corps in 1955, he returned to his hometown of Monroe, North Carolina and joined the local chapter of the NAACP. Growing threats of violence from the White Citizens Council and the Ku Klux Klan, which had its southeastern regional headquarters in Monroe, had whittled the membership of the local NAACP chapter down to six, and the well-off middle-class black leadership was proposing to dissolve the chapter altogether. When Williams objected, he was elected president and the rest of the members, except a Dr. Albert E. Perry, a newcomer, all resigned. Perry became vice-president, and by 1957 he and William had rebuilt the local chapter with a membership of working-class people—laborers, farmers, domestics—and a large contingent of returned veterans who, according to Williams, "didn't scare easy.'"

In 1956 Williams began a drive to integrate Monroe's swimming pool, which had been built with federal funds, and which was closed to blacks. The city officials refused to let black children use the pool; nor would they build a pool in the black community. Williams took legal action. While he was preparing the groundwork for court proceedings, the Klu Klux Klan began a campaign against the NAACP chapter. After holding mass rallies, KKK members would drive through the black neighborhood in motorcades, honking their horns and firing pistols out of the car windows.

A group of pacifist ministers asked the city officials to stop the Klan from driving through the black community, but the request was rejected on the grounds that the Klan was a legal group having "as much constitutional right to organize as the NAACP."

Appeals to the Governor of North Carolina and President Eisenhower followed, but no aid was forthcoming. It was at this time that the Monroe chapter of the NAACP started to arm itself. It applied for, and received, a charter from the National Rifle Association. Within a year it had sixty members.

In the summer of 1957 an armed motorcade of Klan members opened fire on Dr. Perry's house on the outskirts of the black community. Williams and his followers shot it out with the Klan and turned them back.

Two incidents in the following year brought Williams and the city of Monroe into national prominence. In October, 1958, a seven-year-old white girl kissed a nine-year-old black boy on the cheek. The girl innocently told her mother she had kissed the boy because he was a friend she hadn't seen for a long time and she was so glad to see him again that she kissed him. The mother called the police. The boy, and a friend who was with him at the time, were arrested for rape. Williams reported that he called the national office of the NAACP for help, but they refused to have anything to do with it because they did not like to get involved in a "sex case." The boy and his friend were sentenced to fourteen years in the reformatory. The story first appeared in a London paper, then spread over Europe, where it became a cause for riots and demonstrations. Finally, American papers began to write about the "Kissing Case." The boys were released on February 13, 1959, through the intervention of President Eisenhower.

The national office of the NAACP was thoroughly embarrassed. Roy Wilkins offered Williams a job in Detroit if he would leave Monroe, but Williams refused.

A second court case occurred in 1959. It involved the acquittal of a white man who had raped and beaten a black woman, eight months pregnant. The case incited Williams to reaffirm the right of self-defense. Williams told reporters that black men in Monroe would meet violence with violence if the courts failed to protect them.

Because of his statements to the press concerning the injustice of the Southern courts and the right of black men to defend their homes and families, Williams was suspended by the NAACP. All over the country news broadcasts reported that Williams had received a six-month suspension for advocating violence. Some white pacifist members of Williams chapter sent a telegram to the national office of the NAACP stating that they were white Southerners, but they protested Williams' suspension because "they understood the problems of the community and . . . the national office did not."

The NAACP never made the telegram public. Despite national publicity, not a single newspaper reported that the Union County (Monroe) NAACP was an interracial branch nor that its white Southerner members supported Williams' position.

Williams appealed to the NAACP convention but his suspension was upheld, even though the issue created enough debate sentiment to force the national leadership to insert an endorsement of the concept of self-defense in the NAACP's constitution.

At the end of the six months, instead of going back in office automatically, Williams held an election and was voted back as president. "I didn't want the NAACP national office to think they were doing me any special favor," he said.

In 1960, Williams began to hold sit-ins and to demonstrate for school integration, but he was unable to get any assistance from the national office of the NAACP. In June, 1961, after four years of protest, the Monroe chapter of the NAACP decided to picket the city swimming pool. The picket line closed the pool, and when the pool closed, violence broke out.

Whites fired pistols and rifles over the heads of the picketers, but the local chief of police turned his head and did nothing to stop it. Williams sent a telegram to the U.S. Justice Department, which referred him to the local FBI, which in turn told him it was not a matter for the Justice Department. The FBI men in Monroe told Williams it was a police matter, and they said they had checked with the chief of police, who assured them he would provide ample protection for the pickets.

Two attempts on Williams' life followed, yet the picket line continued. Finally, in a dramatic last-minute rescue from a near-riot confrontation with white citizens, the state police came on the scene. State troopers successfully enforced law and order in Monroe.

The city closed the pool for the rest of the year, and Williams withdrew the picket line. It was at this time that the civil rights Freedom Riders came to Monroe. In their first few hours there, so many Freedom Riders and blacks were arrested that prisoners with legitimate charges against them were set free to make room in the city jail. The shootings and beatings continued, and Monroe's citizens began to arm themselves to defend their lives and their homes.

In his book *Negroes with Guns* Williams describes the ensuing events. He reports that shortly after receiving a call from a police official saying, "In thirty minutes you'll be hanging in the courthouse square," he saw police cars forming a cordon around his block. Gathering together his wife and children, he fled to Canada. Eventually he went to Cuba, where he wrote *Negroes with Guns*. He has since gone on to permanent exile in China, where today he is an active Maoist. The following excerpt from his book is one of the first explicit advocations recorded in the 20th century of the value of violence for the black man in America.

THE DOCUMENT

Chapter titled "Self-Defense: An American Tradition," from *Negroes with Guns* by Robert F. Williams, Marzani & Munsell Inc., New York, 1962

The stranglehold of oppression cannot be loosened by a plea to the oppressor's conscience. Social change in something as fundamental as racist oppression involves violence. You cannot have progress here without violence and upheaval, because it's struggle for survival for one and a struggle for liberation for the other. Always the powers in command are ruthless and unmerciful in defending their position and their privileges. This is not an abstract rule to be meditated upon by Americans. This is a truth that was revealed at the birth of America, and has continued to be revealed many times in history. Self-defense is an American tradition that began at Lexington and Concord.

We have come to comprehend the nature of racism. It is a mass psychosis. When I've described racial conditions in the United States to audiences of foreign newsmen, Cubans and other Latin Americans, they have been shocked to learn of the depths of American race hatred. When I have cited as illustrations such extreme situations as the segregation of telephone party-lines in Union County, or the segregated pet-animal cemetery in Washington, D.C, where an Afro-American cannot bury his dog, they find such things comic as well as pathetic.

Such extreme examples of the racist mentality only appear comic when looked upon as isolated phenomena. In truth they are perfectly logical applications of the premises that make up the racist mentality. Look at the phenomena this way and they are the logical inventions of a thoroughly diseased mind. The racist is a man crazed by hysteria at the idea of coming into equal human contact with Negroes. And this mass mental illness called racism is very much a part of the "American Way of Life."

When Afro-American liberation is finally achieved in the USA, one of the many new developments in such a society will be some sort of institution that will correct those Americans whose minds are thoroughly warped by racism. Somehow a way will be found so that these insane people will be made whole, will be made well again.

This is the time for the Afro-American to act. Our sense of national consciousness and militancy is growing. I speak of the masses of people, the masses of Afro-Americans that I know and have visited; in Jacksonville, Florida; in Atlanta, in Savannah, and in Macon, Georgia; in Columbia, in Charleston, and Greenville, South Carolina. The oppressed and exploited black men that I've met on the streets of Harlem, the streets of Detroit, and in Chicago. And I speak of the people in Monroe where five years ago, when I started talking about self-defense, I would walk through the streets and many of my black neighbors would walk away to avoid me. Today, despite the FBI manhunt and my exile, despite the frame-up arrests and the shooting since, despite the intimidation campaigns like the one to drive Mrs. Johnson of the *Crusader* staff from Monroe, despite all of this, black Monroe continues its struggle.

As editor of *The Crusader*, I went south in the fall of 1960, deep into Jim Crowland, to observe the freedom struggle. I was confronted with this new wonderful spirit rising throughout Dixie—this determination to break the chains of bondage and the spirit of valor of a people who just a few years ago were submissive peons in civilization's no-man's-land. Daily, I saw the old myth about Afro-Americans being incapable of unity and action exploded.

In Savannah an NAACP leader had contributed $30,000 to the local branch. The branch has a full-time worker and a suite of office space. Pickets and sit-iners and jobs have been lost, but the struggle goes on. The leader is not afraid of violence to himself because the people are with him. In that city an Afro-American union leader said that it had come to pass that the masses of Afro-Americans can see that "We must defend ourselves against violence with violence." That many of them now say that the American white racist needs a good "whipping" to bring them down to earth and to break his white supremacy mania.

I learned in Atlanta that Mr. Elijah Muhammed had made quite an impression and that many Afro-Americans are learning, to the consternation and embarrassment of the black respectable leadership, that he has more to offer than weak prayers of deliverance. A prominent minister in South Carolina said, "Our biggest stumbling block is the Uncle Tom minister—the people must stop paying these traitors." In Atlanta, a university professor, energetic about the new spirit on the part of the negroes, was very hopeful that a new militant leadership would replace the old Uncle Toms, whose days, he was confident, were numbered.

There are exceptions among us. The Uncle Toms, the Judases, and the Quislings of the black "elite" would deny this rising consciousness. They do everything possible to make white Americans think that it is not true, while apologizing to us for the very people who oppress us. Some of these "responsible" Negroes are afraid that militant action damages "amiable race relations." They complain that race relations may deteriorate to a point that many Negroes may lose jobs. What they mean is that they may lose *their* jobs. For the black workers, who are the first to be fired, and last, if ever, to be hired, the situation is so bad it can't deteriorate.

We realize that there must be a struggle within our own ranks to take the leadership away from the black Quislings who betray us. Then the white liberals who are dumping hundreds of thousands of dollars into our struggle in the south to convert us to pacifism will have to accept *our* understanding of the situation or drop their liberal pretensions.

Why do the white liberals ask us to be non-violent? We are not the aggressors; we been victimized for over 300 years. Yet nobody spends money to go into the South and ask the racists to be martyrs or pacifists. But they always come to the downtrodden Negroes, who are already oppressed and too submissive as a group, and they ask them not to fight back. There seems to be a pattern of some sort of strange coincidence of interest when whites preach a special doctrine to Negroes. Like the choice of theology when the plantation owners saw to the Christianization of the slaves. Instead of the doctrines which produced the rugged aggressively independent and justice-seeking spirit that we associate with Colonial America as the New England Conscience, the slaves were indoctrinated in the most submissive "trust-your-master," pie-in-the-sky after-you-die form of Christianity.

It is because our militancy is growing that they spend hundreds of thousands of dollars to convert us into pacifists. Because our militancy is growing they come to us out of fear.

Of course, the respectable Negro leadership are the most outspoken exponents of non-violence. But if these people, especially the ministers, are such pure pacifists, why is it that so few, if any, criticize the war preparations of this country? Why is it that so few speak out against the Bomb? Isn't that the sort of preaching one expects and *hears* from sincere pacifists? The responsible Negro leadership is pacifist in so far as its one interest is that we do not fight white racists; that we do not "provoke" or enrage them. They constantly tell us if we resort to violent self-defense we will be exterminated. They are not stopping violence—they are only stopping defensive violence against white racists out of a fear of extermination.

This fear of extermination is a myth which we've exposed in Monroe. We did this because we came to have an active understanding of the racist system and we grasped the relationship between violence and racism. The existence is at the very heart of a racist system. The Afro-American militant is a "militant" because he defends himself, his family, his home, and his dignity. He does not *introduce* violence into a racist social system—the violence is already there, and has always been there. It is precisely unchallenged violence that allows a racist social system to perpetuate itself. When people say that they are opposed to Negroes "resorting to violence" what they really mean is that they are opposed to Negroes defending themselves and challenging the exclusive monopoly of violence practiced by white racists. We have shown in Monroe that with violence working *both ways* constituted law will be more inclined to keep the peace.

When Afro-Americans resist and struggle for their rights they also possess a power greater than that generated by their will and their hands. With the world situation as it is today, the most racist and fascist United States government conceivable could not succeed in exterminating 20,000,000 people. We know there is a great power struggle going on in the world today, and the colored peoples control the true balance of power. We also know, from the statistics of the Detroit race riots, that production in this country would fall in forty-eight hours. People everywhere in the world would be ready to support our struggle.

Nor should we forget that these same deceiving pacifist-preaching well-to-do southern blacks profit from the struggle, living lives of luxury while most Afro-Americans continue to suffer. Are they any better than the Negro Quisling in neighboring Charleston, North Carolina—a black man who rode around in a new pink Cadillac with anti-NAACP and anti-integration literature, a huge roll of money, and an expense bank count, all the blessings of the White Citizens' Council? It is an ironic sign that black Judases are becoming more expensive as the white racist becomes desperate—though it is a small consolation to those of us who suffer from his betrayals.

In Monroe, where we fought the Klan, we were being penalized. There are children there growing up without any education, children without shoes, children without food. Old people without medical attention. For the Monroe Negro, there is no work; there is no welfare. From all the money raised in the North by the official black leadership, no one would send a penny to Monroe, because the white liberals who gave this money considered us to be outlaws and thugs. They preferred to let us suffer rather than to identify themselves with our position. They sent truck convoys into other places in the South, but penalized us because we took a militant stand.

But our children who are growing up without shoes are also growing up with a sense of direction they cannot obtain in the Jim Crow schools. There once was a threat, in Monroe, of Negro teen-age gang war. It abated as the teen-agers resolved their difficulties by coming to understand the problem. It is only natural to expect the black youth to be infected with a desire to do something. Frustrated by less active adults, this desire may be projected in the wrong direction. The vigor of the youth can be channeled into constructive militant actions. It is simply a matter of common sense to have these young Negroes constructively fight racial injustice rather than fight among themselves. Danger is not a respecter of color lines; it is better to bleed for a just cause than to bleed just for the thrill of the sight of blood. Rebellion ferments in modern youth. It is better that it expend itself against its true enemies than against teen-age schoolmates who can't even explain the reasons for their dangerous skirmishes.

The Montgomery bus boycott was perhaps the most successful example of completely pacifist action. But we must remember that in Montgomery, where Negroes are riding in the front of buses, there are also Negroes who are starving. The Montgomery bus boycott was a victory—but it was limited. It did not raise the Negro standard of living; it did not mean better education for Negro children, it did not mean economic advances.

Just what was the issue at hand for the white racists? What sacrifice? Remember that in Montgomery most of the white Americans have automobiles and are not dependent on the buses. It's just like our own experience in Monroe when we integrated the library. I just called the chairman of the board in any county, I told him that I represented the NAACP, that we wanted to integrate the library, and that our own library had burned down. And he said, "Well, I don't see any reason why you can't use the same library that our people use. It won't make any difference. And after all, I don't read anyway." Now, this is the attitude of a lot of white Southerners about the Montgomery bus boycott. The white people who control the city didn't ride the buses anyway; they had their own private cars, so it didn't make any difference to them.

But when Afro-Americans get into the struggle for the right to live as human beings and the right to earn the same amount of money, then they meet the greatest amount of resistance, and out of it will come police-condoned or inspired violence. When that happens, the racist must be made to realize that in attacking us he risks his own life. After all, his life is a white life, and he considers the white life to be superior; so why should he risk a superior life to take an inferior one?

Now I believe, and a lot of other Negroes do too, that we must create a black militancy of our own. We must direct our own struggle, achieve our own destiny. We must realize that many Afro-Americans have become skeptical and extremely suspicious of the so-called white liberals who have dominated "Negro" freedom movements. They just feel that no white person can understand what it's like to be a suppressed Negro. The traditional white liberal leadership in civil rights organizations, and even white radicals, generally can not understand what our struggle is and how we feel about it. They have always made our struggle secondary and after all these years we really never got any place.

They have a patient sense for good public relations. But we're not interested in a good press. We're interested in becoming free. We want to be liberated. To me, oppression is harmful. It is painful. I would wake up in the morning as a Negro who was oppressed. At lunchtime, I would eat as a Negro who was oppressed. At night, I would go to bed as a Negro who was oppressed. And if I could have been free in thirty seconds, it would not have been too soon.

"Too long have others spoken for us," began the first editorial in the first Afro-American newspaper, which began publication in 1827. The truth of these words has not dimmed in the century and a half since they first appeared in *Freedom's Journal*. They are more appropriate than ever.

There are white people who are willing to give us aid without strings attached. They are willing to let us direct our own struggle; they are genuinely interested in the liberation of the Negro. I wouldn't have been able to remain in the South as long as I did if it had not been for the support that I got from some white people in the North. And I might never have succeeded in escaping the legal-lynching manhunt fomented by the FBI, nor have reached Cuban sanctuary but for the help of whites. They will be willing to continue helping us for the sake of justice, for the sake of human decency. . . .

The tactics of non-violence will continue and should continue. We too believed in non-violent tactics in Monroe. We've used these tactics; we've used all tactics. But we also believe that any struggle for liberation should be a flexible struggle. We shouldn't take the attitude that one method alone is the way to liberation. This is to become dogmatic. This is to fall into the same sort of dogmatism practiced by some of the religious fanatics. We can't afford to develop this type of attitude.

We must use non-violence as a means as long as this is feasible, but the day will come when conditions become so pronounced that non-violence will be suicidal in itself. The day is surely coming when we will see more violence on the same American scene. The day is surely coming when some of the same Negroes who have denounced our using weapons for self-defense will be arming themselves. There are those who pretend to be horrified by the idea that a black veteran who shouldered arms for the United States would willingly take up weapons to defend his wife, his children, his home, and his life. These same people will one day be loud advocates of self-defense. When violent racism and fascism strike at their families and their homes, not in a token way but in an all-out bloody campaign, then they will be among the first to advocate self-defense. They will justify their position as a question of survival. When it is no longer some distant Negro who's no more than a statistic; no more than an article in a newspaper; when it is no longer their neighbors, but it means them and it becomes a matter of personal salvation, then will their attitude change.

As a tactic, we use and approve non-violent resistance. But we also believe that a man cannot have human dignity if be allows himself to be abused; to be kicked and beaten to the ground, to allow his wife and children to be attacked, refusing to defend them and himself on the basis that he's so pious, so self-righteous, that it would demean his personality if he fought back.

We know that the average Afro-American is not a pacifist. He's not a pacifist and he has never been a pacifist and he's not made of the type of material that would make a good pacifist. Those who doubt that the great majority of Negroes are not pacifists, just let them slap one. Pick any Negro on any street corner in the USA and they'll find out how much he believes in turning the other cheek.

All those who dare to attack are going to learn the hard way that the Afro-American is not a pacifist; that he cannot forever be counted on not to defend himself. Those who attack him brutally and ruthlessly can no longer expect to attack him with impunity.

The Afro-American cannot forget that his enslavement in this country did not pass because of pacifist moral force or noble appeals to the Christian conscience of the slaveholders.

Henry David Thoreau is idealized as an apostle of non-violence, the writer who influenced Gandhi and through Gandhi, Martin Luther King, Jr. But Thoreau was not dogmatic; his eyes were open and he saw clearly. I keep with me a copy of Thoreau's *Plea For Captain John Brown*. There are truths that are just as evident in 1962 as they were in 1859 when he wrote: [Editor's note: Here Williams gives an excerpt from Thoreau's "Plea for Captain John Brown."]

It is in the nature of the American Negro, the same as all other men, to fight and to try to destroy those things that block his path to a greater happiness in life.

Whenever I speak on the English-language radio station in Havana (which broadcasts for an audience in the United States), I hope in some way to penetrate the mental barriers and introduce new disturbing elements into the consciousness of white America. I hope to make them aware of the monstrous evil that they are party to by oppressing the Negro. Somehow, I must manage to clearly reflect the image of evil that is inherent in a racist society so that white America will be able to honestly and fully see themselves as they really are. To see themselves with the same clarity as foreigners see them and to recognize that they are not champions of democracy. To understand that today they do not really even *believe* in democracy. To understand that the world is changing regardless of whether they *think* they like it or not.

For I know that if they had a glimpse of their own reality the shock would be of great therapeutic value. There would be many decent Americans who would then understand that this society must mend its ways if it is to survive; that there is no place in the world now for a racist nation.

As an individual, I'm not inclined toward "politics." The only thing I care about is justice and liberation. I don't belong to any political party. But I think that as long as the present politics prevails the Negro is not going to be integrated into American society. There will have to be great political changes before that can come about.

Those Americans who most deny the logic of the future are the ones who have driven me into exile. Those people have been cruel. Yet cruel as it may be, this exile was not the end those people had planned for me. But it is not in the hands of today's oppressors to determine any end. Their role in history denies to them an understanding of this, just as their role will not allow them to understand that every true nationalist leader in Africa has been imprisoned or exiled, and that the future leaders of Latin America and Asian national liberation today are experiencing imprisonment, exile, or worse.

The future belongs to to-day's oppressed and I shall be witness to that future in the liberation of the Afro-American.

UNIT 10-10

LETTER FROM BIRMINGHAM CITY JAIL

Martin Luther King, Jr.

My dear Fellow Clergymen,

While confined here in the Birmingham city jail, I came across your recent statement calling our present activities "unwise and untimely." Seldom, if ever, do I pause to answer criticism of my work and ideas. If I sought to answer all of the criticisms that cross my desk, my secretaries would be engaged in little else in the course of the day, and I would have no time for constructive work. But since I feel that you are men of genuine good will and your criticisms are sincerely set forth, I would like to answer your statement in what I hope will be patient and reasonable terms.

I think I should give the reason for my being in Birmingham, since you have been influenced by the argument of "outsiders coming in." I have the honor of serving as president of the Southern Christian Leadership Conference, an organization operating in every southern state, with headquarters in Atlanta, Georgia. We have some eighty-five affiliate organizations all across the South—one being the Alabama Christian Movement for Human Rights. Whenever necessary and possible we share staff, educational and financial resources with our affiliates. Several months ago our local affiliate here in Birmingham invited us to be on call to engage in a nonviolent direct-action program if such were deemed necessary. We readily consented and when the hour came we lived up to our promises. So I am here, along with several members of my staff, because we were invited here. I am here because I have basic organizational ties here.

Beyond this, I am in Birmingham because injustice is here. Just as the eighth century prophets left their little villages and carried their "thus saith the Lord" far beyond the boundaries of their hometowns; and just as the Apostle Paul left his little village of Tarsus and carried the gospel of Jesus Christ to practically every hamlet and city of the Graeco-Roman world, I too am compelled to carry the gospel of freedom beyond my particular hometown. Like Paul, I must constantly respond to the Macedonian call for aid.

Moreover, I am cognizant of the interrelatedness of all communities and states. I cannot sit idly by in Atlanta and not be concerned about what happens in Birmingham. Injustice anywhere is a threat to justice everywhere. We are caught in an inescapable network of mutuality, tied in a single garment of destiny. Whatever affects one directly affects all indirectly. Never again can we afford to live with the narrow, provincial "outside agitator" idea. Anyone who lives in the United States can never be considered an outsider anywhere in this country.

You deplore the demonstrations that are presently taking place in Birmingham. But I am sorry that your statement did not express a similar concern for the conditions that brought the demonstrations into being. I am sure that each of you would want to go beyond the superficial social analyst who looks merely at effects, and does not grapple with underlying causes. I would not hesitate to say that it is unfortunate that so-called demonstrations are taking place in Birmingham at this time, but I would say in more emphatic terms that it is even more unfortunate that the white power structure of this city left the Negro community with no other alternative.

In any nonviolent campaign there are four basic steps: (**1**) collection of the facts to determine whether injustices are alive, (**2**) negotiation, (**3**) self-purification, and (**4**) direct action. We have gone through all of these steps in Birmingham. There can be no gainsaying of the fact that racial injustice engulfs this community.

Birmingham is probably the most thoroughly segregated city in the United States. Its ugly record of police brutality is known in every section of this country. Its unjust treatment of Negroes in the courts is a notorious reality. There have been more unsolved bombings of Negro homes and churches in Birmingham than any city in this nation. These are the hard, brutal and unbelievable facts. On the basis of these conditions Negro leaders sought to negotiate with the city fathers. But the political leaders consistently refused to engage in good faith negotiation.

Then came the opportunity last September to talk with some of the leaders of the economic community. In these negotiating sessions certain promises were made by the merchants—such as the promise to remove the humiliating racial signs from the stores. On the basis of these promises Rev. Shuttlesworth and the leaders of the Alabama Christian Movement for Human Rights agreed to call a moratorium on any type of demonstrations. As the weeks and months unfolded we realized that we were the victims of a broken promise. The signs remained. Like so many experiences of the past we were confronted with blasted hopes, and the dark shadow of a deep disappointment settled upon us. So we had no alternative except that of preparing for direct action, whereby we would present our very bodies as a means of laying our case before the conscience of the local and national community. We were not unmindful of the difficulties involved. So we decided to go through a process of self-purification. We started having workshops on nonviolence and repeatedly asked ourselves the questions, "Are you able to accept blows without retaliating?" "Are you able to endure the ordeals of jail?" We decided to set our direct-action program around the Easter season, realizing that with the exception of Christmas, this was the largest shopping period of the year. Knowing that a strong economic withdrawal program would be the by-product of direct action, we felt that this was the best time to bring pressure on the merchants for the needed changes. Then it occurred to us that the March election was ahead so we speedily decided to postpone action until after election day. When we discovered Mr. Connor was in the run-off, we decided again to postpone action so that the demonstrations could not be used to cloud the issues. At this time we agreed to begin our nonviolent witness the day after the run-off.

This reveals that we did not move irresponsibly into direct action. We too wanted to see Mr. Connor defeated; so we went through postponement after postponement to aid in this community need. After this we felt that direct action could be delayed no longer.

You may well ask, "Why direct action? Why sit-ins, marches, etc.? Isn't negotiation a better path?" You are exactly right in your call for negotiation. Indeed, this is the purpose of direct action. Nonviolent direct action seeks to create such a crisis and establish such creative tension that a community that has constantly refused to negotiate is forced to confront the issue. It seeks so to dramatize the issue that it can no longer be ignored. I just referred to the creation of tension as a part of the work of the nonviolent resister. This may sound rather shocking. But I must confess that I am not afraid of the word tension. I have earnestly worked and preached against violent tension, but there is a type of constructive nonviolent tension that is necessary for growth. Just as Socrates felt that it was necessary to create a tension in the mind so that individuals could rise from the bondage of myths and half-truths to the unfettered realm of creative analysis and objective appraisal, we must see the need of having nonviolent gadflies to create the kind of tension in society that will help men to rise from the dark depths of prejudice and racism to the majestic heights of understanding and brotherhood. So the purpose of the direct action is to create a situation so crisis-packed that it will inevitably open the door to negotiation. We, therefore, concur with you in your call for negotiation. Too long has our beloved Southland been bogged down in the tragic attempt to live in monologue rather than dialogue.

One of the basic points in your statement is that our acts are untimely. Some have asked, "Why didn't you give the new administration time to act?" The only answer that I can give to this inquiry is that the new administration must be prodded about as much as the outgoing one before it acts. We will be sadly mistaken if we feel that the election of Mr. Boutwell will bring the millennium to Birmingham. While Mr. Boutwell is much more articulate and gentle than Mr. Connor, they are both segregationists, dedicated to the task of maintaining the status quo. The hope I see in Mr. Boutwell is that he will be reasonable enough to see the futility of massive resistance to desegregation. But he will not see this without pressure from the devotees of civil rights. My friends, I must say to you that we have not made a single gain in civil rights without determined legal and nonviolent pressure. History is the long and tragic story of the fact that privileged groups seldom give up their privileges voluntarily. Individuals may see the moral light and voluntarily give up their unjust posture; but as Reinhold Niebuhr has reminded us, groups are more immoral than individuals.

We know through painful experience that freedom is never voluntarily given by the oppressor; it must be demanded by the oppressed. Frankly, I have never yet engaged in a direct action movement that was "well-timed," according to the timetable of those who have not suffered unduly from the disease of segregation. For years now I have heard the word "Wait!" It rings in the ear of every Negro with a piercing familiarity. This "Wait" has almost always meant "Never." It has been a tranquilizing thalidomide, relieving the emotional stress for a moment, only to give birth to an ill-formed infant of frustration. We must come to see with the distinguished jurist of yesterday that "justice too long delayed is justice denied." We have waited for more than 340 years for our constitutional and God-given rights. The nations of Asia and Africa are moving with jetlike speed toward the goal of political independence, and we still creep at horse and buggy pace toward the gaining of a cup of coffee at a lunch counter. I guess it is easy for those who have never felt the stinging darts of segregation to say "Wait." But when you have seen vicious mobs lynch your mothers and fathers at will and drown your sisters and brothers at whim; when you have seen hate-filled policemen curse, kick, brutalize and even kill your black brothers and sisters with impunity; when you see the vast majority of your twenty million Negro brothers smothering in an airtight cage of poverty in the midst of an affluent society; when you suddenly find your tongue twisted and your speech stammering as you seek to explain to your six-year-old daughter why she can't go to the public amusement park that has just been advertised on television, and see tears welling up in her little eyes when she is told that Funtown is closed to colored children, and see the depressing clouds of inferiority begin to form in her little mental sky, and see her begin to distort her little personality by unconsciously developing a bitterness toward white people; when you have to concoct an answer for a five-year-old son asking in agonizing pathos: "Daddy, why do white people treat colored people so mean?"; when you take a cross-country drive and find it necessary to sleep night after night in the uncomfortable corners of your automobile because no motel will accept you; when you are humiliated day in and day out by nagging signs reading "white" and "colored"; when your first name becomes "nigger" and your middle name becomes "boy" (however old you are) and your last name becomes "John," and when your wife and mother are never given the respected title "Mrs."; when you are harried by day and haunted by night by the fact that you are a Negro, living constantly at tiptoe stance never quite knowing what to expect next, and plagued with inner fears and outer resentments; when you are forever fighting a degenerating sense of "nobodiness"; then you will understand why we find it difficult to wait. There comes a time when the cup of endurance runs over, and men are no longer willing to be plunged into an abyss of injustice where they experience the blackness of corroding despair. I hope, sirs, you can understand our legitimate and unavoidable impatience.

You express a great deal of anxiety over our willingness to break laws. This is certainly a legitimate concern. Since we so diligently urge people to obey the Supreme Court's decision of 1954 outlawing segregation in the public schools, it is rather strange and paradoxical to find us consciously breaking laws. One may well ask, "How can you advocate breaking some laws and obeying others?" The answer is found in the fact that there are two types of laws: there are *just* and there are *unjust* laws. I would agree with Saint Augustine that "An unjust law is no law at all."

Now what is the difference between the two? How does one determine when a law is just or unjust? A just law is a man-made code that squares with the moral law or the law of God. An unjust law is a code that is out of harmony with the moral law. To put it in the terms of Saint Thomas Aquinas, an unjust law is a human law that is not rooted in eternal and natural law. Any law that uplifts human personality is just. Any law that degrades human personality is unjust. All segregation statutes are unjust because segregation distorts the soul and damages the personality. It gives the segregator a false sense of superiority and the segregated a false sense of inferiority. To use the words of Martin Buber, the great Jewish philosopher, segregation substitutes an "I-it" relationship for the "I-thou" relationship, and ends up relegating persons to the status of things. So segregation is not only politically, economically and sociologically unsound, but it is morally wrong and sinful. Paul Tillich has said that sin is separation. Isn't segregation an existential expression of man's tragic separation, an expression of his awful estrangement, his terrible sinfulness? So I can urge men to disobey segregation ordinances because they are morally wrong.

Let us turn to a more concrete example of just and unjust laws. An unjust law is a code that a majority inflicts on a minority that is not binding on itself. This is difference made legal. On the other hand a just law is a code that a majority compels a minority to follow that it is willing to follow itself. This is sameness made legal.

Let me give another explanation. An unjust law is a code inflicted upon a minority which that minority had no part in enacting or creating because they did not have the unhampered right to vote. Who can say that the legislature of Alabama which set up the segregation laws was democratically elected? Throughout the state of Alabama all types of conniving methods are used to prevent Negroes from becoming registered voters and there are some counties without a single Negro registered to vote despite the fact that the Negro constitutes a majority of the population. Can any law set up in such a state be considered democratically structured?

These are just a few examples of unjust and just laws. There are some instances when a law is just on its face and unjust in its application. For instance, I was arrested Friday on a charge of parading without a permit. Now there is nothing wrong with an ordinance which requires a permit for a parade, but when the ordinance is used to preserve segregation and to deny citizens the First Amendment privilege of peaceful assembly and peaceful protest, then it becomes unjust.

I hope you can see the distinction I am trying to point out. In no sense do I advocate evading or defying the law as the rabid segregationist would do. This would lead to anarchy. One who breaks an unjust law must do it *openly, lovingly* (not hatefully as the white mothers did in New Orleans when they were seen on television screaming, "nigger, nigger, nigger"), and with a willingness to accept the penalty. I submit that an individual who breaks a law that conscience tells him is unjust, and willingly accepts the penalty by staying in jail to arouse the conscience of the community over its injustice, is in reality expressing the very highest respect for law.

Of course, there is nothing new about this kind of civil disobedience. It was seen sublimely in the refusal of Shadrach, Meshach and Abednego to obey the laws of Nebuchadnezzar because a higher moral law was involved. It was practiced superbly by the early Christians who were willing to face hungry lions and the excruciating pain of chopping blocks, before submitting to certain unjust laws of the Roman Empire. To a degree academic freedom is a reality today because Socrates practiced civil disobedience.

We can never forget that everything Hitler did in Germany was "legal" and everything the Hungarian freedom fighters did in Hungary was "illegal." It was "illegal" to aid and comfort a Jew in Hitler's Germany. But I am sure that if I had lived in Germany during that time I would have aided and comforted my Jewish brothers even though it was illegal. If I lived in a Communist country today where certain principles dear to the Christian faith are suppressed, I believe I would openly advocate disobeying these anti-religious laws. I must make two honest confessions to you, my Christian and Jewish brothers. First, I must confess that over the last few years I have been gravely disappointed with the white moderate. I have almost reached the regrettable conclusion that the Negro's great stumbling block in the stride toward freedom is not the White Citizen's Councilor or the Ku Klux Klanner, but the white moderate who is more devoted to "order" than to justice; who prefers a negative peace which is the absence of tension to a positive peace which is the presence of justice; who constantly says, "I agree with you in the goal you seek, but I can't agree with your methods of direct action"; who paternalistically feels that he can set the timetable for another man's freedom; who lives by the myth of time and who constantly advised the Negro to wait until a "more convenient season." Shallow understanding from people of good will is more frustrating than absolute misunderstanding from people of ill will. Lukewarm acceptance is much more bewildering than outright rejection.

I had hoped that the white moderate would understand that law and order exist for the purpose of establishing justice, and that when they fail to do this they become dangerously structured dams that block the flow of social progress. I had hoped that the white moderate would understand that the present tension of the South is merely a necessary phase of the transition from an obnoxious negative peace, where the Negro passively accepted his unjust plight, to a substance-filled positive peace, where all men will respect the dignity and worth of human personality. Actually, we who engage in nonviolent direct action are not the creators of tension. We merely bring to the surface the hidden tension that is already alive. We bring it out in the open where it can be seen and dealt with. Like a boil that can never be cured as long as it is covered up but must be opened with all its pus-flowing ugliness to the natural medicines of air and light, injustice must likewise be exposed, with all of the tension its exposing creates, to the light of human conscience and the air of national opinion before it can be cured.

In your statement you asserted that our actions, even though peaceful, must be condemned because they precipitate violence. But can this assertion be logically made? Isn't this like condemning the robbed man because his possession of money precipitated the evil act of robbery? Isn't this like condemning Socrates because his unswerving commitment to truth and his philosophical delvings precipitated the misguided popular mind to make him drink the hemlock? Isn't this like condemning Jesus because His unique God-consciousness and never-ceasing devotion to his will precipitated the evil act of crucifixion? We must come to see, as federal courts have consistently affirmed, that it is immoral to urge an individual to withdraw his efforts to gain his basic constitutional rights because the quest precipitates violence. Society must protect the robbed and punish the robber.

I had also hoped that the white moderate would reject the myth of time. I received a letter this morning from a white brother in Texas which said: "All Christians know that the colored people will receive equal rights eventually, but it is possible that you are in too great of a religious hurry. It has taken Christianity almost two thousand years to accomplish what it has. The teachings of Christ take time to come to earth." All that is said here grows out of a tragic misconception of time. It is the strangely irrational notion that there is something in the very flow of time that will inevitably cure all ills. Actually time is neutral. It can be used either destructively or constructively. I am coming to feel that the people of ill will have used time much more effectively than the people of good will. We will have to repent in this generation not merely for the vitriolic words and actions of the bad people, but for the appalling silence of the good people. We must come to see that human progress never rolls in on wheels of inevitability. It comes through the tireless efforts and persistent work of men willing to be co-workers with God, and without this hard work time itself becomes an ally of the forces of social stagnation. We must use time creatively, and forever realize that the time is always ripe to do right. Now is the time to make real the promise of democracy, and transform our pending national elegy into a creative psalm of brotherhood. Now is the time to lift our national policy from the quicksand of racial injustice to the solid rock of human dignity.

You spoke of our activity in Birmingham as extreme. At first I was rather disappointed that fellow clergymen would see my nonviolent efforts as those of the extremist. I started thinking about the fact that I stand in the middle of two opposing forces in the Negro community. One is a force of complacency made up of Negroes who, as a result of long years of oppression, have been so completely drained of self-respect and a sense of "somebodiness" that they have adjusted to segregation, and, of a few Negroes in the middle class who, because of a degree of academic and economic security, and because at points they profit by segregation, have unconsciously become insensitive to the problems of the masses. The other force is one of bitterness and hatred, and comes perilously close to advocating violence. It is expressed in the various black nationalist groups that are springing up over the nation, the largest and best known being Elijah Muhammad's Muslim movement. This movement is nourished by the contemporary frustration over the continued existence of racial discrimination. It is made up of people who have lost faith in America, who have absolutely repudiated Christianity, and who have concluded that the white man is an incurable "devil." I have tried to stand between these two forces, saying that we need not follow the "do-nothingism" of the complacent or the hatred and despair of the black nationalist. There is the more excellent way of love and nonviolent protest. I'm grateful to God that, through the Negro church, the dimension of nonviolence entered our struggle. If this philosophy had not emerged, I am convinced that by now many streets of the South would be flowing with floods of blood. And I am further convinced that if our white brothers dismiss us as "rabble-rousers" and "outside agitators" those of us who are working through the channels of nonviolent direct action and refuse to support our nonviolent efforts, millions of Negroes, out of frustration and despair, will seek solace and security in black nationalist ideologies, a development that will lead inevitably to a frightening racial nightmare.

Oppressed people cannot remain oppressed forever. The urge for freedom will eventually come. This is what happened to the American Negro. Something within has reminded him of his birthright of freedom; something without has reminded him that he can gain it. Consciously and unconsciously, he has been swept in what the Germans call the *Zeitgeist*, and with his black brothers of Africa, and his brown and yellow brothers of Asia, South America and the Caribbean, he is moving with a sense of cosmic urgency toward the promised land of racial justice. Recognizing this vital urge that has engulfed the Negro community, one should readily understand public demonstrations. The Negro has many pent-up resentments and latent frustrations. He has to get them out. So let him march sometime; let him have his prayer pilgrimages to the city hall; understand why he must have sit-ins and freedom rides. If his repressed emotions do not come out in these nonviolent ways, they will come out in ominous expressions of violence. This is not a threat; it is a fact of history. So I have not said to my people "get rid of your discontent." But I have tried to say that this normal and healthy discontent can be channelized through the creative outlet of nonviolent direct action. Now this approach is being dismissed as extremist. I must admit that I was initially disappointed in being so categorized.

But as I continued to think about the matter I gradually gained a bit of satisfaction from being considered an extremist. Was not Jesus an extremist in love—"Love your enemies, bless them that curse you, pray for them that despitefully use you." Was not Amos an extremist for justice—"Let justice roll down like waters and righteousness like a mighty stream." Was not Paul an extremist for the gospel of Jesus Christ—"I bear in my body the marks of the Lord Jesus." Was not Martin Luther an extremist—"Here I stand; I can do none other so help me God." Was not John Bunyan an extremist—"I will stay in jail to the end of my days before I make a butchery of my conscience." Was not Abraham Lincoln an extremist—"This nation cannot survive half slave and half free." Was not Thomas Jefferson an extremist—"We hold these truths to be self-evident, that all men are created equal." So the question is not whether we will be extremist but what kind of extremist will we be. Will we be extremists for hate or will we be extremists for love? Will we be extremists for the preservation of injustice—or will we be extremists for the cause of justice? In that dramatic scene on Calvary's hill, three men were crucified. We must not forget that all three were crucified for the same crime—the crime of extremism. Two were extremists for immorality, and thusly fell below their environment. The other, Jesus Christ, was an extremist for love, truth and goodness, and thereby rose above his environment. So, after all, maybe the South, the nation and the world are in dire need of creative extremists.

I had hoped that the white moderate would see this. Maybe I was too optimistic. Maybe I expected too much. I guess I should have realized that few members of a race that has oppressed another race can understand or appreciate the deep groans and passionate yearnings of those that have been oppressed and still fewer have the vision to see that injustice must be rooted out by strong, persistent and determined action. I am thankful, however, that some of our white brothers have grasped the meaning of this social revolution and committed themselves to it. They are still all too small in quantity, but they are big in quality. Some like Ralph McGill, Lillian Smith, Harry Golden and James Dabbs have written about our struggle in eloquent, prophetic and understanding terms. Others have marched with us down nameless streets of the South. They have languished in filthy roach-infested jails, suffering the abuse and brutality of angry policemen who see them as "dirty nigger-lovers." They, unlike so many of their moderate brothers and sisters, have recognized the urgency of the moment and sensed the need for powerful "action" antidotes to combat the disease of segregation.

Let me rush on to mention my other disappointment. I have been so greatly disappointed with the white church and its leadership. Of course, there are some notable exceptions. I am not unmindful of the fact that each of you has taken some significant stands on this issue. I commend you, Rev. Stallings, for your Christian stance on this past Sunday, in welcoming Negroes to your worship service on a non-segregated basis. I commend the Catholic leaders of this state for integrating Springhill College several years ago.

But despite these notable exceptions I must honestly reiterate that I have been disappointed with the church. I do not say that as one of the negative critics who can always find something wrong with the church. I say it as a minister of the gospel, who loves the church; who was nurtured in its bosom; who has been sustained by its spiritual blessings and who will remain true to it as long as the cord of life shall lengthen.

I had the strange feeling when I was suddenly catapulted into the leadership of the bus protest in Montgomery several years ago that we would have the support of the white church. I felt that the white ministers, priests and rabbis of the South would be some of our strongest allies. Instead, some have been outright opponents, refusing to understand the freedom movement and misrepresenting its leaders; all too many others have been more cautious than courageous and have remained silent behind the anesthetizing security of the stained-glass windows.

In spite of my shattered dreams of the past, I came to Birmingham with the hope that the white religious leadership of this community would see the justice of our cause, and with deep moral concern, serve as the channel through which our just grievances would get to the power structure. I had hoped that each of you would understand. But again I have been disappointed. I have heard numerous religious leaders of the South call upon their worshippers to comply with a desegregation decision because it is the law, but I have longed to hear white ministers say, "Follow this decree because integration is morally right and the Negro is your brother." In the midst of blatant injustices inflicted upon the Negro, I have watched white churches stand on the sideline and merely mouth pious irrelevancies and sanctimonious trivialities. In the midst of a mighty struggle to rid our nation of racial and economic injustice, I have heard so many ministers say, "Those are social issues with which the gospel has no real concern," and I have watched so many churches commit themselves to a completely otherworldly religion which made a strange distinction between body and soul, the sacred and the secular.

So here we are moving toward the exit of the twentieth century with a religious community largely adjusted to the status quo, standing as a taillight behind other community agencies rather than a headlight leading men to higher levels of justice.

I have traveled the length and breadth of Alabama, Mississippi and all the other southern states. On sweltering summer days and crisp autumn mornings I have looked at her beautiful churches with their lofty spires pointing heavenward. I have beheld the impressive outlay of her massive religious education buildings. Over and over again I have found myself asking: "What kind of people worship here? Who is their God? Where were their voices when the lips of Governor Barnett dripped with words of interposition and nullification? Where were they when Governor Wallace gave the clarion call for defiance and hatred? Where were their voices of support when tired, bruised and weary Negro men and women decided to rise from the dark dungeons of complacency to the bright hills of creative protest?"

Yes, these questions are still in my mind. In deep disappointment, I have wept over the laxity of the church. But be assured that my tears have been tears of love. There can be no deep disappointment where there is not deep love. Yes, I love the church; I love her sacred walls. How could I do otherwise? I am in the rather unique position of being the son, the grandson and the great-grandson of preachers. Yes, I see the church as the body of Christ. But, oh! How we have blemished and scarred that body through social neglect and fear of being nonconformists.

There was a time when the church was very powerful. It was during that period when the early Christians rejoiced when they were deemed worthy to suffer for what they believed. In those days the church was not merely a thermometer that recorded the ideas and principles of popular opinion; it was a thermostat that transformed the mores of society. Wherever the early Christians entered a town the power structure got disturbed and immediately sought to convict them for being "disturbers of the peace" and "outside agitators." But they went on with the conviction that they were a "colony of heaven," and had to obey God rather than man. They were small in number but big in commitment. They were too God-intoxicated to be "astronomically intimidated." They brought an end to such ancient evils as infanticide and gladiatorial contest.

Things are different now. The contemporary church is often a weak, ineffectual voice with an uncertain sound. It is so often the arch-supporter of the status-quo. Far from being disturbed by the presence of the church, the power structure of the average community is consoled by the church's silent and often vocal sanction of things as they are.

But the judgment of God is upon the church as never before. If the church of today does not recapture the sacrificial spirit of the early church, it will lose its authentic ring, forfeit the loyalty of millions, and be dismissed as an irrelevant social club with no meaning for the twentieth century. I am meeting young people every day whose disappointment with the church has risen to outright disgust.

Maybe again, I have been too optimistic. Is organized religion too inextricably bound to the status quo to save our nation and the world? Maybe I must turn my faith to the inner spiritual church, the church within the church, as the true *ecclesia* and the hope of the world. But again I am thankful to God that some noble souls from the ranks of organized religion have broken loose from the paralyzing chains of conformity and joined us as active partners in the struggle for freedom. They have left their secure congregations and walked the streets of Albany, Georgia, with us. They have gone through the highways of the South on tortuous rides for freedom. Yes, they have gone to jail with us. Some have been kicked out of their churches, and lost support of their bishops and fellow ministers. But they have gone with the faith that right defeated is stronger than evil triumphant. These men have been the leaven in the lump of the race. Their witness has been the spiritual salt that has preserved the true meaning of the gospel in these troubled times. They have carved a tunnel of hope through the dark mountain of disappointment.

I hope the church as a whole will meet the challenge of this decisive hour. But even if the church does not come to the aid of justice, I have no despair about the future. I have no fear about the outcome of our struggle in Birmingham, even if our motives are presently misunderstood. We will reach the goal of freedom in Birmingham and all over the nation, because the goal of America is freedom. Abused and scorned though we may be, our destiny is tied up with the destiny of America. Before the Pilgrims landed at Plymouth we were here. Before the pen of Jefferson etched across the pages of history the majestic words of the Declaration of Independence, we were here. For more than two centuries our foreparents labored in this country without wages; they made cotton king; and they built the homes of their masters in the midst of brutal injustice and shameful humiliation—and yet out of a bottomless vitality they continued to thrive and develop. If the inexpressible cruelties of slavery could not stop us, the opposition we now face will surely fail. We will win our freedom because the sacred heritage of our nation and the eternal will of God are embodied in our echoing demands.

I must close now. But before closing I am impelled to mention one other point in your statement that troubled me profoundly. You warmly commended the Birmingham police force for keeping "order" and "preventing violence." I don't believe you would have so warmly commended the police force if you had seen its angry violent dogs literally biting six unarmed, nonviolent Negroes. I don't believe you would so quickly commend the policemen if you would observe their ugly and inhuman treatment of Negroes here in the city jail; if you would watch them push and curse old Negro women and young Negro girls; if you would see them slap and kick old Negro men and young boys; if you will observe them, as they did on two occasions, refuse to give us food because we wanted to sing our grace together. I'm sorry that I can't join you in your praise for the police department.

It is true that they have been rather disciplined in their public handling of the demonstrators. In this sense they have been rather publicly "nonviolent." But for what purpose? To preserve the evil system of segregation. Over the last few years I have consistently preached that nonviolence demands that the means we use must be as pure as the ends we seek. So I have tried to make it clear that it is wrong to use immoral means to attain moral ends. But now I must affirm that it is just as wrong, or even more so, to use moral means to preserve immoral ends. Maybe Mr. Connor and his policeman have been rather publicly nonviolent, as Chief Pritchett was in Albany, Georgia, but they have used the moral means of nonviolence to maintain the immoral end of flagrant racial injustice. T. S. Eliot has said that there is no greater treason than to do the right deed for the wrong reason.

I wish you had commended the Negro sit-inners and demonstrators of Birmingham for their sublime courage, their willingness to suffer and their amazing discipline in the midst of the most inhuman provocation. One day the South will recognize its real heroes.

They will be the James Merediths, courageously and with a majestic sense of purpose facing jeering and hostile mobs and the agonizing loneliness that characterizes the life of the pioneer. They will be old, oppressed, battered Negro women, symbolized in a seventy-two-year-old woman of Montgomery, Alabama, who rose up with a sense of dignity and with her people decided not to ride the segregated buses, and responded to one who inquired about her tiredness with ungrammatical profundity: "My feet is tired, but my soul is rested." They will be the young high school and college students, young ministers of the gospel and a host of their elders courageously and nonviolently sitting-in at lunch counters and willingly going to jail for conscience's sake. One day the South will know that when these disinherited children of God sat down at lunch counters they were in reality standing up for the best in the American dream and the most sacred values in our Judeo-Christian heritage, and thusly, carrying our whole nation back to those great wells of democracy which were dug deep by the Founding Fathers in the formulation of the Constitution and the Declaration of Independence.

Never before have I written a letter this long (or should I say a book?). I'm afraid that it is much too long to take your precious time. I can assure you that it would have been much shorter if I had been writing from a comfortable desk, but what else is there to do when you are alone for days in the dull monotony of a narrow jail cell other than write long letters, think strange thoughts, and pray long prayers?

If I have said anything in this letter that is an overstatement of the truth and is indicative of an unreasonable impatience, I beg you to forgive me. If I have said anything in this letter that is an understatement of the truth and is indicative of my having a patience that makes me patient with anything less than brotherhood, I beg God to forgive me.

I hope this letter finds you strong in the faith. I also hope that circumstances will soon make it possible for me to meet each of you, not as an integrationist or a civil rights leader, but as a fellow clergyman and a Christian brother. Let us all hope that the dark clouds of racial prejudice will soon pass away and the deep fog of misunderstanding will be lifted from our fear-drenched communities and in some not too distant tomorrow the radiant stars of love and brotherhood will shine over our great nation with all of their scintillating beauty.

Yours for the cause of Peace and Brotherhood,
Martin Luther King, Jr.
April 16, 1963

UNIT 10-11

IS VIOLENCE NECESSARY TO COMBAT INJUSTICE?

Robert F. Williams and Martin Luther King, Jr.

EDITOR'S NOTE

The great debate in the integration movement in recent months has been the question of violence vs. nonviolence, as instruments of social change. The nonviolent way was brought dramatically to the public consciousness by the successful Montgomery bus protest of 1955–56. The debate, long smoldering under the surface, was precipitated last spring when Robert Williams, Negro leader of Monroe, N.C., made his much-publicized statement that Negroes must "meet violence with violence." Much misunderstanding of both positions has followed. In the opinion of Patriot editors, the most meaningful and enlightening discussion of the issue was presented in the September and October issues of the pacifist publication, Liberation, in the form of articles by Mr. Williams and by Dr. Martin Luther King, Jr., leader of the non-violent movement. We reprint excerpts from both articles here.

FOR THE POSITIVE

WILLIAMS SAYS "WE MUST FIGHT BACK"

Robert F. Williams

In 1954, I was an enlisted man in the United States Marine Corps. . . . I shall never forget the evening we (heard) the historic Supreme Court decision that segregation in the public schools is unconstitutional. . . .

At last I felt that I was a part of America and that I belonged. That was what I had always wanted, even as a child.

I returned to civilian life in 1955 and the hope I had for Negro liberation faltered. . . . Acts of violence and words and deeds of hate and spite rose from every

Southern Patriot, January 1960.

quarter. . . . There is open defiance to law and order throughout the South today. . . . I have become disillusioned . . .

What Will Deter?

Laws serve to deter crime and protect the weak from the strong in civilized society. Where there is a breakdown of law. . . . where is the force of deterrent?. . . . Only highly civilized and moral individuals respect the rights of others. . . . The Southern brute respects only force. Nonviolence is a very potent weapon when the opponent is civilized, but nonviolence is no repellent for a sadist. . . .

I have great respect for the pacifist, that is, for the pure pacifist. . . . I am not a pacifist and I am sure I may safely say most of my people are not. Passive resistance is a powerful weapon in gaining concessions from oppressors, but I venture to say that if Mack Parker had had an automatic shotgun at his disposal, he could have served as a great deterrent against lynching. . . .

In 1957 the Klan moved into Monroe and Union County (N.C.). . . . Their numbers steadily increased to the point wherein the local press reported 7500 at one rally. They became so brazen that mile-long motorcades started invading the Negro community.

These hooded thugs fired pistols from car windows. . . . On one occasion they caught a Negro woman on the street and tried to force her to dance for them at gun point. . . . Drivers of cars tried to run Negroes down. . . . Lawlessness was rampant. . . . instead of cowing, we organized an armed guard. . . . On one occasion, we had to exchange gunfire with the Klan.

Each time the Klan came on a raid they were led by police cars. We appealed to the President of the United States to have the Justice Department investigate the police. We appealed to Governor Luther Hodges. All our appeals to constituted law were in vain . . .

A group of nonviolent ministers met the City Board of Aldermen and pleaded with them to restrict the Klan from the colored community. The city fathers advised these cringing, begging Negro ministers that the Klan had constitutional rights to meet and organize in the same way as the NAACP.

Not having been infected by turn-the-other-cheekism, a group of Negroes who showed a willingness to fight caused the city officials to deprive the Klan of its constitutional rights after local papers told of dangerous incidents between Klansmen and armed Negroes. Klan motorcades have been legally banned from the City of Monroe. . . .

"Sick Inside"

On May 5, 1959, while president of the Union County branch of the NAACP, I made a statement to the United Press International after a trial wherein a white man was supposed to have been tried for kicking a Negro maid down a flight of stairs in a local white hotel. In spite of the fact that there was an eyewitness, the defendant failed to show up for his trial, and was completely exonerated.

Another case in the same court involved a white man who had come to a pregnant Negro mother's home and attempted to rape her. In recorder's court the only defense offered for the defendant was that he's not guilty. "He was just drunk and having a little fun." . . . A white woman neighbor testified that the woman had come to her house excited, her clothes torn, her feet bare and begging her for assistance; the court was unmoved. . . .

This great miscarriage of justice left me sick inside, and I said then what I say now. I believe Negroes must be willing to defend themselves, their women, their children and their homes. They must be willing to die and to kill in repelling their assailants. . . . Negroes must protect themselves, it is obvious that the federal government will not put an end to lynching; therefore it becomes necessary for us to stop lynching with violence. . . .

TAUGHT TO FIGHT

Some Negro leaders have cautioned me that if Negroes fight back, the racist will have cause to exterminate the race. . . . This government is in no position to allow mass violence to erupt, let alone allow twenty million Negroes to be exterminated. . . .

. . . . it is instilled at an early age that men who violently and swiftly rise to oppose tyranny are virtuous examples to emulate. I have been taught by my government to fight. . . . nowhere in the annals of history does the record show a people delivered from bondage by patience alone.

FOR THE NEGATIVE

KING SEES ALTERNATIVE IN MASS ACTIONS

Martin Luther King, Jr.

Paradoxically, the struggle for civil rights has reached a stage of profound crisis, although its outward aspect is distinctly less turbulent and victories of token integration have been won in the hard-resistance areas of Virginia and Arkansas.

The crisis has its origin in a decision rendered by the Supreme Court more than a year ago which upheld the pupil placement law. Though little noticed then, this decision fundamentally weakened the historic 1954 ruling of the Court. It is imperceptibly becoming the basis of a *de facto* compromise between the powerful contending forces. . . .

Token integration is a developing pattern. This type of integration is merely an affirmation of principle without the substance of change. . . . Full integration can easily become a distant or mythical goal. . . .

"NO COMPROMISE"

The Negro was the tragic victim of another compromise in 1878, when his full equality was bargained away by the Federal Government. . . . There is reason to believe that the Negro of 1959 will not accept supinely any such compromises in the contemporary struggle for integration. . . .

It is axiomatic in social life that the imposition of frustrations leads to two kinds of reactions. One is the development of a wholesome social organization to resist with effective, firm measures any efforts to impede progress.

The other is a confused, anger-motivated drive to strike back violently, to inflict damage. . . . It is punitive—not radical or constructive. The current calls for violence have their roots in this latter tendency.

Here one must be clear that there are three different views on the subject of violence. One is the approach of pure nonviolence, which cannot readily or easily attract large masses, for it requires extraordinary discipline and courage.

The second is violence exercised in self-defense, which all societies, from the most primitive to the most cultured and civilized, accept as moral and legal.

The third is the advocacy of violence as a tool of advancement, organized as in warfare, deliberately and consciously. To this tendency many Negroes are being tempted today.

VIOLENCE CONFUSES

There are incalculable perils in this approach. . . . The greatest danger is that it will fail to attract Negroes to a real collective struggle, and will confuse the large uncommitted middle group, which as yet has not supported either side. . . .

It is unfortunately true that however the Negro acts, his struggle will not be free of violence initiated by his enemies, and he will need ample courage and willingness to sacrifice to defeat this manifestation of violence. But if he seeks it and organizes it, he cannot win.

Does this leave the Negro without a positive method to advance? Mr. Robert Williams would have us believe that there is no effective and practical alternative. He argues that we must be cringing and submissive or take up arms. To so place the issue distorts the whole problem. There are other meaningful alternatives.

The Negro people can organize socially to initiate many forms of struggle which can drive their enemies back without resort to futile and harmful violence. . . . Many creative forms have been developed—the mass boycott, sitdown protests and strikes, sit-ins,—refusal to pay fines and bail for unjust arrests—mass marches—mass meetings—prayer pilgrimages, etc.

There is more power in socially organized masses on the march than there is in guns in the hands of a few desperate men. Our enemies would prefer to deal with a small armed group rather than with a huge, unarmed but resolute mass of people.

However, it is necessary that the mass-action method be persistent and unyielding. Gandhi said the Indian people must "never let them rest," referring to the British. He urged them to keep protesting daily and weekly, in a variety of ways. This method inspired and organized the Indian masses and disorganized and demobilized the British. It educates its myriad participants, socially and morally.

It is this form of struggle—non-cooperation with evil through mass actions—"never letting them rest"—which offers the more effective road for those who have been tempted and goaded to violence.

Boldness Needed

It needs the bold and the brave because it is not free from danger. . . . It requires dedicated people, because it is a backbreaking task to arouse, to organize, and to educate tens of thousands for disciplined, sustained action.

Our present urgent necessity is to cease our internal fighting and turn outward to the enemy, using every form of mass action yet known—create new forms and resolve never to let them rest. This is the social lever which will force open the door to freedom.

Our powerful weapons are the voices, the feet, and bodies of dedicated, united people. . . . Greater tyrants than Southern segregationists have been subdued and defeated by this form of struggle. We have not yet used it, and it would be tragic if we spurn it because we have failed to perceive its dynamic strength and power. . . .

UNIT 11

MISSISSIPPI, VOTER EDUCATION PROJECT, FREEDOM SUMMER, AND 1964 CIVIL RIGHTS ACT

	INTRODUCTION	599
11-1 •	111 ARRESTS MARK MISSISSIPPI FREEDOM DAY	600
11-2 •	MISSISSIPPI: THE CLOSED SOCIETY *James W. Silver*	601
11-3 •	THE GENERAL CONDITION OF THE MISSISSIPPI NEGRO	621
11-4 •	MISSISSIPPI STRUCTURE OF THE MOVEMENT, PRESENT OPERATIONS AND PROSPECTUS FOR THIS SUMMER	642
11-5 •	FREEDOM SCHOOLS, MISSISSIPPI	650
11-6 •	FREEDOM SCHOOL DOCUMENT	652
11-7 •	MISSISSIPPI NEGRO VOTE CURTAILED IN CONGRESSIONAL PRIMARY	659
11-8 •	SOVEREIGNTY COMMISSION (MS) MEMO, SEPTEMBER 23, 1965	662
11-9 •	FIELD REPORTS—TELLING IT LIKE IT WAS	663
11-10 •	SOVEREIGNTY COMMISSION (MS) MEMO, JUNE 26, 1964	678
11-11 •	THE ROAD TO MISSISSIPPI	679
11-12 •	AFFIDAVITS FROM MISSISSIPPI BLACK PAPER	693

11-13 • LIFE IN MISSISSIPPI **703**
AN INTERVIEW WITH FANNIE LOU HAMER
J. H. O'Dell

11-14 • CIVIL RIGHTS LAW COMPLIANCE VARIES **710**

11-15 • MAPS, CHARTS ON 1964 CIVIL RIGHTS ACT **712**

11-16 • SNCC FUND-RAISING LETTER **714**

INTRODUCTION

Unit 11 looks at life in Mississippi and the Freedom Summer of 1964. The unit is framed by James Silver's famous essay on Mississippi, "The Closed Society" (11-2). In its impact, this piece can be likened to *The Strange Career of Jim Crow*—an essay by an historian that helped affect the way Americans saw their society. SNCC's report (11-3) complements Silver's essay by demonstrating the extreme material impoverishment of African Americans in rural Mississippi. The rest of the unit considers what Silver meant by calling Mississippi "the closed society."

The next three documents (11-4, 11-5, 11-6) describe the structure and operations of Freedom Summer, explaining the workings of the Council of Federated Organizations (COFO) broadly and freedom schools specifically.

As seen in 11-7, 11-8, and 11-10, segregationists placed numerous obstacles in front of the Freedom Summer workers. Pay special attention in 11-7 to the article in the lower center: "Mississippi Prepares for Summer Project." The Sovereignty Commission Memo (11-8) reveals how deep the paranoia ran in some white Mississippians about the arrival of hundreds of young black and white students. The second Sovereignty Commission Memo (11-10) demonstrates this state sponsored organization's ability to infiltrate the movement.

Civil rights workers and black Mississippians recount their experiences in four documents (11-9, 11-11 to 11-13). The Voter Education Project (VEP) Field Reports (11-9) include more than just dispatches from Mississippi Freedom Summer; they reveal similarities in the experiences of VEP workers across the South. Started in 1962, the VEP was a Kennedy Administration inspired, Northern foundation funded, and Southern Regional Council directed project to register African Americans to vote. A number of SNCC efforts, such as in Albany, Georgia, were formally VEP projects. "The Road to Mississippi" (11-11) includes excerpts from the letters of Freedom Summer volunteers. In the "Affidavits from Mississippi Black Paper" (11-12), black Mississippians tell in their own words how difficult and frightening life could be for African Americans in the South. Fannie Lou Hamer, best known for her eloquent words at the 1964 Democratic Convention, talks about her life and work in Mississippi in a 1965 *Freedomways* interview (11-13). *Freedomways* was a magazine devoted to the African-American struggle for civil rights.

From a national perspective, the most important accomplishment of 1964 was the Civil Rights Act that went into effect on July 2, 1964. 11-14 graphically describes the four most important provisions of the law; 11-15 details some difficulties faced by African Americans despite the passage of the Civil Rights Act of 1964.

John Lewis, the Chairman of SNCC, summed up the first five frenetic years of the 1960s in a November, 1965, fundraising letter to SNCC supporters across the country. By November, the fight against *de jure* discrimination in the South had been won, but, as Lewis reminds SNCC's supporters, black Southerners still faced serious *de facto* economic, political, and social discrimination.

INTIMIDATION IN ALABAMA

ON PAGE TWO

THE STUDENT VOICE

VOL. 5 NO. 17 STUDENT VOICE, INC. 6 Raymond Street, N. W. Atlanta, Georgia 30314 JULY 22, 1964

RUINS OF JERUSALEM BAPTIST AND BETHEL METHODIST CHURCHES in Kingston, near Natchez. The two churches are among 10 burned or bombed in Mississippi since the Mississippi Summer Project began.

CHURCH BURNINGS STILL UNCHECKED

FLASH! At press time STUDENT VOICE learned that three more churches have been bombed in Mississippi. Details and pictures next week.

GREENWOOD, MISS - Another church burning in Mississippi on July 17 raises the total burned or bombed to 10, SNCC reported this week.

The most recent burning occured in McComb, July 17 when the Zion Hill Baptist Church burned to the ground. The church, located west of McComb on Route 44, had not been used for civil rights activity.

Two other burnings occurred

CONTINUED ON PAGE 3

IN GREENWOOD

111 ARRESTS MARK MISS. FREEDOM DAY

FORMAN CALLS FOR FEDERAL PROTECTION

GREENWOOD, MISS. - In what SNCC Executive Secretary James Forman described as "flagrant violations of the 1960 and 1964 Civil Rights Acts and the First Amendment," 111 local Negroes, SNCC workers, and Mississippi Summer Project volunteers were arrested here after a Freedom Day on July 16.

On July 17, the cases were removed to Federal court.

SNCC has been working in Greenwood since 1962. Greenwood's first "Freedom Day" was held March 25, and resulted in the arrests of 14 workers and local residents. A second "Freedom Day" was held April 9; 46 persons were arrested.

The jailings were made as integrated groups picketed the Leflore County Courthouse, carrying signs urging Negroes to reg-

CONTINUED ON PAGE 4

GREENWOOD POLICE drag pregnant rights worker during a Freedom Day to increase Negro voter registration.

UNIT 11-2

MISSISSIPPI: THE CLOSED SOCIETY

James W. Silver

Between 1938 and 1947 three Mississippi professors, Percy Lee Rainwater, John K. Bettersworth, and Vernon L. Wharton, published scholarly volumes which laid great stress on Mississippi's poverty-stricken leadership in secession, Civil War, and Reconstruction to 1890. It is quite likely that if these studies were put on the market today, their authors would be run out of the state.

The search for historical truth has become a casualty in embattled Mississippi where neither the governor nor the legislature, in their hot pursuit of interposition, indicates any awareness that Mississippians were Americans before they were Southerners or that Magnolia State politicians once stood firm against nullification and secession. The state's present-day exploiters of federal munificence, however, should applaud the cleverness of their ancestors in the 1850s who interpreted state rights as requiring the use of national power to destroy local self-government in the territories and to thwart Northern state nullification of the fugitive slave law.

The striking parallel between people and events of the 1850s and the 1950s reminds us that Mississippi has been on the defensive against inevitable social change for more than a century, and that for some years before the Civil War it had developed a closed society with an orthodoxy accepted by nearly everybody in the state. The all-pervading doctrine then and now has been white supremacy—whether achieved through slavery or segregation—rationalized by a professed adherence to state rights and bolstered by religious fundamentalism. In such a society a never ceasing propagation of the "true faith" must and has gone on relentlessly with a constantly reiterated demand for loyalty to the united front demanding that nonconformists be hushed, silenced with a vengeance, or in crisis situations driven from the community. Violence and the threat of violence have reinforced the presumption of unanimity.

An expanded version of the presidential address delivered at the annual meeting of Southern Historical Association at Asheville, North Carolina, November 7, 1963.

By 1861 Mississippians had been thoroughly prepared for secession by their shortsighted politicians, their chauvinistic press, their political preachers, and their blind philosophers, all operating within the authoritarian society. Even to the present generation the people have been paying for and *eulogizing* their most unwise decision of all time. In fact the romanticism associated with the Old South, the glorification of the Confederacy, and the bitter remembrances of Reconstruction have played their witless and powerful role in preserving a social order based on neither fact nor reason. According to Citizens Council literature, Mississippi is now the innocent victim of a second vicious Reconstruction from which its stalwart citizenry, demonstrating ancestral courage, will emerge triumphant as it did in 1875.

One of today's little sophistries asserts that equality must be earned, can never be achieved by force or law. The forgotten truth is that between 1875 and 1890 *inequality* was effected by force and regularized by law. By the end of the century Negroes had long since learned that Mississippi freedom included neither political nor any other kind of equality. The caste system had once and apparently for all been substituted for slavery, the Negro was in his place, and the society was once more closed and sacrosanct.

No meaningful challenge to the caste system was possible in Mississippi in the first half of the twentieth century. In public life no white man, demagogue or patrician, proposed to do anything constructive about the Negro. Preferring corrupt and inefficient government to participation by the black man, the whites got a one-party system without competition between recognizable groups, with no continuity of existence even of factions, and no means of checking the wild-eyed—in sum, a series of Bilbonic plagues and Barnett blights. Whether The Man Bilbo was just the "slick little bastard" described by his admirers, or represented "nothing save passion, prejudice, and hatred," as claimed by Fred Sullens, is of small importance as compared with his career as symptomatic of the chaos and bankruptcy of Mississippi politics and its social order. In such a demoralized wasteland the sharp-eyed Snopeses have grasped their petty gains, to the greater glory of laissez faire, which ironically has in turn produced the much damned transfer of state functions to the federal government and a diminution of state sovereignty.

Today the totalitarian society of Mississippi imposes on all its people an obedience to an official orthodoxy almost identical with the proslavery philosophy—this in the teeth of the nearly universal dissipation of whatever intellectual sanction white supremacy had among the enlightened at the turn of this century. Every Mississippi politician not only denies the validity of the Fourteenth Amendment but in his heart hungers for the negative days of the Articles of Confederation. Governor Ross Barnett, whose personal constitution stops with the Tenth Amendment, is conveniently ignorant of the incompatibility of state rights and modern industrialization.

On the racial question, the Governor's views are now well known. "If we start off with the self-evident proposition," Barnett says, "that the whites and colored are different, we will not experience any difficulty in reaching the conclusion that they are not and never can be equal." It was his appointee to the Mississippi Supreme Court, Justice Tom Brady, who became for awhile the metaphysician of the master racists with the publication of the hastily written and scholastically barren *Black Monday* (1955). In turn this was outmoded by *Race and Reason* (1961) by Carleton Putnam, Roosevelt biographer and successful airline executive, become, by his own admission, expert theologian, psychologist, and anthropologist within a two-year period. To the enchantment of Mississippians, Putnam exposed the Franz Boas conspiracy which, he asserted, had held the scientific world in a climate of terror and fear of persecution for half a century. Mississippians did not read the book (they just sent it to their friends, as instructed by the Citizens Council), else they would have discovered that, even by Putnam's logic, the white race was already doomed inasmuch as more than half the country's Negroes lived in integrated situations. But who would argue with the new messiah? With a flourish of trumpets he was brought to Jackson on October 26, 1961 (proclaimed by the Governor as Race and Reason Day) and feted at a $25-a-plate dinner attended by five hundred patriots.

There was no Dickens to point out that there never had been another such day in Mississippi. It could, Barnett believed, "mark the turning point in the South's struggle to preserve the integrity of the white race." Putnam had indeed provided an Article of Faith that Mississippians could live by. Denouncing the "left-wing pseudo-scientists" for creating the fallacy that "has gained complete possession of the Northern and Western mind," he designated Mississippi as "the heartland of the struggle for racial integrity" and in his best Bryan manner exclaimed, "You don't crucify the South on a cross of equalitarian propaganda." Calling on the South to produce more Barnetts, Putnam identified equalitarianism with Communism and segregation with Christianity.

In one respect Putnam's racist argument was not anachronistic. At the very time when the Negro was in the lengthy process of becoming a civilized being, he appeared to be and demonstrably *was* a cultural inferior, carefully trained for that status by every controllable factor in his environment. Faulkner has the Mississippian say: "We got to make him a nigger first. He's got to admit he's a nigger." From birth to death the Negro was exposed to an irresistible pressure for deferential behavior, and when he failed to conform he was driven out or even killed. By and large he played the role of Sambo well, giving little indication of any hope or desire to share in the white man's privileges.

One of the privileges he has seldom had in Mississippi is that of voting. In the twentieth century never so much as 10 per cent and normally less than 5 per cent of the Negro voting population has been allowed to register. Governor Barnett has repeatedly asserted that Negroes in Mississippi just don't want to vote, that they could if they so desired. Since 1954, Mississippi law, Barnett to the contrary, has required the voter applicant to read and write and interpret any section of the state constitution and (since 1960) to be of good moral character and to have his name and address published in a local newspaper for two weeks. At the moment, a substantial Negro vote would embarrass any white candidate in Mississippi. But the future is also plain. As Senator Bilbo once reminded an organizer for the Amalgamated Clothing Workers, "Son, when you can show me that you can control any sizable number of voters in Mississippi, I'll be the damnedest champion you've ever had."

Gradual improvement of white schools has until very recently been shared by the Negroes only to a remote degree. But, as James K. Vardaman had understood, any Negro education spelled the eventual doom of the caste system. There may have been rumblings before, but the summer of 1954 brought a shock from which Mississippi's Old Guard will never recover. Having checked with his retinue of Uncle Toms, Governor Hugh White called in a hundred Negroes to get their anticipated endorsement for "separate but equal" school facilities. But a few young Negro radicals arranged for a caucus the night before the big meeting and after a heated debate carried the timid along with them.

Speaker Walter Sillers opened the momentous conference. Governor White spoke of the amicable race relations of the past. As planned, when the preliminaries were over, Charlie Banks got the floor and argued for the abolition of segregation. Five or six others followed suit. A conservative Negro publisher made a last stand for the old regime but was roundly denounced by a woman delegate as being a classic example of the effects of segregation. In desperation, Sillers called on another known friend of the white man, the Reverend H. H. Humes. As he walked to the front of the room the old minister was the center of all attention. "Gentlemen," he told the Governor and his friends, "you all should not be mad at us. Those were nine *white* men that rendered that decision. Not one colored man had anything to do with it. The real trouble is that you have given us schools too long in which we could study the earth through the floor and the stars through the roof." At this point, Governor White, mumbling that you couldn't trust Negroes any more, called the meeting to an end. It was also the end of an era. "For the first time," one of the delegates later said, "I was really proud to be a Negro in Mississippi."

Yet in the years since 1954 the state's Negroes have made few gains. The Establishment is entrenched so strongly that without the help of external forces (channeled through the federal government) Mississippi Negro leadership is for the short run in a helpless position. For, with varying degrees of enthusiasm, the makers of the orthodoxy—the press, the pulpit, the politicians, the philosophers, and the patriots—have since the Brown decision rushed to the successful defense of their way of life.

Moderation is expressed in the daily newspapers of Greenville, Tupelo, and McComb, and in an occasional weekly; nevertheless, the Mississippi press as a whole mounts vigilant guard upon the closed society. Happy with what a news director of a Jackson television station called their home grown version of news management," the Hederman family newspapers manipulate information with little regard for accuracy or integrity. Negro crime and immorality in the North, Negro complicity in Communism, even Negro support for Barnett are given the headlines day after day. Shotgun blasts fired into a Negro home become a NAACP plot, the assassination of Medgar Evers is turned into a sacrificial offering to rekindle racial unrest, Mississippi is victimized by hate peddlers jealous of the state's economic progress. The Jackson *Clarion-Ledger* makes a revealing historical comparison: "Never was Hitler, nor Mussolini, nor the Mikado, nor even Kaiser Wilhelm attacked so venomously" as Mississippi—which invariably represents the South, with the South always a solid and unfaltering unit. But this leading state newspaper will find it difficult to approach ever again the imagination of its most famous headline, inspired by the arrest of Byron de la Beckwith, scion of an old Delta family, born on the Pacific coast but who had lived in Mississippi for thirty-eight years: "CALIFORNIAN IS CHARGED WITH MURDER OF MEDGAR EVERS."

To such editors and their heavy-banded associates the Fifth Circuit Court becomes "the nine judicial baboons in New Orleans," President Kennedy "regards himself as a Jesus whose infinite wisdom represents mankind's only real hope of salvation," and Ross Barnett is twisted into a modern combination of David, Horatius, and Leonidas. Tougaloo College, a center of integrationist activity, is rechristened "Cancer College," with a new summer course in "Rapid Hate," and the slanderous *Rebel Underground*, having recommended the execution of the President of the United States, emerges as "an innocuous handbill." By March 1963, the Jackson *Daily News* adds up the "price tag" on the federal invasion of Mississippi as coming to $14 million because of 130 bonus accidental deaths on the state's highways attributed to "a frame of mind, an atmosphere of anger, a period of bayonet-point frustration" which lowered the morale of the highway patrol. For the University faculty members who had the temerity to treat James Meredith as a human being, editor Jimmy Ward predicts crushed spirits, bitterness, even self-imposed tragedy.

In times of trial the Jackson papers lose all semblance of perspective. For example, on the day that Judge Sidney Mize ordered Meredith enrolled in the University, the *Daily News* front page carried these headlines:

ROSS RISKS JAIL TO HALT MIXING

Note Bares Negro Plan to Agitate

Hattiesburg Agitation Order [photostat]

We Support Gov. Barnett [editorial]

Negroes Purchased Shot, Says Mayor

President Deplores Shooting in State

Judge Mize Issues Permanent Injunction [bulletin] Meredith Effigy Hanged at Oxford

Barnett During and After Broadcast [pictures]

Moses' Automobile [picture]

Editor's Column: All Loyal Mississippians Support Him [Barnett]

There was still room for a small cartoon about a Mississippi College football game and the index.

The role of the church since 1954 is more difficult to assess than is that of the press. Some churches have taken exceptional action, notably the Mississippi diocese of the Episcopal Church which issued a general call for support of the Supreme Court's decision and eventual integration. And in the past year many preachers and a few ministerial groups have made courageous stands. But the church as a whole has remained loyal to the status quo. Ministers who led the discussion about segregation were for it, prompted no doubt by "an echo from the pew." In annual session, the Mississippi Baptist convention refused to endorse a series of resolutions reaffirming "our intelligent good will toward all men" and calling upon Christians to pray "that we may live consistent with Christian citizenship." A Baptist missionary, second cousin of Governor Barnett, wrote from Nigeria that Mississippians were making her work extremely difficult: "You send us out here to preach that Christ died for all men. Then you make a travesty of our message by refusing to associate with some of them because of the color of their skin. You are supposed to be holding the lifelines for us, and you are twisting them into a noose of racism to strangle our message. Communists do not need to work against the preaching of the Gospel here; you are doing it quite adequately." The missionary's mother expressed regret: "Antonina doesn't understand that Ross has been doing the best he can."

Other groups in Mississippi society, supporters of the orthodoxy, hold a position comparable to their predecessors of the Civil War period. The conservative men of large property holdings considered secession a doubtful though perfectly legal remedy for their troubles; it was a much larger group of active, restless lawyer-politicians, petty planters, and small-town editors, successful enterprisers on the make, who took Mississippi out of the Union in 1861. After World War II another crowd of "new men," bold entrepreneurs enamored as their forefathers had been of the prevailing social order, too busy making money to think deeply about changes bound to accompany progress, pleased with the "right-to-work" principle embedded in the constitution and with a colossal program of state socialism to entice the Yankee carpetbagger industrialist, sat by quietly and acquiesced in the building of the Citizens Council juggernaut.

Constitutional questions, on which so much controversy has centered since 1954, continue to bring a response in keeping with the quality of Mississippi leadership. There seems to be some confusion in the minds of the state's lawyers and jurists as to whether Mississippians must obey the law of the land as interpreted by the federal courts. Dean Robert J. Farley of the Ole Miss law school repeatedly warned in public that lawyers were acting irresponsibly in permitting by their silence the Citizens Council and irreconcilable politicians to interpret the law for them. The chief dereliction, it seems clear, came in *allowing the people of Mississippi to believe that they could get away with an outright defiance of the courts*. "We as Mississippians," declared Justice Brady in 1959, "will not bow down to a court of nine old men whose hearts are as black as their robes." Brady castigated Governor Coleman, who had frowned upon interposition as so much "legal poppycock," as a moderate—"a man who is going to let a little sewage under the door." But the classic statement regarding law and order came in 1963 from the very top of Mount Olympus. Indignant over the "sickening" conduct of Negro parents and ministers in Birmingham in permitting boys and girls to run "afoul" of the law by "using these children for ignoble and loathesome ends and deliberately and contemptuously inciting them to become juvenile delinquents," Governor Barnett declared in a burst of emotion: "What do these degenerates know of freedom? True freedom consists of and is founded upon the observance of law and the power of law to make those who would break the law conform to it. History tells us that freedom can exist only under the protection of constitutional law. These agitators seek to defy constitutional law under the name of freedom." Once again Ross was doing the best he could.

The new legislature convening in January 1962 was met by a request from the Governor to (1) outlaw the Communist party (years before, the FBI had found one Communist in Mississippi), (2) pass "an enforceable sedition act," and (3) compel state employees to take an oath of allegiance to the United States and Mississippi. (Barnett did not explain whether this could be accomplished in a single oath.) In any event, when Mississippi legislators get together their herd instinct drives them to resolving the fate of the world. If they hate Hodding Carter or the President of the United States, or love Elvis Presley, Dizzy Dean, the Mississippi State basketball team, or South Africa, or feel that a former Miss America is an accomplished actress, they are not inhibited from saying so. Senator Hugh Bailey, who had ridden a bull from Canton to Jackson to fulfill a campaign promise, offered a resolution urging the United States to substitute turnip seed for cash in the foreign aid program. Such action, be asserted, "would relieve pressure in this country's economy and give the world's population necessary vitamins, minerals, and bulk." A mere handful of the seed would feed a hundred people and could be mailed overseas for planting.

Legislators spend much of their time devising legal subterfuges to keep the Negro in his place. When it appeared that the number of "smart alecks" telephoning "white ladies" had reached "epidemic stages," the House voted a $10,000 fine and five years imprisonment for cursing into the telephone. Objection to such stiff punishment brought the assurance that judges would know how to use the law. The House unanimously called for a constitutional amendment barring from voting persons guilty of vagrancy, perjury, and child desertion, and concurred in the addition of adultery, fornication, larceny, gambling, and crimes committed with a deadly weapon. A still further addition of habitual drunkenness was defeated when a member suggested that it "might even get some of us." There was some objection, also, to the inclusion of adultery. Reprisal legislation is common, like that bill which the committee chairman said was "concerned with a woman editor who has been writing things which don't go along with the feelings in the community" or another condemning land belonging to Campbell College after Representative McClellan explained, "Jackson has had a cancer in its midst long enough." The cancer will be removed to Mound Bayou in 1964.

One legislator was sorely impressed with the power of the Citizens Council:

> It's hard for us sometimes to consider a bill on its merits if there is any way Bill Simmons [executive secretary of the Citizens Council] can attach an integration tag. For instance, a resolution was introduced in the House to urge a boycott of Memphis stores because some of them have desegregated. I knew it was ridiculous and would merely amuse North Mississippians who habitually shop in Memphis. The resolution came in the same week that four Negroes were fined in court for boycotting Clarksdale stores. Yet the hot eyes of Bill Simmons were watching. If we had voted against the resolution he would have branded us. So there we were, approving a boycott while a Mississippi court was convicting Negroes for doing what we lawmakers were advocating. It just didn't make sense.

As is characteristic of a closed society, the schools, too, are pressured by organized voices of the orthodoxy: the Citizens Council, the American Legion, and the patriotic ladies' groups. A case in point was the withdrawal of a film called "The High Wall," donated to the state by the Anti-Defamation League and shown in Mississippi schools for more than six years. The Citizens Council interpreted the film as teaching "children to pity their prejudiced parents who did not enjoy the enriching experience of intermingling with persons of different racial, ethnic and cultural backgrounds." At the end of the film the Council was saddened to find "Americans and Poles walk arm-in-arm into the setting sun." An "alert state senator" sounded the alarm, a private exhibition was given for Council and Mississippi Sovereignty Commission officials who agreed "The

High Wall" was "unfit for showing to Mississippi school children," and the menace was removed.

The state Daughters of the American Revolution have time and again gone directly to the legislature, predictably with the encouragement of the Governor who comes down hard for cleaning up the books "so that children can be truly informed of the southern way of life." The *Daily News* was acutely disturbed by such "oblique propaganda as 'gives evidence that Negro people have done much to develop themselves.'" The DAR is understandably unhappy when first-graders are no longer exposed to "the story of the squirrel storing nuts," since it "helped to make America a great nation populated by men and women steadfast in their ability to put into effect their early training for adult life." All but the headiest fans of Lord Keynes may look upon such a lament with sympathy. But listen to what the Citizens Council officially suggests for the third and fourth grades:

> God wanted the white people to live alone. And He wanted colored people to live alone. The white men built America for you. White men built America so they could make the rules. George Washington was a brave and honest white man. The white men cut away big forests. The white man has always been kind to the Negro. We do not believe that God wants us to live together. Negro people like to live by themselves. Negroes use their own bathrooms. They do not use white people's bathrooms. The Negro has his own part of town to live in. This is called our Southern Way of Life. Do you know that some people want the Negroes to live with white people? These people want us to be unhappy. They say we must go to school together. They say we must swim together and use the bathroom together. God had made us different. And God knows best. Did you know that our country will grow weak if we mix the races? White men worked hard to build our country. We want to keep it strong and free.

And some recommendations for the fifth and sixth grades:

> The Southern white man has always helped the Negro whenever he could. Southerners were always their best friends. The South went to war to prevent the races from race-mixing. If God had wanted all men to be one color and to be alike, He would not have made the different races. One of the main lessons in the Old Testament of our Bible is that your race should be kept pure. God made different races and put them in different lands. He was satisfied with pure races so man should keep the races pure and be satisfied. BIRDS DO NOT MIX. CHICKENS DO NOT MIX. A friend had 100 white chickens and 100 reds. All the white chickens got to one side of the house, and all the red chickens got on the other side of the house. You probably feel the same way these chickens did whenever you are with people of a different race. God meant it to be that way.

With the makers of the ideology in control and economic opportunity at a minimum, it is not strange that large numbers of the most ambitious Mississippians, the ablest and the most adaptable to change, have left the state year after year. Such constant attrition of potential leadership (proven by the eminence achieved by Mississippi exiles) must be a major reason for the people's unwillingness to discard their ancient folkways. One cannot help speculating as to what degree Mississippi's story would have been more heartening if a sizable proportion of those thousands of bright, perceptive *natural leaders* among the men and women who have left the state had in some miraculous way found it possible to remain.

Some of those who have left had no choice. They were victims of a state now deservedly famous for its incredible past of police brutality and for the harassment, even to death, of those who defy the code. The state retains a good deal of the frontier recklessness toward human life found by William Howard Russell who noted that casual Mississippi conversations had "a smack of manslaughter about them." In the year after the Brown decision, four Negroes were openly slain, with no conviction for any crime; it would almost seem that when these atrocities had served their purpose, murder as an instrument of policy was then put in cold storage for a time.

On March 31, 1963, the Voter Education Project of the Southern Regional Council released a chronological list of sixty-four acts of violence and intimidation against Negroes since January 1961. The thirty-page indictment of man's inhumanity to man, with its accusations of whippings, shootings, murder, and outrageous debasement of the courts, admittedly came from an interested party, but it is characterized by understatement.

Mississippi acts of savagery have often been publicized throughout the world, some beyond their merit. The following examples of harassment by the closed society have been examined with caution and some thoroughness.

For twelve years Eugene Cox and Dr. David Minter, both Southerners, had worked closely together as manager and physician for the white and black families making up the Providence Cooperative, a 2,700-acre farm in Holmes County. On September 27, 1955, at a mass meeting called by leading members of the Citizens Council, Cox and Minter were ordered out of the community, mainly on the basis of evidence recorded in two hours of questioning by Council and county officials of four Negro boys accused of making obscene remarks about a white girl. Allegations of the intermingling of the races at the farm were denied, though it was conceded freely that white and Negro patrons did attend meetings of the credit union together. Threats of violence were made against both men and their families, and, Minter's patients having been intimidated, his medical practice fell off about fifty per cent. An economic boycott was less effective. Professional segregationist Edwin White said, "We just can't afford to have them up there teaching what they are teaching—which will lead to violence unless it is stopped." At the mass assembly Cox admitted his belief that segregation is un-Christian. A planter whose father had been a minister spoke out, "This isn't a Christian meeting." Cox and Minter continued to deny all accusations and offered to make their records available for investigation. White commented, "I do not say these men are Communists, but I do say they are following the Communist line." With threats of arson increasing, and a roadblock arranged by the sheriff, Cox sat up, a rifle across his knees, from midnight to dawn for ten straight nights. Minter stuck it out until July 1956. Cox left for Memphis a month later. In their joint Christmas greeting that year, they recalled: "Only two members of our church wrote to us. A few others have voiced their faith in us, but above these small voices is the frightening SILENCE. It is frightening—not only for us, but for any Christian and American who may wake up some morning to find himself persecuted because of his beliefs, or for unfounded rumors and 'guilt by association.'"

When James Meredith made his painful entry into Ole Miss, the "forgotten man" who had tried to break down the Mississippi education racial barrier without federal aid was languishing in the state penitentiary at Parchman, having been sentenced to a seven-year term for stealing by proxy $25 worth of chicken feed. Much of the evidence points to the conclusion that Clyde Kennard was "framed," though no one seems to know who did it. Born in Hattiesburg, moved to Chicago at twelve, discharged from paratroop service in Korea and Germany in 1952, Kennard meritoriously attended the University of Chicago for three years. Upon the death of his stepfather, he returned to Mississippi to help his mother run a chicken farm in Forrest County. For years he discussed with the president of Mississippi Southern University his possible admission on a voluntary basis. In 1958 he turned down Governor Coleman's offer of education outside the state but obligingly agreed to delay his formal application until after the 1959 Democratic primary. On September 15 he was officially refused admission in a fifteen-minute interview witnessed by the chief investigator for the Sovereignty Commission. Within minutes Kennard was arrested for speeding, then fined for possession of liquor (probably planted) in his car. By

1961 when the Mississippi Supreme Court disposed of this summary justice, Kennard had been convicted as an accessory in the theft of three bags of chicken feed and sentenced to one year's imprisonment for each $3.57 worth of feed allegedly stolen. At most the penalty, assuming guilt, would normally have been ninety days. The illiterate boy who made the theft, if there was one, continued in his job with the feed co-operative.

Though President William D. McCain refused Kennard's application on specious claims of "irregularities" and "questionable moral character, and is alleged to have said that he could do more to "develop honesty, culture, and individual integrity as president of Mississippi Southern than he can in a silly martyrdom for one Negro," Kennard himself refused to believe that McCain "had anything to do with what happened to me." The subsequent career of Clyde Kennard is a sad one. It includes surgery for cancer at the University Hospital in Jackson in June 1962, unconscionable treatment at Parchman in the months following his operation when he was refused periodic checkups recommended by University doctors, the rapid development of his malignancy, an eight-hour operation in the Billings Hospital at the University of Chicago, and his death in the early summer of 1963. Not long before he died, Kennard was planning to return to his chicken farm and, as he saw it, to help Mississippi "co-ordinate" her race relations. One of his last statements was, "I still think there are a few white people of good will in the state and we have to do something to bring this out."

The most likely candidate,in Mississippi for the next Medgar Evers treatment is the president of the state NAACP, Aaron Henry, one-time porter and shoeshine boy in the Old Cotton Bowl Court Hotel in Clarksdale and now owner of a drugstore on Fourth Street. He walks the earth with the sure step and upright carriage of a younger version of another Mississippian, Archie Moore, and he is not likely to be run out of Coahoma County. He does not know how many times the windows in his place of business have been smashed, but the last time, in March 1963, he left for all to see the bricks, the broken glass, and the displays—one of the Declaration of Independence and the other of the Emancipation Proclamation. In 1962 he was convicted of leading a boycott of Clarksdale stores after it had been determined there would be no Negro float in the Christmas parade.

In March, Henry was fined $500 and sentenced to six months' in jail by an eighty-year-old justice of the peace for allegedly molesting a white hitchhiker. According to the *Daily News* reporter, the Bolivar County attorney "during the final arguments, took the Mississippi statute and read to Judge Rowe the disturbing the peace law, explained it to him and told him the maximum sentence and fine." Before defining the sentence, the judge said, "The evidence shows this young man could not have described the interior of the defendant's car unless he was in it." There was no other witness.

When Henry accused the county attorney and police chief of plotting the charge against him, they countered with a libel suit in the Coahoma Circuit Court where the jury awarded them damages of $40,000. All these cases are still in the higher courts. On March 13, 1963, Henry's living room picture window was demolished and his home set afire at two in the morning by gasoline, bombs thrown by two young thugs who said they were "just having fun" and were not aware of being in the Negro section of town. Not only did they admit the bombing, but a filling station attendant heard them planning the attack and commenting afterwards that Henry "was lucky to be alive." The first man tried was acquitted of arson by an all-white jury which deliberated for fifteen minutes, and an identical charge against the other was dropped. One of those involved later asked Henry's forgiveness, saying he had been tricked into the nasty business.

In May 1963 the Henry drugstore was rocked by an explosion which ripped a hole in the roof. Sheriff Ross and Deputy State Fire Marshal Hopkins investigated and found that the blast "was caused by a bolt of lightning." Henry wrote: "I am not really sure as to the cause. The hole on top of the roof is much smaller than the rupture in the ceiling. The experts I have talked with contend that lightning does not act that way." It would appear that Henry is not only courageous but more literate than his opposition.

Harassment by the closed society can be savage even when it is not violent. Twenty-eight young Methodist ministers, feeling that they had "a particular obligation to speak," issued by way of the *Mississippi Methodist Advocate* of January 1963 a "Born of Conviction" statement that still has the state and church in an uproar. They affirmed their belief in the freedom of the pulpit, the brotherhood of man, an unalterable opposition to the closing of the public schools, and an unflinching antagonism toward Communism. Within two weeks the Mississippi Association of Methodist Ministers and Laymen, displaying more churchmanship than religion, had repudiated the "Born of Conviction" pastors, submitted their own "declaration of conscience on racial matters" (drawn up by Medford Evans, Citizens Council consultant, and published in the January issue of the Citizen), and called for a secret referendum on whether or not Methodists wanted their church integrated. Later these conservatives declared integration a "crime against God." The lament of one of the young ministers, that "The power clique which dominates the conference has aligned itself with the Methodist Ministers and Laymen and with the Citizens Council," was corroborated by subsequent events.

The closed society battered the outspoken young preachers upon the anvil of public opinion. By summer ten had left the state, and at least half a dozen more were shifted to urban pulpits. At least half volunteered the feeling that they had not been sufficiently supported by their superintendents and their bishop. Methodists in general, with professional assistance, were reflecting an opinion that had driven from Mississippi sixty-eight of their seminary-trained men since 1954. Dr. W. B. Selah, for eighteen years pastor of the largest Methodist congregation in the state, who had supported the "Born of Conviction" statement and had declared "there can be no color bar in a Christian church," resigned in protest when five Negroes were refused admission to his church.

The Mississippi Advisory Committee to the United States Commission on Civil Rights made, in January 1963, a report on the administration of justice within the state. In a period of fourteen months it had held six open meetings in which a hundred or so Mississippians had testified, though "actively opposed by agents and instrumentalities of the State Government." The legislature in 1960 "passed an act," the committee stated, "to intimidate persons who might wish to assert their rights as citizens by altering the requirement of proof for prosecution of perjury solely in cases where the defendant has testified before this Committee."

In its published findings, the committee declared that "in all important areas of citizenship, a Negro in Mississippi receives substantially less than his due consideration as an American and as a Mississippian." They found that "a pattern exists in our State that leads to the denial of Constitutional rights and, in some instances, to brutality and terror. From the moment a Negro adult is hailed as 'boy' or 'girl' by a police officer, through his arrest, detention, trial—during which his Negro lawyer is treated with contemptuous familiarity by the judge and other officers of the court—and eventual imprisonment, he is treated with a pernicious difference. This difference is incompatible with Christian ideals about the dignity of man and with principles of Anglo-Saxon criminal law." Declaring that "justice under law is not guaranteed for the Negro in Mississippi in the way that it is for the white man," the committee reported that "42.3% of the citizens of this State must either accept an inferior station in life and an attitude of servility or endanger themselves and their families by protesting. We find that terror hangs over the Negro in Mississippi and is an expectancy for those who refuse to accept their color as a badge of inferiority; and terrorism has no proper place in the American form of government." The committee found that "in general the press is failing to meet its obligation to our society. The people of Mississippi are largely unaware of the extent of illegal official violence and the press is partly to blame. . . . When a State disregards a large segment of its population, the Federal Government is compelled to intervene in behalf of the victims."

And the federal government has intervened at the state's best known institution of higher learning, the University of Mississippi. The University has had its moments of greatness, its faculty and administrators of integrity and virtue, and a long history of genteel poverty. In the presidency of Alfred B. Butts (1935–1946) Ole Miss began a precarious climb from the depths of depression despair and the shame of the Bilbo spoliation. For at least a decade after World War II, under the leadership of Chancellor John D. Williams, the University seemed on the verge of living up to the dreams and hopes of its founders and directors of exactly a century before. A tremendous building program on the already beautiful, wooded campus, an expansion of libraries and laboratories, the addition of new departments, and, most exciting of all, the gathering together of an excellent faculty dedicated to good teaching and fruitful research, all of these developments and more were taking place. The new chancellor was adept not only at selling the University to the people but in making it an integral part of many schemes designed to raise the horizons of a long submerged society.

It was increasingly evident in the middle fifties, however, that changes were taking place in the state that would adversely affect the University. In a series of crises from Kershaw (1955) to Kerciu (1963), the administration became more and more appeasement-minded, more and more involved (like a woman constantly professing her virtue) in presenting the Ole Miss story to the state as if it were a bar of soap.

More serious was a 1955 edict of the Board of Trustees requiring the screening of all speakers brought to the campus, a ruling steadfastly opposed by the chancellor at its inception but stoutly defended some years later when he refused even to pass along to the Board a petition of the AAUP calling for an end to the screening. A clergyman was turned away from Religious Emphasis Week when it became known that he had contributed to the NAACP, and the incoming president of the Southern Historical Association was paid his full fee for not delivering a history lecture after the shocking disclosure that his wife had written in the *Saturday Evening Post* of her teaching experiences with Negro students in Atlanta.

The handling of absurd charges of apostasy and subversion against fourteen members of the University community in 1958 was brought off expeditiously and with a flair for public relations. Faculty members involved in this tempest, which was kept going in the press for almost a year, were asked to remain silent (which most of them did) while the chancellor affirmed his belief in the Bible, an omnipotent God, immortality of the soul, state sovereignty, segregation, and the right of private property. In August 1959 the Board dismissed the allegations against the chancellor and the faculty and stated its policy that "there should prevail at our universities and colleges an atmosphere of freedom in their research, teaching programs and services and that there should be no political or subversive propagandizing in the academic program."

In the past year or so the University of Mississippi has desperately needed the help of all those concerned with its welfare, but, far from being consulted, these friends have been told that things were under control, the situation was returning to normal, enrollment was holding up in great style, just a few professors were leaving. On the anniversary of the insurrection, the director of the University News Service insulted "some few professors" by accusing them of having leveled "bitter attacks" against it to "make national headlines" for the purpose of securing better positions, and it belittled the intelligence of those who remained by stating that "the vast majority" of these had refused more lucrative job offers elsewhere. In a state where higher education is expendable, this bowing before and in fact anticipating every wind may have had a soothing effect on the legislature, but it also indicated a chronic inability to face reality. After all, General Ulysses S. Grant has been the only man in history to make a positive decision not to destroy the University.

Until 1962 the University successfully avoided integration. In that year, on June 26, almost exactly eighteen months after he had first written to the registrar, James Howard Meredith, the "man with a mission and with a nervous stomach," was ordered admitted to the University of Mississippi. Speaking for the Fifth Circuit Court in New Orleans Judge John Minor Wisdom later said that "A full review of the record leads the Court inescapably to the conclusion that from the moment the defendants discovered Meredith was a Negro they engaged in a carefully calculated campaign of delay, harassment, and masterly inactivity. It was a defense designed to discourage and defeat by evasion tactics which would have been a credit, to Quintus Fabius Maximus." Tartly reprimanding Judge Sidney Mize of the United States District Court for the Southern District of Mississippi for "Continuances of doubtful propriety and unreasonably long delays," Judge Wisdom viewed the case as one "tried below and argued here in the eerie atmosphere of never-never land." He might have added, of the closed society." The contention of the Board of Trustees and of University officials, accepted as fact by Judge Mize, "that the University is not a racially segregated institution" and that "the state has no policy of segregation ... defies history and common knowledge." There was nothing in the case "reaching the dignity of proof" to make the court think otherwise. "We find that James Meredith's application for transfer to the University of Mississippi was turned down solely because he was a Negro."

Many members of the faculty expressed dismay when Ole Miss officials made uncalled-for affirmations which the court deemed frivolous and when they followed "a determined policy of discrimination by harassment" and assigned as a reason for rejecting Meredith "a trumped-up excuse without any basis except to discriminate." It was hard, too, to comprehend why an administrator would deny that "he understands and interprets the policy of the State of Mississippi as being that negroes and whites are educated in separate institutions of higher learning." More than a hundred years ago Chancellor F. A. P. Barnard had declared that the University's destiny was "to stamp upon the intellectual character of Mississippi the impress it is to wear. . . . "

From September 13, 1962, when Mississippi's long court battle against Meredith reached "the end of the road" in Judge Mize's sweeping injunction and Governor Barnett read his antiquarian interposition proclamation, it was evident to all that the showdown was imminent. In, those last hectic days the "power structure" of the state made a rather impressive attempt to control the Barnett juggernaut, but it was too late, and the people were largely unaware of the effort. Moderate statements by Oxford ministers appeared in the Memphis but not the Jackson papers which thundered about taking note "of those who stand with courage in an hour of crisis." The closed society was operating efficiently and almost automatically, as it does in times of great stress, as if it were some malicious Frankenstein monster.

On the Ole Miss campus was circulated a broadside, *The Liberty Bulletin*, urging students to "Place yourself under the direction of Gov. Barnett. Do not engage yourself in force or violence unless he calls for it." *Clarion-Ledger* columnist Hills reported that "the governor will watch with a jaundiced eye any attempt to apply punitive action against Mississippi's patriots. College presidents are standing ready to fight alongside the governor, or else."

In the upper house of the legislature on September 25, Senator E. K. Collins arose to remark, "We must win this fight regardless of the cost in time, effort, money and in human lives." Senator Hayden Campbell thought "they would have to open the doors to murder and rape." Senator Hilbun barked that "these are the same people who won't let our children pray in school." In Washington, Senator Eastland was sure that the next few days would "determine whether a judicial tyranny as black and hideous as any in history exists in the United States."

On Thursday, September 27, the *Clarion-Ledger* carried a sensational headline to the effect that a "gunbattle was possible at the University. Representative Walter Hester told the UPI it was "likely" that state officials would attempt to fight off the marshals if they tried to enroll Meredith, but he did not prophesy an all-out insurrection. The situation was "extremely tense and there are some people who don't mind dying for an honorable cause." Either Senator McLaurin or Senator Yarbrough told Senator Lambert that "they were going to provoke the Kennedys into sending troops into Mississippi." Months later,

Attorney General Patterson called McLaurin and the "CC & Co." a "little band of would-be ruthless dictators seeking to promote all-out riot and bloodshed on the campus by encouraging the people of Mississippi to pick up their rifles, shotguns and slingshots and go to fight it out with the armed forces of the United States." This could result only in "bloodshed, death, destruction and heartaches."

Barnett talked about jailing any federal officer attempting to arrest a state official. The *Daily News* was accused by the campus paper, the *Mississippian*, of distortion, fabrication, "screaming and sensational stories." On the day of the Ole Miss-Vanderbilt football game the hysteria whipped up in Jackson was unbelievable. The press and radio added their bluster to the normal uproar of a conference game. At the half-time ceremonies that night when he still might have turned the populace aside from its madness, the Governor achieved his greatest triumph of oratorical lunacy: "I love Mississippi—I love her people—I love her customs!" Understandably, the man was overcome by his own hoarse eloquence and the reasonless, incoherent, delirious response. He could not go on. The people were bewildered. Television carried the infection statewide, and former Major General Edwin Walker was on his way to Oxford.

The propaganda machine never faltered. The next day, the Sunday that began so peacefully, a joint legislative committee pronounced nine frivolous reasons for denying Meredith admission and cunningly announced that his registration would jeopardize the accreditation of the University to the point of expulsion from the Southern Association of Colleges. In the afternoon and early evening, fatigued students were driving back to the campus, listening to their blaring radios tuned to the appeals of the Citizens Council to "form a human wall around the mansion" to protect the Governor from arrest by federal marshals. Thousands of citizens swarmed the streets of Jackson. Few knew that the Governor, called by an Episcopal priest the "living symbol of lawlessness," had already sold out his closest advisers. Word came that planeloads of marshals had flown out of Memphis. For some time their destination was in doubt. Unknown to most Mississippians, Meredith was, before supper, unpacking his bag in his room in Baxter Hall on the Ole Miss campus.

It was impossible that he could stay without help from the federal government. When Mississippi officials blocked by physical might on four separate occasions Meredith's court-ordered enrollment, and the Fifth Circuit Court wearily acknowledged that it had come to the end of its resources, the President was faced with the alternative of acceptance of the breakdown of law or the employment of force. The admission of Meredith was not negotiable. Kennedy performed his constitutional obligation in the same spirit George Washington had exhibited in the Whisky Rebellion. Having apparently learned the lesson of Little Rock, he insisted upon the use of civilian federal marshals rather than paratroopers. Certainly there had been no stated objection to marshals accompanying Meredith on those expeditions when they had been overcome by superior state power. Whatever "deals" he may have made with the Governor behind the scenes, the President gently and eloquently appealed to the patriotism and sense of sportsmanship of Mississippi citizens in asking them to obey unpopular court decrees. But former Major General Walker having called for 10,000 volunteers to go to the aid of Barnett, and it being general knowledge that hundreds and perhaps thousands were converging on Oxford, there would have been a serious evasion of responsibility had the Army high command not prepared for the emergency. Troops were moved to Memphis. The President earnestly hoped that the job could be done by civilians, and the United States Army was not ordered to the University of Mississippi until it became evident that the marshals were fighting for their lives, and the Army's first contingent arrived just in time to prevent a disaster.

From the arrival of the marshals at the Lyceum Building shortly before five o'clock until the firing of the tear gas at eight, it became increasingly apparent that there was a serious lack of liaison between federal and state officials on the scene. At six the chancellor (at this time not much more than a spectator himself) believed the deal had been made and the game would have to be played out, and the gathering students and faculty were so informed. By, seven all observers knew that for whatever reason, the Mississippi Highway Patrol had abandoned its enforcement of law and order and was in fact in some cases encouraging the restless crowd to demonstrate against the marshals. Twice these agents of the federal government donned their masks as the crowd closed in. The campus chief of police and four highway patrolmen had moved back part of the surly crowd (which promptly surged forward again when the officers left that part of the scene) and were achieving some little success in front of the Lyceum Building when the marshals opened fire with gas and drove what almost instantly became a bowling mob back to the Confederate monument. Whether Chief Marshal McShane was justified in giving the order to fire at precisely the moment he did is a question for the professionals to answer. It is relevant, however, that two score of faculty members and their wives later testified that the marshals had undergone for at least an hour a constant harassment of obscene language and an increasingly heavy barrage of lighted cigarette butts, stones, bottles, pieces of pipe, and even acid. It is a small matter whether the gas should have come fifteen minutes earlier or later, but rather ironic that a full-scale insurrection should get underway at the exact moment that the President was appealing to Mississippians for fair play in the name of Lucius Quintus Cincinnatus Lamar.

Before the work was done that night the Army brought more troops to Mississippi than General Sherman had had in the environs of Oxford exactly a hundred years before. Several hundred reporters soon concentrated on the Mississippi campus to ferret out the facts about what actually had taken place and to inquire into the background for the state's turmoil. By and large the reportage was accurate and the interpretation sound and temperate. Those who have wished to know have had spread before them a reasonably trustworthy record of events.

This is true for all the world except Mississippi. With its long history of being on the defensive against outside criticism and a predisposition to believe their own leaders can do no wrong, the people have been almost completely sold on a palpable and cynical hoax. The closed society immediately projected (in fact, it had foreshadowed) the orthodox version that the insurrection resulted from federal encroachment, deliberately planned by the Kennedys and callously incited by McShane when he called for tear gas. What did happen in front of the Lyceum Building in that crucial hour before eight o'clock on the night of September 30? Truth cries out that the orthodox Mississippi view is false, that cleverness in shifting the culpability for defiance of law from those creating the violence to those enforcing the law could succeed only among a people suffering from a touch of paranoia.

The genesis of the deception which shifted the blame for the insurrection from Mississippians to federal officials came from the University administration. A singularly inaccurate story blaming the "trigger-happy, amateurish, incompetent" marshals and suggesting examples of diabolical brutality toward male and female students was in the hands of Barnett and Eastland within an hour or so of the firing of the gas. These opportunists took up and grossly exaggerated the cry and called for state and federal investigations. By October 2, David Lawrence was to devote his syndicated column to the "official" view of the University. Long after it was made abundantly clear that many faculty members had witnessed the inception of the riot and knew for a certainty about the fraud against the federal government, the administration did not deviate from its original position but, on the contrary, continued to search for evidence condemning the marshals.

On the morning of October 1, Governor Barnett ordered the Mississippi flag at half-mast because "there had been an invasion of our state resulting in blood." The riot, he said, had been touched off by those "inexperienced, nervous and trigger-happy" marshals who had "deliberately inflamed" the people "In order that the resulting resistance can be cited as justification for military force against a sovereign state." Next day the *Clarion-Ledger* headline, "Eastland, Others Charge [3/8 in.]/Marshals Set Off Ole Miss Rioting [7/8 in.]" was serenity itself compared to a featured column which elaborated the official view: "Our state is labeled insurrectionist because it does not care to be negroid in totality." The columnist did admit a temporary defeat: "So watch the peace-lovers come to the fore, grab a nigger-neck and start bellowing brother love. The Mississippi Junior Chamber of Commerce distributed almost a half million copies of a 24-page pamphlet entitled *Oxford: A Warning for Americans*, which put the blame for the insurrection squarely on the shoulders of John and Robert Kennedy. The most specious implication of the pamphlet was that Meredith would have been allowed to enroll peacefully if only the Attorney General had awaited "the completion of the judicial processes, most unlikely result in a state which had already indulged in so much legal quackery and whose Governor had made it so evident that he would never accept the desegregation of the University. John Satterfield, probable author of the pamphlet and certainly an intimate counselor of Barnett, was now apparently defending his own bad advice which in part came straight from John C. Calhoun. Satterfield has tried to place the mantle of respectability on Barnett's unlawful conduct and to cast doubt on the legality an propriety of the United States government's actions. He threw his weight as past president of the American Bar Association and prime mover in the Citizens Council into the intellectual propaganda barrage directed at Mississippians, who were unlikely anyhow to pay attention to the statement made on October 2 by the incumbent president of the ABA: "The paramount issue was whether or not the judgment of the court was to be upheld. The executive branch had a clear duty to see that the courts were sustained."

Mr. Satterfield maintained an Olympian objectivity compared to Judge W. M. O'Barr, who in his charge to the LaFayette County grand jury investigating the death of two persons on the night of the insurrection, spoke of the United States Attorney General as "stupid little brother" and described the Supreme Court as made up of "political greedy old men" who "together with the hungry, mad, ruthless, ungodly, power-mad men [in Washington] would change this government from a democracy to a totalitarian dictatorship." The grand jury responded appropriately with an indictment of McShane for precipitating the riot, and for good measure taunted University professors (who had previously defended the marshals) for talking too much.

Support for the state administration came, too, just one month after the insurrection, from Mississippi's Women for Constitutional Government. One of the state's more active groups, they were assembled in Jackson by the sister of the speaker of the House of Representatives to adopt a "bill of grievances" against the "unwarranted and unlawful use of military force" and the alleged violation of Mississippians' civil rights resulting from "the collusion of the President of the United States, the Justice Department, and the Federal courts." The high-flown language of "the thousand angry women" obscured, for Mississippians at least, their exquisitely imaginative account of what had taken place at the University.

In the months after the insurrection, many engaged in the pleasant pastime of guessing whether the Governor was at the moment taking instructions from the "resistance to the death" counselors (the White Muslim clique in the Citizens Council) or from the more cautious who, as one observer put it, had planned only a little riot, who didn't really want to see anybody killed. The Council sent up trial balloons suggesting the closing of the University, called upon faculty moderates (to Simmons, "gutless liberals") to accept segregation or resign, and conducted a postcard campaign directing the Board to fire "quislings and scalawags [who] betray our state and our people in the time of crisis." The extent of the Council's responsibility for open defiance of University authorities by extremist students who returned from weekends at home with suitcases filled with cherry bombs and minds filled with rebellion is still an open question. The Oxford council, whose leaders were dedicated if not brilliant, distributed a mimeographed list of faculty members who were to be harassed with anonymous telephone calls—which did cause some inconvenience because the sleeping habits of the daring dialers did not mesh with those of their victims.

The Mississippi Municipal Association prepared a model speech to be used in winning friends and thwarting enemies. After touching lightly on the notion that court decisions, after all, are not the law of the land and warning of the danger of centralization, the orator was then to rise eloquently to the defense of Mississippi's official conduct: "This action is not a defiance of the law or the courts. Such action is an exercise of the heritage of freedom and liberty under the law preserved for us by our fathers." Although it was not suggested, the more gifted ambassadors could also have sung some lines from the "Ballad of the Ole Miss Invasion":

> They came rolling down from Memphis and dropping from the skies
> With bayonets for our bellies and tear gas for our eyes
> Some resisted them with brickbats, while others ran and hid,
> Some tangled with the marshals—who can blame them if they did?

For months it was believed that the General Legislative Investigating Committee would quietly abandon its inquiry into the insurrection as it ran into more and more unpalatable material. Having sent investigators from Washington, Senator Stennis made no report and Senator Eastland shifted his effort to the collection of tall tales by disgruntled students against their instructors. The Mississippi Senate of course did not need facts to plead with the country to "join our State in defiance of all who would destroy our freedoms, heritage and constitutional rights." Only one senator called for secession, a few more demanded Kennedy's impeachment, while others galloped up and down the land to warn their countrymen of the coming of the orange-jackets, those federal fiends whose savage brutalities at Oxford had "stopped short of Nazi atrocities only in that there were no deaths."

The legislative committee took six months to put together from the sworn statements of more than ninety witnesses its masterpiece of sententious fiction. For reasons never explained, faculty witnesses and even legislators who had been at Ole Miss with the federalized national guard had not been called upon to testify. There was no minority report. How scores of the world's crack reporters had been kept from seeing the blundering and the repeated brutalities and "planned physical torture" of the marshals, the women students bit by projectiles fired at point-blank range, the deliberate gassing of seven dormitories, the "torture slab," the army truck set on fire by "a folded paper airplane," and dozens of other Alice-in-Wonderland concoctions will remain one of the mysteries of twentieth-century journalism. It was the sad commentary of an eyewitness that the "young gentlemen of the New Confederacy," who were able to glorify insurrectionist conduct as "freedom fighters" in the "Brick and Bottle Brigade"—attacking the armed forces of their own country—would have small compunction about lying to a legislative investigating committee, especially one that made perfectly clear what it wanted to hear.

The legislative report was "verified" in advance by a documentary film, "Oxford, USA," depicting "how the federal government violated the constitution in the invasion of Mississippi last fall." Just before he sold three copies to the Sovereignty Commission for almost $7,000, the producer asserted the picture was "based strictly on the Constitution" and had been endorsed by Governors Barnett and Wallace. According to billboard advertising, it "EXPOSES FEDERAL ATROCITIES." Actually, about half of the fifty-minute extravaganza is taken up with poorly filmed statements from Barnett, Johnson, Attorney General Patterson, Chief of the Highway Patrol Birdsong, and a legislator who makes some disparaging and untrue remarks about the University and Meredith. The opening action shot shows motorized troops moving into Oxford, which they did—about eight hours after the beginning of the insurrection. By implication the viewer gets the impression that marshals had fired shotguns (which they did not have) at innocent students and even that they had killed the French reporter. Altogether the film is a shabby conglomeration of falsehood, distortion, and political dissemblance unlikely to convince the fair-minded who may be left in the membership of the Citizens Council.

The people of Mississippi have thus once again been victimized, this time by a gigantic hoax perpetrated on them by their own timeserving leaders whose sense of loyalty is only to the false orthodoxy of the closed society.

The closed society is never the absolute society. There always have been and there always will be the dissenters, the doubters who point to the road not taken. In the past year more than fifty professors have departed from the University of Mississippi, many of them literally driven from the state. The best of them, particularly the native Mississippians, would have remained if there had been any prospect of an atmosphere of freedom or a decent chance to fight for one.

No, the closed society is not absolute. In Mississippi there are legislators, editors, lawyers, labor leaders, educators, and ordinary citizens who sometimes protest against the prevailing orthodoxy. The day that Barnett let loose his interposition blast, Ira Harkey pointed out in the Pascagoula *Chronicle* that it was not the Kennedys but "the United States of America, democracy itself, the whole of humanity" that was making demands upon Mississippi. In a series of five short, logical articles, Representative Karl Wiesenburg demonstrated conclusively that Barnett's course was "the road to riot," that the Governor had violated his oath of Office, that the bloodshed on September 30 was the "price of defiance," and that states have responsibilities as well as rights. The *Mississippi Methodist Advocate* accepted for the church part of the guilt for the riot.

Three days after the insurrection, the Ole Miss chapter of the American Association of University Professors adopted a ringing statement protesting the fraud against the marshals. Without a campaign in its favor more than seventy faculty members signed the document as their way of "standing up to be counted." A professor of anthropology made his protest by putting into writing the conclusions of those in his profession concerning the validity of Putnam's *Race and Reason*, and this was serialized in the Pascagoula *Chronicle*. The exemplary conduct of more than 3,000 federalized Mississippi national guardsmen is worth the scrutiny and praise of all Americans. General W. P. Wilson said, "There were absolutely no incidents of any individual wilfully refusing to report for mobilization." George Fielding Eliot paid high tribute to the state guard: "In its ranks are men who, as citizens, share some of the views and even the prejudices of their fellow Mississippians. But when the call to duty came, they laid all else aside. After that they were soldiers of the United States, summoned by the President to aid in enforcing the laws of the Union, as the Constitution provides." One guardsman who had suffered rough treatment at the hands of the hoodlums, went right to the heart of the matter: "It was just the matter of an oath I took."

There are many thousands of "men of good will" in Mississippi, mild-mannered people for the most part, who in their day-to-day affairs do what they can to ameliorate the difficult conditions imposed upon their fellowmen by the closed society. But because of a strong desire to live in peace or because of one kind or another of fear, these men will not openly protest what they know in their hearts are gross evils all about them. These are the individuals who, when one of their own number speaks out or in some little way defies the orthodoxy and is pilloried as a result, shrug their shoulders and say, "Well, he asked for it."

Men of good will are not enough. In his article in the *Saturday Evening Post* after the riot, John Faulkner professed surprise at a plea to return to law and order: "this to us, the responsible people of Oxford, who raised no finger against any man." In high indignation he refused to see the need for penitence: "If all the sin I have to answer for is my part in bringing on what happened here Sunday and Monday, then I relinquish my place to someone more needful of forgiveness than I." Perhaps Mr. Faulkner said more than he intended, perhaps he was speaking for all the good men who to whatever degree had abandoned the feeling of accountability for conditions in Mississippi. These same men were shocked to learn, probably at Leslie's drugstore, the price of defiance as well as the fact that some of their neighbors were throwing rocks at other neighbors in the uniform of the United States government. But they were not moved by the riot—they were solidified. They had forgotten, if they had ever known, that it was not Gavin Stevens who had prevented the lynching of Lucas Beauchamp, but Miss Habersbam, Chick Mallison, and Aleck Sander.

The more embattled the closed society becomes, the more monolithic, the more corrupt, and the more willing to engage in double-think and double-talk. There is Mississippi's institutionalized hypocrisy that the Negro can freely vote and freely attend the university of his choice. There is the casuistry of Governor Barnett that he is preserving law and order and upholding the Constitution by physically obstructing the execution of an explicit directive of the Fifth Circuit Court of Appeals of the United States. There is the legislature shamefully passing laws which the judges "will know how to handle" or for the purpose of "getting, certain individuals. The idea that this is a nation of laws and not of men, constantly reiterated within the state, has a hollow ring in Mississippi. How few of its leaders can come into court with clean hands!

Hostility to authority and disrespect for law are commonplace in Mississippi. How could it be otherwise in a state which tolerates the cynical disregard of prohibition and collects the black-market tax? How can anything else be expected when the state itself brazenly tells the world it has achieved "separate but equal" school facilities, when in 1959–1960 local school expenditures were $81.86 for the white child as against $21.77 for the colored? Or when, as in 1951, the county superintendents of education, looking greedily toward the allocation of equalization funds, reported 895,779 children of educable age (6–20) while the United States census of 1950 listed the number of children from 5 to 19 as only 651,600? What respect can there be for the legal process when one standard of justice prevails when a Negro commits a crime against a Negro, another when a Negro commits a crime against a white, still another when a white commits a crime against a white, and a fourth when a white commits a crime against a Negro?

What can be said about the morality of a social order that sends a teen-age colored girl to a long term in an institution for delinquents because, by walking from school to the courthouse, she is held to have violated an injunction against demonstrations? And, when questioned, justifies the exorbitant penalty on the basis of previous abortions—which up to the time of her sentence the society had ignored? Which is immoral, the girl or the society?

In spite of the closed society the Negro has made *some* gains since his emancipation a century ago. In the same period, the white man, determined to defend his way of life at all costs, has compromised his old virtues, his integrity, his once unassailable character. He has so corrupted the language itself that he says one thing while meaning another. He no longer has freedom of choice in the realm of ideas because they must first be harmonized with the orthodoxy. New currents of thought he automatically distrusts, and if they clash with the prevailing wisdom he ruthlessly rules them out. He cannot allow himself the luxury of thinking about a problem on its merits. In spite of what he claims, the white Mississippian is not even conservative—he is merely negative. He grows up being against most things other men at least have the pleasure of arguing about. All his life he spends on the defensive. The most he can hope for is to put up a good fight before losing. This is the Mississippi way, this is the Mississippi heritage. It will ever be thus as long as the closed society endures.

Although there have been moments of enlightenment, the spiritual secession of Mississippi from history has never ended. For more than a century Mississippians have refused to be bound by the national will. Perhaps this recalcitrance could be borne with in the past, as have been many other excesses of democracy. But with the sanctuary provided by the oceans gone, the national interest, the instinct for survival, demand discipline. They demand also that attitudes or "principles" growing out of racial situations not be allowed to intrude themselves into the country's policy making decisions. Since Reconstruction Mississippians have had no real reason to believe that they were not free to handle the race question as they wished, without meaningful interference from the federal government; and, when they now discover that all their bluster and subterfuge and intransigence will avail them nothing, they have little to fall back on except blind rage and fierce hatred.

In committing itself to the defense of the biracial system, Mississippi has erected a totalitarian society which to the present moment has eliminated the ordinary processes by which change may be channeled. Through its police power, coercion and force prevail, instead of accommodation, and the result is social paralysis. Thus, the Mississippian who prides himself on his individuality in reality lives in a climate where nonconformity is forbidden, where the white man is not free, where he does not dare to express a deviating opinion without looking over his shoulder. Not only is the black man not allowed to forget that he is a nigger, but the white moderate must distinctly understand that he is a "nigger-lover."

Mississippi has long been a hyperorthodox social order in which the individual has no option except to be loyal to the will of the white majority. And the white majority has subscribed to an inflexible philosophy which is not based on fact, logic, or reason. Nonwhite Mississippians and all others are outlanders. Close contiguity with a large repressed population and fear of what these "inferior" people might do have held the society near the point of unanimity. Especially in times of stress the orthodoxy becomes more rigid, more removed from reality, and the conformity demanded to it more extreme. Today the advocacy or even the recognition of the inevitability of change becomes a social felony, or worse. Mississippi is the way it is not because of its views on the Negro—here it is simply "the South exaggerated"—but because of its closed society, its refusal to allow freedom of inquiry or to tolerate "error of opinion." The social order that refuses to conform to national standards insists upon strict conformity at home. While complaining of its own persecuted minority station in the United States, it rarely considers the Negro minority as having rights in Mississippi.

Perhaps the greatest tragedy of the closed society is the refusal of its citizens to believe that there is any view other than the orthodox. In recent years there has been a hardening attitude among college students who do not want to hear the other side. In such a twilight of nondiscussion, minds not only do not grow tough, they do not grow at all. Intelligent men with ideas are isolated from the rest of the community, and what little interracial communication existed in the past is now destroyed. One reason the Ole Miss faculty failed to protest an ugly situation before the insurrection was that through one means or another freedom of speech had long since been curtailed, This was at least a partial cause for from eight to ten members of the history department leaving in the two years *before* the troubles of last year. The jolt of the violence on the campus and the obvious fraud against the federal government initiated a spurt of resistance to ignorance, stupidity, and conformity. For the moment many of the faculty developed a healthy scorn for expediency and security. In the light of Mississippi's history it was probably already too late to expect anything more than an occasional stand, such as that put up by the ministers who were willing to count the cost and pay the price. With the great silence from the men of good will, and the disposition of the good people to let things run their courage, there can be little hope for anything constructive in Mississippi in the next decade.

It can be argued that in the history of the United States democracy has produced great leaders in great crises. Sad as it may be, the opposite has been true in Mississippi. As yet there is little evidence that the society of the closed mind will ever possess the moral resources to reform itself, or the capacity for self-examination, or even the tolerance of self-examination. Inasmuch as a nation marching swiftly in the direction of the fulfillment of the promise of the Declaration of Independence and the Emancipation Proclamation is at the same time fighting for survival against Communism, it will not much longer indulge the frustration of its will. Nevertheless, it would seem that for the foreseeable future the people of Mississippi will plod along the troubled road of resistance, violence, anguish, and injustice, moving slowly until engulfed in the predictable cataclysm.

And yet, in spite of all that has been presented in this paper, it seems inescapable that Mississippians one day will drop the mockery of the late Confederacy and resume their obligations as Americans. It is just that there is small reason to believe that they will somehow develop the capability to do it themselves, to do it, as William Faulkner said, in time. If not, the closed society will become the open society with the massive aid of the country as a whole, backed by the power and authority of the federal government.

Mr. Silver is professor of history at the University of Mississippi.

UNIT 11-3

THE GENERAL CONDITION OF THE MISSISSIPPI NEGRO

This paper is a report published by the Student Nonviolent Coordinating Committee. It is general and extensive in scope rather than specific and detailed. The report's purpose is threefold:

1. To give SNCC's Mississippi field workers a handy reference source detailing statistically some of the general facts relating to the status of the Negro in Mississippi,
2. To indicate the dire necessity for support of community centers and county workers, and
3. To serve as a guideline for more detailed studies to be made in the near future.

In this study, the term "nonwhite people" is used instead of the term "Negro" in many instances. Because of the high proportion of Negroes in the nonwhite category, it is not a distortion to use data that refers to "nonwhites" as data that refers particularly to Negroes. In 1960, in Mississippi, 99.6 percent of the nonwhite population was Negro, and 99.7 percent of the nonwhite farm operators were Negroes.

STUDENT NONVIOLENT COORDINATING COMMITTEE
6 RAYMOND STREET, N.W.
ATLANTA, GEORGIA
688–0331

October, 1963 Labor Donated

PERTINENT BACKGROUND DATA

GROWTH IN THE POPULATION, 1940–1960

NUMBER AND PROPORTION

915,722 Negroes constituted, in 1960, roughly 42% of the total 2,178,000 population in Mississippi. Between 1940 and 1960, the total population remained nearly the same (percent change: –0.2), with a more than 7% decrease in the Negro population compared with an increase of more than 6% among the non-Negro population. (See Chart 1 and Table 1)

Although birth rates among Negroes have been consistently higher than those among whites, mortality rates are higher, average life expectancy is lower and migration out of the state is considerably higher among Negroes than among whites.

BIRTH RATES

The higher birth rates among Negroes, in comparison with whites, are shown in Table 2. In 1949, the rate per 1,000 among the Negro population was 34.8, compared with 21.8 among whites. Since 1945 there has been a significant rise in the birth rate for Negroes. During the depression '30s, sharp declines in birth rates occurred among both Negroes and whites. (Chart 2)

DEATH RATES

Death rates among Negroes continue to be higher than the rates for whites, though the difference in the rates has consistently narrowed. (Table 3) It it still a fact, however, that the death rate among Negroes today is not as low as it was for whites in 1913, the first year for which we have death rate data. This is largely a reflection of the continued low standard of living under which Mississippi Negroes exist, in addition to a lack of access to adequate hospital care. (Chart 3)

INFANT MORTALITY

Infant mortality rates since 1920 for both races have generally gone downward. The rate for nonwhites, however, swung upward in 1957 and continued upward until 1961 when it started downward again (Chart 4). It takes no statistical genius to understand what the figures reflect: In Mississippi the chances of a Negro baby dying within the first year of life are at best twice those of a white baby. Though most babies of both races do survive, Negro babies have a greater chance of starting life with a health handicap. In communities where Negroes are subject to major segregation and discrimination, the Negro baby is much more likely to be born prematurely. Premature babies may get excellent care *if* they are born in or near a hospital with a modern center for premature infants, but Negroes in Mississippi are largely denied this. (Table 4)

SIGNIFICANT POPULATION CHARACTERISTICS, 1950–1960

AGE DISTRIBUTION

Table 5 compares the changes in the Negro and white population which have occurred among different age groups between 1950 and 1960. During this decade the total population of Mississippi remained almost the same. There was a net increase in the white population and a net decrease in the nonwhite population. Most significant for Negroes is the large decrease in the group aged 20 to 34. Because workers in this age group are traditionally preferred in hiring for new employment, this change in age composition of the population may contribute to increased employment opportunity for younger Negroes. The situation may also add to the dilemma of employers whose hiring policies continue to favor white workers and workers under 35 years of age. (Chart 5)

URBAN-RURAL DISTRIBUTION

In 1960, the Negro population was largely rural, there being over two-thirds of the Negroes in the State living in rural areas. Of the 79,545 persons who migrated from rural areas into Mississippi cities, only 5 percent were non-white. There obviously has been no significant rural-urban redistribution of the non-white population within the state during the last decade. This is largely a reflection of the fact that employment opportunities for rural non-whites in the state's towns and cities are poor. (Table 7)

COUNTY VARIATIONS

Table 8, showing the Negro and white population in 1950 and 1960 for each county, reveals the high percentage of Negroes in some counties and the considerably high out-of-state migration taking place. There are 29 counties wherein Negroes constitute more than 50% of the population. Hinds, Calhoun and Coahoma are the counties with the largest numbers of Negroes. Tunica, Clairborne, and Jefferson have the largest percentages of Negroes. The area commonly referred to as the "Gulf Coast" has shown the only consistent increases in population during the last decade. Significantly, this is the most affluent economic area or region in the state.

CITIES OF 10,000 OR MORE

Table 9 shows the 18 cities in Mississippi that have a population of greater than 10,000. In all of these cities, with the exception of Biloxi, Negroes constitute 20 percent or more of the total population.

EDUCATIONAL ATTAINMENT

As shown in Table 10, in 1960 *all* Negroes aged 25 and over had completed an average of only six years of school. This is five years less than the average for whites. The average is even less in the rural-farm areas where a high proportion of Negroes live.

RECENT LABOR FORCE AND EMPLOYMENT TRENDS

NEGROES IN THE LABOR FORCE

PROPORTION IN THE LABOR FORCE

The proportion of Negroes in the labor force is very similar to the proportion for whites. There is a noticeable difference in the proportions when the races are divided into sexes, however. There is a greater percent of Negro women, particularly urban married Negro women, in the labor force, than white women. The proportion of Negro men in the labor force is noticeably lower than the proportion of white males. (Table 11 and Chart 7)

UNEMPLOYMENT

Table 12 shows that in 1960 the average unemployment rate for Negroes was more than 50 percent greater than that of whites. Changes in the rates for the two races from 1950 to 1960 were relative—the same. This change has been an unfavorable one, resulting in an unemployment rate for Negroes of 7.1 percent. (Chart 8)

STATUS AMONG DIFFERENT AGE GROUPS

Table 13 shows, for 1960, the variations at different ages in the labor force status of Negroes in comparison with white men and women. About 67% of all Negro men ages 14 or over were in the labor force compared to roughly 75% of all white men. A significantly higher proportion of Negro men under age 24 and over age 65 were in the labor force. For both Negro men and white men between the ages of 20 and 64 the rates of labor force participation were comparable. The pattern among women shows some significant contrasts. The proportion of Negro women in the labor force was higher than for white women in every age group except ages 14–19 and 20–24. Among white women, the rate of labor force participation drops after age 24 (about the average age of marriage), whereas for Negro women the rate increases through the 45–49 age group.

INDUSTRY DISTRIBUTION

In Table 14, it is apparent that of the roughly one-half million employed Negroes in the State, more than a third are employed in agriculture with more than another third employed in service industries. Unbelievable as it may seem, though Negroes comprise almost 40% of the total employed labor force, only about 4 1/2% are employed in manufacturing and even less than that in construction employment.

PATTERN OF EMPLOYMENT

Table 15 reveals that of those Negroes unemployed, not more than 8% can be categorized as skilled workers. Though 21.1% of those unemployed were previously semi-skilled operatives or kindred workers, 31.9% were non-agricultural laborers and 21.55% were farm laborers. Thus, over 50% of the unemployed Negroes were unskilled laborers.

INCOME

INCOME OF FAMILIES, 1950–1960

Table 16 and Chart 9 present the median income of all Negro and white persons for the years 1950–1960. In 1960 Negroes had an average annual income of $606, only 29% of the average income of $2,023 among whites. The difference seems particularly wide in view of the fact that a higher proportion of Negro family members are in the labor force. The data in the previous section on labor force and employment show that a higher proportion of Negro males under age 24 and women over age 24 are in the labor force than is the case among whites.

There is a relatively smaller differential between Negroes and whites for urban as compared with rural persons. In 1960, the average income of urban Negroes was 33% of the average among whites, a decline from 38% in 1950. The urban Negro family in 1960 had an average income of $871, compared with an average of about $2,600 for whites. Between 1950 and 1960 the average income of urban whites increased some $800, whereas among Negroes it increased less than $200. Among rural persons the median income of Negroes increased from $390 in 1950 to $474 in 1960 when it was about 31% of the average for white persons. This represented a relative decline form the $390 average of 1950 when the rural Negro's average income was 41% of the average among rural whites. The money income of both Negroes and white persons living on farms remained low and increased relatively less than that of rural non-farm and urban families in the years 1945–1949.

HOUSING CONDITIONS

Statistics revealing housing conditions for Mississippi Negroes are somewhat shocking. In 1960 there were 207,611 housing units for Mississippi Negroes. Of these, 38.1% were owner-occupied, and 61.9% were renter-occupied (significantly out of line with the national proportion of owner- and renter-occupied housing). Of the 207,611 houses, only one-third can be classified as being in sound condition; the others have been classified as either deteriorating or dilapidated. Of the homes in rural areas, over 75% are without any piped water at all and over 90% of these rural homes had no flush toilets, no bathtub and no shower. (see Table 17)

Chart 1: Population, 1940 & 1960, in Thousands

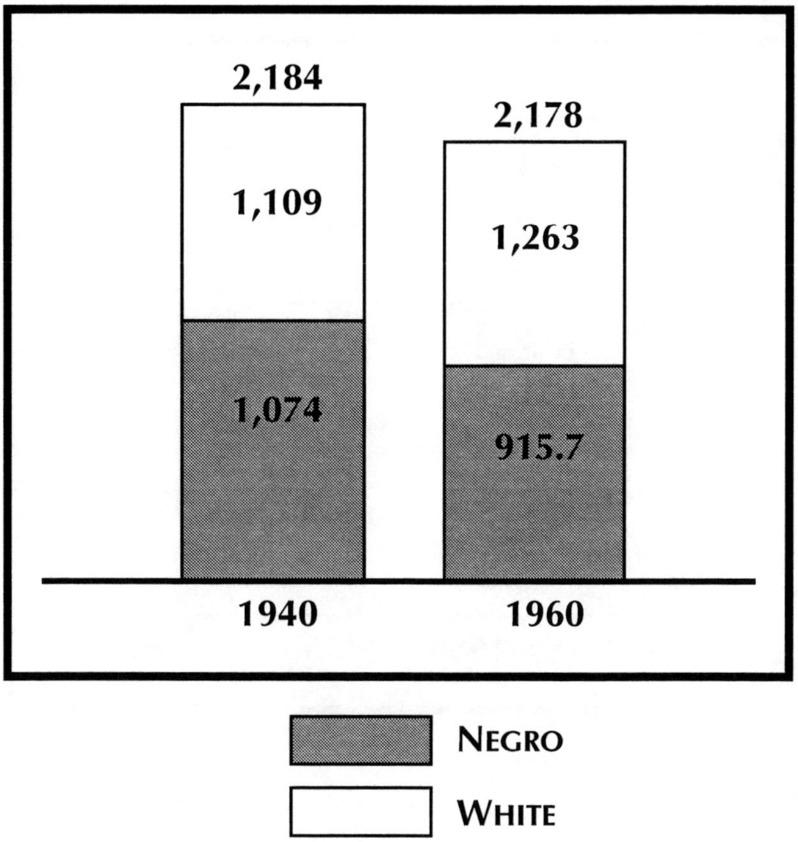

CHART 2: BIRTH RATES, SELECTED PERIODS

Rate Per 1,000 Population

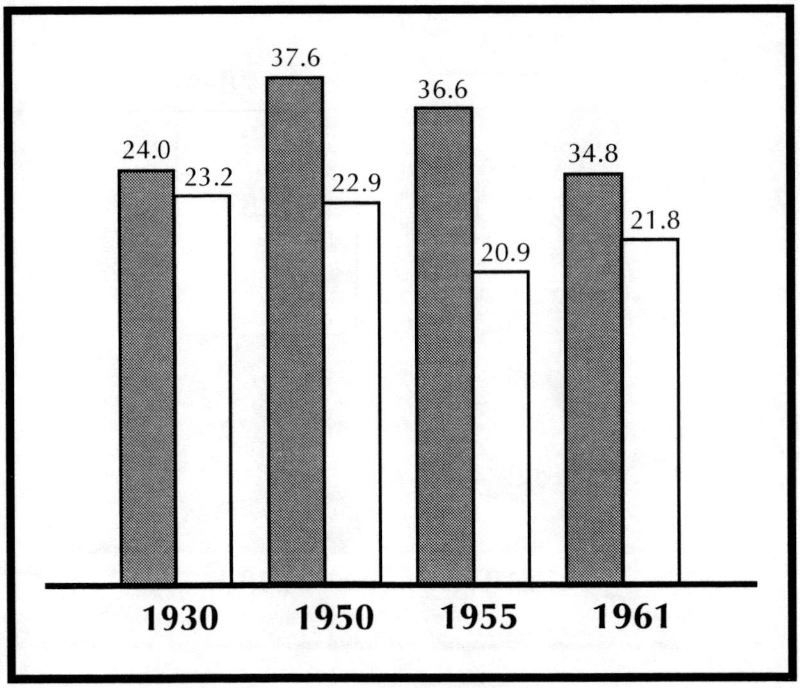

CHART 3: DEATH RATES

Rate Per 1,000 Population

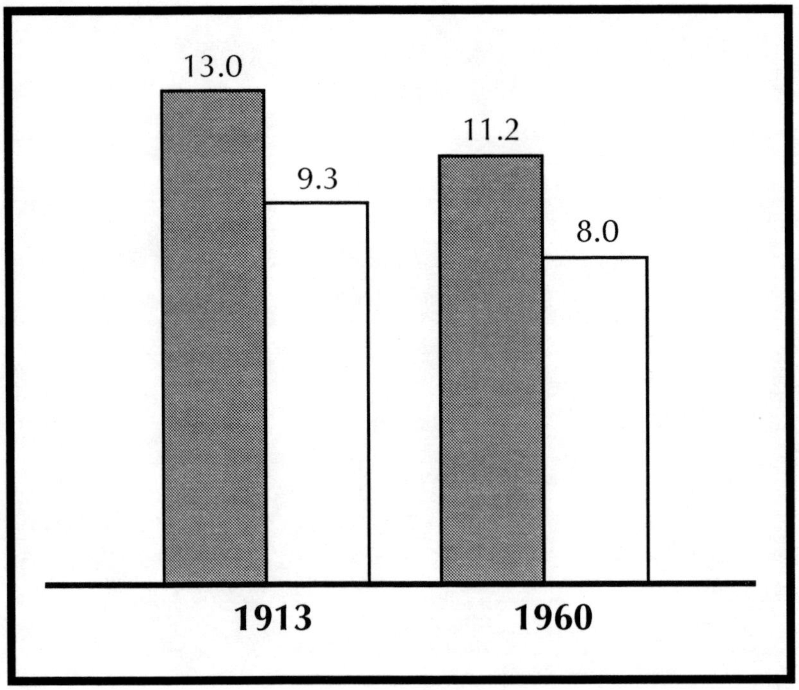

CHART 4: INFANT MORTALITY

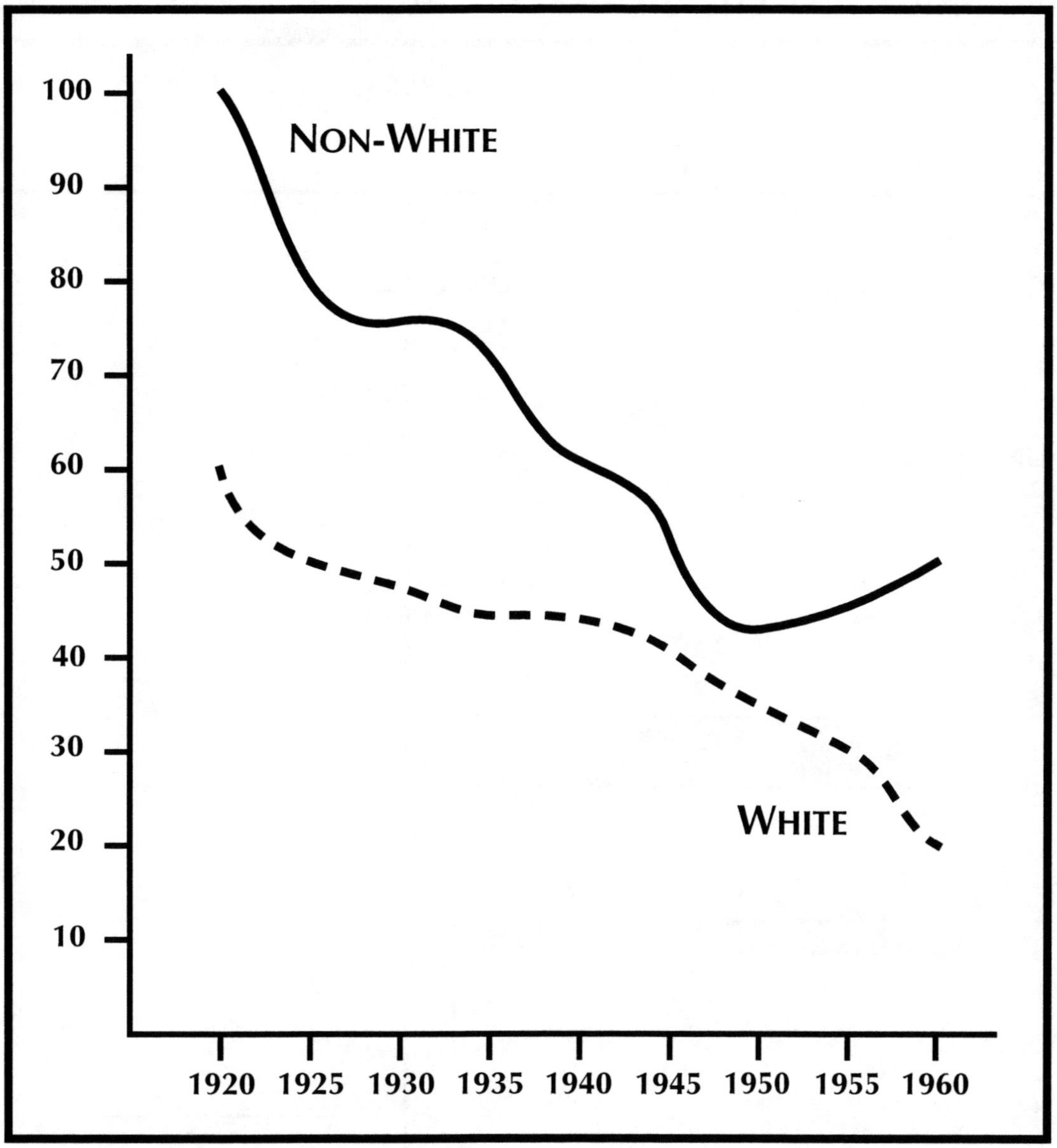

Source: U.S. Bureau of the Census and Mississippi State Board of Health

CHART 5: PERCENTAGE CHANGES IN NEGRO AND WHITE POPULATION BY AGE (1950–1960)

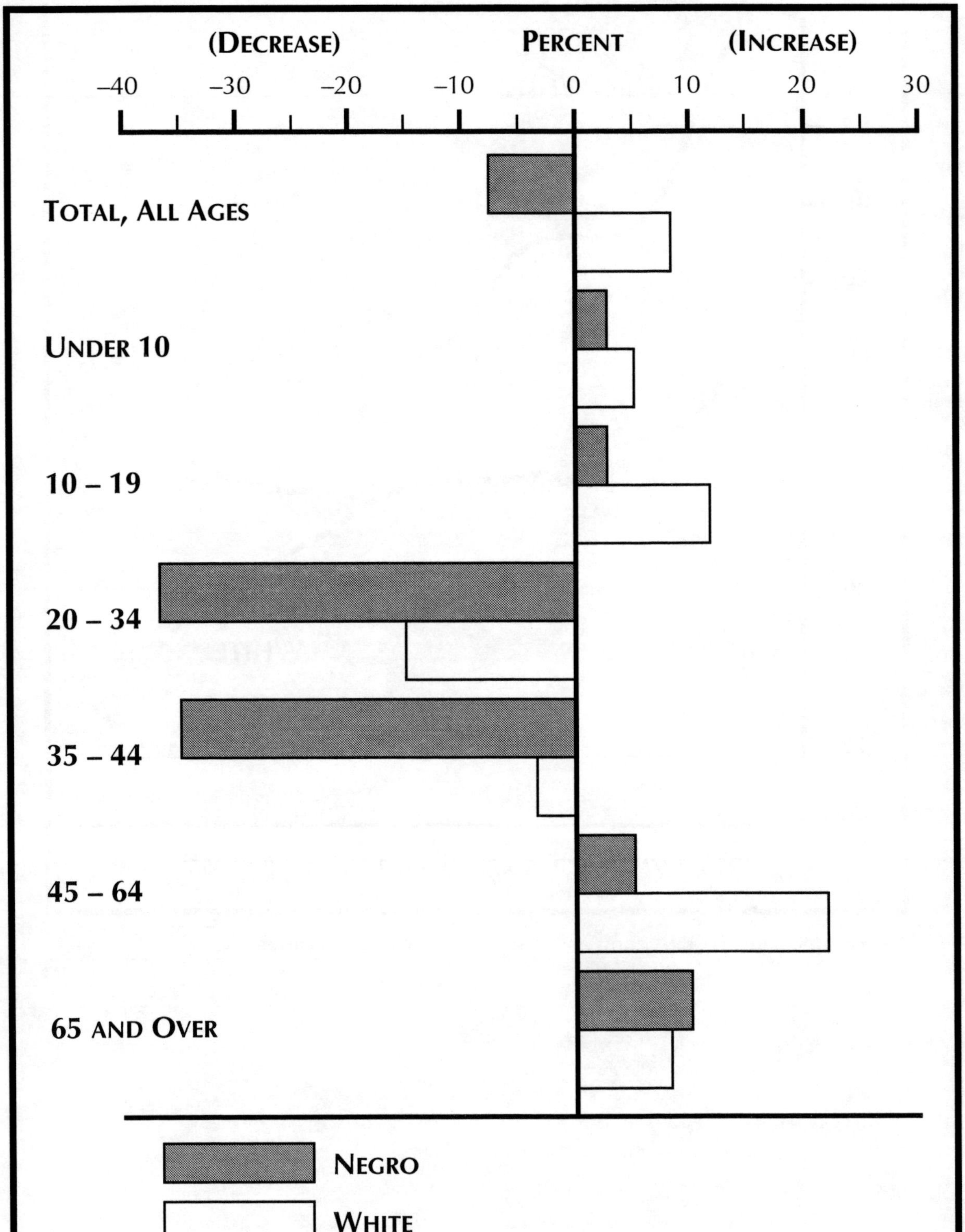

Source: U.S. Bureau of the Census

CHART 6: NEGRO POPULATION, BREAKDOWN BY COUNTY

(Percentage Distribution)

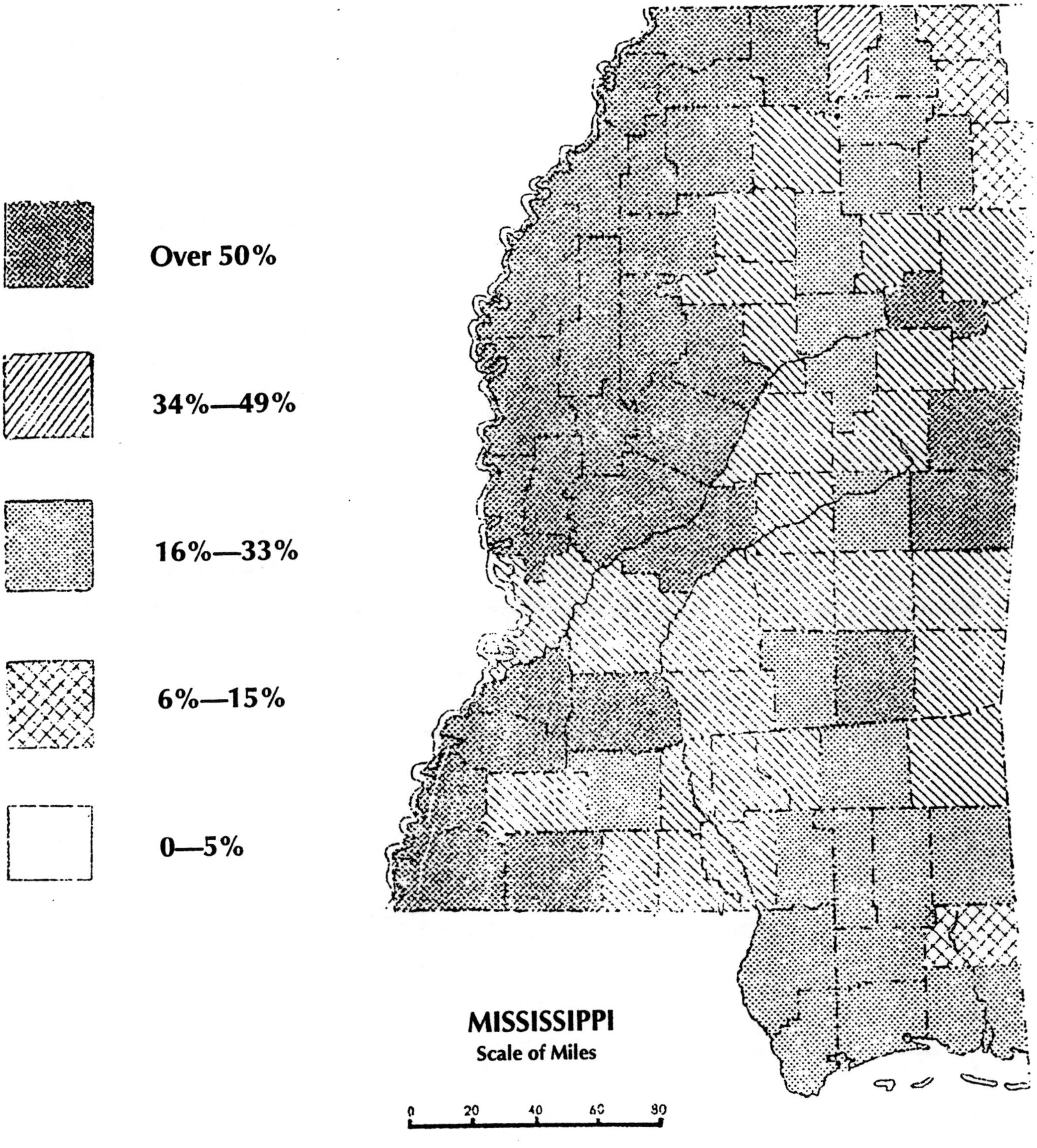

CHART 7: PERCENT OF NEGRO AND WHITE POPULATION IN THE LABOR FORCE, 1960

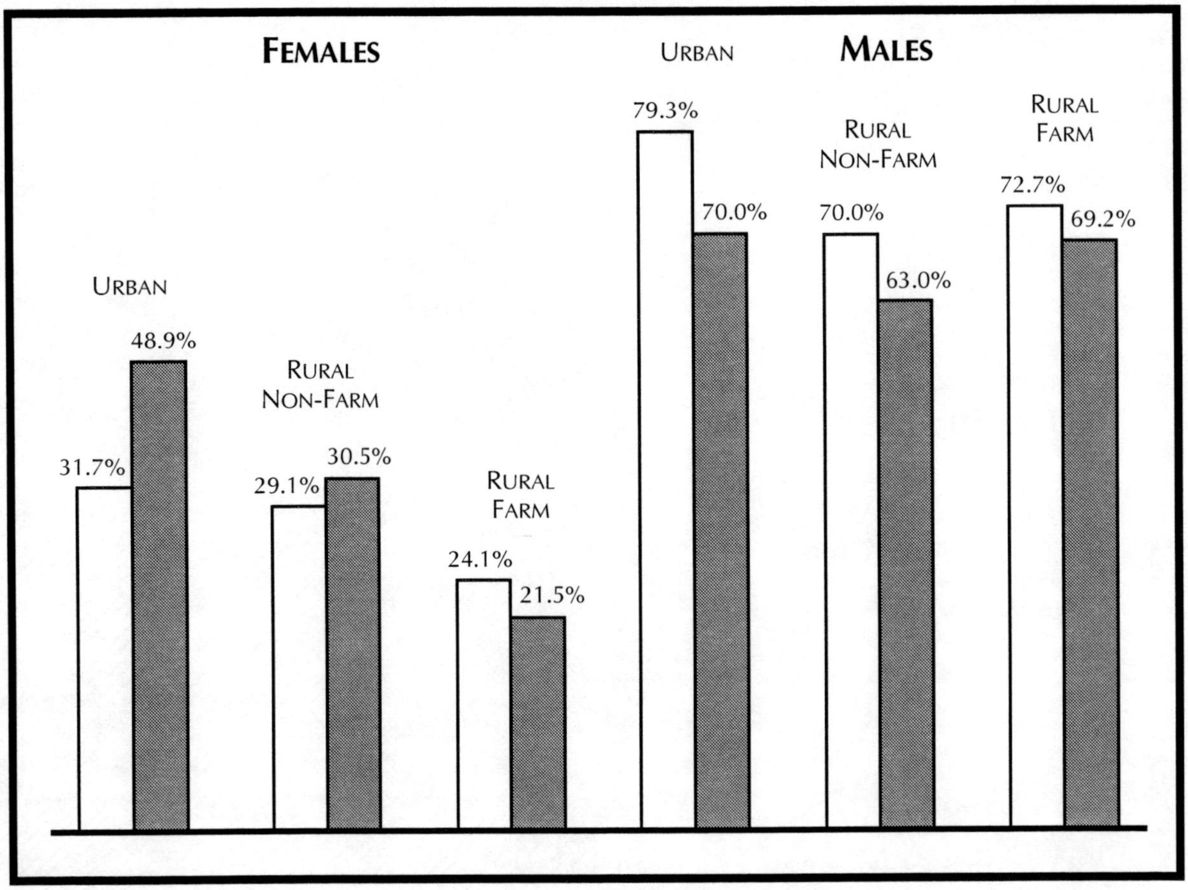

CHART 8: PERCENT OF NEGRO AND WHITE WORKERS IN THE LABOR FORCE UNEMPLOYED, 1950 AND 1960

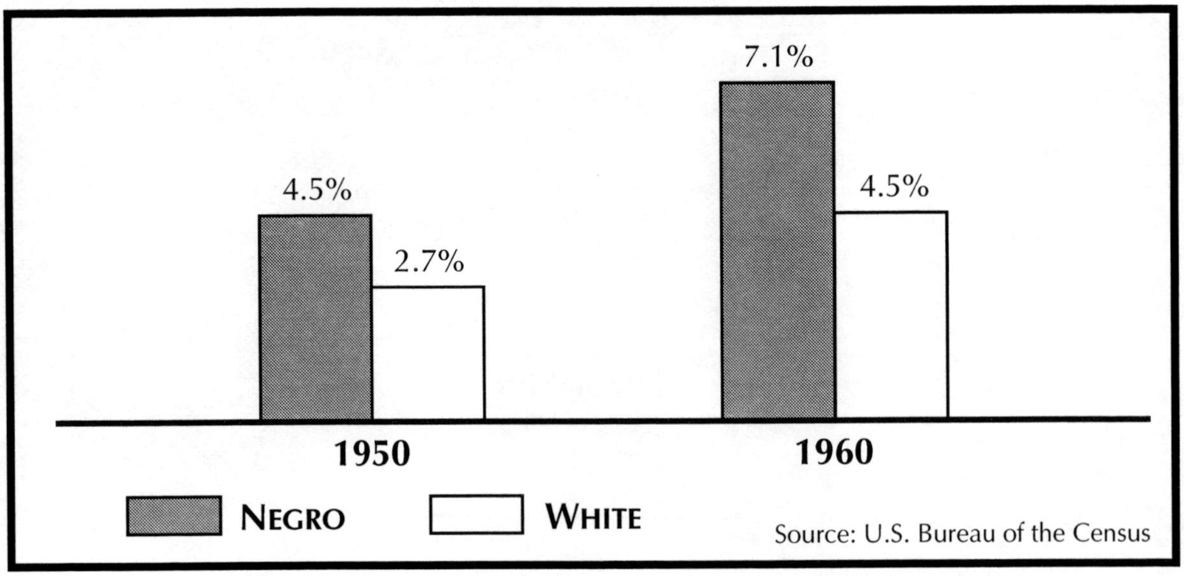

Appendix Tables

Table 1: Population of Mississippi, by Color, 1900–1960

Year	Total	Nonwhite	
		Number	Percentage
1960	2,178,141	920,595	44.4
1950	2,178, 914	990,282	45.5
1940	2,183,796	1,077,469	49.1
1930	2,009,821	1,011,744	50.5
1920	1,790,618	936,656	52.5
1910	1,797,114	1,011,003	56.2
1900	1,551,270	910,070	58.6

Source: U.S. Bureau of the Census

Table 2: Estimated Birth Rates, by Color; Selected Years, 1920–1961

Births Per 1,000 Population

Year	Nonwhite	White
1961	34.8	21.8
1959	36.6	20.9
1955	36.6	23.2
1950	37.6	22.9
1940	27.3	20.9
1935	25.1	20.8
1930	24.0	23.2
1925	23.4	24.1
1920	22.7	26.3

Source: Mississippi State Board of Health

Table 3: Death Rates, by Color, Selected Years, 1920–1961

Deaths Per 1,000 Population

Year	Nonwhite	White
1961	11.0	8.8
1959	11.4	8.1
1955	10.2	8.7
1950	11.2	8.0
1940	12.6	8.6
1935	11.6	8.7

YEAR	NONWHITE	WHITE
1930	14.8	9.0
1925	14.4	8.8
1920	15.1	9.3

TABLE 4: DEATHS UNDER 1 YEAR; SELECTED YEARS, 1920–1961

Deaths Per 1,000 Population

YEAR	NONWHITE	WHITE
1961	50.0	23.5
1960	54.4	23.5
1955	46.4	24.7
1950	42.6	28.1
1945	44.7	36.1
1940	60.9	46.4
1935	58.6	47.5
1930	84.5	51.0
1925	85.7	53.0
1920	101.1	59.9

Source: Mississippi State Board of Health

TABLE 5: POPULATION OF MISSISSIPPI, BY COLOR, AGE, AND SEX 1950–1960

AGE & SEX	NEGRO		NATIVE-BORN WHITE		CHANGE: 1950–1960			
					NUMBER		PERCENTAGE	
	1950	1960	1950	1960	NEGRO	N. B. WHITE	NEGRO	N.B.W.
TOTAL	987,935	915,722	1,179,964	1,250,282	–72,213	70,318	–7.3	6.2
Under 10	270,685	276,403	250,315	260,678	5,746	10,363	2.1	4.1
10–19	203,905	206,586	208,785	231,572	2,681	22,787	1.3	10.9
20–34	188,975	130,405	264,085	236,908	–58,514	–28,177	–38.5	–10.7
35–44	114,475	79,386	244,450	157,199	–35,089	–4,930	–33.8	–2.1
45–64	143,430	149,447	206,455	251,383	6,017	44,927	4.2	21.8
Over 65	66,605	72,528	85,680	92,043	5,923	6,363	8.9	7.4
MALE TOTAL	479,580	440,641	589,869	621,656	–35,939	37,787	–8.1	5.4
Under 10	135,685	138,456	128,310	133,140	2,771	4,830	2.0	3.8
10–19	100,490	105,074	107,490	120,351	4,584	12,861	4.5	1.3
20–34	86,520	57,893	129,785	117,612	–28,621	–12,173	–33.1	–9.4
35–44	52,755	33,923	79,810	77,181	–18,832	–2,628	–35.7	–3.3
45–64	70,940	70,053	101,770	122,485	–887	20,715	–1.2	20.7
Over 65	33,270	35,284	41,200	50,886	2,014	9,686	6.1	23.4

AGE & SEX	NEGRO		NATIVE-BORN WHITE		CHANGE: 1950–1960			
FEMALE TOTAL	508,355	475,081	590,095	628,626	–33,274	38,531	–6.6	6.5
Under 10	135,000	137,947	122,005	127,538	2,947	5,533	2.2	4.4
10–19	103,415	101,512	101,295	111,221	–1,903	9,926	–1.9	9.8
20–34	102,395	72,512	135,300	119,296	–29,883	–16,004	–29.1	–11.9
35–44	61,720	45,463	82,320	80,017	–16,257	–2,303	–26.4	–2.8
45–64	72,490	79,394	104,685	128,897	6,904	24,212	9.6	23.1
Over 65	33,335	37,244	44,480	41,157	3,909	–3,323	11.7	–7.5

Source: U.S. Bureau of the Census

TABLE 6: POPULATION OF MISSISSIPPI, BY RACE AND URBAN-RURAL RESIDENCE, 1960

RESIDENCE	NATIVE-BORN WHITE		NEGRO	
	MALE	FEMALE	MALE	FEMALE
Urban	245,006	266,507	134,907	158,765
Rural; Non-Farm	243,385	243,131	156,597	167,778
Rural; Farm	124,265	118,988	149,137	148,588

Source: U.S. Bureau of the Census

TABLE 7: URBAN AND RURAL MIGRATION, BY RACE, IN MISSISSIPPI, 1950–1960

AREA	POPULATION		NET MIGRATION		NATURAL INCREASE %	NET CHANGE %
	1950	1960	NUMBER	%		
STATE	2,178,914	2,178,141	–424,158	–16.3	19.4	–0.03
White	1,188,632	1,257,546	–108,470	–7.9	14.9	5.8
Nonwhite	990,282	920,595	–315,688	–25.5	24.8	–7.0
URBAN	607,162	820,805	79,545	10.7	22.1	35.2
White	374,320	525,853	75,476	16.8	20.3	40.5
Nonwhite	232,842	294,952	4,069	1.4	24.9	26.7
RURAL	1,571,752	1,357,336	–503,703	–27.1	18.4	–13.3
White	814,312	731,693	–183,946	–20.1	12.4	–10.1
Nonwhite	757,440	625,643	–319,757	–33.8	24.8	–17.4

Source: Mississippi State Board of Health

TABLE 8: COUNTY BREAKDOWN OF POPULATION AND MIGRATION

COUNTY	POPULATION	NUMBER NONWHITE	% NONWHITE	NET CHANGE OF NONWHITES, 1950–1960
Adams	37,730	18,695	49.5	–16.1
Alcorn	25,282	3,333	13.2	–14.6
Amite	15,573	8,443	54.2	–19.1
Attala	21,335	9,546	44.7	–17.5
Benton	7,723	3,609	46.7	–6.3
Bolivar	54,464	36,943	67.8	–14.4
Calhoun	15,941	4,346	27.3	1.3
Carroll	11,177	6,500	58.2	–26.4
Chicksaw	16,891	6,511	38.5	–22.7
Choctaw	8,423	2,520	29.9	24.3
Clairborne	10,845	8,245	76.0	–7.7
Clarke	16,493	6,492	39.4	–17.6
Clay	18,993	9,719	51.3	–3.7
Coahoma	46,212	31,582	68.3	–11.4
Copia	27,051	14,059	52.0	–13.7
Covington	13,637	4,741	34.8	–9.1
Desoto	23,891	14,643	61.3	–11.4
Forrest	52,722	14,752	28.0	13.0
Franklin	9,286	3,800	40.9	–11.7
George	11,098	1,287	11.6	4.5
Greene	8,366	1,923	23.0	27.9
Grenada	18,409	9,057	49.2	–7.9
Hancock	14,039	2,255	16.1	10.6
Harrison	119,489	19,256	16.1	43.5
Hinds	187,489	74,840	40.0	17.1
Holmes	27,096	19,501	72.0	–20.3
Humphreys	19,093	13,335	69.8	–17.2
Issaquena	3,576	2,400	67.1	–28.3
Itawamba	15,080	874	5.8	–6.7
Jackson	55,522	10,864	19.6	61.3
Jasper	16,909	8,507	50.3	–12.5
Jefferson	10,142	7,653	75.5	–9.1
Jefferson Davis	13,540	7,414	54.8	–13.9
Jones	59,542	15,447	25.9	2.9
Kemper	12,277	7,449	60.7	–21.0

COUNTY	POPULATION	NUMBER NONWHITE	% NONWHITE	NET CHANGE OF NONWHITES, 1950–1960
Lafayette	21,355	7,245	33.9	–10.4
Lamar	13,675	2,232	16.3	6.0
Lauderdale	67,119	23,484	35.0	0.4
Laurence	10,215	3,861	37.8	–18.9
Leake	18,660	8,101	43.4	–11.6
Lee	40,589	10,289	25.3	–3.5
Leflore	47,142	30,443	64.6	–13.8
Lincoln	26,759	8,352	31.2	–9.1
Lowndes	46,639	17,768	38.1	–3.5
Madison	32,904	23,637	71.8	–5.2
Marion	23,293	7,885	33.9	–6.0
Marshall	24,503	17,239	70.4	–2.8
Monroe	33,953	12,021	35.4	–12.3
Montgomery	13,320	5,971	44.8	–4.1
Neshoba	20,927	5,901	28.2	–11.5
Newton	19,517	6,567	33.6	–16.4
Noxubee	16,826	12,102	71.9	–18.8
Oktibbeha	26,175	11,448	43.7	–2.6
Panola	28,791	16,226	56.4	–7.2
Pearl River	22,411	5,190	23.2	15.5
Perry	8,745	2,412	27.6	9.1
Pike	35,063	15,408	43.9	–1.9
Pontotoc	17,232	3,286	19.1	–13.9
Prentiss	17,949	2,186	12.2	–6.3
Quitman	21,019	13,304	63.3	–15.3
Rankin	34,322	12,818	37.3	–6.2
Scott	21,187	8,137	38.4	–13.2
Sharkey	10,738	7,491	69.8	–18.5
Simpson	20,454	7,200	35.2	–1.0
Smith	14,303	3,247	22.7	–4.2
Stone	7,013	1,711	24.4	25.3
Sunflower	45,750	31,020	67.8	–18.7
Tallahatchie	24,081	15,501	69.4	–20.1
Tate	18,138	10,442	57.6	0.7
Tippah	15,093	2,756	18.3	–18.8
Tishomingo	13,889	679	4.9	–15.8

COUNTY	POPULATION	NUMBER NONWHITE	% NONWHITE	NET CHANGE OF NONWHITES, 1950–1960
Tunica	16,826	13,321	79.2	–24.8
Union	18,904	3,312	17.5	–8.9
Walthall	13,512	6,100	45.1	–14.9
Warren	42,206	19,759	46.8	–1.7
Washington	78,638	43,399	55.2	–7.8
Wayne	76,258	5,809	35.7	–6.6
Webster	10,580	2,642	25.0	–1.9
Wilkinson	13,235	9,428	71.2	–3.4
Winston	19,246	8,393	43.6	–9.7
Yalobusha	12,502	5,540	44.3	–16.8
Yazoo	31,653	18,791	59.4	–14.9

Sources: United States Bureau of the Census and Mississippi State Board of Health

TABLE 9: URBAN PLACES OF MORE THAN 10,000 PERSONS, 1960

PLACE	TOTAL POPULATION	WHITE AND NONWHITE		NONWHITE	
		MALE	FEMALE	MALE	FEMALE
Biloxi	44,053	26,606	17,447	2,748	2,809
Clarksdale	21,105	9,834	11,271	5,056	6,148
Cleveland	10,172	4,902	5,270	1,841	2,042
Columbus	24,771	11,022	13,749	4,542	5,396
Corinth	11,453	5,334	6,119	1,042	1,275
Greenville	41,502	19,636	21,866	9,186	11,002
Greenwood	20,436	9,303	11,133	4,675	5,826
Gulfport	30,204	15,064	15,140	3,030	3,306
Hattiesburg	34,989	16,644	18,345	5,189	6,026
Jackson	144,422	67,619	76,803	23,854	27,702
Laurel	27,889	13,169	14,720	4,615	5,352
McComb	12,020	5,574	6,446	1,531	1,882
Meridan	49,374	22,715	26,659	7,501	9,260
Natchez	23,791	11,073	12,718	5,633	6,710
Pascagoula	17,155	8,599	8,556	1,924	1,961
Tupelo	17,221	8,158	9,063	1,847	2,300
Vicksburg	29,143	13,422	15,721	6,098	7,436
Yazoo	11,236	5,109	6,127	2,745	3,441

Source: U.S. Bureau of the Census

TABLE 10: YEARS OF SCHOOL COMPLETED BY PERSONS 25 OR OLDER, 1960

COLOR	NUMBER 25 AND OVER	YEARS COMPLETED						
		GRADE SCHOOL					HIGH SCHOOL	
		NONE	1–4	5–6	7	8	1–3	4
NONWHITE								
Number	383,017	24,318	92,063	61,525	37,729	67,239	42,547	16,273
Percentage		8.4	31.3	20.2	9.1	12.4	11.1	4.2
WHITE								
Number	681,959	8,444	40,274	51,865	38,450	98,287	156,554	168,058
Percentage		1.2	5.9	7.6	5.6	14.4	23.0	24.6

Median Grade: Nonwhite — Grade 6
White — Grade 11

Source: U.S. Bureau of the Census

TABLE 11: EMPLOYMENT STATUS OF THE CIVILIAN, NONINSTITUTIONAL POPULATION IN MISSISSIPPI, BY COLOR AND SEX, 1960

(% Distribution)

EMPLOYMENT STATUS AND SEX	WHITE			NONWHITE		
	URBAN	RURAL NON-FARM	RURAL FARM	URBAN	RURAL NON-FARM	RURAL FARM
BOTH SEXES						
Total, 14 years and over	100	100	100	100	100	100
In labor force	57.6	49.3	48.9	58.1	45.7	45.1
Not in labor force	42.4	50.7	51.1	41.9	44.3	44.9
In labor force						
Employed	96.0	94.6	96.3	91.2	92.9	95.3
Unemployed	4.0	5.4	3.7	8.8	7.1	4.7
FEMALES						
Total, 14 years and over	100	100	100	100	100	100
In labor force	37.7	29.1	24.1	48.9	30.5	21.5
Not in labor force	62.3	70.9	75.9	51.1	69.5	78.5
In labor force						
Employed	95.3	95.0	95.0	92.0	91.7	90.2
Unemployed	4.7	5.0	5.0	8.0	8.3	9.8
MALES						
Total, 14 years and over	100	100	100	100	100	100
In labor force	79.3	70.0	72.7	70.0	63.0	69.2
Not in labor force	20.7	30.0	27.3	30.0	37.0	30.8
In labor force						
Employed	96.3	94.5	96.7	94.5	93.5	96.9
Unemployed	3.7	5.5	3.3	5.5	6.5	3.1

Source: U.S. Bureau of the Census

TABLE 12: RATE OF UNEMPLOYMENT, 1950–1960

1950		1960	
WHITE	NONWHITE	WHITE	NONWHITE
2.7	4.5	4.5	7.1

Source: U.S. Bureau of the Census

TABLE 13: TOTAL IN LABOR FORCE, 1960

(Percentage, by Ages)

AGE	MALE		FEMALE	
	NONWHITE	WHITE	NONWHITE	WHITE
Total, 14 years and up	100	100	100	100
14–19	33.0	34.5	15.1	16.5
20–24	80.3	64.3	38.6	40.8
25–29	89.5	92.4	43.4	39.4
30–34	91.2	94.3	47.2	42.6
35–39	91.2	93.9	48.8	44.0
40–44	91.2	93.2	49.1	46.6
45–49	90.4	92.1	49.6	45.3
50–54	87.2	89.1	46.3	41.9
55–59	81.9	83.9	40.4	35.3
60–64	72.4	71.0	30.7	26.0
65–69	49.0	44.9	18.2	14.8

Source: U.S. Bureau of the Census

TABLE 14: INDUSTRY GROUPING OF EMPLOYED PERSONS, 1960

(Percentage)

INDUSTRY	NONWHITE				WHITE			
	STATE	URBAN	RURAL NON-FARM	RURAL FARM	STATE	URBAN	RURAL NON-FARM	RURAL FARM
Agriculture	34.9	3.1	36.0	76.5	12.8	1.2	8.4	47.1
Manufacturing	4.6	6.7	4.4	2.0	23.3	20.1	29.1	20.2
Wholesale Trade	1.3	2.4	1.1	0.2	3.2	4.6	2.5	1.1
Mining	0.1	0.2	0.1	0.1	1.3	1.3	0.9	0.8
Transportation, Communications, and Other Public Utilities	4.0	3.6	3.3	1.5	4.8	6.1	3.3	2.8
Retail Trade	8.5	14.4	7.4	1.7	16.9	20.9	16.9	7.5
Service Industries	35.9	55.1	31.7	12.4	26.1	31.1	23.0	10.8
Industry Not Reported	2.1	2.6	1.9	1.5	1.9	2.2	1.7	1.8

Source: U.S. Bureau of the Census

TABLE 15: MAJOR GROUP OCCUPATION OF THE EXPERIENCED UNEMPLOYED, 1960

(Percentage)

GROUP	MALE		FEMALE	
	WHITE	NONWHITE	WHITE	NONWHITE
Professionals	2.4	0.6	5.5	1.2
Farmers and Farm Managers	3.2	3.5	0.4	3.2
Managers, Officials, Proprietors	3.5	0.2	2.5	0.1
Clerical and Kindred Workers	4.4	0.9	18.6	0.6
Sales Workers	4.0	0.2	10.9	0.5
Craftsmen, Foremen and Kindred	28.5	10.4	1.2	0.1
Operatives and Kindred Workers	29.1	21.1	35.2	5.6
Private Household Workers	0.1	0.7	2.4	39.8
Service Workers, Except Private Household Workers	3.0	6.1	12.5	12.8
Farm Laborers and Foremen	4.8	21.5	2.4	31.5
Laborers, Except Farm and Mine	13.3	31.9	0.7	1.0
Occupations Not Reported	3.7	3.0	7.6	3.7

Source: U.S. Bureau of the Census

TABLE 16: MEDIAN INCOME FOR PERSONS, 1950 AND 1960

RACE	1950			1960		
	STATE	URBAN	RURAL	STATE	URBAN	RURAL
WHITE	$1,236	$1,826	$973	$2,023	$2,622	$1,065
NONWHITE	$440	$693	$390	$606	$871	$474

Source: U.S. Bureau of the Census

TABLE 17: NEGRO HOUSING IN MISSISSIPPI, 1960

	STATE TOTAL	URBAN	RURAL
TOTAL HOUSING UNITS	207,611	77,824	129,787
Owner-Occupied (#)	79,059	32,913	46,146
Owner-Occupied (%)	38.1%	42.3%	35.6%
Renter-Occupied (#)	128,552	44,911	83,641
Renter-Occupied (%)	61.9%	57.5%	64.4%
CONDITION			
Owner-Occupied			
Sound	36,656	17,677	18,979
Deteriorating	27,545	10,055	17,540

	State Total	Urban	Rural
Dilapidated	14,858	5,231	9,627
Renter-Occupied			
Sound	33,168	15,294	17,874
Deteriorating	52,629	15,937	36,692
Dilapidated	42,755	13,680	29,075
Water Supply			
Hot and Cold Piped Inside	40,870	33,181	7,689
Cold Only, Piped Inside	39,101	30,376	8,725
Piped Water Outside	27,502	10,229	17,273
No Piped Water	100,138	4,038	96,100
Toilet Facilities			
Flush Toilet, Exclusive Use	62,160	52,481	9,679
Flush Toilet, Shared Use	7,570	6,965	605
None	137,881	18,378	119,503
Bathing Facilities			
Bathtub or Shower, Exclusive Use	44,991	36,333	8,658
Bathtub or Shower, Shared	2,207	1,807	400
No Bathtub or Shower	160,413	39,684	120,729

Source: U.S. Bureau of the Census

UNIT 11-4

MISSISSIPPI

STRUCTURE OF THE MOVEMENT, PRESENT OPERATIONS AND PROSPECTUS FOR THIS SUMMER

WHAT IS COFO?

The Mississippi Council of Federated Organizations is a federation of all the national civil rights organizations active in Mississippi, local political and action groups and some fraternal and social organizations. Anyone active under any of these groupings is entitled to attend COFO conventions and participate in policy-making decisions of the organization. The COFO staff, consisting of anyone working full time with any civil rights organization in Mississippi, implements the decisions of the COFO conventions, and prepares recommendations for the consideration of the COFO convention. Below the level of the statewide COFO convention, there are district organizations corresponding to the five Congressional districts. These district organizations are presently in the planning stages for practical purposes. The staff, however, is broken down into Congressional districts, with five district directors; this organization structure actually functions. The state organization has four standing committees: Welfare and Relief, Political Action, Finance and Federal Programs. The district organizations have, or will have, similar standing committees. Dr. Aaron E. Henry of Clarksdale, State President of the NAACP, is President of the Council of Federated Organizations. Robert Moses, Field Secretary and Mississippi Project Director for SNCC, is the Program Director, who supervises the Mississippi staff and is elected by it. David Dennis, Mississippi Field Secretary for CORE, is Assistant Program Director, and is similarly elected.

HOW IS COFO FINANCED?

The expenses for COFO's projects are paid by direct grants from national civil rights groups as these groups volunteer to contribute. This accounts for nearly all of COFO's income. Expenses of staff workers are paid by the national civil rights groups also, the arrangements varying with the group. At present, the Student Nonviolent Coordinating Committee supports COFO projects in the First, Second, Third, and Fifth Congressional Districts as well as the state COFO office in Jackson. The Congress of Racial Equality assumes responsibility on a direct-to-the-project basis for the Fourth Congressional District. COFO does not solicit funds for itself, by agreement with the civil rights organizations which support it, for it is felt that it would thus compete with the supporting groups. Negligible amounts are sent directly to COFO, however, and these moneys are not credited to any national civil rights organization. Usually such small donations are earmarked for particular projects, such as the book drive or welfare relief (Food for Freedom) funds, and are dispensed according to the direction of the donor.

WHAT IS COFO'S RELATIONSHIP TO NATIONAL CIVIL RIGHTS ORGANIZATIONS?

COFO represents the effort of all civil rights workers in Mississippi to coordinate their efforts in one direction for maximum efficiency. Staff members, however, are paid by separate organizations and do not lose the organizational identity or their affiliation with the national office of whatever organization they work for. SNCC and CORE workers work together on joint "COFO" projects, and thus must make all plans and decisions in common; on the project they are not separate. But they maintain their special relationship with the organization which hired and pays them.

COFO—SHORT HISTORY

COFO has evolved through three distinct phases in its short history. In its first phase it was little more than an ad hoc committee called together after the Freedom Rides of 1961, in a successful effort to obtain a meeting with Governor Ross Barnett. This committee of Mississippi civil rights leaders proved a convenient vehicle for channeling the voter registration programs of the Voter Education Project into Mississippi. This injection of funds led to the second phase of COFO as an umbrella for voter registration drives in the Mississippi Delta, and other isolated cities in Mississippi. During this period, beginning in February 1962, COFO added a small full-time staff, mostly SNCC and a few CORE workers, and developed a voter registration program. The staff worked with local NAACP leaders, and SCLC citizenship teachers in an effort to give the Mississippi Negroes the broadest possible support. COFO continued essentially as a committee with a staff and a program until the fall of 1963. There were many doubts about the validity of COFO during this period; some thought it should be abandoned. But always, we come back to the inescapable fact that the Negro people in Mississippi needed some organization which could belong to them (as opposed to their belonging to it) which would serve as a unifying force among the isolated Negro communities. The emergence of the Ruleville Citizenship group, and the Holmes County Voters League, testified to the possibility of starting strong local groups. We felt the need to develop horizontal ties among these groups, with the strongest common denominator possible within the general aims of the Civil Rights Movement. Thus there was continuing effort on our part to cut across county and organizational lines and have people from different areas meet with each other, to sponsor county, regional and statewide meetings, to bring students together from different parts of the state for workshops, to help send groups outside of the state to meetings, conferences, workshops and SCLC citizenship schools—anything to help break the despair of aloneness the isolated Mississippi Negro feels. During this second phase we began to feel more and more that the "Committee" could be based in a network of local adult groups sprung from the movement as we worked the state.

We are presently in the third stage which really began with the Freedom vote for Governor campaign of the fall of 1963. This marked our first state wide effort and coincided with the establishment of a state wide office in Jackson and a trunk line to reach into the Mississippi Delta and hill country. During this stage we have broadened the staff to include more CORE and SNCC workers and more citizenship of the Southern Christian Leadership Conference, have established working relations with a great many local organizations, and have established in our own minds the validity and necessity of COFO.

We envisage the fourth stage in which the funds, program and staff for the long pull are worked out with the major civil rights groups and other interested organizations and individuals across the Country, in which we reach down into every Negro community to organize and train local people to lead Mississippi through the next difficult years of transition.

WHAT ARE COFO'S PROGRAMS?

COFO works in two major areas. Most of its resources are directed toward various voters' activities. It has a large and growing number of programs, however, which came under a classification of "educational and social." Each program can be described briefly.

The "educational and social" programs are the Freedom Schools, Federal Programs, Literacy, Work-Study, Food and Clothing, and Community Centers projects.

A. The Freedom Schools are planned for the summer of 1964. Freedom schools will be geared to high-school aged children and will run for six weeks during the summer. The students will be given remedial instruction in basic educational skills and exposed to cultural influences which are not normally available to them, but the main emphasis of the schools will be to implant habits of free thinking and ideas of how a free society works. Hopefully, too, the schools will lay the groundwork for a statewide youth movement, which would coordinate projects of special interest to young people, such as a statewide school boycott in sympathy with voter registration efforts.

B. The goal of the federal programs is to make the programs of the federal government which are designed to alleviate poverty and ignorance reach the people of Mississippi. Such programs as the Area Redevelopment Act, the Manpower Development and Training Act, and such bureaus as the Farmers Home Administration and the Office of Manpower, Automation and Training cannot benefit the people of Mississippi as things now stand because the normal channels of information, the State agencies, do not properly present these programs. The federal government insists that any federal aid be given on a nondiscriminatory and integrated basis, and the State of Mississippi is not reconciled to this. So private agencies must act as liaison between the federal programs and the people they are designed to help. COFO projects in this program so far have included a Conference on Jobs and Job Training, where leading industrial and governmental officials discussed the expansion of job training opportunities in Mississippi in connection with the space facility now being built by the National Aeronautics and Space Administration, and a planned conference with the National Sharecroppers Fund to present agricultural opportunities to Mississippi farmers scheduled for the end of February.

C. The literacy project at Tougaloo College is a research project under the direction of John Diebold and Associates company, and is financed by an anonymous grant to

Tougaloo College. The goal of the project is to write self-instructional materials which will teach adult illiterates in lower social and economic groups to read and write. Such educational materials do not now exist, and they must be developed before there can be any comprehensive program to eliminate illiteracy in Mississippi. Staff workers are being trained to develop these materials under the direction of the Diebold group.

D. The Work-Study project is an attempt to solve one of the more pressing staff problems in the Southern Movement, that of the conflict between full-time civil rights work and school for the college-age worker. Under the work-study program, students spend a year in full-time field work for the Student Nonviolent Coordinating Committee, under the direction of COFO field staff, and with special academic work designed to complement their field work and keep them familiar with learning and intellectual discipline. After this year of field work, they get a full scholarship to Tougaloo College for one year. The academic expenses of the project, both the Tougaloo scholarships and the first year scholastic program, are financed by a grant from the Field Foundation. Project and personal expenses of the work-study group during the first year of field work are financed by SNCC. The group plans to expand next year to other campuses, but this year it is based in Jackson and Tougaloo.

E. The food and clothing program is a privately-financed distribution program of the necessities of life for persons whose needs are so basic that they cannot feed their families one meal a day per person.

FOOD

The adequacy of dietary levels is measured by two criteria: caloric intake (quantity) and nutritional content (quality). The caloric intake of some—not all—poor rural Mississippians is at some—not all—times sufficient. These times are usually (**1**) when they receive government commodities, (**2**) when the tenant or low-income farmer receives money from his cotton and other minor crops, usually in early and mid-fall, and (**3**) when landlords give credit to tenant families, usually from late March to July. The rest of the time the poor rural families, the under and un-employed, fare as best they can. Usually this means tightening their belts, surviving off one meal a day, adults going without so that children may eat—in short, it means starving. Even when people get enough food, it is largely starches and fats. There is great reliance on corn bread, sweet potatoes, rice and fat or side pork. Even the government commodities are not sufficient for adequate nutrition. The poor in Mississippi do not get enough protein, calcium, essential vitamins and minerals for proper nutrition.

Our goal, of course, is to see that these people are ultimately paid a living wage—but malnutrition can be cut down by distribution of a few food commodities and massive distribution of inexpensive vitamins.

CLOTHING

The clothing situation of both the urban and rural poor is desperate. Mothers do not go around the house in dirty robes or ragged dresses or even in their slips because they are basically unclean, but because they have nothing to change into. Fathers don't lounge around in the filthy, smelly overalls they work in during the day because they are too lazy to change their clothes, but because they have nothing else to put on. Children do not walk around barefoot because they want to pat their feet in the Mississippi mud, but because their parents cannot buy them shoes. And in the winter the Mississippi mud becomes hard frozen ground.

SHELTER

Many people in the deep South live in housing unfit for human habitation. The 1960 census showed that in Mississippi over 50% of the rural occupied farm housing was classified as either deteriorating or dilapidated. Furthermore, more than 50% of the rural occupied homes have no piped water and more than 75% have no flush toilets, bathtubs or showers. For Negroes the housing situation is even worse. The 1960 census showed that in Mississippi, 66% of all Negro housing was "dilapidated or deteriorating"—71% in rural areas. More than 90% of rural Negro homes in Mississippi have neither flush toilets nor bathing or shower facilities.

COFO's food and clothing program cannot cope with poverty this serious (State welfare aid is totally inadequate), but it helps, especially in some especially pressing areas. The program gives special consideration to persons in need because of their participation in other COFO programs, such as attempting to register to vote. Food distribution is along the same lines as government commodity programs administered by the counties. There is presently no vitamin distribution, but it could probably be arranged if administrative difficulties could be resolved (*i.e.*, securing the cooperation of doctors). Clothing distribution involves a national coordinating effort. Sympathetic persons and groups collect clothing in drives all over the country and ship them to Mississippi with the cooperation of a national relief agency. At present COFO has no program to deal with the housing conditions of Mississippi, but when the community centers are better organized, COFO can begin a program of home-repair workshops and volunteer youth corps assisting people to repair their homes, all working out of a community center.

F. The community centers program projects a network of community centers across the state. Conceived as a long-range institution, these centers will provide a structure for a sweeping range of recreational and educational programs. In doing this, they will not only serve basic needs of Negro communities now ignored by the state's racist political structure, but will form a dynamic focus for the development of community organization. The educational features of the centers will include job training programs for the unskilled and unemployed, literacy and remedial programs for adults as well as young people, public health programs such as prenatal and infant care, basic nutrition, etc. to alleviate some of the serious health problems of Negro Mississippians (for instance, Negro infant mortality rates in some counties are so high as to invite comparison with "underdeveloped" nations), adult education workshops which would deal with family relations, federal service programs, home improvement and other information vital to the needs of Negro communities, and also extracurricular programs for grade school and high school students which provide opportunity for critical thought and creative expression. Each center would have a well-rounded library—to which Negroes in many communities now have no access.

Though the community centers program is primarily educational, some of each center's resources would be used to provide much-needed recreational facilities for the Negro community. In most communities in Mississippi the only recreation outside of taverns is the movies, and for Negroes this means segregated movies. If there is a movie theater in the Negro community, it is old, rundown, and shows mostly out-of-date, third-rate Hollywood films. The film program of the centers will not only provide a more agreeable atmosphere for movies, it will bring films of serious content which are almost never shown in Mississippi, where ideas are rigidly controlled. Other recreational offerings will be music appreciation classes, arts and workshops, drama groups, discussion clubs on current events, literature and Negro achievement, etc., pen pal clubs, organized sports (where equipment allows), and occasional special performances by outside entertainers, such as folk festivals, jazz concerts, etc. Organized story-telling for young children will be entertaining, and will introduce them to the resources of the center's library and to reading for pleasure in general.

The development of this wide range of social and educational programs has emerged almost inevitably out of the urgent necessity to create institutions outside the existing structure to meet the vastly neglected needs of the Negro communities of Mississippi. But COFO's primary objective remains in the area of voter education, because it is only by the creation of a broadly-based and informed electorate that Mississippi's system of racial oppression can be destroyed ultimately. Thus, most of COFO's staff work is presently in the area of voter registration. Through neighborhood canvassing, mass meetings, and citizenship classes teaching the difficult registration form, COFO's staff members work continuously to encourage as many Negroes as possible to register to vote. In areas where there are already local organizations COFO workers provide incentive and technical skill to voting efforts. But often the COFO worker must work in areas where there are no established community groups and in such places he must undertake the organization of the local people into a durable civic structure.

All this voter activity must operate under extremely hostile conditions. In the past two years alone, hundreds of civil rights workers have been arrested in the course of promoting registration efforts: for distributing leaflets ("littering the sidewalks," "publishing libel," etc.), for picketing, and for an untold variety of trumped-up charges ranging from armed robbery to traffic violations. In addition, workers have been beaten frequently, often by local or state officials, and sometimes even shot. (One, Jimmy Travis, missed death by inches last winter when he was hit with a bullet in the neck.) But local citizens are often the worst victims of the atmosphere of political oppression which exist in Mississippi, for they are not only subject to harassment, intimidation and arrest, but economic reprisals as well. Countless numbers have lost their jobs, been evicted from plantations, or had their credit suddenly discontinued for the simple act of attempting to register. But despite these conditions, thousands of Negroes, in the past two years have filed into county courthouses around the state in an effort to become qualified voters. In Mississippi, however, to attempt to register is rarely a guarantee of gaining the right to vote. By means of arbitrary powers endowed in local registrars, the state was ensured the systematic rejection of Negro applicants. For instance, one requirement for successful registration is a correct interpretation of a section of the Mississippi constitution. As a result, of some sixty thousand Negroes who have attempted to register in the past four years, only about six thousand have been inscribed on the voting rolls.

The frustration of regular efforts to register voters led to the "Freedom" concept of political action. In the fall of 1963, COFO held a statewide nominating convention to choose a candidate for Governor of Mississippi. Dr. Aaron Henry, state president of the NAACP, was nominated. His campaign was, of course, unofficial—COFO provided its own machinery for voting—but it served a number of very important purposes.

> The first was to lay a groundwork for political organization around the state for serious candidates for public office. Secondly, the campaign dramatized a few basic truths about Negro participation in Mississippi politics.
>
> **1.** The first contention was that Negroes do not vote because of justified fears of physical and economic intimidation and also because of discriminatory registration practices, not because they are apathetic and have no idea of where their political interests lie. The Freedom Vote clearly supported this contention: when they were given a chance, 83,000 Negro Mississippians did in fact vote.
>
> **2.** The second contention was that if Negroes were registered without discrimination and intimidation, they not only would vote, but that their votes would change the results of Mississippi elections, and therefore of the political structure of the state, now dominated by white, conservative racists. Aaron Henry's 83,000 votes certainly would have influenced an election where the losing official candidate received only about 130,000 votes, and the winner about 200,000, if they had been registered.

The third reason for the campaign was to provide a forum for discussion of the real issues in Mississippi; discussion of this kind is not possible in the context of regular Mississippi political campaigns.

Perhaps the most significant result of the Freedom Vote campaign was in the area of organizational development. For the first time, a genuinely statewide operation took effect. A central office was set up in Jackson to coordinate activities around the state. The five congressional district offices, established in September, became organizational bases for penetration of neighboring cities and towns and in practice expanded their operational scope beyond the city in which they were based. The campaign workers made contact with cities and towns previously untouched by the movement.

The Freedom Registration program grew logically out of the Freedom Vote idea. The plan of the Freedom Registration is to register a large proportion of the 425,000 Negroes of voting age in Mississippi on the COFO Freedom Registration books using COFO requirements, rather than the official state registration requirements. The COFO requirements would be the same as the state requirements concerning age, residence good moral character, but COFO registration would have no literacy or poll tax requirements. Local people will serve as registrars in every community, under the supervision of a County Board of Registrars. Polling places will be put where people normally go—churches, business places, lodge halls, beauty parlors and barbershops, etc. Registration books would be open in the evenings and on Saturday and Sunday. The idea would be to encourage registration, not to make it difficult and inconvenient.

In the fall elections, those persons who are freedom registered and who produce their freedom registration cards, will be entitled to vote in the freedom elections. Negro candidates will run against the regular party candidates in both the freedom and the official elections, and the comparison of totals is expected to prove that Negroes are now denied what would be a significant voice in Mississippi political affairs. In these political campaigns, where there is no question of actually winning public office, the question is raised as to why put forth all the effort. Besides the value of the campaigns in organizing Negro communities, and the dramatic demonstration of the denial of the right to vote, there is one more important reason. One of the most effective ways to create interest in voter registration is to have candidates running who discuss the real issues publicly, and who attract the attention and interest of the Negro community simply because there is great novelty in a Negro candidate for public office. The discussion of the issues is especially important because regular party campaigns do not normally allow a forum for honest debate of the state's real problems. Also the mass communications media do not permit those who oppose the official economic and racial policies a wide audience for their views. A political campaign with federal guarantees of equal time is one of the few opportunities to reach a large audience with an accurate presentation of the COFO goals and programs. Negro candidates in this fall's elections will create this discussion, at least in the Negro community.

Related to the Freedom election activity is a planned challenge of the Mississippi Democratic party. In 1960, both parties abolished civil rights platforms which, if implemented, would have brought racial and economic justice closer to reality. They were, however, not enacted. In 1964, the civil rights organizations must bring this discrepancy of promise and accomplishment to the attention of the American public. There will be activity at the national conventions around this theme. COFO in Mississippi plans to send a "freedom" delegation to challenge the right of Eastland Democrats to represent the people of Mississippi. Beginning with precinct conventions in February which send delegates to the county conventions, then to the district and state conventions and finally to the Democratic National Convention, COFO plans to challenge the segregationist Democratic delegates on all levels and over as large an area as possible. The challenge will be based on: **(1)** attempts to participate in the regular party conventions, **(2)** presumed expulsion, (3) duplication of party conventions in rival, "freedom" proceedings, (4) election of rival, freedom delegates at all levels, and (5) presentation of the State Freedom delegates at the National Democratic Convention to challenge the seating of the regular delegates. The most recent COFO convention also voted to challenge the Republican National Convention in some more modified manner, but more specific plans have not yet been made.

Much of this projected political and educational activity depends upon a staff much larger than is now in operation, or could be in permanent operation, on COFO's budget. COFO plans to provide the necessary man-power with a massive summer project, using college students from all over the country, but especially from Southern Negro colleges to organize the Mississippi Negro community, register voters both on the county and the Freedom books, operate the Freedom Schools, begin the community centers projects. The participants will be divided into three categories for administrative feasibility. The Freedom Schools would have one overall director for the state and district supervisors for each congressional district. The community centers would be organized on the same basis. Political activity is already organized this way; the summer project would add to the present structure of political activity, besides a general beef-up, two new categories: mobile unites of four men and a car which would fill gaps in the state political program plus moving into crisis areas if the regular staff is depleted; also two or three "saturation" areas where masses of field workers would concentrate on a city (as many as one worker to every twenty eligible Negroes) to register every possible Negro, both official and freedom, and promote other protest activities.

COFO; 1017 Lynch, Jackson, Miss.

PAGE 2 AUGUST 5, 1964 STUDEN

FREEDOM SCHO

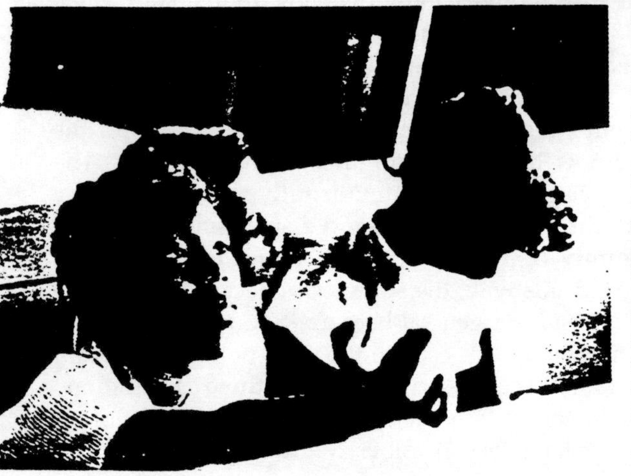

"I am Mississippi bred, I am Mississippi fed,

I asked for your churches, and you turned me down,
But I'll do my work if I have to do it on the ground,
You will not speak for fear of being heard,
So you crawl in you shell and say, "Do not distrub,"
You think because you've turned me away,
You've protected yourself for another day.
But tomorrow surely will come,
And your enemy will still be there with the rising sun,
He'll be there tomorrow as all tomorrows in the past,
And he'll follow you into the future if you let him pass.

*** from a poem by Joyce Brown, 16. Freedom School pupil in McComb, Mississippi

This poem was written by a 16-year old Negro girl in McComb Miss. She and approximately 1,825 other Negroes — children, teen-agers and adults — are attending the 39 Freedom Schools of the Mississippi Summer Project, sponsored by the Council of Federated Organizations (COFO), a statewide organization of local groups aided by field secretaries of the Student Nonviolent Coordinating Committee (SNCC), CORE, NAACP, and the Southern Christian Leadership Conference. These students -- going to "school" in churches, private homes, and backyards — are learning Negro history, civics, American history, arts and crafts drama, music, English, arithmetic, algebra and chemistry They are being taught by 250 Negro and white summer volunteers from 40 states in schools which have been set up in every Mississippi city or town of considerable size, as well as in rural counties where Negroes have been shot to death for attempting to register to vote.

Project coordinators state that the Freedom School program is an unqualified success. Rev. Thomas Wahman, a coordinator of religious activities at New York University, and a Freedom School coordinator, terms the project a "completely unexpected phenomenon." Despite the fear which prevails in most Negro communities throughout the state, "several are demanding that COFO come in and set up schools," says Wahman.

Ralph Featherstone, a 25-year old Negro speech teacher from Washington, D.C., is director of the McComb Freedom School. Featherstone explains that the opening of the school was delayed for two weeks after three civil rights workers disappeared in Philadelphia, Miss. and advance scouts prepared the way in the dangerous Southwest area of Mississippi.

But Featherstone found the students ready and waiting. In fact, Featherstone says, "They'd heard about the school and they felt left out because we didn't arrive on time."

Now the registration in McComb is up to 105, with a daily attendance of 75. Many of the students are the younger brothers and sisters of the 110 high school students who walked out of school when four of their number were arrested on a sit-in charge at the Greyhound bus station in 1961.

"I think the Freedom School is inspiring the people to lend a hand in the fight," Featherstone reports. "The older people are looking to the young people, and their courage, is rubbing off. The school makes the kids feel they haven't been forgotten. It makes them feel that at last something is coming down to help them. They feel the school is for them."

The McComb school started in the backyard of the SNCC Freedom House a week after it was bombed. For one week, students conducted classes in the blistering heat only yards away from the spot where three explosions ripped away one wall. Now they are in a church.

The Hattiesburg Freedom School system (there are five) has the highest registration and the most varied curricula in the state. Some 575 young people and adults attend morning and evening classes in the usual academic subjects, plus music programs, discussion groups, slide exhibitions, and art classes. Three of the five schools are putting out a newspaper, and Mrs. Carolyn Reese, a Negro Detroit school teacher and administrator of the Hattiesburg Freedom Schools, reports that the other two will begin putting theirs out soon.

To understand what the Freedom Schools mean to those attending them, it is first necessary to understand several facts about the regular system of education in Mississippi.

The Mississippi educational system is geared to teach the Mississippi Way of Life: Dissent is heresy. Ignorance is safer than inquiry. Fear pervades the academic atmosphere.

Example: in the spring of 1961, a number of Negro students in Jackson were expelled from (Negro) high school because they stood up in their classrooms and inquired pointedly about the Freedom Rides and their significances.

Example: More than 800 students at Alcorn A&M College (Negro) in Southwest Mississippi were tossed out of school in the spring of 1964 by the college pre-

... nothing but

Mississippi slave, ...

sident because they protested social conditions on the campus. The president enlisted the aid of the much-feared Mississippi Highway Patrol to load the students into busses so that they could be sent home without ever the opportunity to collect their belongings.

Example: also during this spring, an issue of the student newspaper at the University of Southern Mississippi (white) was confiscated by campus police under the direction of school president W.D. McCain because it carried an article about the school administration's refusal to grant admission to a Negro applicant. (McCain is a strong supporter of the White Citizen's

OLS MISSISSIPPI

ı poor black boy. "I am a

Council, and an advisory board member of the Patriotic American Youth, a campus youth organization which shares space with the John Birch Society in a Jackson bookstore. He also received a special commendation from the state legislature for refusing admittance for the fifth time to John Frazier, a student at predominantly Negro Tougaloo College.

There are many other such examples of suppression of student rights, and even of faculty rights, e.g., the constant persecution of Ole Miss Professor James W. Silver. However, what is even more chilling is the economy of school segregation in Mississippi.

Despite the fact that Alabama spends less per pupil, black and white, than any state in the nation, the expenditure in the Mississippi Delta is even less. More important, the disparity between funds spent per white student and funds spent per black student is even greater.

In Mississippi, the county appropriates funds for education --- according to its own budget --- in addition to the funds contributed by the state. The following is the county appropriation, above the state minimum, for instruction per pupil in 1960-61:

North Pike County
(44 % non-white)
(McComb)

white	$30.89
Negro	.76

South Pike County
(Magnolia)

white	$59.55
Negro	1.35

Forrest County
(28% non-white)

white	$67.76
Negro	34.19

Hattiesburg Separate

white	$115.96
Negro	61.69

Whites who control Mississippi have little respect for education, but use it unscrupulously to prevent Negroes from obtaining the basic democratic right, the right to vote.

For instance, while the State Penitentiary Reform Bill was still in the Senate, Sen. Howard McDonnell of Biloxi proposed an amendment which would require that the superintendent of the penitentiary have two years of college education. Foes of the amendment said the requirement would force the ouster of the present superintendent, C.E. Breazeale. The amendment failed McDonnell then asked that the Superintendent be required to have a high school education. That amendment was also defeated.

Yet, the Mississippi legislature has established voter registration requirements which lawyers contend would be extremely difficult for anyone without a law degree to pass, if the tests are honestly administered.

.... I will be buried in a Mississippi grave, nothing but a poor dead boy."

. . . These words were penned by a 13-year-old youngster

The Freedom Schools are a war against this academic poverty. It is not just the courses provided, but the fact that the schools are a focal point for personal expression against the oppression, on the one hand, and for personal growth and creativity, on the other. The regular Mississippi schools are fundamentally opposed to this approach.

Mrs. Reese says, "The Freedom Schools mean an exposure to a totally new field of learning new attitudes about people, new attitudes about self, and about the right to be dissatisfied with the status quo. The children have had no conception that Mississippi is a part of the United States; their view of American history is history with no Negroes in it. It's like making a cake with no butter."

Mrs. Reese explains that "Mississippi has sold itself short. There are many good minds here which are being used as sacrificial lambs. The children are alert and eager to learn. If they had something to learn, they'd be happy to learn it."

Both Mrs. Reese and Featherstone find themselves faced with the unexpected problem of a pupil-teacher ratio which is growing too large. Mrs. Reese tells of one teacher who is so popular that her class has increased from 15 to 27 students -- who come every day. Wahman is now recruiting an additional 100 teachers for the month of August and expects that schools in five new communities will be opened then.

Both Featherstone and Wahman point to the Negro history curriculum as possibly the most valuable legacy of the Freedom Schools this summer. "The only thing our kids knew about Negro history," Featherstone says, "is about Booker T. Washington and George Washington Carver and his peanuts."

But subjects like chemistry and algebra are also popular. Featherstone told by pupils in the McComb school that Negro children are taught algebra in high school, but white children begin the subject in the sixth grade. Wahman says that when the chemistry teacher left the Gulfport Freedom School, his 15 students also left in protest, and return only when another was sent into the school.

Mrs. Reese gives an idea what the Hattiesburg schools are accomplishing: "The children are learning that somebody is supposed to listen to them. They are writing letters to the editor of Hattiesburg newspapers, and learning where to direct their complaints. At first, the children were somewhat awe-stricken with the white teachers, at their whiteness, their hair, but many are learning to appreciate them as human beings. "When you get an appreciation of yourself, then you can put the other individual into his proper focus."

UNIT 11-6

FREEDOM SCHOOL DOCUMENT

Freedom Schools in Mississippi were proposed late in 1963 by Charles Cobb, a student at Howard University until he joined the COFO staff, and a gifted creative writer. Cobb proposed the creation of a statewide network of schools as part of the Mississippi Summer Project, then being planned. He describe the Freedom School as a place where students could freely ask questions about all those things, political as well as academic, which troubled and excited them. Calling attention to the fear of dismissal which restrains teachers in the Negro Public schools from exploring controversial topics, and noting also that the per capita expenditure of Mississippi local school boards for the white child is almost four times the figure for the Negro child,[1] this first Freedom School prospectus affirmed that help from outside Mississippi was needed if the Negro youngster were to have any chance of access to a larger world.

On June 21, 1964, Michael Schwerner, James Cheney and Andrew Goodman were killed as they attempted to create a Freedom School in Neshoba County. The purpose of their trip to Philadelphia that Sunday was to inspect the ruins of the Mt. Zion Church, burned to the ground two days previously because it was intended for a Freedom School, and to seek a new site for the school. They never returned.

As of July 26, 1964, there were 38 functioning Freedom Schools in 20 communities across the state with an enrollment of 2135 students, twice the figure projected in planning for the summer.[2] Approximately 175 persons were teaching full-time in the schools, and recruitment of 50–100 more was in process.

Thus, out of a dream, and death, and dedication, the Mississippi Freedom Schools came into being.

The classic instance of a successful school in an urban setting—indeed the Mecca of the Freedom School world—is Hattiesburg, with 600-odd students in five schools. Here, as in Canton, there can be no doubt that the success of the schools stemmed from the intensive civil rights campaign in the community during the months of late winter and spring.

The RELATIONSHIP OF FREEDOM SCHOOLS TO THE COFO POLITICAL PROGRAM varied from school to school. In some communities, such as Shaw, the politically-conscious teenagers for whom the schools were particularly intended were too wrapped up in canvassing to be bothered with Freedom School. In such situations the Freedom School staff typically assigned some teachers to full-time canvassing in an effort to take the school to the youngsters if the youngsters were not interested in coming to school. Thus at Shaw

---

July 1964.

I participated in role-playing a picket-line in preparation for actual (and highly successful) picketing at the Cleveland court house the next day.

Elsewhere the Freedom School proved its political value as an instrument for building confidence in the Negro community when canvassing was impractical. McComb provides a noteworthy example. In this southwestern town, mass registration is, for the time being, simply too dangerous. But Freedom school is possible, and the McComb school now has nearly a hundred students. On the first day of school it was necessary to meet on the lawn in front of the bombed McComb Freedom House, for no Negro church would open its doors. Joyce Brown, chairman of the student committee planning the Freedom School Convention (see below), wrote a moving poem about the occasion, called "The House of Liberty". This poem, read to a meeting of Negro adults, persuaded them to make a church available to the school. Thus the presence of a Freedom School helped to loosen the hard knot of fear and to organize the Negro community.

As the first Freedom School session ended, a number of STATEWIDE SPECIAL PROGRAM—a travelling drama group and circulating film programs, for example—were just coming into operation.

PROSPECT: SHORT-RUN

The most important planed events for the second Freedom School session (Aug. 3–Aug. 21) are: (**1**) The opening of Freedom Schools in Jackson; (**2**) The tour of the schools by the Mississippi-made Free Southern Theater, playing *In White America;* (**3**) Most important, the Freedom School Convention which will take place in Meridian.

The JACKSON FREEDOM SCHOOLS will begin in five-to-ten local churches on August 5. To meet the anticipated demand for up to thirty teachers, as well as present demands for 25-plus additional teachers from existing Freedom Schools, 50–100 teachers for the August session are presently being recruited by Friends Of SNCC groups in the Northeast. These new teachers will be oriented in Washington, D.C., the week-end of August 1.

The actors constituting the FREE SOUTHERN THEATER—Gilbert Moses, Susan Wahman, John O'Neal, Eric Weinberger, and others—are of professional caliber. Their aim is the creation of a fresh theatrical style which will combine the highest standards of craftsmanship with a more intimate audience rapport than modern theater usually achieves. Each playing of *In White America* will be accompanied by theater workshops designed to introduce youngsters to the experience of theater through participation.

The purpose of the FREEDOM SCHOOL CONVENTION is to stimulate a sustained process of group thinking about a political program among the young people who are the future leaders of Mississippi. This process arises spontaneously in the Freedom Schools: see the Declaration of Independence of the Palmer's Crossing school of Hattiesburg (Appendix C). Each of the twenty-odd communities which have Freedom Schools will send three delegates to Meridian. Each school will conduct preparatory discussions, draft its own program, and send this program with its representatives. At Meridian approximately 75 delegates, together with the Freedom School coordinators acting as advisors, will participate in eight workshops leading toward the formulation of a young people's program for Mississippi. The young people themselves are planning the convention through an executive committee chosen by delegates meeting in Jackson on July 25. Joyce Brown of McComb is chairman of this committee. Robert Moses and Mrs. Fannie Lou Hamer have been invited to address the Freedom School Convention. *In White America* will be played the first night of the convention.

As the first three-week session of the Freedom Schools came to an end, a number of generalizations were possible:

The TYPICAL FREEDOM SCHOOL had an enrollment of 25–100 and a staff of five or six teachers. It met in a church basement, often using an adjoining outdoor area as well. In addition to the 10th-11th-12th grade youngsters for whom the schools were principally intended, the typical Freedom School also acquired a sizeable number of Junior high school and even elementary school students, as well as some adults. In the typical school, the morning curriculum was built around a core of citizenship and Negro history. More specialized classes, such as French and typing (both very popular), were held in the late morning or afternoon; in these hours also, projects such as drama and student newspaper took place.[3] After a late-afternoon break, the typical school also held evening classes for adults and for those teen-agers who worked during the day.

This typical picture can be broken down into THREE CHARACTERISTIC SCHOOL SITUATIONS: (**1**) Isolated rural; (**2**) Urban or semi-urban, strong previous civil rights activity; (**3**) Urban or semi-urban, weak previous civil rights activity. The most successful schools were in categories (**1**) and (**2**). Thus in Holmes County and Carthage where there are few alternative attractions, students travelled long distances over hot dusty roads to attend Freedom School. In Holmes County, at the Mileston Freedom School, school adjourned at 2 P.M. each afternoon and moved down the road to the community center for an all-ages football game. When the Freedom School staff arrived at Carthage, the entire Negro community was assembled at the church to greet them; when, two days later, the staff was evicted from its school, the community again appeared with pickup trucks to help move the library to a new school site; as this is being written, the Carthage community, with the help of summer volunteers, is building it own community center. These are examples of isolated rural situations with successful Freedom Schools.

PROSPECT: LONG-RUN

Long-run prospects for the Freedom Schools can be discussed under two headings: assistance to individual students, and continuance of the Freedom Schools themselves.

We have opened up a promising channel for ASSISTANCE TO INDIVIDUAL STUDENTS with the help of the National Scholarship Service and Fund for Negro Students (NSSFNS). Standardized tests will be administered to the most promising Freedom School students in mid-August under the direction of the College Entrance Examination Board.[4] Upon evaluation of the scores and other data by NSSFNS, some Freedom School students will enter a program involving (**a**) a transitional educational experience in the summer after high school graduation, (**b**) a reduced load in the freshman year at college, (**c**) financial aid arranged by NSSFNS, all proceeding on the assumption that there are some students who with the proper help can make the big jump from a Mississippi Negro high school to an integrated Northern college.

Other Freedom School students can be helped by the already-existing Work-Study Program, which makes a full tuition, room and board scholarship at Tougaloo College near Jackson available to students who take a year out from college, or prior to college to work for the civil rights movement.

The question of CONTINUING FREEDOM SCHOOLS is the heart of this report. It is the unanimous recommendation of the entire Freedom School administration and staff, and I believe of the Summer Project Executive Committee, too, that Freedom Schools be continued after August. This recommendation is based on the following considerations:

1. In several places (Shaw, Holly Springs, Carthage) the Freedom Schools are now running concurrently with a public school summer session. The students *are* interested in attending Freedom School classes after regular school. Partly they feel that Freedom School provides instruction in subjects not available in public school, such as foreign

languages; more centrally, they are attracted to a school conducted in an informal, questioning spirit and built around the students' experience in the movement.

2. There is widespread apprehension among Mississippi Negroes as to what will happen to them when the Summer Project volunteers leave. We want to be able to tell them that the program will *not* end, that the momentum cumulated during the summer months will not be permitted to slack off.
3. In situations like McComb (see above), the Freedom School has proven its value to the overall COFO political program as an organizing instrument.
4. Among the various COFO programs, the Freedom School program is one which holds out particular hope of communication with the white community. In at least two situations (Vicksburg and Holly Springs), white children have attended for short periods.
5. The possibility of private-school legislation by the Mississippi legislature designed to sidestep public-school integration (already ordered for Fall 1964 in Jackson, Biloxi, and Leake County) also opens the possibility that COFO may want to erect a parallel school structure in some counties, just as it has created a parallel political structure through the Freedom Democratic Party.

If, then, the desirability of continuing Freedom Schools is accepted, the next question is, How?

The FORM OF INSTRUCTION, so the coordinators think, would be evening classes in the local community center. Already in many communities the Freedom School and community center programs are combined, and often in the same building. A POOL OF TEACHERS can be expected from the following four sources:

(1) *Summer volunteers* who decide to stay on. A poll of four Freedom School staffs indicated that one teacher in four is seriously considering staying on through the winter. If one in five actually stays, this would yield 50 teachers.

(2) *The Work-Study Program* (see above) should make available a substantial number of Southern Negro students; some of whom could be assigned to teaching. This is especially important since at present only 1 teacher in 10 is Negro (almost half of the coordinators are Negroes, however).

(3) *Negro adults* may in some cases volunteer for Freedom School teaching. In Hattiesburg, every Freedom School teacher has been asked to find and train a local resident to take his place when the Summer Program ends.

(4) If Freedom Schools are accepted as a valid part of the permanent COFO program, the assignment of *regular COFO staff* to part-time teaching should be considered. I believe that teaching could represent a refreshing change-of-pace for many voter registration workers.

If manpower is available, the remaining question is MONEY. In Appendix E will be found a tentative budget for the Mississippi Freedom Schools for the period September 1964 to June 1965. Beyond this looms the further challenge of Summer 1965. Freedom Schools throughout the Deep South? Residential Freedom Schools bringing together the best student leaders from all over a state or region? Those who have seen the faces of students brighten and come alive this summer will want to answer these questions, Yes.

APPENDIX A

Freedom School enrollment July 26, 1964:

1st Congressional District		
Columbus (2 schools)	60	
		60
2nd Congressional District		
Clarksdale (4 schools)	60	
Holmes County (3 schools)	105*	
Holly Springs (3 schools)	155	
Greenville (2 schools)	35	
Greenwood (2 schools)	60	
Ruleville (2 schools)	50	
Shaw (1 school)	35	
		490
3rd Congressional District		
Vicksburg (1 school)	60	
McComb (1 school)	75	
		135
4th Congressional District		
Canton (3 schools)	110	
Rural Madison (5 schools)	225 *	
Carthage (1 school)	75	
Meridian (1 school)	150	
		560
5th Congressional District		
Hattiesburg (5 schools)	675	
Laurel (1 school)	65	
Moss Point (1 school)	40	
Biloxi (1 school)	35	
Gulfport (3 schools)	75	
		890
Grand Total		2135

* CORRECTION: In the Introduction it is stated that as of July 26 there were 38 functioning Freedom Schools. This total was based on the erroneous assumption that there were 2 schools in Holmes County and three schools in rural Madison County. Actually, there are 3 and 5, respectively. The correct total of functioning Freedom Schools is therefore 41.

APPENDIX B

A budget for evening Freedom Schools in 25 communities, Sept., 1964–June, 1965

I. Supplies and Books

A. On the assumption that the cost of supplies for one Freedom School for a two-month full-time program would approximately equal the cost of supplying a part-time school for half the winter, then $200 x 2 x 25 comes to

$10,000

B. Several thousand books are in the state, but new acquisitions will be necessary in Negro history. At the very minimal figure of $25 per school, then $25 x 25 would come to

$625

II. Special Programs

A. If four films circulate continuously at a rental $25 per film per month, then for the winter the film budget would be about

$1,000

III. Administrative Expenses

The principal expenses this summer have been A. Postage and B. Gas. Setting each of these at the admittedly arbitrary sum of $500 for the winter, overhead administrative expenses total

$1,000

IV. Subsistence and Scholarships for Teachers

A. At the standard COFO rate of $10 per week per person, subsistence for two teachers at each school for forty weeks would come to

$20,000

B. If, on the same principle that applies in the Work-Study Program, scholarship aid for return to college is made available, then if 50 teachers were offered a 50% scholarship and if this is assumed to be $1000 in a typical Northern college, then this would add to the budget

$50,000

V. Bail

If the Summer Project figure of $500 cash bail be accepted, and if COFO undertakes to provide half of this sum (if necessary for 50 teachers, then 50 x 250)

$12,500

VI. Emergency Reserve

$4,875

Grand Total

$100,000

ENDNOTES

1. See James W. Silver, "Mississippi: The Closed Society," *Journal of Southern History,* XXX, (1964); p. 31. Silver gives the per capita expenditures in 1959–1960 as $81.86 for the white child and $21.77 for the Negro.

2. See Appendix A for a statistical breakdown.

3. For sample Freedom School newspapers, see Appendix B.

4. Appendix D for the application form NSFFNS is using for the Freedom Schools.

THE STUDENT VOICE

VOL. 5 NO. 14 STUDENT VOICE, INC. 6 Raymond Street, N. W. Atlanta, Georgia 30314 JUNE 9, 1964

MISS. NEGRO VOTE CURTAILED IN CONGRESSIONAL PRIMARY

Rev. John Camuron votes in Congressional primary in Hattiesburg. Rev. Cameron was a candidate for the Democratic House seat in the 5th Congressional District.

JACKSON, MISS. - Clever timing and scant publicity combined to help a newly passed state law curtail the number of votes cast for Mississippi's four Negro candidates who ran for nomination to U.S. Congress in the June 2 Democratic primary.

Only 6.6. percent of Mississippi's voting age Negroes are registered to vote - about 25,000. Four hundred thousand are eligible.

Incomplete election figures showed that 4,314 votes from across the state were returned for Victoria Jackson Gray who ran against Sen. John C. Stennis for the Senatorial nomination.

On e thousand one hundred-ninety ballots were cast for James Houston who ran for the Congressional nomination in the 3rd District, and the Rev. John Cameron received 1,071 votes in the 5th District.

Mrs. Fannie Lou Hamer, who opposed Rep. Jamie Whitten in the 2nd district, composed mainly of the Delta, received 389 votes. Most of the Delta's counties are located in the so-called Black Belt where a majority of the population is Negro.

None of the candidates, who were backed by the Mississippi Freedom Democratic Party, expected to win. But all of theml hoped to c onduct active campaigns to educate the state's voters and the nation to unconstitutional denial of the vote to Mississippi's Negro and lower class whites.

The candidates also sought to raise political issues obscured by the campaigns of candidates seeking election on the basis of who will most ardently uphold segregation.

A newly passed bill which appears to comply with the 24th Amendment added to the obvious hurdles Negro candidates would have to getting nominated.

On June 1, the night before the primary election, U.S. District Judge Harold Cox issued a re-

CONTINUED ON PAGE 3

Brutality Hearing Held In Capital

WASHINGTON, D.C. - A public hearing on Mississippi will be conducted here June 8.

The hearing, sponsored by the Mississippi Council of Federated Organizations (COFO), will be held at the National Theater. Testimony will be heard from Mississippians who are victims of various kinds of reprisal, discrimination, police or unofficial brutality, before a panel of distinguished persons.

The panel includes authors Michael Harrington, James Baldwin, Paul Goodman, Lorraine Hansberry, and Joseph Heller; educator Harold Taylor; Judge Justine Polier; and Gresham Sykes of the American Sociological Association. Testimony will also be heard from Robert Coles, research psychiatrist at Harvard University, and others who will speak about the necessity for presidential action in Mississippi.

According to SNCC communications director Julian Bond who is coordinating the hearing, Mississippians are being brought to Washington to testify since the U.S. Civil Rights Commission has never conducted a hearing in the state.

FLASH! *FLASH!* *FLASH!*

Riders Throw Bomb At Freedom House

CANTON, MISS. - A bomb thrown from an automobile exploded outside the Canton Freedom House early Monday morning.

The bomb, thrown at the house, bounced off, rolled 20 feet away and exploded. The windows in the house were shattered. No one was injured. There were two people in the house at the time of the bombing, 1:30 A.M.

Later that night somebody called the Freedo m House and asked "How many did we get."

The Freedom House has been under constant harassment from callers for the last few weeks."

Over 50 people were arrested and a Negro youth was beaten unconscious during a Freedom Day, here, May 29.

Canton, located in the 4th Congressional District, has been the site of a concentrated voter registration drive by the Council of Federated Organization a coalition of major civil rights groups in Mississippi.

MISSISSIPPI PREPARES FOR SUMMER PROJECT

JACKSON, MISS. - As civil rights workers complete plans for the Mississippi Summer Project, the state has been tightening legislative screws to halt as many phases of the project as possible.

As a Mississippi newspaper put it, there is a "statewide movement to erect a bulwark against anticipated racial demonstrations in Mississippi this coming summer." Part of this bulwark has been the recent enactment of six new laws aimed at the project by the state legislature.

An AP story in the Jackson Daily News April 20 explained that the Mississippi legislature's program of "quietly arming the state for an expected invasion"

CONTINUED ON PAGE 2

BACKGROUND NEWS-

LEGAL BARRIERS TO GREET WORKERS

CONTINUED FROM PAGE 1

by civil rights workers had received little notice because state solons "do not discuss racial bills on the floor and give only a minimum of explanation." The reason, the AP story continued, was that state legislators were fearful such speeches would be used by the Federal government in civil rights cases to show the intent of the law was to maintain segregation and was therefore unconstitutional.

New Laws Passed

1. RIOT CONTROL. Authorizes cities to "pool" personnel, manpower and equipment, and ingeneral, give "mutual assistance." Introduced in the state Senate as bill #1526, the measure as enacted and signed into law by Governor Paul B. Johnson, facilitates exchange of jail space as well as the pooling of city police forces.

It is assumed the city of Jackson will be prominent in assisting other cities in "riot control". In recent months the city has strengthened its police force and laid in an extra supply of gas masks, shotguns and helmets according to Jackson newspapers. A $15,000 tank known locally as "Thompson's Tank will be part of the equipment of "Allen's Army" - both namesakes of Jackson Mayor Allen Thompson.

2. CURFEW. Authorizes cities to "restrict the movements of individuals and groups" and to set curfew hours. (House bill #64.)

3. A law which BOOSTS THE STATE HIGHWAY PATROL to almost double its present size gives state police full power in civil disorders as well as undercover investigations. Prior to the enactment, those officers were restricted to traffic law enforcement. The law has had special backing from the governor since he requested the legislation in a speech before a joint session of the state legislature March 3. The new law gives the governor personal power to send state police into areas, even over the heads of local law enforcement. Originally introduced in the House as bill #564, the controversial measure passed despite opposition from some states solons who feared it might be used to control illegal liquor practices in this dry state.

In referring to the law which expands the patrol from 275 to 475 men a Greenville daily, the Delta Democrat-Times said, "A private army which can be used at the governor's own discretion is not a healthy kind of temptation to have around."

It was reported in January that every member of the state police then on the force had been trained in riot control techniques. Colonel T.B. Birdsong, commissioner of public safety, said these men in turn trained police and sheriff's officers across the state.

4. ANTI-PICKETING. Prohibits picketing of all public buildings, streets and sidewalks and other places belonging to the city, county and state. The maximum penalty on conviction is $500 and /or six months in jail. The constitutionality of the new law is presently being tested in Federal court by 44 persons arrested in Hattiesburg April 10-11.

House bill #546 was introduced as an "emergency bill for Greenwood" March 25 - the same day as Greenwood's first Freedom Day - by a state representative from Forrest County where a Freedom Day was held in January Picketing of the Forrest County courthouse has occured almost daily since then.

5. INCREASED PENALTIES. Larger penalties may be assessed by municipal courts as a result of enactment of Senate bill #1517. Maximum fines by be raised from $100 to $300 in city courts and maximum jail terms from 30 to 90 days. This would apply to traffic violations which have been lodged with increasing frequency against rights workers as the summer approaches.

6. OUTLAWS DISTRIBUTION OF BOYCOTT LITERATURE. Senate bill #1545 was introduced by a state senator from Canton, where a boycott to pressure for an end to discriminatory pratices by merchants and businesses has been underway since January. The new law provides for a maximum penalty of $500 and / or six months in jail for printing or circulating materials concerning boycotts.

Rights workers maintain this law, and the anti-picket provision, are flagrantly unconstitutional.

***

State Legal Code

The state Sovereignty Commission - official watchdog agency to perpetuate segregation - has mailed a "handy" reference digest of statutes already on the books to law enforcement officers throughout the state with the suggestion that they be used to halt civil rights acitivity.

State code sections suggested by the state subsidized group for use in racial matters are the following:

* Congregating and refusing to disperse when so ordered by a law officer (maximum fine $200 and/ or four months in jail),
* Interfering with customers or the operation of restaurants stores, hotels and theaters (maximum fine $500 and / or six months in jail),
* Making false statements to Federal authorities-FBI, courts, Justice Department, Civil Rights Commission - about denial of constitutional rights by the state or its agents (maximum fine $1, 000 and/ or six months in jail),
* Encouraging anouther person to remain on the premises of another "when forbidden to do so" (maximum fine $500 and/ or six months in jail).

***

Laws Considered

1. OUTLAWS FREEDOM SCHOOLS. Senate bill #1969 makes it a misdemeanor to teach in or conduct a school not licensed by the state. Rights workers contend it is explicity directed at curbing Freedom Schools.

2. ANTI-INVASION. House bill $270 prohibits entry into the state with the intention of violating state laws, and sets the penalty at a fine of up to $1,000 and as much as two years in prison.

3. CRIMINAL SYNDICALISM. Senate bill #2027 prohibits "criminal syndicalism" which is defined as the doctrine which advocates or teaches "the commission of crime, violence and force as a means of accomplishing or affecting a change in agricultural or industrial ownership or control . . . or in affecting any political or social change." That measure, now passed by the Senate and before the House, makes it a felony to teach or "justify" such a precept. It is claimed by state solons that the law could be used against "extremists'" of either persuasion on the question of race.

4. OUTLAWS COMMUNITY CENTERS. - Senate bill #2136 if passed would require certification by the state of all clinics or schools where general education and general health subjects would be taught. Summer project plans call for community centers where instruction in child care, dietary health and housing repair would be offered. The measure also arms the attorney gneral with injunctive power to "dissolve any operation" which does not have permits.

***

Other Laws

1. Two bills passed in the House which would keep Negroes from serving on juries in the state by restricting selection to resident landowners and / or registered voters. Only 6.6. percent of the voting age Negroes in Mississippi are registered to vote.

2. A juvenile demonstration measure provides that youths arrested in racial demonstrations be excluded from juvenile courts.

SIT-IN CASES NEAR HIGH COURT HEARING

ATLANTA, GA. - "Sit - in" cases resulting from SNCC - led anti-segregation protests here last January are a step nearer to a hearing by the U.S. Supreme Court.

Attorneys Donald L. Hollowell and Howard Moore, acting for demonstrators, filed a response June 1 to an earlier petition by state court authorities who are asking the tribunal to order the 5th Circuit Court of Appeals to remand the cases back to state jurisdiction.

The cases go back almost a year. One hundred-one cases that have been removed to the Federal courts stemmed from indictments handed down here by a grand jury in August. The 101 were charged with violating the anti-trespass law.

Judge Durwood T. Pye ordered the cases brought before him, but only three defendants - Thomas Taylor Tolg, the Rev. Ashton Jones, and Mardon Walker, all white- actually went to trial and were convicted. Each received the maximum penalty.

Attorneys for the others petitioned a Federal judge for removal. The judge refused and Hollowell and Moore sucessfully appealed his refusal to the 5th Circuit Court of Appeals.

Judge Pye then ordered the solicitor general of the Atlanta circuit to file a petition with the Supreme Court for a order directing the 5th Circuit to send the cases back to the state courts.

The Negro lawyers' June 1 petition was an answer to this petition.

BIAS GROUP FORMED

NATCHEZ, MISS.-SNCC workers report the formation of another white racist organization in Southwest Mississippi.

A new group called the Adams County Religious Association recently published a leaflet charging communist influence of a local priest and a Yale University student who was shot at last fall while working on a mock ballot campaign.

Southwest Mississippi has traditionally been the stronghold of white terrorist groups. During the past few weeks an upsurge in activity by white supremacist groups has been reported in the Mississippi press.

Discontented Ku Klux Klan and White Citizens Councils members are apparently forming their own new groups in this part of the state.

PRIMARY

CONTINUED FROM PAGE 1

straining order against election officials to prohibit use of newly enacted Senate bill #1783 which banned the poll tax in Federal elections but required presentation of a receipt marked "Poll Tax Not Paid" in order to vote.

In an attempt to challenge both the new law and the court ruling which established similar means for exclusion at the polls, many Negroes went to election places without either stamped poll tax receipts or affidavits.

State elections required poll tax receipts for the past two years. Mississippi poll tax is $2.00 a year, and automatically exempts many for financial reasons.

The newly enacted "non-payment" provision bill received almost no coverage in Mississippi newspapers. This, in addition to the fact that only 30 days were allowed to obtain the receipts, meant that those Negroes who had been able to register were in many cases unable to cast ballots in this election.

"In view of the many obstacles thrown up, including what appears to be collusion between the press and the state legislature, we consider the results of the June 2 primary election a good showing," one SNCC worker said here.

SNCC has conducted a voter registration project in that state since 1961 and has encouraged Negroes to run for public office. A major emphasis of the Mississippi Summer Project will be voter registration.

All four Negro candidates intend to run as independents in the general elections in November.

The Mississippi Freedom Democratic Party plans to contest the seating of delegates from the regular Democratic Party at the National Democratic Convention in Atlantic City, N. J. in August. A program of "Freedom Registration" will seek to show that 400,000 Negroes in Mississippi would vote if they were allowed.

In the 1960 presidential election votes cast in Mississippi totalled 266,000. Connecticut, with approximately the same population, returned 966,000 ballots.

THE STUDENT VOICE
Published Once A Week
On Mondays At Atlanta,
Fulton County, Ga.
By STUDENT VOICE, INC.
6 Raymond Street, N. W.
Atlanta, Georgia 30314

Less than 7% of Mississippi's voting age Negroes are registered. This summer, a concentrated vote drive will be held as part of the Mississippi Summer Project.

SUPPORT THE MISSISSIPPI SUMMER PROJECT!

Enclosed is my contribution of $ ______________.

I pledge $ _____ per month to the Student Nonviolent Coordinating Committee (SNCC).

NAME ______________

ADDRESS ______________

CITY ______________

STATE ______________

Contributors to SNCC receive a subscription to the STUDENT VOICE. Send to: SNCC, 6 Raymond Street, N.W., Atlanta, Ga. 30314.

UNIT 11-8

SOVEREIGNTY COMMISSION (MS) MEMO

September 23, 1965

MEMORANDUM

TO: File

FROM: Director, Sovereignty Commission

SUBJECT: Venereal Disease

We have been reliably informed that in the membership of the Mississippi Freedom Democratic Party, now composed of SNCC and COFO workers, the rate of venereal disease is 39.2 percent.

We have also been informed that some of the doctors and nurses imported to treat these have resigned in disgust and returned to their respective homes in the north and east.

Erle Johnson, Jr.

cc: Honorable Herman Glazier
EJ/ea

UNIT 11-9

FIELD REPORTS—TELLING IT LIKE IT WAS

The large file of regular narrative field reports of voter registration workers in VEP projects constitutes a unique contribution to the literature of American history. What follows are excerpts selected almost at random from some five thousand or more pages of such material. The attempt has been not only to pull out some of the more dramatic, or apt or particularly colorful narratives, but also to give a representative feel of the whole of these files. In this way, it is hoped that the flavor, spirit, and reality of the movement during these years will be conveyed.

There has been no effort to edit or clean up the excerpts. It is therefore appropriate to remind the reader that they were written often under the most stressful of conditions, and that while some indicate less than adequate education, others more nearly reflect momentary inattention to details of grammar and punctuation. They were written to convey information (and, certainly, often feeling), not as finished compositions. As often is the case with such writing, there is probably more communication in them than most prose consciously set down for print.

From Charles M. Sherrod, project coordinator, *Southwest Georgia Voter Registration Project,* December 1962—

Since our last report, 13 meetings have been held in the three counties of our area: In Sumter on the Thursday nights of Nov. 15, 22, 29, and Dec. 6, in Terrell on Wednesdays Nov. 14, 21, 28, and Dec. 5, in Lee on Saturdays Nov. 10, 17, 24, and Dec. 1 and 8. The meetings are at present absolutely essential to the program and every effort is made that they should be attended not only by the protect coordinator and the staff working in the particular county, but by the staff from other counties and from Albany.

Our faithful friend the Rev. Samuel B. Wells of East Albany never fails to drive out, which helps us provide transportation for those citizens of Albany who wish to accompany us . . .

The importance of this "outside" attendance can hardly be overstressed as a morale-builder. The sense that "we are not alone" is important, and so is the practical usefulness of the sharing of experience . . .

We are hoping to change the emphasis of the meetings slightly. In the early days their primary purpose was to enhearten the wavering, to encourage the unregistered voters who attended to move on from the first crucial step of summoning up the courage to come, to the decisive step of going to the courthouse and making the effort to register. The sense of fellowship, the heartening influence of the prayers, the songs, the scripture readings, the tales of hardship bravely borne, all these must stay with us. But by now a large proportion of the local attendance at any mass meeting is made up of people who have already registered.

In the context of the legitimate emotion of the meeting, they should be given more than the simple instructions and exhortations concerning the registration procedure, and the exchanges of information on progress in the counties, which have been the bulk of the content of the meetings to date.

From Charles M. Sherrod, *Southwest Georgia Project,* December 1962—

We have placed almost total allegiance to the group in the areas of strategy and practice. In the group the individual finds the strength he cannot or rather does not see outside of its jurisdiction. One of the reasons the white man with the segregationist attitude has been somewhat successful in blocking the black man in the past has much to do with the effectiveness of isolation . . .

From Jack Chatfield, *Southwest Georgia Project,* December 1962—

Talked to one ancient man on the porch of his home, and he said, "Looks like they tried to scare some of those fellows away, but it weren't no spo't." He was speaking of the fellows in the movement, whom he said he had seen "on the television." We told him they wouldn't pull no spo't with us either.

He told us he was from Florida and has lived in north Georgia. "I said 'Yas' and 'No' down Florida . . . and north too. . . . "

Southwest Georgia is "Yassuh" country.

He was an intelligent man and his hands were scarred hideously. I suspect his intelligence was scarred too.

"And after all that" he said, "three dollar a day."

Somewhere in Bronwood, in a house with a green roof, there is a blind man who wants us to talk to him. . . .

Faith Molsaert, *Southwest Georgia Project*—

Right now, it's a big step if people, instead of complaining to themselves of harassments, tell us. But *some day, they won't even need the students.*

Jack Chatfield, *Southwest Georgia Project,* December 1962—

It is shocking upon consideration that the night air above the red roads of the colored section is not filled with furtive hymns of plot and overthrow, of philosophy and abstract design. Since September (the registration drive began officially in January and reached a height during the torrid summer), I have not heard report of a single unofficial gathering of citizens whose discussion topic was: "What can be done?" There are no doubt countless dinner conversations, but nothing which remotely approaches a loose "organization" or "conspiracy" of any sort.

As for Mrs. Silas, whom we recommended contact Mr. Henderson about getting transportation to the tent in Sasser, she "ain't seen him." As for Mr. Henderson, whom we recommended contact Mrs. Silas (who was "interested" in attending a voter registration meeting with Mr. Henderson), he "ain't seen her."

As for Mrs. Nelson, whom we recommended speak to Deacon Green (who had recently attended his first meeting), she "ain't spoke to him." As for Deacon Green whom we recommended contact Mrs. Nelson (who shared his fears), he "sho' ain't stopped by."

Sometimes, under the weight of the awful impotence I have encountered spasmodically, you find yourself hollering, "How the hell do you make them move? Where is the courage, where is the wisdom? Why don't they move?"

Ten o'clock and you have resolved that they have failed; eleven o'clock and you have resolved that you have failed. Twelve o'clock and you don't know a damn thing. . . .

Ruleville and Sunflower County, Mississippi, January 4–12, 1963,
by Charles McLaurin—

On January 4, 1963, we made it back to Ruleville, that night we went to the home of Mrs. Bessie Lee Green, who lives in Ruleville. She have attempted to register and have attended most of the meetings. She did not make enough money picking or chopping cotton to carry her through the winter, she have bills to pay on her stove water lights and gas and an addition to her house. Mrs. Green have a daughter that have a small child sometime the child don't have milk to drink. Her daughter's husband don't have a steady job he is 23 years of age and have not tried to register because he feel the person he is working for would fire him. Mrs. Green needs $260 or she will not have a stove to cook on and the lumber company could take her bathroom fixtures . . .

On January 5, we went from door to door trying to find people to go down to register, we found three persons who said they would go down Monday January 7th.

On Sunday, January 6, 1963 the Ruleville Christian Citizenship Club met, there were 19 persons present. This group is made up of people who have gone to Indianola and took the test, at this meeting was Mrs. Irean Johnson chairman of the group and one of the four persons to pass the voters test. Each member said they would try to get at least two new persons to come to the meeting, the meetings are open to everyone. We played the record (Freedom In The Air), and talked about it.

January 7th we helped needy persons fill out COFO Welfare and Relief applications, those people need help other than commodities and the small Welfare checks that they receive. COFO is giving clothes, shoes, to them, this will inable the people to use money that they would buy clothes with to pay bills and other needed items.

Tuesday, January 8, 1963, we did not take the three people down to register because they wanted to wait and see if others would go from the meeting that night. In the meeting four more said they would go down Thursday January 10th. So on the 9th we gave out some of the clothing we had for the people. Thursday night we attended a mass meeting in Shaw, Mississippi. Rev. James Bevel gave a class on Voter Registration, there was about 50 to 75 people there. Meetings will be held in Shaw every Thursday night.

We are going to Drew, Miss. Wednesday January 16, to start canvassing. On Sunday January 13, one of us will go to church in Drew, this way we meet some of the leading people.

Mrs. Vera Pigee, Clarksdale, Mississippi, January 16–23, 1963—

I carried 20 or more to the Circuit Clerk Office here in Coahoma County, 17 was processed, however, I don't know if they passed the literary test or not but I will know in the next 30 days.

The reason the 3 out of 20 didn't get to take the test was because the Clerk deputy only processed (1) one at a time, by this way the time ran out before they got a chance. . . . the room she used can seat 20.

I have also seen [the] Circuit Clerk let people who are not Negroes put their name on the book without taking the test.

Fear plays a part also, some women say if they try to register their husband will lose their job, they will lose theirs, their children are teachers and will [lose] their job . . .

Frank Smith, Holly Springs, Mississippi, January 4–15, 1963—

After returning to Mississippi from the retreat, we found things to be in reasonably good shape. I think we were beginning to shake off the effect of the "Ole Miss" crisis and become our normal selves again. . . .

On Sunday it was raining and muddy and our Speaker's Bureau didn't get out. I went to the County to see Mr. Pegues and got stuck. Man what a predicament, scared to ask anyone to give me a push and damned sure I was not going to walk from out there. My partner, Beamon, and I had a pushing good time.

From Reginald Robinson, Orangeburg, South Carolina, January 1963—

Friday 11, January, 1963—Most of today I have been putting all of the notes from interviews together. I called Mrs. Rackely about 5:30. She had talked with Mr. Earl Middleton and he did not know of a place in which I would work out of, and he told her he want to see me. Mrs. Rackely went on to say she had about three more place to call . . . Went to see Mr. Earl Middleton. We talked about what I had been doing all week. Mr. Middleton said the reason I was being sent from person to person and could not get their support was, because they want the credit of anything done in Orangeburg. They [NAACP] does not like for anybody coming in using the local chapter. The local chapter here in Orangeburg will not work with another group; because they have there own project. The only help you can get is from the people as individuals not as the NAACP. Middleton told me I could get anything I needed to work with. I asked him for a map of the city or county. He gave me a map broken down by ward & precinct. There was a list made of all the registered Negro sometime back. I asked Middleton if I could have a copy. Middleton said "he was told by one of the NAACP heads not to let me have this list." He also said he did not understand why I could not have a copy, and that if I come back to see him Monday, he would have a copy for me. This is when I left, because I had taken as much as I could. I knew now the only way I was going to get anything was to make my own group, and the hell with these people.

From Mrs. Colia Lafayette, Selma, Alabama, February 1963—

The people from Browns, Ala., have to drive 18 miles into town to attend the voter classes. Five of the people from Browns have been trying to register since 1956. They are Mrs. Rebecca Anderson, Mrs. Lillian Tean Kimbrough, mother of 13, Mrs. Ethel Washington, 76, had six sons to serve at the same time during World War II, Mr. Eddie Criffin . . . and Mr. Gus Tabb.

From Jack Chatfield, *Southwest Georgia Project*—

We strolled round the colored section, and at one point during the afternoon we were buzzed by a pick-up; he turned around and buzzed us again at about 50 miles per hour. My lungs runneth over with dust. There was a colored boy in the front seat with him, admirably demonstrating, I believe, "the white man's" total lack of comprehension in the area of Negro affairs.

We had been told by Mr. Henderson that Les Holly, a blind man, wanted us to stop by. We stopped by.

Les Holly was sitting on a tiny porch on the front of his home, surrounded by all appearances by a retinue of relatives or visitors. Chico introduced himself and I did the same. A lady whom I took to be his wife or daughter repeated, "This is Mr. Chatfield."

I was holding Mr. Holly's hand and he asked, "Is this Chatfield?"

He said that he wanted us to stop back, so that he could sit and talk with us for a long spell. I was in love with this guy: his eyes, shielded with dark glasses, were facing in our general direction; he became the symbol of the human tragedy, this waste of human lives, and it was as though he had been waiting for us a very long time—and the wait was not for someone who could lift him out of the tragedy, but who would understand it. He is over the hill—blind, ancient, surrounded by cackling kin; it was as if we were the only ones who would know him.

These are the times when the man is reduced, in human terms, to the myth, the legend. But in human terms—so that he is saved from destruction.

"I wish I could have seen you before my sight went," he said. His sight had gone in August of this year.

I said that sight did not matter, and I told him that we would sit and read the constitution of the United States together. He smiled.

"The radio said all Chatfield would say was the fourth constitution. He wouldn't tell'em anything except the fourth constitution."

He was talking about the fourteenth amendment, which Holly's whole life has been a violation of.

So now in Bronwood, there is Les Holly, who has been waiting a long time, who perhaps up until Saturday was happy with the myth, and who now we shall have to make happy with the reality, which is tough.

From Ida Holland, Greenwood, Mississippi, February 1963,
on food distribution by COFO—

Some of them had walked from as far as 20 miles to get here. Some were so cold they could hardly talk. Others were without proper clothes and shoes. Some didn't believe; it was "too good to be true." I asked the people if they would like to vote. Some didn't know what voting was. Others couldn't read or write. Some said no, but the majority said yes.

From Essie Lee Marks of Greenwood, another helper—

On Feb. 20, we distributed more food and we didn't get to everyone. There were hundreds who didn't receive anything and really needed it. We just didn't have enough food and clothing to get around to everyone.

The people were very nice and attentive when we told them, we just couldn't get to them.

On Feb. 21, we went to the church and sorted the clothes and shoes into sizes. On Feb. 22, we started distributing the clothes and shoes to the needy people. These people were in bad shape. Some of them didn't have shoes on. They were wearing raggedy dirty old clothes. Most of the ladies had on men pants, big shoes, and some type of rag on their head.

We gave all the clothes out to these people. Still there were many more who needed things badly. We need more clothes for these children. Lots of them are out of school on account of no clothes and shoes. These children are between the ages of six and fourteen years of age.

From James Austin, Selma, Alabama, February 1963—

On January 22, 1963, 1 started my first class with only one student, on January 24 I had two students, January 29, I had four students and January 31 I had six students. Starting the month of February, the students began to come in more and more. February 5 I had six students and February 14, I had 14 students. I am also sending the names of students to go down Monday 24 of February and register. They are as following: Charles Mazey, Sadia Mitchell, Eddie Criffin, Gus Tabb, Rebecca Anderson.

From Frank Smith, Holly Springs, February 1963—

Saw Mr. Pegues Tuesday, January 15, and gave him some forms for our welfare relief program. He said, "I think you ought to give these to Reverend Echols he would be a better person." He offered the excuse he had to do business and didn't want to become involved. He said he was scared for his wife and family.

Mrs. Loullen asked me for some names and addresses because she said that she knew that she was going to be "messed with." She is a great lady. She carries people down to register, tries to get them welfare and just worries them to death if they don't. She is a valuable person or asset. Boy does she live in the country, when it rains, the only way we can communicate is by mail.

Mr. Ingram took a family the other day that had been put out. The man didn't have any place to stay and Ingram provided him one.

From Wallace Harvey, Greenwood, Mississippi—

On off time from my job, one day in August I met two young men, they were strangers to me. Then and there I noticed something different about these two men. They introduced themselves and told me things about their movement, and I had that feeling of intellect. I was impressed with that extra boost. I saw the green light on and that means go, and I have been going since.

I started that week working on Voters Registration. It was hard to get my people to cooperate. The first and most important was fear. When questioned, 7 out of 10 of the people stated they had not worked since cotton time. . . .

Coahonw County, Mississippi, Branch NAACP, February 26, 1963,
Aaron Henry, president—

The Clarksdale Police Department has the task of explaining the death of a Negro prisoner in the City Hall. The attitudes and actions, by both the Clarksdale Police Department and the City Administration, against Negroes all along, makes a thorough investigation in this death necessary by both local and federal authorities.

It appears the most sure remedy to this kind of treatment is a sustained "Registration to Vote Drive." We must be willing to go, time and time again, to the Circuit Clerk's office and offer to register, regardless of how many times we are denied the right to register; most of our problems can be cleared up with the vote.

We can vote for decent treatment of Negro Prisoners by voting for a Mayor and City Commissioners that will not tolerate abuse of prisoners. The chief of police and all other policemen are employees of the city administration. We can vote for better and fair law enforcement by voting in men and women who will administer the law fairly without regard to race or creed.

We can vote for employment by.voting into office and administration those that will secure industry which will employ *all of the unemployed* and not just industry that will employ the *white unemployed*.

We can vote for a better school system—one that will obey the laws of the nation—by voting in a city administration that will respect the law of the nation. We can vote for better streets and lights in Negro neighborhoods by voting in men that can be fair in their administration if the popular vote will support them.

We can vote for the right to vote by supporting men who will not make it so difficult for Negroes to become registered voters. The vote will help tremendously in our struggle to gain dignity, respect, and employment from the downtown merchants. In the meantime we must rely on the boycott. Let us plan now to wear our old clothes for Easter. Those items we cannot do without, let us purchase them on this side of the railroad track or go into other communities to purchase them. The NAACP is still supplying transportation to Memphis, Helena, Arkansas, and other cities where more courtesy and employment are available to Negroes.

The votes will, in time, help the local press refrain from its continual discourtesy in refusing to refer, in print, to adult Negroes with court titles. The personnel of the local press is really sympathetic to our cause for freedom. They disagree with many of our methods, which is understandable, none of them being Negroes . . .

The Negro is not without fault in this whole affair. Citizenship schools have been set up to help the Negro improve himself in every facet of livelihood. These schools are under the direction of Mrs. Vera M. Pigee, and are held every Monday and Tuesday night from 6:00-8:00 p.m. The schools are conducted at: Chapel Hill Baptist Church Rayford Chapel Baptist Church, Silent Grove Baptist Church, Pigee Beauty Salon, and Johnson's Sandwich Shop. All citizens are invited an encouraged to attend these schools to effect self betterment in every facet of life.

From Carver Neblett, *Southwest Georgia Project*, early 1963—

I have been after Joe to register for almost a month now. His excuse has been that I work out of town. And that he is off from work at 6:00. When I heard that he was off from work Monday, December 24, jumped on him with all four feet. Joe has been coming to meetings the past month.

I predict that when Mr. Holly, Bronwood, Mrs. Beasley, Parrot school teacher who plans to register against the county superintendent's will, and Joe registers, maybe we will start a few of the more reluctant people such as Mr. Henderson, Mrs. Silas, Mrs. Collier, Etc., to thinking an maybe coming to meetings. WE SHALL OVERCOME . . .

From Elizabeth Wyckoff, Albany, Georgia—

East Albany is largely a working class area, and many residents are fairly recent immigrants from the adjacent rural areas, and still have relatives there. While it is apparently true that in Albany itself simply applying for registration does not expose one to reprisals, and the registrars, both at City Hall and the Court House, are not overtly obstructive, many East Albany residents are convinced that it is dangerous to attempt to register. Others believe that voting is futile. Still others are (often rightly) uncertain that their degree of literacy is sufficient to pass the test, and almost equally alarmed at the prospect of the test for illiterates. Only a few of these people react positively to the suggestion of attending citizenship school . . . The area has been canvassed several times in the last few years, so that most of the unregistered voters are people who have at some time been urged to "become first-class citizens," and have decided against it, whether consciously, or by procrastination. They are therefore harder to persuade than those not unearthed before, to whom the idea is a new one . . .

There is also in the area a hard core of registered voters. These are those who have served Rev. Wells as street and block workers in the past, and besides these one meets, again and again, even on blocks where it may be that no one else is registered, people who look one in the eye and say firmly that they have been registered "ever since the colored could vote." These are the people on whom we must build.

From Charles Sherrod, *Southwest Georgia Project*, February 1963—

Terrell,—As you know, a white policeman was summoned before the throne of justice in the presence of people of the counties around. We have been talking about this case and the possibilities of his conviction for some time. The people had built their hopes up high. Actually, they were prepared to see him eaten by the lions. He was to be a sacrifice of appeasement. They wanted to see his blood. They came to Americus, Georgia, each day of the week during the period in which the trial was to come up. From each county they came, Terrell, Lee, Dougherty, and Sumter. On Wednesday night, they turned out to the mass meeting at Sasser, on Thursday they turned out to the meeting in Sumter, and on Saturday after the acquittal ruling was made they turned out in large numbers at Lee County. They were broken in spirit but they made us feel ashamed that we were all so despondent, not openly, but the people love us and though they respect their leaders, they love and understand us as they do children for we are what they hope their children will become (they don't know do they). The meeting in the tent on Wednesday night after the decision of the court was the most inspirational of my memory. Some of the people went up to such an emotional pitch that they arose together when it was suggested by one lady about fifty that we march on Dawson's City Hall. Of course, the opinion was respected and treated with consideration, and then we moved on to the issue at hand.

It was amazing how some of the people with whom we work have not been discouraged by this defeat in our opinion. They said that it was a victory even to have been able to get the policeman to stand in judgment before a judge and jury . . .

We were told by John Martin, an attorney of the justice Department, that the case of the *United States v. Z. T. Mathews* may not come up in court. This was again very disappointing to us. The people need to see blood. This is bad but they must have a victory in the courts. A white man must be punished for doing harm to a black man, a white man with a badge on must bow to justice. And this is different. The officials in Terrell think that they can put on a badge and do anything they like and the black men of this section think that the badge is magic too. Anybody wearing a badge can do anything. It's about time that these sons learn that they stand under the judgment of the same badge that they wear. Anyway, Martin of the Justice Department told us that the county officials did not want to go to the court but rather wanted a settlement out of the courts.

From Leflore County, Greenwood, Mississippi, *Report of Registration Campaign* by Mrs. Monetta Hancock, Reporter—

On February 26, 1963, we accompanied large numbers of people to the county court house of Greenwood, Mississippi, to register to become qualified voters of Mississippi.

I arrived about 15 minutes until 10:00 with a small group. I was accompanying John H. Ball who is leader of the Voting Committee. At the time I arrived, I was told that at least 49 people had already taken the test. New people were coming in to register also. I took some of their names and John Ball was taking some of their names too . . .

After about an hour or so the jailer and a prisoner came out with a buffer to buff the floor where these people were standing. Because of this, the people had to move and scatter about. After he buffed the area where the people were standing, he came over where they were standing in the beginning. So, I decided to follow the people and stand in line with them. After a while the prisoner came back to where we were standing. I asked the boy if we moved over this time would he be through this time? He came closer to me and told me, "Look, lady, I'm not doing this on my own. I am doing this because they (the jailor) told me to do this. They don't want you all to vote; but you all stick right here." I told him thank you and proceeded to tell John Ball about this incident. He said that he was already aware of what was going on. So the floor was being buffed all while we were there.

From John O'Neal, Lee County, Georgia, March 6, 1963—

Mr. C. . . . deserves some comment. [He] is 25 years old, married and has one child. He himself has experienced quite a bit of difficulty in his attempts to register. He has gone down about four times and each time has been unable to complete the process because of . . . [the official in charge]—sometimes he sick or absent for some other reason and sometimes he's just plain cantankerous.

[Mr. C.] has personally been responsible for getting at least ten or twelve people to go down, however, including his wife and three other ladies whose husbands live and work on the plantation. He is important because of the fact that so many people in exactly the same position refuse to cooperate because of their positions—being directly dependent on a white man's judgment of his worth. There ought to be some way to provide for the economic security of people in such positions. They could be fired for simply leaning on the wrong tree.

Mr. C. is a very effective worker and is very persuasive. I worry sometimes if his enthusiasm might not override his better judgment. He has invited us to his home several times which is situated right in the middle of the plantation in plain view of everyone. His home is one of several places that Negroes are permitted to use in order that the guests of the plantation can see how well the good negroes are treated down heah. This favor is also a symbol of the high status that the dog trainer occupies on a sports ranch. (The place is owned by a North Carolina textile manufacturer who vacations there three months out of the year. There are 11,000 acres in the place, which is used primarily for bird hunting.) If we become too regular as visitors, surely our presence, even all Black, will be noticed and our identity already is too well known to remain secret to inquisitive Brothers. If [Mr. C.] is fired or hurt in any way, the Plantation types will quickly turn back to their shriveled existence with no more than a mournful host of "I told you so's." Many of the gains that we are beginning to make in this area would be lost.

From Cleveland Banks, Leflore County, Mississippi—

On March 26, 1963, about 50 people went to Wesley Chapel to go down town [Greenwood] and register. We walked down Howard, and went by the city hall to talk to Chief Lary about some protection. Before going to the courthouse. Instead of talking to Chief Lary, Mayor Simpson was standing in the door of the city hall, he told us to get out, but no one moved, he gave two minutes to leave, still no one moved, then he stepped back inside the door and told the policeman with the dog to come out, he came out and repeated what the mayor had said "You have two minutes to leave." If not he was going to let go of the dog. The people started moving backward after the policeman let the dog have some slack in his lease he snapped at the people. Bob said "I would like to sec Chief Lary." The dog tore his trousers from the cuff to the knee. Jim Forman said "Let's leave and go to the courthouse." Jim had taken several pictures of the policeman with the dog, and the policeman tried to take the camera. McLaurin took the camera from Jim and ran with it. The police picked up Jim and Bob at the post office and arrested them. After they had picked up Jim and Bob the people formed in small groups and some came to the courthouse and the others went back to the church . . .

From Charles Sherrod, *Southwest Georgia Project*—

But we are having a couple of problems here with the young girls' parents. At least one parent has told his three children that it would be impossible for them to continue to work with us. The young girls told us that all kinds of allegations had been made—we were teaching them immoral codes of ethics and practices of the same. The girls who work with us are the best looking and brightest at the high school and junior high in Albany. But they are picking us out as "boy friends" and so on. Although the opinion of this particular father is wrong, we have run into the problem of boy-girl relations, yea, sexual relations. This is a hell of a problem! It meets us squarely every day so much so that it is our idea now to ask the help of the young girls who work with and swing those hips so unmercifully before us. They must understand what could happen if some mishap should occur among us and many of the girls are under seventeen-jailbait summa cum laude. We elected to call a meeting and ask for their help. We would call their attention to our codes and call their attention to the many ways in which they frustrate them, pointing out further that they do so with cold and calculated forethought. Finally, we intend to start them to making reports for the week, also. This will help them and us . . .

From Prathia Hall, *Southwest Georgia Project*, February 23-March 8, 1963—

Rev. Wells never ceases to amaze me. But when he showed up last Saturday at our 7:30 AM canvass meeting with Mrs. Otis Holloway the dean of Women at Albany State, I just stared. Mrs. Holloway is a friend of McCree Harris'—Rutha's sister. She was willing to risk her job to help us. She promised to help us by doing some research on voting statistics and voting rights on the political structure of this area. Already Rev. Wells had her making phone calls for canvassers and registrants.

The technique of sending canvassers down in front of City Hall to "snatch folks off the streets" and taking them in to register was extremely good. It served its purpose for voter registration and also served to physically and psychologically confront people with the movement—a type of direct action. We might well have been picketing. Some people were frightened to death—like the woman who pushed me away as she ducked into a store to avoid giving me her name which I asked her for when she hastily told me she had been registered for years. I don't know, some I believe, and some I don't. Some were quiet about their fear and sheepishly hauled their excuses out of moth balls. And, of course, other people were willing: they were either already convinced or were just on the border line. I found two such people. As a group we found 15 who more than anything else, needed an invitation.

From Mrs. Colia Lafayette, Selma, Alabama, April 1963—

Cleopbus Hobbs [a youth leader] . . . said he just had to keep up with us because if we had not come to town he probably would have gotten his boys to rob a bank or something.

From Ruby Tyler of Biloxi, Mississippi, NAACP—

Three out of every five people contacted actually has no intention of registering, and merely says so to get rid of the worker. Especially when a worker abolishes all their excuses. We have had as many as 15 people which say they would go and when the driver comes, they're sick, or have to go to work and maybe five will go. Our only tactic has been to get the block worker to go with the driver when the person sees the worker, they're usually ashamed not to go. This has worked fairly well for us. We still have a large percentage of people who feel there is no need to register. My only suggestion is, instead of an annual drive, try and keep the program before the public. . . .

From Charles Sherrod, *Southwest Georgia Project*, March 10, 1963—

As you can see when you go through the reports, some of the ideas which we have had for a long time are beginning to materialize. Let us take the idea that the most effective way to organize communities in this area is to widen the identification of "community." In essence, this idea is directly in opposition to the development of the community as the tradition of the system of segregation had dictated in this area. It (the system of segregation) has called for rigid control of the mobility of the person in accord with color, of course. It operates in the attitude of persons located in one geographical to another geographical area. In practical terms, for example, the people in Albany have been afraid to go to Terrell County; the people in Terrell are afraid to go to Leesburg; the people in Sumter County feel that the people in Leesburg and Dawson are the victims of merciless situations in everyday life, and the people are therefore afraid to associate freely at any time of day or night. In Albany it has always been hard to get people to take us to either of these places, until now . . .

This sense of the "new community" has given birth to other ideas. Take for an example, the idea of Mr. Vinson Collier—he proposes that we instigate a loan association. He proposes to have five base members to begin with. Each base member would earn four shares and no more at five dollars per share. This accumulative one hundred dollars would be the capital on which the association would operate initially. The loan system would operate on this wise—one could borrow five dollars every two weeks, the interest would be fifty cents and the insurance or dues would be twenty-five cents. An additional one-dollar and twenty-five cents could be given toward a share of stock. The interest would be shared with the stockholders at the end of the year. This is the idea of a man who hardly has a high school education. This is, as you know, the general arrangement made by any credit union but this idea is original because it came out of this man. His wife works with us in our Voter Registration drive and this is his contribution to the drive.

Of course he does other things for us; he is an auto-mechanic and does work on our cars for free . . .

From Lee County, Georgia, spring 1963—

One agriculture teacher registered last week, whatever that may mean. That is sort of like seeing a flying saucer in Lee County.

The teachers were really stumped at having to face their own students (some of whom were registered) as if they themselves were students, and at being asked things like, "Don't you feel any responsibility for what goes on over at that school?" We can now use the students as a sort of reserve weapon.

SNCC Report, local worker, Greenwood, Mississippi, March 1963—

One thing here in this city of Greenwood, the older people are a bad influence on the younger people. On Tuesday, I went canvassing and talked to some. About six out of seven are afraid of the white man.

John Due of VEP staff, field report—

Mr. Robinson, by his very own words, is typical of a growing number of Negroes, although to me few in number, who in their early '50s are now willing to die. They have "Uncle Tommed" enough now that their children are out of school.

From Weldon Rougeau of CORE, Dade County, Florida, September 2, 1963—

Preparations for a county-wide voter registration drive involving most community organizations began on July 8 and initial steps were taken to contact leaders from the Negro and white communities at that time.

The intensified portion of the drive is scheduled to last until October 5, when the registration books are expected to close for the November 4 election. Our goal is to get at least 40,000 as the number of registered Negroes in the county.

Our areas of concentration are North Miami Beach, Opa-Locka, Liberty City, Brown's Sub, Downtown Miami, Coconut Grove, Richmond Heights, Goulds, Perrine, and Homestead. My main purpose in each community has been to get existing organizations to get active and begin assuming the responsibilities for engineering their phase of the drive in their community.

The organizations contacted to help generate an adult-youth effort are the League of Women Voters, the National Conference of Christians and Jews, the B'nai B'rith youth organization, the American Jewish Committee, the Greater Miami Council of Churches, the Florida Labor Council, CORE, NAACP, Community Relations Council of Dade County, The Women's International League for Peace, and several other organizations from the community. Each pledged to help in whichever way it could.

In many ways this is not an opportune time for a registration drive due to the lack of political appeal in the upcoming election. However, I still believe that with a concerted effort we can obtain significant results. I hope we are able to have a banner drive.

The people have been very receptive towards the drive but rather apprehensive about working. This is the time when they feel the students should do the hard work. However, I remain very optimistic about the results of the drive. I guess when one is committed to this line of duty, optimism must be prevalent for encouragement . . .

From Carl Arnold, Hattiesburg, Mississippi, September 1963—

They come by the office and I sit down with them and we go over the voter registration form together and then I go down and stand beside them as they take the test. Determination is the thing that makes them go down, and the thing that overcomes their fear of not being able to handle the questions on the form. You know to be patient with them; you have to coach them and when their fear of the written form causes them to panic and fall into a state of indecision and confusion, you have to lead them out.

From Jack Chatfield, Southwest Georgia Project—

We never got to Bronwood, though we planned to go. Chico was typing and I walked to Deacon Green's store to arouse discontent, much like opening a safe with your teeth. (The book reads, "The Negro's social misery, heretofore a kind of paralytic disability, is in this mid-century being tapped and directed into victory after countless victory.")

I said "Hi" and Deacon Green said "Hi" and I said, "'Bout meetin' time" and Deacon Green said, "'Fraid I cain't make it around tonight" and I fished around for change for to buy me a soda for to give me time to gather my defense. No change. "Why not, Deacon?"

"'Fraid I jest cain't make it round tonight."

Actually, what had preceded all this is interesting: An insurance man had called me into the store by name (I was waiting for him to conclude his business) and when I came in I saw that he was eating a Baby Ruth and not selling insurance at all, so I said, "Did you call me?"

"You don't have to be afraid to come in just because I'm here," he said.

I said I was merely waiting for him to finish his business, which was a half-truth (I'm tremendously self-conscious around whites).

At any rate, he was a New Yorker who joined the Air Force and was sent South and learned Karate and twenty-eight ways of killing a man with the nipples of your breasts, shorn of hair; learned that justice for all men was okay stuff and why not justice for the colored man? because that was okay stuff, too; had outsold every insurance man in the state of Georgia, had killed the enemy in Guam (1957, which must have been a war this county never knew it was fighting) with piano wire thrice or more and was prepared to show me with string how it was done. I declined the gambit, feigned fatigue, but he succeeded in getting the string around my ersatz neck (forefinger) and we pranced around in a little murderer-murdered game for a while. He had defused bombs at Turner that Cyrus Citizen would never know existed and had run down a Yugoslavian spy with a fire truck after watching him toss a napalm bomb into the cockpit of an airplane that Alvin Average would never know existed ("I meant to kill him. That was orders").

He excused himself after a time, and John O'Neal and Eddie Brown happened by from Lee and I excused myself.

It had been an exhilarating afternoon. . . .

From Weldon Rougeau, Dade County, Florida—

The month of September proved to be a productive one for voter registration here. Through a community effort, we were able to add 5,593 persons on the registration rolls.

The highlight of the drive was from September 16 to September 28. During that time, we registered 5,567 persons. Of that total approximately 100 were whites.

Registration was conducted in eleven predominately Negro areas which had sub-stations placed in them by the county for the convenience of the people living in these areas . . .

These locations were opened from Monday to Saturday, from 8:00 a.m. to 5:00 p.m., with the exception of Tuesdays and Thursdays when they remained open until 9:00 p.m. The turnouts on Tuesdays and Thursdays were very heavy despite rain in some areas.

The personnel for these sub-stations came from the eleven areas and were hired by the county. They were all Negroes who were registered voters. In most instances, there was representation of the two major political parties.

The task of getting the sub-stations was not an easy one. Initially, there was considerable opposition because of the nature of the registration drive which was supposed to be in the Negro areas only. Only after I brought the matter up at a meeting with the Catholic

Bishop of the Diocese of South Florida did the leadership of the county begin to seriously consider rendering this service to the community.

Several members of the Community Relations Board [official bi-racial committee] took the matter before the County Manager. He was very receptive towards this and asked that preferential locations for registration sub-stations be submitted to him by the Board. I was asked to name the locations for this and after I had consulted with residents and leaders I submitted a list of locations for the books to be placed.

Again, there was the omnipresent problem of getting the organizations in the Negro community to take an active part in the drive. We were given too many promises from the recognized giants in the community. A few organizations did get members to work with us, but the number from these organizations was not representative of the active membership in them.

The organizations that helped were: The National Conference of Christians and Jews, the B'nai B'rith Youth Organization, the Boy Scouts (Goulds), CORE, the League of Women Voters, the Florida Labor Council, several local organizations both youth and adult, and countless individuals who were not direct representatives of organizations . . .

In conducting our drive, we were given publicity by the two Negro newspapers, a Negro radio station, and several nightclubs in the county who constantly announced where the registration sub-stations were, the times they were open, and the qualifications for one to register.

In following our publicity phase of our drive, we also had persons to go into churches on Sundays and make announcements about the registration drive and the need for a good showing to insure our getting the books again at a subsequent date or pre-election period. We also had persons going to theaters and making announcements and appealing for help with the drive.

We were able to get the principals of all the schools in these areas to send memorandums to the parents, make daily announcements about the location of the books in the community, and also instruct the leaders of the student organizations to help in the distribution of leaflets, canvassing, and office work. About 50 of each student body participated in one way or another.

Several weeks before the acquisition of the books, we had persons canvass each area we were anticipating having the books. The information gathered was whether the persons of voting age were registered, their name and address, and telephone number if they had one. We also informed them that there was a possibility of getting the books in their community and if we were successful, we would inform them of the location, times, and give them transportation to the sub-station if they did not have any.

When we were officially notified that the books would be in the areas we had selected, we had leaflets, posters, and placards printed with the 11 locations, times for registering, qualifications, and reasons why one should register. We distributed over 125,000 leaflets, 1,000 posters, and 1,550 placards. This proved to be very effective in notifying the people we had contacted while canvassing.

Money continues to be a problem here. CORE does not get enough from VEP to amply meet the needs of Dade County when there are so many other areas with vociferous opposition confronting our staff in trying to perform their duties. Therefore, I hope you will be able to include more money or enough money to meet the necessary needs of Dade County—a county with a population of over one million people.

Respectfully submitted this 10th day of October, 1963.

Field Report, September 1963, Ronnie Moore—

The Congress of Racial Equality has 15 task force workers and two field secretaries working on voter registration in Louisiana, covering seven parishes; namely, West Baton Rouge, St. Helena, Iberville, Tangipaboa, East Feliciana, West Feliciana, and Pointe Coupee . . .

We are aiming at registering 1,550 people in the named parishes by October 31, 1963. The number is based on imagination and optimism . . .

IBERVILLE—Voter registration has not been its very best, but we anticipate better results for October. We have 12 Negro candidates seeking election to office of sheriff, police jury, coroner, parish Democratic committee, constable, justice of peace, and state Democratic central committee. CORE has workers in 7 of the 9 wards, and SCLC is working in the remaining two wards, since Major Johns is running for state representative . . .

We have set a quota of 900 as our October voter registration goal. PRAY FOR US.

ST. HELENA—The story is about the same. The registrar is still turning Negroes down 4–1. Community interest in voter registration is still good. Negroes are still attempting to register. However, because the registrar in this parish . . . and others like him, have used the (LR-l) application form to turn down 90% of the persons denied registration, we anticipate the federal government's filing a suit in the next few days against the use of the LR-1 forms as a test. On the basis of numerous complaints filed by CORE, this suit was possible, so say federal officials. Ha! Ha! Nevertheless, we are sitting tight, waiting for the suit to get to court . . .

POINTE COUPEE—From the standpoint of cooperation of leaders, this is a good parish . . . The registrar is nice but a wizard at turning Negroes down in large numbers. However, we shall continue to work in the same areas with the hope that the recent racial and political developments will give the local people the shot they need to overcome apathy.

WEST BATON ROUGE—Voter registration is moving without interference from the white power structure. We anticipate registering large numbers when we overcome the large degree of apathy and illiteracy.

WEST FELICIANA—September has been a month of canvassing and setting up and conducting clinics. We have had persons in large numbers attending clinics and I think I didn't include the number of clinic participants: 85-115. People are waiting until later October before attempting to register, because of "sweet potato" contracts with the all-white canning company . . .

Only the naked eye can convince you of the economic problems in housing, education, and political attitude of the local people. I invite you to come to Louisiana and see Hardwood, of this parish.

EAST FELICIANA—As indicated in the past, intimidation by parish officials continues to hinder voter registration efforts. The registrar is worse than the registrar in St. Helena because he is turning Negroes down in larger proportions . . .

At voter registration rallies, policemen and sheriff deputies stand guard in cars around the area. Negroes fear both political and economic reprisals if they attempt to register and vote. However, we still canvass on plantations, back woods, and dusty roads in Wilson, La., Clinton, La., and Jackson, La., and throughout the parish.

TANGIPAHOA—Voter registration is still rough because the registrar is still turning Negroes down in large numbers. Community interest is good. Local voters leagues are active with CORE in sending lines of Negroes to the registrar's office daily, so reports CORE worker Galway Kinnell.

CONCLUSION—At one time I thought that some parishes were better than others. I still believe this to some extent. Nevertheless, when you look at the total situation, in one parish we find apathy, in another fear, and yet another illiteracy. In every parish it is discrimination by nature in the Louisiana voter registration system, but from one registrar to another discrimination varies.

In short, we are doing our best, but unless this damn system is obliterated, the task of developing the Negro voting potential in Louisiana is a lost cause.

From Dickie Flowers, regarding arrests in Indianola, Mississippi, October 1963—

The jail was the filthiest one I ever been in. The floor was dirty, the bathtub was in bad shape, and there was a split pipe in the tank of the commode. There was a hole in the floor and clothes were filthy, the mattresses raggedy with half the cotton on the floor under the bed. No water to drink unless we wanted to drink from the bathtub. We had to eat from tin pans which were rusted. There were 18 of us in that bad place, and we were obliged to share 4 bunks . . . Although there were 8 beds, there were only 4 mattresses, so we had to put the mattress on the floor in order for a maximum number of us to sleep at one time.

From W. C. Patton, March 1964—

In Atlanta, Texas, we had the sad experience of having one of our prize winners return his check because he was afraid to cash it over the signature of the NAACP. We are trying to adjust this by having him endorse the check and return it to us and we, in turn, will send him a postal money order.

From Ronnie Moore, Plaquemines Parish, Louisiana, April 1964—

CORE has been active in the parish for a period of two months. Due to a mass rally held in New Orleans, Perez began cracking down on the Negro community. Up to that time, contacts had been made to start a voter registration clinic at a Catholic Church. Since Perez's intimidation, the Negro Community has withdrawn and activity has been at a standstill. I would say that in this parish, official and unofficial opposition is great and quite hazardous, to say the least.

UNIT 11-10

SOVEREIGNTY COMMISSION (MS) MEMO

June 26, 1964

MEMORANDUM

TO: Honorable A.D. Morgan, Administrative Assistant
Mississippi Public Safety Commission

FROM: Director, Sovereignty Commission

SUBJECT: Protection for Informant

We would appreciate cooperation of the Highway Patrol in assuring safe passage of one of our informants back into Mississippi from Oxford, Ohio.

Subject is a colored male, who will be driving a 1957 Cadillac with green top and beige body, Hinds County tag No. HD 8942. He will be accompanied by his wife and a white male. It is likely they will be the only occupants of the car. He will travel on Highway 45 to Corinth and then on Highway 45 from Tupelo to the Natchez Trace. He expects to arrive in Mississippi between 12:00 noon and 2:00 P.M., Saturday, June 27, and get into Jackson Saturday night.

It is very important that you understand that the white male does not know about the informant's connection with the Sovereignty Commission. It is suggested that since an integrated group in a car might provoke some reaction that Highway Patrolmen merely keep an eye on the car at intervals to make sure it is still proceeding as planned. No surveillance will be needed after the car leaves the Natchez Trace. Subject has been advised that if the car is stopped for any traffic violation, etc., that whatever fines are imposed be paid without question.

This information is not being passed to any law enforcement officers other than the Highway Patrol.

Your cooperation will be appreciated.

Erle Johnston, Jr.

cc: Honorable Herman Glazier

EJ/ea

UNIT 11-11

THE ROAD TO MISSISSIPPI

And that freedom train's a-comin', comin', comin'
And that freedom train's a-comin', comin', comin'
And that freedom train's a-comin', comin', comin'
Get on board.

It'll be bringing nothing but freedom, freedom, freedom
It'll be bringing nothing but freedom, freedom, freedom
It'll be bringing nothing but freedom, freedom, freedom
Get on board.

They'll be coming by the thousand, thousand, thousand
They'll be coming by the thousand, thousand, thousand
They'll be coming by the thousand, thousand, thousand
Get on board.

They were called "the volunteers": 650 young people, mostly Northerners and mostly white and mostly students. They were the largest single group of the many people who went to Mississippi in the summer of 1964. They were the nonprofessionals. The kids. And they wrote the letters that make up this book.

Most of them knew why they wanted to go to Mississippi before they left home or school to join the project. Some found out at the orientation sessions held in Ohio, Tennessee and other nearby states. Some learned the best reasons in Mississippi itself. And perhaps a few understood only when they had left.

All of them realized that the eyes of the nation were fixed upon their undertaking: from almost every side came the voices of skepticism as well as admiration. Hostility was not limited to white Mississippians like Mayor Allen Thompson of Jackson, who stood ready to greet the "invaders" with his specially built tank and riot squads. A Louis Harris public opinion poll taken in June among Americans across the nation indicated that 65% opposed the Mississippi Summer Project. The doubts and criticisms ranged wide:

Why Mississippi when there is so much racial injustice in their own backyards?

Let Mississippi do its own house cleaning.

Let the government do the job.

Letters from Mississippi, Elizabeth Sutherland, ed. (1965).

They'll just stir up a lot of resentment among the whites and make matters worse.
They are being used to foster violence and thus force federal intervention.
They're just doing it for publicity.
They're wild-eyed radicals, they're naive idealists, they're beatniks, they're misfits.
But some voices said: They are the cream of our youth. The hope of this nation.

The first contingent of volunteers—about 250 strong—poured in from all parts of the country for orientation at Western College for Women in Oxford, Ohio during the weekend of June 13–14. A second orientation period began the following week when the first group left. The lush, 200-acre Oxford campus included an oddly symbolic bird sanctuary; the dormitory rooms were attractive and the modernistic dining hall of glass and wood served unusually good food. In these surroundings the volunteers spent a week learning how to avoid being beaten or killed.

A hundred facts of Mississippi life were thrown at them one day, real tear gas another. They learned how the racist Citizens Councils operate, what sort of work they might be doing, how to talk to a group of threatening whites, how not to dress. But their first real discovery had little to do with all this.

Dear Mom and Jo, Oxford, Ohio, June 14

The reception at Western College was not warm. I was surprised at how unfriendly and unextending people were. Small groups formed or had been formed and people seemed concerned with "fitting in." I went to bed. Later that day (today) I went to register. I still felt uncomfortable but attempted to shake a few hands. (It wasn't too bad.) Some people were friendly and helpful. Tremendous enthusiasm was generated when we all began singing after dinner. It was the spiritual revival type singing and you know how I love that. We all must have sung for about 2 hours, and the previous in-grouping of Negroes and reservedness of whites seemed to disappear—but not really. . . . Maybe we'll be able to at the end of the summer, but right now we don't know what it is to be a Negro and even if we did, the Negroes here would not accept us. It's the old case of having to prove ourselves. In their eyes we're rich middle or upper-class whites who've taken off a summer to help the Negro.

Intellectually, I think many of us whites can understand the Negroes' resentment but emotionally we want to be "accepted" at face value. We want this acceptance because this is part of our reason for going down south, i.e., the basic worth of the individual. I've always thought that my relations with Negroes have been fairly honest. I've gone to a predominantly Negro high school and participated in athletics with them. I've gotten to know Negroes in college . . . I haven't gone out of my way to meet them but those I have met I have gotten along well with, if not intimately. What I mean to say is that I never detected a "difference," or an inability to communicate with one another. . . . But what I am finding here is a different situation and perhaps a more honest one . . .

Love,
Lew

June 15

. . . Us white kids here are in a position we've never been in before. The direction of the whole program is under Negro leadership—almost entirely. And a large part of that leadership is young people from the South—Negroes who've had experience just because they're Negroes and because they've been active in the movement. And here "we" are, for the most part never experiencing any injustice other than "No, I won't let you see your exam paper . . ."

Dear Peggy:

. . . All whites who read Baldwin ask, "Is he right? Do they really hate us?" I have never before talked to a Negro about his feelings toward whites. A wonderful Negro man from Detroit named Joe Harrison told me here at Oxford, "I always feel much more comfortable with Negroes than with whites. But I can become good friends with white people."

And one SNCC [Student Nonviolent Coordinating Committee] worker—Frank Smith—said, "I grew up hating all white folks. It wasn't till a couple of years ago that I learned that there could be good whites—and even now I sometimes wonder."

So, there is this great reluctance and distrust, born of generations of oppression and slavery . . . It seems that if more whites understood this—especially white liberals—race relations might be a lot less strained.

I have also discovered a lot about my own feelings about race. I grew up in an upper middle-class Westchester home, where my parents were good liberals, but I never knew any Negroes except the woman who cooked and cleaned for us. I loved her very much and she, me. . . . We all called her "Sarah" while she called me "Ellen" and my parents "Mr. and Mrs."

Consequently, although my parents told me that Negroes were just as good as whites—I must have seen them in the role of servants. Once, my mother tells me, when I was little, we were driving along a road near our house and passed a Negro woman waiting for a bus. "There's somebody's maid," I said.

To arrive in Ohio, where there were 60 or 70 Negro kids my age—all close friends and rather cliquish at first—was a frightening experience. It was not that I looked down on them at all—quite the contrary: I was awed by them. For the first few days, I mostly hung around with the kids from Harvard. I sat with them at meals or in meetings, walking by the groups of Negro kids who also sat together at the table or under a tree on the grass. . . . But as the week wore on, things began to change.

Ellen

The turning point came with the showing of a film, on June 16.

Dearest,

For the first two days there was a noticeable tension between the volunteers and the staff. . . . Then, Tuesday night we saw a movie made by CBS Reports ["Mississippi and Fifteenth Amendment"] describing how the Negro was discriminated against in Mississippi with regard to voting. Some of the film was absolutely ridiculous and ludicrous—a big, fat really fat and ugly white county registrar prevents Negroes from voting; the stupid, really completely irrational and dishonest views of some white Southerners and so on. Six of the staff members got up and walked out of the movie because it was so real to them while we laughed because it was so completely foreign to us—if anyone had said what they did in the movie, we in the North would lock them up or dismiss them completely, but this is the way many white Southerners think.

After the movie one of the staff told us why they had walked out and it shook some of us up. We were afraid the whole movement was going to fall apart . . .

Love,
Wally

Dear Folks, June 16

We had the whole thing out in the living room, with everybody sitting on the floor or standing along the walls. The kids brought out their gripes: the staff was distant, they didn't let us know what was going on or who would be assigned where, or how we would be assigned, and they looked down on us for not having been through what they had. They shouldn't walk out like that, saying in effect you white people are too stupid to understand how serious all of this is.

Other people argued that we should take into account all of the hardships they were going through, and the fact that they had a lot on their minds. Others again demanded that the staff respect us more: we were after all products of our environments, and did not understand Mississippi, and had not been beaten. Could we do something really concrete down there, or are we just pawns? If so, why should we go down there indeed? Did the staff trust us, could we learn?

Staff members began drifting in from a meeting and entered the discussion. "We did not walk out because of you, necessarily. We have seen too much of that stuff in the flesh. We know that bastard and don't have to see him on the screen." One guy said "if you get mad at us walking out, just wait until they break your head in, and see if you don't have something to get mad about. Ask Jimmy Travis over there what he thinks about the project. What does he think about Mississippi? He has six slugs in him, man, and the last one went right through the back of his neck when he was driving a car outside Greenwood. Ask Jesse here—he has been beaten so that we couldn't recognize him time and time and time and time again. If you don't get scared, pack up and get the hell out of here because we don't need any favors of people who don't know what they are doing here in the first place."

"We cried over you in the staff meeting because we love you and are afraid for you. We are grown men and women who have been beaten and shot at, and we cried for you. Somebody walked out of a movie, but you won't see anybody walk out on your picket line. When you get beaten up, I am going to be right behind you. The song we sang yesterday was dedicated to a couple of the people now in jail, and they know we are singing and thinking about them. As long as there is one person alive wearing a SNCC pin they know. And you had better know it too, or else get out. I was a good soldier in Korea. I can stick a bayonet in your back in the right spot so that you don't make a sound. I know how to use piano wire around your neck and then let you fall to the ground soft. And all the time in Korea I was sick to the gut because I was being taught to kill so good. Don't tell me that you are coming down to help me because you are saving your selves. We are proud of you, and love you. Don't worry when we don't have time to shake hands, because that's not the SNCC greeting anyway. We hug and kiss you because we love you."

Here is what I said: people have been talking about Americans, and how there is more than just the black man's problem. Somebody said that we sounded like a sick bunch of people with all of our complaints. Well, we are all sick, black and white, because we are Americans, and that fat bastard on the screen has poisoned all of us. The whole god damn country has gone to hell, and we are the only ones who can save it. Isn't it sick when we have to see an in-group sitting together at lunch and feel that they are suspicious of us because we are white? That is why we are going down, not to help the Negro, but to get rid of those guys for all of us. It is natural that these things should come out, because that bastard put it into all of us. That is why the training is a week long and not just two days . . .

Then some of the staff people came in singing, and we all sang together, and the first time *really* together. The crisis is past, I think.

Love,
Bill

With the tension between Negro staff and white volunteers broken, if not resolved, the volunteers began to see Mississippi through the eyes of those who knew it all too well. Their understanding of what lay ahead grew stronger—as did their fear.

Dear People at home in the Safe, Safe North, June 17

Mississippi is going to be hell this summer. Monday Jim Forman, executive secretary of SNCC stood up during one of the general sessions and calmly told the staff (who already knew) and the volunteers that they could all expect to be arrested, jailed, and beaten this summer, and, in many cases, shot at. There is a quiet Negro fellow on the staff who has an ugly scar on his neck and another on his shoulder where he stopped .45 slugs. . . . Another fellow told this morning how his father and later his brother had been shot to death. . . . I'd venture to say that every member of the Mississippi staff has been beaten at least once and he who has not been shot at is rare. It is impossible for you to imagine what we are going in to, as it is for me now, but I'm beginning to see. . . .

Please talk up Mississippi up North, pass around the materials I am sending, and begin petitioning the Federal government for intervention . . .

Love,
Xtoph

Dear God, also dear me, and anyone else interested, June 19

I want to write everything down now, while I have time and can and before I leave Oxford. . . .

My feelings are many and mixed and are not always the same. . . . When I began this letter I was feeling quite calm and relaxed, then the butterflies started in the pit of my stomach, they subsided somewhat and then continued to my hands.

Whenever I am scared or terribly excited about something, I have always gotten this feeling in my stomach and then often even in my hands. But this afternoon I felt it so that I ached—my whole stomach, my chest, my arms, hands, legs and even down to my feet. That is pretty nearly all of me. . . .

A Negro girl said to me in the john a few minutes ago that she wondered if I had a match. I said No. And she said "You don't smoke yet?" I replied, "no." "You will before the end of the summer," she said.

She went on to tell me, "I do because I'm nervous. No, I'm going to quit saying I'm nervous. I'm scared. Sometimes I smoke two packs a day."

She also said she had been told that many of the girls, especially in a certain other dorm, cried all by themselves at night, that they really didn't want to go. "If I didn't really want to go I wouldn't go" she said. And I said "Sometimes there isn't a really don't and a really do." She continued, "And sometimes you've told the people back home you were going to help and what will they think if you come home now." I said "Well, that would present a problem too."

Perhaps I should have said "that does present a problem too." I actually have thought about the feelings or thoughts of others should I back out. So this is one of the pressures. But only one, and who can say how large or small . . .

With much love, a very (calm right now) me,
Virginia

Monday night, June 15

I turned down a chance to work in the southwest part of the state, the most dangerous area. I talked to a staff member covering that area for about fifteen minutes and he told me about the five Negroes who have been taken into the woods and shot in the last three months. . . . I told him that I couldn't go in there because I was just too scared. I felt so bad I was about ready to forget about going to Mississippi at all. But I still wanted to go; I just didn't feel like giving up my life. After thinking about this seeming contradiction, I decided that I have not discovered just how dedicated I am to the civil rights cause and that is the purpose of the trip. . . .

Amidst the apprehension, the volunteers went on listening and learning. The days were packed from morning to night, the week from beginning to end, with new knowledge and new songs and especially new people.

Dear family and friends, June 18

Sunday evening, the first program was a solemn memorial service for Medgar Evers conducted by Ed King, a native Mississippian who is Methodist chaplain and dean at Tougaloo—the Negro college outside of Jackson. Monday morning King led off the first session with a run-down of some of the factors which contribute to making Miss. a police state. King is a soft-spoken man with large scars from an auto accident disfiguring one side of his face. He ran for Lieutenant Governor in the Freedom Election run last year by SNCC. He told about the techniques the White Citizens Council, which receives state funds, has used to keep control of the state. No politician can afford to be a moderate. Three were voted out recently for voting against an extreme piece of anti-Negro legislation. In the past six years over 60 Methodist ministers have been forced out of the Southern half of the state alone. Merchants who meet the terms of the civil rights groups are economically coerced to change or leave. All widely read newspapers simply deny the white guilt for violence and usually ignore incidents entirely. National news on TV is interrupted by local commercials or by saying, "The following is an example of biased untrue Yankee reporting." King says that he sees how there can be some truth to the contention that many Germans didn't know about the treatment of the Jew under Hitler.

Next Bob Moses talked to us in his quiet, reasoned manner about the project and the situation in various parts of the state. Bob warned us that we are all victims of the plague of prejudice but must not make the mistake that the authorities in Camus' *Plague* made by resisting the recognition of the disease because recognition would have made action necessary. . . . He then sketched some of the goals of the summer. He said that the mere fact of our spending the summer in Negro homes would be a very important victory. It is also hoped that we, through our connections back home will give the project more projection, and bring the Justice Dept. into Mississippi in a bigger way.

In the next session the body was broken down into small groups in which project directors from the local projects described in some detail the conditions in their counties. I happened to be assigned to a group where Charles McLaurin was talking about Sunflower and Bolivar counties. He is a dynamic, clear speaker whose determination, good humor and calmness are massively impressive. These SNCC staff people must really stand out against the background of a lazy dead-end society. It becomes almost understandable how they can persuade people to risk house, job and life to go down and attempt to register.

That evening we went back into the same groups and discussed race relations. This was a painful rather intimate discussion. . . . One boy from West Virginia confessed that he is quite embarrassed when confronted by a group of Negroes and asked how he should act. A little blond Smith girl said she knew what he meant though she didn't have the problem herself, in fact she didn't know whether it was environment or heredity but she found Southern Negroes quite attractive. The discussion was very valuable in posing the problem of how does one adapt without selling out his own identity . . .

Tuesday we had more regional briefings. Then there was an informal general session to discuss various problems. The most interesting discussion was about how we should confront the white kids in Mississippi who want to talk to us and persuade us to go back home. Should we insist that a Negro come along. If their minds are closed what is the use of talking to them. . . . On the other hand it is so important, I feel, to get into the white community and let somebody know what we are like. I imagine the rumors about the invasion of Communists are getting pretty wild.

Tuesday evening was a talk by Charles Morgan, the courageous Birmingham attorney who stood up at the time of the bombings and made a strong public statement in favor of sanity. He has since been forced out of Birmingham by economic coercion and published a book, *A Time to Speak*. He warned us gravely about the dangers of Mississippi. Said he thought that atrocities don't soften but harden the local people. . . . He said one thing that might help was that Mississippi is very concerned about its image. He laid the slow movement of the civil rights cause in the South not to the strength of Southern opposition but to the weakness of the North on the issue. . . . He ended by solemnly stating that he admired our courage. From a guy like that who has seen a lot of fire, this was really frightening. We have all lived under the increasing weight of fear and the struggle to come to terms with the possibility of death consumes much of our emotional energy . . .

Just the security precautions are scary: beware of cars without tags—they are always danger; never go out alone; never go out after dark, never be the last out of a mass meeting; watch for cops without their badge; listen for an accelerating car outside; if you wake up at night thinking there is danger, wake everybody up. There seems to be a very good type instinct for preservation. Some of the Negro field secretaries I was talking to informally told how they played like real Uncle Toms to the cops when in danger. . . .

Wednesday, Rev. James Lawson presented and skillfully defended Christian revolutionary nonviolence as a way of life. Most of the staff and volunteers were agnostic nonviolent technicians. The discussion was hot but very real. It became clear that not all nonviolent techniques could be practised by certain personality types. Only perhaps 10% can talk successfully with someone who is going to beat you. For the rest, withdrawal seems the best reaction. . . .

Thursday we got some practical legal counsel from one of three Negro lawyers in Mississippi who takes civil rights cases. He is a witty old fox with a wonderful sense of humor and a great gift for diplomacy (no, not Uncle Tomming). Also heard from head of legal defense fund and others. There will be 150 lawyers in the state this summer! Friday morning we heard John Doar, Burke Marshall's assistant in the Justice Department, talk about what they would be doing there. He said they would keep very close watch on us and try to watch for trouble brewing. However, he said unless there is a Federal court order to bring Federal troops into an area, responsibility for maintaining law and order is left up to the local law enforcement agencies. The kids' questions and statements were quite burning. There is a law which gives the FBI power to arrest and protect people from intimidation of their right to vote. . . .

Love,
Mike

P.S. A word about the group. A surprising number of young married couples. One school teacher who left wife and kids at home. Maybe a majority of Young Democrat types with a good representation of people from the left. It is hard to tell how we will turn out till we have seen action.

Dear Folks,

A great deal of tension and a great deal of camaraderie here at Oxford. Workshops and role-playing are constant. We staged one situation, a screaming mob lining the steps to the courthouse while a small band of registrants tried to get through. The inevitable happened—what will actually happen in Mississippi happened. The chanting mob (instructed to be as brutal as possible, and to pull no punches) turned into a clawing, pounding mob, and we volunteer registrants were down in our crouched-up ball. Casualties? A couple of scratches, a sprained ankle, and one cameraman who got swept up was a little bit shaken. It seems like brutal play, and it is. We've got to be ready for anything, and we must prepare for it ourselves. Once we get south we are nonviolent; we must get whatever there is in our systems out now, and we must also learn to take the worst. Some of the staff members walk around carrying sections of hose. This strangely terrible training in brutality may well save lives. (I must confess, I have not been able to take part in even the screaming of a mob scene, much less the pummeling. Wherever possible, I am among the victims.)

We have registration workshops, too. And lecturers came from all over the country to speak to us. And we sing. What "We Shall Overcome" is to the national movement, "We'll never turn back" is to the Mississippi workers. It is a slow song, measured out in grief and determination. The final verse goes,

We have hung our head and cried,
Cried for those like Lee[1]
who died
Died for you and died for me,
Died for the cause of equality,
But we will never turn back
Until we've all been free
And we have equality, and we have equality.

Love,
Jim

THE OTHER COUNTRY

Mississippi is really two countries—Negro Mississippi and white Mississippi, and the difference is startling . . .

THE KLAN LEDGER

An official Publication of the White Knights of the Ku Klux Klan of Mississippi (July, 1964)

We are now in the midst of the "long, hot summer" of which was promised to the Innocent People of Mississippi the savage blacks and their community masters. . . .

The recent events in Neshoba County and Statewide call for a message to the general public and the citizens of the State of great Mississippi. The arch-traitor and long-time betrayer of patriots the world over, Dulles, has used his lying tongue to try and convince the American public that this organization was involved in the so-called "disappearance."

We were *NOT* involved, and there was *NO DISAPPEARANCE*. Anyone who is so simple that he cannot recognize a communist hoax which is which is as plain as the one they pulled on Kennedy in Dallas (and which Earl Warren is working so hard to cover-up), had better do a little reading in J. Edgar Hoover's primer on communism, "MASTERS OF DECEIT" . . .

There is no racial problem here in this state. Our system of strict segregation permits the two races to live in close proximity and harmony with each other and eliminates any racial problem . . . Bi-racial groups are the greatest danger we face in this State today. These groups have absolutely no legal standing whatsoever . . . Bi-racial groups have brought violence and bloodshed to every area in which they have been recognized. The surest way to have violence in Mississippi is to give any weight or recognize the authority of a bi-racial group. . . .

We are not going to recognize the authority of any bi-racial group, NOR THE AUTHORITY OF ANY PUBLIC OFFICE WHO ENTERS INTO ANY AGREEMENT WITH ANY SUCH

SOVIET ORGANIZATION. We Knights are working day and night to preserve Law and Order here in Mississippi, in the only way that it can be preserved; by strict segregation of the races, and the control of the social structure in the hands of the Christian, Anglo-Saxon White men, the only race on earth that can build and maintain just and stable governments. We are deadly serious about this business. We have taken no action as yet against the enemies of our State, our Nation and our Civilization, but we are not going to sit back and permit our rights and the rights of our posterity to be negotiated away by a group composed of atheistic priests, brain-washed black savages, and mongrelized money-worshippers, meeting with some stupid or cowardly politician. Take heed, atheists and mongrels, we will not travel your path to Leninist Hall, but we will buy *YOU* a ticket to the Eternal if you insist. Take your choice, *SEGREGATION, TRANQUILITY AND JUSTICE, OR BI-RACISM, CHAOS AND DEATH*. . . .

Moss Point, Monday, July 6

Tonight the sickness struck. At our mass meeting as we were singing "We Shall Overcome" a girl was shot in the side and in the chest. We fell to the floor in deathly fear; but soon we recovered and began moving out of the hall to see what had happened . . . When I went out I saw a woman lying on the ground clutching her stomach. She was so still and looked like a statue with a tranquil smile on her face. I ran to call an ambulance and police . . .

It seemed as though a signal had been given. Two days later, the Project headquarters in McComb was bombed. On Friday, a Molotov cocktail was thrown at the Freedom House in Canton; in Hattiesburg a visiting Rabbi and two volunteers were severely beaten. On Saturday night, the Shaw project workers learned of a bombing plot as whites surrounded their office. The next day in beautiful old Natchez, a Baptist and a Methodist church were destroyed by fire—two of five Negro churches burned to the ground that week.

The week of July 6 showed that while there were relatively "good" and "bad" areas, violence could explode anywhere. Natchez and McComb had always been trouble, and there was originally some debate as to whether volunteers should go there at all. Eventually a few Negro and white male volunteers went to McComb, but no white women until the summer was over. Hattiesburg and Moss Point on the other hand were considered fairly peaceable. But in the end they all added up, as the song says, to Mississippi Goddam.

Each of the incidents had something to teach the volunteers about the attitude of Mississippi police and the pattern of law enforcement. In Moss Point, on the Gulf Coast, the victim was a local Negro girl of 17, Jessie Mae Stallworth. The occasion was a voter registration rally.

Moss Point, July 9

On Monday night we had a mass meeting, and the fifth district director, Lawrence Guyot, gave a terrific speech. The gist of his speech was that people say Moss Point is an easy area, "we have nice white folks here," that everyone has what they want already. But we don't have such nice white folks here, he said, and even if we did it shouldn't make us apathetic, it should make us want to take advantage of that extra little space . . . He kept saying, "What will it take to make you people move? A rape? A shooting? A murder? What will it take?"

At the very end of the meeting we were singing the last verse of "We Shall Overcome," 300 people in a huge circle. Suddenly there were gunshots, and all these people including me, hit the floor in a wave . . . A few seconds later we all got up trembling. A car of whites had gone by on the road outside and fired three shots through the open door. One Negro girl was hit in the side. She is in the hospital and is going to be all right, but nobody knew that at the time. The whole thing was additionally frightening because during the confusion when everybody was taking cover under tables etc., a piece of wire or something got caught in an electric fan and made a noise like a machine gun.

All during the meeting, the deputy sheriff was sitting there and the police patrol outside. The sheriff left shortly before the meeting was over and with him the police protection. At the time of the shooting there were no police anywhere around. Instead, they came fifteen minutes later, long after the whites had gotten away. . . .

. . . The boy who had been standing next to her, just outside the door of the meeting hall, said that there were four white men in the car. Kids were walking around saying, "They can't do that to us any more." It was only with much persuasion on the part of some of their friends and the COFO workers that they calmed-down a little and went home. That night, the police arrested five Negro men. No white men!

MR. CHARLIE AND MISS ANNE

Aside from the hate stares and the traffic tickets, the conversations which weren't conversations and the beatings, the volunteers had little contact with whites as they walked from Negro homes to Negro farms or churches or Freedom School. Many of them fell that it must be possible to do more, that somewhere in Mississippi minds could be opened.

Canton

We had thought that perhaps our one chance for making contact was through the churches. Members of our group (all white) have tried to make contact with both the white Methodist and Presbyterian Churches in Canton. The first time some of them went to the Methodist Church they had a chance to talk to a few people who really seemed to be interested in finding out what the project was all about. . . .

. . . The next Sunday they were met at the door and told by the preacher, "You are not welcome here." The third Sunday, they were again turned away at the door and beaten up on the way home. Local Negro preachers said, "Yes, that was a white man's church. It was not God's church". . . .

. . . Then a new man joined our project, Bill Monnie, who is a Methodist and is planning to study for the ministry. He wanted to make one last attempt to get into the Methodist Church. When he and several others got to the church in his car, and stepped out, a number of men rushed down off the church steps and shoved them back into the car energetically enough so that one of the car windows got broken. Two women from our group, who had gone in another car, went into the church and signed the guest book. A few minutes later an usher called them out and asked if they were connected with the COFO project. When they replied that they were, they were told they were not welcome. When they returned to the car, they found the tires slashed. . . .

. . . Our contacts with the Presbyterian Church have been more encouraging. Three of our group have been going there regularly. . . .

In Clarksdale on July 5 two white volunteers went to the First Christian Church (Disciple of Christ) and were refused admittance. A six-page statement was read to them in front of the church by a member of the church's board of directors while a police car circled the area.

Clarksdale, July 6th

Yesterday afternoon, Dave B. called the pastor of the First Christian Church (Dave is a disciple and plans to become a minister) and asked him for an explanation of what happened. The pastor met with us, and we had a very friendly, understanding, and mutually informative conversation. He said that he had not known anything about the incident until after church, nor had he known any such statement had been prepared. He appeared to be one of the few white moderates who is seriously concerned with the social situation, and he has been trying for five years to negotiate with some of his parishioners. . . .

Another Sunday, another church . . .

Clarksdale, July 14th

Four of us (white) went to the Episcopal Church last Sunday, and I have never felt so much outside the Episcopalian club! I tried to look nice and smile a little at everyone, so that the returning stares were discomforting. I think two people did say good morning to us. Half a block away from the church a man came up and without introductions asked us, "You won't bring any niggers next week, will you?"

If they couldn't get very far with church-goers and ministers, perhaps the "intellectuals"? Hattiesburg had its University of Southern Mississippi, a number of Jewish residents, and for sixteen years a rabbi who was known to be progressive.

Aug. 1

. . . I talked to a psychology prof at Mississippi Southern. This man is Jewish from New York, but southern orientation: schooled in Atlanta and Florida, wife from Atlanta, here since 1958. He too seemed very sympathetic, but not very willing to say anything; in fact I don't think he made any positive remarks, but he didn't make any negative remarks and smiled in the right places. I invited him to the Freedom Schools; he didn't say yes, but he did say maybe (I don't expect him). . . .

. . . Bob Beech got some Southern Mississippi prof to have an interracial group to his house, and what a comedy, with not turning on the porch lights when we came in so no one would see, and the general nervousness that none of his friends would unluckily drop by, etc. And everybody admired his courage for having us at all, which only shows what things are like . . .

Dear Mom and Dad, July 25

Mississippi liberals are almost without exception scared stiff. Deviation from the proud old rebel flag and Our Southern Way of Life is obvious to all, and a threat or two—perhaps a few bullets fired at a house or a cross burning—is likely to leave two alternatives: silence or pulling up stakes. Boycotts are illegal in Mississippi as is handing out boycott literature, but of course this applies only to the Negroes. The Forrest County Citizens Council had no difficulty getting out a sheet calling for the boycott of several stores in Hattiesburg which had desegregated their lunch counters rather than close them down as did other merchants (after the Civil Rights Act passed) . . .

I was also told that the students did not seem to get excited about much of anything; that they were for the most part apathetic. One student told about trying to get a liberal club of some sort started last fall . . . It was about ready to go into action at the time of Kennedy's assassination but after that it died. The campus was stirred up; in some cases they cheered and gave parties celebrating the murder of the President. . . .

Bill

Dear Friends: Aug. 5

Another volunteer from the project and I sat and talked for about four hours with a dozen students; asking and answering questions. They were great kids, and most would be considered liberal in Mississippi terms—in other words, they recognize that there might be a problem, but it must be solved by the people here and the method of solution would be separate and equal. They were open and honest and we did communicate in some ways, but I could not seem to impress upon them the very basic fact of the humanity of the Negro people; their need for dignity and escape from the "great white father" relationship. As I came away from this mental beating, I cried, for it all seemed so hopeless. . . .

In freedom and love,
Beth

To the north of Hattiesburg, at Oxford, volunteers made a special effort to establish contact with people at the University of Mississippi.

REPORT ON A VISIT TO THE UNIVERSITY OF MISSISSIPPI

On Thursday, July 22nd, I went with George McClain, the minister assigned to our project, to the University of Mississippi—in Oxford. We went first to meet the Methodist Chaplain on the campus, whom George had met on a previous visit. He had offered to take George around the campus.

We talked with the Episcopal Chaplain, who has been active in the Movement. His great concern is for the whites of Mississippi. He emphasized that, for many people, standing up and stating their position would simply mean being forced to leave the state.

The Chaplain's feeling is that people who do believe in integration are too valuable in their communities working underground with other whites to lose if they make a principled stand and are forced to leave the state. The reason why his job is not in jeopardy, as are the jobs of ministers from congregational churches, is that he is responsible only to the Bishop of Mississippi and not to a board of local people. . . .

After eating lunch in the school cafeteria we went to visit Professor Russell Barrett of the Political Science Department. He had been James Meredith's advisor . . . He stated that he felt that there was a real lack of communication between the COFO workers and the white community. We discussed with him some of the things we were doing in Holly Springs. We then talked about getting more Negro students into Ole Miss. He said that they would all need court orders and that if we could get together some who would be interested in going to Ole Miss they could use the same lawyer and come in under the same order. He said that the Dean of Women was especially anxious to get some girls. . . .

We then went to the home of a Professor where we met a student, Phil Patterson, and his wife . . . Phil Patterson had been identified as a "nigger-lover" and was eventually forced out of first one and then another dormitory by the students. The Saturday before, an attempt at a "K" bad been slashed in the front seat of his car and a threatening note left. . . . The Professor's wife suggested that we come back another day and speak in some of the classes as a way of communicating to some of the students the purpose of our project. She said that she would contact some of the professors. . . .

At the Journalism Building we talked with the editors of the campus newspaper "The Mississippian." We met the girl who is editor of the paper during the regular school year, Kathryn Webb, and one of the summer co-editors, plus a few more students who were around at the time. We talked for about half an hour about why we had come to Mississippi when there were problems in so many other places, etc. Kathryn Webb was one of the most vocal in the group and one of the most open-minded. She admitted honestly that she was prejudiced and that she resented Mississippi being put in the spotlight for the summer. But she was interested in talking with us and hearing what we had to say. The others lost interest before she did and we ended just talking with her.

To sum up, we learned that there were professors on the campus actively concerned about what was happening in Mississippi. One family keeps a harassment map in their living room. The students we talked with were friendly to us although dialogue could be carried on only so far before minds began to close.

A week later, the volunteers went back—this time without their minister.

July 30

Yesterday, July 29, two of us (both white) went to speak in two Sociology classes . . . We spoke about our project in Holly Springs and then answered questions. While some questions were relevant, many were of the nature of: "Would you marry a Negro?" "Is your organization Communist?" and "Why are Negroes so immoral?" Both Alvin and I felt that it was fairly successful. We were able to answer most of the questions in sociological terms. The second class which we attended was an advanced class in Urban Sociology. Their questions were for the most part more sophisticated. Both classes treated us respectfully and were very attentive to what we had to say . . .

A few girls came up and invited us to eat lunch in the cafeteria with them. I was told later by a professor that this move was fairly courageous on their part, as students who had eaten with two people involved with the Movement a month before had been under pressure from their fellow students. . . . We spoke with about seven students, though none stayed with us more than 15 minutes and none offered to renew contact. There were catcalls of "queer" and "communist"; a boy who came up and said, "I heard you were on campus and I just came up to say, "I won't shake hands with you sons of bitches." Eventually we found ourselves sitting alone in a crowded cafeteria. . . . Our conversations at lunch depressed me but I could not really put my finger on why until after we had left.

When our car came to take us back to Holly Springs, two police cars followed our car to the outskirts of Oxford. They waited until we were at the edge of town. Then they stopped us—three cars, four policemen. They asked for all our identifications . . . Before he let us go, the policeman gave us a lecture about why we should notify the police when we come to Oxford, so that they could protect us from any harassment.

Even as he was uttering these words, three burly characters were walking up and down in front of us. If we had not been stopped, we would never have been seen by these guys. When we left, a green truck pulled out *right* behind us and began to follow us. We recognized the three who had marched up and down before us as we were talking to the police. Our driver picked up speed and so did they. Soon we were driving at 90 and 100 miles per hour, with them right behind us. We finally lost them when a police car passed us coming from the opposite direction and probably stopped them. . . .

Later, I realized what had been bothering me about those people at lunch. It was that they were patting themselves on the back for recognizing and admitting that conditions in Mississippi were bad. . . .

I find it hard to care about people who say they are concerned but will not take small risks to help prevent the deaths of many other people . . . I am beginning to understand why people who work in the Movement come to not really care too much about the kind thoughts of some "liberal" southern and, for that matter, northern whites.

I try to fight the bitterness . . .

But the Summer Project did assign twenty-five volunteers to work exclusively on finding white allies. Eighteen of them, including a good number of white Southerners, went to Biloxi—a "moderate" town on the Gulf Coast. Some of the group worked on making contacts with "poor whites," the rest with middle-class residents.

In midsummer, one volunteer evaluated the job they had done thus far.

Greetings from the sovereign state of Mississippi, July 30

It looks like the pilot phase of our White Community Project is pretty much over. We had a war council over the weekend to hash out what we had learned thus far. First of all, the group of 18 of us dropped into the community of Biloxi was too big. Eighteen people, in one place, in a community which already expects all manner of chicanery from the "invaders," and watches every move so closely that little could be done. A more subtle and selective approach needs to be taken, working with smaller groups. Second, the groups should have a more specific focus. Groups attempting to be involved in the power structure and business and religious community have to maintain a different image to be effective from a group in the poor white community. We have worked against one another in this area. Those whose interest is the poor white community enabled the rest of the white community to consider us a bunch of beatniks (which they probably would have done anyway!) and at the same time, those of us involved in the middle class were always after the others to improve their appearance for the sake of our success, causing tensions within the group.

Third, in the middle class white community, a more selective approach must be taken. With few exceptions, people in business and politics and in the churches feel they cannot speak out . . . This being the case, our approach must change from the attempt to involve them in action NOW, but to explain the nature of the coming changes. . . . This new approach would be much more quietly done. It would not consider time spent with people of commitment rigidly opposed to us as very worth while.

Soren

Fear, fear, fear: the same story over and over again. It was no white myth; the volunteers themselves saw intimidation in action.

ENDNOTES

1. Herbert Lee, Negro voter registration worker killed in Liberty, Miss., in 1961.

UNIT 11-12

AFFIDAVITS FROM MISSISSIPPI BLACK PAPER

COUNTY OF AMITE

I am 56 years old, a Negro, and a resident of Amite County, Mississippi. I have lived in Amite County all my life.

In 1954 I organized the Amite County Chapter of the NAACP. We held several meetings in Liberty, and in other places in Amite County. One night, while we were having a meeting in a school building in the 5th District of the county, the sheriff, Ira Jenkins, his deputy, and a member of the school board, and 15 or 20 other white men came out and surrounded the building. Then the sheriff, deputy, and school board member came into the meeting. This was about 8 P.M. These three did not take off their hats or anything, they just sat down. Then the school board member turned to different people and asked them what they were doing at the meeting. They didn't answer him. Then he said: "My advice to you is to take this money and put it into the school building." He apparently thought the group was collecting some money, though this was not the case. When they were ready to leave, the sheriff without asking reached on the table and took the secretary's book. Then they left the building and drove off. Because of their presence, the people were frightened and the meeting ended.

Ever since that time, whenever we have held meetings, the sheriff or his deputy drives around, and the people are frightened by this. We discuss voter registration at these meetings, and that is why they want to frighten us. It is hard to get people to come to the meetings because they are so afraid. Before 1954 it was easy to get people to any kind of meeting or to take part in any kind of organization.

I live very far off the highway, and the white people have never come out to threaten me at my house. But in September, 1963, a cross was burned where the road to my house leads off from the highway. I believe that the Ku Klux Klan is operating in Amite County. It is extremely dangerous for anyone to work for civil rights there without protection from outside the county. We don't have any protection from inside the county—we can't depend on it there. I feel that my life is in danger. There is not an hour which passes when I do not feel my life is in danger. I have felt this since I began working for the NAACP in 1954, and it has gotten worse all the time. I feel this because I hear about people being beaten and threatened in Amite County. They do not say much, because they are afraid, and they do not have anyone they can appeal to for help.

SIGNED: *E. W. Steptoe*

LEFLORE COUNTY

On Feb. 28, 1963, I attended a voter registration meeting in the office of the Student Nonviolent Coordinating Committee in Greenwood, Mississippi. At about 8:30 I noticed a white 1962 Buick circling the block. I checked further and discovered that there were no license plates on the car. At 10:15 that night, the car was still around the office and I notified the rest of the office people that it was still there and to be careful.

At about 10:30 that night, Robert Moses, Randolph Blackwell, and myself left the meeting to go to Greenville, Mississippi. The three of us first stopped at a gas station where we filled up the gas tank and got something to eat.

We then drove onto Highway 82 going to Greenville. As we were going onto the highway, we noticed the same white 1962 Buick that had been driving around the office coming off the highway. There were three white men in the car. As soon as they saw us, they turned around and pulled onto the highway behind us. I believe they were able to recognize us because our car had been parked in front of the SNCC office during the time they had been driving around it.

When I noticed their car following us on Highway 82, I slowed down to 35 m.p.h., the minimum speed limit on that 60 m.p.h. highway. I slowed down in order to let their car pass and also, if possible, to avoid being run off the road by them. When I slowed down, they also slowed down and remained behind us. They followed us for about seven miles, during all of which time there were many other cars on the road. At this point, there were no other cars in sight. They speeded up and pulled even with us. When they were right beside us, one of the men in the car opened fire with a submachine gun. He fired for about three or four seconds and then the car sped away.

I felt something hit me in the neck. I said, "I'm hit." Bob Moses, who was sitting beside me, grabbed the wheel from me and I then slumped in his lap. Bob was able to stop the car safely. I was then taken and laid in the back seat. Randolph got into the back seat with me. Bob then drove to Itta Bena, which was the closest town. We knew that there was an infirmary at Mississippi Vocational College which was located there.

When we got there, there was no doctor present and we called to Greenwood to have one sent up. When he got there he took one look at me and told them to rush me to the hospital in Greenwood. I had been shot once in the neck and once in the shoulder. When our car was later examined, eleven to thirteen bullet holes were found in it.

I was then rushed to a Greenwood hospital where I stayed overnight, and then to Jackson, where the bullet that was still in me (a .45 caliber bullet) was removed from my neck. I stayed in the hospital two more days before I was released.

At the time I was shot, I was twenty years old and a field secretary for SNCC. Bob Moses was also a SNCC field secretary and Randolph Blackwell was the field director of the Voter Education Project being run by the Southern Regional Conference. All three of us are Negro.

SIGNED: *James Travis*

MONTGOMERY COUNTY

I am a Negro, 46 years of age, and reside in Ruleville, Sunflower County.

On the 9th of June, 1963, I, Miss Annell Ponder, and eight other women were returning from a voter registration workshop in South Carolina. We were on a Continental Trailways bus that stopped at Winona, Montgomery County, at the bus station. Annell Ponder and others of our party, including James West from Itta Bena, Rosemary Freeman from near Greenwood, and June Johnson, a 15-year-old girl, got off the bus to go to the restaurant. Two, Euvester Simpson and Ruth Day, also of our party, got off the bus to use the rest room. I remained on the bus.

The four that got off the bus to go to the restaurant—and had gone to the "white" side of the restaurant—were coming back to the bus. I got off the bus and asked them what happened. They said that there were some policemen and highway patrolmen in there. Annell said policemen with billy clubs told them to get out of there. I said that this can be reported and Annell said, "Yes, I am going to get the tag number." The four of them were standing outside to get the tag number, and Euvester Simpson was standing with them talking, when all five of them were put in the patrol car, which I think was the highway patrolman's car; he was also the one giving orders.

I got off the bus when all at once an officer from the patrol car said, "Get that one too." A county deputy, Officer A_____ , and one more got out of the car and opened the door to his car and said, "You are under arrest." I was going into the car when Officer A_____ kicked me into the car. While driving me to the jail, they were questioning me and calling me "bitch."

We got to the jail, and I saw all five of the above [Annell Ponder, Rosemary Freeman, June Johnson, James West, and Euvester Simpson] in the booking room. As soon as I got to the booking room, a tall policeman walked over to James West and jumped hard on James West's feet.

I was led into a room—a cell—with Euvester Simpson. While I was in the cell, I could hear screaming and the passing of kicks. Pretty soon I saw several white men bringing Annell Ponder past my cell. She was holding on to the jail walls, her clothes all torn, her mouth all swelled up, and her eyes were all bloody—only one eye looking like itself.

After a while they came for me: Officer B_____ , a highway patrolman (his name on a metal plate on his pocket); the policeman who had jumped on James West's feet; and another policeman with a crew-cut haircut.

They came into my cell and asked me why I was demonstrating, and said that they were not going to have such carryings-on in Mississippi. They asked me if I had seen Martin Luther King, Jr. I said I could not be demonstrating—I had just got off the bus—and denied that I had seen Martin Luther King. They said "Shut up" and always cut me off. They then asked me where I was from. I said Ruleville. They then left, saying that they were going to check it out.

They then returned. Officer B_____ said: "You damn right you are from Ruleville. We are going to make you wish that you were dead, bitch." They led me to another cell. Before I had been led out of the cell, I saw a Negro—who I reckoned was a trusty, who stayed around the jail—bring a mop and bucket to take somewhere. Doctor Searcy, Cleveland, Mississippi, said that I had been beaten so deeply that my nerve endings are permanently damaged, and I am sore.

Signed: *Fannie Lou Hamer*

MONTGOMERY COUNTY

I am 31, Negro, and a resident of Atlanta, Georgia.

I was returning on June 9, 1963, from a workshop in voter education and community development held in John's Island, South Carolina. I was returning on a Trailways bus together with Mrs. Fannie Lou Hamer, June Johnson, Euvester Simpson, James West, Rosemary Freeman, and four other people.

When we got to the Winona bus station at about 12 noon, the five people named above, excepting Mrs. Hamer, got off the bus, and June Johnson, James West, and Rosemary Freeman and I went into the lunchroom. This lunchroom was the one normally reserved for white people (all of the party were Negroes). We sat down at the counter and the waitress behind the counter wadded up some paper and threw it against the wall and said: "I can't take no more."

By this time a member of the Winona city police (apparently _____) and a member of the highway patrol entered the back of the room. They came up behind where we were sitting and tapped each of us on the shoulders and said: "Get up and get out of here." I was the last one on the line, and I asked him if he didn't know it was against the law to put us out. (This was after the ICC ruling against discrimination in ICC facilities.) He said: "Ain't no damn law, get up and get out of here."

So we went outside. We stood outside discussing what happened. Mrs. Hamer saw us and got off the bus and asked us why we had come out so quick. So we told her what happened, and she said: "Yeah, this is what we have to put up with. This is what we have to go against here in Mississippi."

Then we agreed that we would include what had happened here in a report we were going to make about incidents during the trip. Mrs. Hamer got back on the bus and the rest of us stayed in front of the station talking, saying that it didn't look good to get up and walk out of the lunchroom when we knew we had a right to be in there. We said if anything like that happened again, we would just go to jail.

Then I went back to the door and looked inside to get a better look at the police officers, so I could identify them. But they crouched back against the wall so I couldn't see them. So I decided I would get the number off the patrolman's car. It didn't have a number on the side so we walked around to the back, to get the license plate number.

As I was taking that down, the officers came out of the restaurant and said that we were under arrest, and said: "You all get in that car," indicating the highway patrol car. Mrs. Hamer saw us getting in the car and she got off the bus, and she called out to me and asked me what I wanted them to do. I told her to go ahead on the bus.

The officer driving the car we were in called out to another policeman and said: "Get that other one too." Mrs. Hamer was then placed in another car which followed us to the Montgomery County jail.

When we got there they started questioning us and one of them asked me something and I said "Yes" or "No." Then he wanted to know if I had enough "respect" for him to say "sir" when I answered his questions. So I asked him what he said, and he repeated his question, using the term "nigger" to refer to me. I told him I didn't know him that well. He looked very angry and confused. Then the highway patrolman walked over and stepped hard on James West's foot and ground on it, though James had not done anything.

Then they questioned us more about the civil rights work, about the Greenwood voter registration project, and said we had come to demonstrate. After a while they put us in cells, two of us together in a cell. James West and June Johnson were kept out.

After we were in awhile, I heard them questioning June Johnson, asking her what did she think they were supposed to do about it, apparently referring to our presence in Winona and our activities in civil rights. June said that she felt they were supposed to protect us and take care of us. Then I began to hear sounds of violence. There was a whiskey still (metal) in the booking room and I could hear people scraping against this and the floor and walls, and could hear June screaming.

After a while they came to get me, bringing June to put in my cell. She was bleeding from the face and neck and crying. They took me into the booking room, and made me stand several different places consecutively. Finally I was standing in a corner. There was blood on the floor in this place. I started to tell the four white men and police officers in the room that we wanted them to understand that we didn't hate them. When I told them that they turned toward me and one of them (in blue uniform) said he wanted to hear me say "sir." I ignored him. Another young man in a crew-cut said: "You just came up here to stir up trouble." The man slapped me in the head with his fist. Then the officer in blue uniform hit me. Then the highway patrolman wanted to know why I took down his license plate number. I told him I wanted to make an accurate report if there was trouble. They wanted to know who we would make a report to. I told him the federal government.

They said: "Who do you mean, Bobby Kennedy?" and there was contempt in their voices. I said: "No, the federal government." Then they started again insisting I say "sir." Through all this conversation they kept hitting me. The policeman in blue uniform at one point took a sort of blackjack from the man who I believe was _____ and from then on he used that in beating me. This went on for about 10 minutes, with questioning and my being beaten to the floor and getting up and being beaten down again. At one point the highway patrolman hit me in the stomach. They finally stopped beating me and put me in a maximum security cell. One of my teeth had been chipped and my lip was bleeding, and later when I tried to walk I staggered and fell.

When I was brought to another cell I saw two Negroes who were in their 20s or a little younger. Officer B_____ said, "Take this," talking to the youngest Negro. Officer B_____ had in his hand a long, two-foot blackjack made out of leather, wider at one end, and one end being filled with something heavy. The young Negro said: "You mean for me to beat her with this?" Officer B_____ said, "You damn right. If you don't, you know what I will do for you."

The young Negro told me to get on the bunk and he began to beat me. I tried to put my hands to my side where I had polio when I was a child, so that I would not be beat so much on that side. The first Negro beat me until he got tired. Then the second Negro was made to beat me. I took the first part of it, but couldn't stand the second beating. I began to move and the first Negro was made to sit on my feet to keep me from kicking. I remember that I tried to smooth my dress which was working up from all of the beating. One of the white officers pushed my dress up. I was screaming and going on, and the young officer with the crew-cut began to beat me about the head and told me to stop my screaming. I then began to bury my head in the mattress and hugged it to kill out the sound of my screams. It was impossible to stop the screaming. I must have passed out—I remember trying to raise my head and heard one of the officers, Officer B_____ who said, "That's enough."

He said, "Get up and walk." I could barely walk. My body was real hard, feeling like metal. My hands were navy blue, and I couldn't bend the fingers. I was taken back to the cell.

While I was back in the cell, I could talk to June Johnson, Annell Ponder, and Rosemary Freeman, who were in their cells. I learned that June Johnson had a hole in her head from her beating. I learned that the trusty had used the bucket and mop to mop the blood.

Then they got us up one night to take our pictures and Officer B_____ , who had taken the pictures, forced me to sign a statement which they already had made me write, that I had been treated all right. That night was the following Monday night. I tried to write the statement in such a way that anybody would know that I had been forced to write the statement.

The following Tuesday, we had our trial. There was no jury. We had no lawyer.

We were charged and were found guilty of disorderly conduct and resisting arrest.

When we were put in the jail, and when I was put in the jail, I told them that nothing is right around here. The arresting officer had lied and said that I was resisting arrest. I told them that I was not leaving my cell, and that if they wanted me they had to kill me in the cell and drag me out. I would rather be killed inside my cell instead of outside the cell.

On that Tuesday, I heard some white men talk to Officers C_____ and D_____ and that they were FBI and had to report what they said. I was able to see Lawrence Guyot, a field secretary of SNCC who I had known before in voter registration work, and saw him in the booking room and saw that he had been beaten.

On the following Wednesday, James Bevel, Andrew Young, and Dorothy Cotton of SCLC (Southern Christian Leadership Conference) came to see us and to get us (the people who had been on the bus and were arrested) out. But before I left the jail I was able to see that Lawrence Guyot's head had been beaten out of shape.

On the 31st of August, 1962, I had been fired from my plantation job, Dee Marlow's Plantation, Ruleville, because I attempted to register to vote. I had been working for SNCC and SCLC before I had been beaten. At the present time, I am a candidate for Congress in the coming primary, for the Second Congressional District.

I was kept in the cell for three days and no doctor was brought to see me.

After three days I was charged in a trial with disorderly conduct and resisting arrest. We were found guilty, and appealed. And the next day we were released. We would have been fined $100 on each charge, but we got out on $200 appeal bond.

Since then the Justice Department brought suit against the officers. They denied the charge and an all-white male jury found them innocent.

Signed: *Annell Ponder*

MONTGOMERY COUNTY

I am 16 years old and live in Greenwood, Mississippi. A group of civil rights workers was traveling from Charleston, South Carolina, to Greenwood, Miss., by bus on June 9, 1963. The group consisted of Mrs. Fannie Lou Hamer, Miss Annell Ponder, Mr. James West, Miss Euvester Simpson, Miss Rosemary Freeman, and myself. On the trip from Columbus, Miss., to Winona, Miss., our group sat in the front of the bus and occasionally sang freedom songs.

When we got to Winona, the bus stopped at the terminal there. Everybody went into the terminal except Mrs. Hamer. When we got inside the terminal, our group sat down on the "white" side. [A] Winona [police officer] came in and told us to "get over where you belong." We got up and went outside the terminal. Soon the [police officer] and a state trooper came outside and arrested us. When she saw us getting into the trooper's car, Mrs. Hamer got out of the bus and asked us, "Should I go on to Greenwood?" We told her to go ahead, but the trooper called out, "Get that woman," and an unidentified white man grabbed her and put her in his car. The trooper took us to the Montgomery County jail. Mrs. Hamer arrived in the other car about the same time.

We were taken inside. The trooper said, "What you niggers come down here for—a damn demonstration?" We all shook our heads and answered "No." Then he said, "You damn niggers don't say 'No' to me—you say 'Yes, sir.'" While he was saying this, Officer A_____ and the Winona [police officer] came in, accompanied by the same white man that brought Mrs. Hamer in.

Officer walked over and stamped James West's toe and hit Euvester in the side with a ring of heavy keys. Then the trooper questioned us. While questioning Annell Ponder, he found out that she lived in Atlanta, Ga. He told her, "I knew you wasn't from Mississippi 'cause you don't know how to say 'Yes, sir' to a white man." Then he turned to the rest of us and said, "I been hearing about you black sons-of-bitches over in Greenwood, raising all that hell. You come over here to Winona, you'll get the hell whipped out of you."

He opened the door to the cell block and told everybody to get inside. I started to go in with the rest of them and he said, "Not you, you black-assed nigger." He asked me, "Are you a member of the NAACP?" I said yes. Then he hit me on the cheek and chin. I raised my arm to protect my face and he hit me in the stomach. He asked, "Who runs that thing?" I answered, "The people." He asked, "Who pays you?" I said, "Nobody." He said "Nigger, you're lying. You done enough already to get your neck broken." Then the four of them—Officer A_____, the [Winona police officer], the state trooper, and the white man that had brought Mrs. Hamer in—threw me on the floor and beat me. After they finished stomping me, they said, "Get up, nigger." I raised my head and the white man hit me on the back of the head with a club wrapped in black leather. Then they made me get up. My dress was torn off and my slip was coming off. Blood was streaming down the back of my head and my dress was all bloody. They put me in a cell with Rosemary Freeman, and called Annell Ponder. I couldn't see what they did to Annell, but I could hear them trying to make her say "Yes, sir." When they brought her back, she was bloody and her clothes were torn.

About 5 minutes later the trooper came in and yanked Rosemary Freeman off the bed and bumped her up against the brick wall of the cell two or three times. Then he turned to me and said, "Pull your dress down and wash off. When I come back in 5 minutes, you'd better be clean." I started to wash up but a man in a blue uniform told me to wait until we left.

Then we heard the policemen shouting at Mrs. Hamer in her cell. Then they took her somewhere into a different part of the building.

A little while later we heard Mrs. Hamer hollering, "Don't beat me no more, don't beat me no more." Later they brought her back to her cell crying. She cried at intervals during the night, saying that the leg afflicted with polio was hurting her terribly.

We stayed in that jail day and night from Sunday till Tuesday, when they booked us and informed us that we were charged with disorderly conduct and resisting arrest. We then went back to jail until Wednesday afternoon, when a group of SNCC people came from Greenwood to get us out of jail. We got back to Greenwood about 7 P.M. on June 12, 1963.

SIGNED: *June E. Johnson*

NESHOBA COUNTY

I am 22 years old and the wife of Michael H. Schwerner, one of the three civil rights workers who have been missing in or near Philadelphia, Miss., since June 21, 1964. Michael and I came to Mississippi on about January 16 this year as field staff workers for the Congress of Racial Equality, assigned to the Council of Federated Organizations. On about January 21 we went to Meridian, Mississippi, with the purpose of establishing a community center in that city which would provide such services which the state and local authorities would not provide for Negro citizens. From that time until June 21, 1964, we worked continually in and around the area of Meridian and other counties in the eastern half of the Fourth Congressional District. To my knowledge, the only times that Michael left the state in those six and a half months were for a four-day conference in New Orleans in February, a one-day trip the two of us took to New York in March, and the Oxford orientation session in Oxford, Ohio, immediately prior to his disappearance. The only additional time that I was out of the state was for a ten-day visit to New York City from May 24 to June 2.

Shortly after we arrived in Meridian in January, we met Mr. James E. Chaney, a 21-year-old Negro man who worked with us and eventually became part of the Congress of

Racial Equality staff. From about the middle of February to the end of March, James was out of Meridian, working first in Canton and then, for a short time, in Greenwood. At the end of March, he returned to Meridian to work with us.

In the first few weeks that Michael and I were in Meridian, we had to change our place of residence some three or four times, because the Negro families who took us in received intimidating phone calls and became afraid to house us. In February we were able to rent a house from a Negro, Mr. Albert Jones, which he rented from a white woman, Mrs. Roy Cunningham. We lived in that house until the beginning of June, when Mrs. Cunningham insisted that we leave. Prior to our eviction, we had had our rent raised by her.

In the first few weeks that we were in Meridian, we received no threats, nor did we suffer harassment at the hands of the local authorities. However, as people came to know us better, to recognize us, and to know what we were attempting to do, the tension increased. On several occasions my husband was picked up by the local police and taken to the police station, where he was questioned as to our activities, asked to show proof of ownership of our car, etc. They never did pick me up for questioning.

As we achieved some success in establishing the community center, the threats and intimidation began to increase. By May we received so many phone calls at late hours of the night that in order to get some sleep we were forced to remove our telephone receiver before going to bed. We finally resolved this problem by obtaining an unpublished telephone number when we moved to our new apartment after being evicted. The phone calls at the office during the day and evenings continued. They were of several forms. Some were extremely unpleasant in that when I picked up the phone the party at the other end of the line would use extremely offensive language towards me. Other calls we received were threats of violence, such as someone calling and telling me that he was planning to kill my husband, or that my husband was already dead. Michael received anonymous calls telling him that they intended to kill me or that I was already dead.

A man by the name of Mr. _____ , who runs an _____ shop a few doors down the block from our office, used abusive language directed towards me and my husband continually. He constantly referred to my husband as "Jew-boy" and "nigger-lover." I have been told by workers in Meridian that on at least one occasion in the last month, several of them were threatened by Mr. _____ with an axe handle.

As the car which we drove became well known, we were followed by the police and by white citizens on many occasions. We became extremely cautious about driving at night, and would not do so unless it was a necessity. The white cab drivers took to following us, and did so even when I returned for the hearing on July 23.

At the end of April, my husband was arrested on two counts of blocking a crosswalk. He was held in the Meridian City jail from Monday until after his trial on Wednesday. When he was released he told me that he had narrowly escaped a beating. The police officer who took him to his cell on Monday afternoon called one of the other prisoners out of the cell. My husband could not hear what the police officer said to the other prisoner, but when that man returned to the cell he took Michael aside and told him that he didn't know who he, my husband, was, or what he did, but that he better keep quiet about it while in the jail, because the police officer had said that if this prisoner got the others to beat Michael, no action would be taken by the police.

On Friday, April 18, my husband and I were visiting Reverend R. S. Porter, when he received word that a cross was burning in front of his church. We arrived at the First Union Baptist Church as the fire department was extinguishing the flames, but the cross was still smoldering.

In the beginning of June, a large group of people were arrested in Meridian when they attempted to form a picket line in front of three of the five-and-ten-cent stores. They were charged with obstructing traffic. My husband went down to the police station to find out the charges on the arrested persons. Officer A_____ , who I believe was the desk sergeant that day, threatened my husband. From what Michael told me, his words were something like this: "If you get any more of these damn kids arrested, Schwerner, I'm going to get you, and that's a promise."

Working so closely with my husband and James Chaney, I was able, over the course of the months, to observe their habits and attitudes as workers. I have had the opportunity to observe other civil rights workers at their job, but I do not believe that there are any other workers in the state any more cautious or meticulous in their work than were Michael and James. Michael's concern about the danger to other people and the importance of minimizing it came from his experience as a rights worker and his feeling of responsibility as the Project Director. James undoubtedly derived much of his feeling of caution from the experiences he underwent in the 21 years of his life as a Mississippi Negro, subject to all the whims and capricious acts of the white citizens of this state.

Michael started making trips into Neshoba County in February and, in all, made about 30 such expeditions. Every time he went into that county to work, I remained in the office in Meridian to receive his phone calls when he checked in, or in the event that anything went wrong and he needed to contact someone. The only times that I did not serve in that capacity were the few trips he made into Neshoba County when I was out of the state. Because the county was known to be so dangerous, I insisted on assuming that job myself, out of obvious concern for my husband's safety. When James Chaney returned to Meridian at the end of March, the two of them usually traveled to Neshoba together, although there were one or two occasions when one of them went alone or with another person. Neshoba County has had a reputation for being so volatile that it has been nicknamed "Bloody Neshoba," and many experienced civil rights workers, for very good reason, declined to work in that territory.

My husband believed very strongly in security precautions, such as phoning in one's whereabouts, and on several occasions I heard him reprimand others who did not call in to the office when they were supposed to. I remember only one incident prior to his disappearance when Michael was two hours late returning from Neshoba County and did not call to tell me why. I was frantic and at the point of calling the jails, but refrained because I knew that if he had not been picked up, this would inform the authorities of his whereabouts and make the situation far graver. When he and James returned that particular evening, they said that they had been detained in talking with a contact who had no telephone, and that they were fearful of stopping on the road to call in and advise me of their delay.

On one occasion, I believe at the beginning of May, the two men, James and Michael, were planning to drive to Philadelphia during the day to see some people. As I had met several of the Neshoba County contacts in Meridian, and I had information to relate to them about community center programs which I believed would benefit them, I requested permission of the two men to accompany them. At first they both refused, but when I persisted, Michael finally agreed, and I believe that he agreed because he felt he might have been overprotective of me as his wife. James, however, did not have any of these personal involvements, so that he was able to rationally say that if I went, he would not, as he said that if he was seen in Neshoba County with a white woman we would all be killed. His sound advice was heeded and I did not enter Neshoba County on that day, or at any other time until after the disappearance of my husband, James Chaney, and Andrew Goodman.

On one or more occasions, James told me that the car had been followed in Neshoba County by white persons in cars with the license plates either covered or removed. On one occasion he said he had been followed by an official car, either that of police or sheriff's department, but I don't know which.

On June 21, 1964, Michael and James made another trip to Philadelphia, this time accompanied by Andrew Goodman, one of the volunteer COFO summer workers. I was in Oxford, Ohio, at the time, but before my husband left Oxford at 3 A.M., Saturday, June

20, he told me of his intention to go on Sunday to Philadelphia to investigate the burning of the Mt. Zion Church in the Longdale community. The three men never returned to Meridian, nor did they call in their whereabouts. All knowledge I have of my husband's habits and training indicates that, given the opportunity, he certainly would have called in. It is foolish to assert that he would have turned down the opportunity to do so. The information from officials is vague and contradictory, and all knowledge of the situation in Neshoba County would lead me to believe that the three men have been murdered.

On June 25, at about 3 P.M., I went to the State Capitol building in Jackson with John Robert Zellner, a Student Nonviolent Coordinating Committee field secretary, and Reverend Edwin King, the Tougaloo College chaplain. I attempted to see Governor Johnson to ask for his promise of help in the search for the three men. We were told by Senator Barbour that the governor was out for the afternoon and could not be contacted. He was extremely rude in his treatment of me. We then walked over to the Governor's Mansion, arriving just as Governor Johnson walked up the steps with Governor Wallace of Alabama. We followed them up the steps and Mr. Zellner introduced himself by name to Governor Johnson and they shook hands. Mr. Zellner then turned towards me and introduced me as the wife of Michael Schwerner, one of the three missing men. He said that I would like to speak for a moment with the Mississippi governor. The moment Johnson heard who I was, he turned and bolted for the door of the Mansion. The door was locked behind him and a group of Mississippi highway patrolmen surrounded the three of us. An officer with the name plate "Harper" refused to allow us to request an appointment with the governor. Harper said that he would not convey our request to Johnson.

On June 26, 1964, when I went to Neshoba County to speak with Sheriff Rainey, the car which I was in was followed by a blue, late-model pick-up truck without license plates. There were two white men in the truck. At one point the truck blocked us off in front and a white, late-model car blocked us from behind. We turned our automobile around and were able to get by the white car; the pick-up truck followed us awhile farther. We reported this to the FBI agents who were working in Philadelphia on the investigation. After I spoke with Sheriff Rainey, who denied knowledge of the circumstances of the disappearance of the three men, we obtained permission from Rainey and the FBI to follow the sheriff's car to the garage where the station wagon (which the men had driven on June 21) was being kept, in order that I could see it. Several young white men, who I believe were workers at the garage, laughed and made screams which are usually referred to as rebel yells when they realized who I was. When we left the garage the sheriff's car was close behind ours, and the blue pick-up truck once more followed after us to the outskirts of town, with the sheriff making no attempt to stop it or question the occupants about the lack of license plates.

SIGNED: *Rita L. Schwerner*

UNIT 11-13

LIFE IN MISSISSIPPI

AN INTERVIEW WITH FANNIE LOU HAMER

J. H. O'Dell

O'Dell: Mrs. Hamer, it's good to see you again. I understand you have been to Africa since we last talked; I would like for you to talk about your African trip today.

Hamer: It was one of the proudest moments in my life.

O'Dell: That is a marvelous experience for any black American particularly for anyone who has lived here all of his life. Then, too, we want to talk about some of your early childhood experiences which helped to make you the kind of person and provide the basis for your becoming so active in the freedom movement.

Hamer: I would like to talk about some of the things that happened that made me know that there was something wrong in the south from a child. My parents moved to Sunflower County when I was two years old. I remember, and I will never forget, one day—I was six years old and I was playing beside the road and this plantation owner drove up to me and stopped and asked me "could I pick cotton." I told him I didn't know and he said, "Yes, you can. I will give you things that you want from the commissary store," and, he named things like crackerjacks and sardines—and it was a huge list that he called off. So I picked the 30 pounds of cotton that week, but I found out what actually happened was he was trapping me into beginning the work I was to keep doing and I never did get out of his debt again. My parents tried so hard to do what they could to keep us in school, but school didn't last but four months out of the year and most of the time we didn't have clothes to wear. My parents would make huge crops of sometimes 55 to 60 bales of cotton. Being from a big family where there were 20 children, it wasn't too hard to pick that much cotton. But my father, year after year, didn't get too much money and I remember he just kept going. Later on he did get enough money to buy mules. We didn't have tractors, but he bought mules, wagons, cultivators and some farming equipment. As soon as he bought that and decided to rent some land, because it was always better if you rent the land, but as soon as he got the mules and wagons and everything, somebody

---

Mrs. Fannie Lou Hamer is Vice-Chairman of the Mississippi Freedom Democratic Party (MFDP), and is its candidate for Congress from the Second Congressional District of that state. Mrs. Hamer has traveled widely, speaking on behalf of the Movement. She was recently named by the University of Mississippi School of Journalism as one of the five outstanding women in the state doing the most to bring about changes in Mississippi.

went to our trough—a white man who didn't live very far from us-and he fed the mules Paris Green, put it in their food and it killed the mules and our cows. That knocked us right back down. And things got so tough then I began to wish I was white. We worked all the time, just worked and then we would be hungry and my mother was clearing up a new ground trying to help to feed us for $1.25 a day. She was using an axe, just like a man, and something flew up and hit her in her eye. It eventually caused her to lose both her eyes and I began to get sicker and sicker of the system there. I used to see my mother wear clothes that would have so many latches on them, they had been done over and over and over again she would do that but she would try to keep us decent. She still would be ragged and I always said if I lived to get grown and had a chance, I was going to try to get something for my mother and I was going to do something for the black man of the south if it would cost my life; I was determined to see that things were changed. My mother got down sick in '53 and she lived with me, an invalid, until she passed away in 1961. And during the time she was staying with me sometime I would be worked so hard I couldn't sleep at night. . . .

O'Dell: What kind of work were you doing?

Hamer: I was a timekeeper and sharecropper on the same plantation I was fired from. During the time she was with me, if there was something I had to do without, I was determined to see that she did have something in her last few years. I went almost naked to see that my mother was kept decent and treated as a human being for the first time in all of her life. My mother was a great woman. To look at her from the suffering she had gone through to bring us up—20 children: 6 girls and 14 boys, but still she taught us to be decent and to respect ourselves, and that is one of the things that has kept me going, even after she passed. She tried so hard to make life easy for us. Those are the things that forced me to try to do something different and when this Movement came to Mississippi I still feel it is one of the greatest things that ever happened because only a person living in the State of Mississippi knows what it is like to suffer; knows what it is like to be hungry; knows what it is like to have no clothing to wear. And these people in Mississippi State, they are not "down"; all they need is a chance. And I am determined to give my part not for what the Movement can do for me, but what 1 can do for the Movement to bring about a change in the State of Mississippi. Actually, some of the things I experienced as a child still linger on; what the white man has done to the black people in the south!

One of the things I remember as a child: There was a man named Joe Pulliam. He was a great Christian man; but one time, he was living with a white family and this white family robbed him of what he earned. They didn't pay him anything. This white man gave him $150 to go to the hill (you see, I lived in the Black Belt of Mississippi) . . . to get another Negro family. Joe Pulliam knew what this white man had been doing to him so he kept the $150 and didn't go. This white man talked with him then shot him in the shoulder and Joe Pulliam went back into the house and got a Winchester and killed this white man. The other white fellow that was with him he "outrun the word of God" back to town. That gave this Negro a chance to go down on the bayou that was called Powers Bayou and he got in a hollowed-out stump where there was enough room for a person. He got in there and he stayed and was tracked there, but they couldn't see him and every time a white man would peep out, he busted him. He killed 13 white men and wounded 26 and Mississippi was a quiet place for a long time. I remember that until this day and I won't forget it. After they couldn't get him, they took gas—one man from Clarksdale used a machine gun—(Bud Doggins)—they used a machine gun and they tried to get him like that and then they took gas and poured it on Powers Bayou. Thousands of gallons of gas and they lit it and when it burned up to the hollowed-out stump, he crawled out. When they found him, he was unconscious and he was lying with his head on his gun but the last bullet in the gun had been snapped twice. They dragged him by his heels on the back of a car and they paraded about with that man and they cut his ears off and put them in a showcase and it stayed there a long, long time—in Drew, Mississippi. All of those things, when they would happen, would make me sick in the pit of my stomach and year after year, every time something would happen it would make me more and more aware of what would have to be done in the State of Mississippi.

O'Dell: What do you think will have to be done?

Hamer: The only thing I really feel is necessary is that the black people, not only in Mississippi, will have to actually upset this apple-cart. What I mean by that is, so many things are under the cover that will have to be swept out and shown to this whole world, not just to America. There is so much hypocrisy in America. This thing they say of "the land of the free and the home of the brave" is all on paper. It doesn't mean anything to us. The only way we can make this thing a reality in America is to do all we can to destroy this system and bring this thing out to the light that has been under the cover all these years. That's why I believe in Christianity because the Scriptures said: "The things that have been done in the dark will be known on the house tops."

Now many things are beginning to come out and it was truly a reality to me when I went to Africa, to Guinea. The little things that had been taught to me about the African people, that they were "heathens," "savages," and they were just downright stupid people. But when I got to Guinea, we were greeted by the Government of Guinea, which is *Black People*—and we stayed at a place that was the government building, because we were the guests of the Government. You don't know what that meant to me when I got to Guinea on the 12th of September. The President of Guinea, Sekou Touré, came to see us on the 13th. Now you know, I don't know how you can compare this by me being able to see a President of a country, when I have just been there two days; and here I have been in America, born in America, and I am 46 years pleading with the President for the last two to three years to just give us a chance—and this President in Guinea recognized us enough to talk to us.

O'Dell: How many were in your delegation?

Hamer: It was eleven of us during that time, and I could get a clear picture of actually what had happened to the black people of America. Our foreparents were mostly brought from West Africa, the same place that we visited in Africa. We were brought to America and our foreparents were sold; white people bought them; white people changed their names . . . and actually . . . here, my maiden name is supposed to be Townsend; but really, what is my maiden name . . . ? . . . What is my name? This white man who is saying "it takes time." For three hundred and more years they have had "time," and now it is time for them to listen. We have been listening year after year to them and what have we got? We are not even allowed to *think* for ourselves. "I know what is best for you," but they *don't* know what is best for us! It is time now to let them know what they owe us, and they owe us a great deal. Not only have we paid the price with our names in ink, but we have also paid in blood. And they can't say that black people can't be intelligent, because going back to Africa, in Guinea, there are almost 4 million people there and what he, President Touré, is doing to educate the people: as long as the French people had it they weren't doing a thing that is being done now. I met one child there eleven years old, speaking three languages. He could speak English, French and Malinke. Speaking my language actually better than I could. And this hypocrisy—they tell us here in America. People should go there and see. It would bring tears in your eyes to make you think of all those years, the type of brain-washing that this man will use in America to keep us separated from our own people. When I got on that plane, it was *loaded* with *white* people going to Africa for the Peace Corps. I got there and met a lot of them, and actually they had more peace there in Guinea than I have here. I talked to some of them. I told them before they would be able to clean up somebody else's house you would have to clean up yours; before they can tell somebody else how to run their country, why don't they do something here. This problem is not only in Mississippi. During the time I was in the Convention in Atlantic City I didn't get any threats from Mississippi. The threatening letters were from Philadelphia, Chicago and other big cities.

O'Dell: You received threatening letters while you were at the Convention?

Hamer: Yes. I got pictures of us and they would draw big red rings around us and tell what they thought of us. I got a letter said, "I have been shot three times through the heart. I hope I see your second act." But this white man who wants to stay *white,* and to think for the Negro, he is not only destroying the Negro, he is destroying himself, because a house divided against itself cannot stand and that same thing applies to America. America that is divided against itself cannot stand, and we cannot say we have all of this unity they say we have when black people are being discriminated against in every city in America I have visited.

I was in jail when Medgar Evers was murdered and *nothing,* I mean *nothing* has been done about that. You know what really made me sick? I was in Washington, D.C. at another time reading in a paper where the U.S. gives Byron de la Beckwith—the man who is charged with murdering Medgar Evers—they were giving him so much money for some land and I ask "Is this America?" We can no longer ignore the fact that America is NOT the "land of the free and the home of the brave." I used to question this for years—what did our kids actually fight for? They would go in the service and go through all of that and come right out to be drowned in a river in Mississippi. I found this hypocrisy is all over America.

The 20th of March in 1964, I went before the Secretary of State to qualify to run as an official candidate for Congress from the 2nd Congressional District, and it was easier for me to qualify to run than it was for me to pass the literacy test to be a registered voter. And we had four people to qualify and run in the June primary election but we didn't have enough Negroes registered in Mississippi. The 2nd Congressional District where I ran, against Jamie Whitten, is made up of 24 counties. Sixty-eight percent of the people are Negroes, only 6-8 percent are registered. And it is not because Negroes don't want to register. They try and they try and they try. That's why it was important for us to set up the "Freedom Registration" to help us in the Freedom Democratic Party.

O'Dell: This was a registration drive organized by the Movement?

Hamer: Yes. The only thing we took out was the Constitution of the State of Mississippi and the interpretation of the Constitution. We had 63,000 people registered on the Freedom Registration form. And we tried from every level to go into the regular Democratic Party medium. We tried from the precinct level. The 16th of June when they were holding precinct meetings all across the state, I was there and there was eight of us there to attend the meeting, and they had the door locked at 10 o'clock in the morning. So we had our own meeting and elected our permanent chairman and secretary and regulars and alternates and we passed a resolution as the law requires and then mailed it to Oscar Townsend, our permanent chairman. This is what's happening in the State of Mississippi. We had hoped for a change, but these people (Congressmen) go to Washington and stay there 25 and 30 years and more without representing the people of Mississippi. We have never been represented in Washington. You can tell this by the program the federal government had to train 2,400 tractor drivers. They would have trained Negro and white together, but this man, Congressman Jamie Whitten, voted against it and everything that was decent. So, we've got to have somebody in Washington who is concerned about the people of Mississippi. After we testified before the Credentials Committee in Atlantic City, their Mississippi representative testified also. He said I got 600 votes but when they made the count in Mississippi, I was told I had 388 votes. So actually it is no telling how many votes I actually got.

O'Dell: In other words, a Mr. Collins came before the Credentials Committee of the Democratic National Convention and actually gave away the secret in a sense, because the figure he gave was not the same figure he gave to you as an official candidate?

Hamer: That's right. He also said I had been allowed to attend the precinct meeting which was true. But he didn't say we were locked out of the polling place there and had to hold our meeting on the lawn.

O'Dell: So now you have a situation where you had the basis for a Freedom Democratic Party. You have had four candidates to run for Congress. You had a community election where 63,000 of our folk showed their interest in the election. How do you size up the situation coming out of Atlantic City? What impressions did you get from your effort in Atlantic City to be seated, and how do you feel the people back home are going to react to this next period you are going into?

Hamer: The people at home will work hard and actually all of them think it was important that we made the decision that we did make *not to compromise;* because we didn't have anything to *compromise* for. Some things I found out in the National Convention I wasn't too glad I did find out. But we will work hard, and it was important to actually really bring this out to the open, the things I will say some people knew about and some people didn't; this stuff that has been kept under the cover for so many years. Actually, the world and America is upset and the only way to bring about a change is to upset it more.

O'Dell: What was done about the beating you and Miss Annelle Ponder, your colleague in the citizenship school program, experienced while in jail? Was any action taken at all?

Hamer: The Justice Department filed a suit against the brutality of the five law officials and they had this trial. The trial began the 2nd of December 1963 and they had white jurors from the State of Mississippi, and the Federal Judge Clayton made it plain to the jurors that they were dealing with "nigras" and that "who would actually accuse such upstanding people like those law officials"—be careful what they was doing because they are law-abiding citizens and were dealing with agitators and niggers. It was as simple as that? And those police were cleared. They were on the loose for about a week before I left for Atlantic City. One of those men was driving a truck from the State Penitentiary. One night he passed my house and pointed me out to one of the other men in the State Penitentiary truck and that same night I got a threat: "We got you located Fannie Lou and we going to put you in the Mississippi River." A lot of people say why do they let the *hoodlums* do that? But it is those people supposed to have *class* that are doing the damage in Mississippi. You know there was a time, in different places, when people felt safe going to a law official. But I called them that day and got the answer back, "You know you don't look to us for help."

O'Dell: This threat: the man called you up and said "we've got you spotted"; I gather from that that the river has some special meaning to us living there in Mississippi?

Hamer: Yes. So many people have been killed and put in the Mississippi River. Like when they began to drag the river for Mickey and Chaney and Andy.[1] Before he was to go to Oxford, Ohio, Mickey was telling me his life had been threatened and a taxi driver had told him to be careful because they was out to get him.

When they (the sailors) began to drag the river they found other people and I actually feel like they stopped because they would have been shook up to find so many if they had just been fishing for bodies. The Mississippi is not the only river. There's the Tallahatchie and the Big Black. People have been put in the river year after year, these things *been* happening.

O'Dell: The general policy of striking fear in people's hearts. In other words, it is like lynching used to be. They used to night ride. . . .

Hamer: They still night ride. The exact count was 32 churches they had burned in the State of Mississippi and they still ride at night and throw bombs at night. You would think they would cut down with Mrs. Chaney. But since they murdered James Chaney, they have shot buckshot at his mother's house. And hate won't only destroy us. It will destroy these people that's hating as well. And one of the things is, they are afraid of getting back what they have been putting out all of these years. You know the Scripture says "be not deceived for God is not mocked; whatsoever a man sow that shall he also reap." And *one day,* I don't know how they're going to get it, but they're going to get some of it back. They are scared to death and are more afraid now than we are.

O'Dell: How active is the White Citizen's Council? Has it the kind of outlet through TV and radio and so forth that Negroes are aware of its presence?

Hamer: They announce their programs. In fact, one day I was going to Jackson and I saw a huge sign that U.S. Senator John Stennis was speaking that night for the White Citizens Council in Yazoo City and they also have a State Charter that they may set up for "private schools." It is no secret.

O'Dell: Does it seem to be growing? Is the white community undergoing any change as a result of all the pressure that has been put now with the Mississippi Summer Project and the killing of the three civil rights workers. What effect is it having on the white community?

Hamer: You can't ever tell. I have talked to two or three whites that's decent in the State of Mississippi, but you know, just two or three speaking out. I do remember, one time, a man came to me after the Students began to work in Mississippi and he said the white people were getting tired and they were getting tense and anything might happen. Well, I asked him "how long he thinks *we* had been getting tired"? I have been *tired* for 46 years and my parents was tired before me and their parents were *tired;* and I have always wanted to do something that would help some of the things I would see going on among Negroes that I didn't like and I don't like now.

O'Dell: Getting back just for a minute to Atlantic City. You all were in the national spotlight because there was nothing else happening in the Democratic National Convention other than your challenge to the Mississippi delegation and I would like to go back to that and pull together some of the conclusions you might have drawn from that experience.

Hamer: In coming to Atlantic City, we believed strongly that we were right. In fact, it was just right for us to come to challenge the seating of the regular Democratic Party from Mississippi. But we didn't think when we got there that we would meet people, that actually the other leaders of the Movement would differ with what we felt was right. We would have accepted the Green proposal. But, when we couldn't get that, it didn't make any sense for us to take "two votes at large." What would that mean to Mississippi? What would it have meant to us to go back and tell the Mississippi people? And actually, I think there will be great leaders emerging from the State of Mississippi. The people that have the experience to know and the people not interested in letting somebody pat you on the back and tell us "I think it is right." And it was very important for us not to accept a compromise and after I got back to Mississippi, people there said it was the most important step that had been taken. We figured it was right and it *was* right, and if we had accepted that compromise, then we would have been letting the people down in Mississippi. Regardless of leadership, *we have to think for ourselves!*

O'Dell: In other words, you had *two* battles on your hands when you went to Atlantic City?

Hamer: Yes. I was in one of the meetings when they spoke about accepting two votes and I said I wouldn't dare think about anything like this. So, I wasn't allowed to attend the other meetings. It was *quite* an experience.

O'Dell: There will be other elections and other conventions and the people in Mississippi should be a little stronger.

Hamer: I think so.

O'Dell: Well, it's good to know that the people you have to work with every day are with you.

Hamer: Yes, they are with us one hundred percent.

O'Dell: That's encouraging because it makes the work that much easier. Is there any final thing you want to say that is part of this historic statement of life in Mississippi for yourself as a person who lives there?

Hamer: Nothing other than we will be working. When I go back to Mississippi we will be working as hard or harder to bring about a change, but things are not always pleasant there.

O'Dell: You will probably have the support of more people than you have ever had, all around the country.

Hamer: Yes, actually since the Convention I have gotten so many letters that I have tried to answer but every letter said they thought this decision, not to accept the compromise, was so important. There wasn't one letter I have gotten so far that said we should have accepted the compromise—not one.

O'Dell: So, those are the people who are interested in your work, and as you get back into the main swing of things you will be keeping in touch with those people so that they should be asked to help in any way they can regardless of where they live. It is national and international public pressure that is needed.

Are you aware that there has been any coverage of the African trip by the Mississippi press? Have they made any comments on it?

Hamer: I don't know about the press, but I know in the town where I live everybody was aware that I was in Africa, because I remember after I got back some of the people told me that Mayor Durr of our town said he just wished they would boil me in tar. But, that just shows how ignorant he is, I didn't see any tar over there. But I was treated much better in Africa than I was treated in America. And you see, often I get letters like this: "Go back to Africa."

Now I have just as much right to stay in America—in fact, the black people have contributed more to America than any other race, because our kids have fought here for what was called "democracy"; our mothers and fathers were sold *and* bought here for a price. So all I can say when they say "go back to Africa," I say "when you send the Chinese back to China, the Italians back to Italy, etc., and you get on that Mayflower from whence you came, and give the Indians their land back, who really would be here at home?" It is our right to stay here and we will stay and stand up for what belongs to us as American citizens, because they can't say that we haven't had patience.

O'Dell: Was there a lot of interest in your trip among the African People that you met?

Hamer: Yes. I saw how the Government was run there and I saw where black people were running the banks. I saw, for the first time in my life, a black stewardess walking through a plane and that was quite an inspiration for me, It shows what black people can do if we only get the chance in America. It is there within us. We can do things if we only get the chance. I see so many ways America uses to rob Negroes and it is sinful and America can't keep holding on, and doing these things. I saw in Chicago, on the street where I was visiting my sister-in-law, this "Urban Renewal" and it means one thing: "Negro removal." But they want to tear the homes down and put a parking lot there. Where are those people going? Where will they go? And as soon as Negroes take to the street demonstrating, one hears people say, "they shouldn't have done it." The *world* is looking at America and it is really beginning to show up for what it is really like. "Go Tell It on the Mountain." We can no longer ignore this, that America is not "the land of the free and the home of the brave."

O'Dell: Thank you, Mrs. Fannie Lou Hamer, Vice-Chairman of the Freedom Democratic Party of Mississippi; courageous fighter for human rights.

ENDNOTES

1. Michael Schwerner, James Chaney and Andrew Goodman.

THE STUDENT VOICE

Vol. 5, No. 16 STUDENT VOICE, INC. 6 Raymond Street, N. W. Atlanta, Georgia 30314 July 15, 1964

CIVIL RIGHTS LAW COMPLIANCE VARIES

Over Sixty Arrested in Registration Drive

SELMA REGISTRATION, TESTING TO CONTINUE

SELMA, ALA. - Organized testing of public facilities here and a stepped up voter registration drive will continue, a Student Nonviolent Coordinating Committee spokesman announced this week.

On July 10, an injunction prohibiting assembly of more than three people, meetings where violations of law are suggested, or encouraging impeding justice, was issued against SNCC, CORE, COFO, NAACP, the Southern Regional Council, Alabama Council on Human Rights, the Dallas County Voter's League and Improvement Association, SNCC Executive Secretary James Forman, SNCC Chairman John Lewis, SNCC Selma Project Director John Love, the Reverend Ralph Abernathy, SNCC workers Benny Tucker, Alvery Williams, Karen House, Willie C. and Charles Robertson and James Austin, attorneys Bruce Boynton and Charles Chestnut, 27 local residents and the Ku Klux Klan and the National States Rights Party.

Only SNCC has had an active program in Central Alabama. The National States Rights Party has been holding meetings in the Selma area.

Over 60 people, including John Lewis, SNCC Chairman, have been arrested here since July 3, when the rights bill was signed into law. City and county policemen and members of a special Sheriff's posse, under the direction of Dallas County Sheriff Jim Clark, beat and jailed Negroes making integration tries on Saturday, July 4. Clark's men also arrested four members of a SNCC - aided Literacy Project here.

Thomas Brown, 24, a SNCC worker, said organized teams of Negroes would test whether Selma's eating places and movie

CONTINUED ON PAGE 3

A GEORGIA STATE TROOPER (left) tries to reach SNCC worker Chuck Neblett being beaten with metal chairs at a July 4th rally in Atlanta. Neblett, Wilson Brown, and Matthew Jones were beaten when they entered outdoor stands to hear Alabama Governor George E. Wallace and ex-Mississippi Governor Ross Barnett speak.

PROJECT GOES ON DESPITE BOMBING

McCOMB, MISS. - Despite three blasts that rocked a Negro home here July 8 and a history of violence, a Student Nonviolent Coordinating Committee (SNCC) voting and educational project will continue.

Ten voter registration workers in the home at 702 Wall Street here were not seriously injured. One, Curtis Hayes, 22, a SNCC worker, was cut by flying glass. Another, SNCC Mississippi Summer Project Volunteer Dennis Sweeny, 21, of Portland, Oregon, suffered a mild concussion.

Others in the home were SNCC workers George and Freedye Greene, 20, and 19, both from Greenwood, Mississippi; SNCC worker Julius Samstein, 25, of New York City; SNCC worker Jesse Harris, 22, of Jackson, Mississippi; SNCC worker Sher-

CONTINUED ON PAGE 4

Court Order, SNCC Drive - Registration Jumps from 1 to 237

BATESVILLE, MISS. - A federal court has erased double standards for Negro and white voters here.

Two SNCC workers helped 237 Negroes register at the Panola County Courthouse here in one week.

The current registration drive began after the Fifth Circuit Court of Appeals overturned a decision by the District Court of North Mississippi "opening" registration books to Negroes. In effect, the court said the same standards that had been applied to whites must be applied to Negroes.

The court ruled registration applicants must be 21 years or over, may apply for registration without paying a poll tax, may try to register without the registrar or his deputy being present, and that as many applicants

CONTINUED ON PAGE 3

SANCTIONED TERROR HINDERS COMPLIANCE

ATLANTA, GA. - Successful attempts to integrate formerly all-white public places in four deep South states were reported this week by SNCC.

But the SNCC said "a clear pattern of extra-legal and officially sanctioned violence, condoned or initiated by local policemen, is evident in Arkansas, Alabama, Florida, Georgia and Mississippi where Negroes have tried to exercise their rights under the 1964 Civil Rights Act."

The SNCC office here reported the following incidents:

Georgia establishments in Atlanta, Albany, Thomasville, Tifton, Savannah and Americus integrated quietly on July 3, but on the days following, SNCC worker John Perdew, 22, of Denver, Colorado, was beaten in Americus four times by a white mob on July 4 after leaving a newly integrated restaurant; mobs of whites drove through Americus' Negro neighborhoods shooting and throwing bricks; four SNCC workers, Donald Harris, Randolph Battle, Roy Shields and Dale Smith and nine other Negroes were arrested on July 5 for trying to enter a public swimming pool in Albany; a mob of 250 whites and police chased Negroes away from an integrated movie theatre in Americus.

In Laurel, Mississippi on July 4, a group of Negroes attempting to enter a restaurant were repulsed by a white mob and two Negro youths were slashed with razor blades.

In Selma, Alabama, Negroes peacefully integrated a movie theatre on July 4 until the owner stopped selling tickets. Mobs of whites and policemen attacked the Negroes waiting outside.

In Pine Bluff, Arkansas, members of a SNCC testing team were served in two of four places they entered. At one, Ray's

CONTINUED ON PAGE 3

STUDENT VOICE July 15, 1964 PAGE 3

PROGRESS REPORT I

SUMMER PROJECT

JACKSON, MISS. - "There are now 1,500 students ranging in age from eight years to 82 years enrolled in 25 Freedom Schools in Mississippi," a SNCC spokesman reported.

Six more schools are planned bringing enrollment to over 2,000 students. By mid-summer more than 900 full-time workers will be engaged in the "Mississippi Freedom Summer Project," a statewide educational and voter registration effort growing out of a pilot voter registration project started by SNCC in 1961 in McComb.

450 summer volunteers are in the state now. 100 additional workers are expected in the next ten days. They are joining close to 100 SNCC staff members and other civil rights groups that make up the coordinating agency of the three-month drive.

Some 150 lawyers and law students, plus 100 clergymen who will serve as counselors to the volunteers, make up a complement of 900 workers in the state.

The second group of volunteers, arriving here June 27 from a training session in Oxford, Ohio, man community centers and teach in Freedom Schools located in cities and towns across the state. The first group, which arrived June 20, is engaged mainly in voter registration.

Each school will have a low teach-student ratio. The "Freedom Schools" will offer courses in leadership development, remedial academic programs (reading, writing, mathematics, history), and contemporary issues.

SNCC STAFF MEMBER DICK FREY (left) explains SNCC's Mississippi Summer Project plans to Representative Augustus Hawkins (D-Calif.), Rep. Philip Burton (D-Calif.) and Rep. William Fitts Ryan (D-N.Y.). The three congressmen and Rep. Don Edwards (D-Calif.) toured Mississippi last week with SNCC staff members to inspect summer project activity.

The first "Freedom Schools" opened Thursday, July 2 in Vicksburg, Clarksdale and Mileston with approximately 30 students each. Schools opening Monday, July 6 included Sharon, with 100 students; Camden, 100; Valley View, 100; Canton, 60; Hattiesburg, 575 (five schools); Greenville, 60; Moss Point, 60; Greenwood, 50 (three schools); and Ruleville, 30. Total enrollment at all schools is expected to top 1,000.

Director for the SNCC "Freedom School" program is Dr. Staughton Lynd, former social studies professor at Atlanta's Spelman College, who will join the Yale University faculty this fall. The United Federation of Teachers assisted in recruiting

CONTINUED ON PAGE 4

SELMA

CONTINUED FROM PAGE 1

theatres would obey the 1964 Civil Rights Act. Brown said a "Freedom Week," during which Negroes made registration attempts here in large numbers, would continue, with increased canvassing of Negro neighborhoods for potential voters.

Observers who saw Lewis jailed said police crowded the young integration leader into an alley with others arrested with him and "treated them with excessive brutality." The witness said policeman pushed electric cattle prods under girls' dresses to shock and burn them.

Lewis' arrest here July 6 was his 33rd. He was arrested here September 25, 1963, and again this week while carrying signs urging Negroes to register.

On Sunday night, July 5, posse members and local policemen beat and clubbed Negroes leaving a weekly mass meeting. Four persons were hospitalized, including two white newspaper reporters attacked by the officers.

Law officers refused to let Negroes seeking to register enter the front door of the county courthouse July 6 and made one SNCC staff member, a Selma resident, leave a line at the rear of the building. Fifty other Negroes seeking to register, plus Lewis and three other SNCC staff members, were jailed on charges they interfered with a court session.

Nine Negroes were jailed July 7 while walking down a Selma street.

16 more were jailed July 8, including Ernest McMillian, 19, a SNCC staff member from Dallas, Texas. Police have also impounded two automobiles belonging to SNCC.

VOTER DRIVE

CONTINUED FROM PAGE 1

as possible may take the test as physical space allows.

Over 85% of the eligible white voters in Panola County are registered voters. Of 7250 eligible Negroes, however, only 1 was registered before the SNCC drive began.

The Fifth Circuit Court of Appeals said a Negro Voters League, formed in 1955, had attempted to register 10 Negroes and had only registered one, while local white people could register "without distraction" even when many white voters "were not qualified to be registered according to Mississippi law."

In addition, the court found many Negroes had been intimidated by local whites.

The suit was originally filed against Leonard C. Duke, Circuit Clerk and Registrar of Panola County, and the state of Mississippi.

In other Mississippi voting cases, U.S. District Judge Sidney Mize took under advisement a request from the Department of Justice for a preliminary injunction to halt discrimination against Negroes in Lauderdale County. District Judge Claude Clayton will hear voter discrimination cases against Carroll County registrar George W. Tuberville and Humphreys County registrar G. H. Hood.

In addition, a three-judge federal panel has been appointed to hear a suit challenging the state's election laws, and asking for an injunction preventing all county registrars from giving Negro voting applicants tests not given to whites. The suit also asks the three-judge panel to set aside state Democratic precinct and county meetings and to delay the state Democratic convention until Negroes are assured a greater role in state Democratic party activity.

RIGHTS LAW

CONTINUED FROM PAGE 1

Truck Stop, where comedian Dick Gregory and Arkansas Project Director Bill Hansen were arrested earlier this year, a white customer hit a Negro SNCC worker. At another eating place, a white man threatened the group with a shotgun.

In Helena, Arkansas, three Negroes - including two SNCC workers - were arrested July 7 near a swimming pool after integrating a formerly all-white library and restaurant. SNCC worker Hansen reported that two of the arrested men were beaten by Helena police.

In Jackson, Mississippi, Negroes integrated a movie theatre and two hotels. In Texarkana, Texas, four people were injured in an exchange of gunfire over an integration attempt at a beach. In St. Augustine, Florida, 15 white youths attacked five Negroes, including a woman and a child, while they were fishing. In Ocala, Florida, four restaurants served Negroes but a fifth refused to serve an all- Negro group. A Fort Smith, Arkansas swimming pool was peacefully integrated by eight Negro boys. In Baton Rouge, Louisiana, a white government worker hit a Negro who took part in integrating a cafeteria at the state capitol.

In other Georgia incidents, Negroes were admitted to a previously all-white pool in East Point and five eating places in Warner Robins, but were turned away from three eating places in Perry and a Winder movie theatre by mobs of whites. The East Point pool was later closed after a fight at the pool's parking lot. In Brunswick, city and county pools were closed down.

THE CIVIL RIGHTS BILL—FOUR KEY PROVISIONS

PUBLIC ACCOMMODATIONS: Discrimination in hotels and places of entertainment is forbidden.

■ States without laws against discrimination in public accommodations

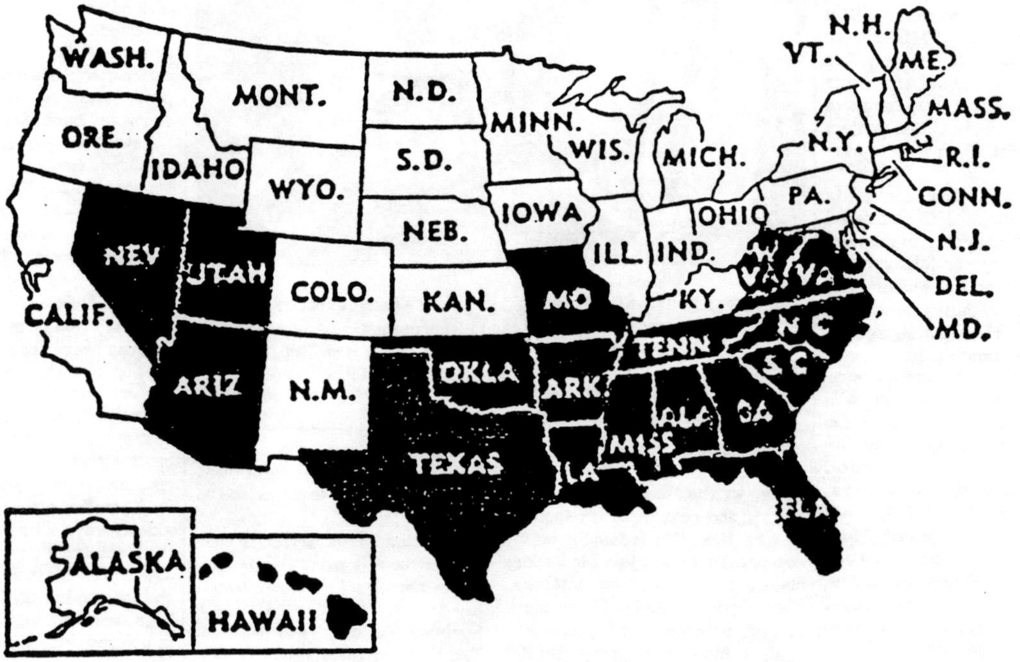

SCHOOL INTEGRATION: Attorney General is authorized to initiate suits on behalf of individuals.

■ Counties having both white and Negro school children but none attending the same schools

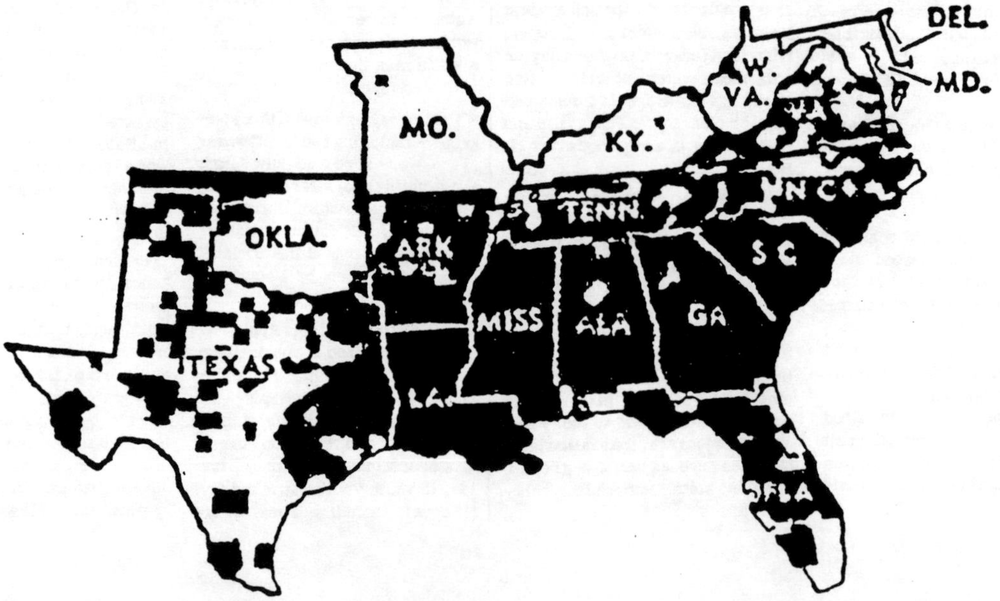

AND THE PROBLEMS THEY ARE DESIGNED TO CORRECT

FAIR EMPLOYMENT: A Federal commission is to be set up to investigate discrimination in hiring.

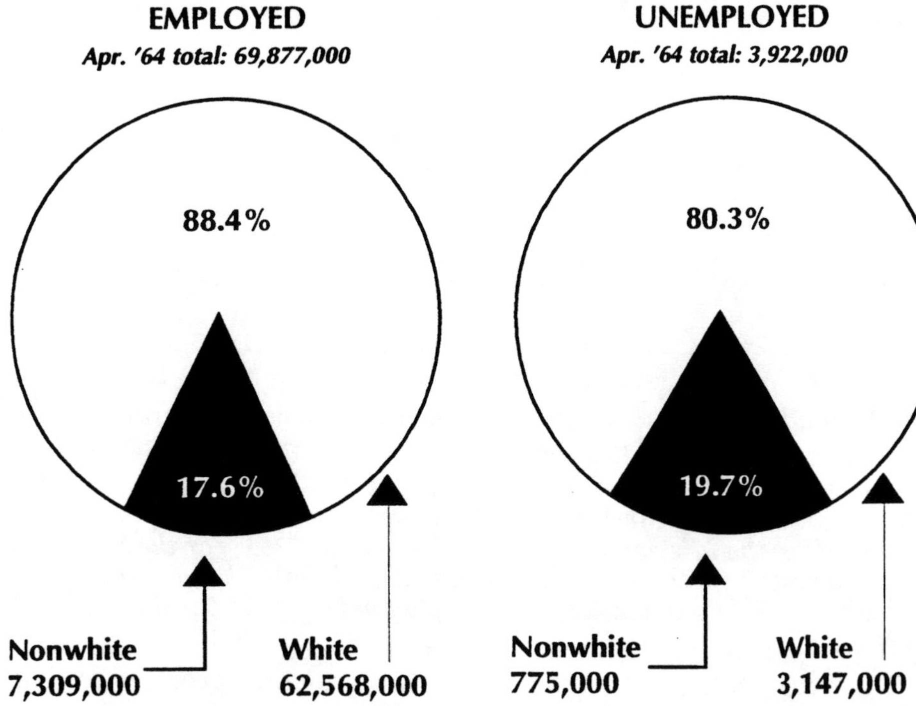

VOTER REGISTRATION: Tactics used by some in South to keep Negroes from voting are barred.

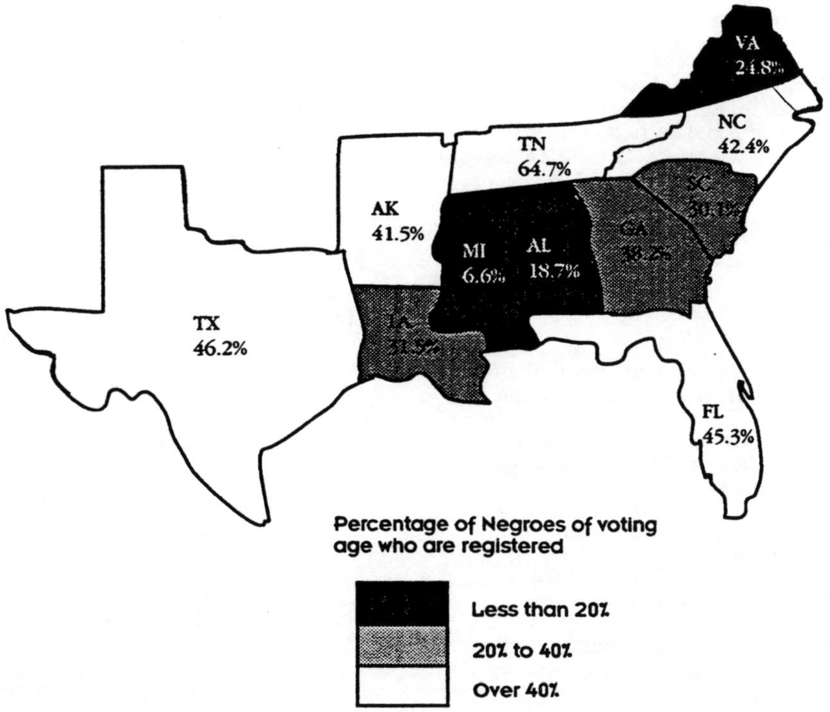

Student Nonviolent Coordinating Committee

360 NELSON STREET S.W., ATLANTA, GEORGIA • 688-0331
100 FIFTH AVENUE, NEW YORK, NEW YORK 10011 • YUKON 9-1313

November, 1965

Dear Friend:

This letter brings a simple but heartfelt message: thank you.

As the holiday season draws near, we want to express our gratitude for your past support of the Student Nonviolent Coordinating Committee.

In one emergency after another, we asked for help and received it—sometimes without having the time or resources to convey our appreciation. Aid was needed for the Mississippi Summer Project of 1964, for the Selma crisis of 1965—and it was forthcoming. Thanks to individuals like yourself, it has been possible for SNCC to continue the struggle for justice in the South.

But you may be less aware of our work as it goes on behind the scenes. We would like to offer you, as a supporter, this up-to-date report on some aspects of that work:

SNCC PROGRAMS: A REPORT FOR 1965

"When, in calmer times, men come to write the history of our raucous era; when they seek the cry that called a New Left, the rasp that twitched the nerves of Negro youths and the image that convulsed American campuses; when they try to set down in words once and for all the forces that pushed America to a desperate confrontation with herself, it seems likely that they will devote a considerable amount of attention to the Student Nonviolent Coordinating Committee which has emerged within the last year as a major force of the Freedom movement, to the dismay of many persons of power—not all of them white."

Lerone Bennet, in Ebony

Background

SNCC was founded in 1960 as a loose network of militant Southern Negro students who sought to find a new dignity by ending Jim Crow, primarily in public accommodations. Out of the sit-in struggle came an awareness that in many of the Black Belt counties of the Deep South, where Negroes often outnumber whites, the basic political structure must be changed. The right to vote was basic to this. By October, 1961, SNCC had taken on staff for a voter registration campaign; it had more full-time workers in the South than any other civil rights organization. Two years later, voter registration and direct action were SNCC's two main weapons in a frontal attack on segregation.

It may seem easy to say "register to vote." But before a Negro can take that walk to the courthouse, he must conquer a century of fear and oppression. Therefore, the first task of a SNCC worker is to live in the community in which he works for as long as necessary; to listen and talk and persuade and gradually help that community achieve the confidence to begin creating its own organizations and programs. SNCC workers bring people ideas, information, and tools; they seek not to lead but to bring forth leadership. In turn, they receive information, ideas, and renewed commitment.

This, of course, is the job of an organizer and that is what SNCC has become: a band of organizers, of catalysts for the release of human energy and strength. On the national level, that energy has become pressure upon the federal government. It is no exaggeration to say that without such pressure as SNCC has mustered, there would not have been a Civil Rights Act in 1964 nor a Voting Act in 1965.

Political Organization

On the final night of the Selma-Montgomery march, Mrs. Viola Liuzzo was murdered by Klansmen in Lowndes County. SNCC's answer to her murder was to send Field Secretaries into that terror-ridden area, to organize people for political action. The murder of the young Episcopal seminarian, John Daniels, did not stop the newborn freedom movement.

A few months ago, not a single Negro was registered to vote in Lowndes County. Today, as a result of the Voting Act and SNCC's presence, 2000 have registered out of an eligible 5000 and Negroes have their own action group: the Lowndes County Christian Movement for Human Rights. Its activities include work on economic, social and educational problems as well as political participation.

This brief history of SNCC "shock-troops" at work has been repeated many times in Alabama, Mississippi, and Southwest Georgia– another Klan-infested area, where SNCC has been working for the vote since the fall of 1961. Across the South, SNCC has helped thousands to register. But there is no point in getting the right to vote—for racist candidates. More and more, SNCC has been urging Negroes to run for office while at the same time working to avoid the creation of black machines which would be as unresponsive to people's needs as the whites in power.

In Georgia, SNCC was active in the 1964 campaign to elect C. B. King of Albany to Congress. This year, Julian Bond—a SNCC staff member—ran successfully in Atlanta for the State Legislature.

In Alabama, local law provides that a group of registered voters in a particular county can select and run its own candidates for both county and state offices. By winning a certain number of votes, the group can become a political party of the county and eventually of the state. SNCC workers are therefore helping to establish freedom parties in a number of the poorest counties with a view to creating a new Alabama political party from the ground up.

In September, 1965, SNCC workers in Arkansas helped 30 Negroes to run for seats on School Boards across the state. All but one were defeated. Contrary to popular impression, Arkansas has proven to be as dangerously racist as any area in which SNCC operates. SNCC workers believe that the Negroes would have won many of the contests if it had not been for intimidation and fraud, and they have submitted a special report on this to Washington. Meanwhile, Arkansas continues to be one of SNCC's most active and growing projects, with workers in 31 counties.

For the Southern farmer and share-cropper, the elections which affect his life most directly are those for the county committees of the Agricultural Stabilization and Conservation Service (a branch of the Dept. of Agriculture). The ASCS committees strongly influence how much land a man may plant with certain crops, who gets loans, etc. In 1965, SNCC workers helped get Negroes on the ballot in Alabama, Mississippi, Georgia, North Carolina and Arkansas. In Green County, Alabama, for example, Negroes were nominated this fall for 36 out of 40 available committee seats. As in the Arkansas School Board elections, Negro ASCS candidates have been frustrated by suspected fraud. But the experience of organizing for such elections can be the beginning of political participation.

The most concrete result of SNCC's organizing work has been the Mississippi Freedom Democratic Party. The MFDP was set up April, 1964, when it seemed clear that the total denial of Negro participation in Mississippi politics called for creation of a special organism—a "parallel structure." SNCC, whose roots in the state go back to 1961, threw its resources behind the new party and has continued to do so.

At the 1964 national Democratic convention in Atlantic City, the MFDP challenged the regular Mississippi delegation and in 1965 went on to challenge the seating of the five Congressmen. Although both efforts failed, they focussed national attention on Negro disenfranchisement as never before. And in late 1965, the MFDP drew up a new program which includes a crash voter registration drive—now under way in the 9 counties where there are federal registrars—and campaigns in the 1966 primaries for all five Congressional seats.

Primaries for state and national offices are also coming up in 1966 in Alabama, Georgia, and North Carolina. SNCC is drawing up a 4-year political program for these states and has also demanded that the Democratic National Committee carry out the mandate of the Atlantic City Convention to end exclusion of Negroes from party activity and elections in the South.

Jobs and Income

By 1965, the right to organize had been sufficiently established and enough restrictions on voting removed to free SNCC energy for dealing with the economic problems of the Southern Negro.

A crucial development was the birth of the Mississippi Freedom Labor Union. It began in the Delta last January when a number of tractor drivers and cotton choppers decided they had had enough of a plantation system which kept men perpetually hungry and in debt. The choppers were tired of working a 10 or 12 hour day for $2.50 to $3.00; the drivers, skilled workers, knew they should get more than $6.00 per day. They simply stopped, and soon were joined by others.

By late spring over 1000 men had quit. Some were evicted and are still living in tents. Union members have been arrested. But small increases were won in some cases and the MFLU grew until today it has chapters in some 10 communities. The union now seeks to strengthen its organization and legal status, with a massive strike planned for the spring.

The idea of saying NO to economic slavery proved contagious. In McComb, maids at the Holiday Inn walked out. Cooks in a Cleveland cafe, some of them working 77 hours a week at 42¢ an hour, walked out. Bus drivers in Marshall City struck. The idea spread to Tennessee, where a Freedom Labor Union was born consisting mainly of tractor drivers and skilled workers in cotton gins; by October, it had 300 members.

SNCC worked closely with community people to build the FLU. In more urban areas, it has helped mount protest against job discrimination. In Natchez recently, SNCC helped to create a boycott of white-owned stores which devastated business in that city. Albany and Americus, Georgia have seen large demonstrations and boycotts this year against several white-owned stores in the Negro neighborhood to get Negroes hired. Negro women, who work as domestics for $10 a week throughout the Black Belt, have also been organizing; in Americus, 40 of them formed a maids' union and at least one got an increase. At a lingerie plant in North Carolina, SNCC workers are pressing for better working conditions. And on the Eastern Shore of Maryland, SNCC worked this past year with Negro employees of a crab canning factory as well as with migrant workers.

SNCC has not only sought to improve existing job conditions; it has also helped to create work that pays. In 1965, the Poor People's Corporation—an idea of SNCC staffer Jesse Morris—was set up in Mississippi to create and assist new light industry as well as independent farming. At its first membership meeting on Aug. 29, the Corporation made small loans to a new sewing firm created by women who were tired of working as maids; to an okra cooperative; to several new leather-working shops for which young people had been trained during the summer.

In Alabama and Georgia, SNCC has worked this year on such new enterprises as a quilting co-op, a credit union, a retail food market. Like the labor union and the Corporation, these could not be considered "SNCC projects" but they are almost always the result of SNCC presence.

Schools

Across the Black Belt, school integration has been little more than token. Facilities in the Negro schools usually range from bad to terrible. The schools fail to give black children either decent academic training or any knowledge of their own heritage; they are prepared only for the cotton field and the kitchen. SNCC has worked on all these aspects of the education problem.

In Alabama, Georgia, Mississippi and Tennessee, SNCC workers have helped people find the courage merely to apply for transfer of their children to white schools last fall. Parents who did apply have been evicted, had their homes shot into, and had crosses burned outside. In Tennessee, children were sprayed with disinfectant when they went to the white school and in Greensboro, Alabama, Negro pupils were turned back by whites with guns.

SNCC has helped people to pressure school boards for integration plans and in some cases succeeded. It has organized many boycotts of Negro schools to protest bad facilities—from books to bathrooms—and tuition fees, split sessions, failure to integrate.

The most dramatic of these took place last September in Forrest City, Arkansas, when a group of Lincoln High School students demonstrated against conditions and demanded total integration of the school system. A boycott began which was 90% effective. Over 200 students and SNCC workers were arrested. Some later went to Washington to petition the Office of Education but no action followed. They then set up a Freedom Center where they have been attending regular classes and plan to do so until conditions are improved probably by some form of federal pressure.

Workers in Arkansas maintain half a dozen other Freedom Schools which were established primarily to teach Negro history and other subjects not offered in the black schools. In Lowndes County, Alabama, a tutorial program is being set up which will emphasize academic needs but also include Freedom School techniques and material.

Schools have not been the only target for integration by SNCC this year. Restaurants and movie theaters have been tested; hospitals have been integrated. In Americus, Georgia, twenty of us were arrested when we sought to attend services at "white churches." In Arkansas, SNCC workers who tried to integrate the cafeteria in the State Capitol were beaten.

* * * *

Violence and police brutality continue to be daily realities in SNCC's work. The unpublicized and mysterious deaths of local Negroes continue. The beatings and shootings, the bombings and church burnings, have not let up.

To inform the nation of these events and their causes, to maintain contact with the field, to service the needs of workers—all this calls for resources which often do not exist or are very expensive. SNCC has therefore created its own photo unit, research department, printing plant, and communication system. It maintains a central administrative staff in Atlanta as well as seven Northern offices to mobilize support and raise funds. Space does not permit description of SNCC's educational program for its own staff, nor its campus program, but these too are vital.

SNCC now has 150 full-time staff workers, and a program for 1966 which includes intensified political action, economic self-help projects, and school integration. Though many people here and abroad believe the problem of racism has been resolved by federal legislation, those working in the South know that it is only the beginning. Many months of struggle lie ahead.

A long winter has begun, and it is a cold one in the South. We are deeply grateful for your past support; we hope you may help us through this winter. Meanwhile, please accept our thanks and best wishes for 1966 as a year of progress, justice, and peace.

Yours in freedom,

John Lewis

John Lewis, Chairman

UNIT 12

COMPETING FORCES I

INTRODUCTION 720

12-1 • "WHICH SIDE ARE YOU ON," SONG 721

12-2 • QUESTIONS RAISED BY MOSES 722
TRANSCRIPT OF THE TALK GIVEN BY BOB MOSES
AT THE 5TH ANNIVERSARY OF SNCC
Bob Moses

12-3 • SNCC POSITION PAPER: WOMEN IN THE MOVEMENT 725

12-4 • THE ROLE OF BLACK WOMEN IN THE CIVIL RIGHTS MOVEMENT 727
Anne Standley

12-5 • SHOULD CIVIL RIGHTS WORKERS TAKE A STAND ON VIETNAM? 741
Howard Zinn

12-6 • THE WAR IN VIETNAM 743

12-7 • THE FREEDOM MOVEMENT AND THE WAR IN VIETNAM 745
Robert S. Browne

12-8 • SNCC POSITION PAPER: VIETNAM 755

12-9 • SNCC VIETNAM COMIC BOOK 757

INTRODUCTION

With the end of legalized discrimination in the South, many civil rights activists turned to a number of other problems affecting African Americans. Two of the most contentious issues were gender relations and the escalating conflict in Vietnam.

As the movement progressed, many women activists became disillusioned by a struggle for equal rights for African Americans that relegated women to minor roles in its day-to-day operations. Written by Mary King and Casey Hayden, two well known SNCC activists, the position paper (12-3) is the most famous contemporary criticism of the treatment of women in the movement. Some scholars consider this document pivotal in the modern renaissance of feminism.

The relationship between civil rights activism and the Vietnam War was a central concern of movement activists during the late 1960s. The last five documents in this unit examine the contemporary debate over Vietnam and civil rights. In 1965, Howard Zinn, a well known historian and SNCC advisor, argued that young people involved in the movement should oppose the Vietnam War. "The Freedom Movement and the War in Vietnam" (12-7), an article that appeared in the Spring 1965 issue of *Freedomways*, provides an overview of the questions raised by civil rights activists about the war. The magazine's editorial stance on the war is presented in 12-6. SNCC's position on Vietnam is represented by two documents: the 1966 position paper that articulated the organization's opposition to the war (12-8) and a SNCC comic book that set forth in words and pictures the reasons behind the position paper (12-9). SNCC distributed the comic book widely to convince young Americans, black and white, to oppose the war.

Which Side Are You On?

Original verses by Florence Reese, new verses by James Farmer (CORE).

"I rewrote the old labor song by Florence Reece 'Which Side Are You On?' on the spur of the moment in the Hinds County Jail, after the Freedom Riders who were imprisoned there had been discussing and speculating about the attitude of local Negroes regarding the Freedom Rides. We had learned through trustees in the jail that most local Negroes were with us, but afraid to do anything because of fear of reprisals. They told us that, of course, there were a lot of Uncle Toms around and it was hard to tell who was and who was not."

— James Farmer

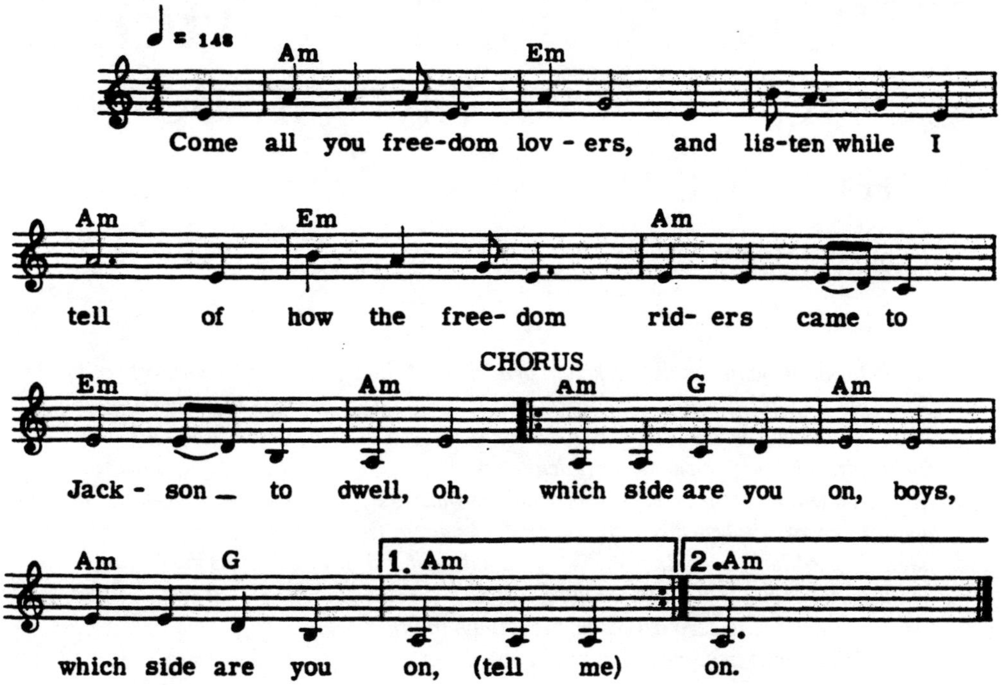

My daddy was a freedom fighter and
I'm a freedom son
I'll stick right with this struggle until
the battle's won.

Captain Ray will holler 'move on', but
the Freedom Riders won't budge
They'll stand there in the terminals
and even before the judge.

Don't 'tom for Uncle Charlie', don't
listen to his lies
'Cause black folks haven't got a
chance until they organize.

They say in Hinds County, no neutrals
have they met
You're either for the Freedom Ride
or you 'tom' for Ross Barnett.

Oh people can you stand it, tell me
how you can
Will you be an Uncle Tom or will you
be a man?

UNIT 12-2

QUESTIONS RAISED BY MOSES

TRANSCRIPT OF THE TALK GIVEN BY BOB MOSES AT THE 5TH ANNIVERSARY OF SNCC

Bob Moses

James Forman, John Lewis, Stokely Carmichael, Julian Bond, and many others have been in the SNCC leadership because they were able to win the respect of the other organizers and, more important, of the Negro people. But Robert (Moses) Parris was, more than any other SNCC leader, the inspiration for thousands of students and poor people now in The Movement. He resigned from SNCC in 1965, partly because he was afraid that a cult was developing around him, and this was against his principles. He even changed his name from Moses to Parris to put an end to this adoration. Although the division is somewhat artificial, it might be useful to think of Moses-Parris as the poet-visionary, which does not mean he lacks tactical or common sense; rather, he is a utopian thinker who touches deep nerves and emotions in other people.

The following document is a speech about fear given by Bob Moses at SNCC's fifth anniversary.

What you should suppose about SNCC people is that they are not fearless. You'd have a better idea about them if you would suppose that they were very afraid and suppose that they were very afraid of the people in the South that they have to fight and struggle against. And suppose also that they are very afraid of this country. But suppose, then, that they had no choice, that is they can, through many different ways, see that their backs, so to speak, were against the wall and they had to move within that fear. And then suppose that what they are trying to do is explore how to move within the boundaries of fear and that what they've got to learn about fear is that it paralyzes you so that you don't move—you don't do what you think you should, be it ask a question or take a person down to register. And suppose also about the Mississippi people that they're not heroes and that we're not heroes, that we're trying very hard to be people and that is very hard. If anything, what we're trying to do, or have to do, is to see how you can move even though you are afraid.

I have just one thing that I would like to share with you. It's a question, it's a problem, that our country faces tangled up with thousands of other problems. We suppose that the

From *Movement* [the SNCC California newspaper], April 1965.

people who murdered Mickey and Andrew and James were not like us, not like most people in the country. And I think that that's a deep mistake, that we don't understand the implication of that. People keep asking me, "Do you think that they will get convicted?" and I keep saying, "No." But I also wonder why they keep asking because if you think about that, it seems that our experience will tell us that they cannot be convicted, that they will not be convicted, that the chance of their being convicted is almost zero. For them to be convicted would be for society to condemn itself and that's very hard for society to do, any society. Condemnation seems to have to come from outside or from the ranks within that are not a part of it.

So the jury that votes together to decide whether or not the people, the eighteen or twenty-one people who evidently got together and sat down and then planned and then got up and then murdered, that jury is like them. That's a hard thing to understand in this country.

The only place where they can be tried for murder is by a jury, a local jury, called together in Neshoba County. They're being tried now, not for murder, but for depriving people of their civil rights in the act of murdering them. That's the actual charge. People don't understand that.

That jury, that local jury, if you called it together, would presumably be the murderers' jury because the juries in the counties in the South are called together under the auspices of the sheriffs and the sheriff is presumably one of the persons indicted for the conspiracy to murder. I am fascinated with that. It's a very, very clear kind of thing. Suppose the sheriff killed somebody; then to have his trial, he calls the jury together. So you have the murderer's jury. And the problem seems to me to be, how can a society condemn itself?

I think that that question is a question for the country in this sense. The country refuses to look at Mississippi, and at the white people down there, as like them. So, therefore, they miss the main point, it seems to me, about the Deep South and about the people there and, also, about ourselves.

Life magazine had a picture of the people who did the murder and they pictured them eating and laughing and joking and talking as though they were morally idiots. And I think most people in the country reading that got that impression. But you don't put yourself in that classification so they're other people—they're not like you or like us. The *Saturday Evening Post* had a picture of a Ku Klux Klan on the front page just recently and at the end of the article talked about them as outcasts, as people who are in no way like most Americans, as rejects from the society. I think that's a false interpretation which people are getting and, therefore, they analyze the problem wrongly and, therefore, they look for wrong solutions.

The problem is so deep, all you can do is raise these questions. We feel that if we're going to get to the bottom, if we're going to go down there and try and create anything new, then we have to do this because it seems that right within our country you have that problem where everybody can focus on it and say what are the conditions which create a society in which people sit down and plan and kill and then pat themselves on the back as patriots. Because they're defending their liberties and what they hold most dear and their civilization?

That, it seems to me, is the point about us as a country where we are with the bomb and what we do in terms of Vietnam. We are not over there killing people primarily but defending liberty and defending our concept of what is democracy, civilization and so forth. There's no forum to raise those questions.

I raise them because I don't think we're going to escape that easily, because they're going on killing in Mississippi. At the same time that everyone knows about the three who were killed and the people who are on trial for that, no one asks about the two Negro boys whose bodies were severed in half, who were found while they were looking for the other three, because nobody knows about them. And nobody asks why did that grand jury let those people off who were indicted for that crime, on the same day that they indicted the people who were supposed to have killed the other three. And nobody asks because, again, nobody knows about it.

I have one other thing that I'd like to share. What we have begun to learn and are trying to explore about people is how they can come together in groups, small groups and large groups, and talk to each other and make decisions about basic things, about their lives. I think that that has application everywhere in the country. Whatever we currently mean by democracy, we don't mean that people should come together, discuss their main problems that they all know about and be able to do something about themselves. That was what the Free Speech Movement meant, as I understand it, as it unfolded in part.

One problem with people who might want to try to do this, say in S.F. or anyplace, is that they would first think that in order to go to people and get them together, they would have to have something for them to talk about. So they would have to have a program to carry to them or they would have to have something to organize them around. But it doesn't turn out to be true, from our experience. You could in the North, in the ghettos, get together ten or twenty people and out of their getting together and giving them a chance to talk about their main problems would come some programs, that they themselves decided on, that they thought about. If that happened and began to happen around the country, that would be the key to spreading some of the things that have happened in the South to the rest of the country. That not only goes for poor people but for the professional people as well. The last meeting where I was, where I was partially hooted down, was at a doctors' Medicare. The concept that doctors should discuss Medicare, pro and con, in their meetings seems to be alien to democracy.

UNIT 12-3

SNCC Position Paper: Women in the Movement

1. Staff was involved in crucial constitutional revisions at the Atlanta staff meeting in October. A large committee was appointed to present revisions to the staff. The committee was all men.
2. Two organizers were working together to form a farm league. Without asking any questions, the male organizer immediately assigned the clerical work to the female organizer although both had had equal experience in organizing campaigns.
3. Although there are women in Mississippi project who have been working as long as some of the men, the leadership group in COFO is all men.
4. A woman in a field office wondered why she was held responsible for day to day decisions, only to find out later that she had been appointed project director but not told.
5. A fall 1964 personnel and resources report on Mississippi projects lists the number of people in each project. The section on Laurel, however, lists not the number of persons, but "three girls."
6. One of SNCC's main administrative officers apologizes for appointment of a woman as interim project director in a key Mississippi project area.
7. A veteran of two years' work for SNCC in two states spends her day typing and doing clerical work for other people in her project.
8. Any woman in SNCC, no matter what her position of experience, has been asked to take minutes in a meeting when she and other women are outnumbered by men.
9. The names of several new attorneys entering a state project this past summer were posted in a central movement office. The first initial and last name of each lawyer was listed. Next to one name was written: (girl).
10. Capable, responsible, and experienced women who are in leadership positions can expect to have to defer to a man on their project for final decision-making.
11. A session at the recent October staff meeting in Atlanta was the first large meeting in the past couple of years where a woman was asked to chair.

SNCC Papers, January 1966.

Undoubtedly this list will seem strange to some, petty to others, laughable to most. The list could continue as far as there are women in the movement. Except that most women don't talk about these kinds of incidents, because the whole subject is [not] discussable—strange to some, petty to others, laughable to most. The average white person finds it difficult to understand why the Negro resents being called "boy", or being thought of as "musical" and "athletic", because the average white person doesn't realize that *he assumes he is superior.* And naturally he doesn't understand the problem of paternalism. So too the average SNCC worker finds it difficult to discuss the woman problem because of the assumption of male superiority. Assumptions of male superiority are as widespread and deep rooted and every much as crippling to the woman as the assumptions of white supremacy are to the Negro. Consider why it is in SNCC that women who are competent, qualified, and experienced, are automatically assigned to the "female" kinds of jobs such as typing, desk work, telephone work, filing, library work, cooking, and the assistant kind of administrative work but rarely the "executive" kind.

The woman in SNCC is often in the same position as that token Negro hired in a corporation. The management thinks that it has done its bit. Yet, every day the Negro bears an atmosphere, attitudes and actions which are tinged with condescension and paternalism, the most telling of which are when he is not promoted as the equally or less skilled whites are. This paper is anonymous. Think about the kinds of things the author, if made known, would have to suffer because of raising this kind of discussion. Nothing so final as being fired or out right exclusion, but the kinds of things which are killing to the insides—insinuations, ridicule, over-exaggerated compensations.

This paper is presented anyway because it needs to be made know[n] that many women in the movement are not "happy and contented" with their status. It needs to be made known that much talent and experience are being wasted by this movement when women are not given jobs commensurate with their abilities. It needs to be known that just as negroes were the crucial factor in the economy of the cotton South, so too in SNCC, women are the crucial factor that keeps the movement running on a day-to-day basis. Yet they are not given equal say-so when it comes to day-to-day decision-making. What can be done? Probably nothing right away. Most men in this movement are probably too threatened by the possibility of serious discussion on this subject. Perhaps this is because they have recently broken away from the matriarchal framework under which they may have grown up. Then too, many women are as unaware and insensitive to this subject as men, just as there are many Negroes who don't understand they are not free or who want to be part of white America. They don't understand that they have to give up their souls and stay in their place to be accepted. So too, many women, in order to be accepted by men, on men's terms, give themselves up to that caricature of what a woman is—unthinking, pliable, an ornament to please the man.

Maybe the only thing that can come out of this paper is discussion—amidst the laughter—but still discussion. (Those who laugh the hardest are often those who need the crutch of male supremacy the most.) And maybe some women will begin to recognize day-to-day discriminations. And maybe sometime in the future the whole of the women in this movement will become so alert as to force the rest of the movement to stop the discrimination and start the slow process of changing values and ideas so that all of us gradually come to understand that this is no more a man's world than it is a white world.

UNIT 12-4

THE ROLE OF BLACK WOMEN IN THE CIVIL RIGHTS MOVEMENT

Anne Standley

The role of black women in the civil rights movement has received scant attention from historians. Most studies of the movement have examined such organizations as the Southern Christian Leadership Conference, the Student Nonviolent Coordinating Committee, the Congress of Racial Equality, and the National Association for the Advancement of Colored People, and accordingly have focused on the black ministers who served as officers in those organizations, all of whom were men. Harvard Sitkoff's list of the leaders of the movement, for example, consisted exclusively of men—Martin Luther King, Jr., of SCLC, James Forman and John Lewis of SNCC, James Farmer of Core, Roy Wilkins of the NAACP, and Whitney Young of the National Urban League. The accounts of other historians, such as Aldon Morris, Clayborne Carson, and August Meier, also showed male preachers spearheading the various protests-boycotts of bus companies and white-owned businesses, voter registration drives, and marches—that constituted the movement. Likewise, the vast majority of students leading the sit-ins and freedom rides named by Sitkoff were men. He cited only two of the many women who held positions of leadership in the movement—Fannie Lou Hamer, who was elected delegate to the Democratic National Convention by the Mississippi Freedom Democratic Party in 1964, and Ella Baker, executive secretary of SCLC—and understated their influence.

The omission of women from many of the histories of the movement is also apparent in the widespread use of the metaphor of reaching manhood to describe the self-confidence that blacks gained from the movement. Sitkoff, for example, observed:

"Sit-ins transformed the young blacks' image of themselves . . . Each student had his own way of expressing 'I became a man.'"[1] Although this image accurately described the emergence of a new, male-defined black identity, historians' use of this analogy reveals their failure to consider the impact of the movement on black woman's consciousness, and to recognize the contributions of women in making this racial pride possible.

Women in the Civil Rights Movement: Trailblazers and Torchbearers, 1941–1965, Crawford, Rouse, Woods, ed. (1990).

The argument that men were the principal leaders of the civil rights movement is not wholly inaccurate. According to women who achieved prominence within the movement, such as Septima Clark, who trained teachers of citizenship schools for SCLC, or Ella Baker, and historians Jacqueline Jones and Paula Giddings, the ministers' sexism and authoritarian views of leadership prevented women from assuming command of any of the movement organizations. Indeed, in light of the advantages men possessed in establishing themselves as leaders of the movement—the preachers' virtual monopoly on political power within the black community and the exclusion of women from the ministry in many black churches—it is remarkable that any women achieved positions of authority.

Yet, in fact, women exerted an enormous influence, both formally, as members of the upper echelon of SNCC, SCLC, and the Mississippi Freedom Democratic Party, and informally, as spontaneous leaders and dedicated participants. Many of the protests that historians describe as led by ministers were initiated by women. For example, Martin Luther King, Jr., is usually cited as the leader of the Montgomery Bus Boycott, since it was King who was appointed director of the organization that coordinated the boycott, the Montgomery Improvement Association. Yet the boycott was started by a woman, Jo Ann Robinson, and by the women's group that she headed, the Women's Political Council. Black women directed voter registration drives, taught in freedom schools, and provided food and housing for movement volunteers. As members of the MFDP, women won positions as delegates to the national Democratic convention in 1964 and as representatives to Congress. They demonstrated a heroism no less than that of men. They suffered the same physical abuse, loss of employment, destruction of property, and risk to their lives.

Black women also deserve credit for the refusal within the movement to accept halfway measures towards eradicating Jim Crow practices. Fannie Lou Hamer's rejection of the compromise offered the MFDP delegation at the Democratic National Convention in 1964 typified the courage of black women, who formed the majority of the preachers' congregations and whose pressure forced the ministers in SCLC, CORE, and the other movement associations to persist in the face of white opposition to their demands. Paula Giddings reported that when the minsters of Montgomery met after the first day of the bus boycott to discuss whether to continue the boycott, they agreed on the condition that their names not be publicized as the boycott leaders. E. D. Nixon, former head of the Montgomery NAACP, shamed them into giving their public endorsement by reminding them of the women to whom they were accountable: "How you gonna have a mass meeting, gonna boycott a city bus line without the white folks knowing about it? You guys have went around here and lived off these poor washerwomen all your lives and ain't never done nothing for 'em. Now you got a chance to do something for 'em, you talking about you don't want the White folks to know about it."[2]

As well, black women were responsible for the movement's success in generating popular support for the movement among rural blacks. Ella Baker convinced SCLC to jettison plans to take control of SNCC, allowing the student-run group to remain independent of the other movement organizations and to adopt, with Baker's encouragement, an egalitarian approach to decision-making. Because SNCC workers formulated the organization's objectives by soliciting the views of members of black communities in which the volunteers worked, they were able to build considerable grass-roots support for the movement.

Despite the exclusion of black women from top positions in movement organizations and the little recognition they received from either blacks or whites for their contributions, the published accounts of black women activists suggest that the movement gave women as well as men a sense of empowerment. Bernice Reagon, who was suspended from Albany State College for participating in civil rights demonstrations, and who sang with the Freedom Singers of Albany, credited the battle for equal rights with giving her the confidence necessary to combat all forms of oppression. For Reagon, the significance of the movement lay not in the abolition of specific forms of discrimination, nor in the impact of particular protests on the strategic position of the movements official leaders, but rather in its liberating effect on her sense of self.

> There was a sense of power, in a place where you didn't feel you had any power. There was a sense of confronting things that terrified you, like jail, police, walking in the street—you know, a whole lot of Black folks couldn't even walk in the street in those places in the south. So you were saying in some basic way "I will never again stay inside these boundaries." There were things asked for like Black police and firepeople and sitting where you wanted on the bus . . . But in terms of what happened to me and what happened to other people I know about, it was a change in my concept of myself and how I stood . . . When I read about: the Albany movement, as people have written about it, I don't recognize it. They add up stuff that was not central to what happened. Discussion about Pritchett [the police chief]; discussion about specific achievements; discussion about whether it was a failure or success for King. For me, that was not central. I had grown up in a society where there were very clear lines. The older I got, the more I found what those lines were. The Civil Rights Movement gave me the power to challenge *any* line that limits me . . . [3]
>
> I learned that I did have a life to give for what I believed. Lots of people don't know that; they feel they don't have anything. When you understand that you do have a life, you do have a body, and you can put that on the line, it gives you a sense of power. So I was empowered by the Civil Rights Movement.[4]

Similarly, Anne Moody, who grew up in Centreville, Mississippi, and who began working for SNCC in the summer of 1963 after her junior year at Tougaloo College, reported that the movement became an inseparable part of her identity that prompted her to fight segregation wherever she went. She described her attempts to take a vacation from the movement:

> Before the train pulled in, I found myself sitting in the white waiting room . . . Sitting there in the station, I got the same feeling I had in all the other sit-ins I had participated in. I remember getting up once, and going to the Negro section to ask the Negroes there if they knew the white section was desegregated. Then I knew that I would never really be leaving the Movement.[5]

The other women activists who wrote about their experiences in the battle for equal rights confirmed Moody's and Reagon's observation that the movement raised their self-esteem. Yet these women differed in their analyses of the cause of the racial oppression that they combatted. Two of the older women leaders—Daisy Bates, who was president of the NAACP State Conference of Branches, and who led the integration of Central High School in Little Rock, Arkansas, and Jo Ann Robinson and a younger leader, Diane Nash, who organized sit-ins and freedom rides for SNCC, viewed racism as politically motivated. They believed that if blacks could obtain the vote, white politicians would be forced to act against racial discrimination at the polls, segregated schools, and the varied forms of extralegal violence carried out against blacks. Blacks could use their political influence to improve their economic status, which in turn would enhance their image among whites.

Because they saw themselves as having to convince whites to support the movement, and because they identified so completely with the struggle for civil rights, Bates, Robinson, and Nash refrained from making critical judgments about the movement or their roles within it. Nor did they, according to their memoirs, question or challenge the other black leaders who were mostly men, leading one to infer that as Morris, Sitkoff, and other historians maintained, they played subordinate roles to the ministers in the black community. Consequently their behavior showed contradictions—on the one hand a boldness in initiating protests and applying pressure on whites in power, while at the same time a submissiveness in their acceptance of the authority of the black male clergy.

Jo Ann Robinson was born in 1916 in Colloden, Georgia, twenty-five miles from Macon. She was the youngest of twelve children. Her family subsequently moved to Macon, where she graduated first in her class from an all black high school. Robinson received a bachelor's degree from Georgia State College in Fort Valley, taught for five years at a public school in Macon, and earned a master's degree in English literature from Atlanta University. In 1949, after teaching for a year at Mary Allen College in Crockett, Texas, she moved to Montgomery to join the faculty at Alabama State University. Robinson chaired the Women's Political Council in Montgomery, an organization of professional women that sought to raise the status of blacks by working with juvenile and adult delinquents and organizing voter registration. She also served on the Executive Board of the Montgomery Improvement Association and edited the MIA newsletter.

Robinson declared that in publishing her memoir, she hoped to improve whites' image of blacks by demonstrating blacks' courage, dedication, and self-discipline in their fight for their rights. Robinson saw the movement as blacks' attempt to overcome the circumstances that degraded them—to secure the same living conditions and opportunities as whites—so as to live decently and thereby prove their equality with whites.

> I have chosen to record the facts of the Montgomery Bus Boycott for several reasons . . . so that the world will know that black people of America are not, as stereotypes have depicted them for generations, a 'Happy-go-lucky,' self-satisfied, complacent, lazy, good-for-nothing race that has nothing good or worthwhile to offer society. People the world over should know that any group, if given equal opportunity in education, employment, civil rights, and the like can be desirable citizens anywhere, with as much . . . to offer as any group. Debasement or degeneracy of character is not confined to one race, but is found in all races. From this record future generations may know that black Americans are just people like other people, wanting the same things, doing the same things, enduring the same things, and fighting against the same things that destroy the soul as well as the mind and body. When this is understood, a pure democratic government may survive in the American land of freedom, with justice and opportunity for all . . . [I am also writing this book] . . . to show that black Americans can endure hardship and suffering for the cause of justice. If given the same chance to get an education and to obtain jobs on all levels for which they are trained, oppressed people can control emotion and discipline feeling, even when tension is high and justice is derelict.[6]

Robinson's view of the movement as the first step towards black redemption in the eyes of whites, and the role she assumed as the movement's publicist, left little room for a candid evaluation of the male leadership or for challenging its authority. She briefly criticized the ministers in Montgomery for their timidity, stating that only when they read a circular advertising the bus boycott and realized that "all the city's black congregations were quite intelligent on the matter and were planning to support the one-day boycott with or without the ministers' leadership" did they endorse it. She offset this reproach, however, with praise for the preachers' work, and attributed the boycott's success to the clergymen.

> Had it not been for the ministers and the support they received from their wonderful congregations, the outcome of the boycott might have been different. The ministers gave themselves, their time . . . and their leadership . . . which set examples for the layman to follow. They gave us confidence, faith in ourselves,

> faith in them and their leadership, that helped the congregations to support the movement every foot of the way.[7]

In her memoir, *The Long Shadow of Little Rock*, Daisy Bates displayed similar contradictions between her readiness to confront her white oppressors, which she demonstrated both as a child and as an adult, and her acceptance of what she regarded as a flawed black leadership. Bates grew up in southern Arkansas, in a town controlled by a sawmill company. She first experienced discrimination at the age of eight, when a white grocer refused to serve her until he had waited on all of the white customers. Bates also learned, at about the same age, that the couple who raised her were not her real parents, and that her mother had been raped and murdered by three white men. Her anger led her to reject all whites in her community, including a white friend, and to search for her mother's killers. When she discovered that one of them was a drunk who slept on a bench outside the commissary, she walked every day to stare at the man and to torment him with her resemblance to her mother. One day she shook him awake and glared at him.

> I don't know how long we stayed there, staring at each other. Finally he struggled to his feet in a low, pleading voice, he said "In the name of God, leave me alone."[8]

Bates not only challenged whites while growing up; she also defied the authority of her parents and members of the black community. Although her mother believed in leniency, Bates frequently succeeded in provoking her wrath. "I was often clobbered, tanned, switched and made to stand in the corner. The floor in the corner was slightly worn from the shuffling of my feet."[9]

In another anecdote, Bates described making fun of a group of devout and prominent women. These "Church Sisters" had come to pray for Bates while she lay sick in bed. Bates secretly let loose her guinea pigs, which proceeded to run across the legs of one of the women.

> That night the Church Sisters, who met each week at the church or at the home of some sick person to pray, gathered at our home. They knelt around my bed and prayed for my soul. I noticed the fat knees of one praying lady. It gave me an idea I couldn't resist. I eased the box [of guinea pigs] to the floor and released [them]. One of them ran across the fat lady's leg. Unable to lift her weight upon the chair beside her, she lumbered around the room, screaming hysterically. The other ladies, managing to keep a few paces ahead of her, joined in the wild demonstration.

Bates admitted her own amusement at the woman's distress. 'Helpless with laughter, I could not reply . . . I got my behind properly spanked."[10]

Bates's narrative showed that as an adult, she continued to challenge those in power. She met with the governor of Arkansas and the U.S. Attorney to urge them, unsuccessfully, to respond to the whites' violence. In contrast, however, she appears to have deferred to the male leadership in the black community. She made only a passing reference to her irritation at the black ministers' silence in the face of the whites' violence carried out against the black students, suggesting that she suppressed her frustration.[11] In her conclusion, she assailed Congress and the Eisenhower administration for their lackluster support of desegregation, but like Robinson, refrained from placing any blame for the movement's slow progress on its leadership.

One can see similar inconsistencies in the actions of Diane Nash, a SNCC volunteer. Nash grew up in Chicago and came to Nashville to attend Fisk University. Nash's shock at the segregation of restaurants, water fountains, and other public facilities in the south prompted her to join SNCC.[12] In 1965, Nash wrote an article for *Ebony* that implied that she accepted the prevailing view that the civil rights movement, and specifically SCLC, should be led primarily by men. Nash's article, "The Men Behind Martin Luther King" profiled the male staff members of SCLC. She depicted the women on the staff, who numbered three out of a total of twelve, as important but peripheral figures. She reported, "Although most of SCLC's programs constitute 'men's work,' a few of the 'men' behind King are women. In addition to SCLC wives who do a lot of reading for their husbands and keep in touch with the public reaction to SCLC projects, a few women provide major leadership in the various education programs."[13] In describing the different points of view expressed in staff meetings, Nash mentioned only those of the male staff members, suggesting that the men's opinions carried the most weight, and that the women were not included in the inner core of the staff. At no point did Nash question the women's secondary status within SCLC.

Nash's prominence in protest efforts, however, seemed to contradict the unspoken assumption of her article that men should lead the movement. Nash chaired the central committee of the sit-in movement in Nashville. She also assembled a second group of freedom riders to continue the journey when harassment forced the first group to disperse in Birmingham before they reached their destination of New Orleans. Juan Williams' quotation from Nash shows her determination.

> If the freedom riders had been stopped as a result of violence, I strongly felt that the future of the movement was going to be cut short. The impression would have been that whenever a movement starts, all [you have to do] is attack it with massive violence and the blacks [will] stop.[14]

While Bates, Robinson, and Nash attributed racism to blacks' lack of representation in the political process, the majority of black women leaders who left accounts of their experiences regarded racial oppression as symptomatic of a structurally flawed society. Disheartened by the movement's fragmentation in the late sixties and by what they regarded as its limited success, they concluded that racial oppression formed part of a larger system of inequities that characterized American society and that could not be eradicated without addressing the other injustices to which it was connected. One activist who became disillusioned was Jean Smith, a student at Howard University who registered voters for SNCC in 1963 and who organized the MFDP meetings that elected an integrated delegation to the Democratic National Convention in 1964. Smith maintained that the right to vote, while unifying the black community and giving blacks the confidence to assert themselves and challenge racist laws or customs, had proved ineffectual in diminishing white hegemony and improving the living conditions of blacks

> The best way to understand is to look at what the Negro people who cast their lot with the Movement believed. They believed, I think, that their participation in the drive for voting rights would ultimately result in the relief of their poverty and hopelessness. They thought that with the right to vote they could end the exploitation of their labor by the plantation owners. They thought they could get better schools for their children; they could get sewers dug and sidewalks paved. They thought they could get adequate public-health facilities for their communities. And of course they got none of these . . . They believed there was a link between representation in government and making that government work for you. What they—and I—discovered was that for some people, this link does not exist. For most black people, voting has not much more benefit than the exercise of walking to the polls. Why is this the case? Because the link between voting and partaking of the benefits of society exists at the pleasure of society. The society must be willing to respond to the legitimate needs of the people; only then can the channels for the expression of these needs, such channels as voting, be meaningfully employed.[15]

Anne Moody expressed similar bitterness.

> I came to see through my writings that no matter how hard we in the Movement worked, nothing seemed to change; that we made a few visible little gains, yet at the root, things always remained the same; and that the Movement was not in control of its destiny—nor did we have any means of gaining control of it. We were like an angry dog on a leash who had turned on its master. It could bark and howl and snap . . . but the master was always in control. I realized that the universal fight for human rights, dignity, justice, equality, and freedom . . . [is] the fight of every ethnic and racial minority . . . every one of the minions who daily suffer one or another of the indignities of the powerless and voiceless masses. And this trend of thinking is what finally brought about an end to my involvement in the Civil Rights Movement . . . [16]

Joyce Ladner, a SNCC volunteer, decided at an early age that the deprivation and degradation she suffered formed part of a larger system of oppression. Ladner grew up in Hattiesburg, Mississippi. Her father worked as a diesel engine mechanic. Her mother stayed at home, because her father "insisted that she not work for whites and be subjected to the abuse his mother had experienced."[17]

Ladner helped organize the first NAACP Youth Council in Hattiesburg in 1959, when she was a junior in high school. In the summer of 1963, she registered voters for SNCC in Albany, Georgia.

> Growing up in the segregated South meant that I had severe restrictions placed on almost every facet of my life. I did not have the freedom to express myself and to explore many of those things in which I was interested. I felt like a caged animal . . . It is very difficult to describe how oppressed I felt during those years: to be stifled, to be poor and subjugated, to be humiliated by ignorant whites whom we regarded as the scum of the earth and to realize that people in powerful positions didn't care what happened to you. I was acutely sensitive to those less fortunate than ourselves. I always defended the underdog. When I was in the sixth grade I had a classmate named Hattie Mae Naylor. Hattie Mae was one of about 18 children from a very poor family . . . I remember going off into the comer crying when the other children made fun of Hattie Mae because of her tattered clothing and her worn, dusty shoes . . . In some sort of way I understood that Hattie Mae and her parents were victims of the same system that created both the abject poverty in which they lived and [our] vicious [white] bus driver [who Ladner recalled "frequently swore at the black passengers."][18]

This disenchantment with the civil rights movement led some activists to temporarily embrace separatism. Smith, for example, in 1968 argued for a self-sufficient black community as the solution to blacks' political impotence.

> . . . the call for black-power . . . I consider the other side of the coin of black consciousness. One cannot exist without the other . . . We have to build a broad-based black consciousness so that we can begin to depend on one another for economic, political, and social support. We have to build our own businesses to put money into the development of the Negro community . . . We have to make our politicians responsible to us so that either they improve our communities or they go . . . Our immediate objective must be the strengthening of the black community instead of the apparently unattainable goal of diffusion of all black people into the mainstream of American life. We have to become strong so that we can depend on one another to meet our needs and so that we'll be able to deal with white people as we choose to, not as we are obliged to.[19]

Two years earlier, in 1966, Ladner had also abandoned integration as a goal, convinced by the unrelenting brutality of whites that black power offered the most effective means of improving the status of blacks.

> When Vernon Dahmier [Ladner's mentor] was killed, my faith in integration was shaken. I found myself trying to justify my belief that "Black and white together" was still the solution to the race problem . . . What Blacks needed to do, I thought, was to unite as a group and develop their own institutions and communities. What they needed was Black power! Only then, I felt, would whites give in to our demands. I gave up on trying to appeal to the conscience of whites. Racial power politics seemed to be a more viable way to effect fundamental changes. Institutional racism became the target instead of individual racial prejudice . . . I suppose the most painful time of all came when I rejected long-time white friends solely because they were white . . . I felt that my ideological commitment to integration had never brought the freedom and dignity [I had been told to] fight for when I was a young child.[20]

In addition to embracing separatism, Ladner turned to marxism for a diagnosis and a solution to racial oppression, along with Frances Beal, a former SNCC activist. Ladner asserted that in aspiring to middle-class goals of upward mobility and wealth, blacks condoned a structure of economic inequality. For Ladner, it was not blacks' lowly position in the hierarchy, but their acceptance of a capitalist economy which required a hierarchy, in which the fortunes of a few came from the exploitation of many, that oppressed them.[21] Similarly, Frances Beal claimed that the feminists who sought only to improve their own position, demanding, for example, equal pay for equal work, failed to attack capitalism as the root of inequality and thus perpetuated an unjust system.[22]

Perhaps because they published their views twenty years after the movement, when American society had become significantly more integrated, Bernice Reagon and Septima Clark did not share the disillusionment of Moody, Smith, Ladner, or Beal, although they shared those activists' opinion that racism was inseparable from other forms of oppression. They expressed hope in the possibility of progress, and emphasized the power of ideas to bring about social change. They argued that the movement succeeded because it increased consciousness of a variety of social problems, which in turn would prompt the necessary broad based reform.[23]

> For many Civil Rights Movement organizers and supporters, leaving a specific project or struggle didn't mean the end of political activity. These people came away from their Civil Rights Movement experience with a greater facility for seeing a wide range of questions. For many, there was no end nor rest. The Civil Rights Movement was only a beginning. Its dispersion continues to be manifested in ever widening circles of evaluation of civil and human rights afforded by this society . . . The movement continues . . . People are being threatened in almost every way. If it runs its course, no institutions or values will be left unexamined or untested.[24]

Robinson, Bates and Nash sought to present a united front to white authorities. Consequently, they suppressed their differences with the male leadership. In contrast, the other activists aired their disagreements with the men managing the movement organizations, although most did so only in hindsight.

Only two of the women, Ella Baker and Septima Clark, confronted the male leaders of the movement while working with them to challenge their policies. Baker, like Robinson and Bates, belonged to the older generation of women civil rights leaders. She was 57 when SCLC appointed her as executive secretary in 1960. Baker was born in 1903 in

Norfolk, Virginia. Her family moved to Littleton, North Carolina when Baker was seven. Baker's father waited on tables for the Norfolk-Washington ferry; her mother tended to the sick in the community.[25] After graduating from Shaw University in Raleigh, Baker began a long career of activism. She worked for a WPA consumer education project in New York City during the depression. The NAACP hired her in 1938 to recruit members and raise money in the south, and five years later named her national director of branches. Baker helped found SNCC in 1960. In 1964 she gave the keynote address at the MFDP convention in Jackson and established the MFDP Washington office.

Baker's readiness to confront the male officers in SCLC may have come in part from her commitment to participatory decision-making. She disapproved of King's autocratic style of leadership, insisting that a true leader gave others the opportunity to acquire skills in managing and speaking for an organization or effort. Baker said of SNCC, "I had no ambition to be in the leadership. I was only interested in seeing that a leadership had a chance to develop. My theory is strong people don't need strong leaders."[26]

Baker's account of the debate within SCLC on a strategy to bring SNCC under SCLC's control showed her opposing SCLC's hierarchical style of management-her efforts to democratize the leadership of the movement by lobbying for an autonomous SNCC, and her refusal to defer to King.

> The Southern Christian Leadership Conference felt that they could influence how things went. They were interested in having the students become an arm of SCLC. They were most confident that this would be their baby, because I was their functionary and I had called the meeting. At a discussion caused by the Reverend Dr. King, the SCLC leadership made decisions [about] who would speak to whom to influence the students to become part of SCLC. Well, I disagreed. There was no student at Dr. King's meeting. I was the nearest thing to a student, being the advocate, you see. I also knew from the beginning that having a woman be an executive of SCLC was not something that would go over with the male-dominated leadership. And then, of course, my personality wasn't right, in the sense I was not afraid to disagree with the higher authorities. I wasn't one to say, yes, because it came from the Reverend King. So when it was proposed that the leadership could influence the direction by speaking to, let's say, the man from Virginia, he could speak to the leadership of the Virginia student group, and the assumption was that having spoken to so-and-so, so-and-so would do what they wanted done, I was outraged. I walked out.[27]

Septima Clark, the other activist who challenged the male staff of SCLC, was also a member of the older generation of women civil rights leaders. Clark was born in 1898 in Charleston, North Carolina. She taught in the Charleston public schools until she lost her job in 1956 when the legislature passed a law prohibiting state employees from belonging to the NAACP. The Highlander Folk School, which brought blacks and whites together to discuss social issues at a farm in Tennessee, hired Clark to lead workshops with members of rural communities to teach their neighbors to read and to register to vote. In 1961, when the Tennessee legislature moved to close Highlander, SCLC and the United Church of Christ provided the funds to enable Clark to continue organizing citizenship schools, which in 1964 numbered 195.

Clark talked freely about what she saw as the sexism of the SCLC staff.

> I was on the executive staff of the SCLC, but the men on it didn't listen to me too well. They like to send me into many places, because I could always make a path in to get people to listen to what I have to say. But those men didn't have any faith in women, none whatsoever. They just thought that women were sex symbols and had no contributions to make. That's why Reverend Abernathy

> would say continuously, "Why is Mrs. Clark on this staff?" Dr. King would say, "Well she has expanded our program. She has taken it into eleven deep south states." Rev. Abernathy'd [*sic*] come right back the next time and ask again.
>
> I had a great feeling that Dr. King didn't think much of women either . . . when I was in Europe with him, when he received the Nobel Peace Prize in 1964, the American Field Service Committee people wanted me to speak. In a sort of casual way he would say "Anything I can't answer, ask Mrs. Clark." But he didn't mean it, because I never did get the chance to do any speaking to the AFS committee in London or to any of the other groups.[28]

Like Baker, Clark communicated to King her differences with his style of leadership, urging him in a letter to run SCLC more democratically by delegating authority. She also attacked other ministers for their dependence on King, in which they assumed that only King could lead the movement, and for their belief that to suggest expanding the leadership of the movement cast doubt on King's own capabilities.

> When I heard the men asking Dr. King to lead the marches in various places, I'd say to them, "You're there. You going to ask the leader to come everywhere? Can't you do the leading in these places?"
>
> I sent a letter to Dr. King asking him not to lead all the marches himself, but instead to develop leaders who could lead their own marches. Dr. King read that letter before the staff . . . they just laughed. I had talked to the secretaries before about it, and when the letter was read they wouldn't say a word, not one of them. I had a feeling that they thought Dr. King would have to do the leading. If you think that another man should lead, then you are looking down on Dr. King. That was the way it was.[29]

Clark insisted that her capacity to criticize King and the other SCLC staff members came from the influence of the National Organization for Women (NOW) which she joined in 1968. She observed that while she worked for SCLC in the early and mid-sixties, she was blind to its leadership's sexism.

> . . . in those days I didn't criticize Dr. King, other than asking him not to lead all the marches. I adored him. I supported him in every way I could because I greatly respected his courage, his service to others, and his nonviolence. The way I think about him now comes from my own experience in the women's movement.[30]

Yet Clark also stated that she joined NOW because she resented the subordination of women to men in the south, which suggests that she was not as unaware of sexism in the movement as she later claimed to be. "I found all over the South . . . whatever the man said would be right, and the wives would have to accept it."[31] Clark first attended a NOW conference in 1968 at the request of Virginia Durr, a white southern liberal. She spoke to its members about

> . . . the women of the South who failed to speak up when they knew what they wanted, about white women who would see their husbands doing wrong but dared not tell them, about black women who wouldn't speak at all because the husband had the right to say whatever.[32]

Kathleen Cleaver also discussed her perceptions of sexism in the movement. She reported in 1971 that she joined the women's movement because she observed while working for SNCC, beginning in 1966, that women did most of the work but that few women held positions of authority. Those women who obtained administrative posts,

Cleaver noticed, carried the double burden of their jobs and their duties as wives and mothers, and also had to contend with the male staff members' refusal to accept them as their equals. Cleaver attributed the death of Ruby Doris Smith, Executive Secretary of SNCC, to sheer exhaustion from the many demands and from having to fight racism and sexism simultaneously. "What killed Ruby Doris was the constant outpouring of work, work, work, with being married, having a child, the constant conflicts, the constant struggles that she was subjected to because she was a woman."[33]

A letter written in 1977 by Cynthia Washington, who directed a freedom project for SNCC in Mississippi in 1963, suggested that the position of black women in the movement was more ambiguous than the deference of Robinson, Bates, or Nash to the male leadership, or the anger of Baker, Clark, or Cleaver at women's subordinate status indicated. Washington contended that she did not recognize sexism in the movement because, although women were rarely appointed to senior positions, they were frequently given jobs with responsibility, such as the job Washington herself held of project director. Although she recalled observing that white women were typically assigned the most menial tasks, Washington reasoned at the time that it was because they lacked the competence required for more challenging jobs.

> During the fall of 1964, I had a conversation with Casey Hayden about the role of women in SNCC. She complained that all the women got to do was type, that their role was limited to office work no matter where they were. What she said didn't make any particular sense to me because, at the time, I had my own project in Bolivar County, Mississippi. A number of other black women also directed their own projects. What Casey and other white women seemed to want was an opportunity to prove they could do something other than office work. I assumed that if they could do something else, they'd probably be doing that.[34]

Washington said that while some black men viewed the women as inferior—she quoted Stokely Carmichael's jeer that the only position for women in SNCC was prone—she believe that the authority she enjoyed as project director demonstrated that few shared his view. "Our relative autonomy as projects directors seemed to deny or override his statement. We were proof that what he said wasn't true—or so we thought."[35]

In addition, according to Washington, women who participated in the movement may not have been aware of sexism because they assumed that black men did not question their abilities, for historically, the poverty of blacks had forced the women to work as well as the men in order to support their families, while also caring for their children. These multiple responsibilities, said Washington, were not seen as evidence of an inferior status. On the contrary, women were honored for their labor.

> I did not see what I was doing as exceptional. The community women I worked with on projects were respected and admired for their strength and endurance. They worked hard in the cotton fields or white folks houses, raised and supported their children, yet still found the time and energy to be involved in struggle for their people. They were typical rather than unusual.[36]

Yet Washington also implied that she later concluded that sexism did exist, despite her lack of awareness of it at the time. "In fact, I'm certain that our single-minded focus on the issues of racial discrimination and the black struggle for equality blinded us to other issues."[37]

The ambiguity in the status of women in the movement brought out by Washington's letter paralleled the activists' ambivalence towards the male leaders, in which even those women who criticized the male activists for their condescending attitudes towards women did not hold the men responsible for their sexism. Some, such as Clark, saw the men's treatment of women as reflecting their hostility towards a racially oppressive society that put down black men even more than black women. Clark thought that black men's sexism was a reaction against their overprotective mothers, who tried to shield their sons from the violence of whites to which black men were particularly susceptible. Clark's insights shed light on one source of the stereotype, expressed by Andrew Young, that " . . . a system of oppression tends to produce strong women and weak men."[38]

> I see this as one of the weaknesses of the civil rights movement, the way the men looked at women. I think I know how the men got that way. I think about my mother, who had a feeling that black boys in the south could be conspired upon. She wanted to keep her boys right under her nose; she never wanted them away from her. She would always say, "A girl will bring you one trouble, but a boy can bring so many others. He can be arrested for stealing. He can be arrested for looking at a white." She'd name all these things that I think caused black mothers to feel as if black boys have to be very docile. Because they resented that, the black boys grew up feeling that women should not have a say in anything.[39]

Other movement workers, such as Beal and Cleaver, blamed capitalism as well as racism for black men's discrimination against women. Sexism, like racism, they argued, was a device by which whites reinforced the exploitation of the masses. Just as racism perpetuated lower-class whites' poverty by preventing them from joining forces with blacks to overthrow their oppressors, so too, by internalizing the sexism of whites, black men contributed to the marginal economic status of blacks. Their complicity in the segregation of jobs by sex, which limited black women's access to all but the lowest paid jobs, and which treated women as a source of surplus labor and as strikebreakers, impoverished blacks as a group.

Cleaver agreed with Clark that black men developed sexist attitudes because they were oppressed, although Cleaver saw their oppression as economic. The black men, according to Cleaver, resented the "strong role black women had had to assume as breadwinners as well as mothers. They vented their frustration by asserting their power over women—treating them as inferior, abusing them—or by abandoning their families to escape their guilt at their inability to find employment.

> The oppression of the woman by the black man is something that is perpetuated and encouraged by the system of colonialism run by the white man. We must always remember that the basic enemy of the black woman is not her own man because her own man, the black man, is not the creator or perpetrator of the system that is dedicated to depressing women. However, as black men move to assert themselves . . . to regain a sense of dignity . . . of manhood . . . of humanity, and to become strong enough and powerful enough and manly enough to fight against the oppressor, they many times take out their resentment of their position against their own black women. And many times flee from the guilt that they know is theirs in their refusal and inability to protect the black woman . . . the violence that black men direct toward their own women, the brutality, the hostility, the bitterness, the antagonism, and all this resentment, is something that black women are subjected to as a result of the colonization of the man.[40]

All of the women leaders agreed that discrimination against women was of secondary importance to the subjection of all blacks and the inequitable distribution of power in society. Cleaver, for example, insisted that to focus on sexism diverted blacks from attacking the root of all injustice, "colonization", or economic exploitation of white women and minority men and women.[41] Likewise, Reagon believed that the basic structure of the country . . . as it's set up, cannot sustain itself without oppressing someone"[42] and Fannie Lou Hamer asserted that the liberation of one required the liberation of all.[43]

Moreover, these activists held differing views of the relationship between the status of black women and that of blacks as a whole. Cleaver thought that women's equality was a necessary precondition to achieving the equality of all blacks—a means of ensuring the full utilization of blacks' resources.

> As long as the men deny the women their full role and their full respect in that struggle (to destroy the system of colonialism) . . . they are cutting themselves short and they're selling the struggle short because the women have as much to give as the men . . . therefore the black woman must be given her full respect in life and not hampered in her abilities, in her desires, and her activities towards forwarding the liberation of her people.[44]

Ladner, on the other hand, feared that the assertiveness of women made black men look relatively weak as Andrew Young suggested, and hindered the men from proving their equality to whites.

> What is clear, however, is that an alteration of roles between Black males and females must occur. The traditional "strong" Black woman has probably outlived her usefulness because this role has been challenged by the Black man, who has demonstrated that the white society acknowledge his manhood and deal with him directly instead of using his woman—considered the weaker sex—as a buffer . . . I am not suggesting that the distinctive positive character of Black womanhood forged by centuries of oppression be abolished . . . I am proposing, however, that the stereotyped "Sapphire" ("Sapphire" is the name applied to the typical strong Black woman) cannot continue to operate in the traditional manner but must make the necessary adjustments that will allow for the full development of male and female.[45]

The inconsistencies in the behavior of these women leaders, in which they challenged white authorities but deferred to black ministers, or criticized the male activists, but only in hindsight, or directly challenged the male officers of movement organizations, yet nevertheless accepted their leadership, cannot entirely be explained by their various theories on the source of racism. Indeed, only in the case of three of the activists, Robinson, Bates, and Nash, do their ideologies seem consistent with their actions. A more plausible explanation for their contradictory behavior is that these women, for the reasons given by Washington, did not consider themselves oppressed by black men, either in or out of the movement, and in some respects believed that black men were worse off than black women. Consequently they did not seek to change their roles in the movement. In addition, the women had conflicting feelings about whom to hold responsible for sexism, if they thought that it did exist, and were uncertain as to how the assertion of their rights as women would affect the status of blacks as a group. These women leaders' reflections suggest that the role of black women in the civil rights movement, largely ignored by historians, was complicated by their ambivalence about what it ought to be and defies a definitive answer.

ENDNOTES

1. Harvard Sitkoff, *The Struggle for Black Equality,* (New York: Hill and Wang, 1981), p. 90.
2. Paula Giddings, *When and Where I Enter* (New York: Bantam Books, 1984), p. 266.
3. Dick Cluster, ed., *They Should Have Served that Cup of Coffee,* (Boston: Sought End Press, 1979), pp. 22–23.

4. *Ibid.*, p. 29.

5. Anne Moody, *Coming of Age in Mississippi* (New York: Dial Press, 1968), p. 310.

6. David Garrow, ed., *The Montgomery Bus Boycott and the Women Who Started It. The Memoir of Jo Ann Gibson Robinson* (Knoxville: University of Tennessee Press, 1987), pp. 10–11.

7. *Ibid.*, pp. 53–54.

8. Daisy Bates, *The Long Shadow of Little Rock* (New York: David McKay, 1962), p. 22

9. *Ibid.*, p. 25.

10. *Ibid.*, p. 13.

11. *Ibid.*, pp. 85–86.

12. Juan Williams, *Eyes on the Prize*, (New York: Viking Penguin, 1987), p. 130.

13. Diane Nash, "The Men Behind Martin Luther King", *Ebony*, 1965, p. 170, as cited in Mary Mace Spreading, ed. *In Black and White*, Vol. 2, (Detroit: Gale Research Company, 1980), p. 211.

14. Williams, *Eyes on the Prize*, p. 149.

15. Jean Smith, "I Learned to Feel Black," in Floyd Barbour, ed., *The Black Revolt*, (Boston: Porter Sargent, 1968),p. 211.

16. Quoted in Jane E. Bowden, ed., *Contemporary Authors*, (Detroit: Gate Research Company, 1977), vol. 65–68, p. 418.

17. Joyce Ladner, "Return to the Source," *Essence*, June 1977, p. 126.

18. *Ibid.*, p. 127.

19. Smith, "I Learned to Feel Black," pp. 214–217.

20. Ladner "Return to the Source," p. 129.

21. Joyce Ladner, *Tomorrow's Tomorrow*, (New York: Doubleday, 1971), pp. 273–275.

22. Frances Beal, "Slave of a Slave No More: Black Women in Struggle." *Black Scholar*, March, 1975, p. 9.

23. Septima Clark, *Ready From Within*, (Navarro, California: Wild Tree Press 1986), p. 126.

24. Cluster, *They Should Have Served*, p. 36.

25. Ellen Cantarow, *Moving the Mountain*, (Old Westbury: The Feminist Press. 1980), pp. 59–60.

26. *Ibid.*, pp. 86, 53.

27. *Ibid.*, p. 84.

28. Clark, *Ready from Within*, p. 77.

29. *Ibid.*, p. 77.

30. *Ibid.*, p. 78.

31. *Ibid.*, p. 79.

32. *Ibid.*, p. 80.

33. Sister Julia Herve, "Black Scholar Interviews Kathleen Cleaver, *The Black Scholar*, December 1971, p. 55.

34. Cynthia Washington, "We Started From Different Ends of the Spectrum," *Southern Exposure*, Vol. 4, No. 4, 1977, p. 14.

35. *Ibid.*, p. 15.

36. *Ibid.*, p. 14.

37. *Ibid.*, p. 15.

38. Giddings, *When and Where I Enter*, p. 313.

39. Clark, *Ready from Within*, p. 79.

40. Herve, "Black Scholar Interviews Kathleen Cleaver," p. 59.

41. *Ibid.*

42. Cluster, *They Should Have Served*, p. 25.

43. Fannie Lou Hamer, interview with Anne Romaine and Howard Romaine, 1966, Fannie Lou Hamer papers, Wisconsin State Historical Society, p. 14.

44. Herve, "Black Scholar Interviews Kathleen Cleaver," p. 59.

45. Ladner, *Tomorrow's Tomorrow*, p. 285.

UNIT 12-5

SHOULD CIVIL RIGHTS WORKERS TAKE A STAND ON VIETNAM?

Howard Zinn

The question has burst out suddenly in The Movement, with varying responses. The NAACP, through Roy Wilkins, says "Let's not take a stand." The Urban League says very much the same. CORE obviously has a strong rank-and-file sentiment for opposing American policy in Vietnam, but James Farmer pressured them into silence at their recent convention. The SCLC, at its annual meeting, showed great concern, with James Bevel speaking of using non-violence to somehow stop the war. FDP workers in McComb came out with a hot anti-war leaflet, and SNCC people participated in several Washington demonstrations against American policy.

Clearly, people in the movement are torn and troubled, and I would like to initiate a discussion in SNCC on this question.

Let me start by reversing the situation. Suppose one of the peace organizations is approached by a member of the Freedom Democratic Party and asked to take a stand on behalf of the Challenge. And suppose the organization says: "Well, we are really with you, but we don't want to commit ourselves openly because our primary concern is peace, not civil rights. We think it may hurt our work for peace if we get tangled up in issues like the Challenge." I think Movement people would be indignant, and rightly so. They would ask: "Isn't *all* human suffering our concern? Aren't war and discrimination twin evils of modern society? What if all people of conscience separated into many different causes, and insisted on sticking only to their own cause, not giving aid to the others?"

The point is not that a civil rights group should stop what it is doing on racial equality and turn to the issue of world peace. But why can't it continue its main work, and at the same time support to whatever extent it can, people in other parts of the world who are poor and oppressed? I am talking not only about Vietnam, but about the Dominican Republic, South Africa, or anywhere else where there is a burning issue of injustice.

Student Voice, August 30, 1965.

Vietnam right now is the critical spot in the world, just as Mississippi was the critical spot in the United States in the 1964 summer.

Movement people are perhaps in the best position to understand just how immoral are this nation's actions in Vietnam. One reason, as Bob Parris said recently in Washington, is not that civil rights workers understand so much about foreign policy, but that they understand so much about the United States. They understand just how much hypocrisy is wrapped up in our claim to stand for "the free world." They know how much they had to endure in beatings and bombings and murder before the American government acted to pass civil rights legislation that was a century overdue (and which is still only the first small step towards real equality). And so, to put it bluntly, Movement people don't have that much faith in what the government says.

Events in Vietnam become easier to understand in the light of recent experience in the South. For instance: the cry of "outside agitator" is raised in *both* places. Just as the white South finds it hard to believe that Southern Negroes are genuinely dissatisfied, and so attributes the Negro revolt to "outsiders," the U.S. finds it hard to believe that the Vietnamese peasant really is in revolt against the old way of life, and so blames the rebellion on "outsiders" from the Communist nations.

Now it is true that "outsiders" support the Southern Negro, and even come South to help out. And it is true that North Vietnamese have come South to help the Vietcong rebels. But these facts don't alter the fundamental issue: that in both cases there is a homemade uprising against an oppressive system. President Johnson again and again muddies this basic fact with talk about "aggression" when all the people fighting against the U.S. are in their own country and American soldiers are ten thousand mile away from home.

There is another interesting analogy between the plight of the Southern Negro and the crisis in Vietnam. In both situations there is the use of special words that arouse hatred and distort reality. In the South the word is "nigger." It destroys the individual human being of tan or brown or black color, who is a man or woman, a farmer or a teacher, who is a *single* person, unlike any other person in the world. The word "nigger" is designed to abolish that individuality, to put millions of people into one inhuman category which makes them an object of hatred and murder.

In American foreign policy, the word is "Communist." The word is a blanket which smothers the true complexity of the world and the individuality of human beings. A "Communist" in Russia is not quite the same as a Communist in Yugoslavia or in China or in Italy. Stalin was a Communist, who used terrorism against his critics, but his critics were Communists today, and there are Communists today who oppose such terrorism. And inside each "Communist" country there are wide variations of belief. Yet, American marines shoot Vietnamese women and children, our planes destroy the homes of farmers and their supplies of food. All of this is justified by the use of the word "Communist" while the facts indicate that the average Vietcong fighter is an ordinary peasant tired of being ruled in the old way.

And so, young people in the Movement can see through the Vietnamese situation with a quick clarity that middle-class intellectuals often do not have. That is why a number of SNCC people have been taking part in demonstrations against American policy in Vietnam. SNCC always prided itself on a special honesty, on not playing it "safe," in saying exactly what it felt like saying. Shouldn't it now say, at this crucial moment, the *freedom now* must be international?

UNIT 12-6

THE WAR IN VIETNAM

In what is one of the most tragic and morally unjustifiable adventures in our nation's history, the American people find themselves at war with the 30,000,000 people of Vietnam. Whatever the face-saving euphemisms, this is the fact of life. The African-Asian block of independent countries in the United Nations prevents the U.S. from using that body as a screen, behind which to hide its naked intervention, as was the case in the Korean War. Obviously, this is not 1950! Consequently, the present military build-up of American forces in the Vietnam Civil War cannot be passed off as a "police action" or by any other semantic magic. This is a full scale war using conventional weapons, costing the American people 1 1/2 billion dollars per year and tens of thousands of human lives, both Vietnamese and American.

The familiar picture of an American soldier painting an inscription on a bomb intended to be dropped on Vietnam villages, with an inscription reading *"from Raleigh, North Carolina"* speaks eloquently enough of the real nature of American involvement in Vietnam. Nor is it purely a coincidence that among the loudest supporters of this unjust adventure are such ardent segregationists as Senator Long of Louisiana and the Goldwater Republicans. This is not the first racist war in which the American people have been dragged by their political leaders. This country, indeed, is peculiarly shaped, in part, by its history of wars—against the Indian population, Mexico, the Philippines, Cuba, Haiti and the Korean people.

The current military adventure against the people of Vietnam, by the Johnson-McNamara Administration, with napalm bombs, gas and chemical warfare is but one more chapter in a sordid record of (in the words of Frederick Douglass, a century ago)—"crimes that would disgrace a nation of savages." The fundamental reason why our government can so arrogantly violate the right of the Vietnamese people (and the people of Santo Domingo), to settle their disputes in their own way, is because the government of the United States has a "tradition," over the past 90 years, of never having upheld and defended the right of the black people of the southern states to choose the kind of government they wish to live under, by guaranteeing to them the ballot and free elections. This is the link that connects Selma and Saigon.

History has its own way of boldly asserting its priorities. The very day that 3,500 U.S. troops were landing in Vietnam, the Negro citizens of Selma, Alabama, were being beaten, tear-gassed, and smoke-bombed by Alabama State police for trying to march in peaceful

---

Freedomways, 1965.

protest against being denied the right to vote. This began the Second Battle of Selma, whose real origins go back to our own Civil War of a hundred years ago.

We commend Sen. Wayne Morse and Sen. Ernest Gruening for the stand they have taken; and those students and other citizens who organized and participated in the significant Peace March on Washington. Increasingly, there must be a fuller cooperation between the grass-roots participants and leaders of the Peace Movement and the Civil Rights Movement. Each has a stake in the goals of the other. For the good of the American people, both racism and war must be rooted out of the contemporary life of our country.

THE EDITORS

UNIT 12-7

THE FREEDOM MOVEMENT AND THE WAR IN VIETNAM

Robert S. Browne

During the several years which I lived in Vietnam, I enjoyed an intimacy with Vietnamese life which was probably unique for an American. Although I could never escape the obvious truth that I was a foreigner, the fact that I was a non-white, Vietnamese-speaking member of a Vietnamese family, frequently made me privy to conversations intended only for Vietnamese ears [Negro readers will readily understand what I mean] and provided me an unusual measure of insight into the depths of Vietnamese thinking and emotions. Unquestionably, it is this unique insight which led me as early as 1960 to become a constant and vigorous critic of the United States policy in Vietnam.

Although the stimulus for this disaffection with the American effort in Vietnam derived primarily from my awareness of what suffering we were inflicting upon the Vietnamese people by imposing upon them the hated dictatorship of President Diem and his family, my lifelong interest in international political affairs had made me extremely skeptical of the American official policy in Southeast Asia long before I ever went to live there. America's acquiescence in France's 1946 re-occupation of her former Indochinese empire had early alerted me to our government's unwillingness or incapacity to extend the idea of freedom to the non-white peoples of this part of the world, and after 1950 the open support by the United States of the French colonial war in Indochina had clearly placed America in opposition to the aspirations of the Vietnamese, Laotian and Cambodian peoples.

When, in 1954, the French finally decided to sue for peace in Vietnam, the United States took upon itself the responsibility of attempting to fill the so-called vacuum which America typically assumed would be created by the departure of the white colonizers. In large measure, it is the Vietnamese peoples' resistance to this paternalistic approach to them, with its implicit assumption that they are incapable of resolving their own problems, which lies at the base of the United States-Vietnam conflict. The myriad domestic problems of Vietnam have been completely overshadowed by America's insinuation of its presence into the Vietnam political scene, which has aggravated the existing factionalism amongst

Freedomways, 1965.

the Vietnamese and elevated their internal quarrel into an international *cause celebre,* with the resultant massive destruction which we see taking place today.

The belief that there was a "white man's burden" in Indochina which America was obliged to assume was clothed, not in the 19th century garment of protecting commercial or religious interests, but in the modern cloak of resisting the spread of international communism. Using the pretext that communism was the worst fate which could befall the Vietnamese people, but stubbornly refusing to submit this value judgment to a plebiscite amongst the Vietnamese people, Washington proceeded to assume major responsibility for directing Vietnamese affairs. That the Vietnamese were reluctant to accept either Washington's direction of their country or its assessment of what was best for their welfare, however, was strikingly illustrated by President Eisenhower's comment on the failure of the Vietnamese peasants to cooperate with the U.S. program. As late as 1960, *i.e.,* after 6 years of massive American influence in Vietnam, Eisenhower remarked that "our biggest problem is to convince the Vietnamese people that communism is their number one enemy." But in 1965, after yet an additional 5 years of United States interference on a ferocious scale, the Vietnamese people are even less ready than before to do Washington's bidding. Having brought only strife, suffering, and unimaginable destruction to their country, the U.S. has become the object of undisguised scorn for these people who only 10 short years ago had hardly heard of America. What they perhaps resent most is that there are now only two alternatives remaining available to them—communism, or a continuation of the wholesale slaughter of their people—the opportunity to neutralize their country having been lost to them by the United States' interference.

DULLES POLICY DISCREDITED

Not surprisingly, the political thinking which initially rationalized our Vietnam policy back in 1954–55 has been discredited by events as well as by most responsible persons in Washington itself. The basic plank of this policy, the Dulles proposal to contain Chinese communism by ringing China with a network of pro-American states "pending China's collapse from within," has proved to be both unworkable and falsely premised. A neutralized S.E. Asia, free of cold war pressures, for which Nehru, Sukarno, and Sihanouk pleaded at Bandung and subsequently, was dismissed as "immoral" by Secretary Dulles as he proceeded to pit Vietnam against Cambodia, Thailand against Indonesia, and within Vietnam, to pit a pro-American, largely capitalist and Christian faction against a nationalist, largely socialist and Buddhist one. The ultimate guarantee of continued western control of the region, however, was supposed to lie in a so-called mutual assistance organization in which five European nations joined with three Asian nations to determine the future of Southeast Asia. It was misleadingly called the Southeast Asia Treaty Organization.

As the unworkability of the policy became apparent, President Diem, the politician whom the U.S. had supported to assume the leadership of the South Vietnamese government, resorted to terror to impose his will upon the Vietnamese people. Not surprisingly, this provoked a counteraction which, being denied any legal means of protest, organized itself into a rebel movement and adopted guerrilla tactics to establish its position. Alarmed at the speed and effectiveness with which this resistance movement began to grow, the United States decided in 1961 to commit itself to a major military stance to defend the government of President Diem in Vietnam. (Although President Johnson attributes this decision basically to President Eisenhower, Eisenhower denies the charge and claims that his administration's commitment to President Diem was economic and political, but not military.)

It was not possible for the Vietnamese guerrilla forces, dubbed "Viet Cong" by Diem, to match the build-up in sophisticated arms and trained men which the United States provided to the South Vietnam government. However, these U.S. arms increasingly served to supply the rebel forces as well, some of them being captured from the American and Vietnamese government troops and others reaching the rebels via black market sales or as gifts from defecting government troops. These defections, as well as the increasing sympathy for the rebels arising as a protest against such American-backed outrages as the strategic hamlet programs, which summarily uprooted the villagers from their homes, and the wholesale burnings of villages, substantially swelled the ranks of the rebels. The politically severed northern half of Vietnam, under communist rule, also increasingly supplied small arms assistance to the southern rebel forces. Not unexpectedly, the rebels' growing dependence on the North to enable them to withstand the United States' build-up strengthened the degree of communist influence within their movement, a fact which may have surprised Washington but which surprised no one else.

Modern planes, the latest in United States weaponry, chemicals, and gas were turned against the rebels, and even more so against the innocent Vietnamese peasants from whom the rebels are indistinguishable. Four more years of warfare, however, failed to turn the tide in favor of the United States' government forces. In 1963, the myth of Diem's popular democracy had been exploded by a half dozen Buddhist monks who, in self-sacrificing protest, had dramatically cremated themselves in the streets of Vietnam, forcing the United States finally to admit Diem's unpopularity and to withdraw its support from him. This led to his rapid overthrow and assassination, to the undisguised, if unbecoming, glee of millions of Vietnamese people who declared three days of festivities in celebration.

In early 1965, the United States materially changed the character of the war by extending its aerial bombardment into North Vietnam, and then in the summer of 1965 President Johnson finally admitted the obvious: the Vietnamese were either unable or unwilling to win this war and the United States must do it for them. A major American military commitment was made, with some 125,000 men to be sent to Vietnam by year's end. A few days later the new United States Ambassador to Vietnam was reported by the *New York Times* to have stated that we wouldn't withdraw from Vietnam even if the Vietnamese government asked us to do so. South Vietnam's transformation into an undisguised American colony was thus complete, except that control of most of South Vietnam's territory was daily being bloodily disputed.

In South Vietnam itself, which I revisited in 1965 after a four-year absence, I found the people crying out for surcease from the sorrow which the ill-conceived American involvement in their affairs had brought them, but despairing because they saw no way to exert any influence over the events taking place in their country. The general feeling was that the Americans had gained so much control over Vietnamese affairs that any genuine expression of the people's wishes was absolutely impossible. With the exception of the small but influential northern refugee segment of the Catholic community, there seemed to be virtually no support for the American effort to impose a military solution to the Vietnamese quarrel. Catholics and Buddhists, students and workers, intellectuals and peasants were as one in their desire to bring a halt to the destruction of their country by the massive American military machine. The National Liberation Front, as the rebels are more properly called, had won wide respect for itself because of its ability to frustrate the efforts of the most powerful country in the world. The degree of communist influence in the NLF was a hotly debated question among the Vietnamese, but even among those who most loudly condemned the NLF for its communist orientation there was general admission that it was the only genuinely nationalist movement in the country. Many of those with whom I talked believed that a victory by the NLF would eventually lead to a communist government in South Vietnam, but this seemed generally to be preferable to the continued destruction of their country. Indeed, most every one felt that the National Liberation Front would ultimately be victorious *in any case* because the rebels had so wide and devoted a following whereas few people had any real respect for the succession of corrupt Saigon governments, whose basic allegiance to a foreign power [the United States] seemed to be quite well known. What particularly frustrated the people was the insistence by the Americans that the war continue to be fought out year after year, at such a high toll in Vietnamese life and property, when the ultimate outcome was already so plain to see.

PROTEST OF U.S. POLICY INCREASING

As American military involvement in Vietnam has grown more massive and as aerial bombing has expanded into neighboring Laos, Cambodia, North Vietnam and up to the very frontiers of China, a groundswell of protest and indignation has arisen from amongst the intellectual and religious segments of the American populace and from many foreign quarters previously not openly opposed to American policy. Reports of indiscriminate burnings and bombings of Vietnamese villages, often gleefully confirmed in morbid detail by sadistic American officers boasting with obvious satisfaction of the numbers of the "yellow bastards" which they have bagged, send waves of horror through the more sensitive segments of the American public.

The Vietnam war is gradually replacing civil rights as the top story of the mid-sixties, and because the protest against the United States policy in Vietnam has been primarily made on moral grounds, as was the demand for civil rights, there has been an inevitable coincidence of the two movements on various levels. This has been particularly noticeable on the organizational circuit, where many of the groups which have been most vocal in their support of civil rights are the same ones which are most outspoken against the worst aspects of United States involvement in Vietnam. Especially prone to this double involvement have been the northern-based student movements, the pacifist organizations, and the more militant religious institutions. Inevitably, this duality of interests led to growing pressure upon the major civil rights organizations to extend their scope sufficiently to encompass a position on the vital Vietnam question. Martin Luther King, as a Nobel Peace Prize winner and world symbol of non-violent resolution of conflicts, was particularly urged to take a public position on Vietnam. As the personification of America's moral conscience, his endorsement was viewed as especially significant for the moral protest against United States atrocities in Vietnam.

These pressures introduced a new and potentially revolutionary dimension into the civil rights movement, and perhaps into Negro thinking generally. Traditionally, the American Negro has been single-minded to a fault insofar as his social consciousness was concerned. He has bestirred himself solely about problems directly involving his welfare *as a Negro*. Issues involving him only as a citizen, but not as an ethnic group, were of little interest to him; and certainly foreign policy, one of the most sophisticated of public affairs, was generally beyond his sphere of interest. No wonder then that the effort to involve the civil rights movement in the Vietnam crisis met strong resistance. Roy Wilkins, the leader of the National Association for the Advancement of Colored People, adopted the curious position that foreign policy was not a proper sphere for public analysis and criticism. On the other hand, James Farmer of the Congress of Racial Equality was willing to offer his critical judgment of the Administration's foreign policy, but insisted on doing it as an individual, vigorously opposing his organization's taking a public stand on Vietnam. The Southern Christian Leadership Conference and the Student Non-Violent Coordinating Committee have openly supported efforts to seek a peaceful solution to America's involvement in the Vietnam conflict and perhaps the most durable tie between the civil rights and the peace movements is the growing tendency for the peace movement to adopt the non-violent techniques perfected by the latter two organizations. Following publication of a moving "open letter to Martin Luther King" from the Vietnamese Buddhists, a letter in which he was urged not to remain silent in this moment of great "suffering caused by this unnecessary war," Dr. King publicly added his great prestige to the burgeoning nationwide moral condemnation of the ungodly American activities in Vietnam.

The principal arguments against the civil rights movement's involvement in the Vietnam protest hinge on: (**1**) the risk of losing significant financial support from civil rights contributors who either support the United States policy in Vietnam or who for other reasons do not favor popular opposition to American foreign policy; (**2**) the risk of causing dissension among activists in the civil rights movement who may hold differing views on Vietnam; (**3**) the risk of the civil rights movement's being smeared as communist-oriented; and (**4**) the risk of dissipating scarce energy and resources in a peripheral activity.

Of these four reasons, the first would appear to be the most serious. With the Negro still far, far short of achieving anything approaching first class citizenship status, the civil rights leaders could be held irresponsible if they permitted their organization to become financially impoverished except for the most compelling of reasons: Since the principal business of these organizations is to fight for civil rights, a direct linkage between the Vietnam protest and the success of the civil rights program would have to be demonstrated to warrant risking a significant cut-off of funds. Whether in fact any noticeable loss of contributors would indeed result is problematic at this stage and would probably depend on which organization one is thinking about. Undoubtedly, the NAACP would be the most vulnerable to this sort of retaliation, its more conservative approach to problems presumably being a reflection of generally more conservative sources of financial support.

The second objection, the risk of dissension among the civil rights workers themselves, is probably slight. Although the liberals who do oppose the Vietnamese war usually act from a strong position of moral indignation, the others appear relatively ambivalent or indifferent to the war and are unlikely to be antagonistic to those who do come out against it.

Red-baiting is a real risk, of course. It is, however, one which the civil rights organizations have been failing increasingly in any case. The more popularly based civil rights movements have advanced to the place where traditional middle class approval and respectability are no longer given priority over program achievements. Their organizations are perhaps sufficiently self-secure to ignore the hysteria of the red-baiters, although recognizing the threat which such attacks represent to their fund-raising capabilities. As with the first reason, the more conservatively based organizations are likely to be the more sensitive to this menace.

The extent to which scarce resources, other than leadership, would be transferred from the civil rights struggle to the Vietnam protest would appear to be largely under the control of the civil rights organizations themselves. A simple statement of support shifts no resources and while there is a growing tendency for some civil rights activists to devote a portion of their energy to the peace movement, this trend is likely to proceed independently of the organizational position which is adopted. Naturally, to the extent that the leaders choose to play a continuing role in the Vietnam protest, there will be a diluting of their principal function and it is to be hoped that they would refrain from overextending themselves in this way.

GROWING ALLIANCE OF CIVIL RIGHTS AND PEACE MOVEMENT

On the other hand, there are strong arguments favoring a civil rights alliance with the Vietnam protest, or with the peace movement generally. These also fall under four headings:

1. The recognition that the civil rights movement represents the moral conscience of America and therefore naturally belongs in the vanguard of the Vietnam protest, felt now to be the number one moral issue confronting American society.
2. The argument that the billions of dollars being diverted to the Vietnam war represent funds which might otherwise be available for giving substance to the programs necessary for raising the Negro to a level of real equality in American life.
3. The belief that the civil rights objectives are unachievable under the present organization of American society and therefore must necessarily be fought for as part of a larger effort to remake American society, including its foreign policy.
4. The view that the Vietnam war is intimately involved in American racist attitudes generally, and therefore falls naturally within the range of American Negroes' direct sphere of interest.

That the civil rights movement has reinvigorated and restored a strain of morality to an increasingly purposeless and alienated American society is generally conceded, and it is also probably safe to predict that as the American public becomes aware of the true nature of its government's role and activities in Vietnam, the Vietnam involvement may well become the leading moral issue in America. Comparison of United States atrocities in Vietnam with the Nazis' extermination of Jews in Germany are being made increasingly and by responsible moral leaders, so that an explosive potential is already developing. That the presence of a powerful moral strain in the two issues leads automatically to their joining forces is not axiomatic, however, although it is certainly highly desirable to have the perennially weak voices of morality being raised in unison and gaining strength from mutual reinforcement.

The argument that funds spent in Vietnam can be used for constructive projects at home is indisputable. The only matter for question here is whether the funds would, in fact, be used for the poverty program if they were not being used in Vietnam. Our Congress is notoriously more generous in voting funds for military purposes than for programs of social welfare.

The viewpoint that achievement of full civil rights for the Negro requires ultimately a thorough going revision in American society has a variety of rationalizations. Its mildest formulation is probably contained in the manifesto entitled, *The Triple Revolution*, a scholarly document prepared by a group of leading American intellectuals who envisioned a revamping of American society around three foci: peace, civil rights, and automation. Civil rights as well as international peace were viewed as inseparable from the economic ordering of our society, and the dynamic of automation was seen as both the challenge and the hope for the necessary reordering of our society so as to make peace and civil rights an achievable reality.

The more extreme approaches to the remaking of American society derive from the various Marxian interpretations of human existence which view the Negro's low status as a necessary facet of American capitalism and which places Vietnam in a comparable slot in the global capitalist arrangements to which the United States is partisan. The tendency of the economic position of the Negro in America to go backward despite the efforts currently being made in his behalf is duplicated by the growing relative impoverishment of most of the underdeveloped [colored] nations of the world. These parallel phenomena strongly reinforce the demand for dramatic new approaches to the organization of economic affairs domestically as well as internationally. Some form of socialist organization is most frequently advocated.

However, the complexity and controversiality of such proposals render them unpromising rallying cries for arranging an immediate marriage between the civil rights and the peace movements. In any case, the United States interference in Vietnam is not a particularly convincing case of the classical Marxist argument that the foreign policy of American capitalism is explainable solely in terms of seeking markets and sources of primary products to exploit for American benefit. It is not primarily the dollar which is sending 125,000 American troops to Vietnam: it is fear of a strong, independent China, and although the basis of this fear may be partly in the ultimate economic threat which a revitalized China portends, one suspects that America's racist obsession—in this case, with the "yellow peril"—plays the significant role in the anti-Chinese hysteria.

IS RACISM INVOLVED IN VIETNAM WAR?

We are thus brought to the final consideration: whether or not there is a racist aspect to the Vietnam war, and if so what implications this has for American Negroes. Speculation on this topic opens a Pandora's box of considerations and can predictably arouse the greatest interest among Negroes themselves for it confronts them with their most difficult contemporary dilemma, that of identity. The dual streams of thought historically running through American social development—the plural society versus the melting pot—are currently reflected within Afro-American society in the separatism of the Black Muslims and other black nationalist groups versus the integrationist objectives of the Negro middle class. The emergence of Africa has raised the negritude concept—a mystic bond tying together all peoples of Negroid descent, transcending national boundaries. Amongst the much larger community of all colored peoples the common heritage of subjugation and exploitation which has been their lot until the post World War II era has created a vague sense of community which finds special nourishment in the problems of underdevelopment which they all share and in their common revulsion to any expression of white racial superiority and colonialism, of which they have all been victims. The so-called "wars of liberation," which the communists praise and the Americans condemn are well understood by the American Negro, who has faced similar struggles himself.

American Negroes inescapably feel a pull toward this mass of colored people, even as they attempt simultaneously to win acceptance into American society, for they know that America will forever be a white society, and they are instinctively skeptical that their full acceptance into it can ever be achieved. Fearing that a move to Africa may demand too great an adjustment of them, but doubtful about achieving a satisfactory role in American society, Negroes are already groping toward some new cosmopolitan political arrangements which would relieve them of their *dilemma*. During a series of visits to a number of Negro college campuses last year, I was interested to note how many of the students recoiled from the hypothetical prospect of taking up arms against Ghana, with whom United States relations were particularly strained at that time. (The rescue of the American flag from desecration at the hands of rioting Ghanaians by a Negro United States embassy employee, which had occurred shortly prior to my visit, was soundly criticized by many of the Negro students.)

Whether such sentiments will crystallize into a political position or not is impossible to predict, but the Vietnam conflict could certainly become a catalyst in that direction.

Certainly, no one will deny the growing international implications of race. That the spectacle of white Americans bombing and burning Asians has an explosive potential has been frequently alluded to by the State Department itself, and the U.S. government has worked diligently to try to convince other Asian nations to send combat troops to Vietnam so as to minimize the stark racial appearance of the conflict. General De Gaulle has publicly warned of the racial polarization which he saw developing in the world, and China has made frequent reference to race in her competition with the USSR for influence with the non-white nations.

To see innocent, uprooted American youths being incited to maim and murder women and children in Vietnam last summer was indescribably depressing to me, but to see American Negroes forced to engage in such atrocities absolutely enraged me. I was further appalled by what seemed to be a disproportionately large number of Negro faces among the United States troops and I could only wonder if this were the Pentagon's way of attempting to deflect the accusations of whites killing non-whites—and at the same time a way of driving a wedge between American Negroes and the colored people of Asia[1] I have noted other racial manifestations which give one cause for reflection. On August 17, 1965, the *New York Herald Tribune* carried a front-page column which concerned itself with the views of Negro troops in Vietnam. The purpose of the column seemed to be to prove that the American G.I.'s in Saigon found the Vietnamese to be anti-Negro. (Similar charges were publicized by The *New York Times* three weeks later.) These allegations are completely at variance to my own lengthy experience in Vietnam where I encountered no racism whatsoever on the part of the Vietnamese but on the contrary found many of them sympathetic with the Negro struggle in America. Indeed, considering the prominence afforded these anti-Negro allegations one wonders why so little publicity was given to the fact that in May of 1964 the Saigon taxi drivers' union called for a one week boycott of all foreign passengers *except American Negroes*.

One does not wish to be overly suspicious in this matter. Yet, one of the most depressing aspects of contemporary American diplomacy is America's obsessive fear of the American Negro's intimacy with other colored nationals. I have written elsewhere of the attempts to convince the Negro that he has nothing in common with the African. Although the Asian is a virtual stranger to the American Negro, a base for friendship and understanding between them certainly exists, I personally recall how, on the occasion of my first encounter with the venerable Tri Quang, leader of the Vietnamese Buddhists, I was momentarily thunderstruck at his appearance for, with his hair clipped short in the traditional style of the Buddhist monk, he looked exactly like any Negro whom one might meet on 125th Street in Harlem. Just as I question how it can be in America's interest to continue its futile effort to dominate and rule South Vietnam, even so do I question whether it is in the best interest of the American Negro to accept with equanimity the role which he is perhaps being obliged to play in this racially charged struggle. As a minimum, some effort should be made by Negroes to determine whether Negroes are in fact being used in excessive numbers in Vietnam so as to deflect the growing Asian accusations that the Vietnamese war is a confrontation between whites and non-whites. If such practices are substantiated, they will indeed be grave ones.

Whether or not any organized Negro protest against the Vietnamese war should take the suggested form of a refusal to do military service deserves considerable thought. Such a call appeared last summer in Mississippi, and later a similar call was circulated by a group entitled Afro-Americans for Freedom. The Mississippi protest was based primarily on the inappropriateness of American Negroes going off to kill unknown Vietnamese with whom they had no quarrel at a time when they had real, visible enemies who were murdering their families and friends in Mississippi, Alabama and Georgia. The latter protest had a slightly different philosophical basis in that it urged American Negroes to refuse to fight any other colored peoples. It, too, cited the substandard treatment of Negroes in America, but it was unclear if this were being offered as the rationale of the protest or if the ideological foundation lay more in the negritude concept mentioned earlier.

Verbalized objection by Negroes to military service is by no means new to the American scene. Although the position historically taken by the majority of Negro spokesmen has been a demand for full and nondiscriminatory participation for Negroes in America's military establishment, there has long been open expression of the contrary opinion as well. The advent of the Vietnam conflict, however, finds the American Negro for the first time in a position where his decision on this matter could be of serious national, and even international significance. It is only with the 1960s that the Negro finds himself with adequate sophistication and self-involvement, with adequate organization and leadership—black, grass roots leadership—so that mass collective action could be even remotely possible.

SHOULD NEGRO AMERICANS REFUSE MILITARY SERVICE?

Whether or not the time has come to utilize Negro power in this way promises to become a major topic of controversy. When I first read of the Mississippi statement urging Negroes not to fight in Vietnam I greeted it as a worthy first step toward bringing the beleaguered Vietnamese people the peace and self-determination which they so desperately want. A moment's reflection, however, caused me to realize that the implications of the proposed military service boycott were much broader in scope than a simple moral objection to the wanton murder which we are committing in Vietnam. Although such a boycott, if it caught hold amongst both whites and Negroes, might well offer some relief to the Vietnamese peoples, it holds equally the potential for creating of America a true force for peace at this critical moment for human survival. It could become the first step in promoting a genuine human community surpassing the narrow boundaries of the nation-state, which is basically a European concept in any case. By the same token, however, so drastic a step poses a severe risk to the entire Negro struggle to win acceptance into the "Great Society" of President Johnson and obviously should not be taken without sober thought.

James Baldwin has bemoaned the fact that the Negro is working so hard to gain acceptance into a society which is basically sick and in decline, an observation with which many will agree. But certainly our glorious struggle is for something greater, something more substantial than merely to win for Negroes an opportunity to imitate their white compatriots—to immerse themselves in a color television or to kill themselves in an overpowered automobile. Hopefully, our vision of a better world relies as much on the spiritual values as on the material ones. Is it not conceivable, then, that the Negro people, who understand the white man's hypocrisy better than any one else and who are already applying an enema to the rot which has for so long contaminated America's domestic social organization, may spark an international purification as well?

Whether we are indeed ready to undertake this ambitious task or not, there should be no disagreement regarding the urgency of insuring that, as non-whites, we are not being inadvertently manipulated into an untenable position within the global framework. We must amass all of our wits so as to steer a careful course between the Scylla of American racism and the Charybdis of foreign intrigue. We intend to be tools of neither. Rather, Afro-Americans can perform no greater service to their country and to humanity than to use their unique position to encourage international racial amity and to prevent international racial conflict. They can do mankind no greater disservice than to allow themselves to be used as tools in precipitating such as catastrophe.

ENDNOTES

1. The following interesting item was reported in April in the liberal Parisian weekly, *L'Express*, by veteran French reporter Georges Chaffard, who traveled extensively behind the lines, *i.e.*, in Vietcong territory, in the Vietnamese war. Commenting on the abundant supplies of American weapons in the hands of the Vietcong, he quotes a French planter in the rebel territory: "These are weapons sold to the Vietcong by soldiers of the National Army or by some Negroes in the U.S. Army. . . . It's as simple as that."

The Negro GI's may be more astute politicians than their Pentagon bosses!

Robert S. Browne teaches Economics at Fairleigh Dickinson University. He lived in Vietnam and Cambodia from 1955–1961, while working for the U.S. foreign aid program. In 1965 he returned to Vietnam to lecture at the Buddhist University in Saigon, to evaluate the current Vietnamese political situation, and to visit friends and (his wife's) relatives.

UNIT 12-8

SNCC POSITION PAPER: VIETNAM

"THE U.S. GOVERNMENT HAS DECEIVED US"

The Student Nonviolent Coordinating Committee has a right and a responsibility to dissent with United States foreign policy on any issue when it sees fit. The Student Nonviolent Coordinating Committee now states its opposition to United States' involvement in Vietnam on these grounds:

We believe the United States government has been deceptive in its claims of concern for the freedom of the Vietnamese people, just as the government has been deceptive in claiming concern for the freedom of colored people in such other countries as the Dominican Republic, the Congo, South Africa, Rhodesia, and in the United States itself.

We, the Student Nonviolent Coordinating Committee, have been involved in the black people's struggle for liberation and self-determination in this country for the past five years. Our work, particularly in the South, has taught us that the United States government has never guaranteed the freedom of oppressed citizens, and is not yet truly determined to end the rule of terror and oppression within its own borders.

We ourselves have often been victims of violence and confinement executed by United States governmental officials. We recall the numerous persons who have been murdered in the South because of their efforts to secure their civil and human rights, and whose murderers have been allowed to escape penalty for their crimes.

The murder of Samuel Young in Tuskegee, Alabama, is no different than the murder of peasants in Vietnam, for both Young and the Vietnamese sought, and are seeking, to secure the rights guaranteed them by law. In each case, the United States government bears a great part of the responsibility for these deaths.

Samuel Young was murdered because United States law is not being enforced. Vietnamese are murdered because the United States is pursuing an aggressive policy in violation of international law. The United States is no respecter of persons or law when such persons or laws run counter to its needs or desires.

We recall the indifference, suspicion and outright hostility with which our reports of violence have been met in the past by government officials.

The Movement, January 1966.

We know that for the most part, elections in this country, in the North as well as the South, are not free. We have seen that the 1965 Voting Rights Act and the 1966 Civil Rights Act have not yet been implemented with full federal power and sincerity.

We question, then, the ability and even the desire of the United States government to guarantee free elections abroad. We maintain that our country's cry of "preserve freedom in the world" is a hypocritical mask behind which it squashes liberation movements which are not bound, and refuse to be bound, by the expediencies of United States cold war policies.

We are in sympathy with, and support, the men in this country who are unwilling to respond to a military draft which would compel them to contribute their lives to United States aggression in Vietnam in the name of the "freedom" we find so false in this country.

We recoil with horror at the inconsistency of a supposedly "free" society where responsibility to freedom is equated with the responsibility to lend oneself to military aggression. We take note of the fact that 16% of the draftees from this country are Negroes called on to stifle the liberation of Vietnam, to preserve a "democracy" which does not exist for them at home.

We ask, where is the draft for the freedom fight in the United States?

We therefore encourage those Americans who prefer to use their energy in building democratic forms within this country. We believe that work in the civil rights movement and with other human relations organizations is a valid alternative to the draft. We urge all Americans to seek this alternative, knowing full well that it may cost them their lives—as painfully as in Vietnam.

VIETNAM
T.G. Lewis '67

WHO IS AGAINST THE WAR IN VIET NAM?
MARTIN LUTHER KING, JR.
AND THE SOUTHERN CHRISTIAN LEADERSHIP CONFERENCE ARE AGAINST IT.
THE SOUTHERN CONFERENCE EDUCATIONAL FUND, AN INTERRACIAL CIVIL RIGHTS GROUP, IS AGAINST IT.

JOHN LEWIS, STOKLEY CARMICHAEL AND THE STUDENT NONVIOLENT COORDINATING COMMITTEE ARE AGAINST IT.
ONE SNCC MEMBER, JULIAN BOND, WAS THROWN OUT OF THE GEORGIA HOUSE OF REPRESENTATIVES BECAUSE HE IS AGAINST THE WAR IN VIETNAM.
CASSIUS CLAY-MUHAMMED ALI- AND ELIJAH MUHAMMED AND THE BLACK MUSLIMS ARE AGAINST IT.
MALCOMB X WAS AGAINST THE WAR IN VIETNAM.

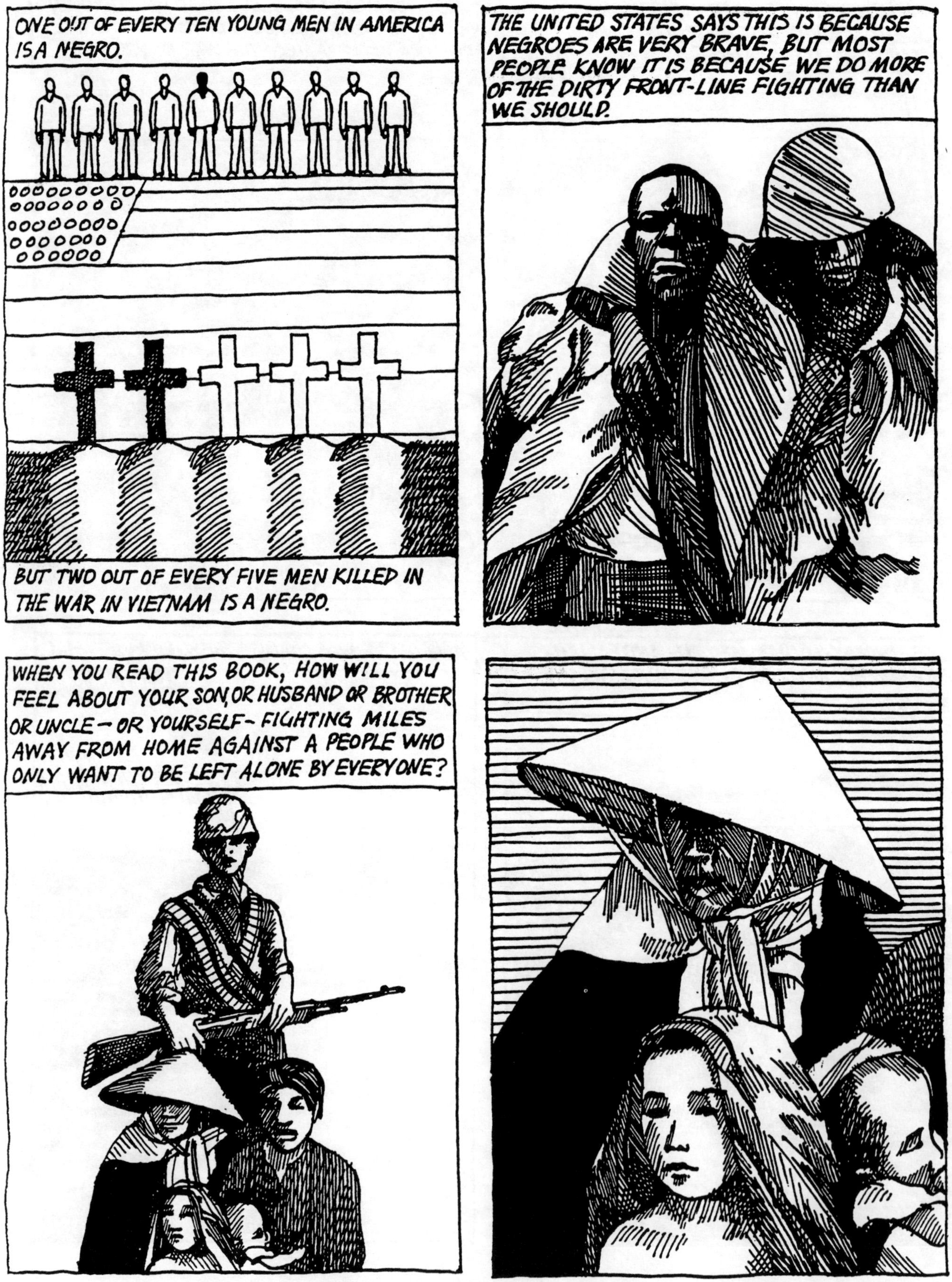
ONE OUT OF EVERY TEN YOUNG MEN IN AMERICA IS A NEGRO.
BUT TWO OUT OF EVERY FIVE MEN KILLED IN THE WAR IN VIETNAM IS A NEGRO.
THE UNITED STATES SAYS THIS IS BECAUSE NEGROES ARE VERY BRAVE, BUT MOST PEOPLE KNOW IT IS BECAUSE WE DO MORE OF THE DIRTY FRONT-LINE FIGHTING THAN WE SHOULD.
WHEN YOU READ THIS BOOK, HOW WILL YOU FEEL ABOUT YOUR SON, OR HUSBAND OR BROTHER OR UNCLE – OR YOURSELF – FIGHTING MILES AWAY FROM HOME AGAINST A PEOPLE WHO ONLY WANT TO BE LEFT ALONE BY EVERYONE?

IN 1860, WHEN THE UNITED STATES WAS FIGHTING A WAR TO FREE THE SLAVES,
THE FRENCH WERE FIGHTING A WAR TO MAKE SLAVES OF THE PEOPLE WHO LIVE IN VIETNAM. THE VIETNAMESE PEOPLE WANTED TO RUN THEIR OWN COUNTRY, BUT COULD NOT DEFEAT THE STRONG FRENCH ARMIES.
DURING THE SECOND WORLD WAR, ONE GROUP OF FRENCHMEN WAS FRIENDLY TO JAPAN AND GERMANY. THESE MEN SURRENDERED VIETNAM TO JAPAN WITHOUT FIRING A SHOT.
THE JAPANESE TOLD THE VIETNAMESE PEOPLE THEY COULD BE FREE UNDER JAPANESE RULE, BUT A GROUP OF VIETNAMESE UNDER A MAN NAMED HO CHI MINH WANTED FREEDOM UNDER THEIR OWN RULE. THESE MEN FOUGHT THE JAPANESE.

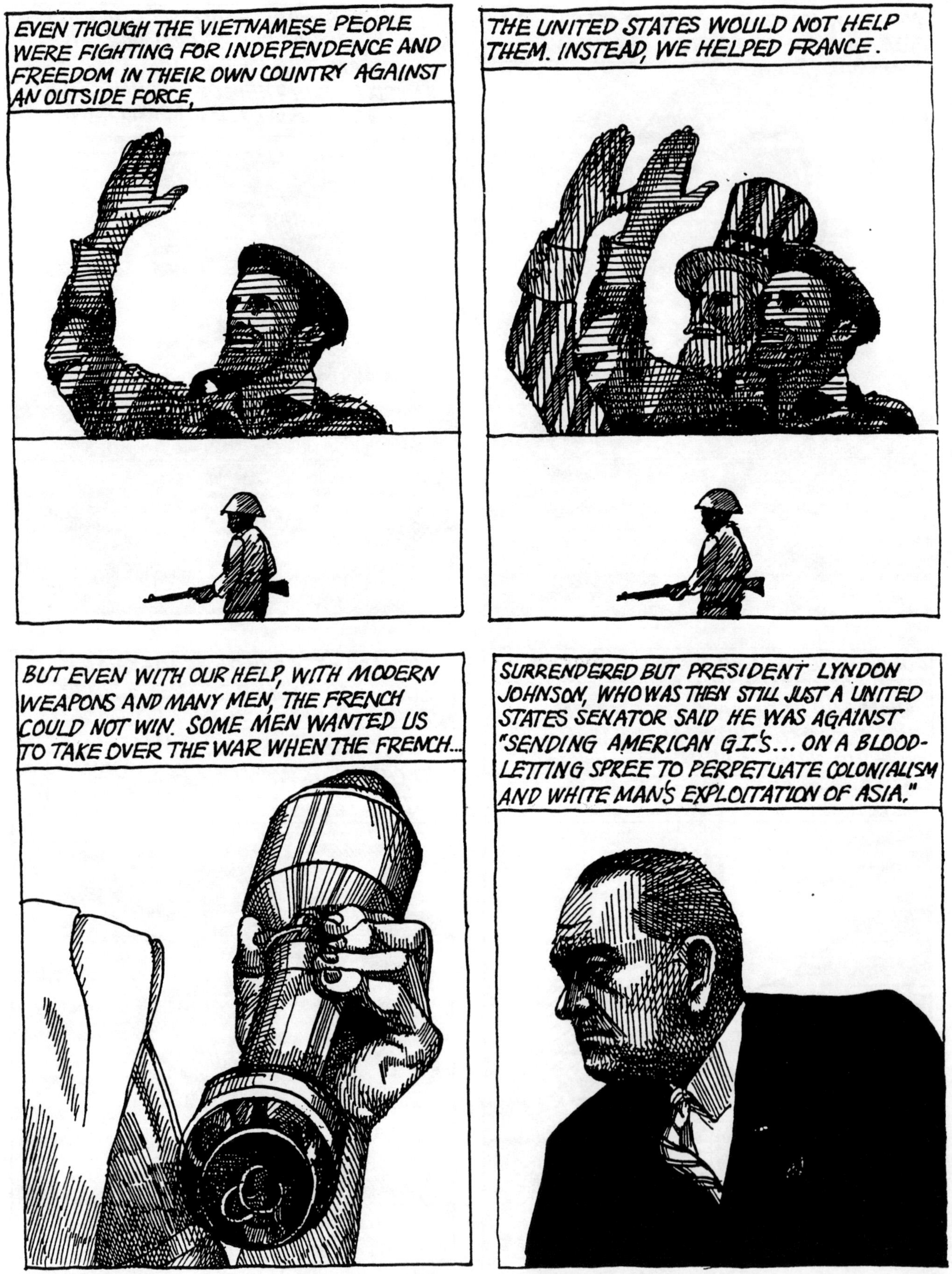
EVEN THOUGH THE VIETNAMESE PEOPLE WERE FIGHTING FOR INDEPENDENCE AND FREEDOM IN THEIR OWN COUNTRY AGAINST AN OUTSIDE FORCE,
THE UNITED STATES WOULD NOT HELP THEM. INSTEAD, WE HELPED FRANCE.
BUT EVEN WITH OUR HELP, WITH MODERN WEAPONS AND MANY MEN, THE FRENCH COULD NOT WIN. SOME MEN WANTED US TO TAKE OVER THE WAR WHEN THE FRENCH...
SURRENDERED BUT PRESIDENT LYNDON JOHNSON, WHO WAS THEN STILL JUST A UNITED STATES SENATOR SAID HE WAS AGAINST "SENDING AMERICAN G.I.'S... ON A BLOOD-LETTING SPREE TO PERPETUATE COLONIALISM AND WHITE MAN'S EXPLOITATION OF ASIA."

BECAUSE WE DIDN'T WANT THE PEOPLE OF VIETNAM TO SELECT A MAN WE DIDN'T LIKE, WE SET UP A MAN NAMED NGO DINH DIEM AS PRESIDENT OF SOUTH VIETNAM AND HELPED HIM HOLD TWO ELECTIONS IN THE SOUTHERN PART OF THE COUNTRY.
THE ELECTIONS VIOLATED THE AGREEMENT WHICH HAD ENDED THE FIGHTING.
THE DIEM GOVERNMENT IN SOUTH VIETNAM ARRESTED, TORTURED AND KILLED MANY PEOPLE WHO DID NOT AGREE WITH IT.
IN DECEMBER, 1960, THE NATIONAL LIBERATION FRONT WAS FORMED.
SOME PEOPLE HERE CALLED IT THE "VIET CONG" LIKE PEOPLE WHO DON'T LIKE NEGROES CALL US "NIGGERS."

BUT WE ALSO SAY WE WANT THE VIETNAMESE PEOPLE TO CHOOSE THEIR OWN GOVERNMENT, AND THEN WE WON'T EVEN LET COMMUNISTS RUN FOR OFFICE.
WE SAY THE NORTH [redacted] GOVERNMENT WILL NOT NEGOTIATE WITH US, BUT THEY HAVE TRIED TO TALK WITH US SEVEN TIMES SINCE SEPTEMBER, 1964.
WE ARE WORRIED ABOUT FIGHTING A WAR AGAINST POVERTY IN AMERICA.
BUT WE SPEND $499,999.96 FOR EVERY ENEMY SOLDIER WE KILL OR CAPTURE WHILE PEOPLE STARVE AND GO WITHOUT GOOD JOBS AT HOME.

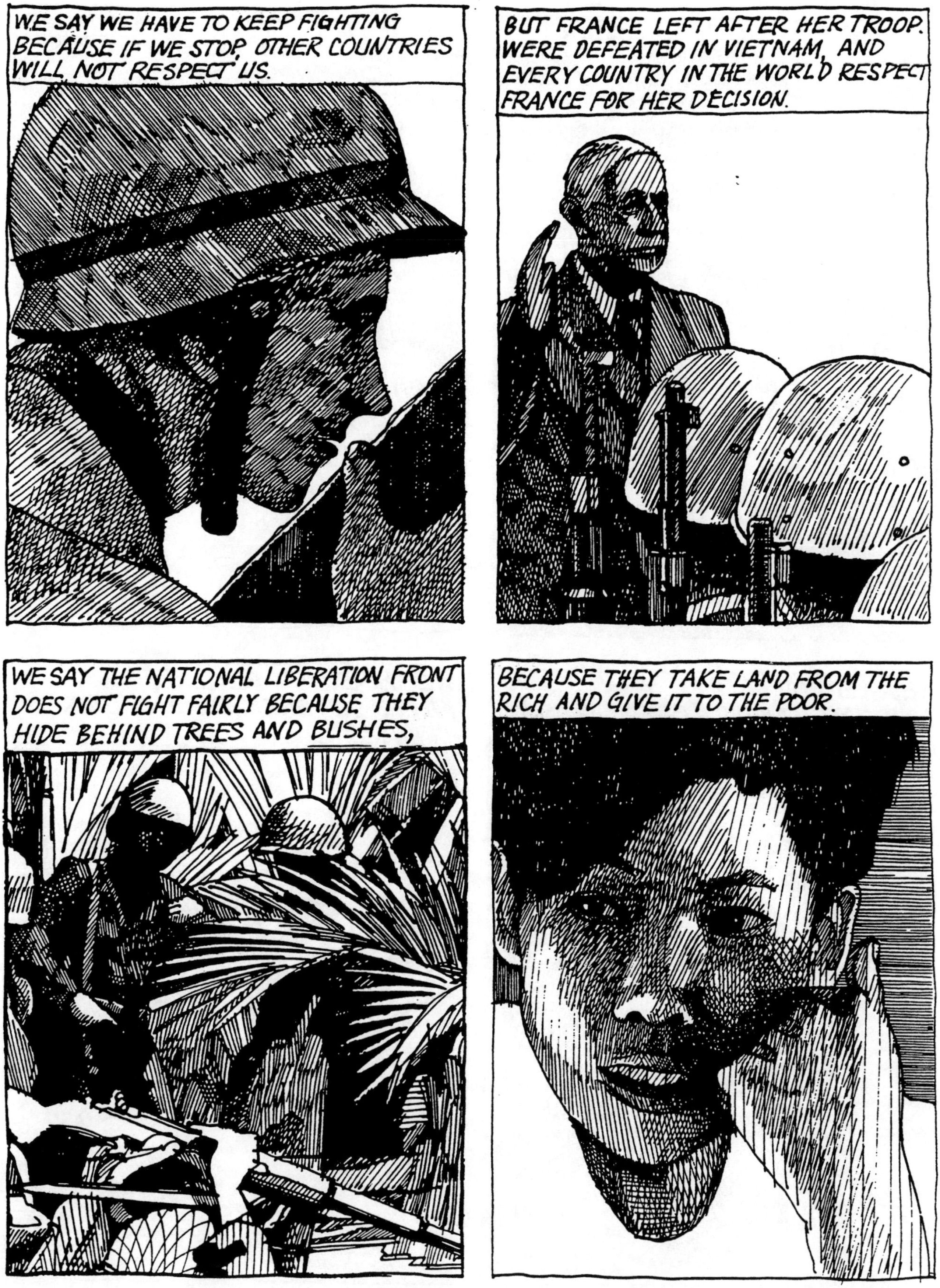
WE SAY WE HAVE TO KEEP FIGHTING
BECAUSE IF WE STOP, OTHER COUNTRIES
WILL NOT RESPECT US.
BUT FRANCE LEFT AFTER HER TROOP.
WERE DEFEATED IN VIETNAM, AND
EVERY COUNTRY IN THE WORLD RESPECT
FRANCE FOR HER DECISION.
WE SAY THE NATIONAL LIBERATION FRONT
DOES NOT FIGHT FAIRLY BECAUSE THEY
HIDE BEHIND TREES AND BUSHES,
BECAUSE THEY TAKE LAND FROM THE
RICH AND GIVE IT TO THE POOR.

BECAUSE THEY KILL THEIR ENEMIES.
BUT WE HID BEHIND TREES AND BUSHES WHEN WE FOUGHT THE BRITISH FOR OUR INDEPENDENCE.
WE ASKED FOR HELP FROM ANY COUNTRY THAT WOULD GIVE IT TO US (FRANCE, SPAIN AND HOLLAND DID GIVE US TROOPS AND AID).
WE TARRED AND FEATHERED AND KILLED OUR ENEMIES, AND TOOK THEIR LAND.

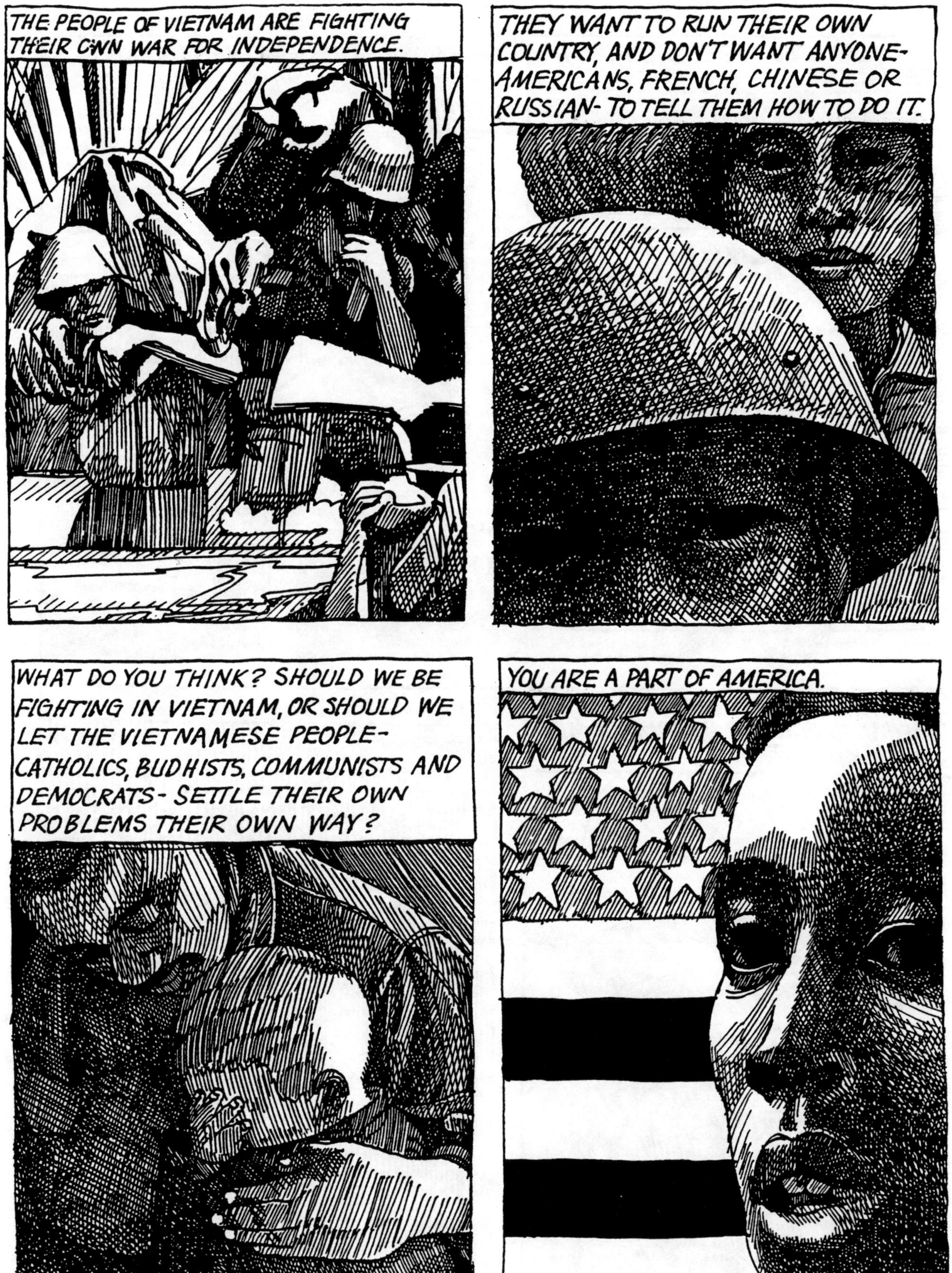
THE PEOPLE OF VIETNAM ARE FIGHTING THEIR OWN WAR FOR INDEPENDENCE.
THEY WANT TO RUN THEIR OWN COUNTRY, AND DON'T WANT ANYONE- AMERICANS, FRENCH, CHINESE OR RUSSIAN- TO TELL THEM HOW TO DO IT.
WHAT DO YOU THINK? SHOULD WE BE FIGHTING IN VIETNAM, OR SHOULD WE LET THE VIETNAMESE PEOPLE- CATHOLICS, BUDHISTS, COMMUNISTS AND DEMOCRATS- SETTLE THEIR OWN PROBLEMS THEIR OWN WAY?
YOU ARE A PART OF AMERICA.

YOU ARE SUPPOSED TO BE A PART OF THE GOVERNMENT.
REGISTER TO VOTE
MEN YOU VOTE FOR HELP MAKE THIS WAR POSSIBLE. WILL YOU VOTE FOR THEM AGAIN?
OR WILL THE WAR IN VIETNAM - THE WAR THAT IS FOUGHT IN YOUR NAME - KEEP ON KILLING?
WHAT DO YOU THINK?

UNIT 13

COMPETING FORCES II

INTRODUCTION 770

13-1 • FROM CIVIL RIGHTS TO BLACK POWER: THE CASE OF SNCC, 1960–1966 771
Allen J. Matusow

13-2 • SCLC TACKLES ECONOMIC PROBLEMS 788

13-3 • A MOVEMENT TURNS TO ECONOMICS 790
MISSISSIPPI REVISITED
Liz Shirah

13-4 • THE SNCC TRENDS: CHALLENGE TO WHITE AMERICA 793
Anne Braden

13-5 • BLACK—WHITE RELATIONS: A TIME OF SEARCHING 800
Virginia Collins and Ed Hamlett

13-6 • BLACK POWER: ITS NEED AND SUBSTANCE 804
Stokely Carmichael and Charles V. Hamilton

13-7 • LIBERATION BY ANY MEANS NECESSARY 815
ADDRESS TO A MEETING IN NEW YORK, 1964
Malcolm X

INTRODUCTION

By the mid-1960s many activists in the civil rights movement realized that integrated public accommodations and voting rights left other basic problems of a long segregated society untouched. As the 1960s wore on, more and more activists confronted the numerous economic problems that hobbled African Americans in the South. 13-2 and 13-3 sample the views of a major civil rights organization and of local activists in Mississippi on economic equality.

After passage of the 1964 Civil Rights Act and the 1965 Voting Rights Act, long simmering tensions between white and black activists over the role of whites in the movement rose to the surface. "From Civil Rights to Black Power" (13-1) provides one overview of SNCC's history with an emphasis on the development of a "black power" ideology in the group. 13-2 from the *Southern Patriot* examines Martin Luther King's and the Southern Christian Leadership Conference's shift toward an emphasis on economic issues. 13-3 focuses on the Mississippi movement's focus on economics.

Two 1966 *Southern Patriot* articles from the special issue on black-white relations are reprinted as 13-4 and 13-5. The first article is a long review of the issues involved by the *Patriot's* editors; the second contrasts the opinions of a white student activist and a black student activist concerning the role of whites in the movement.

13-6 is Stokely Carmichael's and Charles Hamilton's description of Black Power, and 13-7 is Malcolm X's speech "By Any Means Necessary."

UNIT 13-1

From Civil Rights to Black Power: The Case of SNCC, 1960–1966

Allen J. Matusow

The transformation of black protest in the 1960s from civil rights to black power has seemed in retrospect an inevitable development. When the inherent limitations of the civil rights movement finally became apparent and when the expectations that the movement created met frustration, some kind of militant reaction in the black community seemed certain. However predictable this development may have been, it tells little about the concrete events that led to the abandonment of the civil rights program and to the adoption of a doctrine that is in many ways its opposite. For black power was not plucked whole from impersonal historical forces; nor was its content the only possible expression of rising black militancy. Rather, black power both as a slogan and a doctrine was in large measure the creation of a small group of civil rights workers who in the early 1960s manned the barricades of black protest in the Deep South. The group was called the Student Nonviolent Coordinating Committee (SNCC). Through its spokesman, Stokely Carmichael, SNCC first proclaimed black power and then became its foremost theoretician. Others would offer glosses on black power that differed from SNCC's concept, but because SNCC had contributed so much to the civil rights movement, no other group could speak with so much authority or command a comparable audience. Although SNCC borrowed freely from many sources to fashion black power into a doctrine, the elements of that doctrine were in the main the results of SNCC's own history. An examination of that history reveals not only the roots of black power but also the sad fate of the whole civil rights movement.

Founded in 1960, SNCC was an outgrowth of the historic sit-in movement, which began in Greensboro, North Carolina, on February 1 of that year. Four freshmen from a

---

Allen J. Matusow, "From Civil Rights to Black Power: The Case of SNCC, 1960–1966," in Barton J. Bernstein and Allen J. Matusow, eds., *Twentieth Century America: Recent Interpretations*, Harcourt Brace Jovanovich, 1969, pp. 531–536.

local Negro college attempted to desegregate the lunch counter at a Woolworth's five and ten store. The example of these four sent shock waves through the black colleges of the South and created overnight a base for a campaign of massive civil disobedience. The new generation of black students seemed suddenly unwilling to wait any longer for emancipation at the hands of the federal courts and in the next months supplied most of the recruits for the nonviolent army of 50,000 that rose spontaneously and integrated public facilities in 140 Southern cities. For the students on the picket lines, the prophet of the sit-in movement was Dr. Martin Luther King, the leader of the successful Montgomery bus boycott of 1955–56. The students found in King's nonviolent philosophy a ready-made ethic, a tactic, and a conviction of righteousness strong enough to sustain them on a sometimes hazardous mission.[1] It was King's organization, the Southern Christian Leadership Conference (SCLC), that first suggested the need for some central direction of the sit-in movement. At the invitation of SCLC's executive secretary, some 300 activist students from throughout the South met in Raleigh, North Carolina, in April 1960, to discuss their problems. The students agreed to form a coordinating body. which became SNCC, and in May 1960, hired a secretary and opened an office in Atlanta. In October the organization decided to become a permanent one, and 235 delegates approved a founding statement inspired by King's philosophy:

> We affirm the philosophical or religious ideal of nonviolence as the foundation of our purpose, the presupposition of our belief, and the manner of our action. . . . Through nonviolence, courage dissipates fear. Love transcends hate. Acceptance dissipates prejudice; hope ends despair. Faith reconciles doubt. Peace dominates war. Mutual regards cancel enmity. Justice for all overwhelms injustice. The redemptive community supersedes immoral social systems.[2]

In truth, the Christian rhetoric of SNCC's founding statement was not appropriate. The author of the statement was James Lawson, a young minister who never actually belonged to SNCC.[3] Most of the students who rallied to the sit-ins in 1960 accepted King's teachings more out of convenience than conviction and respected his courage more than his philosophy. For while King believed that Christian love was an end in itself and that Negro nonviolence would redeem American society, the students preferred to participate in America rather than to transform it. Sociologists who examined the attitudes of protesters in the black colleges found not alienation from American middle-class values but a desire to share fully in middle-class life.[4] In a perceptive piece written for *Dissent*, Michael Walzer supported these findings from his own first-hand impressions of the sit-ins. Walzer concluded that the students were materialistic as well as moral, were "willing to take risks in the name of both prosperity and virtue," and had as their goal "assimilation into American society." As for nonviolence, Walzer wrote, "I was told often that 'when one side has all the guns, then the other side is non-violent.'"[5]

In the beginning, the philosophical inconsistencies of the sit-ins did not trouble SNCC, for it stood at the forefront of a movement whose ultimate triumph seemed not far distant. But within months, as mysteriously as it began, the sit-in movement vanished. By the spring of 1961 the black campuses had lapsed into their customary quiescence, their contribution to the civil rights movement at an end. As for SNCC, since October 1960, the student representatives from each Southern state had been meeting monthly to squander their energies trying to coordinate a movement that was first too amorphous and then suddenly moribund. SNCC's attempts in early 1961 to raise up new hosts of students proved ineffectual, and lacking followers, the organization seemed without a future.[6] Then in May 1961, the Freedom Rides restored a sense of urgency to the civil rights movement and gave SNCC a second life.

On May 14, 1961, members of the Congress of Racial Equality (CORE) began the Freedom Rides to test a Supreme Court decision outlawing segregation in transportation terminals. On May 20, after one of CORE's integrated buses was bombed near Anniston, Alabama, and another was mobbed in Birmingham, CORE decided to call off its rides. But amid sensational publicity, students from Nashville and Atlanta, many associated with SNCC, rushed to Birmingham to continue the journey to New Orleans. After mobs assaulted this second wave of riders, the Federal Government stepped in to protect them, and they were permitted to go as far as Jackson, where local authorities put them in jail for defying segregation ordinances. Throughout the summer of 1961 some 300 citizens from all over America took Freedom Rides that brought them to the jails of Jackson.[7] For SNCC the Freedom Rides provided a temporary outlet for activism and, more important, inspired radical changes in the structure and purpose of the organization.

Perhaps the most important result of the Freedom Rides for SNCC was to focus its attention on the Deep South. Most of the sit-ins had occurred in the cities and larger towns of the Upper South, and the victories there had come with relative ease. Now the magnitude of the task confronting the civil rights movement became clearer. As some in SNCC had already perceived, sit-ins to desegregate public places offered no meaningful benefits to poverty-stricken tenant farmers in, say, Mississippi. In order to mobilize the black communities in the Deep South to fight for their rights, sporadic student demonstrations would be less useful than sustained efforts by full time field workers.[8] In the summer of 1961, as SNCC was beginning to grope toward the concept of community action, the Federal Government stepped in with an attractive suggestion.

Embarrassed by the Freedom Rides, Attorney General Robert F. Kennedy moved to direct the civil rights movement into paths that, in his view, were more constructive. Kennedy suggested that the civil rights organizations jointly sponsor a campaign to register Southern black voters. Such a drive, its proponents argued, would be difficult for even extreme segregationists to oppose and eventually might liberalize the Southern delegation in Congress. When the Justice Department seemed to offer federal protection for registration workers and when white liberals outside the Administration procured foundation money to finance anticipated costs, the civil rights groups agreed to undertake the project.[9] Within SNCC, advocates of direct action fought acceptance of the project, but the issue was compromised and a threatened split was averted. SNCC's decision to mobilize black communities behind efforts to secure political rights decisively changed the character of the organization. It thereafter ceased to be an extracurricular activity of student leaders and became instead the vocation of dedicated young men and women who temporarily abandoned their careers to become full time paid workers (or "field secretaries") in the movement. Moreover, as SNCC workers drifted away from the black campuses and began living among Deep South blacks, they cast aside the middle-class goals that had motivated the sit-ins of 1960 and put on the overalls of the poor. Begun as middle-class protest, SNCC was developing revolutionary potential.[10]

In Mississippi the major civil rights groups (NAACP, SCLC, CORE, and SNCC) ostensibly joined together to form the Council of Federated Organizations (COFO) to register black voters. But in reality, except for one Mississippi congressional district where CORE had a project of its own, COFO was manned almost entirely by SNCC people. The director of COFO was SNCC's now legendary Robert Moses, a product of Harlem with a Masters degree in philosophy from Harvard, whose courage and humanity made him the most respected figure in the organization. Moses had entered Pike County, Mississippi, alone in 1961, stayed on in spite of a beating and a jail term, and in the spring of 1962 became COFO's director in charge of voting projects in Vicksburg, Cleveland, Greenwood, and a few other Mississippi towns.[11] Although SNCC also had registration projects in Arkansas, Alabama, and Georgia, it concentrated on Mississippi, where the obstacles were greatest.

Throughout 1962 and into 1963 SNCC workers endured assaults, offered brave challenges to local power structures, and exhorted local blacks to shake off fear and stand up for freedom. But SNCC scored no breakthroughs to sustain morale, and while its goals remained outwardly unchanged, its mood was turning bitter. To SNCC the hostility of local racists was not nearly so infuriating as the apparent betrayal that it suffered at the hands of the Justice Department. SNCC believed that in 1961 the Kennedy Administration had guaranteed protection to registration workers, but in Mississippi in 1962 and 1963, SNCC's only contact with federal authority consisted of the FBI agents who stood by taking notes while local policemen beat up SNCC members. SNCC and its supporters insisted that existing law empowered the Federal Government to intervene, but the Justice Department contended that it was in fact powerless. SNCC doubted the sincerity of the Government's arguments and became convinced that the Kennedys had broken a solemn promise for political reasons.[12] Thus by 1963 SNCC was already becoming estranged from established authority and suspicious of liberal politicians.

SNCC's growing sense of alienation cut it off even from other civil rights organizations and most importantly from Dr. King, who by 1963 had become a fallen idol for SNCC workers. They believed that King was too willing to compromise, wielded too much power, and too successfully monopolized the funds of the movement. Doubts about King had arisen as early as the Freedom Rides, when students turned to him for advice and leadership and received what they considered only vague sympathy. In fact, after CORE called off the first ride, King privately supported Robert Kennedy's plea for a "cooling-off" period. But much to SNCC's annoyance, when militant voices prevailed and the rides continued, the press gave King all the credit.[13] In Albany, Georgia, in December 1961, after SNCC aroused the black population to pack the local jails for freedom, King came to town, got arrested, monopolized the headlines, and almost stole the leadership of the Albany campaign from SNCC.[14] In SNCC's view, dependence on King's charisma actually weakened the civil rights movement, for it discouraged development of leadership at the grass-roots level. Why, SNCC asked, did King use his huge share of civil rights money to maintain a large staff in Atlanta, and why did he never account for the funds that he so skillfully collected?[15] As King lost influence on SNCC, dissenting attitudes about nonviolence, implicit since 1960, came to be frankly articulated. When Robert Penn Warren asked Robert Moses what he thought of King's philosophy, Moses replied,

> We don't agree with it, in a sense. The majority of the students are not sympathetic to the idea that they have to love the white people that they are struggling against. . . . For most of the members, it is tactical, it's a question of being able to have a method of attack rather than to be always on the defensive.[16]

During the March on Washington in August 1963, the nation almost caught a glimpse of SNCC's growing anger. John Lewis, the chairman of SNCC and one of the scheduled speakers, threatened to disrupt the harmony of that happy occasion by saying what he really thought. Only with difficulty did moderates persuade Lewis to delete the harshest passages of his address. So the nation did not know that SNCC scorned Kennedy's civil rights bill as "too little and too late." Lewis had intended to ask the 250,000 people gathered at the Lincoln Memorial,

> What is there in this bill to insure the equality of a maid who earns $5 a week in the home of a family whose income is $100,000 a year? . . . This nation is still a place of cheap political leaders who build their careers on immoral compromises and ally themselves with open forms of political, economic, and social exploitation. . . . The party of Kennedy is also the party of Eastland. The party of Javits is also the party of Goldwater. Where is *our* party? . . . We cannot depend on any political party, for the Democrats and the Republicans have betrayed the basic principles of the Declaration of Independence.

In those remarks that he never delivered, Lewis used both the language of Christian protest and images alive with the rage of SNCC field workers. "In the struggle we must seek more than mere civil rights; we must work for the community of love, peace, and true brotherhood." And,

> the time will come when we will not confine our marching to Washington. We will march through the South, through the heart of Dixie, the way Sherman did. We shall pursue our "scorched earth" policy and burn Jim Crow to the ground—nonviolently. We shall fragment the South into a thousand pieces and put them back together in the image of democracy.[17]

The crucial milestone of SNCC's road to radicalism was the Freedom Summer of 1964. Freedom Summer grew out of a remarkable mock election sponsored by SNCC in the autumn of 1963. Because the mass of Mississippi's black population could not legally participate in choosing the state's governor that year, Robert Moses conceived a freedom election to protest mass disfranchisement and to educate Mississippi's blacks to the mechanics of the political process. COFO organized a new party called the Mississippi Freedom Democrats, printed its own ballots, and in October conducted its own poll. Overwhelming the regular party candidates, Aaron Henry, head of the state NAACP and Freedom Democratic nominee for governor, received 70,000 votes, a tremendous protest against the denial of equal political rights. One reason for the success of the project was the presence in the state of 100 Yale and Stanford students, who worked for two weeks with SNCC on the election. SNCC was sufficiently impressed by the student contribution to consider inviting hundreds more to spend an entire summer in Mississippi. Sponsors of this plan hoped not only for workers but for publicity that might at last focus national attention on Mississippi.[18] By the winter of 1963–64, however, rising militancy in SNCC had begun to take on the overtones of black nationalism, and some of the membership resisted the summer project on the grounds that most of the volunteers would be white.

Present from the beginning, by mid-1964 whites made up one-fifth of SNCC's approximately 150 full time field secretaries. Though whites had suffered their fair share of beatings, some blacks in SNCC were expressing doubts about the role of white men in a movement for black freedom. At a staff meeting at Greenville, Mississippi, in November 1963, a debate on the proposed Freedom Summer brought the issue of white-black relations into the open. In his book *SNCC: The New Abolitionists*, Howard Zinn, who attended this meeting, summarizes the views of the militants:

> Four or five of the Negro staff members now urged that the role of whites be limited. For whites to talk to Mississippi Negroes about voter registration, they said, only reinforced the Southern Negro's tendency to believe that whites were superior. Whites tended to take over leadership roles in the movement, thus preventing Southern Negroes from being trained to lead. Why didn't whites just work in the white Southern community? One man noted that in Africa the new nations were training black Africans to take over all important government positions. Another told of meeting a Black Muslim in Atlanta who warned him that whites were taking over the movement. "I had the feeling inside. I felt what he said was true."

But Fannie Lou Hamer disagreed. Mrs. Hamer had been a time-keeper on a cotton plantation and was one of the local Mississippi blacks whom SNCC discovered and elevated to leadership. Speaking for the majority of the meeting, she said, "If we're trying to break down this barrier of segregation, we can't segregate ourselves." Thus in February 1964, SNCC sent an invitation to Northern college students to spend their summer vacation in Mississippi.[19]

In retrospect, the summer of 1964 was a turning point in the civil rights movement. When the summer began, SNCC was still operating within the framework of liberal

America, still committed to integration and equal political rights for all citizens. But by the end of the summer of 1964, the fraying cords that bound SNCC to liberal goals and values finally snapped. In a sense, much of later black power thought was merely a postscript to SNCC's ill-fated summer project.

In June 1964, more than 700 selected students, judged by a staff psychiatrist at MIT to be "an extraordinarily healthy bunch of kids,"[20] came to Oxford, Ohio, for two week-long orientation sessions conducted by veteran SNCC workers. The atmosphere in Oxford, tense from the outset, became on June 22 pervaded with gloom. Robert Moses quietly told the volunteers that three workers had gone into Neshoba county in Mississippi the day before and had not been heard from since. One was Michael Schwerner, a CORE staff member; the second was James Chaney, a black SNCC worker from Mississippi; and the third was Andrew Goodman, a student volunteer who had finished his orientation in Ohio a few days before.[21] (In August the bodies of these three were discovered in their shallow graves near Philadelphia, Mississippi.)

The volunteers in Ohio had to face not only their own fear but also unanticipated hostility from the SNCC workers whom they had come to assist. Tensions between black workers and white volunteers seethed under the surface for some days and then finally erupted. One night SNCC showed a film of a grotesque voting registrar turning away black applicants. When the student audience laughed at the scene, six SNCC people walked out, enraged at what they considered an insensitive response. There followed an exchange between the workers and the volunteers, in which the students complained that the staff was distant, uncommunicative, and "looked down on us for not having been through what they had." A SNCC worker replied,

> If you get mad at us for walking out, just wait until they break your head in, and see if you don't have something to get mad about. Ask Jimmy Travis over there what he thinks about the project. What does he think about Mississippi? He has six slugs in him, man, and the last one went right through the back of his neck when he was driving a car outside Greenwood. Ask Jesse here—he has been beaten so that we wouldn't recognize him time and time and time and time again. If you don't get scared, pack up and get the hell out of here because we don't need any favors of people who don't know what they are doing here in the first place.

The bitter words seemed to have a cathartic effect, and the meeting culminated in emotional singing. Said one volunteer a bit too optimistically, "The crisis is past, I think."[22]

From one perspective the story of the two months that followed is one of the human spirit triumphant. Though three more people were killed, eighty others were beaten, thirty-five churches were burned, and thirty other buildings bombed, few turned back; black and white together, the civil rights workers in Mississippi worked for racial justice.[23] The student volunteers taught in Freedom Schools, where 3,000 children were given their first glimpse of a world beyond Mississippi. They organized the disfranchised to march on county courthouses to face unyielding registrars. Most importantly, they walked the roads of Mississippi for the Freedom Democratic Party (FDP). Denying the legitimacy of the segregated Democratic party, COFO opened the FDP to members of all races and declared the party's loyalty to Lyndon Johnson. The goal of the FDP in the summer of 1964 was to send a delegation to the Democratic convention in Atlantic City to challenge the credentials of the regular Democrats and cast the state's vote for the party's nominees. To mount this challenge against the racist Democrats of Mississippi, COFO enrolled 60,000 members in the FDP and then organized precinct, county, and state conventions to choose 68 integrated delegates to go north. The FDP, in which tens of thousands of black Mississippi citizens invested tremendous hopes, was a true grass-roots political movement and the greatest achievement of Freedom Summer.[24]

Although the FDP brought to Atlantic City little more than a sense of moral outrage, it nevertheless managed to transform its challenge of the Mississippi regulars into a major threat to the peace of the national party. Mrs. Hamer helped make this feat possible by her electrifying (and televised) testimony before the credentials committee on how Mississippi policemen had beaten her up for trying to register to vote. As Northern liberals began rallying to the FDP, the managers of the convention sought a compromise that would satisfy the liberals and at the same time keep the bulk of the Southern delegations in the convention. President Johnson favored a proposal to seat all the Mississippi regulars who pledged their loyalty to the party, to deny any voting rights to the FDP delegates, but to permit them to sit on the floor of the convention. In addition, he proposed that at future conventions no state delegations chosen by racially discriminatory procedures would be accredited. But because this compromise denied the FDP's claims of legitimacy, the FDP and many liberals declared it unacceptable and threatened to take their case to the floor of the convention, a prospect that greatly displeased the President. Johnson then sent Senator Hubert Humphrey to Atlantic City to act as his agent in settling the controversy. Unsubstantiated rumors had it that if Humphrey's mission failed, the President would deny the Senator the party's vice-presidential nomination. In close touch with both the White House and the credentials committee, Humphrey proposed altering the original compromise by permitting two FDP delegates to sit in the convention as delegates at large with full voting rights. This was as far as Johnson would go, and at the time it seemed far enough. Though the Mississippi white regulars walked out, no Southern delegations followed them, and, at the same time, most liberals felt that the Administration had made a genuine concession. Black leaders, including Dr. King. pleaded with the FDP to accept Humphrey's compromise. But the FDP denied that the compromise was in any sense a victory.[25] Angered at Humphrey's insistence that he alone choose the two at-large delegates, the FDP announced that it had not come to Atlantic City "begging for crumbs."[26] Mrs. Hamer, by now a minor national celebrity, said of Humphrey's efforts, "It's a token of rights on the back row that we get in Mississippi. We didn't come all this way for that mess again."[27]

To the general public the FDP appeared to be a band of moral zealots hostile to reasonable compromise and ungrateful for the real concession that the party had offered. The true story was more complicated. Aware that total victory was impossible, the FDP had in fact been quite willing to accept any proposal that recognized its legitimacy. At the beginning of the controversy Oregon's Congresswoman Edith Green offered a compromise that the FDP found entirely acceptable. Mrs. Green proposed that the convention seat every member of both delegations who signed a pledge of loyalty and that Mississippi's vote be divided between the two groups according to the number of seated delegates in each. Since only eleven members of the credentials committee (10 percent of the total) had to sign a minority report to dislodge the Green compromise from committee, the FDP seemed assured that its case would reach the convention floor, where many believed that the Green compromise would prevail over Johnson's original proposal. FDP's hopes for a minority report rested chiefly on Joseph Rauh, a member of the credentials committee, leader of the Democratic party in the District of Columbia, veteran of innumerable liberal crusades, and, happily, adviser and legal counsel of the FDP. But Rauh was also a friend of Hubert Humphrey and an attorney for Humphrey's strong supporter, Walter Reuther. After Humphrey came on the scene with his compromise, Rauh backed away from the minority report.

In his semi-official history of the Mississippi Summer Project, *The Summer That Didn't End*, Len Holt presents the FDP and SNCC interpretation of what happened. Presumably pressured by his powerful friends, Rauh broke a promise to the FDP and would not support the Green compromise. One by one the FDP's other allies on the committee backed away—some to protect jobs, others to keep alive hopes for federal judgeships, and one because he feared the loss of a local antipoverty program. In the end the FDP failed to collect the needed signatures, and there was no minority report. The angry rhetoric that the FDP delegates let loose in Atlantic City was in reality inspired less by Humphrey's compromise than by what the FDP regarded as its betrayal at the hands of the white liberals on the credentials committee. By the end of the Democratic convention SNCC was convinced that membership in the Democratic coalition held little hope for Southern blacks and that, lacking power, they would always be sold out by the liberals. In Atlantic City the phrase "white power structure" took on concrete meaning. Freedom Summer, which began with SNCC fighting for entrance into the American political system, ended with the radical conviction that that system was beyond redemption.[28]

In the end the Freedom Summer Project of 1964 not only destroyed SNCC's faith in the American political system; it also undermined its commitment to integration. Within the project racial tensions between white and black workers were never successfully resolved. Though many white volunteers established warm relationships with the local black families that housed them,[29] healthy communication between students and veteran SNCC workers proved difficult at best. Staff members resented the officious manner of better-educated volunteers and feared that the white students were taking over the movement. "Several times," one volunteer wrote, "I've had to completely re-do press statements or letters written by one of them."[30] Said a SNCC worker, "Look at those fly-by-night freedom fighters bossing everybody around."[31] SNCC people found it hard to respect the efforts of volunteers who they knew would retreat at the end of the summer to their safe middle-class world. One sensitive white female volunteer wrote that SNCC workers "were automatically suspicious of us, the white volunteers; throughout the summer they put us to the test, and few, if any, could pass. . . . It humbled, if not humiliated, one to realize that *finally they will never accept me*."[32] By the end of the summer a spirit akin to black nationalism was rising inside the SNCC organization.

The overall failure of Freedom Summer administered a blow to SNCC's morale from which the organization almost did not recover. In November 1964, Robert Coles, a psychiatrist who had worked closely with SNCC, wrote about the tendency of veteran workers to develop battle fatigue. Even heroic temperaments, he said, could not escape the depression that inevitably results from long periods of unremitting dangers and disappointments. But by the fall of 1964 battle fatigue was no longer just the problem of individual SNCC members; it was pervading the entire organization. One patient told Coles,

> I'm tired, but so is the whole movement. We're busy worrying about our position or our finances, so we don't do anything. . . . We're becoming lifeless, just like all revolutions when they lose their first momentum and become more interested in preserving what they've won than going on to new challenges. . . . Only with us we haven't won that much, and we're either holding to the little we have as an organization, or we get bitter, and want to create a new revolution. . . . You know, one like the Muslims want which is the opposite of what we say we're for. It's as if we completely reverse ourselves because we can't get what we want.[33]

Uncertain of their purpose, SNCC workers in the winter of 1964–65 grew introspective. Months were consumed in discussing the future of whites in the movement and the proper structure of the organization. Fresh from a trip to Africa where he met the black nationalist Malcolm X, John Lewis, Chairman of SNCC, spoke for the majority in early 1965 when he demanded that blacks lead their own movement.[34] At the same time, quarrels over organization almost tore SNCC apart. Some workers became "high on freedom" and advocated a romantic anarchism that rejected bureaucratic structure and leadership. Robert Moses, for instance, believed that SNCC workers should "go where the spirit say go, and do what the spirit say do." Moses was so disturbed by his own prestige in the movement that he changed his name, drifted into Alabama, and thereafter was only vaguely connected with SNCC. Meanwhile SNCC's field work tended to fall into neglect.[35]

In the summer of 1965 SNCC brought 300 white volunteers into Mississippi for its second and last summer project. The result was a shambles. Racial tensions caused some projects to break up and prevented serious work in others. Problems only dimly perceived a year before assumed stark clarity, and SNCC's resentment of the volunteers became overt and unambiguous. At staff meetings blacks would silence white students with such remarks as "How long have you been here?" and "How do you know what it's like being black?" and "If you don't like the way we do it, get the hell out of the state."[36] Not all the blame for the final breakdown of race relations in SNCC, however, belonged to the black staff. The questionable motivation of some of the white students led Alvin Poussaint, a black psychiatrist close to SNCC, to add a new neurosis to medical terminology—the white African Queen or Tarzan complex. The victim of this neurosis harbored repressed delusions of himself as an "intelligent, brave, and handsome white man or woman, leading the poor down-trodden and oppressed black men to freedom and salvation."[37]

But the most serious obstacle to healthy race relations inside SNCC was sex, and in this dimension, as really in all others, the villain was neither black worker nor white student, but rather the sad and twisted history of race relations in America. The white girl who came South to help SNCC found herself, according to Dr. Poussaint, "at the center of an emotionally shattering crossfire of racial tensions that have been nurtured for centuries."[38] In the summer of 1965 a veteran black civil rights worker in SCLC tried to warn white girls of the perils that awaited them in their dealings with black men in the movement:

> What you have here is a man who had no possible way of being a man in the society in which he lives, save one. And that's the problem. The only way or place a Negro man has been able to express his manhood is sexually and so you find a tremendous sexual aggressiveness. And I say quite frankly, don't get carried away by it and don't get afraid of it either. I mean, don't think it's because you're so beautiful and so ravishing that this man is so enamoured of you. It's not that at all. He's just trying to find his manhood and he goes especially to the places that have robbed him of it. . . . And so, in a sense, what passes itself as desire is probably a combination of hostility and resentment—because he resents what the society has done to him and he wants to take it out on somebody who symbolizes the establishment of society.[39]

At the end of the summer a white girl spoke of her experiences:

> Well, I think that the white female should be very well prepared before she comes down here to be bombarded. And she also has to be well prepared to tell them to go to hell and be prepared to have them not give up. . . . I've never met such forward men as I have in Mississippi.[40]

The problem was complicated by the jealousy of black girls toward their white rivals, and by neurotic whites who sought to ease their guilt by permitting blacks to exploit them sexually and financially.[41] On leaving their projects to go home, a few white girls told Poussaint, "I hate Negroes."[42] By the end of the summer of 1965 no one could any longer doubt that the blacks reciprocated the feeling.

The year 1965 was a lost one for SNCC. For the first time since its founding, it was no longer on the frontier of protest, no longer the keeper of the nation's conscience, no longer the driving force of a moral revolution. The civil rights acts of 1964 and 1965 brought the civil rights movement, for which SNCC had suffered so much, to a triumphant conclusion, but SNCC had lost interest in integrated public accommodations and equal political rights. SNCC seemed to be losing its sense of mission and after years of providing heroes for the black protest movement, it now needed a hero of its own. Significantly it chose Malcolm X, the black nationalist who had been assassinated by Muslim rivals in February 1965.[43] Only a few years before, SNCC and Malcolm X had seemed to occupy opposite poles of black protest. Thus while SNCC's John Lewis was toning down his speech at the March on Washington, Malcolm X was saying,

> Who ever heard of angry revolutionists all harmonizing "We Shall Overcome . . . Suum Day . . . " while tripping and swaying along arm-in-arm with the very people they were supposed to be angrily revolting against? Who ever heard of angry revolutionists swinging their bare feet together with their oppressors in lily-pad park pools, with gospels and guitars and "I Have a Dream" speeches?[44]

While policemen were clubbing SNCC workers in Mississippi, Malcolm X was saying, "If someone puts a hand on you, send him to the cemetery."[45] While SNCC was pondering the meaning of Atlantic City, Malcolm X was saying, "We *need* a Mau Mau. If they don't want to deal with the Mississippi Freedom Democratic Party, then we'll give them something else to deal with." While black nationalists were still a minority in SNCC, Malcolm X was calling for black control of black politicians in black communities, black ownership of ghetto business and black unity "to lift the level of our community, to make our society beautiful so that we will be satisfied in our own social circles and won't be running around here trying to knock our way into a social circle where we're not wanted."[46] This was the language that had made Malcolm X the hero of the urban ghetto, and it was the language appropriate in 1965 to SNCC's militant mood. In a certain sense Malcolm X was the link that connected SNCC with the black radicalism that was arising in the North.

Unlike SNCC, the ghetto masses never had to disabuse themselves of the colorblind assumptions of the civil rights movement. Trapped permanently in their neighborhoods, the poor blacks of the North have always been painfully conscious of their racial separateness. As Essien-Udom, a historian of black nationalism, has written, blackness "is the stuff of their lives and an omnipresent, harsh reality. For this reason the Negro masses are instinctively 'race men.'"[47] But the civil rights movement nevertheless had its consequences in the ghetto. The spectacle of Southern blacks defying their white tormentors apparently inspired among Northern blacks race pride and resurgent outrage at the gap between American ideals and black realities. Thus the civil rights movement had the ironic effect of feeding the nationalist tendency in the ghetto to turn inward, to separate, and to identify the white men outside as the enemy. SNCC's frustrations exploded intellectually in the formulation of black power doctrines, but ghetto rage took the form of riot.

The riot of August 1965, in Watts (the sprawling ghetto of Los Angeles) dwarfed the violent outbursts of the previous year and awakened America to the race crisis in her big cities. A social trauma of the first order, the Watts riot resulted in 35 deaths, 600 burned and looted buildings, and 4,000 persons arrested.[48] Above all it revealed the dangerous racial hatred that had been accumulating unnoticed in the nation's black ghettos. The official autopsy of Watts denied by implication that it was a revolt against white oppression. The McCone Commission (after its chairman, John McCone), appointed by California's Governor Pat Brown to investigate the riot, estimated that only 10,000 Watts residents, or 2 percent of the population in the riot area, had actually been on the streets during the uprising. This minor fraction, the Commission contended, was not protesting specific grievances, which admittedly existed in abundance, but was engaged in an "insensate rage of destruction" that was "formless, quite senseless."[49] Critics of the McCone report have ably challenged these findings. (For example, Robert Fogelson points out that "to claim that only 10,000 Negroes rioted when about 4,000 were arrested is to presume that the police apprehended fully 40 percent of the rioters.")[50] In reality, a rather large minority of the riot-age population in Watts was on the streets during the riot, and as one of the Commission's own staff reports revealed, the riot had significant support inside the ghetto, especially in the worst slum areas.[51]

On the crucial question of the riot's causes, observers on the scene agreed that the rioters were animated by a common anger against whites.[52] Robert Blauner, a staff member for the McCone Commission and its severest critic, has written,

> Most of the actions of the rioters appear to have been informed by the desire to clear out an alien presence, white men, rather than to kill them. . . . It was primarily an attack on property, particularly white-owned businesses. . . . The spirit of the Watts rioters appears similar to that of anti-colonial crowds demonstrating against foreign masters.[53]

Said Bayard Rustin, a moderate black intellectual who was in Watts during the riot, "The whole point of the outburst in Watts was that it marked the first major rebellion of Negroes against their masochism and was carried on with the express purpose of asserting that they would no longer quietly submit to the deprivation of slum life."[54] Thus in 1965, for different reasons, both the ghetto masses and the members of SNCC were seized by militant anti-white feelings, and it was this congruence of mood that would shortly permit SNCC to appeal to a nation-wide black audience.

After a year on the periphery of the black protest movement, SNCC in 1966 moved again to the forefront. In May 1966, at a time when the organization was apparently disintegrating, 135 staff members (25 of them white) met in Nashville to thrash out their future. Early in the emotional conference, by a vote of 60 to 22, John Lewis, the gentle advocate of nonviolence, retained the chairmanship of SNCC by defeating the challenge of the militant Stokely Carmichael. But as the conference went on, the arguments of the militants began to prevail. When the staff voted to boycott the coming White House conference on civil rights, Lewis announced that he would attend anyway, and the question of the chairmanship was then reopened. This time SNCC workers chose Carmichael as their new leader by a vote of 60 to 12. The conference next issued a statement calling, among other things, for "black Americans to begin building independent political, economic, and cultural institutions that they will control and use as instruments of social change in this country."[55]

A few weeks later the full meaning of Carmichael's election became clear to the whole nation. The occasion was the famous Meredith march through Mississippi in June of 1966. James Meredith, the man who integrated the University of Mississippi in 1962 with the help of the United States Army, embarked on a 200-mile walk from Memphis to Jackson to show the black people of Mississippi that they could walk to the voting booths without fear. On June 6, 28 miles out of Memphis, a white man felled Meredith with buckshot. Erroneously believing that Meredith had been killed, civil rights leaders immediately flew to Mississippi to continue his walk against fear. So it was that arm in arm, Martin Luther King of SCLC, Floyd McKissick of CORE, and Stokely Carmichael of SNCC marched down U.S. Highway 51.

Early efforts of the three leaders to maintain surface unity rapidly broke down. Significantly, the first issue that divided them was the role of white people in the Meredith march. King's workers publicly thanked Northern whites for joining the procession. McKissick also thanked the Northerners but announced that black men must now lead the civil rights movement. And Carmichael mused aloud that maybe the whites should go home. As the column moved onto the back roads and Southern white hostility increased, the leadership of the march failed to agree on how to respond to violence. In Philadelphia, Mississippi, Dr. King conducted a memorial service for Goodman, Chaney, and Schwerner and told a crowd of 300 jeering whites that the murderers of the three men were no doubt "somewhere around me at this moment." Declaring that "I am not afraid of any man," King then delivered a Christian sermon. But after the service was over and local whites got rough, the marchers returned punch for punch.

The real spokesman for the march, it soon developed, was not King but Stokely Carmichael. In one town, after spending a few hours in jail, Carmichael told a crowd, "I ain't going to jail no more. I ain't going to jail no more," and he announced, "Every courthouse in Mississippi ought to be burned down to get rid of the dirt." Carmichael then issued the cry that would make him famous. Five times he shouted "Black Power!" and, the *New York Times* reported, "each time the younger members of the audience shouted back, 'Black Power.'" Informed of this new slogan, Dr. King expressed disapproval, and SCLC workers exhorted crowds to call not for black power but for "freedom now." Nevertheless, by the end of the Meredith march, black power had become a force to reckon with.[56]

At its inception in June, 1966, black power was not a systematic doctrine but a cry of rage. In an article in the *New York Times Magazine*, Dr. Poussaint tried to explain the psychological origin of the anger expressed in the new slogan:

> I remember treating Negro workers after they had been beaten viciously by white toughs or policemen while conducting civil rights demonstrations. I would frequently comment, "You must feel pretty angry getting beaten up like that by those bigots." Often I received a reply such as: "No, I don't hate those white men, I love them because they must really be suffering with all that hatred in their souls. Dr. King says the only way we can win our freedom is through love. Anger and hatred has never solved anything."
>
> I used to sit there and wonder, "Now, what do they really do with their rage?"

Poussaint reported that after a while these workers vented their mounting rage against each other.

> While they were talking about being nonviolent and "loving" the sheriff that just hit them over the head, they rampaged around the project houses beating up each other. I frequently had to calm Negro civil rights workers with large dose of tranquilizers for what I can describe clinically only as acute attacks of rage.

In time the civil rights workers began to direct their anger against white racists, the Federal Government, and finally white people in the movement. Said Poussaint:

> This rage was at a fever pitch for many months, before it became crystallized in the "Black Power" slogan. The workers who shouted it the loudest were those with the oldest battle scars from the terror, demoralization, and castration which they experienced through continual direct confrontation with Southern white racists. Furthermore, some of the most bellicose chanters of the slogan had been, just a few years before, examples of nonviolent, loving passive resistance in their struggle against white supremacy. These workers appeared to bc seeking a sense of inner psychological emancipation from racists through self-assertion and release of aggressive angry feelings.[57]

In the months following the Meredith march, SNCC found itself at the center of a bitter national controversy and spokesman for an enlarged constituency. The anger implicit in the slogan "black power" assured SNCC a following in the ghettos of the North and ended its regional confinement. Through its leader, Stokely Carmichael, SNCC labored through 1966 and into 1967 to give intellectual substance to the black power slogan, seeking especially to frame an analysis that would be relevant to black Americans of all sections. Although his speeches were often inflammatory, Carmichael in his writing attempted serious, even restrained, argument suitable for an educated audience. But the elements of black power were not, in truth, derived from rational reflection but from wretched experience—from the beatings, jailhouses, and abortive crusades that SNCC veterans had endured for six years. SNCC had tried nonviolence and found it psychologically destructive. (The "days of the free head-whipping are over," Carmichael and his collaborator Charles Hamilton wrote. "Black people should and must fight back."[58]) SNCC, for example, had believed in integration and tried it within its own organization, but black and white together had not worked. (Integration, said Carmichael, "is a subterfuge for the maintenance of white supremacy" and "reinforces, among both black and white, the idea that 'white' is automatically better and 'black' is by definition inferior."[59]) SNCC had allied with white liberals in the Democratic party and had come away convinced that it had been betrayed. (In dealing with blacks, Carmichael said, white liberals "perpetuate a paternalistic, colonial relationship."[60]) SNCC had struggled for equal political rights but concluded finally that political inequality was less oppressive than economic exploitation. In 1966 SNCC felt it was necessary to go beyond the assertion of these hard conclusions and to attempt to impose on them systematic form. So it was that after years of activism divorced from ideology, SNCC began to reduce its field work and concentrate on fashioning an intellectual rationale for its new militancy. At a time when the black protest movement was floundering and its future direction was uncertain, SNCC stepped forward to contribute the doctrines of black power, which were really the culmination of its career. No history of SNCC would be complete, therefore, without some consideration of those doctrines.

According to Stokely Carmichael, the black masses suffer from two different but reinforcing forms of oppression: class exploitation and white racism. To illustrate this point, he relies on an analogy apparently inspired by Franz Fanon's *Wretched of the Earth*, a book with considerable influence in black power circles. The black communities of contemporary America, Carmichael says, share many of the characteristics of African colonies under European rule. Thus as Africa once enriched its imperialist masters by exporting valuable raw materials to Europe, so now do the American ghettos "export" their labor for the profit of American capitalists. In both Africa and America, white men own local businesses and use them to drain away any wealth somehow possessed by the subject population. As in Africa, there exists in the ghetto a white power structure that is no abstraction, but is a visible and concrete presence—the white landlords, for instance, who collect rent and ignore needed repairs, the city agencies and school systems that systematically neglect black people, the policemen who abuse black citizens and collect payoffs from white racketeers. By far the most insidious method devised by the white imperialists for perpetuating class exploitation has been the use of race as a badge of inferiority. Colonial masters, says Carmichael, "purposely, judiciously, and with reckless abandon relegated the black man to a subordinated, inferior status in society. . . . White America's School of Slavery and Segregation, like the School of Colonialism, has taught the subject to hate himself and deny his humanity." As the colonies of Africa have done, black Americans must undergo "political modernization," liberate their communities, and achieve self-determination. And like Africa, the ghetto must win the struggle by its own effort.[61]

For Carmichael, liberation begins with eradication of the effects of white racism. To overcome the shame of race bred in them by white men, blacks must develop a cultural identity, rediscover the rich African civilization from which they originally came, and learn from their history that they are a "vibrant, valiant people."[62] Freed of their damaging self-image, they can begin to challenge the capitalist values that have enslaved them as a class. The white middle class, says Carmichael, has fostered esteem for "material aggrandizement," is "without a viable conscience as regards humanity," and constitutes "the backbone of institutional racism in this country." Black men, however, will develop values emphasizing "the dignity of man, not . . . the sanctity of property," "free people," not "free enterprise."[63] "The society we seek to build among black people, then, is not a capitalist one. It is a society in which the spirit of community and humanistic love prevail."[64] To complete the process of liberation, black men will have to purge the ghetto of exploiting institutions and develop structures that conform to their new values.

The reconstruction of the black community, Carmichael contends, should be in the hands of black people in order to "convey the revolutionary idea . . . that black people are able to do things themselves." Among other acts of liberation that they can perform, ghetto blacks should conduct rent strikes against slum landlords and boycotts against the ghetto merchant who refuses to "'invest' say forty to fifty percent of his net profit in the indigenous community." Governmental structures that have violated the humanity of blacks will have to be either eliminated from the ghetto or made responsive to their black constituency. The school system must be taken from professionals, most of whom have demonstrated "insensitivity to the needs and problems of the black child" and given to black parents, who will control personnel and curriculum. The indifference of the existing political parties to black people necessitates formation of separate (parallel) black organizations, both in the 110 Southern counties with black majorities and in the ghettos of the North.[65] According to Carmichael, it is simply naive to think that poor and powerless blacks have anything in common with the other components of the Democratic coalition. White liberals inevitably fall under the "overpowering influence" of their racist environment, and their demands for civil rights are "doing for blacks." Labor unions accept the existing order and, in the case of the AFL, even discriminate against black workers. Black political parties, Carmichael believes, will alone be devoted to real change and will in fact make possible emancipation from dominant American values and power centers.[66]

Carmichael professes to believe that black power is not really a departure from American practice. "Traditionally," he writes, "for each new ethnic group, the route to social and political integration into America's pluralistic society has been through the organization of their own institutions with which to represent their communal needs within the larger society."[67] Once in possession of power, blacks then could reenter the old coalitions for specific goals. But "let any ghetto group contemplating coalition be so tightly organized, so strong, that . . . it is an 'undigestible body' which cannot be absorbed or swallowed up." Given Carmichael's scheme for a radical reconstruction of American society, it is not surprising that the only group that he someday hopes to make his ally is the poor whites.[68]

As several critics have pointed out,[69] Carmichael's version of black power is hardly more than a collection of fragments, often lacking in clarity, consistency, and conviction. Thus, for example, Carmichael talks about the need for parallel institutions but offers only one example—black political organizations. He claims that these organizations can regenerate the entire political system but typically neglects to explain concretely how this regeneration is to be achieved. He calls for radical rejection of American values and institutions but at the same time portrays the black community as merely another ethnic group turning temporarily inward to prepare for later integration into American society. According to Carmichael, ghetto blacks are an exploited proletariat kept in bondage to enrich America's capitalist class; yet black workers seem more like a *lumpenproletariat* threatened with loss of economic function and forced to the margin of the American economy. Carmichael fails to reveal the mechanisms by which big business keeps the black man exploited, and indeed it seems doubtful that big business especially profits from the depressed condition of such a large group of potential consumers. But the real criticism of black power is not that as a body of thought it lacks coherence and sustained argument. Its greatest weakness is its failure to propose adequate solutions.

Carmichael began his argument by maintaining that black men suffer from two separate but related forms of discrimination—racial and economic. When Carmichael proposes ways for black men to undo the effects of racism, he makes good sense. Certainly black men should uncover their cultural roots and take pride in what has been of worth in their heritage. Certainly liberal paternalism is now anachronistic and black men should lead their own organizations. Nonviolence probably was psychologically damaging to many who practiced it, and integration into a hostile white society is not only an unrealistic goal but demeaning to a self-respecting people. Furthermore, some middle-class values, as Carmichael maintains, are less than ennobling, and elements of the black man's life style do have intrinsic merit. But it is doubtful whether black self-respect can ever be achieved without a solution of the second problem confronting ghetto blacks, and it is here that Carmichael's version of black power is most deficient.

Concerned primarily with humanizing social and governmental structures inside the ghetto, Carmichael has little to say about ending poverty in black America. Although more responsive policemen and schoolteachers and less dishonest slum lords and merchants will no doubt be a great step forward, these aspects of ghetto life are of less consequence than unemployment or poverty wages. Within the ghetto the resources for economic reconstruction are simply not available and since Carmichael rejects coalitions outside the ghetto, he is barred from offering a realistic economic strategy. It is this weakness that led the black intellectual and long-time civil rights leader Bayard Rustin to oppose black power. Pointing to the futility of separatist politics in a society in which the black man is a minority, Rustin calls for "a liberal-labor-civil rights coalition which would work to make the Democratic party truly responsive to the aspirations of the poor, and which would develop support for programs (specifically those outlined in A. Philip Randolph's $100 billion Freedom Budget) aimed at the reconstruction of American society in the interest of greater social justice."[70] Rustin's goals are considerably less apocalyptic than Carmichael's, but they are far more realistic. Carmichael's radical ruminations about a socialist alliance of poor whites and poor blacks seem fantasies irrelevant to American social realities. Although Carmichael's vision holds out hope for some distant time, it offers no meaningful proposals for the present.

The true significance of black power lies not in the doctrines into which it evolved but in the historical circumstances that gave it birth. The real message of black power is that after years of struggle to make America an open and just society, an important group of civil rights workers, instructed by the brute facts of its own history, gave up the fight. Black power was a cry of rage directed against white bigots who overcame righteous men by force, a cry of bitterness against white liberals who had only a stunted comprehension of the plight of the black poor, and a cry of frustration against gains that seemed meager when compared to needs. It is possible, however, that even rage can perform a useful function, and if the black power slogan brings about a constructive catharsis and helps rouse the black masses from apathy, then the intellectual shortcoming of black power doctrines may seem of little consequence, and what began as a cry of despair may yet play a creative role in the black protest movement. Therefore, whether the history of SNCC in this decade will be considered triumph or tragedy depends on events yet to occur.

Endnotes

1. For accounts of the sit-ins see Howard Zinn, *SNCC: The New Abolitionists* (Beacon, 1965), Chapter 2; Jack Newfield, *A Prophetic Minority* (Signet, 1966). Chapter 3; August Meier, "The Successful Sit-Ins in a Border City: A Study in Social Causation," *The Journal of Intergroup Relations*, II (Summer, 1961), 230–37; Charles U. Smith. "The Sit-Ins and the New Negro Student," *ibid.*, 223–29; James Peck, *Freedom Ride* (Simon & Schuster, 1962), Chapter 6.

2. Quoted in Newfield, *A Prophetic Minority*, p. 47.

3. Emily Schottenfeld Stoper, "Student Nonviolent Coordinating Committee: The Growth of Radicalism in a Civil Rights Organization," unpublished dissertation, Harvard University, 1968, pp. 35–36.

4. Ruth Searles and J. Allen Williams, Jr., "Negro College Students' Participation in Sit-Ins," *Social Forces* (Dec., 1966), 215–20.

5. Michael Walzer, "The Politics of the New Negro," *Dissent*, VII (Summer, 1960), 235–43.

6. Anne Braden, "The Southern Freedom Movement in Perspective," *Monthly Review*, XVII (July-Aug., 1965), 31–32; also James Howard Laue, "Direct Action and Desegregation: Toward a

Theory of the Rationalization of Protest," unpublished dissertation, Harvard University, 1965, p. 128.

7. For accounts of the Freedom Rides, see Zinn, *SNCC*, Chapter 3; and Peck, *Freedom Ride*, Chapters 8 and 9.

8. Laue, "Direct Action and Desegregation," pp. 154, 160, 167–68.

9. On origins of the voter registration drive, see Pat Watters and Reece Cleghorn, *Climbing Jacob's Ladder* (Harcourt, Brace & World, 1967), pp. 44–59; and Louis Lomax, *The Negro Revolt* (Signet, 1963), pp. 246–50.

10. Braden, "Southern Freedom Movement," p. 36; Laue, "Direct Action and Desegregation," p. 171; Stoper, "The Student Nonviolent Coordinating Committee," pp. 6 and 8.

11. For an account of Moses in Mississippi, see Zinn, *SNCC*, Chapter 4.

12. See *ibid.*, Chapter 10, and Watters and Cleghorn, *Climbing Jacob's Ladder*, p. 58.

13. Laue, "Direct Action and Desegregation," pp. 179, 338.

14. Stoper, "The Student Nonviolent Coordinating Committee," p. 104; *New York Times* (Dec. 24, 1961), section IV, 5.

15. "Integration: Hotter Fires," *Newsweek*, LXII (July 1, 1963), 19–21.

16. Robert Penn Warren, *Who Speaks for the Negro* (Random House, 1965), p. 91.

17. Quoted in Watters and Cleghorn, *Climbing Jacob's Ladder*, pp. xiv–xv.

18. On freedom ballot, see Len Holt, *The Summer That Didn't End* (William Morrow, 1965), pp. 35–36, 152–53.

19. Zinn, *SNCC*, pp. 8–9, 186–88; see also Calvin Trillin, "Letter from Jackson," *New Yorker*, XL (Aug. 29, 1964), 80–105.

20. Quoted in James Atwater, "If We Can Crack Mississippi . . . ," *Saturday Evening Post*, CCXXXVII (July 25, 1964), 16.

21. Sally Belfrage, *Freedom Summer* (Viking, 1965). p. 11.

22. Elizabeth Sutherland, ed., *Letters from Mississippi* (McGraw-Hill, 1965), pp. 5–6.

23. Watters and Cleghorn, *Climbing Jacob's Ladder*, p. 139.

24. Holt, *The Summer That Didn't End*, Chapter 8; Zinn, *SNCC*, p. 251.

25. Holt, *The Summer That Didn't End*, pp. 16–17; Watters and Cleghorn, *Climbing Jacob's Ladder*, pp. 290–92; *New York Times* (Aug. 25, 1964), 23.

26. William McCord, *Mississippi: The Long Hot Summer* (Norton, 1965), p. 117.

27. Mrs. Hamer is quoted in Holt, *The Summer That Didn't End*, p. 174.

28. *New York Times* (Aug. 25, 1964), 23; Holt, *The Summer That Didn't End*, pp. 171–78; see also Zinn, *SNCC* pp. 251–56; and Stoper, "The Student Nonviolent Coordinating Committee," pp. 74, 77–79, 81.

29. See, for instance, Sutherland, *Letters from Mississippi*, p. 48.

30. Quoted in *ibid.*, p. 202.

31. Quoted in Pat Watters, *Encounter with the Future* (Southern Regional Council, May, 1965), p. 32.

32. Belfrage, *Freedom Summer*, p. 80.

33. Robert Coles, "Social Struggle and Awareness" *Psychiatry*, XXVII (Nov., 1964), 305–15.

34. Watters, *Encounter with the Future*, pp. 29–31; see also Lerone Bennett, Jr., "SNCC, Rebels with a Cause," *Ebony*, XX (July, 1965), 146–53.

35. For the Moses quote, see Gene Roberts, "From Freedom High to 'Black Power,'" *New York Times Magazine* (Sept. 25, 1966). 21; see also Bruce Payne. "The Student Nonviolent Coordinating Committee: An Overview Two Years Later," *The Activist* (Nov., 1965), 6–7; and Stoper, "Student Nonviolent Coordinating Committee," pp. 126–27.

36. These quotations are from transcripts of informal taped interviews conducted in the South in 1965 by students of Stanford University. The tapes are stored at Stanford.

37. Alvin F. Poussaint, "Problems of White Civil Rights Workers in the South," *Psychiatric Opinion*, II (Dec., 1966), 21.

38. Alvin F. Poussaint, "The Stresses of the White Female Worker in the Civil Rights Movement in the South," *American Journal of Psychiatry*, CXXIII (Oct., 1966), 401.

39. Taped by Stanford students in 1965.

40. *Ibid.*

41. Poussaint, "Problems of White Civil Rights Workers in the South," 20–21.

42. Poussaint, "Stresses of the White Female Worker," 404.

43. On influence of Malcolm X on SNCC, see Stoper, "The Student Nonviolent Coordinating Committee." p. 181.

44. *The Autobiography of Malcolm X* (Grove Press, 1966), pp. 280–81.

45. *Malcolm X Speaks: Selected Speeches and Statements* (Merit, 1965), p. 12.

46. *Ibid.*, 38–39.

47. E. U. Essien-Udom, *Black Nationalism* (Univ. of Chicago Press 1962), p. 3.

48. A Report by the Governor's Commission on the Los Angeles Riot, *Violence in the City—An End or a Beginning?* (Dec. 2, 1965), pp. 1–2. (Referred to hereafter as the McCone Report.)

49. McCone Report, pp. 1, 4–5.

50. Robert M. Fogelson, "White on Black: A Critique of the Mccone Commission Report on the Los Angeles Riots," *Political Science Quarterly*, LXXXII (Sept., 1967), 345.

51. E. Edward Ransford, *Attitudes and Other Characteristics of Negroes in Watts, South Central and Crenshaw Areas of Los Angeles* (a staff study prepared for the McCone Commission), p. 2.

52. See, for instance, Robert Conot, *Rivers of Blood, Years of Darkness* (Bantam Books. 1967), p. 204.

53. Quoted in Robert Blauner, "Whitewash over Watts: The Failure of the McCone Commission Report," *Transaction*, III (March-April, 1966), 9.

54. Bayard Rustin, "The Watts 'Manifesto' and the McCone Report," *Commentary*, XLI (March, 1966), 30.

55. This account of Carmichael's election and the quotations from SNCC's statement are from Newfield, *A Prophetic Minority*, pp. 75–77.

56. For the Meredith march, see *New York Times*, June 7, 1966, p. 1; June 8. pp. 1 and 26; June 9, p. 1; June 12, pp. I and 82; June 17, p. 1; June 21, p. 30; June 22, p. 25.

57. Alvin F. Poussaint, "A Negro Psychiatrist Explains the Negro Psyche," *New York Times Magazine* (Aug 20, 1967), 55 ff.

58. Stokely Carmichael and Charles V. Hamilton, *Black Power: The Politics of Liberation* (Vintage, 1967), p. 52.

59. Stokely Carmichael, "What We Want," *New York Review of Books* (Sept. 22, 1966), 6.

60. Carmichael and Hamilton, *Black Power*, p. 65.

61. For the colonial analogy, see *ibid.*, Chapter 1.

62. *Ibid.*, pp. 37–39.

63. *Ibid.*, pp. 40–4.

64. Carmichael, "What We Want," 7.

65. Carmichael and Hamilton, *Black Power*, Chapter 8 and p. 166.

66. *Ibid.*, pp. 60–66.

67. Stokely Carmichael, "Toward Black Liberation," *The Massachusetts Review*, VII (Autumn, 1966), 642.

68. Carmichael and Hamilton, *Black Power*, pp. 80, 82.

69. For critiques of black power, see, for instance, Paul Feldman, "The Pathos of 'Black Power,'" *Dissent* (Jan.-Feb., 1967), 69–79; Bayard Rustin, "'Black Power' and Coalition Politics," *Commentary*, XLII (Sept., 1966), 35–40, Christopher Lasch, "The Trouble with Black Power," *New York Review of Books*, X (Feb. 29. 1968), 4 ff.

70. Bayard Rustin, "'Black Power' and Coalition Politics," 36.

UNIT 13-2

SCLC TACKLES ECONOMIC PROBLEMS

SAVANNAH, Ga.—The job of the civil rights movement now is to develop a program that can change the economic conditions of the American Negro and to build the political strength to make such a program a reality.

This was the central theme that emerged from the annual convention here of the Southern Christian Leadership Conference (SCLC).

The turn toward economics and politics has been a growing tendency in the civil rights movement for the past two years. That this turn is now becoming a central focus of SCLC is especially significant, because SCLC was originally born out of the direct-action attacks on segregation in public accommodations.

Direct action means sit-ins, stand-ins, picketing and other mass demonstrations; political action means votes and running for office and, in its most highly developed form, a shift in political power.

The public accommodations aspect of the drive against segregation meant assault on the segregated buses, lunch counters, restaurants, motels, etc.—the visible symbols of second-class citizenship; the assault on economic problems means attacking job discrimination, slum housing, poor schools, etc.

The two aspects are not mutually exclusive, but there is a definite difference in emphasis.

Partly the declining emphasis on public accommodations results form the fact that with the passage of the 1964 Civil Rights Act this battle, except for some mopping-up action, was essentially won.

But the shift started at least two years before passage of this law. The deeper reason for it is a growing realization that integrated public accommodations leave the basic problems of a segregated society untouched and unsolved.

Dr. Martin Luther King, Jr., who is president of SCLC, set the keynote here when he said in his annual report to the convention:

"Of what advantage is it to the Negro to establish that he can be served in integrated restaurants or accommodated in integrated hotels, if he is bound to the kind of financial servitude which will not allow him to take his wife out to dinner?

Southern Patriot, November 1964.

"What will it profit him to be able to send his children to an integrated school if the family income is insufficient to buy them school clothes? . . . "

The Rev. Wyatt Tee Walker, long-time leader of SCLC, spoke of thousands forced to live in slum conditions in the nation's cities. Dr. King noted that one half of all Negro families in the United States are "poor" when measured by the figure used by the Federal Government to determine poverty, income under $3,000 a year.

What is needed, Dr. King said, is a gigantic Federal program to combat these conditions—of which the current "war on poverty" can be considered only a minute and cautious beginning.

The Negro, he said, becomes "cynical and skeptical about 'war on poverty' when he reads about expenditures to photograph the moon which are many-fold larger than the cost of the anti-poverty bill . . . "

Two weapons emerged in the speeches and discussions at this convention as necessary to the civil rights movement if there is to be any national program against poverty on the scale needed.

One is more political action and political power. Dr. King said SCLC will continue to encourage mass demonstrations where they seem effective. But he said this is no longer enough.

Demonstrations alone often opened public accommodations, he noted, because they called attention to the evil, aroused the conscience of the community, and additionally eliminated the evil itself.

But when you are battling slums and poverty, demonstration can only call attention to the evil and arouse conscience; it can't present a program for removing the evil.

"For example," Dr. King explained, "demonstrations can be useful in calling attention to the fact that Negroes are tragically unemployed. . . . But billions of dollars are needed to insure full and fair employment. This is a question of creating political power to induce Congress to appropriate such a sum of money."

The second necessary weapon that got attention here is the building of new alliances with sections of the white population. This convention specifically rejected black nationalism, which holds that the Negro must go it alone.

This is significant because in some places—as Negro activists have realized that the lunch counter is not so important after all when people still live in rat-infested ghettos—the tendency has been toward militant nationalism.

SCLC has always been for unity of Negro and white but previously mainly as a moral call. That is still there but now there is also an element of practical necessity.

"The Negro people," Dr. King said, "do not themselves possess the political power to that of other groups (the religious communities, Catholic, Protestant, and Jewish, to labor, to the liberals and intellectuals) in order to create a broad and strong political force . . . "

He noted that although a greater percentage of Negroes than whites are poor by the $3,000 standard, 78 percent of the total 9 million families classified as poor in America are white. Thus if the civil rights movement can provide some motor power for a drive to win a real war on poverty, whites will benefit too. The practical necessity exists on both sides of the color line.

Bayard Rustin, a key strategist in the civil rights movement, hammered at this same theme at last fall's conference of the Student Nonviolent Coordinating Committee (see December, 1963, Patriot). He was at this SCLC meeting helping to map ways of implementing these ideas, as were the Rev. C. T. Vivian, the Rev. James Bevel and other key leaders of the nonviolent movement.

UNIT 13-3

A MOVEMENT TURNS TO ECONOMICS

MISSISSIPPI REVISITED

Liz Shirah

JACKSON, MISS.—A visit to Mississippi nearly one year after the much-publicized Summer Project reveals an array of new organizational forms, Programs and purposes, and a degree of activity little dreamed-of a year ago.

One of the most significant developments is the formation of the Mississippi Freedom Labor Union, centered in the Delta town of Shaw. This union called a strike of farm workers in several Delta counties this spring.

However, Mississippi is still a land of segregation and police terrorism, notwithstanding the increased moderation of some officials (see March *Patriot*).

As one COFO spokesman put it, "A year ago we were fighting for the right to organize in Mississippi. Now we are facing the problems of what organization and power mean, and what political power is going to mean when we get it."

Last summer's activity was largely carried out under a single structure, the Council of Federated Organizations (COFO), a united front of most civil rights groups working in the state.

Today, initiative is dispersed among the old components of COFO, new organizations such as the Mississippi Freedom Democratic Party (MFDP) and its county committees, and groups of local people organized on an ad hoc basis for specific purposes. Many of the needs these groups are trying to meet are still political, but there is a new emphasis on economic activity.

This new emphasis has come about largely because local people are defining their own goals more and more, and because much of the movement's thrust is now directed toward rural areas, especially the tough Delta region, where the most severe poverty exists. There is growing recognition that the vote will be relatively meaningless where economic bondage remains.

Southern Patriot, May 1965.

This is the significance of the recently organized Mississippi Freedom Labor Union (MFLU). Shaw, its headquarters, lies well inside the Delta, where cotton is still the mainstay of the economy. Nearly all the Negroes in the community work in the fields or in the homes of whites.

Laborers have received about $3 a day for chopping or picking cotton from sunrise to sundown. This year cotton growers decided to lower wages to $1.75 a day. Many people live in shacks on the plantations, some paying rent to the owner and buying on credit in his store. Surplus commodities are given to the most destitute during five winter months; they are cut off in April.

The Freedom Labor Union was the outgrowth of several factors. A woman from Shaw attended a workshop in Biloxi last winter, returned home and declared, "I'm not going to work for three dollars a day this summer. I'm going to school."

She and others attended daily discussion meetings during the spring at COFO centers.

COFO workers Bill Weil and Mary Sue Gellatly worked closely with Shaw residents, especially George Shelten, a nineteen-year-old farm worker. Shelton developed rapidly as an organizer; with other militant people, he has been spreading news of the union to people living on plantations.

In April, 60 people from Shaw and surrounding communities went to Greenville to picket an invitational meeting sponsored by the U.S. Department of Agriculture. The conference was scheduled to discuss the Delta labor surplus, wages, transfer of workers, and other matters affecting hundreds of Delta farm workers. No Negroes were invited.

Pickets demanding admission to the conference confronted participants at the Downtowner Motor Inn the first day of the conference. When they returned the second day, directors of the conference at first offered to admit seven; when this offer was rejected, the entire group was allowed to come in.

Encouraged by the results of this first encounter with the "powers-that-be," union people began active canvassing in Shaw, Greenville, Rosedale, and other places. People were asked to sign pledges indicating that they would support the union and a strike effort. A few signers promised to strike whether or not their action was seconded by others.

Strike demands include payment of the federal minimum wage of $1.25 an hour, adequate support for those who cannot find jobs, an end to use of workers under 16 and over 60.

The dramatic nature of these commitments is clear in the perspective of the almost totally dependent lives led by plantation people.

The Freedom Labor Union faces real difficulties. Cotton production is being automated rapidly, and no alternative source of jobs is available. New chemical weed killers have almost eliminated the need for chopping, and estimates are that in two more years no hand labor will be required on the plantations.

A three-day workshop in Shaw began to tackle some of the problems in sight. People with no experience or familiarity with trade unions groped their way toward a concept of unionism relative to their needs.

As one elderly man remarked, "We have said we would strike and now each of us wonders whether our neighbors will strike along with us. It is time to consecrate this union. We have to plan, yes, but first of all, we have to consecrate this union."

The group discussed ways of starting a strike fund. One young girl offered to do hairstyles for a dollar each. Another woman said she would throw an entertainment for teens. Someone else volunteered to do ten-cent shoe shines. In addition they offered suggestions for telling the rest of the nation about their struggles, in the hope of getting outside help.

So far, the MFLU is very broad in its concept. It is intended to be a union for all kinds of workers who are underpaid—field hands, tractor-drivers, maids and others.

Pledges have been obtained in large numbers wherever canvassers have been, and in very little time.

The implications of a broadly inclusive union militant enough to influence working conditions, pay scales, and welfare programs are important for poor people throughout the state, white as well as Negro.

The MFLU is only one manifestation of the interest in economic self-betterment.

Several kinds of economic programs have been tried in Canton. An effective boycott of white retailers in this 70 percent Negro community forced the White Citizen's Council to bargain with the movement and to create a bi-racial committee.

A farmer's cooperative in Canton has been formed to buy fertilizer and seed and is now looking for a location.

Women in Canton have taken steps to turn their Ladies Sewing Club into a profitable undertaking. They are applying for a corporation charter and plan to sell custom-made shirts.

Another phase of the Mississippi movement has centered around this year's elections for the Agricultural Stabilization and Conservation Service, boards which control crop allotments. Elections have traditionally excluded Negroes as candidates or voters.

Protests during the winter directed to the U.S. Department of Agriculture brought promises of remedial action. These promises, however, have so far produced little in concrete results.

Panola County has formed a co-operative of okra growers which has purchased seed and fertilizer. The co-op is now looking for market outlets—a broker, or, ideally, a contract.

Through movement channels, especially the Freedom Democratic Party, each of these experiments is made known to people throughout the state.

The youth phase of the movement is still primarily concerned with voter registration and direct action protests. Mississippi high school students, many of them drawn into the movement by last summer's Freedom Schools, have built an active organization, called the Mississippi Student Union. Most chapters hold weekly discussions, publish newsletters, and send delegates to monthly state-wide meetings.

The young people are also beginning to participate in the national movement of students. A chartered bus recently carried a group of MSU members to take part in the Washington march against the War in Vietnam, sponsored by Students for a Democratic Society. Like the senior Freedom Democratic Party, the youth organization is seeking a charter from the National Young Democrats, so far without success.

Ironically, some places which were very active last summer are now inactive—and this is most true in areas where organizing has met with the least harassment and violence. But new movement is appearing in areas never touched before, and even in remote areas people have an increasing sense of organization and politics which is new.

This summer county MFDP groups will determine the program and staff needs for each county and will obtain volunteer staff and program assistance through the Freedom Democratic Party. So far, most requests are for political education programs and technical or legal help in setting up economic programs.

UNIT 13-4

THE SNCC TRENDS: CHALLENGE TO WHITE AMERICA

Anne Braden

EDITOR'S NOTE

The simmering question of black-white relations in the Southern freedom movement has recently erupted into the consciousness of many people. Most of this issue of The Patriot is devoted to articles related to this question. We apologize for the length of the articles, the shortage of pictures and omission of other important news we did not have space to cover. We will try to correct this in the next issue. Meantime, the editors feel the questions discussed here are of such vital importance that they had to take precedence.

The most talked-about matter in the freedom movement in recent weeks has been developments in the Student Nonviolent Coordinating Committee (SNCC).

Most of the discussion has centered on SNCC's calls for "black power"—by which it is saying that Negroes, where they have the numbers to do so, should organize themselves into independent political groups that can win elections.

This phrase has frightened many white people. There have been new attacks on SNCC in the daily press of the country. There have been many distortions, half-truths and rumors about SNCC's policies, some of which are simply not true and others of which are gross over-simplifications.

Thus, even among some people who have been ardent supporters of SNCC since its beginning in 1960 and who want to understand its position, there has been confusion and questioning about where the organization is going.

The Southern Patriot, also long a supporter of SNCC, has delayed publication of this issue in an effort to interview as many people connected with SNCC as possible and thus bring its readers a report that can shed light where there has been mostly heat.

Southern Patriot, May 1966.

The first thing to note is that the so-called "new directions" of SNCC do not represent any sudden change of policy. Rather they are trends that have been developing over a period of years.

All that has happened recently is that certain surface events have suddenly brought these trends into public view and focus.

The surface events were that in May SNCC held a week-long staff meeting near Nashville, Tenn., tried to define its positions on basic questions. and elected new officers.

The election was widely interpreted as a "change in command." In part it was, and in part it was not.

John Lewis, who has served as SNCC chairman since 1963, was replaced by Stokely Carmichael, a young man reared in the slums of the West Indies and New York City, educated at Howard University, and now identified in the public mind with the new all-Negro political organizations he has sparked in the Black Belt Of Alabama, with the symbol of the Black Panther.

Thus his election was interpreted as a new turn toward militancy by SNCC. But Carmichael has been a part of SNCC from its earliest days and was one of the key organizers in Mississippi, where he developed many of the ideas he is now putting into effect in Alabama.

(It should be recalled that SNCC has always been militant and has long been attacked or admired for it, depending on the attitude of the viewer. Three years ago it was John Lewis who was being attacked as "too militant" at the time of the March on Washington.)

Jim Forman, who has been executive secretary of SNCC since 1961, did not run for re-election but remains a key figure in the organization. He simply decided that instead of spending most of his time fund-raising in the North he wanted to concentrate on developing new leadership among young Southern Negroes.

He was replaced as executive secretary by Mrs. Ruby Doris Robinson, former Spelman College student in Atlanta, one of the earliest sit-in leaders and an original founder of SNCC who has been a leader in the organization ever since. Cleveland Sellers, who was named program secretary in 1965, was re-elected to that post; he too is a long-time SNCC worker and was a key organizer in Mississippi.

These three—Carmichael, Sellers, and Mrs. Robinson—make up the present governing "secretariat" of SNCC. They are important as individuals in that they obviously represent the long-developing trends in SNCC that are now being brought into public focus.

These trends are the product of SNCC experiences as it has worked in the deeply racist communities of the Deep South over the past five years, and anyone with the courage to face truth must see that they represent the developing thought of the majority of Negroes in those areas.

Patriot readers are probably familiar with most of these trends, as they have been reported at intervals in these pages since 1961. The current call for "black power" is only one of these trends, and it cannot really be understood except in the context of at least three others:

1. The first is the movement of SNCC toward an increasingly close identification with the poor and disinherited Negroes of the South and of the entire country.

This began when SNCC moved from campus to community organizing in 1961, and began to work with people who were very poor and very hungry.

Obviously, this didn't happen in 1966 at the Nashville staff meeting but it helps to explain why SNCC in 1966 is rejecting the concept of coalitions with so-called moderate forces in the South.

Some SNCC people deny that white moderates exist in the Deep South. This probably depends on how the term "moderate" is defined. But one essential fact is that the people usually described as "moderate"—the white people and the Negroes who form coalitions with them—are generally people who never knew or have forgotten what it is to be poor.

SNCC simply does not believe that these people, even if they were strong enough to win elections in Alabama or elsewhere, are going to make the social and economic changes necessary to improve the life conditions of poor people. They think poor people have to do it themselves.

2. The second basic trend in SNCC is the movement away from dependence on the federal government—either for protection or action that can change poor people's lives.

THE DISILLUSIONED

That started back down the road too—when civil rights workers' calls for help brought much talk but little action, when FBI agents kept taking endless notes but people kept getting shot and beaten and killed, when new laws were passed but scantily enforced and nothing really changed in the South

Obviously this disillusioning process did not happen in 1966 at the Nashville staff meeting either, but it helps to explain why, soon after the Nashville conference, SNCC issued its statement refusing to take part in the White House Conference on civil rights because it considered it a farce and a hoax that was not going to accomplish anything.

3. The third basic trend has been SNCC's slow but steady move toward independent political organization—independent, that is, of the old political parties.

SNCC spokesmen now are saying this has always been the organization's goal—to help previously powerless people organize their own Political vehicles.

"The only difference now is that it has become possible to do it," one SNCC leader said. "Until recently the struggle had to focus on the simple right to vote and organize. Now we are to the point where we can think about what to do with the vote."

The Mississippi Freedom Democratic Party (MFDP) was actually a move toward independent polities. It was people organizing for themselves—even though at that point they hoped to work within the framework of the national Democratic Party.

Most of them concluded they couldn't do it. The rejection of MFDP at the Democratic National Convention in Atlantic City in 1964 and the failure of the congressional challenge in 1965 had a profound influence on SNCC workers. Many decided then and there that there was no way for Negroes to build political strength within the American two-party system.

The next logical step was to try building their own parties where they had the numbers and conditions to do it—and that is what has developed with the independent parties in Alabama Black Belt counties.

It is significant that these parties, which held their own nominating conventions on primarily day in Alabama, will have their candidates on the ballot in November, whereas almost all Negro candidates who ran for nominations in Democratic primaries have now been eliminated from the races.

The idea of independent political parties is sure to spread—both through the Black Belt areas of the South and the ghettos of the North.

This does not mean that SNCC is rejecting the idea of coalitions for all time to come. It is rather obvious that in a country where Negroes represent only 11 percent of the population and even in the South do not have a majority in any state and only in a limited number of counties there must someday be coalitions with someone.

The question SNCC is asking at this point is coalition where, when, and with whom. It is saying that in order for a meaningful coalition to take place, at least two conditions must exist: (1) the people who have been powerless must create a power of their own, else there will be no coalition but only a situation in which they will be absorbed and controlled by those who have all the power; and (2) there must be groups with kindred interests with whom to make a coalition.

Since SNCC orientation is to a politics of power for poor people, this makes meaningful coalition with white people impossible at this moment, since organized groups of poor white people resisting oppression simply do not exist.

This brings us to the matter of SNCC's position on black-white relations.

The phrase that is being used widely in Negro organizations today in "black consciousness," and that is one of the things SNCC is saying must be built.

With this phrase, SNCC is saying to Negroes that they need to eliminate from their thinking and feeling the patterns that have been put there by a society that is essentially built on the concept of the superiority of the white man.

It is saying that Negroes need to reject the unconscious idea that what is white is better. And because they do live in a society that holds to that idea, they will begin to think and feel differently only when they realize their own history, their own worth as a people, their own ties with dark, skinned people elsewhere in the world.

As one SNCC leader put it: "It's really just a new way of saying an old thing—don't be ashamed of yourself. It is a matter of human dignity."

With this phrase of "black consciousness" SNCC is also saying some crucially important things to white people within the movement.

FALSE RUMOR

It is not true, as has been falsely rumored, that SNCC is asking all of its white staff members to leave. Rather it is saying to them that they simply cannot, because of objective conditions, attempt any longer to organize in Negro communities.

SNCC in saying that this is impossible because if Negroes are ever to achieve the "black consciousness" that is necessary to human dignity they must organize themselves—that as long as white people are there doing the work the idea is perpetuated that only white People can do things.

They are saying further that the very presence of white organizers in black communities has an intimidating effect on Negroes who have known white people only in the role of oppressors. This happens, SNCC says, even if the white organizers have the best of attitudes, even if they don't actually do anything to make it happen.

It happens because we live in a racist society that has conditioned the thinking of black people as well as white, and the white person who cares about the freedom movement must accept the truth about the consequences of that racist society of which he is a part.

Thus RNCC is saying, in effect, to its white organizers: "Sure you served an important function in the Negro communities of the South. You helped break the ground and establish the right to organize. But now this in done, and if you really mean what you said about why you came here in the first place that you wanted to help people win the power to control their own lives—you must now step aside and let them do it in the manner that they decide to do it."

Beyond this, and maybe more important, SNCC is saying something else to white people in the movement. It is saying that instead of giving their time and their energy—and maybe their lives-in the Negro communities it is now time (and long overdue) that they turned to the essential task of working in the white community.

DELAYED TASK

It is there, SNCC points out, that the basic problem in race relations in America exists because the basic problem is white racism. It is time that white people who care address themselves to the task of confronting this racism on its home ground, combatting it, and of organizing white America for a new kind of world.

Especially, SNCC says, white people must get to the task of organizing the poor white people of the South who are also oppressed but have been bypassed by the civil rights movement and thus left prey to their fears, to white racist groups and their propaganda. Unless someone with a belief in the freedom movement organizes these people there is no hope of those meaningful coalitions for the Negro movement that have been talked about.

The Southern Patriot agrees with this concept and SCEF, which publishes it, has long taken the position that the job of white people who believe in freedom is to confront white America. SCEF has been laying the basis for efforts to organize poor white Southerners in alliance with Negroes with its Southern Mountain Project in Appalachia.

SNCC workers will soon be attempting similar work. Many Negroes in SNCC are frankly doubtful that the poor white people of the South can be organized for such coalition, but they have not reached the point of rejecting the hope of trying. How long they maintain that hope may depend on how much effort whites are willing to put into such work.

(Whether the correct method of organizing white people is in groups separate from Negroes is still a subject of debate within the movement. The *Patriot* does not agree that it is correct, and this will be the subject of later articles.)

In addition to all these trends, there are two other developments in SNCC that must be noted.

One is simply a matter of organizational structure. SNCC is trying to tighten it up.

From the beginning SNCC has been loosely organized. This has been in a way its genius, since it gave free rein to individual creativity, but it has also been its weakness.

Creativity sometimes became over-weighted by wasted effort when many people came into SNCC seeking the "new world" and were more interested in finding their own freedom there than in doing what might be needed at the moment to build that new world. This became known as the "freedom-high" movement in SNCC.

Now they are rejecting the "freedom-high" idea and are saying that if people are serious about making a social revolution there are certain organizational disciplines that are necessities of the struggle. How well this will work out remains to be seen.

The other development—and it is a basic one—is that most people in SNCC have rejected the idea of nonviolence as a philosophy and in most situations are becoming more critical of it even as a tactic.

Like the other trends, this one has been developing over the last five years, but has just now been brought into public focus.

It is important to add quickly, however, that this in no way means that SNCC has turned to advocating violence.

As a matter of fact, those who jump to this conclusion should stop to realize that SNCC's emphasis on serious political organization is the direct opposite of advocacy of violence. Effective independent political organization may be the last, best, and only hope of avoiding widespread violence as a means of attacking the racial situation in America.

But most people who work with SNCC in the Deep South—and for that matter with other civil rights groups—simply reject the idea of turning the other cheek. They believe in people's right to defend themselves against the continuing and unrelenting violence of white racists.

The idea of nonviolence as an aggressive weapon of Social change—the concept of nonviolent revolution—has, at least for the time being, disappeared as a significant factor in the South.

WHEN AND WHY?

Just when and why this happened will be the subject of a future article in the Patriot. Suffice it to say here that those who believed in this concept missed the historic moment in which it might have been effectively projected, and such a moment is not likely to come again in the near future.

With the decline of this concept, certain other concepts and phraseology have fallen into disrepute within the movement. As Ed Hamlett points out in an article elsewhere in this issue, nobody talks about "the beloved community" anymore. Words like "love", "Morality" and I. Conscience" are rarely heard in the Southern movement today, and if they are heard they are laughed at.

Stokely Carmichael has been widely quoted as saying recently that "integration is irrelevant." His entire quote, which was not used in the press but which sheds considerable light on what he meant, was:

"Integration is irrelevant when initiated by black people in the present society. It does nothing to solve their basic problems."

Most people in SNCC agree with him. What white people must realize is that integration has been presented as a matter of Negroes being "integrated" (or absorbed) into white society. On the face of it this says plainly that what is white is better. This is a raw insult to Negroes; many have long sensed this and now they are saying it.

Asked recently how he defined integration, Jim Forman said: "It means moving Negroes into the mainstream of American life and its accepted value system. I reject this."

This is not what everyone in the movement has meant by integration. To some it has meant the literal meaning of the word integrate: "to make whole, that is, to make whole the human race.

It meant integration of peoples not into the existing society but into a new society that the movement would build where different groups of people could enrich each other's lives, where all men could be free, and where it was possible for men to live as brothers.

The Patriot is among those who believed in this concept of integration—and it still does.

But as a publication which promotes this belief, *The Patriot* feels it has both the right and the obligation to point out certain realities to others who hold to this belief.

The basic reality is that this concept of integration is yet only a dream in the minds of some people. It does not square with the world as it now is. And until the world is different the dream cannot be realized.

The fact that many people in the movement now laugh at words like "love" and "conscience" does not mean they would not like to see a world where these words could have meaning. It is simply that talk of love is hollow mockery when so little of it is evident and hate runs rampant not only on the South but in the entire county.

White people who believe in integration must see that it can never exist until there is equality in strength between different groups of people that the human race can never be "made whole" until those who have been oppressed can create for themselves their own strength. The concept of white supremacy which we must realize has been the cornerstone of our society makes this impossible today.

That is why white people who really believe in a united human race should not be frightened when SNCC and other groups talk about "black power." Our society has lived by white power. Unless black people create their own power there can never be a meeting ground.

This is a time of great flux in the Southern movement. Many white people who have worked in Negro communities in the South are being hurt because they now feel rejected. There are individual instances in which they feel overt hostility which for some reason they did not realize was there before.

Of course it *was* there, and if it is now coming to the surface it is a much healthier situation than when it was repressed. The individuals who are feeling hurt and rejected must try to see that what SNCC is doing may be the only way that the conditions can be created whereby a meaningful unity of black and white can come into being.

SNCC is not rejecting white people. Rather, by forcing them out of the black communities and back into the white communities where so much work needs to be done, it may be providing this generation with the last chance white people may ever have to overcome the racism and white supremacy by which western man has come close to destroying this planet.

A Time to Help

The new attacks on SNCC have cut its income, as people who disagree with or do not understand its policy cancel contributions. We urge our readers to stop and think where the South would be today if there had never been a SNCC and where it will be tomorrow if SNCC, which has provided the pioneering thrust toward change, should be destroyed.

The thing to remember is that while many honest friends of SNCC may disagree with its current policies the forces attacking it want to utterly destroy the organization—and not basically because of the black-white question but because SNCC represents real political dissent. No other civil rights organization—and no individual who realizes the importance of political dissent—can stand by and let this happen. SNCC's address is $360 Nelson St., S.W., Atlanta, Ga. 30313.

No Monolith

It seems to be characteristic of the United States politics—whether left, right or center—that no organization is quite monolithic, although most at some time consider themselves so. Certainly SNCC is not. For example, SNCC leaders in Arkansas recently issued a public statement disagreeing with the policy of forming all-black political parties. They said it wouldn't work in Arkansas, were Negroes make up 22 percent of the population.

UNIT 13-5

BLACK—WHITE RELATIONS: A TIME OF SEARCHING

Virginia Collins and Ed Hamlett

TWO MEETINGS . . . TWO REPORTS

On a weekend in May two meetings took place in the South at the same time. One, in New Orleans, was attended only by Negroes. It was called an Afro-American Festival. The other, in Pensacola, Fla., was attended only by white people, all of them civil rights people, some of whom had turned over their New Orleans apartments to persons attending the Afro-American Festival. They met to discuss organizing in the white community. On this page we print a report from the New Orleans meeting and excerpts from an essay prepared during the Pensacola meeting by one of the participants. Taken together, these two documents shed considerable light on the current period of searching in the matter of black-white relations in the South. The author of the New Orleans report, Mrs. Virginia Collins, is a long time civil rights leader in that city. Ed Hamlett, a native Southerner, is a former staff member of the Student Nonviolence Coordination Committee and a founder of Southern Student Organizing Committee (SSOC), in whose newsletter the text of this essay appeared. Both are SCEF board members.

AFRO-AMERICAN FESTIVAL SEEKS WORLD TIES WITH BLACK PEOPLE

Virginia Collins

NEW ORLEANS, La.—"Our aims in participating in this conference are: (1) to communicate the fact that we Afro-Americans are the most strategically placed people in the world at this moment in history, (2) to reconnect our people with land, history, and culture, and (3) to begin our decolonization."

Southern Patriot, May 1966.

With this as their stated purpose, a group of some 200 "black" militants from both the North and South met in New Orleans one weekend in May.

The conference, which was billed as an Afro-American Festival, disturbed many "whites" who are active in the freedom movement, coming as it did on the heels of an emerging tendency toward "black nationalism" or "black exclusionism."

Nevertheless, many white activists in New Orleans spent the weekend in Pensacola, Fla., in order that their homes might be open to the delegates.

"A Dream Deferred"

The conference opened with remarks by Bob Parris. [Editor's Note: Bob Moses Parris launched the new movement in Mississippi in the early 1960s. Last year he was active in the national peace movement.]

Parris highlighted the history of the Afro-American in this country. He also spoke of the impasse in the civil rights movement caused by the deferment, either temporary or permanent, of the "beloved community."

The first part of the conference was devoted to African history. Speakers attempted to show the significance of African history to Afro-Americans. They invalidated the myth of the docility of the slaves and also the myth of the savagery, inferiority, and backwardness of the African prior to and including the dawn of European exploitation.

The second part of the conference Concerned itself with the American Negro, or the "Africans in Exile." It was stated that the Constitution is totally irrelevant to the Afro-American and that the English language is inadequate for the needs of Afro-Americans and in fact is used to degrade them.

Speakers discussed the inability of critics to find adequate adjectives to describe Afro-American music, art, and poetry. They pointed out the connotations of such words as "black-ball," "black sheep," and "black market."

Following these two phases of the festival, a third phase came on Sunday morning-a phase which was at once more tense, more contemporary, more practical, and less formal. Sandwiched in between these two parts was some soulful entertainment by the Afro-American Folkloric Troupe of San Francisco and the Free Southern Theater of New Orleans.

A World Alliance

The last phase of the festival was more tense in that it was here that the suppressed controversy over integrated organizing in black communities was brought into the open through the appearance of a paper prepared by a small group of conference participants.

Although this issue was never debated due to an abundance of more pressing problems, it did cause many individuals to analyze carefully the arguments against integrated organizing in black communities.

The last part was more contemporary in that the situation of the Afro-American was related to the situations of the emerging nations of color in a very graphic way. It was pointed out that Asians, Africans, and Latin Americans are fighting against the same American economic and political denomination of their lives as the Afro-American is fighting against.

Therefore, it was said, the Afro-American should contemplate joining some type of alliance with these nations, or at any rate he shouldn't be fighting against these nations with the American military.

Taking note of the fact that the Afro-Americans were being brought to this country at the same time that Africa was being partitioned by the European powers, one participant suggested that "maybe our presence in America should be thought of as a sort of domestic colonization." In this light, it was said, the "assimilation" of the Afro-American into the mainstream of American life is unrealistic.

For assimilation, as it is now practiced, attempts to introduce the Afro-American into American society on the basis of an accepted inferior position and not on the basis of a significant and contributing member of the family of man.

The "assimilationists" were further attacked when it was pointed out how the communications media constantly advertize goods which will brighten one's complexion and/or straighten one's hair, and how the prevailing beauty standards in this country are diametrically opposed to the features of most Afro-Americans.

THE TWO CAMPS

The widening debate over the desirability or the undesirability of assimilation tended to polarize the festival into two camps: the one adhering to the "Black Revolution" which is international and seeks to affiliate with radical groups in Africa, Asia, and Latin America; the other adhering to the "Negro Revolution," which is national and generally seeks to become a part of the American consensus which condemns revolutionary movements in these countries.

Having reached a stalemate, the conference concluded with both sides admitting the need for further study of the economic and political forces which dominate the lives of Afro-Americans and with both sides agreeing to meet again.

ONE WHITE SOUTHERNER LOOKS AT NEW "BLACK CONSCIOUSNESS"

Ed Hamlett

PENSACOLA, Fla.—A bunch of white folks from New Orleans, Nashville, and Alabama are here to talk about white community organizing. The informal meeting was called by people in New Orleans who gave up their apartments to black folks for a weekend meeting to talk about Black Consciousness.

I said *Black Consciousness*, not *Beloved Community*. Movement people in the South don't talk about the latter so much anymore.

The reasons for the dampening of idealism are not difficult to discover: . . . a few hundred thousand newly registered voters, with the same old "Segs" running and winning; a few thousand Negro kids in previously all-white schools—learning about the blessings of the white man's civilization. . . .

SEASON OF HOPE

But, you protest, the Beloved Community was to have been built first within the Movement, if not immediately in the larger society, So what about that "band of brothers and circle of trust"? The Student Nonviolent Coordinating Committee (SNCC), which is what I'm talking about mainly, has always had whites on its staff.

They were there initially for at least two reasons: (1) to demonstrate in the South that whites and Negroes could work together, and (2) to utilize their vitally needed skills and labor. In early days there was a good deal of talk about and feeling for the Beloved Community which, everyone hoped, was being built.

In the fall of 1963, it was discovered in the Freedom Vote campaign in Mississippi that the presence of northern whites in fairly large numbers brought protection to the work from the federal government that it had never given black workers.

The call went out for 1,000 northern volunteers to help open up Mississippi in the summer of 1964.

Second Thoughts

By the previous spring many local Negroes had begun to carry on the day-to-day work of their own freedom organizations—doing mimeographing, typing, and leg work. And then the volunteers came. They were more "efficient" in almost every way. They meant well; they tried hard . . . but some of the hosts soon had second thoughts.

The flood of whites produced serious problems. It took almost a year for local participation in daily work to be built up again. . . . Now some say that for whites to remain (in Southern Negro communities) would be extremely detrimental.

Here we must look at the question of Black Consciousness and what it in.

Blacks, all blacks, must be aware that they are not inferior to whites. They must know that black people have made significant contributions to world civilization over the centuries, including here in the United States. . . . It is not only having facts and knowledge about history, and sociological statistics, *etc.*; *it is also believing and feeling in one's GUTS* that they are true. . . .

Many blacks assert that this will not happen if whites continue to help to do the organizing, and all the other things.

It is increasingly contended that the very presence of whites has a very serious intimidating effect on the masses of black people. Because they have been taught it all their lives, many continue to believe that "if you're black, stay back." and "white is right."

If you do not readily take to this line of reasoning, as I did not, you are offered other compelling arguments for confining your work to the white community. For example:

There is much talk by whites about an interracial movement of the poor. But there is no movement of poor whites, with whom the thousands of organized Negroes may ally themselves.

Most blacks in the Movement realize that poor Negroes need allies. . . . But they question whether poor whites, who do the dirty work of bombing and beating, can be organized.

None of us whites are demonstrating to them that they are wrong. . . . (Many Negroes argue that disaffected middle. class whites have been taking the easy route and escaping to the black community.)

There is also the problem of racism in America which pervades all classes of whites. . . . This means that whites too must be made conscious of Negro history. . . . And whites must forcefully make this confrontation, no small task.

Furthermore, those of us who cherish the idea of an integrated society, whether we be white or Negro, must ask ourselves if it is integration or assimilation that we are about at present. . . . The whole discussion of integration has to do with absorption, not with sharing. This must stop!

Rough Road Ahead

In the last analysis, I must admit that I have serious questions about much of what I have tried to relate in the above. When I heard about the all-black meeting in New Orleans, I was not half-joking when I suggested that we whites must hold "sit-ins" at the affair to protest an "obviously unjust situation."

The injustice is not so obvious to me now. . . .

Much rough road will be traveled in the threshing out of this whole thing in the South. . . . Wailing and gnashing of teeth is senseless. What is needed is a serious attempt at understanding and openness; and much work in the white community.

UNIT 13-6

Black Power: Its Need and Substance

Stokely Carmichael and Charles V. Hamilton

"To carve out a place for itself in the politico-social order," V. O. Key, Jr. wrote in *Politics, Parties and Pressure Groups*, "a new group may have to fight for reorientation of many of the values of the old order" (p. 57). This is especially true when that group is composed of black people in the American society—a society that has for centuries deliberately and systematically excluded them from political participation. Black people in the United States must raise hard questions, questions which challenge the very nature of the society itself: its long-standing values, beliefs and institutions.

To do this, we must first redefine ourselves. Our basic need is to reclaim our history and our identity from what must be called cultural terrorism, from the depredation of self-justifying white guilt. We shall have to struggle for the right to create our own terms through which to define ourselves and our relationship to the society, and to have these terms recognized. This is the first necessity of a free people, and the first right that any oppressor must suspend.

In Politics Among Nations, Hans Morgenthau defined political power as "the psychological control over the minds of men" (p. 29). This control includes the attempt by the oppressor to have his definitions, his historical descriptions, accepted by the oppressed. This was true in Africa no less than in the United States. To black Africans, the word "Uhuru" means "freedom," but they had to fight the white colonizers for the right to use the term. The recorded history of this country's dealings with red and black men offers other examples. In the wars between the white settlers and the "Indians," a battle won by the Cavalry was described as a "victory." The "Indians' " triumphs, however, were "massacres." (The American colonists were not unaware of the need to define their acts in their own terms. They labeled their fight against England a "revolution"; the English attempted to demean it by calling it "insubordination" or "riotous.")

The historical period following Reconstruction in the South after the Civil War has been called by many historians the period of Redemption, implying that the bigoted southern slave societies were "redeemed" from the hands of "reckless and irresponsible" black rulers. Professor John Hope Franklin's Reconstruction or Dr. W.E.B. Du Bois' Black Reconstruction should be sufficient to dispel inaccurate historical notions, but the larger society persists in its own self-serving accounts. Thus black people came to be depicted as "lazy," "apathetic," "dumb," "shiftless," "good-timers." Just as red men had to be recorded as "savages" to justify the white man's theft of their land, so black men had to be vilified in order to justify their continued oppression. Those who have the right to define are the masters of the situation. Lewis Carroll understood this:

> "When I use a word," Humpty Dumpty said in a rather scornful tone, "it means just what I choose it to mean—neither more nor less."
>
> "The question is," said Alice, "whether you can make words mean so many different things."
>
> "The question is," said Humpty Dumpty, "which is to be master—that's all."[1]

Today, the American educational system continues to reinforce the entrenched values of the society through the use of words. Few people in this country question that this is "the land of the free and the home of the brave." They have had these words drummed into them from childhood. Few people question that this is the "Great Society" or that this country is fighting "Communist aggression" around the world. We mouth these things over and over, and they become truisms not to be questioned. In a similar way, black people have been saddled with epithets.

"Integration" is another current example of a word which has been defined according to the way white Americans see it. To many of them, it means black men wanting to marry white daughters; it means "race mixing"—implying bed or dance partners. To black people, it has meant a way to improve their lives—economically and politically. But the predominant white definition has stuck in the minds of too many people.

Black people must redefine themselves, and only they can do that. Throughout this country, vast segments of the black communities are beginning to recognize the need to assert their own definitions, to reclaim their history, their culture; to create their own sense of community and togetherness. There is a growing resentment of the word "Negro," for example, because this term is the invention of our oppressor; it is his image of us that he describes. Many blacks are now calling themselves African-Americans, Afro-Americans or black people because that is our image of ourselves. When we begin to define our own image, the stereotypes—that is, lies—that our oppressor has developed will begin in the white community and end there. The black community will have a positive image of itself that it has created. This means we will no longer call ourselves lazy, apathetic, dumb, good-timers, shiftless, etc. Those are words used by white America to define us. If we accept these adjectives, as some of us have in the past, then we see ourselves only in a negative way, precisely the way white America wants us to see ourselves. Our incentive is broken and our will to fight is surrendered. From now on we shall view ourselves as African-Americans and as black people who are in fact energetic, determined, intelligent, beautiful and peace-loving.

There is a terminology and ethos peculiar to the black community of which black people are beginning to be no longer ashamed. Black communities are the only large segments of this society where people refer to each other as brother-soul-brother, soul-sister. Some people may look upon this as *ersatz*, as make-believe, but it is not that. It is real. It is a growing sense of community. It is a growing realization that black Americans have a common bond not only among themselves, but with their African brothers. In *Black Man's Burden*, John O. Killens described his trip to ten African countries as follows:

> Everywhere I went people called me brother " . . . Welcome, American brother." It was a good feeling for me, to be in Africa. To walk in a land for the first time in your entire life knowing within yourself that your color would not be held against you. No black man ever knows this in America.

More and more black Americans are developing this feeling. They are becoming aware that they have a history which pre-dates their forced introduction to this country. African-American history means a long history beginning on the continent of Africa, a history not taught in the standard textbooks of this country. It is absolutely essential that black people know this history, that they know their roots, that they develop an awareness of their cultural heritage. Too long have they been kept in submission by being told that they had no culture, no manifest heritage, before they landed on the slave auction blocks in this country. If black people are to know themselves as a vibrant, valiant people, they must know their roots. And they will soon learn that the Hollywood image of maneating cannibals waiting for, and waiting on, the Great White Hunter is a lie.

With redefinition will come a clearer notion of the role black Americans can play in this world. This role will emerge clearly out of the unique, common experiences of Afro-Asians. Killens concludes:

> I believe furthermore that the American Negro can be the bridge between the West and Africa-Asia. We black Americans can serve as a bridge to mutual understanding. The one thing we black Americans have in common with the other colored peoples of the world is that we have all felt the cruel and ruthless heel of white supremacy. We have all been "niggerized" on one level or another. And all of us are determined to "deniggerize" the earth. To rid the world of "niggers" is the Black Man's Burden, human reconstruction is the grand objective.

Only when black people fully develop this sense of community, of themselves, can they begin to deal effectively with the problems of racism in *this* country. This is what we mean by a new consciousness; this is the vital first step.

The next step is what we shall call the process of political modernization—a process which must take place if the society is to be rid of racism. "Political modernization" includes many things, but we mean by it three major concepts: **(1)** questioning old values and institutions of the society; **(2)** searching for new and different forms of political structure to solve political and economic problems; and **(3)** broadening the base of political participation to include more people in the decision-making process. These notions (we shall take up each in turn) are central to our thinking throughout this book and to contemporary American history as a whole. As David Apter wrote in *The Politics of Modernization*, ". . . the struggle to modernize is what has given meaning to our generation. It tests our cherished institutions and our beliefs. . . . So compelling a force has it become that we are forced to ask new questions of our own institutions. Each country, whether modernized or modernizing, stands in both judgment and fear of the results. Our own society is no exception."

The values of this society support a racist system; we find it incongruous to ask black people to adopt and support most of those values. We also reject the assumption that the basic institutions of this society must be preserved. The goal of black people must *not* be to assimilate into middle-class America, for that class—as a whole—is without a viable conscience as regards humanity. The values of the middle class permit the perpetuation of the ravages of the black community. The values of that class are based on material aggrandizement, not the expansion of humanity. The values of that class ultimately support cloistered little closed societies tucked away neatly in tree-lined suburbia. The values of that class do not lead to the creation of an open society. That class *mouths* its preference for a free, competitive society, while at the same time forcefully and even viciously denying to black people as a group the opportunity to compete.

We are not unmindful of other descriptions of the social utility of the middle class. Banfield and Wilson, in *City Politics*, concluded:

> The departure of the middle class from the central city is important in other ways. . . . The middle class supplies a social and political leavening in the life of a

> city. Middle-class people demand good schools and integrity in government. They support churches, lodges, parent-teacher associations, scout troops, better-housing committees, art galleries, and operas. It is the middle class, in short, that asserts a conception of the public interest. Now its activity is increasingly concentrated in the suburbs.

But this same middle class manifests a sense of superior group position in regard to race. This class wants "good government" *for themselves;* it wants good schools for *its children.* At the same time, many of its members sneak into the black community by day, exploit it, and take the money home to their middle-class communities at night to support their operas and art galleries and comfortable homes. When not actually robbing, they will fight off the handful of more affluent black people who seek to move in; when they approve or even seek token integration, it applies only to black people like themselves—as "white" as possible. *This class is the backbone of institutional racism in this country.*

Thus we reject the goal of assimilation into middle-class America because the values of that class are in themselves anti-humanist and because that class as a social force perpetuates racism. We must face the fact that, in the past, what we have called the movement has not really questioned the middle-class values and institutions of this country. If anything, it has accepted those values and institutions without fully realizing their racist nature. Reorientation means an emphasis on the dignity of man, not on the sanctity of property. It means the creation of a society where human misery and poverty are repugnant to that society, not an indication of laziness or lack of initiative. The creation of new values means the establishment of a society based, as Killens expresses it in *Black Man's Burden,* on "free people," not "free enterprise" (p. 167). To do this means to modernize—*indeed, to civilize*—this country.

Supporting the old values are old political and economic structures; these must also be "modernized." We should at this point distinguish between "structures" and "system." By system, we have in mind the entire American complex of basic institutions, values, beliefs, etc. By structures, we mean the specific institutions (political parties, interest groups, bureaucratic administrations) which exist to conduct the business of that system. Obviously, the first is broader than the second. Also, the second assumes the legitimacy of the first. Our view is that, given the illegitimacy of the system, we cannot then proceed to transform that system with existing structures.

The two major political parties in this country have become non-viable entities for the legitimate representation of the real needs of masses—especially blacks—in this country. Walter Lippmann raised the same point in his syndicated column of December 8, 1966. He pointed out that the party system in the United States developed before our society became as technologically complex as it is now. He says that the ways in which men live and define themselves are changing radically. Old ideological issues, once the subject of passionate controversy, Lippmann argues, are of little interest today. He asks whether the great urban complexes—which are rapidly becoming the centers of black population in the U.S.—can be run with the same systems and ideas that derive from a time when America was a country of small villages and farms. While not addressing himself directly to the question of race, Lippmann raises a major question about our political institutions; and the crisis of race in America may be its major symptom.

Black people have seen the city planning commissions, the urban renewal commissions, the boards of education and the police departments fail to speak to their needs in a meaningful way. We must devise new structures, new institutions to replace those forms or to make them responsive. There is nothing sacred or inevitable about old institutions; the focus must be on people, not forms.

Existing structures and established ways of doing things have a way of perpetuating themselves and for this reason, the modernizing process will be difficult. Therefore, timidity in calling into question the boards of education or the police departments will not do. They must be challenged forcefully and clearly, If this means the creation of parallel community institutions, then that must be the solution. If this means that black parents must gain control over the operation of the schools in the black community, then that must be the solution. The search for new forms means the search for institutions that will, for once, make decisions in the interest of black people. It means, for example, a building inspection department that neither winks at violations of building codes by absentee slumlords nor imposes meaningless fines which permit them to continue their exploitation of the black community.

Essential to the modernization of structures is a broadened base of political participation. More and more people must become politically sensitive and active (we have already seen this happening in some areas of the South). People must no longer be tied, by small incentives or handouts, to a corrupting and corruptible white machine. Black people will choose their own leaders and hold those leaders responsible to *them*. A broadened base means an end to the condition described by James Wilson in *Negro Politics*, whereby "Negroes tended to be the objects rather than the subjects of civic action. Things are often done for, or about, or to, or because of Negroes, but they are less frequently done *by* Negroes" (p. 133). Broadening the base of political participation, then, has as much to do with the quality of black participation as with the quantity. We are fully aware that the black vote, especially in the North, has been pulled out of white pockets and "delivered" whenever it was in the interest of white politicians to do so. That vote must no longer be controllable by those who have neither the interests nor the demonstrated concern of black people in mind.

As the base broadens, as more and more black people become activated, they will perceive more clearly the special disadvantages heaped upon them as a group. They will perceive that the larger society is growing more affluent while the black society is retrogressing, as daily life and mounting statistics clearly show (see Chapters I and VIII). V. O. Key describes what often happens next, in *Politics, Parties and Pressure Groups*: "A factor of great significance in the setting off of political movements is an abrupt change for the worse in the status of one group relative to that of other groups in society. . . . A rapid change for the worse . . . in the relative status of any group . . . is likely to precipitate political action" (p. 24). Black people will become increasingly active as they notice that their retrogressive status exists in large measure because of values and institutions arraigned against them. They will begin to stress and strain and call the entire system into question. Political modernization will be in motion. We believe that it is now in motion. One form of that motion is Black Power.

The adoption of the concept of Black Power is one of the most legitimate and healthy developments in American politics and race relations in our time. The concept of Black Power speaks to all the needs mentioned in this chapter. It is a call for black people in this country to unite, to recognize their heritage, to build a sense of community. It is a call for black people to begin to define their own goals, to lead their own organizations and to support those organizations. It is a call to reject the racist institutions and values of this society.

The concept of Black Power rests on a fundamental premise: *Before a group can enter the open society*, it must first close ranks. By this we mean that group solidarity is necessary before a group can operate effectively from a bargaining position of strength in a pluralistic society. Traditionally, each new ethnic group in this society has found the route to social and political viability through the organization of its own institutions with which to represent its needs within the larger society. Studies in voting behavior specifically, and political behavior generally, have made it clear that politically the American pot has not melted. Italians vote for Rubino over O'Brien; Irish for Murphy over Goldberg, etc. This phenomenon may seem distasteful to some, but it has been and remains today a central fact of the American political system. There are other examples of ways in which groups in the society have remembered their roots and used this effectively in the political arena.

Theodore Sorensen describes the politics of foreign aid during the Kennedy Administration in his book *Kennedy*:

> No powerful constituencies or interest groups backed foreign aid. The Marshall Plan at least had appealed to Americans who traced their roots to the Western European nations aided. But there were few voters who identified with India, Colombia or Tanganyika [p. 351].

The extent to which black Americans can and do "trace their roots" to Africa, to that extent will they be able to be more effective on the political scene.

A white reporter set forth this point in other terms when he made the following observation about white Mississippi's manipulation of the anti-poverty program:

> The war on poverty has been predicated on the notion that there is such a thing as a community which can be defined geographically and mobilized for a collective effort to help the poor. This theory has no relationship to reality in the deep South. In every Mississippi county there are two communities. Despite all the pious platitudes of the moderates on both sides, these two communities habitually see their interests in terms of conflict rather than cooperation. Only when the Negro community can muster enough political, economic and professional strength to compete on somewhat equal terms, will Negroes believe in the possibility of true cooperation and whites accept its necessity. En route to integration, the Negro community needs to develop a greater independence—a chance to run its own affairs and not cave in whenever "the man" barks—or so it seems to me, and to most of the knowledgeable people with whom I talked in Mississippi. To OEO, this judgment may sound like black nationalism . . . [2]

The point is obvious: black people must lead and run their own organizations. Only black people can convey the revolutionary idea—and it is a revolutionary idea—that black people are able to do things themselves. Only they can help create in the community an aroused and continuing black consciousness that will provide the basis for political strength. In the past, white allies have often furthered white supremacy without the whites involved realizing it, or even wanting to do so. Black people must come together and do things for themselves. They must achieve self-identity and self-determination in order to have their daily needs met.

Black Power means, for example, that in Lowndes County, Alabama, a black sheriff can end police brutality. A black tax assessor and tax collector and county board of revenue can lay, collect, and channel tax monies for the building of better roads and schools serving black people. In such areas as Lowndes, where black people have a majority, they will attempt to use power to exercise control. This is what they seek: control. When black people lack a majority, Black Power means proper representation and sharing of control. It means the creation of power bases, of strength, from which black people can press to change local or nation-wide patterns of oppression—instead of from weakness.

It does not mean *merely* putting black faces into office. Black visibility is not Black Power. Most of the black politicians around the country today are not examples of Black Power. The power must be that of a community, and emanate from there. The black politicians must start from there. The black politicians must stop being representatives of "downtown" machines, whatever the cost might be in terms of lost patronage and holiday handouts.

Black Power recognizes—it must recognize—the ethnic basis of American politics as well as the power-oriented nature of American politics. Black Power therefore calls for black people to consolidate behind their own, so that they can bargain from a position of strength. But while we endorse the *procedure* of group solidarity and identity for the purpose of attaining certain goals in the body politic, this does not mean that black people should strive for the same kind of rewards (i.e., end results) obtained by the white society. The ultimate values and goals are not domination or exploitation of other groups, but rather an effective share in the total power of the society.

Nevertheless, some observers have labeled those who advocate Black Power as racists; they have said that the call for self-identification and self-determination is "racism in reverse" or "black supremacy." This is a deliberate and absurd lie. There is no analogy—by any stretch of definition or imagination—between the advocates of Black Power and white racists. Racism is not merely exclusion on the basis of race but exclusion for the purpose of subjugating or maintaining subjugation. The goal of the racists is to keep black people on the bottom, arbitrarily and dictatorially, as they have done in this country for over three hundred years. The goal of black self-determination and black self-identity—Black Power—is full participation in the decision making processes affecting the lives of black people, and recognition of the virtues in themselves as black people. The black people of this country have not lynched whites, bombed their churches, murdered their children and manipulated laws and institutions to maintain oppression. White racists have. Congressional laws, one after the other, have not been necessary to stop black people from oppressing others and denying others the full enjoyment of their rights. White racists have made such laws necessary. The goal of Black Power is positive and functional to a free and viable society. No white racist can make this claim.

A great deal of public attention and press space was devoted to the hysterical accusation of "black racism" when the call for Black Power was first sounded. A national committee of influential black churchmen affiliated with the National Council of Churches, despite their obvious respectability and responsibility, bad to resort to a paid advertisement to articulate their position, while anyone yapping "black racism" made front-page news. In their statement, published in the *New York Times* of July 31, 1966, the churchmen said:

> We, an informal group of Negro churchmen in America, are deeply disturbed about the crisis brought upon our country by historic distortions of important human realities in the controversy about "black power." What we see shining through the variety of rhetoric is not anything new but the same old problem of power and race which has faced our beloved country since 1619.
>
> . . . The conscience of black men is corrupted because having no power to implement the demands of conscience, the concern for justice in the absence of justice becomes a chaotic self-surrender. Powerlessness breeds a race of beggars. We are faced with a situation where powerless conscience meets conscienceless power, threatening the very foundations of our Nation.
>
> We deplore the overt violence of riots, but we feel it is more important to focus on the real sources of these eruptions. These sources may be abetted inside the Ghetto, but their basic cause lies in the silent and covert violence which white middle class America inflicts upon the victims of the inner city.
>
> . . . In short, the failure of American leaders to use American power to create equal opportunity in life as well as law, this is the real problem and not the anguished cry for black power.
>
> . . . Without the capacity to participate with power, i.e., to have some organized political and economic strength to really influence people with whom one interacts, integration is not meaningful.
>
> . . . America has asked its Negro citizens to fight for opportunity as *individuals*, whereas at certain points in our history what we have needed most has

> been opportunity for the whole group, not just for selected and approved Negroes.
>
> . . . We must not apologize for the existence of this form of group power, for we have been oppressed as a group and not as individuals. We will not find our way out of that oppression until both we and America accept the need for Negro Americans, as well as for Jews, Italians, Poles, and white Anglo-Saxon Protestants, among others, to have and to wield group power.

It is a commentary on the fundamentally racist nature of this society that the concept of group strength for black people must be articulated—not to mention defended. No other group would submit to being led by others. Italians do not run the Anti-Defamation League of B'nai B'rith. Irish do not chair Christopher Columbus Societies. Yet when black people call for black-run and all-black organizations, they are immediately classed in a category with the Ku Klux Klan. This is interesting and ironic, but by no means surprising: the society does not expect black people to be able to take care of their business, and there are many who prefer it precisely that way.

In the end, we cannot and shall not offer any guarantees that Black Power, if achieved, would be non-racist. No one can predict human behavior. Social change always has unanticipated consequences. If black racism is what the larger society fears, we cannot help them. We can only state what we hope will be the result, given the fact that the present situation is unacceptable and that we have no real alternative but to work for Black Power. The final truth is that the white society is not entitled to reassurances, even if it were possible to offer them.

We have outlined the meaning and goals of Black Power; we have also discussed one major thing which it is not. There are others of greater importance. The advocates of Black Power reject the old slogans and meaningless rhetoric of previous years in the civil rights struggle. The language of yesterday is indeed irrelevant: progress, non-violence, integration, fear of "white backlash," coalition. Let us look at the rhetoric and see why these terms must be set aside or redefined.

One of the tragedies of the struggle against racism is that up to this point there has been no national organization which could speak to the growing militancy of young black people in the urban ghettos and the black-belt South. There has been only a "civil rights" movement, whose tone of voice was adapted to an audience of middle-class whites. It served as a sort of buffer zone between that audience and angry young blacks. It claimed to speak for the needs of a community, but it did not speak in the tone of that community. None of its so-called leaders could go into a rioting community and be listened to. In a sense, the blame must be shared—along with the mass media—by those leaders for what happened in Watts, Harlem, Chicago, Cleveland and other places. Each time the black people in those cities saw Dr. Martin Luther King get slapped they became angry. When they saw little black girls bombed to death in a *church* and civil rights workers ambushed and murdered, they were angrier; and when nothing happened, they were steaming mad. We had nothing to offer that they could see, except to go out and be beaten again. We helped to build their frustration.

We had only the old language of love and suffering. And in most places—that is, from the liberals and middle class—we got back the old language of patience and progress. The civil rights leaders were saying to the country: "Look, you guys are supposed to be nice guys, and we are only going to do what we are supposed to do. Why do you beat us up? Why don't you give us what we ask? Why don't you straighten yourselves out?" For the masses of black people, this language resulted in virtually nothing. In fact, their objective day-to-day condition worsened. The unemployment rate among black people increased while that among whites declined. Housing conditions in the black communities deteriorated. Schools in the black ghettos continued to plod along on outmoded techniques, inadequate curricula, and with all too many tired and indifferent teachers. Meanwhile, the

President picked up the refrain of "We Shall Overcome" while the Congress passed civil rights law after civil rights law, only to have them effectively nullified by deliberately weak enforcement. "Progress is being made," we were told.

Such language, along with admonitions to remain nonviolent and fear the white backlash, convinced some that that course was the only course to follow. It misled some into believing that a black minority could bow its head and get whipped into a meaningful position of power. The very notion is absurd. The white society devised the language, adopted the rules and had the black community narcotized into believing that that language and those rules were, in fact, relevant. The black community was told time and again how *other* immigrants finally won acceptance: that is, by following the Protestant Ethic of Work and Achievement. They worked hard; therefore, they achieved. We were not told that it was by building Irish Power, Italian Power, Polish Power or Jewish Power that these groups got themselves together and operated from positions of strength. We were not told that "the American dream" wasn't designed for black people. That while today, to whites, the dream may seem to include black people, it cannot do so by the very nature of this nation's political and economic system, which imposes institutional racism on the black masses if not upon every individual black. A notable comment on that "dream" was made by Dr. Percy Julian, the black scientist and director of the Julian Research Institute in Chicago, a man for whom the dream seems to have come true. While not subscribing to "black power" as he understood it, Dr. Julian clearly understood the basis for it: "The false concept of basic Negro inferiority is one of the curses that still lingers. It is a problem created by the white man. Our children just no longer are going to accept the patience we were taught by our generation. We were taught a pretty little lie—excel and the whole world lies open before you. *I obeyed the injunction and found it to be wishful thinking.*" (Authors' italics)[3]

A key phrase in our buffer-zone days was non-violence. For years it has been thought that black people would not literally fight for their lives. Why this has been so is not entirely clear; neither the larger society nor black people are noted for passivity. The notion apparently stems from the years of marches and demonstrations and sit-ins where black people did not strike back and the violence always came from white mobs. There are many who still sincerely believe in that approach. From our viewpoint, rampaging white mobs and white night-riders must be made to understand that their days of free head-whipping are over. Black people should and must fight back. Nothing more quickly repels someone bent on destroying you than the unequivocal message: "O.K., fool, make your move, and run the same risk I run—of dying."

When the concept of Black Power is set forth, many people immediately conjure up notions of violence. The country's reaction to the Deacons for Defense and Justice, which originated in Louisiana, is instructive. Here is a group which realized that the "law" and law enforcement agencies would not protect people, so they had to do it themselves. If a nation fails to protect its citizens, then that nation cannot condemn those who take up the task themselves. The Deacons and all other blacks who resort to self-defense represent a simple answer to a simple question: what man would not defend his family and home from attack?

But this frightened some white people, because they knew that black people would now fight back. They knew that this was precisely what they would have long since done if *they* were subjected to the injustices and oppression heaped on blacks. Those of us who advocate Black Power are quite clear in our own minds that a "non-violent" approach to civil rights is an approach black people cannot afford and a luxury white people do not deserve. It is crystal clear to us-and it must become so with the white society—*that there can be no social order without social justice.* White people must be made to understand that they must stop messing with black people, or the blacks *will* fight back!

Next, we must deal with the term "integration." According to its advocates, social justice will be accomplished by "integrating the Negro into the mainstream institutions of the society from which be has been traditionally excluded." This concept is based on the assumption that there is nothing of value in the black community and that little of value could be created among black people. The thing to do is siphon off the "acceptable" black people into the surrounding middle-class white community.

The goals of integrationists are middle-class goals, articulated primarily by a small group of Negroes with middle-class aspirations or status. Their kind of integration has meant that a few blacks "make it," leaving the black community, sapping it of leadership potential and know-how. As we noted in Chapter I, those token Negroes—absorbed into a white mass—are of no value to the remaining black masses. They become meaningless show-pieces for a conscience-soothed white society. Such people will state that they would prefer to be treated "only as individuals, not as Negroes"; that they "are not and should not be preoccupied with race." This is a totally unrealistic position. In the first place, black people have not suffered as individuals but as members of a group; therefore, their liberation lies in group action. This is why SNCC—and the concept of Black Power—affirms that helping *individual* black people to solve their problems on an *individual* basis does little to alleviate the mass of black people. Secondly, while color blindness may be a sound goal ultimately, we must realize that race is an overwhelming fact of life in this historical period. There is no black man in this country who can live "simply as a man." His blackness is an ever-present fact of this racist society, whether be recognizes it or not. It is unlikely that this or the next generation will witness the time when race will no longer be relevant in the conduct of public affairs and in public policy decision-making. To realize this and to attempt to deal with it does not make one a racist or overly preoccupied with race; it puts one in the forefront of a significant *struggle.* If there is no intense struggle today, there will be no meaningful results tomorrow.

"Integration" as a goal today speaks to the problem of blackness not only in an unrealistic way but also in a despicable way. It is based on complete acceptance of the fact that in order to have a decent house or education, black people must move into a white neighborhood or send their children to a white school. This reinforces, among both black and white, the idea that "white" is automatically superior and "black" is by definition inferior. For this reason, "integration" is a subterfuge for the maintenance of white supremacy. It allows the nation to focus on a handful of Southern black children who get into white schools at a great price, and to ignore the ninety-four percent who are left in unimproved all-black schools. Such situations will not change until black people become equal in a way that means something, and integration ceases to be a one-way street. Then integration does not mean draining skills and energies from the black ghetto into white neighborhoods. To sprinkle black children among white pupils in outlying schools is at best a stop-gap measure. The goal is not to take black children out of the black community and expose them to white middle-class values; the goal is to build and strengthen the black community.

"Integration" also means that black people must give up their identity, deny their heritage. We recall the conclusion of Killian and Grigg: "At the present time, integration as a solution to the race problem demands that the Negro foreswear his identity as a Negro." The fact is that integration, as traditionally articulated, would abolish the black community. The fact is that what must be abolished is not the black community, but the dependent colonial status that has been inflicted upon it.

The racial and cultural personality of the black community must be preserved and that community must win its freedom while preserving its cultural integrity. Integrity includes a pride—in the sense of self-acceptance, not chauvinism—in being black, in the historical attainments and contributions of black people. No person can be healthy, complete and mature if he must deny a part of himself; this is what "integration" has required thus far. This is the essential difference between integration as it is currently practiced and the concept of Black Power.

The idea of cultural integrity is so obvious that it seems almost simple-minded to spell things out at this length. Yet millions of Americans resist such truths when they are applied to black people. Again, that resistance is a comment on the fundamental racism in the society. Irish Catholics took care of their own first without a lot of apology for doing so, without any dubious language from timid leadership about guarding against "backlash." Everyone understood it to be a perfectly legitimate procedure. Of course, there would be "backlash." Organization begets counter organization, but this was no reason to defer.

The so-called white backlash against black people is something else: the embedded traditions of institutional racism being brought into the open and calling forth overt manifestations of individual racism. In the summer of 1966, when the protest marches into Cicero, Illinois, began, the black people knew they were not allowed to live in Cicero and the white people knew it. When blacks began to demand the right to live in hordes in that town, the whites simply reminded them of the status quo. Some people called this "backlash." It was, in fact, racism defending itself. In the black community, this is called "White folks showing their color." It is ludicrous to blame black people for what is simply an overt manifestation of white racism. Dr. Martin Luther King stated clearly that the protest marches were not the cause of the racism but merely exposed a long-term cancerous condition in the society.

We come now to the rhetoric of coalition as part of the traditional approach to ending racism: the concept of the civil rights movement as a kind of liaison between the powerful white community and a dependent black community. "Coalition" involves the whole question of how one approaches polities and political alliances. It is so basic to an understanding of Black Power that we will devote an entire chapter to the subject.

ENDNOTES

1. Lewis Carroll, *Through the Looking Glass*, New York: Doubleday Books, Inc., p. 196.
2. Christopher Jencks, "Accommodating Whites: A New Look at Mississippi," *The New Republic* (April 16, 1966).
3. *The New York Times* (April 30, 1967), p. 30.

UNIT 13-7

LIBERATION BY ANY MEANS NECESSARY

ADDRESS TO A MEETING IN NEW YORK, 1964

Malcolm X

Malcolm X (formerly Malcolm Little) was born in Nebraska in 1925. His father was a militant Baptist clergyman who was also an organizer for Garvey's UNIA. When Malcolm was a child, the family was threatened by the Ku Klux Klan and other racist groups. Eventually, his father was murdered "by person or persons unknown," in the words of the law-enforcement officials who investigated the case.

In his late teens, Malcolm drifted into a life of petty crime and then into a career as a successful hustler. He was caught, arrested, and jailed, and it was while in jail that he was converted to Elijah Muhammad's Nation of Islam. After his release, his remarkable talents led him straight to the number-two spot in the Muslim organization. In 1964, he withdrew from the Nation of Islam and set up an orthodox Muslim mosque as well as a black protest organization, the Association of Afro-American Unity. The last year of his life was spent trying to develop a comprehensive program for black liberation.

The speech printed here was given by Malcolm X at a meeting sponsored by the Militant Labor Forum, a socialist organization in New York City, on April 8, 1964, less than a month after his break with Elijah Muhammad. In the speech can be seen the growing internationalism of Malcolm's outlook as well as his critical view of the various civil rights organizations active at the time.

According to Malcolm X, a revolution is necessary to free the black man in America, and though it is possible that this can be accomplished without bloodshed, it is unlikely that it will happen so. Less than a year after he delivered this speech, Malcolm himself was dead, felled by an assassin's bullet.

Friends and enemies, tonight I hope that we can have a little fireside chat with as few sparks as possible being tossed around. Especially because of the very explosive condition that the world is in today. Sometimes, when a person's house is on fire and someone

---

From Malcolm X, "The Black Revolution," *Two Speeches by Malcolm X* (New York: Merit, 1965). Reprinted by permission of Merit Publishers and Betty Shabazz.

comes in yelling fire, instead of the person who is awakened by the yell being thankful, he makes the mistake of charging the one who awakened him with having set the fire. I hope that this little conversation tonight about the black revolution won't cause many of you to accuse us of igniting it when you find it at your doorstep.

I'm still a Muslim, that is, my religion is still Islam. I still believe that there is no god but Allah and that Muhammad is the apostle of Allah. That just happens to be my personal religion. But in the capacity which I am functioning in today, I have no intention of mixing my religion with the problems of 22,000,000 black people in this country. Just as it's possible for a great man whom I greatly respect, Ben Bella, to be a Muslim and shall be a nationalist, and another one whom I greatly respect, Gamal Nasser, to be a Muslim and still be a nationalist, and Sukamo of Indonesia to be a Muslim and still be a nationalist, it was nationalism which enabled them to gain freedom for their people.

I'm still a Muslim but I'm also a nationalist, meaning that my political philosophy is black nationalism, my economic philosophy is black nationalism, my social philosophy is black nationalism. And when I say that this philosophy is black nationalism, to me this means that the political philosophy of black nationalism is that which is designed to encourage our people, the black people, to gain complete control over the politics and the politicians of our own community.

Our economic philosophy is that we should gain economic control over the economy of our own community, the businesses and the other things which create employment so that we can provide jobs for our own people instead of having to picket and boycott and beg someone else for a job.

And, in short, our social philosophy means that we feel that it is time to get together among our own kind and eliminate the evils that are destroying the moral fiber of our society, like drug addiction, drunkenness, adultery that leads to an abundance of bastard children, welfare problems. We believe that we should lift the level or the standard of our own society to a higher level wherein we will be satisfied and then not inclined toward pushing ourselves into other societies where we are not wanted.

All of that aside, tonight we are dealing with the black revolution. During recent years there has been much talk about a population explosion and whenever they are speaking of the population explosion, in my opinion they are referring primarily to the people in Asia or in Africa—the black, brown, red, and yellow people. It is seen by people of the West that as soon as the standard of living is raised in Africa and Asia automatically the people begin to reproduce abundantly. And there has been a great deal of fear engendered by this in the minds of the people of the West, who happen to be, on this earth, a very small minority.

In fact, in most of the thinking and planning of whites in the West today it's easy to see the fear in their minds, conscious minds and subconscious minds, that the masses of dark people in the West, in the East rather, who already outnumber them, will continue to increase and multiply and grow until they eventually overrun the people of the West like a human sea, a human tide, a human flood. And the fear of this can be seen in the minds, in the actions, of most of the people here in the West in practically every thing that they do. It governs political views and it governs their economic views and it governs most of their attitudes toward the present society.

REASON FOR FILIBUSTER

I was listening to Dirksen, the Senator from Illinois, in Washington, D.C., filibustering the civil-rights bill and one thing that he kept stressing over and over and over was that if this bill is passed it will change the social structure of America. Well, I know what he's getting at, and I think that most other people today, and especially our people, know what is meant when these whites who filibuster these bills, and express fears of changes in the social structure, our people are beginning to realize what they mean. Just as we can see that all over the world one of the main problems facing the West is race, likewise here in America today, most of your Negro leaders as well as the whites agree that 1964 itself appears to be one of the most explosive years yet in the history of America on the racial front, on the racial scene. Not only is this racial explosion probably to take place in America, but all of the ingredients for this racial explosion in America to blossom into a world-wide racial explosion present themselves right here in front of us. America's racial powder keg, in short, can actually fuse or ignite a world-wide powder keg.

And whites in this country who are still complacent when they see the possibilities of racial strife getting out of hand and you are complacent simply because you think you outnumber the racial minority in this country, what you have to bear in mind is wherein you might outnumber us in this country, you don't outnumber us all over the earth.

And any kind of racial explosion that takes place in this country today, in 1964, is not a racial explosion that can be confined to the shores of America. It is a racial explosion that can ignite the racial powder keg that exists all over the planet that we call earth. Now I think that nobody would disagree that the dark masses of Africa and Asia and Latin America are already seething with bitterness, animosity, hostility, unrest, and impatience with the racial intolerance that they themselves have experienced at the hands of the white West.

And just as they themselves have the ingredients of hostility toward the West in general, here we also have 22,000,000 African-Americans, black, brown, red, and yellow people in this country who are also seething with bitterness and impatience and hostility and animosity at the racial intolerance not only of the white West but of white America in particular. And by the hundreds of thousands today we find our own people have become impatient, turning away from your white nationalism, which you call democracy, toward the militant uncompromising policy of black nationalism. I point out right here that as soon as we announced we were going to start a black nationalist party in this country we received mail from coast to coast, especially from young people at the college level, the university level, who expressed complete sympathy and support and a desire to take an active part in any kind of political action based on black nationalism, designed to correct or eliminate immediately evils that our people have suffered here for 400 years.

The black nationalists to many of you may represent only a minority in the community. And therefore you might have a tendency to classify them as something insignificant. But just as the fuse is the smallest part or the smallest piece in the powder keg it is yet that little fuse that ignites the entire powder keg. The black nationalists to you may represent a small minority in the so-called Negro community. But they just happen to be composed of the type of ingredient necessary to fuse or ignite the entire black community. And this is one thing that whites—whether you call yourselves liberals or conservatives or racists or whatever else you might choose to be—one thing that you have to realize is, where the black community is concerned, although there the large majority you come in contact with may impress you as being moderate and patient and loving and long suffering and all that kind of stuff, the minority who you consider to be Muslims or nationalists happen to be made of the type of ingredient that can easily spark the black community. This should be understood. Because to me a powder keg is nothing without a fuse.

1964 will be America's hottest year; her hottest year yet; a year of much racial violence and much racial bloodshed. But it won't be blood that's going to flow only on one side. The new generation of black people that have grown up in this country during recent years are already forming the opinion, and it's a just opinion, that if there is to be bleeding, it should be reciprocal—bleeding on both sides.

It should also be understood that the racial sparks that are ignited here in America today could easily turn into a flaming fire abroad which only means it could engulf all the people of this earth into a giant race war. You cannot confine it to one little neighborhood, or one little community, or one little country. What happens to a black man in America today happens to the black man in Africa. What happens to a black man in America and Africa happens to the black man in Asia and to the man down in Latin America. What happens to one of us today happens to all of us. And when this is realized I think that the whites—who are intelligent even if they aren't moral or aren't just or aren't impressed by legalities—those who are intelligent will realize that when they touch this one, they are touching all of them, and this in itself will have a tendency to be a checking factor.

The seriousness of this situation must be faced up to. I was in Cleveland last night, Cleveland, Ohio. In fact I was there Friday, Saturday and yesterday. Last Friday the warning was given that this is a year of bloodshed, that the black man has ceased to turn the other cheek, that he has ceased to be non-violent, that he has ceased to feel that he must be confined to all these restraints that are put upon him by white society in struggling for what white society says he was supposed to have had a hundred years ago.

So today, when the black man starts reaching out for what America says are his rights, the black man feels that he is within his rights—when he becomes the victim of brutality by those who are depriving him of his rights—to do whatever is necessary to protect himself. And an example of this was taking place last night at this same time in Cleveland, where the police were putting water hoses on our people there and also throwing tear gas at them and they met a hail of stones, a hail of rocks, a hail of bricks. Couple weeks ago in Jacksonville, Florida, a young teenage Negro was throwing Molotov cocktails.

Well Negroes didn't do this ten years ago. But what you should learn from this is that they are waking up. It was stones yesterday, Molotov cocktails today; it will be hand grenades tomorrow and whatever else is available the next day. The seriousness of this situation must be faced up to. You should not feel that I am inciting someone to violence. I'm only warning of a powder-keg situation. You can take it or leave it. If you take the warning perhaps you can still save yourself. But if you ignore it or ridicule it, well death is already at your doorstep. There are 22,000,000 African-Americans who are ready to fight for independence right here. When I say fight for independence right here, I don't mean any non-violent fight, or turn-the-other-cheek fight. Those days are gone. Those days are over.

If George Washington didn't get independence for this country non-violently, and if Patrick Henry didn't come up with a non-violent statement, and you taught me to look upon them as patriots and heroes, then it's time for you to realize that I have studied your books well.

POWER OF MINORITY

Our people, 22,000,000 African-Americans, are fed up with America's hypocritical democracy and today we care nothing about the odds that are against us. Every time a black man gets ready to defend himself some Uncle Tom tries to tell us, how can you win? That's Tom talking. Don't listen to him. This is the first thing we hear: the odds are against you. You're dealing with black people who don't care anything about odds. We care nothing about odds.

Again I go right back to the people who founded and secured the independence of this country from the colonial power of England. When George Washington and the others got ready to declare or come up with the Declaration of Independence, they didn't care anything about the odds of the British Empire. They were fed up with taxation without representation. And you've got 22,000,000 black people in this country today, 1964, who are fed up with taxation without representation, and will do the same thing. Who are ready, willing and justified to do the same thing today to bring about independence for our people that your forefathers did to bring about independence for your people.

And I say your people because I certainly couldn't include myself among those for whom independence was fought in 1776. How in the world can a Negro talk about the Declaration of Independence when he is still singing "We Shall Overcome." Our people are increasingly developing the opinion that we just have nothing to lose but the chains of segregation and the chains of second-class citizenship.

STRUGGLES WILL MERGE

So 1964 will see the Negro revolt evolve and merge into the world-wide black revolution that has been taking place on this earth since 1945. The so-called revolt will become a real black revolution. Now the black revolution has been taking place in Africa and Asia and in Latin America. Now when I say black, I mean non-white. Black, brown, red or yellow. Our brothers and sisters in Asia, who were colonized by the Europeans, our brothers and sisters in Africa, who were colonized by the Europeans, and in Latin America, the peasants, who were colonized by the Europeans, have been involved in a struggle since 1945 to get the colonialists, or the colonizing powers, the Europeans, off their land, out of their country.

This is a real revolution. Revolution is always based on land. Revolution is never based on begging somebody for an integrated cup of coffee. Revolutions are never fought by turning the other cheek. Revolutions are never based upon love your enemy, and pray for those who spitefully use you. And revolutions are never waged singing, "We Shall Overcome." Revolutions are based upon bloodshed. Revolutions are never compromising. Revolutions are never based upon negotiations. Revolutions are never based upon any kind of tokenism whatsoever. Revolutions are never even based upon that which is begging a corrupt society or a corrupt system to accept us into it. Revolutions overturn systems, and there is no system on this earth which has proven itself more corrupt, more criminal than this system, that in 1964 still colonizes 22,000,000 African-Americans, still enslaves 22,000,000 Afro-Americans.

There is no system more corrupt than a system that represents itself as the example of freedom, the example of democracy and can go all over this earth telling other people how to straighten out their house, and you have citizens of this country who have to use bullets if they want to cast a ballot. The greatest weapon the colonial powers have used in the past against our people has always been divide and conquer.

America is a colonial power. She has colonized 22,000,000 Afro-Americans by depriving us of first-class citizenship, by depriving us of civil rights, actually by depriving us of human rights. She has not only deprived us of the right to be a citizen, she has deprived us of the right to be human beings, the right to be recopied and respected as men and women. And in this country, the black can be 50 years old and he is still a "boy."

I grew up with white people. I was integrated before they even invented the word and I have never met white people yet—if you are around them long enough—who won't refer to you as a "boy" or a "gal," no matter how old you are or what school you came out of, no matter what your intellectual or professional level is. In this society we remain "boys."

AMERICA'S STRATEGY

So America's strategy is the same strategy as that which was used in the past by the colonial powers: divide and conquer. She plays one Negro leader against the other. She plays one Negro organization against the other. She makes us think we have different objectives, different goals. As soon as one Negro says something, she runs to this Negro and asks him what do you think about what he said. Why anybody can see through that today— except some of the Negro leaders.

All of our people have the same goals. The same objective. That objective is freedom, justice, equality. All of us want recognition and respect as human beings. We don't want to be integrationists. Nor do we want to be separationists. We want to be human beings. Integration is only a method that is used by some groups to obtain freedom, justice, equality and respect as human beings. Separation is only a method that is used by other groups to obtain freedom, justice, equality or human dignity.

So our people have made the mistake of confusing the methods with the objectives. As long as we agree on objectives, we should never fan out with each other just because we believe in different methods or tactics or strategy to reach a common objective.

We have to keep in mind at all times that we are not fighting for integration, nor are we fighting for separation. We are fighting for recognition as human beings. We are fighting for the right to live as free humans in this society. In fact, we are actually fighting for rights that are even greater than civil-rights and that is human rights.

We are fighting for human rights in 1964. This is a shame. The civil-rights struggle has failed to produce concrete results because it has kept us barking up the wrong tree. It has made us put the cart ahead of the horse. We must have human rights before we can secure civil rights. We must be respected as humans before we can be recognized as citizens.

Among the so-called Negroes in this country, as a rule the civil-rights groups, those who believe in civil rights, they spend most of their time trying to prove they are Americans. Their thinking is usually domestic, confined to the boundaries of America, and they always look upon themselves as a minority. When they look upon themselves upon the American stage, the American stage is a white stage. So a black man standing on that stage in America automatically is in the minority. He is the underdog, and in his struggle he always uses an approach that is a begging hat-in-hand, compromising approach.

Whereas the other segment or section in America, known as the nationalist, black nationalists, are more interested in human rights than they are in civil rights. And they place more stress on human rights than they do on civil rights. The difference between the thinking and the scope of the Negroes who are involved in the human rights struggle and those who are involved in the civil rights struggle—those so-called Negroes involved in the human rights struggle don't look upon themselves as Americans.

They look upon themselves as a part of dark mankind. They see the whole struggle not within the confines of the American stage, but they look upon the struggle on the world stage. And, in the world context, they see that the dark man outnumbers the white man. On the world stage the white man is just a microscopic minority.

So in this country you find two different types of Afro-Americans, the type who looks upon himself as a minority and you as the majority, because his scope is limited to the American scene; and then you have the type who looks upon himself as part of the majority and you as part of a microscopic minority. And this one uses a different approach in trying to struggle for his rights. He doesn't beg. He doesn't thank you for what you give him, because you are only giving him what he should have had a hundred years ago. He doesn't think you are doing him any favors.

NO PROGRESS

He doesn't see any progress that he has made since the Civil War. He sees not one iota of progress because, number one, if the Civil War had freed him, he wouldn't need civil-rights legislation today. If the Emancipation Proclamation, issued by that great shining liberal called Lincoln, had freed him, he wouldn't be singing "We Shall Overcome" today. If the amendments to the Constitution had solved his problem, still his problem wouldn't be here today. And even ff the Supreme Court desegregation decision of 1954 was genuinely and sincerely designed to solve his problem, his problem wouldn't be with us today.

So this kind of black man is thinking, he can see where every maneuver that America has made—supposedly to solve this problem—has been nothing but political trickery and treachery of the worst order. So today he doesn't have any confidence in these so-called liberals. Now I know that you—all that have come in here tonight don't call yourselves liberals. Because that's a nasty name today. It represents hypocrisy. So these two different types of black people exist in the so-called Negro community and they are beginning to wake up and their awakening is producing a very dangerous situation.

So you have whites in the community who express sincerity when they say they want to help. Well how can they help? How can a white person help the black man solve his problem? Number one: you can't solve it for him. You can help him solve it, but you can't solve it for him today. One of the best ways that you can solve it—or to help him solve it—is to let the so-called Negro, who has been involved in the civil rights struggle, see that the civil rights struggle must be expanded beyond the level of civil rights to human rights. Once it is expanded beyond the level of civil rights to the level of human rights, it opens the door for all of our brothers and sisters in Africa and Asia, who have their independence, to come to our rescue.

CRIMINAL SITUATION

Why, when you go to Washington, D.C., expecting those crooks down there to pass some kind—and that's what they are—to pass some kind of civil rights legislation to correct a very criminal situation, what you are doing is encouraging the black man, who is the victim, to take his case into the court that's controlled by the criminal that made him the victim. It will never be solved in that way. Just like running from the wolf to the fox. The civil rights struggle involves the black man taking his case to the white man's court. But when he fights it at the human rights level, it is a different situation. It opens the door to take Uncle Sam to the world court. The black man doesn't have to go to court to be free. Uncle Sam should be taken to court and made to tell why the black man is not free in a so-called free society. Uncle Sam should be taken into the United Nations and charged with violating the UN charter on human rights.

You can forget civil rights. How are you going to get civil rights with men like Eastland and men like Dirksen and men like Johnson? It has to be taken out of their hands and taken into the hands of those whose power and authority exceed theirs. Washington has become too corrupt. Uncle Sam's conscience—Uncle Sam has become bankrupt when it comes to a conscience—it is impossible for Uncle Sam to solve the problem of 22,000,000 black people in this country. It is absolutely impossible to do it in Uncle Sam's courts—whether it is the Supreme Court or any other kind of court that comes under Uncle Sam's jurisdiction.

The only alternative that the black man has in America today is to take it out of Senator Dirksen's and Senator Eastland's and President Johnson's jurisdiction and take it downtown on the East River and place it before that body of men who represent international law and let them know that the human rights of black people are being violated in the country that professes to be the moral leader of the free world.

Any time you have a filibuster in America, in the Senate, in 1964 over the rights of 22,000,000 black people, over the citizenship of 22,000,000 black people or that will effect the freedom and justice and equality of 22,000,000 black people, it's time for that government itself to be taken before a world court. How can you condemn South Africa?

There are only 11,000,000 of our people in South Africa, there are 22,000,000 of them here. And we are receiving an injustice which is just as criminal as that which is being done to the black people of South Africa.

So today those whites who profess to be liberals—and as far as I am concerned it's just lip profession—you understand why our people don't have civil rights. You're white. You can go and hang out with another white liberal and see how hypocritical they are. While a lot of you sitting right here know that you've seen whites up in a Negro's face with flowery words and as soon as that Negro walks away you listen to how your white friend talks. We have black people who can pass as white. We know how you talk.

We can see that it is nothing but a governmental conspiracy to continue to deprive the black people in this country of their rights. And the only way we will get these rights restored is by taking it out of Uncle Sam's hands. Take him to court and charge him with genocide, the mass murder of millions of black people in this country—political murder, economic murder, social murder, mental murder. This is the crime that this government has committed and, if you yourself don't do something about it in time, you are going to open the doors for something to be done about it from outside forces.

I read in the paper yesterday where one of the Supreme Court Justices, Goldberg, was crying about the violation of human rights of 3,000,000 Jews in the Soviet Union. Imagine this. I haven't got anything against Jews, but that's their problem. How in the world are you going to cry about problems on the other side of the world when you haven't got the problems straightened out here? How can the plight of 3,000,000 Jews in Russia be qualified to be taken to the United Nations by a man who is a Justice in this Supreme Court, and is supposed to be a liberal, supposed to be a friend of black people and hasn't opened up his mouth one time about taking the plight of black people down here to the United Nations?

POLITICALLY MATURE

Our people are becoming more politically mature. Their eyes are coming open. They are beginning to see the trend in all of the American politics today. They notice that every time there is an election it is so close among whites that they have to count the votes over again. This happened in Massachusetts when they were running for governor, this happened in Rhode Island, it happened in Minnesota, and many other places, and it happened in the election between Kennedy and Nixon. Things are so close that any minority that has a bloc vote can swing it either way.

And I think that most students of political science agree that it was the 80 percent support that Kennedy got from the black man in this country that enabled him to sit in the White House. Sat down there four years and the Negro was still in the doghouse. The same ones that we put in the White House have continued to keep us in the doghouse. The Negro can see that he holds the balance of power in this country politically.

It is he who puts in office the one who gets in office. Yet when the Negro helps that person get in office the Negro gets nothing in return. All he gets is a few appointments. A few handpicked Uncle Tom handkerchief-head Negroes are given big jobs in Washington, D.C. And then those Negroes come back and try and make us think that that administration is going to lead us to the promised land of integration. And the only ones whose problems have been solved have been those handpicked Negroes. A few big Negroes got jobs who didn't even need the jobs. They already were working. But the masses of black people are still unemployed.

The present administration, the Democratic administration, has been there for four years. Yet no meaningful legislation has been passed by them that proposes to benefit black people in this country, despite the fact that in the House they have 267 Democrats and only

177 are Republicans. They control two thirds of the House. In the Senate there are 67 Democrats and only 33 Republicans. The Democrats control two thirds of the government and it is the Negroes who put them in a position to control the government. Yet they give the Negroes nothing in return but a few handouts in the form of appointments that are only used as window-dressing to make it appear that the problem is being solved.

TRICKERY AND TREACHERY

No, something is wrong. And when these black people wake up and find out for real the trickery and the treachery that has been heaped upon us you are going to have revolution. And when I say revolution I don't mean that stuff they were talking about last year about "We Shall Overcome." The Democrats get Negro support, yet the Negroes get nothing in return. The Negroes put the Democrats first, yet the Democrats put the Negroes last. And the alibi that the Democrats use—they blame the Democrats.

A Dixiecrat is nothing but a Democrat in disguise. You show me a Dixiecrat and I'll show you a Democrat. And chances are, you show me a Democrat and I'll show you a Dixiecrat. Because Dixie in reality means all that territory south of the Canadian border. There are 16 Senatorial committees that run this government. Of the 16 Senatorial committees that run the government, ten of them are controlled by chairmen that are from the South. Of the 20 Congressional committees that help run the government, 12 of them are controlled by Southern segregationists.

Think of this: ten of the Senatorial committees are in the hands of the Dixiecrats, 12 of the 20 Congressional committees are in the hands of the Dixiecrats. These committees control the government. And you're going to tell us that the South lost the Civil War? The South controls the government. And they control it because they have seniority. And they have seniority because in the states that they come from, they deny Negroes the right to vote.

If Negroes could vote south of the—yes, if Negroes could vote South of the Canadian border—if Negroes could vote in the southern part of the South, Ellender wouldn't be the head of the Agricultural and Forestry Committee, Richard Russell wouldn't be head of the Armed Services Committee, Robertson of Virginia wouldn't be head of the Banking and Currency Committee. Imagine that, all of the banking and currency of the government is in the hands of a cracker.

In fact, when you see how many of these committee men are from the South you can see that we have nothing but a cracker government in Washington, D.C. And their head is a cracker President. I said a cracker President. Texas is just as much a cracker state as Mississippi—and even more so. In Texas they lynch you with a Texas accent and in Mississippi they lynch you with a Mississippi accent.

And the first thing this man did when he came in office was invite all the big Negroes down for coffee. James Farmer was one of the first ones—the head of CORE. I have nothing against him. He's all right—Farmer, that is. But could that same President have invited James Farmer to Texas for coffee? And if James Farmer went to Texas, could he have taken his white wife with him to have coffee with the President? Any time you have a man who can't straighten out Texas, how can he straighten out the country. No, you're barking up the wrong tree.

If Negroes in the South could vote, the Dixiecrats would lose power. When the Dixiecrats lost power, the Democrats would lose power. A Dixiecrat lost is a Democrat lost. Therefore the two of them have to conspire with each other to stay in power. The Northern Democrat puts all the blame on the Southern Dixiecrat. It's a con game, a giant political con game. The job of the Northern Democrat is to make the Negro think that he is our friend. He is always smiling and wagging his tail and telling us how much he can do for us if we vote for him. But, at the same time he's out in front telling us what he's going to do, behind the door he's in cahoots with the Southern Democrat setting up the machinery to make sure he'll never have to keep his promise.

This is the conspiracy that our people have faced in this country for the past 100 years. And today you have a new generation of black people who have come on the scene who have become disenchanted with the entire system, who have become disillusioned over the system and who are ready now and willing to do something about it. So in my conclusion in speaking about the black revolution, America today is at a time or in a day or at an hour where she is the first country on this earth that can actually have a bloodless revolution. In the past revolutions have been bloody. Historically you just don't have a peaceful revolution. Revolutions are bloody, revolutions are violent, revolutions cause bloodshed and death follows in their paths. America is the only country in history in a position to bring about a revolution without violence and bloodshed. But America is not morally equipped to do so.

Why is America in a position to bring about a bloodless revolution? Because the Negro in this country holds the balance of power and if the Negro in this country were given what the Constitution says he is supposed to have, the added power of the Negro in this country would sweep all of the racists and the segregationists out of office. It would change the entire political structure of the country. It would wipe out the Southern segregationist that now controls America's foreign policy, as well as America's domestic policy.

And the only way without bloodshed that this can be brought about is that the black man has to be given full use of the ballot in every one of the 50 states. But if the black man doesn't get the ballot, then you are going to be faced with another man who forgets the ballot and starts using the bullet.

Revolutions are fought to get control of land, to remove the absentee landlord and gain control of the land and the institutions that flow from that land. The black man has been in a very low condition because he has had no control whatsoever over any land. He has been a beggar economically, a beggar politically, a beggar socially, a beggar even when it comes to trying to get some education. So that in the past the type of mentality that was developed in this colonial system among our people, today is being overcome. And as the young ones come up they know what they want. And as they listen to your beautiful preaching about democracy and all those other flowery words, they know what they're supposed to have.

So you have a people today who not only know what they want, but also know what they are supposed to have. And they themselves are hearing another generation that is coming up that not only will know what it wants and know what it should have, but also will be ready and willing to do whatever is necessary to see that what they should have materializes immediately. Thank you.

SELECTIVE CHRONOLOGY

Julian Bond

1900	July 24–27	Black homes and schools destroyed in New Orleans race riot.
	August 12	Whites attack blacks in New York.
	November 6	William McKinley reelected President; Theodore Roosevelt elected Vice-President.
1901	March 4	North Carolina's George H. White leaves Congress; last black member for more than 25 years.
	September 6	President McKinley assassinated. Roosevelt succeeds him.
	October 16	Booker T. Washington (BTW) dines with President Roosevelt at the White House, creating an uproar.
1903		W.E.B. Du Bois' (WEBD's) *Souls Of Black Folk* is published, helping to organize criticism of BTW.
1904	August 16	Paul Reed and Willis Cato seized from jailers at their murder trial in Statesboro, Georgia, and burned alive.
1905	July 11–13	A group of black intellectuals meets near Niagara Falls and adopts resolutions demanding racial equality.
1906	April 13	Clashes erupt after white civilians taunt black soldiers in Brownsville, Texas; three white men die. President Roosevelt dishonorably discharges the soldiers.
	September 22–24	Twenty-one die in Atlanta race riot.
1908		White anti-black riot in Abraham Lincoln's hometown, Springfield, Illinois, prompts concerned whites to call for a conference which leads to founding of the National Association for the Advancement of Colored People (NAACP) in 1909.
	November 3	William Howard Taft elected President.

1909	February 12	White liberals and black intellectuals, including Jane Addams, Mary White Ovington, WEBD, Oswald Garrison Villard, and John Dewey form the NAACP.
	March 31	U.S. occupation of Cuba ends.
	November 18	U.S. warships ordered to Nicaragua.
1910	April	The National Urban League (NUL) is formed in New York.
1911	March 7	Twenty thousand U.S. troops dispatched to Mexican border.
1912	November 5	Woodrow Wilson elected President.
1914	April 21	U.S. forces seize customs house at Vera Cruz, Mexico; Marines occupy the city.
	June 28	Austrian Archduke Francis Ferdinand assassinated.
1915	January 14	Two hundred whites storm jail in Monticello, Georgia, and lynch four blacks, members of Daniel Barber family.
	June 21	Supreme Court outlaws "grandfather clauses" used to deny blacks the franchise in *Guinn v. United States.*
	December 4	Dormant Ku Klux Klan revived under new charter granted by Georgia.
1916	March	U.S. troops enter Mexico in search of Pancho Villa.
	May	U.S. Marines land in Santa Domingo, remain until 1924.
	November	Woodrow Wilson reelected President.
1917	April 2	Jeannette Rankin of Montana becomes first woman seated in House of Representatives.
	April 16	United States enters World War I. Three hundred thousand blacks will serve in the war; 1400 will be commissioned as officers.
	July 1–3	At least 40 blacks killed in East St. Louis, Illinois, race riot.
	July 28	NAACP organizes a silent march of 10,000 down Fifth Avenue to protest racism.
	August 23	Black soldiers and white civilians clash in Houston, Texas; 17 whites, two blacks are killed. Thirteen blacks are later executed.
1918	February 19–21	Organized by WEBD, the first Pan-African Congress meets in Paris, concurrently with the Paris Peace Conference.
	July 13– October 1	More than 25 race riots occur across U.S., leaving over 100 dead and thousands wounded. Eighty-three lynchings recorded in 1918.
	November 11	World War I ends.

1920	August 1–2	Marcus Garvey's (MG's) Universal Negro Improvement Association's (UNIA's) National Convention meets in New York; MG speaks to 25,000 at Madison Square Garden.
	November 2	Warren G. Harding elected President.
1922–23		
	October to October	An estimated 500,000 blacks leave the South. Klan violence increases. Oklahoma placed under martial law because of terrorist activity by Klan.
1925	May 8	A. Philip Randolph (APR) organizes the Brotherhood of Sleeping Car Porters.
	August 8	Forty thousand Ku Klux Klansmen march down Washington's Pennsylvania Avenue.
1926	May 10	U.S. Marines land in Nicaragua.
1927	March 7	In *Nixon v. Herndon*, the Supreme Court strikes down a Texas law excluding blacks from Democratic primaries.
	December	MG, convicted in 1925 for mail fraud, released from federal prison and deported.
1928	November 6	Herbert Hoover elected president. Illinois Republican Congressman Oscar DePriest elected, the first black since 1901.
1929	January 15	Martin Luther King Jr. (MLK) born in Atlanta.
	October 29	Stock market crashes, beginning the Great Depression.
		Ten lynchings recorded in 1929.
1930	March 31	After President Hoover nominates North Carolina Judge John J. Parker to the Supreme Court, the NAACP leads a successful campaign against his nomination.
	June 7	The *New York Times* announces that the word "Negro" will be spelled with a capital "N."
1931	April 6	Nine black youths accused of raping two white women go on trial in Scottsboro, Alabama.
1932	November 8	Franklin Delano Roosevelt (FDR) is elected President, promising a "New Deal" to fight the Depression.
1934	July	Southern Tenant Farmers' Union organized.
	November 7	Black Democrat Arthur Mitchell defeats Rep. DePriest in Chicago.

1934		Elijah Muhammad—born Elijah Poole in Georgia in 1897—succeeds W. D. Fard as leader of the Nation of Islam.
1935	June 25	Joe Louis defeats Primo Carnera at Yankee Stadium.
1936	August 9	American Olympian Jesse Owens wins four Gold medals at the Summer Olympics in Berlin, embarrassing Adolph Hitler.
	December 8	NAACP successfully files *Gibbs v. Board of Education* in Montgomery County, Maryland, equalizing white and black teachers' salaries.
	November 3	FDR reelected.
1937	March 26	William H. Hastie becomes the first black federal judge.
	June 22	Joe Louis becomes the heavyweight champion by defeating James J. Braddock.
1938	December 12	In *Missouri ex rel. Gaines* the Supreme Court rules states must provide equal, if separate, facilities within their boundaries.
1939	March	Daughters of the American Revolution refuses Marian Anderson permission to sing at Washington's Constitution Hall; Secretary of the Interior Harold Ickes arranges her appearance on Easter Sunday at the Lincoln Memorial, where 75,000 gather to hear her.
	September 3	Great Britain and France declare war on Germany.
	October 11	NAACP Legal Defense and Educational Fund is organized.
1940	February	Richard Wright's *Native Son* becomes a best seller.
	March	Hattie McDaniel becomes the first black to receive an Oscar for her role as "Mammy" in "Gone With The Wind".
	April	Virginia Legislature adopts black composer James A. Bland's "Carry Me Back To Old Virginny" as the state song.
	May 26–June 4	British Expeditionary Forces retreat from Dunkirk.
	June 10	MG dies in London.
	September 27	FDR meets with black leaders to discuss discrimination in the military.
	October 8	Senate kills anti-lynching bill.
	October 9	White House declares War Department policy is "not to intermingle colored and white enlisted personnel in the same regimental organizations."
	October 16	Benjamin O. Davis Sr. makes Brigadier General, becoming the highest ranking black in the armed services.
	October 25	FDR meets with Committee on Participation of Negroes in the National Defense Program.
	November 5	FDR reelected; Henry Wallace elected Vice-President.

1941	April 12	APR announces "plans for an all-out March of ten-thousand Negroes on Washington are in the making" to protest discrimination in defense industries and the military.
	April 28	Supreme Court rules that separate railroad facilities must be substantially equal.
	May 1	March on Washington (MOW) Committee issues a formal call for a July 1 march.
	June 13	New York Mayor Fiorella LaGuardia and Eleanor Roosevelt met with APR and MOW leadership.
	June 15	FDR issues a memorandum saying "I shall expect the Office of Production Management to take immediate steps to facilitate the full utilization of our productive manpower."
	June 18	FDR meets with MOW Committee leaders.
	June 22	Nazi Germany invades the Soviet Union.
	June 25	FDR issues Executive Order 8802 establishing the Fair Employment Practices Commission (FEPC).
	June 28	APR announces the MOW will be postponed.
	October 20–21	FEPC holds its first hearings in Los Angeles.
	December 7	Japanese attack Pearl Harbor; U.S. enters World War II December 8.
1942	March	Fifty black organizations declare "that the Negro people were cool to the war effort because of continued racial discrimination."
	June 16	Eighteen thousand blacks pack a New York MOW rally.
	June 26	Twenty-six thousand overflow Chicago MOW rally.
	June	Congress of Racial Equality (CORE) is organized by an interracial group in Chicago.
	November 3	Democrat William L. Dawson elected to Congress from Chicago.
1943	May 12–August 2	Forty killed in race riots; troops called out in Mobile and Detroit.
1944	April 3	In *Smith v. Allwright* the Supreme Court rules the white-only primary unconstitutional.
	August 1	New York Democrat Adam Clayton Powell elected to Congress.
	November 7	FDR reelected President.
	December 13	Black women permitted to enter the Women's Naval Corps (WAVES).
1945	March 12	New York establishes the first state FEPC.
	April 12	FDR dies; Harry S. Truman (HST) succeeds him.
	May 7	Germany surrenders.
	June	United Nations Charter approved.
	July 16	First atomic bomb exploded.
	August 6	Hiroshima destroyed by U.S. atomic bomb.
	September 2	Japan surrenders; World War II ends. More than one million blacks served.

1946	February 7	Senate filibuster kills bill for permanent FEPC.
	February	Malcolm Little sentenced to ten years in Massachusetts prison for burglary.
	June 3	In *Morgan v. Virginia* the Supreme Court outlaws segregation in interstate bus travel.
	December 5	HST names Committee on Civil Rights to investigate racial injustice.
1947	April 9	CORE sends "Freedom Riders" on a Journey of Reconciliation through the upper South to test *Morgan v. Virginia.*
	April 10	Jackie Robinson joins the Brooklyn Dodgers.
	October 29	HST's President Committee on Civil Rights releases "To Secure These Rights."
1948	January 12	In *Sipuel v. University of Oklahoma* the Supreme Court rules a state must provide a legal education for blacks if it offers a legal education to whites.
	March 31	APR tells a U.S. Senate Committee he will urge black youth to refuse induction in the armed services unless discrimination in the Selective Service System is ended.
	May 3	In *Shelley v. Kraemer* the Supreme Court rules restrictive housing covenants unenforceable.
	June 9	Attorney Oliver Hill elected to the Richmond, Virginia, City Council.
	July 14	Southerners walk out of the Democratic National Convention to protest a civil rights plank.
	July 26	HST issues Executive Orders 9980 and 9981 creating a Fair Employment Board to end racial discrimination in federal employment and a President's Committee on Equality of Treatment and Opportunity in the Armed Services.
	November 2	HST elected President.
1950	June 5	In *Sweatt v. Painter* the Supreme Court rules that equality in education requires more than identical physical facilities. In *McLaurin v. Oklahoma* the Court rules that, once admitted to a previously all-white school, a black student cannot be segregated within the school.
	June 27	U.S. enters the Korean War.
1951	February 2	Martinsville Seven executed in Richmond for raping a white woman.
	April 24	University of North Carolina admits its first black student.
	May 8	Willie McGee executed in Mississippi for raping a white woman.
	May 24	Washington, D. C., court outlaws segregation in District restaurants.
	July 12	Illinois Governor Adlai Stevenson calls out the National Guard to suppress a riot against a black family who moved into an all-white neighborhood in Cicero, Illinois.
	October 1	The 24th Infantry, the last all-black Army unit, deactivated.
	December 25	NAACP leaders Harry T. and Harriet Moore assassinated in Mims, Florida.

1952	January 12	University of Tennessee admits black students.
	August	Malcolm Little released from Massachusetts prison.
	November 4	Dwight D. Eisenhower (DDE) elected President; Richard M. Nixon (RN) elected Vice-President.
	December 30	Tuskegee Institute reports 1952 was the first lynching-free year in seventy-one years.
1953	March 5	Joseph Stalin dies.
	May 7	French forces surrender at Dien Bien Phu in Vietnam.
	June 8	In *District of Columbia v. John R. Thompson Co., Inc.* the Supreme Court upholds desegregation of Washington's restaurants.
	June 19	Bus boycott protesting unequal treatment begins in Baton Rouge, Louisiana.
	June 27	Korean armistice signed.
	June	Dr. Walter Ridley becomes first black graduate of a University of Virginia professional school.
	August 4	Riot against integrated housing begins in Chicago.
	August 20	Soviet Union announces the explosion of a hydrogen bomb.
1954	May 17	In *Brown v. Board of Education* the Supreme Court rules unanimously that segregated public schools are inherently unequal and unconstitutional, overturning 1896's *Plessy v. Ferguson.*
	June 29	Central Intelligence Agency (CIA) sponsored coup overthrows the government of Guatemala.
	July	First "White Citizens Council" organized in Indianola, Mississippi.
	July 21	U.S. refuses to sign Geneva Accord on Indochina.
	September 7–8	Public schools in Baltimore, Maryland, and Washington, D. C., desegregated.
	September	Bobby Bland enters the University of Virginia Engineering School.
	November 2	Black Detroit Democrat Charles Diggs elected to Congress.
	October	White Citizens Council chapter organized in Selma, Alabama.
1955	January 18	DDE establishes President's Committee on Government Policy to enforce a non-discriminatory policy in federal hiring.
	April 11	Roy Wilkins becomes the NAACP's Executive Secretary.
	May 7	NAACP leader Rev. George Wesley Lee killed in Belzoni, Mississippi.
	May 31	In *Brown II*, the Supreme Court orders schools integrated "with all deliberate speed."
	July 22	Alabama enacts a "Pupil Placement Law" to circumvent school desegregation.
	August 1	Georgia teachers are ordered by the State Board of Education to resign from the NAACP or face firing.
	August 13	Political activist Lamar Smith killed in Brookhaven, Mississippi.
	August 28	Fourteen-year old Emmett Till kidnapped and murdered in Money, Mississippi.

1955	November 25	Interstate Commerce Commission (ICC) prohibits segregation in public vehicles and waiting rooms used in interstate travel.
	October 10	Supreme Court orders Autherine Lucy admitted to the University of Alabama.
	October 22	John Earl Reese killed in Mayflower, Texas, by nightriders opposed to black school improvements.
	December 1	Rosa Parks arrested for refusing to give up her seat to a white man on a Montgomery, Alabama, bus.
	December 5	Parks convicted; a successful one-day boycott held to protest her arrest. MLK is elected leader of boycott organization, the Montgomery Improvement Association (MIA).
1956	January 30	MLK home bombed in Montgomery.
	February 1	MIA files lawsuit against bus segregation.
	February 3	Autherine Lucy admitted to the University of Alabama.
	February 7	Alabama students riot; Lucy suspended.
	February 21	Montgomery grand jury indicts 115 boycott leaders. Bayard Rustin arrives in Montgomery to advise MLK.
	February 28	Rustin, Stanley Levison, Ella J. Baker organize "In Friendship" in New York to assist southern activists.
	February 29	Lucy expelled for making "false" and "outrageous" statements about university officials.
	March 11	Nineteen senators and 81 representatives, in Southern Manifesto, promise to use "all lawful means" to reverse *Brown v. Board of Education.*
	March 22	MLK convicted of leading illegal boycott.
	April	South Carolina State College students boycott classes to protest official harassment of NAACP.
	April 11	Singer Nat "King" Cole attacked on stage in Birmingham.
	April 23	Supreme Court overturns South Carolina bus segregation law.
	May 27	Florida A & M University students in Tallahassee begin boycott of segregated busses.
	June 1	Alabama outlaws NAACP.
	June 5	Rev. Fred Shuttlesworth and others organize the Alabama Christian Movement for Human Rights (ACMHR) in Birmingham.
	June 5	In *Browder v. Gayle* three-judge district court rules Montgomery's bus segregation is illegal.
	June 30	Tallahassee bus service suspended.
	October 23	Hungarian uprising begins.
	November 4	Soviet troops attack Budapest and crush Hungarian revolt.
	November 6	DDE defeats Stevenson soundly.
	November 13	Supreme Court affirms Montgomery bus segregation ruling.
	December 20	MIA ends bus boycott.
	December 23	Tallahassee boycott ends; city continues segregation.
	December 25	Bomb destroys Shuttlesworth's home.

1956	December 26	Shuttlesworth, others arrested for breaking Birmingham's bus segregation law.
	December 27	Tallahassee bus segregation declared illegal.
1957	January 10–11	Sixty meet at Atlanta's Ebeneezer Baptist Church to form "Southern Leadership Conference on Transportation and Nonviolence"; MLK is chosen Chairman.
	January 23	Willie James Edwards forced by Klansmen to jump to his death from a railroad bridge in Montgomery.
	February 14	MLK is elected President of Southern Negro Leadership Conference in New orleans.
	March	MLK visits Ghana to attend independence ceremonies.
	May 17	MLK addresses 15,000 at Prayer Pilgrimage in Washington at Lincoln Memorial.
	June	MLK meets Vice President RN. Blacks in Tuskegee, Alabama, begin boycott to protest gerrymander removing nearly all blacks from city limits.
	August	Southern Christian Leadership Conference (SCLC) holds first convention in Montgomery.
	September 9	1957 Civil Rights Act becomes law.
	September 24–25	DDE orders federal troops into Little Rock to halt interference with integration of Central High School.
	October 4	Soviet Union launches artificial satellite Sputnik.
1958	January	Baker sets up SCLC offices in Atlanta.
	January 31	U.S. launches satellite Explorer.
	February 12	SCLC begins "Crusade for Citizenship."
	May	Rev. John Tilley becomes SCLC Executive Director.
	June 23	MLK, Roy Wilkins, APR and NUL's Lester Granger meet with DDE.
	July 15	DDE sends U.S. Marines to Lebanon.
	August 19	NAACP Youth Council members in Oklahoma City begin lunch counter sit-in demonstrations.
	September 3	MLK arrested in Montgomery.
	September 20	MLK stabbed while autographing *Stride Toward Freedom* in New York.
	October 12	Atlanta synagogue bombed.
1959	April 15	Tilley resigns; Baker replaces him on temporary basis.
	April 25	Mack Charles Parker, accused of rape, is taken from his jail cell and lynched in Poplarville, Mississippi.
	September 7	U.S. Civil Rights Commission asks DDE to appoint federal registrars in areas where blacks are denied vote.
	December	Fidel Castro's revolutionaries overthrow Cuban dictator Fulgencio Batista.

1960	February 1	Four Greensboro students stage sit-in at Woolworth's Department store.
	February 17	Alabama grand jury indicts MLK for tax evasion.
	March	National Liberation Front (NLF) steps up war against U.S. backed Diem regime in South Vietnam.
	March 3	Vanderbilt University expels James Lawson for sit-in participation.
	March 7	Felton Turner of Houston beaten and hung-upside down in a tree, initials "KKK" carved in his chest.
	March 19	San Antonio becomes first city to integrate lunch counters.
	March 20	Florida Governor Leroy Collins calls lunch counter segregation "unfair and morally wrong."
	April 8	Weak civil rights bill survives Senate filibuster.
	April 15–17	Student Nonviolent Coordinating Committee (SNCC) organized at SCLC-sponsored conference at Shaw University, Raleigh, North Carolina.
	April 19	Nashville civil rights lawyer Z. Alexander Looby's home bombed.
	April 21	1960 Civil Rights Act becomes law.
	May 5	Soviet Union announces it has shot down a U.S. U-2 spy plane.
	May 28	All white Alabama jury acquits MLK.
	June 24	MLK meets Senator John F. Kennedy (JFK).
	June 28	Rustin resigns from SCLC after condemnation by Rep. Powell.
	July	SCLC volunteer Robert Moses, traveling for SNCC, meets Amzie Moore in Mississippi Delta.
	July 31	Elijah Muhammad calls for an all-black state. Membership in Nation of Islam estimated at 100,000.
	August	Rev. Wyatt Tee Walker replaces Baker as SCLC's Executive Director.
	September	North Vietnam backs NLF against U.S. backed Diem regime.
	October 19	MLK, fifty others arrested at sit-in at Atlanta's Rich's Department Store.
	October 26	MLK's earlier probation revoked; transferred to Reidsville State Prison.
	October 28	After intervention from Robert F. Kennedy (RFK), King is freed on bond.
	November 8	JFK defeats RN, winning by 119,000 votes out of 68,800,000 cast.
	December	In *Boynton v. Virginia*, Supreme Court prohibits segregation in waiting rooms and restaurants serving interstate bus passengers.
1961	January 11	Riot suspends two black students desegregating University of Georgia.
	January 18	DDE's farewell address warns against "acquisition of unwarranted influence . . . by the military-industrial complex."
	January 31	CORE's Tom Gaither, nine students arrested in Rock Hill, South Carolina.
	March 13	CORE announces Freedom Ride.
	April 17	CIA trained Cuban exiles unsuccessfully invade Cuba.
	May 4	CORE Freedom Ride begins from Washington, D. C., to New Orleans to test *Boynton v. Virginia*.
	May 14	Freedom Riders attacked by mobs in Anniston, Alabama, and Birmingham.
	May 17	Nashville students take up Freedom Ride.
	May 20	Riders assaulted in Montgomery.

1961	May 21–22	Riders besieged in Montgomery church; RFK sends federal marshals.
	June–August	Justice Department initiates talks with civil rights groups, foundations on beginning Voter Education Project (VEP).
	July	SCLC begins citizenship classes; Andrew J. Young hired to direct the program. Moses arrives in McComb.
	September	James Forman becomes SNCC's Executive Secretary.
	September 23	ICC, at RFK's insistence, issues new rules ending discrimination in interstate travel, effective December 1, 1961.
	September 25	Voter registration activist Herbert Lee killed in McComb, Mississippi.
	October	SNCC workers Charles Sherrod and Cordell Reagon arrive in Albany, Georgia.
	November 17	Albany Movement formed.
	December 1	Albany "Freedom Riders" arrested.
	December 11–15	Five hundred arrested in Albany.
	December 16	MLK arrested in Albany.
	December 18	Albany truce; MLK leaves town.
1962	January 18–20	Student protests over sit-in leaders' expulsions at Baton Rouge's Southern University, the nation's largest black school, close it down.
	February 26	Segregated transportation facilities, both interstate and intrastate, ruled unconstitutional by Supreme Court.
	March	SNCC workers sit-in RFK's office to protest jailings in Baton Rouge.
	March 20	FBI installs wiretaps on Levison's office.
	April 3	Full racial integration of military reserve units, except the National Guard, ordered by the Defense Department.
	April 9	Corporal Roman Duckworth shot by a police officer in Taylorsville, Mississippi.
	June	Leroy Willis becomes first black graduate of the University of Virginia College of Arts and Sciences.
	June	Secretary of Defense Robert McNamara visits South Vietnam, says, "We're winning this war."
	June	SNCC workers establish voter registration projects in rural Southwest Georgia.
	July 10–August 28	SCLC renews protests in Albany; MLK in jail July 10–12 & July 27–August 10.
	September 9	Two black churches used by SNCC for voter registration meetings burned in Sasser, Georgia.
	Sept 30–Oct 1	Supreme Court Justice Hugo Black orders James Meredith admitted to Ole Miss. Meredith enrolls; riot ensues. French photographer Paul Guihard and Oxford resident Ray Gunter are killed.
	October	Leflore County, Mississippi, supervisors cut off surplus food distribution in retaliation against voter drive.
	October 23	Federal Bureau of Investigation (FBI) begins Communist Infiltration (COMINFIL) investigation of SCLC.
	October 14–28	Cuban missile crisis.

1962	November 7–8	Edward Brooke elected Massachusetts Attorney General, Leroy Johnson Georgia State Senator, Augustus Hawkins first black from California in Congress.
	November 20	RFK authorizes wiretap on Levison's home telephone.
	November 20	JFK upholds 1960 campaign promise to eliminate housing segregation with "stroke of a pen."
1963	January	SNCC's Moses, six others, sue RFK and J. Edgar Hoover, FBI Director, for failure to enforce laws demanding protection of civil rights workers.
	January 9–10	SCLC meets in Dorchester, Georgia, to plan Birmingham campaign.
	January 28	Harvey Gantt enrolls in Clemson College.
	February	SNCC workers begin project in Selma.
	February 6	MLK and Walker meet in Birmingham with ACMHR Board.
	February 28	SNCC worker Jimmy Travis shot outside Greenwood, Mississippi.
	March 5	Mayoral results delay Birmingham campaign until run-off.
	April 2	Albert Boutwell defeats Eugene "Bull" Connor for Mayor of Birmingham.
	April 3	SCLC and ACMHR begin Birmingham protests.
	April 12–20	MLK writes "Letter From Birmingham City Jail."
	April 23	Baltimore postal worker and CORE volunteer William Moore killed in Atalla, Alabama, while on a march from Baltimore to Jackson, Mississippi.
	May	Buddhist revolt begins against Diem regime in South Vietnam.
	May 2–7	SCLC organizes children's demonstrations in Birmingham.
	May 8	SCLC suspends demonstrations.
	May 10	ACHMR and SCLC sign Birmingham desegregation agreement.
	May 31	Danville, Virginia, demonstrations begin.
	June 11	Alabama Governor George C. Wallace fails to halt admission of black student at University of Alabama; JFK federalizes National Guard and promises additional civil rights legislation.
	June 12	Mississippi NAACP Field Secretary Medgar Evers is assassinated in Jackson, Mississippi.
	June 12	After night rioting, SCLC suspends demonstrations in Savannah, Georgia.
	June 21	Danville grand jury indicts SNCC workers for "inciting the colored population to acts of violence against the white population."
	June–August	Civil rights protests in almost every American city.
	July 12	Modified martial law declared in Cambridge, Maryland.
	July 22	MLK and other civil rights leaders meet JFK to discuss March on Washington. Burke Marshall, RFK and JFK tell King to end relationship with Jack O'Dell and Levison.
	July 22	FBI requests wiretaps on New York home of SCLC lawyer Clarence Jones; RFK approves.
	August 2	Savannah desegregation agreement reached.
	August	Three SNCC workers and CORE worker indicted for inciting insurrection in Americus, Georgia. Federal grand jury in Macon indicts nine Albany Movement leaders and SNCC worker for conspiracy to obstruct justice.

1963	August 28	Two hundred and fifty thousand gather at March on Washington as MLK gives "I Have A Dream" speech.
	September 15	Birmingham's 16th Street Baptist Church bombed; four girls—Addie Mae Collins, Carole Denise McNair, Carole Rosamond Robertson, Cynthia Diane Wesley—are killed. Later that day, a white youth shoots and kills 13-year-old Virgil Ware.
	October 21	RFK approves wiretap on MLK's home, New York and Atlanta SCLC offices.
	October 22	Two hundred and fifty thousand school children boycott Chicago's segregated schools.
	November 2	U.S. sanctioned coup in South Vietnam leads to Diem's overthrow and murder.
	November 22	JFK assassinated in Dallas.
	December 3	MLK meets President Lyndon B. Johnson (LBJ).
	December 23	FBI holds Washington meeting to discuss discrediting MLK.
1964	January 5–7	FBI conducts microphone surveillance of MLK's room at Washington's Willard Hotel; 14 other "bugs" are used against him between January, 1964 and November, 1965.
	January 27	FBI installs "misur" (microphone surveillance) at MLK's Milwaukee hotel room.
	January 31	Louis Allen, witness to September 25, 1961 Herbert Lee slaying, killed in McComb.
	January–February	James Bevel and Diane Nash draft plan for massive Alabama right-to-vote demonstrations.
	March 12	Malcolm X announces withdrawal from the Nation of Islam.
	March 28–April 4	SCLC demonstrations in St. Augustine, Florida.
	April 26	Mississippi Freedom Democratic Party (MFDP) founded in Jackson.
	Spring	Alabama Governor Wallace enters Democratic Presidential Primaries in Maryland, Wisconsin and Indiana.
	June 13	Summer volunteers begin training in Oxford, Ohio.
	June 21	CORE worker Mickey Schwerner, volunteer Andrew Goodman & CORE volunteer James Chaney disappear near Philadelphia, Mississippi.
	July 2	1964 Civil Rights Act—integrating public accommodations—becomes law.
	July 7	FBI installs three additional "technical surveillances" at Atlanta SCLC office.
	July 11	Ku Klux Klansmen shoot and kill Lt. Colonel Lemuel Augustus Penn near Colbert, Georgia.
	July 12	The lower half of Charles Eddie Moore's body and the headless body of Henry Hezekiah Dee pulled from Mississippi River near Tallulah, Louisiana; FBI believes they were murdered by Klansmen May 2.
	July 18–August 30	Racial disturbances sweep urban America.
	July 29	SCLC, NAACP and NUL agree to demonstration moratorium until after presidential election; SNCC and CORE reject moratorium.
	July	Walker leaves SCLC; Young becomes Executive Director.

1964	August 2–3	North Vietnamese boats allegedly attack U.S. ships in Gulf of Tonkin; LBJ orders retaliatory attack.
	August 4	Bodies of Schwerner, Goodman, and Chaney are found in an earthen dam near Philadelphia, Mississippi.
	August 7	House (416–0) and Senate (88–2) pass "Gulf of Tonkin Resolution," approving U.S. action in Southeast Asia.
	August 22–27	MFDP contests seating of all-white regular Democrats at Atlantic City convention.
	August 28	Rioting breaks out in Philadelphia, Pennsylvania.
	August 30	LBJ signs Economic Opportunity Act of 1964.
	September 6	14-year-old Herbert Oarsby's body pulled from the Big Black River near Canton, Mississippi, dressed in CORE tee-shirt.
	September 11	SNCC delegation visits Guinea, West Africa.
	September 25	LBJ says "We don't want our American boys to do the fighting for Asian boys. We don't want to . . . get tied down in a land war in Asia."
	September 28–30	SCLC Convention endorses LBJ.
	October 14	MLK wins Nobel Peace Prize.
	October	SNCC's John Lewis and Don Harris meet with Malcolm X in Nairobi.
	October	Nikita Krushchev falls from power in Soviet Union.
	November 3	LBJ defeats Barry Goldwater with 61% of the popular vote.
	November 18	Hoover calls MLK "the most notorious liar in America."
1965	January 2	MLK, SCLC join Selma vote campaign.
	January 5	MLK discovers FBI blackmail letter and tape.
	February 1–5	MLK in Selma jail.
	February 3	Malcolm X speaks in Selma.
	February 6	Viet Cong attack U.S. base at Pleiku; LBJ orders bombing of North Vietnam.
	February 9	MLK discusses need for voting legislation with Attorney General Nicholas Katzenbach, Vice President Hubert Humphrey and LBJ.
	February 18	State troopers attack marchers in Marion, Alabama, wounding Jimmie Lee Jackson.
	February 21	Malcolm X assassinated at New York's Audubon Ballroom.
	February 26	Jackson dies; Bevel proposes Selma to Montgomery March.
	March 2	LBJ orders continuous bombing of North Vietnam.
	March 7	Police, troopers attack marchers at Selma's Edmund Pettus Bridge.
	March 8	Three thousand five hundred U.S. Marines land at Da Nang.
	March 9	MLK leads marchers to site of March 7 attack, turns around.
	March 11	Rev. James Reeb dies after attack by Selma whites.
	March 15	LBJ announces voting rights legislation.
	March 16	SNCC Montgomery marchers attacked by mounted police.
	March 22–25	Selma to Montgomery march. Detroit housewife Viola Liuzzo murdered as she drives marchers back to Selma.
	April 17	Twenty-five thousand march against war in Washington; SNCC's Moses speaks.

1965	April 28	LBJ sends Marines to Dominican Republic.
	June 2	Black deputy sheriff Oneal Moore killed by nightriders near Varnado, Louisiana.
	July 18	Willie Brewster killed by nightriders in Anniston, Alabama.
	August 20	Seminary student Jonathan Daniels killed by deputy in Hayneville, Alabama.
	June–September	SCLC runs SCOPE program, registering voters in 51 Southern counties.
	July 28	LBJ announces 50,000 additional U.S. troops will go to Vietnam.
	August 6	1965 Voting Rights Act becomes law.
	August 11–16	Watts riot in Los Angeles; 35 die.
	August 12	MLK calls for negotiated end to Vietnam war; offers to act as negotiator.
	October 15–16	Nationwide anti-war demonstrations held.
	Oct–Dec	Bevel establishes SCLC presence in Chicago.
1966	January 3	Student civil rights activist Samuel Younge killed in dispute over whites-only restroom in Tuskegee, Alabama.
	January 3	North Carolina civil rights attorney Floyd McKissick succeeds James Farmer as Director of CORE.
	January 6	SNCC condemns U.S. policy in Vietnam as neocolonialist aggression.
	January 7	MLK announces Chicago Freedom Movement.
	January 10	NAACP President Vernon Dahmer killed in dynamite blast in Hattiesburg, Mississippi.
	January 10	Georgia legislature refuses to seat SNCC staff member Julian Bond.
	March 22	Seven SNCC workers arrested in anti-apartheid protest at South African Consulate in New York.
	May 16	Stokeley Carmichael succeeds Lewis as Chairman of SNCC.
	June 6	James Meredith shot while on "March Against Fear" in Mississippi.
	June 7–26	MLK, Carmichael, McKissick and others continue Meredith's march. SNCC's Willie Ricks leads cries for "Black Power."
	June 10	Ben Chester White killed by Klan in Natchez, Mississippi.
	July 1–9	CORE's national convention endorses "Black Power."
	July 5	LBJ criticizes "Black Power." Roy Wilkins calls it "a reverse Ku Klux Klan."
	July 12–15	West side riot in Chicago.
	July 18–23	Cleveland riot.
	July 30	Clarence Triggs slain by nightriders in Bogalusa, Louisiana.
	July 30–August 25	Chicago Freedom Movement demonstrations.
	August	Eighty member police strike force raids Philadelphia, Pennsylvania, SNCC office.
	August 26	Chicago agreement ends protests.
	October 14	MLK refuses to sign statement condemning "Black Power."
	November 14–16	At SCLC staff retreat, MLK urges shift toward socialism.
	December 5	Supreme Court unanimously rules Bond must be allowed to take his seat in Georgia legislature.

1967	February 25	MLK delivers first public attack on war in Vietnam.
	February 27	NAACP activist Wharlest Jackson killed by bomb after promotion to a "white" job in Natchez, Mississippi.
	March 25	MLK and Dr. Benjamin Spock lead anti-war march in Chicago.
	April 4	Two hundred thousand attend Spring Mobilization against the war; MLK speaks. Four hundred thousand march in New York April 15.
	April 9	Carmichael and SNCC's George Ware arrested in Nashville for inciting to riot; SNCC office raided.
	May 11	National Guard fires on black student protest at Jackson State, killing civil rights worker Benjamin Brown.
	May 12	H. Rap Brown succeeds Carmichael as SNCC Chairman.
	May 16	Police fire "several thousand rounds" on dormitories at Texas Southern University; 481 arrested.
	July	LBJ authorizes increase in U.S. Vietnam forces from 480,000 to 525,000.
	July 12–15	Riot in Newark leaves 26 dead; in Detroit July 23–27, 43 dead.
	July	H. Rap Brown arrested on federal charges of inciting Cambridge riot; Dayton, Ohio, charges Brown with "criminal syndication;" Maryland indicts him on arson charge. He is arrested in New York for carrying a weapon across state lines while under indictment.
	July 27	LBJ appoints National Advisory Commission on Civil Disorders.
	August 26	FBI extends Counter Intelligence Program (COINTELPRO) to "Black Nationalist Hate Groups" including SCLC.
	October 2	Thurgood Marshall becomes first black Supreme Court justice.
	November 30	Senator Eugene McCarthy announces his candidacy for the Democratic Presidential nomination.
1968	January 15–16	SCLC staff meets to prepare for Poor People's Campaign.
	January 16	Lucius D. Amerson takes office in Macon County, Alabama, first black Southern sheriff since Reconstruction.
	January 21	North Vietnamese troops attack U.S. base at Khe Sahn.
	January 23	North Korea seizes the USS Pueblo.
	January 31	Viet Cong guerrillas and North Vietnamese regulars launch the Tet offensive.
	February 8	South Carolina State students Samuel Ephesians Hammond, Delano Herman Middleton and Henry Ezekial Smith killed, three wounded by South Carolina law enforcement officials firing at protestors.
	February 12	Memphis sanitation workers strike for higher pay and union recognition.
	February 23	Memphis police break up march of sanitation workers.
	February 29	Kerner Commission, named by LBJ to investigate riots, condemns white racism in U.S.
	March 4	FBI plans to disrupt Poor People's Campaign.
	March 12	McCarthy wins 42% of the vote in New Hampshire primary.
	March 16	RFK announces he will be a Presidential candidate.
	March 18	MLK speaks to Memphis sanitation workers and promises to lead a support march.
	March 28	Sanitation workers march turns violent.

1968	March 31	LBJ says he will not run for reelection.
	April 4	MLK assassinated in Memphis. Ralph Abernathy succeeds him as SCLC President.
	April 5–9	Widespread rioting across the U.S.; 39 die.
	April 9	MLK buried in Atlanta.
	April 10	Congress passes Civil Rights Act.
	April 15	Chicago Mayor Richard Daley orders police to "shoot to kill."
	April 16	Memphis sanitation workers win recognition, call off strike.
	May 12	Poor People's Campaign opens in Washington, D.C.
	June 5	RFK shot in Los Angeles hotel.
	June 6	RFK dies.
	June 17	Supreme Court rules against discrimination in the purchase or lease of property.
	June 24	Police close down Poor People's Resurrection City.
	July 16	Poor People's Campaign ends.
	November 5	RN elected president, defeating Humphrey and Wallace. Democrat Shirley Chisholm defeats Republican James Farmer, becoming the first black women ever to serve in Congress. Eighty blacks elected across the South.